Fifth Edition

Human Resource Management: Global Strategies for Managing a Diverse Workforce

Michael R. Carrell
University of Nebraska

Norbert F. Elbert
Bellarmine College

Robert D. Hatfield
West Virginia State College

Prentice Hall, Englewood Cliffs, NJ, 07632

Library of Congress Cataloging-in-Publication Data

Carrell, Michael R.
   Human resource management: global strategies for managing a
diverse workforce / Michael R. Carrell, Norbert F. Elbert, Robert D.
Hatfield. — 5th ed.
      p.   cm.
   Prev. ed. published under title: Personnel/human resource
management. 4th ed. 1992.
   Includes bibliographical references and index.
   ISBN 0-02-319533-9
   1. Personnel management. I. Elbert, Norbert F. II. Hatfield,
Robert D. III. Carrell, Michael R. Personnel/human resource
management. IV. Title.
   HF5549.C295 1995
   658.3 — dc20   94-6286
                                                          CIP

Acquisitions Editor: Natalie Anderson
Assistant Editor: Lisamarie Brassini
Editorial Assistant: Nancy Proyect
Manufacturing Buyer: Paul Smolenski
Cover Designer: Patricia Wosczyk
Cover Director: Jayne Conte
Project Manager: Alana Zdinak

 © 1995, 1992, 1989, 1986, and 1982 by Prentice-Hall, Inc.
A Simon & Schuster Company
Englewood Cliffs, New Jersey 07632

Printed in the United States of America

10   9   8   7   6   5   4   3   2   1

ISBN 0-02-319533-9

Prentice-Hall International (UK) Limited, *London*
Prentice-Hall of Australia Pty. Limited, *Sydney*
Prentice-Hall Canada Inc., *Toronto*
Prentice-Hall Hispanoamericana, S.A., *Mexico*
Prentice-Hall of India Private Limited, *New Delhi*
Prentice-Hall of Japan, Inc., *Tokyo*
Simon & Schuster Asia Pte. Ltd., *Singapore*
Editora Prentice-Hall do Brasil, Ltda., *Rio de Janeiro*
Prentice Hall Inc., *Englewood Cliffs, New Jersey*

Dedications

Frank Kuzmits, colleague and friend who started this project with me many years ago, and whose camaraderie is sorely missed!

M.R.C.

In this age of dual careers and work-family conflicts not many wives would sacrifice a job and time away from family and friends to accompany a spouse to far flung parts of the globe, often for months at a time. Barb, thanks for joining me in my "great" adventures and for your constant and loving source of inspiration.

N.F.E.

This book is dedicated to four special individuals. First, it would be uncommon to be blessed with a wonderful wife, or enthusiastic research partner, or supportive collaborator. Melanie Fitzpatrick Hatfield is all three of these for me. Second, I was lucky twenty years ago to learn about managing people with your head and your heart from a very wise business manager, mentor, and friend, Walt Jones. Third, I owe what ability, thoughtfulness, and ambition that I possess to my Creator and the encouragement and patience of my extraordinary parents, Norma and Bob Hatfield.

R.D.H.

BRIEF CONTENTS

v

CONTENTS

PART VI
Special Issues 731

PREFACE

The first edition of this appeared over a decade ago. And what a decade it has been. We have observed a world that has been turned upside down. Who could have guessed ten years ago the sudden demise of communism and the complete break-up of the old Soviet Union? Western companies are pouring money, technology, and management expertise (especially HRM) into regions that were once off-limits, acquiring state enterprises, forming joint ventures, or creating new businesses from the ground up. And if that wasn't enough global change, consider the new markets in Canada and Mexico created from the North American Free Trade Agreement. Closer to home, companies are going through some painful changes including downsizing and reengineering, benefiting from diversity, using self-managed work teams, flattening organizations, and turning routine work over to automation and computers. Every day newspapers carry stories of new job losses. Employees are told the only way to protect their jobs is to increase productivity. It is no wonder the added stress and strain on people make it increasingly difficult to create and maintain a work environment that motivates and satisfies human resources.

Regardless of size or type of business, people really are the most important asset of any organization. There is no doubt successful human resource management, and its emphasis on the well-being of employees, enhances the organization's bottom line. This text is not written as much for the HRM Specialist (although they will find it useful) as for non-HRM personnel. All managers need to understand HRM concepts, especially practical techniques, if they are to build high performance organizations. The fifth edition presents an up-to-date resource of ideas, concepts, and techniques for anyone who works in any organization and who will be influenced by the human resource function.

The fifth edition has undergone major changes, much like the world we live in. One of the original authors, Frank Kuzmits, has decided to "move on" in pursuit of other academic interests. However this edition incorporates many of Frank's ideas, and we continue to be grateful for his contributions. His replacement, and a good one, is Bob Hatfield. Bob brings HRM experience and a very lively writing style that our readers will appreciate.

The fifth edition has been completely rewritten yet retains its highly praised easy readability, lively examples, and unique **HR In The News** boxes. And, there are **two new chapters** that reflect our secondary title: **global strategies for managing a diverse workforce.** The global economy, cultural diversity, and regulatory forces are major topics of the first three chapters. And, these issues are further integrated into subsequent chapters.

Content Highlights

A Global Perspective of Human Resources (new Chapter 2) examines the special challenges of integrating new foreign acquisitions into an existing corporate culture. The global economy enables us to present HRM in a **strategic** context. Questions are raised about transferring HRM practices into the foreign subsidiary, and how it should be done. Major geographical regions are reviewed in terms of identifying important cultural and HRM differences, specifically: Canada, Mexico, Japan,

Western Europe, Central/Eastern Europe, and China. Moreover the section on Central and Eastern Europe is unparalleled because attention is given to the timely issue of how to create HRM strategies for transitioning from communism to market systems.

The other new chapter, **Workforce Diversity and Regulatory Challenges** (Chapter 3), presents strategies for cultivating differences in a way that results in achieving multicultural synergy. It examines the legal environment, which plays a large role in organizations' efforts to respond to diversity regulations. Many of these issues are further integrated in subsequent chapters. This new emphasis provides the coverage necessary to meet the new diversity and international curriculum requirements adopted by the American Assembly of Collegiate Schools of Business (AACSB) which is the national accreditation organization for U.S. Business Schools.

While every chapter was extensively updated, major revisions were made on the following six chapters. **Job Design** (Chapter 5) explores the emerging new models of working together including telecommuting, groupshare technology, and temporary and contract work. And, of course, the radically new Total Quality Management (TQM) and Process Reengineering programs are explained.

Chapter 8, **Performance Appraisal and Performance Management** moves from the traditional supervisor-rater appraisal to the latest in performance management techniques appropriate for TQM and other team organizations. Some of the most exciting changes are discussed in new sections on team appraisal techniques, reverse appraisals, along with customer-, peer-, and self-ratings. A new section on employee monitoring creates interest for this controversial topic. Concerns expressed by Deming and other TQM proponents about the failure of PAs in the U.S. are explored in this new edition. A chilling new section on violence related to appraisals demonstrates the seriousness of the appraisal. New PA forms il-

lustrate both new and traditional techniques. Students will enjoy the opportunity to "rate the President of the U.S." in a new PA exercise.

Employee Training and Management Development (Chapter 9) combines two chapters from the old edition into one comprehensive and updated chapter. Students will learn why HRM professionals believe there is a "skill gap" in the 1990s and what approaches will have to be taken in basic skills training. The latest examples of cutting-edge training programs are combined with the current trends in training design and evaluation. New sections on learning highlight the latest in whole brain theories, sensory learning, and other adult learning theories. The role of humor in training is discussed along with the challenges for the "second wave" of diversity training programs. A new case and group exercise complete the updating of this exciting chapter.

Chapter 10, **Internal Staffing and Career Management** focuses upon the challenges created as organizations' continue to flatten their hierarchies in the mid-1990s. This theme of employers' "going horizontal" leads to new expanded discussions on telecommuting, early-retirement programs, HRM balancing, lateral transfers, and the "contingency workforce." The latest projections on which industries are on the rise and which employers will be hiring can help students form realistic career expectations. The special concerns of women and minorities in management are updated and fit more naturally into this chapter rather than the training chapter as in the old text. A challenging new exercise which requires students to design a diversity training program can be used to enliven class discussion.

Chapter 16, **Computers, HRISs, and the HR Department** is substantially rewritten because of the technological improvements and ubiquity now of computers. Students at any level of computer literacy will be comfortable and, indeed, may use this chapter as a computer reference—especially the popular and updated "talking computerese" section. There are new discussions about switching and decentralizing information systems, computer security, increasing system use by employees (e.g., to get benefits information), and the continuing demands for information required by new employment laws (e.g., the Family Medical Leave Act of 1993). Students are given the latest listing of HRIS software topics from *HRMagazine* as well as two new exercises.

The final chapter, **HR Research and Problem Solving** (Chapter 17) is one of the most practical. After students learn about the domains and sources for HR research, they are given information on the latest techniques HR professionals are using to gather information and make decisions in five critical areas — performance, absenteeism, turnover, dissatisfaction, and fairness. We have added time-tested advice on exactly how to more effectively perform the common employee survey. New details on "performance surveys" integrate well with TQM approaches. Students are asked to find a way to stop Taco Bell employees from "Heading for the Border" in a stimulating new role-play exercise on turnover.

Pedagogical Features

Each chapter contains several features designed to enhance student learning.

- Each chapter opens with a list of behavioral **learning objectives** that inform the reader of the key terms and concepts to be presented. This feature is intended to help the student gain an overview of the chapter material.

- **HR In The News** — a unique feature, usually a brief article about current HRM activities whose purpose is to help students relate current events to the HRM practices discussed in the chapter.

- A balance of HRM theory with practice.

- **Conclusions and Applications** emphasizing the important points and their relationship to the management of human resources.

- **Key Terms and Concepts** including much of the vocabulary unique to the HRM filed.

- **Review and Discussion Questions** which focus on the major areas covered and which stimulate and enhance classroom discussion of chapter concepts and practices.

- A **Case Study** appears at the end of each chapter. Over half are new, and showcase the "hottest" issues in HRM today, such as work-family conflicts, cultural diversity, downsizing and creating a high performance work force in transition economies.

- Two New **Experiential Exercises** appear at the conclusion of each chapter. Many promote teambuilding, improved face-to-face communication skills, and problem-solving skills — an important element for meeting AACSB accreditation guidelines.

SUPPLEMENTS

Instructor's Manual/Test Bank

A comprehensive Instructor's Manual to accompany this book is available from the publisher. The manual includes:

- a chapter outline for ease in preparing lecture materials,

- answers to review and discussions questions,

- experiential exercise supplements,

- additional and more comprehensive cases that can be reproduced and distributed to students, and

- an all-new test bank (fifth edition) of multiple-choice, and true/false questions.

Acknowledgments

Like so many others caught in a turbulent industry, the world of mergers and acquisitions finally hit home for us. Macmillan Publishing was acquired by Paramount Publishing and our text **Human Resource Management, fifth edition,** unfortunately lost some valuable production time. Nevertheless, we were able to make good use of this added time by updating ideas and techniques. All of this would not have been possible without the extraordinary efforts of many people. The project was initiated with the support of our former editor, Nina McGuffin. It was completed under the guidance of Prentice Hall and our current editor, Natalie Anderson. We are especially indebted to two outstanding professionals: Helen Wallace for her persistence in Faxing to Eastern Europe and to Tom Dorsaneo for his encouragement during the project's final tense moments.

Several reviewers made very helpful suggestions for improving previous editions, including: Edwin Arnold, Auburn University, Montgomery; Gerald Benzchawel, University of Wisconsin, Oshkosh; Donald Caruth, East Texas State University; Kermit R. Davis, Jr., Auburn; Kack L. Dustman, Northern Arizona University; Ann Harriman, California State University, Sacramento; Thomas C. Head, Clarkson University; Herff L. Moore, University of Central Arkansas; Herbert S. Parker, Kean College of New Jersey; Velma Pomrenke, University of Akron; Abdullan Pooyan, University of North Dakota; George S. Roukis, Hofstra University; William C. Sharbrough, The Citadel; Mark Sherman, University of Houston, Clear Lake; Charlotte Sutton, Auburn; Alfred W. Travers, Indiana Vocational Technical College; Michael J. Vest; Richard E. Wolfe, Golden Gate University; Robert Alexander, Marshall University; Sinclair E. Hugh (SPHR), Cal Poly-Pomona, Irvin A. Zaenglein, Northern Michigan University; Thomas J. Liesz, Western State College of Colorado; Howard Smith, University of New Mexico; Richard Discenza, University of Colorado at Colorado Springs.

For the fifth edition, we would like to mention the following individuals: Joseph Blasi, Rutgers University; Jason Schweizer, Motorola; Brad Hobbs, Bellarmine College; Jerald Smith, Florida State; Nancy Higgins, Montgomery College; Clyde Scott, University of Alabama.

The global transformation could not have occurred without the help and support of truly international HRM colleagues. Among the most helpful we would include: Susan Karoliny and Ferenc Farkas, Janus Pannonius University in Pecs, Hungary; Andras Nemeslaki and Robert Kovack, International Management Center, Budapest, Hungary; Rudolf Galik, Juraj Koman, and Viki Murphy, Czechoslovak Management Center; Dorothy Marcic, Metropolitan State; William Pendergast, Monterey Institute of International Studies; Daniel Fogel, University of Pittsburgh; and Earl Gibbons, Thunderbird. And, a very special thanks must go to an experienced world traveler himself, Jason Schweizer (Motorola), whose ideas and encouragement were appreciated almost as much as his friendship. Closer to home, special thanks should go to Jay McGowan and David House (Bellarmine College) for the opportunity to internationalize, and to Ed Popper for supporting global thinking.

Special thanks to Tim Baldwin, Steve Grover, Mike Bedell, James Wimbush, Bill Bommer, Jon Johnson, and other colleagues at Indiana University for their thoughts and help in locating materials during the writing of this edition. Gratitude is due to research partner Chun Hui at the Hong Kong University of Science and Technology for allowing the use of our work concerning discrimination against the disabled and other support. Many organizations helped by sharing their current practices and HR policies. Special among these are Jim Way and Luke Armstrong of the Marley Cooling Tower Company and John Galloway with the Indiana State Government. And certainly this book would not have been possible without the encouragement and cooperation of Donald Darton, West Virginia State. Finally, since no text could be written without the help of many library professionals, thanks goes to all, and special thanks to Stuart Fraxer at the Drain-Jordon Library in West Virginia and Louise Walker at the Data Courier Center at Bellarmine.

Michael R. Carrell   Norbert F. Elbert (PHR)   Robert D. Hatfield
Omaha, NE   Louisville, KY   Charleston, WV

PART I

THE ENVIRONMENT FOR HUMAN RESOURCES

CHAPTER **1**

THE FOUNDATION AND CHALLENGES OF HUMAN RESOURCE MANAGEMENT

3

CHAPTER OBJECTIVES

1. To recognize the importance of environmental forces in the management of people, the design of work, and the organization's capacity to compete effectively.

2. To trace the history of personnel/human resource management.

3. To define the connection between successful companies and strategic human resource management.

4. To understand the organizational structure of the typical human resource department.

5. To describe the major functions and roles of the human resource department.

6. To recognize HR's critical responsibility for designing and maintaining two-way communication systems.

7. To identify the major issues and challenges faced by HR professionals today, particularly increasing worker productivity and quality, downsizing, work force diversity, work-family conflicts, and global competition.

8. To describe the career opportunities within the human resource field.

The twentieth century is rapidly coming to an end. The traditional corporation is also becoming a thing of the past. Efficiency and economies of scale, two dominant twentieth-century themes, have been replaced by new values: teamwork over individualism, global markets over domestic ones, and customer-driven focus over short-run profits. Only fluid, flexible, highly adaptive organizations, like the Eaton Corporation highlighted in the opening HR in the News, will thrive in the fast-paced global economy.[1]

For HR professionals, one thing is certain: traditional personnel approaches that were conceived in cultures emphasizing command and control are giving way to new approaches characterized by greater employee commitment, cooperation, and communication. Companies with rigid structures will be swept away.[2] By contrast, companies like the Eaton Corporation (see HR in the News: "Working Together") are empowering employees, letting workers manage everything from budgets to inventory control, often without direct oversight from top management.

Has there really been that much change in the way employees need to be managed? In short, yes. For example, the issue of workplace flexibility has emerged in response to the needs of today's companies and the diversity of its employees. Before the 1980s, standardization was the norm in personnel administration. Consistency and conformity were once hallmarks of management policy. Today, developing the capacity for flexibility is considered a vital component of the company's corporate human resource strategy.[3]

What makes an organization effective? Is it the land, buildings, capital, patents, and technology it owns? An organization's tangible assets are certainly important factors in its success, but managers today recognize that an

Working Together

It's 7:30 A.M., time for the morning quiz at Eaton Corporation's factory in Lincoln, IL. Ten union workers, each representing work teams, sit around a boardroom table. "What were our sales yesterday?" asks a supervisor at the head of the table. A worker, glancing at a computer printout, replies.

The review continues, covering other vital statistics: the cost of materials and supplies used the day before; the cost of labor, shipping and utilities.

The aim of the exercise isn't simply to help workers understand the bottom line but also to get their help in enhancing it. Eaton encourages workers to take thousands of small steps that incrementally improve the products they make and the processes used to make them. The penny pinching extends to office workers, who haggle over utility rates, challenge local tax assessments, scrutinize inventory, and eliminate paperwork.

Eaton is obsessive about costs because it has to be. Its chief customers, the auto makers, are just as obsessive about their costs and pay as little as possible for parts even in the best of times.

"You can't expect price increases anymore, so getting productivity improvements every day is critical," says John Rodewig, Eaton's president. In the past decade, the company's productivity—its output per hour worked—rose 3 percent a year, better than the 1.9 percent average for all U.S. manufacturers, but, Eaton executives say, still not good enough. Now managers are told to aim for annual gains of at least 4 percent.

Some of Eaton's belt-tightening efforts are conventional. The four factories it closed last year eliminated 897 workers, reducing its work force to 38,000 in 110 facilities around the world. But Eaton's experience shows that the best way to control costs is to get employees to understand how that effort can benefit them. At one unionized plant, which for years was mired in labor–management animosity, Eaton rewarded 10 percent productivity gains by offering to relocate 70 low-wage jobs from Mexico.

Getting people to think for themselves—and in work teams—is important to Eaton. The company starts by hiring managers who aren't autocratic and training them to accept encroachments on their authority. Not everyone can work this way. Managers who adjust, however, tend to stay at one plant for a long time. Managers are encouraged to be flexible and give people as much freedom as they can handle.

That style was certainly evident when a human resources (HR) position opened up and a joint labor–management task force was asked to whittle the field of eighteen down to three candidates. When it came time for a final decision, the plant manager asked the task force to decide on its own. "Our opin-

(continued)

5

ions matter here," one member said. "What we say counts—and it's not just to appease us."

SOURCE: Reprinted by permission of *Wall Street Journal*. Adapted from Thomas O'Boyle, "A Manufacturer Grows Efficient by Soliciting Ideas from Employees," *Wall Street Journal,* June 5, 1992: A5. Dow Jones & Company, Inc. All rights reserved worldwide.

organization's people—its HR—are its most critical assets. How should this critical human resources be managed? What are effective HR policies and practices? Which methods of HR management can lead to maximum productivity, quality, and customer satisfaction? The answers to questions such as these, and many more, are the focus of this book. Without question, the successful management of an organization's human resources—its people—is an exciting, fluid, and challenging field.

HUMAN RESOURCES: PAST AND PRESENT

Modern HR management is radically different from personnel management of decades ago. Since the turn of the century, the managerial philosophy that has defined the personnel function has undergone significant changes. In the last eighty years, both the scientific management approach and the human relations approach have appeared and declined; today what has popularly become known as the *human resource* approach has emerged.

Scientific Management

The technique of **scientific management** was the first radical change in what most owners and managers of the early 1900s generally considered the most effective means of managing employees— constant supervision and threats of the loss of their jobs (similar to that of Dickens's Ebenezer Scrooge). Before the advent of scientific management, all employees were considered equally productive, and if their

productivity did not measure up, they deserved to be quickly terminated. The founders of the scientific management movement believed differently. Instead of simply relying on the use of fear and intimidation, Frederick Taylor, Frank and Lillian Gilbreth, and Henry Gantt believed that managers should take a scientific and objective approach in studying how work can be most efficiently designed. Taylor, the "father of scientific management," and the others employed scientific data collection and analysis methods often found in research laboratories at that time. He emphasized the study of the motions required for each job, the tools utilized, and the time required for each task. Then, based on scientific data instead of a boss's subjective judgment, fair performance standards for each job could be determined. Workers who produced output above the standard would receive additional incentive pay. At the time, all employees were generally given the same daily or weekly wage, regardless of their individual efforts. The results of scientific management techniques received widespread praise in the newspapers and even in a series of congressional hearings on commerce held in 1914. Scientific management principles spread quickly, generally with success. However, the movement's treatment of the worker—someone motivated solely by money—led to problems.

Frederick Taylor declared that "one of the very first requirements for a man who is fit to handle pig iron as a regular occupation is that he shall be so stupid and so phlegmatic that he more nearly resembles in his mental makeup the ox than any other type."[4] Taylor's oft-quoted comment underscores a widespread managerial attitude of the early twentieth century: along with raw materials, capital, and machinery, the employee is simply another factor of production. As such, the scientific management approach resulted in work methods and techniques that showed great concern for employee output but little concern for employee satisfaction. So-called time-and-motion studies replaced "rule-of-thumb" work methods with the "one best way" to perform a task. Typically, the one best way to do the job was highly specialized and routine, involving little mental effort and few opportunities to make decisions or use judgment. Proponents of scientific management are quick to point out that the average turn-of-the-century worker had little formal education and few skills or abilities that could be applied to organizational problems.

The concept of the *economic man,* embraced by many managers and administrators during the early part of the century, held that a worker is motivated primarily by economic gain and that a worker's output can be maximized only through financial incentives. With that concept in mind, Taylor created the *differential piece-rate system,* whereby workers would receive a higher rate of pay per piece produced after the daily output standard had been achieved. Through the differential piece-rate system (along with other techniques), workers were expected to produce at a maximum level to satisfy what was believed to be their only work-related need: money.

The personnel departments of large manufacturing companies during the early years of the century had the traditional responsibilities of recruiting, selection, training, and health and safety. But the main focus of their activities was the implementation of scientific management techniques. For example, the personnel staff conducted time-and-motion studies and fatigue studies, performed job analyses, prepared job specifications, and created wage incentive programs.[5] During this period, many

personnel departments also actively supported welfare programs that addressed the needs of the worker: vacations, personal hygiene, job training, instruction in English for the purpose of naturalization (many factory workers were immigrants), lunchrooms, company housing, employee loans, insurance plans, and recreational programs. Such welfare programs generally reflected the paternalistic attitude of management common at the time: "We know what is best for you." But paternalistic practices often failed to bring about unquestioned acceptance of authority. Primarily for that reason, the popularity of employee welfare programs declined during the 1920s and 1930s.

Human Relations

During the 1930s and 1940s, with impetus provided by the classic Hawthorne studies, management's attention shifted from scientific management to **human relations.** The Hawthorne studies demonstrated that employee productivity was affected not only by the way the job was designed and the manner in which employees were rewarded economically but also by certain social and psychological factors.[6] Hawthorne researchers Elton Mayo and F. J. Roethlisberger discovered that employees' feelings, emotions, and sentiments were strongly affected by such work conditions as group relationships, leadership styles, and support from management.[7] And those feelings could, in turn, have a significant impact on productivity. Thus, it was asserted, treating employees with dignity would both enhance employee satisfaction and enable the achievement of higher productivity. The Mayo-Roethlisberger research led to the widespread implementation of behavioral science techniques in industry, including supervisory training programs that emphasized support and concern for the workers. The personnel staff was primarily responsible for designing and implementing such programs.

The shift to human relations was also influenced by the growing strength of unions during the period. The rise of unionism was largely the result of passage of the Wagner Act of 1935, which gave workers the legal right to organize and to bargain collectively with employers in disputes about wages, job security, benefits, and many other work conditions. Although the Wagner Act did not legislate good human relations, it did compel many employers to improve their personnel programs (i.e., employee relations) in an effort to keep unions out. With unionization came formal grievance procedures, which provided employees with a measure of protection against arbitrary or despotic supervision. Although unionization led to an erosion of labor–management relations in some firms, in many other companies it resulted in greater acceptance of the principles of human relations.

The human-relations approach was no doubt instrumental in improving the working environment of many workers, but it achieved only minimal success in increasing worker output and enhancing job satisfaction. The lackluster performance of the approach is attributable to the following:

- The approach was based on an oversimplified concept of human behavior in an organizational setting. The notion that "a happy worker is a hard worker"—generally presented to management as an untested hypothesis—is now recognized to be valid for only part of the work force.

- The approach failed to consider the concept of individual differences. Each worker is a unique and complex person with different wants, needs, and values. What motivates one worker may not motivate another; being happy or feeling good may have little or no impact on the productivity of certain employees.

- The approach failed to recognize the need both for job structure and for controls on employee behavior, and it largely neglected the importance of procedures, standards, and work rules in guiding employees toward the goals of the organization.

- The approach failed to recognize that good human relations are but one of many conditions necessary to sustain a high level of employee motivation. For instance, productivity may also be improved with performance appraisal systems, career development programs, job enrichment programs, and selection and placement systems that successfully match the employee with the job.

The human relations approach fell out of favor with management during the 1950s and 1960s and is considered passé today. While good human relations is still an important organizational objective, the human relations approach is no longer the predominant one guiding leadership style within organizations. Good feelings are necessary but certainly not sufficient to ensure peak levels of employee satisfaction and productivity.

Human Resources (HR)

The emerging trend in **human resource (HR) management** is clearly toward the adoption of the human resource approach, through which organizations benefit in two significant ways: an increase in organizational effectiveness and the satisfaction of each employee's needs. Rather than addressing organizational goals and employee needs as separate and exclusive, the human resources approach holds that organizational goals and human needs are mutual and compatible: one set need not be gained at the expense of the other.

The human resource approach is relatively new in the management of people. The term became popular during the 1970s as research in the behavioral sciences showed that managing people as resources rather than as factors of production or as human beings who act solely on the basis of emotions could result in real benefits to both the organization and the employee. As important as the approach has

FIGURE 1-1 Human resource approach.

EMPLOYEE

HIGHER
Employee Motivation
and Applied Ability

Leads to

GREATER
Quality, Quantity
of Work

Leads to

Leads to

GREATER
Employee Rewards,
Recognition

HIGHER
Organizational
Productivity, Profits

ORGANIZATION

Leads to

become, the term *human resources*—like many other terms in the management literature—is hard to define with clarity. Nonetheless, a number of principles provide the basis for a human resources approach:

- Employees are investments that will, if effectively managed and developed, provide long-term rewards to the organization in the form of greater productivity.

- Policies, programs and practices must be created that satisfy both the economic and emotional needs of employees.

- A working environment must be created in which employees are encouraged to develop and utilize their skills to the maximum extent.

- HR programs and practices must be implemented with the goal of balancing the needs and meeting the goals of both the organization and the employee. As Figure 1-1 indicates, this can be achieved through a circular process in which the organization and employees enable each other to meet their goals.

STRATEGIC HUMAN RESOURCE MANAGEMENT

In a fast-paced global economy, change is the norm. Environmental, social, and technological change, the increased internationalization of business, and the increased scarcity and cost of HR, can only mean that long-term planning is risky but absolutely essential. How do organizations make decisions about their future in this complex, rapidly changing world? The process is called *strategic management*. It involves making those decisions that define the overall mission and objectives of the organization, determining the most effective utilization of its resources, and crafting and executing the strategy in ways that produce the intended results.

Business strategy is management's game plan.[8] Without one, management would have no road map to follow and no action plan to produce desired results. Strategic human resource management activities address a wide variety of people issues relevant to business strategy. HR management crosses all the functional areas and is fully integrated with all the significant parts of the organization: operations, marketing, finance, and so on. Lastly, the process is led and coordinated by top management, usually the vice-president of human resources.

In the past, people issues were the sole province of the personnel department. Today strategic HR problems are the responsibility of every manager in every department. The HR staff are themselves resources to be called on in support of operating managers. Whether managers are in charge of sales, accounts payable, or information systems, if they are responsible for people, then they are HR managers.

Successful firms have at least one commonality. They have developed a strategy for developing and maintaining superiority in critical technical and organizational skills. Wal-Mart's competitive advantage, for example, is to offer lower prices and better services than its rivals. It can accomplish this feat by having a better distribution system (building within easy driving distance of warehouses), information management systems (transmitting point-of-sale data by satellite to suppliers), good supplier relations (no hassles and quick payment, access to satellite communication system, authority to reorder automatically based on sales), and good customer service (e.g., greeting customers as they enter the store).

Wal-Mart refuses to leave to chance the development of critical skills that will give them a competitive edge. Identifying the mix of talents and skills needed to achieve desired results, and matching that mix to what is currently available, is a big part of strategic HR planning. Each HR function (training, recruitment, performance appraisal, etc.) can then be examined to consider how it supports the strategic thrust. Any gap between desired and existing human resource skills, knowledge, and abilities (SKA) necessitates the adoption of changes in HR policies and practices, such as hiring people with needed skills, creating new training programs, and so on.

Well-conceived HR strategies are an important basis for competition. How important depends entirely on the industry and on the extent to which people play a vital role in the success of the business. The bigger the role, the greater the potential payoff for having well-conceived HR strategies for maximizing talents. While this philosophy applies to most industries, there are situations in which success or failure is governed by market and financial forces that have little to do with human resources. Low-skill manufacturing, for example, may not depend on people's creative juices as much as on low wages. Nevertheless, this book rests on the premise that effective strategic HR management is a powerful competitive weapon.

HUMAN RESOURCE FUNCTIONS

Because the **human resource function** within each organization is unique to that organization, the activities included in the HR department will vary from organization to organization. However, as Table 1-1 indicates, approximately sixty-four *different* management activities can be assigned to the personnel/human resource department, either exclusively or in conjunction with other departments in the organization. Among the activities that are most likely to be assigned exclusively to the HR department are:

1. Compensation and benefits issues, such as insurance administration, wage and salary administration, unemployment compensation, pension plans, vacation/leave processing, and flexible benefits accounts.

2. Employee services such as outplacement services, employee assistance plans, health and wellness programs, savings plans, and relocation services.

3. Affirmative Action and Equal Employment Opportunity.

4. Job analysis programs.

5. Preemployment testing, including drug testing.

6. Attitude surveys (research).

In addition, the HR department is likely to carry out some activities jointly with other departments in the organization, including interviewing, productivity/motivation programs, training and development, career planning, disciplinary procedures, and performance appraisals.[9]

Table 1-1 Personnel/Human Resource Activities in U.S. Organizations

Activity	Company Has Activity	Responsibility for the Activity Is Assigned to:		
		P/HR Dept. Only	P/HR and Other Dept(s).	Other Dept(s). Only
Interviewing	99%	38%	59%	3%
Vacation/leave processing	99	77	21	2
Insurance benefits administration	99	86	9	5
Recruiting (other than college recruiting)	99	74	25	1
Personnel recordkeeping/information systems	99	74	26	1
Promotion/transfer/separation processing	99	65	33	1
Induction/orientation	99	63	34	3
Wage/salary administration	99	82	16	2
Workers' compensation administration	99	73	12	15
EEO compliance/affirmative action	99	90	8	2
Unemployment compensation	99	82	9	9
Job descriptions	99	68	31	1
Payroll administration	98	30	28	42
Performance appraisal, management	98	56	38	7
Disciplinary procedures	98	43	55	2
Purchasing	97	3	8	89
Job evaluation	97	70	27	3
Performance appraisal, non-management	96	53	42	5
Administrative services	96	13	20	66
Maintenance/janitorial services	96	6	7	87
Exit interviews	95	84	15	2
Job analysis	94	78	20	2
Award/recognition programs	94	69	25	5
Complaint procedures	94	57	40	3
Skills training, non-management	94	26	48	26
Supervisory training	93	50	41	9
Security/property protection	93	23	16	61
Safety training/OSHA compliance	93	44	30	26
Employee communications/publications	93	42	41	17
Public/media relations	90	13	23	64
Risk management/business insurance	90	11	17	72
Human resource forecasting/planning	89	54	40	6
Travel/transportation services	89	8	16	76
Community relations/contribution programs	89	27	33	40
Management development	89	48	42	10

In this text we discuss all these HR activities, whether they are performed solely by the HR department or together with other departments. The following is a brief summary of the text's chapters and of HR activities discussed in each chapter.

Job Analysis and Design

For an employee to perform satisfactorily, his or her skills, abilities, and motives to perform the job must match the job's requirements. A mismatch may lead to poor performance, absenteeism, turnover, and other problems.

Table 1-1 continued

Activity	Company Has Activity	Responsibility for the Activity is Assigned to:		
		P/HR Dept. Only	P/HR and Other Dept(s).	Other Dept(s). Only
Pension/retirement plan administration	88%	71%	18%	11%
Tuition aid/scholarships	86	85	11	4
Recreation/social programs	84	58	33	9
Pre-employment testing (other than drug tests)	81	90	9	2
Executive compensation	81	53	30	17
Office/clerical services	79	26	22	52
Employee assistance plan/counseling	76	82	11	7
Organization development	76	41	44	15
Productivity/motivation programs	76	31	57	12
Thrift/savings plan administration	73	72	19	9
Incentive pay plans	72	49	41	10
Relocation services	70	76	20	5
Career planning/development	70	53	43	5
Food service/cafeteria	69	27	10	63
College recruiting	67	79	18	3
Suggestion systems	61	53	33	14
Health/wellness program	60	76	14	10
Attitude surveys	57	82	13	5
Outplacement services	56	91	8	0
Drug testing	55	85	12	3
Pre-retirement counseling	51	89	7	4
In-house medical services	51	54	11	35
Library	51	12	9	79
Flexible benefits plan administration	50	84	10	5
Union/labor relations	48	75	21	3
Flexible-spending account administration	47	70	15	15
Profit-sharing plan administration	43	60	25	15
Mergers and acquisitions	38	45	40	15
Stock plan administration	32	53	23	24
International personnel/HR administration	19	69	26	6
Child-care center	10	29	10	60

SOURCE: Survey of 477 members of the Society for Human Resource Management (SHRM). *Bulletin to Management* (BNA Policy and Practice Series), Vol 41, no. 26—Part II, SHRM-BNA Survey no. 54 (June 28, 1990). Copyright 1990 by the Bureau of National Affairs, Inc., Washington, D.C. 20037. Used by permission.

Through a process called *job analysis,* the skills and abilities to perform a specific job are determined. In Chapter 4, we will present various job analysis techniques and discuss how job analysis data are used to create effective HR programs.

When scientific management was popular, jobs were designed to be simple and routine so that unskilled workers could be quickly trained to do the work. A primary assumption of such job design was that the average worker had no need to gain satisfaction from work and had neither the skill nor the inclination to participate in work decisions. No doubt many assumptions about turn-of-the-century workers were valid. But though employee needs and motives have experienced many changes since the formative years of industrialization, job design in many organizations still resembles that of scientific management. Organizational research shows that employees are not only demanding more satisfying and rewarding work but also demonstrating that their involvement in decision making can enhance rather than impair organizational effectiveness. In Chapter 5 we will explore job design, as well as various strategies for scheduling the workweek and improving the quality of work life.

Recruitment and Selection

To a great degree, the effectiveness of an organization depends on the effectiveness of its employees. Without a high-quality labor force, an organization is destined to have mediocre performance. For this reason, the recruitment of human resources is a critical HR function. Recruiting and selecting a qualified labor force involves a variety of HR activities, including analysis of the labor market, long-term planning, interviewing, and testing. Chapters 6 and 7 focus on these topics.

Appraisal, Training, and Development

The growth of an organization is closely related to the development of its human resources. When employees fail to grow and develop in their work, a stagnant organization most likely will result. A strong employee development program does not guarantee organizational success, but such a program is generally found in successful, expanding organizations.

One important developmental function is the appraisal of employee performance. During an appraisal process, employees become aware of any performance deficiencies they may have and are informed of what they must do to improve their performance and thus become promotable. Various methods and techniques of performance appraisal, with their advantages and disadvantages, will be described in Chapter 8.

For many organizations, the heart of the development process is composed of on-the-job and off-the-job activities that teach employees new skills and abilities. Because modern managers recognize the benefits derived from the training and developmental process, expenditures for employee education are at an all-time high. This rise in employee education has been accompanied by growing professionalism in the training field and a demand for competent, qualified trainers.

Training and development offer many rewards but also pose many problems for training personnel: Who should be trained and why? What training techniques should be used? Is training cost-effective? The training and development of both managerial and nonmanagerial personnel are the focus of Chapter 9.

Chapter 10 deals with a relative newcomer to the personnel field: career management. HR managers are giving increasing attention to processes and activities that enhance career advancement and solve problems employees encounter along their career paths. While career management is difficult to implement, advances in recent years have brought about improvements in the decision-making processes that affect employees' careers.

Compensation and Health

The issue of compensation has long posed problems for the HR manager: How should jobs be evaluated to determine their worth? Are wage and salary levels competitive? Are they fair? Is it possible to create an incentive compensation system tied to performance? Techniques for evaluating the financial worth of jobs and other issues pertaining to the design of pay systems are discussed in Chapter 11.

An increasingly important part of compensation is employee benefits. Because the cost of benefits for many organizations now averages as much as 40 percent of total payroll costs, employers are trying to control benefit costs without seriously affecting the overall compensation program. The kinds of benefits that employers may offer and the considerations that should be given to planning a total benefits package are discussed in Chapter 12.

A newer area of concern to the employee today is health and safety. Each year accidents, injuries, and occupational diseases cost billions of dollars in medical expenses, medical insurance, equipment damage, and production problems. Although much is being done to improve the workplace environment, there is still considerable room for improvement. In Chapter 13 we will explore important health and safety legislation and describe various strategies for strengthening an organization's health and safety program.

Labor Relations

Labor unions exert a powerful influence on employers and help shape the HR policies and programs for union employees. Because union participation in personnel decision making may have great impact on the economic condition of the firm, managers must understand a union's philosophies and goals and explore ways in which a cooperative rather than an adversarial relationship may be achieved. Union goals, union organizational structure, the union-organizing drive, the collective bargaining process, and techniques for handling employee grievances are examined in Chapter 14.

Chapter 15 focuses on a problem that has plagued managers for centuries: the unsatisfactory employee. The employee who fails to perform up to expectations not only can be costly to management but can also create stress, frustration, and tension within the work group. For these reasons, managers must recognize the causes of unsatisfactory performance and be able to bring about a permanent improvement in job behavior. This chapter emphasizes the philosophies and techniques of discipline and counseling.

Special Issues: HRIS and HR Problem Solving

The HR department has been transformed by the computer in more ways than were even *imagined* only twenty years ago. A former personnel director—one of the authors—recalls: "The activities that required about 75 percent of our total staff time, such as employee records, payroll, benefits, administration, vacation scheduling, and so on, could be accomplished on a PC today in about 10 percent of the total staff time. What is even more remarkable is that all these functions can be performed far better and with more capabilities than we could have even dreamed about."

Today all the activities just mentioned, and many more, can be accomplished with a human resources information system (HRIS) package, often on a mainframe and increasingly on a personal computer (PC). With the right areawide network and database server, PCs can be configured to handle the HRIS needs of almost all organizations, regardless of size.[10] These common HR computer techniques are discussed in Chapter 16.

Many HR problems—such as absenteeism, turnover, job dissatisfaction, and unfair employee treatment—are costly and slow an organization's productivity rate. Today's administrators must create strategies to resolve these problems. In Chapter 17, we will describe ways in which common problems may be researched and solved.

HR Department Roles

The primary task of the HR department is to ensure that the organization's HR are utilized and managed as effectively as possible. HR administrators help design and implement policies and programs that enhance human abilities and improve the organization's overall effectiveness. Top executives have learned—sometimes the hard way—that inattention to personnel relations and neglect of HR programs are often causes of poor labor–management relations, excessive absenteeism and turnover, lawsuits charging discrimination, and substandard productivity. More and more, leaders of public and private organizations recognize that *people* are the organization's primary resource and acknowledge the HR department's role in developing that resource.

Does the HR Function Affect the Success of an Organization?

Managers, owners, and even college professors sometimes question whether the HR department can really affect the financial success of an organization. Without a doubt, organizations wishing to remain competitive in today's rapidly changing global marketplace need to address the issue of achieving productivity through their employees. The question that is often asked, however, is how important the HR function is in that achievement, given other critical factors such as the leadership provided by top management, product line, market advantage, and research and development.

The importance of the HR function in the organization's efforts to achieve financial success was solidly supported by a 1990 report. The top one hundred rapid-growth companies as identified by *Inc. Magazine* were included in a study of twelve HR practices. The results indicated a strong relationship between HR practices and bottom-line profits. A second finding was that company size, measured by number of employees, did not affect the re-

sults: companies of all sizes were equally affected. The results generally indicated that more successful companies engaged in more HR practices than did less successful companies. Successful rapid-growth companies were generally able to use the HR function to solve problems and achieve success in the following ways:[11]

- Having the HR directors report directly to the president.
- Placing a major company emphasis on employee recruitment, selection, and training.
- Using team building and creating an environment of rapid decision making at lower levels.
- Communicating key company performance objectives through all programs and linking them to goals at all levels.
- Including HR planning as part of management's strategic planning.

Throughout this book, you will find many of these points repeated and discussed in detail. Employers who have successfully integrated the HR function into the top level of management and strategic planning, and who have placed a strong emphasis on employee recruitment, selection, motivation, and team building, can expect greater employee productivity and thus greater overall company success.

To acquire and retain employees, HR administrators perform five critical roles: create and implement policy, maintain communication, offer advice, provide services, and control personnel programs and procedures. Let us examine the multiple roles of the personnel staff more fully.

HR Policies

HR policies are guides to management's thinking, and they help management achieve the organization's HR objectives. Policies also help define acceptable and unacceptable behavior and establish the organization's position on an issue. Top HR officials—the vice-president or the HR department heads—are generally responsible for policy making. In critical HR matters, such as equal employment or management development, the policies may be drafted by an HR committee for approval by the chief executive officer. HR committees generally include members from both line and staff departments. A *line function* is one that is directly related to the achievement of an organization's goals. In a typical manufacturing enterprise, line functions include production and sales. In a university, teaching is a line function and the faculty members are line personnel. *Staff* generally refers to a department that provides specialized services for the entire organization. Staff departments normally include engineering, research and development, purchasing, quality control, legal, finance, and HR. Line managers not only bring experience to the HR committee but are also more likely to support the policies they help create.

To be maximally effective, HR policies should be in writing and should be communicated to all employees. To ensure that employees are familiar with HR policies, many organizations—particularly large firms and government agencies—publish an HR policy manual. Each manager receives a copy of the manual, with instructions to review it in detail with all new employees. Updates of the manual may be posted on bulletin boards, and supervisors may be required to discuss policy revisions with their employees. A well-written and well-used policy manual can be a valuable aid not only in orienting new employees to the workplace but also in settling differences between supervisors and subordinates.

Critical Policy Issues

Most of the critical issues facing HR management are included in four broad areas: employee influence, personnel flow, reward systems, and work systems. Each of these areas must be addressed regardless of the industry, size of the firm, or types of employees in-

volved. By developing critical HR policies with those four areas in mind, decision makers can create HR programs in a unified and systematic manner rather than by accident or by gut reaction to problems and pressures. Such decisions involve choices, and choices are most effectively made through planned policies and practices.[12]

Employee Influence With the increasing popularity of reengineering, total quality management, cooperative labor–management relationships, and other forms of worker participation, more and more organizations are developing policies that define the scope and breadth of employee influence in managing the organization. Such policies specify the degree of authority and responsibility that are delegated to employees and employee groups, and the way in which those relationships (e.g., quality circles vs. self-managed work groups) may most effectively be institutionalized. Policies defining the degree of employee influence deal with such diverse matters as organizational goals, compensation, working conditions, career advancement, and job design.

Personnel Flow Attention must be paid to the task of ensuring that *personnel flow*—the management of people into, through, and out of the organization—meets the organization's long-term requirements for the number and kinds of human resources. Decisions about selection, promotion, job security, career development and advancement, fair treatment, and termination must be made in light of profits, growth, and other critical organizational goals.

Reward Systems The objectives of reward systems include the attraction, motivation, and retention of employees at all organizational levels. The accomplishment of these objectives forces management to consider a number of critical policy issues: Should pay incentives reward individual or group behavior? Should profits or reductions in operating costs be shared by employees? If so, how? Should employees be involved in the design and administration of the pay system? What is the most effective mix of pay and nonpay rewards to motivate performance? Answers to these questions will define a critical aspect of the employee–employer relationship.

Work Systems Work systems are concerned with the design of work: how tasks and technologies are defined and arranged, the quantity and kinds of decisions that people make, and the extent to which quality of work life is an important organizational goal. Policy decisions that affect work systems include the kinds of manufacturing and office technologies implemented and the way in which labor is divided.

Communication

All business organizations depend on communication. Communication is the glue that binds various elements, coordinates activities, allows people to work together, and produces results. It is more important today—given current trends—because companies are larger than ever, and more mergers and acquisitions are on the way. Departments within a company may be spread throughout the country or even throughout the world. Trends in management style—away from the strictly authoritarian and toward the more collaborative —also make communication more important than ever.

Often it is the HR staff who plays a pivotal role in the design and maintenance of good companywide communication flows to and from all employees. HR communication efforts, of course, can occur in a variety of ways. **Downward communication** methods, from management to employees, include orientation sessions, bulletin boards, newsletters, and employee handbooks. **Upward communication** methods usually include suggestion programs, complaint procedures, electronic mail, attitude surveys, and open-door meetings.

- *New Employee Orientation.* Consider the impression made on new employees during their first few days and weeks in a company. The HR staff is usually the first contact employees have when they come on board. First impressions are usually the most important. How HR comes across in terms of defining the employee's role, explaining critical policies, procedures and rules, as well as benefits regarding vacations, health, and so on, can set the tone for encouraging future participation and involvement.

- *Bulletin Boards.* Communications of a general nature, including official notices of policy changes, and personal employee news such as marriages or births may be posted on an employee bulletin board. However, electronic bulletin boards are increasingly replacing traditional boards.

- *Communication Meetings.* Top management can hold open meetings with small groups of employees to answer questions and provide an opportunity for employees to raise questions of interest to them. These regular meetings may also be used to present special issues such as a new health insurance program. If such meetings are held regularly and employees develop a sense that management has a sincere interest in their concerns, they can provide an excellent source of upward communication.

- *Newsletters.* The widespread use of computers and newsletter software programs has made the employee newsletter a popular communication technique. A company may use the company newsletter to explain and promote organizational and industrywide changes; for instance, see Figure 1-2, which shows how one company introduces TQM to its employees. News of a general nature, such as the beginning of a new medical plan or the announcement of employees' civic accomplishments, can be easily and effectively communicated in an informal style. Newsletters are often mailed to retirees, laid-off

FIGURE 1-2 An employee newsletter.

Energizer

A Team Oriented Company Dedicated to Customer Satisfaction

A Publication for Employees & Retirees   July 1991

Total Quality in Everything We Do . . .

Quality. Japan.

Do you realize that these two words are linked through good old American know-how? And that this know-how is now seen as the key to improving quality in American businesses?

It's ironic that American businessmen began looking to Japanese industry in the 1980s to learn a system that was used so successfully by the United States to help defeat Japan in World War II. And it's even more ironic that one of the world's most prestigious awards for quality, which is sponsored by the Japanese government, is named for the American who helped to turn around Japanese industry.

This same system, which has been highly refined over the years, is at the root of LG&E's exploration of Total Quality Management (TQM) that is headed by Craig Pickett, Manager, Quality Assurance. But before he discusses the new effort, Craig likes to go into the background on the subject.

In the late 1940s, cheap and shoddy imports had turned the label "Made in Japan" into a synonym for "junk." There were jokes that Japanese toys, appliances and even cars were made out of old beer cans. It was the height of sarcasm to call the Japanese the "perfectionists of the Orient."

Japanese leaders recognized the problem and hired American quality expert W. Edwards Deming to help them. His principles had been used by the U.S. government and American arms manufacturers during World War II. Today, thanks in part to the system that Dr. Deming set up, Japanese cameras, cars, appliances, electronic devices and other products are among the best in the world.

To encourage quality in manufacturing, the Japanese established the Deming Prize in 1951. Competition for the prize was limited to Japanese companies until 1985, when it was opened to companies from other nations. Four years later, Florida Power and Light became the first "foreign" company to win the Deming Prize.

In the 1980s, the United States established its own award for

quality—the Malcolm Baldridge National Quality Award. This honor has been bestowed on Federal Express, Xerox, Motorola and parts of IBM, as well as on smaller companies.

As might be expected, the search for quality has created a whole new area of business, which is complete with its own experts (including Deming, who's still active), consultants, training programs, management models, computer software, magazines, newsletters and conventions. All this activity, Craig says, is aimed at achieving one basic goal, which can be summed up in this definition.

"Quality—meeting or exceeding customer requirements [at the lowest cost]."

Total Quality Management (TQM), he explains, can be defined as "the system that produces continuous improvement, while focusing on meeting or exceeding customer requirements [at the lowest cost]."

Craig refines these definitions in three ways.

continued on page 2

employees, and others who normally would not be up-to-date on company and employee events.

- *Employee Handbooks.* A well-written, up-to-date handbook can address important policies, procedures, and rules that apply to employees, such as wage and benefits information, general personnel policies concerning vacation, sick leave, insurance, and so on. In addition, the company's history and philosophy are usually included.

- *Suggestion Programs.* The suggestion box has existed in the American workplace for nearly a century. However, for most of that time, it has been considered a joke. Workers viewed it with skepticism and, sad to say, management's interest was not always genuine. Of course, it probably didn't matter anyway. Until the tumultuous 1980s, employees were often conditioned to let management do all of the thinking and problem solving; workers were not expected to think independently or creatively. Today these are the very qualities that are crucial to a company's success in a globally competitive environment.

The suggestion box can work, as many organizations are learning. Over 1000 companies comprise the National Association of Suggestion Systems, which claims that its member organizations saved $2.3 billion in 1991 alone. The association recorded that 328,000 employee ideas were implemented, which doubles the savings over 1985.[13] Why the increase in employee suggestions?

Certainly, incentives for particularly good suggestions are more generous today than they were decades ago. Kodak's George Eastman, for example, awarded a $20 prize in 1898—the first time an award was given. Perhaps the most widely publicized award, however, was that of A. P. Giannini, Bank of America's founder, who in 1928 gave his chauffeur a Scrooge-like $1 bonus for proposing the concept of traveler's checks. If employees submitted a good idea back then, it was generally not for money but for recognition.

Today companies are more generous. IBM, Lilly, and AT&T, for example, give back to employees a percentage of the savings. An IBM employee, Jesse Corbett, received $150,000 for designing a new tool that ended up saving $1.4 million in the first year alone.

- *Complaint Procedures.* A critical communication need is to provide employees with a comfortable and effective means for bringing problems or complaints to management. Organizations are becoming more sensitive to employees' complaints about supervisors, jobs, and organizations. A few organizations have developed **whistle-blowing** procedures for addressing illegal or unethical acts before they reach the point where outside investigators are brought in. To encourage more employees to speak up without fearing retribution from their supervisors or management, many organizations are adopting systems that protect the individual's identity. One popular system involves appointing an ombudsman, who investigates reported complaints.

In addition, most companies have implemented formal grievance procedures. The first step is usually to present the problem to the immediate supervisor. If the problem concerns the supervisor or the employee is not satisfied with the first step, the second step is usually to approach the supervisor's superior. The HR department is often a third party available to the employee. Union-negotiated grievance procedures almost always include the use of outside arbitrator as a fourth and final step, a practice being increasingly used by nonunion employers.

- *Electronic Mail.* Almost unheard of a decade ago, electronic mail is quickly becoming the method of choice for rapid, informal, and accessible intercompany communication. Access to a computer terminal connected to a larger mainframe is the usual requirement, but with personal computers becoming more powerful, the need for a mainframe is rare. Employees can be linked together either through a local electronic mail system or connected to outside systems such as Internet or Bitnet for communicating over great distances. A local system, such as IBM's Professional Office System (PROFS) or its competitive equivalent, gives each user instant ability to (1) send notes and messages to other users, (2) perform electronic calendaring and meeting scheduling, and (3) create and process documents and a variety of other PC functions. Global PC networks are emerging that enable people to "connect" and work in teams (see Chapter 5) over vast distances.

- *Surveys.* The employee survey is the most widely used research technique among HR professionals. The most common surveys include the wage survey and the job satisfaction survey. The job satisfaction survey is often referred to as an *attitude* or *morale* survey. It may either be developed internally or prepared by an outside consulting firm. Survey results communicate information upward, telling management how employees view their jobs, work conditions, management and supervision, and so on.

- *Open-door Meetings.* A popular management practice and an excellent upward communication technique is the open-door policy. Usually at a specified time each week or month, a manager's door is open to any employee who has a suggestion, question, or complaint. If over time the manager makes employees feel comfortable using this process and each action receives a follow-up investigation (often by the HR office), this technique can effectively open lines of communication between employees and management.

Advice and Services

Over the past several decades, management has become increasingly complex. A restrictive legal environment, sophisticated technologies, a restive labor force, and demands by various societal groups for more socially responsible activities are a few of the pressures felt by managers. To cope with complex issues, managers often turn to staff experts for advice and counsel. Some questions that personnel staff members may be asked to answer include the following:

- How do I deal with an employee who I suspect is on drugs?

- How do I meet my equal employment goals without raising cries of "reverse discrimination"?

- How do I tell a high-achieving employee that the budget will not allow a merit increase this year?

- How do I counsel a manager who is suffering a midcareer crisis?

- How do I deal with an employee who has been with the company for twenty-five years but now can no longer perform effectively?

- How can I increase employee morale?

In theory, advice from the HR staff may be accepted or rejected. Line managers who think the advice is not sound have the prerogative to disregard it. Of course, the rejection of staff advice will be inversely proportional to the confidence a manager has in staff experts. Thus, all staff members have an obligation to ensure that their advice is sound, objective, and fair and will contribute to the goals of the organization.

An unexpected problem can occur in an organization when line managers rely heavily on the advice of HR specialists and transfer the major responsibility for dealing with people issues from themselves to the HR department. This is counterproductive because everyday people problems should generally be solved by the organization's supervisors. It is, in fact, a critical aspect of their job. A survey of supervisors at Roy Rogers, a division of Marriott Corporation, indicated the supervisors believed that almost 60 percent of unwanted turnover by managers who reported to them was caused by factors beyond their control. Yet they believed that the HR department was almost three times more responsible for the causes of the turnover. They cited human resources as responsible for recruiting, training, and locating employees—all frequent causes of turnover. One supervisor even held the HR function responsible for his own poor supervision practices: "Human resources doesn't train us to manage properly!"[14]

Of course, supervisors who are generally responsible for many decisions affecting their employees should be the first to identify unmet needs or problems and, perhaps with assistance from the HR department, find a solution. The daily involvement with employees must be the responsibility of line managers, yet the HR department should be able to give them advice and assistance in meeting the needs of their employees.

Control Functions

Like the quality control department in many manufacturing concerns, the HR department performs important control functions for the management of human resources. For example, a written policy on equal employment opportunity is ineffectual unless executives are aware of the policy and adhere to it. HR administrators are responsible for monitoring personnel goals and guidelines to ensure their achievement. Common control activities include the following:

- Collection and analysis of hiring, selection, placement, and promotion data to ensure that equal employment opportunity laws and policies are being observed.

- Analysis of performance appraisal records to determine if appraisals are being conducted in an unbiased manner.

- Analysis of statistics on absenteeism, grievances, and accidents to determine where problems are most critical and what may be done to reduce them.

Because of the nature of these activities, HR staff members generally possess the authority necessary to carry out control functions. In theory, line managers and other leaders must cooperate with those HR officials, but the latter must ensure that decision makers fully understand all HR policies, procedures, and standards so that resentment and conflict are not created when control activities are performed. Further, HR administrators should be tactful when putting pressure on managers to conform to guidelines. Harmonious relationships between the HR department and other organizational units will ensure compliance with guidelines, with a minimum of stress to the organization.

STRUCTURE OF THE HUMAN RESOURCE DEPARTMENT

The HR department normally contains clerical (support), professional, and managerial jobs. Clerical employees include clerks, typists, receptionists, and lower-level administrative assistants. Professional employees are specialists in fields such as counseling, benefits, employee development, employee testing, and labor relations. They often possess college degrees in business administration and may have concentrated their studies in HR. Lower-level employees are occasionally promoted to professional positions and are given both on- and off-the-job training for their new roles. The managers oversee the clerical and professional employees and coordinate the organization's personnel activities. Top HR managers formulate personnel policies and create important personnel programs.

The HR department in medium-sized to large companies contains individual work groups organized by function. An HR manager heads each group, providing leadership to the professional and clerical employees. The HR department may be headed by a vice-president of human resources who reports to the president. An example of the HR structure for a medium-sized or large organization is shown in Figure 1-3.

Large corporations generally have divisions in many states and foreign countries. Each division is usually run independently as a decen-

tralized profit center. Division managers have their own staff services, such as engineering, accounting, finance, legal, and HR. The corporate HR staff, however, generally creates major HR policies and programs for recruiting, management development, equal employment opportunity, and wages and salaries. Divisional HR managers put the policies into operation so that there is consistency across all divisions. Each HR manager has some flexibility in his or her division's program.[15] No doubt, the average day in the HR profession is never dull, as Madelyn Jennings found out (see *HR in the News:* "A Day in the Life of an HR Professional").

FIGURE 1-3 Organizational structure of an HR department. Abbreviations: AA, Affirmative Action; EAP, Employee Assistance Program; HRIS, human resource information system; OSHA, Occupational Safety and Health Administration.

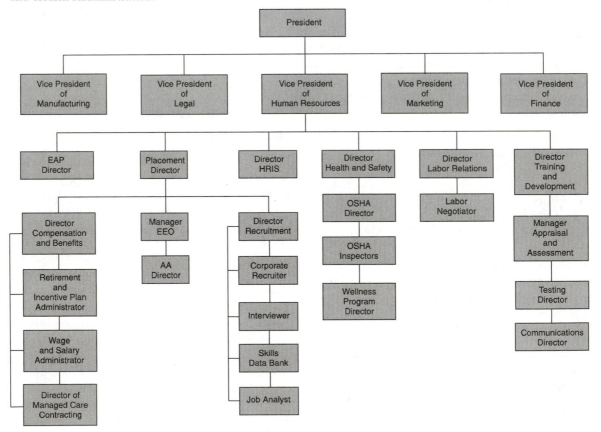

A Day in the Life of an HR Professional

Madelyn Jennings, Senior Vice-President of Personnel at Gannett Company, the publishing giant, says: "One moment I'm dealing with a major overhaul of the medical plan or a discussion of whether this person is the right person to go into a job, and the next moment I'm having a telephone conversation with a manager who doesn't have the budget to pay the clerks or reporters who can't use their computers because of wrist problems." Jennings received the 1990 Society for Human Resource Management Award of Professional Excellence. What is she most proud of? "Helping create a culture where when we say we have an open-door policy, we really do; where many new recognition programs have been developed to enhance morale; where your sex or color means little—it's our results that are what count.

SOURCE: "Madelyn Jennings Wins Excellence Award." *HR News* (July 15, 1990): 12.

Responsibilities for HR Functions

The responsibility for performing the HR function does not reside only in the HR department; all managers at all levels of the organization share in that responsibility. For example, the branch manager of a bank will normally interview job applicants, orient new employees, train and develop new and current employees, evaluate employee performance, and so on. In most organizations, particularly larger ones, the HR staff designs HR policies and procedures and the operating managers implement them. On occasion, line managers help design HR policies and HR staffers help implement them. But the primary responsibility for implementation of HR policies and procedures rests with those who are responsible for day-to-day supervision of subordinates.

CURRENT ISSUES AND CHALLENGES

It is generally accepted that the quality of an organization's human resources represents a critical factor. One HR challenge is how to attract, retain, motivate, and develop individuals with talent. And, if that isn't enough of a challenge, consider the impact a turbulent business environment presents, the difficulty of managing a diverse work force, and the ever-changing legal climate and government regulations. The external environment presents, at times, a bewildering array of challenges. What are these external challenges, and how have companies responded?

Worker Productivity

The U.S. dominance in the international economy began to deteriorate markedly in the late 1970s, reflecting the increasing lack of competitiveness of many U.S. companies. The economic weakness was particularly evident in heavy manufacturing, such as steel, which was almost eliminated. Free trade and globalization placed many firms in fiercely competitive markets, where factors such as world-class quality, flexible manufacturing, and shortened product life cycles are prerequisites for survival. Rigorous quality standards, such as **ISO**

23

HR IN THE NEWS

Western Europe: Changing the World's Standards

Founded in the aftermath of World War II, the International Organization for Standardization (ISO), Geneva, Switzerland, has evolved into the decision making body for international standards. **ISO 9000** is a series of approved standards relating to a purchaser/supplier contractual relationship. The standards seek to harmonize the quality process in both product oriented companies as well as service oriented companies. The key is the emphasis on "process" not on "product." Companies seeking compliance must successfully complete a rigorous external audit. A third party auditor must be used to conduct official assessments. Once a company has been certified as being in compliance, it may use the quality stamp on all literature but not on the actual product. The Human Resource function is typically the unit responsible for monitoring ISO 9000 standards.

Membership is growing rapidly with over 90 nations already participating. Currently, all EC countries subscribe to ISO. And 51 member nations have adopted the ISO 9000 quality standards as their own national standards—including the U.S. Any American company that expects to compete on quality had best be prepared to meet more rigid world standards.

9000, are catching on throughout the industrialized world (see *HR in the News*: "Western Europe: Changing the World's Standards") as the standard of factory quality performance.

Can American workers deliver the kind of quality world-class organizations promise? Not long ago, a member of the old-guard Japanese political establishment made a critical comment regarding the American worker that inflamed the American public. He said that American workers were lazy and illiterate. Another Japanese politician added that American workers were too carefree and casual in their approach to work and therefore not suited to produce products that require meticulous workmanship.[16] Could these statements be true? Is American productivity in a state of decline?

Actually, the statistics tell quite another story. No doubt, Japan, Germany, and many other countries are constantly challenging the United States for economic preeminence. And, at least for the moment, American workers are performing impressively. Their productivity, the industrial world's highest, is growing faster than Germany's and as fast as Japan's. Even in the automotive industry, Japan's most visible symbol of success, American workers are producing at roughly the same pace.

As to the issue of laziness, again the statistics tell a different story.[17] In reality, Ameri-

24

cans work longer hours (average, 1890 per year) than ever, second in the industrial world to Japan (average, 2173 hours per year). The Germans, for example, work on the average only 1668 hours per year and take an average of 30 paid vacation days. Americans, on the average, take only 12 vacation days per year. While the Japanese get slightly more vacation days (15.5), they actually take only 8.2 days and work the remainder.

The American response to unprecedented competition, often from overseas, is heartening. Companies are turning themselves inside out to stay competitive. One radical step many have taken is calling on all the workers' abilities and genuinely democratizing the workplace to do so. Companies are abandoning management practices that have often let alienation replace motivation in the workplace. The Taylorism that was successful in companies sixty years ago no longer works. Hierarchical systems designed to command and control workers, which divided work into small, easily supervised tasks, is becoming obsolete—except in government. Companies are cracking down on excessive absenteeism, high defect rates, and idleness on the job by picking, training, and rewarding subordinates differently.[18]

HR professionals are often leading the workplace revolution. Their goal is get everyone thinking constantly about how the job they know best could be done better. Employees like Urban Bianchi (see *HR in the News:* "Shake the Dust Off the Suggestion Box") care about quality and constantly strive to improve the process. By giving them more autonomy and responsibility, management is attempting to enlist their pride, judgment, and creativity.

Other approaches are used as well. Self-managed teams are being implemented. Typically, a team replaces the supervisor by controlling everything from scheduling to hiring and sometimes firing. Building flexible teams is what empowerment is all about.

While HR professionals will play an important role, line managers will be expected to spend more time on HR issues. That will create yet another challenge: how to train and develop the great mass of operating and general managers to assume HR responsibilities.

Quality Improvement

American workers fully recognize the importance of quality in the workplace. Although it may have been the Japanese who shocked U.S. companies out of their complacency, the quality focus today is less of an "us versus them" mentality and more of a new philosophy: excellence should be the norm, not the exception.

Improved quality means survival.[19] As trade barriers come down, worldwide competition will intensify. Only companies with the best quality will thrive—and not because of quality alone. Two by-products of making or doing things better are almost always lower costs and higher productivity. Quality means conforming to customer requirements, preventing errors and accidents, and striving toward error-free output.

A quality orientation signals an important change in corporate culture. It involves more than a technical function or department. It is an operating system that extends throughout the organization. In the past, quality efforts suffered from a lack of top management commitment. Quality circles, for example, were the rage a decade ago, but faded into the sunset because top management generally failed to empower employees to fully implement them.[20]

Getting employees to support quality efforts can be a major challenge. Too many workers and managers dismiss quality efforts as inappropriate to their tasks until they are convinced that such efforts produce important results. Eastman Kodak's scientists resisted until studies proved that they were spending less

Shake the Dust Off the Suggestion Box: Employees' Ideas Save Billions

Urban Bianchi is the undisputed king of the suggestion box. His output is unparalleled. In ten years with Parker Hannifin Corporation's aerospace plants, Bianchi has proposed more than 800 cost-cutting suggestions. And, incredible as it seems, most have been accepted by his bosses.

A machinist who works as a supervisor in quality control, Bianchi's unending stream of written suggestions, often accompanied by detailed diagrams, have been known to drive company engineers batty. He has been called a nit picker. More often he has been called a gem—particularly in an economy in which companies are desperate to cut costs.

Bianchi is prized not simply for his ideas, which tend to be unspectacular, nuts-and-bolts notions that save the company a few hundred dollars at a time. He is also cherished for his bulldog attitude.

"Look here." He held up a small, thin piece of metal with six identical holes. It was part of a new idea he was submitting: a fixture to hold six gear levers so that the levers could be computer-inspected simultaneously rather than one at a time.

"The fixture'll cost twenty dollars to make. In the long run, it'll save 'em six, seven thousand dollars a year" in employee inspection time, he said. "I'm just making my job easier. I'm making the machine do the work."

While many companies offer cash incentives, Bianchi has instead been rewarded with microwave ovens, bicycles, ice chests, food processors, house tools, and portable phones, plus scores of free-dinner coupons—$17,000 worth in the last four years alone.

He believes it is more than enough. "If the company can't save money, the company can't stay in business," he said. "I've got to save money."

SOURCE: Adapted from Bob Baker, "Employee Suggestions Take on Weight in Lean Times," *Los Angeles Times* September 15, 1991: A 1.

---

than one-quarter of each day in the lab and the rest of the time on trivial organizational activities such as going to staff meetings, writing reports, and ordering supplies.[21]

Many U.S. companies are meeting the quality challenge by implementing long-term programs. Florida Power and Light Company began a small-scale quality improvement program in 1981. In 1990, this company became the first non-Japanese company to win the prestigious Deming Prize for quality (i.e., Japan's highest award for quality).[22]

In the United States over the past few years, quality training programs have begun to be actively encouraged by government and by industry associations. In 1987, the U.S. Congress established the Malcolm Baldridge National Quality Award. The award recognizes the excellence of a company's total quality management processes and results. Past winners of the "Baldy Award" include Westinghouse's Commercial Nuclear Fuel Division, Federal Express Corporation, Cadillac, Xerox, and Motorola.

Critical success factors in quality improvement are education and training, teamwork, employee involvement, and so on. These factors are listed in Figure 1-4. The common thread evident in all successful programs, however, is a strong companywide commitment involving all levels of management and labor in all departments and functions.

Downsizing, Delayering, and Decruiting

No matter what you call it, as corporations trim costs and the nation shifts from a manufacturing economy to a service economy, companies are laying off employees at a pace reminiscent of that of the Great Depression (see Table 1-2). Among them are such giants as IBM, Kodak, and Procter and Gamble, whose former guarantees of job security are only memories. These massive layoffs are not happening in the United States alone; more than half of Europe's largest corporations plan to cut their work forces as global competition and high wages take their toll.[23]

Companies cite many reasons for cutting payrolls: plant and store closings, cost-cutting measures, restructuring, slowdowns in military and commercial aircraft programs, and acquisitions.[24] And it isn't just low- or unskilled workers who are being let go. Layoffs are happening just as often to people once thought to have very marketable skills.

FIGURE 1-4 Key characteristics of successful quality improvement programs

Education and training (problem solving, technical improvement including hands-on training, case studies, role playing)

Teamwork (especially across functional areas)

Total systems approach

Employee involvement (at all levels of the organization)

Top management commitment and encouragement

Establishment of customer-driven standards

Long-term perspective

Allocation of resources to the program

If this trend isn't depressing enough, consider what some experts are predicting. Doomsayers are convinced that companies will continue to let people go because, unlike earlier downsizing periods in which employers simply wanted to cut costs until business picked up, today an operation that does not create value is permanently squeezed out.[25] The methods being used are total quality management and process reengineering efforts. The goal is clear

Table 1-2 Downsizing—An Industry Ranking (As of July 1993)

Industry	Total Layoffs Announced
Aerospace	86,890
Computers	86,257
Retailing	62,090
Consumer products	23,504
Transportation	12,073
Communications	10,329
Utilities	10,266
Insurance and real estate	10,009
Food	8,349
Pharmaceuticals	6,322
Health care	6,285

SOURCE: Challenger, Gram and Christmas, Inc. (Chicago, 1993).

and unambiguous: continuous improvement is needed to prepare for global competition.

It is understandable why so many workers, both employed and unemployed, are less loyal today. Many feel hurt, and far too many have a sense of betrayal by their employers. However, despite these anxieties about their employers, workers continue to express high commitment to their jobs. The typical American worker takes pride in and personal responsibility for his or her work.

The Changing Work Force

The demographics of North American workers are creating a new, diverse, changing work force. There are more single parents, working couples, women, and minorities. In fact, the Bureau of Labor Statistics estimates that by the year 2000, the only group that will be smaller is the white male group. Only 10 percent of new American workers will be a white male (compared to 45 percent in 1985).[26]

How does such a diverse population view work, management, and the future? And what are companies doing to meet the changing demographics and the growing emphasis on worker competitiveness?

The Families and Work Institute surveyed a national sample of employed individuals (approximately 3000 people) and sought their opinions about work, bosses, and organizational efforts to address employees' concerns. Their results depict a U.S. work force that has little loyalty to the company, is concerned about issues of race and gender, and perceives a growing conflict between work and family life.[27] The study also suggests that the typical American workers' definition of success is the personal satisfaction that comes from doing a good job, independent of any feeling of loyalty to the employer.

As to the issue of loyalty, there is clearly a trend toward workers being less loyal to employers than in the past. The results are understandable, considering that 42 percent of those surveyed had already experienced corporate restructuring, downsizing, or unacceptable job relocations.[28] Even more discouraging, 20 percent of the sample perceived they were currently extremely vulnerable to being fired. However, while overall trends are discouraging, there remain a few places where job loyalty is strong (see *HR in the News*: "Is Job Loyalty a Thing of the Past?").

Another constant challenge is work force diversity. While laws are in place and gains are being made, progress across ethnic groups is still slower than it ought to be. There is evidence that today's workers are no better equipped to cope with a more diverse workplace than were their parents. Over half of the Families and Work Institute sample, for example, said they prefer working with people of the same race, sex, gender, and level of education.[29] There is one positive note: the survey suggests that once people acquired experience living or working with diverse groups, they showed a stronger preference for diversity in the workplace.

Gender discrimination continues to occur. Although progress is being made, there still exists a "glass ceiling" for women who aspire to top management. Although many more women are working today than in the past, women managers perceive their career opportunities as far fewer than those of their male colleagues. But society may have turned at least one corner regarding gender. Workers' preference for male managers is declining.[30] The typical male employee, for example, is just as comfortable working for a female manager as for a male manager, and vice versa.

Another work force change is that more men spend time at home. One survey of male managers indicated that they were not as willing to work long hours as they were in 1987.[31] The primary reason: a desire to spend more time with their families. However, few compa-

Is Job Loyalty a Thing of the Past?

Not at Motorola and Xerox. The significance of the individual employee to building a "total quality" culture is communicated by the company's perspective on job security. Employees who establish a ten-year record of successful performance become "Service Club" members. Membership virtually guarantees future job security. According to Motorola, job security and the freedom it affords employees contribute to a culture that supports innovation, flexibility, and acceptance of change—important elements in achieving a commitment to total quality.

SOURCE: Richard Blackburn and Benson Rosen, "Total Quality and Human Resources Management: Lessons Learned from Baldridge Award-Winning Companies," *Academy of Management Executive*, Vol. 7 No. 3 1993: 50–51.

---

nies encourage workers to seek flexible schedules or family leave.

With more single parents, dual-career couples, and a growing population of elders, balancing the demands of home and work has become the *great challenge* of the typical American worker and his or her employer. When there is conflict between work and family, the family is three times more likely to suffer than the employee's job performance.[32] But how productive can an employee really be when there is a sick child at home with a sitter, or when an aged parent is hospitalized and long-term care is needed, or when a spouse is told of an impending job transfer to a remote location?

Companies need to become more family friendly, although a few already are. Companies such as Johnson & Johnson, U.S. West, and AT&T are discovering that family-friendly work environments more than pay for themselves. Each of these companies has discovered that "workplace flexibility is not an accommodation to employees but a competitive weapon."[33] Absenteeism is reduced, turnover is cut, efficiency is improved, and the bottom line is more attractive.

Although family-friendly programs are addressed later in this book, they generally include information and counseling services, time off and flexible schedules, and financial assistance, usually in the form of dependent-care support.

Middle managers are the people most responsible for implementing family policies and rules. Unfortunately, most managers still resist efforts to make the workplace more family friendly. These traditionalists continue to rely on **face time**—the number of hours spent under the watchful eyes of the boss—as their primary method for getting results.

Perhaps the biggest challenge is persuading managers not to penalize employees—many of them single parents—who miss work because they have to tend to sick children. There is also some resentment among childless workers, many of whom feel exploited because they perceive themselves losing out in benefit

Diverse by Design

Levi's is recognized as among the most ethnically and culturally diverse companies in the U.S., if not the world. At the end of 1991, 56% of its 23,000 U.S. employees belonged to minority groups. Its top management level was 14% non-white and 30% female. Since the mid-1980s, the company has worked to eliminate a "glass ceiling" that prevented some qualified minorities and women from reaching the company's top ranks.

As the economy rebounds and the job market improves, workers are bolder about bringing up issues of fairness and flexibility. Where previous generations grappled with labor-management battles and such basics as safety on the job, today's wars rage around diversity, opportunity, and attitudes.

The company's diverse educational programs are designed to get employees thinking about how to become more tolerant of personal differences, and, ultimately, how to see the importance of them.

Taking the moral high road does have its price, however. Costly and time-consuming disagreements abound in a company where everyone's ideas are encouraged. Some managers feel uncomfortable with the wide-open organization. "Lots of key managers got there by command and control," says Sue Thompson, director of human resource development. "Some see [that] the direction we are going is not for them."

SOURCE: Adapted from *Business Week/Reinventing America,* Special Issue 1992, p. 72.

---

packages that favor families with children. Childless workers complain that they are automatically given the most time-consuming assignments, or targeted to go out of town or work weekends. And while maternity leave has become a standard benefit, personal leave for serious matters unrelated to having children is much harder to win.

Experts are in agreement on one thing: any solution that addresses both productivity goals and help in family situations must involve work flexibility. For example, telecommuting, job sharing, and time compression (working four-day, forty-hour weeks) make a lot of sense for people with families, as well as for increasing numbers of employees without them.

Given the long-term outlook on layoffs and decline in company loyalty, it would appear that companies are not as concerned about changing demographics and workers' personal needs as perhaps they should be. However, evidence is beginning to show that companies are getting better productivity and good results not by ignoring work force diversity and workers' personal needs but rather by specifically addressing them (see *HR in the News:* "Diverse by Design").

Global Economy

The changing **global economy** is placing new and increasing demands on the human resources in companies. This marketplace is marked by increased competition worldwide: a new European economy, expanding Asian markets, a reformed Russia and a reformed Central Europe, a developing South America, and a capital-rich Japan. The new global economies have brought competitive changes unequaled in U.S. history.

Because the perceived quality of U.S. goods has declined in many foreign markets, simply exporting goods made in the United States is no longer enough to make American firms competitive in the global economy. They must match foreign competition if they are to take advantage of the opportunities presented by new markets in Asia, Latin America, and Europe. As foreign investors determine where to build new international operations, workers in the United States are continually measured against those of other nations, not only in terms of the products and services they produce, but also in terms of their skills and motivation. Globalization brings new opportunities, such as joint ventures, but it also puts increasing pressure on U.S. workers and management to meet the challenge presented by foreign competition. New trading agreements and national partnerships will have great impact on the U.S. economy. The 1992 unification of the European market, the U.S.–Canada Trade Agreement, the North American Free Trade Agreement, and China's takeover of Hong Kong in 1997 are examples of dynamic shifts in world markets that will create shifts of capital and work force.[34]

The Impact of Government
The HR profession has felt the great impact of government policies and programs. Beginning in the 1960s, with major antidiscrimination laws including the Civil Rights Act (1964), the Equal Pay Act (1963), and the Age Discrimination Act (1967), the federal government and many state governments became involved in setting HR policy through legislation. That expansion has continued with the Occupational Safety and Health Act (1970), the Americans with Disabilities Act (1990), and the Family and Medical Leave Act (1993), just to list the major ones! U.S. Senator Orrin G. Hatch (Republican, Utah) believes the future will bring even more regulations for HR professionals since Congress has "an ever increasing desire to have more and more federal government control over business." Issues that will likely be the subject of new federal laws include employment at will, parental leave, child-care availability, health-care insurance, and additional opportunities.[35]

Quality of Working Life
Sociologists have spoken of the quality of life. Behavioral scientists have also begun using a related term, *quality of working life (QWL).* This term refers to the extent to which employees' personal needs are met through their work. One's QWL improves as one's work meets more and more personal needs, such as security, responsibility, and self-esteem.[36] Making work more rewarding, reducing employees' anxieties, encouraging more participation in decisions relating to work and employment, and team building are examples of QWL approaches.

Increasing numbers of organizations are providing a good QWL for employees, for example through family-friendly programs, in order to take advantage of a demographically diverse society. It may also make employees more loyal to their employers, helping to reverse the trend discussed earlier.

There are strong indications that improvements in QWL favorably affect organizational performance and enable companies to compete in a global environment. The Japanese, for example, are ardent supporters of QWL and design work around teams and a strong company culture. The result is not only high productivity but lower absenteeism and turnover.

While most American companies are following the Japanese lead, some are branching out

Office Stiffs Told to Let Loose, Lighten Up

Ask most people about their jobs and you'll probably find that work is not high on their list of fun things to do. Making the experience a little less miserable has become a priority for top managers in many fields. And what they're finding is that lightening up is an effective way to boost morale and worker productivity.

The theory is simple. Laughter makes people happy. Happy employees work harder, get to work earlier and don't call in sick as often as unhappy employees.

Workers at Boca Raton First National Bank are encouraged to "dress down" on Fridays and "dress up" on major holidays. Staff members at *Boca Raton Magazine* relieve stress by starting water gun fights or playing with the company intercom. And one manager in a cable company will occasionally slip into different voices, earning him the honor of being designated the "Robin Williams" of the office.

If it's true that about 85 percent of the population gets up every morning and goes to a job they hate, then some silliness at work is a good thing. Laughter not only helps employees feel better about work, it has physical benefits as well. When a person laughs, the brain releases endorphins, chemicals that reduce pain and relieve depression. And, if it's true that one can be silly and still do a good job, then it appears that it's not only OK to laugh but necessary.

SOURCE: *Sunday World-Herald,* Omaha, Nebraska, September 26, 1993:G1

---

into new QWL territory. A few companies are even rearranging offices and using decor that encourages employees to let loose, have fun, and approach work creatively. They believe that office design reflects management style the same way that fashion style can be a statement of personality. Individual personalities are allowed to emerge and are given precedence over traditional job and office configurations (see *HR in the News:* "Office Stiffs Told to Let Loose, Lighten Up"). Instead of working elbow to elbow at desks arranged in military rows, with minimal fraternizing between management and the lower ranks and an atmosphere best described as rigid, staid, and uninspired, QWL advocates adhere to the notion that office design should inspire creativity.

Another facet of QWL is having fun at what you are doing. Watch children at play and you notice their endless energy, joy derived from simple pleasures, and simple youthful feeling of fun. Many adults feel very serious about their work, which is to be expected. However, the youthful joy of having fun in what you are doing can help employees to be mentally healthier, more alert, and more creative. It also may increase their motivation to work and thus their productivity. Almost anything can be fun. In a survey of workers, for example, a few even reported that giving a performance appraisal can be fun. Fun at work depends on three elements: people's personal intentions, the organizational culture, and the behavior of top management. The communications from top management are most critical. Gary Rogers, chief executive officer of Dreyer's Grand Ice Cream, has three company goals: quality, profits, and having fun. Rogers reminds us that "everyone only goes around the track once in life, and if you don't enjoy the trip, its pretty pathetic."[37]

What are some practical examples of adding fun to the workplace? Here are a few.[38]

1. *Bulletin board.* Install a bulletin board near the coffee pot and encourage people to post their best jokes, with prizes going to monthly winners.

2. *Theme days.* On specific holidays, employees can dress according to a theme and have a pot-luck lunch. Award best-costume certificates at the lunch.

3. *Fun committee.* Establish a volunteer fun committee to plan programs; provide a small annual budget.

4. *Company roast.* As an alternative to the traditional holiday dinner, have a company roast, with those roasted selected by employees.

5. *Baby picture contest.* On the bulletin board or in the employee newsletter, conduct a "name this baby" contest with a prize for the winner.

6. *Calling cards.* Print "You Made My Day: Thank You!" cards and make them available for employees to pass on to others who add fun to their day.

7. *Birthday celebrations.* Allow small working groups to take their members to lunch on their birthdays.

8. *Celebrate achievements.* When goals, such as completing a project on time, are achieved, throw an afternoon party and say "thank you" to all who helped.

9. *Recognize personal achievements.* Include articles in employee newsletters or send special memos recognizing an employee's son who is quarterback of the high school team, an employee who finishes a triathalon, or an employee's fifth wedding anniversary.

10. *Encourage humor.* Managers can encourage humor by creating a relaxed atmosphere. Practical jokes, goofing off, or cartoons that downgrade the workplace are not needed to have fun.

Creating a work environment that minimizes the likelihood of an accident or injury has long been a goal of QWL programs. In the modern workplace, a number of safety and health issues have proved difficult to resolve in both manufacturing and service industries.

First, many employers have established wellness programs or simply provide employees critical health-care checkups, such as cholesterol and blood pressure checks, and weight and nutrition education. Employees who participate in such programs are more likely to be healthier and happier and to lower employer-provided health-care costs.

Second, there is evidence that some work environments are responsible for cancer, infertility, lung disease, and other illnesses.[39] Unlike an accident or injury, occupational diseases are difficult to detect, and often they remain undetected until it is too late for a remedy. More and more often the workplace is being labeled as hazardous to one's long-term health.

Third, job stress can be just as hazardous as an unsafe workplace. Unlike accidents and injuries—which are of most concern in the construction, manufacturing, mining, and transportation industries—job stress can be a problem in any kind of firm in any job, whether it be blue-collar, clerical, managerial, or professional. Extreme stress can lead to ulcers, heart failure, nervous conditions, and other physiological or psychological impairments.[40] The potential impact of stress on job performance is obvious. Managers are now beginning to recognize potential personal and organizational job stress dangers and are seeking ways to recognize and reduce the problem.

Technology and Training

An organization's **technology**—the methods and techniques used to produce goods and services—profoundly affects the skills and abilities that an organization's employees must possess. Until recently, however, technology has done little to affect how people worked together. But that is changing. A new area of computer software technology has emerged to address the issues of working together and to support lateral communication and collaboration. This software is called **Groupware** (for more information, see chapter 5).

Technology has dramatically increased the skills and **training** necessary to perform many of the jobs in today's organizations. At the same time, employers are faced with fewer workers entering the labor market and an increase in underprepared workers. Thus, skilled workers who are able to fill high-technology jobs are increasingly in short supply. The answer, of course, is an increase in worker reeducation and training programs. A common problem, however, is that skills that are taught through training programs in one industry are specialty skills: training programs often teach workers narrow job skills and not broad basic skills that are transferable to other jobs. However, this situation is the result of increasing technology, which requires more job-specific skills. Employers are therefore providing both broad basic-skills education programs and job-specific technology training.

HR Career Opportunities

Students often ask: what are the best strategies for entering HR careers? Can someone with no HR work experience enter the profession?

What are the most important skills HR people need in order to succeed? Serious students are asking these questions much earlier in their educations, and wisely so, given the increasingly tighter prospects for meaningful employment.

Despite the gloomy job projections for employment overall, the future still holds numerous opportunities for students who seek careers in HR management. However, it will demand diligent preparation.

HR professionals consider academic preparation a necessity. Years ago, this was not always the case. HR staff members were often selected largely because of their personalities; those with people-oriented traits were preferred. Certainly, liking people is important, but it does little to describe the skills and knowledge of the modern HR professional.

The future HR professional will almost certainly be expected to hold a college degree. A recent survey of HR managers concluded that the most preferred academic background was business administration, followed by the social sciences (communication and psychology), humanities (art, English, history), education, and science.[41] As to whether it is better to pursue a master's degree (without experience), the evidence seems to suggest that it depends on the position being sought. If the HR job opening requires detailed technical knowledge or skills that a particular graduate degree can provide, such as a master's degree in compensation systems, then probably it would be an advantage.

Useful HR-related academic courses include organizational behavior and change, training and development, employee selection, labor–management relations, and compensation. While successful academic work is a big plus, recruiters also look for applicants who can demonstrate the specific skills identified in Figure 1-5. The ability to communicate and work with people will open up a lot of opportunities.

FIGURE 1-5 What Recruiters Are Looking For

Most Important Skills Needed	
Skill	**Frequency**
Communication skills	79
Interpersonal skills	65
Analytical skills	35
Listening skills	34
Organizational skills	25
HR knowledge	23
General business knowledge	22
Planning skills	22
Management skills	20
Good judgment/common sense	18
Flexible/resilient	16
Leadership	13
HR law knowledge	12
Interviewing/selection skills	11
Practical experience	9
Action oriented	9
Innovative thinking	8
Group dynamics	8
Problem solving	8

SOURCE: T. Bergman, "Preparing to Enter and Succeed in Human Resource Management," *SAM Advanced Management Journal* (Winter 1992): 37.

Can skills such as those in Figure 1-5 be acquired through academic preparation? Certainly; for example, active participation (i.e., demonstrated by holding a leadership position) in campus organizations, such as student government, is an excellent strategy for preparing to enter the HR profession.

While technical knowledge and critical communication and interpersonal skills can be acquired through academic preparation, other competencies, such as organizational and management skills, are best developed outside the classroom.[42] Students who work off campus, either part- or full-time, rather than thinking of this situation as a limitation, should reframe it and use it to acquire the critical skills. Many recruiters consider a student's work experience a plus, especially if it shows increasing levels of responsibility and initiative. Job experience, such as assistant manager of a fast-food restaurant, can be an excel-

lent strategy for demonstrating many HR skill competencies.

Perhaps the most prevalent strategy for entering and succeeding in the HR profession is networking. The results of surveys of Society for Human Resource Management (SHRM) members suggest that HR managers depend on their networks for referrals and internal transfers to fill HR management openings. Otherwise, entry-level positions are filled about half the time by applicants coming through college placement services. Executive HR openings are frequently filled through search firms.

The trend is clearly toward staffing entry-level HR positions with internal applicants before going outside. Indeed, some firms, such as Toyota's Georgetown, Kentucky, facility, prefer that new employees first prove themselves on the operational side of the business, such as on the assembly line, before being selected for specific staff assignments.

Another strategy for entering the HR profession is to obtain work experience in a specific industry. HR internships are one way of gaining valuable experience of this type. That experience, plus the contacts, may provide the edge for gaining entry into HR. While an attractive resumé is always an advantage, it would appear that professional contacts and networks are important—some experts argue that they are the most important—strategies for finding an HR job in a tight labor market.

A practical strategy for building an HR network is through the local SHRM. There are hundreds of SHRMs throughout North America. Many universities and colleges have SHRM-sponsored student chapters. The link between student chapters and SHRMs is strong. Students often attend monthly meetings with HR professionals and are included in major functions. A SHRM is an excellent place to begin networking. SHRMs also sponsor an accreditation program to certify professional competency. Students who pass the Personnel Accreditation Institute exams and who then

Table 1-3 HR Salaries by Company Size in the United States for 1992

HR Job Title	Total Employment	
	Fewer than 250 People ($ thousands) $	More than 10,000 People ($ thousands) $
Top HR manager	$90	$221
Top organizational development	86	109
Top compensation/benefits	62	124
Top division/regional HR	66	103
Top employee relations	64	91
HR generalist	34	47
EEO specialist	40	44
Benefits administrator	27	37
Compensation analyst	32	36
Recruiter	26	34

SOURCE: Adapted from Kate Beatty, "The 1992 HR Pay Picture," *HR Magazine* (June 1992): 63.

work in the HR field for two years will be designated as Professional in Human Resources (PHR). There is also a Senior Professional in Human Resources (SPHR) designation. For those already working in the HR field, accreditation is becoming one method for rising to the top.

Other associations and societies that promote HR professionalism include the Academy of Management, the American Society of Training and Development (ASTD), the American Management Association, the American Compensation Association, and the Society for the Advancement of Management. These organizations meet regularly to discuss important topics and new developments in HR and related fields. In addition, they publish journals and conduct educational seminars on new developments, as well as on methods and techniques for improving traditional functions.

Layoffs, corporate restructuring, and hiring freezes have taken their toll on HR professionals, as on everyone else. So far, however, HR professionals have seen their pay rise significantly over the past two decades. This trend reflects the increasing responsibilities HR professionals are given.

The average compensation for top HR executives is $126,000.[43] Large companies pay more than small companies. Average base pay for different HR specialties will vary, as indicated in Table 1-3. The figures represent only national averages and should be interpreted loosely; what HR people in a specific region or locale earn may differ substantially from these figures.

CONCLUSIONS AND APPLICATIONS

- Strategic HR activities address a broad range of issues relevant to the successful implementation of operational plans. The more critical the HR to an organization's success, the more important strategic planning becomes.

- The management of people has seen three distinct approaches since the turn of the century: scientific management, human relations, and HR. The trend has been toward the HR approach, whereby two complementary goals are sought: increased organizational effectiveness and the satisfaction of individual employee needs. HR policies and programs strive to achieve both goals.

- A number of critical issues face HR managers and administrators today. Improving worker productivity through HR programs, policies, and techniques remains a challenge. Increasing the quality of working life (QWL) is a goal of many organizations, and programs such as the redesign of jobs have been implemented to enhance QWL.

- Hiring and motivating today's changing work force is a major HR challenge. Innovative HR programs must meet the needs of a diverse labor force while enabling the corporation to compete successfully in a global economy.

- Although the HR programs of different organizations will vary, the HR departments of most organizations have these common responsibilities: job design and analysis; recruitment and selection; appraisal, training, and development; compensation; and employee relations.

- HR managers and administrators play a number of roles in achieving effective HR management. These include creating HR policies, offering advice to line managers, providing services (e.g., recruiting, training, and research), and controlling activities to ensure that employment legislation and HR policies are being followed. Also, it is usually HR's responsibility to design and maintain effective companywide communication flows.

- Jobs in the HR department include clerical (support), professional, and managerial positions. The number of HR and labor relations employees is expected to grow as fast as the average for all occupations throughout the 1990s, with most growth occurring in the private sector.

- Free trade and globalization are putting most firms in fiercely competitive markets where factors for success depend on the quality of HR. The scope of HR functions has broadened to include attracting, training, and motivating a heterogeneous work force from a wide variety of cultures. Management styles, selection, appraisal, training, and reward systems need to be reevaluated in terms of the local culture if the company is to operate effectively. International HR managers are faced with the challenge of balancing corporate long-term HR policies and practices with the work force needs of their international subsidiaries.

CASE STUDY

Family Feud

It was Friday evening and Tom Bennett's turn to prepare the family meal. He had not given this task much thought; actually, he didn't want to think about it all, and only at the last moment decided to grill some hamburgers. "Keep it simple" was his motto—a decision his family appreciated too. Tom took off early in order to squeeze in some time with his kids and to meet with their teachers.

Tom and his wife, Margie Vintner (she kept her maiden name), were a successful dual-career couple, living in Denver for the past five years with their two children—Jacob, nine, and Emily, seven. By most measures, the couple had achieved the American dream—a healthy income, a beautiful home, vacations in the mountains for skiing, and a housekeeper. Normally, a housekeeper would help with the cooking tonight, but the family is without one at the moment, thus the need for Tom to prepare the evening meal.

What was unusual about this couple is that Tom and Margie were both in the HR profession at separate companies in the Denver area. Margie worked at one of the banks downtown, and Tom worked with one of the airlines based in the city. Although both jobs required long hours and some travel (more in the case of Tom), Margie's job had recently become more intense since her bank was recently acquired by National Bank Corporation (NBC) in San Francisco. It was during their graduate school days, back in New York, that the couple met and married.

The couple often found themselves discussing work-related issues at home. Tom worked in the benefits area, and Margie's job was in employee relations. The fact that they shared the same profession has presented few problems. Each partner always gave the other morale support, and on more than a few occasions, one partner would provide the other with specific, useful professional, assistance. Margie's superior had even bragged to top management that they were getting two professionals for the price of one. Ironically, while it was their mutual interest in the profession that initially brought them together, recently it had become a source of tension. Tonight would be no exception.

Margie, in an afternoon phone conversation with Tom, announced that she had something important to tell him this evening. Tom had become increasingly ambivalent and didn't really like surprises, so his anxiety level was a bit higher than normal as he flipped the hamburgers and watched Margie slowly walk onto the deck, carrying two glasses of wine. Tom winced. Margie normally drank only on special occasions or when she was angry about something. Which one would it be tonight?

"Hi, Tom. How did it go for you and the kids today?" Margie's tone lacked genuineness—a bad sign, Tom concluded correctly.

Tom gave her a quick summary of the kids' day as he accepted a glass of wine. He mentioned Jacob's invitation (pleading was more accurate) to attend his Little League game in the morning and Emily's school play next Monday afternoon. It was the latter that sparked Margie's attention.

"They never consider the parents who work during the day and who have schedules to maintain," she replied. "It's frustrating that the schools are dragging their heels on moving into the twenty-first century with regard to single parents or dual-career couples."

There she goes again, thought Tom. She hasn't been home more than ten minutes, and she's already knocking the system. For the past couple of years, the two had had a friendly debate over many HR issues, but none had raised more passion than the role of the corporation in resolving work–family conflicts.

Margie was an advocate for businesses taking a more activist stance on behalf of workers with family duties. Doing nothing, which is what she believed traditional businesses like her own practice, can only lead to loss of the best talent.

Tom came from the traditional school of thought. He hesitated when it came to breaching the traditional wall between work and family. Employers had no business involving themselves more deeply in workers' family lives. The corporate culture should be values neutral, not pro-family. Emphasis should stay on what companies do best—creating jobs—and avoid opening the Pandora's box of raised expectations, employer liability, invasion of privacy, and even accusations of unfairness that work–family programs could cause. Tom was also afraid that expensive programs would hurt a company's global competitiveness—a situation that he saw occurring in the airline industry. In fact, his particular airline was already looking at ways to cut such core benefits as health insurance and pensions.

Margie's comments also triggered memories of his conversation at lunch that day with a group of airline employees who had complained to management about the airline's new policy on flexible hours. He gave Margie a quick account.

"They presented a senior manager with a list of grievances," he said, "including complaints that childless employees are expected to work more hours than their counterparts who have children. Some resented having to

forfeit more weekends. One person even accused Jane Busby of using her children as a convenient copout. The jealousy is much more serious than you can imagine."

Margie conceded that change was a problem, but one that could and must be overcome. "Companies say they want to be family friendly; some may actually mean it." She paused for effect. "But the way they do business runs contrary to it."

"Tom, certainly you agree that there is a push for balance between work and home," Margie continued, "even at the cost of lost promotions and pay. But the reality is that respect for the individual in most companies is biased against certain people. People are managed very, very rigidly. The traditional system still puts much more emphasis on face time at the office instead of results. And people who can achieve results, but in nonconventional ways, are constantly having roadblocks put in their way between doing their best at work and taking care of their families."

"And Tom, the prevailing corporate culture in most businesses is far from values neutral. If anything, it reflects the traditional family structures of the 1950s: a wife who cares for the children at home while the husband goes off to work. Top management has a hard time sympathizing with work–family conflicts because it is male dominated and rarely has them. And whether you want to believe it or not, Tom, there is a glass ceiling, and I think it is getting thicker—not thinner."

"I think that's bogus," Tom rebutted. "You've been watching too many *Current Affairs* and *Oprah Winfrey* shows. Yes, I agree that some managers demand long hours and seven-day workweeks. But that is because those jobs cannot be restructured, and it is so impractical to permit the kind of flexibility you're touting. I shouldn't need to remind you that my own company and industry are downsizing; our managers are under intense pressures, much of it from huge waves of change. Expecting them to be flexible when reducing staff is just not realistic. And besides, there is no proof that these programs help the bottom line.''

"Okay, Tom." Margie accepted the challenge. "Where's the research that says that taking a client out for an expensive dinner and entertainment has a payoff—or memberships in the country club, for that matter?"

"You're applying a double standard," she said. "Work–family programs are being held to higher standards. Everyone knows that these programs increase our ability to attract, retain, and motivate skilled employees. But getting management to sign on is next to impossible. Which, by the way, hit home for me today."

Margie then proceeded to tell Tom that she had learned that the new owner of her bank, NBC, had offered the recently vacated vice-president for HR position to Larry Wellington, not her. It would have meant a much higher salary, more responsibility, and a move to San Francisco.

Although Tom and Margie had discussed relocation before, and had agreed to consider it should it be offered to either of them, it was a sensitive topic because it raised the ultimate work–family conflict: whose career is more important? And tonight, Tom wisely concluded, was not the night to tackle *that* issue.

"Larry is a competent guy," Margie added, bringing Tom back to the immediate topic. "but I cannot help but think that when it came down to it, Larry got the job because there is another double standard operating as well. Tom, who is most likely to succeed in *your* company? Honestly, isn't it the person who can transfer at a moment's notice or who puts in the most face time at the office? Larry is single, I'm not. Isn't it the person with the least number of things to keep him or her from moving around, from being available at

a moment's notice, from working any hours—all things that don't really have a valid business rationale?"

Tom understood that Margie's questions were rhetorical. He also understood why Margie was on edge and uncharacteristically embittered. Margie's comments did stir his own conscience, leaving him to wonder: Is Margie right? Is management's concern for work–family issues all talk, no action? And is the entire structure of work biased in favor of those who can come in early, leave late, and travel at a moment's notice instead of those who are most effective?

QUESTIONS

1. Even though both Margie and Tom are HR professionals, their views about what companies should do about easing work–family conflicts are quite different. Describe their differences. What do you think is the source of their differences?

2. Work–family proponents cite a number of barriers in the workplace that prohibit employees who want to maintain a balance between work and family from achieving their goals. Describe the barriers. What is the price of corporate inaction in failing to address these employees' personal and family needs?

3. Tom raised the issues that family support programs may have a negative side effect: resentment among childless workers. Is this true, and if so, what solution would you recommend?

4. What evidence is available that work–family conflict causes workplace problems? Do you agree or disagree with Tom's claim that these programs do not help the bottom line? Is Margie's response ("Everyone knows that these programs increase. . .") a sufficient answer for top management? What effect will corporate inaction have on employee morale and productivity?

EXPERIENTIAL EXERCISES

1. Sources of Personnel/HR Information

PURPOSE

To learn how to research a personnel/HR topic and to gain practice in researching personnel-related issues in the library.

THE TASK

A number of topics related to the field of personnel/HR management follow. Choose a topic of interest to you (or your instructor may assign a topic for you to research). After you have chosen a topic, do the following:

1. Find at least six recent references (or more, depending on your instructor's wishes) that pertain to your topic. Do not use a reference (e.g., *Personnel Journal*) more than once.

2. For each reference, indicate the title of the book, journal, and so on; the title of the journal article (if applicable); the author's name; and the publisher and publication date. In addition, indicate how you located each reference (e.g., *Business Periodicals Index*).

3. Write a one-paragraph abstract for each source (if your source is a book, review at least one important chapter and write the abstract for that chapter).

Personnel/HR Topics

- Absenteeism: Causes and Cures
- Age Discrimination in Industry
- Americans with Disabilities Act of 1990

- Profit Sharing
- Recruiting Problems and Issues
- Sexual Harassment: How to Prevent and Control It
- Social Security: Is It Failing?
- Stress: What Causes It, How to Reduce It
- Test Validation Techniques
- Assessment Centers: How Effective?
- Benefit Plans (Flexible)
- Career Opportunities in Personnel/HR Resource Management
- Child-Care Programs
- Collective Bargaining Issues in Current Negotiations
- Compensation: Problems and Issues
- Disciplinary Methods and Techniques
- Drug Usage and Testing
- Dual-Career Couples
- Employee Rehabilitation Programs
- Employee Stock Option Plans (ESOPs)
- Employment at Will
- Executive Compensation Techniques
- Flextime Programs
- Grievance Procedures (Union and Nonunion Employers)
- Health Care Cost Containment Methods
- Immigration Reform Act of 1986: Is It Working?
- Incentive Compensation Systems
- Job Enrichment: Successes and Failures
- Labor Relations: Current Trends and Issues

- Management by Objectives (MBO)
- Negligent Hiring
- Occupational Safety and Health Act (OSHA): How Effective?
- Employee Orientation Programs
- Outplacement Programs for Managerial and Nonmanagerial Personnel
- Part-time Employees

- Polygraph and Honesty Testing
- Turnover: Causes and Cures
- Union–Management Relations: Current Trends and Issues
- Wellness Programs
- Women and Work: Problems and Perspectives
- Work Force Diversity

2. Predicting Work in the Year 2000

PURPOSE

To understand the potential influence of trends and changes occurring in North America that will influence the design and implementation of HR management practices.

TIME: Thirty minutes of class time

PROCEDURES

This exercise should be done in groups of four to five students. The year 2000 is not far away. One prediction seems certain to occur: the next century promises to bring even more rapid advances in technology, more intense global competition, and increased pressures on workers to be more productive. Review each of the trends that are predicted to occur and list ideas about the impact of each on major HR management functions: global strategic planning, job design, recruitment and selection, performance appraisal, training and development, career planning, compensation and benefits, health and safety, and labor relations.

Each group will then present its ideas to the class.

Trends	Impact on HRM
1. The average company will become smaller, employing fewer people.	
2. The traditional hierarchical organization will give way to a variety of other structures.	
3. Business will shift from producing or manufacturing to providing a service.	
4. Work itself will be redefined: constant learning, more high-order thinking, less nine-to-five work.	
5. Increasing numbers of dual-career and single-parent families.	
6. More technicians, professionals, and specialists than manufacturing workers.	

KEY TERMS AND CONCEPTS

Changing work force
Command and control cultures
Diversity
Face time
Global economy
Human relations
Human resource functions
Human resource (HR) management
Human resource policies
Human resource roles

ISO 9000
Productivity
Quality
Quality of working life (QWL)
Scientific management
Strategic human resource management
Strategic management
Technology
Training

REVIEW QUESTIONS

1. How do scientific management, human relations, and HR approaches to managing people differ? Why is the HR approach considered by many to be better than the traditional ways of managing people?

2. What are the traditional personnel functions performed by almost every HR department? Describe the different roles performed by HR managers. What HR functions and roles are performed by all managers, line as well as staff?

3. Describe the variety of ways top management might communicate important information to its employees. Which communication methods are effective for passing information from employees to managers?

4. What are the most critical challenges facing HR professionals today? What changes in society and within organizations have been instrumental in reshaping the HR role?

5. Describe the forces that make up the global environment.

6. What is the career outlook for those who wish to enter the HR field? What is a good strategy for students with no experience who want to break into the field?

DISCUSSION QUESTIONS

1. One often hears that the scientific management approach is still widely used in manufacturing and other forms of unskilled or semiskilled work. Why might this be so? Will scientific management principles still be used in the year 2000? Explain.

2. Why did the human relations approach decline in popularity? How important are good human relations? What else must a good manager do in addition to practicing good human relations?

3. The question of government interference in private enterprise has long been a hot topic for businesspeople. In general, have equal employment opportunity laws been good or bad for business? Good or bad for women or minorities? Do you feel that more equal employment opportunity legislation will be enacted in the coming decade?

4. Much more professionalism is demanded from HR officials today than in the past. Why is this so?

5. What types of HR programs are needed to attract, retain, and motivate today's culturally diverse work force?

6. Much has been said about global competition. What will it mean to managers and HR professionals in the decades to come in terms of HR functions, roles, and policies?

ENDNOTES

Chapter 1

1. Michael Hammer and James Champy, *Reengineering the Corporation* (New York: HarperBusiness, 1993), pp. 7–14

2. *Business Week/Reinventing America,* Special Issue 1992: 60–63.

3. Sue Shellenbarger, "Work-Force Study Finds Loyalty Is Weak, Divisions of Race and Gender Are Deep," *Wall Street Journal* (September 4, 1993): B1.

4. Frederick W. Taylor, *Scientific Management* (New York: Harper & Brothers, 1947), pp. 45–46.

5. For a description of personnel functions and activities undertaken by large companies during the scientific management era, see Ordway Tead and Henry C. Metcalf, *Personnel Administration* (New York: McGraw-Hill, 1920).

6. For a detailed description of the Hawthorne studies, see F. J. Roethlisberger and W. J. Dickson, *Management and the Worker* (Cambridge, MA: Harvard University Press, 1939).

7. Not all researchers agree that changes in employee behavior were caused by changes in the work environment. For an alternative explanation, see H. M. Parsons, "What Happened at Hawthorne?" *Science* (March 8, 1974): 922–32.

8. Arthur Thompson, Jr, and A. J. Strickland III, *Strategic Management,* 6th ed. (Boston: Irwin, 1992), pp. 2–3.

9. "The Personnel/Human Resources Department: 1989–90." *Bulletin to Management* (July 28, 1990) pp. 1–3.

10. Stephen Perry, "An HRIS for the '90s," *Personnel Journal* 69, no. 8 (August 1990): 75–78.

11. Michael Alvert, "HR Profit Power," *Personnel* 67, no. 2 (February 1990): 47–49.

12. This discussion is taken from M. Beer, B. Spector, P. Lawrence, D. Mills, and R. Walton, "Managing Human Assets," *Personnel Administrator* (January 1985): 60–69.

13. Bob Baker, "Employee Suggestions Take on Weight in Lean Times," *Los Angles Times* (September 15, 1991): A1.

14. Barbara Whitaker Shimko, "All Managers Are the HR Managers," *Human Resource Magazine* 35, no. 1 (January 1990): 67–70.

15. Linda Thornburg, "Madelyn Jennings Wins Excellence Award," *HR News* (July 15, 1990): 12.

16. George Fields, "How the Japanese Really See Us," *Wall Street Journal* (January 31, 1992): A12.

17. Myron Magnet, "The Truth About the American Worker," *Fortune* (May 4, 1992): 48–65.

18. Ibid.: 65.

19. "Questing for the Best," *Business Week* (October 25, 1991): 11.

20. Ibid.: 13.

21. Lloyd Dobyns, "Ed Deming Wants Big Changes, and He Wants Them Fast," *Smithsonian* 21, no. 5 (August 1990): 74–82.

22. Linda S. Vines, "FP&L Pursues the Prize," *Human Resource Executive* 4, no. 4 (April 1990): 28–29.

23. Fred R. Bleakley, "Over Half of Europe's Big Firms Are Planning Work Force Cuts," *Wall Street Journal* (September 21, 1993): A19.

24. Louis S. Richman, "When Will the Layoffs End?" *Fortune* (September 20, 1993): 54–56.

25. Ibid.: 56

26. Tammy Brecht-Dunbar, "Diverse Work Force Will End Discrimination," *HR News* (March 1990): 1.

27. For more information, see Sue Shellenbarger, "Work-Force Study Finds Loyalty Is Weak, Divisions of Race and Gender Are Deep," *Wall Street Journal* (September 4, 1993): B1. Note: the Families and Work Institute, a nonprofit New York research and consulting company, surveyed a national sample of 2958 workers about their work attitudes and personal lives.

28. Ibid.

29. Ibid.

30. Ibid.

31. Michael Galen, "Work and Family," *Business Week* (June 28, 1993): 80–88.

32. Sue Shellenbarger, "Work and Family," *Wall Street Journal* (February 12, 1992): B1.

33. Michael Galen, "Work and Family," *Business Week* (June 28, 1993): 82.

34. Joseph F. Coates, J. Jarratt, and J. Mahaffie, "Workplace Management 200" *Personnel Administrator* 34, no. 12 (December 1989): 51–55.

35. Stephenie Overman, "Government Steers HR's Future," *Personnel Administrator* 34, no. 12 (December 1989): 61–63.

36. See J. R. Hackman and J. L. Suttle, *Improving Life at Work* (Santa Monica, CA: Goodyear, 1977).

37. David J. Abramis, "Fun at Work," *Personnel Administrator* no. 11 (November 1989): 60–63, and "Building Fun in Your Organization," *Personnel Administrator* 10 (October 1989): 68–72.

38. Unpublished manuscripts by Patrick Arnold, CherAmi Calderwood, Molly Hensen, Michele Marotta, and Staci Wilkins, 1990.

39. E. Price, "Occupational Diseases: The Scope," *Cleveland Plain Dealer* (September 3, 1979): E-2.

40. A. Brief, R. Schuler, and M. Van Sell, *Managing Job Stress* (Boston: Little, Brown, 1981).

41. T. J. Bergmann, M. J. Close, and T. Will, "Preparing to Enter and Succeed in Human Resource Management," *SAM Advanced Management Journal* (Winter 1992): 36–40.

42. T. J. Bergmann and M. J. Close, "Entry Level Human Resource Positions: What Is the Employer Looking For?" *Personnel Journal* 66, no. 1 (January 1987): 124–125, and "Preparing for Entry Level Human Resource Management Positions," *Personnel Journal* 29, no. 4 (April 1984): 95–100.

43. Kate Beatty, "The 1992 HR Pay Picture," *HR Magazine* (June 1992): 62–64.

A GLOBAL PERSPECTIVE OF HUMAN RESOURCES

CHAPTER OUTLINE

CHAPTER OBJECTIVES

1. To become aware of economies in transition and of the effect
this transition has on culture, government, and labor

2. To learn how culture, both national and corporate, can
influence HR management

3. To recognize ethnocentric, polycentric, and geocentric HR management strategies

4. To understand why people from different cultures work and what it will take to motivate people to work harder

5. To understand differences in national cultures across several world regions

6. To be able to design HR strategies for postsocialist economies

7. To become aware of global downsizing patterns

The disintegration of the Soviet Union has had a profound effect on the world. The former Iron Curtain nations of Hungary, Poland, and the newly created Czech and Slovak states, as well as many of the former Soviet republics, are now struggling to become democracies with **free market systems**. And as if that isn't enough change, China is beginning to open up; with over a billion people, it has the potential to be the largest consumer market in the world. While reforms are occurring in each of these countries, the pace at times is excruciatingly slow. A few countries are changing rapidly, such as Poland's "shock therapy," but most are being very deliberate.

In American newspapers, **capitalism** is conceived almost as a form of spontaneous combustion. This is not true. The challenge isn't simply how to educate the new breed of managers, but how to educate average citizens, most of whom are asking some very basic questions: What does it mean to live in a free market system? Why must bread prices go up? Why should we pay more for housing? The vast majority of citizens in these transition economies still do not understand how capitalism works.

The new governments and their leaders cannot shoulder the burden alone and must look to the West for direction and support. But Western governments can do only so much. Low-interest loans, grants, improved trade agreements, and technical assistance are being offered, but these will never be enough. Western corporations are getting into the act, with a few doing as much as, and maybe more than, their governments.

Critical technologies are being transferred. Perhaps the West's most important contributions, however, are its efforts to retrain managers and workers. In effect, they are transforming organizations and their members' behaviors with modern HR management skills, thus enabling them to take advantage of their human capital and begin to compete in a global environment. But that goal represents an immense undertaking, with substantial risk that even the giants fall prey to. IBM, AT&T, and Honeywell had disastrous beginnings in China in the 1980s. In each case, the mistakes were the same: not understanding the business culture and available work force, and being unable to transfer core competencies to a new environment.

The fall of communism was not the only major event taking place. Trade barriers are falling all over the world, thanks to successful NAFTA (North American Free Trade Agreement) and GATT (General Agreement on Tariffs & Trade) negotiations. The world has undergone massive technological and consumer changes. The Chinese cannot get enough KFC fried chicken, the Japanese are beginning to eat American rice (and liking it), and the

From Comrade Director to HR Director

During April 1992, Rita Van Vranken, vice-president of Cooperative Marketing Concepts, traveled to Russia as part of the Citizen Ambassador Program. These are her impressions.

"I came to Russia with very little knowledge of the country and left in awe of the Russians' ability to work under today's conditions. I also brought home a new appreciation for the way the U.S. works. The HR issues and procedures that are standard and commonplace in the States are, in many cases, truly foreign to our Russian counterparts.

"Among the interesting and sometimes amusing differences and similarities between our two countries is the term *human resources.* It is a completely foreign and unusual concept to them. For them, the personnel function had been closely linked to the Communist Party and existed solely to monitor workers' efforts. It wasn't surprising, then, to find them highly receptive to our concept and anxious to receive our guidance and advice.

"One of the most serious concerns their personnel people are confronting is downsizing. Under communism everyone was entitled to a job, even if there was really nothing to do. Unemployment is a completely new experience. It already is above 7 percent—and climbing. At the moment, an unemployed worker receives benefits that last about a year. The government is responsible for paying benefits, although employers do contribute 1 percent of payroll costs.

"At the other extreme is the overabundance of workers in many areas. Since everyone was entitled to a job of some sort, work forces across all sectors were bloated. On the other hand, layoff laws are very strict. A few groups are even exempt from layoffs, for example, women with children under 3, and families with three or more children.

"Women make up only a small percentage of the managerial levels. At one company I visited in St. Petersburg, which was a rather progressive company, only 1 percent of the management staff was female. In most every meeting my group attended, the Russians commented about how beautiful the women delegates were and said things you would be uncomfortable and offended to hear, had they been said in a U.S. office environment. And in most of these meetings, the only Russian women were the ones who brought in coffee and tea. These women watched us with keen interest. Our interpreter said she thought we U.S. women had such great opportunities.

"One state committee we met with was particularly interested in the way we handled job safety conditions as well as environmental concerns. As we discussed OSHA and EPA requirements, they told us that their organization was more in the research phase than in actual enforcement—a metaphor for nothing more than

(continued)

never having to leave the research lab. My colleagues just looked at each other. There are environmental laws now on the books and a stiff fine for violators, although no firm has yet to be penalized. Given the mess in their environment, and it's a lot worse than here in the States, it is almost incredible that at least one enterprise hasn't been cited. I guess enforcement isn't high on their list.

"I don't think I can ever take for granted my good fortune to be in the United States. It's sobering to face each work day knowing how different even the everyday things would be if I were living in another country."

SOURCE: Adapted from "An American HR Professional in Russia . . . ," *HR News* (January 1993): C10. Used by permission.

Germans are building their best cars in Alabama and South Carolina. The very concept of domestic business has disappeared. Modern organizations no longer have any place to hide; national boundaries are not the sanctuaries they once were. Organizations do not have the luxury of focusing on their own little world; they must adopt a global perspective.

THE IMPACT OF THE ENVIRONMENT ON HR MANAGEMENT

As recently as 1980, international HR management was more fiction than fact. Global firms superimposed on their international subsidiaries the HR practices of the corporate home office. This **ethnocentric** philosophy presumed that the organization's culture, management styles, and procedures for selection, appraisal, and reward systems would transfer to any other area in the world. The logic at the time was that all people share the same basic needs and values. Today evidence is fairly conclusive that national culture guides people's actions even when it is opposed by a strong corporate culture.

It is not only a question of different cultures. Many forces operating in the environment influence the selection and implementation of various HR systems. As Figure 2-1 depicts, forces in the environment may include differences in economic systems, government policies and laws, and the quality of labor–management relations. Environmental forces influence each other too; unions in Europe are inclined to take an active role in both government and business. In turn, both business and government are heavily influenced by economic conditions.

In Western Europe, for example, societies are accustomed to governments providing cradle-to-grave human services and employers to paying generous wages. But declining global competitiveness is forcing governments, labor, businesses, and societies to reevaluate and separate real needs from costly (and unaffordable) traditions. The increasing movement of trade across national borders will ultimately influence national cultures. Most of these changes will be subtle and occur gradually, except in the former Iron Curtain societies. The same types of tough decisions are being made all over the world, even in culturally insulated societies such as Japan.

With the continuing globalization of business, it is more imperative than ever that managers expand their horizons across national boundaries. This chapter focuses on global HR management approaches from the perspective of people and culture. Effective worldwide HR

FIGURE 2-1 Environmental forces.

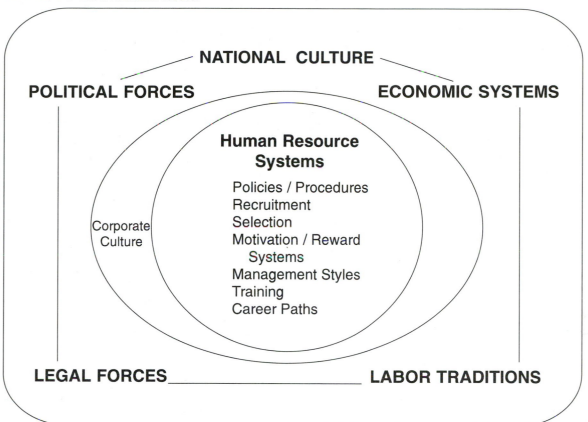

management depends on acquiring knowledge of specific cultures and other environmental forces. While many of the same HR practices are found throughout the world, there is wide variation in *how* and *when* each should be implemented.

Several major regions are identified and reviewed (space prevents mention of all of them). Important cultural differences are noted. **Culture** is defined as the shaping of the mind that distinguishes the members of one group or category of people from those of another.[1] The group or category may be a nation (i.e., national culture), an occupation, or an organization (i.e., corporate culture).

Organizations tend to be culture bound, and management practices reflect elements of the national culture. Even across nations with relatively similar cultures, important differences remain; and the greater the disparity, the more difficult it will be to implement effective HR management practices. In those regions where national culture suffered from decades of tyranny, as in the cases of Russia and China, the challenges are immense because there are minimal advantages to be gained from local adaptation. For other regions, different cultures simply mean that managers must manage differently; that is, there are many equally effective ways to manage, with the most effective depending, among other contingencies, on the cultures involved.

Understanding differences across cultures is important but hardly sufficient. Today the accent is on developing **multicultural teams**. The organizational pyramid is gradually giving way to horizontal structures. Bureaucracies are quickly fading, and teamwork is taking their place. Tough competition, changing technology, budget cuts, resource scarcity, and similar constraints have stimulated the use of teams within single domestic markets. Going global only adds to the challenge; now there are foreign partners, foreign suppliers, and multiple markets. The conclusion is obvious: multicultural teams are needed to improve coordination and cooperation.

GLOBAL HR STRATEGIES

Global corporations have missions and strategies that are worldwide in scope, and their revenues abroad are substantial. Global HR strategies must coincide with corporate strategies. Like any strategy, these begin with the three basic questions: Where are we now? Where do we want to be? How are we going to get there? The answers, along with a **SWOT analysis** (strengths, weakness, opportunities, and threats), will lead to development of strategic objectives and a master strategy—the blueprint for accomplishing the mission. Human resources plays a pivotal role in all phases.

Global strategies are necessary when a firm decides that the kind of business it wants to be in ultimately takes it out of its domestic market. The strategic process remains the same, however—only more complicated. The global organization must coordinate and integrate people, products, and business functions across countries.

Mission and strategy drive the type of organizational structure created, which, in turn, drives the degree of **centralization** or **decen-**

tralization adopted. A centralized global company tends to retain authority for important decisions within the home office. An ethnocentric multinational will put home office staff in charge of critical functions and operate abroad the same way it does at home. Policies and procedures, rules, rewards—in effect, large portions of the corporate and national cultures influencing management practices at home are replicated in the subsidiaries. The first wave of Japanese companies venturing into the United States tended to operate **ethnocentrically.**

Decentralized multinationals transfer important decisions to the subsidiaries in different countries. As long as the subsidiary is profitable, the home office leaves it alone. When local nationals in the subsidiary are placed in key positions and allowed to appoint and develop their own people, the approach is called **polycentric**. Products are modified to fit the peculiar needs of the local market, suppliers and distribution channels are adjusted, and staffing needs are filled through local networks. There are disadvantages to polycentric organizations; subsidiaries may be so loosely affiliated that valuable opportunities for economies of scale, joint marketing efforts, or shared technology may be lost. If only Americans work in the United States, Mexicans in Mexico, and the Japanese in Japan, the company loses the input of talented individuals with different backgrounds and perspectives.[2]

When organizations are truly globalized, they adopt strategies that totally integrate operations and resources, particularly human resources. Such organizations are called **transnational** corporations, and what separates them from multinationals is their complete dedication to global concerns and perspectives. National considerations are secondary. Ethnocentric tendencies are minimized due to the placement of personnel from different countries in key positions in the home office. The strategy reflects a **geocentric** approach. As Alvin Toffler, the futurist, said in a speech,

The Price of Cultural Misunderstanding

On a sea voyage, you are traveling with your wife, your child, and your mother. The ship develops problems and starts to sink. Of your family, you are the only one who can swim and you can only save one other individual. Who would you save?

This question was posed to a group of men in Asia and the United States. In the United States, more than 60 percent of those responding said they would save the child, 40 percent would choose to save the wife, and none would have saved the mother. In the Asian countries, 100 percent said they would save the mother. Their rationale? You can always remarry and have more children—but you cannot have another mother. . . .

When doing business overseas, Americans can't rely only on American values and behavior patterns. . . . What is good in one place ("Father is getting about the age where he would probably be happier in the senior citizens home in Arizona") is scandalous in another ("Look at how they treat older people in this country—it's awful"). . . .

Cross-cultural mistakes are expensive. Companies spend a minimum of $125,000 a year to have a U.S. manager working in an overseas position. Another less obvious factor is the human cost accrued when someone does poorly or comes home early from an overseas assignment. Premature return of an employee and family sent on overseas assignment may cost the company between $50,000 to $200,000 when replacement expenses are included. Mistakes of corporate representatives because of language or intercultural incompetence can jeopardize millions of dollars in negotiations and purchases, sales and contracts, as well as undermine customer relations. No doubt, managerial failures to be culturally skillful at work can weaken both productivity and profitability.

The price of providing employees with education and training for intercultural effectiveness is minuscule compared to the financial losses that can occur because of personnel "faux pas" in cross-cultural business relations. The benefits from developing human resources can be enormous.

"The transnational corporation may do research in one country, manufacture components in another, assemble them in a third, sell the manufactured goods in a fourth, deposit its surplus funds in a fifth, and so on." To develop and manage a transnational organization necessitates developing and managing people who can think, lead, and act from a global perspective, who possess a global mind as well as global skills.[3]

GLOBAL HR ACTIVITIES FOR NEW ACQUISITIONS

A few HR activities are essential components of the strategy implementation process. This is especially true when foreign companies are acquired. Global organizations are well advised to establish an appropriate and lasting role for HR management from the very beginning. One important HR role is preparing the buyer's negotiating team. There are many differences from culture to culture that influence negotiations—for example, language, approaches to problem solving, implicit assumptions, gestures and body language, and the role of ceremony and formality.

Furthermore, an understanding of local HR and personnel management practices is needed, preferably prior to acquisition. A company should want to know what it is buying in terms of core competencies, morale, and potential for change. What are the qualifications and expertise of the acquired staff? An assessment of the strengths and weaknesses of personnel will influence the decision on whether to decentralize operations. Important management practices need to be identified, especially how employees are recruited, retained, and rewarded. In China, for example, the government takes responsibility for providing workers and makes it difficult to discharge incompetent people. Yet there are no minimum wage laws, and an employer can pay whatever the market will bear.

Finally, plans should be made for the post-acquisition transfer of managers to and from the local sites. How will personnel from both organizations be integrated in a way that supports the overall global mission? Who and how many management personnel need to be transferred from the buying to the acquired firm directly after the takeover? What type of training program must be implemented to improve cooperation between the global organization and its new acquisition?

Selecting and training management staff for the foreign operation is expensive and time-consuming. Making it more complicated are the families involved. A spouse who must sacrifice a career, finding schools for the children, and many other difficult international transfer issues have to be addressed.

HR policies are implemented in light of their applicability to specific cultures and laws. Today global managers are asking corporate officers many tough questions: Which HR management policies should be global? Which ones should be local? How much expatriation (sending employees to foreign countries) should occur? In the developing countries, how does the global firm train local people in even the simplest technologies and management methods? How can the global company attract, retain, and motivate the local labor force? Not only reward systems, but also benefit packages, grievance channels, and career paths should be examined.

GLOBAL IMPLICATIONS FOR MOTIVATION AND JOB DESIGN

Because a global firm has to operate in different countries, understanding why people work and how they are motivated to work harder is important. Undesirable, sometimes disastrous, consequences can occur when international HR managers assume that people in other countries think, feel, and act the same way they do in the United States.

Global HR managers need to use caution before applying U.S. management theories, such as Maslow's hierarchy of needs, as a model for analyzing the reward preferences of workers in other parts of the world. Hofstede, for example, found that people from different cultures attach different importance to various needs and even give different priorities to some of Maslow's higher-order needs.[4] Nevertheless, it would be fairly safe to assume that unsatisfied lower-order needs will motivate, regardless of culture. In very poor countries, most workers may be so deprived that an employer can expect workers to perform if work means food, shelter, and other basic necessities. Any motivational differences among higher-order needs can usually be traced to culture or the collective mental programming of an entire group of people.[5]

In industrial nations such as the United States, personal economic achievement is presumed to be the prevailing notion that drives people's behaviors. Furthermore, people will usually work harder at any task when the reward is worth winning and their chances are realistic. Is this belief about people's motivations true even for European nations? Unfortunately, no. In the former Soviet Union and some Eastern European nations, the collective mental programming from decades of communism has taken a heavy toll. Consider these questions: Why work hard when wages won't change and, even with money, there is little to buy? Why work hard when corruption is king and quality is nonexistent? And, most disturbing, why work hard when a society's moral code is: do not trust anyone beyond a tight circle? Plainly, the differences between socialist economies and free market economies are of considerable significance for HR professionals.

Cultural Dimensions

For anyone planning to become a U.S. expatriate manager, one prerequisite is to learn the customs, traditions, and cultures of the host country because it is these things that influence reward preferences, job designs, managerial styles, gender role expectations, and much more. Expatriate managers are repeatedly influenced by incorrect cultural stereotypes. One such stereotype is that people from developing countries lack a strong work ethic. In fact, the economic failures of many Third World countries are often attributed to the easygoing temperament of the local population. Who hasn't seen a television commercial or advertisement depicting Caribbeans, Africans, Latin Americans, or others as people who lie idle on a nearby beach? Only when one considers what the true outcomes of hard work are for these people—a hostile climate, discrimination, or nearly worthless currency—will old stereotypes disappear.

Monetary incentives in the form of higher wages and promotions for superior work will do wonders to motivate apparently lethargic people to become hard-working and ambitious. People who do not seem ambitious in their native country work hard and do very well if they migrate to the United States. For many people, it is *the opportunity to achieve,* and not temperament, that is missing. National or ethnic "temperament," if it exists, is vastly overrated as an explanation for the failure to motivate people from developing countries.

While the need to achieve would appear to be widely shared, there are cultures in which rigid class hierarchy restrains people from improving their social standing. In some Mediterranean and Latin American countries, an individual is accepted largely on the basis of the social status of his or her family rather than on individual achievement.[6]

In many cultures, being competent is not enough to merit desired rewards. Rather, factors such as seniority, sex, or social standing will largely determine who is eligible to fill certain positions and how compensation will be determined.[7]

Attitudes toward women make it extremely difficult for women to work in certain countries. In Saudi Arabia, for example, women cannot legally drive, show their faces, or venture out alone. In some African countries, very few women are allowed to work in manufacturing organizations. A U.S. manufacturer in Japan learned the hard way that in order to get its workers and their spouses to a company dinner, they had to call it a "family day." Otherwise, neither wives nor female employees would attend.[8]

Motivating in Different Cultures

It would appear that management theories popular in the United States will provide some direction in designing productive and satisfying work in other countries once the local culture is understood. Group affiliations based on sex, family, and other factors often reflect a person's degree of access to material and economic opportunities, but once factored in, the motivation to work is largely explained by fulfillment of higher-order needs and opportunities for achievement. Clearly, a host country's culture must be reflected in the visitor's management practices.

In terms of success stories, one of the best concerns the use of participatory management at a Paris hotel. The French (along with other Western European nations) have long had a law requiring all businesses with fifty or more employees to give workers a voice in running things and a share of the profits. When a British fast-food and motel chain acquired the hotel, a great deal of anxiety occurred among the hotel's employees. Would the new owner continue with work participation or merely make it quasi-involvement (i.e., superficial and nonsubstantive decision making)? The new owners actually improved on the system, and gave the workers greater freedom of expression and decision-making ability in running the hotel. The results were striking: a 35 percent increase in efficiency and a 15 percent increase in occupancy, despite significant hikes in room rates. One employee said: "Money is not the main thing, you know—especially for the young people. For them it is to be happy. But [money] is not the center of their lives."[9]

An example of one popular U.S. management practice used inappropriately is the open-door policy. It was implemented in a U.S. firm in Germany and resulted in a serious office conflict between American and German co-workers. The Germans repeatedly kept their office doors closed, which made the Americans believe they were shut out and created a conspiratorial atmosphere. But to the Germans open doors were unprofessional and unbusinesslike, making them feel exposed.[10]

Hofstede reported that in the Scandinavian countries and the Netherlands, more importance is placed on social needs and less on self-actualization than in the United States. What this means for job design remains to be seen, but it clearly suggests that attempts at individual job enrichment should be reconsidered.[11]

In a study of reward perceptions of American, English, and Ghanaian (West Africa) workers, Earley found several differences among the three cultures:[12] It was believed that social interaction of workers with their supervisors would be highly valued. However, after all the employees received specialized training that encouraged supervisors and shop floor workers to interact, management in the three countries observed mixed results. It became evident that English workers resented, rather than appreciated, new opportunities to interact on a social level with their supervisors. In fact, they viewed the attempt as a management means of spying on the workers. Ghanaian workers, on the other hand, responded very favorably to this change. American workers fell somewhere between the two extremes. Earley concluded that the English shop floor workers are part of a class-oriented society that structures the nature of acceptable interactions, whereas the Ghanaians are from a largely tribal society that places great value on family life and social interaction.[13]

In recent years, much has been written about the Japanese and their view of work. In Japan, the individual is seen primarily as a member of a group. This difference may help explain why jobs are designed more with the group than with the individual in mind.

Being aware of and adapting to the special characteristics of each country's culture will make the multinational HR professional more effective and efficient in that environment. In open market societies, HR management must stimulate employees to be flexible and highly motivated. Lack of attention to this factor has contributed greatly to the decreased competitiveness of some global corporations.

CANADA

Labor markets around the world are as diverse as the people who make them up. In many ways, two that are more alike than different are those of the United States and Canada. They share many economic, political, demographic, and societal characteristics. And, of course, the U.S.–Canada free trade agreement has only brought them closer together. Standard HR functions such as recruitment, selection, compensation, and training and development are performed in similar ways.

Still, the typical Canadian company will design HR management policies more in tune with Canada's stronger emphasis on **social justice**. In most Canadian jurisdictions, Ontario for example, the Employment Standards Act prohibits employers from paying male and female employees differently for substantially the same kind of work that requires substantially the same skill, effort, and responsibility.[14] An executive secretary should receive a salary comparable to that of a senior cost accountant or a machinist first class. While the United States does have the Equal Pay Act, it is effective only in cases involving pay discrimination among people performing similar tasks.

Canadian HR management is distinct in another important way. Universal health care coverage is practiced in Canada, while it is only being proposed in the United States. The financial and administrative burden is assumed by the Canadian government, not the employer. Of course, there are various proposals in the U.S. Congress that address the current health care crisis, but at this moment, most people continue to depend on their employers for coverage, thus making health care benefits a major HR management responsibility (and nightmare).

Labor markets in Canada, with the exception of farm, domestic help, and white collar work, are extensively organized and, in many cases, affiliated with international unions headquartered in the United States. One result of the stagnant Canadian economy in the 1980s was a significant drop in union membership from its high of 37 percent.[15] Recently, however, global competition has contributed to a more cordial relationship between union and management.

As to cross-cultural differences, English-speaking Canadians tend to be slightly more reserved and formal than their American counterparts in the United States. Perhaps this is due to their strong British heritage. Standards of etiquette are more pronounced; for example, subordinates seldom address their superiors on a first-name basis and practice strict punctuality. In Quebec, the French culture is prevalent. French language, food, and social customs are dominant. French Canadians are considered more easygoing and less time-conscious than their English-speaking countrymen.[16]

MEXICO

Events are moving rapidly in Mexico. This country is undergoing dramatic change and is one of the United States' most important cus-

"Here I Have a Real Career"

Arturo Arriaga closes the sheet of steel he uses for a door, fastens a chain, and snaps shut the padlock. The 23-year-old Monterey worker can't afford much more than a sparse cinder-block house with no phone. Still, he considers himself on the fast track program at Galvak, a specialty steel company; he and his co-workers have seen productivity skyrocket and their pay nearly double, to $13.38 a day. If Arriaga passes his next test, he'll get another promotion. Sure, Arriaga says, Mexican dishwashers and farm workers earn more in the United States, "but here I have a real career."

Indeed Arturo is much like other Mexican workers who are employed within Mexico's interior. While wages are low and living conditions close to primitive, workers like Arturo are at least optimistic about their futures, particularly their careers. Most plants along the U.S.-Mexican border do not invest in programs for up-grading workers' skills. Mexican companies located away from the border are more willing to train workers like Arturo.

There are 300,000 Mexicans who work in 1500 manufacturing plants along the U.S.-Mexican border. The working arrangement is called **Maquiladora**, a Mexican term for production sharing. Initially created to take advantage of plentiful labor and low wages, both countries offer tax incentives to encourage manufacturers to assemble products in Mexico and then ship them to the U.S.

Because jobs are easy to find, Maquiladora workers don't feel obligated to work long hours. Many workers quit in order to take care of family members. Attempts to control the high turnover have not been particularly effective. Rather than raising wages or providing training and development opportunities, most Maquiladoras encourage employees to participate on the company's baseball or soccer teams and hope that some sort of team spirit is created. So far, this approach doesn't appear to be working.

SOURCE: Adapted from "The Mexican Worker," *Business Week* (April 19, 1993): 85–91.

---

tomers. With a growing, dynamic economy, Mexicans spend more per person on U.S. goods than either the Europeans or the Japanese—over $40 billion in 1993 alone. NAFTA is already making many U.S. citizens take notice of their southern neighbor. With a population expected to be over 100 million by the year 2000, Mexico has enormous social and business implications for the United States.[17]

The Mexican economy resembles an Asian model more than a Western one. It is a top-down, market system economy in which the president has immense control. President Carlos Salinas de Gortari and his successors are leading the country through a major transition. Their aim is to broaden the industrial base by moving away from state-owned enterprises, create more and better-paying jobs, and improve the standard of living for their citizens. Although events are still being shaped, the plan appears to be working.

In government and corporations, Mexican leaders tend to make decisions without much concern for consensus. Unlike the U.S. culture, which discourages authoritarian leadership styles, there is little risk of antagonizing Mexican subordinates. Most Latin Americans respect power and a central authority. They prefer the "strong man" image.[18] Latinos generally approve of a strong, decisive leader (usually a male) as long as his power is not abused. Unlike North Americans, they see the leader as a "patron"—a man of power (or wealth) who maintains the loyalty of those of lower status.[19]

Mexican and Latin American social behavior, as a whole, is influenced by *personalismo, machismo, hierarchy and rank, and kinship ties.* These traits approximate charisma, virility, decisiveness, patriotism, and a strong family orientation. Latinos tend to respond better to strength and heroism than to persuasion, logic, or consensus.[20] On first encountering North Americans in any sort of business relationship, a Mexican will likely be suspicious and cautious. Generally speaking, trust can develop only over time, through a series of frequent, warm interpersonal transactions.

The Mexican labor market is immense, with approximately 10 million skilled and semi-skilled workers.[21] North Americans often perceive the Mexican as lazy and unconcerned about productivity. But the "siesta" stereotype is far from accurate. Companies such as GE, Cummins Engine, Kodak, Goodyear, and Nissan are convinced that the Mexican labor force is eager to work and certainly capable of producing world-quality goods. The work force is

young and open to new ideas, methods, and technologies. But their attitudes toward *time* are different from those of North Americans. Mexicans do not allow schedules to interfere with experiences involving family and friends. In business, they take time to talk and socialize. The Latin culture, in general, is *people oriented* rather than task oriented.[22] Labor unions are playing an increasingly important role. More than 25 percent of Mexico's labor force is unionized. There is much more popular support for collective bargaining than there was in the early 1980s. Historically, Mexican unions, were not aggressive, conceding to management if jobs were put in jeopardy. Currently, unions are becoming more vocal and assertive, no doubt because the government is supportive. The current government policy is to support strikes when workers' productivity is high. If the workers meet world standards—as the Ford employees who struck at Hermosillo in 1993 did—then the government is inclined to support their wage demands by putting immense pressure on management.[23]

Other notable HR management differences include employee selection and placement laws. For example, a thirty-day probationary period is law.[24] After an individual has been employed for one year, that employee may not be justifiably dismissed except for causes specifically identified by law. While there are no unemployment benefits, laid-off workers are legally entitled to three to six months' severance pay.

Overall, employee wages and benefits are much less than in the United States. The average 1992 manufacturing wage was $2.35 an hour in Mexico compared with $15.10 in the United States. Retirement programs are rare. A Social Security–type system is Mexico's primary mechanism for providing retirement income, addressing illness, and dealing with calamities, but it is woefully underfunded. Employee incentives such as profit sharing are becoming quite popular in Mexico. Large employers set aside a minimum of 8 percent of taxable profits for distribution to workers. There is concern that corporations are short-changing workers by underreporting earnings. The presence of a long-term housing shortage resulted in legislation that requires large employers in the industrial, mining, and agricultural sectors to provide, free of charge, shelter for employees and their families. Other government-mandated employee benefits are vacation premiums (at 125 percent of usual pay) and Christmas bonuses equaling at least fifteen days' pay.[25]

JAPAN

Japan is the industrial world's second largest economy. Although the nation has taken a fall recently, perhaps its worse since the oil embargo shock in 1974, don't count the Japanese out. While some wholesale rethinking is underway, the Japanese will find a way to make themselves more competitive. One management practice sure to go is Japan's social contract that promises **lifetime employment** (see *HR in the News:* "Guaranteed Lifetime Employment in Japan: Not Anymore!"). On the other hand, if national interests such as protecting their agricultural base were at stake, Japanese consumers wouldn't think twice about personal sacrifices. An example is their willingness to pay twice the amount necessary for rice, their primary food staple, rather than purchase cheaper and equally good foreign rice.

The Japanese share many cultural characteristics with other East Asians, and all of these groups contrast notably with North Americans. Some of the more obvious differences are reflected in Figure 2-2. There are many unwritten rules governing the workplace in Japan. For example, employees are expected to stay until the work is done, even if this practice violates wage and hour laws. The company and work comes first; family comes second. Con-

FIGURE 2-2 A comparison of cultural differences.

East Asian Countries

- Social concerns are more important than wealth.
- The group is the fundamental building block of society and is critical to motivating individual behavior.
- Family extends beyond siblings and parents, including distant relatives and even the nation.
- Work is valued, and employees are highly disciplined and organized.
- Education is a goal of parents for their children; it brings great prestige and economic security to the family.
- Status, social standing, and protocol are important.
- Harmony is more important than personal conflicts.

North America

- Economics (i.e., achieving wealth) is the primary motivator.
- Individual rights are the most fundamental concerns.
- Historically, the nuclear family was the building block of society.
- The importance of work has decreased and that of leisure has increased.
- Education is an investment in personal development/success.
- Rank and status are less important; competence is more important.
- There is nothing wrong with conflict; in fact, the energy it produces can lead to positive changes.

sequently, employees end up sleeping at their desk, socializing late into the evening, or playing golf on the weekends with colleagues and customers.

But Japan is no longer so insulated that what happens in the outside world cannot reverberate in their own society. The younger generations are choosing parts of Western culture as their own, such as putting their families

Guaranteed Lifetime Employment in Japan: Not Anymore!

TOKYO—As Japan's economy remains mired in a grim downturn, a debate is widening over whether big business still can afford Japan's paternalistic labor practices, including its vaunted guaranteed lifetime employment. And fears are spreading that major corporations will soon be forced to lay off workers—perhaps on a large scale.

Japan's blue-chip corporations have weathered downturns mainly by cutting overtime and bonuses, reducing hiring and asking employees—sometimes firmly—to take early retirement.

In previous downturns, it was assumed that a drop in business was cyclical, that sales would soon grow again, and that hiring would expand. The government even subsidized corporations to protect the no-layoff policy. While Western governments give money to workers after they lose their jobs, Tokyo pays distressed companies not to lay off workers.

But such policies may have boosted complacency at corporations and may mask the true scale of unemployment in Japan. Experts estimate that there are millions of "in-house unemployed" workers on company payrolls.

Some critics say that Japan's conventional labor practices actually hurt the economy by making it harder for corporations to go through much needed changes. In a recent bank survey, more than a third of the companies said that the biggest obstacle to restructuring was the inability to lay off workers. "In the long run we are going to have to have a fluid labor market," said one Japanese economist. "To some extent, there is something we can learn from the U.S. experience."

first, and over time this will make Japan look and feel very different.

HR Practices in Japan

As noted, the Japanese taboo against layoffs is ending. Toyota, for example, is creating a new category of temporary professional workers. The company is hiring a limited number of *one-year* automotive designers instead of offering them a customary lifelong job. In another break with tradition, Toyota pays them a higher salary based on individual merit, rather than linking pay to seniority and company performance.

63

Nevertheless, most males who work for major corporations will stay with their employer for their entire work lives. The "lifetime" offer is good only until age fifty-five, at which time executives are expected to retire. In fact, the system never covered more than one-third of the work force, and it has always omitted most of the people working in small companies, retirees who return to the work force, and all women. Historically, women tended to leave their jobs when they married, but even that practice may be changing due to economic changes.

Good benefits, automatic raises and promotions (although slower than in the United States), and early retirement benefits, not to mention job rotation and a lot of training, help to stabilize the company work force. It is important to note that what a Japanese corporation practices in Japan is not necessarily how it manages in another country. Toyota in the United States, for example, never offers lifetime job guarantees.

The Role of Women   Japanese women represent 40 percent of the total work force, but the vast majority are relegated to clerical or service jobs. Approximately half of managerial posts of all kinds in the United States are held by women; the ratio in Japan is less than 1 in 10. Women are responsible for all family duties, including child raising, housekeeping, and care of the elderly and sick. But that position also gives the wife leverage over her spouse. It is the wife who controls the husband's paycheck and the children's education, the latter being one of the most important measures of status and success in Japan (see Figure 2-2).[26]

While many more women are opting for careers, they are finding it tough to compete with males. Even women graduating from Japan's most elite universities are being forced to scale back their expectations. Statistics for 1993 show that 66 percent of graduating women have job commitments compared with 85 percent of men; half of the firms hiring refused to hire women as career workers despite a new law requiring it; and part-time workers, nearly all of whom are women, work up to 43 hours a week but get paid 44 percent of the hourly wages of a full-time male worker.[27]

Equal Opportunity Laws   By 1986 Japan had passed equal opportunity laws that were intended to protect women from unfair hiring practices, wage discrimination, and discharge. It was hoped that doors would be opened and women would have access to meaningful jobs that would free them from serving tea and answering telephones, the traditional duties of the "office ladies." Unfortunately, the laws had no teeth and only urged companies to treat women fairly and consistently.[28]

Without even the threat of penalties, there is little hope that Japanese women can make significant progress. And the declining economy has only aggravated the situation. The recession is forcing some corporations to lay off workers, and women, it is turning out, are the primary victims. Hoping to save the jobs of management-track *sarimen,* most of whom are male, companies are shedding clerical workers—99 percent of whom are female.[29] While positive changes have occurred for women, such as the so-called two-track system described in the accompanying *HR in the News:* "Japanese Track System Isn't Working," most are superficial and designed only to enhance the company's international image by appearing to be in step with efforts to ensure women's equality.

Recruitment and Selection   A normal practice is to begin recruiting certain university applicants well before the time they actually begin employment. These applicants for management and technical positions are often expected to pass an examination covering Japanese language skills, mathematics, English, and one or two specialized functions. Going to work for foreign firms, particularly early in a

Japanese Track System
Isn't Working

TOKYO—As part of the bargain to keep "teeth" out of Japan's Equal Employment Opportunity Act, businesses agreed to offer new workers their choice of job path.

They could opt for "sogo shoku," the career track, or "ippan shoku," the general employee system. That way, business leaders claimed, any woman (or man) could get onto the fast track simply by asking.

But the much ballyhooed two-track system is in danger of going belly-up.

Because the law carries no penalties, many companies blatantly deny women access to the career track with no fear of recrimination. Meanwhile, women themselves are turning down the career-path option.

"The two-track system is silly," said veteran journalist Mitsuko Shimomura, who works for the 8 million circulation Asahi Shimbun. "It's just another way to discriminate against women."

Seven years after the law came into force, it is now becoming clear that its impact is negligible.

In a survey of 8,000 companies by the Japan Productivity Center in November, 51 percent said they never hire women for career positions and 18 percent said they do so only occasionally.

Tokyo University professor Chizuko Ueno surveys personnel departments and has found that while all men opt for the career track (it's automatic for them), only 1 percent of women do. Moreover, women's survival rate is dismally low.

Under the plan, women who opt for the career track are to be treated equally with men, getting the same promotions, opportunities, training and salaries. But it rarely works out that way, said Ueno.

Her survey shows that women aren't given the same responsibilities and power and, in fact, often are nothing more than glorified "office ladies," or general track employees who do clerical work. They may even have to wear the same uniform as office ladies while men dress in street clothes.

Also, because so many big decisions are made outside the office—on the golf course or in bars at night, places to which women aren't often invited or able to go—they are left out of the decision-making loop.

"I'd come in the next day and say, 'What are we going to do about such and such,' and they'd say, 'Oh, we settled that last night,' " said one career-path woman whose family responsibilities kept her from weekend and evening activities.

Moreover, many young women simply don't want the grueling life of the corporate samurai. Newspapers report regularly on the new syndrome of "burnout" among professional women racing to keep up with their male counterparts but without the help of a wife or mother to cook, clean and pack their bags.

Japan's seniority and life-time employment systems virtually preclude career-track women from marriage and a family, particularly since women are responsible for nearly all child care, elderly care and housekeeping. Once off the track for family leave, it is impossible to get back on. *(continued)*

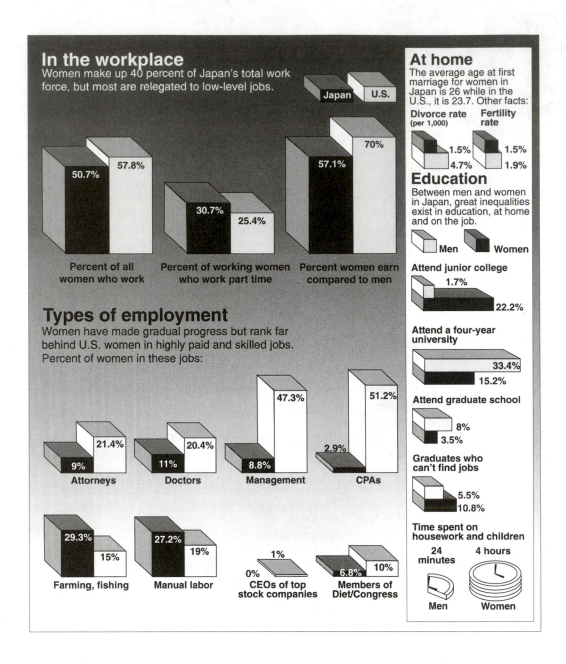

In the workplace
Women make up 40 percent of Japan's total work force, but most are relegated to low-level jobs.

Japan | U.S.

Percent of all women who work: 50.7% / 57.8%

Percent of working women who work part time: 30.7% / 25.4%

Percent women earn compared to men: 57.1% / 70%

Types of employment
Women have made gradual progress but rank far behind U.S. women in highly paid and skilled jobs. Percent of women in these jobs:

Attorneys: 9% / 21.4%
Doctors: 11% / 20.4%
Management: 8.8% / 47.3%
CPAs: 2.9% / 51.2%
Farming, fishing: 29.3% / 15%
Manual labor: 27.2% / 19%
CEOs of top stock companies: 0% / 1%
Members of Diet/Congress: 6.8% / 10%

At home
The average age at first marriage for women in Japan is 26 while in the U.S., it is 23.7. Other facts:

Divorce rate (per 1,000): 1.5% / 4.7%
Fertility rate: 1.5% / 1.9%

Education
Between men and women in Japan, great inequalities exist in education, at home and on the job.

Men | Women

Attend junior college: 1.7% / 22.2%

Attend a four-year university: 33.4% / 15.2%

Attend graduate school: 8% / 3.5%

Graduates who can't find jobs: 5.5% / 10.8%

Time spent on housework and children:
Men: 24 minutes
Women: 4 hours

In spite of the rampant violation of the law, however, nothing is being done to correct it. Not a single test lawsuit has been filed, according to leading feminist attorney Mizuho Fukushima.

"Young women in Japan are so reluctant," said Fukushima. "But I am waiting."

SOURCE: Ellen Hale, "Japanese Track System Isn't Working," Gannett News Services, reprinted by *The Courier-Journal* (January 16, 1994): E1. Copyright 1994, Gannett Co., Inc. Reprinted with permission.

career, is risky. If it doesn't work out, the employee may have a harder time finding employment later with a Japanese organization.[30]

Performance Appraisal The Japanese concept of performance varies from that of the West and includes not only the achievement of actual results but the expenditure of good faith effort. Job duties are generally broader and more ambiguous than in North America. There are no clear-cut job descriptions.[31] New employees are expected to learn by doing rather than from a written description, and they are expected to do anything. The national culture encourages a sense of collectivity and precludes a strong identification with occupational expertise; for example, employees do not see themselves in terms of their skills, such as marketer or HR management professional, but rather as a Toyota family member.

Compensation is not considered a measure of personal worth, as in the United States. Salary increases and promotions are generally automatic and result from time on the job, not necessarily exceptional performance. There does appear to be a movement away from the seniority system. While bonuses are common, the principal motivators are interesting assignments, training opportunities, and eventual promotion to a higher grade or managerial position.[32]

Benefits Japanese companies provide various fringe benefits, including transportation allowances, housing subsidies, meals at work, family allowances, and use of company-owned recreation facilities. There is a Social Security program that covers health insurance, unemployment, disability, and a state pension insurance plan. Employees may contribute up to half of the premiums, and the employer pays the difference.[33]

Labor Unions Labor relations are distinctly different from North American practices. In Japan, unions are organized on a company basis

rather than on an industry or trade basis. These company-based "enterprise unions" restrict membership to company employees, including lower-level managers. In the past, as much as 90 percent of eligible employees joined; that proportion has been declining in recent years.[34]

Another difference is that labor unions and management are partners, not adversaries. They act together to solve problems, such as productivity declines and personnel transfers.

Enterprise unions are grouped into national federations. Every spring, labor unions act in unison to negotiate wage increases with management. This spring offensive is known as *shunto*, and is the most important nationwide labor activity. The final contract between organized labor and management is then used as a yardstick by employers of unorganized labor to determine wage increases for their employees.[35]

Japanese HR Management Practices in the United States

The Japanese presence in the United States is strong. Over 300,000 Americans hold jobs in Japanese-owned companies. Most of the jobs are in the manufacturing sector, principally the automotive industry. As more Americans find themselves working for a Japanese company, questions arise as to how these companies train and motivate their employees.

Toyota USA, for example, has a large operation in Georgetown, Kentucky, employing more than 5000 employees, with expansion expected by 1996 that will double this capacity. The chief product at Georgetown is the Camry. The manager is Japanese, as are most of the top management staff. The HR management philosophy is depicted in Figure 2-3 and is built around one pervasive theme: the Toyota production system. Emphasis is given to various methods of selecting employees, developing their skills, and creating a support system that reinforces the desired behaviors.

FIGURE 2-3 HR management in the Toyota production system.

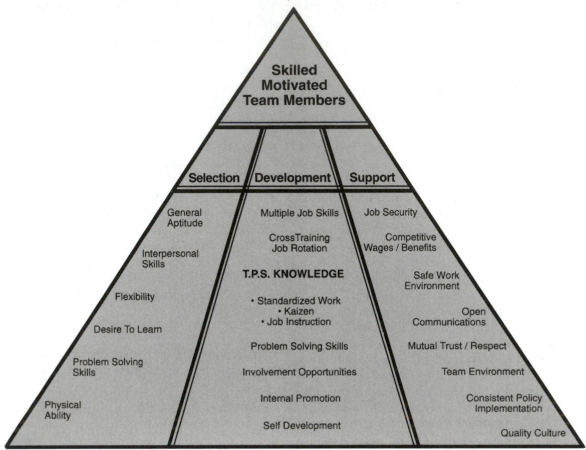

Taken together, the result is a company culture that is strong, pervasive, and focused on quality, continuous learning, and cooperation.

A number of HR management practices are designed to support teams. The company provides uniforms to almost everyone. The only distinction between leaders and their groups is a small insignia on the leaders' hats. Calisthenics are part of the morning regimen but are not mandatory. Except for production schedules, virtually no computers are used. They don't rely on electronic mail either, and they encourage face-to-face communication whenever possible.

Everyone starts out as a team member. All production workers belong to a team and a group. There are three to five people in a team, and they usually rotate jobs within the team every two hours. Groups are composed of three to five teams. Each group has its own meeting area where important information is posted on walls, floors, or anywhere there is space. Teams meet at least twice per day. If the team meets over lunch, the company will cover for the lunch—but will not compensate them for their time.

Quality circles (QC) are a big part of the Toyota culture. They are independent of teams

Shifting Gears:
Americans Are Less
Enamored of Japanese
Techniques

After spending billions of dollars refitting and automating their factories, many American manufacturers are coming to the conclusion that some of the Japanese systems, however useful in Japan, haven't achieved much here in the States. Companies such as GE and Whirlpool have abandoned efforts to implement quality circles because it hasn't made them really competitive. The reason comes down to cultural differences—these methods work in Japan because the culture supports them.

Some American companies also invested heavily in copying Japanese automation and are now reversing themselves. Federal-Mogul, an auto-parts company in Lancaster, PA, was burdened with high labor costs in 1987. After investing in state-of-the-art automation—and with ideas imported from Japan—the company started turning out parts faster than ever. But there was one big problem. It couldn't shift gears fast enough. And changing product lines quickly and efficiently was more important to the company's customers than the speed of parts being produced. Out went the automated equipment, the robots, and most production-line computers. Now, when product change-overs occur, the company relies on its workers to make the important decisions.

Another "fad" biting the dust is quality circles. No doubt, the concept has merit—workers brainstorm ideas to improve quality, and management provides the training to make it happen. The Whirlpool Corporation invested heavily in quality circles but concluded that they weren't sufficiently focused. Their QC's ended up discussing a lot of unrelated issues that are often referred to as "creature comforts," such as what vending machines to include in employees' lounges. Now Whirlpool has shifted gears and adopted "gainsharing" methods, under which employees participate in savings resulting from quality improvements.

Another company disembarking off the quality circles boat is GE, but for different reasons. They found it too rigid and narrow for freewheeling American workers. The QC idea doesn't lend itself to interrelating functions and still depends too much on direction from the top. GE has refined the QC concept into something they call "**work-out**." Workers and managers will get together, usually away from the work setting, to discuss radically new ideas. Instead of members coming from an already intact work group, these members represent different functions which impact the process. And instead of only incremental changes, work-outs are capable of making significant improvements that may require major investment. Managers are expected to respond to workers' suggestions on the

(continued)

69

spot. Rewards are allocated on an individual basis, a purely American characteristic, rather than the Japanese approach of giving recognition only to the group.

Certainly there is a lot we can learn from everyone, not just the Japanese. Yet whatever methods are adopted, each must fit the existing culture. Simply mechanically copying what works in Japan, Sweden, or Timbuktu isn't going to fly anymore.

SOURCE: Reprinted by permission of *Wall Street Journal*. "Some Manufacturers Drop Efforts to Adopt Japanese Techniques," *Wall Street Journal* (May 7, 1993): A1. Dow Jones & Company, Inc. All rights reserved worldwide.

and groups. Employees who want to participate can choose their own theme to work on. Over 50 percent of the work force participates. Employees whose suggestions are implemented are rewarded a percentage of the savings. Included are suggestions from anyone, whether he or she is a member of a QC or not. So far, the awards have varied from $5 to $10,000.

With so many positive factors in place, it might appear that the Japanese have discovered the secret to successful HR management practices in the United States. Not quite. Japanese firms have been the targets of litigation on race, age, and sex discrimination. One study concluded that the location pattern of Japanese automobile facilities in the United States pointed to a systematic effort to avoid heavily nonwhite regions.[36] There has also been some concern that the Japanese are reluctant to fully integrate locally hired managers into the corporations' upper hierarchy. Last, there are concerns that the Japanese techniques being used in the United States are not culturally compatible. Once popular, QCs are being dropped by American companies (see *HR in the News:* "Shifting Gears"). And concerns are being raised in Japan's U.S. organizations regarding the lack of clear performance standards and performance appraisal procedures.

WESTERN EUROPE

Western Europe is an area with great diversity among national cultures. Three of the larger cultures—the British, French, and Germans—are as different from each other as Americans are from Mexicans. Although efforts toward a United States of Europe have met resistance, most experts believe that by the turn of the century there will be a free flow of goods, workers, and services throughout the Economic Community.

Europeans, as a whole, do share many traditions. One is that it is government's duty to care for those in need. The cradle-to-grave **social welfare** system, which was designed for the needs of earlier generations, may not be wholly appropriate to today's conditions. It is also contributing to Europe's inability to compete in the global marketplace (see *HR in the News:* "Economic Hardships Taking Toll in Europe"). Reforms are currently underway, and by the year 2000, Europe and North America may be more alike than different when it comes to welfare programs.

Another tradition under attack is the widely held notion that every worker is entitled to a "just wage"—even when market forces drive down the cost of labor. In the past, some countries (notably France, Germany, and Italy) refused to use wages as the primary strategy

Economic Hardships
Taking Toll in Europe

Europeans have a long tradition of extending generous welfare protection benefits to their citizens, such as universal coverage for health care, pensions, and unemployment compensation. However, a recession, soaring budget deficits, aging populations, increasing medical costs, and a lack of global competitiveness are some of the immediate factors driving Europeans to shrink their welfare states. This is important to private enterprises because they are expected to shoulder most of the expense; in Italy, for example, employers cover more than half the cost.[1] Predictably, corporations are leading the fight to trim expensive social programs.

As the European market becomes more open and global competition heats up, odds are that the social justice principle will erode or perhaps become completely unattainable. Governments and societies, without business support, are reluctant to continue to foot the bill. But the 1993 recession, including an unheard-of 10 percent unemployment rate, is forcing all the countries of Western Europe to reassess their entitlement programs and, for a few, a hasty retreat. All over Europe, governments are taking measures to reduce burdens on the public purse and to encourage workplace flexibility.[2]

SOURCES: [1]"Europe's Social Cushion Is Looking Rather Frayed," *Business Week* (July 5, 1993): 50. [2]"French Flounder," *Wall Street Journal* (October 29, 1993): A16.

for gaining a competitive advantage. French unions and their former socialist government, for example, insisted that companies refrain from cutting wages simply to lower costs and gain market share over rivals.

One principle of all market economies is the importance of gaining a competitive advantage over rivals. In most Western European countries, labor costs are high; thus, advantages must come from elsewhere, such as technology, manufacturing processes, and so on. For many Third World nations, trade advantages often come from lower labor costs. European competitiveness is suffering from some of the highest labor costs in the world, as Table 2-1 clearly illustrates. In order to protect their

workers' wages, these governments intrude in the market economy and subsidize an inefficient industry (e.g., French farming) or, in the case of foreign competition, slap a tariff on imported goods. Businesses understand that labor costs must come down, but as with their welfare programs, they are fighting a century-old tradition.

The role of European trade unions is shifting. As companies become more able to move freely anywhere in the Economic Community and into low-wage Central and Eastern European countries, unions are coming under increasing pressure to abandon socialist ideals. The auto makers Daimler-Benz, Opal, and Volkswagen have announced plans to cut

Table 2-1 Comparative Labor Costs Approximate

Country	Hourly Manufacturing Labor Cost ($)	Paid Holidays per Year (days)	Total Hours Worked per Week	Total Taxes as a Share of GDP
Germany	$26.40	30	37*	40%
Japan	17.29	11	41	29
France	16.36	25	38	43
U.S.	15.1	12	40	30
United Kingdom	14.9	27	38	32

*The workweek is guaranteed not to exceed thirty-five hours by 1995.

SOURCE: *U.S. News & World Report* (October 25, 1993): 42–43.

thousands of jobs in Germany and shift some production to Eastern Europe.

European wages and benefits are generous even by U.S. standards. German manufacturing workers, for example, receive an average hourly wage of $26.40 (see Table 2-1), work only a thirty-seven-hour week, and receive lengthy vacations.[37]

One particular union, Germany's IG Metall (metalworkers), has won for its members some of the highest wages and shortest work weeks in the world.

France

The French have a reputation for being proud and nationalistic. Given their heritage and accomplishments, this attitude is understandable. France has a market economy in which individual and private ownership are valued. Historically, government was the primary driver in the workings of the economic system through legislation, monetary policy, and social policy.[38] However, as global competition heats up, the government is finding itself in the unpleasant position of having to sell off many of its state-owned enterprises.

The French motto "Liberty, Equality and Fraternity" expresses the essence of their culture. It also has influenced many other cultures, such as those of Canadians, Mexicans, and Americans. Nevertheless, the French culture is different from the U.S. culture in several noticeable ways. The French, typically, are not as competitive as Americans and do not feel comfortable when put in a competitive position.[39] Paradoxically, the French do not mind conflict and sometimes enjoy it. A conversation between two screaming Frenchmen may seem unpleasant to the casual American observer, but to the French such an argument is interesting and stimulating.[40]

Another obvious difference from the U.S. culture is the French attitude toward politeness and business etiquette. The French put special importance in greeting people with such terms as *bonjour,* using proper addresses such as *Madame* or *Monsieur,* and shaking hands frequently. First names are used only by intimate associates.[41]

The French are productive and hard workers. They take great pride in their work but do not like to work overtime. Quality of life is more important than achievement, which may explain the lengthy vacations the French like to take.

As to decision making, the typical French worker is more comfortable letting top executives do it. There is less delegation of responsibility than in the United States, and tight reins of authority contribute to a rigid organizational structure.[42]

The population is highly skilled and multilingual; approximately 80 percent speak a second language.[43] Employee training and development is given high priority by the government and by French corporations. The most prestigious educational institutions, know as the "grandes ecoles," prepare most of the country's managers and administrators. These institutions promote management as a state of mind rather than a set of techniques. In fact, France is often called the Japan of Europe because what Japan achieves through consensus, France achieves through a core of like-minded people.[44] The relationship between business and state has always been close. The government provides financial and technical assistance for the unemployed or for those industries where jobs have become obsolete.

Recruitment and selection methods and laws are not very different from those of the United States; for example, certain protected groups (e.g., the disabled, veterans) are given employment preferences. Surprisingly few restrictions or limitations exist in terms of what the interviewer may ask of job applicants.

The French have a reputation for mixing business and pleasure at the office. Consequently, when the Clarence Thomas/Anita Hill hearings occurred in the United States, the French press made humorous note of the event, even suggesting that Americans might be taking office relationships too seriously. Since then, many French women (and a few men) have come forward with their own stories of being sexually harassed. There now appears to be a movement advocating the abolishment of unwanted sexual advances at work. Whether legislation is passed protecting employees from sexual harassment remains to be seen.

Most employees are hired on a probationary basis, subject to collective bargaining agreements. Dismissing an employee in the private sector is not very different from the practice in the United States. Usually ample justification must be provided and strict procedural steps followed. Discharging a worker in the French public sector is almost impossible.[45] However, downsizing is becoming more prevalent, and special procedures must be followed.

Individual performance appraisals and peer evaluations do not occur regularly. Furthermore, goal setting and management by objectives are not widely accepted in France as useful management techniques. The reason may be the notion that goals, appraisals, and performance feedback tend to encourage the competitive spirit of Americans but do little to motivate the typical French worker. Job security and leisure time are more important to the French.[46]

Labor unions are prevalent throughout all French industries and make up about 15 percent of the work force.[47] French unions are unique, even in Europe, because their orientation is political rather than social or economic. French labor unions are notorious for striking at inappropriate moments—as many unsuspecting tourists visiting Paris have discovered the hard way.

Germany

The rebuilding of West Germany following World War II into the third largest worldwide economic giant—behind the United States and Japan—is one of the world's great achievements. Now the Germans are faced with another formidable challenge. The fall of the Berlin Wall on November 9, 1989, and the subsequent reunification of West and East Germany was a triumph for the free enterprise system over communism. However, early expectations for a quick economic transition in the East have been dampened by the European recession. While the most serious obstacles are economic, there is also a vast array of problems rooted in social, cultural, political, and organizational differences.

An HR management perspective raises questions on how to change the national and corporate cultures of the East, influenced by more than forty years of communism, into efficient organizations that can compete effectively in global markets. Even under ideal conditions it is an arduous task. Unfortunately, the German government is faced with other daunting challenges: high interest rates, brutal global competition, labor strife, and the most severe unemployment since World War II.

Will the Germans weather the storm? Can they reinvent industry in the East? Will they come to grips with an economic crisis on a scale they have not seen in decades? The answers lie in their history. The Germans have long held the respect of the world when it comes to being focused, industrious, hardworking, and exact. Other German strengths are a highly trained and literate work force, an efficient national infrastructure, years of export savvy, and a strong social contract among government, labor, and business.

A characteristic unique to Germany is the legally defined role of labor in all business decisions. The arrangement is called **codetermination**. Employees are given certain rights and obligations in relation to the employer and, as a group, are given the right to participate in matters concerning plant operations.[48]

Every business, except the very smallest, is expected to have a **workers' council** that represents the employees, addresses complaints, and ensures that management adheres to labor laws. The net effect is that workers' councils have a major say on everything from the selection of CEOs to restructuring and layoffs.[49]

In no other industrialized country is labor so involved in management decision making. Management must be able to work with and through the workers' council when it comes to HR planning, recruiting, restructuring, and downsizing. Job analysis is thorough, and unions are sensitive to any attempt to reclassify or change established ways of performing work tasks.

With so much emphasis on employees' rights, it is surprising that equal employment and antidiscrimination laws are much weaker than in the United States. However, employers are limited in the range of questions they may ask job applicants; for example, they may not inquire about marital status, political party, trade union membership, or religious affiliation.[50]

Performance appraisals are an accepted practice in Germany. They are usually annual and very formal. They are always done in private. Custom dictates that evaluations are the responsibility of managers; thus, peer evaluations and self-evaluations are uncommon. German managers have a reputation for being cautious, conservative, and less flexible than American managers—but that situation may be changing.[51]

Labor, management, and government put great emphasis on training. An extensive **apprenticeship** program is available to qualified youths. About 65 percent of middle school graduates (equivalent to U.S. high school graduates) enter apprenticeship training in fields ranging from skilled manufacturing to office work. Over three years, these apprentices spend four days per week in on-the-job training and at least one day per week at a state-supported vocational school.[52] The partnership also allows employees to upgrade existing skills. The German model for training young people in various crafts, particularly through apprenticeship programs, is considered the best in the world.

However, while the labor–management partnership worked with near-perfection for four decades, there are signs that it is beginning to unravel. Germany's workers are now the highest paid in the world (see Table 2-1). Their unions have negotiated extremely generous benefits, including six weeks of vacation a year and a thirty-five-hour workweek. Although Germany does not provide a lifetime employment guarantee, there are strict rules for termination of labor contracts.

Recently, the German economy has begun to decline in terms of global competitiveness. Unlike U.S. companies, which started much earlier, German companies have only recently begun eliminating layers of management and making the painful transition to flatter, leaner structures. Labor was not affected because the unions were too powerful and resisted. Now many hourly workers will pay a painful price too as their companies struggle to catch up with their global rivals. Unemployment in 1993, for example, was 10 percent—16 percent in the East.[53]

Most experts believe that the key to German productivity is the partnership between labor, management, and government. Government and management recognize what needs to be done to regain a competitive edge. The question remains: Will Germany's unions face up to the realities of a recession and a bloated, inflexible work force? While some unions continue to push their traditional demands, such as IG Metall, others recognize the futility of it and are trading wage moderation and greater job flexibility for job security.[54]

United Kingdom

The United Kingdom is one of the most industrialized nations in the world. It was also the first industrial nation. It is composed of England, Scotland, Wales, and Northern Ireland, as well as some smaller possessions throughout the world. Two world wars and the loss of colonies have sapped the nation's once mighty industrial strength. Nationalization of key industries, such as steel, failed to revitalize an economy plagued by labor disputes and low worker productivity. The government reversed its nationalization course and began privatizing during the 1980s.[55] It now appears that the country is moving forward again and will continue to be a major force in the global arena.

The United Kingdom and United States have always been close economic traders. And, of course, the United Kingdom has strong economic ties with its continental neighbors through the European Community. Customs and language make the United Kingdom an attractive springboard into Europe for U.S. and Canadian investors.

As to customs, it would seem that the United States and United Kingdom, thanks to

common language and laws, share many traditions, and that is true. But there are many distinctions too. The British are more punctual and polite than the Americans. While they are not as serious or conservative as the Germans and appreciate humor when it is natural, they do want to get down to business.[56]

The U.S. preoccupation with making money and efficiency is generally not prevalent in the United Kingdom. Tradition is important, and time-honored conventions such as high tea have been preserved. Tradition also explains why the British tend to rely on old school ties for recruiting, selecting, and promoting within their management ranks. Conversely, a somewhat exclusive educational system makes it difficult for children from working-class families to attend a university.[57]

Although HR management practices across the United States and United Kingdom are quite similar, labor relations are very different. One difference is that in the United Kingdom, many more people belong to labor unions. Organized labor represents nearly half of the working population. Another difference is philosophical. Labor—management conflict in the United States has been called adversarial and usually comes down to the bread-and-butter issues of wages, benefits, and working conditions. In the U.K. the conflict is closer to a class struggle.[58]

Since the birth of the Industrial Revolution, there has existed a fairly rigid social class system separating workers, management, and owners. The struggle among them led to the birth of militant trade unionism, which favored nationalization of private property while regarding profit and productivity as irrelevant.[59] Labor relations have improved in recent years, however, due to global economic competition and a history of a people who respond best to adversity.

In contrast to the United States, labor relations in the United Kingdom are characterized by the relative absence of legal constraints and structuring. Trade unions are voluntary associations, not legal entities. Collective bargaining agreements are understandings, not contracts; they have no legal status.

Collective bargaining is conducted at both industry and company levels. A typical agreement reflects an understanding between the parties at a given time. If conditions change, a new understanding is required. Agreements typically cover wages (or minimum piece rates), job classification, pay for overtime and shift work, the standard workweek, and procedures for settling disputes and changing the agreement.

Employee benefits, for the most part, are covered by a generous social welfare system called the *National Health Service* (NHS). This system is available to all residents, whether they hold jobs or not. As in the rest of Europe, the NHS's million-member work force is being pruned. Employers are being pressured to provide additional benefits such as pensions.

Employee participation is beginning to take hold in the United Kingdom. Many unions are working with management to create shop floor democracy as a strategy for reducing production costs and improving product quality. It is doubtful if codetermination, or legally mandated industrial democracy, will ever exist in the United Kingdom as it does in Germany.

CENTRAL/EASTERN EUROPE

"Where were you when the Wall came down?"
Business Week (November 27, 1989)

If there was one single day that captures the collapse of Communism, it was the day the Berlin Wall fell. Events moved rapidly once the wall came down. Map makers had a hard time keeping up with new national boundaries (Figure 2-4). Beginning in Poland, then in Hungary, and ultimately in the former Soviet Union, governments were toppled and new forms of government were introduced. The Czechoslovaks (even their name has changed) refer to this period as the *Velvet Revolution* because it was relatively free of violence. Thankfully, the public and many of the leaders recognized the inevitability of change by refusing to resort to repressive tactics.

The transition to market systems has not been easy. All of the countries in the region have been the victims of centralized socialistic planning that has left them with ill-prepared, unproductive workers, obsolete factories, a devastated infrastructure, double-digit unemployment, and runaway inflation (30–100 percent).

The good news is that democracy has taken root in Central Europe, including Hungary, Poland, and the Czech and Slovak republics (i.e., formerly Czechoslovakia). Having historic links with the West, these countries have asked for admission to the European Community. They currently hold associate status, but odds are that most will achieve full status by the year 2000.

The transition is not proceeding as smoothly in Eastern European countries such as Russia, Ukraine, Bulgaria, and Rumania (see Figure 2-4).[60] These countries are still in the earliest stages of market reform, and some, such as Russia, keep tilting toward turning the clock back to communism. It may be hard for Americans to accept, but there was a positive side to communism. In Communist societies, for example, the bottom 40 percent of the population had a higher relative income than they do under capitalism. As Westerners know firsthand, in market systems there are both winners and losers (economically speaking). Income differences will now be obvious, with the newly affluent acquiring big homes and cars. There is a real risk that people will reject a market economy out of resentment and because the quality of their lives has diminished rather than improved.

FIGURE 2-4 What will Europe look like in 2000?

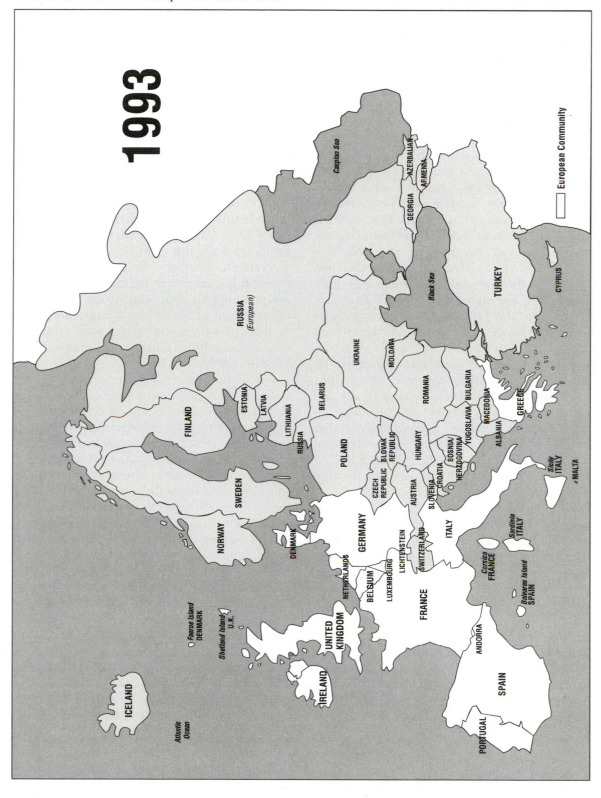

"I'll Pretend to Work if You Pretend to Pay Me"

The idea behind command economies was that everything could be planned, and if the plan was sufficiently comprehensive, there would be no crisis that could not be met. Every factory was nationalized, categorized by industry, and controlled by a particular ministry.

The ministries and planners collected data from technicians and then devised a central plan. Then they "commanded" each factory what to produce, what to sell, how much it should cost, where supplies and raw materials could be found, the number of people employed, their pay and their bonuses, their job titles and their promotions. There was little opportunity for managers and workers to provide input. However, that did not matter as long as everything and everyone functioned according to the plan.

Clearly, a centralized plan depended on workers who would cooperate. Promotions were awarded on the basis of party loyalty and connections. If the worker happened to be educated and was qualified, chances are that that particular combination was an accident. In fact, management was not considered to be a respectable or relevant profession because Marxism had all the answers anyway.

Unfortunately, the best people were discouraged from taking risks and making tough decisions. Instead, they spent their working lives as paper pushers or fixers. The former group concentrated on writing regulations, completing endless reports, and negotiating with the ministry about quotas, production targets, and prices. The latter were good at locating suppliers, raw materials, and replacement parts and at trading for hard currencies. Under communism, making connections, networking, and depending on relationships for favors were refined and valued skills.

The Communist system discouraged initiative and action. More often, it was compliance that enabled ambitious managers to move up the socialist ladder. Many managers were paralyzed by the fear of making a mistake. Whenever possible, managers held endless meetings, requested additional research and data, and, in the end, pushed the decision upstairs, leaving the task for their bosses to complete.

Trade unions existed under Communism but were actually only extensions of the government. Apart from Solidarity in Poland, few trade unions operated independently of the Communist Party. It was not unusual for more than 90 percent of the workers to participate in trade unions. But those numbers have declined since 1989 to less than half. Most people have even less faith in trade unions than they do in their new governments. Now a new breed of union leaders are at the helm. Most unions are pursuing an independent course and, at the moment, appear to have more interest in market economics and privatization proposals than in the political and social agendas of their Western European cousins.

Since the fall of Communism, millions of citizens have gone into business for themselves, the majority being modest mom-and-pop operations. Governments are selling off (or trying to) their best state-owned companies. And Western companies, many of them from the United States, are shopping for bargains that offer them the best opportunities for making the transition to profitability. Realistically, the majority of state-owned enterprises will go it alone once state subsidies are terminated. A few state enterprises will be sold to the employees and managers, thanks to long-term but very high-interest loans from the government and investors. And, of course, some enterprises are not viable under any conditions and will simply disappear. The speed of the transition varies by country, from Poland's attempt to get it over with as quickly as possible to the go-slow approaches of Hungary and Slovakia.

For most countries (the former East Germany is the sole exception), the road from Communism to capitalism has been fraught with detours and delays. One hurdle is the creation of laws and financial systems that make it possible for citizens to buy and sell property. Another is the need to educate the average citizen about market systems. Under Communism, for example, the customer was never king. A sales clerk would not hesitate to intimidate any customer who requested a simple service. That tradition will be difficult to overcome.

The Need for Management Reeducation

Another vital need is for management reeducation. Communist managers adhered to Communist dogmas. They were more concerned about following the official party line and less about quality and productivity. They often lacked the most basic skills, attitudes, and mind sets considered normal in a market economy.[61]

Financial management, cost accounting, pricing, market research, product and customer service, quality control, and human resource management were skills not in great demand or necessary to run a state company. Universities refused to offer courses in these areas because the state considered their "social value" to be minimal.[62] A Czech colleague of one of the authors sums up how management was viewed:

> The political regime believed that Marxism had all the answers, and management, both as a theoretical discipline and as a practice, was considered superfluous at best and, at worst, a threat to the system. Much more attention was devoted to meticulous planning than management. The Communists hoped that state control would take care of all the nuts and bolts of the economy. People in the companies were simply expected to carry out the orders from above. The planners considered ridiculous the assumption that any education or training, let alone one in management, would help the managers carry out their responsibilities or improve the efficiency of the economy.
>
> Michal Cakrt, Czechoslovak Management Center

Obviously, management training and development is a top priority. A number of American companies are joining with Central and Eastern Europeans as partners in a variety of endeavors.[63] But changing the old Communist culture and replacing it with something new—a culture that blends the best of each partner—is not going to be easy. One major hurdle is language. If an American multinational acquires a Czech company, for example, which language should take precedence? Most Americans would respond that English makes most sense; after all, that is the language in which most global business communication occurs. Yet that kind of thinking is arrogant.

Americans often think that English is the universal language of commerce, and it is true that it is spoken throughout the world. But do not tell that to the French or to people of other nationalities. If there is a stereotype the world holds of Americans, it is that they are language illiterates who know only one language. If Americans are to compete globally, some foreign language skills will be necessary.

Once language difficulties can be overcome, transnationals such as Philip Morris, GE, and Digital often choose to send critical host staff to the West for training. Living and working in the West is a powerful change strategy, but it is so costly that only a few ever have the opportunity. As another option, Western companies may offer specialized management training to their host employees by importing trainers from the West, preferably those who can speak the local language. But that is not always possible because some languages are spoken by only a small percentage of people. For example, locating a competent management trainer, who speaks fluent Romanian and who would be willing to accept a hardship assignment in Bucharest is not easy.

The last option, and the least preferred, is to use interpreters with training. Some Western companies depend on host interpreters to translate into their host's language. Anyone who has ever used interpreters will attest to the number of errors that inevitably occur, particularly when the material is technical and new to the interpreters themselves.

China

The most populous country in the world, and probably the oldest, China is changing with breathtaking speed. Yet this change is occurring under unusual circumstances. China remains a Communist country. Its economy is purely Chinese—neither capitalistic nor socialistic, and the means of production (i.e., capital, raw materials, labor, and land) remain in the public sector. The country's leaders continue to retain control of all major industrial sectors.

But China needs massive amounts of hard currency to survive, and that means opening up its markets to the West. Opening the door also allows the Chinese Communist Party to cling to power by relaxing controls and making a limited amount of foreign consumer goods available. The old leadership is betting that the Chinese people will continue to accept party rule if their lives improve economically.

Doing business in China, as anyone who remembers the events at Tiananmen Square (June 4, 1989) will verify, is not for the faint of heart. Business failures far outnumber successes. The fragile and unpredictable economy explains why there have been many burps and hiccups along the path to open market systems.

One of the most serious obstacles to overcome is **corruption**. It is pervasive. The government has entirely too many bureaucrats, and most of them are on the take. But before judging them, consider that **bribery** is an old and normal method of conducting business. One foreign businessman in China relates his story: "To get a small contract, say $20,000, I figure it's a couple of dinners out and bowling. For a $250,000 contract, it's a 'familiarization'

trip for the official in the States. A contract of a million and above? Then we're talking about helping get a visa for the guy's son."[64]

Payoffs are part of almost every business venture in China's freewheeling atmosphere. Only a few companies avoid them, usually because the size of the venture draws too much negative attention to the Chinese government. For example, when GE first ventured into China, its managers were approached by scores of public officials, all of whom wanted a piece of the action. It was the host government that quickly got the word out to leave GE alone. Evidently, only the magnitude of GE's involvement in China, not ethics, spurred the government to action. Of course, U.S. antibribery laws discourage any U.S. company from giving or receiving payoffs, but this doesn't mean that the company is not permitted to give gifts and provide special favors. One popular perk that local Chinese officials accept without violating U.S. law is a trip to the States for training, or so-called inspection trips.

But getting into China is only the first problem. Staffing and motivating an effective work force is an ongoing challenge. The labor market is controlled by the government, which promises all workers lifelong employment and free housing. Employee benefits do not exist, and wages, even for the best workers, may only be around $100 to $200 per month.

The government controls hiring decisions for all businesses except joint ventures and the few companies that own and operate their own factory. Moreover, the vast majority of workers are employed by the state. Anyone who chooses to work for a foreign operation must apply to leave his or her job—a process that often takes months. And the foreign operator must reimburse the state for having already "trained" any new employees.

When it becomes necessary to discharge an employee, stringent rules must be followed. A worker who feels that the company was unfair will go to the labor grievance board, which is almost always sympathetic to his or her cause. Most employers provide generous severance packages in the hope of avoiding untimely and costly legal hassles.

Retaining good workers is also a problem and demands a bit of ingenuity on the part of management. One American couple, Stacy and Paul Condrell, have been in China since 1986 and own a small mail order company. They pay triple wages for an average worker and as much as six times average wages for good performers. And even then they have a hard time keeping them. For example, Zhang Pingyu, the Condrell's accountant, left a government job and accepted the Condrells' offer that quintupled her salary. Is she happy with her move? Not quite. "I was overwhelmed with the work and responsibility here," she says. "I couldn't believe one person had to do all this."[65] At her old government job, expectations were so low that a full day's work was required only about twice a month. She has since gone back to her old government job.

After more than forty years of Communism, workers have forgotten what it is like to work hard. "They're not ambitious because all jobs are dead-end and all work is treated the same," Paul Condrell explains. "Climbing the ladder and going places are not in the vocabulary." The biggest challenge for private Western employers is competing with the idea of the *iron rice bowl*—the belief that the government will care for its workers forever. "We can't get a lot of people out of the state companies," he says, "because they're afraid we'll go under or they'll be fired."[66]

The emerging Chinese corporations also tend to be highly centralized. CEOs refuse to delegate authority and make most decisions, even down to signing every check. Consequently, workers expect guidance at every step, another habit picked up in a Communist society, where managers insist on having a say in everything. Clearly, China has a long way to go in terms of creating a work ethic that will enable it to compete globally.

HR MANAGEMENT CHALLENGES IN TRANSITION ECONOMIES

Because human systems have been neglected, the role of HR is particularly critical in leading state-owned and private enterprises to profitability. In free market systems, employees and management look to the HR management department for leadership. This is not a practice in transition economies. The personnel director in a socialist country was often closely linked to the Communist Party for two reasons: to maintain political control and to meet production goals.[67]

While many old-guard Communist bureaucrats will never be effective in the HR role and are only waiting for retirement, there are many talented, ambitious, and people-sensitive replacements waiting in the wings. Top management, whether Western or local, must work hard to redefine the role of HR, making it credible as a positive, supportive discipline. Identifying those individuals who fit the new role is easy; giving them the tools to succeed will be challenging.

Do not be misled into thinking that this region's labor pool is devoid of effective personnel managers. For the moment, there may be a shortage of highly skilled HR professionals, but that situation will soon change. In the meantime, these individuals have excellent technical educations. Their mathematics and engineering backgrounds are every bit as good as those of persons from the West, probably better. They are also known for their craftsmanship. But their most underrated talent is to *improvising in a very uncertain environment*—a talent necessary for surviving in a depleted economy.[68]

The most pressing HR management challenge is to transform the stagnant bureaucratic state enterprise into one that encourages employees to be self-reliant. Another challenge is to train managers to be leaders who will take an occasional risk and who will listen to and motivate their subordinates. The old system rewarded workers for their passivity, conformity, and poor work habits. New systems, whatever form they take, cannot ignore the fact that workers are burdened by severe problems in their daily lives (substandard housing, food shortages, and the like), which, no doubt, have a strong effect on their ability to motivate their employers.

GLOBAL DOWNSIZING

Much has been said about downsizing in the United States. But unemployment is growing in Europe and Japan too. More than half of Europe's largest corporations and many of Japan's plan to cut their work forces over the next few years as global competition and high wages take their toll. While the rising yen is making Japanese exports more expensive, Europe's problems are the result of a costly labor market. Diamler-Benz AG, Germany's largest industrial group, plans to reduce its work force by 40,000. Toyota, Japan's top auto maker, also plans to let thousands of workers go.[69]

But don't look for unannounced plant closings and sudden cutbacks because there are laws to protect workers and a generous social cushion for those who are affected. Both Europe and Japan will rely on normal attrition and voluntary early retirement, rather than dismissals, to achieve rightsizing. And as in the U.S. labor market, downsizing will spur the trend toward the use of part-time workers and fewer commitments for lifetime guarantees.

Unemployment may be a new phenomenon for Japanese white-collar workers, but blue-collar workers, women, and foreigners have been experiencing it for some time. The recession has hit these groups hardest because the unemployed also lose important benefits, such as health and retirement.

Unemployment is subsidized in most industrial nations, but benefits are particularly good in Europe. In France and Germany, the unemployed worker receives about 59 percent of his or her wages compared to about 50 percent in the United States. In the Netherlands, the rate rises to 70 percent. Not only are benefits more generous, they extend well over a year (in France, over two years; in the Netherlands, three years).[70]

The European Community, as a whole, has failed to come to terms with high unemployment. Unions have been reluctant to change, adhering to traditional work arrangements. European societies continue to follow old customs by looking to government for assistance and paying for it by taxing employers. On average, Social Security–type taxes account for 60 percent of European payroll costs compared to around 40 percent in the United States. And the unemployed themselves add to the problem by their refusal to shift to more promising job markets.[71]

Job mobility may appear to be a realistic option to unemployed U.S. workers, but it holds little appeal for most European workers. "American workers take a chance by being willing to travel hundreds or even thousands of miles for a job that may involve an entirely new line of work for them," says the former French Economics Minister Jean-Pierre Fourcade. Job relocation is a rare event in Europe.[72]

European job protection laws are so stringent that companies are reluctant to hire, knowing that once they have added workers to their payrolls, it may take months of expensive legal wrangling to let them go if they are incompetent or if market conditions deteriorate. In addition, there is a pervasive expectation that it is the obligation of government to provide jobs. European hourly workers prefer to remain near family and friends, believing that their governments will come through. Managerial and professional workers, however, are more inclined to relocate.

CONCLUSIONS AND APPLICATIONS

- The pace of change in the world is picking up. As companies move beyond their own domestic borders, HR management practices will have to be reviewed and modified to fit the existing national cultures. How much and which parts of the corporate culture should be transferred to the foreign subsidiary can only be determined after the new market has been studied and any disparities identified. For cultures that have been subjected to Communism, the transition to free market systems will be even more difficult. For others, it may simply mean that managers must manage differently.

- Multinationals are companies that operate principally out of one country. The strategy they tend to follow is either ethnocentric or polycentric. At the other extreme are transnational, or global, companies with totally integrated operations and staff. A transnational company may have manufacturing facilities in one country, research and development in another, and markets in a third country.

- Global HR activities include assisting in the development of strategic plans, particularly when acquiring foreign companies. Negotiations often depend on the HR staff's knowledge of the culture, language, approaches to problem solving, body language, and the role of ceremony and formality. The HR staff may also be expected to analyze the personnel management practices of the acquired firm and to assess its strengths and weaknesses. Once an assessment is made, a plan can be created for transferring the critical core competencies that will make the new acquisition competitive and compatible with the larger organization.

- If the United States is to operate effectively at a global level, its global managers need to recognize that there are different ways of thinking, behaving, managing, and doing business. For that recognition to take place, the corporate headquarters must recognize that its ways of managing people reflect its own values, culture, management styles, and laws.

- Canada's approach to HR management is similar in most ways to that of the United States. Differences do occur in the government's larger role in providing national health care coverage and its greater emphasis on social justice, as is evident in Canada's comparable-worth legislation.

- Mexico's top-down economy is undergoing rapid transformation to a free market economy. The recent passing of NAFTA will only add to the momentum of this movement. The culture of Mexicans is quite different from that of their North American neighbors. More emphasis is put on charisma, virility, decisiveness, and a strong family orientation. In business, a people orientation is evident.

- Japan is one of the most modern countries in the world. The quality of life of its citizens rivals that of the United States. Japanese HR management is sophisticated, with many of its practices being copied by companies all around the world. Quality circles, group emphasis, and job rotation, are just a few of the methods Japanese society has refined and utilized to achieve significant productivity and quality gains. However, some U.S. companies are reevaluating the compatibility of Japanese methods with American workers, whose culture emphasizes individualism. In addition, although Japan may be as modern, educated, and productive as any in the world, Japanese women remain largely defenseless in their fight against discrimination and harassment at work.

- Western Europe is a land full of contrasts and different cultures. The quality of life is excellent. The easing of trade restrictions in the Economic Community suggests that eventually the various nations will converge and form an even stronger bond. One tradition all European nations do share is a cradle-to-grave welfare system. Declining competitiveness may force these nations to reduce their generous benefits, but social justice will always represent a significant fabric of their culture. The relationship between labor unions and governments is one of partnership, rather than adversarial, in most of Europe, except for the United Kingdom. The three largest Western European nations—France, Germany, and the United Kingdom—are very different from one another.

- Central and Eastern Europe, following the fall of Communism, is presenting the West with many serious challenges. For those Western companies willing to venture into the "Wild East," the risks and rewards are high. One of the biggest hurdles is transforming the old Communist state enterprises into profitable, viable, and thriving operations. The national cultures have been pulverized by as many as ninety years of Communist ideology. This tradition is not easy to overcome.

- China, like Central and Eastern Europe, is opening its doors to the West, but unlike the Europeans, it is still ruled by an old Communist hierarchy. Nevertheless, in its drive to remain firmly in command, the government needs hard currency, and that means doing business with the West. This situation involves the highest political risk. All the important factors of production are controlled by the government: land, labor and capital.

- One challenge facing all of these economies is how to achieve global competitiveness. Regions of the world, such as Western Europe and Japan, have achieved a high level of competitiveness on the basis of technological innovations or protective trade agreements. But as markets open up (and tariffs come down), these advantages are either lost or offset, leaving the cost of labor, in many cases, as the determining factor. Companies in the United States have been downsizing for the past few years, and although this has been and continues to be a painful process, it has enabled many companies to recapture market share. Other countries are now going through this painful stage, which appears to be an increasingly acceptable and ongoing global business practice.

CASE STUDY

How Does Japanese Management Play in Hungary?

After a difficult start, industrial relations have settled down at Suzuki of Hungary, a car factory run by Suzuki of Japan at Esztergom in northern Hungary. Suzuki founded the plant in April 1991 and sent some of its staff to Japan for training courses. Many of them reacted coolly to the Japanese approach to work. Discontent festered when Suzuki imposed a smoking ban in most areas of the factory.

Relations have improved since then, and Japanese management and Hungarian employees are now working well together—although the Hungarians appear to be making all the compromises.

Says Szabolcs Foldvari, chairman of the workers' council at the plant: "We are having to adopt the Japanese way of thinking about work on the production line. We have to concentrate on making good cars. So it is not only about technology but a way of thinking, an emphasis on quality. The Japanese think it most important that everybody moves continuously."

Nine of Suzuki's 600 employees sit on the workers' council, but the employees are not represented by trade unions. Says Foldvari: "By Hungarian law, we have the opportunity to join any trade union. We have not decided whether we want one. The workers' council functions like a trade union." However, about one hundred workers have joined the iron and metalworkers union.

Workers on the production line find the speed quicker than anything they have ever experienced. Clerical staff have also had to change their work habits to comply with the practices of their owners. Says Bela Baka, an assistant manager in the maintenance and utilities division: "It's working rather well, with no big problems. It was strange at first, working in such big, open offices. It was quite noisy, but now people are used to it. Before, we were used to having small offices with just two or three people."

Work hours are dictated by Hungarian labor law—eight hours per day. Overtime is paid at one and one-half times the hourly rate.

Wages average Ft 23,000 ($251) a month, close to the Hungarian average, but they vary each week and are determined by several factors. A basic salary is supplemented by additional payments based on a worker's attendance rate and productivity, as determined by a complicated formula. In addition, workers are assessed by their managers every six months and can receive a discretionary increase as a result of that appraisal.

The workers' council generally meets every month, but it can meet at short notice to deal with an emergency. Management attends if the problem is relevant to them. The last meeting concerned the way workers are able to buy cheaper cars from the factory. A plan devised by managers allows employees a 10 percent discount from cost, with 20–50 percent paid in a lump sum and four years to pay off the balance.

However, workers are not very happy with this arrangement. Says Foldvari: "It takes up a large part of our wages. In the future, I think we will have more meetings about this issue."

QUESTIONS

1. Describe the changes taking place that reflect Japanese management practices. Would American automotive companies such as Ford or GM do things differently? Explain.

2. What are the chances of a trade union being established in the factory? What is the Japanese strategy regarding unions?

3. Based on the information presented, what approach is Suzuki's management taking with its Hungarian factory—ethnocentric, polycentric, or geocentric? Explain.

4. What do the Hungarian workers seem most interested in? What other incentives might the Suzuki management use?

EXPERIENTIAL EXERCISES

1. Working Abroad

PURPOSE

This exercise is intended to familiarize students with the concept of *culture*. Teams will gather information on what life would be like in a different country and culture, and will examine the need for administration and coordination of HR systems throughout global organizations.

THE TASK

Students will be grouped into teams. Each team should select a country, preferably a non-English-speaking one, and gather materials on what life would be like if one were transferred for a three-year assignment. Assume that the spouse and two children, ages nine and fifteen, would accompany their parents.

Each team will present oral reports, including maps, to the class. The project will involve some outside work. Your instructor will tell each team how much time is allotted.

1. Using the criteria identified here, what are the differences between your national culture and the one to which you will be moving?

   Criteria:

   Relation to nature: (1) domination over nature, (2) harmony with nature, (3) subjugation to nature

   Time: (1) emphasis on the future, (2) concentration on the present, (3) preoccupation with the past

   Relationships: (1) individualistic, (2) group, (3) hierarchical (e.g., as in the Middle East)

   Space: (1) private, with emphasis on barriers and closed doors; (2) public, open, frequent touching, physically close.

   Important nonverbal communication signals (facial expressions, gestures, etc.)

   Humor (what is considered funny and what is thought odd behavior)

2. What type of economic system is practiced (free market, socialism, etc.)? Explain the relationship between government and business: Does the government control land, labor, and capital? What role does the government have in maintaining the welfare of its citizens, particularly the aged, unemployed, and minorities? What is the role of men and women? Are there differences in the way women are treated at work?

3. What is the role of religion and education in the daily life of citizens? Does religion affect the type of government and the everyday work life? Is education encouraged? If so, explain why. Compare their educational system to yours; what are the differences? How are foreigners treated?

4. Identify important indicators of personal success (e.g., salary, title, power). Is a particular type of management style expected? How are rewards given (e.g., individual monetary reward, group recognition)? How are poor performers disciplined?

5. Assume that your company has decided to organize a subsidiary in this country. What

philosophical approach would your team recommend: ethnocentric, polycentric, or geocentric? How much control should the home office exercise in establishing important HR policies, procedures, and systems (hiring, compensation, evaluation, training and career paths, etc.)? Which HR systems ought to be decentralized?

2. Performance Appraisal Across Cultures

PURPOSE

This exercise is designed to illustrate how one particular HR function is performed in different countries. The function is performance appraisal, and the countries are the United States, Saudi Arabia, and Japan.

THE TASK

Experts have noted that one important cross-cultural communication distinction is *context*. Cultures that have high-context communications emphasize the environment in which the information is conveyed; that is, the meaning comes less from the words that are used and more from the physical context. The Spanish, Chinese, Japanese, and Saudi Arabians put extensive effort into interpreting what is not said—nonverbal communication or body language, silences and pauses, and relationships and empathy. North American cultures engage in low-context communications. The emphasis is on sending and receiving accurate, articulate messages.

Global managers are expected to evaluate people and situations, just as domestic managers are. However, how individual performance information is observed, gathered, described, communicated, and evaluated depends largely on the underlying assumptions prevalent in the local culture. Performance appraisal is a routine function performed universally by every global company. But the why, when, what and how of performance appraisal will vary. Test your cross-cultural knowledge of three cultures and the performance appraisal process.

Your task is to match each culture (United States, Saudi Arabia, and Japan) to the performance appraisal dimensions. For each of the ten dimensions, select the alternative that best matches your impression of how performance appraisal is handled in the United States, Japan, and Saudi Arabia. Every alternative matches one of the three countries, although some practices are shared across cultures.

Cultural Variations: Performance Appraisal

1. The objective or purpose of performance appraisal is:
  a. Direction of the company/employee development.
  b. Placement.
  c. Evaluation of past performance and development for the future.

(continued).

2. Who conducts appraisal:
   a. Immediate superior.
   b. Manager several levels above the employee who is very familiar with the employee's personal situation.
   c. Mentor and immediate superior, both of whom know the employee well.

3. Authority of the appraiser (where does it come from?):
   a. Reputation (prestige is determined by nationality, age, sex, family, tribe, title, education).
   b. Presumed by superior's position or title.
   c. Respect accorded by the employee to the superior.

4. How often appraisals are performed:
   a. Once per year or periodically.
   b. Once per year.
   c. Developmental appraisal as often as once per month; evaluative appraisal at much longer intervals, sometimes of several years.

5. Assumptions behind the appraisal process:
   a. Connections are important; who you know is more important than what you did.
   b. Superior's subjective performance appraisal is acceptable because the employee trusts the process.
   c. Objective appraisal is fair; subjective appraisal is a problem.

6. Manner of communicating and feedback:
   a. Formalities are observed, and any criticism is subtle and given verbally.
   b. Criticism is direct, given in writing, and based on authenticated, objective facts.
   c. Criticism is subtle and never written.

7. Most popular motivators:
   a. Internal excellence.
   b. Money and promotion.
   c. Loyalty to management or the desire to become a group leader or manager.

8. Praise is:*
   a. Given individually.
   b. Given to entire group.

9. Rebuttals (rejection or appeal):*
   a. Would rebut appraisal.
   b. Would rarely rebut appraisal.

10. If a problem arises in the office, it is handled by:
   a. Asking the superior for advice.
   b. Learning to depend on yourself to solve the problem.
   c. Requesting an office meeting, politely mentioning that there may be a problem, and patiently discussing alternative methods for solving it.

*Two cultures share the same practice

KEY TERMS AND CONCEPTS

Apprenticeship
Capitalism/free market systems
Centralization/decentralization
Codetermination
Communism/socialism
Corruption/bribery
Culture
Ethnocentric
Geocentric
Global downsizing
Global strategies
Lifetime employment

Maquiladoras
Multicultural teams
Polycentric
Quality circles
Social justice
Social welfare
SWOT analysis
Transitional economies
Transnationals
Workers' councils
work-out
Unions in Western Europe

REVIEW QUESTIONS

1. What steps are Western governments and global corporations taking to ease the transition problems in Central and Eastern Europe?

2. Define *culture*. How might national culture influence the effectiveness of HR management practices?

3. In addition to culture, what other environmental factors influence individual and group behavior in organizations? Explain how these other forces tend to interact with each other.

4. What is the difference between ethnocentric, polycentric, and geocentric approaches to managing a company operating in several countries?

5. Compare manufacturing labor costs across Western Europe, Japan, and the United States. Which region has the most expensive labor? Which region emphasizes the quality of work life? Why? What region(s) appear to have a competitive edge in terms of less costly labor?

6. Explain what *machismo, personalismo, hierarchy and rank,* and *kinship ties* mean in the Latin culture.

7. Compare the cultural differences between North Americans and East Asians.

8. Describe the problems Japanese women have when they choose to work in a Japanese corporation.

9. As impossible as it may sound to North Americans, what was the positive aspect of Communism? What are *fixers* and *paper pushers?*

DISCUSSION QUESTIONS

1. Assume that you are in charge of global HR management for a large transnational automotive corporation. Your company has decided, after much deliberation, to begin operations in Moscow. But the corporation is having difficulty deciding whether to begin fresh (new factory, new employees, etc.) or to acquire the large state-owned enterprise that produces the Lada car. You have had preliminary discussions and negotiations with the Russian State Property Agency (SPA) and with officials at the Lada facility. One person who has been very friendly and helpful was your Russian personnel counterpart. However, you have just learned that he was previously a high-level official in the Communist Party. This is causing you to be apprehensive. The SPA is eager to sell, and you suspect that the factory can be purchased for a bargain basement price. You know that converting an old factory, and an existing work force, to an efficient, modern operation is a major undertaking. Your top management is waiting for your recommendations before deciding. Should you be concerned about this person's former affiliation with the Communist Party? What are some of the advantages and disadvantages of acquiring an existing facility versus starting a new operation? What would you do?

2. Americans have been hearing a lot about maquiladoras operating along the U.S.– Mexican border. What advantages did they have before the passage of NAFTA? Now that NAFTA has passed, will HR practices in Mexico begin to resemble those of North Americans?

3. How do Japanese HR management practices, policies, and systems differ when managing a factory in Japan versus managing American workers at a Japanese-owned facility in the United States? Which method best describes the Japanese approach at the Toyota manufacturing facility in Georgetown, Kentucky: ethnocentric, polycentric, or geocentric?

4. Describe the relationship of Western European labor unions with government and business. How does it differ from the U.S. and Japanese relationships?

5. Global corporations, through their HR professionals, have been leading major change efforts to streamline production processes and improve quality. One such industry is the auto industry. Innovative methods such as lean manufacturing processes, low inventory, just-in-time parts delivery, flexible teams of workers, *Kaizen* (or continuous improvement), total quality management, and reengineering have been implemented with great fanfare. Will these methods work in the former Soviet bloc nations? Explain your reasoning.

ENDNOTES

Chapter 2

1. Geert Hofstede, "Cultural Dimensions in People Management," *Globalizing Management*, edited by Vladimir Pucik, Noel Tichy, and Carole Barnett (New York: John Wiley, 1992), p. 139.

2. Ellen Brandt, "Global HR," *Personnel Journal* (March 1991): 38.

3. Hofstede, "Cultural Dimensions," p. 3.

4. For an interesting discussion of specific motivation theories and their applicability to different cultures, see Geert Hofstede, "Motivation, Leadership, and Organization: Do American Theories Apply Abroad?" *Organizational Dynamics* (Summer 1980): 42–63.

5. Ibid.

6. For a discussion of how management styles vary across cultures, see Andre Laurent, "The Cross-Cultural Puzzle of International Human Management," *Human Resource Management* 25, no. 1 (Spring 1986): 91–102.

7. H. C. Triandis, "Dimensions of Cultural Variation as Parameters of Organizational Theories," *International Studies of Management and Organization* (Winter 1982–1983): 143–44.

8. Kenneth Dreyfack, "You Don't Have to Be a Giant to Score Big Overseas," *Business Week* (April 13, 1987): 63.

9. B. Nelson, "Participative Management at a Paris Hotel," *Business and Society Review* 41 (1982): 29–32.

10. Edward Hall, *Hidden Differences* (Garden City, NY: Doubleday, 1987), p. 77.

11. "Volvo's Radical New Plant: The Death of the Assembly Line?" *Business Week* (August 28, 1989): 92–93.

12. C. Earley, "Compensation in International Settings," *Global Business Management in the 1990's* (Washington DC: Beacham Publishing, 1990), pp. 428–33.

13. Ibid., p. 430.

14. "Pay Equity Gets a Tryout In Canada—and U.S. Firms are Watching Closely," *Wall Street Journal* (December 28, 1988): A-1.

15. Philip Harris and Robert Moran, *Managing Cultural Differences*, 3rd ed. (Houston: Gulf Publishing, 1991), p. 345.

16. Ibid., p. 346.

17. "The Mexican Worker," *Business Week* (April 19, 1993): 84–92.

18. *Manufacturing in Mexicali: The In-Border or Maquiladora Industry Handbook* Industrial Development Commission of Mexicali, (1988).

19. Ibid.

20. Harris and Moran, *Managing Cultural Differences*, pp. 373–77.

21. "The Mexican Worker," p. 86.

22. Hofstede, "Motivation, Leadership, and Organization," pp. 42–63.

23. "The Mexican Worker," p. 90.

24. Susan Lefler, *Doing Business in*

Mexico (Southern Methodist University, Mirror Times Books, 1988).

25. "The Mexican Worker," Fort Worth Business Week, April 19, 1993: 91.

26. Tomasz Mroczkowski and Masao Hanaoka, "Continuity and Change in Japanese Management," *California Management Review* (Winter 1989): 39–53. See also, Karen Lowry Miller, "The Mommy Track, Japanese Style," *Business Week* (March 11, 1991): 46.

27. Ellen Hale, "Still on the Outside," *The Courier-Journal* (January 16, 1994): E1.

28. David E. Sanger, "In Japan, Unequal Opportunity," *International Herald Tribune* (December 2, 1992): A1.

29. Anne Fisher, "Japanese Working Women Strike Back," *Fortune* (May 31, 1993): 22.

30. Refik Culpan and Orsay Kucukemiroglu, "A Comparison of U.S. and Japanese Management Styles and Unit Effectiveness," *Management International Review* 33 (1993): 27–42.

31. James Bowman, "The Rising Sun in America (Part 1)," *Personnel Administrator* 31, no. 9 (September 1986): 67.

32. Ibid.

33. Tomasz Mroczkowski and Masao Hanaoka, "Continuity and Change in Japanese Management," *California Management Review* (Winter 1989): 47–48.

34. White Paper of Labor (Tokyo: Department of Labor of Japan, 1988).

35. Ibid.

36. "Some Manufacturers Drop Efforts to Adopt Japanese Techniques," *Wall Street Journal* (May 7, 1993): A1.

37. "Germany Fights Back," *Business Week* (May 31, 1993): 48.

38. John Ardagh, *France in the 1980s* (New York: Penguin Books, 1987), pp. 25–46.

39. *France: Industrial Investment File,* Issue No. 22. Paris French Industrial Development Agency (April 1987) and Special Issue (August 1988).

40. Michael Emerson, *What Model for Europe?,* (Cambridge MA: MIT Press, 1988), pp. 13–66.

41. Harris and Moran, *Managing Cultural Differences,* p. 466.

42. Ibid., p. 468.

43. Ibid., pp. 471–72.

44. Ibid., pp. 469–70.

45. Nancy J. Adler, *International Dimensions of Organizational Behavior* 2nd ed. (Boston: PWS-Kent, 1991), pp. 72–73.

46. Jean-Louis Barsoux and Peter Lawrence, "The Making of a French Manager," *Harvard Business Review* (July-August 1991): 58–67.

47. Harris and Moran, *Managing Cultural Differences,* pp. 465–720.

48. Ibid., p. 470.

49. Emerson, *What Model for Europe?,* pp. 81–122.

50. Harris and Moran, *Managing Cultural Differences,* p. 475.

51. Ibid.

52. Friedrich Furstenberg, "Recent Trends in Collective Bargaining in the Federal Republic of Germany," *International Labour Review* (September-October 1984): 615–30.

53. "Laying off Nanny," *U.S. News & World Report* (October 25, 1993): 41–44.

54. Fred Bleakley, "Over Half of Europe's Big Firms Are Planning Work Force Cuts," *Wall Street Journal* (September 21, 1993): A10.

55. Harris and Moran, *Managing Cultural Differences*, p. 454.

56. Ibid., pp. 457–58.

57. Ron Johnson, "Are the British Qualified to Join Europe?", *Personnel Management* (May 1990): 50–53.

58. Tony Horwitz, "Working Class Culture Erodes Britain's Rank in a Unified Europe," *Wall Street Journal* (February 11, 1992): A1.

59. Harris and Moran, Managing Cultural Differences, p. 458.

60. It is difficult to draw a line between what is called Central Europe and Eastern Europe. Generally, both would include (in alphabetical order) Albania, Belarus, Bulgaria, Croatia, the Czech Republic, Estonia, Hungary, Latvia, Lithuania, Moldava, New Yugoslavia (Serbia), Poland, Romania, Russia, Slovakia, Slovenia, and the Ukraine.

61. Michal Cakrt, "Management Education in Eastern Europe: Toward Mutual Understanding," *Academy of Management Executive* 7, no. 4 (1993): 63–68.

62. Jozsef Voros and John Schermerhorn, "Institutional Roles in Higher Education for Business and Management in Hungary," *Management Education and Development* 24, part 1 (1993): 70–82.

63. Norbert F. Elbert, "Reflection on Life Outside the HRM Mainstream: One Year's Experience in Hungary," *Academy of Management Annual Meeting*, Atlanta, August 1993.

64. "Cracking the China Market," *Wall Street Journal* (December 10, 1993): R1.

65. Dana Milbank, "Workers, Workers Everywhere," *Wall Street Journal* (December 12, 1994): R6.

66. Ibid.

67. Jone L. Pearce, "From Socialism to Capitalism: The Effects of Hungarian Human Resource Practices," *Academy of Management Executive* 5, no. 4 (1991): 75–88.

68. Michal Cakrt, "Management Education in Eastern Europe."

69. Peter Gumbel, "Western Europe Finds That It's Pricing Itself Out of the Job Market," *Wall Street Journal* (December 9, 1993): A1.

70. Ibid., p. A6.

71. Bernard D. Kaplan, "Europeans Look to U.S. for Ways to Cut Long-term Unemployment," *The Courier-Journal* (December 21, 1993): E5.

72. Ibid.

CHAPTER **3**

WORKFORCE DIVERSITY AND REGULATORY CHALLENGES

CHAPTER OBJECTIVES

1. To understand the impact the diversification of the American labor force is having on the workplace.

2. To learn the value of a diversified work force that mirrors the population.

3. To identify the primary principles of the federal employment discrimination laws.

4. To understand the key role HR professionals play in the development and enforcement of policies that protect employees from unlawful discrimination.

5. To appreciate the need for employers to develop sexual harassment policies and complaint procedures.

6. To identify the key elements of the Americans with Disabilities Act and the Civil Rights Acts of 1964 and 1991.

7. To describe the purpose and advantages of employment arbitration agreements.

8. To identify common forms of religious discrimination in the workplace.

9. To appreciate the role the U.S. Supreme Court has played in defining employment discrimination laws.

10. To recognize the differences and similarities between affirmative action and equal employment opportunity.

WORKFORCE DIVERSITY
The 1990s and a New Century

It's the '90s, and the United States is experiencing an enormous challenge. The demographics of its work force has changed dramatically, and the turn of the century heralds a revolution in the way work will be done in America.

Sound familiar? With the recent advent of *cultural diversity* as an HR concept, it should. But the 1990s just referred to are not the 1990s, they're the 1890s. Before the turn of the century, America faced the challenge of converting from an agrarian to an industrial nation, and of accepting and accommodating over 20 million immigrants who had come to this country during the half-century after the Civil War.[1] At first, these immigrants were primarily Western European—Irish, Scandinavian, English, and German. Soon, however, word spread of the opportunities for work and religious freedom, and masses of immigrants came from Italy, Poland, Austria, Hungary, and Russia. From all of these countries, groups migrated to escape direct and persistent discrimination in their native lands.[2] This second wave of immigrant workers from Southern and Eastern Europe also came about because of America's need for cheap, plentiful labor to fill the factories and mines that multiplied during the Industrial Revolution.

Through World War I, the Depression, and World War II, America's production continued, and after World War II it flourished. Unlike Europe and Japan, the United States emerged from World War II with its industrial base intact. Our production system was geared to turn out standard, assembly-line products in high volume. For the United States, it was a seller's market. There were plenty of customers, domestically and internationally, ready to absorb our goods.

But while the United States continued to organize and produce in the same way for most of the twentieth century, other countries were rebuilding, using the technology of the twenty-first century in that rebirth. Their postwar recovery was slow and, out of necessity, was designed to supplant the United States as the main producer of goods worldwide. This buildup of industry in sync with the latest technology during the last quarter of this century placed the United States at a competitive disadvantage. The need to meet this global competition and to utilize new technology has made U.S. companies reassess their most important asset—their work force.

In this chapter, we will examine the American work force as a diverse work force, how the diversity came about, and the legal environment that affects the way employers interact with this new work force. We will explore approaches to managing work force diversity and review real-life programs by employers on the leading edge of diversity training.

DEFINING DIVERSITY

In 1987, the Hudson Institute, funded by the U.S. Department of Labor, released the study *Workforce 2000: Work and Workers for the 21st Century*. The predictions of that study startled corporate America. While probably not the first indication of a changing American work force, the study certainly brought the future composition of America's work force into clear and dramatic focus. Almost overnight the HR field began to view the recruitment, selection, and management of the emerging diverse work force as a key issue in long-term survival.

The study predicted that the homogeneous work force, long composed of and led by white males born in America, was rapidly changing (Figure 3-1). New entrants into the labor force by the year 2000 would consist of only 15 percent native white males. Women (white and of color) would make up 61 percent of the new workers, and people of color (including women of color) would provide 29 percent of the *new* century's beginning work force. Coupled with the changing faces of the work force will be a reduction in the numbers of new entrants. In the 1970s, when baby boomers were still joining the employment lines, the labor force grew by 2.9 percent a year. Growth of only 1 percent a year is predicted for the 1990s.[3] Ironically, a new wave of immigrants into the American work force will be the solution to the shrinking labor pool, just as it had been in the late 1890s.

To meet the challenge of the twenty-first century, America businesses must have access to the best and brightest employees. The work force must be willing and able to provide the skills and commitment necessary to compete in the world economy. They must be trained in new technologies, sometimes two or three times during their careers, just to stay even.

Leaders must emerge from the work force to motivate and direct the workplace. As in the past, these leaders must be able to understand the organization's and the employees' needs and see that both are met. Table 3-1 gives examples of just some of the changes that can be expected in the workplace by the year 2000.

If American business is to succeed, it must recognize the emergence of the diversified work force and find the means to harness its energies, talents, and differences for tomorrow's challenges. The major groups that provide diversity in the work force will now be considered.

FIGURE 3-1 The workforce 2000.

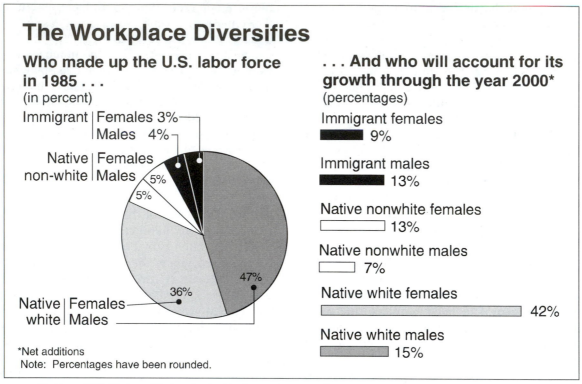

The Workplace Diversifies

Who made up the U.S. labor force in 1985 . . .
(in percent)

Immigrant | Females 3%
          | Males 4%

Native | Females
non-white | Males 5%
          5%

47%

36%

Native | Females
white | Males

*Net additions
Note: Percentages have been rounded.

. . . And who will account for its growth through the year 2000*
(percentages)

Immigrant females
█████ 9%

Immigrant males
██████ 13%

Native nonwhite females
☐☐☐☐☐ 13%

Native nonwhite males
☐☐☐ 7%

Native white females
▨▨▨▨▨▨▨▨▨▨▨▨▨ 42%

Native white males
▨▨▨▨ 15%

SOURCE: *Workforce 2000: Work and Workers for the 21st Century* (New York City) The Hudson Institute, (1987).

Table 3-1 Changes in the Year 2000 and Beyond

Technological	By the year 2015, 1 million Americans will be over the age of one hundred.
Productivity	28 million American workers will work out of their homes.
Globalization	Successful executives will need a working knowledge of four languages.
Organization	Management layers will compress from an average of twelve to an average of six.
Competition	Workers will shift careers more frequently, some as often as every five years.
People	Companies will discover that their employees are their biggest asset, and diverse individuals will be able to make professional contributions to the workplace.

Racial and Ethnic Groups

Currently, racial and ethnic groups—people of color—make up one-fourth of America's population. If current trends in immigration and birth rates continue, by the year 2050 these groups will outnumber whites in the general population. More specifically, African-Americans now comprise 11 percent of the labor force and are projected to reach 12 percent by 2000. Hispanics make up 7 percent of the work force today and will be 10 percent by the year 2000 if they contribute the projected 23 percent of new work force entrants by that date. Three percent of the work force now consists of Asian-Americans, Pacific Islanders, and native Americans. By 2000 these Asian/American groups will represent 4 percent of the work force.[4]

Immigrants who contribute to this increase in the proportion of people of color are generally underrepresented in the growth occupations, which require technical skills and education. They are overrepresented in slow-growing or declining occupations such as farm and factory work. Since they are protected against employment discrimination, which is discussed later in the chapter, these underrepresented groups present great recruitment opportunities and challenges to the HR professional (see *HR in the News,* "Profile of a Diversity Trainer").

Women

Women are expected to provide almost two-thirds of the 15 million new entrants into the job market by the year 2000. The availability of women will likely offset the decline in the number of younger male workers. But female workers are still not utilized by many employers in top management positions. Also, women are concentrated in occupations that have been seen as female occupations and that pay less than traditionally male occupations.

Older Workers

Of the 26 million people in the United States who are sixty-five years or older, 4 million are still in the work force. In the year 2000 the average age of American's worker will be thirty-nine years, up from today's average of thirty-six years.[5]

Americans with Disabilities

Depending on the definition used, the U.S. Department of Health and Human Services has estimated that the number of Americans with one or more disabilities could be as high as 43 million. Approximately 21 million of them are able to work, but fewer than 6 million have jobs. That leaves 15 million, or nearly 72 percent of this population, unemployed.[6]

Sexual/Affectional Orientation

The famous Kinsey Report on the sexual attitudes of men and women in America estimated that at least 10 percent of the population is homosexual. If that estimate is correct, then 10 percent of the men and women in the work force are gay and constitute a greater percentage of the work force than some other minorities.[7]

Exactly What Is Diversity?

The change in the demographic structure of the U.S. work force mirrors the diversity of the U.S. population as a whole. This diverse customer base and the increased importance of globalization for U.S. industry will challenge organizations to appeal to a diversified marketplace. The challenge of recruiting, selecting, and managing a diverse work force involves more than complying with federal and state employment laws; it is necessary for organizational survival. The technological revolution that replaces unskilled laborers with machines is changing the way companies design work in America. More skilled workers demand a more receptive environment. Companies that want to succeed in the twenty-first century must form pluralistic organizations.[8]

The term **diversity** is not contained in the *Workforce 2000* report or any law; instead, it grew out of academic and popular press usage. Every individual is unique. At the same time, every individual shares biological and environmental characteristics with any number of others. *Diversity* in the workplace can be generally defined as recognition of the groups of people who share such common traits. These traits—the properties and characteristics that constitute a whole person—both unite and divide us. In the HR field and in U.S. organizations, however, the term *diversity* has three major working definitions:[9]

- The politically correct term for equal employment opportunity/affirmative action.

Profile of a Diversity Trainer

Daisy Wood enjoys her work. Her voice, her eyes, and her hands capture your attention, and what she says can surprise and amaze any group of business professionals. Ms. Wood tells the future! No, she is not a fortune teller, she's a human resource professional and a talented, knowledgeable cultural diversity trainer. Recently promoted to manager of the Recruiting and Diversity Division of GE Appliances, a General Electric Company, Ms. Wood is responsible for all recruitment for the over 25,000 GE appliance employees as well as its diversity programs. The future she foretells is about the American workplace in the next century.

Ms. Wood first approaches a group who wants to manage diversity by challenging them to imagine. Imagine a culture of the future where twenty-nine body parts can be replaced in the human body, where national leaders will need to be fluent in four languages, where one million of the people in the U.S. will be over 100 years old!

The audience she is addressing is going to be asked to open their minds to such possibilities and to realize that if they and their organization are to survive in such a world, *all* of their talents must be harnessed.

As Ms. Wood leads the group through various "awareness raising" exercises, the force of her conviction that we must value all people within an organization spills over onto the participants. It is not of question of "why?" anymore, but of "how?".

- The recruitment and selection of racial and ethnic minorities and women.
- The management of individuals sharing a broad range of common traits.

The first of these definitions represents a very narrow view of diversity and is more likely to be found in organizations without formal diversity policies or programs. The second definition reflects the reality that many diversity programs focus on employment law concerns. The third definition is the broadest and is likely to be used in organizations with diversity programs that include many of the activities in Figure 3-2.

Primary dimensions are those human differences that are inborn and that exert a major impact on us. Age, ethnicity, gender, race, physical abilities/qualities, and sexual/effectual orientation are primary dimensions at the core of individual identities. All of us view the world and experience the world through the filter of these dimensions.

Secondary dimensions are more mutable and can be changed, discarded, or modified throughout our lives. Secondary dimensions add depth and individuality to our lives. Education, geographic location, income, marital status, military experience, religion, work experience, and parental status are examples of secondary dimensions. One can view the primary and secondary dimensions as a circle, as

Since January 1990, Daisy Wood has been responsible for developing communication and monitoring a company-wide minority/female recruiting and development plan for the General Electric Company. In other words, she is supposed to insure that the "GE Is Me" slogan in fact reflects the cultural diversity of the world GE serves. To hear her tell it, it is a labor of love. "Yes, I like it because it's the kind of work that makes a difference both individually and collectively. I'm helping individuals reach their potential and I can enjoy the euphoria the group feels when they realize the advantages to treating the business environment like a salad, instead of a melting pot."

Ms. Wood's expertise comes from over 28 years of experience in personnel issues which were not minority or women oriented. She was with Exxon Corporation for 22 years developing a number of employee training and development programs. It was only in her last four years with Exxon that she focused on the "Year 2000 Project," which involved defining and planning for the influx of women and people of color into the work force.

A product herself of affirmative action goals in the early 1960s, Ms. Wood knows the need to move past equal employment opportunity and affirmative action to a society which values and uses the diversity around us. "Eventually I would like to drop 'diversity' from my title. Recruiting new employees, bringing them into the company fully aware of GE's diversity culture will eventually totally change the workplace. Diversity will be a way of life, not a goal."

SOURCE: Interview with Christina Heavrin, March 17, 1993.

shown in Figure 3-2, with the primary dimensions at the center and the secondary dimensions on the outside ring.

People are grouped and identified most often, and certainly in any initial encounter, by the primary dimensions that are most readily observed: age, gender, race, and physical abilities/qualities. Many of us live in homogeneous communities, or at least in communities far less diverse than our society as a whole. Therefore, our entry into the workplace may be our first encounter with a diverse population.

In a national survey of U.S. organizations of all types and sizes, employers were asked about diversity issues. In response to the question "What is meant by 'diversity' to decision makers in your organization?" the characteristics of diversity were ranked as seen in Table 3-2.

Some employers further volunteered the additional characteristics of language, education, and sexual preference as also constituting diversity. The survey confirmed the recognition of HR officials of the primary dimensions of diversity.

Stereotypes and Prejudices

A *stereotype* is a fixed, distorted generalization about members of a group. Stereotyping that stems from the primary dimensions of diversity—race, gender, age, physical abilities/qualities, or sexual orientation—attributes

HR IN THE NEWS

"Ugly People" Gain Protection

An anti-discrimination law passed in Santa Cruz, California, expanded the protections typically reserved for women and minorities to a new class of people. By forbidding job and housing discrimination against people on the basis of their weight, height, or physical characteristics, Santa Cruz became the first American City to actually grant legally enforceable protection to ugly people.

The law was in response to a newspaper story about a 300-pound woman who was refused a job in a health foods store because she could not navigate narrow aisles to restock shelves. The City Councilman who sponsored the law believed that women were often the target of unfair job discrimination because of their weight or looks.

SOURCE: Richard C. Paddock, "Santa Cruz Grants Anti-Bias Protection to the Ugly," *Los Angeles Times* CXI, no. 174 (July 21, 1993): D1.

FIGURE 3-2 Primary and secondary dimensions of diversity.

SOURCE: Marilyn Loden and Judy B. Rosener, *Workforce America* (Homewood, IL: Business One-Irwin, 1991), p. 20.

Table 3-2 Characteristics of Diversity (included in employer definitions)

Rank	Characteristic	Percentage Yes	Percentage No	Percentage Uncertain
1	Race	94.1%	4.2%	1.7%
2	Culture	86.3	8.4	5.3
3	Gender	84.5	11.6	3.9
4	Natural origin	83.6	11.4	5.0
5	Age	70.6	24.7	4.7
6	Religion	57.5	34.6	7.9
7	Physical abilities	56.0	20.4	23.6
8	Regional origin	36.9	48.4	14.7

SOURCE: Michael R. Carrell and Everett E. Mann, "Defining Workforce Diversity Programs and Practices in Organizations," *Labor Law Journal* no. 12 (December 1993):

incomplete, exaggerated, or distorted qualities to members of this group.

As human beings, we process information by using learned knowledge. A child whose fingers are burned when touching a stove learns not to touch the stove again. Such generalizations about the world around us are arrived at through logic, experience, and available facts. *Stereotyping is not generalization.* A stereotype usually comes from outside sources, not individual experiences. A belief is formed early in life by contact with our parents, teachers, neighbors, and contemporaries. It might be stated that "A woman's place is in the *home.*" In itself, such a statement may not threaten a woman's right to equal employment. Nonetheless, it becomes a stereotype when exaggerated beliefs about a woman's ability to function in the workplace are told and retold and begin to be believed. A stereotype requires that the exaggerated beliefs about a group be sustained by selective perception and/or selective forgetting of facts and experiences inconsistent with the stereotype. All the years of experience each of us have had with women teachers, for example, are suddenly forgotten when one questions a woman's ability to succeed.

Stereotyping negates people's individuality and limits their potential. To a great extent, people perform according to the expectations placed on them. If the stereotype is that the person is not competent, then he or she may not perform competently.

Clinging to negative stereotypes about people different from ourselves results in prejudice. *Prejudice* consists of processing our stereotypes in such a way as to reinforce one's own sense of superiority to the members of that group. Stereotyping and prejudice against diverse groups have been institutionalized in the workplace. Therefore, one function of the organization is to recognize and eradicate both stereotyping and prejudice.

Assimilation

In the past, the workplace response to an influx of people who are different was assimilation. *Assimilation* assumed that the dominant group's performance and style were superior to those of persons who are not in the dominant group. This assumption devalued diversity in the organization and reinforced the value of homogeneity. "The problem with measuring everyone against that white male standard," says Gerald Adolph, a management consultant and principal at Booz, Allen, and Hamilton, "is that you set up a sizable portion of your work force for failure."[10]

Organizations may contend that assimilation is a proper response to diversity. Some companies believe they have been successful because the homogeneous ideal—a Lee Iacocca or a Ross Perot—made them succeed due to their tough, no-compromise, macho approach to management. They believe that if diverse employees conform to those traits, they too will be successful.

But for companies that value diversity, assimilation is not the ideal. The basis for assimilation is bias. Pressuring diverse employees to conform diminishes them as individuals. In trying to gain acceptance by the dominant group, they may lose touch with their own cultural backgrounds. An example is a woman manager who has been told to be more assertive and is accused later of being pushy and unfeminine.

When diversity is not valued, the diverse employee's accomplishments may not be noted and mistakes may be magnified. African-American managers often complain that they are expected to prove themselves before getting a promotion, while white managers are promoted on the basis of their potential.[11] There are few role models for diverse employees, and to a great extent, those diverse employees who have assumed positions of authority in an organization do not have the clout of white male authority figures. Women and minority managers find themselves frozen in middle management positions or advancing only in staff positions.[12]

Finally, the energy and effort used by diverse employees to assimilate drains them of enthusiasm for reaching the goals of the organization. More and more diverse people are giving up the struggle to succeed in corporations and creating their own businesses. Between 1974 and 1984, women started their own businesses at six times the rate of men. Companies like Corning Glass Works, in an effort to stem the flow of women and minorities, have had to devise specific programs to retain a diverse work force.[13]

Pushing assimilation does not benefit the dominant work force group either. It reinforces the bias that spawns this approach, and it perpetrates stereotyping and prejudice in the workplace. Companies whose work force cannot adapt to the new century will not survive. And if the organization fails, the current dominant group will find itself jobless, along with fellow diverse employees. With the breakup of AT&T in 1984, the eliminating of more than 100,000 employees caused some white men to rethink their biases. They became pragmatic when they realized that it was going to take everyone, people of color and women included, to keep the corporation functional.[14]

Valuing Diversity

The first step in getting an organization to value diversity is to acknowledge the fundamental difference between valuing diversity, on the one hand, and equal employment opportunities and/or affirmative action, on the other. As stated earlier, equal employment opportunity is a legal approach to workplace discrimination. It is against the law to deny a person a job or a job advantage because of race, gender, age, or other primary characteristics. Affirmative action is a response to underutilization of protected groups in various job categories in which a business attempts to attract and advance people from such groups because of their failure to do so in the past due to discrimination. Valuing diversity moves past both of these concepts and results in management designed to reap the benefits that a diverse work force offers.[15]

Unfortunately, for some companies, managing diversity is still seen as part of its affirmative action/equal employment opportunity policies. Equal employment opportunity and affirmative action, however, are government initiated, legally driven efforts to change—

Valuing Diversity at Kinney Shoes

John Kozlowski, senior vice-present of human resources of Kinney Shoes, believes that serving a diverse customer base requires a diverse workforce. He also believes that compliance with equal employment laws is not enough. "When we say equal employment opportunity is a good business practice, but all we do is compliance, we demean it," Kozlowski says.

In a proactive approach to diversity, Kozlowski created Kinney's Office of Fair Employment Practice, which is not part of their human resource EEO/AA compliance arm. Through education of their managers, Kinney is trying to instill within the corporate culture the best hiring and management practices so that the *best* candidates for hiring or promoting are identified, regardless of race, culture, or gender.

The program used by Kinney includes an 8-hour "Valuing Diversity" seminar for executives and store managers which focuses on managing persons from different cultural backgrounds. Through a number of problem solving situations, the training teaches the managers how different persons react to the same workplace situation. One example is to show how a native American is embarrassed by public praise from a supervisor, while a white American is honored.

Kinney Shoes, a wholly owned subsidiary of Woolworth Corporation, recognizes that its customer base, as well as its work force pool, will be made up of a greater number of women and minorities by the year 2000. Kozlowski sums it up, "If you're going to be in a business that serves this mix of people, you had better have a mix of people who understand them. Today's retail environment needs a diverse workforce to service a diverse customer base."

SOURCE: Joyce E. Santora, "Kinney Shoe Steps into Diversity," *Personnel Journal* 70 (September 1991): 72–77.

---

from a quantitative standpoint—the makeup of a company's work force. From their inception, the emphasis was on numbers and assimilation. By contrast, valuing diversity is a company-specific, necessity-driven effort to change—from a qualitative standpoint—the utilization of the company's work force. From its inception, the emphasis was on performance by individuals as individuals. In an organization that values diversity, managing diversity becomes a substitute for assimilation.

An excellent example of such an organization is Kinney Shoes, which is discussed in *HR in the News*.

MANAGING DIVERSITY

An organization must be clear about its motivation in managing diversity. Being in compliance with equal opportunity laws is not enough. The organization must recognize the business necessity of having a diverse work force and tapping the potential of that work force.

Typically, such motivation is articulated in organizations mission statement or strategic plan. Figure 3-3 is a vision statement of U.S. West, a corporate leader in diversifying its work force.

There may be considerable benefits to be gained by managing diversity and considerable costs for not doing so. Organizations that cannot change will be faced with higher employee turnover and higher recruitment and training costs. Employee conflicts that may result in sabotage or high absenteeism can be expected. Misunderstandings can lead to expensive discrimination litigation.[16]

Potential benefits for an organization that successfully manages diversity include the following:

- *Bottom line* Companies that experienced high absenteeism and job turnover rates in diverse employee populations have found that frustration over career growth and cultural conflict with the dominant white male culture were most often the cause of employee unrest. As these populations grow within the work force, companies that satisfy their diverse needs will have a competitive advantage. Success in return for such accommodation can be seen in a study of one company that instituted four benefit-liberalization changes for pregnant workers. The higher the company's score for accom-

FIGURE 3-3 U.S. West's Diversity Vision statement.

OUR CULTURE WILL BE DEVOID OF RACISM, SEXISM, AND ALL OTHER FORMS OF DISCRIMINATION: EQUAL OPPORTUNITY WILL MAXIMIZE THE CONTRIBUTIONS OF ALL INDIVIDUALS TO THE PROFITABILITY OF THE BUSINESS.

modation, the lower the number of sick days taken by the pregnant workers. Instituting company-sponsored day-care centers reduced absenteeism in two companies dramatically. Flextime work scheduling has also reduced absenteeism and increased workers' performance.[17]

- *Getting the Best Person for the Job* For many organizations, diversity is a question of HR and the ability to attract the best employees in a predominantly female, nonwhite work force. Some employers are already having difficulty in recruitment. A survey of 645 HR professionals conducted as a follow-up to the *Workforce 2000* report found that 55 percent of the respondents cited problems in hiring entry-level secretaries and 53 percent had difficulty hiring entry-level professionals.[18]

- *Valuing the Diverse Customer* Diversity in the work force mirrors the diversity in the consumer market. The organizations that know how to manage a diverse work force will be able to sell to a diverse customer base. Low profitability in inner-city markets gave Avon Corporation the motivation to adopt diversity. Those markets are now among their most profitable.[19] U.S. West realized that its English-speaking employees were not communicating with a large proportion of its customer base in the southwestern part of the United States—Spanish-speaking Hispanics. Because of its groundbreaking approach to diversity, the company now boasts that people of color constitute 13 percent of its managers.[20] U.S. companies cannot ignore the need to compete in a global market. With the diversity of the general population to rely on companies in the United States should have a competitive edge if it manages that diversity (Table 3-3).

- *Understanding That Innovation Means Profits* To compete in the next century, companies will have to be creative, innovative, and flexible. Studies have shown that

Table 3-3 Competitive Advantages of Cultural Diversity

1. Cost argument	As organizations become more diverse, the cost of a poor job in integrating workers will increase. Those who handle this well will thus create cost advantages over those who don't.
2. Resource	Companies develop reputations on favorability as prospective employers for women and ethnic minorities. Those with the reputation for managing diversity will win the competition for the best personnel. As the labor pool shrinks and changes composition, this edge will become increasingly important.
3. Marketing argument	For multi-national organizations, the insight and cultural sensitivity that members with roots in other countries bring to the marketing effort should improve these efforts in important ways. The same rationale applies to marketing in sub-populations within domestic operations.
4. Creativity argument	Diversity of perspectives and less emphasis on conformity to norms of the past (which characterize the modern approach to management of diversity) should improve the level of creativity.
5. Problem-solving	Heterogeneity in decision and problem solving groups potentially produces better decisions through a wider range of perspectives and more thorough critical analysis of issues.
6. System flexibility argument	An implication of the multicultural model for managing diversity is that the system will become less determinant, less standardized, and therefore more fluid. The increased fluidity should create greater flexibility to react to environmental changes (i.e., reactions should be faster and at less cost).

SOURCE: Reprinted with permission from Taylor H. Cox and Stacy Blake, "Managing Cultural Diversity: Implications for Organizational Competitiveness," *Academy of Management Executive* 5, no. 3 (March, 1991): 47.

heterogeneous groups have more creativity and better problem-solving skills than homogeneous groups. The broader, richer base of experience provided by people with diverse backgrounds improves problem solving and decision making. While complete diversity might be disruptive and complete homogeneity unstimulating, cohesive groups of diverse people provide an increased number of alternative ideas that are then subjected to a high level of critical analysis, resulting in a much better product.[21] As organizations become more flexible in their basic employment practices in order to respond to the changing work force, they become more flexible in their practices. This flexibility can be seen in a company like Levi Strauss. This San Francisco–based apparel manufacturer developed a mission statement whose goal was to create a company that supported employees balancing their work and personal lives. In reaching this goal, it experimented with telecommuting and flexible work schedules, job sharing, and part-time work, programs unheard of in the garment industry.[22]

Diversity Programs

Organizational diversity programs have been in existence for only a few years and substantially vary in their content, cost, and effectiveness. The most common policies or programs that employers classify as diversity are those required by federal and state laws—sexual harassment policies; providing physical access for employees with disabilities; parental leave policies; and the recruitment and selection of minorities and women. Most organizations provide such policies since they are required by law. U.S. organizations also provide more extensive diversity policies and programs, listed in such as the ones in Figure 3-4. While the percentage of organizations providing these policies and programs may appear low, it should be remembered that virtually none

FIGURE 3-4 Organizations providing broad diversity initiatives.

Managing Diversity Policies/Programs

Policy/Program	Percentage Policy Exists	Percentage Believe They Need to Do More
Awareness and Valuing Diversity		
Discussion groups to promote tolerance and understanding	49.9%	75.1%*
Diversity training for supervisors	38.0	74.5
Efforts to change corporate culture to value differences	37.0	61.4
Team building for diverse groups that must work together	35.3	68.8
Diversity task force to recommend policy changes where needed	34.6	44.9
Holding managers accountable for increasing diversity in the managerial ranks	32.7	65.5
Educational Initiatives		
Incentives for younger workers to complete their education	65.6	72.7
Basic education classes (reading, math)	29.8	57.1
Classes in English for non-English-speaking employees	21.4	64.8
Career Support		
Minority internships	58.5	62.2
Networking among minority groups	41.7	70.3
Programs to steer women and minorities into "pivotal" jobs—key positions critical to rapid advancement	25.7	61.8
Specific goals to diversity middle and upper management	27.7	57.1
Accommodating Special Needs		
Scheduled days off to accommodate religious preferences	58.2	40.5
Policies to hire retirees for temporary assignments	45.1	51.6
Day-care arrangements or benefits	24.5	48.8
Work-at-home arrangements	19.5	32.7
Job redesign to accommodate disabled employees	17.3	49.4
Translation of written materials (manuals, newsletters) into several languages.	12.6	21.0

SOURCE: Benson Rose and Kay Lovelace, "Piecing Together the Diversity Puzzle," *HR Magazine* 36 (June 1991): 56–59.

existed before the 1987 Hudson Institute report and that they continue to grow rapidly in number. The awareness and valuing-diversity training programs have not met with great success. In fact, a national survey of HR professionals found that only 32 percent of companies rated their training programs as a success, 50 percent were neutral, and 18 percent rated them as unsuccessful. The possible reasons for their lack of success include (1) no follow-up activities after the initial training; (2) few or no incentives for managers to increase the diversity of their work groups; and (3) top management's view of diversity as an HR issue, not as a key to the organization's long-term success.[23] Furthermore, attitudes toward diversity within organizations depend on the people being asked. HR professionals are generally positive about diversity and recognize the need for a diverse work force. Line managers are generally more skeptical and believe that diversity has made their jobs more difficult. Top managers' attitudes fall between those of HR professionals and line managers (Figure 3-5).

Diversity Awareness Training

Education begins the process of cultural change within an organization that has the mo-

tivation and the requisite leadership to change attitudes. The first group to undergo this training should be top management. General manager and employee training should soon follow, focusing primarily on stereotyping and the dimensions of diversity. Education in managing diversity as a resource is ongoing and will be unique to each organization's needs.

Awareness training seeks to motivate employees to recognize the worth and dignity of

FIGURE 3-5 The effect of training programs on managers' attitudes.

Attitudes Toward Diversity Management			
Favorable Attitudes	**HR View**	**Line Mgrs' View**	**Top Mgrs' View**
Diversity programs help companies project a positive public image	62.6	33.9	54.8
Diversity management is no longer a choice for us: our employees are too diverse to ignore this issue	61.5	20.3	35.3
A more diverse work force will better enable us to serve our clients and customers	60.0	21.0	40.8
In our industry, diverse organizations will be more successful and innovative	58.8	16.8	37.3
Diversity programs are socially desirable activities	50.3	17.8	34.7
Without a diversity program, we risk losing some of the best employees in our company or industry	40.8	11.7	25.9
Diversity programs are necessary because there are still a lot of insensitive or discriminatory employment behaviors	25.0	11.3	24.8
Unfavorable Attitudes			
Greater work force diversity has made the manager's job more difficult	41.1	65.1	46.9
Valuing diversity is a "politically correct" term for affirmative action	25.8	28.8	26.7
Special treatment for various subgroups of workers reinforces negative stereotypes of these groups	23.3	43.0	29.3
Diversity programs are motivated primarily by a desire to comply with regulations and avoid costly lawsuits	18.1	42.7	34.1
Greater work force diversity increases the cost of doing business	11.6	26.1	23.7
Overall, the costs of a more diverse work force outweigh the potential benefits	10.9	15.3	15.4
As diversity increases among employees, group cohesiveness typically decreases	9.5	22.2	13.4
Greater work force diversity leads to more employee grievances	9.3	29.1	18.9
The existence of a diverse work force makes it more difficult to uphold performance standards	6.6	20.9	12.9
Diversity management programs are just a passing fad	6.5	20.5	17.0
Diversity training programs discriminate against white males	5.8	26.6	14.0

SOURCE: "1993 SHRM/CCH Survey," *Human Resources Management* (Washington, DC: CCH, Inc., May 26, 1993): 10.

everyone in the workplace and to treat them with respect. It also seeks to diminish the negative impact of individual prejudices by getting each person to *accept responsibility for the problem.* Role playing and/or listing commonly held stereotypes are two methods trainers use to get employees to see themselves through their fellow workers' eyes. Unlearning biases is a long-term process. Individuals must be willing to reevaluate and reprogram many deeply held beliefs. Awareness is the first step. Awareness training may, however, cause a backlash among some employees (as described in *HR in the News:* "Diversity Training May Cause Backlash") if not carefully developed and implemented.

Diversity training takes various forms. It may involve encounter-type retreats or quiet consciousness-raising sessions. Following are some exercises that may be used in diversity training:

1. *Values Clarification*   A checklist of values—like punctuality, honesty, acceptance, and financial success—is prioritized by all individuals in terms of their own preference and how they believe the organization ranks the values. The group then discusses the differences and similarities in the priorities.

2. *Perceptual Differences*   The participants are asked to give a precise percentage definition of such as *always, frequently,* and *almost always.* This exercise uncovers the imprecise communication that may exist in the workplace.

3. *Problem-solving Case Studies*   The participants are given a partial description of a job applicant and are told to come up with a complete profile. Depending on the limited facts given, the profile may uncover any number of biases when the group completes the picture. For example, one group was told to profile a woman who was returning to the work force and was responsible for two children. The group profiled her as a recently divorced woman who had stopped working to raise her children. The group leader pointed out that she may in fact have been out of the work force completing her education and that she may be married.

4. *Exploring Cultural Assumptions*   The participants can openly explore assumptions that one group may make about another. For example, at one such awareness session, there was a lively discussion on whether or not it was ever acceptable for women—or men, for that matter—to cry in the workplace.

5. *Personalizing the Experience*   The awareness trainer may try to make everyone aware of their own uniqueness and of the possibility that they can be different. One trainer had the group members describe the first time they became aware that there were people different from themselves—in color, in gender, perhaps in religion, or in economic status. By doing this, even white males can experience the difference that surround them.

At a labor–management legal seminar attended by an equal number of male and female professionals, a luncheon speaker warned the audience of the impact of diversity in the work force by saying, "I'm sorry to say this, but by the year 2000, the work force will be made up of nearly 50 percent women." There were audible objections by a number of the women present and embarrassed looks by the men. The speaker seemed totally unaware of the impact of this statement on the audience.

This incident points to the powerful role language plays in reinforcing stereotypes and in dividing workers in the work force. While the message sent by the speaker was that U.S. companies were not prepared for *Workforce 2000* and had to become prepared, the message received was that a work force made up of more than 50 percent women was something to be sorry about.

Diversity Training May Cause Backlash

In the 1990s diversity training came into the mainstream of the U.S. workplace. About 65 percent of medium and large U.S. employers have conducted some form of diversity training program. The programs generally consist of 1–2 day classroom sessions involving lectures, film and role-playing. The objectives of the program are to increase employees' sensitivity towards others and inform them of organizational diversity policies.

The programs have not always succeeded in changing employee attitudes and behaviors towards others. In fact, in some cases they have produced a backlash and resulted in employees feeling more polarized than before the training.

A good example of diversity training backlash occurred at the Washington State Ferry System in Seattle. All 1500 employees of the ferry system were required to participate in day-long seminars. It was intended to provide "shock therapy" or a "cultural boot camp" for the deckhands, seamen, captains and mates. One year later, as intended, the training did produce some work place changes—the girlie calendars were taken down and some female and black workers reported that they were treated with greater respect.

However, a "huge backlash" of anger and polarization was the most significant result, according to one of the program's supporters. The training increased tension among groups of workers. One supervisor summarized this result: "We used to all be just ferry workers, but now everyone's divided up into little groups: blacks, women, gays, even white males." The training also failed to achieve a primary objective—reduction of sexual harassment and racial incidents. Instead the number increased.

Some critics of diversity training programs believe the ferry system experience is similar to that of other organizations. They believe it is futile to try and change attitudes by forcing people to sit in all-day seminars or giving them lists of forbidden words. While participants may agree with the goals of such training, they often find the process condescending, especially when white-collar trainers try to tell blue-collar workers how to behave and talk.

One backhoe operator in Portland, Oregon, may have summed up the situation with his comment: "Let's face it—I'm a middle-aged guy, and my mind is made up. Sitting in a classroom all day isn't going to change me one iota."

What's the solution for organizations trying to improve their diversity environment? According to some managers: hiring a diverse work force, enforcing policies and laws on discrimination, and leaders setting the right example.

SOURCE: "Sensitivity Class Causes Backlash," *The New York Times,* as reprinted in the *World Herald* (October 24, 1993): D1–D4.

Table 3-4 Appropriate Diversity Terms

When Referring To:	Use:	Instead Of:
Women	Women	Girls, ladies, gals, females
Black people	African-Americans, Caribbean-Americans, black people, people of color	Negroes, minorities
Asian people	Asian-Americans, Japanese, Koreans, Pakistanis, etc.; differentiate between foreign nationals and American born; people of color	Minorities
Pacific Islanders	Pacific Islanders, Polynesians, Maoris, etc.; use island name (e.g., Cook Islanders, Hawaiians); people of color	Asians, minorities
American Indians	American Indians, Native Americans, name of tribe (e.g., Navajo, Iroquois), people of color	Minorities
People of Hispano– Latin American origin	Latinas/Latinos, Chicanas/Chicanos; use country of national origin (e.g., Cubanos, Puerto Ricans, Chileans); people of color, Hispanics	Minorities Spanish-surnamed
Gay men and lesbians	Gay men, lesbians	Homosexuals
Differently abled people	Differently abled, developmentally disabled, physically disabled, physically challenged	Handicapped, crippled
White people	European-Americans; use country of national origin (e.g., Irish-Americans, Polish-Americans); white people	Anglos, WASPS
Older/ younger adults	Older adults, elderly, younger people, younger adults	Geriatrics, kids, yuppies

SOURCE: Marilyn Loden and Judy Rosener, *Workforce America! Managing Employee Diversity As a Vital Resource* (Homewood, IL: Business One Irwin, 1991), pp. 85–90.

Language sensitivity and guidelines for appropriate language help managers value a divers work force. Some rules would seem to be so obvious as to not need repeating, but unfortunately they do.

- Don't tell jokes directed at a group of people stereotyped because of their primary or secondary characteristics.

- Use metaphors and analogies from diverse sources and diverse disciplines, like the arts and sciences, as well as sports.

- Avoid terms that devalue people—*crippled, boy, girl*—or that spotlight differences— *black doctor, old supervisor.*

- Be aware of and sensitive to the preferences of members of diverse groups regarding titles

or terminology. *People of color* seems to be the most acceptable reference for those who have been called minorities. *Physically disabled* is the current term used most often to refer to differently abled people.

Table 3-4 contains a list of appropriate words used to communicate in a diverse environment.

RESPONSE TO DIVERSITY: FEDERAL LEGISLATION

During the civil rights movement of the 1960s, it became apparent that prejudice against African-Americans would not disappear easily.

In every area of society—education, religion, and politics—the challenge was to change the way white Americans thought and felt about black Americans. More important, there was an urgent need for white Americans to change the way they treated black Americans.

Changing hearts and minds would take generations. Changing behavior became a matter of legislating rights and responsibilities. Thus, Congress and the courts initiated reforms to ensure that all individuals have an equal chance of being selected for employment and that they will be treated equally once they are hired. Special emphasis was given to veterans and to minorities, which had experienced discrimination in past decades. The various acts of Congress that apply to recruitment and selection must be understood in detail by HR administrators and line managers. Todays "IAW lingo" can be confusing. (See Figure 3-6 to help you gain a basic understanding of it.)

While the American work force is becoming increasingly diversified, discrimination is still a problem. In fact, two national surveys report that almost one-third of employers admit that discrimination still exists in their organizations, and one-fourth of American workers reported experiencing employment discrimination. HR professionals are the key individuals within organizations who must develop and enforce policies and procedures that protect members of the diversified work force against unlawful discrimination.[24]

Equal Pay Act

Because of many publicized cases of female employees being paid substantially less than their male counterparts while performing identical work, the **Equal Pay Act** (EPA) was passed by Congress in 1963. The act requires organizations of all sizes to pay men and women substantially the same wages for **substantially equal** work or approximately equal "skill, effort, responsibility, and working conditions." Substantial equality is the basis on which jobs should be compared. In practice, this means that jobs do not have to be identical to command the same basic wage; nor do employers have to pay a different wage for each different job. They must pay equal wages for substantially equal work. Has the EPA achieved equal pay? See *HR in the News:* "30 Years After the Equal Pay Act, Women's Wages Still Lag Behind."

When an employer has employees in two or more establishments (separate businesses or locations), employees of the different establishments need not be compared for purposes of pay comparisons. But if the employer controls all employees centrally and their work is integrated, then under the act, employees should be compared for purposes of pay equity. The EPA is administered by the Equal Employment Opportunity Commission.[25]

The EPA has had wider application than many other pieces of legislation dealing with employment because the act does not stipulate a statutory minimum number of employees. It applies to all organizations with two or more employees.[26]

Of particular importance are the exceptions allowed by the EPA: differences in pay can be based on seniority, merit, quality of work, or quantity of work. Therefore, paying different wages to men and women performing the same job can be justified by these differences.

This act has caused many organizations to develop a wage and salary system based on formal job evaluation plans. Under such plans, employees are paid according to the jobs they are performing and not other factors, such as sex or supervisory bias. Organizations that adopt or amend their wage and salary plan cannot, according to the EPA, reduce the wage rate of any employee in order to comply with the act.[27]

Civil Rights Act

The primary federal law that regulates employment practices is the **Civil Rights Act** of 1964, an act passed while the nation mourned the

FIGURE 3-6 Employment law lingo.

Using the wrong word, not fulfilling the duties required by new statutes, or inadvertently taking on responsibilities that are not actually required by law can lead to a variety of harsh consequences for today's employers. Employers need to learn employment law "lingo" to best protect themselves from litigation. Below are just a few definitions to help clarify some common misunderstandings.

- **Equal Employment Opportunity.** Equal Employment Opportunity is an umbrella term that encompasses all laws and regulations prohibiting discrimination and/or requiring affirmative action. More specifically, Title VII, the Americans with Disabilities Act, and the Age Discrimination in Employment Act are all federal Equal Employment Opportunity statutes. Most states also have statutes that prohibit discrimination. Some are broader than the federal laws. For example, in many states, marital status is protected. Also, in a few jurisdictions, sexual preference and orientation are protected.

- **Civil Rights Act of 1991.** For the most part, the Civil Rights Act of 1991 does not make anything illegal that was not already illegal. What the act does is increase the likelihood that employees will sue by making their discrimination cases easier to win and by making the damages they can be awarded even more substantial.

  The act makes it easier for them to win by relaxing the burdens of proof and introducing jury trials. Moreover, an employee's recovery is no longer limited to lost earnings. A successful litigation now can recover damages for pain and suffering, and in some cases, punitive damages.

- **Harassment.** Sexual harassment is a form of sex discrimination that violates federal, state and most local laws. Sexual harassment can take two forms. The first, quid pro quo, occurs when a supervisor conditions the granting of some economic benefit on a subordinate's providing sexual favors or punishes the subordinate for not providing such favors.

  The second, hostile work environment, occurs when supervisors and/or co-workers create an atmosphere so infused with unwelcome sexually oriented or otherwise hostile conduct that an employee's reasonable comfort level or ability to perform is undermined.

- **The Americans with Disabilities Act.** The Americans with Disabilities Act prohibits discrimination against a qualified person with a disability with regard to all aspects of employment. An applicant or employee is qualified for employment if, with or without a reasonable accommodation, the applicant or employee can perform the essential functions of the job.

- **Quotas.** A quota is a fixed, inflexible percentage or number of positions that an employer agrees or decides can be filled only by members of a certain minority group. Quotas are a form of reverse discrimination and are strictly scrutinized by the courts for reasonableness and necessity. Quotas are almost always illegal, notwithstanding the laudatory goals of enhancing diversity.

- **Affirmative Action.** Affirmative action usually does not involve the setting of specific quotas, but rather general aspirational goals to increase the number of minorities and women in specific positions. Affirmative action is lawful if ordered by a court as a remedy for past discrimination.

  Affirmative action is also required of certain federal contractors. Compliance with such affirmative action obligations is monitored by the Office of Federal Contract Compliance Programs. Finally, voluntary affirmative action programs may be upheld where there has been past discrimination and where the plan is limited in time and scope.

SOURCE: Jode-Trager Planer, "Employment Law Lingo," *HR Magazine* (May 1992): 48. Used by permission.

death of John F. Kennedy. Only months before his assassination, the nation had witnessed demonstrations throughout the country as minorities demanded recognition of their civil rights. **Title VII** of the act requires employ-

ment and compensation of employees without discrimination:

> *Title VII, Section 703*   It is unlawful for an employer to discriminate against an individual with respect to his compensation, terms,

30 Years After the Equal Pay Act, Women's Wages Still Lag Behind

The Equal Pay Act, passed in 1963, was supposed to close the gap between the wages paid to men and women. On the thirtieth anniversary of the act, however, the median annual wage paid to women was only 70 percent of that for men. At least it was an increase from the 1963 median of 60 percent. Minority women in the 1990s fare even worse: the median income for black women is only 62 percent and for Hispanic women it is 54 percent.

Critics and supporters of the Equal Pay Act generally agree that it failed to achieve its goal. The modest 10 percent gain registered by women in thirty years probably would have occurred without the act due to the increased presence of working women. Employers have claimed that the gap in pay is due largely to women's lack of seniority and credentials. However, research has shown that with the same credentials and seniority, men average 18 percent higher pay than women. The gap varies substantially according to occupation, as the following table illustrates:

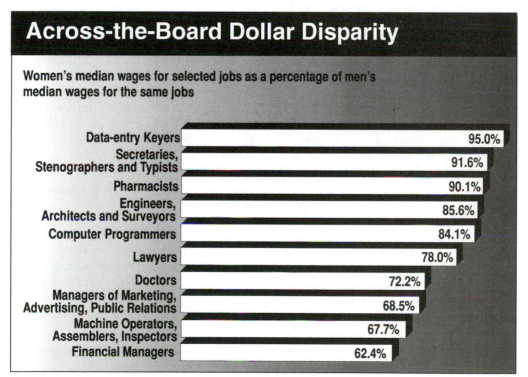

Across-the-Board Dollar Disparity

Women's median wages for selected jobs as a percentage of men's median wages for the same jobs

Job	Percentage
Data-entry Keyers	95.0%
Secretaries, Stenographers and Typists	91.6%
Pharmacists	90.1%
Engineers, Architects and Surveyors	85.6%
Computer Programmers	84.1%
Lawyers	78.0%
Doctors	72.2%
Managers of Marketing, Advertising, Public Relations	68.5%
Machine Operators, Assemblers, Inspectors	67.7%
Financial Managers	62.4%

(continued)

Part of the problem, according to some experts, is that women are more hesitant to ask for a raise and are less likely to engage in self-promotion. The Equal Employment Opportunity Commission may also be part of the problem—in 1992 it filed only *two* lawsuits under the Equal Pay Act.

SOURCE: Joan E. Rigdon, "Three Decades After the Equal Pay Act, Women's Wages remain far from Parity," *The Wall Street Journal* (June 9, 1993): B1, 3; and the Bureau of Labor Statistics.

conditions, or privileges of employment because of such individual's race, color, religion, sex, or national origin; or to limit, segregate, or classify his employees in any way which would deprive or tend to deprive any individual of employment opportunities or otherwise adversely affect his status as an employee, because of such individual's race, color, religion, sex, or national origin.

Two basic forms of discrimination are addressed in Title VII. One, **disparate treatment**, is easier to understand. It refers to intentional discrimination against an individual by an employer. If, for example, a person was not hired because he or she was Hispanic, then disparate treatment occurred. In a disparate treatment case, the plaintiff (protected class applicant or employee) must prove a prima facie case of discrimination, meaning actions taken by the employer that enable one to reasonably infer discrimination. The employer must provide evidence that the employment decision was not motivated by discrimination. The second form, **disparate impact**, occurs when an employment policy or practice that is racially neutral results in a disproportionate number or percentage of protected class individuals not being hired or promoted. Examples include tests, educational requirements, or physical requirements. The intent of the policy or practice may have been nondiscriminatory, but if the result of its utilization is discriminatory, then disparate impact has occurred. The two types of discrimination are not exclusive.[28] In fact, often an individual files a disparate treatment lawsuit that on investigation

becomes a disparate impact case including hundreds or even thousands of persons who may have been affected by a discriminatory policy or practice (see *HR in the News:* "State Farm Insurance Company Pays Record Disparate Impact Settlement").

The Civil Rights Act also established the **Equal Employment Opportunity Commission** (EEOC). The EEOC was given the authority to investigate employee complaints of job discrimination. Where the EEOC finds such complaints justified, it cannot directly order organizations to make personnel changes. But it can bring suit in federal courts against employers if job discrimination is suspected.

Under Title VII, the EEOC is empowered to investigate employee complaints and to act as their attorney. The employer is obligated to show personnel records and other requested material to the EEOC. In addition, all employee applications must be kept for three years in case they are needed in an EEOC complaint or other action. Typically, a discrimination complaint is processed in the following steps:

1. The employee's *inquiry* is filed with the EEOC or a state commission dealing with human rights. The employee is interviewed by a professional, who ascertains all facts of the case. The EEOC then reviews the facts and determines whether the case warrants further investigation.

2. If the EEOC finds that there may be **probable cause**—a reasonable possibility—of discrimination, the commission requests

Jury Awards $20 Million in Sex Discrimination Suit

Janella Sue Martin, a 48-year-old credit supervisor, won $20.3 million in a sex discrimination suit, the largest award in U.S. history. Martin contended that she twice lost promotions to men who were less deserving. In addition, she claimed that Texaco transferred her from Houston to Los Angeles to set up the credit office and become the credit manager. Instead, while she was on vacation, Texaco transferred a man from Houston to become manager.

The jury awarded Martin $2.65 million in actual damages (lost wages and benefits, court costs and legal fees), which was doubled because the employer's action was determined to be fraudulent. The jury also awarded her $15 million in punitive damages. In addition, the judge ordered Texaco to promote Martin.

Martin called the ruling "a great victory for me and other women and minorities who have suffered unlawful discrimination. It's also a victory for Texaco, because it gives them one more opportunity to act in good faith. Now we'll see if they will."

SOURCE: Donna K. H. Walters, "Texaco Is Told to Promote Winner of Sex Bias Case," *The Los Angeles Times* (February 12, 1992): A1.

---

the employer's records. These records may include application blanks, interview results, or test results. The EEOC then determines if there was probable cause for the complaint.

3. The EEOC arranges a *conciliation meeting* with the employer to discuss the employee's complaint if the EEOC feels that it has probable cause. The purpose of the conciliation meeting is to arrive at a mutual agreement that will satisfy both the employer and the aggrieved employee. If this is not possible, then the EEOC weighs the severity of the complaint and discusses alternative actions with the employee.

4. If there is no satisfactory conciliation agreement, the EEOC may issue a **right to sue** to the complainant, indicating that the commission does not feel that it should take the case to court. However, the complaining employee does have the right to sue with a private attorney. Many times this action is an indication that the EEOC does not feel that the complainant has a strong case. The alternative to giving the complainant a right to sue is for the EEOC to take the case of the complainant to court. Title VII covers attorney's fees for complainants if the EEOC does so.

Court Procedures When a disparate treatment complaint is taken to court, the case usually proceeds according to the *McDonnell-Douglas v. Green* case that was litigated in

117

State Farm Insurance Company Pays Record Disparate Impact Settlement

To resolve 814 lawsuits filed with the EEOC, State Farm Insurance Company agreed to pay $157 million to 814 women who applied for sales positions. The suits were based on State Farm's alleged sex discrimination practice of refusing to hire women sales agents in California from 1974 to 1987. During that period 586 agents were hired; only one was female. In 1988 State Farm entered a federal court consent decree in which it agreed that a quota of 50% or more of its new agent hires in California for 10 years would be women.

The 814 women covered by the settlement were mostly secretaries or clerical workers who had become de facto agents in State Farm offices but were turned down for agent positions, which were then given to men. The first suit was filed in 1975 by Muriel Kraszewski, a State Farm secretary, who became a successful agent for Farmers Insurance Group, a State Farm competitor. Kraszewski commented that she filed the case "because I wanted to stop State Farm from treating any woman like they treated me."

By 1993 about 20 percent of State Farm's agents in California were women. The plaintiffs' attorney noted that State Farm, "to its credit, got religion."

SOURCE: Richard B. Schmitt, "State Farm's $157 Million Settlement Caps Discrimination Suit by 814 Women," *The Wall Street Journal* (April 29, 1993): A3.

1972.[29] The complainant must generally prove all of the following:

- **Minority or Female Status** In most cases this is not difficult, though proving that one is of American Indian or Hispanic origin may sometimes be difficult.

- **Qualification for the Position** The complainant must demonstrate minimum qualifications for the position specified in the employer's position announcement or recruitment ad.

- **Failure to Be Hired** Usually this is easily proved except in cases of ongoing recruit-

ment, in which the complainant may still be under consideration for selection.

- **Position Remained Open** In addition, the employer continued to seek applications from persons with similar qualifications.

The organization may put forward one of a number of defenses. For instance, the organization may claim that the employee did not have the requisite **bona fide occupational qualification** (BFOQ). Title VII provides that in certain instances religion, sex, or national origin is a BFOQ if such a qualification is reasonably necessary to the normal operation of the organization. BFOQ is a vague and seldom used defense for discrimination cases. An example of a BFOQ might be a firm's hiring a male to serve as a men's room attendant or a church's refusing to hire someone of a different religion to serve as a minister. The courts have ruled that it is not a BFOQ for flight attendants to be female. Title VII also states that an organization must make reasonable accommodation for employees of specific religious beliefs or employees with handicaps. Exactly how much is "reasonable accommodation" is subject to interpretation.

Another defense is that it was a **business necessity** not to hire the complainant. If safety or profitability requires hiring a specific person, then discrimination could be defended under Title VII. For example, if a company hired an individual to work specific hours during the week, and after being hired the individual could not work those hours due to personal circumstances, management may claim a business necessity as a defense. Another example is a dress shop that claims that it is a business necessity to hire young females as salesclerks so that they may better match the public they are serving.

Still another defense is that the person hired is better qualified for the job than the complainant. This is the most common defense for an organization charged with employment discrimination. HR records should prove that the results of the tests or interviews indicate that the person hired was better qualified. HR departments with standardized and documented records, using proper selection techniques, have a strong defense. If, however, their defense is based solely on what they remember about a case or what they believe occurred, then they have a weak defense.

The EEOC usually hears complaints from applicants who were discriminated against in the process of hiring or promotion, not in matters of unequal pay. Under Title VII, employment discrimination refers to much more than the initial hiring process; it encompasses all

"terms, conditions, or privileges of employment" and includes selection, promotion, transfers, and employee training. Therefore, all organizational decisions that relate to an employee's job classification are included under the Civil Rights Act.

Mixed-Motive Discrimination Mixed-motive discrimination occurs when an employer uses discriminatory criteria, as well as other factors, in making an employment decision. If the employer can prove that it would have made the same decision in the absence of discriminatory criteria, then it cannot be punished. The U.S. Supreme Court, in *Price Waterhouse* v. *Hopkins* (1989), found that Price Waterhouse had the burden of proving that a woman who was denied a partnership because of "sexual stereotyping" would have still been denied the partnership in the absence of any sexual discrimination. The court ruled that Hopkins had been denied a partnership because sexual stereotyping was "a substantial factor" in decision making and not simply "a factor."[30]

Equal Employment Opportunity Act In 1972 the Civil Rights Act of 1964 was amended by the Equal Employment Opportunity Act. The amendment effectively changed Title VII of the 1964 act to include all private employers and labor unions with fifteen or more employees or members, state and local governments, and public and private educational institutions. More important, the Equal Employment Act considerably strengthened the 1964 act by giving the EEOC power to bring suits directly to federal courts when conciliation efforts proved unsuccessful. Previously, the EEOC did not have such power and relied on employers to comply voluntarily with conciliation efforts. State and local EEOC offices were established to provide local-level counseling for complainants who felt they had suffered discrimination.

Pregnancy Discrimination Act A type of sex discrimination openly practiced in the past is one based not entirely on sex but on so-called *sex plus*.[31] A typical example of sex-plus discrimination occurred when a manager openly told all women with small children that they would not be hired because of their child-care responsibilities. The courts found the policy illegal because it was not equally imposed on men.[32] Sex-plus discrimination has also been used against pregnant women. The U.S. Supreme Court had held that such discrimination was legal. But the Pregnancy Discrimination Act of 1978, an amendment to the 1964 Civil Rights Act, prohibited sex discrimination, including but not limited to pregnancy, childbirth, and related medical conditions. The 1978 act also required employee medical insurance to cover pregnancy as fully as it covers other long-term disabilities.[33]

Sexual Harassment

Sexual harassment has developed into one of the most controversial, complex, and perhaps widespread HR problems in the United States. One of the first attempts to measure the extent of sexual harassment was undertaken by *Redbook* magazine. Of the 9000 women workers who responded to a survey, 80 percent reported that they had experienced some form of unwanted attention on the job.[34]

A national study of over 13,000 workers found that 42 percent of the women and 14 percent of the men had experienced some form of sexual harassment in a three-year period. The study also found that only 5 percent of the men and women who had experienced harassment chose to report it. The primary reasons why the other 95 percent did not report their harassment include the following:[35]

- The fear of losing one's job.
- The need for a future job reference.
- The possibility of being considered a trouble-maker.
- The assumption that nothing would change if harassment was reported.

- Concern about being accused of inviting the harassment.
- A reluctance to draw public attention to private lives.
- The prospect of emotional stress for filing a lawsuit and undergoing long, costly legal procedures.

Clearly, the magnitude of the problem demands that HR administrators seek ways to minimize sexual harassment in their organizations.[36]

The EEOC has set forth guidelines that declare sexual harassment a form of illegal sex discrimination because sexual harassment constitutes a form of behavior directed toward an employee specifically because of his or her sex. (Most incidents of sexual harassment are directed toward women, but research shows that male employees are also sexually harassed on the job, though such incidents are few compared to the problems reported by women.) The EEOC also issued guidelines that set forth a working definition of sexual harassment:[37]

> Unwelcome sexual advances, requests for sexual favors, and other verbal or physical conduct of a sexual nature constitute sexual harassment when (1) submission to such conduct is made either explicitly or implicitly a term or condition of an individual's employment, (2) submission to or rejection of such conduct by an individual is used as the basis for employment decisions affecting such individual, or (3) such conduct has the purpose or effect of unreasonably interfering with an individual's work performance or creating an intimidating, hostile, or offensive working environment.

Points (1) and (2) of the EEOC guidelines describe the types of harassment known as *quid pro quo:* sex in exchange for favors and/or to avoid adverse actions. Point (3) of the guidelines describes a type of harassment that results in a hostile work environment. Regardless of which type of harassment is involved, the same criterion applies: the conduct, whether physical or verbal, must be both unwelcome and of a sexual nature.

Unwelcome Sexual Advances   It is critical to understand what *unwelcome* means in the EEO guidelines. A person may have acquiesced in some type of conduct, but the conduct can still be unwelcome. Acquiescence to the conduct may have happened because the person feared loss of the job or some other retaliation. If the conduct was unsolicited, or if the victim viewed the conduct as undesirable or offensive and did nothing to initiate it, even if it was agreed to, it could still be considered unwelcome. Questions about *welcome* and *unwelcome* sexual advances are fact based and particular to each case. Consider, for instance, a woman who went out of her way to visit her supervisor in the hospital and in his brother's home and allowed him to visit her home. Later, this woman may not be able to convince a jury that the supervisor's conduct of which she complained was unwelcomed. Nor, in another example, might a woman who claimed that a *hostile work environment* existed be able to prove it when she began most of the discussions about sex herself.

Sexual Nature   For harassment to be based on sex, as that term is used in the Civil Rights Act, there must be something of a sexual nature in the conduct. Usually that test is met when a person is propositioned, comments or jokes are made about the person's anatomy, or pictures of people nude and/or in sexually suggestive poses are displayed. Conduct of a sexual nature can also be found when a *but for* situation arises. In one case, male crew members harassed female crew members by pulling such pranks as locking the restroom door at the work site and disabling their trucks.[38] "But for" the harassed victim being women and unwanted by this particular male work crew, the harassment they experienced would not have happened. This, then, became a "but for their sex" situation.

Quid Pro Quo

Quid pro quo sexual harassment occurs when a threat or promise is made in exchange for a sexual favor. In order to threaten or promise, the harasser has to be in a position to follow through. Usually the harasser is the immediate supervisor, but sometimes he or she is higher up on the organizational ladder.

Monetary damages must be provable. Generally in a quid pro quo situation, actual losses can be demonstrated. The victim may have been denied a promotion or raise or may have been fired for refusing the harasser.

This type of harassment need happen only once to be actionable. If the truth of the harassment can be demonstrated, there is no necessity to show a pattern of other violations. *Once is enough* in quid pro quo cases.

Employers have been held *strictly liable* for the sexual harassment of one of their supervisors under a *respondeat superior* theory, which states that the employer is responsible for his or her agents. Actual knowledge on the part of the employer about how the supervisor acts is not required.[39] The employer has placed the supervisor in a position of authority and has given the supervisor the opportunity to misuse the authority.

Employers must ensure that there is a policy prohibiting sexual harassment, that the policy is communicated to all employees, that an effective complaint procedure exists, and that all managers have been trained in the policy.

Hostile Environment

Harassing conduct that interfere with an individual's work performance can come from anyone in the workplace: supervisors, coworkers, and even outsiders such as visitors or customers. One incident of harassment cannot establish a hostile work environment. Generally, the offensive conduct is frequent, repetitive, and part of an overall pattern that cannot be explained by coincidence. A victim may not be able to prove a particular monetary loss through a demotion or any specific job action. In fact, money damages may not have occurred. Unlike quid pro quo, job or money losses are not required; hostile environmental harassment includes unwelcome sexual advances, requests for sexual favors, verbal or physical conduct of a sexual nature, and actions that alter the conditions of the victim's employment and create an abusive working environment. In general, the courts have determined that a hostile environment was created when (1) the actions were unwelcome; (2) serious actions were repeated (an isolated sexual advance that was not repeated and that resulted in no retaliation is usually not sufficient); and (3) the actions were so severe as to alter the conditions of employment.[40]

In a hostile environment case, the conduct complained of is so offensive as to be objectionable to an uninvolved third party. Courts have traditionally used what was known as the *reasonable person* standard to judge what the community as a whole considers acceptable, despite individual peculiarities. For purposes of sexual harassment, the EEOC advised investigators to view the conduct as a reasonable person would, keeping the victim's perspective in mind.

A Florida court went further and decided the case on a *reasonable woman* standard because the court felt that men viewed sexual harassment as a comparatively harmless amusement.[41] Another court, in using a reasonable woman standard, relied on research that found that two-thirds of males interviewed would be flattered by a sexual approach in the workplace, while only 15 percent would be insulted. The response from women to the same question was reversed.[42]

In another example of differing perspective, a survey was conducted of fifty-one employees of a company, and a comparison was made of male and female attitudes toward sexual harassment. Most employees, both male and female, did not think sexual harassment was a major problem at their company, although nearly 25 percent of the women had experienced it and only 3 percent of the men had. When a man joked "Who's the lucky guy?" when the 3 percent figure was announced, men tittered but women did not.[43]

The employer's liability in a hostile environment case is not automatic.[44] The facts in each case must be examined to see if the employer had notice, either actual or constructive, of the offensive conduct. Did the victim complain, either formally through a complaint system or informally to the employer, of the harassment? Was the conduct so open and pervasive that the employer could not claim ignorance of it? And when the employer learned of the harassment, what was the response? Did the employer move quickly to investigate and resolve the problem? Or did the employer disregard the harassment and, by doing so, encourage it?

In fact, did the employer have *preventive* measures in place to discourage such conduct? Was there a strong policy prohibiting sexual harassment, as well as training on the issue, not only of supervisors but of all employees?

Under Title VII, a plaintiff must file a charge of discrimination with the EEOC within 180 or 300 days of the alleged unlawful employment practice. An exception to this rule allows other alleged violations to be considered if the offense is a *continuing violation.* Hostile environment claims usually involve a continuing violation. In a hostile environment an individual feels constantly threatened, even in the absence of constant harassment. In such a case, the court will apply the *reasonable woman* doctrine: would a reasonable woman feel that the environment was hostile throughout the period? If the answer is yes, then a hostile environment existed. Court decisions in continuing violation cases have produced a set of circumstances that are often present in continuing violation cases:[45]

1. Failure by management to discipline alleged perpetrators.

France Adopts
Harassment Law

France joined seven other European countries that followed the example of the United States in making sexual harassment in the workplace illegal. The French law makes anyone found guilty of using a position of authority to demand or extract sexual favors subject to a year in jail and a $2000 fine. The penalties might have been more severe, but many European legislators are reluctant to go far "toward what they see as the desexualization of the United States." Veronique Neierty, the French Secretary of State for Women's Rights, said the new law in France avoided "American excesses"—turning all sexual advances into potential criminal offenses.

While polls indicate that, depending on the country, between 20 percent and 70 percent of European working women reportedly have suffered harassment, very few file complaints. Women are generally afraid to speak up or file a complaint, and the problem is even worse in a recession because they are afraid of losing their jobs.

SOURCE: Adopted from Alan Riding, "Europeans Discover Sexual Harassment, But Don't Complain Much," *Herald Tribune* (November 4, 1992): 1, 7.

---

2. Failure to take aggressive measures to eliminate overt methods of harassment.

3. Shifting the blame to the harassed employee and requiring the employee to collect all of the evidence and data before management acts.

4. Requesting the harassed employee to change his or her behavior while ignoring the behavior of the alleged perpetrators.

5. Stereotyping the role of women in the workplace.

6. Not conducting a meaningful or effective investigation.

In *Waltman* v. *International Paper Company* (1989)[46] the court outlined three factors needed to determine if a continuing violation exists:[47]

1. *Subject Matter* Did the acts involve similar types of discrimination?

2. *Frequency* Were the acts recurring (versus a single employment decision or an isolated incident)?

3. *Degree of Permanence* Did the acts have a degree of permanence, which would notify the employee to assert his or her rights?

The hostile environment created by a continuing violation may be the result of an organizational policy that is discriminatory or a series of related acts against an individual.

While many women and men are reluctant to report incidents of sexual harassment (See *HR in the News*: "France Adopts Harassment Law"), those who do file "win" as many as 90 percent of their cases. Winning, in this context, was defined as receiving a financial award, being reinstated in the job or receiving a promotion, or receiving a guarantee from the employer that the harassment would cease.[48]

The chances of a favorable court decision or out-of-court decision, however, are greatly enhanced (1) if the sexual harassment involved sexual assault, unwanted physical contact, or propositions linked to employment, (2) if witnesses supported the charge, and (3) if management was previously notified of problems by the complainant. Complaints that courts have agreed to hear generally have involved clear-cut instances. Less serious behaviors such as crude jokes, offensive language, or unwanted gestures, stares, or whistles have generally not been litigated successfully.[49]

Measuring and Researching Sexual Harassment Because of the sensitivity of the subject, it may be difficult to get an accurate reading of the extent of sexual harassment in an organization. Nonetheless, certain techniques may provide HR administrators with estimates about the nature, extent, and location of sexual harassment. These include the following:

- Grievance data.
- Oral complaints to management and HR officials.
- Exit interviews.
- Survey data.

Perhaps the most accurate and comprehensive technique for measuring sexual harassment is a well-designed anonymous employee survey. An example of a survey to discover the extent of sexual harassment is shown in Figure 3-7.

Reducing Sexual Harassment The Anita Hill testimony during well-publicized U.S. Senate confirmation hearings for Supreme Court nominee Clarence Thomas awakened many employers to the need for clear policies and guidelines in the area of sexual harassment. Employers realized that developing procedures and training supervisors in how to investigate a claim after it is filed is too late. Once a person complains, emotion rather than reasoning is likely to dominate, and thus an objective investigation is often impossible. It is important to establish policies and investigation procedures in cases of alleged sexual harassment that.[50] For example:

- *Don't Presume Guilt* All claims should be taken seriously, but if the investigation is influenced by a presumption of guilt, the employer may be subject to a viable defamation suit. Few allegations are potentially more damaging to one's professional and home lives than a claim of sexual harassment. Individuals once charged usually fight back and, if the process appears unfair, may countersue the employer. Employers should be considerate of the rights of both the victim and the accused and conduct an impartial investigation.

- *Use the Reasonable-woman Standard* This standard is significant in court cases (See *HR in the News*: "Supreme Court Issues Firm Decisions on Sexual Harassment"). Investigations conducted only by men may reach invalid conclusions and lack credibility with a jury that must determine if the conduct would have been offensive to a reasonable woman. Thus women should play a key role in all phases of any investigation and decision making.

- *Maintain Confidentiality* To minimize potential defamation claims by alleged harassers, the allegations should only be made known to people on a need-to-know basis. In general, an HR official, not supervisors, should conduct harassment investigations to maximize confidentiality. Any personnel questioned in the process should be strongly warned to not discuss the case with others.

- *Document All Complaints* Employees often discuss a hostile environment situation informally with someone but then plead with this person to take no action. Even if no action is taken at the employee's request, the

FIGURE 3-7 A survey to discover the extent of sexual harassment in an organization. All respondents remain anonymous.

Sexual Harassment Questionnaire

Circle the best response listed after each question. Please answer each question.

1. Are you aware that sexual harassment has been deemed illegal by guidelines set forth by the Equal Employment Opportunity Commission?
   a. yes
   b. no

2. Which of the following do you feel constitute sexual harassment? (circle all letters that apply)
   a. Sexually offensive comments
   b. Sex-oriented jokes
   c. Staring or leering
   d. Touching, grabbing, pinching
   e. Sexual propositions
   f. Rape
   g. Other forms of sexual harassment
   h. None of the above constitutes sexual harassment

3. Which of the following have you experienced on your job from co-workers or supervisors? (circle all letters that apply)
   a. sexually offensive comments
   b. sex-oriented jokes
   c. staring or leering
   d. touching, grabbing, pinching
   e. sexual propositions
   f. rape
   g. other forms of sexual harassment
   h. have not experienced sexual harassment

4. How many times in the last twelve months have you personally experienced sexual harassment in the organization where you are presently working?
   a. none
   b. 1–2 times
   c. 3–4 times
   d. 5–6 times
   e. more than 6 times

5. How did you react to a co-worker or supervisor's sexual advances?
   a. ignored it
   b. enjoyed it
   c. asked them to stop
   d. reported it to a company official or government agency
   e. have not received sexual advances

6. If you reported sexual harassment to a supervisor or union representative, what do you think would most likely happen?
   a. nothing
   b. an investigation would be made but no actual results obtained
   c. an investigation would be made, and action would be taken to stop it
   d. I would be transferred
   e. I would be fired

7. Have you ever used your sexual attractiveness at work for any of the following?
   a. to gain a promotion
   b. to get in good with the superior
   c. to obtain other advantages
   d. not applicable

---

continued

complaint should still be filed, with all pertinent information noted. A copy given to the employee may prevent the employee from changing his or her story later or denying the request that no action be taken. In addition, the employer must consider investigating such complaints even when the employee requests otherwise because the employer has a duty to protect other employees who may be affected. The employer may be held liable for

FIGURE 3-7 *continued*

---

8. How has sexual harassment affected you? (circle all letters that apply)
  a. economically
  b. work opportunities
  c. mental and physical health
  d. Self-esteem
  e. Have not experienced any sexual harassment

9. You would hesitate to report sexual harassment for any of the following reasons?
  a. feel it would not do any good
  b. would be afraid of being punished in some way
  c. would fear the publicity
  d. would not hesitate to report it

10. Which sex do you feel has a problem with sexual harassment?
  a. women only
  b. mostly women and very few men
  c. women and men about equally
  d. mostly men and very few women
  e. sexual harassment is not a problem

11. Which individuals in your organization are most involved with sexual harassment?
  a. an immediate supervisor harasses a subordinate
  b. a company representative harasses a prospective employee
  c. a coworker harasses another coworker
  d. an employee harasses another employee who is neither a subordinate nor a coworker
  e. a subordinate harasses a superior
  f. sexual harassment is not a problem

12. To what extent do you consider sexual harassment a problem in your organization?
  a. Sexual harassment is a frequent, troublesome part of the organization's working environment. Organizational effectiveness is definitely affected by sexual harassment problems.
  b. Sexual harassment is an occasional problem, with sexual harassment situations occurring only periodically. Organizational effectiveness is affected only to a minor degree.
  c. Sexual harassment is a minor problem, with sexual harassment situations occurring infrequently. Organizational effectiveness is affected hardly at all.
  d. Sexual harassment is not a problem in this organization. It does not affect the organization's effectiveness.

Please feel free to write below any additional comments you have on sexual harassment. We are particularly interested in learning about any situations in which you have personally experienced sexual harassment. Please do not sign your name or identify your employer. Thank you for your cooperation.

_____
_____
_____

---

a hostile environment if the company failed to take appropriate action.

▪ *Establish Clear Policies* Policies should define and prohibit sexual harassment and provide an explicit code of conduct for all employees. All written and oral complaints should be investigated. Any refusal to provide a written complaint does not release the employer from the responsibility to investigate.

▪ *Provide Training* Training is essential, and can increase awareness among all employees and reduce the number of incidents. A growing number of companies are training most or all of their employees including DuPont, Digital Equipment, Honeywell,

Supreme Court Issues Firm Decisions on Sexual Harassment

- "9-Zip"
- "27 days!"
- "I love it"

Those were the first reactions by Teresa Harris when she heard she had won her sexual harassment suit by a 9 to 0 decision that was handed down in only twenty-seven days—an unprecedentedly short period for the Supreme Court. By acting quickly and unanimously, the Court sent a dramatic message to the lower courts and the American workplace: sexual harassment claims are serious, and such acts should not be tolerated by victims.

Harris had been harassed by her former boss, the company president, until she quit her job. Justice Sandra Day O'Connor, writing for the Court, stated that offensive remarks and conduct break the law if a reasonable person would find that the workplace had become a hostile and abusive environment. Thus the Court solidified these important principles of sexual harassment litigation.

The importance of the decision was summarized by Helen Newborne, executive director of the National Organization for Women Legal Defense Fund: "We are thrilled with the Court's strong message that when women suffer sexual harassment, they will be treated exactly the same as any other group discriminated against based on race, religion or national origin."

SOURCE: Adapted from Andrea Sachs, "'9-Zip! I Love It!'," *Time* (November 22, 1993): 44–45.

Corning, and Pacific Gas & Electric. Sexual harassment can be an uncomfortable and tough subject, according to Corning's HR Manager, Tom McCullough, who has directed awareness seminars. Videos are effective tools because they can show subtle actions better than words alone. Employees generally want to discuss the entire range of harassment behaviors (Figure 3-8), as well as the gray areas of relationships. Discussing all the examples cited in Figure 3-8 can be critical because sexual harassment does not mean the same thing to everyone. But by viewing each act as a point on a continuum, people better understand the seriousness of all acts, as well as how some minor actions may lead to more serious ones or become part of a hostile environment. The desired outcome is that some unintentional harassment may be stopped.[51] It is also important to make employees aware that a *continuing pattern* of the acts on the left of the spectrum in Figure 3-8 may constitute a hostile environment.

Religious Discrimination

Discrimination based on religion is prohibited by Title VII of the 1964 Civil Rights Act, Executive Order 11246, the 1991 Civil Rights

127

FIGURE 3-8 Sexual harassment

Sexual Harassment
A Spectrum of Behavior Patterns

Visual	Verbal	Written	Touching	Power	Threats	Force
•Ogling	•Requests for dates	•Love poems	•Violating Space	•Relationships	•Quid pro quo	•Rape
•Staring	•Questions about	•Love letters	•Patting	•Using position	•Demands	•Physical
•Posters	personal life	•Obscene poems	•Grabbing	to request	•Loss of job	Assault
•Magazines	•Lewd comments	•Obscene letters	•Pinching	dates, sex, etc.	•Selection process	
•Flyers	•Dirty/sexual jokes	•Cards	•Caressing			
	•Whistling		•Kissing			

←————————— **Offensive Conduct**————————————————————————— **Demands** ————————→
                (May be illegal)   **(Illegal in all cases)**

•Individual perceptions and reactions determine harassment   •Behaviors are intentional; goal is to intimidate, harass
•Behaviors unwanted by recipient are harassment   or hurt another person
•Behaviors may not be intended to harass, but that is often the result
•Illegal if the result is perceived as harassment

SOURCE: *Sexual Harassment Manual,* General Electric Corporation.

Act, and various state and local laws. All aspects of the employment process are included in these acts. In the past, the number of cases based on religious discrimination was relatively few. However, with the work force becoming more culturally diverse, it is expected that the number will increase. The federal laws define *religion* to include "all aspects of religious observance, practice, and belief." However, the legitimacy of some religions and their practices has been questioned.[52] Thus, to clarify the definition, the courts have identified three major characteristics that should be present: (1) the belief is based on a theory of "man's nature or his place in the universe," (2) which is not merely a personal preference but has an institutional quality about it, and (3) which is sincere.[53]

Religious discrimination issues have mostly focused on one of the following issues:[54]

▪ *Dress Policies* Many employers have grooming and dress policies designed to maintain an appropriate image or provide employee safety. The courts have generally upheld these policies if they have been fairly and uniformly enforced. Restaurants, for example, have successfully defended the policy of no facial hair and have required uniforms as a business necessity to maintain a public image of cleanliness.

▪ *Work Schedules* Employees requesting time off for religious observances are a problem for many employers. In general, employers are required to make reasonable accommodations if no undue hardship is placed on the business or on other employees. In one case, for example, the U.S. Supreme Court upheld TWA's firing of an employee who refused to work on Saturday for religious reasons. In a previous TWA position, the employee had had enough seniority to avoid Saturday work. After requesting for and receiving another position that required Saturday hours, the employee started on a new seniority list and thus was scheduled to work Saturdays. He repeatedly failed to report on Saturday and was terminated. The Court upheld TWA's decision and cited the seniority system as a reasonable means of meeting employees' religious and secular needs.

- **Harassment** Prohibited religious discrimination also includes jokes, slurs, taunts, or tricks by coworkers and/or supervisors. If such activities occur repeatedly, the situation is viewed as a hostile environment and may violate the law.

- **BFOQ** Church-run organizations may consider religion a bona fide occupational qualification (BFOQ). Employees can then be required to be members of the church, and nonmembers can be discriminated against on the basis of religion.

- **Atheists** Discrimination against atheists is also legally prohibited because religion has been found to include belief and nonbelief. For example, an atheist bank employee refused to attend staff meetings because they opened with a prayer. She eventually felt forced to resign due to her absences. The Court found in her favor, noting that her quitting was not voluntary.

Age Discrimination in Employment Act

The **Age Discrimination in Employment Act** (ADEA) was passed in 1967 and amended in 1978 and 1986. The act makes it illegal for employers with twenty or more employees, governmental bodies, and labor unions to discriminate against individuals over age forty. Employers cannot refuse to hire or discriminate in terms of compensation, promotion, or other conditions solely due to an individual's age. Nor can age be used as a preferential criterion in recruitment.

Section 4(f) of the ADEA allows employers to discipline or terminate an employee for a job-related reason such as incompetence,

theft, or some other just cause that is "not age related." The courts have upheld employers' age policies where health and safety are of concern. In a landmark case, *Hodgson* v. *Greyhound Lines, Inc.,* a court of appeals upheld Greyhound's policy of barring applicants over the age of thirty-five for the job of bus driver.[55]

The 1986 amendment prohibits any mandatory retirement age for workers (previously set at age seventy [1978 amendment] and originally at age sixty-five [1967 act]). The 1986 amendment also requires employers to continue the same group health insurance for employees over age seventy that is offered to younger employees. The elimination of the mandatory retirement age has received ardent support from senior citizens, labor leaders, and civil rights groups.[56]

At least three areas of HR costs may be significantly affected by the 1986 amendment.

First, the requirement that employers continue to provide health coverage for older employees will most likely increase health care costs significantly. Medical plan rating manuals show increased claims for older workers; thus, health care premiums can be expected to rise. A critical factor will be how many employees choose to work beyond the normal retirement age. Conceivably, the amendment's requirement that employers continue health care coverage for older employees could influence their decision to continue working beyond the age at which they would like to retire. Thus, the new amendment gives them an additional incentive to continue working.

The second area likely to be affected by the amendment is pension funding. In theory, if employees work longer, their retirement base and, therefore, their pension checks will be increased. However, if the average age of Americans does not continue to increase, choosing to work longer may mean that future retirees will collect retirement pensions for fewer years. It may well be the year 2000 before the actual impact on pension costs is known, and then the results may differ from organization to organization.[57]

The third area affected will likely be Social Security. The Congressional Budget Office concluded that Social Security retirement benefits and Medicare may decrease by $25 million annually due to employees choosing to work longer. They will be contributing a greater amount and withdrawing less from the Social Security system, which should slow the rise in Social Security tax rates for both employers and employees.[58] Jerome Rosow, president of the Work in America Institute, Inc., supported the 1986 amendment by predicting that it will decrease the threat of intergenerational conflict if older workers continue to pay into the Social Security system longer and reduce the number of years they withdraw benefits.[59]

The 1978 amendment to the ADEA transferred the enforcement responsibility to the EEOC and provided for jury trials. The change to jury trials greatly increased the number of cases that go to court. Jurors tend to be sympathetic to individuals who are generally the same age as themselves, and they are often prejudiced against large corporations. At the same time, companies began "retiring" many older employees due to economic pressures. Increased pressure from the baby-boom generation to make room for their upward mobility also put pressure on companies to force early retirement of older workers.[60]

How can employers help their employees plan their retirement? An American Society for Personnel Administration survey of American employers found that they can provide the following:[61]

- *Early Retirement Options* In addition, early retirement incentive programs (ERIPS) may be offered to encourage eligible employees to volunteer for early retirement by speeding up their benefits.
- *Written Retirement Planning Information* This should be provided for employees of all ages. Of particular value is retirement program design and administration, as well as key personal issues such as Social Security, health, legal, and emotional adjustment.

- *Postretirement Benefits* In addition to monthly retirement checks, retirees may receive health insurance, life insurance, special activity discounts, and retiree newsletters. In recent years, more employers have also provided part-time and consulting work.

The result of these different forces has been a large increase in age discrimination cases. The typical complainant in ADEA cases is a managerial or professional employee over age fifty. Most cases involve mandatory retirement, demotion, or direct termination.[62] An analysis of over 300 cases filed showed that while the EEOC was involved in less than 25 percent of the cases, it was able to win 79 percent of the cases it chose to pursue. Employees generally had a greater likelihood of winning cases that contested mandatory retirement and pension-related employer actions. Age-conscious remarks by employers can help an employee's case, (see Figure 3-9). Employers can increase their chances of winning age discrimination cases if they do the following:[63]

- Make all decisions on the basis of documented performance appraisals.
- Eliminate organizational policies that might indirectly be age discriminatory and formalize HR policies that are not.
- Train managers and other personnel to refrain from making references to age, especially in front of potential witnesses.
- Chart ages and any other employee characteristics protected against discrimination and analyze any possible discrimination by age.
- Document employee responses to early retirement programs that may be needed as evidence of their voluntary participation.

FIGURE 3-9 Age-conscious remarks that can be used against you.

In 1985 the EEOC reported a record number of age-discrimination charges against employers. Employees have clearly become more aware of employer age-discrimination practices—and they know their rights under the Age Discrimination in Employment Act (ADEA). Unlike most race-discrimination cases, age-discrimination cases are decided by juries, which may be more sympathetic to the worker. Age-conscious remarks by managers can influence a jury's decision.

Examples of age-conscious communications that have been found to be discriminatory included:

- A piece of paper with the official reason for layoff that says: "Lay off—too old."
- Memo recommending a reduction in [the work] force to promote "a younger image."
- Job advertisements seeking: "college student," "recent college graduate," or "retired person."
- Direct comments by supervisors who affect employment decisions: "for men your age, there isn't going to be a future in the new [company]"; or the company was "going to get rid of the 'good old Joes' and get some younger folks in."

In lawsuits involving age discrimination the employee must prove that age . . . was a determining factor in an employment action—but age need *not* have been the sole reason for the action taken. Employers can avoid liability by eliminating age-conscious remarks in official communications and by documenting a well-organized campaign to sensitize all managers to the need to avoid age-conscious remarks and thinking.

SOURCE: John J. Coleman, III, "Age-Conscious Remarks: What You Say Can Be Used Against You," *Personnel* 62, no. 9 (September 1985): 22–29. Used by permission.

Separation Agreements

An employer and an employee may both benefit from the employee's early retirement. In fact, employers often offer "retirement windows" to employees close in age and seniority to retirement. The window is a fixed period of time, usually a month, during which the employee must decide whether or not to accept and sign a **separation agreement** that provides enhanced retirement benefits such as continued health care coverage or a higher monthly pension. The 1986 ADEA amendment requires early retirement programs to be voluntary.

In a landmark case, *Sullivan* v. *Boron Oil Company* (1987),[64] an employee's written separation agreement was upheld as legal and binding. In this case, an employee of the Standard Oil of Ohio (SOHIO) Company signed an agreement titled "Release of Claims," which stated that "In consideration of the benefit provided me . . . , I release the Standard Oil Company . . . from all claims." The employee claimed age discrimination because he was

mentally and physically fatigued when he signed the release. The U.S. Court of Appeals applied a five-part test to determine the validity and fairness of the agreement and found that (1) the release was clear and unambiguous, (2) the plaintiff knew his rights as stated in the agreement, (3) the plaintiff understood the agreement, (4) the plaintiff had an opportunity to negotiate, and (5) the plaintiff voluntarily accepted the release for personal compensation. This decision provides employers with specific guidelines for developing voluntary early retirement plans that can be legally executed without fear of successful litigation.

Older Workers Benefit Protection Act

The ADEA was again amended in 1990 by the **Older Workers Benefit Protection Act** (OWBPA). Title I of the OWBPA effectively nullified the 1989 *Betts* decision by the U.S. Supreme Court. That court decision had allowed age discrimination in the administration of benefit plans, thus allowing employers to offer benefit plans of greater value to younger workers, regardless of cost considerations. Title I of the OWBPA includes employer benefit plans under the ADEA. Therefore, an employer cannot make age-based distinctions in designing employee benefit plans unless the costs are greater for older workers than for younger ones. In addition, early retirement plans are permitted as long as they are voluntary and employees receive a financial incentive for electing to participate.

Under Title II of the OWBPA,[65] an individual may not waive any right or claim under the ADEA unless the waiver is "knowing and voluntary." In general, the most common scenario involves an employee over age forty who is told that his or her position is no longer needed due to downsizing (or rightsizing), merger, or reorganization. The HR director offers the employee a separation agreement, reviews it with the employee, and provides time for it to be reviewed by the employee's attorney. In general, the release offers the employee more compensation than he or she would normally receive in pension benefits in exchange for a written release and covenant not to sue under the ADEA or OWBPA. The employee may later decide that he or she was discriminated against because of age and coerced to sign the agreement. The employer's attorney, however, may file a countersuit based on the employee's breach of the agreement. A court must then decide if someone was wronged. Decisions have been made in favor of both sides, but more often in favor of employees if age was a factor in their being selected for termination. Here is an example of separation agreement:[66]

> In consideration of these undertakings by the company, the employee agrees to release from, and covenants not to sue the company for any and all claims, including but not limited to those arising out of the employee's employment with the company and cessation thereof, and also including but not limited to any and all

claims of discrimination on account of . . . age. . . . I [each employee] understand that by signing this release I am releasing the company from any and all claims I may have against the company to date. I certify that I do so knowingly and voluntarily in exchange for the company's agreement to perform the actions outlined above.

Vocational Rehabilitation Act

Under the **Vocational Rehabilitation Act** of 1973, employers with government contracts of $2500 or more must have approved affirmative action programs for the handicapped. Programs include special recruitment efforts for the handicapped, as well as procedures to promote and develop the handicapped within the organization. Employees are also required to make environmental changes, such as adding ramps to make their business more accessible to the handicapped. The act is administered by committee members from the Civil Service Commission, the U.S. Department of Veterans' Affairs, the U.S. Department of Labor, and the U.S. Department of Health and Human Services. Handicapped individuals who feel that their rights have been violated under the act may file complaints with the U.S. Department of Labor.

Although the term *handicap* is usually associated with physical impairments, the act also covers such mental impairments as retardation and emotional disorders. In addition, the act covers certain illnesses sometimes used by employers as grounds for rejecting applicants, including diabetes, heart disease, epilepsy, and cancer. Individuals who are alcohol or drug users are included unless their illness affects their ability to perform their job.[67] In practice, the Department of Labor's guidelines for contractors require them to make a "reasonable accommodation" for the handicapped, which generally includes the following:[68]

- *Job Accessibility* Adding wheelchair ramps, Braille signs on elevators, air conditioning for workers with respiratory problems, and so on.

- *Job Design*   Eliminating tasks that a handicapped person cannot perform but that are not really necessary to do the job.

- *Qualifications*   Eliminating unnecessary job specifications, such as a physical exam that might limit the entry of handicapped applicants.

- *Unprejudiced Treatment*   Eliminating hiring decisions based on people's fear or uneasiness about handicaps such as epilepsy or speech impairment.

Vietnam Era Veterans Readjustment Act

This act was a special effort to help Vietnam War veterans who had particular difficulty in securing jobs when they returned to the United States. The **Vietnam Era Veterans Readjustment Act** of 1974 requires all organizations holding government contracts of $10,000 or more to hire and promote Vietnam War veterans. The act is administered by the Veterans Employment Service of the U.S. Department of Labor. Employers holding government contracts are required to list their job openings with local state employment offices in order that these offices may contact unemployed veterans as well as other individuals. One side effect of the act has been a demonstrated increase in job openings listed by state employment offices, which has increased their effectiveness in many communities.

Immigration Reform and Control Act

Congress in 1986, after years of debate, passed a comprehensive federal immigration-control law. In effect, the **Immigration Reform and Control Act** (IRCA) shifted much of the burden of immigration enforcement from the federal government to employers (see *HR in the News:* "Why Employer Sanctions in Immigra-

tion?"). This shift was accomplished by making it illegal for an employer to hire, recruit, refer for a fee, or continue to employ an alien whom the employer knows is not eligible to work in the United States. Employers are required to verify and maintain records of each new employee's identity and work eligibility for three years of employment or for one year after termination. Thus, in practice, employers will require of all new employees one of the following as documentation of legal employment status:[69]

- Social Security card or certificate of birth with current driver's license.

- Alien Registration Receipt Card (green card).

- Valid United States passport.

- Valid certificate of citizenship or United States identification card.

- Valid certificate for naturalization.

- Unexpired Immigration Naturalization Service (INS) work permit.

- Unexpired foreign passport bearing an appropriate unexpired endorsement of the United States Attorney General.

- Resident alien card.

- Form I-94 bearing an employment authorization stamp.

A second major feature of the IRCA makes it unlawful for employers to discriminate against individuals who look or sound "foreign" but are legally in the United States. This section of the act was passed in response to concerns of Hispanic-American groups and others who feared that the new employer requirements might lead to unintentional employment discrimination.[70] Specifically, Section 274B(a)(1) of the act provides the following:

> It is an unfair immigration-related employment practice for a person or other entity to discriminate against any individual (other than an unauthorized alien) with respect to the hiring, or recruitment or referral for a fee, of the individual for employment or the discharging of the

Why Employer Sanctions in Immigration?

Immigration is an expression of one of the most fundamental human aspirations: the desire for a better life, a new start, a clean slate.

And, as long as people see these opportunities lying just across a border, they will continue to move toward them, whether someone says it is legal to do so or not.

This phenomenon of migration is a central element of the American experience and of our heritage. In recent years, however, a lack of control of illegal movement across our national borders—allowing the unfettered entry of millions of illegal aliens—has strained our national patience and placed at risk the long-standing American tradition of a fair, humane, and generous welcome for legal aliens.

It also highlighted the patent unfairness of an immigration system that allowed a flood of illegal entries into the United States but that allowed only a comparative trickle of legal aliens.

Finally, uncontrolled illegal immigration had created an underclass in the United States: a class of law-abiding persons who had been in the United States for many years, but whose illegal status made them afraid and fearful of asserting their legal and moral rights lest they be deported. This class was especially vulnerable to the most shameful and degrading exploitation.

It was quickly clear to those of us on congressional panels with jurisdiction over immigration that the magnitude and complexity of the illegal immigration problem were such that a single solution was not possible.

A multifaceted approach was needed if the problems as well as the benefits

---

individual for employment—(a) because of such individual's national origin, or (b) in the case of a citizen or intending citizen . . . , because of such individual's citizenship status.

The preamble to the regulations emphasizes that policies such as "English-only" rules, lengthy residence requirements, or unnecessary documents for employee verification can be challenged if adopted for discriminatory purposes.

Employers of four or more employees are covered by the act. The Department of Justice is charged with its enforcement. The act re-

quires employers to refuse employment to unauthorized aliens. It is unlawful to continue to employ individuals whom the employer knows are using fraudulent documents or whose temporary work authorization has expired. The act specifically excludes union hiring halls from any documentations or certification requirements. Employers of union referrals, however, are covered by the act.

The act includes civil penalties of $250 to $2000 per alien for the first offense of knowingly hiring an unauthorized alien. Subsequent offenses may bring penalties of $2000 to

posed by illegal immigration were to be dealt with by our government in a balanced, effective way.

This approach had to be stern enough to end illegal entry into the United States. At the same time, it had to be generous enough to legitimize the status of many of the undocumented who were already in the country, in keeping with the magnanimous and humane traditions of the United States. . . .

Woven into employer sanctions is a protection against any discrimination that might be directed against prospective employees. It is precisely to avoid this possibility of discrimination that employers must ask all prospective employees to show the proper documentation—not just those who look or sound "foreign," but all employees. Employees and prospective employees are further protected from employment-related discrimination by a special counsel of the Justice Department.

Employer sanctions are a key element in the comprehensive strategy and national policy to control illegal immigration into the United States and to do justice to the illegal aliens who are already here.

It is hoped that by reducing the incentive for the undocumented aliens to enter, by enhancing the security of our borders to stop those who remain undeterred, and by providing a clean slate for certain illegal aliens who have already established themselves here in the United States, the new Immigration Act can help resolve the problem of illegal immigration in a pragmatic, principled way.

Thus, with the cooperation of employers and employees across the country, the borders of the United States will be made more secure, legal immigration policies will continue to be humane and generous, the American labor force will be protected from job displacement and depressed wages, and undocumented aliens can become full-fledged, productive members of U.S. society.

SOURCE: Unpublished paper by U.S. Congressman Romano L. Mazzoli (D–KY). Used by permission.

$5000. Penalties of $100 to $1000 can be imposed on employers who fail to comply with the documentation requirements. Employers who engage in a "pattern or practice" of violations may be charged with additional fines and up to six months' imprisonment.[71]

Another major provision of the act is amnesty for aliens who entered the country illegally before January 1, 1982, and have resided here continuously since that time. The act allows "brief, casual, and innocent absences" from the United States without loss of amnesty, but not absences due to lack of work or vacation. Employers may assist individuals seeking to obtain amnesty by offering payroll records as evidence of continuous residence.

Americans with Disabilities Act

The **Americans with Disabilities Act** (ADA) was enacted in 1990, and full coverage of all of its wide-ranging provisions (see Figure 3-10) became law in 1994. In general, the ADA prohibits discrimination against persons with disabilities in four broad areas:[72] employment (Title I); governmental programs and services (Title II); public accommodations and ser-

FIGURE 3-10 ADA employer obligations.

The following points summarize employers' legal obligations under the Americans with Disabilities Act.

1. An employer must not deny a job to a disabled individual because of a disability if the individual is qualified and able to perform the essential functions of the job, with or without reasonable accommodation.

2. If an individual who has a disability is otherwise qualified but unable to perform an essential function without an accommodation, the employer must make a reasonable accommodation unless the accommodation would result in undue hardship.

3. An employer isn't required to lower existing performance standards for a job when considering the qualifications of an individual who has a disability if the standards are job-related and uniformly applied to all employees and candidates for that job.

4. Qualification standards and selection criteria that screen out or tend to screen out an individual on the basis of a disability must be job-related and consistent with business necessity.

5. Any test or other procedure used to evaluate qualifications must reflect the skills and abilities of an individual rather than impaired sensory, manual or speaking skills, unless those are the job-related skills that the test is designed to measure.

With respect to the recruitment and job application process, including pre-employment inquiries, employers:

1. Must provide an equal opportunity for an individual who has a disability to participate in the job application process and to be considered for a job.

2. May not make pre-employment inquiries regarding any disability, but may ask questions about the ability to perform specific job functions and, with certain limitations, may ask an individual who has a disability to describe or demonstrate how he or she could perform these functions.

3. May not require pre-employment medical examinations or medical histories, but may condition a job offer on the results of a post-offer medical examination, if all entering employees in the same job category are required to take such an examination.

4. May use tests for illegal drugs, which are not considered medical examinations under ADA.

SOURCE: Wayne E. Barlow and Edward Z. Hane, "A Practical Guide to the Americans with Disabilities Act," *Personnel Journal* (June 1992): 59. Used by permission.

vices, including hotels, restaurants, retail stores, service establishments, and other public facilities (Title III); and telecommunications (Title IV).

The act was passed after a 1988 federal study of workers with disabilities showed a sharp decline in the proportion of disabled men who were employed to only 23 percent; it also found that only 13 percent of disabled women were employed. The study clearly indicated the disabled to be the group of Americans that had suffered the greatest employ-ment discrimination.[73] The ADA provides assistance to the over 43 million American workers who have disabilities by acknowledging "that they have a role in the work force," according to Alan Emery, a San Francisco health specialist. It will also help the nondisabled become more aware of the ability of many disabled to be productive on the job and therefore end many myths concerning the disabled. Much of the compliance required by the ADA simply involves sensitivity and common sense, as described in Figure 3-11. As nondis-

FIGURE 3-11 Disability etiquette in the workplace.

How to Treat Disabled Employees with Respect

Interviews. Interviews offer a time when courtesy and reasonable accommodation work together. The interviewer needs to know the essential functions of the job (thus job descriptions are important), questions related to essential functions, and the ability to determine the person's skill level as it relates to the job.

The initial interview is the first time many will have contact with a person who has a disability, and they may be unfamiliar with how to approach these individuals. Be aware of:

- **Greetings.** Treat the person who has a disability as you would anyone else: maintain eye contact, sit at the interviewee's eye level, maintain proximity and attention. Give that person the same orientation and assistance you would a nondisabled individual. Do you shake hands with someone who has no use or limited use of arms? What if he or she has short arms or a prosthesis or is visually impaired? The answer is yes. If you usually shake hands, that's what you would expect to do in these situations.

- **Eye contact and eye level.** It's important to maintain eye contact and eye level because it gives a person who has a disability a nonverbal message that creates the tone of the interaction and lets that person know that you're comfortable in his or her presence; that you're focused on the individual, not the disability; and that you're extending the same courtesies you would to anyone else. Maintain eye contact at all times with someone who's hearing impaired even when he or she is looking at the interpreter and when the interpreter is repeating the person's words to you. Pretend the interpreter isn't there.

- **Proximity and attention.** During a conversation or interview, sit as you do when you're interviewing other candidates. For example, some people choose to have a barrier (i.e., a desk) between themselves and the interviewee; others choose to have none. Regardless of the disability of the person, maintain the same level of attentiveness.

- **Assistance.** Usually a disabled person will ask for help if it is needed; otherwise don't offer or assist without first asking if help is needed.

- **Information access.** This is one of the most important aspects of the work day. It's crucial for everyone to have access to vital information in the organization—and at the same time. With employees who have a disability, the form of communication may be one that hasn't been used before. For example, if your company uses a public address system, [use] a "buddy system" in which a hearing person can transmit the information. If there's going to be a meeting the next day that involves a 40-page report and a person who's visually impaired, give that person an audiotape.

- **Physical space.** Consider the person's disability and be aware of the environment as it affects that person. Think in terms of what the person can and can't do for him or herself, how long it will take and the safety factors involved. For instance, if the mail slots are far from the desk of an individual who uses a wheelchair, other arrangements might be made, or co-workers might regularly check his or her slot as well as their own.

SOURCE: Patricia Morrissey, *Disability Etiquette in the Workplace,* as reported in "How to Treat Disabled Employees with Respect," *Personnel Journal* (June 1992): 71.

abled workers see and work with more disabled workers, they may at first feel uneasy or uncomfortable. However, over time, they will likely change their attitudes and appreciate the skills and motivation of disabled coworkers.[74]

The ADA's employment discrimination provisions (Title 1), administered by the EEOC, primarily include the following:

- ***Disability Defined*** Section 1630 defines *disability* as "a physical or mental impairment that substantially limits one or more of the major life activities." The act also includes individuals with a history of physical impairment such as cerebral palsy and muscular dystrophy; or of diseases such as mental illness, cancer, epilepsy, or AIDS. In addition, it includes individuals who are

Obese Workers: The Newest Protected Group

If a person's appearance does not meet the standards set by an employer, can he or she be terminated for being significantly overweight? Past decisions of relevant court cases indicate that the answer is "yes." Such cases include the following:

- *Greene* v. *Union Pacific Railroad.* The judge found the required physical examination and weight requirement to be justified as a business necessity. The judge also noted that "obesity was not an immutable condition such as blindness or lameness."

- *Underwood* v. *TransWorld Airlines.* A flight attendant's excess weight was judged by her supervisor to detract from her physical appearance. She was given five months to reach a weight goal. When she did not, she was terminated. While Underwood, the attendant, did not win her case, all major airlines re-evaluated their requirements and eased their weight restrictions over the next five years.

- *Krien* v. *Marian Manor Nursing Home.* A nurse's aide was fired for obesity. She filed suit, claiming that her condition was a physical handicap and thus that she had been illegally discriminated against. The state supreme court did not agree and noted that obesity does not make a person a member of a protected class.

Obese people, however, have been given new protection from discrimination by the EEOC under the ADA. The ADA defines an individual with a disability differently from other discrimination laws. And since obesity was found to fall under the act's definition of limiting "one or more of the major life activities," the EEOC in 1993 determined that people who have been extremely overweight for a long period of time may qualify for protection under the ADA. This protection applies even if the individual was given a goal and time to lose weight (as in the *Underwood* v. *Trans World Airlines* case) but was unsuccessful. The EEOC noted

---

regarded as having a substantial impairment—meaning that their disability is not substantially limiting but is perceived to be so by others. It does not include transvestites, homosexuals, or people with emotional disorders. Are obese workers covered? See *HR in the News*: "Obese Workers: The Newest Protected Group."

- ***Discrimination*** (Section 102(a)) No covered employer shall discriminate against a qualified individual with a disability. This in-

cludes the following employment practices:[75]

Application	Medical examinations
Testing	Compensation
Hiring	Leave
Assignment	Benefits
Evaluation	Layoff
Disciplinary actions	Recall
	Termination
Training	Promotion

that while obesity is not a "traditional" disability and can be altered, "it is a chronic, lifelong condition . . . and, it is not necessary under the ADA that a condition be involuntary or immutable to be covered." Final determination may come from a Supreme Court ruling.

Employers, however, are becoming increasingly concerned about overweight employees due to their skyrocketing health care costs. Some employers have begun health screening programs:

- *Hershey Food Company.* The candy company started a program that tests employees' health in five categories. Employees can lose over $1400 per year in health benefits if they do not meet the standards.

- *Metropolitan Life Insurance Company.* Employees must stay within 20 percent of their ideal weight to avoid additional health care insurance charges of $384 per year.

- *U-Haul International.* Smokers and overweight employees are required to pay an additional insurance premium.

- *Adolph Coors Company.* The company will pay 90 percent of an employee's medical bills *only if* he or she is found to be fit.

Peter Floyd, a partner with Personnel Corporation of America, has stated that "Anyone who's supposed to meet with customers is going to have a big problem [in finding a job] if they are overweight." His remarks were sustained by a research team from the University of Vermont that found that overweight people often suffer job discrimination. Should the courts allow them to be legally discriminated against by employers?

SOURCE: Adopted from Wade Lambert, "Obese Workers Win On-the-Job Protection Against Bias," *The Wall Street Journal* (November 12, 1993): B1; Sharlene A. McEvoy, "Fat Chance: Employment Discrimination Against the Overweight," *Labor Law Journal* (January 1992): 3–14; and James G. Frierson, "Obesity as a Legal Disability Under the ADA, Rehabilitation Act, and State Handicapped Laws," *Labor Law Journal* (May 1993): 286–296.

Qualified individuals with disabilities include those who have a disability and meet the skill, experience, education, and other job-related requirements.

Step 1. The individual possesses the prerequisites for the position, such as experience, license, skill, and education. Any requirement must be demonstrably job related.

Step 2. The individual can perform the *essential* job functions, with or without reasonable accommodation. Essential job functions can be identified through job analysis and are often found in job descriptions. The descriptions should, however, distinguish between essential and marginal job functions and be current. An essential job function is

139

one that is critical to the success of the job and that must be performed by the incumbent (see Figure 3-12). Marginal job functions may be performed by the incumbent or others and are incidental to the main purpose of the job.

- **Reasonable   Accommodation**   (Section 102(b)(5)(A)   Discrimination includes not making **reasonable accommodation** to the known physical or mental limitations of an otherwise qualified individual with a disability who is an applicant or employee, unless the employer can demonstrate that the accommodation would impose an undue hardship on the operation of the business. . . .

Under the ADA, however, the employer is not required to provide employees with personal items such as hearing aids, wheelchairs, corrective lenses, or prosthetic devices that people use in their daily lives. The Job Accommodation Network at West Virginia University has estimated that of those items that must be provided under the reasonable accommodation statute, about half cost less than $50. Some, however, such as a new portable reading machine for the blind, can cost over $5000. Common low-cost items include:[76]

- Modification of doorknobs with a lever-type handle; Cost: $11.
- Telephone headsets to replace the handset for people with mobility limitations; cost: $25 to $150.
- Use of a lazy susan type of file folder system on a desk for people with impaired mobility; cost: $150.

The ADA has caused some larger employers to hire an assistive technology coordinator to help them make reasonable accommodations. Small employers, however, are also responding to the ADA (see *HR in the News*: A Small Company's Response to the ADA").

FIGURE 3-12 Essential job functions under the ADA.

To comply with the ADA employers must determine which job functions are essential to a position and which are marginal. The ADA regulations specify several factors which should be considered when making this determination. These factors can be evaluated by answering the following:

1. Does the position exist to perform these functions? If the performance of a particular function is the principal purpose for hiring a person, it would be an essential function.

2. Would the removal of the function fundamentally alter the position? If the purpose of the position can be fulfilled without performing the function, it isn't essential.

3. What's the degree of expertise or skill required to perform the function? The fact that an employee is hired for his or her specialized expertise to perform a particular function is evidence that the function is essential.

4. How much of the employee's time is spent performing the function? The fact that an employee spends a substantial amount of time performing a particular function is evidence that the function is essential.

5. What are the consequences of failure to perform the function? The fact that the consequences of failure are severe is evidence that the function is essential.

6. How many other employees are available among whom the function can be distributed? The smaller the number of employees available for performing a group of functions, the greater the likelihood that any one of them will have to perform a particular function.

SOURCE: Wayne E. Barlow and Edward Z. Hane, "A Practical Guide to the Americans with Disabilities Act," *Personnel Journal* (June 1992): 54. Used by permission.

A Small Company's Response to the ADA

A company needn't be large to offer assistance to its workers. Tusco Manufacturing in Gnadenhutten, Ohio, which has only 68 employees and manufactures point-of-purchase displays, is a perfect example.

President Michael Lauber is the person behind the company's progressive stance in relation to the Americans with Disabilities Act. In Tusco's case, the emphasis is on HIV/AIDS, which some employers don't realize is included in provisions of the ADA.

Lauber started his educational program for employees in 1990 after attending a business conference. Two of 22 CEOs disclosed that they had employees who had AIDS on the payroll. They were stumped as to how to handle the number of challenges that this presented to them.

"Ordinarily when you put 22 CEOs together in one room, you have 22 different opinions—ardently felt," says Lauber. "But in this case, no one spoke. It was the most dumbfounded interminable silence you've ever heard. None of us ever thought we'd have any HIV cases." As a result, Lauber became active in the National Coalition on AIDS.

"Small businesses have no idea about what the ADA is all about," he says. "They think it's strictly about access, and that's only a small part. For the first time, a disease is classified as a disability, and it's called HIV/AIDS."

Lauber holds monthly, company-wide meetings. He addresses the HIV/AIDS issue every few months within the context of safety, trying to foster an environment in which the education he provides will enable his employees to feel comfortable if the situation arises.

"We've made a written, public statement that we're going to treat people with respect, people who have heart disease or cancer. If someone who has heart disease needs an absence, they've got it. It's the same thing with HIV."

Lauber's biggest fear, though, is that someone will discover a fellow employee who had HIV/AIDS and refuse to work with him or her. Under the ADA, that employer would have to allow the other worker to quit. It couldn't fire the person who has the disability. So Lauber is trying mightily to re-educate people who have prejudices and fears, so the situation won't arise.

SOURCE: Charlene M. Solomon, "What the ADA Means to the Nondisabled," *Personnel Journal* (June 1992): 75.

- *Selection Criteria* (Section 102(b)(6)) Discrimination includes using qualification standards, employment tests, or other selection criteria that screen out or tend to screen out an individual with a disability; or a class of individuals with disabilities unless the standard, test or other selection criteria is shown to be job-related for the position in question and is consistent with business necessity.

- *Medical Examinations* (Section 102(c)) Employers shall not conduct a preemployment medical examination or make inquiries of a job applicant as to whether the applicant has a disability or as to the nature of such disability. An employer may make preemployment inquiries into the ability of an applicant to perform job-related functions. In addition, an employer may require a medical examination after an offer of employment has been made, and the employer may condition an offer on the results of an examination if all employees are subjected to such an examination.

- *Drug Testing* Section 1630.3 states that "employers may discharge or deny employment to persons who illegally use drugs, on the basis of such use, without fear of being held liable for discrimination." Illegal drug use is defined to include both the use of unlawful drugs and the unlawful use of prescription drugs. Employers are specifically permitted wide latitude in regulating drug and alcohol use in the workplace. Employers may prohibit alcohol as well as the use of drugs. In addition, a drug test is *not* considered a medical examination (as discussed in the previous section); thus, requiring a drug test prior to an employment offer is permissible. It should be noted, however, that individuals disabled by alcoholism are included in the ADA definition of disability.[77]

The general purpose of the ADA is to prohibit job discrimination against individuals with disabilities. In the past, such discrimination typically occurred in the form of application blanks or job interviews that inquired into the *existence of a disability* rather than the *ability to perform* the functions of a job. Another common form of discrimination consisted of slotting the disabled into menial or dead-end jobs.[78]

While the ADA has received praise for its intention to prohibit employment discrimination, critics complain that it is replete with vague terms, such as *reasonable accommodation* and *undue hardship,* which will likely be interpreted by the courts. Section 10(A) simply defines undue hardship as "an action requiring significant difficulty or expense" when considered in light of four factors: (1) the nature and cost of the accommodation needed; (2) the overall financial resources of the facility, the number of persons employed, and the impact of such accommodation; (3) the overall size of the business; and (4) the type and geographic separateness of the facilities. Under the ADA, reasonable accommodation may include eliminating nonessential job duties, permitting part-time or modified work schedules, and acquisition of new equipment or devices that would enable the disabled employee to perform the job. Examples of such equipment include adaptive computer hardware, braille devices, and hearing aids or amplifiers. The act does not provide guidelines for employers to follow in determining which job duties are nonessential to a job and therefore should be transferred to another employee as part of an employer's reasonable-accommodation requirement. As an example, a federal district judge, in applying a similar California statute, found that 12 percent of a telecommunications equipment installer's functions were insignificant and thus should be eliminated so that an asthmatic applicant could be hired. Employers who fail to comply with the ADA may be required to hire disabled applicants or provide back pay and reinstate employees who have suffered discrimination, as well as to pay court costs and attorneys' fees.[79]

Title III of the ADA has also had significant impact on employers who serve the public, including hotels, restaurants, bars, theaters, stadiums, retail stores, banks, gas stations, professional offices, schools, day-care facilities, parks, zoos, and other public buildings. All such facilities, regardless of size, must make their premises accessible to the disabled by removing architectural and communication barriers.

Cases filed under the ADA are decided by juries. This substantial change provided by the Civil Rights Act of 1991 will undoubtedly alter the course of history in the area of employment discrimination. Previously, for over twenty-five years, judges (who were typically white, male, and middle-aged or older) decided discrimination cases. The change will occur because, as one attorney noted, "Juries decide cases with their guts and hearts, not necessarily with their heads." A mock ADA trial with over 300 attorneys proved this to be a valid conclusion. The critical terms in the ADA—*qualifications, essential job functions, reasonable accommodations,* and *undue hardship*—are only vaguely defined in the act. Jurors used their own definitions of these terms and almost always tended to see themselves as the employee—never as the employer. One juror even seriously argued that reasonable accommodation should have included providing a disabled employee his own airplane and pilot. The following was clear from the mock trial that should be of interest to employers: (1) all jurors were sympathetic to the employee if no one from the company had ever sat down with the employee and discussed the employee's needs or performance problems—this lack of dialogue really "stuck in the craw" of the jurors; (2) the jurors decided the case not by judging the employee's job performance, but by the extent to which the employer had tried to assist the employee.[80]

Civil Rights Act of 1991

In response to several U.S. Supreme Court decisions on civil rights and employment discrimination, the U.S. Congress passed the Civil Rights Act of 1991.[81] It is the most important federal employment legislation to be enacted since the 1964 Civil Rights Act. Supporters claimed it was needed to eradicate the U.S. Supreme Court decisions (Table 3-6) they believed had turned back the clock on employment discrimination practices.[82] The signing of the act ended a bitter two-year struggle between President George Bush and Congress. The central issue was whether the bill required employers to resort to quotas as the only way of avoiding discrimination claims. The act does not contain such a requirement.[83] It does, however, include a significant number of major provisions:[84]

1. *Disparate Impact* The act requires that an employer justify an employment practice that has been shown to have disparate impact. The employer must show that the practice is a business necessity, which is defined to be job related for the position(s) in question. This provision overturns the 1989 *Wards Cove* decision by the U.S. Supreme Court and supports the 1971 *Griggs* v. *Duke Power Co.* court decision (Table 3-6). The *Wards Cove* decision had shifted the burden of proof to the employee at all times during a case. Under the 1991 Civil Rights Act, a disparate impact claim is established if[85]

a complaining party demonstrates that a respondent uses a particular employment practice that causes a disparate impact on the basis of race, color, religion, sex, or national origin and the respondent fails to demonstrate that the challenged practice is job related for the position in question and consistent with business necessity.

2. *Race Norming* The act prohibits the adjustment of test scores on the basis of the

religion, national origin, gender, or race of the test takers (race norming). Race norming is the employment practice of adjusting job-test scores according to separate racial percentiles. In practice, test results are separated into racial groups, and then whites, blacks, and Hispanics are ranked by percentile against members of their own race alone. Then the results are combined without reference to race and listed by rank. Effectively, a person whose real score on the test was high could be listed at a lower percentile than someone whose real score was lower but whose within-race percentile was higher. The justification for race norming generally was that it was needed to compensate for tests that were biased against minority groups.

3. *Mixed Motives*   An employer is prohibited from allowing race, sex, religion, or national origin to be a "motivating factor" in an employment decision. This provision overturns the 1989 U.S. Supreme Court decision in *Hopkins* v. *Price-Waterhouse,* which allowed an employer to avoid liability by showing that the same decision would have been reached even though gender had been a factor (Table 3-6). For example, assume that Jones, Chevy, and Rydell were all finalists for a position and Rydell was hired. Jones files a discrimination suit and the employer admits that her sex was a factor in the decision. However, the employer also proves that Rydell would have been selected even if sex had not been a factor.

4. *Foreign Personnel*   The act applies Title VII of the 1964 Civil Rights Act and the ADA to employment practices by U.S. employers in foreign countries. Thus employees of U.S. companies are allowed to return to the United States and file suit against their employer for "foreign" discrimination. This provision overturns the *Boureslan* v. *Aramco* decision of the U.S. Supreme

Court, which held that Title VII did not protect employees of U.S. companies who worked outside of the country and where the decision was wholly foreign.

5. *Jury Trials*   Perhaps the most significant provision is the introduction of jury trials in cases involving Title VII or the ADA. Previously, plaintiffs had no right to a jury trial, which is generally more sympathetic to their cases. Also significant is the introduction of compensatory and punitive damages in cases involving intentional discrimination (not caused by an employment practice or test applied to all applicants or employees). These damages are not available in disparate impact cases, and are limited by caps:

$50,000   (employers with 15–100 employees)

$100,000   (employers with 101–200 employees)

$200,000   (employers with 201–500 employees)

$300,000   (employers with over 500 employees)

6. *Seniority Systems*   Employees may file suits claiming discrimination in the operation of a seniority system, either on its adoption or on its impact on an employee. This provision overturns the 1989 *Lorrance* v. *AT&T Technologies* decision by the U.S. Supreme Court, which allowed challenges only within 180 days of the date that a seniority system was implemented.

7. *Intentional Discrimination*   In the 1989 *Pattersen* v. *McLean Credit Union* case, the U.S. Supreme Court held that intentional discrimination was illegal under the 1866 Civil Rights Act in hiring decisions alone. The 1991 act overrode the *Pattersen* decision by amending Section 1981 of the 1866 Civil Rights Act to apply to *all* employment decisions, including promotions, discharges, and demotions. This change was

also significant because the 1866 act applies to employers of fewer than fifteen employees who are protected from racial and ethnic discrimination. The 1964 Civil Rights Act only applies to employers of fifteen or more employees.

The significant provisions of the 1991 Civil Rights Act increased the number of employment discrimination claims, largely due to the change in the burden of proof provision in disparate impact cases, the introduction of jury trials, and the introduction of compensatory and punitive damages. At the same time, the direction set by the U.S. Supreme Court in its 1986–1989 employment law decisions was clearly reversed.

Employment Arbitration Agreements

The number of employment discrimination cases filed each year was increasing rapidly *before* passage of the ADA of 1990 and the Civil Rights Act of 1991. With the addition of these two new laws, the estimated 100,000 employment discrimination case backlog in state and federal courts is expected to increase. An alternative to the court process is the arbitration of employment disputes, which can reduce the number of court cases following a 1991 U.S. Supreme Court decision.[86]

In *Gilmer* v. *Interstate/Johnson Lane Corp.*[87] the court required the arbitration of an age discrimination suit. The employee, Gilmer, in a New York Stock Exchange application, had signed an agreement to arbitrate any dispute, claim, or controversy with his employer. After being terminated, he had filed a discrimination suit with the EEOC. The employer moved to compel arbitration as provided in the agreement, which a district court denied but the U.S. Supreme Court approved. Several lower courts have ordered the use of arbitration in similar cases on the basis of the *Gilmer* decision.[88]

The use of arbitration to settle disputes is usually a voluntary arrangement between two parties. For many years, labor unions and employers, for example, have voluntarily agreed to resolve most grievances with arbitration as the last of a series of steps. Section 118 of the Civil Rights Act of 1991 encourages the use of arbitration or some alternative dispute method:

Where appropriate and to the extent authorized by the law, the use of alternative means of dispute resolution, including settlement negotiations, conciliation, facilitation, mediation, factfinding, minitrials, and arbitration, is encouraged to resolve disputes arising under the Act or provisions of federal law amended by this title.

The use of arbitration to settle employment cases, in comparison to the court process, has several potential advantages:[89]

- Faster resolution of disputes (multiple lengthy court appeals are avoided).
- Less expensive.
- Avoidance of jury trials (sympathetic juries often side with employees).
- Improved supervision and employee morale (as supervisors act more reasonably in accordance with established policies).

Employers can be expected to expand the use of arbitration in employment disputes by (1) requiring the signing of an arbitration agreement on an employment application; (2) including the arbitration process in an employee handbook or personnel manual; or (3) including an arbitration clause in a severance agreement.[90] In any potential use of arbitration agreements, employers, to be fair to their employees and to maximize the likelihood that the process will be upheld by a court, should do the following:[91]

- Ensure that the agreement is voluntarily executed.

- Describe the arbitration process in precise, nonlegalistic terms detailing key issues such as what kinds of claims will be disputed, how the arbitrator will be selected, who bears the expense, and when the hearing will occur.

- Require the employee to sign a statement that he or she has read and understood the agreement and freely accepts it.

Employment arbitration agreements may not always be upheld by the courts. However, the courts have generally required that the process be followed if it has been voluntarily agreed to by both parties, and arbitration awards may be given significant weight by a court if the case is pursued.

AFFIRMATIVE ACTION

By **Executive Order 11246**, President Lyndon B. Johnson created what is known today as **affirmative action**. Since 1965 this order has been amended several times by later presidents. An *executive order* is not a law and, therefore, does not have the wide impact of federal laws such as the Civil Rights Act of 1964. An executive order directly affects only governmental agencies and contractors or subcontractors of federal government programs. But organizations may be ordered by a court to develop an affirmative action plan. Unlike the previously discussed laws passed by Congress, which may be referred to as *neutrality laws* because they require only that organizations obey them, executive orders relating to affirmative action require that certain organizations take specific positive actions to improve the employment opportunities of minorities.

In employment an *affirmative action plan* (AAP) is a formal, written process that includes the hiring and promoting of members of targeted groups. The AAP is based on an analysis of an organization's work force. The analysis compares the gender and racial composition of the available qualified labor pool to that of the organization and determines if there is an imbalance. Where an imbalance (or underutilization) exists, goals and timetables for hiring additional females and minorities are established for the purpose of ending the imbalance. These hiring goals are not rigid quotas. Only courts can impose a hiring quota (a specified percentage of new hires that must be female or minority), and they have done so where employers have been found guilty of substantial past discrimination practices.

Affirmative action may be remedial or preferential. *Remedial affirmative action* refers to efforts to ensure equality of access to all employment opportunities for those denied access or overlooked in the past. Targeted recruiting or training programs may be remedial. *Preferential affirmative action* refers to preferential treatment given to someone because of his or her race, gender, disability, or veteran's status. An *affirmative action employer* is one that gives preferential treatment to minorities, women, the handicapped, and Vietnam veterans. The purpose of preferential treatment is to end an imbalance of minority representation in an organization's work force. The differences between affirmative action and equal employment opportunity (EEO) are outlined in Table 3-5. Affirmative action does not require an employer to hire or promote an unqualified or less qualified individual. It does mean that when there are comparably qualified applicants for a position, affirmative action considerations may be the determining factor.[92]

Employers practice affirmative action because they (1) are so ordered by a court, (2) are government contractors or subcontractors, or (3) do so voluntarily. AAPs must be approved by the Office of Federal Contract Compliance Programs (OFCCP) and must include the entire organization, not only one branch office or unit. Generally, valid plans must meet four conditions:[93]

Table 3-5 Major Differences Between EEO and Affirmative Action

Enforcement Agency	Basic Requirement	Factors Included	Employers Covered
EEOC OFCCP	Prohibit discrimination in employment based on any factor(s) (EEO)	Minorities Women Handicapped Veterans Aged Religion	2 or more (EPA) 25 or more (Title VII) 15 or more (ADA and governments) 20 or more (ADEA)
OFCCP	Best good-faith efforts to achieve balance between local labor force and employers (Affirmative Action)	Minorities Women Handicapped Veterans	Court ordered Government contractor/ subcontractor Voluntary

SOURCE: Adapted from John A. Gray, "Preferential Affirmative Action in Employment," *Labor Law Journal* (January 1992): 23–30.

1. Have the remedial purpose of ending statistical imbalances within certain job categories.

2. Exist only temporarily to achieve a balanced work force (not for maintenance).

3. Not totally bar hiring and/or promotion opportunities for white males.

4. Not include layoffs or other actions that would harm current employees.

Program Development

Development and administration of an affirmative action program usually requires an organization to perform specific acts.

First, an organization must give a copy of the EEO policy to all employees and applicants. The policy must specify a commitment to EEO and affirmative action. The organization must reaffirm these commitments in all ads and employee notices.

Second, an organization must give a specific, top-ranking company official the authority and responsibility for affirmative action program implementation. This manager or coordinator should have the authority to secure necessary information and demand assistance in developing and carrying out an AAP. This person must receive complete support from top management to ensure cooperation from lower-level employees, who may not place affirmative action problems at the top of their daily agenda.

Third, an organization must complete a *work force analysis* of the organization. The first step is to count the employees in the organization by number and percentage of minorities and women in each major job classification. The next step is to determine whether the organization has **underuse of minorities or women** in any job classification. Underuse can be defined as having fewer minorities or women in a particular job category than would be found in the relevant labor market. The next step for the organization is to compare its own employment figures with those of the Metropolitan Statistical Area (MSA); these data are available from the local U.S. Department of Labor office. The work force analysis should also identify any concentration of minorities or females in a particular job category. A *concentration* exists when there are more members of a particular minority group in a job category than would be expected when compared to the labor market figures. The final step in the work force analysis is to determine which job categories have an underuse or concentration of minorities or women. If either underuse or concentration occurs, then management must take affirmative actions in order to end the discriminatory activities that caused the situation.

Fourth, an organization must establish goals and timetables. Once managers have determined where an organization may have discriminated in the past, they can develop specific goals and timetables to improve performance in those job categories. Managers then determine if any discrimination barriers may have limited participation of minorities and women in certain job categories and decide how to ensure that sufficient minority group members and women will be hired in the future. As Figure 3-13 illustrates, the goals should establish specific numbers and percentages to be hired in specific job categories, and the timetable should set dates by which these goals should be accomplished.

And fifth, an organization must develop recruitment plans. Such plans may include advertising at colleges and universities that traditionally have large minority and female enrollments. Current minority and female employees are also usually good sources of information about reaching interested female and minority applicants.

Required Records

Adequate records must be kept to meet EEOC requirements. Even if the organization's statistics show no problems with underutilization or concentration, these records can provide a defense in court cases or in compliance reviews by federal agencies. The EEOC recommends

FIGURE 3-13 EEOC instructions to organizations about goals and timetables.

Goals and Timetables

Each manager will establish goals and timetables to rectify underutilization of minorities and women. This is the heart of each unit's affirmative-action program. Goals should be significant, measurable, and attainable given the commitment of the organizational unit and its good faith efforts. The internal work force analysis and the analysis of the relevant external labor area provide the basic data on which goals and timetables are formulated, in combination with the company's goals and timetables. Goals and timetables must meet the following descriptions:

1. Goals and timetables will be determined for women and minorities separately.
2. In establishing timetables to meet goals, each organizational unit will consider the anticipated expansion, contraction, and turnover of its work force.
3. Specific goals and timetables for women and minorities will be established for each category of employment (e.g., office, factory, apprenticeship, college, professional).
4. Specific goals and timetables for women and minorities will be established for each promotional category (e.g., hourly to exempt, office, factory, professional).
5. The nature of the goals and timetables established are a function of:
   a. The degree of underutilization within the specified job family.
   b. The scope of the relevant recruitment area.
   c. The availability of qualified or qualifiable minorities and women in the area.
   d. The number of job openings available, determined by turnover, expansion, etc.
   e. The commitment of the organization unit to correct underutilization of minorities and women.
   f. The AAP and EEO policy of the company.
6. The one-year and five-year goals will be recorded on Form XX, by completing Columns 37–61 per the instructions.

SOURCE: Adapted from *Affirmative Action and Equal Employment, A Guidebook for Employees,* U.S. EEOC (Washington, DC: U.S. Government Printing Office, 1974), p. A-14.

that the following records and supporting data be kept for affirmative action purposes:[94]

- Information about the employer, including job categories and the number of employees—male and female—in each, including trainees; the EEOC requires all employers with one hundred or more employees to file this form each year; a copy of the most recent report must be kept at each reporting unit (i.e., separate facility) and presented to EEOC officials on request.[95]

- Number of applications for each major job category and hires by sex and minority group for the previous twelve months (Form P).

- Chronological list of all hires by name, sex, minority group, job, rate of pay, and recruitment source for the previous twelve months (Form P).

- List of schools, date, name, sex, and minority group of those interviewed (if there is a college recruitment program), indicating those to whom offers were extended and the disposition (Form P).

- List of all promotions and transfers, giving the date, name, sex, minority group, previous job department and pay, and new job department and pay for the previous twelve months (Form Q).

- List of all terminations by department for the previous twelve months, giving the name, sex, minority group, job and department, date of hire, date of termination, and reason (Form S).

- List of various ongoing or completed training programs during the previous twelve months, with the name, sex, minority group of participants, date of completion, and job and pay before and after training (Form R).

- Copies of any agreements pursuant to investigations of charges of discrimination by federal, state, or local agencies and copies of any outstanding charges and present status.

- Copies of all current labor agreements.

- Seniority lists or computer printouts showing all employees by name, sex, minority group, date of hire, other job-related dates, original job, date of last promotion, present job and category, rate of pay, and (if available) education or special training or both. Data must be provided in seniority order within departments, along with all interpretive materials, including organization charts, promotional sequences, and lines of progression. Those on layoff status should be designated.

- AAP goals, along with current status of attainment.

- Material on testing.

- Written job descriptions and related qualifications.

Program Implementation

Many managers and employees still do not recognize the importance and impact of antidiscrimination laws. Often EEO coordinators and affirmative action program managers do not get complete cooperation from department heads and employees. Sometimes coordinators must resort to coercion to get information and assistance from employees.

The affirmative action program manager may find it more productive to implement three basic strategies. First, try to make the recruitment and selection of employees job related instead of trying to change employees' attitudes toward the recruitment and selection of members of minorities and women. Second, encourage participation in the design and implementation of the program from all levels of management. Third, relate organizational goals to each department's goals and timetables.[96] A specific letter of instruction to department heads concerning goals and timetables may help to accomplish this third strategy.

UNIFORM GUIDELINES ON EMPLOYEE SELECTION PROCEDURES

In 1978, the Uniform Guidelines on Employee Selection Procedures were adopted by four federal agencies: the EEOC, the Civil Service Commission, the U.S. Department of Labor, and the U.S. Department of Justice. In order to comply with suggested practices and avoid potentially costly litigation, both managers and HR practitioners must be familiar with the guidelines' basic principles. The more significant sections are printed here and then interpreted in light of practical experience.

> *Section 2. B. Employment Decisions* These guidelines apply to tests and other selection procedures which are used as a basis for any employment decision. Employment decisions include—but are not limited to—hiring, promotion, demotion, membership (for example, in a labor organization), referral, retention, and licensing and certification to the extent that licensing and certification may be covered by federal equal employment opportunity law. Other selection decisions, such as selection for training or transfer, may also be considered employment decisions if they lead to any of the decisions listed above.

Remember that guidelines apply to tests of the paper-and-pencil variety and "other selection procedures." Thus, the guidelines apply to any reference check, interview, application blank, or other selection instrument utilized by an organization. In recent years, due in part to the guidelines, the use of written tests has declined and the use of interviews in selection has increased. Ironically, the interview, which may be subject to even more personal bias, is just as vulnerable to EEO pressures.[97]

> *Section 3. Discrimination Defined* Relationship between use of selection procedures and discrimination. Procedure having adverse impact constitutes discrimination unless justified. The use of any selection procedure which has an adverse impact on the hiring, promotion, or other employment or membership opportunities of members of any race, sex, or ethnic group will be considered to be discriminatory and inconsistent with these guidelines, unless the procedure has been validated in accordance with these guidelines, or the provisions of Section 6 . . . are satisfied.

In Section 3 the guidelines link discrimination directly to adverse impact. **Discrimination** occurs when an individual who has an equal probability of being successful on a job does not have an equal probability of getting the job.

An **adverse impact** (or disparate impact) on an employment practice causes members of any race, color, sex, religion, or national origin to receive unequal consideration for employment. If an employer's selection procedure, such as an interview, results in an applicant's not having an equal chance to be hired or promoted, then that procedure caused the organization to discriminate against that applicant. A selection procedure or policy that has adverse impacts on the employment opportunities of any race, sex, or ethnic group is normally illegal under Title VII unless the employer can offer a legal defense.

Section 3 states that a properly validated selection procedure is not discriminatory. **Validity in testing** means that a test actually measures what it is intended to measure. If a test is valid, then the employer knows that it is directly measuring the applicant's ability to perform the job and not something else. A valid test is not influenced by personal bias. For example, a person measuring a sapling with a yardstick and finding it to be 38 inches high thinks that is a valid measurement. The yardstick could not measure a friend's ability to estimate the height of the same tree correctly. The friend's point of view—size and proximity to the tree—influences the guesstimate. The same type of influence occurs when individuals' points of view consciously or unconsciously influence decisions concerning job applicants. Since there once were no standard means available to measure the validity of employment tests, the guidelines offer standards for test validity.

Section 5. General Standards for Validity Studies. A. Acceptable types of validity studies. For the purposes of satisfying these guidelines, users may rely upon criterion-related validity studies, content validity studies, or construct validity studies in accordance with the standards set forth in the technical standards of these guidelines. B. Criterion-related content and construct validity. Evidence of the validity of a test or other selection procedure by a criterion-related validity study should consist of empirical data demonstrating that the selection procedure is predictive of or significantly correlated with important elements of job performance. Evidence of the validity of a test or other selection procedure by a content validity study should consist of data showing that the content of the selection procedure is representative of important aspects of performance on the job for which the candidates are to be evaluated. Evidence of the validity of a test or other selection procedure through a construct validity study should consist of data showing that the procedure measures the degree to which candidates have identifiable characteristics which have been determined to be important in successful performance in the job for which the candidates are to be evaluated.

Criterion-related validity can be established by collecting data from job applicants and employees. This form of validation correlates test scores with employee success on the job. There are many measures of employee productivity that may be used, such as absenteeism, sales levels, supervisory evaluations, or quantity of production. Two primary methods of establishing criterion-related validity are predictive validation and concurrent validation.

Predictive validity, preferred by the EEOC, is usually the most difficult to determine. Establishing predictive validity requires testing the entire pool of job applicants, hiring them, and then correlating their test scores with their criterion scores.

For example, to determine the predictive validity of a test given to applicants for sales representative positions, all applicants during the previous month are tested. All applicants are then hired, given equal training, and assigned to sales routes. After one year, the total commission sales of the new employees (the criterion of job success) are correlated with their test scores. The resulting figure, called a *correlation coefficient,* can vary from -1 to $+1$. For example, if the correlation coefficient (r) is .67, then the test is valid for sales representatives because individuals' test performances have been shown to be related to job performance.

If the comparison of the applicants' test scores with their criterion scores produces a high correlation coefficient, then the organization may use the test for future applicants because it has evidence that the test is a valid predictor of employee performance.

Concurrent validity is similar to predictive validity in that test scores are compared to job performance measures. But to establish concurrent validity, both test scores and performance measures are collected at the same time.

This is accomplished by testing current employees, for whom the organization already has performance scores, such as supervisory ratings. The major difference between predictive validity and concurrent validity is that the former concerns applicants and the latter concerns present employees. This difference is very important because, in establishing predictive validity, the firm gets test scores from the total range of individuals who might apply for the job. By contrast, in establishing concurrent validity, the firm tests only those individuals who have been kept as employees. For practical reasons, establishing concurrent validity is preferable. One important reason is that administrators do not like to hire all applicants, some of whom very likely will fail as employees. Another reason is time. Concurrent validity can be established within a few weeks; predictive validity requires at least six months to a year to be established.

Content validity is a nonempirical (nonstatistical) approach to validation. To establish content validity, the organization shows, often through job analysis, that the content of the test is actually a sample of the work performed on the job. For example, a typing test could be given to applicants for clerical positions that require typing. Another example would be testing bank teller applicants' speed and accuracy with figures.

Construct validity is another nonempirical approach to validation. This type of validation is based on the theoretical relationship between a test and a construct, a characteristic in which an employee should have to be successful. Giving store manager applicants a general IQ test because management believes they need a certain level of intelligence to be successful is an example of construct validity. Giving sales clerks "personality" tests to determine if they will work well with customers could be considered construct validation.

In general, the EEOC gives the greatest preference to predictive validity and the least to construct validity. Both empirical validations, predictive and concurrent, are strong because they involve empirical data collection and statistics, which generally are not discriminatory. Content validity is at least a direct test of individuals' ability to perform some—usually not all—of the tasks required on the job. Construct validity is often management's last choice and may be hard to defend in court.

Section 4.D. Adverse Impact and the Four-fifths Rule   A selection rate for any race, sex, or ethnic group which is less than four-fifths (4/5) (or eighty percent) of the rate for the group with the highest rate will generally be regarded by the federal enforcement agencies as evidence of adverse impact, while a greater than four-fifths rate will generally not be regarded by federal enforcement agencies as evidence of adverse impact.

The **four-fifths rule** or *80 percent rule* in the guidelines raised serious questions by private industry. The rule provides a quantitative definition of adverse impact, not a legal definition.[98] For example, if eight out of fifty white male applicants (16 percent) and three out of twenty black male applicants (15 percent) were hired, the four-fifths rule has been met because four-fifths of 16 percent (12.8 percent) is less than the 15 percent hiring rate for blacks. No evidence of adverse impact is present.

Section 1.B. Purpose of Guidelines   These guidelines do not require a user to conduct validity studies of selection procedures where no adverse impact results. However, all users are encouraged to use selection procedures which are valid, especially users operating under merit principles.

These sections of the guidelines permit one component of the selection process to have an adverse impact if the total selection procedure does not produce an adverse impact. If an employer's total selection process meets the four-fifths rule but the interview, one of several components, violates it, the federal government usually will not take action or require validation of the interview process as part of the entire selection procedure.

Section 4.A. Information Required   Records concerning impact. Each user should maintain and have available for inspection records or other information which will disclose the impact which its tests and other selection procedures have upon employment opportunities of persons by identifiable race, sex, or ethnic group . . . in order to determine compliance with these guidelines. Where there are large numbers of applicants and procedures are administered frequently, such information may be retained on a sample basis, provided that the sample is appropriate in terms of the applicant population and adequate in size.

The guidelines require that certain records be kept by employers. Private employers must annually complete an EEO-1 form, which includes the number of applicants and employees by minority group and sex. The format is quite similar to that required in affirmative action reports.

The employer must indicate on the EEO-1 form if the selection process for any job has had an adverse impact on any group that constitutes 2 percent of the relevant labor force. This section indicates that employers are not required to maintain records for minority groups that constitute less than 2 percent of the relevant labor force.

SUPREME COURT DECISIONS

The federal employment laws passed by Congress and the affirmative action executive orders have been interpreted through landmark decisions by the U.S. Supreme Court. Those decisions, as summarized in Table 3-6, have had a significant impact on HR practices as employers strive to follow the intent of the decisions, which is likely to be applied in the lower courts, where the great majority of cases are decided. For many years, employers generally applied the court's decisions in the

Table 3-6 Significant EEO/AA U.S. Supreme Court Decisions

Case	Year	Decision/Effect
Griggs v. *Duke Power Co.*	1971	Provided first interpretation of the 1964 Civil Rights Act. Established that (1) the employer must prove that any job requirement is job related; (2) tests must be validated; and (3) the absence of discriminatory intentions does not absolve an employer.
Albermarle Paper v. *Moody*	1975	Required employer to prove test validation if the test had adverse impact on any minority group. Tests included performance appraisals.
Kaiser Aluminum v. *Weber*	1979	Upheld race-conscious AAPs that require certain positions to be filled by minorities, thus voiding the concept of reverse discrimination.
Firefighters Local 1784 v. *Stotts*	1984	Maintained the use of a bona fide seniority system in the case of layoffs and recall actions, even when conflicting with affirmative action.
Wygant v. *Jackson Board of Education*	1986	Upheld the use of seniority systems in layoffs unless prior discrimination existed. Also endorsed underutilization as a basis for an AAP.
Sheet Metal Workers v. *EEOC*	1986	Supported court-ordered quotas to overcome a history of discrimination.
Firefighters v. *City of Cleveland*	1986	Upheld a voluntary union–employer agreement to promote minorities on a one-to-one basis.
Johnson v. *Transportation Agency*	1987	Established the use of sex-based hiring goals in affirmative action programs.
Martin v. *Wilks*	1989	Allowed the use of reverse discrimination theory by permitting white firefighters to challenge the promotion of black firefighters in a court-approved consent decree. Narrowed the *Weber* (1979) decision.
Price Waterhouse v. *Hopkins*	1989	Ruled that even if gender was one factor in an employment decision, if the same decision would have been reached in the absence of discrimination, it can be allowed.
Wards Cove Packing v. *Antonio*	1989	Reversed *Griggs* by ruling that the ultimate burden of proof in a Title VII disparate impact case is on the plaintiff (employee).
Lorrance v. *AT&T Technologies*	1989	Required those adversely affected by a discriminatory seniority system to sue within 180 days of the time when the system takes effect.

INTERNATIONAL HR IN THE NEWS

Japanese Firms May Create a "Bamboo Ceiling"

In *Fortino* v. *Quasar Co.* the Seventh Circuit Court of Appeals ruled that Japanese businesses operating in the United States may legally hire only Japanese citizens in top management positions. The ruling clarified that Title VII of the U.S. Civil Rights Act, which prohibits discrimination based on national origin, does not apply to Japanese-owned firms. Instead Title VII is preempted by a treaty between Japan and the United States which permits companies of either country to prefer their own citizens for top tier positions.

The decision created a legally enforceable "bamboo ceiling" for American employees working in Japanese-owned companies and those working for any foreign-owned company whose country has a similar treaty. Foreign-owned companies which elect to create a bamboo ceiling run the risk of alienating American workers and customers. They also limit the effectiveness of foreign investment in the U.S., which some economists claim is good because it creates U.S. jobs.

SOURCE: "Court Rules Japanese-Owned Company Not Bound by Title VII," *Issues in HR* (March-April 1992): 1–2.

Griggs (1971) and *Albemarle* (1975) cases in matters of employment selection. The need to validate tests, determine possible adverse impacts of selection criteria, and utilize job analysis to develop job-related position requirements was firmly established. The 1978 EEOC Selection Guidelines provided substantial additional guidance for employers striving to comply with federal selection laws.

Reverse Discrimination

The term *reverse discrimination* generally refers to situations in which minorities and/or females are given preference over white males beyond affirmative action requirements. The Supreme Court has directly addressed this concept only in cases involving a seniority system and the layoff and recall of employees. In

the *Stotts* (1984) decision, the Court upheld the use of seniority systems even when they adversely affect an employer's affirmative action program.

In other cases involving a white male claiming illegal discrimination under Title VII, several circuit courts have generally not given claimants the same rights as minorities and females. Instead, the white male plaintiff must show either a discriminatory intent or highly unusual circumstances. The general theory applied in reverse discrimination cases has been that while members of majority groups are protected, historically they as a group have shown no need for additional protection. Thus, white males must show evidence, apart from race and sex, that an employer discriminated against them.[99]

154

In 1986–1987, in a series of cases, the Supreme Court upheld and extended the general principles of affirmative action as they had evolved since the 1960s. The Court upheld voluntary and court-ordered AAPs, including numerical standards to address the underutilization of minorities and women. Such plans could require employers to hire or promote women and minorities over more qualified white males. In cases of layoff and recall, however, seniority system plans continued to be upheld.

Then the Court, whose membership was changing, in 1989 decided four landmark cases that appeared to signal a new direction. The theory of reverse discrimination was given new life, the burden of proving discrimination in disparate impact cases was shifted from the employer to the plaintiff, and bias as one factor in an employment decision was allowed if the same decision would have been reached without any bias. Considering that these cases were all decided in one year, only a few years after the 1986–1987 cases, and that they appeared to partly overturn some earlier landmark cases, it seemed clear that the Court was changing course.

Therefore, the U.S. Supreme Court has, at least as perceived by some civil rights advocates, handed down rulings that lessen the impact of the 1964 Civil Rights Act. These cases and their new direction caused Congress to enact the 1991 Civil Rights Act, which largely overturned the 1989 cases and reaffirmed the federal government's commitment to the 1964 Civil Rights Act.

Discrimination Against Smokers

One area in which the states have taken the lead in prohibiting employment discrimination involves smokers. Starting in 1991, the Tobacco Institute began pushing state legislatures to enact laws that prohibit employers from discriminating against smokers (Figure 3-14). The push resulted from the decision of an increasing number of employers to ban smoking in the workplace and refuse to hire smokers. Newly enacted state laws generally follow one of two formats: (1) they broadly bar discrimination against employees who use any lawful product (including tobacco and alcohol) in their off hours; (2) alternatively, in New Hampshire and Wyoming, smoking outside the workplace is a declared civil right. The second type of law has angered some civil rights leaders who believe it is demeaning to equate civil rights legislation laws on smoking with those that protect minorities and women. The state laws do not affect an employer's right to ban or restrict smoking in the workplace. Chuck Crawford, president of Kimball Physics, Inc., a Wilton, New Hampshire, electronic optics manufacturing company, believes employers should be able to fire and refuse to hire employees who smoke. He cites as reasons (1) the need to maintain clean working conditions in his electronic optics firm; (2) insurance benefits; and (3) some employees' allergy to smoke. Even if employers do not smoke at work, Crawford believes that residue from their clothes and breath contaminates the workplace.[100]

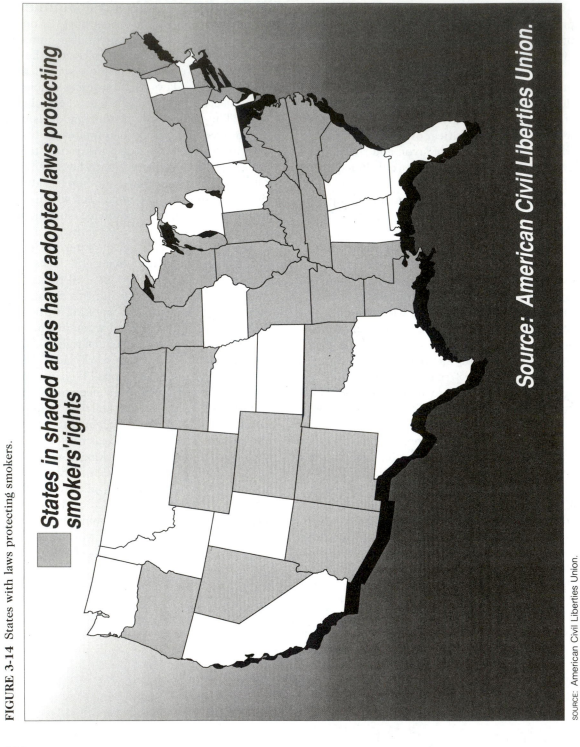

FIGURE 3-14 States with laws protecting smokers.

States in shaded areas have adopted laws protecting smokers' rights

Source: American Civil Liberties Union.

156

CONCLUSIONS AND APPLICATIONS

- The rapid diversification of the American work force is changing how managers succeed in administering organizations. They must be able to harness the energies, talents, and differences of a more diversified work force. This requires an ability to recognize value and to manage individuals from diverse cultures and perspectives.

- Diversity awareness training and diversity programs strive to increase employees' recognition of the value of everyone in the workplace. Some programs, however, have caused problems among certain employees. To achieve diversity, HR managers must (1) hire a diverse work force; (2) enforce policies and laws on discrimination; and (3) learn to value and manage employees' differences.

- Federal laws and court decisions have greatly affected the selection process. Employers must ensure that their hiring practices are nondiscriminatory and that each applicant is given an equal opportunity.

- In recent years, many more discrimination suits have been filed under the ADEA and ADA. Employers have increased their efforts to guard against age discrimination by making employment decisions on the basis of documented performance data and by offering early retirement programs only on a voluntary basis. In addition, reasonable accommodations must be made for employees with a disability who can successfully perform essential job functions.

- Affirmative action programs by employers seek to determine areas of underuse of women and minority group members. Employers establish goals and timetables to increase recruitment and selection of women and minorities in underutilized job categories.

- Sexual harassment has developed into a complex but critical HR issue. Both quid pro quo and hostile environment forms of harassment are clearly prohibited by the Civil Rights Act. Employers realize that developing complaint investigation procedures and training supervisors to respond must be done before a complaint is filed to provide objectivity.

- Employment arbitration agreements can provide a faster, less expensive means to settle employer–employee disputes. The 1991 Civil Rights Act encourages the use of arbitration or other methods of dispute resolution that are effective and provide relief to the overburdened court system.

CASE STUDY

Fire Department Promotion

Everett Mann is the HR director of the fire department in a metropolitan area. Today he must make a decision that will greatly affect the morale of the entire department and quite possibly lead to a major lawsuit. Mann must recommend to the mayor one of two finalists for the position of captain of the Third District. The promotion decision has become highly controversial both within the fire department and at City Hall. Mann knows that his recommendation will be accepted by the mayor and implemented, but he must be ready to defend it to critics and, if necessary, in the courts.

The two finalists are both qualified and deserving of the position. Both graduated from local high schools the same year, and both come from good middle-class backgrounds. Both are forty years old and have worked together in the Third District. Now for the differences:

Michael Wines	Twenty-two years' experience with the fire department; excellent record. Joined after graduating from high school.
James Barlow	Twelve years' experience with the fire department; excellent record. Joined ten years after graduating from high school
Michael Wines	White, male.
James Barlow	Black, male. (Joined the fire department the first year blacks were eligible.)
Michael Wines	Ranks first in seniority in the Third District and first among those who applied for the position.
James Barlow	Ranks second in seniority in the Third District and second among those who applied for the position.
Michael Wines	Ranked ninth among those who took the Civil Service Promotion Examination.
James Barlow	Ranked eighty-sixth among those who took the Civil Service Promotion Examination.
Michael Wines	Promoted to lieutenant three years ago.
James Barlow	Promoted to lieutenant four years ago.

Michael Wines	On affirmative action: "The Civil Rights Act passed twenty-five years ago, and a whole generation has come up since then. Where's affirmative action going to end? I say end it now. My kids shouldn't have to pay for it."
James Barlow	On affirmative action: "It's not totally fair, but was it fair that I couldn't be a fireman back in the 1960s? If there had been black firemen then, there wouldn't have been a consent decree in the first place."

The consent decree Barlow refers to was issued by a federal court to settle a discrimination suit against the city for not hiring blacks as firefighters. In the past, the city had a whites-only hiring policy and, after it was dropped, promoted the first black fire department supervisor only eight years ago. The consent decree, agreed to by the city, black firefighters, the U.S. Department of Justice, and the NAACP, provides that the city will give half of each year's jobs and promotions to blacks. That was eight years ago, and since then the percentage of black firefighters has increased from 10 to 24 percent and the percentage of black lieutenants and captains from 0 to 28 percent. The consent decree provides that the long-term hiring and promotion goals should be equal to the percentage of black civilians in the county—28 percent.

Mann, then, must recommend that either Wines, the top-ranked white candidate, or Barlow, the top-ranked black candidate, receive the promotion.

QUESTIONS

1. If you were Everett Mann, whom would you recommend? Why? What would be the legal basis of your defense?

2. Are AAPs with hiring quotas, such as the one in this case, still appropriate more than thirty years after the Civil Rights Act?

3. Does the consent decree's quota system, in fact, require reverse discrimination? Is that legal?

4. Are consent decree hiring goals the same as quotas?

SOURCE: Adapted from Barry Siegel, ''Battling to Climb the Ladder,'' *The Los Angeles Times* (February 7, 1990): A1, A14, A15.

EXPERIENTIAL EXERCISES

1. What Do *You* Think Is Sexual Harassment?

PURPOSE

The concept of sexual harassment is not one which everyone can agree on when specific examples are discussed. Open, honest examination of the following questions can help all parties better understand the views of others and realize this is not a simple issue.

TASK: Part A

Answer each of the following questions according to *your personal beliefs*. The instructor will then provide the answers according to experts' interpretations of the law.

T/F

_____ **1.** Unwanted sexual attention will usually stop if no one pays attention to it.

_____ **2.** It isn't sexual harassment if I don't mean to impose on another worker.

_____ **3.** Some people won't complain about another person's behavior even though it bothers her/him just so the other person won't get in trouble.

_____ **4.** Most healthy people will usually tell you that you said or did something that bothers her/him.

_____ **5.** To avoid sexually harassing a woman worker in a traditionally male work place, men should not haze her.

_____ **6.** A sexual harasser may be told by a court to pay part of a settlement to the employee he/she harassed.

_____ **7.** My employer has a policy which says that employees who sexually harass other employees can be fired.

_____ **8.** A sexually harassed man does not have the same legal rights as a harassed woman.

_____ **9.** Men who offend women coworkers usually know that their comments/attention is not welcome.

_____ **10.** Men are more likely than women to be flattered by sexual comments and overtures.

_____ 11. About 90% of all sexual harassment is done by males to females.

_____ 12. Telling a person to stop his/her unwanted sexual behavior usually doesn't do any good.

_____ 13. Mature men and women interpret social signals such as compliments and touching in the same way.

_____ 14. Most cases of sexual harassment involve a supervisor requesting sexual favors in exchange for preferential treatment.

_____ 15. A person who has been harassed usually could have done something to prevent the incident.

_____ 16. Men in male-dominated workplaces usually have to change their behavior when a woman begins working there.

_____ 17. A sexual harasser may be told by a court to pay part of a settlement to the employee he/she harassed.

_____ 18. An employer is not liable for the harassment of one of its employees unless it knows about the incident.

_____ 19. A policy forbidding sexual harassment protects an employer from liability for incidents of which it is unaware.

_____ 20. Sexually suggestive visuals or objects in a work place don't create liability unless an employee complains about them and management doesn't remove them.

SOURCE: *Sexual Harassment in the Workplace*, Litigation and Administrative Practice Series, No. 426, Jana Howard Carey-Chair, Practicing Law Institute 1992.

TASK: Part B

The instructor will give you two 3 × 5 cards. On the first card, describe an episode of sexual harassment that involved you or that you are aware of from another person who was involved in the incident. If you are not aware of any such incidents, leave the card blank; do not create a hypothetical situation. On the back of the card, write "serious" and explain why you considered the incident to be one of serious sexual harassment.

On the second card, describe an actual harassment incident that *you* would not consider serious, but only a joke, a casual comment, or an innocent compliment. If you are not aware of an innocent situation, leave the card blank. On the back of the card, write "innocent."

The instructor will collect the cards, randomly select one, and read the description of the incident. The class will then be asked to decide whether it was serious or innocent. The instructor will then read the back of the card and *may* ask the author to explain his or her evaluation.

2. Exploring Differences

PURPOSE

To explore differences in personal values among diverse coworkers.

TASK

Step 1: Divide into small groups that are diversified as much as possible by gender, race, age, and so on. Complete *as a group.* the following "Personal Values Inventory." Consensus must be reached on a "yes" or "no" answer, with *no* change in the numbered statements.

Step 2: The instructor will ask each group to report its answers and lead a discussion of them.

DO YOU BELIEVE THAT . . .

Yes   No

1. It is acceptable for women to cry at work

2. It is okay for men to cry at work

3. It is okay for women to leave work early to coach Little League

4. It is okay for men to leave early to coach Little League

5. The company should provide day care

6. Women and minorities should change for the organization's needs

7. The organization should change for the needs of women and minorities

8. A woman or minority could become the CEO of the organization within the next ten years

9. Women have a higher absentee rate than men

10. There are some jobs or markets in which women and minorities cannot be effective

11. There are jobs in your area that women and minorities cannot perform

12. There are many women or minorities who can effectively take over your job

13. The organization should provide separate programs for special groups

14. Minorities will always have primary loyalty to their group, not to the company

15. Our society is suffering because women are not at home

16. Men should alter their careers to raise children

17. Native dress and behaviors should affect advancement for minorities

18. Intelligence is ethnically based (i.e., blacks are less intelligent, Japanese are more intelligent)

19. Children from different backgrounds should be educated together

20. Certain groups can handle certain jobs more effectively

21. All people have a right to live in any place of their choice

22. Integrated neighborhoods are beneficial

23. Socializing with people of other cultures is appropriate

24. Business associates should socialize

25. We should have private (exclusive) clubs that restrict women and minorities

26. Women and minorities want to socialize with majority males   ____ ____

27. Minorities should be sponsored to join your most intimate circles   ____ ____

28. You should try to avoid putting minority men and majority women into social and travel situations for their own good   ____ ____

29. Interracial dating/marriage is acceptable   ____ ____

30. You would accept an interracial marriage in your family   ____ ____

KEY TERMS AND CONCEPTS

Adverse impact
Affirmative action
Age Discrimination in Employment Act (ADEA)
Americans with Disabilities Act (ADA)
bona fide occupational qualification (BFOQ)
Business necessity
Civil Rights Act (1964 and 1991)
Discrimination
Disparate impact
Disparate treatment
Diversity
Employment arbitration agreements
Equal Employment Opportunity Commission (EEOC)
Equal Pay Act (EPA)
Essential job functions
Executive Order 11246

Four-fifths rule
Immigration Reform and Control Act (IRCA)
Older Workers Benefit Protection Act (OWBPA)
Probable cause
Reasonable accommodation
Reasonable person (woman) standard
Religious discrimination
Reverse discrimination
right to sue
Separation agreement
Sexual harassment
substantially equal
Title VII
Underuse of minorities or women
Validity in testing (types of)
Vietnam Era Veterans Readjustment Act
Vocational Rehabilitation Act

REVIEW QUESTIONS

1. Describe the demographic differences between the U.S. work force of the 1960s and the year 2000.

2. What is the purpose of providing diversity awareness training to employees? Should such a program be mandatory or voluntary for employees?

3. What is the approximate median annual wage paid to working women expressed as a percentage of that paid to men? What was

the percentage in 1963 when the EPA was passed? Has progress been made?

4. Define the two major types of sexual harassment—quid pro quo and hostile environment. Which occurs more often? Which is more serious?

5. What prompted Congress to pass the 1991 Civil Rights Act? What are its major provisions?

6. Why should employment arbitration agreements be used to resolve employer–ployee disputes? Should employers be allowed to require employees to sign them?

7. List common employer policies that might cause unlawful religious discrimination.

8. How should employers be prepared to meet the provisions of the ADEA?

9. What is the primary purpose of the Immigration Reform and Control Act?

10. What are the employment provisions of the ADA?

DISCUSSION QUESTIONS

1. In some cases, diversity awareness training has caused a backlash among some employees. Why? Should organizations provide such training?

2. What are the potential benefits to an organization that successfully manages work force diversity?

3. Federal laws designed to prohibit workplace discrimination have existed for over thirty years. Have they been effective? Will they ever be unnecessary?

4. What actions should an employer take to prevent sexual harassment in the workplace and comply with the law?

5. Do you agree with the EEOC's decision to include obese workers as a disabled group under the ADA? What about employers' concerns that obese workers increase their health care costs?

6. If you believed you were discriminated against, under what circumstances would you contact the local EEOC or let the situation ride? Why?

7. Do you agree with the Seventh Circuit Court in the *Fortino* v. *Quasar Co.* case? Explain your position.

8. Is there a group of American workers that you believe suffers employment discrimination, yet is not protected by federal law? Should a new law be passed to provide such protection?

ENDNOTES

Chapter 3

1. Ralph K. Andrist, ed., *The American Heritage History of the Confident Years* (New York: American Heritage, 1991), p. 306.

2. Alistair Cooke *America* (New York: Alfred A. Knopf, 1973), pp. 273–288.

3. Beverly Geber, "Managing Diversity," *Training* 27 (July 1990): 23–30.

4. The Hudson Institute, *Workforce 2000: Work and Workers for the 21st Century* (New York: 1987).

5. Sami M. Abbasi and Kenneth W. Hollman, "Managing Cultural Diversity: The Challenge of the 90s," *Records Management Quarterly* (July 1991): 24–32.

6. Wayne E. Barlow, "Act to Accommodate the Disabled," *Personnel Journal* (November 1991): 119.

7. George K. Kronenberger, "Out of the Closet," *Personnel Journal* (June 1991): 40–44.

8. Linda Thornburg, "What's Wrong with Workforce 2000," *HR Magazine* (August 1991): 38.

9. Michael R. Carrell and Everett E. Mann, "Defining Workforce Diversity Programs and Practices in Organizations," *Labor Law Journal* (December 1993): 755–765.

10. Lennie Copeland, "Learning to Manage a Multicultural Workforce," *Training* (May 1988): 51.

11. Floyd Dickens, Jr., and Jacqueline Dickens. *The Black Manager* (New York: AMACOM, 1991), pp. 96–97.

12. Ann M. Morrison and Mary Ann Von Glinow, "Women and Minorities in Management," *American Psychologist* 45, no. 20 (February 1990); 200–8.

13. Ann Morrison and Carol Hymowitz, "One Firm's Bid to Keep Blacks, Women," *Wall Street Journal*, Marketplace Section, (1993): June 21 201.

14. Charlene Marmer Solomon, "Are White Males Being Left Out?" *Personnel Journal* (November 1991): 88–94.

15. Copeland, "Learning to Manage," pp. 49–56.

16. Marilyn Loden and Judy B. Rosener, *Workforce America! Managing Employee Diversity As a Vital Resource* (Homewood, IL: Business One Irwin, 1991), p. 12.

17. Taylor Cox and Stacy Blake, "Managing Cultural Diversity: Implications for Organizational Competitiveness," *Academy of Management Executive* 5, no. 3 (1991): 53.

18. Jerry Beilinson, "Workforce 2000: Already Here?" *Personnel* (October 1990): 3–4.

19. Cox and Blake, "Managing Cultural Diversity," p. 49.

20. Shari Caudron, "U.S. West Finds Strength in Diversity," *Personnel Journal* (March 1992): 40–44.

21. Cox and Blake, "Managing Cultural Diversity." p. 51.

22. Charlene Marmer Solomon, "24-Hour Employees," *Personnel Journal* (August 1991): 61–62.

23. "1993 SHRM/CCH Survey," *Human Resources Management* (Washington, DC: CCH, Inc., May 26, 1993), pp. 1–12.

24. Ann C. Wendt and William M. Slenacker, "Discrimination Reflects on You," *HR Magazine* (May 1992): 44.

25. Paul S. Greenlaw and John P.

Kohl, "The EEOC's New Equal Pay Act Guidelines," *Personnel Journal* 61, no. 7 (July 1982): 517–21.

26. George Wendt, "Should Courts Write Your Job Descriptions?," *Personnel Journal* (September 1976): 442–44.

27. Ibid., pp. 443–50.

28. Paul S. Greenlaw, "Proving Title VII Discrimination," *Labor Law Journal* (July 1991): 407–17.

29. *McDonnell-Douglas Corp.* v. *Green,* 441, U.S. 792 (1972), SEPD.

30. Michael J. Lotilo, "The Civil Rights Act of 1990: Practical Considerations for Business," *HR News* (July 1990): 10–11.

31. James Ledvinka, *Federal Regulation of Personnel and Human Resource Management* (Boston: Kent, 1982), pp. 62–63.

32. *Phillips* v. *Martin Marietta,* 400 U.S. 542 (1971).

33. Public Law 95–955, 92 Stat. 2076–77 (1978).

34. C. Safran, "What Men Do to Women on the Job: A Shocking Look at Sexual Harassment," *Redbook* (November 1976): 419.

35. Donald J. Peterson and Douglas P. Massengill, "Sexual Harassment Cases Five Years After *Meritor Savings Bank v. Vinson,*" *Employee Relations Law Journal* (Winter 1992–1993): 489–515.

36. T. L. Leap and E. R. Gray, "Corporate Responsibility in Cases of Sexual Harassment," *Business Horizons* (October 1980): 58.

37. Equal Employment Opportunity Commission, *1980 Guidelines* (Washington, DC: Government Printing Office, 1980).

38. *Hall* v. *Guss Construction Co.,* 46 FEP Cases 573 (8th Cir. 1988).

39. Stacey J. Garvin, "Employer Liability for Sexual Harassment," *HR Magazine* (June 1991): 101–7.

40. Petersen and Massengill, "Sexual Harassment Cases Five Years After *Meritor Savings Bank v. Vinson.*"

41. *Ellison* v. *Brady,* 924 R. 2d 871 (9th Circuit 1991).

42. *Robinson* v. *Jacksonville,* 86-927-CIV-J-12 (MD Fla., January 18, 1991).

43. M. G. Fine, F. L. Johnson, M. S. Ryan, "Cultural Diversity in the Workplace," *Public Personnel Management* 19, No. 3 (Fall 1990): 315.

44. Garvin, "Employer Liability," p. 106.

45. Frederick L. Douglas, "The Civil Rights Act of 1991: Continuing Violation and the Retroactivity Controversy," *Labor Law Journal* (March 1993): 153–61.

46. *Waltman* v. *International Paper Company,* 875 F. 2d 468, 474 (1989).

47. Douglas, "Civil Rights Act," p. 155.

48. I. Goering and C. Kleiman, "Fighting Harassment Pays, Experts Say," *Chicago Tribune* (October 29, 1991): Sec. 2, p. 1.

49. David E. Terpstra and Douglas D. Baker, "Outcomes of Sexual Harassment Charges," *Academy of Management Journal* 31, no. 1 (March 1988): 185–94.

50. Jonathan A. Segal, "Proceed Carefully, Objectively to Investigate Sexual Harassment Claims," *HR Magazine* (October 1993): 91–94.

51. Ann Meyer, "Getting to the Heart of Sexual Harassment," *HR Magazine* (July 1992): 82–84.

52. Teresa Brady, "The Legal Issues Surrounding Religious Discrimination in the Workplace," *Labor Law Journal* (April 1993): 246–51.

53. 398 U.S. 300 (1970).

54. Brady, "Legal Issues Surrounding Religious Discrimination," pp. 246–51.

55. *Hodgson* v. *Greyhound Lines, Inc.,* 499 F. 2d 859, 7th Circuit (1974).

56. Michael R. Carrell and Frank E. Kuzmits, "Amended ADEA's Effects on HR Strategies Remain Dubious," *Personnel Journal* 66, no. 5 (May 1987): 111–20.

57. Ibid.

58. "Retirement Age Law to Keep 200,000 on Job," *Resource* (November 1986): 3.

59. Edmund R. Hergenrather, "The Older Worker: A Golden Asset," *Personnel* (August 1985): 56.

60. Nicholas J. Mathys, Helen La Van, and Frederick Schwerdtner, "Learning the Lessons of Age Discrimination Cases," *Personnel Journal* 63, no. 6 (June 1984): 30–32.

61. Malcolm H. Morrison and M. Kathryn Jedrziewski, "Retirement Planning: Everybody Benefits," *Personnel Administrator* 33, no. 1 (January 1988): 74–80.

62. Herbert Field and William Holley, "The Relationship of Performance Appraisal System Characteristics to Verdicts in Selected Employment Discrimination Cases," *Academy of Management Journal* 25, no. 2 (March 1982): 392–406.

63. Mathys, La Van, and Schwerdtner, "Learning the Lessons," pp. 30– 32.

64. *Sullivan* v. *Boron Oil Co. et al.*, no. 86–00076 (3rd Cir. 1987).

65. Public Law No. 101-433, 104, Stat. 978.

66. Philip M. Halpern, "Age Discrimination in Employment: Releases Protect Employers Too!" *Labor Lawyer* (1992): 948–50.

67. Ledvinka, *Federal Regulation*, pp. 71–81.

68. Ibid.

69. Bruce D. May, "Law Puts Immigration Control in Employers' Hands," *Personnel Journal* (March 1987): 106–11.

70. Lawrence Lorber and Craig Freger, "Employment Discrimination Under the IRCA of 1986," *HRM Legal Reporter* (Winter, 1987): 4–7.

71. May, "Law Puts Immigration Control in Employers' Hands," p. 108.

72. *Americans with Disabilities Act of 1990*, Congressional Report 101-596 (July 12, 1990): 3–12.

73. *Labor Force Status and Other Characteristics of Persons with a Work Disability: 1981–1989* (U.S. Government Printing Office: Washington, DC, 1989).

74. Charlene M. Soloman, "What the ADA Means to the Nondisabled," *Personnel Journal* (June 1992): 70–76.

75. Wayne E. Barlow and Edward Z. Hane, "A Practical Guide to the Americans with Disabilities Act," *Personnel Journal* (June 1992): 53–59.

76. Neville C. Tompkins, "Tools That Help Performance on the Job," *HR Magazine* (April 1993): 87–91.

77. Samuel J. Bresler and Roger D. Sommer, "Take Care in Administering Tests Under ADA," *HR Magazine* (April 1992): 49–51.

78. J. Freedley Hunsicker, Jr., "Ready or Not: The ADA," *Personnel Journal* 69, no. 8 (August 1990): 81– 83.

79. Ibid.

80. Jack Raisuer, "How to Survive

the New ADA Litigation," *HR Magazine* (June 1992): 78–83.

81. Civil Rights Act of 1991, Public Law No. 102-166, 105 Stat. 1071 (1991).

82. Thomas J. Piskorski and Michael A. Warner, "The Civil Rights Act of 1991: Overview and Analysis," *The Labor Lawyer* (1992): 9–17.

83. W. Randall Kanmeyer, "Disparate Impact Cases Under the Civil Rights Act of 1991," *Labor Law Journal* (October 1992): 639–50.

84. David A. Cathcart and Mark Snyderman, "The Civil Rights Act of 1991," *The Labor Lawyer* (1992): 849–922.

85. Civil Rights Act of 1991, Section 105(a).

86. Evan J. Spelfogel, "New Trends in the Arbitration of Employment Disputes," *Arbitration Journal* (March 1993): 6–15.

87. 111 S. Ct. 1647 (1991).

88. Robert A. Shearer, "The Impact of Employment Arbitration Agreements on Sex Discrimination Claims: The Trend Toward Nonjudicial Resolution," *Employee Relations Law Journal* 18, no. 3 (Winter 1992–1993): 479–89.

89. Spelfogel, "New Trends," pp. 6–15.

90. Todd H. Thomas, "Using Arbitration to Avoid Litigation," *Labor Law Journal* (January 1993): 3–13.

91. Ibid.

92. John A. Gray, "Preferential Affirmative Action in Employment," *Labor Law Journal* (January 1992): 23–30.

93. Ibid.

94. U.S. Equal Employment Opportunity Commission, *Affirmative Action and Equal Employment, A Guidebook for Employers* (Washington, DC: U.S. Government Printing Office, 1974), pp. 47–48.

95. David Gold, "In Response to . . . ," *HR News* (July 1990): 5.

96. David Brookmore, "Designing and Implementing Your Company's Affirmative Action Program," *Personnel Journal* (April 1979): 232–37.

97. Robert Gatewood and James Ledvinka, "Selection Interviewing and EEO: Mandate for Objectivity," *The Personnel Administrator* (May 1976): 15–18.

98. "Uniform Guidelines on Employee Selection Procedures (1978)," *Federal Register* (August 25, 1978): 38291.

99. Sue Ann Unger, "Should Men Benefit from the Same Presumption of Unlawful Sex Discrimination That Helps Women Claimants Under the Equal Pay Act?" *Labor Law Journal* (March 1993): 186–91.

100. Junda Woo, "Employers Fume Over New Legislation Barring Discrimination Against Smokers," *The Wall Street Journal* (June 4, 1993): B1, B2.

PART II

ATTRACTING HUMAN RESOURCES

CHAPTER **4**

JOB ANALYSIS

CHAPTER OBJECTIVES

1. To understand the basic elements of a job analysis program.
2. To describe the end products of an analysis.
3. To identify the major methods of job analysis.
4. To discuss the future use and updating of analysis information.
5. To recognize the major elements of job descriptions.
6. To cite techniques useful in writing job descriptions.
7. To understand the uses of job descriptions.
8. To explain the legal requirements of job descriptions.

"That's Not My Job"

Gloria Gomez's job for a telephone company in central Texas was driving her nuts. Because she spoke Spanish, she was always being interrupted by co-workers who had non-English-speaking customers on the line. Some days, translations made up half her workload.

Gomez (not her real name), a customer service representative, hadn't been hired because of her bilingual ability and nothing was mentioned about it being a required skill when she interviewed for the job. It was not in her job description and she wasn't being paid more for it. In fact, she felt she was being penalized: Her company's worker-productivity formula gave her no credit for the time she spent helping others with their Spanish calls. And so one day in 1987, the middle-aged widow flatly refused to translate a call.

That isolated gripe was soon translated into something more serious when the telephone company was notified by the U.S. Equal Employment Opportunity Commission that charges were being filed in federal court. The government charged that the employer was violating the Civil Rights Act of 1964 by requiring Gomez to speak Spanish without additional compensation.

SOURCE: Adapted from "Bilingual Skills Spark Worker Suit," *Denver Post,* October 1, 1989.

The Equal Employment Opportunity Commission (EEOC) lawsuit (see *HR in the News:* "That's Not My Job") contains implications that frighten some organizations—and rightly so. What steps would have prevented this case from reaching lawsuit proportions? How far must an employer go in analyzing a job and preparing descriptions and specifications? How much detail must be included in a job description? What if a manager learns after hiring that the new employee has a special talent, such as being able to speak another language, and then begins to add translation to her assignments? And, most important, at what point does the job's worth change and higher wages are due? Clearly, however, the employer in question could have avoided most of these problems had it been more thorough in providing accurate, comprehensive, de-tailed job information. This chapter examines popular job-analysis methods.

Job analysis is the process by which management systematically investigates the tasks, duties, and responsibilities of the jobs within an organization. The process includes investigating the level of decision making by employees within a job category, the skills employees need to do a job adequately (such as bilingualism), the autonomy of the job in question, and the mental effort required to perform the job. Machines operated, reports completed, and specific financial or other responsibilities must be included in an analysis of a job. Also examined are the working conditions of the job, such as the levels of temperature, light, offensive fumes, and noise.

The process of job analysis is also known as *job review* or **job classification**. Whether one

Job Descriptions for the 21st Century

There are many theories about what happened to the dinosaurs. The one thing most of these theories have in common is the belief that somehow they didn't adapt to change.

Because everyone realizes that hierarchy gets in the way of speed and innovation, the organizational pyramid is becoming a dinosaur. Savvy CEOs are developing flatter organizations and empowered employees who can make decisions unencumbered by multiple layers of approval. As the hierarchy begins to crumble—aided by the information explosion, a great leveler—another relic looks shaky as well: the job description.

One organization that has given a new twist to job descriptions is British Petroleum (BP). In fact, BP has abandoned the traditional job descriptions in favor of skills matrices. Within each matrix are cells that describe skills and levels of performance that apply to a particular job family. They are not descriptions of specific jobs. For example, under technical expertise, the bottom level might include "Is acquiring basic knowledge and has awareness of the key skills," while a higher level in the matrix might say, "Conducts and/or supervises complex tasks requiring advanced knowledge of key skills or a thorough working knowledge of a range of key skills."

BP identified those employee skills it needs to have to enhance its performance and to be successful in the future. The matrices, which are distributed throughout the company, are so detailed that employees can see precisely what types of roles are available in BP and what levels of performance are required at each level.

The advantages the skills matrices offer are important. It is no longer necessary for an individual to be promoted into a new position to receive a higher salary—an employee can upgrade his or her skills and productivity within the current role and be rewarded accordingly. It also saves time, because employees don't have to wait for the HR staff to re-evaluate a job. Finally, managers know what to expect of their employees, and employees know what the organization expects of them.

But don't count traditional job descriptions out yet. As long as the environment remains relatively stable, job descriptions will continue to work well. It is when markets, products and technology cycles change with dizzying speed, however, that job descriptions drive down the road toward obsolescence.

SOURCE: Adapted from Milan Moravec and Robert Tucker, "Job Descriptions for the 21st Century," *Personnel Journal* (June 1992): 37–44.

term or another is used by an organization is not important because management will perform job analysis—either indirectly through various techniques or directly through an intentional job analysis program.

IMPORTANCE OF JOB ANALYSIS

For many organizations, especially those undergoing restructuring, downsizing, or other changes, job analysis and subsequent changes in job descriptions are a core management issue. As the two preceding *HR in the News* stories suggests, HR professionals frequently need to drastically overhaul existing job descriptions to reflect the new realities. What are these *new realities?*

- Organizational restructuring due to downsizing that call for basic changes in "who does what, where, and with what."

- The need to motivate and reward people, especially managers and professionals, on the basis of what they know along with traditional job objectives.
- The impact of technology, particularly information systems technology, on jobs throughout the organization.
- A new regulatory requirement (ADA and Civil Rights Act of 1991) which together put renewed emphasis on the rights of the disabled.[1]

Although organizations respond to these factors in different ways, all of them engage in the same basic activities. A number of activities—specifically recruitment, selection, job design, job worth, training, and appraisal—depend on information collected through job analysis (see Figure 4-1).

What that information is, and how it is collected and used is of critical importance, because such information directly affects em-

FIGURE 4-1 Job analysis.

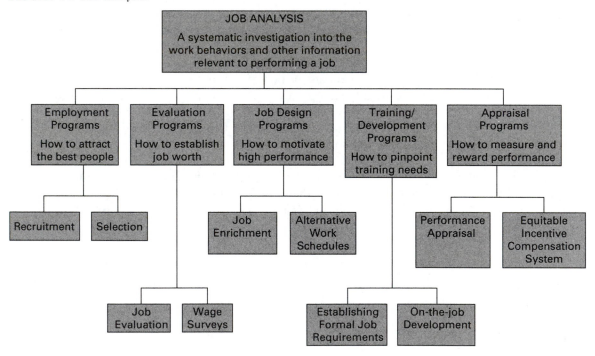

ployees' working conditions, such as pay or work assignments. Thus, job analysis may indirectly affect an employee's satisfaction and productivity.

The federal government, in particular the courts, has encouraged the use of job analysis and job descriptions so that organizations have specific, objective methods of determining HR decisions. Fuzzy, vague, or obsolete job descriptions make it hard to document and defend a company's HR policies.

The 1978 *Uniform Guidelines* of the EEOC clearly require a systematic job-analysis program to provide information for employee recruitment and selection.[2] The legal burden of proof is on the employer to provide evidence of proper job-related validation information, which is usually collected through job analysis.[3]

A job analysis is seldom the end product; instead, it provides the input to obtain end products systematically. A job analysis determines both the minimum and the desirable qualifications necessary to perform in a job. Such information is crucial in putting together a recruitment plan. In the selection process, an employee's relative abilities and skills must be evaluated. A job analysis may indicate what tasks, duties, and responsibilities the job will entail, how repetitive the job may be, or how much independence the job requires. By using that information during an interview, the HR interviewer can evaluate the qualifications of the person being considered for the job.

Once hired, the new employee needs to be oriented to the organization as quickly as possible. A job analysis informs the new employee about what must be learned to complete the job successfully. Often management will give new employees such information when hired. A complete job analysis will reveal if a new employee needs additional training in certain areas to complete the job successfully. This can usually be discerned by comparing the employee's past work history and training to the tasks specified in the job analysis.

Job analysis can also help management determine an equitable pay system. Almost all organizations desire to base a pay system on the relative value of each job to the organization. Difficult jobs, those that require specific abilities, or those that are more hazardous should receive more pay than less difficult jobs. While the United States has no comparable-worth legislation yet, other countries, such as Canada, do. Canadian organizations depend on job analyses to restructure pay rates so that women and men are compensated equally for comparable work.

Through job analysis, management can find out exactly what tasks are performed on each job and can compare individual tasks for similar jobs across the organization.

Performance appraisal—determining how well employees have performed their jobs in the past—as well as promotion decisions can be facilitated by a system that evaluates specific tasks that employees perform. Job analysis can be helpful in determining which duties and responsibilities should be considered in an evaluation.

A good job-analysis system is important to the HR function, the primary focus of which is to maintain a high level of employee productivity and efficiency. Job analyses affect most areas of employment and therefore indirectly affect performance appraisal, compensation, and training, which in turn affect employee performance and productivity.

PROGRAM IMPLEMENTATION

Larger firms typically have specially trained HR staff, called *job analysts,* whose primary function is to collect and process job information. Job analysts may conduct the review on their own or in consultation with job incumbents (i.e., employees who perform the work) and their supervisors.

The creation and implementation of a job analysis program varies from firm to firm.

Nonetheless, most organizations follow a standard format in conducting a job analysis that generally includes committee review, information collection, choosing a job-analysis method(s), product completion, and updating.

Committee Review

Experience indicates that the best way to initiate an effective program is through a representative committee. The committee must make the critical decisions in choosing the appropriate job-analysis technique and the important job elements to be evaluated.[4] Working with the HR department and the job analyst, the committee reviews information about each job within the organization and then makes difficult decisions in comparing job factors, such as relative responsibility or working conditions.

Committee membership should represent all the major departments to be studied in the job-analysis system. That is, if jobs to be analyzed are from six departments, then each department should have representatives on the committee who understand the department's jobs and procedures. The committee should include HR staff members who collect and evaluate job-analysis information on a firsthand basis. All the people assigned to this committee should understand the standard operating procedures within the organization and be able to work well together.

The quality of the job analysis will depend on the accuracy of the information gathered by the job analyst, the consistency and objectivity of the job analyst's evaluation of the information, and the ability of the committee members to make critical decisions when necessary. In this first step, the committee should decide the end products of the job analysis: Will the information be used to write job descriptions? Will the analysis be the basis for a system of job evaluation? Will it be used to determine minimum specifications for jobs in the organization? There may be more than one end product of job analysis.

The committee needs the cooperation of both employees and supervisors during information gathering. One reason for having each department represented is to allow committee members to report back to their departments about how the job analysis will proceed and to reassure fellow employees that the program is accurate and fair.

Information Collection

As noted previously, job analysis is a systematic investigation into the tasks, duties, and responsibilities of one or more jobs. Information involving job content is collected, analyzed, and interpreted. There is a variety of ways to collect this information; but the most common ones include the *Dictionary of Occupational Titles (DOT)*, site observation, interviews, and questionnaires.

Background research must always be among the first steps in a job analysis. Learning something about job-analysis techniques employed by other organizations, the problems they encountered, and their results could save the analyst an enormous amount of time, not to mention money. One of the best sources of job-relevant documents is the *DOT*.

U.S. Department of Labor   The U.S. Department of Labor (DOL) has developed a standardized method for job analysis that uses four major categories.[5]

1. *Worker Function*   What the worker does in relation to people, data, and things.
2. *Work Fields*   The methods by which the worker carries out the technological, sociological, or scientific requirements of the job.
3. *Equipment Utilization*   The tools, machines, and equipment that the worker must utilize.
4. *Products and Services*   The materials worked on, products produced, knowledge assembled, or services rendered.

Table 4-1 General Occupation Code of the *DOT*

DOT First Digit	Occupation
0,1	Professional, technical, managerial
2	Clerical, sales
3	Service
4	Farming, fishery, forestry
5	Processing
6	Machine trades
7	Bench work
8	Structural work
9	Miscellaneous

SOURCE: U.S. Department of Labor, *Dictionary of Occupational Titles,* 4th ed. (Washington, DC: U.S. Government Printing Office, 1977).

One advantage of the Department of Labor method is that it utilizes the U.S. Employment Service's *Dictionary of Occupational Titles (DOT).* The *DOT* classifies jobs by field of work, tasks performed, and the relationship of the job to data, people, and things. Each job title in the *DOT* system is given a six-digit code. The first digit indicates the general occupation, as shown in Table 4-1. The second and third digits provide a finer breakdown with respect to industry and function. The last three digits of the code are derived from the work-function code, as illustrated in Table 4-2. A tax accounting job, for example, is given the code 160.162; where 1 indicates professional; 60 indicates the accounting field; 1 indicates data coordinating; 6 indicates speaking or signaling (people contact); and 2 indicates operating or controlling.

Internal Methods In addition to external research, job analysts have to use a variety of internal sources to obtain job information, including documents such as technical manuals, training materials, organization charts, and previous job analyses.

Job incumbents represent the most common internal source because they probably know best how to perform a job. Of course, what incumbents report may reflect how a task is done rather than the best way. Other subject matter experts (SMEs), such as supervisors, can provide additional perspectives. Whether one source or several sources are used, there are several methods of collecting this type of information.

Table 4-2 Work Function Code of the *DOT*

Data (Fourth Digit)	People (Fifth Digit)	Things (Sixth Digit)
0 Synthesizing	0 Mentoring	0 Setting Up
1 Coordinating	1 Negotiating	1 Precision working
2 Analyzing	2 Instructing	2 Operating-controlling
3 Compiling	3 Supervising	3 Driving-operating
4 Computing	4 Diverting	4 Manipulating
5 Copying	5 Persuading	5 Tending
6 Comparing	6 Speaking-signaling	6 Feeding-offbearing
	7 Serving	7 Handling
	8 Taking Instructions–helping	

SOURCE: U.S. Department of Labor, *Dictionary of Occupational Titles,* 4th ed. (Washington, DC: U.S. Government Printing Office, 1977).

Site Observations Observing people at work permits the analyst to pinpoint precise details about the timing, frequency, and complexity of various tasks and duties; gather information about work flow, production efficiencies, work conditions, materials, and equipment used on the job; and assess the actual physical tasks that make up the job. When several employees perform the same job, the analyst would observe only the one or two who perform the job most effectively. Site observations minimize the likelihood of job incumbents' biasing the data by misleading, embellishing, or overlooking important aspects of the job. It can be accomplished by having a job analyst review film or tape of a job being performed, as well as by site observations.

One problem with site observation is that it can be used only on jobs that are easily discernible or measurable. An analyst would not learn much from observing an accountant who manipulates figures all day or a systems analyst who creates an accounts receivable program. Another problem is that some employees may resent being observed or may be uncomfortable, and thus may not perform in their normal manner. Such changes caused by observation are examples of the Hawthorne effect, first discovered in the early Hawthorne studies of human motivation. [6]

Work Sampling One variation on site observation is work sampling, in which a job analyst randomly samples the content of a job instead of observing all of an employee's behavior. Work sampling is particularly useful for highly repetitive, mostly mental jobs, as are often found in clerical and service concerns. The job analyst must take care to ensure that what is observed is representative of the entire domain of tasks involved and not simply isolated or one-of-a-kind job behaviors. [7]

Interviews A common alternative to observation is to interview either job incumbents or the job supervisor. Usually the analyst will ask similar questions regarding a particular job, thus giving the interview some structure. One-on-one sessions, meetings with a sample group of incumbents or supervisors, or discussions with SMEs are a few of the interview options available. This method of collecting job information is particularly valuable when the primary purpose of the job analysis is for designing performance appraisal standards, identifying training needs, and determining job worth. Interviews, unlike observation, offer the opportunity to probe and clarify areas of confusion about complex portions of the job.

The primary disadvantage of the interview method is that the analyst must spend a great deal of time with each employee. Some employees may not respond to questions carefully because they feel on the spot during an interview. Also, comparison of information gathered from different interviews is difficult. Even structured interviews result in a lack of standardized information, particularly if more than one analyst is conducting interviews. Caution must be exercised to ensure that the final summary of interview findings adequately reflects day-to-day job duties. Nevertheless, the interview can capture the complexity and uniqueness of some jobs better than standardized methods when basic guidelines such as those in Figure 4-2 are followed.

Questionnaires Perhaps the most efficient method of gathering job information is to use a questionnaire. Use of the questionnaire is faster and easier than an interview, and it almost always results in standardized, specific information about the jobs in an organization. Figure 4-3 is a sample of a job analysis questionnaire that has been used by

FIGURE 4-2 Job analysis interview guidelines.

1. *Consult the supervisor* of the job before deciding which persons to interview. If six or eight employees perform the same job, ask the supervisor which two perform the job best and thus would respond accurately.
2. *Make sure the interviewee understands the purpose* of the job analysis. Many times employees fear that the interview will be used against them, for example, to increase a job's expected output. Develop rapport with the employee as soon as possible, and express the stated goals of the job-analysis program before the interview begins. Often it will be necessary to emphasize that there will be no increase in work load or reduction in pay as a result of the job analysis.
3. *Structure the interview* as much as possible; decide what questions will be asked of all employees before any interviews begin. A structure assures standardization of format and comparability of information gathered. It also helps keep the interviews from deteriorating into bull sessions or complaint sessions.
4. *Complete a rough draft* of the interview and then go back to the employee to verify that your interpretation of the employee's statements is correct. After verification, contact the supervisor to check the accuracy of the information.
5. *And above all, prepare beforehand* by studying the job in order to ask the right questions.

both service and manufacturing organizations.

Whenever information gathered through a questionnaire is insufficient, follow-up interviews can be scheduled with certain employees. Thus, the advantage of the interview—exploring specific topics the analyst is unclear about or gaining information not in the standardized questions—can often be achieved with a questionnaire.

Constructing the questionnaire demands thoughtful planning and may require numerous revisions to ensure that the desired information is accurately pinpointed. Keep in mind that rigorous legal requirements apply when the purpose of the questionnaire is to gather data for selection decisions such as staffing or promotion. Figure 4-4 provides guidelines for compiling the job analysis questionnaire.

Job Analysis Methods

After the initial review, the committee or analyst must decide whether information should be collected by a method developed specifically for use in that organization or by a standardized method of job analysis. Standardized methods have the advantage of being previously tested and utilized, which increases their general validity. But one significant drawback of standardized methods is that they are not designed for use by a specific organization. Each method, whether standardized or not, has various strengths and weaknesses. Thus, a combination of methods may be used in an attempt to realize the strength of each.[8]

The DOL Although designed more for information collection than as a method of job analysis, the DOL method is used by smaller firms, where personnel specialists can quickly classify each job and use the *DOT* job descriptions; over 12,000 job titles are included. In other firms, specialists use the *DOT* as a starting point, modifying the standardized descriptions to fit their jobs.

The *DOT's* greatest asset is its acceptance by federal employment agencies. According to the *Uniform Guidelines on Employee Selection Procedures,* "It is desirable to provide the

FIGURE 4-3 A job-analysis questionnaire.

1. EMPLOYEE'S NAME: _____ Date Completed: _____

   Position Title: _____ Department: _____

   Title of Immediate Supervisor: _____

2. List the names and job titles of persons that you supervise, and the percentage of time spent in supervision.

Name	*Title*	*Hrs. Per Day/Week Supervising*
_____	_____	_____
_____	_____	_____

3. What is the lowest grade of grammar school, high school, or college that should have been completed by a person starting in your position?

   _____

4. What special type of training, skill, or experience should a person possess before starting in your position?

   _____

5. What training or experience have you received in your position, and how long would it take the average person to perform this work satisfactorily without close supervision?

   _____

   _____

6. What machines or equipment do you operate in your work and for what percentage of your time per day, week, or month?

Machine	*%*	*Period*
_____	_____	_____
_____	_____	_____

7. What do you consider to be the most important decisions that you alone make in the course of your work, and what percentage of your time is devoted to making such decisions?

   _____

   _____

8. What responsibility do you have for handling money, securities, inventory, or other valuables, and what is your estimate of their worth?

Responsibility	*$ Worth per Week*
_____	_____
_____	_____

FIGURE 4-3 *Continued*

9. What responsibility do you have in dealing with customers or other persons outside the company?

Person Contacted	Position	Nature of Contact	Frequency of Contact
_____	_____	_____	_____
_____	_____	_____	_____
_____	_____	_____	_____

10. What unusual aspects about your work and your work surroundings (working conditions, hours, out-of-town travel, physical requirements, etc.) should be included in a description of your job?

_____

_____

_____

11. What activities do you perform only at stated periods (weekly or monthly) or at irregular intervals?

Activity	Purpose	Interval
_____	_____	_____
_____	_____	_____
_____	_____	_____

12. List the specific duties you perform in the usual course of your daily work, and approximately what percentage of your workday is spent in each activity. (Please try to use active verbs such as type, file, interview, etc. On the following page you will find a sample list of duties that may be helpful in preparing your answer to this question.)

_____

_____

_____

13. Discuss any considerations not covered in this questionnaire that you consider important in writing a description of your job.

_____

_____

_____

THANK YOU FOR FILLING OUT THE QUESTIONNAIRE

FIGURE 4-4 Job analysis questionnaire guidelines.

1. *Review questionnaires used by organizations, professional groups, or university researchers.* Many items on other questionnaires may not have occurred to you. You can learn from other analysts' experiences.
2. *Keep the questionnaire short.* Most people do not like completing questionnaires. Thus, the longer the questionnaire, the less attention will be paid to the items during its completion.
3. *Have each questionnaire completed at work.* Questionnaires completed at home often are not done earnestly. Because job analysis is important to the organization, it should be done on company time so that employees have adequate time to provide the information and do not look upon completion as an extra burden they must bear.
4. *Categorize answers.* Structure questions so that responses can be categorized as much as possible. Whenever possible, design closed-end questions; have employees check one of several responses or indicate numbers or percentages for responses. Such a design avoids gathering information that is hard to compare or cannot be used by the analyst.
5. *Test the questionnaire with several trusted employees.* Many times the analyst will find that questions may be vague and misleading, or that important aspects of the jobs have been omitted.
6. *Include one open-ended question.* Always include at least one question that allows the employee to give any additional information that has not been elicited in the rest of the written questionnaire. In that way, the analyst may discover important information about particular qualities of some jobs.

user's job title(s) for the job(s) in question and the corresponding job title(s) and code(s) from the U.S. Employment Service's *Dictionary of Occupational Titles*.[9] It is also considered a fundamental mechanism by which different occupational job families are related to each other.[10]

Position Analysis Questionnaire   Ernest J. McCormick's **Position Analysis Questionnaire (PAQ)** is another standardized method of job analysis that describes jobs in terms of worker activities. The PAQ contains job elements that fall into twenty-seven job dimensions, which in turn fall into six major job categories (shown in Figure 4-5).[11]

The twenty-seven dimensions are the job families most common to organizations. Examples of the job families include use of decision making, tools, interpersonal associations, and working conditions (see Figure 4-5). Use of the PAQ requires that job incumbents and job supervisors be familiar enough with the job being analyzed to check the questionnaire items that apply to the job in question. Figure 4-6 shows one page from the PAQ concerning information input.

The PAQ has the obvious advantage of being quantitative. Having a quantitative system is helpful because the job analyst can easily

FIGURE 4-5 Position Analysis Questionnaire Job Categories.

Information input: How information to do the job is received.
Mental processes: The extent and type of decision making, planning, and organizing.
Work output: Tools, machines, and physical activity associated with the job.
Relationships: Associations with co-workers, supervisors, customers, and so on.
Work situation and job context: Working conditions, including hours and physical surrounding.
Other job characteristics: Work schedules, method of pay, responsibility, job demands, and the like.

SOURCE: Adapted from E. J. McCormick, P. R. Jeanneret, and R. C. Mecham, "A Study of Job Characteristics and Job Dimensions As Based on the Position Analysis Questionnaire (PA/q)," *Journal of Applied Psychology* 56 (1972): 349.

FIGURE 4-6 A page from the PAQ.

NA	Does not apply
1	Nominal/very infrequent
2	Occasional
3	Moderate
4	Considerable
5	Very substantial

1 INFORMATION INPUT

1.1 Sources of Job Information

Rate each of the following items in terms of the extent to which it is used by the worker as a source of information in performing the job.

1.1.1 Visual Sources of Job Information

1. **4** Written materials (books, reports, office notes, articles, job instructions, signs, etc.)
2. **4** Quantitative materials (such as graphs, accounts, specifications, tables of numbers, etc.)
3. **1** Pictorial materials (picturelike materials used as sources of information, for example, drawings, blueprints, diagrams, maps, tracings, photographic films, X-ray films, TV pictures, etc.)
4. **NA** Patterns/related devices (templates, stencils, patterns, etc., used as sources of information when observed during use; do not include here materials described in item 3 above)
5. **1** Visual displays (dials, gauges, signal lights, radarscopes, speedometers, clocks, etc.)
6. **1** Measuring devices (rulers, calipers, tire pressure gauges, scales, thickness gauges, pipettes, thermometers, protractors, etc., used to obtain visual information about physical measurements; do not include here devices described in item 5 above)
7. **NA** Mechanical devices (tools, equipment, machinery, and other mechanical devices which are sources of information when observed during use or operation)
8. **NA** Materials in process (parts, materials, objects, etc., which are sources of information when being modified, worked on, or otherwise processed, such as bread dough being mixed, workpiece being turned in a lathe, fabric being cut, shoe being resoled, etc.)
9. **NA** Materials not in process (parts, materials, objects, etc., not in the process of being changed or modified, which are sources of information when being inspected, handled, packaged, distributed, or selected, etc., such as items or materials in inventory, storage, or distribution channels, items being inspected, etc.)
10. **NA** Features of nature (landscapes, fields, geological samples, vegetation, cloud formations, and other features of nature which are observed or inspected to provide information)
11. **NA** Features of environment created by people (structures, buildings, dams, highways, bridges, docks, railroads, and other altered aspects of the indoor or outdoor environment which are observed or inspected to provide job information; do not consider equipment, etc., that an individual uses during work, which are covered by item 7).

SOURCE: Adapted from the *Position Analysis Questionnaire*: Visual Sources of Job Information. PAQ Services, Inc., Logan, UT. Used with permission.

differentiate between jobs by comparing the point totals of one job to those of another and, therefore, can assign jobs to different pay grades. The PAQ also has the advantage of being standardized: each job is looked at with the same criteria in mind. The PAQ has demonstrated a high degree of reliability even when the level of cooperation of employees is quite low or when attempts are made to manipulate the information provided. Furthermore, the PAQ is supported by a considerable number of human resources information system (HRIS) software programs already on the market. The PAQ is perhaps the most widely used job analysis method. [12]

Critical Incident Technique John Flanagan proposed two criteria to define a job activity as critical: (1) it was complete enough to allow someone to make an inference about a job incumbent's performance, and (2) it was crucial to either outstanding or poor job performance.[13] When all the critical acts (i.e., behaviors) in a job are compiled, the results provide an accurate portrayal that can focus on both the action of the worker and the context in which the behavior occurs.

The **critical incident technique (CIT)** method is an excellent job analysis technique when the primary purpose is performance appraisal, training, selection, or job design. Moreover, the method appears to adhere to legal requirements because it is job related and systematically designed.[14] We will leave the actual explanation of CIT design, as well as examples, to Chapter 8.

Critical incidents can be collected through interviews or questionnaires. Job incumbents typically provide the information, although job supervisors can be consulted. It helps to have multiple points of view on a single job, which means that the technique is limited to jobs performed by a dozen or more people. Obviously, such a restriction limits the use of CIT to jobs that are routine—tasks that are usually found at the lower levels of the organization's structure.

Functional Job Analysis   A modification of the DOL method was developed by Sidney A. Fine, at one time a member of the employment services division of DOL. Fine named his standardized system **Functional Job Analysis (FJA)**.[15] In FJA the job analyst gathers background research, interviews job incumbents and supervisors, makes site observations, and then prepares detailed task statements with a standard questionnaire that specifies what a worker *does* and what gets *done* on a job. These statements are reviewed and verified by subject matter experts. Once approved, the job analyst uses the FJA questionnaire to rate each job.

In addition to tasks statements, worker functions are identified. Like the *DOT,* the function level describes differing levels of complexity in three areas of task performance: data, people, and things. For each task within a job, a measure of complexity of data, people, and things is taken. For example, a scale for measuring worker instructions is depicted in Figure 4-7.

TI/CODAP   The **Task Inventory/Comprehensive Occupational Data Analysis Program (TI/CODAP)** was devised by R. Christal and colleagues for Air Force personnel.[16] It contains two parts: the first is a comprehensive inventory of up to 500 task statements, and the second is a computerized statistical package for analyzing the responses of job incumbents who completed the task inventories. The TI/CODAP defines a task as any meaningful unit of work or activity specified by the job incumbent.

The TI/CODAP process is quite similar to that of the FJA. Background research, interviews, and site observations begin the process. They are followed by the construction of an initial task inventory questionnaire that includes other items such as work experience, education, race, sex, and equipment needs. Each task contained in the inventory is rated on "relative time spent" or whatever scale is deemed appropriate. When information has been collected from all or most of the job incumbents, it is subjected to the CODAP part of the process. Given that thousands of pieces of information from thousands of people might be involved, only a computer analysis is feasible. The job activities are grouped into occupational clusters or families. Further analysis is performed that identifies similar tasks with equivalent "relative time spent" distributions.

While the CODAP method is superb for yielding job descriptions, specifications, and job evaluations, it is the potential for other applications that really excites the HR

FIGURE 4-7 The worker instructions scale of the FJA.

Worker Instructions Scales: Levels of Responsibility

The worker instructions scale defines *responsibility* in terms of the mix of specifications (that which is prescribed) and judgment (that which is specifically left to discretion) assigned to the worker. A worker's responsibilities may encompass several levels, depending on the activity(ies) involved.

Level 1

Inputs, outputs, tools, equipment, and procedures are all specified. Almost everything the worker needs to know is contained in the assignment. The worker is to produce a specified amount of work or a standard number of units per day.

Level 2

Inputs, outputs, tools, and equipment are all specified, but the worker has some leeway in the procedures and methods used to get the job done. Almost all the information needed is provided in the daily assignment. Production is measured on a daily or weekly basis.

Level 3

Inputs and outputs are specified, but the worker has considerable freedom in procedures and timing, including the use of tools and equipment. The worker may have to refer to several standard sources for information (handbooks, catalogs, wall charts). Time to complete a particular product or service is specified, but this varies up to several hours.

Level 4

Output (product or service) is specified in the assignment, which may be in the form of a memorandum or of a schematic (sketch or blueprint). The worker must work out ways of getting the job done, including selection and use of tools and equipment, sequence of operations (tasks), and acquisition of important information (handbooks, etc.). The worker may either do work or set up standards and procedures for others.

Level 5

Same as Level 4, but in addition the worker is expected to know and employ theory—the whys and wherefores of the various options available for dealing with a problem—and can independently select from among them. Reading in the professional and/or trade literature may be required to gain this understanding.

Level 6

Various possible outputs are described that can meet stated technical or administrative needs. The worker must investigate the various possible outputs and evaluate them in regard to performance characteristics and input demands. This usually requires creative use of theory well beyond referring to standard sources. There is no specification of inputs, methods, sequences, sources, or the like.

Level 7

There is some question about what the need or problem really is or what directions should be pursued in dealing with it. In order to define it, to control and explore the behavior of the variables, and to formulate possible outputs and their performance characteristics, the worker must consult largely unspecified sources of information and device investigations, surveys, or data-analysis studies.

Level 8

Information or direction comes to the worker in terms of needs (tactical, organizational, strategic, financial). The worker must call for staff reports and recommendations concerning methods of dealing with them. The worker coordinates organizational and technical data in order to make decisions and determinations regarding courses of action (outputs) for major sections (divisions, groups) of the organization.

SOURCE: Adapted from the scale developed by Sidney A. Fine, Ph.D., Advanced Research Resources Organization, Washington, D.C. Used by permission.

profession. For example, CODAP analyses provide the frequency of task performance by job incumbents as well as differences in frequency of task performance by employees in different jobs. However, it is time-consuming—sometimes taking months—and can be done only on large numbers of job incumbents.

Information Review

Regardless of the method selected to collect information, the next step is to assemble and review that information with the employees and the job analysis committee. After writing a first draft of the standardized information collected, the analyst needs to make sure that the data are factually correct and complete and that a clear picture of the job is being presented. After checking with the employees and supervisors involved in gathering information, the analyst must take these first drafts to the job analysis committee, which reviews each analysis to make sure that it is both objective and easily comparable with analyses of other jobs. The establishment of standardized categories of information about the jobs—such as work environment, decision making required, and supervision—makes comparisons among jobs easier. The more effort put into these first drafts, the easier it will be to determine the desired end products.

Product Completion

The fourth step involves the completion of whatever end products are desired by management. For example, job analysis data may be used to write job descriptions or job specifications, to conduct a job evaluation for wage and salary purposes, to determine training and development needs, and to create tests for employee selection.

Future Use and Updating

The last step in the job analysis procedure will be to determine how the information will be stored for future use. The HR department should have access to this information in case additional end products are desired. Also, the job analysis committee will need to determine how to update the information periodically because information gathered in the job analysis process has a tendency to become obsolete over time. Changes will occur as supervisors train employees to accept more responsibility, as additional tasks are developed, or as organizational changes are made. Updating the information in the job analysis program maintains its accuracy and guarantees its usefulness in the future.

Job Analysis Problems

Any job analysis will run into certain problems, regardless of the size of the organization, the status of employee relations, or the abilities of those performing the analysis. Particularly in an era of continuous delayering and downsizing, one of the most common problems is employee fear. Often employees see a job analysis as a threat to their current jobs or pay levels or both. In the past, job analysis was used as a means of expanding jobs while reducing the total number of employees. Job analysis has also been used to increase production rates and, therefore, decrease employees' pay. Organizations must overcome employees' fears so that employees and their supervisors will give accurate information.

One of the most successful methods of reducing employee fear is to involve employees or their representatives in as many aspects of the job analysis procedure as possible. Before the procedure begins, employees should be told why it has to be instituted, who will initiate it, how the employees will be affected, and why their input is critical. Management may want to make a written commitment that the organization will not terminate any employee, lower the pay of any employee, or decrease the total number of jobs because of the results of the job analysis. Such measures may enable the job analysts to obtain complete information from employees. It is unfortunate for job analysts that in past years job analysis was sometimes used improperly.

A second problem of job analysis is the need to update the information gathered. While any job analysis is being completed, jobs will be changing as the organization changes. As jobs expand, as work is reassigned within a department, and as supervisors develop, the description of their jobs will necessarily have to change. The problem, then, becomes how to keep the information current. One method is the annual review of the job analysis information, in which the HR department sends the information to supervisors, asking them to note any changes that have occurred during the past year. A second method is to have managers submit proposed changes in jobs or reclassifications. This method is especially important when the reclassification may result in a change in pay.

Both methods have their problems. The annual review is quite time-consuming because every job must be reanalyzed each year. Also, when jobs are reviewed annually, employees sometimes expect that their jobs will always be reclassified—with accompanying pay increases. Another problem with an annual review is that whenever the content of a job is substantially increased only a week or two after the initial job analysis, employees in that job may be underpaid for the next forty or fifty weeks. Finally, the annual review looks at all jobs, even those that have not changed. Possibly 90 percent of the jobs do not need to be reexamined; only the 10 percent that have changed during the year need to be reviewed.

Constant updating by managers implies that only those jobs that need to be changed will be looked at. Also, this method produces more current data and ensures that employees will not have to wait for months to have their jobs reclassified, with a possible change in salary or other benefits. A primary disadvantage of this method is that management may forget to keep up with changes. Thus, employees become frustrated, feel underpaid, or do not realize

what must be done to have their jobs reclassified.

The two methods may be combined in some form, such as having biennial performance reviews with constant updates by managers who want to reclassify jobs. Yet combining the two methods contains the advantages as well as the disadvantages of the two methods separately, and therefore combinations are less common than using one method or the other.

Another problem with job analysis occurs when a job is held by only one or two employees. In such a case, the analysis is often of the person's performance and not of the job itself. The analyst must look at what the job should entail and not at how well or how poorly one employee is performing the job.

A problem commonly occurs when job analyses form the basis for job descriptions handed out to new employees. Employees often feel that the description is a contract describing what they should and should not do on the job. When asked occasionally to do extra work or an unusual task, employees may respond, "It's not in my description"—and by that reasoning resist performing the task. Management can change job descriptions by assigning added tasks to employees, but if a task is done rarely or is never to be repeated, changing the job description for a single situation is unnecessary. Many organizations use **elastic clauses** in job descriptions, such as "performs other duties as assigned." An elastic clause allows supervisors to assign employees duties different from those normally performed without changing the job descriptions.

JOB DESCRIPTIONS

The most common end product of a job analysis is a written **job description**. One of the oldest HR tools, job descriptions have attracted renewed interest in recent years, primarily because of governmental regulatory guidelines. Job descriptions have no exact format and are often used for many different purposes. Indeed, some cultures, like the Japanese (Figure 4-8) prefer broad, but less precise description, whereas Americans prefer clear, detailed, and unequivocal description.

Uses of Job Descriptions

Over one hundred major uses of job descriptions in the HR function have been identified. Most employers, however, typically use them for five or six functions.[17] Job descriptions serve a variety of purposes for HR professionals. Several employment and compensation activities depend on job information normally included in the organization's job descriptions. In addition, the basic job information needed for such legal requirements as equal employment opportunity, affirmative action, overtime qualifications, and employee safety can be included in job descriptions. Collective bargain-ing agreements may also specify which duties are to be performed by each union employee covered by the agreement.

Recruitment Job descriptions may be used to develop recruitment advertisements and to provide applicants with additional information about the job openings.

Interviewing Job descriptions are often used when they include job specifications as a means of providing the interviewer with concise, accurate information about the job. The interviewer can then better match the applicant to the job opening and make sure that the minimum qualifications of the job are met by the applicant.

Orientation New employees may be given job descriptions to spell out job requirements and areas to be evaluated.

FIGURE 4-8 Job analysis Japanese style.

In Japan, job duties are generally broader, more ambiguous job responsibilities than those customarily found in the United States. It is assumed that those who are good enough to be hired can develop the necessary skills and versatility to perform in a variety of positions, much like players on a volleyball team.

Work is organized around groups of people instead of around individual skills. Employees work in teams, so that each shares a common point of view and learns all the duties of the unit. This means that workers use slack times to do other jobs, and if business falls off, they are able to fill in elsewhere as needed. There are, then, no clear-cut job specifications and duties; the Japanese sense of collectivity precludes a strong identification with occupational expertise. Once employees grasp the company's philosophy, it is believed that they can deduce for themselves the necessary role as work situations arise; there is, therefore, little need for detailed instruction manuals and predetermined job rules. . . .

The difference in classification systems between a Japanese affiliate and an American-owned operation is aptly illustrated by an official in a Japanese motorcycle company. "Our hourly work force is almost exactly the size of theirs (the U.S. firm's), yet we have only 20 different job descriptions versus 150 for them." By following relatively nonspecialized career paths, employees become experts in the organization rather than experts in one functional specialty. This person-centered (as opposed to position-centered) system places a high premium on adaptability, a critical requirement in rapidly changing technologies that require integration of the whole company. . . .

SOURCE: Adapted from James S. Bowman, "The Rising Sun in America (Part One)," *Personnel Administrator* 31, no. 9 (September 1986): 67, 114. Copyright 1986, The American Society for Personnel Administration, Alexandria, VA.

Training Organizations use job descriptions to specify both the training an employee requires for effective performance and the type of training current employees may need to become promotable.

Job Evaluation Job descriptions often specify comparable factors in the process of **job evaluation** so that a job evaluator can compare various jobs and make pay decisions. HR practices and federal laws require that such comparisons be based on job-required skill, effort, responsibility, and working conditions. The required documentation of such information is usually found in job descriptions. Thus, there is an inevitable link between pay and job descriptions. That link sometimes tempts managers to use fancy language and elaborate generalities to describe job duties in order to justify higher pay levels. HR professionals are then forced to act as police officers to guard against such problems. The growth of computerized personnel systems has greatly assisted the personnel manager in maintaining descriptions and evaluations that accurately match the job content within an organization.[18]

Wage Compensation Survey Job descriptions give the HR administrator the opportunity to estimate whether the wages being paid for a job are equitable in comparison with wages for similar jobs in other organizations in the community or throughout the country. Thus, job descriptions provide information for both internal comparisons (through job evaluation) and external comparisons (through survey analysis).

Performance Appraisal Job descriptions may specify the basis on which an employee will be judged during performance appraisal. If employees are told which areas and duties they are responsible for performing, they are forewarned about what will eventually be evaluated.

Outplacement Job descriptions may also play an important role in the career change process. Organizations that lay off workers temporarily or downsize permanently often want to assist affected employees. The HR staff can use an employee's job description to help prepare a resume that gives detailed information. The HR staff may also refer to the description when providing reference information to prospective employers.[19]

Legal Requirements

Job descriptions can be a great help to an organization as it attempts to comply with a number of important federal laws.

Americans with Disabilities Act (ADA) Recently, the ADA and the Civil Rights Act of 1991 were passed. The ADA prohibits discrimination against disabled persons if they can perform the "essential functions" of the job they are applying for or wish to retain. And the new Civil Rights Act puts the burden of proof on employers to demonstrate that these essential functions are, in fact, essential to job performance. Together these regulations put new emphasis on the importance of job analysis for identifying and defining fundamental job duties. (See the accompanying *HR in the News:* "Job Descriptions Under the ADA."[20])

The ADA requires that employers make a "reasonable accommodation" to qualified individuals with a disability. Therefore, identifying and defining the essential functions are critical in order to determine if someone is a qualified individual with a disability and, if so, what if any reasonable accommodations will be required.

For example, the job of hospital laboratory technician may require the in-person delivery of lab tests to many different medical facilities in different buildings over a one-square-mile area, daily trips to the post office, and emergency trips to patients' rooms throughout the

Job Descriptions Under the ADA

Under the ADA, employers will make the initial determination of what constitutes an essential function. If challenged, an employer must be able to substantiate that its determinations are reasonable. While not required under the ADA, current job descriptions will be given considerable weight, especially if they are prepared before advertising for the position or interviewing applicants.

Whether job descriptions should be developed will become very important under the ADA. Many employers now do not use job descriptions in an effort to avoid the "that's not my job" syndrome. The ADA presents an important question to that thinking and employers should carefully consider all sides of the question as they prepare for ADA compliance.

Detailing the essential functions of the job in job descriptions decreases the likelihood that individuals responsible for hiring will violate the law by basing decisions on an applicant's ability to perform marginal functions.

SOURCE: Adapted from David Israel and Debra Scott, "Hiring Under the ADA," *HRMagazine* (November 1991): 88–89.

hospital, usually by walking or taking the stairs to save valuable time instead of waiting for the slower elevators. The hospital has only a few lab technicians, so this job cannot reasonably be filled by someone in a wheelchair or otherwise unable to perform these essential travel functions.

In another hospital, with a larger laboratory staff, certain positions may require little or no travel. The position of lab director, for example, may essentially involve managing the staff and sending others to pick up or deliver lab test results. In this case, a person using a wheelchair could handle the essential functions of the job, and the ADA may require that the company make a reasonable accommodation, such as the installation of ramps to ease access to the lab workstations.

How essential functions are determined, and the extent to which an employer is ex-

pected to accommodate the disabled, are tricky issues. Basically, the "reasonable accommodation" provisions of the ADA require employers to make workplace changes that permit the employment of disabled persons—as long as the changes are reasonable in terms of cost and business necessity. While written job descriptions are an important consideration in determining what are essential functions, other factors may also play a role, such as specific terms in a collective bargaining agreement.[21]

Fair Labor Standards Act of 1938 This act, which was amended in 1974, created the initial demand for job descriptions and made them popular in the 1940s. The act specifies, among other things, that employees must be paid a minimum wage. It also sets a forty-hour workweek by dividing employees into two categories—exempt and nonexempt. *Nonexempt* employees must be paid time and a half when they work more than forty hours per week. *Exempt* employees do not have to be paid overtime wages. Thus, an organization must determine whether each job is exempt or nonexempt through job analysis or by analyzing job descriptions. Basically, exempt positions are managerial, supervisory, technical, professional, and certain sales positions. Statutes similar to the federal Fair Labor Standards Act have been enacted in most states.

Equal Pay Act of 1963   This act requires that organizations give "equal pay for substantially equal work requiring equal skill, effort, responsibility, and working conditions." Job descriptions may be an organization's defense against charges of discrimination filed under the Equal Pay Act. Descriptions can be used to show that jobs are not substantially equal in terms of skill, effort, responsibility, or working conditions and, therefore, can be paid at different rates.

Title VII of the 1964 Civil Rights Act   Title VII prohibits discrimination in employment based on race, sex, age, creed, religion, or national origin. Job descriptions provide documentation that employees are hired and paid according to necessary job requirements.

Occupational Safety and Health Act of 1970   Job descriptions are required by this act to specify "elements of the job that endanger health, or are considered unsatisfactory or distasteful to the majority of the population." Providing a job description to employees as an advance notice is a good defense against possible legal actions by employees.

Collective Bargaining Demands   A long-standing union demand is "equal pay for equal work." Thus, job descriptions specifying work to be performed often stipulate certain pay for specific duties. Such pay considerations have been a critical area in labor negotiations for many years.

Elements of Job Descriptions

Although there is no universal format for job descriptions, most have certain common elements. A list of job duties is one element found in all job descriptions. Most will contain some identification and a brief job summary. They often contain job specifications, though it is also common practice to list specifications on separate forms.

Job Identification   The first part of a job description, the identification section, usually includes the title of the job, the location of the job (e.g., plant, department, or division), the title of the immediate supervisor, the job status (exempt or nonexempt), and the pay grade or pay range. This information is needed for general administrative and record-keeping functions. Job titles can be used to identify a particular job within an organization, but generally they cannot legally be used to compare jobs for pay purposes. The content of the job is described in the duties and responsibilities section. The content must be evaluated for pay considerations because job titles can be misleading; an administrative assistant in one organization may be quite different from one in another organization. A statement of location is required by the 1978 *Uniform Guidelines* when the job description is used to provide evidence of legality in an organization's selection procedures.[22]

Other useful elements sometimes included in the identification section are the name of the job analyst who approved the description, the name of the employee who provided the basic information, the date the description was approved, and, if applicable, the standard code number published in the *DOT,* the equal employment and affirmative action (EEO-1/AAP) reporting category, and the point total in a point system of job evaluation.

Figure 4-9 is a sample job description. That description of a chief quality control engineer contains a particularly good example of job identification. The identification includes not only the usual information—such as job title, department, and title of the immediate supervisor—but also the job code or the *DOT* job number. The exempt status of the job indicates a salaried position that does not pay overtime wages. The inclusion of a date on which the description was approved and the name of the person who approved it eliminates future questions or conflicts concerning accuracy or completeness. A pay grade is given so that employees or applicants can estimate the pay range for a job and its level within the

FIGURE 4-9 A sample job description.

Chief Quality Control Engineer		*156.132*		
Job Title		Job Code		
Manager of Quality Control		*Quality Control*		
Title of Immediate Supervisor		Department		
7	*Louisville*	*Exempt*	*August 12, 1990*	
Bldg.	Plant	Status	Date	
Robert Myers	*Kathy Johnson*	*16*	*751*	*1/2*
Approved by	written by	Grade	Points	EEO/AAP

SUMMARY

Supervises six salaried quality control personnel; plans, organizes, coordinates, and administers manufacturing activities.

JOB DUTIES

1. Establishes and maintains supplier contacts to assist in solving quality problems by evaluating contacts' quality capabilities, facilities, and quality systems. (10%)
2. Establishes and reviews goals, budgets, and work plans in the areas of quality, cost schedule attainment, and operator/equipment utilization. (10%)
3. Reviews product and process designs, identifying problems which might result in customer dissatisfaction or failure to meet established goals or allocated costs. (20%).
4. Specifies quality control methods and processes to support quality planning. Provides cost estimates and procures necessary tools and equipment to support overall project schedule. (10%).
5. Supplies input to manufacturing engineers on producibility and other quality matters. (20%)
6. Provides feedback on quality levels and costs during test runs and during production to measure system effectiveness. (10%)
7. Supervises six to eight salaried personnel assigned to the quality control engineering area. Trains new personnel in proper procedures and policy. Completes performance appraisals of subordinates. (20%)

organization. The 751 points refers to evaluation points; if the point total is close to the next highest pay grade, future reclassifications may move it up to the next highest pay grade.

Job Summary A job summary is a one- to three-line description of the essence of the job. Job summaries usually start with a verb, such as *supervises, coordinates,* or *directs.* Job summaries should emphasize either the most common function, the primary output, or the objective of the job.

Job Duties and Responsibilities Job duties and responsibilities are the heart of the job description. There are two common formats for the duties section. One is a paragraph describing the job. The problem with this format is that a reader may find it difficult to recognize immediately which functions are important. A more popular format is grouping the tasks of a job and listing them separately, as for example in Figure 4-9. The tasks might be grouped by functional categories, such as "supervision given," "organization of work," "physical demands," and "financial accountability." As with job summaries, each duty or responsibility should begin with a verb, such as *supervises* or *performs.* The intention of the duties section is to give the reader a complete and concise account of what is being performed on the job—though it is not intended to be a training instrument to teach a novice how to perform the job. The estimated time spent on each duty often appears in parentheses after each duty is explained.

Job Specifications Job specifications, or minimum qualifications, state the qualifications job applicants must possess to be considered for the job. These qualifications are often grouped into three categories: **skills, knowledge,** and **ability (SKAs).** *Skills* include observable capabilities performed on the job. *Knowledge* constitutes the body of information in a particular subject area that is required by a new employee to perform the job satisfactorily. *Ability* refers to any mental or physical activities required of a new employee. For example, a section supervisor might be required to know the safety regulations that affect the plant, to have the skill to operate a quality-control laser machine, and to have the ability to write daily work assignments. SKAs are most useful in personnel decision-making situations, such as selection, training, and performance evaluation.[23]

Job specifications may also include required education, experience, and training, as well as any specific certification required for the job. As a job specification, *effort* might encompass specific physical tasks the job holder must be able to perform or some necessary experience in a supervisory position. *Responsibility* might encompass reporting responsibility, supervisory responsibility for inventory maintenance, or financial responsibility such as making up shortages in a cash drawer. Job specifications might also include working conditions, such as the hours the employee must be available, as well as other unusual conditions, such as high levels of noise or fumes.

Figure 4-10, a description of a word processing secretary's job, contains job specifications that would allow an interviewer to decide easily and objectively if an applicant meets the qualifications. Although a specification may not always be quantitative in nature, it should be whenever possible. The first three specifications for the job are examples of measurable or **verifiable qualifications;** the interviewer can verify that a person has a high school degree or college experience and can measure an applicant's typing and filing ability with standardized tests. The fourth and fifth specifications are important but are more vague and subjective—and thus subject to interviewer bias. Notice that the sample job description shown in Figure 4-9 does not contain a section on job specifications.

FIGURE 4-10 A sample job description.

Job Title: *Word Processing Secretary*
Department: *Branch Administration*
Position of Immediate Supervisor: *Branch Administrative Manager*

I. GENERAL SUMMARY OF RESPONSIBILITIES:
Types, edits, and distributes various correspondence to clients and internal staff. Transmits and proofs various essential status reports for day-to-day operations.

II. SPECIFIC JOB RESPONSIBILITIES:
Types daily correspondence and sales orders from nine representatives from machine dictation and hard copy. (40%)

Proofreads and prepares final copies for distribution. (10%)

Receives handwritten copies and maintains priority file of reports and correspondence. (5%)

Types special projects, such as proposals, quotations, systems, analyses, and office surveys for marketing department. (20%)

Transmits computer programs via magnetic card typewriter and other telecommunication equipment. (10%)

Logs and maintains records of completed staff and client work. (4%)

Receives and assigns priority to special client and staff requests and special projects. (5%)

Serves as backup for receptionist. (5%)

Performs other duties as assigned. (1%)

III. JOB SPECIFICATION:
High school diploma required, with one or two years of college preferred.

Training or one year's experience on magnetic card typewriter. Type 50 wpm.

Able to file ten documents per minute without error.

Must be able to consistently produce accurate, professional-quality documents.

Ability to work well with people in developing proposals is essential.

CONCLUSIONS AND APPLICATIONS

- A sound job analysis program produces many benefits for an organization. Information critical to employment and compensation is collected on a systematic basis. Job descriptions, job specifications, and job evaluations can easily be produced from the job, analysis data. Thus, critical HR practices such as hiring, wage determination, and administrative record keeping are assisted by job analysis.

- Information collection should always begin by conducting background research. One excellent source is the DOL, especially the *DOT*. Internal sources can be either standardized or unstructured and include previous job analyses, interviews with job incumbents and job supervisors, site observations by the analyst, and questionnaires.

- There is a variety of standardized job analysis methods, with each having certain advantages, depending on the purpose, cost, and time. For smaller companies, the *DOT* is often the basis for constructing job descriptions. The most popular method is the PAQ. When performance appraisals drive the job analysis, the CIT is frequently used. More complex methods that demand computer analysis and which can handle thousands of jobs and people are the FJA and TI/CODAP.

- The methods of information collection are two: standardized and internal. Internal written questionnaires are often faster and easier and can be tailored to the needs of the organization. Interviews with employees and supervisors can also be used to ensure complete and accurate information.

- Job analysis is necessary to comply with the primary employment provisions of the ADA.

It requires all selection criteria that tend to screen out the disabled to be job related and consistent with business necessity. The process itself helps to determine essential functions and whether an individual can carry out the essential functions with or without reasonable accommodation.

- The federal government and the courts have increased the pressure on HR managers to utilize job analysis as a means of producing job-related job descriptions, hiring criteria, and compensation systems.

- Job descriptions generally should contain a complete identification of the job and its location within the organization. The section on duties and responsibilities should group all tasks into major functional categories, and each entry should begin with verbs. Job specifications should include all SKAs needed to perform the job, as well as other minimum qualifications.

CASE STUDY

Good Intentions Aren't Enough

Melanie's company downsized four times in three years, and each time management made an effort to find a job for her. She had always been a dependable and productive employee, and her bosses did not want to lose her. In their efforts to keep Melanie, she was assigned three different jobs in two different work groups over the three-year span. Ted, Melanie's current boss, thought Melanie was particularly resourceful and smart. She was the kind of employee the company had to retain once the difficult times were over.

Ted and the other managers also thought Melanie knew how lucky she was that she still had her job. Ted and his colleagues were wrong. As far as Melanie was concerned, the last three years had been a nightmare.

Every time she began to catch on to a new job, the company announced more restructuring, and she ended up with another assignment. She desperately wanted to do a good job, but she did not completely understand what she was supposed to do until weeks into each new assignment. There were occasional pats on the back encouraging her to hang in there, but there was also the increasing pressure to do more.

Each day, Melanie reported to a work space designed for ten people and now home to just three. Abandoned files and photos of bygone office parties haunted her. Making matters worse, her own work load soared, partly as a result of the work group's shrinking to three from sixteen.

Melanie could not help but feel at least a pang of "survivor's guilt" whenever she moved into a new job once held by a dismissed co-worker. Despite her success in still holding on to a job, she felt distrustful toward management, overworked, and more insecure than ever. In addition, she sensed resentment from other survivors and co-workers who wanted to know what skills and knowledge she was expected to bring to the job. A question kept popping up in her mind: "Why was I any better than the person I replaced?"

Melanie was afraid to tell Ted how she felt. She could not handle the stress of constantly figuring out what was expected of her. Admitting her faults to Ted could only jeopardize her already precarious future. Talking to Ted about the confusing nature of her work, she reasoned, would be the straw that would break the camel's back and result in her own organizational demise. It would be better to hide these frustrations until things improved. So she plodded to work each day, did what she could, and asked no questions.

Melanie attempted to vent her frustrations by combing through the help-wanted ads in the local paper. And while the number of possibilities was smaller than in years past, eventually Melanie's search paid off. She interviewed for another job and was made an offer at less pay, which she quickly accepted.

Melanie's boss was flabbergasted. Ted had no idea she was any more unhappy about her job than any of the other survivors. And for her to leave abruptly after he had bent over backward to make sure she wasn't laid off was simply ingratitude. Ted thought that what he and the other managers had done to protect Melanie from a layoff was a marvelous act of allegiance to employees.

QUESTIONS

1. Did Ted and the other managers do Melanie any favors by protecting her from a layoff?

2. What did Melanie suffer from? What should Ted and the other managers have done to encourage Melanie to communicate her frustrations?

3. How might job analysis have prevented Melanie's defection?

4. In terms of job analysis, what steps should Ted have taken to rescue the survivors, such as Melanie, following the restructuring?

1. Writing Job Descriptions

PURPOSE

To conduct a brief job analysis and to create a job description.

PROCEDURE

Break the class into small groups of four or five each. Each group must include at least one student who is currently employed or has recently been employed.

THE TASK

Using the information in this chapter, group members will perform a perfunctory job analysis with the student concerning his or her job. Once the job analysis has been performed, write a job description for that job. Be sure that your job description conforms to the characteristics of good job descriptions discussed in this chapter. Once the assignment has been finished, your instructor will lead a discussion concerning each group's job analysis and job description.

2. Job Analysis for Recruiting

The job analysis is the foundation for a number of important activities. One of the most important is recruiting. Information gathered about a job can provide a solid foundation regarding specific openings. When designed with recruiting in mind, the job description can serve as a road map detailing who the candidate is and where you can look for the best people. This exercise is designed to give students a chance to search for the unique, detailed information necessary for attracting the best people in today's recruitment marketplace.

Form teams of four or more. Contact an HR representative in a nearby company and request an interview with any person whose position is being advertised. It is important to talk with a person who is most familiar with the open position—not necessarily the hiring HR officer or even the manager because they may be too far removed from the position to have an accurate idea of what this person will be doing from day to day.

The first question addresses the position title, duties, and description of an average workweek. This information is useful but, for recruitment purposes, hardly enough to sell an applicant. Request information on the salary range, including all bonuses, perks, and company benefits. Be prepared for refusals because compensation is a sensitive issue (but there is no harm in asking).

Second, request recruiting information, including the background of the ideal candidate, what level of education is necessary, how much experience is needed, what kind of person best fits the job, and where the best applicant might be found (industries, companies, departments within those companies, big or small businesses, etc.).

Third, what are the long-term opportunities for the applicant? Why would someone who is happily and securely employed leave his or her job and come to work here? Are there any negative aspects of the job? What happened to the previous people holding this position? Depending on the answers, this may be the most important recruiting information for persuading an applicant to work here.

Finally, ask the person what types of questions (with answers that require knowledge, skill, or experience regarding the open position) may be asked of the applicant fairly early in the selection process. In technical fields this is a critical stage because it will help the HR staff decrease the interview-to-hire ratio and the time spent with unqualified applicants.

After gathering all of this information, the team will present its findings to the class. The team should be prepared for questions from the instructor and other students.

KEY TERMS AND CONCEPTS

ADA
Critical incident technique (CIT)
Dictionary of Occupational Titles (DOT)
Elastic clauses
Functional job analysis (FJA)
Job analysis
Job classification
Job descriptions

Job evaluation
Job specifications
Position Analysis Questionnaire (PAQ)
Skills, knowledge, ability (SKAs)
Task Inventory/Comprehensive Occupational Data Analysis Program (TI/CODAP)
Verifiable qualifications

REVIEW QUESTIONS

1. Define the practical relationship among job analysis, job descriptions, and job specifications.

2. What information is necessary to develop job descriptions? What are some of the qualities of a well-constructed job description?

3. How can a firm benefit from having a complete and accurate system of job descriptions and job specifications?

4. Outline the advantages and disadvantages of the various methods of job analysis.

5. How do governmental influences affect the process of job analysis?

6. If an organization has no formal system of job analysis, how might the objectives of job analysis be obtained?

DISCUSSION QUESTIONS

1. If you were an HR specialist in a company that was introducing job analysis, how would you reassure employees who felt threatened?

2. When faced with the problem of updating job analysis information, would you favor an annual review or reclassification? Explain why.

3. Describe the methods you would use to gather job information in a bank, a small manufacturing firm, or a newspaper.

4. Discuss how job analysis could or could not resolve the following problems: (a) an employee who produces less than others doing the same job; (b) an employee who complains about a dirty work environment; (c) an employee who feels passed over when promotions are announced.

5. As an HR manager, you must describe job analysis to employees. Which ideas would you stress for blue-collar workers? For white-collar workers?

6. Assume that you are the director of a medium-sized HR department and happen to be attending a staff meeting with all the department heads and the CEO. During the meeting, suppose that a manager from the manufacturing division suddenly and forcefully starts criticizing the need for job descriptions of managers. He says that they reflect a set of static, predetermined duties created by management and evaluated by the HR department, which also assigns salary levels to them based on the number of people he supervised. He goes on to say that these job descriptions tend to be snapshots of what is needed at a particular point in time. He points out a few that he says have been frozen in place, even as technological advances and competitive challenges occur. You have heard his criticisms and note that the CEO is now looking to you to respond to his comments. Are job descriptions unnecessary? If so, what would take their place?

7. How would an HR professional define and determine the essential functions of a job in accordance with the ADA?

ENDNOTES

Chapter 4

1. Robert J. Sahl, "Pressing New Reasons for Accurate Job Descriptions," *The Human Resources Professional* (Fall 1992): 18.

2. "Uniform Guidelines on Employee Selection Procedures," *Federal Register* (August 25, 1978): 38302, 38306.

3. T. M. Stutzman, "Within Classification Job Differences," *Personnel Psychology* 36 (1983): 503–16.

4. Edward C. Brett and Charles M. Canning, "Job Evaluation and Your Organization: An Ideal Relationship?" *Personnel Administrator* 29, no. 4 (April 1984): 115–24.

5. U.S. Department of Labor, Manpower Administration, *Handbook for Analyzing Jobs* (Washington, DC: U.S. Government Printing Office, 1972), pp. 340–51.

6. Alex Carey, "The Hawthorne Studies: A Radical Criticism," *American Sociological Review* 32, no. 3 (1967): 403–16.

7. W. H. Weiss, "How to Work-Sample Your People," *Administrative Management* (June 14, 1982): 37–38, 49–50.

8. E. L. Levine et al., "Evaluation of Job Analysis Methods by Experienced Job Analysts," *Academy of Management Journal* 26 (1983): 339–48.

9. "Uniform Guidelines," pp. 38304, 38306.

10. P. Geyer, J. Hice, K. Hawk, R. Boese, and Y. Brannon, "Reliabilities of Ratings Available from the Dictionary of Occupational Titles," *Personnel Psychology* 42 (1989): 547–60.

11. Ernest J. McCormick, Paul J. Jeanneret, and Robert C. Mecham, "A Study of Job Characteristics and Job Dimensions As Based on the Position Analysis Questionnaire (PAQ)," *Journal of Applied Psychology* (August 1972): 347–68.

12. R. D. Arvey et al., "Narrative Job Descriptions As Potential Sources of Job Analysis Ratings," *Personnel Psychology* 35 (1982): 618–29.

13. John Flanagan, "The Critical Incident Technique," *Psychological Bulletin* 51 (1954): 327–58.

14. R. D. Gatewood and H. S. Feild, *Human Resource Selection* (Hinsdale, IL: Dryden, 1987).

15. Sidney A. Fine and Wretha Wiley, *An Introduction to Functional Job Analysis: A Scaling of Selected Tasks from the Social Welfare Field*, Methods for Manpower Analysis no. 4 (Kalamazoo, MI: Upjohn Institute for Employment Research, 1979), pp. 3–20.

16. R. Christal, "The United States Air Force Occupational Research Project," *JSAS Catalog of Selected Documents in Psychology* Vol. 4 (Manuscript no. 651, 1974), p. 61.

17. Philip Grant, "What Use Is a Job Description?" *Personnel Journal* 67, no. 2 (February 1988): 45–53.

18. E. James Brennan, "Job Descriptions and Pay: The Inevitable Link," *Personnel Journal* 63, no. 7 (July 1984):

19. Grant, "What Use Is a Job Description?" pp. 48–49.

20. David Gold and Beth Unger, "Written Job Description Not Only Factor for ADA," *HRNews/Society for Human Resource Management*, (January 1992): A5; also Kenneth Pritchard, "Job Analysis Is the Key to ADA Compliance," *HRNews/Society for Human Resource Management* (June 1992): A8.

21. Ibid.

22. Mark A. Jones, "Job Descriptions Made Easy," *Personnel Journal* 63, no. 5 (May 1984): 31–34.

23. Ibid.

JOB DESIGN

CHAPTER OBJECTIVES

1. To be aware of the dramatic changes occurring in most corporations and their effect on the design of work.

2. To recognize that old industrial models of job design, while achieving efficiency and control, may occur at a very high human price.

3. To understand how the design of a job affects employee motivation and performance.

4. To show various methods of designing motivating jobs.

5. To understand how motivating jobs can be created by building work teams.

6. To become aware of radically new organizational programs such as TQM and reengineering.

7. To learn why the office environment cannot be left to chance.

8. To review the many alternatives to work scheduling that better optimize human and organizational needs.

Work has changed relentlessly from nineteenth-century factories. Established systems of mass production, which once could be counted on to last for decades, now last only for years.[1] For example, on numerous occasions, GM attempted to cut its labor costs—generally by using robots to replace the human work. But the effort did little to reduce the cost of production, and GM's market share continued to decline.[2] Recent history of GM suggests that only dramatic changes can save conventional companies operating in chaotic industries.

Traditional factory work was packaged into clusters called jobs. After two hundred years, the world of work is changing again, perhaps more radically than ever before. New models of working together are emerging, thanks to technology, fast-moving economies, part-time and temporary work situations, and project teams.

Fast-moving organizations, like Motorola, will likely hire a person, assign her to a project, and when the project changes (as most do), the person's responsibilities and tasks change with it. Then the person will probably be assigned another project (well before the first project is finished), and then maybe another. This person can expect to work under several team leaders (at the same time), being in various places, and performing a number of different tasks.

Look for the eight hour job to vanish. Work will be governed partly by the demands of the task and partly by other economic factors. For example, the availability of technological linkages through Video Conferencing via desktop machines will significantly increase the number of face-to-face interactions in daily work even when the individuals "meeting" are thousands of miles apart (see *HR in the News:* "Groupware Beware"!). All the experts agree, tomorrow's worker will be far more independent and self-directed than today's.

OLD PARADIGMS

In the old industrial paradigm—laid out by Adam Smith, Frederick Taylor, and Henry Ford—success was based on efficiency and economies of scale, not quality or customer service.[3] Companies were organized by function—sales, manufacturing, finance, marketing, and the like. Complex work was broken down into simple, repetitive tasks that were performed in sequence by specialists until the good or service was delivered to the customer. The primary job of supervisors was to control the quantity, quality, and cost of the work performed. Creativity and flexibility were insignificant goals. And there certainly was no emphasis on adaptability.

Old habits are hard to break, however. Industrial methods, such as scientific management, for managing labor took deep root in North America's manufacturing sectors.[4] For example, the US. automotive industry prior to the 1980s concentrated on designing

Groupware Beware!

When Tom Jacobs walks into his office, located in his Hollywood home, the first thing he does is check his PC for E-mail messages that may have come in from Europe during the night. Being on the West Coast, there is a nine hour time difference between his office and the one in Vienna, Austria. The only opportunity he has to communicate by phone is when his Austrian colleagues stay late, which is not a common occurrence. In the old days this job would have been impossible; now it's simply challenging.

On any given day Tom will have dozens of E-mail messages awaiting him—not surprising, since Tom is in charge of his company's North American distribution of U.S.-made movies to Europe. A few of the messages demand immediate responses, which he quickly handles. The others he will address later. But Tom is just getting started on his computer. He snaps his mouse on a particular icon, and instantly he sees various articles on topics about the film industry. His computer has standing orders to track topics from various data bases, and Tom takes a few minutes to catch up on current events in his industry. He spots two articles that he wants his London staff to read and quickly sends them electronically.

His company invested in "groupware." While most computer software has been written for people working alone, groupware programs make it easier for groups to work together *through a PC network*. By giving employees access to information previously unavailable or restricted to top management, groupware spreads information power far more widely than before. Where E-mail focused on person-to-person, groupware permits many-to-many.

Employees within his company, including the far-flung Paris staff, have access to these same groupware electronic boards—thanks to satellite communication technology and software programs such as Lotus Notes. Tom calls up one board that holds messages about doing business in DC. A Washington lobbyist his company employs reports on an upcoming Congressional hearing regarding proposed French tariffs on American-made films. Tom has some thoughts about that and quickly sends an E-mail message to the lobbyist. The system will coordinate colleagues' electronic datebooks and figure out when he and the lobbyist can get together—not an easy thing to do when one colleague is three time zones away. Tom is also hoping that other employees will check into this board and take an interest in the subject, creating a kind of corporate Internet of the office.

From the moment he turns on his computer, Tom is helping to define the future of corporate computing. He is also defining the way work is already being performed. Office or home, individual contributor or team player, Los Angeles or Paris, networking is making computers more and more interpersonal. Thanks to global communication technologies, the world is getting smaller while the employee is getting more powerful.

low-skilled, assembly-line, "idiot-proof" jobs that required a minimum of training and individual decision making. It is important to note that the old industrial model worked then and, under certain conditions, will continue to function. It created a highly centralized, structured, and efficient system that enabled companies to raise productivity and lower costs. Understandably, many companies continue to design work with this model in mind.

But, while efficiency and control clearly have a place, they come at a human cost. Employee job dissatisfaction, absenteeism, and turnover—factors that can make a great difference in a competitive, labor-intensive industry—tend to be high. And in a world where companies are forced to continually reinvent themselves, nineteenth-century paradigms are woefully out of date in certain industries because they do not allow for worker initiative or problem solving.

Old paradigms, such as scientific management, are still practiced throughout North America and in many developing countries. A few experts even caution against premature dismissal of Taylor's ideas.[5] Scientific management fueled the engine that dominated the industrial world for most of this century. In its philosophy lay the secret for making money—efficiency and control—at least until the Japanese entered the picture in the late 1970s.

Manufacturers in the United States had few economic rivals following World War II. Flush with success after success, U.S. companies concentrated on producing as much as they could as quickly as possible, with little regard to quality. The tactic paid huge dividends in a world of war-ravaged competitors and eager consumers. Eventually that tactic backfired when the Japanese, using such methods as flexible manufacturing and lean production, started producing high-quality, low-cost products.[6] In a quest for global competitiveness, U.S. companies began—called by various names—restructuring, reengineering, delayering, downsizing, rightsizing, and decruiting.

The result has been many changes in job design. Not only are companies moving toward quality and customer satisfaction, they are empowering their employees to make decisions that only their bosses once made. There will be closer links not only between management and employee, but also between producer and supplier and between company and customer. All of these changes have been made possible by the explosive growth in information technology. This chapter will examine several approaches that organizations might follow in their efforts to foster productivity and quality improvements.

The success of any organization depends on its employees. No job, regardless of its design, can overcome an employee's lack of interest or willingness. If the employee doesn't care about his or her job, then no effort will be exerted, and nothing else matters—*not even a boss who cracks a whip*. Motivation is the engine for driving the human resource and the foundation of job design.

MOTIVATION

Many HR managers have theories regarding the motivation of employees' performance. Some believe that only one motivational theory is enough to develop productive employees. Others may claim that no technique works because employees are born either achievers or loafers. Undoubtedly, no single theory will address all motivational problems; however, something can be learned from each theory.

Maslow's Hierarchy of Needs

Perhaps the most intuitively appealing theory for HR professionals today is Abraham **Maslow's hierarchy of needs**. According to Maslow, when a need occurs, motivational tension develops and is directed toward satisfaction of the felt need. The intensity of the effort is a function of how strong the need is.[7]

The hierarchy comprises five levels of needs (see Figure 5-1). *Physiological needs* are the primary needs for food, shelter, and clothing that can be directly satisfied by compensation; employees who are adequately paid can provide for their basic needs.

Once the physiological needs have been satisfied, the safety or *security needs* become a motivational factor. Many employees' most important security need is job security. Other security factors include increases in salary and benefits.

On the third level are *social needs*. At this level, employees desire social relationships inside and outside the organization. Peer group acceptance within the work force is often an important psychological need for employees.

Once employees have formed friendships within the organization and feel a part of the peer group, the *need for self-esteem* takes precedence. Organizational factors such as job title, status items within the organization such as parking spaces or office size, and level of responsibility become important to the employee.

Finally, the highest need is *self-actualization*. At this level, employees seek a fulfilling, useful life in the organization and in society. Employees seek challenging and creative jobs to achieve self-actualization. Maslow contends that individuals will climb the ladder of need fulfillment until they have become self-actualized. If any need is not fulfilled, the individual will continually strive to fill that need, that is, the need becomes a motivational factor. At any level, needs may be fulfilled outside the organization as well as within the organization.

Alderfer's ERG Theory

Closely related to Maslow's hierarchy of needs is C. P. **Alderfer's ERG** theory (existence, relatedness, and growth), especially in terms of the needs included.[8] Differences do exist, how-

ever. Alderfer proposes that when one need is frustrated, we simply concentrate on the others. For instance, if the way a task is designed deprives the worker of all forms of casual conversation, then that worker may tend to want more money. Thus, the theory does seem to offer a plausible explanation for what may seem like greedy pay demands or petty demands for changes in working practices.

Goal Setting

Research has shown that job performance can be increased through **goal setting**—when individuals are given measurable goals rather than vague performance standards. Another conclusion is that when individuals are given specific goals that they perceive to be difficult but reasonable, the result will be higher performance.[9]

The best-known expression of goal setting theory is management by objectives (MBO).

Basically, goal-setting strategies involve a systematic process whereby the manager and subordinate discuss and agree on a set of jointly determined goals. With proper preparation, each party should be able to present a case for or against each goal. If the process is functioning effectively, the final result will be a set of goals that is in keeping with the overall goals of the organization. Moreover, the manager will have something concrete on which to gauge the subordinate's performance. Feedback on progress is periodically supplied, enabling the worker to make necessary corrections. Above all, the link between performance and rewards is made explicitly clear to the subordinate, with emphasis on *what* was achieved rather than on *how* it was accomplished or how hard the subordinate tried to meet the goals.

Positive Reinforcement

The concept of **positive reinforcement** is central to most motivation techniques. It is the practice of giving valued rewards to someone who has just engaged in a desired behavior.

FIGURE 5-1 HR practices that satisfy various levels of human needs in Maslow's Hierarchy.

Physical Needs

1. Furnish pleasant and comfortable environment.
2. Provide for ample leisure.
3. Provide for "comfortable" salary.

Security Needs

1. Adhere to protective rules and regulations.
2. Minimize risk-taking requirements.
3. Provide strong directive leadership and follow chain of command policy.
4. Provide well-defined job descriptions.
5. Minimize negative stroking and threatening behavior.
6. Provide information about firm's financial status and projections.
7. Provide "just" compensation and supportive fringe benefits.

Social Needs

1. Encourage the team concept.
2. Systematically use organizationwide feedback survey.
3. Use task groups to execute projects.
4. Provide for firm and/or office business and social meetings.
5. Provide close personal leadership.
6. Encourage professional-group participation.
7. Encourage community-group participation.
8. Compensate on basis of total team performance.

Self-Esteem Needs

1. Include employees in goal-setting and decision-making processes.
2. Provide opportunity to display skills and talents.
3. Provide recognition of advancement—e.g., publicize promotions
4. Provide recognition symbols—e.g., name on stationery.
5. Assign associates and support staff for coaching and development.
6. Provide personal secretary to associates.
7. Use positive-reinforcement program.
8. Pay attention to office size, office location, parking spaces, etc.
9. Institute mentor system.
10. Compensate as recognition of growth.

Self-Actualization Needs

1. Provide for participation in goal-setting and decision-making processes.
2. Provide opportunity and support for career-development plan.
3. Provide staff job rotation to broaden experience and exposure.
4. Offer optimum innovative and risk-taking opportunities.
5. Encourage direct-access communication to clients, customers, suppliers, vendors, etc.
6. Provide challenging internal and external professional development opportunities.
7. Provide supportive leadership that encourages a high degree of self-control.
8. Compensate as reward for exceptional performance.

SOURCE: Norbert F. Elbert and Richard Discenza, *Contemporary Supervision* (New York: McGraw-Hill, Inc. 1985), pp. 81-82. Used by permission.

The technique is based on the **law of effect**, which means that behavior that leads to a pleasant response will be repeated, whereas behavior that results in an unpleasant response tends not to be repeated.[10] Reinforcement is at the heart of merit increases. In order for reinforcement to continue to affect employees' future behavior, a manager must make certain that rewards are meaningful and desired by each employee.[11] As Maslow points out, each employee's needs are different; therefore, the manager must tailor the reward, whether it be recognition, pay, or changing job requirements, to fit the employee. In addition, the manager must be sure that employees realize that rewards are contingent on correct behavior.

Herzberg's Two-Factor Theory of Motivation

Perhaps one of the most interesting, and controversial, theories is Frederick Herzberg's concept of motivator-hygiene factors.[12] Whereas Maslow applied the hierarchy of needs theory to motivation in general, Herzberg applied his specifically to the workplace and job design. After asking a large number of accountants and engineers about their feelings toward their jobs, Herzberg noticed that respondents identified different things as sources of work dissatisfaction—subsequently called *hygiene*—than they did as sources of satisfaction—which he called *motivators*. Herzberg concluded that satisfaction and dissatisfaction were not simple opposites.

Poor working conditions resulted in dissatisfaction, yet ideal working conditions did not necessarily lead to satisfaction or motivation. Herzberg referred to the factors that prevented dissatisfaction as *hygiene factors*. He reasoned—by analogy—that a town's poor sewage system will lead to greater health problems for its citizenry; however, a good sewage system does not ensure that the users will be free of disease and ill health. The same principle holds for job design, he concluded.

Hygiene factors, such as salary and working conditions (see Figure 5-2) reflect the **context** of the job. They are external to the employee and to the job. For this reason, they can be thought of as extrinsic conditions. In other words, they are factors that are essentially controlled by someone other than the employee. Herzberg contends that hygiene factors are difficult to control effectively, and, more important, they do not provide long-run motivation. But they are necessary for preventing dissatisfaction, and their absence keeps the employee from concentrating on higher-level needs. Hygiene factors may include attendance rules, vacation schedules, grievance and performance appraisal procedures, noise levels, customer and co-worker relations, and hourly wages. Herzberg argues that none of these factors will motivate people.

Furthermore, the two-factor theory states, the more resources that are poured down the hygiene drain (e.g., by increasing fringe benefits), the more resources will be required in the future because, with hygiene factors, ever-increasing amounts are needed to produce the same effect. Indeed, this argument makes sense when considering how salary issues never appear to be resolved (e.g., who has not heard of workers' discontent over wages even after concluding salary negotiations?).

Motivators are intrinsic in nature. They reflect the **content** of the job. No superior dispenses them to employees; instead, each employee controls and administers them personally. No one can give another person the satisfaction that comes from accomplishing a particularly challenging job.

The two-factor theory has received a great deal of attention and criticism. Legitimate questions have been raised regarding the theory's methodology, as well as about the confusing relationship between satisfaction and motivation. Nevertheless, managers should

FIGURE 5-2 Herzberg's theory: factors affecting job satisfaction.

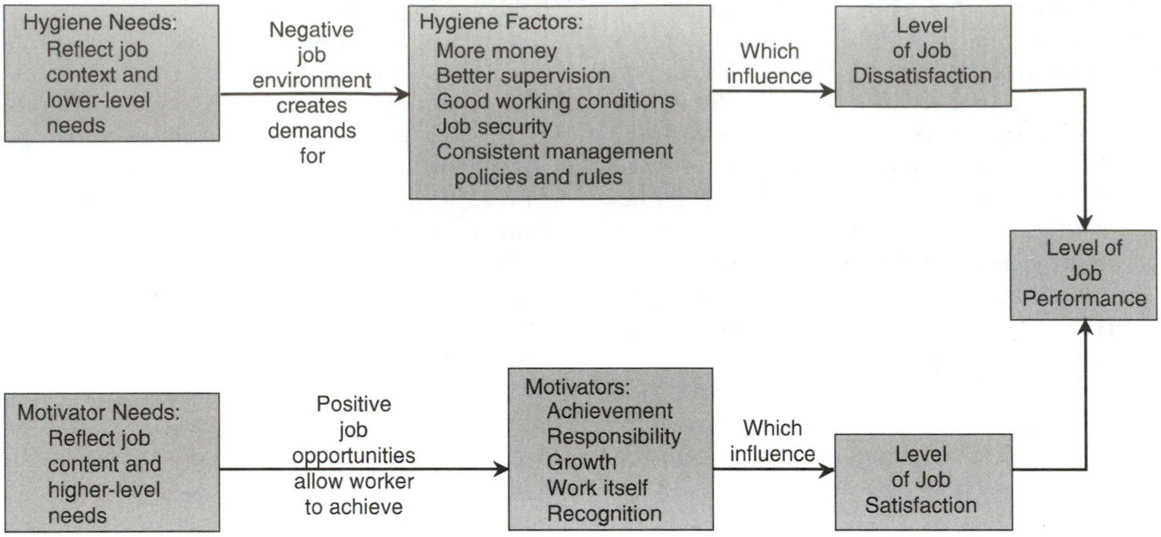

pause and consider the questions the theory raises. For example, are attempts to use money to motivate effective? Are an organization's precious resources effectively used when they are pumped into such hygiene factors as fancy lounges for breaks, expensive office furniture, or business-class air travel? Experts do agree, however, that the two-factor theory provides guidance for building motivators into job content, an approach called **job enrichment**.

The Great Debate: For Love or Money

There is an intense academic debate over the roots of human motivation. The behaviorists, including noted psychologists such as the late B. F. Skinner, believe that human behavior is the product of consequences. They promote the liberal use of positive reinforcers, including raises, promotions, bonuses, and prizes, as incentives for improving performance. American industry, no doubt, has listened to their ideas and techniques.

At the other extreme is a group that might be labeled antibehaviorists, including such noted psychologists as Frederick Herzberg. They believe that monetary rewards will not bring employees' happiness and may even work against the employer who uses them. How might incentives such as a bonus become a negative motivator?

The risk occurs when the task itself takes on secondary importance to the incentive, becoming almost a chore, something one has to get through in order to win the prize (e.g., a bonus). Herzberg has argued for years that monetary incentives, even when they work, work only over the short term. Who would not get excited about a trip to Hawaii for winning a sales contest? But over time, Herzberg claims, the most successful salespeople will grow tired of trips to Waikiki Beach and require a motive closer to their sense of themselves or lose their spark altogether.

Behaviorists offer a number of rebuttals, but their most persuasive argument is that money can mean many things to many people. Certainly, the monetary motivation is a compli-

"Well . . . on the Other Hand . . ."

An interesting story, if true, is that Herzberg, while negotiating over a lecture fee on why pay motivation doesn't work, suddenly had the tables turned. A perceptive business agent, who had obviously done his homework and was familiar with Herzberg's point of view, politely pointed out that the lower offer ought to stand because "after all, money doesn't motivate, so why haggle over it?"

"Money in fact doesn't motivate me," Herzberg said without embarrassment, "but it sure as hell helps me sort out my priorities."

---

cated process. Issues such as how much money it takes to excite someone or whether the desired results are measurable influence money motivation performance.

Antibehaviorists prefer natural rewards. Give each person a chance to do his or her best, they say, find ways for them to work in teams, give them variety and a sense of worthwhile work, and give them as much choice as possible in what they do and how they do it. This argument seem simple, but critics argue that even when the new job designs are in place and seem to be working, they are still tied to other motivators that include money.

What is the answer? How successful is the pay increase in solving motivational problems? The answer of most HR professionals is "not very." Much of the answer has to do with the mechanics and less with what money means as an extrinsic motivator. Perhaps it is useful to remember that different situations produce different motivational requirements. Thus, the best path for managers to take depends on a balance of both types of rewards—natural and extrinsic. Even Herzberg would agree; see *HR in the News:* "Well . . . on the Other Hand . . ."

DESIGNING JOBS

Two of the most important concerns of HR managers are employee productivity and job satisfaction. A critical factor affecting these areas is the type of work performed by the employee. Job design determines how work is performed and, therefore, greatly affects how an employee feels about a job, how much authority an employee has over the work, how much decision making the employee performs on the job, and how many tasks the employee should complete. Managers realize that job design determines both their working relationship with their employees and the relationship among the employees themselves. Job design determines the nature of social relationships that exist on the job, as well as the relationship between the employee and the work.

Job design is the manipulation of the content, functions, and relationships of jobs in a way that both accomplishes organizational purposes and satisfies the personal needs of individual job holders.[13] The content of a job encompasses the variety of tasks performed, the autonomy of the job holder, the routineness of tasks performed, the difficulty of the tasks performed, and the identity of the job

211

FIGURE 5-3 A framework for job design.

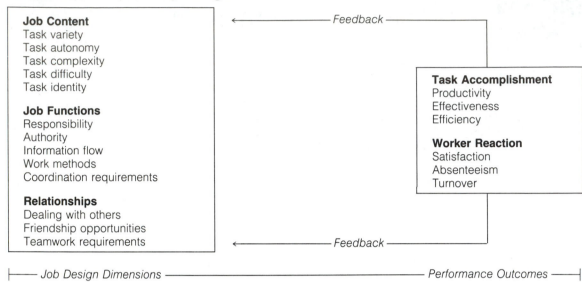

SOURCE: *Organizational Behavior and Performance*, 2d ed., by Andrew D. Szilagyi and Marc J. Wallace (p. 149). Copyright © 1980 by Goodyear Publishing Company. Reprinted by permission.

holder, or the extent to which the whole job is performed by the person involved.[14] The functions of a job encompass the work methods utilized, as well as the coordination of the work, responsibility, information flow, and authority of the job. The relationships of a job encompass the work activities shared by the job holder and other individuals in the organization.[15]

Figure 5-3 shows the importance of job design to both the worker and the organization. The design determines the way in which and the extent to which tasks are accomplished by a job holder. At stake is a worker's satisfaction with the job situation—that is, the work itself. A worker's favorable reaction to job design means greater accomplishment, greater job satisfaction, less absenteeism, fewer grievances, and less turnover.

How should jobs be designed? This topic has been discussed widely since the Industrial Revolution. Traditional approaches to job design have been seriously questioned in recent years. Some job design problems in the last

twenty-five years have been the result of workers' increasing dissatisfaction with jobs designed for robots or mindless machines. Henry Ford's assembly line is an excellent example of the job design method known as *job specialization.*

Specialization-Intensive Jobs

Job specialization is characterized by jobs with very few tasks, tasks that are repeated often during the workday and require few skills and little mental ability. These are called **specialization-intensive jobs**. Job specialization was the primary component of the scientific management developed by Frederick Taylor, who described management's role in job design as a three-step process:[16]

1. The manager determines the one best way of performing the job.

2. The manager hires individuals according to their abilities, which must match the needs of the job design. For example, a strong per-

son is hired to carry heavy loads and a diligent person is hired to file records.

3. Management trains workers in the one best way the job should be performed. All planning, organizing, and control of the job are done by the manager.

Scientific management, which for many years was quite popular in the United States, has many advantages. First, management can hire unskilled labor for almost all operative jobs in the organization. Since highly specialized jobs are designed for people with very few skills or experience, most members of the work force can perform most of the lower-level jobs in a company. Second, unskilled workers are among the lowest-paid members of the work force. This was particularly true in the early 1900s, when unskilled workers were moving from agricultural areas to industrial centers and few unions protected them. Third, workers tend to make very few errors when performing simple, routine jobs. There are very few chances for mental errors, since managers organize the work flow so that the employee makes few decisions. Fourth, the average cost per unit decreases as jobs become highly specialized. As Henry Ford discovered, it is far more cost efficient to build cars on an assembly line where workers are trained to perform one or two routine tasks than to hire engineers or mechanics to assemble a complete automobile. This principle of reduced average cost per labor-dollar spent has long motivated industrial engineers to design highly specialized jobs.

At United Parcel Service (UPS), the principles of scientific management are clearly evident—even at the close of the twentieth century. Most of the work is routine, repetitive, and easy to learn. The supervision can only be described as tight. Front-line employees are typically part-time workers, many of them college students, who earn wages ranging from $8 to $15 per hour, plus generous benefits. There are no applicant shortages. In fact, many of the part-timers are long-term employees. One reason is job security. Another reason is UPS's policy of giving preferential treatment to internal candidates applying for management openings.

The industrial engineers at UPS continue to devise efficient systems of work simplification and work standardization, including sorting packages and loading/unloading delivery vehicles and cargo planes. The company is profitable and growing. Productivity and customer service are rated high. And—what may surprise a few people—employee absenteeism and turnover are not problems.

The Problem of Overspecialization Job specialization evolved from a preoccupation with command and control systems. Jobs are narrowly designed to achieve standardization, simplification, and division of labor. Maximum efficiency is the goal. There is no doubt that specialization offers economic benefits, especially when there is an abundant supply of unskilled labor.[17] Why, then, are many organizations dropping specialization and redesigning work around human needs?

The answer is found in overspecialization—or going to extremes. It is a frequently cited reason for workers feeling alienated from work and their bosses. Overspecialization hampers what people can do in several ways.[18]

Repetition Employees performing only a few tasks, which must be repeated many times during a work shift, will quickly become bored. Most people need to be stimulated and challenged.

Mechanical Pacing Employees who are restricted by an assembly line, and required to maintain a certain pace of work, will soon divert their attention to anything other than the task at hand. Identifying the optimum pace is not easy, however; what is just right for one may be too fast for another.

No End Product Overspecialization makes it difficult for employees to identify the end product. Consequently, they will have little pride in and enthusiasm for their work.

Little Social Interaction Employees will complain that because the assembly line requires constant attention, there is little chance to interact on a casual basis with co-workers. This makes it difficult for employees to develop significant social bonding at work.

No Input Employees tend to complain that they have little chance to determine how they perform their jobs, the tools they use, or their work procedures. The lack of personal control creates a lack of interest in the job because there is nothing they can improve or change.

Job Dimensions   The degree to which a job is highly specialized can be determined by measuring two dimensions of the job, scope and depth. The first dimension is **job scope**— how long it takes a worker to complete the total task. For example, an assembly line worker in an early Ford plant might have taken five minutes to add a wiring harness to an automobile as it moved down the assembly line. After the wiring harness was added to one automobile, the worker had five minutes to add a harness to the next car. Thus, the scope of the job, or the job cycle, was five minutes.

The second dimension measured to determine the degree of specialization is **job depth**. This dimension is more difficult to determine because it cannot be measured in easily identifiable terms. *Depth* refers to how much planning, decision making, and controlling the worker does in the total job. For example, to what extent can a worker vary the methods utilized on the job? How many decisions can the worker make without supervisory approval? If various techniques and tools are determined solely by management, the job is said to have very little depth. At the other end of

the continuum, a job in which a worker performs independently has great depth, or a great deal of autonomy.

Motivation-Intensive Jobs
Modern management has found that the increased cost of employee absenteeism and turnover, as well as the decreased productivity and quality, may outweigh the advantages of highly specialized jobs. The challenge is to balance the employees' human needs and the employer's economic goals. Table 5-1 shows the advantages of each of the two approaches to job design.

The category referred to as **motivation-intensive jobs** includes a broad range of approaches. Job rotation, enlargement, enrichment, and work teams represent a variety of methods for rearranging work in a way that creates enough interest to motivate workers yet simple enough for most members to perform. The more specialized a job, the lower the likelihood that the worker will find it motivating. When this happens, HR professionals must identify other means for motivating employees, usually by rearranging work schedules in ways that better optimize employees' needs and staffing requirements.

Job Rotation
Another technique designed to enhance employee motivation is **job rotation**, or periodically assigning employees to alternating jobs or tasks. For example, an employee may spend two weeks attaching bumpers to vehicles and the following two weeks making final checks of the chassis. During the next month, the same employee may be assigned to two different jobs. Therefore, the employee would be rotated among four jobs. The advantage of job rotation is that employees do not have the same routine job day after day.

Does job rotation solve the problem of boringly repetitive jobs? No. Job rotation only

Table 5-1 Advantages of the Major Approaches to Design

Specialization-Intensive Jobs	Motivation-Intensive Jobs
High productivity of unskilled workers	High productivity of challenged workers
Less training time required	Less absenteeism
Easy to replace workers	Less turnover
Few mental work errors	Higher product quality
Greater manager control of operations	More employee ideas, suggestions
	Greater employee job satisfaction

addresses the problem of assigning employees to jobs of limited scope; the depth of the job does not change. The job cycle of the actual daily work performed has not been lengthened or changed. Instead, employees are simply assigned to different jobs with different cycles.

Because job rotation does not change the basic nature of jobs, it is criticized as nothing more than having an employee perform several boring and monotonous jobs rather than one. Some employees dislike job rotation more than being assigned to one boring job because when they are assigned to one job they know exactly where to report and what work to expect each day. Workers quickly realize that job rotation does not increase their interest in their work.

Why, then, is job rotation still common practice? Although it seldom addresses the lack of employee motivation, it does give managers a means of coping with frequent absenteeism and high turnover. Thus, when absenteeism or turnover occurs in the work force, managers can quickly fill the vacated position because each employee can perform several jobs.

Job rotation is often effectively used as a training technique for new, inexperienced employees. At higher organizational levels, rotation also helps develop managerial generalists because it exposes them to several different operations.[19]

Job Enlargement

Another means of increasing employees' satisfaction with routine jobs is **job enlargement**, or increasing the number of tasks performed (i.e., increasing the scope of the job). Job enlargement, like job rotation, tries to eliminate short job cycles that create boredom. Unlike job rotation, job enlargement actually increases the job cycle. When a job is enlarged, either the tasks being performed are enlarged or several short tasks are given to one worker. Thus, the scope of the job is increased because there are many tasks to be performed by the same worker. Job enlargement programs change many methods of operation—in contrast to job rotation, in which the same work procedures are used by workers who rotate through work stations. Although job enlargement actually changes the pace of the work and the operation by reallocating tasks and responsibilities, it does not increase the depth of a job.

The focus of designing work for job enlargement is the exact opposite of that for job specialization. Instead of designing jobs to be divided up into the fewest number of tasks per employee, a job is designed to have many tasks for the employee to perform. An enlarged job requires a longer training period because there are more tasks to be learned. Worker satisfaction should increase because boredom is reduced as the job scope is expanded. However,

Tuesday Afternoon

Dear Judith,

As usual, it's been a while between letters. But, I have to say, I don't think that much new has happened. I'm terribly bored at work. I mean, I have absolutely no motivation. For the past week and a half my boss has been away on business. Unfortunately, he didn't really leave me with anything to do. So, I've spent the time editing a friend's manuscript for a book he's writing. That's finished, and I really should get to work developing a class for our clerks on telephone skills—after all, that's my job as a trainer—but you can just imagine how exciting that will be. Tomorrow I'll start developing it and, hopefully, be able to finish it by the end of the week. Then it will seem like I've been wrapped up in that all this time. In truth, it sounds like I have a really great job, but it's very frustrating.

I hate sitting around staring at the clock all day. You are probably asking yourself why? The answer is very simple. I have nothing to do.

Last week I asked my boss if I could have off Tuesday, since Monday I had nothing to do (I didn't tell him that part). Only one problem: If I don't work, I don't get paid. It becomes a very expensive proposition to take time off. There is so little work for me here that I wonder if I will remember how to really work when I get another job. All this leads me to believe that I should look for another job come January, but (1) the job market is so bad, (2) job hunting stinks, (3) this company has great benefits including automatic six weeks' vacation, (4) the money is good, (5) wedding plans take precedence.

I guess I've decided to hold off looking until after I'm back from my honeymoon. (That is, if this job becomes a staff position in January, for there is always the chance that it will be eliminated and I won't have any job at all.)

The pathetic thing is, they all think I do so much more than the woman who had the job before me for six years. I do nothing, and I do more than her! What did she do—come in and sleep? Anyway, I guess I shouldn't be complaining. I'm sure a lot of people would think I have it great as a trainer: they pay me a fortune, and I don't have to work. But it's really very stressful.

Enough for now. See you soon.

Your friend,
Maria

SOURCE: Jason Schweizer. Used with permission.

job enlargement programs are successful only if workers are more satisfied with jobs that have increased scope; such workers are less prone to resort to absenteeism, grievances, slowdowns, and other means of displaying job dissatisfaction. Consider, for example, the employee described in *HR in the News,* "Tuesday Afternoon." This person might positively respond to an enlarged job.

An early job enlargement program at the Maytag Company is a good example of this approach. Maytag undertook fifteen job enlargement projects during a three-year period. At the conclusion, Maytag managers observed the following:[20]

- Quality of production was improved.

- Production costs were lower.

- Employees reported higher job satisfaction. They especially preferred the slower work pace that resulted from an enlarged job that did not have a repetitive cycle and that required a greater variety of skills.

- Greater efficiency arose because of reduced materials handling and the stability of production standards being met.

Although job enlargement is still considered a valid means of addressing specialization problems, it has been augmented by a more sophisticated technique known as **job enrichment**. Most modern redesign projects involve job enrichment rather than job enlargement, although the two techniques have distinctly different applications.

Job Enrichment

Organizations with employees who have high levels of knowledge and skills should consider job enrichment programs. With job enrichment, jobs are redesigned in both scope and depth. Typically, the worker decides how the job is performed, planned, and controlled and makes decisions concerning the entire process. The overall purpose is to improve a job by making it more exciting and challenging.

Job enrichment goes further than job enlargement by grouping a set of tasks of sufficient complexity to require choices (discretion) about how to bring together the varied operations and get the job done. It is usually quite comprehensive. When one job is enriched, typically the functions of supervisors and other employees are altered. For example, instead of simply feeding material into a machine, the worker with an enriched job might perform machine setup, feed the machinery, inspect the output, accept or reject the output, and, if necessary, adjust or perhaps even repair the machine. Not only are more tasks added, thus increasing *variety,* but the worker can see the process through from start to finish, what is called *task identity.* Prior to the change, the worker probably had a hard time believing that quality of workmanship really mattered; now the worker can take *responsibility* for a *significant* portion of the overall product. And by inspecting the completed product, the worker receives timely *feedback* on whether it was made properly or not.[21]

Clearly, this type of program requires a great deal of commitment and planning by top-level management, retraining of employees, and substantial changes in leadership styles from supervisors and managers. The last change is particularly difficult for managers who are accustomed to tight controls. Convincing these types of leaders to change their styles is perhaps the most critical step when implementing job enrichment programs.

Labor leaders are skeptical of job enrichment programs. Typical responses range from mild skepticism to total opposition. Such negative feelings are not completely unjustified. In the past, managers introduced programs under the guise of job enrichment that increased output standards for employees or decreased the number of jobs by increasing the work each employee performed. Since most job enrichment programs result in the employees' taking on additional responsibilities, determining whether a program will result in increased job autonomy or simply increase work loads is difficult. A well-known labor leader stated what many of his colleagues believe:[22]

> Studies tend to prove that workers' dissatisfaction diminishes with age. That's because older workers have accrued more of the kinds of job enrichment that unions have fought for—better wages, shorter hours, vested pensions, a right to have a say in the working conditions, a right to be promoted on the basis of seniority, and all the rest. That's the kind of enrichment that unions believe in.

Job enrichment programs can also be used successfully in service organizations. The First National Bank of Chicago, for example, redesigned the "paperwork assembly line" in a credit department. The 110-member department had been designed with highly specialized jobs. Tasks were fragmented for 80 percent of the employees; one person, for example, had only one task—feeding tape into a Telex machine. Over a six-month period, the employees and outside consultants totally redesigned all jobs by consolidating tasks to be performed by broadly trained workers. The employees then received training to upgrade their skills and were assigned to new, enriched jobs with 20 percent higher salaries. The result? The first year with the redesigned jobs produced the following:[23]

- Substantial increases in profits for the department ($2 million) and in total volume sales.
- Higher job satisfaction and salaries for employees.
- Improved customer relations due to the shorter credit application approval time.

Work Teams

The methods discussed to this point, scientific and motivation-intensive, reflect jobs designed for individuals. Yet job enrichment may involve organizing employees in work teams. In addition to satisfying important higher-level needs, work teams offer the potential for satisfying the individuals' social needs.

Generally, when these teams are first created, they are closely monitored by management. Ultimately, the objective is for employees to participate and assume greater job responsibilities. As the group gains experience, management tends to give them more freedom and discretion. For an example of how such teams work, see *HR in the News:* " 'Platform Teams' Bring Chrysler Back from the Brink."

If everything goes as planned, teams are empowered to manage themselves and the work they do. Controlling schedules, dividing up tasks, learning multiple jobs, and training one another are typical responsibilities of work teams. The members may even elect their own leader (usually called the *coordinator* or *facilitator* but seldom the *supervisor*), so the idea of a boss becomes almost an anachronism.[24] When teams reach this level of independence, they are referred to as **self-managed work teams** or **autonomous work groups**. Highly successful teams may even evaluate one another's job performance. If technology permits, some teams will follow the product all the way to completion (for an example of what happens when teams go beyond existing technology, see *HR in the News:* "Update on Volvo").

Members are often expected to perform, or rotate to, more than one job for the team. This is called **multiskilling** and usually involves being paid for the variety of skills mastered rather than for the job actually being performed. Motorola implemented multiskilled teams in order to solve critical quality problems with its cellular phone manufacturing process. Two major obstacles to creating multiskilled teams, however, are a rigid job classification system and union resistance. Motorola had to dissolve six pay categories at its Arlington Heights, Illinois, cellular telephone factory. Employees received pay increases only when they learned new skills and maintained the quality at their workstations at zero defects

Update on Volvo

In previous editions of this book, the Volvo AB Car Corporation's efforts to redesign the automotive assembly line were examined (i.e., "Volvo's Radical New Plant: The Death of the Assembly Line?" *Business Week,* August 28, 1989: 92–93). Volvo's management strategy at that time was clearly concentrated on attracting and retaining a work force. This approach was not unusual in socialistic societies, like Sweden's, where the country's well-trained, highly educated labor force loathed factory work.

Volvo had established a reputation as an industry leader in experimenting with new work systems. First at its Kalmar plant, which opened in 1974, and later in the ultramodern Uddevalla facility, which came onstream in 1989. At the Uddevalla facility there were no assembly lines. Cars were assembled by teams—from frame to finish. This facility was expected to avoid the decades' old problems of high worker absenteeism and turnover and lead to improved quality in its cars. Volvo hoped to avoid traditional assembly line problems, particularly alienation created by short work cycles of one or two minutes (e.g., the time it might take to attach upholstery to a car's interior)—often resulting in mind-numbing routines and worker dissatisfaction.

The Uddevalla plant revolutionized auto assembly operations. It employed teams of seven to ten hourly workers. Each team worked in one area and assembled four cars per shift. Since members were trained to handle all assembly jobs, they worked an average of three hours before repeating the same task. The goal was to produce 40,000 cars a year by 1991, significantly less than the 120,000 of an average traditional assembly operation.

Did the company succeed in attracting and retaining highly skilled workers? Yes, it did. Unfortunately, the company's efforts to create happy workers didn't improve the bottom line. Volvo, citing overcapacity, was forced to close the Uddevalla plant in 1993—only four years after its opening. Furthermore, the Kalmar plant closed in 1994. The company is letting 4500 workers go.

Only a few years ago, Sweden was regularly cited as a model society—a nearly perfect combination of economic success and social justice. But that model is slowly coming apart. Swedish unemployment has recently gone from 3 percent to 8 percent. As in most of northern Europe, generous unemployment benefits discourage work.

Ironically, the only Volvo operation still running is its oldest plant, at Torslanda, on the west coast of Sweden. It still produces cars the old-fashioned way. And while the Swedes may not like working in a factory, it does appear that the assembly line, at least, will be around for a few more years.

for five consecutive days. This arrangement worked, and defects were reduced by 77 percent.[25]

Work teams are emerging in every industry as the *primary* motivational vehicle for improving productivity and quality while lowering costs.[26] Employees tend to be more committed; they do not simply come to work and do what someone tells them to do. Instead, they have a sense of ownership. Work teams are also proving to be an essential element for organizations contemplating major restructuring, either through total quality management or reengineering strategies.

Total Quality Management

One of the fastest-growing productivity improvement programs in the United States has been **total quality management** (TQM). And why not? In today's global marketplace, only those companies that are able to deliver what customers want in terms of quality, service, and cost will prosper. What TQM can do is to ensure that an organization is committed to **continuous improvement** and to **meeting customers' needs** completely.

The idea of continuous improvement is particularly difficult for Americans, who traditionally have reacted poorly to programs geared to perfection, according to the American Quality Foundation.[27] Management's insistence on quality can lead to a sense of guilt—hardly a sensible way of motivating workers. Change is always more threatening to people when they do not control it, which is often the way it comes down from top management. When every individual understands what it means on the job, and what exactly needs to be done to achieve perfection, and that failing to do so could lead to unhappy customers, only then will continuous improvement be real.

Used correctly, the concept of quality becomes a competitive weapon. Companies that embrace quality have an edge of up to 10 cents on every sales dollar over rivals, says one quality consultant.[28] That is because fewer defects mean less rework and wasted management time, lower costs, and higher customer retention rates.

The challenge facing HR professionals attempting to implement quality initiatives is serious. And never is the task more daunting than when the organizational culture must be transformed to support the dedication to quality and customer service. Paulin Brody, chairwoman of Xerox's Quality Forum, described how difficult that transformation can be:

> TQM requires a change in organizational culture, a fundamental change in the way individuals and groups approach their work and their roles in the organization, that is, from an environment of distrust and fear of reprisal to one of openness and trust where creativity can flourish; from working as individuals to working as teams; from protection of organizational turfs to the breakdown of departmental barriers; from an autocratic management style of direction and control to a softer style of team leader and coach; from power concentrated at the top to power shared with employees; from a focus on results to a focus on continuous improvement of the processes that deliver the results; and finally a change from making decisions based on gut-feel to an analytic, fact-based approach to management.[29]

As Brody pointed out, culture counts big. At Motorola, one strategy for ensuring a supportive "total quality" culture is communicated by the company's perspective on job security. Employees who can demonstrate a consistent track record of high performance will be admitted into the company's "Service Club," which virtually guarantees future job security. And when employees are more comfortable about their future, they tend to be more innovative, flexible, and approving of change. Companies like Motorola understand that change does not occur merely because management wills it.[30]

Reengineering

It is the most popular new managerial idea around.[31] **Reengineering**, also called **process**

redesign, can yield productivity improvements unmatched by any other method. The central idea is to turn companies around, away from traditional functional departments such as marketing or finance. It almost always begins with a clean sheet of paper. But rather than examining what exists and then fixing it, reengineering begins with the future, and from there works backward. In effect, the process starts with the question "If we were a new company, how would we run this place?" Then, doing whatever is necessary, such as eliminating whole departments or adopting new technologies, management reconfigures the company to their vision.[32]

Is it a management fad? No less an authority than Peter Drucker says that it is for real and "has to be done."[33] Properly applied, reengineering enables a company to do much more with far fewer resources—less investment, less time, and fewer people. But it is not limited to restructuring, downsizing, or automating, although any of these actions may occur.

Nearly every reengineering project involves using technology to allow people to work more quickly and intelligently. Purchasing officers at Procter & Gamble, for example, do not wait to receive an order before sending diapers to Wal-Mart. P&G's computer talks directly to Wal-Mart's and does the reordering automatically.[34]

When the drive-up line starts to back up at Taco Bell, an employee with a hand-held computer walks down the line to take orders and sends them electronically to the kitchen. The restaurants can double their lunchtime capacity without having to add expensive seating areas or drive-up windows that sit unused most of the time.[35] Not every change involves technology, however. Taco Bell has also begun selling burritos and sodas on sidewalks using pushcarts.

Like TQM, reengineering stirs fears in many employees: Hourly workers see it as a cover for layoffs, and middle managers sense a threat to their jobs and status. Their fears are not unfounded. One of the chief architects of reengineering is Michael Hammer, who admits that reengineering typically takes 40 percent of the labor out of most processes. And for middle managers, the rate of attrition is even higher.[36]

With fewer managers, it is understandable for reengineering to rely heavily on teams. And with the help of better information systems and more training, teams make more decisions on their own. Teamwork may also restore a sense of community within the company, a feeling of belonging shattered by waves of restructurings and downsizings, as was the recent case with Chrysler (see *HR in the News:* "Platform Teams' Bring Chrysler Back from the Brink").

Quality will continue to play a critical role. Quality, however, may be less a competitive tool in any company's future than an absolute necessity to compete. "Quality is your ticket into the stadium," says Arnold Nemirow, CEO of Wausau Paper Mills. "You can't even come to the game unless you have a quality product and process in place. You have to compete on other dimensions today."[37]

The Office Environment

Designing and developing an office environment may seem of small importance, but do not be fooled. How an office looks is no coincidence. Most large corporations give office design considerable weight. Decisions about who goes where and gets what perk are deliberate, or at least they should be.

The work environment—space, workstations, light, furnishings, and so on—affects employee morale, productivity and quality, absenteeism, and turnover. Consider, for example, the recent interest in **managing by walking around**. If an office is located away from the action, how effective can that manager be? What about people who perform the same functions: shouldn't they be grouped together? After all, aren't accountants and salespeople segregated for efficiency? With so many orga-

"Platform Teams" Bring Chrysler Back from the Brink

As recently as 1991, the Chrysler Corporation was near insolvency. Financial and Wall Street analysts were predicting the company's demise. Today Chrysler just may be the world's most successful automaker. The numbers for 1993 were so good, in fact, that Chrysler earned more from the auto business than GM and Ford combined! The turnaround is one of the most amazing events in the history of the auto industry.

Experts point to a number of factors, including luck, but one they all can agree on is the implementation in 1989 of autonomous work groups—or platform teams. These teams consisted of skilled employees from a wide variety of functions required to design and manufacture a new vehicle. But don't give Lee Iacocca too much credit. The creation of platform teams occurred not out of some preconceived management plan. It was a serendipitous discovery.

It all began in 1988 when Chrysler purchased the old American Motor's Corporation (AMC). Critics were claiming it was a bad decision. And financially speaking, no doubt it was. Indeed, Chrysler management soon regretted it as well. Included within the acquisition were some 700 AMC engineers. What would the company do with so many engineers? If industry traditions were followed, these professionals would have been farmed out to their respective functions; designers would go to the drawing group, and engineers to fabricate, steering, or powertrain departments. But someone suggested keeping the entire group together and assigning them the project of redesigning the 1993 Grand Jeep Cherokee. It was a masterful decision.

Platform teams were created. Members consisted of professionals from the major functions, including marketing, finance, purchasing, and even outside suppliers—a first time for the auto industry. The teams were given much more independence and control than ever before. Considerable thought and planning

---

nizations being transformed through TQM and reengineering, the old management principles of division of labor and the advantages of specialization are, for them, anachronisms. It would make more sense to assume that people in different jobs will learn from each other and apply what they learn to their own jobs.

A good idea is not always born at a desk. Creativity can occur anywhere. It is as likely to occur during informal conversations with co-workers in the coffee room or with an employee who happens to work at home as with the person at the desk next door. In the right office environment, work will continue during breaks and meals, when employees are theoretically on their own time. Modern organizations are more interested in encouraging encounters outside the immediate work group,

went into keeping teams fast and efficient. They physically shared the same work space—a single floor. One important parameter each team was required to maintain included holding costs down. This was something new. Prior design teams only considered costs at the end of the process, not during it. And the only way this was achieved was through the active involvement of key suppliers, most of whom contributed market intelligence and critical skills that Chrysler lacked.

Furthermore, each team was required to maintain frequent, informal communication within the team and even with outsiders. As to the outcome, the Grand Cherokee was delivered on time and below cost. Evidently the platform concept worked so well that Chrysler has reorganized most of its functional departments into four platform teams: small car, large car, minivan, and Jeep/truck. More evidence of its success: the 1994 Dodge and Plymouth Neon, an $11,000 subcompact, went from design to production in only 31 months and at a bargain basement cost of $1.3 billion. GM and Ford have never come close to these goals.

Ford and GM have begun implementing platform teams as well. But their teams tend to follow more traditional designs. Ford teams are not quite as integrated, preferring to retain functional groups in such areas as electronics and emission. GM still does not provide its teams with the independence and control that Chrysler, or even Ford, lavish on their employees.

Although the Chrysler financial picture is much improved, there remain serious challenges on the horizon. It remains the weakest of the Big Three financially. Perhaps the most serious challenge, however, is the questionable quality of its cars. While the company has delivered a variety of attractive vehicles that customers are buying, the quality of Chrysler products has not caught up with their popularity. Their cars are consistently rated in the bottom half of the J.D. Power & Associates surveys in the number of defects. So far, customers have been willing to overlook this problem, but how long will this generosity last? Odds are that when the luster begins to fade off of those "hot" new cars, the American consumer will not be so forgiving.

SOURCE: Adapted from Alex Taylor, III, "Will Success Spoil Chrysler?" *Fortune* (January 10, 1994): 90.

for example, by weaving a path to the elevator through workstations.

Even selecting such mundane work elements as lighting can be complicated and should be done with extreme care. As almost everyone is aware, there are several types of artificial light. Often not considered, however, are the different and aggravating light—reflection—glare combinations that can result from ambient light, wall surfaces, computer screens, and glass (from either windows or mirrors).[38]

It is probably wise to retain the services of an architect or a design consultant. Most will invite input from employees anyway. A good designer will recommend colors that enliven the area, an optimal layout of work space, and adequate rest areas. Glare and reflections will be studied. In addition, the designer will check for excessive sneezing and illnesses that are possible indicators of poor air quality. Design consultants can guide businesses through the tricky waters of planning an office, from sensitive issues of distributing offices to the nuts and bolts of choosing curtain fabrics or lighting fixtures. These are important questions that every business should consider before redoing office space.

Robotics

Some experts believe that the technological revolution of the late twentieth century rivals the Industrial Revolution of the nineteenth century.[39] One of the most dramatic areas of development has been in **robotics**, the use of robots to perform routine tasks. Industrial robots are often divided into two classes: *anthropomorphic* robots approximate the appearance and functions of humans, and *nonanthropomorphic* robots are machinelike and have limited functions.[40]

The first generation of robots, which were built in the 1950s, performed simple jobs and had limited capabilities. Second-generation robots were built with the senses of vision and touch, making them more anthropomorphic in their complex capabilities and more adaptable to production needs. Carl Remick, a General Motors official, believes that second-generation robots also have decision-making capabilities, enabling them to react to their environment in a humanlike way.[41] Robots are particularly desirable for hazardous and dangerous jobs.

At General Electric Company's Appliance Park in Louisville, Kentucky, refrigerator and dishwasher operations have been upgraded with $144 million in robots and other new assembly equipment. The new technology produced a 30 percent drop in field-service quality problems and a 20 percent drop in end-of-line repairs. The new robots perform most of the shaping, bending, and drilling work previously performed by workers. While employment was initially cut when the robots replaced workers, increased market share (already 10 percent for dishwashers) is actually expected to increase total employment over time.[42]

In general, unions have not been opposed to robots if the affected workers are provided with the training necessary for the new jobs created by technological change. Although unions realize that robotics will reduce their membership, this is preferable to losing all jobs due to foreign competition.

Ergonomics

Taking into account the human factor in designing the employee's workstation is often termed **ergonomics**. The relationship between the employees and their workstations is considered to include the machines used, lighting, noise, chairs, and so on. All these factors can ultimately affect employee productivity. The IBM Corporation's *Ergonomics Handbook* (see Figure 5-4) stresses the need to design the job to fit the person in several respects, including the following:[43]

- *Posture*. Incorporate enough movement in the design of the job to prevent prolonged immobility in the same position, which causes fatigue and discomfort.

- *The back*. About 80 percent of the U.S. population suffers from back pain. The best way to reduce back injuries is to design lifting tasks carefully. Often a simple change in the layout of common lifting tasks can eliminate twisting of the torso when lifting, the most common cause of back injuries.

- *The hand*. Excessive back-and-forth movement can cause inflammation of the hand. Women are three times more susceptible to repetitive-motion injury than men. An effective means of eliminating such injuries is to avoid the use of hand tools that cause constant compression of the palm of the hand.

FIGURE 5-4 Examples of ergonomics.

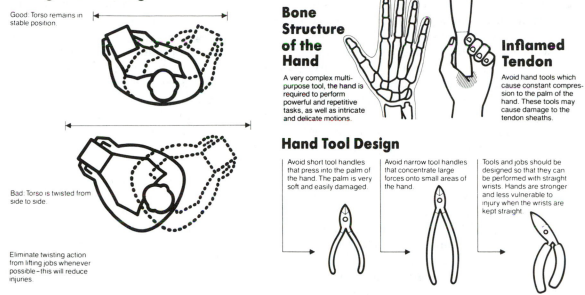

Lifting and Twisting

Good: Torso remains in stable position.

Bad: Torso is twisted from side to side.

Eliminate twisting action from lifting jobs whenever possible–this will reduce injuries.

Bone Structure of the Hand

A very complex multi-purpose tool, the hand is required to perform powerful and repetitive tasks, as well as intricate and delicate motions.

Inflamed Tendon

Avoid hand tools which cause constant compression to the palm of the hand. These tools may cause damage to the tendon sheaths.

Hand Tool Design

Avoid short tool handles that press into the palm of the hand. The palm is very soft and easily damaged.

Avoid narrow tool handles that concentrate large forces onto small areas of the hand.

Tools and jobs should be designed so that they can be performed with straight wrists. Hands are stronger and less vulnerable to injury when the wrists are kept straight.

SOURCE: International Business Machines Corporation. *Ergonomic Handbook*. Used by permission.

- *The environment.* Noise can be distracting and harmful when it is higher than routine background noise. The use of sound-absorbing materials and machine covers can reduce many noises. Higher light levels are required for more intricate tasks such as detailed assembly or constant bookwork. Glare is one of the most frequent lighting problems. The position of the work in relation to the light source is critical. Windows and fixed ceiling lights can present difficult job design problems. The use of video display terminals presents significant design problems, since they require sitting for long periods of time and performing few eye, head, and hand movements. Eye strain and general fatigue can easily affect job performance. Thus, it is important to provide operators with ergonomically designed chairs for proper posture, adjustable terminal bases, and diffused lighting.

PRODUCTIVITY MEASURES

Productivity is a popular term. Not a day goes by without the media depicting the U.S. manufacturing and service sector's problems or successes. Inevitably, the numbers used reflect something nebulously called **productivity**, which generally refers to the quantity or volume being produced. An accurate measure of productivity is vital to any organizational improvement effort.

HR professionals frequently implement strategies for improving productivity and quality in their organizations. Most of these strategies depend on employees seeing a link between what they produce and what the company is attempting to achieve. Without this relationship, work may be less meaningful, and ultimately the employee will be less motivated to perform it. Some of the strategies considered highly effective by some organizations are considered ineffective by other organizations and partially effective by still others. Clearly, there is no easy solution to the problem of motivating employees with specialized jobs. Nor is there an easy way to design jobs that will both motivate the employee and maintain maximum levels of productivity. Regardless of the chosen strategy, productivity must be measured so that performance feedback can occur.

Defining specific productivity measures is difficult. Organizations must be careful to avoid measuring the wrong things or overlooking measures that are more accurate or critical to success. For example, many companies have embraced such quality crusades as TQM. They mistakenly believe that merely implementing quality techniques, including employee empowerment and benchmarking, will produce benefits. Teamwork training is usually the first thing that occurs. And often the measure most closely watched is how many people are being trained, not what difference the training is making in performance.

While some have deemed productivity too elusive to be measured, the fact is that every job and every task can be measured. Productivity is the relationship between what is put into a piece of work (input) and what is yielded (output). It is a measure of efficiency.

Productivity naturally increases when more output is derived from the same input or when the same output is derived from decreased input. Productivity measures (number of calls per day, number of completed projects, number of customers handled each day, cycle time, for example) will yield concrete numbers. Productivity, then, is the ratio of some measurable unit of output to some measurable unit of input.

When measuring productivity, the denominator of the ratio is usually the number of hours worked. The numerator changes according to the work being accomplished. That is, the numerator is the unit by which employees' production, such as the units produced per hour, the customers served per day, or the clients contacted per week is measured. In measuring plant output, labor-hour equivalents should be used in measuring productivity. Products should be expressed in terms of the hours required to produce them. This method is preferable to using dollar measures, which change quickly as the values of costs and inflation change.[44]

Managers often rely on measures of productivity to gauge the efficiency of their departments. Supervisors interested in the direct productivity of employees may disregard other indices that increase the unit cost, such as absenteeism, turnover, or product quality. Thus, the advantages of highly specialized jobs are overemphasized when only the direct productivity of specialization is measured. Managers should also consider the indirect costs of job specialization in doing productivity estimates.

How much does turnover cost an organization? Administrators have only begun to measure the cost of turnover accurately. One cost estimate for a firm losing a computer programmer who was on the job for two years is $20,000 or more.[45] (see Figure 5-5). The costs of absenteeism are measured more frequently because it is easier to measure those costs than to measure the costs of turnover, loyalty, or tenure. An example of how the costs of absenteeism are computed is illustrated in a later chapter.

WORKPLACE FLEXIBILITY

In the 1990s and beyond, developing the capacity for flexible work is increasingly a requirement for operating in a competitive environment. It is so important that organizations include it in their strategic plans. What does **workplace flexibility** mean? This concept is relatively new and has emerged in response to the needs of today's companies and employees. The workplace flexibility challenge is to

FIGURE 5-5 One organization's costs associated with the turnover of one computer programmer

Turnover costs = Separation costs + Replacement costs + Training costs

Separation Costs

1. Exit interview = cost for salary and benefits of both interviewer and departing employee during the exit interview = $30 + $30 = $60
2. Administrative and record-keeping actions = $30

Separation costs = $60 + $30 = $90

Replacement Costs

1. Advertising for job opening = $2,500
2. Preemployment administrative functions and record-keeping actions = $100
3. Selection interview = $250
4. Employment tests = $40
5. Meetings to discuss the candidates (salary and benefits of managers while participating in meetings) = $250

Replacement costs = $2,500 + $100 + $250 + $40 + $250 = $3,140

Training Costs

1. Booklets, manuals, and reports = $50
2. Education = $240/day for new employee's salary and benefits × 10 days of workshops, seminars, or courses = $2,400
3. One-to-one coaching = ($240/day/new employee + $240/day/staff coach or job expert) × 20 days of one-to-one coaching = $9,600
4. Salary and benefits of new employee until he or she gets "up to par" = $240/day for salary and benefits × 20 days = $4,800

Training costs = $50 + $2,400 + $9,600 + $4,800 = $16,850

Total turnover costs = $90 + $3,140 + $16,850 = $20,080/turnover

SOURCE: Michael W. Mercer, "Turnover: Reducing the Costs," *Personnel* (December 1988): 38. Copyright 1988 by Michael W. Mercer.

construct the best scheduling mix between employees' needs and the organization's staffing requirements in ways that are consistent with the company's culture and mission.

Workplace flexibility includes programs such as flextime, job sharing, working at home part time, and compressed workweeks. The increased use of temporary workers, hourly part-timers, and rehired senior citizens also fall into this category.

A few years ago it was rare for a company to customize work schedules to accommodate employees' special needs. Most workers were expected to show up at a specific location and at the traditional time, usually from 8:00 A.M. to 5:00 P.M. HR policies that rigid are inappro-

priate and ineffective for today's labor force. But it is not just the diversification of the work force that necessitated change. Other factors include the transition from a manufacturing to a service-oriented job market, problems with commuter gridlock and air quality, and the emergence of a global economy.

Companies as diverse as DuPont and Aetna Life & Casualty have confirmed the need to change. DuPont's survey of 4000 employees was conclusive. "One word that cried out from the responses was *flexibility*," said Faith Wohl, director of the company's Workforce Partnering division. "That one word in neon lights, popping off the pages. They wanted flexibility in schedules, flexibility in benefits, flexibility of career planning. It was just an overwhelming response focused on a single issue."[46]

Aetna was losing 23 percent of the women who had planned to return to the firm after maternity leave. Their HR research confirmed that this group contained some of their best employees. By instituting flextime, part-time, job sharing, and telecommuting, they were able to reduce the turnover to 12 percent.[47] The following section will examine a few popular scheduling tools for creating a flexible workplace.

Telecommuting

New technological opportunities such as electronic mail (E-mail) and groupware networking (see *HR in the News:* "Groupware Beware!") have created a new alternative in work scheduling called **telecommuting**. Workers can complete some or all their assigned duties at home. For example, Tom Jacobs can operate from his home office because the job necessitates staying in touch with his staff, who are located throughout the world. For him, where he makes management decisions is less important than when. There are all sorts of opportunities for people to work at home, and the numbers are growing. The proportion of company employees working at home at least part time rose 15 percent in 1993 to 7.6 million, according to Link Resources, a New York research concern.[48] More would like to join the trend; 20 percent to 40 percent of employees say that they see telecommuting as a desirable option.[49]

But as the number of telecommuters increases, some who work at home find that it does not work for them. It can foster a sense of isolation, stagnation, family problems, and even compulsive overwork.[50] And while some of the skills required to succeed as telecommuters, as described in *HR in the News:* "Home Work," are obvious, others are harder to measure. An ability to solve problems alone and nurture client and co-worker relations

from home, for example, may be essential parts of the job.

In addition, many telecommuters fear that losing visibility at work can lead to derailing a career. No doubt, the old adage "Out of sight, out of mind" is in the minds of many ambitious telecommuters. Suggestions for minimizing this problem include, first, making sure that the "home work" delivers significant benefits to the boss and the business; second, staying flexible; third, cultivating the boss's active support for the home arrangement; and fourth, keeping in touch and interested.[51] Telecommuters should be prepared to use the telephone and E-mail frequently.

Temporary Help and Contract Workers

Global competition, as well as an ongoing campaign to control labor costs and make businesses more flexible, have led to increased dependence on temporary workers. In the past, temporary workers played an insignificant role, but that situation has changed. Firms are beginning to manage their work forces in a just-in-time manner, much like the practice of keeping their inventories lean and ordering as needed. Some employers hire temporary workers to adjust to sharp peaks and valleys of demand, and many workers want more time off to take care of their families, or for other personal needs or interests.

The Wyatt Company, a Washington, DC, consulting firm, reports that approximately 27 percent of U.S. companies hired temporary employees in 1993. This was a 3 percent increase over 1992. They also reported that many more companies are contracting with outside vendors to handle operations formerly performed by the company.[52]

Although temporary workers are a tiny percentage of the overall work force, their share of total employment has risen over the past decade. The National Association of Temporary Services estimates that temporary help jobs

Home Work

When Brian League's employer offered him a chance to work at home, he snapped it up. A planner for the city of Los Angeles, he "thought it would be nice," he says, to work in a quiet place and go jogging on breaks.

Instead, he wound up talking to his dog. "I missed interacting with my colleagues. I found myself walking around my empty house asking Amos, 'Help me with this.'" His Airedale terrier proved a poor source of inspiration, and he soon quit working at home. "It's not for everybody," he says. "If I were a supervisor, you'd have a tough time convincing me of its merits."

Telecommuting workshops typically draw "a roomful of folks who envision all the good sides—not having to shave and put on make-up or go through traffic, and sitting in their bluejeans all day," says Gil Gordon, a consultant. What they don't ask, he says, is, "Can I manage deadlines? What will it be like to be away from the social context of the office five days a week? Can I renegotiate the rules of the family, so that my spouse doesn't come home every night expecting me to have a four-course meal on the table?"

While most people who work at home for long stretches say they like the arrangement, one-third of the 280 participants in a recent one-year study in Washington's Puget Sound region stopped working at home. About 17% said they lacked equipment or other support, 15% cited problems back at the office and 8% said they simply didn't like it.

Careful screening of prospective telecommuters can avert some pitfalls. Qualities to look for include:

- Has little need for face-to-face contact with co-workers or customers.
- Can commute directly from home to customers.
- Has access to quiet office space at home free from interruptions.
- Has access at home to needed equipment.
- Is a self-starter and able to work with little supervision.
- Performs tasks that can be done from home.
- Reports to a supervisor who managers by results, not by surveillance or time clock.
- Works for someone who trusts him or her.

Not even the most committed home employees can keep work from spilling into home life—even when it is a large house. One "home worker" finds that her two-year-old demands full attention—even though she has a full-time nanny. "If I'm on the telephone, the child sees that as competition. It seems to be a mag-

(*continued*)

net—she's right there screaming . . . I think she almost feels more neglected when I'm home and she can see me, but I can't pay attention."

SOURCE: Reprinted by permission of *Wall Street Journal*. Adapted from Sue Shellenbarger, "Some Thrive, But Many Wilt Working at Home," *The Wall Street Journal* (December 14, 1993): B1. Dow Jones & Company, Inc. All rights reserved worldwide.

represented 1.2 percent of total nonfarm employment in 1992, up from 0.9 percent in 1988 and 0.4 percent in 1982.[53]

From top management's perspective, the flexibility to turn a company around "on a dime" has great appeal. Being able to change products or work locations quickly is a strategic core competence that can be attained only with a flexible work force. And with the diminishing power of organized labor, employers are allowed more leeway in using temporary and contract labor to fill in when there are sudden surges in demand beyond the capabilities of the core work force.

But there is a down side. One problem is that more employers are hiring part-timers to become "lean and mean" in a competitive world, regardless of the harm it does to workers and company efficiency as a whole. In fact, involuntary part-time employees—workers who would prefer full-time jobs—account for most of the growth in the part-time sector.[54] Most of these new jobs pay less than regular jobs, and few come with good benefits. The standard U.S. job, with a forty-hour workweek, medical benefits, and a pension at age sixty-five, is on the wane, many labor experts are saying, because of the availability of temporary or contract workers.

Managing temporary and contract workers can be challenging, especially when they are mixed with permanent employees. One difference between the two groups may result from the insecurity involuntary part-time temporaries often show because they are not on the company's regular payroll but want to be. While some may have quietly resigned themselves to this fact, others may be surreptitiously job hunting, looking for a better deal, while giving the company only a minimum of effort or results.

Another difference between these two groups is their agenda. Permanent employees are interested in events that most temporaries will never experience, for example, promotions, new or revised company benefits, news on who is doing what and when, and local gossip. Temporary employees are more interested in issues that directly affect their status and pay because politically "they're not on the food chain".[55] Involuntary temporaries also see themselves as having the worst schedules, the least interesting jobs, and poor long-term expectations. Maintaining a balanced blend of permanent and temporary employees is becoming a constant challenge for managers. Figure 5-6 offers a few suggestions on how it might be done and what to avoid.

Permanent Part-Time Work

Part-time employment makes up a growing share of jobs in the United States. About half of the jobs people found in 1993 were part-time. These employees represent almost one-fifth of the U.S. work force.[56]

Most part-timers work in clerical, sales, and service occupations. These occupations are predominantly low-paid and low-skilled. Perhaps as much as one-third of all permanent part-time work is available for the highly skilled.[57] Retail organizations, for example, rely extensively on a permanent part-time work force while maintaining only a small core of full-time employees.

FIGURE 5-6 Guidelines for managing a mix of permanent and temporary workers.

1. Refer to temporaries as *associates* or *consultants;* avoid the term *temporary* or even *contingent.*

2. Be as consistent in giving out rewards with temps as with permanent employees—particularly praise and interesting work.

3. Communicate to combat slacking off and cynicism—make an extra effort to keep temps in the loop without implying that they're permanent.

4. Include them socially—if the company sponsors a softball team and temps want to play, let them; it can only build esprit de corps;

5. Be careful when discussing the company's future plans and make no sympathy-fueled promises of permanent positions.

SOURCE: Adapted from Marilyn Kennedy, "A Nightmare Scenario," *Across the Board* (July-August 1993): 12.

Organizations create good part-time jobs to attract and retain valued employees whose personal circumstances prevent them from working full-time. Many of these positions are highly skilled. Unlike temporary or contract employment, permanent part-time employment may involve high compensation, high productivity, and low turnover. Employers often accommodate the worker's schedule rather than ask the worker to accommodate the needs of the job.

Job Sharing

In recent years, **job sharing** has evolved as an opportunity for career part-time employment. *Job sharing* generally refers to dividing full-time jobs into two or more part-time positions, often without particular regard for how the full-time job is divided. In personnel work, the term generally means that two employees hold a position together, whether as a team jointly responsible for the position or as individuals responsible for only half of the position. *Leisure sharing* refers to a couple sharing a single

position because they prefer the increased leisure time that two household members gain by sharing a job. In this way, both of them can pursue careers.[58]

Job sharing as an alternative scheduling technique provides the organization with several possible advantages: increased productivity, a greater pool of qualified applicants, and reduced costs. The most common result is an influx of new energy and enthusiasm brought to the job by a second person (see *HR in the News:* "Splitting Up the Work Load"). The company often gets more than twice the talent from having two workers perform the same job. When job sharing was studied in the mass assembly department of a southeastern manufacturing firm, the scrap ratio was 12 percent lower and output was 7 percent higher for the shared-job positions. Workers found four hours to be far less tiring than eight and so were able to work at a faster pace. Also, fatigue-caused errors were greatly reduced.[59]

The supervisor of a Wisconsin state telecommunications department stated that the primary advantage of job sharing is that employees working a few days a week or four hours a day are happier about their jobs than full-time workers. Many times the expenses of training, hiring temporary workers, and overtime are reduced. Training costs are often reduced because one job-sharing employee can give on-the-job training to the other. Turnover costs are often reduced since job sharers with hours specifically tailored to their personal needs are less likely to leave the job for another one.

Job sharing has disadvantages. Communication problems may increase between job-sharing partners and between them and other members of the work force. Job sharing may make it difficult to assign responsibility to a particular individual. Benefit costs to the organization may increase, particularly if the Social Security (FICA) tax or state taxes for unemployment insurance cannot be prorated. Companies employing job sharers whose in-

Splitting Up the Work Load

Diana Bowler and Alisa Michaels Metzner, vice presidents at BankAmerica in San Francisco, had a common dilemma. Both had baby girls and did not want to work full time. Yet neither wanted to sacrifice a promising career at the bank. With the approval of their bosses, they came up with a solution: sharing one management job and salary. Bowler, 32, and Michaels Metzner, 34, were a good match because both worked in strategic planning and analysis. Michaels Metzner now comes in seven hours a day on Monday, Tuesday, and Wednesday, and Bowler works a similar schedule on Wednesday, Thursday, and Friday. The overlap day allows them to coordinate their work.

The rewards are professional and personal. Says Bowler: "It's the best of both worlds." For BankAmerica too, which pays the two part-timers the equivalent of a single 35-hour weekly salary but gets much more work than that from them.

SOURCE: *Time* (October 3, 1988): 53. Used by permission.

comes exceed the FICA ceiling may pay additional FICA taxes. However, benefit costs usually decrease because the two part-time employees do not receive all the benefits of full-time employees. Perhaps the greatest obstacle to job sharing is that surveys show that job sharing is not positively viewed by managers. Generally they feel that job sharers do not take the shared job seriously enough or lack the commitment to a job that a full-time employee would have.

Steelcase, Inc., in Grand Rapids, Michigan, one of the nation's largest manufacturers of office furniture, first offered job sharing in 1983. After several years, Steelcase has concluded that job sharing lowers absenteeism and turnover by retaining employees who want part-time work.[60]

Compressed Workweeks

Compressed workweeks are schedules with fewer than the traditional five workdays a week for forty hours, or 5/40. The hours worked per day are increased so that the hours worked per week still total forty. The most common compressed workweek is the **four-day workweek**. The four-day week is perhaps the oldest alternative work schedule, though there are a number of ways to devise compressed workweeks. Managers of large manufacturing organizations report substantial savings from compressed workweeks because of reduced start-up time and increased energy conservation (see *HR in the News:* "GM Adopts 4-Day Workweek"). Savings typically are also gained from an increase in employee morale.

4/40 Workweek The usual four-day workweek consists of four ten-hour days, or 4/40. Sixty percent of all compressed workweeks fall into the 4/40 category. In practice, some of the forty-hour workweeks have actually become four nine-hour work periods as employees trade coffee breaks and clean-up time for extra hours off. With this scheme, managers believe that they are getting as much work accom-

GM Adopts 4-Day Workweek

There is strong support within the auto industry for the 4-Day workweek. The General Motors Lordstown facility is expected to build more cars than any plant in North America due to an innovative work schedule that also has reduced manufacturing costs and saved jobs. The key to that performance is a three-crew, two-shift work arrangement. Normally, the plant would have used two crews, each working five 8-hour days, plus any overtime. Now each crew works four 10-hour days. The new system greatly reduces the amount of time the plant sits idle, thus making more efficient use of its equipment. While there are occasional murmurs of discontent, most workers seem to like it. One reason is the minimum eight hours of time-and-a-half overtime each week, which conforms to the UAW's national contract. The compressed workweek plan is also being adopted at the GM Saturn facility in Tennessee.

SOURCE: Adapted from "Four-day Week Boosts GM Plant's Output," *Sunday World-Herald* Omaha, Nebraska (August 22, 1993): G-11.

plished in four nine-hour days as they might in a 5/40 workweek because they save start-up time as well as maintenance, which is often scheduled for the fifth day of work.[61]

4/48 and 3/36 Workweeks An alternative to the 4/40 compressed workweek is a week that rotates four-day and three-day shifts. In this arrangement, employees who work four twelve-hour days are off for three days. Then they work three twelve-hour days, followed by four days off. Thus, employees work forty-eight hours one week and thirty-six hours the next, or 4/48 and 3/36. For forty-eight-hour weeks they automatically receive eight hours of overtime pay. This system requires two crews of employees for each shift. One crew works from 9 P.M. to 9 A.M. as the night shift, while the other crew works from 9 A.M. to 9 P.M. as the day shift. In total then, four shifts of employees work twelve-hour days, with three-day workweeks alternating with four-day workweeks throughout the year.[62]

Discretionary Workweeks/Flextime

A second type of alternative work schedule is the **discretionary workweek**, which offers employees greater freedom in regulating their own lives. Retail stores, service agencies, and some manufacturers have met the demands of business with more satisfied, more productive employees working varied schedules. There are three varieties of discretionary workweeks.

Flextime A system of **flextime** provides a true alternative work schedule for employees, who may follow different schedules of work each day of the workweek. Flextime has been particularly beneficial to service organizations such as retail outlets, banks, savings and loan associations, and insurance companies.

Almost every survey shows companies reporting more advantages than disadvantages to flexible work schedules, regardless of type. Savings in employee turnover, absenteeism, and tardiness are reported so often and over

233

such long periods of time that these advantages must be considered valid attributes of flexible schedules.

In a typical flextime system, the employer establishes a core time when all employees must work. For service organizations, core time is a time during which most customers arrive; for example, from 10:30 A.M. to 1:00 P.M. for a retail outlet where most customers come in during their lunch breaks or five-to-nine for suburban shopping locations. As Figure 5-7 shows, the employer also establishes the total hours of operation during which the employee must work. Normally, the employee must work the core hours within the total eight hours worked. If the core time is not worked, the employee does not get credit for the workday; usually an employee does not arrive at work at all if the core time cannot be worked. The employee may choose a different starting and stopping time each day of the week, as long as the core time is worked and the total hours worked are within the hours the organization is open. The organization may alternate core times for different days of the week if this is necessary to meet customers' demands.

Most employees in the United States and elsewhere favor flextime operations. Employees particularly like the control flextime gives them over their personal lives. They can better schedule leisure activities and family responsibilities, and take care of personal business during normal work hours.

Other flextime advantages for employees include reduced commuting time and faster shopping during slack times. Parents enjoy the advantages flextime gives them because they are often responsible for school-age children.

Organizations that have experimented with flextime report many advantages to the system: improved employee morale, increased productivity, and decreased absenteeism and turnover. Tardiness is practically eliminated since employees can start their total workday later and still work the same hours. Flextime also reduces timekeeping by supervisors. Employers report that employees usually arrive ready to begin working since personal needs can be taken care of before work. Another advantage is the reduction of overtime costs. By setting core hours during the busiest periods of the day, managers avoid scheduling overtime or hiring part-time employees for busy periods. Often retail and service organizations must overstaff to be sure that an adequate number of employees is available during a rush period. Overstaffing is less necessary with flextime.[63]

Flextime may be a key factor for employers who successfully attract and retain employees with diverse ethnic backgrounds. Arnold

FIGURE 5-7 Flexible work schedules.

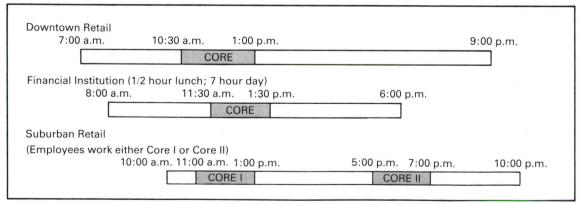

Manseth, director of employee relations at the Pacific Northwest Bell Telephone Company, believes that trust between employer and employees is all that is required to implement flexible work hours. Manseth claims, "Today's employees are no longer content to follow their fathers' footsteps and put the job above everything else. Instead, they have learned to balance the job with other aspects of life, and are asking the employer to understand. For those [employers] who do, they'll find the quality of work will not drop. A happy employee is a productive one.[64]

Creating a flexible work force will also enable employers to retain older employees. In the 1990s, the United States has the oldest work force in its history. Flextime allows older workers the opportunity to ease their work demands while remaining productive.

Gus Tyler, assistant president of the International Ladies' Garment Workers Union, believes that flexible work hours will enhance U.S. competition in the international marketplace. If American companies were more willing to "loosen the boardroom grip" and encourage rather than disdain greater flexibility among their employees, they might find that they do not need to relocate to other countries. Instead, claims Tyler, we could regain paradise in America if companies were more flexible instead of cutting benefits and complaining about government overregulation.[65]

Disadvantages of Workplace Flexibility

The alternatives just discussed are only the beginning of a trend toward new and varied work schedules. Managers, realizing that they cannot redesign all jobs to make them more challenging or interesting, use various scheduling techniques to give employees increased freedom to plan work or leisure time. The major alternatives—compressed workweek, job sharing, flextime, telecommuting, and part-time work—have been successful for the most part. The advantage of workplace flexibility is a substantial gain in employees' satisfaction with their jobs and work environment. However, there are also disadvantages associated with alternative work schedules. These will now be discussed.

Employee Resistance   Employees often resist change of any type. Uncertain of what the new system will bring and at least partially satisfied with the current system, many employees resist possible changes in their basic routine. When asked for their input about a possible change in work schedule, employees are concerned about the new schedule's effect on (1) their personal life, including their family; (2) organizational effectiveness, particularly work coordination; and (3) customer service. Their attitudes toward new work schedules tend to focus not only on personal and family effects, as might be expected, but also on the effects on the employer's cooperation and relations with customers. If such perceived problems materialize, managers will need to take action to alleviate the cause of the concern.[66]

Communication Problems   Possibly the most common disadvantage encountered by any company using alternative work schedules is communication problems. Inconsistent work hours change common communication patterns; at times some employees may be inaccessible for group meetings or casual discussions. This problem can be minimized by proper management planning and correct implementation of the work schedule alternative that has been adopted.

Fatigue   A major complaint of some employees about compressed workweek schedules is fatigue. Obviously, many compressed workweek schemes that involve longer days and mental and physical fatigue may become a real hardship. While many employees may not complain of fatigue directly, the later hours of the workday must be carefully monitored to make sure that fatigue is not becoming a major cause of increased injuries or decreased productivity during a compressed workweek schedule.

Interdependence of Jobs   Real problems for flextime or part-time alternative work schedules are created by the interdependence of jobs. In fact, highly interdependent jobs such as assembly line operations probably make these scheduling procedures impractical. Flextime and other discretionary workweek programs have been utilized primarily by service or small manufacturing organizations that do not have highly interdependent jobs.

JOB DESIGN GUIDELINES

In modern management the problem of designing jobs that are appealing to employees yet result in high productivity is a common one. When implementing a program designed to increase both the motivation and productivity of employees, management should consider the following issues:

- Is the problem one that can be addressed by enlarging the scope of most employee's jobs? Jobs traditionally designed to be routine and dull can often be improved by giving employees more and varied tasks to perform. Job rotation and job enlargement usually require minimal management, planning, and cost. More complete programs increase not only the scope of the job but, more important, its depth to increase the job's motivation for employees. These programs are usually more expensive to develop and implement. Although job enrichment, work teams, and work simplification may involve greater cost and time, they often reap greater returns.

- Any job design program should have two objectives: (1) to increase the general morale of employees in order to bring greater productivity and lower costs to the organization,

and (2) to increase employee job satisfaction because jobs are more interesting and challenging. The objectives of both management and employees must be given equal weight because both must cooperate completely if such a program is to succeed.

- Different employees satisfy different needs in doing their jobs. Any job designer must consider that not all employees want either increased responsibility and authority or increased scope. A certain proportion of the work force prefers specialized jobs so that they can easily learn their work, become proficient, and not worry about their job security. These employees often find personal achievement and growth outside the organization and do not seek high levels of autonomy and achievement through their jobs.

- Before considering a job design program, an organization should carefully investigate the exact causes of employee problems. The design of the work may not be at the heart of those problems; rather, they may be caused by poor supervision, lack of advancement, poor working conditions, or low pay.

- Finally, when embarking on a job design program, management should tap its greatest source of ideas and knowledge: its employees.

Job enrichment, work teams, reengineering, TQM, or any of the flexible work schedules may breathe new life and competitive fire into organizations. There seems to be unabashed optimism in the HR profession for all of them. But while these approaches may promise more motivated employees, improved quality, and better productivity, the results may be less than expected. When this happens, HR professionals must be prepared to tinker with or perhaps abandon these programs.

What may work in one company may not succeed in another. General Electric, for example, has been recognized as a job design innovator for years. One particular GE concept that has drawn acclaim from HR professionals around the world is **benchmarking**. Pacific Gas & Electric embraced it with a passion. The company sent many employees to visit other firms, mostly outside the energy industry, to learn new ways of handling specific problems, such as inventory control or information processing. For PG&E, however, attempts to replicate someone else's best practices ended in disappointment until specific parameters were set describing what the company wanted to find out. As William Blastic, quality improvement manager, said: benchmarking "was a waste of time. We were just industrial tourists."

Even such acclaimed approaches as TQM may need to be modified to fit a particular company with a unique corporate culture. An Atlantic City, New Jersey, casino converted from TQM to something they called the *learning organization* because the TQM teams ran out of steam after key employees became reluctant to suggest any more ways to eliminate bureaucracy. The casino employees were afraid their jobs would be the next to go. Management's antidote was to encourage employees to acquire new skills to promote company growth and enhance their own job security.

While the risk of failed job design is real, the benefits far outweigh the down side for most organizations. Implementing a bad program can lead to mistakes, but doing nothing can lead to extinction. Without a doubt, traditional job designs, particularly those emphasizing overspecialization, will continue giving way to motivation-intensive programs.

CONCLUSIONS AND APPLICATIONS

- A paradigm shift is occurring. Organizations are being designed in terms of processes rather than by functions. The changes are the result of global competitive forces.
- Older industrial engineering models, such as scientific management, concentrated on attaining efficiency and control to achieve economies of scale. Certain industrial sectors, especially manufacturing, depended on specialization using work simplification, standardization, and training to keep costs down. Human concerns were secondary. Companies like UPS continue to design work using scientific management principles.
- Understanding how people are motivated, that is, their needs and goals, is critical to modern job design. Important motivational theories include Maslow's hierarchy of needs, goal setting, positive reinforcement,

and Herzberg's two-factor theory. Herzberg's approach has been the foundation for current job enrichment methods.
- One issue that continues to be controversial is whether money ought to be linked closely to job performance. Does money motivation detract from the intrinsic satisfaction that can come from doing a good job? The evidence is mixed.
- The tasks employees perform on the job and the variety, difficulty level, and autonomy of the job greatly affect job satisfaction and productivity.
- Employees, individually or in work teams, are being asked to take on greater responsibility for the design and control of their jobs. Simple, repetitious tasks are eliminated whenever possible, generally resulting in jobs that are more motivating and challeng-

ing. At the same time, some degree of job specialization is necessary so that new employees can learn their jobs quickly and make fewer errors.

- Programs such as job enrichment, self-managed work groups, TQM, and reengineering have resulted in redesigned jobs that were previously highly specialized and boring. There is also a trend toward multiskilling, whereby team members learn multiple tasks. Organizations are adopting work teams and giving them more freedom and responsibilities.

- Total quality management (TQM) is one of the fastest-growing productivity improvement programs in the world. It is based on the principle of commitment to continuous improvement and meeting customers' needs. It is largely a bottom-up change effort.

- Reengineering is more radical than TQM. It involves more than tweaking old procedures; it is the redesign of business processes to achieve major gains in cost, service, or time.

The process begins with the simple but powerful question: if we could start from scratch, how would we do this? It is different from TQM because it comes from the top down.

- Technology plays an important role in modern job design. Robotics, ergonomics, and the office environment can improve employee creativity, productivity, and quality.

- In addition to job design, organizations may choose to implement programs that increase workplace flexibility. These programs tend to adopt a scheduling mix between employees' needs and the organization's staffing requirements in ways that are consistent with the company's culture. Compressed workweeks, flextime programs, telecommuting, temporary and contract work, and permanent part-time work are the more common approaches. Employees who desire greater control over work hours, who would like easier commuting, or want a different lifestyle will be attracted to organizations that offer these types of programs.

CASE STUDY

And You Thought Your Job Was Bad . . .

Judy Adkins is having a miserable night. The fifty-eight-year-old telemarketer is on her twenty-first phone call on the evening shift, but so far, she has sold just one bank credit card application. She is becoming impatient as she waits for her computer to dial the next prospect. Finally, she hears the beep in her headset and the prospect's name appears on her computer.

"About time," she mutters. There is confusion all around her, but it is rather tame tonight. Everyone except Judy is close to meeting their goals. For some unexplainable reason, tonight is not going well for her.

A young supervisor—not yet thirty, Adkins guesses—has now moved into position just behind her. Adkins knows she is in for some tough comments.

"You're not holding up your end of the wagon tonight, Judy." The supervisor is gone before the words are out of her mouth.

"I don't need to hear that now!" she says.

But Ms. Adkins knows that the pressure goes with the job. She is a seasoned veteran, having over six years experience in a variety of telemarketing industries. Adkins is one of the most senior people in her current job, having just finished her second year. For her and other experienced callers, the daily goal is one hundred calls for an eight-hour shift. The expected "conversion rate" is 15 percent of those who listen long enough to count as a presentation.

Adkins's current supervisor is intense, demanding, and quick to criticize. Frankly, all of them have been that way. "Their job is just as tense as mine," she says. "If they don't fill

their sales targets, they're history, just like us."

Because most supervisors occasionally eavesdrop on calls with cordless phones, they are quick to give feedback. Some are positive, such as "Judy is a goal buster—way to go, Judy!"

More often, however, what employees hear are "suggestions" for improving their sales pitch, such as "Slow the presentation down" or "Don't ad-lib on the script!" While Adkins wants recognition as much as anyone, she has become somewhat jaded from the insincerity and condescending form it takes. She would rather have more pay or benefits, but neither is in the cards.

Most telemarketers are paid an hourly wage plus commissions. For Adkins that amounts to $7.50 per hour plus approximately $5 for commissions, or around $12 per hour on a good day. There are no health benefits, and if you believe telemarketing executives, no prospects for any in the future.

Adding to the tension are the customers. Telemarketing is tough, stressful work. Besides the fact that the boss may well be listening in, some hostile customers will verbally heap abuse on the telemarketer. Profanity is common. And there is nothing to do but continue to be polite and take it.

The constant stress takes a toll on everyone. The turnover in the industry is one of the highest in the country. The average time as a telemarketer is only eleven weeks (not months or years). Those who want to make it a career hope to break into management, where pay and benefits are much better. But that usually requires more education and youth. The last opening for a supervisor's position drew over fifty applications from telemarketers.

QUESTIONS

1. Assume that you are a management consultant called in to analyze the turnover problem. You are told that pay and benefits are fixed and cannot be substantially altered. It is clear that whatever you recommend must not bring productivity down. What would you recommend to management?

2. How might the telemarketer's job be redesigned so that employees are more satisfied and challenged by their work? Is telemarketing a job that can be enriched and remain highly productive or is it more like an assembly line?

3. How might the supervisors be contributing to the problem? What recommendations would you make about changing their styles?

4. How might recruitment be part of the solution?

5. Consider such strategies as team competition and alternative work schedules. What do you think would happen if they were implemented?

EXPERIENTIAL EXERCISES

1. Can This Job Be Enriched?

PURPOSE

To explore the concept of job enrichment by determining whether a routine job has the potential for enrichment.

The basic steps to implement job enrichment include the following:

1. Select the job or jobs to be enriched. Criteria for selection include these:
   a. Can changes be made without costly engineering modifications?
   b. Are job attitudes poor?
   c. Will motivation improve some area or areas of performance?
2. Thoroughly analyze the job and develop a list of ways in which it may be enriched.
3. Screen out ideas that are considered "hygienic": for example, working conditions, pay, benefits, peer and supervisory relationships, and so on. Include only motivators, such as job factors that enable employees to make more decisions and have greater responsibility for their work, as well as increased recognition.

THE TASK

For the following scenario, answer the following questions:

1. *Can* the job be enriched?
2. *Should* the job be enriched?
3. If you decide to enrich the job, *how* would you do so?
4. If you decide to enrich the job, what performance criteria would you use to determine whether your job enrichment strategy was a success?

Bert Garner: Assembly Line Worker

Bert Garner works for General Electronics, Inc., a large manufacturer of home appliances. Garner is employed in a large plant that builds refrigerators. The refrigerators are built on an assembly line that snakes several hundred yards through the plant. Garner is responsible for attaching the freezer door to the refrigerator. As the refrigerator reaches his station, he picks up a door, several screws, and a screwdriver and screws the door to the refrigerator. He does this more than 200 times a day.

Stacks of freezer doors are delivered to Garner's workstation by another employee. Down the line, an inspector checks his work in addition to the work of other operators. Any item that needs to be reworked is removed from the refrigerator and set aside. The speed of the line—and thus the productivity rate—are determined by plant management. Any job changes are generally initiated by the industrial engineering staff.

When asked about his work, Garner responded, "It's a job. I'm not crazy about it, but it puts food on the table. Hell, who likes their job anyway? With the economy the way it is, I feel lucky just to have a job."

General Electronics' refrigerator assembly plant is about thirty-five years old. Capital improvements in the plant are seriously being considered by management to improve plant efficiency. Plans are to install more robot-type machines, particularly for jobs in which quality problems often exist. The labor–management climate is satisfactory, but the union's concern over management's plans for installing advanced technology has strained relations quite a bit.

2. My Ideal Job?

PURPOSE

To help you better understand how the different elements that comprise any job affect job satisfaction and motivation, and that people are motivated by a wide variety of job elements.

Time requirement: thirty to forty-five minutes.

THE TASK

1. The instructor will break the class into small groups. Each group will review and discuss the common job factors from the list to be presented. Each group will be expected to reach a consensus on the top two factors that are most important to the group. The group is not limited to the factors identified on the list.

2. The group will present its list to the class and present a rationale for its selection.

3. Following brief group presentations, the instructor will lead the class through a discussion of the most important job factors.

Job Factors

Job satisfaction is the goal of most workers. What would it take for you to be a satisfied employee? Consider each of the job factors identified here. All of them are commonly found, but it is possible that some other factor not listed is more important to you. If that is the situation, go ahead and list it as well. Place a weight from 1 (least important) to 10 (most important) for each factor.

_____ **1.** Job security

_____ **2.** Good pay

_____ **3.** A friendly boss

_____ **4.** Pleasant office environment or work conditions

_____ **5.** A job with prestige and status

_____ **6.** Challenging, stimulating, and interesting work

_____ **7.** A job you can master and control

_____ **8.** Increased responsibility and authority

_____ **9.** A satisfying, high-quality personal life

_____ **10.** Recognition and appreciation for your work

_____ **11.** Sensible company policies, procedures, and rules

_____ **12.** A desire to continue to learn new skills, gain more knowledge, and so on.

KEY TERMS AND CONCEPTS

Alderfer's ERG
Benchmarking
Compressed workweeks

Content
Context
Continuous improvement

Contract workers
Discretionary workweek
Ergonomics
Flextime
Four-day workweek
Goal setting
Herzberg's two-factor theory
Job design
Job enlargement
Job enrichment
Job rotation
Job scope and job depth
Job sharing
Law of effect
Managing by walking around
Maslow's hierarchy of needs
Meeting customers' needs
Money motivation

Motivation-intensive job
Motivational factors
Multiskilling
Old paradigms
Overspecialization
Permanent part-time work
Positive reinforcement
Process redesign
Productivity
Reengineering
Robotics
Self-managed Work Teams (autonomous work groups)
Specialization-intensive jobs
Telecommuting
Total quality management (TQM)
Work team
Workplace flexibility

REVIEW QUESTIONS

1. Why did old industrial models, such as scientific management, work as well as they did in the United States for most of this century?

2. Why are employees increasingly becoming dissatisfied with specialized jobs?

3. Describe the variety of human needs that could be satisfied through work.

4. Why is it difficult to design highly motivating jobs that can be easily learned by most people?

5. Herzberg's two-factor theory has been widely criticized, yet it seems as popular as ever. What makes it so appealing to managers?

6. How do job enrichment programs differ from job rotation programs?

7. What important factors influence the choice of job design approaches?

8. What can be gained by using part-time workers instead of full-time workers?

9. In what types of organizations could flextime be most effective? Why?

10. Does the Volvo failure with work teams signal the death of motivation-intensive jobs in the automobile industry?

DISCUSSION QUESTIONS

1. Discuss the factors involved in redesigning jobs in an auto assembly plant or insurance agency. Which company would find it easier to redesign jobs?

2. Would you prefer to work flextime, or a four-day, five-day, or eight-day week if you had an assembly line job? If you were a computer programmer? If you were a Fuller Brush salesperson?

3. If you managed a fast-food franchise, would you raise salaries or rotate, enlarge, or enrich jobs to decrease turnover and absenteeism? Explain your choice.

4. Can blue-collar employees on flextime be trusted to keep track of their own hours? Can white-collar workers? What factors would influence both groups?

5. How would you decide which work schedule would be most efficient in a car wash, an accounting firm, a gas station, or a veterinarian's office?

6. Computers and software programs that can link people across vast distances resulted in some companies permitting employees to work at home. What are some of the advantages and disadvantages of this arrangement? How could these obstacles be removed?

ENDNOTES

Chapter 5

1. John A. Byrne, "Paradigms for Postmodern Managers," *Business Week/Reinventing America* 1992: 62.

2. Michael Hammer and James Champy, *Reengineering the Corporation* (New York: HarperBusiness, 1993), p. 14.

3. Christopher Farrell, "A Wellspring of Innovation," *Business Week/Enterprise* 1993: 61.

4. John Schermerhorn, Jr., James Hunt, and Richard Osborn, *Managing Organizational Behavior*, 5th ed. (New York: Wiley, 1994), p. 703.

5. Ibid, p. 706.

6. Richard Blackburn and Benson Rosen, "Total Quality and Human Resources Management: Lessons Learned from Baldridge Award-Winning Companies," *The Academy of Management Executive*, 7, no. 3 (August 1993): 49–66.

7. Abraham Maslow, "A Theory of Human Motivation," *Psychological Review* 50 (1943): 370–96.

8. C. P. Alderfer, *Existence, Relatedness and Growth* (New York: Free Press, 1972).

9. E. A. Locke, "Toward a Theory of Task Motivation and Incentives," *Organizational Behavior and Human Performance* 3 (1968): 157–80.

10. E. L. Thorndike, *Animal Intelligence* (New York: Macmillan, 1911), pp. 1–56.

11. B. F. Skinner, *The Technology of Teaching* (New York: Appleton-Century-Crofts, 1968).

12. Frederick Herzberg et al., *The Motivation to Work* (New York: Wiley, 1959): pp. 59–83.

13. John Ivancevich, Andrew Szilagyi, and Marc Wallace, Jr., *Organizational Behavior and Performance* (Santa Monica, CA: Goodyear, 1977), pp. 141–42.

14. Ibid., p. 141.

15. Ibid., p. 142.

16. F. W. Taylor, *The Principles of Scientific Management* (New York: Harper & Row, 1947).

17. Bernard J. Reilly and Joseph A. DiAngelo, Jr. "A Look at Job Redesign," *Personnel*, 65, no. 2 (February 1988): 61.

18. Although dated, the comprehensive study of the automobile industry by Walker and Guest continues to reflect an accurate assessment of life on the assembly line. See C. R. Walker and R. H. Guest, *The Man on the Assembly Line* (Cambridge, MA: Harvard University Press, 1952).

19. Paul Greenlaw and William Biggs, *Modern Personnel Management* (Philadelphia: Saunders, 1979), pp. 273–75.

20. M. D. Kilbridge, "Reduced Costs through Enlargement: A

Case," *Journal of Business* (October 1969): 357–62.

21. J. R. Hackman and G. R. Oldham, *Work Design* (Reading, MA: Addison-Wesley, 1980). See also "You See the Package from Beginning to End," *Business Week* (May 16, 1983): 103; and R. H. Waterman, *The Renewal Factor* (New York: Bantam Books, 1987), p. 4.

22. William W. Winpisinger, "Job Satisfaction," *AFL-CIO American Federationist,* 80, no. 2 (1973): 9–10.

23. F. K. Plous, Jr., "Redesigning Work," *Personnel Administrator* 32, no. 5 (March 1987): 99.

24. Frank Rodgers, "A Team Approach to Promotions at Rohr Inc.," *Personnel Journal* (April 1992): 44–47.

25. D. Keith Denton, "Multi-skilled Teams Replace Old Work Systems," *HRMagazine* (September 1992): 48–56.

26. Jon R. Katzenbach and Douglas K. Smith, *The Wisdom of Teams: Creating the High-Performance Organization* (Boston: Harvard Business School Press, 1993).

27. *Business Week/Quality* 1991): 164.

28. Armand V. Feigenbaum of General Systems Company in Pittsfield, Massachusetts, October 25, 1991.

29. Pauline N. Brody, "Introduction to Total Quality Management," in *Total Quality Management: A Report of Proceedings from the Xerox Quality Forum II,* August 1990.

30. Blackburn and Rosen, "Total Quality and Human Resources Management," p. 51.

31. Thomas A. Stewart, "Reengineering," *Fortune* (August 23, 1993): 41–48.

32. Ibid., p. 41.

33. Ibid.

34. Hammer and Champy, *Reengineering the Corporation*, p. 22.

35. Ibid., p. 180.

36. Ibid., pp. 29–30.

37. Byrne, "Paradigms for Postmodern Managers," p. 63.

38. *Office Access* (San Francisco: The Understanding Business, 1993).

39. Sar A. Levitan and Clifford M. Johnson, "The Future of Work: Does It Belong to Us or to the Robots?" *Monthly Labor Review* 105, no. 9 (September 1982): 10.

40. George L. Whaley, "The Impact of Robotics Technology Upon Human Resource Management," *Personnel Administrator* 27, no. 9 (September 1982): 61.

41. Carl Remick, "Robots: New Faces on the Production Line," *Management Review* 68 (May 1979): 26.

42. Rick Manning, "GE's Refrigerator Unit Warms Up to Change," *Courier-Journal* (October 14, 1987): B1.

43. International Business Machines Corporation, "Ergonomics," *Personnel Journal* 65, no. 6 (June 1986): 95–102.

44. Leon Greenberg, *A Practical Guide to Productivity Measurement* (Washington, DC: Bureau of National Affairs, 1973).

45. Michael W. Mercer, "Turnover: Reducing the Costs," *Personnel* (December 1988): 38.

46. Barney Olmsted, "Workplace Flexibility: From Employee Accommodation to Business Strategy," *The Human Resources Professional* (Fall 1992): 27.

47. Ibid.

48. Sue Shellenbarger, "Some Thrive, But Many Wilt Working at Home," *The Wall Street Journal* (December 14, 1993): B1.

49. Ibid.

50. Ibid.

51. Sue Shellenbarger, "I'm Still Here! Home Workers Worry They're Invisible," *The Wall Street Journal* (December 16, 1993): B1.

52. "Shift to Temporary Help Appears Permanent," *Sunday World-Herald*, Omaha, Nebraska (September 5, 1993): G-1.

53. Ibid.

54. Marilyn Kennedy, "A Nightmare Scenario," *Across the Board* (July-August 1993): 11.

55. Ibid.

56. Chris Tilly, "Reasons for the Continuing Growth of Part-time Employment," *Monthly Labor Review* (March 1991): 10–18.

57. Ibid., p. 12.

58. Michael Frease and Robert A. Zawacki, "Job-Sharing: An Answer to Productivity Problems?" *The Personnel Administrator* (October 1979): 35–37.

59. Grett S. Meier, *Job Sharing* (Kalamazoo, MI: Upjohn Institute, 1978), pp. 1–3.

60. Kirkland Ropp, "The Solution: Steelcase Inc.," *Personnel Administrator* 32, no. 8 (August 1987): 79.

61. "Flexible Work Schedules," *Small Business Report* (October 1978): 24–25.

62. Ibid., pp. 24–25.

63. Keith Bernard, "Flextime's Potential for Management," *The Personnel Administrator* (October 1979): 51–54.

64. James Fraze, "Preparing for a Different Future," *Resource* 7, no. 1 (January 1988): 1, 10.

65. Ibid.

66. Randall B. Dunham and Jon L. Pierce, "Attitudes toward Work Schedules: Construct Definition, Instrument Development, and Validation," *Academy of Management Journal* 29, no. 1 (March 1986): 170–82.

CHAPTER **6**

EMPLOYEE RECRUITMENT

CHAPTER OUTLINE

CHAPTER OBJECTIVES

1. To explain how the labor market operates.
2. To understand the need for human resources planning.
3. To recognize the advantages of filling vacancies with internal job applicants.
4. To cite the keys to a successful job posting program.
5. To identify the advantages of filling vacancies with external job applicants.

6. To describe methods of recruiting qualified and available job applicants.

7. To evaluate alternatives to recruiting permanent new employees.

Every organization, regardless of its size, product, or service, must recruit applicants to fill positions. *Recruitment* is the process of acquiring applicants who are available and qualified to fill positions in the organization. Most often, HR administrators will actively recruit only as positions become vacant. Through direct applications by individuals and by walk-in applicants, an organization can maintain a large pool of available and qualified applicants without much additional recruitment effort. But because of federal guidelines and the increasing need to hire the very best applicants, HR administrators find it necessary to recruit even when they have a large number of available and qualified applicants. Sometimes the process provides unexpected, humorous events, as presented in Figure 6-1, "Resumania."

Recruiting workers in other countries differs substantially from the American process. Japanese and German employers, for example, develop long-term employee relationships and primarily recruit from the best and brightest high school students. Students in those countries are aware that their final examinations taken at the end of high school determine their job potential, which in turn makes the exams very competitive. Honda and Toyota, for example, select their future workers directly from high school based on their final examination scores. In Germany, half of each high school graduating class goes directly into employers' apprenticeship programs.[1]

RECRUITMENT STRATEGIES IN A DIVERSE WORK FORCE

As discussed in Chapter 3, the often cited landmark study *Workforce 2000* projected the labor force for the year 2000. The study shows that the labor force is experiencing

1. A substantial increase in minority representation (57 percent of all new workers).

2. A substantial increase in female workers (65 percent of all new workers).

3. An older work force (median age of thirty-nine) due to the aging of the baby-boom generation.[2]

These significant demographic shifts in the available labor supply are having a profound impact on recruitment strategies utilized by employers.

Recruiting good applicants has always been challenging; however, demographic and economic factors in today's society require employers to utilize more flexible and innovative recruitment methods. The reality, which was projected by the Bureau of Labor Statistics, is an aging work force that has fewer young people entering the job market to replace retirees; in addition, of those new entrants, 83 percent are women, members of minority groups, or immigrants.[3] This changing work force enables employers to achieve diversity.

To attract and keep good people today requires flexibility. As discussed in *HR in the News:* "What American Workers Value in the

FIGURE 6-1 Resumania

Some time back, while excavating my desk top, I stumbled across an unopened press release of the variety which choke newsroom mailboxes and trash cans almost daily. However, I found this press release—from Robert Half, a New York employment specialist—well worth the reading. Half, who recruits financial executives, accountants, and data processors, has for many years been collecting inappropriate, unintentional, humorous, and self-defeating material that job candidates have included in their résumés. He calls it "resumania."

For example, a Salt Lake City bookkeeper wrote, "I am very conscientius and accurite." A Boston accountant stated, "My consideration will be given to relocation anywhere in the English-speaking world and/or Washington, D.C." A Cleveland computer programmer stipulated, "Will relocate anywhere—except Russia, Red China, Vietnam, or New York City."

Here's what some job hunters had to say when asked why they left their last job: "The sales manager was a dummy." "Responsibility makes me nervous." "The company made me a scapegoat—just like my three previous employers." "They insisted that all employees get to work by 8:45 every morning. Couldn't work under those conditions."

Under the heading of "I don't think they meant to say that," Half includes: "I am also a notary republic." "The firm currently employs 20 odd people."

Prospective employers are still trying to figure out the résumé of a San Jose, Calif., man who wrote, "Please call me after 5:30 P.M., because I am self-employed and my employer does not know I am looking for another job."

Resumania may be avoided, Half advised, by using logic and common sense and by making sure the completed résumé is written in a factual, businesslike, readable, and tactful manner. Examples of what not to do include the résumé of a Pittsburgh job seeker who described her ideal employer: "Perfect would be an organization beset with a variety of problems while simultaneously beginning to stir with the fever of acquisitions and diversification. As the nature of the job declines in the hierarchy of preferences, so obviously would come into play the decisiveness of compensating subordinating factors."

A New York credit manager (who should have pursued a career in law) wrote: "While I am open to the initial nature of an assignment, I am decidedly disposed that it be so oriented as to at least partially incorporate the experience enjoyed heretofore, and that it be configured so as to ultimately lead to the application of more rarefied facets of financial management as the major sphere of responsibility."

Finally, we are left to ponder the fate of an Omaha bank officer whose résumé read, "I can type, pitch hay, and shear sheep. I am also skilled at groundhog hunting and ballroom dancing." And what do you suppose ever happened to the Philadelphia computer operator who bragged, "I was proud to win the Gregg Typting Award"?

Workplace," workers today place a high value on interesting work, open communication, and a positive family/work atmosphere. At IBM, the HR department regularly surveys all employees. "There's a message that comes in loud and clear," according to IBM spokesman Mike Shore, "and that's flexibility." The growing labor shortage caused by the aging work force requires employers to be more flexible. In practice, they must seek people who were not previously recruited—people who have taken early retirement, new immigrants, nonworking women, and the disabled. The largest potential source of workers is the 14 million nonworking women caring for their families at home. To coax these women into the labor force requires employer-sponsored day care, flexible hours, part-time work, job sharing, and extended maternity leave. Women will fill *two-thirds* of the new jobs created in the coming decade. That is

What American Workers Value in the Workplace

A comprehensive survey of American workers revealed important information for recruiters. Unlike their parents and grandparents, today's workers do not place as high a value on factors such as opportunity for management positions, size of employer, salary/wages, and access to decision-makers.

Instead workers place high value on flexible scheduling, attention to personal needs, open communication, interesting work, and quality management. Even more important, 47 percent of workers indicate they are willing to change jobs and accept lower pay to achieve their goals.

American workers are also less loyal to their employers than in the past. That result is not surprising since 42 percent reported they had been laid-off or "downsized," 28 percent witnessed management cutbacks, and another 20 percent feared being fired.

Workers rated men and women managers about the same in areas of communication, recognition, fairness, and support. Women managers were viewed as slightly more sympathetic to family or personal problems. In stark contrast, however, only 60 percent of women managers rated their career opportunities as good compared to 84 percent of the men.

Faith Wohl, Director of Human Resource Initiatives for DuPont, said the results "make you catch your breath" and strongly suggest work-family programs broadened and integrated into the workplace. An impressive two-thirds of employees with children indicated they lack adequate time with their children and often arrive home exhausted.

---

why flexibility is the recruitment motto for the 1990s.[4]

Employers are responding to the labor shortage with a number of nontraditional recruitment strategies, including the following:[5]

- *Minority training programs* At a time when 50 percent of all jobs require a high school diploma and 30 percent a college degree, many minority applicants cannot meet those requirements. To assist minority applicants and achieve a more diverse work force, Aetna Life & Casualty, for example, offers training programs covering basic writing and mathematics skills, as well as job-specific instruction.

- *Internships and mentoring programs* Employers are introducing students to the opportunities available through education by means of internships and mentoring programs. Inroads, Inc., in St. Louis, matches

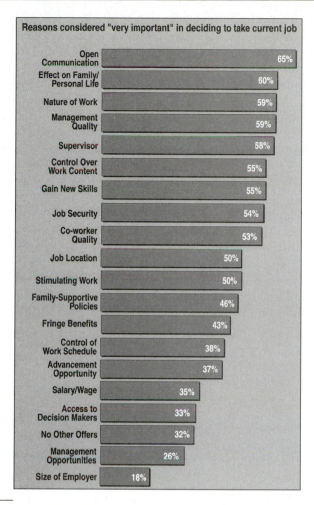

Reasons considered "very important" in deciding to take current job

Reason	Percentage
Open Communication	65%
Effect on Family/Personal Life	60%
Nature of Work	59%
Management Quality	59%
Supervisor	58%
Control Over Work Content	55%
Gain New Skills	55%
Job Security	54%
Co-worker Quality	53%
Job Location	50%
Stimulating Work	50%
Family-Supportive Policies	46%
Fringe Benefits	43%
Control of Work Schedule	38%
Advancement Opportunity	37%
Salary/Wage	35%
Access to Decision Makers	33%
No Other Offers	32%
Management Opportunities	26%
Size of Employer	18%

SOURCE: Sue Shellenbarger, "Work-Force Finds Loyalty Weak," *The Wall Street Journal* (September 3, 1993): B1, 2, and the *National Study of the Changing Workforce* (Families and Work Institute, 1993).

minority students seeking internships in the sciences with employers.

- *Career fairs* Employers are increasingly trying to attract retirees back into the work force. Days Inn of America sponsors national career fairs in locations that are likely to attract retirees. At the fairs, they emphasize special incentives designed to attract older applicants, such as tuition reimbursements for grandchildren. The hotel chain has been able to recruit over one-quarter of its reservation clerks through the program and has experienced a 39 percent reduction in turnover in those positions.

- *Finder's fees* A traditional effective source of new applicants—current employees—is being given a new twist by employers offering bonuses or finder's fees to employees who recruit new hires. Chicago's Continental Bank offers a $300 finder's fee to employees who find new clerical workers. Similar to finder's fees are sign-on bonuses offered to any new employees. Sign-on bonuses have become very popular in hospitals as a means of attracting hard-to-hire nurses and technicians.

- *Telerecruiting* Technology is creating new avenues for recruitment, as well as affecting other HR functions. Cable television has enabled employers to buy time on "employment channels" to air thirty-second want ads on stations such as Chicago's WGBO-TV/Channel 55 (the Television Employment Network) and Channel 21 in Washington, D.C. (the Employment Channel). Interested persons typically call the advertising employer, and the initial interview is conducted over the telephone (i.e., telerecruiting). The résumé information is entered on a computer data bank, which is then accessed when openings occur.

- *Diversity data banks* Employers striving to increase the diversity of their work force often find qualified, culturally diverse candidates difficult to locate since they are less likely to respond to traditional recruitment methods. The need has given rise to national data banks such as Hispan Data, a service specializing in providing recruiters with résumé data on Hispanics for jobs ranging from entry level to MBAs and experienced professionals. Employers, including Mobil Oil Corporation, Apple Computer, Dean Witter Reynolds, Inc., and McDonald's, pay a membership fee for unlimited access to the data bank. Candidates pay only a $5 fee to be included in the file.[6]

LABOR MARKET INFORMATION

An organization's recruitment efforts must compare favorably with its competitors'. A firm's HR department must realize that it is competing with other organizations in the local area for the same good job applicants. In most instances, some type of wage survey is used to maintain labor market information for the local area. Most professional organizations will conduct surveys not only for the local area but for regional and national areas as well. Professional positions require a greater regional and national emphasis because individuals seeking professional jobs are often more willing to relocate to take challenging jobs.

Within the local labor market, a firm can either compile its own survey of wages and positions or use published surveys for semiskilled and unskilled jobs, as well as clerical and other positions. Published surveys can be obtained from union groups, academic groups, and government sources. Local offices of the U.S. Employment Service are probably the most commonly used information source. The survey information available at these local offices is free and presented in a comprehensive, professional manner. The cost of personally compiling survey information for different jobs is prohibitive, even if it could be done completely and professionally. Because the U.S. Employment Service does the same surveying throughout the country and has comparative information for different localities, it is an attractive source of survey information.

One widely used statistic is the **unemployment rate**. Observing changes in the unemployment rate over a period of time can help a firm determine the labor market conditions of a local area. But the **labor force participation rate** for an area is also an important statistic that should be understood and utilized in the recruitment process. On several occasions, the government has claimed that the total number of employees working had increased, while labor unions have indicated that the unemployment rate had increased.[7] Both statements can be true for the same period if many persons who are part of the **labor reserve** decide to join the labor force. Housewives, students, and retired individuals take jobs in hard times to supplement family incomes. The result is that more individuals are employed at the same time that the number of unemployed in an area increases due to lay-offs and economic conditions. Consequently, the unemployment rate increases even though more individuals are working in a labor market area.

The first step in the recruiting process is to determine the relevant labor market and gather information about it. The relevant labor market will determine which strategy and method of recruitment a firm will use. Recruiting methods are quite diverse in their cost and operation. Which one an organization chooses to fill its particular jobs is greatly affected by the survey information available.[8]

Labor Market Sources

The people most available for recruitment are the **unemployed**, who can be contacted through direct application, employment agencies, or advertisements. Other sources often need to be considered when recruiting top candidates.

Part-time employees are good examples of recently developed recruitment sources. In past years, some managers believed that part-time employees were not loyal to the organization and did not produce at the level of full-time employees. However, organizations have found that part-time employees are very productive and that there are qualified applicants who wish to work on a part-time basis. Due to a decrease in benefit costs and lower wages, part-time employees are often less expensive to the organization; if part-time employees can produce at the same level as full-time employees, they then become an attractive alternative. Administrators have also found that part-time employees often have greater enthusiasm for jobs that are traditionally boring and routine because they do not face constant repetition, day after day, for long periods of time.

Underemployed individuals are another group of applicants that can be successfully recruited. Due to a better-educated work force

and a shortage of better-paying positions in many parts of the country and many occupations, some full-time employees feel they are underemployed because their jobs are unrelated to their interests and training. Many of these people are not actively looking for jobs, but they can be recruited by another organization because they would prefer jobs more in line with their training and skills.

Pirating takes place when search firms actively recruit employees from other organizations. Administrators may become aware of an able employee at a competitive firm or at a firm in a related industry. They pirate an individual away from another employer by offering a more attractive salary, better working conditions, or other benefits. In some industries and for some large firms, pirating is preferred to hiring recent college graduates because trained, experienced persons can more quickly become productive and successful.

A rapidly growing labor market source is the **older worker**. Employers are increasingly turning to the recruitment of workers in the expanding forty to sixty-four age group as the number of workers in the sixteen to twenty-four age group continues to decrease. Several industries including fast-food, retailing, insurance, and temporary office help are actively recruiting the older worker.[9] Besides the change in demographics, Jim von Greup, director of public affairs for Wal-Mart Department Stores, believes that there are other valid reasons to recruit older workers: "The older workers have good ethics and work habits. Generally, they have very good skills in dealing with the public, and in many cases they are good teachers for younger workers." Philip Johnson, HR director of the Winn-Dixie supermarket chain, adds, "They have the self-discipline to stick with a job and see it through."[10]

In fact, 1994 was a historic year for older workers in America. That year the median age for all working Americans, which has been steadily climbing, reached forty. Thus, half of the U.S. labor force was included in the "older" category, as defined by the ADEA. Discrimination against older workers continues, largely due to prejudiced thinking and myths, according to Sally Dunaway, attorney for the American Association of Retired Persons. Such unfair stereotypes include the following: "older workers can't learn computer skills," "they get sick more often," "they are closed-minded and won't take direction from younger supervisors," and "they have too many accidents." These myths often lead to discriminatory treatment and over 30,000 age discrimination suits each year. More employers, however, are actively recruiting older workers. Days Inn President John Russell began a campaign to hire older workers because "they are good for business." After eight years the program produced significant results, including lower turnover, better customer relations, and reduced stress. In addition, according to Russell, "if you need someone to stay, the seniors are the first to volunteer."[11]

The Travelers Insurance Company was one of the first to establish a retiree job bank. Bringing back its own retirees to work part-time has become common at Travelers. Small-business owners have also utilized the expertise of retirees (see *HR in the News:* "Entrepreneurs Recruit Retirees"). The Travelers' Retiree Job Bank is a pool of retirees that serves as an in-house temporary agency to fill positions during peak periods, vacations, and illnesses. Travelers has found that 90 percent of its retirees are interested in working part-time and provide an excellent pool of trained, low-cost (few benefits) labor. Similar retiree programs have been successful at Bank of America, Polaroid Corporation, Kentucky Fried Chicken, Lockheed, and Motorola.[12]

What attributes in candidates do recruiters look for most often? According to the recruiters in Figure 6-2, the top criteria include initiative, technical skills, communication skills, analytical skills, and internal motivation.

Operation of the Labor Market

Many economists claim that the labor market operates in a very predictable pattern: to get more individuals into the labor supply, a firm should offer higher wages as an incentive. This economic principle assumes that applicants are aware of the wages and benefits offered by different organizations. It also assumes that a wage and benefit comparison will be the basis of accepting or rejecting job offers. In reality, the labor market does not operate according to the simple economic model of wage levels and labor supply. Instead, most applicants who are looking for jobs or who consider themselves underemployed are not aware of the labor market in their area. Often they have only general notions, at best, of what the going wage rates are, unless they are in a heavily unionized or specialized field. Even if they do know the going wage rates for their jobs, they usually have a difficult time comparing the benefit plans of different organizations. Many do not even consider the benefit plans when comparing organizations. Faced with a lack of information, applicants often concentrate on the nature of the work, whether it is pleasant and desirable, the gross salary, and, perhaps, opportunities for promotion.

There is a tendency for hourly workers to seek jobs informally through newspapers and friends. Typically, hourly individuals do not know what the labor market wage rate is. If they quit one job before finding a new job, they feel compelled to accept the next offer they receive. Hourly workers also tend to stay in one labor market rather than look for jobs in other labor markets.

Professional workers generally know more about the market and have a better idea of the going wage rates. They tend to compare the benefits of various organizations to some degree. Usually professional workers have a broader geographic market, are more willing to relocate, and will interview in other geographic areas. Membership in professional organiza-

Entrepreneurs Recruit Retirees

Janice King of San Jose, California, decided to abandon her career as an electronics component inspector and start her own business. She dreamed of owning a business which would provide true quality care to the elderly, including cooking and housekeeping. But like many entrepreneurs, King had no knowledge of how to develop a business plan, cash-flow analysis, or marketing strategy. Realizing her own limitations, King recruited a 77-year-old retired engineer, businessman Lloyd Michels, who led her through the entire planning process. "He really took his time and got down to the nitty-gritty of how to write a business plan, how to find a target market and everything I needed to know to start a business," Ms. King said. After only two years Michels and King had turned her $3,000 investment into a half-million-dollar business employing 77 employees.

King was not the first entrepreneur to tap the expertise of a retired business executive. She followed thousands of others who have contacted the Service Corps of Retired Executives (SCORE), which provides such assistance to thousands of small business owners in the United States. SCORE is funded by the U.S. Small Business Administration. The volunteer retirees address problems ranging from how to secure capital to selling products to buyers. Owners can receive unlimited counseling from SCORE, which King says "is a service you can't put a price tag on."

When owners contact SCORE, they are matched with a counselor according to the nature of their problem. The most common areas include retailing, developing a business plan, obtaining capital, cash flow, and accounting. The key for the owners, according to SCORE counselors, is for them to "learn and grow on their own," with SCORE providing assistance.

SOURCE: Adapted from "Fledging Entrepreneurs Tap Expertise of Retirees," *The San Jose Mercury News,* reprinted in the *World Herald* (November 7, 1993): B1.

tions that provide national and regional wage surveys helps professional personnel keep abreast of the job market. Typically, professional personnel will stay in their jobs until they find more desirable jobs; thus, they do not feel compelled to take the first new job that is offered to them.

HUMAN RESOURCES PLANNING

How many people will we need? What specific skills will be needed by employees three years from now that they do not currently possess? These are two of the most difficult questions faced by HR managers. Overstaffing causes

FIGURE 6-2 What Recruiters Are Looking For.

SOUTHERN CALIFORNIA GAS COMPANY
Los Angeles-based natural gas supplier
Joyce Ridley, employment manager

> In new employees we look for an ability to take initiative in whatever situation is presented. Our employees should also have a positive attitude and a flexibility in their attitudes and approaches. We also want people with a strong work ethic and a commitment to doing a good job. . . . We are also looking for females to perform jobs that have traditionally been filled by males.

HUGHES AIRCRAFT COMPANY
Westchester County, New York–based defense contractor
Robert Williams, director of employees research, education and development

> The skills we're looking for when we promote someone depends on the level of management we're recruiting for. If it's a fairly low level of management then we're emphasizing technical skills because this person will be supervising workers in a fairly hands-on way. In middle management, we are looking for strong interpersonal skills because these people are supervising the hands-on managers and communicating the results upward in the management chain. At the highest level of management, we look for people who have strong conceptual skills and who are adept at long-range planning and goal setting.

AST RESEARCH INC.
Irvine–based computer maker
Howard Derman, director of human resources

> We like to see people with personal accomplishments and achievements. We want people with creativity and flexibilty in their style and approach to the job. It's nice to have people who are book smart, but it's better to have people who have flexibility and creativity to apply their knowledge in a common-sense kind of way. Unfortunately, a lot of people don't have this. We also look for the personal chemistry between the corporation and the employee. We have to know if the style and aspirations of the applicant match the culture of the company because if they don't the employee won't be happy.

excessive costs, but understaffing causes quality to suffer and opportunities to be missed. Thus, **human resources planning**, also called *manpower planning,* can be important in holding down costs while providing a productive work force.[13] No firm can rely on obtaining critical, highly skilled personnel at a moment's notice.[14]

A survey of over 2000 chief executives showed that 82 percent thought that human resources planning was their organization's most important HR function. Yet many companies have virtually no such planning or provide it only for top administrative positions. Why? Human resources planning has been called a problem waiting for a solution. Some

practitioners say it has seldom been successful, has proven cumbersome and expensive, and lacks specialists in the HR field.[15]

Forecasts

Determining the future supply and demand for human resources is a first step in developing a manpower plan. The *supply forecast* is the result of direct interviews with employees and the use of standard HR data, such as work histories, skills acquired, job progression, and demographics. Modern computerized HR systems have simplified the process of generating supply reports, such as the one in Figure 6-3.

The estimate of the total number of employees needed as well as the skills required is

FIGURE 6-2 *(continued)*

WALT DISNEY COMPANY
Burbank-based entertainment company
Curtis Kishl, manager of employment and professional staffing

We want people who can take an innovative approach to traditional business situations and problems, and we try to find these people by asking a variety of hypothetical questions in our interviews. We're also looking for analytical skills and the ability to present clear solutions to various business situations. Our employees should also be familiar with children's products, possess a feel for the social significance of Mickey and understand that the Disney company stands for family entertainment.

FLOUR CORPORATION
Irvine, California–based engineering and construction firm
Karen Vari, manager of human resources

Beyond the appropriate skills and background for the particular job, we are looking for strong communication skills, a willingness to do the work required by the job, an ability to be a team player and take an innovative and creative approach to the job. We like to hire what we call "committed champions," a term that means internally motivated people who are willing to take some risks. We also look for people who are flexible and can perform many tasks. Because we are a worldwide organization and globalization is an increasingly important part of business, we also look for our employees to be fairly mobile and comfortable with change.

FIRST INTERSTATE BANK
Los Angeles-based bank
Shirley Perkins, senior vice president

Aside from the purely technical skills which vary from job to job, we look for people with good interpersonal skills. We want people who are sales oriented, people who are comfortable selling themselves, selling the corporation and selling the products of the corporation. This means we need people who are self-confident, have the ability to communicate and are able to convey their enthusiasm for their job and the products they are selling.

SOURCE: Adapted from: "What Employers Are Looking For," *The Los Angeles Times* (September 17, 1989): 2, 5. Copyright, 1989, Los Angeles Times. Reprinted by permission.

known as the *demand forecast.* Planners find it difficult to develop precise demand forecasts for various reasons, such as changes in sales patterns, technological innovations, and company reorganizations. Precise demand forecasts are not as important when there is great flexibility in an organization's work force, when employees are mobile and multiskilled, and (most important) when workers are easily found and hired. Why, then, bother with forecasting? Because people are geographically less mobile (less willing to relocate) today than in the past, employees are retiring earlier, and

jobs have often become too specialized to be learned quickly.[16]

Demand forecasts are developed from two main sources: standard statistical data and knowledgeable personnel. Statistical techniques, such as correlation analysis, can be used to detect significant relationships between staffing levels and such variables as the economic climate, the unemployment rate, the competition, and sales levels. But all statistical approaches contain a bias: they predict the future based solely on the past. Thus, critical factors may be omitted. Such factors might

FIGURE 6-3 A Supply Report.

Job Title, Name	Social Security	Date Assigned	EEO	Status	Status Date	Promotable to
Plant Superintendent						
Jackson, Ralph	123-45-6789	05-77		R	10-84	
Plant Engr. Mgr.						
Robinson, Larry	234-56-7891	08-79		P	10-84	Plant Super.
Plant Controller						
Brown, Sarah	345-67-8912	01-78	1F			
Supv. Process 1						
Miles, Jack	456-78-9123	10-67	5M	Q		
Fleming, Mark	567-89-1234	02-69		R	12-82	
Pressler, Roy	678-91-2345	09-77		P	10-84	Plant Engr. Mgr.
Supv. Process 2						
Johnson, Tom	789-12-3456	04-74		R	09-83	
Plant Pers. Mgr.						
Powers, John	891-23-4567	11-78		P	09-83	Supv. Process 2
Indust. Engr. Mgr.						
Rodriguez, Tom	912-34-5678	06-80	3M	P	06-85	Supv. Process 1
Safety Mgr.						
White, Judy	134-56-7891	02-79	2F	P	09-83	Plant Pers. Mgr.
Qual. Cont. Tech.						
Ling, Sam	245-67-8791	11-81	4M	S		

SOURCE: "Manpower Planning Systems: Part I," by Charles F. Russ, Jr., copyright February 1982. Reprinted with the permission of *Personnel Journal,* Costa Mesa, California; all rights reserved.

Status Codes
S = Satisfactory but not moving
P = Place/promote, hence moving
R = Replace/retire, hence moving
Q = Questionable: employee is on probation and is not moving
EEO Codes
F = Female
M = Male
1 = White
2 = Black
3 = Hispanic
4 = Asian
5 = American Indian

include a plan for a new product line, the introduction of new machinery, the loss of an important contract, or a change in government regulations. Thus, knowledgeable personnel must be involved in decisions about future needs.[17] Once the information has been gathered and analyzed, demand reports are generated.

Once the demand-and-supply forecasts have been made, HR administrators can plan on how to address projected shortages or surpluses. Specialized training, early-retirement incentives, and increased outside recruitment are a few of the techniques available to address an organization's needs. Keep in mind that the forecasts are not airtight: not all mismatches are cause for action. It may be preferable to wait for further information or to see if projected changes take place.

Management succession planning (MSP) is commonly used to deal with changes in mid- and top-level personnel. The process involves identifying projected vacancies and choosing replacement candidates for each position, estimating the promotability of each candidate, and, most important, identifying development and training needs to ensure the availability of qualified personnel for future openings.[18]

MSP is a method for career planning designed in part to satisfy Equal Employment Opportunity Commission and affirmative action (EEOC/AA) requirements. The MSP system generates three reports. The first is the supply report, which classifies each individual listed as satisfactory but not ready for promotion or placement on another job; promotable; replaceable or retiring; or questionable because of probation or some other status. The second is the demand report, which shows new positions due to expansion, turnover, or promotion. And the third is the HR report, which shows the supply-demand equation, including the name, job, and location of all those suitable for promotion. The purpose of the HR report is to develop a zero balance between the projected career changes and the expected demand changes.[19]

An excellent example of how human resource planning can be tied to a firm's strategic business planning is provided by Robbins and Meyers, Inc., a multiproduct manufacturer with over 2500 employees. The company instituted an annual planning cycle starting in September, as shown in Figure 6-4. Managers were provided background material, and planning dates were set. The planning process comprised the following steps:[20]

Identify Strategic Issues Managers identified issues that would constrain or enhance a business plan.

Conduct Organizational Analysis Managers developed a one- to two-year organizational plan to deal with structural changes.

Forecast Staffing Requirements Managers identified open positions caused by turnover or growth.

Develop Succession Plans Managers developed individual succession plans for important positions.

Identify Training Requirements Training managers developed programs based on individual and organizational needs.

Identify Development Plans for Selected Employees Those singled out in the succession plans were given individual development plans.

Conduct Organizational Review The HR plan of each division was reviewed by the president and manager of corporate planning.

Develop Budgets Approved plans were given budgets for implementation.

Management at Robbins and Meyers developed their human resources planning as a logical outgrowth of their strategic business planning. Their human resources planning constituted a continuous process—developing from the corporate business plan and helping that plan succeed.[21]

Entry-Level Planning

Human resources planning for mid- and top-level positions focuses on specific individuals—their replacement on retirement or their training, development, and promotion. Human resources planning is also used for entry-level positions, where the focus is not on career planning but on the forecasting of the number of entry-level applicants that will be needed at various times.

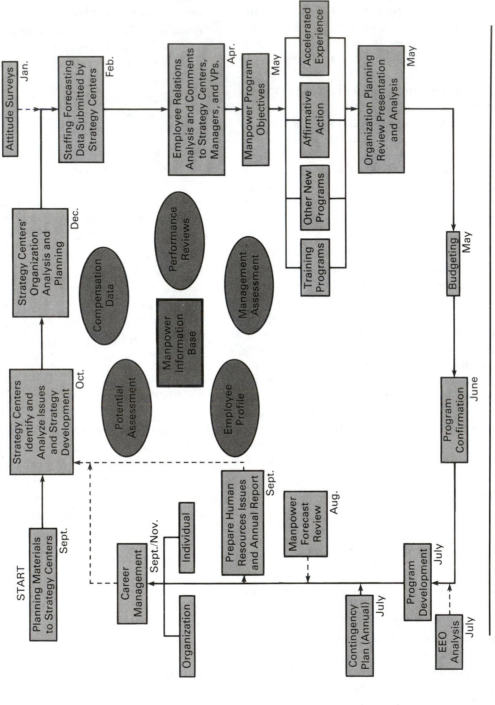

FIGURE 6-4 Robbins and Meyers, Inc., of Dayton, Ohio, instituted human resources planning that was closely tied to the company's strategic business planning. As this flowchart shows, their annual planning cycle begins in September and proceeds through a number of specific steps.

SOURCE: David R. Leigh, "Business Planning Is People Planning," *Personnel Journal* 63 no. 5 (May 1984): 44–50. Used by permission.

The HR manager anticipates the company's needs, the training time that may be required, and employee turnover. As Figure 6-5 indicates, the recruiter with a simple formula can estimate the number of applicants needed in order to fill various entry-level positions. The process can be used for each different entry-level position; thus, four or five different estimates may be made. If a firm typically hires a large number of entry-level clerical workers or sales representatives during the year, such estimates can minimize the time such positions are left open because of a lack of qualified trainees.

Human resources planning balances the long-run demand for employees with the long-run supply of internal and external applicants. Adjustments in training, the transfer of employees, and external recruitment can then minimize severe personnel shortages in future years.

There are a number of steps in determining the number of positions a company will need to fill. First, future customer demands are estimated by examining the market for products and services, the competition, and long-term growth potential. Once customer demands are

estimated, decisions must be made regarding financial resource availability. Those resources determine the two critical inputs in the organization process: capital and materials. Once financial determinations are made, the level of operation must be decided. Management estimates the required level of operation in future months and years so that it can economically purchase materials and equipment. Sometimes overlooked is an estimate of the level of operation and its effect on HR needs. Estimating the level of operation is critical to HR planning because it involves not only the number of employees needed but also the different types of employees required for current and future positions.

RECRUITMENT SOURCES

Once management has determined an organization's staffing requirements, the recruitment process begins. The first decision made is whether a particular job opening should be filled by someone already employed or by an applicant from outside. Normally, firms recruit both internally and externally. In each case,

FIGURE 6-5 Determining how many qualified entry-level applicants are needed annually.

Formula

$$\text{Applicants Needed Annually} = \text{Current and Future Entry-level Positions Needed} \times \text{Turnover Rate} \times \text{Ratio of Applicants Needed to Every Applicant Hired}$$

Example

$$\text{Applicants Needed Annually} = 40 \text{ (clerical positions)} \times 0.5 \text{ (rate)} \times \frac{3}{1} \text{ (ratio)}$$

$$\text{Applicants Needed Annually} = 60$$

If training programs begin on the first of each month, then

$$\frac{60 \text{ Applicants}}{12 \text{ Months}} = 5 \text{ applicants needed to start each training program each month}$$

Table 6-1 Advantages of Recruiting Internally and Externally

Internal Recruitment	External Recruitment
Increases morale of all employees	Applicant pool is greater
Knowledge of personnel records	New ideas, contacts
Chain effect of promotion	Reduces internal infighting
Need to hire only at entry level	Minimizes Peter Principle
Usually faster, less expensive	

the advantages of recruiting outside the organization must be weighed against the advantages of recruiting inside the organization.[22] Table 6-1 shows a few advantages of each type of recruitment. As Figure 6-6 illustrates, however, the use of sources by employers varies by industry.

Internal Applicants

Of the several advantages to recruiting within the organization, probably most important is the increase in morale for employees who believe that the organization will reward successful performance and that they will be promoted to higher positions. The lack of possible promotion and advancement opportunities within an organization can be a major cause of turnover and dissatisfaction.

Managers recruiting within the organization also have the advantage of using HR data maintained by the company. Interviews with supervisors and analysis of employee performance records can be added to the applicant's file during the recruitment process. At best, the organization can only guess at the completeness and objectivity of information received from other organizations. Only after years of interaction with the other organizations can an HR officer begin to measure the accuracy of external applicants' HR files.

A promotion within the organization often leads to a vacant position, which can then be filled from within the organization. This chain effect on promotion means that two or more positions will often be filled at one time when internal recruitment is used. Thus internal promotions have a positive effect on employee morale because each promotion positively affects several employees.

One potential problem associated with internal promotions is the creation of a *glass ceiling* (see *HR in the News*: "Glass Ceiling or Comfort Zone?"). This internal barrier prevents women or minorities from being promoted beyond middle management positions. Employers should carefully review their promotion history and take steps to ensure that such ceilings are not occurring.

When organizations promote from within, often only entry-level vacancies are filled from the outside. The advantage of this approach is that it is not necessary to experiment with unknown people at high levels in the organization; individuals have a chance to prove themselves in lower-level positions first. Rewarding employees for successful performance also can be faster and less expensive than external recruitment. Therefore, because an organization uses its own records and sources of testing, internal recruitment can save money and time.

Employee Relocation Internal promotion with large companies often involves the relocation of an employee from one city to another. The work force of today may be less mobile than that of twenty years ago. The lure of a new home, better job, and higher salary has waned; instead, the prospect of locating in a new city often brings the anticipation of higher house payments, real estate hassles, and unhappy spouses who must find new jobs.

Transferring an employee from one location to another, however, remains one means of filling a vacant position. The obvious advantage is that the employer is well aware of the employ-

FIGURE 6-6 Most prevalent recruiting source by job category.

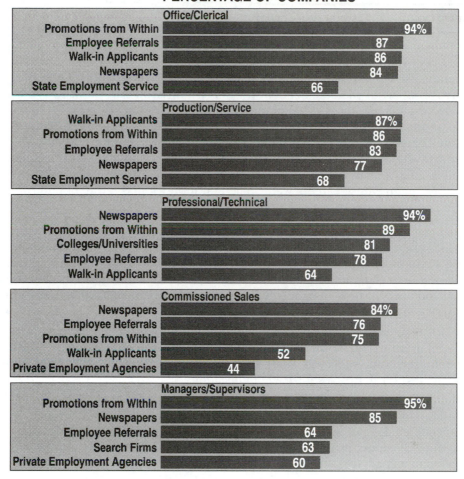

PERCENTAGE OF COMPANIES

Office/Clerical
- Promotions from Within — 94%
- Employee Referrals — 87
- Walk-in Applicants — 86
- Newspapers — 84
- State Employment Service — 66

Production/Service
- Walk-in Applicants — 87%
- Promotions from Within — 86
- Employee Referrals — 83
- Newspapers — 77
- State Employment Service — 68

Professional/Technical
- Newspapers — 94%
- Promotions from Within — 89
- Colleges/Universities — 81
- Employee Referrals — 78
- Walk-in Applicants — 64

Commissioned Sales
- Newspapers — 84%
- Employee Referrals — 76
- Promotions from Within — 75
- Walk-in Applicants — 52
- Private Employment Agencies — 44

Managers/Supervisors
- Promotions from Within — 95%
- Newspapers — 85
- Employee Referrals — 64
- Search Firms — 63
- Private Employment Agencies — 60

SOURCE: Compiled from information provided by the Bureau of National Affairs, Inc.'s *Personnel Management, BNA Policy and Practice Series,* as published in K. Michele Kacman, "Look at Who's Talking," *HRMagazine* (February 1993): 57.

ee's abilities and work record. In addition, the newly transferred employee can quickly become productive on the new job with a minimum of training and orientation.

Employee transfers do have disadvantages. The average cost of relocating an employee within the United States is between $20,000 and $50,000. The costs include direct moving expenses, realtor's fees, temporary housing, travel allowances, and assistance in finding employment for spouses. Another disadvantage often involved is disruption of the spouse's career. In dual-career marriages, women are especially concerned about limiting their own careers to accommodate the transfer of a spouse. Most single parents also dislike relocating because of the disruption in the lives of their children or problems with ex-spouses. Overall, employees are increasingly concerned with their quality of life, and therefore less

Glass Ceiling or Comfort Zone?

The glass ceiling may be the wrong metaphor for what keeps working women from reaching the top levels of management. The term suggests an unbreakable barrier which is a part of the organization. Dawn-Marie Driscoll and Carol R. Goldberg believe the correct term is "comfort zone." Executives may do what is comfortable and familiar to them and thus often make decisions which unintentionally create barriers for women. But hundreds of working women have found ways of entering the "comfort zone" or "breaking the glass ceiling" and Driscoll and Goldberg have analyzed their strategies. Both women are also successful examples of women whose careers were stalled until they found a way of entering an organization's comfort zone.

The strategies, in addition to hard work, that Driscoll and Goldberg believe women can employ to reach the top levels of organizations include:

- Be a *rainmaker*. As early in your career as possible, figure out what jobs will allow you to generate revenues, clients and profits. Then determine what training you need for those jobs and get busy. The rainmakers make their companies survive and grow.

- Work to increase your *personal visibility* inside and outside your company. Develop an expertise on subjects related to your work. Tell your company's public-relations staff you want to field phone calls from the press. Give speeches. Write articles for trade publications.

- Build *relationships* with men. "We have to understand that since the Anita Hill thing, guys are nervous, and don't want to make friends with women," Ms. Driscoll said. "But women need men as business friends." Invite male colleagues, business prospects, and industry members for business breakfasts to talk and ask advice.

- *Play golf together.* It's the perfect sport for socializing because it allows you to converse. The golf course remains one of the most important deal-making venues in America, Ms. Driscoll was surprised to discover. Again and again, women told her of business they lost because men stole their clients over golf, of decisions they were excluded from because they weren't on the links with the guys.

SOURCE: "Glass Ceiling Wrong Metaphor," *The Miami Herald* (November 7, 1993): D1.

266

willing to relocate, even if it means passing up a promotion.[23]

Therefore, employee resistance to relocating has increased in recent years. HR managers must provide even greater assistance in relocation to persuade reluctant employees to move. Complete relocation programs, such as the one at US Sprint, may include the following:[24]

Complete Reimbursement of Costs Costs include shipment of belongings, travel for house-hunting trips, temporary living expenses, realtor's fees, closing costs, and storage costs.

Counseling Stress or psychological counseling for employees and family members may be needed. Why? Relocating is one of the ten most stressful lifetime occurrences. Assistance with matters such as locating school districts, good neighborhoods, and so forth is essential.

Spousal Assistance This may include job-hunting trips, income protection if the job search is not successful, and search firm expenses.

Marketing Assistance Expediting the selling of the old home and buying the new one, including financing assistance, can save the employer money.

Employees' dwindling desire to relocate, which began in the 1970s, continues to increase. The rise in dual-career couples, many with children by previous marriages, and the decrease in company loyalty are the primary reasons more employees refuse to relocate, even when given a promotion and a comprehensive assistance program. Demographics indicate that the number of dual-career couples in the labor force will double from 32 percent of all employees to 64 percent by the year 2000; thus, employee reluctance will likely continue to increase. Employees will also see a continuance of mergers, plant closings, and other factors that will continue to diminish employee loyalty. The traditional male employee of the 1950s and 1960s, who worked for a single employer for most of his career, had a wife who stayed home and raised the family, and relocated when asked, often without hesitation, is rare in the 1990s. Thus, HR managers will need to consider employees in the context of their family unit and develop comprehensive relocation programs similar to the one at US Sprint or Mobil Oil Corporation.[25] Mobil decided to avoid relocating employees by centralizing its operations in four "hub" locations. Employees can, therefore, change jobs without relocation.[26]

External Applicants

One of the advantages of recruiting from the outside is that a greater number of applicants can be recruited than could normally be recruited internally. Outside applicants may bring new ideas, work techniques, production methods, or training to the organization, resulting in increased employee productivity.

External applicants also may have contacts that internal employees do not have. In sales, research and technology, and purchasing, for example, good external contacts are critical, and the recruitment of outside applicants with these contacts may be very helpful.

Recruitment of outside applicants for mid-level and higher positions will eliminate infighting by employees jockeying for promotion. Wherever infighting is severe, organizations begin to do more external recruiting to decrease internal dissension.

In recent years, organizations have sought applicants from the outside to minimize promoting employees to levels where they are unable to perform successfully. The concept that every employee will be promoted beyond his or her level of competence is called the **Peter Principle**. This theory has validity; managers often have promoted employees who cannot perform as expected in their new jobs.[27] This theory may be a self-fulfilling prophecy for policymakers who blame the Peter Principle for their own lack of good internal recruitment methods. However, any firm that promotes exclusively from within will experience the effects of the Peter Principle to some extent.

One common method of avoiding the effects of the Peter Principle—and the resulting dissatisfied employee—is the use of temporary titles. For example, an employee is promoted to "acting department head" for an unspecified period of time. If the employee is not capable of performing the job, a permanent department head can be recruited. Thus, the employee does not suffer the embarrassment of failing to handle the position; nor is a demotion or termination made part of the employee's permanent record. Whenever an acting department head proves capable, that employee can be made the permanent department head.

Whether employees are recruited from inside or outside should be determined by the availability of qualified employees in the organization, the size of the organization, and the desire to keep up with contemporary ideas and methods. Employees should realize that external recruitment does not mean that no one is qualified to fill the position internally. Rather, it indicates the need for fresh ideas and new approaches to old problems.

METHODS OF RECRUITMENT

The two most common methods of internal recruiting are bidding and job posting. Bidding is common with unionized organizations; when an opening exists, qualified employees are notified that they may bid on the position if they wish to be considered for it. The employee with the most seniority receives the promotion. This structured process is usually specified in the union contract; promotions are based on seniority and ability. There are a number of methods of external recruiting, including direct applications, employee referrals, campus recruiting, employment agencies, and overtime and temporary help.

Job Posting

One of the most popular methods of filling positions within organizations is **job posting**. A survey of over 6000 companies indicated that job posting is the most common means of filling open positions. Posting has been used to fill over 75 percent of production openings, over 60 percent of clerical openings, and about 50 percent of professional and lower managerial positions.[28]

Job posting methods include at least three proven, effective processes: (1) traditional bulletin boards, (2) computer electronic mail–based systems, and (3) telephone voice mail–based systems. All three methods can be effective, but the last two offer benefits over traditional bulletin boards that include the following:[29]

- Easy access by all employees.
- Twenty-four-hour availability.
- Minimum paperwork.
- Immediate notification to all employees.

More organizations are developing computer- and telephone-based systems (see *HR in the News:* "Telephone Job Posting Systems at AMP") due to these advantages, as well as positive employee responses.

Although job posting is an effective, useful management tool, it can create severe employee morale problems if not handled properly. Managers should consider several aspects of the job-posting process.

First, the job-posting procedure should be clearly explained to the employees and should be followed to the letter each time a position is open. If the procedure varies according to the job or the particular employee applying for a position, employees may suspect that employer subjectivity is unfairly entering into the process.

Second, job specifications should be clear and should include the years of experience, skills, or training employees must have to apply for the posted position. This will make the

Telephone Job Posting
Systems at AMP

AMP Incorporated Inc., a Harrisburg, Pennsylvania firm, is the world's largest manufacturer of electrical and electronic interconnection products. After over 50 years of utilizing a traditional "bulletin board" job posting system for its 15,000 employees, AMP decided it needed a better system. Problems with the old weekly posting system included:

- Employees weren't made aware of openings
- Supervisors didn't have to inform employees that they were considering them for open positions
- No feedback process existed
- The form limited employees to only three career choices
- Some supervisors and managers believed that employees who participated did so because they were unhappy with their current position
- Some business units refused to allow their employees to be considered for jobs in other units
- The process created a tremendous amount of paperwork

After reviewing traditional systems, computer-based systems, and telephone-based systems at other organizations, AMP chose a voice-mail telephone system. The new *Career Opportunities Program* involves five steps:

1. New openings are input into the system by an HR employee and thus are immediately posted for seven days.
2. Any employee can access the system, which lists all openings by job title and job code 24 hours a day. Using voice response the system guides employees through a series of prompts.
3. To apply for a position an employee leaves their name, employee number, the name of their supervisor, and job number. Additional steps or permission is not required.
4. After seven days all employee responses are listed with the employees' work history and given to the hiring supervisor.
5. After the position is filled the system generates a letter to each applicant which includes positive and negative feedback information.

After a trial period the new posting method produced several impressive results:

- 61 percent of the new vacancies were filled internally compared to 44 percent under the previous system.

(continued)

- Recruitment costs decreased from $311,000 to $87,000, for the year despite more than twice the number of positions being filled.
- Positions stayed open 16 percent fewer days.
- Employees and managers preferred the new system. Employees liked its flexibility, the control they have over their career decisions, and the fairness of the new system.

SOURCE: William C. DeLone, "Telephone Job Posting Cuts Costs," *Personnel Journal* (April 1993): 115–18.

decision process easier for management, assuming that strict seniority will not be used as the only criterion and that other factors such as an employee's HR record and the results of interviews will be considered. When only a few job specifications are included in the posted position, the HR specialist will have a larger number of applicants to review during the selection process.

A study of workers' attitudes toward job-posting programs showed that vague or incomplete job requirements were a major source of employee dissatisfaction. Accurate job specifications that clearly detail the nature of the work, duties and responsibilities, and applicant requirements can significantly improve satisfaction with a job-posting program. The result is fewer and better applicants, fewer rejections, and less chance of employee resentment.[30]

Third, job-posting procedures should specify the exact period during which posted positions will remain open. For example, a position may remain open for fourteen working days after it is first posted, and applications will be taken until 4:30 P.M. on the fourteenth day. Also, the procedure should specify that employees on vacation or laid off will be notified by mail or employee publication of posted positions. The exact media to be used in the job-posting process—that is, bulletin boards, the employee newspaper, and so on—should not only be specified but also consistently used unless employees are notified about a change.

Fourth, the application procedure should be clear. For example, an employee may apply for a posted position through the HR department or a supervisor. If the employee applies directly to the HR department, supervisors feel that the chain of command has not been used. On the other hand, employees going through their supervisors sometimes feel that their supervisors may not wish them to receive the positions. A common compromise is to have employees submit written applications for a posted position to the HR department, with a copy to the supervisor. Finally, and perhaps most important, the HR department should ensure that applicants receive adequate feedback once a selection is made. For example, when nine applicants apply for a posted position and one is accepted, the other eight employees may feel rejected. Although no amount of communication will entirely eliminate this feeling, it is imperative that the rejected employees receive feedback on the selection process. Otherwise, the morale of one employee may increase while the motivation of eight other good employees may significantly decrease.

The rejected employees should be given a counseling interview by the HR department or the hiring supervisor. The interview, which can help cushion the person's disappointment, should include the following:[31]

- Reasons for nonacceptance, but with emphasis on the person's qualifications and strengths that made him or her a strong candidate.

- Suggested remedial measures, such as training and education to improve performance in the person's current job, possible new duties, and so on. Such counseling should be aimed at strengthening any weaknesses of the candidate.

- Information concerning possible openings the candidate might apply for in the future.

- Assistance in the posting process, such as how to bid for a new job and how to conduct a job interview.

If properly used, job posting helps employees feel that they have some control over their future in the organization. Job posting often uncovers employee talent that supervisors would not voluntarily reveal. The supervisors may believe that the undue pressure on the department created by a good employee's loss outweighs the morale gained by having an employee promoted outside the department. Job posting also avoids the awkward situation of recommending an employee for promotion who prefers to remain in his or her current job. When an unwanted promotion is offered by a supervisor, the employee may feel obligated to accept it or risk possibly never being asked again. With job posting, employees not interested in positions do not apply.

Direct Applications

For most organizations, direct applications by mail or by individuals applying in person are the largest source of applicants. In the case of blue-collar jobs, walk-ins are often called **gate hires**. Direct applications can provide an inexpensive source of good job applicants to the organization, especially for entry-level, clerical, and blue-collar jobs. In recent years, direct applications from new college graduates have been used to fill other entry-level positions.

The usefulness of direct applications will often depend on the image the organization has in the community and, therefore, the quality of applicants who will apply directly to the organization. The size of an organization and its reputation determine whether applicants will seek out the organization rather than respond to other recruitment methods. Only the largest, best-known organizations in the labor market will receive a large number of direct applications. Organizations that receive many direct applications must develop an efficient means of screening those applications and keeping a current file of qualified candidates. While the cost of recruitment is low if large numbers of applications are received, the cost of screening and maintaining a file of applicants can be quite high. Medium-sized and smaller firms do not receive a large enough volume of direct applications to fill all their positions with available and qualified candidates without using further recruitment methods.

Some newspapers have increased the advantages of newspaper advertising by utilizing a telephone voice-response system to speed up the process, reduce the number of applicants who provide incomplete information, and provide the employer a computerized data base of applicants for easier screening and sorting. An example of a local newspaper ad that offers voice résumé systems to employers appears in Figure 6-7.

Employee Referrals

In recruiting, **employee referrals** are one of the best means of securing applicants. Employees can be encouraged to help their employers locate and hire qualified applicants by rewards, either monetary or otherwise, or by recognition for those who assist the recruitment process.

Employees who recommend applicants place their own reputations on the line; therefore, they are usually careful to recommend only qualified applicants. When recommended applicants are hired, employees take an active interest in helping new employees become successful in their jobs.

Employee referrals are a quick and relatively inexpensive means of recruitment. In skilled, technical, or professional positions, employee referrals can help the organization

FIGURE 6-7 "Apply-by-phone" newspaper advertising.

How to respond to Apply-By-Phone Voice Resumes

ege degree in ad
an area of specialization ad
vertising or an equivalent of 5
amount of work experience.
Apply-by-Phone
398-4555
24Hrs. Job No. 106
**ADVERTISING
SALES ASSISTANT**

1. Dial 398-4555 on your touch-tone telephone.
2. Enter Job No.
3. Be prepared to answer the following questions:
    1. "Please tell us your name, address and home phone number."
    2. "Please tell us about your educational background."
    3. "Please tell us about the company where you last worked, time frame of employment, and a brief description of your job responsibilities."
    4. "Please tell us your current salary or desired salary."
    5. "Please tell us briefly why you believe you are the best person for the position."
    6. Advertiser's custom question.

Invalid or expired box #? Please check to make sure your touch-tone phone is set on tone rather than pulse. If you have additional questions call 342-6633.

Omaha World-Herald

SOURCE: The *Omaha World-Herald* (July 18, 1993): 15–16.

pirate successful employees from other companies. Newly recruited employees from other organizations often bring new insights or new customers to the organization.

Some administrators avoid employee referrals because inbreeding and nepotism can cause employee morale problems, as well as a lack of successful and productive employees in future years. For example, friends of an employee rejected for promotion will also feel rejected. Naturally, employees who recommend applicants are dissatisfied when their applicants are not hired; they may show their dissatisfaction by not cooperating with the new employee. Typically, employee referrals do not help an organization recruit qualified minority candidates to meet equal employment requirements.

In past years, the **old boy network** filled positions in some organizations with friends and relatives. This hiring of former college friends or neighborhood associates leads to a distorted mix of employees and usually an underrepresentation of minority groups in various job categories. Today **networking** has replaced the old boy network, both in name and in practice. The informal interpersonal network of professional contacts and resources that each employee establishes is an invaluable recruitment source. For example, *The Wall Street Journal* estimates that 70 percent of all executive positions are filled through personal contacts.[32]

Before taking advantage of the relatively inexpensive and easy method of recruiting employees through employee referrals, administrators should minimize possible problems by:

- Conducting objective recruiting, which will ensure compliance with EEO/AA guidelines.
- Ensuring that decisions about the hiring of applicants and their salaries are kept confidential. This process should always be confidential, but it is even more important when applicants are referred by current employees.
- Establishing specific policies on nepotism. For example, the company may not allow relatives to work in the same department or to supervise each other.

Employee referral programs often offer rewards to employees who successfully recruit new co-workers. The relentless national nursing shortage caused the University of Kentucky Hospital (UKH) to develop a "prize" referral program. The hospital realized that it needed to hire 200 nurses during a four-month period. Previous recruitment programs had not been successful. The hospital hired the Bernard Hodes advertising firm to develop an employee referral campaign and offer prizes to employees who participated. The firm developed an attractive visual display featuring a school of dolphins that appeared on posters, buttons, and rule brochures. The campaign hired the needed nurses at an average cost per hire of $837, which was 33 percent less than the hospital's previous average cost per hire. And what were the prizes that encouraged employees to make referrals?[33]

- A beach towel for the name of a qualified nurse.
- A round-trip ticket to any U.S. destination for each referral hired.
- A grand prize (by random drawing from among all employees who made successful referrals), which included five vacation days, $1000 in cash, a round-trip ticket for two to any island in the world, and deluxe accommodations.

Campus Recruiting

A new level of sophistication in campus recruiting began in recent years. Employers' prescreening of students has, in many cases, replaced the old method of selection from the placement office's résumé book. Prescreening programs are designed to identify top students, often as juniors, and to begin to introduce them to employers. Professors may play a critical role in identifying such students. Citibank in New York, for example, hires professors to teach specific programs and involve their students where possible. Texas Instruments encourages company executives to teach at the university level, thereby identifying top students on the basis of firsthand experience.

Students who have difficulty finding their first postgraduation job should use the ten leads discussed in Figure 6-8.

Employers in the expanding Sunbelt states who recruit in other states carefully design recruitment brochures to emphasize quality-of-life factors and cost of living, as well as job-related information. Advanced word processing techniques also allow recruiters to send personal letters quickly to thousands of students. Recruitment videos, (see Figure 6-9), which can be used on campuses or for other recruitment efforts, have been effectively used by employers who want to emphasize the quality of their work environment or community. The videos can be left at the university placement office for weeks and still provide students with a more realistic and personal view of the employer.

Many campus recruiters still use the standard thirty-minute campus interview, handing students a copy of their annual report and playing a passive role in recruiting. These recruiters may be unhappy with their campus recruiting program, possibly because more aggressive recruiters have already signed the top students.[34]

Campus recruiting can be divided into two major sources:

1. The trade or technical school that provides

FIGURE 6-8 Job leads for college students.

College students often have difficulty landing their first real job. A poor economy can make the challenge even greater. Ten proven sources for good leads include the following:

1. *Internships*. Many firms are increasingly hiring only students who have proven themselves through an internship with the employer. It is best to find an internship related to your major; however, if that is not possible, find one with a highly desirable employer in a related type of work.

2. *Referrals*. Former employers, professors, neighbors, and relatives can provide valuable leads. Give them a resume and tell them of your job interests.

3. *Placement Offices*. Don't overlook the obvious! Employers often depend on the college placement office for initial contacts.

4. *Nationalize*. Don't count on opportunities in your local area. Other cities and regions may have stronger economies and more job opportunities. You can always move closer to home after you have gained work experience.

5. *Job Fairs*. Check local and out-of-town newspapers for job fairs; attend as many as possible. An employer may not have open a position of interest, but you might sell yourself to a recruiter who has a new opening in your field within a few weeks.

6. *Volunteer*. If you have a strong desire to work for a particular organization or person, offer to volunteer your services for a few weeks to secure the opportunity to sell yourself.

7. *Part-Time Jobs*. It may not meet your career or financial needs immediately, but a part-time position can give you the opportunity to transfer to a full-time position once you have a good work record.

8. *Nonprofit and Government Employers*. Don't ignore the large percentage of jobs that exist in these important and growing segments of the economy.

9. *Self-Employment*. This may be the best time in your life to start your own business. Consider taking a partner if you need help and encouragement. The U.S. Small Business Administration can provide useful assistance.

10. *Small Towns*. Explore the small towns that offer a reasonable commute from your home. Small-town employers are having increasing difficulty hiring qualified workers and therefore may provide that important first job opportunity.

specialized education such as carpentry or auto mechanics.

2. The four-year college, which produces a wide variety of individuals with varying educational and skills levels.

NCR College Recruiting In many ways NCR Corporation, a 52,000-employee worldwide computer manufacturer headquartered in Dayton, Ohio, is similar to many other corporate recruiters. Almost all of the college graduates hired were once NCR interns or scholarship winners. NCR believes in identifying high-performance students early in their college careers and then grooming them for

success in the corporation. The company spends about $350,000 annually on college scholarships and offers several hundred summer internships, which provide meaningful work assignments and give both parties a chance to evaluate each other. What is unique about NCR is that it hires about 75 percent of its new employees from colleges.

This high percentage is due to an evaluation conducted by NCR that resulted in the conclusion that recent college graduates were more adaptable and stayed longer than other hires. Thus, NCR, after reviewing the success of all of its employees, decided to focus its recruitment on college graduates instead of experienced

FIGURE 6-9 Why Wang?

Wang Laboratories of Lowell, Massachusetts, decided it needed to increase company awareness among the nation's university students. The solution was a recruitment video which is used as Wang's visual "calling card" before on-campus recruitment visits. Copies of the video, as well as company brochures and information packets, are mailed to campuses to encourage students to sign up for on-campus interviews with Wang, a company which offers careers in engineering, marketing, and business administration.

The film is emotional, casual, and upbeat. It includes footage of employees discussing the company, as well as views of the facilities. Employees are seen wearing shorts and tank tops, which, the film emphasizes, is common at Wang. Some of Wang's newest employees, who will be the students' peer group, explain why they chose to work at Wang. Employees were chosen based on articulateness, enthusiasm, and racial diversity. The actual interviews, however, were entirely unrehearsed. Topics of the interviews included:

- Why they wanted to work at Wang
- What they heard about Wang before they started to work
- Why Wang was a good employer for graduating students
- Why they liked working for Wang
- What they would tell their friends about employment opportunities at Wang

Wang reviewed many similar videos and decided to avoid the boring "president gives a tour of the company" approach, and instead emphasize the interviews with recently hired employees who could better relate to students. The video, while continuous, contains eight parts: "Why Wang?" "A Good Place to Start," "Room to Grow," "A Fun Culture," "Personal Development," "Exciting Work," "Great Products," and again, "Why Wang?"

SOURCE: Adapted from Jennifer J. Koch, "Why Video? How Wang Laboratories Artfully Answers the College Recruiting Question," *Recruitment Today* 3, no. 2 (Spring 1990): 30–34.

workers. Then NCR targeted seventy-five to eighty colleges according to several criteria, including the following:[35]

- Faculty quality, measured partly by the number of full-time Ph.D.s on staff.
- Student quality, determined by the schools' entrance requirements.
- The percentage of women and minority enrollments (to support the company's efforts to achieve diversity).
- Supportive services, such as the number of computers in the laboratories compared with the total number of students, research facilities, and so on.

Private Employment Agencies

Although HR departments have increased their use of private employment agencies, some use private agencies only as a last resort, for the expense involved is usually prohibitive. Sometimes the employer pays a percentage of the applicant's first-year salary as a fee to the agency. However, in some cases, a good employment agency can save the personnel office valuable time by screening out unqualified applicants and locating qualified ones. Effective agencies may actually save the organization money by reducing recruitment and selection costs. Use of private employment agencies does not relieve HR departments of any requirements under federal employment laws.

Only two or three competent agencies should be used by one organization; one specific agency should be used for a position when that agency typically has a good number of qualified applicants for that type of position. A **source trust** should be developed with a particular agency counselor so that unqualified applicants are not sent. A counselor will work harder to retain repeat business than to fill just one immediate opening. Repeated contacts also will help the counselor acquire a better understanding of the company and its requirements.[36]

HR managers should limit the number of applicants they allow an agency to send to four or five; this will keep them from being flooded with marginal applicants who probably could have been located without the agency. When limited to only four or five applicants, the agency counselor will do a better job of screening and will send only the people who have the best opportunity to be hired.

The relationship between an employer and an agency may result from one of several situations: (1) a written agreement between the two parties, which specifies the fee and the basis of its obligation—usually when the agency produces an applicant who is hired; (2) an oral agreement such as an HR official asking a recruiter over lunch to "send me some résumés"; (3) an implied agreement, which may occur if two parties continue to operate as they had when a written agreement existed. For example, a recruiter learns of an opening in a firm with which she has conducted business in the past. The recruiter sends several résumés, with a cover letter explaining why they were sent, and one of the applicants is hired; (4) an applicant's résumé includes information about an agency relationship—"property of recruiter Jones, fee expected from employer."[37]

Advertising

In a growing number of fields, including engineering, computer science, aircraft operation and maintenance, and health care, employers are having a difficult time attracting qualified applicants. These employers are increasingly relying on recruitment advertising and have begun using more creative advertisements. A new generation of recruitment ads, such as the one in Figure 6-10, while very different and distinctive, generally have in common the following:[38]

- Images that sell the company first and specific jobs second.
- Recognition of high-tech professionals as people, not just as techno-buffs.
- Strong visuals as attention getters that are "flipper proof"—meaning that the most casual observer cannot flip the page without reading them.
- Humor as well as graphics to attract attention.

Employers who have won *Personnel Journal's* Vantage Award for recruitment advertising excellence include Relational Technology, Inc., a software manufacturer; Hewlett-Packard/Colorado; Belle Aerospace Textron, a Buffalo, New York–based defense systems company; GTE Laboratories, Inc., the Massachusetts engineering firm; Lockheed, the Los Angeles defense industry company (see Figure 6-10); and Mercury Computer, Inc. In the case of Relational Technology, the company was largely unknown to potential applicants even though its database management software, Ingres, was among the best-known products in its field. The Relational ad "Modern Art" shows a photo of art gallery onlookers pondering a framed canvas with the word *Ingres* in bold letters. The ad (which appeared in *Computerworld*) produced the highest response rate in the history of the company and led to the hiring of 110 new employees.[39]

Recruiters can develop successful recruitment advertising for local newspapers, as well as for trade and professional publications, by incorporating the elements of consumer advertising. Often an organization using advertising is not really trying to recruit the unemployed person, who will diligently follow up on most ads, but rather the underemployed person, who if given the right opportunity would welcome a change of jobs. To recruit this type of employee, the ad must be attractive enough to stimulate the employee to respond.

Recruitment advertising, still in its embryonic stage, has begun to use more of the marketing research tools common in consumer ad-

FIGURE 6-10 Award-winning recruitment advertisement.

HIGH PAY, FREE HOUSING, NO TAXES. WHAT'S THE CATCH?

The catch is you'll be living in Saudi Arabia. And while the life-style for Westerners there is very comfortable, it is nevertheless a country where customs are very different from America's. As the tour would also be unaccompanied, you might imagine that the compensation would be generous.

You'd be right.

The benefits for C-130 specialists are extraordinary. We have abundant opportunities in our Mideast Operation for people with the following backgrounds:

C-130 Aircrew (Instructor Qualified)
C-130 Classroom Instructors
C-130 Maintenance Techs

Besides the excellent pay and allowances, the free housing, and tax exemption, you'll also enjoy liberal vacations, travel opportunities, wonderful benefits and a free trip back to the States every year.

For a C-130 experienced professional just leaving the service, this opportunity is a unique and exciting bonanza. Call us toll free, 1-800-472-2203. Or write Lockheed Aircraft Services Company, P.O. Box 33, Dept. 1-782-064, Ontario, California 91761-0033. Lockheed is an equal opportunity, affirmative action employer.

Lockheed-Arabia
INNOVATION: giving shape to imagination

SOURCE: R. M. Dombrowski, Lockheed Aircraft Service Company, Ontario, California.

vertising. The current trend has been toward greater and more sophisticated local and regional recruitment advertising because of the high cost of relocating employees and, more important, the immobility of the work force. Two-career couples have made out-of-town recruiting far more difficult.

According to George Rossi, corporate director of staffing and placement of the Digital Equipment Corporation, people today tend not to want to relocate for technical and professional jobs, whereas people in the past often jumped at the chance to live in a new part of the country at a higher salary. To counter this immobility, Digital continued to recruit nationally but with a coordinated mixture of magazine, radio, television, and newspaper advertising. In addition, a job placement and assistance program for spouses was instituted at Digital.[40]

A successful recruitment advertisement is based on the answers to four questions, according to Bernard Hodes, president of a Chicago advertising firm. The four questions are these:[41]

1. *What do you want to accomplish?* Decide who you want to hire, how many people you want, and in what time frame. Develop accurate, current job descriptions, and summarize critical job functions to be included in an ad.

2. *Who do you want to reach?* Estimate the demographics and motivations of those you want to respond. This helps to select and shape the best media. Develop a psychographic profile of the target audience. The profile can be used to select benefits of the job or organization that would motivate a reader to respond.

3. *What should the advertising message convey?* Identify the facts that must be included, such as job duties and minimum qualifications. Also, decide what image of the organization the ad should convey. Often the general advertising copy, logo, product lines, and the like can be incorporated into the ad so that the reader sees a connection between the common image of the company and the recruitment ad.

4. *How and where should you advertise?* Decide which of the nine major types of advertising media should be used. One or more possibilities may be used after considering the strengths and weaknesses of each, as listed in Table 6-2. After one is chosen, a specific agent must be selected. For example, if a trade magazine is the medium, should *Engineering News-Record, Civil Engineering, Building Digest,* or some other agent be used?

For the job seeker, the number of recruitment ads in a local newspaper is not a reliable indicator of actual job opportunities. *Fortune* magazine editors closely scrutinized ads in a New York State newspaper and found that within a metropolitan area of about 273,000 people the classified ad section contained 228 employment ads. Of the 228 ads, only 131 (57 percent) offered full-time jobs in the immediate area. These ads included eight jobs offered through *blind ads,* which briefly describe a job at an unnamed organization, giving a box number to which an applicant must respond. Only 42 of 228 ads offered full-time jobs in the area to unskilled or semiskilled workers.[42] The number of employment ads in local newspapers has become less indicative of the local economy because more companies are advertising positions not previously advertised. Some of these companies are advertising due to the increased success they have had with advertising positions; others advertise to comply with federal employment guidelines.

Direct Mail   A relatively new tool for recruitment advertising is the direct-mail campaign. This technique is generally used to lure professionals who are employed but willing to consider a job with greater opportunities. For mid- and top-level management jobs, the best

Table 6-2 Advantages and Disadvantages of the Major Types of Advertising Media

Type	Advantages	Disadvantages	When to Use
Newspapers	Short deadlines Ad size flexibility Circulation concentrated in specific geographic areas Classified sections well organized for easy access by active job seekers	Easy for prospects to ignore Considerable competitive clutter Circulation not specialized—you must pay for great number of unwanted readers Poor printing quality	When you want to limit recruiting to a specific area When sufficient numbers of prospects are clustered in a specific area When enough prospects are reading help-wanted ads to fill hiring needs
Magazines	Specialized magazines reach pinpointed occupation categories Ad-size flexibility High-quality printing Prestigious editorial environment Long life—prospects keep magazines and reread them	Wide geographic circulation—usually cannot be used to limit recruiting to specific area Long lead time for ad placement	When job is specialized When time and geographic limitations are not of utmost importance When involved in ongoing recruiting programs
Directories	Specialized audiences Long life	Not timely Often have competitive clutter	Only appropriate for ongoing recruiting programs
Direct mail	Most personal form of advertising Unlimited number of formats and amount of space By selecting names by zip code, mailing can be pinpointed to precise geographic area	Difficult to find mailing list of prospects by occupation at home address Cost for reaching each prospect is high	If the right mailing list can be found, this is potentially the most effective medium—no other medium gives the prospect as much a feeling of being specially selected Particularly valuable in competitive situations

(continued)

candidates may not respond to newspaper or trade journal ads, because those candidates are not actively seeking jobs.

Direct-mail recruitment enables a recruiter to get the attention of desirable candidates and gives the employer an advantage over other employers looking for some prospects.[43] A highly successful direct-mail recruitment program was developed by the Martin Marietta Corporation. The company, which needed to staff a new program, had little success attracting experienced professionals with over two years of experience. Martin Marietta was look-

ing for professionals who were successful in their current jobs, who were not actively looking in the market and thus not responding to conventional ads, and who would be motivated by a new and greater challenge. The company's direct-mail program comprised primarily three steps:[44]

Obtain a Mailing List From various list directories or other firms, a target mailing list was obtained.[45] Martin Marietta used a 10,000-person list that concentrated on targeted disciplines within a 200-mile radius

Table 6-2 (continued)

Type	Advantages	Disadvantages	When to Use
Radio and Television	Difficult to ignore; can reach prospects who are not actively looking for a job better than newspapers and magazines Can be limited to specific geographic areas Creatively flexible; can dramatize employment story more effectively than printed ads Little competitive recruitment clutter	Only brief, uncomplicated messages are possible Lack of performance; prospect cannot refer back to it (repeated airings necessary to make impression) Creation and production of commercials—particularly TV—can be time-consuming and costly Lack of special interest selectivity; paying for waste circulation	In competitive situations when not enough prospects are reading your printed ads When there are multiple job openings and there are enough prospects in specific geographic area When a large impact is needed quickly; a "blitz" campaign can saturate an area in two weeks or less Useful to call attention to printed ads
Outdoor (roadside billboards) and Transit (posters on buses and subways)	Difficult to ignore; can reach prospects as they are literally traveling to their current jobs Precise geographic selectivity Reaches large numbers of people many times at a low cost	Only very brief message is possible Requires long lead for preparation and must be in place for long period of time (usually one to three months)	When there is a steady hiring need for large numbers of people that is expected to remain constant over a long period of time
"Point-of-Purchase" (promotional materials at recruiting location)	Calls attention to employment story at time when prospects can take some type of immediate action Creative flexibility	Limited usefulness; prospects must visit a recruiting location before it can be effective	Posters, banners, brochures, audio-visual presentations at special events such as job fairs, open houses, conventions, as part of an employee referral program, at placement offices or whenever prospects visit at organization's location frequently.

SOURCE: "Planning for Recruitment Advertising: Part II," by Bernard S. Hodes, copyright June 1983. Reprinted with the permission of *Personnel Journal,* Costa Mesa, CA; all rights reserved.

of Baltimore. For discretion, only home addresses were used.

Develop a Mail Package Martin Marietta used a three-part mail package. First, the outer envelope was designed to capture attention. Second, the package contained an attractive company brochure, carefully designed to cover Martin Marietta's growth and technological successes, job descriptions

for open positions, the company's location, and employee benefits. Third, the package contained a response card, a mini-résumé requesting an applicant's name, address, present position, and college degree.

Follow Up Quickly The response card was critical because it facilitated immediate response from individuals who were unlikely to have current résumés. A Martin Marietta representative telephoned each respondent quickly to keep interest high.

The results of Martin Marietta's program were typical of successful direct-mail programs: a high response rate of 4 to 5 percent compared to a 2 percent industry standard; a low cost per hire for executive positions; and the filling of all open positions with highly qualified applicants.[46]

HIRING ALTERNATIVES

In recent years, employers have increasingly sought alternatives to the recruitment and selection of permanent new employees. They are willing to pay a premium to escape the legal responsibilities, paperwork, and commitment required in the traditional hiring of additional employees. The alternatives of assigning overtime to permanent employees, using temporary employees (outside or in-house), or leasing employees, must be carefully reviewed and the criteria included in Table 6-3 considered before one or more are chosen. In recent years, however, an increasing number of employers have chosen alternative methods of adding labor to the workplace, decreasing their dependence on hiring new permanent employees.

The three most immediate sources of additional labor are (1) current employees who work overtime, (2) temporary employees, and (3) leased employees.

Assigning Overtime

Assigning overtime to employees is an attractive alternative because it is a temporary situation rather than a permanent staff increase.

Table 6-3 Comparison of Alternative Methods of Adding Labor

Criteria	Recruit New Permanent Employees	Assign Overtime to Permanent Employees	Outside Temporary Agency	In-House Temporary Service	Leasing
Additional HR administrative activities required	Yes	No	No	Yes	No
Government regulations (OSHA, EEO, etc.)	Yes	Yes	No	Yes	No
Wages and benefits-costs	Normal payroll	1 1/2 time wages	Varies, usually higher	Usually lower benefits	5–10% above normal payroll
Additional training required	Yes (initially)	No	Yes (varies)	No	Yes (initially)
Fast, easy to hire and fire	No	No	Yes	Yes	Yes
Fatigue possibility	No	Yes	No	No	No
Loyalty (potential problem)	No	No	Yes	No	Yes

Choosing overtime means using experienced, knowledgeable employees who do not require any additional training or orientation. But overtime also means additional fatigue for employees who have already worked their full shift and usually the expense of time-and-a-half or double-time pay.

Temporary Help

Temporary help may be less costly than hiring new permanent employees, particularly for companies with great seasonal demands or for an unforecasted temporary absence of important personnel. In office administration, accounting, and engineering, temporary help can quickly be trained to be productive on the job with relatively low start-up costs.

The temporary-services industry in the United States is booming. An estimated nine out of ten American companies use temporary services. Over 800,000 orders are filled *daily*. Why the demand from employers? Temporary-services industry executives offer several reasons. The nature of their business forces them to provide trained personnel who are familiar with the latest office automation technology. Unsatisfactory temporary workers are quickly dismissed, and their companies are seldom contacted again. Thus, the temporary agency offers the employer trained, available personnel who can be put to work quickly and, if necessary, let go just as quickly. The cost and time associated with hiring permanent new employees make this an attractive alternative for many employers. Employers who have highly fluctuating staffing demands due to changes in the economy recognize temporary help as just that—a source of trained staff needed for a temporary period of time.

Employers who use temporary services most often no longer view them as just a source of replacement secretaries. Certainly that is still a large portion of the business, but the downsizing of corporate America has provided temporary services with a large supply of highly trained individuals and many corporate clients, needing temporary manpower, that are wary of adding full-time personnel. Kelly Services, Inc., for example, has a program called Encore that actively recruits people over age fifty. These individuals include many retired executives who can give an organization invaluable assistance without the costs of a full-time, high-level management position. Temporary services have enjoyed substantial growth in the small-business sector. The small entrepreneur who cannot afford or does not need full-time professional assistance can find it readily available on an as-needed basis.[47]

Employers considering using temporary services should review the following suggestions on how best to use the temporary service:[48]

- Develop a partner relationship with one service rather than a vendor relationship. Working primarily with one service allows them to learn your specific needs.

- Invite service representatives into your working environment to assess your needs before submitting orders.

- Before placing an order, compile as much information as possible about your needs—work experience, equipment, software, communication skills, and so on.

- Treat the temporary worker with the same courtesy as you would a permanent employee.

In-House Temporaries   Instead of calling an outside agency to fill a temporary position, larger employers may operate an in-house temporary service. The employer recruits a pool of part-time and full-time workers who are kept available to departments that need to fill a position temporarily due to a regular employee's vacation, illness, or other reasons, or to departments experiencing a seasonal or other sudden increase in work load.

Crestar Bank, headquartered in Richmond, Virginia, operates a large and successful in-house temporary service called Tempo. Out of 1100 positions at Crestar's headquarters, 60 to

100 each week are filled with temporary employees. Tempo, a unit within the bank's HR department, recruits and trains employees to work in all departments. The unit was created to replace Crestar's use of more expensive outside temporary-agency employees. Ellen Barnard, HR vice president at Crestar, sees the greatest advantage of an in-house service as the quality of work. Since the temporaries are employees of Crestar, Barnard believes that they are more committed to their work. Two other advantages of the in-house service, says Barnard, include employees' higher level of skills, since they are already trained, and the lower cost of the benefits package they receive in comparison to full-time employees.[49]

Successful in-house temporary services are also in operation at Aetna Life & Casualty Company in Hartford, Connecticut; Eastern Milk Producers Corporation in Syracuse, New York; Sharp Health-Care in San Diego, California; and Agway, Inc., a farm cooperative in Syracuse. Aetna's program, Aetna Temporary Services, may be the largest in the country, with over 1500 positions filled each year. All the programs report similar advantages: lower costs and higher-quality workers than those of outside agencies. In addition, they report that many of the temporary-unit workers are hired by the departments they serve as permanent positions become available. This process works well for both sides: the temporary employees know in advance if they like the nature of the work and the people they will be working with, and the department is already familiar with their work. Another advantage reported by these companies is the ease of recruiting in today's changing work force. In particular, former employees who retired or left to raise a family can be more easily recruited for part-time or limited temporary jobs, and they are often already trained in the work. The major problem associated with in-house programs is maintaining the pool of workers. It can take as many as six people to fill each job order due to availability, skill requirements, and specific

job needs. In comparison to using outside agencies or leasing, the in-house service also has the disadvantage of being responsible for all required normal HR activities such as hiring, payroll, and benefits. Also, even the largest in-house program must utilize outside agencies when unique skills are needed.[50]

Leasing Employees

A new alternative to the traditional method of recruiting new employees is the practice of **leasing employees**. While the concept of employee leasing is not entirely new, there is a new breed of companies, such as Contract Staffing of America, headquartered in Tustin, California. CSA hires workers and then contracts them out to employers that request employees with certain skills and abilities. Why the new interest in employee leasing? James Borgelt, general manager of Omnistaff, a Dallas leasing firm, believes his customers lease employees for several reasons. For example, small businesses cannot afford a pension program or other benefits that compete with those of large corporations. Thus they lose many good employees to large firms. However, Borgelt contends that his firm offers a competitive salary and benefits to its employees because it can take advantage of group rates. Omnistaff then leases the employees to small employers. Small employers also like not having the EEO/AA administration duties such as payroll, W-2 forms, benefit claims, and so on, which are handled by Omnistaff.[51]

To be considered the common-law employer by the Internal Revenue Service, the leasing company must perform the hiring and firing. The leasing company, as the legal employer, is responsible for all HR functions, including employee records, payroll, complying with government regulations, workers' compensation insurance, and employee benefits. The client employer, however, retains approval of who works in its facility. If a client becomes dissatisfied with an employee or terminates the position, the leasing firm removes the employee and may fire, lay off, or transfer the employee to another client.

The primary advantage to the client employer remains freedom from the administrative burden. This time-saving advantage alone can save the employer 5 to 10 percent of payroll costs generally charged by the leasing company. Another advantage to the client is that management can spend more time running the business and less time on HR functions. The client can also save money by not providing benefits that are provided by the leasing company.

There are also areas of potential advantage to the employees. Leasing companies that provide workers to many clients enjoy the economies of scale that enable them to offer employees benefits that many small employers cannot afford. Employees may also realize greater job security if they work for a successful leasing company. They can be transferred to another client rather than be fired if their relationship with the current client becomes unsatisfactory for either the client or the employee. Thus, employees who simply do not get along with the supervisor have more options than if they were hired directly by the client. Employees of major leasing firms also enjoy greater job mobility since the leasing company usually has clients in cities all over the country. Employees, however, are subject to termination by the leasing company if the client is dissatisfied with their work or if the leasing company believes it can replace them with lower-paid employees. The primary potential disadvantage of leasing for the client employer is loyalty. Since employees are hired and compensated by the leasing firm and may feel a degree of job flexibility with that firm, the lack of loyalty to the client employer can become a problem. Unwanted turnover, poor customer relations, and compromised confidentiality may be caused by employees' lack of traditional employer–employee loyalty. Overall, however, employers, particularly smaller ones,

must believe that the advantages of leasing outweigh the disadvantages since the practice continues to grow.[52]

COST-BENEFIT ANALYSIS OF RECRUITMENT

The basic goal of recruitment is to locate, at the least cost, qualified applicants who will remain with the organization. Therefore, underqualified individuals who will later be terminated should not be hired; nor should overqualified individuals who will become frustrated and eventually leave the organization.[53]

A cost-benefit model illustrates the decision-making aspects of recruitment and stresses the economic implications of selection decisions. In the recruitment process, four outcomes are possible for each applicant, as shown in Figure 6-11. Quadrants I and III indicate correct decisions: hiring applicants who eventually become successes as employees and not hiring applicants who would have eventually become failures as employees. In quadrants II and IV, however, management makes incorrect decisions. In quadrant IV, a hired applicant is not successful on the job. In quadrant II, management rejects an applicant who would have been successful as an employee. The incorrect decision in quadrant IV is called a **false positive** because management was positive about an applicant who turned out to be unsuccessful. The incorrect decision in quadrant II is called a **false negative** because management was negative about an applicant who would have been successful. In quadrants I and III, the managers scored a *hit* in correctly predicting the future performance of the applicant. Of course, management desires to maximize its rate of correct decisions, or **hit rate**, which is its percentage of correct predictions about future performances of employees.

FIGURE 6-11 Four Possible Outcomes in the Recruitment Process.

APPLICANT/ EMPLOYEE PERFORMANCE	SELECTION DECISION	
	REJECT	HIRE
Successful Applicant/Employee	II Incorrect Decision (False Negative)	I Correct Decision (Hit)
Unsuccessful Applicant/Employee	III Correct Decision (Hit)	IV Incorrect Decision (False Positive)

Rate of success (hit rate) is computed as follows:

$$\text{Hit Rate} = \frac{\text{Hits (I + III)}}{\text{Hits (I + III)} - [\text{False Negatives (II)} + \text{False Positives (IV)}]}$$

In order to accomplish a cost-benefit analysis of the recruitment program, several estimates must be made. The cost of the two types of errors that can be made in the recruitment selection process should be considered. The actual dollar costs include advertising positions, reviewing applications, interviewing applicants, and testing a large group of applicants. Also, the cost of orienting and training unsuccessful new applicants (false-positive decisions) must be included.

Perhaps more important than direct costs are potential costs, which cannot be easily measured. False positives include the potential costs of an employee's becoming disenchanted with the organization and spreading low morale. The costs associated with false-negative decisions are also very difficult to estimate. Organizations often do not know, except in extremely costly situations, how much potential they have lost when they reject an applicant who could have been a successful employee. For example, what did it cost the professional baseball team whose scouts originally rejected the young Nolan Ryan?

A perfect recruitment process, of course, would identify which of the four quadrants an applicant falls into and enable the recruiter to choose only those applicants who would be successful employees. Managers can estimate the success of their recruitment by looking at their hit rates and how the rates have changed. The most important cost-benefit analysis associated with recruitment focuses on the sources of recruitment (employee referrals, ad responses, and so on). Each source will produce a different percentage of successful job candidates at differing costs. Managers can easily relate the costs of using a source to the number of applicants located. The disadvantage of compiling direct dollar recruitment costs in this manner is that there is no accounting for the costs to an organization of losing a star performer because one source of recruitment was not utilized. However, that unusual situation should not discourage cost-benefit analysis of recruiting.

INTERNATIONAL HR: STAFFING

One of the more challenging issues facing multinational firms is staffing. Should a firm relocate home-country staff to its foreign operations or hire host-country personnel?[54] The multinational firm can choose to relocate experienced personnel from the United States (i.e., home country) or employ and train nationals (i.e., citizens of the host country). The choice is often determined on the basis of trade-offs between technical expertise that may be available only from the home country and the firm's need to adapt to local customs.

If the type of employee needed to staff the overseas operation is technically or professionally unique (e.g., a computer engineer), chances are high that the person will be transferred from the United States. However, this strategy is very expensive.

The cost of sending personnel overseas (including Central and South America) is estimated at around half a million dollars for a three-year assignment for executives.[55] Of course, this cost will vary in terms of hardship to the employee, distance from the United States, and family obligations. Big-ticket expenditures for relocating personnel may include bonuses for hardship, education of children, visits back to the United States, and additional expenses to maintain an American standard of living. The high cost of expatriates is a major reason why fewer and fewer companies continue this personnel practice.

By and large, international firms are depending more on local labor sources to meet their staffing needs.[56] Figure 6-12 indicates guidelines for recruiting local workers. Recruiting local workers is less expensive and, with the exception of a few countries, there is usually an adequate and available labor pool from which to recruit. An added advantage is that it creates career opportunities, goodwill, and loyalty to the company. It may also be politically astute since governments have been known to impose constraints on the number of foreign managers and specialists brought into their countries. An American mining company in Africa, for example, was required to hire all lower-level workers locally and to phase out all American workers within ten years.

Recruiting productive and loyal local residents is just as challenging as in the United States—maybe even more so.[57] The same concerns can occur with foreign employers; see International HR in the News: "Toyota—On Recruiting American Workers." Perhaps the most sensitive issue is how to screen applicants for loyalty. Everyone who watches the evening news is aware that more and more countries are being swept up in a wave of nationalistic fervor. Certainly patriotism to one's own country is understandable and commendable, but it could cause the company embarrassment sometime in the future. To minimize the potential of a mismatch, a company recruiter might ask applicants the questions found in Figure 6-12.

Global Recruiting at IBM

IBM is a good example of the way in which the multinational enterprise can make effective use of its personnel. IBM has a policy of recruiting and developing host-country nationals for both research and management positions. It even decentralizes much of its research and development (R&D), using local technicians, engineers, and managers while retaining centralized control over the ultimate use of the R&D. IBM also engages in local purchasing and attempts to keep a balance of trade by nation. It has host nationals, including local political figures, on its boards, and it attempts to act as a good corporate citizen in each host nation.

This geocentric concern for the social and economic welfare of all of its managers and workers has resulted in an extraordinary loyalty to IBM among its personnel at all levels. There are excellent management–labor relations and a common corporate culture. Partly because of this method of human resource management, IBM has been successful in the face of ever-increasing global competition.[58]

Over the past few years, world politics have changed quickly. Eastern bloc nations have revolted against over forty years of Communist control, and capitalistic tendencies are being

FIGURE 6-12 Recruiting non-Americans: how to screen for loyalty.

Loyalty is not defined in terms of patriotism or nationalism but in terms of how well that person will understand, empathize with, and relate to the company and its global mission.

Whom do we hire when we take the plunge overseas? Here are eight measures to consider in selecting "locals":

1. How does the applicant view the United States?

If the person is unable to respond to provocative questions about his or her own nation without becoming defensive, don't go any further. Dedication and loyalty to the motherland are to be desired, but not the inability to put them in perspective with the company's historical U.S. orientation.

2. Has the applicant had previous foreign experience?

If this person has not had personal or professional experience outside the native land, take another look: firsthand experience may be critical to your success.

3. Does the applicant demonstrate clear mental flexibility?

Are this person's ideas open to change? Does this person wait to listen to other's ideas before responding, and in responding, does he show understanding of what the other person has said and why? If not, look elsewhere.

4. Can the applicant change his or her behavior in different environments?

Is this person's behavior open to change? Can this person respond to different signals and change behavior? Anyone without this flexibility goes on the waiting list.

5. Does the person have firsthand experience in the Untied States?

Better get someone who's had personal experience here. You wouldn't want to move a persons who'd spent five years in Nairobi to New York unless you were sure he or she understood the differences between them.

6. Does the person display international savvy in general?

Does the applicant show that he or she has learned how to assess the local ground rules before acting in *any* country? This is the sign of the real professional: someone who knows how to learn from experience in another country—*fast*.

7. Can the applicant recognize when behavior is influenced by cultural expectations, as in negotiating situations?

Does the applicant really demonstrate a general awareness and understanding of the patterns of cultural differences in human behavior? If applicant believes that "all people are the same," don't touch!

8. Does the applicant respond to verbal and nonverbal signals from someone different from himself?

If he or she doesn't hold back and wait to find out what the other person is really intending, don't hire.

SOURCE: Adapted from Henry Ferguson, *Tomorrow's Global Executive* (Homewood, IL: Dow Jones-Irwin, 1988), p. 72.

Toyota—On Recruiting American Workers

A worker whose face we could not read—whose heart was a mystery to us. When the time came for us to make a wholesale structural shift and move our manufacturing overseas, this was our greatest fear.

We had developed a very finely tuned production system. What would happen if we turned it over to him?

Everything depended on whether this "foreign" worker would listen to us and learn our ways of doing things.

If he wouldn't, how could we go on making our cars? What kind of cars would they be?

As it turned out, though, there was no problem; these "foreign" workers weren't one bit different than us. They worked just as hard, just as proud, sometimes far more creatively. And they got the same big charge out of being a part of a winning team.

Now we don't think of "foreign" workers anymore. That's nonsense. All of our people not here in Japan are just Toyota, that's all. They're family.

Here it is in the form of one of the teams at our new billion-dollar plant in Georgetown, Kentucky, which came on-line just before our new Ontario, Canada, and Chungli, Taiwan plants.

Can you see it in their faces? Can you see their feeling of family? Of security? Of pride?

That's our spirit.

The first thing we say to anyone we hire is, "Welcome. We are family." We don't just say it, we mean it. And everyone knows we mean it. And that means everything.

The second thing we say is, "We take pride in our work." Those who take pride in their work are always motivated, always on top. They are a source of infinite energy.

That's our spirit.

SOURCE: Annual Report, Toyota (1989), pp. 7, 9.

---

nurtured. Germany is now united, and Hungary, Poland and the Czech Republic are also changing their market systems. Even the former Soviet Union is undergoing social, economic, and political transformations.

Perestroika and HR Perestroika began a new era of HR policies in the Soviet Union. Before President Mikhail Gorbachev's new economic policies were introduced, the HR policy in the Soviet Union was very simple. Everyone was placed in a job chosen by the state and was guaranteed employment. In 1987 laws were adopted to create cooperatives, or privately owned businesses. In 1988 a leasing system was created by law that allows work teams to lease an enterprise for ten to fifteen years and then buy it from the state. Today over 10,000 enterprises have been set up under the leasing system. The management team, instead of the state, makes hiring, production, and wage decisions. The result thus far has been an average work force reduction in leased enterprises (compared to state systems) of 20 percent and increased total productivity. The basic process of people submitting an unsolicited résumé to an employer was completely new in the former Soviet Union. The ability to choose a career, and seek employment without the state, was also new. In the past, all wage rates were set by the state, and both highly skilled and unskilled workers received about the same wage rate. Wage rates were changed only every fifteen years. The average monthly wage for a skilled worker was about 250 rubles, or $40. When an employee made a purchase of food or clothing, the store directly billed his or her employer and the bill was paid through a payroll deduction.[59]

The *International HR in the News,* "Toyota—On Recruiting American Workers," should remind us that HR international policies must consider not only American firms that have operations overseas, but also foreign firms that have operations in the United States.

Coca-Cola's International Recruiting

The Atlanta, Georgia–based Coca-Cola Company operates in 160 countries and employs about 400,000 people. Thus, its HR department must recruit professional and managerial staff that can successfully operate internationally. Mike Semran, director of international resources for Coca-Cola, believes that "As you look to the future, the people who are running companies are going to be people who have operated in more than one culture." Therefore, he has concluded that Coke's management needs to be multilingual and multicultural. While the global language of business is English, according to Semran, applicants who have additional language skills are more valuable to the company. Coca-Cola's managerial recruitment program focuses on candidates at the college level in U.S. schools with strong international programs. A large percentage of its new hires are from the company's formal internship program. According to an International Orientation Resources study, Coca-Cola's international recruitment practices are similar to those of other U.S. companies. In general, the qualities international firms require in recent college graduates include technical expertise, management ability, previous overseas experience, and a second language.[60]

CONCLUSIONS AND APPLICATIONS

- Recruitment requires the HR specialist to acquire a pool of available and qualified applicants. The recruiters can tap a variety of sources including current employees, retirees, part-time workers, the unemployed, and employees of other organizations who feel they are underemployed.

- Human resource planning is a key method by which the HR department can hold down recruitment costs and minimize the time positions remain vacant. By developing demand and supply forecasts, the HR specialist can develop training programs, retirement incentives, management succession planning, and other techniques to aid future recruitment efforts.

- Job-posting programs are widely utilized to recruit applicants for positions. New voice-mail and electronic-mail systems offer several advantages to traditional bulletin boards.

- Effective recruitment advertising has increased due to the use of common marketing research tools. The need for advertising has increased because of two-career couples and a general unwillingness to relocate on the part of professional and technical employees.

- Current employees are the most common source of applicants for higher-level positions. They offer the organization several ad-vantages over external applicants and give all employees the incentive of knowing that they may be promoted as a reward for hard work.

- Overtime, temporary help, and leasing are alternative sources of additional labor. Depending on the number of hours and skills needed, these recruitment sources may be more desirable than hiring permanent employees.

- College campus recruitment has become more competitive and employers more sophisticated in their methods. A poor economy should signal to students the need to use innovative job leads.

CASE STUDY:

An Employee Referral Program

Annabelle Adams is the HR director for Missouri Telemarketing in St. Louis. The company employs about 2500 people, of whom 90 percent are part-time telemarketing sales personnel. Most of these employees are college students, housewives, or retired people who work part-time for $7–10/hour, depending on their seniority and shift. Annual job satisfaction surveys indicate that the employees like their supervisors, wages and benefits, and the workplace facility. Turnover, however, is currently averaging 25 percent due to the hours (evening and weekend shifts must be worked by all employees for at least half of their total hours) and stress due to the constant pressure of meeting sales targets. Employees also complain of the lack of social interaction at work due to their isolation (each employee sits in a small cubicle with a computer that performs the dialing and recordkeeping functions).

The company is growing rapidly, and thus must constantly recruit and train new sales personnel. The president, Mary Anne Ryan, has decided that the company should try an employee prize referral program as a means of recruiting. She has just returned from a conference in Morro Bay, California, where she heard several other CEOs describe how they successfully utilized referral programs. Ryan has directed Adams to develop an employee referral program that will recruit at least 300 new workers in the next three months. She has provided a budget of $150,000 to cover all prizes and expenses directly related to the program (routine HR staff time is not included).

QUESTIONS

1. What prizes should Adams recommend the program offer to employees? Why?

2. How should the program be communicated to the employees?

3. How should the success of the program be determined?

4. Whom should Adams consult for advice in designing the program?

EXPERIENTIAL EXERCISES

1. The Temporary Help Alternative

PURPOSE

To gain an understanding of the temporary help alternative as a method of increasing personnel.

THE TASK

Contact five temporary help agencies and ask each to provide the following information for each of the positions listed: (1) their charge for one week (forty hours); (2) the number of people with at least one year's experience they have available; and (3) how quickly an employee could be provided. If additional information is needed, improvise.

Position	Cost/Week	No. Available	When Available
1. Secretary (experience: WordPerfect, Lotus 1-2-3)			
2. Cashier (must be bonded)			
3. Salesperson (experienced in retail clothing)			
4. Accountant (BS/BA degree)			
5. Driver (current driver's license, experience with delivery trucks)			

2. Effective Help-Wanted Ads

PURPOSE

To understand the criteria for evaluating help-wanted recruiting advertisements and the effectiveness of several actual help-wanted ads.

INTRODUCTION

What are the characteristics of effective help-wanted ads? Consider the following questions and dos and don'ts.

Who Do You Want?

Important information that you will need *before* you write your ad:

- How many people do you need?
- What skills and abilities are required?
- Is this person likely to be working, and if so, where?
- What publications is this person likely to read regularly?
- Which job rewards—compensation, benefits, career opportunities, and so on—is this person likely to be looking for?
- How competitive is the market for this person?
- What is the likely level of job satisfaction the person has with his or her present job?

Once you have answered these basic questions, you will need to create a strategy for effectively communicating the challenges and opportunities of the available job.

Some Dos and Don'ts

- *Headlines are important.* Use a distinctive headline to *sell* the job to the candidate. Don't just list the job title.
- *Use graphics carefully.* Ad graphics vary widely, ranging from the simple to the complex. Graphics that are confusing or misleading are worse than no graphics at all, so make sure that graphics make sense. A basic question to ask is: Do the graphics convey a message that you want to communicate?
- *Don't misrepresent the job.* Don't make promises you cannot keep. Be honest about opportunities for advancement, challenge, responsibility, and so on. Honesty is the best policy.
- *Don't be vague.* Be specific about the job title, salary range, and closing date.
- *"Sell" the employee.* Without tooting your own company horn too loudly, make sure the ad contains the benefits of working for your firm.
- *Avoid stereotypes.* Beware of sexism, racism, and other stereotypes. Make sure it that the ad will not be seen as offensive to anyone.
- *Help prospective candidates identify themselves.* To avoid sifting through countless résumés, define the qualifications you are looking for. You will cut down considerably on unqualified applicants if you specify the three to five key requirements and be specific—for example, "Experience as the manager of ten or more industrial salespeople for at least three years."
- *Use advertising space economically.* Space cost is not cheap. Don't use a full-page ad when a half-page ad will do the job just as effectively. Don't use too many graphics and too little prose; conversely, don't use a space so small that the applicant will get eyestrain from reading. The size of the ad should be in proportion to the size of the firm, impor-

tance of the position, number of candidates sought, and so on.

- *Select recruitment media carefully.* Study the reading habits of potential candidates to determine what they read. Also, study the readership demographics of the various media you are considering. A great-looking ad is no good if the right people are not reading it.

THE TASK

Illustrated are several help-wanted advertisements. All were taken from the same newspaper on the same Sunday morning. Using the criteria listed, evaluate each ad, using the grid provided. Your instructor will lead you in a discussion of the results of your analysis.

SOURCE: Adapted From "Recruitment Ads at Work," by Margaret Magnus, copyright August, 1985. Reprinted with the permission of *Personnel Journal,* Costa Mesa, California; all rights reserved.

Criterion*

	Advertisement						
	1	2	3	4	5	6	7
Distinctive headlines							
Effective graphics							
Clever and creative							
Avoids sounding too glamorous							
Specifies nature of job and qualifications							
"Sells" the employee							
Avoids stereotyping							
Helps candidate identify self							
Uses space economically							
Effective typeface							
Proper recruitment media							
TOTALS:							

Ranking (most effective to least effective)
1.
2.
3.
4.
5.
6.
7.

*Rank each ad for each criterion using the following scale:
5 = Excellent; 4 = Very Good; 3 = Satisfactory; 2 = Below Average; 1 = Very Poor

KEY TERMS AND CONCEPTS

Employee relocation
Employee referrals
False negative
False positive
Gate hires
Hit rate
Human resources planning
Job posting
Labor force participation rate
Labor reserve
Leasing employees
Management succession planning

Networking
Old boy network
Older worker
Part time
Peter Principle
Pirating
Source trust
Temporary help
Underemployed
Unemployed
Unemployment rate

REVIEW QUESTIONS

1. How can an employer recruit a diverse work force?

2. Discuss hourly and professional applicants' knowledge of labor markets.

3. What are the advantages of recruiting applicants internally? Externally?

4. List the three major methods of job posting. Why should an employer consider a voice-mail system?

5. Has advertising increased as a recruitment technique in recent years? Why?

6. Why might hiring temporary help be preferable to assigning overtime or hiring new employees?

7. How can U.S. firms successfully recruit local residents in foreign nations?

DISCUSSION QUESTIONS

1. If you were an underemployed MBA, what steps would you take to find a more satisfactory position?

2. From an inexperienced job applicant's point of view, which recruitment method is more attractive? From the point of view of an applicant with twenty years' experience?

3. How should applicants prepare for job interviews? What questions should they expect to answer?

4. How should the HR director compare alternative recruitment sources?

5. Compared to their grandparents, what factors are important to today's workers as far as the workplace and employer are concerned?

6. How can an employer recruit more older workers if past efforts have not been successful?

ENDNOTES

Chapter 6

1. John Bishop, "High School Performance and Employee Recruitment," *Journal of Labor Research* (Winter 1992): 41–44.

2. Howard N. Fullerton, "Labor Force Projections: 1986 to 2000," *Monthly Labor Review* 110, no. 9 (September 1987): 20.

3. Elizabeth Blacharczyk, "Recruiters Challenged by Economy, Shortages," *HR News* (February 1990): B1, 4.

4. John Naisbitt and Patricia Aburdene, *Megatrends 200* (New York: William Morrow, 1990), pp. 299–34.

5. Blacharczyk, "Recruiters Challenged by Economy, Shortages," p. B4.

6. Jennifer J. Koch, "Finding Qualified Hispanic Candidates," *Recruitment Today* 3, no. 2 (Spring 1990): 35.

7. Mitchell S. Novit, *Essentials of Personnel Management* (Englewood Cliffs, NJ: Prentice-Hall, 1979), pp. 60–64.

8. Paul Greenlaw and William Briggs, *Modern Personnel Management* (Philadelphia: Saunders, 1979), pp. 121–27.

9. Older Workers Rapidly Becoming a New Force in the Labor Market," *Resource* (August 1987): 2.

10. Pat O'Connor, "As the U.S. Grows Up, More Firms Turn to Older Workers," *The Courier-Journal* (July 13, 1987):B12,7.

11. Barry Stavro, "Job-Hunting After 40: Abridged Resumes and Touched-Up Hairs," *The Los Angeles Times* (May 17, 1993): 12.

12. David V. Lewis, "Make Way for the Older Worker," *HRMagazine* 35, no. 5 (May 1990): 75–77.

13. Richard Frantzreb, "Human Resource Planning: Forecasting Manpower Needs," *Personnel Journal* 60, no. 11 (November 1981): 850–51.

14. Norman Scarborough and Thomas W. Zimmerer, "Human Resources Forecasting: Why and Where to Begin," *Personnel Administrator* 27, no. 5 (May 1982): 55–56.

15. Charles F. Russ, Jr., "Manpower Planning Systems: Part I," *Personnel Journal* 61, no. 1 (January 1982): 40–41.

16. Frantzreb, "Human Resource: Planning," pp. 850–54.

17. Ibid.

18. Kendrith M. Rowland and Scott L. Summers, "Human Resource Planning: A Second Look," *Personnel Administrator* 26, no. 12 (December 1981): 73–80.

19. Russ, "Manpower Planning," pp. 44–45. For a complete discussion of commitment manpower planning see Charles F. Russ, "Manpower Planning Systems: Part II," *Personnel Journal* 61, no. 2 (January 1982): 119–23.

20. David R. Leigh, "Business Planning Is People Planning," *Personnel Journal* 63, no. 5 (May 1984): 44–45.

21. Ibid.

22. *Employee Promotion and Transfer Policies*, PPF survey no. 120 (Washington, DC: Bureau of National Affairs, Inc., 1978), pp. 2–4.

23. Linda T. Thornburg, "Relocation Costs Up, Transferees Less Happy," *HR News* (June 1990): 10.

24. Kathryn Scovel, "The Relocation Riddle," *Human Resource Executive*, (June 1990): 46–51.

25. Linda K. Stroh, Anne H. Reilly, and Jeanne M. Brett, "New Trends in Relocation," *HRMagazine* 35, no. 2 (February 1990): 42–44.

26. Christine Kingberg, "More Employees Choosing Family Over Career," *HR News* (April 1990): 9.

27. Lawrence J. Peters and R. Hull, *The Peter Principle* (New York: Bantam Books, 1969), pp. 55–57.

28. Harriet Gorlin, "An Overview of Corporate Personnel Practices," *Personnel Journal* 61, no. 2 (February 1982): 126.

29. William C. De Lone, "Telephone Job Posting Cuts Costs," *Personnel Journal* (April 1993): 115–18.

30. Lawrence Kleiman and Kimberly Clark, "Users' Satisfaction with Job Posting," *Personnel Administrator* 29, no. 9 (September 1984): 104–8.

31. Lawrence S. Kleiman, "An Effective Job Posting System," *Personnel Journal* 63, no. 2 (February 1984): 20–25, 81–84.

32. Gloria Glickstein and Donald C. Z. Ramer, "The Alternative Employment Marketplace," *Personnel Administrator* 3, no. 2 (February 1988): 100–4.

33. Jennifer J. Laabs, "A Prize Referral Program," *Personnel Journal* (May 1991): 95–97.

34. Maury Hanigan, "Campus Recruiters Upgrade Their Pitch," *Personnel Administrator* 32, no. 11 (November 1987): 55–58.

35. Dawn Gunsch, "Comprehensive College Strategy Strengthens NCR's Recruitment," *Personnel Journal* (September 1993): 58–62.

36. Erwin S. Stanton, *Successful Personnel Recruiting and Selection* (New York: AMACOM, 1977), pp. 53–55.

37. J. Jonathan Schraub, "Avoiding Unexpected Fee Liability," *HRMagazine* (October 1993): S2–S3.

38. Beyond Nuts and Bolts," *Personnel Journal* 69, no. 2 (February 1990): 70–77.

39. Ibid.

40. Margaret Nemec, "Recruitment Advertising—It's More Than Just 'Help Wanted,' " *Personnel Administrator* 26, no. 2 (February 1981): 57–60.

41. Bernard S. Hodes, "Planning for Recruitment Advertising: Part II," *Personnel Journal* 62, no. 6 (June 1983): 492–99.

42. Herbert E. Myer, "Jobs and Want Ads: A Look Behind the Words," *Fortune* (November 20, 1978): 88–96.

43. Richard Siedlecki, "Creating a Direct Mail Recruitment Program," *Personnel Journal* 62, no. 4 (April 1983): 304–7.

44. Rick Stoops, "Direct Mail: Luring the Isolated Professionals," *Personnel Journal* 63, no. 6 (June 1984): 34–36.

45. Siedlecki, "Creating a Direct Mail Program," p. 307. Consult the *Direct Mail List Rates and Data*, published by Standard Rate and Data Service, Inc., 5201 Old Orchard Road, Skokie, IL 60077, or contact Direct Mail/Marketing Association (DM/MA), 6 East 43 Street, New York, NY 10017.

46. Stoops, "Direct Mail," pp. 34–36.

47. "The Temporary Services: A Lasting Impact on the Economy," *Personnel Administrator* 33, no. 1 (January 1988): 60–65.

48. Ibid.

49. Steve Bergsman, "Setting Up a Temporary Shop," *HRMagazine* 35, no. 2 (February 1990): 46–48.

50. Ibid.

51. "Leasing Employees," *Changing Times* (May 1985): 50–54.

52. Paul N. Keaton and Janine Anderson, "Leasing Offers Benefits to Both Sides," *HRMagazine* 35, no. 7 (July 1990): 53–58.

53. Greenlaw and Briggs, *Modern Personnel Management*, pp. 122–27.

54. This section draws on A. V. Phatak, *International Dimensions of Management* (Boston: Kent, 1983), pp. 90–96.

55. For more information on the costs of expatriates, see W. E. Green and G. D. Walls, "Human Resources: Hiring Internationally," *Personnel Administrator*, 29 (July 1984): 61–66. See also R. J. Stone, "Compensation: Pay and Perks for Overseas Executives," *Personnel Journal* 65, no. 1 (January 1986): 64–69.

56. For some staffing issues associated with expatriate managers, see G. M. Galiga and J. C. Baker, "Multinational Corporate Policies for Expatriate Managers: Selection, Training, Evaluation," *SAM Advanced Management Journal* 50, no. 4 (Autumn 1985): 31–38.

57. For a more thorough treatment of screening foreign employees, see Henry Ferguson, *Tomorrow's Global Executive* (Homewood, IL: Dow Jones-Irwin, 1988), pp. 70–74.

58. Alan M. Rugman, Donald J. Lecraw, and Laurence D. Booth, *International Business* (New York: McGraw-Hill, 1985), p. 440.

59. Jeanene Whitney, "Perestroika and Human Resource Management," *HR News* (July 1990): 6.

60. Jennifer J. Lambs, "The Global Talent Search," *Personnel Journal* (August 1991): 38–44.

CHAPTER **7**

EMPLOYEE SELECTION

CHAPTER OBJECTIVES

1. To explain the HR department's role in the selection process.

2. To develop a selection decision process.

3. To cite useful application blank information.

4. To develop a structured employment interview.

5. To distinguish among different types of preemployment tests.

6. To understand the need for complete background checks.

7. To identify the significant issues related to staffing operations in foreign countries and the major hiring alternatives.

8. To understand the use of preemployment medical exams and drug tests.

9. To describe negligent hiring and understand its complexity and impact on the selection process.

10. To explain how the final selection decision is made.

The Toyota Selection Process

When Toyota, the Japanese automobile giant, decided to build its first new U.S. automobile plant in Georgetown, Kentucky, it designed a unique selection system. In today's quality-driven auto industry, the stereotyped "nuts and bolts" production worker would not meet Toyota's standards. Instead, Toyota wanted workers who could (1) demonstrate initiative and learn new tasks quickly; (2) take an active role in decision making and problem solving; (3) be flexible, adaptive, and energetic; and, most of all, (4) work well in a team-oriented environment. This would enable Toyota to develop "Kaizen," the gradual, continuous improvement of every member of the work force.

The selection system developed entirely for this one plant focused on potential rather than education and experience. The selection process followed eight phases, with each phase reducing the number of applicants:

1. *Advertising* Jobs were advertised in twenty-eight Kentucky employment offices. Only three job categories were listed—team member, team leader, and group leader—and all production and skilled jobs were in one of the three categories.

2. *Application and Orientation* Applicants completed state and Toyota application forms and viewed an organization video that explained Toyota's management philosophy and selection process.

3. *Technical Skills Assessment* Applicants completed written tests, including the General Aptitude Test Battery (GATB), a validated test of cognitive ability and

---

The selection process begins when there are more qualified and available job applicants than there are open positions. It may be necessary to fill one particular position or several positions as they become open, or to fill positions continuously through training programs so that people are ready to take jobs as they become vacant. In large organizations, which may continuously recruit and select job applicants for future job openings, the time positions remain vacant is minimized.

SELECTION DECISIONS

Human resource selection is the process of choosing qualified individuals who are available to fill positions in an organization. In the ideal personnel situation, selection involves choosing the best applicant to fill a position. After the position opens, the HR manager reviews the available, qualified applicants and fills the position from that pool. The ideal situation, however, seldom occurs. The selection

300

psychomotory skills. Candidates also completed the Job Fit Inventory, a test of people's motivation to work in a highly participatory environment.

4. *Interpersonal Assessment Center (IAC)* Candidates participated in four simulations (eight hours) designed to assess teamwork skills, communication skills, decision-making skills, and manufacturing assembly ability.

5. *Leadership Assessment Center (LAC)* Remaining candidates completed three exercise simulations designed to measure (1) ability to delegate responsibility; (2) ability to write letters and study reports; (3) training and counseling ability; and (4) ability to schedule work.

6. *Technical Performance Assessment* Maintenance applicants took hands-on tests in two technical areas.

7. *The Toyota Assessment* Remaining candidates were interviewed by a team of Toyota HR department and line management. Hiring recommendations were made by the team based on the interview and performance in other phases.

8. *Health Assessment* Recommended applicants were given drug and alcohol tests and a physical exam.

Toyota's selection process has had over 200,000 applicants. Accepted applicants averaged fifteen weeks in assessment. Bill Constantino, group leader, Plastics Section, summarized his feelings about the selection process: " . . . at times I wondered if it would ever end! . . . But a funny thing happened along the way. I noticed how there were fewer and fewer people. . . . I recognized that Toyota was going to end up with high-caliber, motivated people. . . . Over time we developed a real sense of comraderie. . . . Without question, the quality of our people is unmatched."

SOURCE: Adapted from Chuck Cosentino, John Allen, and Richard Wellins, "Choosing the Right People," *HR Magazine* 35, no. 3 (March 1990): 66–70.

process involves making a judgment—not about the applicant, but about the fit between *this* person and *this* job. Almost half of the employees who voluntarily quit their jobs within the first year cited a wrong fit as the reason.[1]

There is no fail-safe method of determining the best person to fill any position. Many subjective factors are involved in the selection process because there is no perfect test or gauge of applicants. But there are objective techniques that increase the validity of the

process. The selection process is perhaps the heart of an organization's HR program. If the selection process is well administered, the employee will be able to achieve personal career goals and the organization will benefit from a productive, satisfied employee.

In the new era of globalization, the key to success is the human factor—people. Unlike products, land, equipment, and money, people experience unique problems when moved across national borders. Thus, even greater care must be taken to select, orient, and assist people who must work in different countries and cultures. Most people are raised, educated, and indoctrinated in only one culture. Yet the magic of successful international business lies in people who have developed knowledge of and respect for more than one culture and thus can interface successfully between two or more cultures. An American Management Association survey of Forbes 500 CEOs found that of the sixty most common problems of international business operations, twelve were related to selecting, training, and developing people (see Figure 7-1).[2] The process also works in reverse, that is, with foreign companies selecting American workers for their U.S. operations. For example, Toyota, the Japanese car manufacturer, developed an extensive, highly successful selection process for its first U.S. assembly plant (see *HR in the News:* "The Toyota Selection Process").

An HR Responsibility

The selection process is usually centered in the HR department, though it involves many individuals from other departments. Particularly in larger organizations, centralizing the recruitment and selection process in the HR department is both efficient and effective. Both current employees and job applicants have one place to apply for jobs, transfers, or promotions, as well as to inquire about related HR matters. In most situations, the cost of recruiting and selecting employees is minimized with centralization because HR specialists can perform these functions more effectively than managers in different departments. The trained HR specialist can also save money by ensuring that an organization's HR selection practices comply with federal laws and restrictions. In addition, the HR manager can ensure that the selection process is objective. Centralizing the selection function minimizes the bias of department managers or others who may wish to promote employees or hire applicants who are not the best qualified.

While the HR department is usually responsible for selection, individual managers are often involved in the interviewing process. Fre-

FIGURE 7-1 Most common HR problems in international business.

An American Management Association survey of CEOs of Forbes 500 companies found twelve of their top sixty most common problems of conducting international business to be HR issues:

1. Selecting and training local managers.
2. Generating companywide loyalty and motivation.
3. Speaking the local language and respecting the culture.
4. Appraising overseas managers' performance.
5. Planning systematic manager development.
6. Hiring indigenous sales personnel.
7. Compensating foreign managers.
8. Hiring and training foreign technical employees.
9. Selecting and training U.S. managers for overseas operations.
10. Dealing with unions and labor laws abroad.
11. Promoting and transferring foreign managers.
12. Compensating U.S. nationals abroad.

SOURCE: S. Hayden, "Our Foreign Legions Are Faltering," *Personnel* (August 1990): 40–44.

quently, the applicant's second or third interview is with the department manager, who has valuable insights about work methods and departmental goals and can evaluate the applicant's qualifications. The selection process also relies on managers to assist in developing job specifications and writing job descriptions, which are critical in determining the needs for a particular position and the best-qualified applicants.

The centralization of the hiring process within the personnel department and the sharing of decision making with line managers have evolved over many years. As outlined in Table 7-1, hiring procedures have been greatly altered by outside influences, such as World War II, federal legislation, and new technology. Many common techniques—such as testing, employee training, and test validation—are the direct result of social movements and government statutes. Yet despite the increased role of the HR department, final selection decisions are often made by line managers.

Table 7-1 A Chronology of Hiring Practices and Influences in the United States

Event or Innovation	Date	Explanation or Significance
First personnel department	1890s	John H. Patterson, president of the National Cash Register Company, Dayton, Ohio, establishes the first personnel department.
Scientific management	1912	Frederick Taylor testifies before a special U.S. House committee on the principles and virtues of scientific management. This approach would reduce waste by hiring the right people and simplifying their jobs. Extremely popular for many years, it was no longer in favor by the end of the 1920s.
Testing	1918	The first group intelligence test, *Army Alpha,* is developed by personnel managers and psychologists to "match each enlisted man to a job." Shortly after World War I, industry and the Civil Service Commission adopt testing as a breakthrough in hiring practices, believing that each job can be scientifically filled with the right person.
	1920s	The first professional journal in personnel, *The Journal of Personnel Research* (forerunner of *Personnel Journal*), describes in issue after issue the profession's infatuation with testing as the means of making hiring decisions with objective and scientific information.
Staff designation	1923	Line managers believe personnel should stay out of day-to-day decisions (including hiring), but personnel offices continue to take over the employment function to make it more scientific. In 1923 the National Personnel Association, in support of line management's views, changed its name to the American Management Association.
Great Depression	1930s	Massive unemployment stops almost all hiring and cruelly shows America that work is not appreciated until it is gone.
Wagner Act	1935	The once unified field of industrial relations is split into two, personnel and labor relations, in the years following enactment of the Wagner Act and the growth of union membership.
World War II	1940s	Organizations rapidly grow in size, and supervisors' preoccupation with production demands often forces them to relinquish all hiring and government-regulations concerns to personnel departments.
		The War Manpower Commission assumes control of most industrial hiring and introduces widespread use of manpower planning and training programs, which remain long after the war. Universities are encouraged to develop "industrial education" personnel programs.

(continued)

Table 7-1 *(continued)*

Event or Innovation	Date	Explanation or Significance
World War II (continued)		Nondiscriminatory hiring orders are first issued by President Roosevelt. By 1945 women account for 36 percent of the work force due to the shortage of men. Both managers and women themselves are confronted with the fact that women are successful in jobs previously closed to them.
The age of Sputnik	1950s	The combination of the GI Bill and the national "space race" with the USSR ignites a trend for organizations to hire college graduates in unprecedented numbers, particularly scientists, engineers, and businessmen.
Federal laws	1960s	The movement toward "fair and open" hiring practices begun during World War II crystallizes into federal legislation: the Equal Pay Act of 1963, the 1964 Civil Rights Act, affirmative action (1965 executive order 11246), and the Age Discrimination in Employment Act (ADEA) of 1967.
		The new hiring legislation forces personnel managers to consider the validity and reliability of selection methods; the use of written tests and the old boy network decline as structured interviews, nondiscriminatory application blanks, assessment centers, and weighted application blanks grow in use.
The new employee	1970s	"Matching the needs of the person with those of the organization" becomes the common hiring practice. A new wave of better-educated, less loyal employees armed with employment laws demands flexible working hours, quality circles, increased leisure time, compressed workweeks, quality of working life, and so on.
		Employers, because of court decisions, become more concerned that their hiring practices must be defensible to their employees and government.
Reagan administration	1980s	Employers perceive a swing of the government-regulation pendulum in their direction. The Supreme Court and federal agencies, inspired by the 1978 EEO hiring guidelines, order less stringent government regulation of hiring practices, except in cases involving age discrimination, due to new "teeth" in the 1978 amendment to the 1967 ADEA. Unions suffer several setbacks from the National Labor Relations Board and the courts.
New round of federal laws	1990s	Congress reaffirms nondiscriminatory hiring practices with the 1990 Americans with Disabilities Act (ADA) and the 1991 Civil Rights Act. The U.S. Supreme Court reaffirms its strong position on sexual harassment.

SOURCE: Adapted from A. S. T. Blackburn, Sam Ervin, Jonathan Glassman, Martha Harris, and John Thelin, "Sixty Years of Hiring Practices," *Personnel Journal* 59, no. 6 (June 1980): 462–82.

THE SELECTION PROCESS

As Figure 7-2 indicates, the selection process pulls together organizational goals, job designs, and performance appraisals, as well as recruitment and selection. The first element in the selection process is the setting of organizational goals, which must include the general hiring policy of the organization. Management can either employ the best people in the marketplace for particular jobs—often involving high salaries and benefits—or pay relatively low wages and salaries, unconcerned with employee turnover or dissatisfaction about wages, benefits, and working conditions. Policymakers must determine how the employees fit into the overall framework of the organization and must establish the relationship among the employees in the organization.

The second element, job design, involves determining what duties and responsibilities each job will entail. How motivating or repeti-

FIGURE 7-2 Basic elements in the selection process.

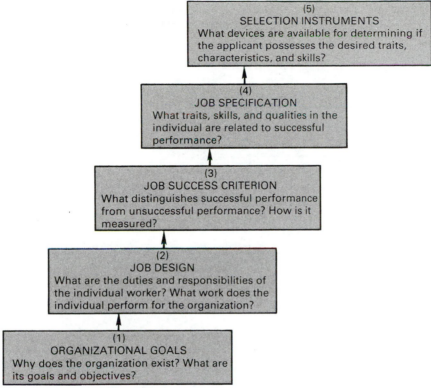

SOURCE: Mitchell S. Novit, *Essentials of Personnel Management,* © 1979, p. 70. Reprinted by permission of Prentice-Hall, Inc., Englewood Cliffs, N.J.

tous each job becomes greatly affects the performance of employees on that job. The performance of employees will be affected by their ability and motivation. The job design will greatly affect both of these factors.

The third element involves the measurement of job success. The discovery of which employees are successful will determine what kinds of employees to recruit and select in the future.

The fourth element, job specifications, comes from the job analysis, which specifies what traits, skills, and background an individual must have to qualify for the job.

Finally, policymakers must determine which combination of interviews, tests, or other selection devices to use in the selection process. There is no magical combination of selection instruments that will minimize the cost of selection and facilitate choosing the best candidates available. Although there are few new selection techniques in HR management, there have been improvements in particular areas. There are also restrictions caused by federal guidelines and other influences.[3] The steps in the selection process are outlined in Figure 7-3. They may change from one organization to another, but all the steps are normally completed at one time or another. The sequence may vary within organizations according to the types of jobs being filled and the size of the organization. The

FIGURE 7-3 The steps in the selection process.

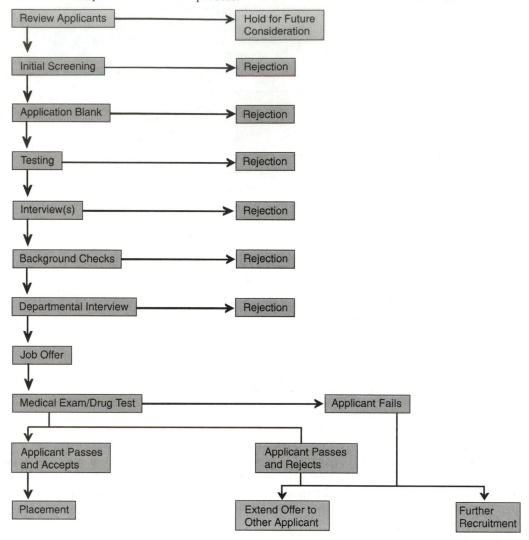

process usually begins by reviewing current applications gathered through the organization's recruitment effort.

Applicants who appear to be qualified for the position are then screened. Initial screening looks for the minimum requirements still available in the job market, as determined by the job specifications. The third step is to have the applicants complete an application blank, which standardizes information about all of the applicants to be considered. Any tests relevant to the job and validated by the organization are then administered to applicants. The next step is usually to interview applicants within the HR department. The background of desirable applicants is checked next, especially their references and employment history. Finally, the few applicants remaining are interviewed by the departmental supervisor or department head. During this in-depth interview, job requirements are discussed so that the applicant as well as the supervisor will be able to judge each other's interest in the job. At this point, a job offer can be made to the applicant best qualified for the job. If that applicant rejects the offer, management can either contact other qualified applicants or begin the recruitment process again if there are no other qualified applicants available. When the applicant accepts the offer, the process of placing the applicant in the organization begins.

Evaluating Ability and Motivation

Maximizing employees' future performance is the objective of the selection process. An employee's performance on the job depends on the employee's ability and motivation to perform the job as is illustrated in Figure 7-4. The entire selection process hinges on determining which applicants have the necessary ability and the greatest motivation to be successful employees.

Often failure on the job is due not to a lack of skill or ability to perform the job adequately but to a lack of motivation. Skills and abilities can be developed in employees through training inside and outside the organization, but motivation cannot be developed to the same extent. For example, 85 percent of the persons who failed to be successful sales representa-

tives in one company lacked motivation rather than ability. The single most important indicator of how a job applicant will perform appears to be past performance. Therefore, during the selection process, obtaining an accurate and verifiable record of the applicant's past job performance is critical, though often very difficult.[4]

The key to assessing accurately a person's motivation may be the measurement of his or her values. If the applicant shares the same values as the employer, they are much more likely to be committed to achieving the same goals. At the Toyota automobile manufacturing plant in Kentucky, for example, over 200,000 applicants have gone through an exhaustive twenty hours of selection, testing, and interviewing to determine if their basic values match those of the company (see *HR in the News:* "The Toyota Selection Process"). Toyota believes that **Kaizen**, a philosophy of continuous improvement, requires employees who are strongly motivated and who place a high value on quality. The Toyota selection process focuses not on skills, which will be given new employees, but on certain traits and values, specifically the following:[5]

- *Problem solving* People who think for themselves and are self-motivated to address problems.

FIGURE 7-4 Job performance is a function of two factors.

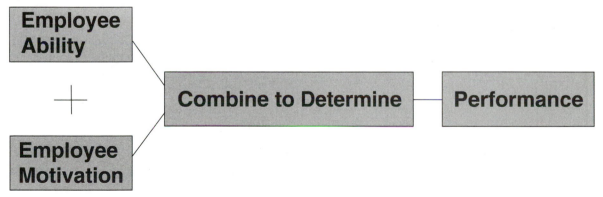

- *Teamwork* Interpersonal skills, diplomacy, and willingness to communicate.
- *Flexibility* Ability to adjust to changing needs.
- *Continual learning* Desire to constantly explore new processes and implement new work methods.

STEPS IN THE SELECTION PROCESS

Initial Screening

Initial screening minimizes the time the HR department must spend during the selection process by removing obviously unqualified or undesirable applicants. For most jobs, many applicants do not deserve the serious attention and time of the HR specialist, particularly if many applications are blind résumés or walk-ins. To maintain a favorable corporate image, every applicant must be given courteous treatment. Primarily, the initial screening determines if the applicant possesses the critical job specifications and expedites the departure of the unqualified applicants to minimize the total cost of the selection process.

In reviewing résumés or letters from applicants, the HR officer must determine which applicants have the minimum qualifications indicated in the job description.

Once the cornerstone of the job search process, the résumé today must be carefully scrutinized. While résumés can provide effective descriptions of individuals' work histories, the validity of their content should be questioned since about 34 percent contain misleading information.[6] To avoid being misled, certain "red flags" should be watched for and investigated (see Figure 7-5).

Qualified applicants are then queried about their interest in the position. If the initial screening can be done by direct contact with the applicant, then the interviewer may pursue a number of strategies. The interviewer can

FIGURE 7-5 Résumé "red flags."

Warning signs that may require further investigation:

- Time gaps in employment
- Vague answers, such as listing the state the employer was in and not the full address
- Vague reasons for leaving previous jobs
- Lack of employment history
- Inconsistencies in salary history
- When all employers listed are out of business

SOURCE: Marlene Brown, "Checking the Facts on a Resume," *Hiring Tips: A Supplement to the 1993 Personnel Journal* (1993): 6–7.

ask so-called knockout questions. Such questions may cause an applicant to withdraw from further consideration. Knockout questions include: What are your salary requirements? Can you work weekends and nights? Can you work shift hours? Can you stay out of town three nights per week? Do you have an RN degree? What is your experience using Word-Perfect 5.1? The interviewer can also give a brief job description. Many applicants will not be interested once they learn the exact nature of the job, salary, or hours.[7]

Applicants who are rejected at this point in the selection process or at any other point must be included in an **applicant flow record**. The Equal Employment Opportunity Commission (EEOC) requires that companies with federal contracts record for each job applicant the name, race, national origin, sex, reference source, date of application, and position applied for. The applicant flow record should also indicate whether a job offer was made to the applicant and the reason why an offer was not made or was rejected. Applicant flow records provide data to be reported in quarterly reports and annual EEO-1 reports.[8]

Résumé Tracking Systems An increasing number of employers are utilizing computer résumé scanning and tracking systems to provide initial screening of résumés. Companies like MCI, Disney, and Nike, Inc., have found that these software systems reduce the administrative and storage costs associated with paper résumés. While such systems vary, in general they involve HR clerks in putting all résumés received into a computer data base. The résumé is then edited and stored according to key words, and a response letter is sent to the applicant. A recruiter can then scan the data base for all applicants who meet certain criteria for positions. If the program produces a list that is too long or short, the criteria can be changed. HR professionals have found that résumé scanning provides several advantages compared to filing, copying, and sorting through paper résumés:[9]

- Reduced utilization of recruitment agencies due to the speed and capacity of the system.
- Ease and speed of storage, which enables all résumés (even thousands of unsolicited ones) to be stored and retrieved.
- Faster recruitment of applicants due to computerized screening of résumés.
- Improved service to applicants.
- A paperless system that eliminates filing, copying, and sorting of résumés.

Application Blank

An **application blank** is a formal record of an individual's application for employment. This record is later used by the HR department and may be reviewed by government agencies. The application blank, which provides pertinent information about the individual, is used in the job interview and in reference checks to determine the applicant's suitability for employment. An example of an application blank appears in Figure 7-6. The agreement section at the end should be read carefully. It contains five critical aspects of a good application blank:

1. The applicant certifies, with his or her signature and the date, that all information provided is correct. Falsification of such information is generally legal grounds for termination.

2. The applicant agrees to submit to a medical examination, with passage being a condition of employment.

3. The applicant authorizes former employers and references to provide background information.

4. The applicant understands and accepts that his or her employment is "employment at will" and thus can be terminated at any time, with or without cause.

5. Only a written employment agreement, signed by the CEO, is a valid offer of employment; thus, any promises or suggestions that may have been casually made by others during the hiring process are not valid.

Discriminatory Practices In recent years, the greatest changes in application blanks have come about after consideration of what questions should be eliminated from the application or very carefully worded. Primarily, these questions concern the following information:

Race, National Origin, Religion Employers have been warned by the EEOC and the courts that application forms that indicate race, national origin, religion, and sex often have been used to discriminate against minorities. Employers eliminated this information from HR records (including the application blank), only to find that to comply with EEO/AA requirements this information had to be gathered in the application process. The EEOC advised that these data should be kept separate from the individual HR files. Such information can be coded,

FIGURE 7-6 An excellent example of a complete application blank from the Kentucky Fried Chicken Corporation. Used by permission.

KFC Management Company — KFC Corporation   Zantigo
Employment Application   MEXICAN RESTAURANT

MO	DAY	YR

All Applicants Will Receive Consideration Without Regard To Age, Race, Color, Religion, Sex, National Origin, Handicap, Or Military Status

PLEASE COMPLETE ALL SECTIONS—FRONT AND BACK

PERSONAL

Last Name	First Name	Middle Name	Social Security#

Present Street Address	City	State	Zip	No. Yrs.	Home Phone (Including Area Code)

Last Address	City	State	Zip	No. Yrs.	If Under 19 Years Of Age, Date Of Birth:

Are You Legally Eligible To Work In The United States? ☐ YES ☐ NO	Have You Ever Been Convicted Of A Felony? ☐ YES ☐ NO	If Yes, Please Explain:

Notify In Emergency: State Name, Complete Address And Phone (Including Area Code):

Minors Indicate Parent or Guardian

JOB INTEREST

Position (Type of Work) Desired:	Starting Monthly Salary Expected: $	Have You Ever Previously Applied To Our Firm? ☐ YES ☐ NO

Date You Can Start Work:	List Any Relatives Or Acquaintances Working For Our Company:

Type Of Employment Desired:
☐ Full Time   ☐ Permanent Part Time   ☐ Temporary Full Time   ☐ Temporary Part Time   ☐ Summer

Are There Any Times When You Are Unavailable For Work? If So, Please Specify:	Are You Known To Schools/References By Another Name? If Yes, By What Name:

Special Interests Or Qualifications That May Help Us In Considering Your Application:

EDUCATION

Circle Highest Grade Completed In Each School Category:	Grade School 1 2 3 4 5 6	High School 7 8 9 10 11 12	College 1 2 3 4	Graduate School 1 2 3 4

Schools	Name And Address	Dates Attended From	To	Diploma Or Degree	Grade Average	Areas Of Specialization
High School						
College						
Graduate School						
Other						

HEALTH

Are you able to perform, with or without accommodation, the essential job tasks?	☐ YES ☐ NO

If hired, could you perform all the tasks in the job description?	☐ Standing	☐ Lifting

If No to the Above, Explain:

VETERANS AND DISABILITY INFORMATION

Answering the questions in this section is completely voluntary and will not affect your chances for employment with the company. They are being asked because the federal government requires the company to maintain records of Vietnam era veterans, disabled veterans, and handicapped individuals seeking employment. The answers to these questions will help fulfill our responsibility in this area, and the company would appreciate your help.

Did you serve in active military duty 180 days or more between August 5, 1964 and May 7, 1975?   ☐ YES   ☐ NO

Were you released from active military duty between August 5, 1964 and May 7, 1975 because of a service connected disability?   ☐ YES   ☐ NO

HR015-REV7/83   **PLEASE CONTINUE ON REVERSE SIDE**

FIGURE 7-6 *(continued)*

EMPLOYMENT RECORD:	List Each Job Held Starting With Your Present Or Last Job. Include Military Service, Summer Employment and Volunteer Activities. If You Need Additional Space, Please Continue On A Separate Piece Of Paper.		

Name Of Company	Type Of Business	From (MO & YR)	To (MO & YR)
Address (Including City And State)		Starting Salary	Last Salary
Name And Title Of Supervisor	Telephone	Titles And Duties:	
Reason For Leaving:			

Name Of Company	Type Of Business	From (MO & YR)	To (MO & YR)
Address (Including City And State)		Starting Salary	Last Salary
Name And Title Of Supervisor	Telephone	Titles And Duties:	
Reason For Leaving:			

Name Of Company	Type Of Business	From (MO & YR)	To (MO & YR)
Address (Including City And State)		Starting Salary	Last Salary
Name And Title Of Supervisor	Telephone	Titles And Duties:	
Reason For Leaving:			

Name Of Company	Type Of Business	From (MO & YR)	To (MO & YR)
Address (Including City And State)		Starting Salary	Last Salary
Name And Title Of Supervisor	Telephone	Titles And Duties:	
Reason For Leaving:			

Name Of Company	Type Of Business	From (MO & YR)	To (MO & YR)
Address (Including City And State)		Starting Salary	Last Salary
Name And Title Of Supervisor	Telephone	Titles And Duties:	
Reason For Leaving:			

REFERENCES — List Names And Addresses Of People Who Have Known You Over 3 Years. (DO NOT LIST RELATIVES.)

Name	Address	Occupation	Phone

AGREEMENT

I certify that all statements given on this application are correct, and understand that falsification or misrepresentation in this or any other personnel record can result in my dismissal if I am employed by the company. If requested to do so, I agree to submit to a physical examination which I must successfully pass as a condition of being accepted for employment. I agree to provide proof of age upon notification of hire. I authorize my former employers and other individuals to give the company information concerning me, whether or not it is part of their written record, and I release them and their companies from any liability whatsoever on account of such information furnished to KFC. I understand that the above noted examination and reference inquiries will be kept confidential and will not be released to anyone by KFC without my written consent. Also, I agree that if I am offered employment by KFC and accept, my employment will be employment at will, that my employment and compensation can be terminated, with or without cause, and with or without notice, at any time, at the option of either KFC or myself. I am hereby informed and I understand that no representative of KFC, other than the Chief Executive Officer, has any authority to enter into any agreement for employment for any specified period of time or to make any agreement contrary to the foregoing and that any such agreement must be in writing and must be signed by the Chief Executive Officer of KFC.

Public Law 91-508 requires that we advise you that a routine inquiry may be made during our initial or subsequent processing which will provide application information concerning character, general reputation and credit, personal characteristics and mode of living. Upon written request, additional information as to the nature and scope of the inquiry, if one is made, will be provided.

Signature:_____ Date: _____

WE APPRECIATE YOUR INTEREST AND THE TIME YOU HAVE TAKEN TO PREPARE THIS APPLICATION.

incorporated into payroll or other records, and kept separate from the individual's HR file. Requesting such information on application blanks is not a violation of the Civil Rights Act per se, but such information recorded on application forms would be carefully reviewed should discrimination charges be filed.[10]

Age, Date of Birth The ADEA prohibits discrimination against applicants over age forty. Therefore, asking the date of birth or age of an applicant is unlawful. However, applicants may be asked if they are of minimum age in order to comply with state and federal child work laws. The employer may also ask if the individual is over age forty.

Marital Status Asking if applicants are married or have children may constitute discrimination. Because such questions can be used to discriminate against women and rarely relate to job performance, they are violations of the Civil Rights Act of 1964.[11] Such information is needed for Social Security and tax records. It may be obtained after the applicant has been employed but not during the selection process.

Education The Supreme Court has prohibited establishing an educational requirement as a condition of employment if such a requirement is not job related. The necessity of requiring a diploma, certificate, or college degree should be determined through job analysis.[12]

Arrest Record The courts have ruled that requesting arrest records is an unlawful selection consideration unless it can be proven to be a business necessity. This ruling was made because a greater proportion of minority-group members than nonminority members are arrested. Therefore, making decisions regarding employment on the basis of arrest records would discriminate against minority members.[13] Federal courts have also ruled that a felony or misdemeanor conviction should not be an absolute criterion for rejecting a job applicant. Instead, the employer should consider the nature of the offense and its relationship to the position.

Photograph Since a photograph would identify an individual's sex, race, or national origin, it can be used to discriminate against minority applicants. The photograph does not provide any job-related information about the applicant. An employer may request a photograph of an employee for identification purposes after the employee is hired.

Height and Weight Requirements Court decisions have determined that height and weight requirements discriminate against Hispanics, Asian-Americans, and women because many persons in these groups are shorter and slimmer than white males. Height and weight requirements should be made only if they are shown by the employer to be a business necessity or a BFOQ.[14]

Disability The 1990 ADA prohibits preemployment inquiries as to whether the applicant has a physical or mental handicap or as to the nature of such a disability. Asking if an individual has the ability to perform essential job-related functions is permissible. Accommodating applicants with disabilities is required (see *HR in the News:* "Meet an Assistive Technology Coordinator").

Union Affiliation The National Labor Relations Act prohibits discrimination on the basis of union affiliation.[15]

Some state EEO laws are more rigid than the federal requirements. An employer could easily be in compliance with federal regulations but not state regulations. A major cause of this problem is the use of appli-

Meet an Assistive Technology Coordinator

Laura Micklus is an assistive technology coordinator with the Center for Independent Living of Southwestern Connecticut in Stratford, Conn., which helps area businesses and educational institutions with ideas to accommodate individuals with disabilities.

"Many business owners are operating out of fear and think only of the costly high-tech end when they should be thinking low-tech," she says. "What does the worker need—that should be focus of the search."

Sometimes it's as simple as helping the person to organize a worker's area to be efficient, providing a work surface with an adjustable tilt or a different type of stool to sit on.

Automating and computerizing factory operations has opened opportunities in plant work for many disabled individuals, Micklus says. Computerized machine shop equipment such as lathes and milling machines can now be operated by individuals with disabilities.

Two of her current projects are recommending work-station equipment for an employer who wants to hire a disabled individual and suggesting computer equipment for an individual with cerebral palsy who has little use of his hands.

Micklus, who has a master of social work degree from the University of Connecticut, can relate well to some of these needs. She has cerebral palsy and uses her $10,000 office computer to retrieve information from her accommodations database. She emphasizes that coordinators like herself in the 600 Independent Living Centers around the country have access to current research in rehabilitation going on in America and around the world. They'll even come on site to conduct job analyses, recommend job modifications or appropriate equipment, if desired by the employer.

SOURCE: Neville C. Tompkins, "Tools That Help Performance on the Job," *HRMagazine* (April 1993): 89. Used by permission.

---

cation forms from national printing firms that generally comply with federal regulations but contain questions that are illegal in some states. Selection officers are sometimes not aware of state laws. Failure to comply with state laws could be costly to employers.

The local branch of the EEOC or the state civil rights commission will review application forms to be sure that any possible discriminatory practices are eliminated. Although future court decisions may alter the items that can lawfully appear on applications blanks, those questions that can appear on the application blanks concern the following:

- Applicant's name.
- Applicant's home address and telephone number.

- Whether the applicant is of minimum working age.
- Whether the applicant can speak or read and write one or more foreign languages (if job related).
- Applicant's educational background (if job related).
- Applicant's work history, including dates of employment, salary progression, job responsibility and duties, and reasons for leaving.
- Whether the applicant can meet special job requirements, such as working in the evening or on weekends.
- Applicant's military experience.
- Applicant's conviction record (if job related).
- Applicant's willingness to travel.
- Applicant's special skills or training.
- How the applicant heard about the position.
- Membership in professional organizations.
- Names of relatives who are employed by the company.
- Other current employment, either full-time or part-time.

Uses of the Application Blank The application blank is a permanent record of the applicant's qualifications for a job. In addition to providing information required for the selection process, the application supplies input for the EEO/AA report. Human resource specialists use the application to develop background checks and interview questions. An important part of the selection process is verification of the applicant's past work history and references. Applicants and their previous employers sometimes disagree about the duties, responsibilities, and importance of previous jobs, length of employment, salary levels, and especially the reason for leaving employment. In an effort to obtain accurate, complete information from the applicant, the HR specialist starts with the application and follows through with background checks and an interview. During the interview, some applicants will give different accounts of prior experience as well as skills from what they provided on their application blanks.

Application blanks can also be used as screening devices to generate **global assessments**, wherein the HR specialist reviews the total applications and determines the general desirability of each applicant. A very subjective technique, global assessment is often used when many applicants are being considered and those lacking an appropriate background or skills can be quickly screened out.

A more objective screening technique using application blanks is to have the HR specialist rate each applicant on particular job-related areas, such as the level of specific skills or experience in particular work areas or in supervisory positions. Such a rating would change from job opening to job opening as different skills and background requirements become more relevant. Generally, if one particularly relevant job specification does not appear on completed application blanks, then these applicants can be screened out.

Preemployment Testing

The use of testing in the selection process has had periods of growth and periods of decline. Once the cornerstone of the selection process, selection tests, particularly paper-and-pencil ones, came under attack by the EEOC and the courts. Some tests were not reliable, and others were found not to predict employee job performance accurately. The primary problem in the past was the use of very general tests for many different jobs without serious thought about their validity. Today most employers are far more careful in the selection and use of tests.

From a 1988 case, *Daniel Construction Company* v. *International Brotherhood of Electrical Workers,* three critical criteria a se-

U.S. Manufacturers Seeking Educated Workers

Thomas Williams quit his high school teaching job to work on the Ford Motor Company assembly line in Avon Lake, Ohio. Why? Williams says, "I've changed my focus, from molding lives to molding products"—to more than double his teaching salary to over $50,000 a year.

Yes, the U.S. automobile industry is hiring again in the '90s, up to 75,000 workers at Ford and Chrysler alone. However, they are hiring a different kind of worker than those hired in the '50s and '60s. The car makers want employees who are quick to learn their job, require limited supervision, and are flexible and productive. Ford and Chrysler have adopted employee selection techniques similar to those used by Toyota (see the chapter opening *HR in the News*) when they select new employees. Applicants are tested in areas such as mathematics and manual dexterity, as well as problem-solving skills and teamwork. Chrysler stopped giving preference to relatives of current employees because of criticism from the United Auto Workers union. The new selection techniques have resulted in a more educated workforce at Ford Motor Company, as can be seen in the accompanying illustration.

Manufacturers in other industries have also adopted selection methods that

Education Profile of Production Workers at Ford Motor Company.

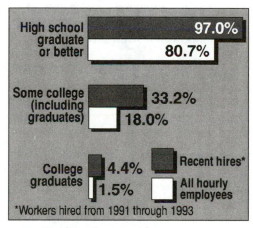

SOURCE: Ford Motor Company.

(continued)

315

hire an educated and skilled workforce. Workers are viewed as "a major capital investment."

The new breed of manufacturing employee views assembly line jobs, which were once disdained, as "plums."

For example in Chrysler's sprawling minivan plant in Windsor, Ontario, you will see Jeffrey Pancheshan, who has a master's degree in business administration from the University of Windsor, tightening catalytic-converter shields to the bottom of each passing minivan. "The reason I got an education was so I could get a good job," declares Mr. Pancheshan, who worked at the plant part time while going to college. "I feel like I have a good job right now."

Twenty-six percent of the new workers at the Windsor plant have college degrees. Only a few years ago many had trouble reading and writing.

The new hires are not quitting after only a few days on the assembly line as they commonly did in previous decades. Arthur Johnson, Supervisor of Training at Ford Motor Company, credits the lower turnover partly to the tight job market, but mostly to Ford's doing a better job of selecting employees.

Ford gives applicants a 3½ hour test in arithmetic, reading, and technical material and dexterity tests, such as quickly attaching washers in the right order to a pole. Ford also tests applicants on their ability to work together in teams, the same exercise the Japanese car makers utilize. Ford then selects applicants who score roughly in the top half and who have solid work histories, which demonstrate their motivation level. Candidates are also interviewed by at least two assembly line employees. They must also pass a drug test and a medical exam.

A major reason for the desire to hire more skilled and educated workers is the new corporate structure, which has fewer supervisors and thus demands more decision making from its workers. Chrysler, for example, had 1 salaried worker for every 25 hourly workers in 1991, 1 per 48 in 1994, and expects 1 per 100 in 1999.

"Before you change the caliber of work force you bring in, you have to change the environment they work in," preaches Mr. Pawley at Chrysler Corporation. "Your have to say to yourself, 'I'm going to pull my people out and turn that assembly line over to an empowered work force.'"

SOURCE: Reprinted by permission of *Wall Street Journal.* Neal Templson, "Auto Plants, Hiring Again, Are Demanding Higher-Skilled Labor," *Wall Street Journal* (March 11, 1994): A1, A4. Dow Jones & Company, Inc. All rights reserved worldwide.

---

lection test should meet to withstand legal challenge can be outlined:[16]

1. The test is a valid predictor of employee performance.
2. The test is developed, administered, and evaluated by professionals.
3. Those who fail a test can appeal the results or have an opportunity to increase their chances through other selection criteria.

Employee testing is generally far more objective than other selection procedures; testing has often proved to be the most valid selection procedure. In fact, one of the most rigorous and complete studies of employment testing concluded that, in general, standardized tests do not discriminate against blacks; blacks and whites with similar test scores do equally well in job performance. Although blacks, Hispanics, and Native Americans as groups do not score as well as white applicants, those differences may be due to less education and other social factors, not to the standardized tests themselves. Most important, no better alternative to a standardized test has been developed. Thus, at least some of the cynicism about testing in recent years has been unfair.[17] Many employers are increasingly using tests to select a skilled workforce. The U.S. manufacturing industry, for example, is generally seeking a more skilled workforce and using tests to select applicants (see *HR in the News*: "U.S. Manufacturers Seeking Educated Workers").

Franciscan Health System of Dayton An example that illustrates how preemployment testing can be effective in the selection process is the Franciscan Health System of Dayton (FHSD). A problem common in the health-care field is employee turnover, yet employees are critical to the service-delivery system in nursing-care facilities like FHSD. Headquartered in Dayton, Ohio, FHSD operates three care facilities with 2700 employees. A few years ago, the organization experienced extremely high turnover (146 percent) and poor employee performance. It was concluded that better employees who would make a long-term commitment to health-care delivery and could excel at difficult and stressful jobs were needed. It was also decided that the selection process, which was based solely on interviews and reference checks, was not effective. At the same time, FHSD implemented a total-quality improvement process and the HR director, Delores Shuermann, concluded that "Getting the right people in the first place is crucial." Thus, a new preemployment series of tests—the

Nursing Assistant Test Battery—was developed, validated, and given a trial period. The battery consists of three separate tests:[18]

1. *Employment Inventory* Measures the motivation level of applicants.
2. *Personality Test* Identifies applicants who are cheerful, tolerant, and don't worry much, all needed qualities in the nursing-care industry.
3. *Job Preference Inventory* Estimates the match between the working conditions of the job and the applicant's preference for certain working conditions. For example, a person who prefers a predictable, stable workday would not be a good match for a nursing assistant position.

The ten-month trial period produced solid results: turnover decreased from 146 percent to 27 percent, employee productivity increased, and supervisors reported that the newly hired employees were "showing more compassion, displaying competence, and collaborating with their co-workers." The test battery was placed in permanent, use and similar batteries were developed for other employee groups. The nursing battery successfully predicted the probability of applicants' becoming above-average employees. Applicants' scores on the tests placed them in one of three categories: hire, don't hire, and proceed with caution (see Figure 7-7). While FHSD would prefer to extend offers only to applicants who fall in the "hire" category, the lack of good candidates or the urgent need to fill positions sometimes forces it to consider applicants in the middle category—hire with caution.[19]

However, a survey of over 7000 HR managers nationwide revealed that many do not use any preemployment tests. The reason is the EEO requirement for validation. Most companies claim that they do not have the time or the money for test validation. Of the tests still in use, achievement tests, or work sample, and

FIGURE 7-7 Using tests in the selection process.

The FHSD utilizes a preemployment test battery. Applicants' scores have been divided into thirds, and successfully predict their performance and turnover.

Outcome	Decision	Predicted Performance
 Red-light candidate (scored in bottom third)	Do not hire	• Shows a less than 50% chance of above-average performance • Estimated annual productivity contribution: − $2204/hire
 Yellow-light candidate (scored in middle third)	Hire with caution	• Shows between a 50% and a 63% chance of above-average performance • Estimated annual productivity contribution: + $727/hire
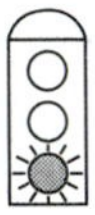 Green-light candidate (scored in top third)	Hire immediately	• Shows a better than 63% chance of above-average performance • Estimated annual productivity contribution: + $1989/hire

SOURCE: Franciscan Health System of Dayton.

psychological tests are the most common (see Table 7-2). In general, entry-level positions require more job-skill testing, while higher-level positions require more psychological testing. Financial officers and sales managers received the most polygraph testing before a 1988 law was passed restricting the use of polygraphs. Before the law was passed, the banking industry accounted for over one-third of all polygraph tests; the wholesale/retail, mineral extracting, and health-care industries were also big users.[20]

General Intelligence Tests Decades ago, general **intelligence tests** were developed to predict the success of young children in school. Testing the success of young school children in their academic careers is still what general intelligence tests are best suited for and they should be utilized.

Aptitude Tests Natural ability in a particular discipline or the ability to learn quickly or

Table 7-2 Preemployment Testing by Employers

Type	Frequency of Employer Use
Achievement and work samples	55%
Clerical and word processing	31%
Physical strength	6%
Writing	6%
Equipment operation	4%
Assessment centers	3%
Personality and psychological	20%
Drug and alcohol abuse	33%
Polygraph/honesty	11%

Use of Test Results	Frequency
Reject applicants who refuse test	52%
Rate test results	35%
Passage required for position	20%

Note: Responses of 142 organizations surveyed.

SOURCE: Adapted from Paul L. Blocklyer, "Preemployment Testing," *Personnel* 65, no. 2 (February 1988): 66–68.

to understand a particular area reveals an aptitude for that area or discipline. **Aptitude tests** indicate the ability of an individual to learn certain skills.[21]

As the official U.S. Employment Services aptitude test, the General Aptitude Test Battery (GATB) is recognized as the basic denominator in estimating aptitude requirements. It is the aptitude test by which jobs are categorized in the *Dictionary of Occupational Titles (DOT)*. Also, many state and local employment agencies use the GATB, which tests the following:

- General intelligence.
- Verbal ability.
- Numerical ability.
- Spatial perception.
- Form perception.
- Clerical perception.
- Motor coordination.
- Finger dexterity.
- Manual dexterity.

The GATB consists of twelve timed tests (parts)—eight paper-and-pencil tests and four apparatus tests. Each part requires performance of familiar tasks such as name comparisons, arithmetic computations, reasoning, pegboard manipulations, and so on. Employer use of the GATB in employee selection is related to its use by the U.S. Employment Service. The Employment Service conducted validity studies of the GATB over a forty-five-year period and found three general abilities (cognitive, perceptual, and psychomotor) to be valid predictors of job proficiency. The Employment Service then began implementing the testing in local Job Service (unemployment) offices. Employers may use the GATB when validated as predictors of employee success.[22]

Personality and Interest Tests Both personality and interest tests seek to measure an individual's motivation in particular fields. Personality tests, such as the Bernreuter Personality Inventory, measure neurotic tendency, self-sufficiency, introversion and extraversion, sociability, and self-confidence. The Thematic Apperception Test (TAT) is a common projective personality test in which the subject is asked to interpret certain situations. The TAT assesses the individual's need for achievement and has been successful in predicting individual motivation. Other personality tests, such as the California Psychological Inventory (CPI) and the Thurstone Temperament Survey (TTS), have been developed to assess specific personality aspects. The Guilford-Zimmerman Temperament Survey is a broad personality measure that assesses the individual's ability to positively interact with others.

Although the use of personality tests has declined, a survey of university graduate students reported about 20 percent had taken a paper-and-pencil personality test. There are three primary problems with personality tests. First, they are generally not reliable or valid predictors of job performance. Second, to be useful, such tests assume that job applicants have sufficient insight to describe themselves accurately—often an unjustified assumption. Third, in a desire to perform well, candidates may give false responses to produce what they believe to be the desired "test score," despite there being no right or wrong answers on personality tests.

Interest tests generally are designed to measure individuals' activity preferences. For example, individuals are asked if they would rather watch a baseball game on television, read a novel, or attend a local Little League game on a Saturday afternoon. Interest tests such as the Strong Vocational Interest Blank (SVIB) have been found to predict the occupations people will enter with reasonable accuracy. By matching the interests of individuals successful in different occupations, the SVIB indicates to applicants which fields most closely match their interests. The SVIB has shown that, within professions, people's interests have been fairly stable over time.

Interest tests like the Job Preference Inventory estimate the match between the working conditions of a job or organization and the extent to which a person likes or prefers to be in a certain type of environment. A match between the actual conditions and those desired by an individual can mean an easier adjustment to a new job and possibly a longer tenure.

Achievement Tests   Aptitude tests assess a person's capacity to learn, whereas **achievement tests** assess the degree to which a person has learned. Because achievement tests measure current behavior, they may be the best predictor of future employee behavior. Therefore, HR departments may use achievement tests to determine whether a person can do the job and aptitude tests to measure whether or not someone can be trained to do the job. Through a job analysis for a specific occupation, a list of questions can be developed that will test an applicant's occupational experience. The U.S. Employment Service has developed a series of trade tests that measure an individual's knowledge of the behavior, tools, and equipment of a particular job. Because achievement tests can be validated, they are useful predictors of job performance where specific knowledge or experience is necessary to perform in a skilled occupation.

Work Samples   One step beyond the achievement test, which measures knowledge of a particular job or occupation, is the use of a **work sample**, in which the applicant performs part of the job as a test. Examples of work samples are typing tests for secretaries, assembly tests for production-line workers, and trial-balances computation tests for accountants. Work samples are generally valid predictors of job performance since they mea-

sure those behaviors required for successful job performance. But work samples have limited use due to their specific nature; that is, they can only test an individual's ability on certain duties within the job setting. Other criteria are measured by other selection devices. Work samples are usually limited to jobs that are physical rather than mental in nature. In the future, more work samples for conceptual jobs may be developed.

Polygraph Tests   The **polygraph** is a device that measures the emotions of an individual by directly measuring galvanic skin response, blood pressure, and breathing rate. A 1988 federal law restricted the use of a polygraph in employment decisions. Before the law was passed, polygraph use in corporations fell into three common areas: (1) verification of employment application information; (2) periodic surveys to determine employee honesty and loyalty; and (3) investigation of a specific instance of theft within the company. About 20 percent of those companies that responded to a survey used the polygraph in some capacity; 50 percent of the commercial banks and retail companies used polygraph examinations. Transportation and industrial firms also indicated heavy use of the polygraph examination.[23]

In 1988, however, Congress passed the *Employee Polygraph Protection Act*, which prohibits the use of polygraphs to screen job applicants or investigate employees' backgrounds. The act also outlaws voice-stress analyzers, psychological-stress evaluators, and deceptographs as applicant screening devices. Exempted employers include security-service firms and pharmaceutical manufacturers and distributors. The act does permit polygraph testing of employees as part of workplace investigations into theft or vandalism, but only under strict regulations.

The passage of the act came after years of congressional debate. Supporters of polygraph testing argued that when operated by a trained professional, the device can be a valuable tool in screening job applicants. Problems occurred, they contended, because no national licensing program existed to ensure professional testing. Opponents (and supporters) of the act maintained that stress detected by the equipment is not proof of untruthfulness and that the test results can be unreliable.[24]

Honesty Tests Preemployment **honesty tests**, as defined by the U.S. government, are written tests designed to identify job applicants who have relatively high propensities to steal money or property on the job or who are likely to engage in behavior of a "counterproductive" nature, including tardiness, sick leave abuse, and absenteeism.[25] While these paper-and-pencil tests have been used in employee selection for over forty years, their widespread use by employers began only after the *Employee Polygraph Protection Act* limited the polygraph's use in selection. Honesty tests were then viewed as logical substitutes. Their use is limited in some states, including Massachusetts, Rhode Island, and Minnesota. The primary concern over their use in employee selection is the lack of sufficient evidence of their validity. The U.S. Office of Technology Assessment (OTA) has not yet been convinced of their validity even though it has conducted extensive research and worked with the publishers of the tests.[26] One credible 1989 review of a large number of validity studies published by test publishers did, however, support their validity.[27] A comprehensive review of a task force of the American Psychological Association concluded that "for those few tests for which validity information is available the preponderance of the evidence is supportive of their predictive validity." The report also noted that many test publishers have not come close to meeting validation standards for their honesty tests.[28]

One major problem with honesty tests reported by the OTA is the high percentage of honest people who fail the test. This result may be caused by the broad range of behaviors covered by the tests, including theft, absenteeism, and falsification of expense records, which make it difficult to define accurately the concept of *honesty* and to predict who is dishonest. A second problem is the disagreement over whether honesty is an individual trait or is something that is situationally determined. If it is situationally determined, then the problem could be addressed by management practices that support honest behavior. The third, and perhaps the most significant, problem with honesty tests is that they fail to predict accurately which persons are likely to engage in theft, generally considered the most critical dimension of employee honesty. Thus, they are not ideally useful as preemployment tests for applicants. At least three major types of honesty tests are currently in use:[29]

1. *Overt* These tests contain items that deal directly with the applicant's attitudes towards theft and dishonesty and admission of past dishonesty.

2. *Personality* These tests strive to predict a variety of counterproductive work behaviors such as low motivation, resistance to following directions, lack of personal pride in work, and unnecessary absences.

3. *Multidimensional* Several scales are measured, including integrity, drug use, property damage, waste, and causes of personnel turnover.

Medical Exam/Drug Tests As indicated in Figure 7-8, a job offer is usually made contingent on the applicant's passing a **medical exam** and a **drug test**. Under the ADA, the medical examination must focus on the applicant's ability to perform the essential job functions. The ADA specifically allows preemployment drug testing (which is not considered a medical examination). To provide maximum validity,

FIGURE 7-8 U.S. preemployment drug screening by industry.

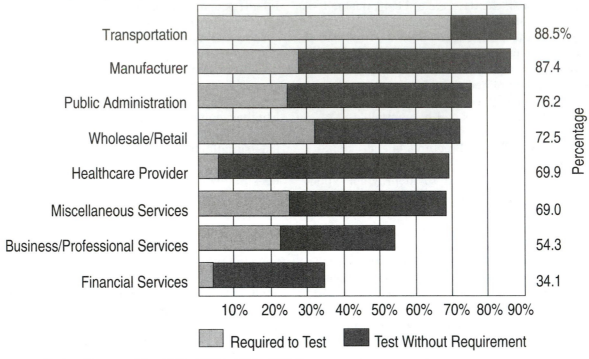

Industry	Percentage
Transportation	88.5%
Manufacturer	87.4
Public Administration	76.2
Wholesale/Retail	72.5
Healthcare Provider	69.9
Miscellaneous Services	69.0
Business/Professional Services	54.3
Financial Services	34.1

☐ Required to Test   ■ Test Without Requirement

SOURCE: American Management Association, *HR Focus* (June 1992): 7.

most employers do not perform in-house drug tests but instead utilize an external laboratory certified by the **National Institute on Drug Abuse (NIDA)**. NIDA standards must be met by federal drug-testing programs and are the recognized industry standards. When testing applicants, NIDA recommends that the drug-testing requirement be included in the position announcement. In addition, the job offer should be made contingent on the applicant's having a negative test result. Applicants who refuse to take the test or who test positive can be rejected. Not all employers require that applicants pass a drug test, and no federal law requires private sector employers to utilize a medical examination or drug test. In addition, seventeen states have passed laws limiting the use of drug testing in the workplace.[30]

A national survey of the American Management Association indicates that 75 percent of major U.S. employers engage in drug testing. Also, about 33 percent of all job applicants offered positions will be tested. The use of preemployment testing varies greatly according to the industry involved (see Figure 7-8). The industries with the highest rates of testing include transportation and manufacturing.[31]

Employer drug-testing programs have contributed to the overall decline in casual drug use, according to experts. About 90 percent of all testing involves job applicants, and employer programs have made drug use more difficult and less socially acceptable. Virtually every employer that has instituted a drug-testing program has witnessed a steep drop in positive test results. Mobile Corporation and Hoffman-

Laroche (a pharmaceutical company), for example, found that about 7 percent of their job applicants failed their tests in the mid-1980s but that ten years later less than 1 percent failed. Tropicana Products, Inc., found 25 percent of its job applicants using drugs when its drug-testing program started. After six years of testing the rate dropped to 5 percent, accidents dropped by 50 percent, and turnover dropped by 20 percent.[32]

HIV-Positive Employees Under the ADA, employers are prohibited from discriminating against a qualified person with a disability. The ADA *Interpretive Guidelines* states that individuals who have AIDS or AIDs-related complex or who are HIV positive are considered disabled and protected from discrimination. Furthermore, the ADA prohibits discrimination against an applicant or employee because he or she has a family member or associate who has a disability. An employer can take action when an HIV-related condition becomes job related. A job-related condition, however, does not result from unfounded fears or prejudices of co-workers, clients, or customers. Generally, an HIV-related condition may become job related and thus allow an employer to take appropriate action under the following conditions:[33]

1. The condition renders the employee incapable of performing the essential job functions.

2. The condition poses a significant risk to others with whom the employee must come in contact in the context of performing his or her job.

Interviews

"I dread it."

"Every time we have a vacancy I fall three weeks behind in my own work."

"I never know what I can say because of all this discrimination stuff."

"We spent over an hour talking . . . but I'm having second thoughts now that he's been here for a week."

Managers realize that the selection process is critical to their organization, yet they often dread the process—particularly the interview. The preceding comments are typical of managers' thoughts about interviewing.[34]

The purpose of the interview is to determine three things about the applicant: (1) Does the applicant have the ability to perform the job? (2) Will the applicant be motivated to be successful? (3) Will the applicant match the needs of the organization? According to a nationwide survey, interviewing is the most widely used selection method. Some employers have reacted to EEOC and court decisions regarding testing by using fewer tests and turning to the interview as the primary selection technique. Ironically, interviewing is just as vulnerable to EEOC guidelines as the written test.

Research has constantly shown that the selection interview is low in both reliability and validity. Reliability is a particular concern with interviews because the interview technique does not have the consistency of form that the written test or the reference check may have. Thus, the interview is not as consistent or reliable a selection technique as other methods.[35]

For many reasons, there is low reliability or consistency in the interview process. First, interviewers must constantly work to reduce personal biases. Even when interviewers recognize their personal biases, an interviewee's sex, race, religion, school, or hobbies may influence the final decision. Biases can be positive as well as negative. The sex of the interviewer or the interviewee affects the total evaluation of the interview situation. This problem occurs even with trained, experienced interviewers.[36]

Second, all interviews are different, as are all interviewees. The content of interviews changes because no two interviewees have the same background and experience; different aspects of the individuals, their skills, and their work histories must be discussed with each individual.

Third, the setting of the interview may affect the outcome. If one interview takes place early in the morning when the interviewer is fresh and the next interview is conducted late in the afternoon when the interviewer is in a hurry to leave, the second interviewee may receive less support when the interviewees are compared. For another example, an applicant interviewed right after an extremely impressive applicant the interviewer has seen is more likely to get a less positive interview evaluation than normal, but an applicant following a poor applicant the interviewer has seen may get a higher evaluation than normal.

Fourth, if the company has established a maximum number of people to interview and a deadline for filling the position, additional pressure is placed on the interviewer. The last applicant to be interviewed may be offered the position if the interviewer is in a hurry to fill it. Thus, the applicant may fill a position that otherwise would not have been offered.

A Structured, Objective Process   The problems with the traditional interview process are well known. They usually result in the interviewer's hiring whoever he or she felt most comfortable with, often a "junior me." Today companies like Johnson Wax, Mobile Corporation, and Marriott Corporation have developed structured, objective interview processes with the goal of achieving "controlled subjectivity." A critical change in this process is the shift from broad, vague questions such as "How would you discipline an employee?", for which applicants can give canned responses, to specific behavioral questions such as "Describe a recent example in which you disciplined an employee with absenteeism or tardiness problems."[37]

Conducting objective interviews is primarily a two-phase process. The first phase is to create a good interview setting before the applicant actually arrives and to prepare for the interview. The second phase is to establish a useful questioning period during the interview. These eight steps encompass the following characteristics of interviewing:

1. *Setting* Prepare a setting that will put the applicant at ease and provide consistent surroundings for each interview. Allow thirty to sixty minutes for an adequate interview.

2. *Documentation* Prepare a system of written records and formalized procedures for the interview. Determine how the interview will be documented at its conclusion to provide a formal record of the outcome.

3. *Standardization* Standardize the interview format. Determine a line of questioning that includes the applicant's prior work history, special abilities, skills, and educational background. This will provide a framework for consistency in the information-gathering process.

4. *Scoring* Determine how the interview will be scored. That is, on what criteria will the applicant ultimately be evaluated as a result of the interview process? An applicant may be scored in each area relevant to the job description, as well as on the basis of the applicant's response to questioning. If several people interview the same applicant, they should compare scores afterward and challenge each other to support their scores.

5. *Reviewing Job Specifications* Review the description and specifications for the particular job before each interview. Since the interviewer may see applicants for different jobs, the important aspects of each job must be fresh in the interviewer's mind.

6. *Reviewing the Application Blank* Review the application before the interview, looking for possible problem areas that require additional information and areas of possible

strengths and weaknesses that should be discussed in more detail during the interview.

7. *Training the Interviewer* Train the interviewer to recognize personal biases and other possible detriments to interview reliability.

8. *Job-Related Questions* Prepare a line of questioning that keeps the interview job related and does not waste time by straying from the subject or delving into personal areas, which could be seen as discriminatory. Questions should require candidates to relate specific examples of their past behavior rather than describe "what I think I would do in that situation."

Conducting an interview is an art as much as a science. Only through experience and training can an interviewer thoroughly question a job applicant and get maximum information in minimum time. Figure 7-9 contains some of the dos and don'ts of effective job interviewing.

The end of the job interview is a critical time. At the end, the applicant should be able to ask questions concerning the job, pay, or working conditions. The interviewer should ask when the applicant will be available to work and tell the applicant when the job will be filled. If more people will be interviewed or if there will be a waiting period for a final decision to be made, the applicant should be given an estimate—such as ten days or two weeks—of when a decision should be reached. The applicant should also be told whether to call to find out the results of the job decision or to wait for notification. Interviewers should be positive toward all applicants, even those who may have to be ruled out, because applicants may be available and suited for other positions at a later date.

Although the interview concentrates on verbal cues, much nonverbal information is given by the candidate that influences the interviewer's perception. Interviewers allow firmness of the handshake, physical appearance, and eye contact during the interview to affect their selection decisions. Body language is a *nonverbal cue* that can greatly influence the interviewer. Candidates who appear nervous or apprehensive do not make a positive impression. The lack of eye contact during the interview can have a strong negative impact on the selection decision if it is interpreted to indicate a person's lack of self-confidence or inability to communicate. Interviewers should be aware, however, that several Oriental cultures discourage direct eye contact, and thus that such action may be a cultural norm. The first few minutes of an interview are often critical.

A board or panel interview can replace the traditional one-on-one interview technique. The panel interview minimizes individual bias since all panel members score the applicant. The final evaluation for each applicant is an average of several individuals' evaluations and, therefore, balances out one individual's bias. The panel technique also forces interviews to become more structured and to the point. The only disadvantage of the panel interview is the increased cost to the organization of having more than one interviewer.

The Structured Interview A structured or patterned interview requires the interviewer to ask a series of predetermined job-related questions. The answers are often scored on a set scale such as 1 for poor, 2 for marginal, 3 for acceptable, 4 for above average, and 5 for outstanding. The interviewer, shortly after the interview is completed, completes an evaluation form, such as the one in Figure 7-10, and includes a brief rationale for the evaluations.

The structured interview can greatly increase the reliability and accuracy of the traditional informal or nonstructured interview. A structured interview usually shows the following characteristics:[38]

Questions The interviewer asks questions exclusively concerned with job duties and requirements critical to the job.

FIGURE 7-9 The dos and don'ts of effective interviews.

Do	Don't
Ask open questions: Why did you apply here? What specific skill do you have?	Ask all closed questions: Could you work here three to five years? Do you enjoy working with figures?
Ask job-related questions: Can you work the 3-to-11 shift? What COBOL experience do you have?	Ask personal questions: Does your husband work? Are your parents Spanish?
Ask reflective or follow-up questions: You said you didn't work the counter. Why? How could you accomplish that?	Ask broad or vague questions: Do you like people?
Open the interview by putting the applicant at ease—discuss an easy topic such as the last job or education.	Do all the talking. Let the applicant talk as much as possible.
Look for areas the applicant is uneasy about and find out why.	Ask judgmental questions: Don't you like flextime? I think a good health insurance plan is critical, don't you?
Ask positive questions: What was your reason for leaving XYZ Company?	Be impatient, constantly hurry the applicant, or look at the clock.
Use summary statements to ensure your understanding: Then you did train employees in COBOL programming?	Ask more than one question at a time: Why did you choose accounting? What courses did you like, dislike?

Questions that may be asked under the ADA

- Are you able, with or without accommodation, to perform the essential tasks required for this job?

- How would you perform the essential job tasks?

- What accommodations would you need to perform the essential tasks?

- If hired, would you be able to perform all of the job tasks outlined in this job description?

Questions that may violate the ADA

- Do you have a disability?

- Have you been treated for the following medical conditions? [Followed by a checklist]

- How many times were you absent from your past job due to illness?

- Have you ever been hospitalized?

- Have you ever filed for worker's compensation benefits?

- Are you taking prescription drugs?

- Have you ever been treated for any mental condition?

- Do you have any disabilities or impairments that may affect your performance?

SOURCE: David Gold and Betty Unger, "How Are Interview Questions Affected by ADA?" *HR News* (August 1992): A4; also, the *ADA Technical Assistance Manual* (EEOC).

Scored Responses The interviewer is provided typical answers to questions on a five-point rating scale.

Interview Committee Responses are discussed and rated by a number of people to minimize bias.

Consistency All applicants for a position are asked the same questions, evaluated with the same scoring method, and reviewed by the same people.

Questions asked in a structured interview are of four types:

Situational Questions The applicant must respond with what he or she would do in a certain situation. For example: "Give me an

FIGURE 7-10 An evaluation form used in a structured interview.

APPLICANT EVALUATION FORM

Applicant's name _____ Pat Wing _____

Date _____ March 15 _____

Requirements (skills, knowledge, and personal traits)	How Applicant Demonstrated Ability	Weight (importance of skill)	Rating of Applicant	Weight × Rating
Ability to supervise.	Was promoted to manage 15 professionals because of success in supervising two paraprofessionals.	5	4	20
Ability to speak before groups.	Evaluated by seminar participants as outstanding; spoke well during interview.	4	5	20
Knowledge of learning theory.	Unable to discuss theory, but had reasonable instincts; diversifies training design.	5	3	15
Knowledge of management theory.	Able to discuss major theorists.	5	5	25
Ability to cooperate in team environment.	Co-trained a few times; usually works independently.	4	3	12
Ability to deal with hostile participants.	Cited specific examples that indicated a great deal of skill.	5	4	20

TOTAL _____ 112 _____

illustration of how you have assigned work when two employees are absent."

Job-Knowledge Questions These are questions that concern the job knowledge the applicant must have before being hired. For example: "Describe a diesel engine that you have overhauled."

Job-Simulation Questions These are questions that approximate the content of the job. For example: "Describe the steps involved in replacing drum-type brakes."

Worker-Requirement Questions These are questions that concern the applicant's willingness or availability for certain working conditions. For example: "Are you willing to relocate after a six-month training program?"

Background Checks
In recent years, thoroughly checking the backgrounds of prospective employees has become increasingly necessary. Such an investigation, a **reference check**, can be both an energy-

FIGURE 7-11 False résumé information.

A study of randomly selected résumés by Equifax Incorporated found deceptive information, including the following:

Résumé Information	Percentage of Sample
Misstated dates of employment (3 months or more)	33%
Misstated why they left previous position	11%
Fudged job titles	4%
Faked employers	3%
Fabricated jobs	3%
Falsified college degrees	3%
Omitted criminal past	2%

SOURCE: Joan E. Rigdon, "Deceptive Résumés," *The Wall Street Journal* (June 17, 1993): B3.

saving procedure and a cost-efficient means of screening out undesirable applicants. Because applicants sometimes misrepresent themselves on their applications or during interviews (see Figure 7-11), checking references has become a common practice in personnel. Between 7 and 10 percent of applicants do not have the experience and background they claim. Thus, employers are turning to a confidential investigation of applicants' backgrounds before proceeding through the selection process.[39]

Falsifying information on job applications is not limited to entry-level applications. In fact Humana, Inc., the national hospital chain, found that thirty-nine (5 percent) physicians seeking jobs during a nine-month period had lied on their job applications. Some doctors who had dropped out of residency training programs claimed that they had completed them. Others falsified board certifications, which indicates that they passed an examination in a particular medical specialty.[40]

There are several methods of checking references. The HR specialist can personally visit previous employers or friends of the applicant. This method should be reserved for candidates being considered for high-ranking positions because of the extra time and expense incurred. A second method is to check references by mail. This method has two disadvantages: several days to weeks are required, and it lacks the depth of information that a personal phone call can provide. In addition, most employers are increasingly wary of putting their perceptions about former employees in writing (see Figure 7-12). The third method, the telephone call, is a time-efficient, accurate means of getting complete information on applicants. Previous supervisors and employers are more likely to give complete information regarding a candidate's background over the phone. The HR specialist can go into detail or ask particular questions concerning the applicant. A final method for checking references involves the use of outside services, which for a fee will investigate the background of applicants. Such services conduct interviews with former employers and check criminal records, credit files, and educational credentials.

Therefore, experienced HR specialists have learned that checking references by telephone provides several advantages:[41]

FIGURE 7-12 The unfavorable but positive recommendation.

For the person who desires to send a letter of recommendation that sounds positive yet contains unfavorable information, Robert J. Thornton of Lehigh University developed the Lexicon of Inconspicuously Ambiguous Recommendations (LIAR):

- To describe a candidate who is woefully inept: "I most enthusiastically recommend this candidate with no qualifications whatsoever."
- To describe a candidate who is not particularly industrious: "In my opinion you will be very fortunate to get this person to work for you."
- To describe a candidate who is not worth further consideration: "I would urge you to waste no time in making this candidate an offer of employment."
- To describe a candidate with lackluster credentials: "All in all, I cannot say enough good things about this candidate or recommend him too highly."
- To describe an ex-employee who had difficulty getting along with fellow workers: "I am pleased to say that this candidate is a former colleague of mine."
- To describe a candidate who is so unproductive that the position would be better left unfilled: "I can assure you that no person would be better for this job."

  Any of the above may be used to offer a negative opinion of the personal qualities, work habits, or motivation of the candidate while allowing the candidate to believe that it is high praise. In any case, whether perceived correctly or not by the candidate, the phrases are virtually litigation-proof.

SOURCE: Robert J. Thornton, "I Can't Recommend the Candidate Too Highly: An Ambiguous Lexicon for Job Recommendations," *The Chronicle for Higher Education* 33 (February 25, 1987): 42. Copyright 1984, The Chronicle of Higher Education. Reprinted with permission.

- *Immediate clarification* of significant issues can be gained.
- *More information* can generally be obtained than through mailed forms.
- *Relatively little expense* is involved, especially when compared to using outside agencies or direct contact.
- *Additional areas* of needed inquiry can be uncovered during the conversation.
- *A structured form* can be utilized, which makes a fast, efficient conversation possible and provides the necessary documentation of the findings.

A major problem with telephone checks is the resistance that may be encountered from some individuals, particularly if the applicant had previous work-related problems. Experi-ence indicates that any such resistance may be minimized if the caller emphasizes that the information is necessary for the applicant to be considered for the position and that the lack of information would probably remove the candidate from further consideration. The caller should begin with "I would like to verify some information given to us by ———— who is a candidate for a job opening." This may put the person at ease because the caller already has information on the applicant and the purpose of the call is to verify that information.[42]

In making reference calls, HR specialists often encounter resistance, regardless of their efforts. After the very first question the response comes: "I am sorry but we only give dates of employment, job title, and wage or salary levels." Why? Employers increasingly refuse to disclose reference information on former employees for fear of incurring liability. Former employees are increasingly suing for defamation of character or invasion of privacy. Unfortunately, if employers refuse to provide information about former employees, other employers increase their exposure to negligent-hiring lawsuits (when the employer fails to investigate an employee's background), an interesting legal paradox.[43] One irate company president recalled:

> "We hired her and after only three months terminated her for frequent absences and tardiness. . . . I talked with her former employer one day who told me they let her go for the same problem! I asked Personnel why they didn't check her references. They said the previous employer would only verify dates of employment, salary and job title. Then I really got mad until, that is, my HR director pointed out that we only give out dates of employment, salary, and job title!

Defamation of character may occur when one person makes a statement, either oral or written, to another person that is false, harms a third person's reputation, and lowers his or her status in the community. Employers who release information about previous employees do have considerable legal protection under the "qualified privilege doctrine," which protects them when the person receiving the information had a need to know. The doctrine states that exchange of information about employees is in the best interest of employers, who have a common interest in hiring desirable applicants, and in the best interest of the public.[44] Employers, however, are protected under the doctrine only under the following conditions:[45]

- The information is given in good faith. Only factual, documented information should be given. If an employee stole inventory, that should be stated. If a supervisor "*thinks* he is a crook," that should not be stated.
- The information should be limited to the inquiry. If asked about the employee's absen-

teeism, do not mention that he or she had poor peer reviews.
- The information must be related to job performance. Do not discuss the employee's personal life.
- The information is valid. The truth is generally an absolute defense to a charge of defamation.

Consumer Credit Reports   Many employers utilize consumer-credit reporting agencies to provide background information on applicants. They must comply with the Fair Credit Reporting Act (FCRA) if such information is used to evaluate job applicants. The FCRA allows employers to use a consumer report as a preemployment measure, but only if the report contains information on the applicant alone—not on a spouse or any other individual. In general, there are two types of reports that an employer may access: (1) *consumer reports,* which contain information on creditworthiness, and (2) *investigative consumer reports,* which contain information on general reputation and character gained through personal interviews with neighbors, friends, or associates. If an applicant is denied employment based solely or in part on report information, the employer under the FCRA must tell the applicant that the report was secured and that the information at least in part caused him or her to be denied employment. In addition, the employer must supply the applicant with the name and address of the agency making the report. Possible penalties for failing to comply with this FCRA disclosure requirement are substantial since they can include damages for humiliation and mental distress, injury to reputation, and injury to creditworthiness.[46]

Negligent Hiring

An employer's liability for the **negligent hiring** and retention of employees who engage in criminal or other illegal acts is a question of significant importance. In negligent hiring cases, the courts have generally found the employer's liability to depend on the soundness of the employer's investigation into the employee's background. If the employee was hired for a job that might include a risk of injury or harm to customers or co-workers, the employer's liability is particularly great. Negligent liability cases are generally decided by a jury, which determines whether the employer should bear all or part of the cost associated with injury or harm to a third party.[47]

In one case, the parents of a young boy received an out-of-court settlement of $440,000 from the employer of the boy's murderer. The employer knew of the employee's extensive criminal background, including a second-degree murder conviction. The employee was hired to provide security in a construction skills training program, where he met the young boy.[48] In another case, a homeowner was assaulted in her home by an employee of a pest-control company. An appellate court ruled that the homeowner had the right to sue for damages on the basis of negligent hiring and retention.[49] Pinkerton's Security Company lost a $300,000 suit for the negligent hiring of a security guard who was convicted of theft. Pinkerton's was found liable because it failed to check adequately the employee's references and previous employers.[50]

How can employers avoid negligent hiring liability? Unfortunately, there are no certain answers. However, following the reasoning of the courts in such cases, employers should do the following:[51]

- Conduct reasonable-effort background checks. Verify dates of employment, the educational record, and residential information.

- Request police and credit records on applicants after checking state laws on hiring applicants with criminal records. These laws vary widely. Reject applicants with criminal records (not arrest, but conviction) according to state law.

- Investigate all complaints employees or customers make concerning an employee's deviant behavior.

In addition to taking these precautions, HR managers should communicate to all HR staff members the risks of negligent hiring and their duty to check applicants thoroughly in order to avoid liability for negligent hiring.[52]

Personal References Many employers continue to request that applicants list the names, occupations, and addresses of three or more individuals who are not previous employers or relatives but who can attest to the applicants' suitability. In reality, almost all applicants list individuals who will say something very positive about them and give good recommendations. Realizing this, the HR specialist does not use a good recommendation to determine the applicant's suitability for the position. A realistic use of personal references includes the following:

- Verifying the data received on the application blank or during the interview. Often personal recommendations can verify information on the application blank. For example, individuals did attend certain schools, do have certain work experiences, or lived at listed addresses for certain periods of time.

- Evaluating the quality of the personal recommendation. Applicants who give professional people or business executives as references have a definite advantage over applicants who use their next-door neighbors or former high school classmates as references.

- Determining how well the person knows the applicant. An HR specialist may call a personal reference and find that the person has little or no knowledge of the applicant other than that the applicant lives down the street or went to the same high school. In some cases, the references do not even give applicants good recommendations, simply saying that they really do not know much about the person. A lukewarm recommendation by a personal reference may be an indication of the applicant's lack of suitability for a position.

Previous Employers   The most important reference check involves the previous employer, co-workers, and supervisor. The use of reference data in the selection process has led to a number of legal challenges under equal employment laws questioning the fairness of such techniques.[53] Thus, many employers have declined to give information to other prospective employers or only provide dates of employment for previous employees. The two legal areas that affect reference checking are equality and privacy. The three relevant federal laws and their major provisions are:[54]

The Privacy Act (1974)   This act applies to federal employees only, though several private organizations have adopted policies similar to those specified in the act. Under the act, individuals may review company records that pertain to them, obtain copies, and have relevant information added to the file. Civil suits may be filed for damages that result from willful action which violates the act.

The Fair Credit and Reporting Act (1970)   Individuals are given the right to know the nature and substance of their credit file. A person has a right to know when an investigative consumer report on his or her credit has been compiled and has a right to have access to the information compiled.

The Family Education Rights and Privacy Act (1974)   Students are given the right to inspect their education records. This act also prevents universities from disclosing education records without prior consent.

Employers can generally provide factual and accurate information that would be useful to other prospective employers. But to protect themselves and the legal rights of former employees, they should follow the guidelines given in Figure 7-13.

As discussed, employees are suing former employers, contending that they have been defamed in a job reference. Many employers have become so concerned over such lawsuits that they will only provide a former employee's dates of employment and job title. This has made the process of checking references by previous employers difficult for HR specialists. Unfortunately, good job applicants can be hurt by their previous employer's reluctance when they cannot prove their previous work records. The law is actually on the side of previous employers. The fundamental legal principle is that neither true statements nor statements of opinion can be defamatory. Employers are generally found liable for defamation only if they knowingly or recklessly spread false information. So, why are employers concerned about defamation cases? Bad publicity and legal fees—whether they win or lose.[55]

Employers should not release the following information without written consent: credit information, medical records, school records or other information, and results of polygraph or honesty tests.

Employers should never release false or unverified reference information, or information that is vague or misleading. For example, a past supervisor's feeling that the applicant did not get along with other employees due to personality conflicts should not be included as reference information. Also, if information would have an adverse impact on a protected class of individuals, then it should not be given as reference information. For example, a supervisor might have commented: "She couldn't handle the job; it was too rough for a woman." Such caution does not preclude or limit most background checking by employers. In fact, rarely

FIGURE 7-13 Guidelines for defensible references from organizations.

Tips on Responding to Reference Checks

1. Don't volunteer information. Respond only to specific company or institutional inquiries and requests. Before responding, telephone the inquirer to check on the validity of the request.

2. Direct all communication only to persons who have a qualified need to know.

3. State in the message that the information you are providing is confidential and should be treated as such. Use qualifying statements such as "providing information that was requested."

4. Obtain written consent from the employee.

5. Provide only reference data that relate and pertain to the job and job performance in question.

6. Avoid vague statements such as "He was an average employee," "She was careless at times," or "He displayed an inability to work with others."

7. Document all released information. Use specific statements such as: "Mr._____ received an evaluation of _____." "Ms. _____ made an average of two errors each week." "This spring, four members of the work team wrote letters asking not to be placed on the shift with Mr. _____."

8. Do not answer trap questions such as: "Would you rehire this person?"

9. Avoid answering questions that are asked "off the record."

SOURCE: Adapted from J. D. Bell, J. Castagnera, and J. P. Young, "Employment References: Do You Know the Law?" *Personnel Journal* 63, no. 2 (February 1984): 32–36.

is a discrimination case based on background checks successful, unless the information released was completely false or vague and misleading.[56]

How employees and employers feel about employees' right to see their own personnel files and the right employers have to that information is a subject of much discussion. A study of HR executives of the *Fortune* 1000, 77 members of Congress, and over 1500 employees provided some interesting results. A majority thought that asking questions of job applicants in several areas is improper. The survey showed that employees, employers, and members of Congress strongly believed that employees should be notified before previous employers release personal information. Only in the area of access to a supervisor's personal notes concerning employees did the employees and employers differ substantially concerning employees' access to their personnel records. Most employees did not believe their

employers were engaged in improper collection and use of their personal data.[57]

The Selection Decision

Deciding which applicant should be offered the position may be accomplished by one of two processes: **compensatory selection** or **multiple hurdles** selection. The multiple hurdles selection process requires the applicant to pass each hurdle: initial screening, application blank, testing, interview, background checks, and departmental interview.

In the compensatory selection process, all applicants who pass the initial screening complete the application blank and are tested; each applicant is interviewed before the final choice is made. The applicants are then compared on the basis of all the selection information. In compensatory selection, an applicant may score low in one area, but the score might be offset by a very high mark in another area. This is particularly beneficial to candidates who receive low interview scores because they are very nervous and lack self-confidence during interviews but perform very well on aptitude and background checks. The disadvantage of compensatory selection is its cost; a larger number of candidates must be processed through the complete selection procedure before a final decision is made. Primarily due to the cost factor, the multiple hurdles selection technique, in which a candidate can be rejected at each stage of the process, is more common.

When the selection decision results in the hiring of an employee who is successful on the job, then the cost of the selection decision is the normal cost of filling a vacant position. But if an erroneous selection decision is made, then additional costs are incurred. Management can make two types of errors in the selection process: selecting someone for a position who fails on the job (false positive) and rejecting an applicant who could have been successful on the job (false negative). Expenses associated with hiring the wrong employee involve the cost of replacing that individual, termination costs, costs of undesirable job behavior, and costs incurred by a lack of morale or cooperation with other employees. These costs must be weighed against the cost of rejecting the individual who could have been successful on the job. Included in these costs are the opportunity costs of having lost a successful employee who could have added to the productivity of the organization and the competitive disadvantage lost if the individual is hired by a competing firm. The cost of recruiting an additional applicant to replace the rejected individual also must be considered.[58]

Although it is difficult to attach dollar values to some of those costs, the decision boils down to estimating the possible losses incurred due to hiring poor employees in comparison with the costs incurred in rejecting employees who could have been successful. The latter cases involve additional recruitment and selection costs.

International Human Resource Management

Expatriate Rights

When Ali Boureslan, a naturalized American citizen, was fired by his Saudi Arabia–based American employer, he sued for discrimination. What Boureslan began as a relatively straightforward case involving one man, one company, and one incident has evolved into an important test case in international employment law. Boureslan's complaint was no longer the central issue. Whether he was discriminated against was no longer the relevant question. Boureslan, a Lebanese native and a Muslim, was hired by ARAMCO in the United States. After he was transferred to ARAMCO's Saudi Arabian operation, he reported that a British co-worker was harassing him because of his religious obligations. The co-worker was eventually fired. Boureslan, however, was later laid off, along with other ARAMCO employees in Saudi Arabia. His suit claims that his termination was really part of the harassment that began with his co-worker.

The issue now concerns the administration of HR policies by American companies with overseas operations. Do Title VII of the Civil Rights Act of 1964 and other employment laws apply to expatriate Americans who are working for U.S. companies?

"The internationalization of the world's economy does not require or even suggest that the domestic social practice of this country or any country be made the standard of practice around the world," said attorney Lawrence Z. Lorber, who argued the Boureslan case.

Boureslan's attorney, James Tyson, agreed that there might be inequality in the treatment of workers of different nationalities, but that is not a sufficient argument, he said, to deny American workers their rights under Title VII. One argument has been used by both sides to support their cases: the chilling effect on Americans' careers if they are guaranteed or denied civil rights protection overseas. Without Title VII protection, said Tyson, few American workers would be willing to accept overseas assignments and expose themselves to the capriciousness of foreign supervisors and foreign cultures.

On the other hand, Lorber said that with the protection—and almost certain resulting cultural conflict—of combined American law and local law, American companies operating abroad would hesitate to hire American workers. This would place an unfair limitation on qualified American employees for whom an overseas assignment would benefit their careers. Lorber added that the combined legal burden would undermine the competitiveness of foreign-based American companies and create unfair conditions that would favor American workers on the job site.

The case was decided in a landmark 1991 decision. In **Boureslan v. ARAMCO, Arabian-American Oil Co.**, the U.S. Supreme Court ruled that the EEOC had no jurisdiction outside the United States and its territories and that Congress did not intend to impose Title VII on American companies employing American citizens outside of the United States.[59] The 1991 Civil Rights Act overturned the Supreme Court decision. Thus employees now have the right to sue an American employer for "foreign" discrimination.

Staffing the New Europe

The economic unification of Europe that occurred in 1992 has caused HR managers in the United States to learn the intricacies of staffing their organizations in countries previously closed to Western businesses. These new operations primarily employ three types of employees:[60]

1. **Local nationals** Citizens of the country where the facility is located, working in their home country.

2. **Third-country nationals** Non-U.S. citizens who are on the payroll in their home country but working in a third.

3. **American foreign-service employees** U.S. citizens who are on the payroll in the United States but working overseas.

Table 7-3 Average First-Year Total Compensation Expenses

Country of Operation	Local National	U.K. Third-Country National[1]		Belgian Third-Country National[1]		U.S. Foreign-Service Employee at $45,000[1]	
		Married	Single	Married	Single	Married	Single
U.K.	$20,916	— —	— —	$66,053 78,458	$57,143 66,039	$93,175 117,039	$76,161 89,383
Germany	$35,860	$60,652 73,968	$51,282 57,141	$87,492 103,373	$78,170 87,035	$134,584 158,678	$115,742 129,021
Italy	$24,305	$42,510 56,042	$28,517 34,430	$74,518 90,635	$58,654 67,378	$97,368 121,612	$74,561 87,878
Belgium	$53,020	$61,484 74,864	$43,770 49,445	— —	— —	$111,831 135,799	$82,073 95,321

[1]The figures on the top line in each box represent the employer's total first-year compensation costs per employee *excluding* relocation expenses. The figures shown on the bottom line *include* relocation expenses.

SOURCE: Neil B. Krupp, "Overseas Staffing for the New Europe," *Personnel* 67, no. 7 (July 1990): 20–25. Used by permission. © 1990, American Management Association, New York. All rights reserved.

The cost differences among the three types of overseas employees can be substantial and must be carefully weighed in planning the work force requirements of foreign operations. Generally, according to Neil B. Krupp, vice-president of the international division of Runzheimer International, a foreign-service employee costs an employer at least three times as much as a local national. It is, of course, more costly to conduct business in some countries, such as Belgium and Germany.

The major factors responsible for cost differences among countries and types of employees are the allowance packages required by foreign-service employees (incentives, housing differentials, goods and services differentials, educational expenses) and taxes. Most employers assume responsibility for all the employee's foreign tax obligation. A Chicago resident earning an annual salary of $45,000 in the United States would incur $38,000 of foreign tax liabilities if relocated to Germany, compared to only about $10,000 in Illinois. Thus, the U.S. employer must pay the $28,000 difference. Table 7-3 provides an indication of the average cost differences of the three types of employees in four European countries.

Note that a German local national can be hired for about one-fourth of what a U.S. foreign service employee must be paid. In each case, the local is less costly.

Employers can potentially reduce their foreign staffing costs by:

1. Employing local nationals when possible.
2. Locating American foreign-service employees in low-allowance and low-tax countries.
3. Minimizing relocation costs by moving foreign-service employees as infrequently as possible.
4. Considering hiring single employees first, without violating federal or state discrimination laws.[61]

CONCLUSIONS AND APPLICATIONS

- The selection process generally centers on the HR office. It is one of the most critical functions in HR because an organization's effectiveness depends on its employees. The selection process is not, however, one of scientific precision. Instead of finding the one best person, managers strive to select an applicant who has the ability and motivation to perform the job for many years.

- Selection screening devices, such as the interview and the application blank, each have advantages and disadvantages. Employers must carefully consider the cost and validity of each method.

- The interview tends to be the most commonly used and decisive selection technique. Subject to reliability problems, the structuring of the interview questions, training, and the scoring of answers can greatly improve reliability and usefulness of the interview as a decision tool.

- Preemployment tests can be effective tools in the selection process. If carefully selected, validated, and monitored, they can help select applicants who will match the position's requirements.

- Reference checking has increased in use but has been subjected to legal challenges. Employers can legally provide factual and accurate information, but they should be able to verify any job-related information they release.

- U.S. employers hiring employees in foreign nations should carefully consider the substantial cost variations related to different staffing alternatives. Most employees were raised, educated, and indoctrinated in only one culture and thus must develop respect for and learn to value another culture to interface successfully between the two cultures.

- Negligent hiring liability has become a major concern for employers. While no practices can guarantee an employer protection, reasonable-effort background checks, requesting police and credit records, and investigating complaints are good precautions.

CASE STUDY:

Blue Grass State University

Blue Grass State University President Glenn Wood had decided that the traditional method of selecting faculty had not been successful. In the past twenty years, when a department had an open position, the chair would attend the regional conference of the appropriate discipline and place a position announcement with the placement service. Interested candidates at the conference would contact the chair and request an initial interview. These professional meetings provided a placement process as a service to faculty and schools. The chair would then return to the campus with vitas and interview notes on several candidates. The department faculty would review this applicant pool and select three to five candidates to be invited to the campus for a formal interview. After all the interviews, an offer was made to the top-rated (by the faculty) candidate. If it was turned down, the offer was extended to the second choice, and so on. Candidates were rated by each faculty member on three factors, with the following weights: (1) teaching interests (specific graduate and undergraduate courses), 40 percent; (2) research interests and publication record, 40 percent; (3) quality of Ph.D. training and fit with departmental

needs, 20 percent. The weighted rating determined each candidate's aggregate score.

President Wood has several problems with the traditional process, and as a former president of a local bank, he was inclined to question it. His specific concerns are the following:

1. The process had produced several faculty members who were not outstanding teachers. Some had poor communication skills, many were satisfactory, but few were outstanding. Wood considered teaching to be the highest priority of the university, and research and community service the other two important priorities.

2. The cost per hire had averaged $5000 per position due largely to the expenses related to bringing several candidates to the campus.

3. Many faculty members hired under this process were unable to work effectively in the community in either the private or the nonprofit sector. Since Blue Grass was an urban community, Wood considered active community involvement to be an important role of everyone employed at the university.

4. The process has produced a faculty that contains only 20 percent women and 4 percent minorities. Wood has set university diversity goals of 40 percent women and 20 percent minorities for each job classification, including faculty.

President Wood has assembled a task force to consider the recruitment and selection process. The task force consists of four students, four faculty members, and two administrators. Wood has given the task force responsibility for developing a new faculty selection process that will address all of his concerns and hire top-quality faculty.

QUESTIONS

1. How should the task force proceed to address the change?

2. Do you agree with President Wood that the problems he listed are probably caused by the faculty selection process?

3. Design a recommended selection process that would meet President Wood's concerns. Consider using each of the selection methods discussed in the chapter. Be specific about what stakeholders (faculty, students, community representatives, alumni, etc.) should be included in using each method.

4. How should President Wood determine whether the new process you proposed (question 3) has been effective after a five-year trial period?

EXPERIENTIAL EXERCISES

1. Is This Application Blank Lawful?

PURPOSE

To recognize the legal issues surrounding the use of application blanks and to analyze an actual application blank for potentially unlawful items.

THE TASK

Illustrated on the opposite page is an actual application blank recently used by a retail clothing chain. How many potentially illegal items on the application blank can you identify? Following your analysis, your instructor will lead you in a discussion concerning this exercise.

2. Interviewer Perspectives

PURPOSE

To recognize the difficulty of conducting effective job interviews and to learn how several interviewers can reach different conclusions on the same applicants.

The Task

The class should be divided into groups of three to five students. An even number of groups is required. Each group will assume the roles of HR professionals or job applicants.

APPLICATION FOR EMPLOYMENT

We are an equal opportunity employer, dedicated to a policy of non-discrimination in employment on any basis including race, creed, color, age, sex, religion or national origin.

PERSONAL INFORMATION

DATE _____

NAME _____		SOCIAL SECURITY NUMBER _____	
LAST	FIRST	MIDDLE	

PRESENT ADDRESS _____
STREET   CITY   STATE

PERMANENT ADDRESS _____
STREET   CITY   STATE

PHONE NO. _____   REFERRED BY _____

DATE OF BIRTH _____   HEIGHT _____   WEIGHT _____   COLOR OF HAIR _____   COLOR OF EYES _____

MARRIED _____   SINGLE _____   WIDOWED _____   DIVORCED _____   SEPARATED _____

NUMBER OF CHILDREN _____   DEPENDENTS OTHER THAN WIFE OR CHILDREN _____   CITIZEN OF U.S.A.   YES ☐   NO ☐

RACE _____   REFERRED BY _____

EMPLOYMENT DESIRED

POSITION _____   DATE YOU CAN START _____   SALARY DESIRED _____

ARE YOU EMPLOYED NOW? _____   IF SO MAY WE INQUIRE OF YOUR PRESENT EMPLOYER? _____

EVER APPLIED TO THIS COMPANY BEFORE? _____   WHERE? _____   WHEN? _____

EDUCATION	NAME AND LOCATION OF SCHOOL	YEARS ATTENDED *	DATE GRADUATED *	SUBJECTS STUDIED
GRAMMAR SCHOOL				
HIGH SCHOOL				
COLLEGE				
TRADE, BUSINESS OR CORRESPONDENCE SCHOOL				

* The Age Discrimination in Employment Act of 1967 prohibits discrimination on the basis of age with respect to individuals who are at least 40 but less than 65 years of age.

GENERAL

SUBJECTS OF SPECIAL STUDY OR RESEARCH WORK _____

DO YOU HAVE ANY PHYSICAL DISABILITIES? IF YES, EXPLAIN: _____

WHAT FOREIGN LANGUAGES DO YOU SPEAK FLUENTLY? _____   READ _____   WRITE _____

U.S. MILITARY OR NAVAL SERVICE _____   RANK _____   PRESENT MEMBERSHIP IN NATIONAL GUARD OR RESERVES _____

[CONTINUED ON OTHER SIDE]

HAVE YOU EVER BEEN ARRESTED? IF YES, FOR WHAT REASON: _____

LAST   FIRST   MIDDLE

Step 1: Members of each HR group will write a brief job description based on a job with which they have some familiarity.

Step 2: The job description developed by the HR group will be given to members of the applicant group, who will then study it and prepare themselves for a job interview. The instructor may wish to allow one or two days to pass before step 3 for the applicants to prepare themselves.

Step 3: Members of the HR group will prepare a list of interview questions to ask the applicants and a list of criteria that they will use to score the interview.

Step 4: The HR group will interview each applicant (other applicants should be out of the room) and individually score the applicant after the interview is completed.

Step 5: All members of each pair of HR and applicant groups will review the interview scores together. Each HR member should be required to explain or defend his or her scoring.

Step 6: If the class contains multiple pairs of groups, one representative of each pair will lead a discussion of the activities of their session.

KEY TERMS AND CONCEPTS

Ability and motivation
Achievement tests
Applicant blank
Aptitude tests
Boureslan v. *ARAMCO*
Compensatory selection process
Defamation
Expatriate
Honesty tests
Intelligence tests
Interest tests

Kaizen
Local nationals
Medical exam/drug test
Multiple hurdles process
National Institute on Drug Abuse (NIDA)
Negligent hiring
Polygraph
Reference check
Third-country nationals
Work samples

REVIEW QUESTIONS

1. Why is the selection process usually centralized in the HR department?

2. Should the HR office ask an applicant for his or her date of birth, marital status, or a photograph?

3. How does the HR specialist use the application blank?

4. What are the real purposes of background checks?

5. How can preemployment tests be utilized in employee selection?

6. What questions may an interviewer legally ask under the ADA to determine if and under what circumstances an applicant could perform a job?

7. Why have employers increased the use of honesty tests in recent years? What are their limitations?

8. How can a battery of tests be utilized to select applicants for jobs?

9. When U.S. companies staff new overseas operations, where can they secure the needed personnel? How can they minimize costs?

DISCUSSION QUESTIONS

1. What inappropriate personality traits would overshadow an employee's skills and abilities enough to cause the dismissal of the following persons: a food-store checkout clerk, a research assistant, an elementary school teacher?

2. If you inherited a shoe factory that had a history of high turnover and low wages, would you attempt to attract only the best workers by raising salaries or continue a minimum wage policy and disregard employees' dissatisfaction? What factors would influence your decision?

3. While interviewing two well-qualified applicants for an accounting manager's position, you notice that one applicant has had one job for seven years and the other has had five jobs in ten years, each change involving a salary increase. Would this information affect your decision?

4. Due to costs and other reasons, some employers require medical exams/drug tests only on applicants for selected jobs. For what types of jobs do you think all employers should be required to test their applicants?

5. You work in a department store's personnel department. The owner requests that all of the store's employees take honesty tests periodically to minimize employee theft. Employees find this approach insulting and demand that you do something. What would you do?

6. How has the U.S. Supreme Court affected the concept of affirmative action in recent decisions? Do you agree with the Court's general direction?

7. Do you agree with the U.S. Supreme Court's decision in the *Boureslan* v. *ARAMCO* case? Explain your position.

8. Some HR professionals believe that Congress should pass a law requiring employers to provide complete, accurate information on their former employees to prospective employers conducting background checks. Do you agree? Why?

ENDNOTES

Chapter 7

1. T. L. Brink, "A Discouraging Word Improves Your Interviews," *HRMagazine* (December 1992): 49–52.

2. S. M. Jameel Hasan, "HRM in a New Era of Globalization," *Business Forum* (Winter 1992): 56–59.

3. Mitchell S. Novit, *Essentials of Personnel Management* (Englewood Cliffs, NJ: Prentice-Hall, 1979), pp. 70–74.

4. Arthur Within, "Commonly Overlooked Dimensions of Employee Selection," *Personnel Journal* 59, no. 7 (July 1980): 573–75.

5. Gary Dessler, "Value-based Hiring Builds Commitment," *Personnel Journal* (November 1993): 98–102.

6. Marlene Brown, "Checking the Facts on a Resume," *Hiring Tips: A Supplement to the 1993 Personnel Journal* (1993): 6–7.

7. Erwin S. Stanton, *Successful Personnel Recruiting and Selection* (New York: AMACOM, 1977), pp. 73–84.

8. U.S. Equal Employment Opportunity Commission, *Affirmative Action* (Washington, DC: U.S. Government Printing Office, 1974) pp. 29–30.

9. Larry Stevens, "Resume Scanning Simplifies Tracking," *Personnel Journal* (April 1993): 77–79.

10. Ibid., pp. 40–60.

11. *Sprogis* v. *United Air Lines*, 444 F. 2d 1194 (7th Cir. 1971).

12. *Griggs* v. *Duke Power Company*, 401 U.S. 424 (1971).

13. *U.S.* v. *Bethlehem Steel Corporation*, 446 F.2d 652 (2nd Cir. 1971).

14. *Castro* v. *Beecher*, 459 F.2d 725, C.A. 1, (1972); *CCH Employment Practices Guide*, para. 6231, 6286.

15. Loretta D. Foxman and Walter L. Polsley, "Select the Right Application Form," *Personnel Journal* 68, no. 10 (October 1989): 28–29.

16. Gerard P. Panaro, "Psychological Testing: Three Key Strategies," *Personnel Practice Ideas* 5, no. 8 (April 1990): 6.

17. Dale Yoder and Paul D. Standohar, "Testing and EEO: Getting Down to Cases," *Personnel Administrator* 29, no. 2 (February 1984): 67–74.

18. Mark Thomas and Harry Brull, "Tests Improve Hiring Decisions at Franciscan," *Personnel Journal* (November 1993): 89–92.

19. Ibid.

20. John Aberth, "Pre-Employment Testing Is Losing Favor," *Personnel Journal* 65, no. 9 (September 1986): 96–104.

21. *Webster's Unabridged Dictionary* (Springfield, Mass., Merriam Co., Pub., 1986): 108.

22. Robert M. Madigan, K. Dow Scott, Diana L. Deadrick, and Jil A. Stodard, "Employment Testing: The U.S. Job Service Is Spearheading a Revolution," *Personnel Administrator* 31, no. 9 (September 1986): 102–12.

23. John A. Bolt and Peter B. Holden, "Polygraph Usage Among Major U.S. Corporations," *Personnel Journal* 57 (February 1978): 80–86.

24. "How to Comply with the Polygraph Law," *Nation's Business* 77, no. 12 (December 1989): 36–37.

25. U.S. Congress, Office of Technology Assessment, "The Use of Integrity Tests for Pre-Employment Screening," OTA-SET-442 (Washington, DC: U.S. Government Printing Office, September 1990), p. 1.

26. Carolyn Wiley and Doria L. Rudley, "Managerial Issues and Responsibilities in the Use of Integrity Tests," *Labor Law Journal* (March 1991): 152–59.

27. Paul R. Sackett, Laura R. Burris, and Christine Callahan, "Integrity Testing for Personnel Selection: An Update," *Personnel Psychology*, 42 (1989): October 491–528.

28. Lewis R. Goldberg et al., *Questionnaires Used in the Prediction of Trustworthiness in Pre-employment Selection Decisions: An A.P.A. Task Force Report*, (Washington, DC: American Psychological Association, 1991), p. 26.

29. Wiley and Rudley, "Managerial Issues," pp. 152–53.

30. Rob Brookler, "Industry Standards in Workplace Drug Testing," *Personnel Journal* (April 1992): 128–32.

31. Eric Rolfe Greenburg, "Test-Positive Rate Drop as More Companies Screen Employees," *HR Focus* (June 1992): 7.

32. Joseph B. Treaster, "As More Companies Test Employees for Drugs, Usage Drops," *The New York Times* (November 21, 1993): D1.

33. Jonathan A. Segal, "HIV: How High the Risk?" *HRMagazine* (February 1993): 93–100.

34. Barbara Felton and Sue Ries Lamb, "A Model for Systematic Selection Interviewing," *Personnel* 59, no. 1 (January–February 1982): 40–48.

35. Ray Forbes, "Improving the Reliability of the Selection Interview," *Personnel Management* (July 1979): 36–67. R. D. Arvey, "Unfair Discrimination in the Employment Interview: Legal and Psychological Aspects," *Psychological Bulletin* 86 (1979): 736.

36. Gerald Rose, "Sex Effects on

Managerial Hiring Decisions," *Academy of Management Journal* 21 (1978): 104–12.

37. Julie Soloman, "The New Job Interview: Show Thyself," *The Wall Street Journal* (December 4, 1989): A1.

38. Elliot D. Pursell, Michael A. Campion, and Sarah R. Gaylord, "Structured Interviewing: Avoiding Selection Problems," *Personnel Journal* 59, no. 11 (November 1980): 907–12.

39. Joan E. Rigdon, "Deceptive Resumes," *The Wall Street Journal* (June 17, 1993): B3.

40. William A. Schaffer, Frank David Rollo, and Carol A. Holt, "Falsification of Clinical Credentials by Physicians Applying for Ambulatory-Staff Privileges," *New England Journal of Medicine* 318, no. 6 (1988): 356–58.

41. Erwin S. Stanton, "Fast-and-Easy Reference Checking by Telephone," *Personnel Journal* 67, no. 11 (November 1988): 123–30.

42. Ibid.

43. Kenneth L. Sovereigns, "Pitfalls of Withholding Reference Informa-tion," *Personnel Journal* 69, no. 3 (March 1990): 116–22.

44. *Circus Hotels* v. *Witherspoon*, 667 P.2d 101 (November 1983).

45. Sovereigns, "Pitfalls of Withholding Reference Information" pp. 116–22.

46. David Israel and Anita Lechner, "Use of Credit Reports Requires Disclosure," *HRMagazine* (April 1992): 93–96.

47. Ronald M. Green and Richard J. Reibstein, "It's 10 P.M. Do You Have to Know Where Your Employees Are?" *Personnel Administrator* 32, no. 4 (April 1987): 71–76.

48. *Henley* v. *Prince George's County*, 305 Md. 320, 503, A. 2d 1333 (1986).

49. *Abbot* v. *Payne*, 457 So. 2d 1156, Fla. Dist. Ct. App. (1984).

50. *Welsh Manufacturing* v. *Pinkerton's, Inc.*, 474 A. 2d 436 R.I. (1984).

51. Green and Reibstein, "It's 10 P.M.," pp. 75–76.

52. Suzanne H. Cook, "How to Avoid Liability for Negligent Hiring," *Personnel* 66, no. 11 (November 1988): 32–36.

53. J. D. Baxter, B. Brock, P. C. Hill, and R. M. Rozelle, "Letters of Recommendation: A Question of Value," *Journal of Applied Psychology* 66, no. 3 (March 1981): 296–301.

54. James D. Bell, James Castagnera, and Jane Patterson Young, "Employment References: Do You Know the Law?" *Personnel Journal* 63, no. 2 (February 1984): 32–36.

55. "When a Boss Says Too Much . . . ," *Denver Post* (December 6, 1987): G1, G6.

56. Ibid., pp. G15–G77.

57. Allan Westin, "What Should Be Done About Employee Privacy?," *The Personnel Administrator* (March 1980): 27–30.

58. Marvin D. Dunnette, *Personnel Selection and Placement* (Belmont, CA: Brooks-Cole, 1966), pp. 173–75.

59. *Boureslan* v. *ARAMCO, Arabian-American Oil Co.*, no. 87–2206 (5th Cir. 1990).

60. Neil B. Krupp, "Overseas Staffing for the New Europe," *Personnel* 67, no. 7 (July 1990): 20–25.

61. Ibid.

PART III

ASSESSMENT AND DEVELOPMENT

CHAPTER **8**

PERFORMANCE APPRAISAL AND PERFORMANCE MANAGEMENT

CHAPTER OUTLINE

CHAPTER OBJECTIVES

1. To explain the evaluative and developmental objectives of performance appraisal.
2. To recognize common appraisal problems.
3. To describe the major performance appraisal methods.
4. To develop an effective appraisal interview.
5. To design and evaluate a program of performance appraisal.
6. To discuss who should perform the appraisal.

PERFORMANCE APPRAISAL AND PERFORMANCE MANAGEMENT

Performance appraisal (PA) is the ongoing process of evaluating and managing both the behavior and outcomes in the workplace. Organizations use various terms to describe this process. *Performance review, annual appraisal, performance evaluation, employee evaluation,* and *merit evaluation* are some of the terms used.

Performance management, a broader term than *performance appraisal,* became popular in the 1980's[1] as total quality management (TQM) programs emphasized using *all* of the management tools, including performance appraisal, to ensure achievement of performance goals. Tools such as reward systems, job design, leadership, and training should join PAs as part of a comprehensive approach to performance. According to a recent study, the number one desire of HR executives is to design performance management systems to achieve business goals. Companies are interested in finding ways to get their strategic goals implemented at lower levels in the organization, especially with the emphasis on TQM and on pushing decision making and responsibility further down in the organizational hierarchy.[2] This chapter examines PA as part of an organization's overall performance management approach.

Although employers may use different names to represent the performance appraisal process, certain processes should not be confused. *Job analysis* (see Chapter 4), a very different process, examines issues such as which tasks, duties, and responsibilities are included in a certain job's design. *Job evaluation* (see Chapter 11), also a very different process, focuses on how much a job is worth to the organization and helps to set ranges of pay for various jobs.

For example, at XYZ, Inc., the job of labor relations manager would first undergo job analysis, in which the responsibilities of conducting the company's union contract negotiations, developing employee involvement programs, and training managers in labor relations might be specified. Job evaluation would then be undertaken to determine the value of these responsibilities to the organization. In many organizations, the pay range might be relatively high for this HR position due to the sensitive nature of the work and the value given today to cooperative labor relations. Separately, a formal performance appraisal of a specific labor relations manager, Mel Fitzpatrick, would be conducted. He would be assessed based on how he has performed the duties and responsibilities of that job during the rating period.

Is Performance Appraisal a Failure?

Performance appraisal in the majority of North American organizations is a resounding failure. The difficulties have become so common that many employees complain that feedback from managers is inadequate, misleading, or violates human rights legislation. Furthermore, HR professionals often report problems in getting managers to carry out performance appraisals.

Evidence to support this negative conclusion has grown in the past decade. Psychological Associates found in a recent survey of 200 large North American companies that over 70% of employees reported that they were more confused than enlightened by the PA feedback they received. Another survey of 3500 companies reported that the organization's PA system was the most frequently mentioned HR concern. Still another survey, by the Society of HR Management (SHRM) concluded that fewer than 10% of PA systems are reasonably successful.[3]

What's wrong? Two causes were cited in a recent article: a) the way PA forms and policies are designed; and b) the lack of adequate training for managers in how to assess and discuss performance constructively.

The authors gave seven guidelines to improve PAs:

1. Involve managers and their employees in the design of the system.
2. Make clear the objectives of PA and place the proper emphasis on each.
3. Focus feedback on observable, job-related results and performance.
4. Avoid giving personal feedback.
5. Listen first and talk later.
6. Be positive first and negative later.
7. Probe first and prescribe later.[4]

PERFORMANCE APPRAISAL OBJECTIVES

Why should management use PAs if, indeed, they are often considered unpleasant and time-consuming processes? See *HR in the News*: "Is Performance Appraisal a Failure?" There are several important objectives of a PA program that cannot be achieved by any other HR program.

PAs are a key element in the use and development of an organization's most vital resource—its employees. Appraisals are used for a wide range of administrative purposes, such as making decisions about pay, promotion, and retention. Effective appraisals can significantly contribute to the satisfaction and motivation of employees—if they are used correctly.[5] For the most part, the objectives of PA fall into two categories: evaluative and developmental. These objectives are illustrated in Figure 8-1.

Evaluative Objectives

As far as employees are concerned, one of the primary purposes of performance appraisals is

349

FIGURE 8-1 Evaluative and developmental objectives in PA.

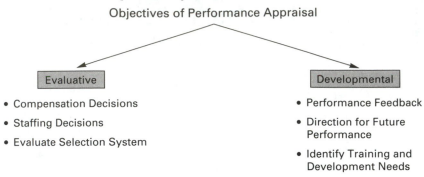

looking at *past* performance. The most common decisions based on **evaluative objectives** concern compensation, which includes merit increases, employee bonuses, and other increases in pay. Thus, the term *merit review* or *merit evaluation* can be found in organizations using the PA to determine pay increases.

PA normally has a two-part effect on future pay. In the short run, it may determine merit increases for the following year; in the long run, it may determine which employees are promoted into higher-paying jobs.

Staffing decisions constitute a second evaluative objective of PA, because the managers and supervisors must make decisions concerning promotions, demotions, transfers, and layoffs. Past PAs normally help determine which employee is most deserving of a promotion or other desirable job changes.

PAs can also be used to evaluate the recruitment, selection, and placement system. The effectiveness of these functions can be partially measured by comparing employees' PAs with their test scores as job applicants. For example, management may find that applicants who scored about the same on selection tests show a significant difference in performance after one year on the job; thus, the tests may not accurately predict behavior. As Table 8–1 illustrates, the evaluative objectives of compensation decisions (merit increases, bo-

Table 8-1 A Ranking of the Uses of PA from a Survey of 256 Companies

Rank	Function of Appraisal	Percentage
1	Merit increases	91
2	Performance results/feedback/ job counseling	90
3	Promotion	82
4	Termination or layoff	64
5	Performance potential	62
6	Succession planning	57
7	Career planning	52
8	Transfer	50
9	Manpower planning	38
10	Bonuses	32
11	Development and evaluation of training programs	29
12	Internal communication	25
13	Criteria for selection procedure validity	16
14	Expense control	7

SOURCE: Charles J. Fombrun and Robert L. Laud, "Strategic Issues in Performance Appraisal Theory and Practice," *Personnel* 601, no. 6 (November–December 1983): 23–31. Used by permission.

nuses) and staffing decisions (promotion, termination, succession planning, transfer, HR planning) dominate the common uses of PA systems, with 7 of the top 10 uses.

Developmental Objectives

The second type of objective of performance appraisal—**developmental objectives**—encompasses developing employee skills and motivation for *future* performance.

Performance feedback is a primary developmental need because almost all employees want to know how their supervisors feel about their performances. Their motivation to improve their current performance increases when they receive feedback that specifies goals, which in turn enhances future career moves.[6]

Developmental performance appraisal is mainly focused on giving employees direction for future performance. Such feedback recognizes strengths and weaknesses in past performances and determines what direction employees should take to improve. Employees want to know specifically how they can improve. See *HR in the News*: "When Is 100% Success Inadequate Performance?" Because PAs are designed to cope with the problem of poor employee performance, they should be designed to develop better employees.[7]

The results of appraisal influence decisions about the training and development (T&D) of employees. Below-average evaluations may signal areas of employee behavior that may be strengthened through on- and away-from-the-job training. Of course, not all performance deficiencies may be overcome through T&D. Supervisors must distinguish performance problems resulting from lack of a critical skill or ability from those caused by low morale or some form of job dissatisfaction.

THE APPRAISAL PROCESS

A variety of appraisal techniques are available to measure employee performance. In creating and implementing an appraisal system, administrators must first determine for what the PAs will be used, and then decide which process should be used. These decisions are just as im-

portant as how the appraisal is conducted or the actual content of the appraisal. If employees believe the appraisal was undertaken lightly or haphazardly, they may take the process less seriously than they should. Possible legal ramifications exist whenever management is not consistent in its PA procedures. A loss of morale or employee productivity may also result from poorly administered PAs.

Steps in Developing a PA System

The specific steps followed in developing a PA system will vary somewhat from organization to organization. Nonetheless, the general guidelines discussed here will be followed by most employers when developing an appraisal system.

1. Determine Performance Requirements In the first step of the process, administrators must determine what skills, outputs, and accomplishments will be evaluated during each appraisal. These may be derived from specific job descriptions or they may be a uniform set of employee requirements included in all PAs. Policymakers must determine exactly what areas of performance are going to be reviewed and how these areas are related to the organization's goals.

2. Choose an Appropriate Appraisal Method Several methods may be used to appraise performance; no one method is best for all organizations. The manner in which a supervisor conducts the PA is strongly determined by the method. Within an organization, different appraisal methods may be used for different groups, such as production, sales, and administrative employees.

3. Train Supervisors A critical step in the PA process is training supervisors (or other raters) so that they prepare fair and accurate appraisals and effectively communicate the evaluation to the employee. Unfair ratings may result in charges of discrimination, loss of

When Is 100% Success Inadequate Performance?

If employees in innovative companies have a 100% new-product success rate, they are not performing up to expectations. Rubbermaid's former chairman, Stanley Gault, said, "In today's world, you just can't afford to be overly conservative."[8] A 100% new-product success rate means that the approach is too conservative, and the innovative company can learn a lot from mistakes.

But, how can companies which must stay on the cutting edge of innovation let their professionals know that it's acceptable to fail?

Encourage risk taking when evaluating performance. When a manager lost a lot of money on a failed new product, Robert Johnson, son of the founder of Johnson & Johnson, congratulated him. Johnson said, "If you are making mistakes, that means you are making decisions and taking risks."[9] In innovative companies, senior management must encourage initiative and risk taking. Performance appraisals must encourage intelligent effort and initiative, and not just short-term success. Dick Liebhaer, executive VP of MCI, says, "We do not shoot people who make mistakes. We shoot people who do not take risks."[10]

Require innovation in the developmental part of PAs. 3M requires that one-fourth of its annual sales come from products introduced in the past five years. In a recent year, 32% of its $10.6 billion sales came from such new products.[11] Setting objectives and goals requiring future innovation combines with evaluating a professional's past innovative performance into a total approach.

Inspire the adapting and modifying of innovations developed by others. Many companies will not work with an innovation if they didn't invent it themselves. Format disagreements in the area of VCRs, DATs, and other technologies are well known. Raychem Corp., a top supplier of high-tech products to telecommunication and aerospace companies, avoids the "not-invented-here" mistake by giving a "Not Invented Here Award." Employees are encouraged to adapt or "steal" ideas from fellow employees in other departments. The "stealer" and the idea originator both receive certificates saying "I stole somebody else's idea, and I'm using it," or "I had a great idea and _____ is using it."[12] The more ideas, wherever they come from, the more chances for testing another innovation.

Performance appraisals can be central in a performance management approach to encourage innovation in companies who live or die based upon a constant flow of new ideas.[13]

employee morale and productivity, or inaccurate appraisals, which lead to poor compensation or staffing decisions.

4. Discuss Methods with Employees Prior to the appraisal interview, supervisors should discuss with employees the method that will be used. This discussion should specify which areas of performance are evaluated, how often, how the evaluation takes place, and its significance to the employee. The use of appraisals varies greatly; some organizations tie pay and promotion directly to the PA; others conduct appraisals only in a perfunctory manner to meet some broad goals or policies.

5. Appraise According to Job Standards The PA should evaluate the employee's work according to predetermined work requirements. Comparison with specific requirements indicates what the employee has or has not done well. The supervisor's feelings about the employee should not affect the appraisal. Feelings cannot be evaluated; they are only mental constructs and may be biased. By discussing the employee's behavior that has been observed and documented, the supervisor focuses the appraisal on concrete, actual performance by the employee.

6. Discuss Appraisal with Employees In some organizations, appraisal discussions are omitted whenever specific evaluative objectives for merit raises or promotions have been met. The general trend, however, is to make sure that supervisors discuss the appraisal with their employees, allowing employees to discuss areas of agreement and disagreement. The supervisor should emphasize positive work performance, those areas in which the employee has met or exceeded expectations, as well as areas that need improvement.

7. Determine Future Performance Goals A critical aspect of PA is the use of goal setting.[14] How specifically or rigidly these goals

are to be pursued is determined by the appraisal method used. Even if goals are only broadly discussed, setting goals for the employee's future appraisal period is critical because it gives the employee direction for continued or improved performance. Leaving the appraisal discussion, the employee feels comfortable knowing how past performance has been viewed and what needs to be accomplished to meet future expectations.

Legal Considerations

The possibility of judicial and agency review of PAs continues to expand in the United States. The expansion of discrimination laws, erosion of the employment-at-will doctrine, and a unending appetite for suing in our society all create a climate where PAs have become a critical legal concern. Policymakers and practitioners must be mindful of the possibility of legal review of terminations, promotions, pay decisions, and other HR decisions.

For instance, a black female manager was discharged as part of a general work force reduction. The employer stated that the reason she was part of the cutback was that she had a tendency to criticize others, which prevented her from achieving management's goals of building morale and encouraging a team spirit. The discharged manager sued, believing that she was a victim of race discrimination. The court held that the employer's stated reason was a *pretext* for racial discrimination. Why? The discharged manager had received consistently good performance ratings and two merit raises. Her only negative ratings were part of a set of appraisals that she had never seen. Further, the supervisor of the discharged manager had been pressured by upper management to lower her ratings on the unseen appraisal after deciding to fire her.[15] Chapter 3 discusses the huge amounts that such a case can cost employers under the Civil Right Act of 1991.

The judgment in EEOC complaints and wrongful-discharge cases often go against the employer because the plaintiff-employee is able to do the following:

- Produce records of consistently favorable PAs showing that there was no warning of trouble.
- Show that no formal PAs criticizing performance were received.
- Prove that the employer's PA system is inherently biased against members of a protected class.[16]

Where EEOC's Uniform Guidelines regulate employment (and other) tests, they regulate PAs as well, since PAs are also measurements affecting employment. In general, such measurements must be valid and administered fairly (refer to Chapter 7). According to other agency regulations and court decisions, the validity and fairness requirements have been interpreted to mean that the instrument measuring performance must be linked to specified job requirements, that a good score means good performance, that the rating reliably predicts future performance, and that the appraisal is a valid measure of motivation and intelligence.[17]

Legal experts suggest several guidelines that, if strictly followed, will help protect a firm from legal problems relating to its PAs.

1. **Written appraisals should be conducted regularly for all employees, not limited to lower-level employees.** These written appraisals should never be backdated or altered at a later time. The Americans with Disabilities Act (ADA) requires any request for reasonable accommodation to be considered and recorded. Such a request might surface during a PA interview.

2. **Supervisors and other appraisers should be trained thoroughly in proper appraisal procedures.** This includes emphasizing that PAs should be truthful, candid but constructive, and not malicious.

3. **Appraisers should apply consistent, explicit, and objective job-related standards when preparing PAs.** Work performance, not the individual, should be judged. The ADA requires that appraisals of an employee or applicant be related to the essential functions of the job. This restriction should emphasize to employers the importance of a good fit among job analysis, job descriptions, and performance appraisals. This fit not only guards against complaints and suits, but integrates these management tools in a logical, predictable fashion.

4. **An audit system should be established to guard against leniency and other rater errors to ensure that the appraisals are unbiased.** For instance, before the PA interview is held with the employee, the PA should be reviewed and approved by another manager or reviewer. The HR department can review ratings by the supervisor to help identify rater errors such as central tendency, harshness, leniency, and so on.

5. **Problem areas should be detailed and documented.** If problems are not specifically identified, the employee will have a hard time knowing exactly what behavior to improve. Documentation of specific problems is crucial.

6. **When problems have been identified in assessing substandard performance, specific goals and timetables should be established for improvement.** PAs are most effective when they contain a compliance timetable and secure the employee's commitment to comply.

7. **Employees should be given a clear opportunity to respond to negative appraisals.** If the employee with substandard performance gives her or his version of the facts, this may smoke out future legal claims and will help gain the employee's involvement in the PA process. An opportunity to appeal ratings within the organization may also help ensure a fair system and provide a real opportunity to respond.

8. **The employer should be able to prove that the employee received the PA.** Employees who disagree with their ratings may be reluctant to sign the PA form, assuming that their signature indicates agreement. Allowing them to sign and indicate that they were "present" or "present but disagree" will still supply the needed proof of receipt. Either the employee should sign indicating receipt or receipt can simply be witnessed by another supervisor.

9. **Circulation of appraisals should be restricted to those in management with a need to know.** Unrestricted access to a PA, including negative ratings, may expose the employer to a defamation suit (see *HR in the News:* "PAs That Make the Case").

10. **Check past PAs.** If termination for unsatisfactory performance is being considered, past PAs should be scrutinized to see if the employee was adequately informed of his or her performance deficiencies and if the PAs are consistent with the stated reasons for the employee's dismissal.[18]

Common Rater Errors

Rating problems should be recognized and minimized by trained supervisors and other raters. Appraisers should not only become aware of the most common rater errors, but should also learn how to avoid committing them. All methods of PA are subject to errors, but training and information can minimize many errors. Raters should not only note the following rater errors, but should be aware that employees use political tactics to capitalize on and create such errors as the halo effect.

Supervisory Bias The most common error that exists in any appraisal method is conscious or unconscious **supervisory bias**. Such biases are not related to job performance and may stem from personal characteristics such as age, sex, disability, or race or from organization-related characteristics such as senior-ity, membership on an organization's athletic team, or friendship with top administrators. For example, a supervisor may give an undeserved high rating to the bowling-team captain.

Halo Effect When a rater lets one particular aspect of an employee's performance influence the evaluation of other aspects of performance, a **halo effect** has occurred. For example, the manager who knows that a particular employee always arrives at work early and helps to open the business may let the halo caused by that employee's dependability influence the appraisal of other areas, such as quality of work or job knowledge. Thus, even though the employee may be only mediocre in terms of quality or quantity of performance, the employee receives all high ratings because he or she is dependable and arrives at work early.

A negative halo, or "devil's horns" effect, also exists. If an accountant, Dwight Hadley, performs poorly only when working directly with plant managers on annual budget projects, the supervisor may allow this one truly negative behavior to cloud the objectivity on ratings given on Hadley's other behaviors. Hadley's ratings on safety, quality, task performance, and all other dimensions may be lowered inaccurately due to an accurately poor rating on one dimension—cooperation.

The halo problem can be minimized by supervisory training. Supervisors should be trained to recognize that all jobs—even routine, low-level jobs—require the application of many different skills and behaviors. Training should also focus on the fact that it is not unusual for employees to perform well in some areas and less effectively in others, and that coaching and training should concentrate on those areas in need of improvement.

Central Tendency When raters evaluate everyone as average, the result is **central tendency**. They may find it difficult and unpleasant to evaluate some employees higher or lower than others, even though performances may reflect a real difference. The problem of

PAs That Make the Case

The following three cases indicate how important following good PA procedure can be in avoiding complaints and lawsuits.

1. An employee with 23 years of service at Bissell, Inc., was fired because of his poor attitude, lack of cooperation, and lack of leadership. The company's own policy said that discharge could occur only if an employee was given notice of performance deficiencies and then was given a chance to improve. The PA given immediately before the termination did *not* indicate any dissatisfaction, even though the employee's supervisor was considering discharging him at that time. The court held that he could sue his former employer for "negligent evaluation" as described by a Michigan law.[19]

2. In another case, a Mr. Dominic complained to his immediate supervisor that he was the victim of age discrimination. A few months later, the supervisor fired Dominic for unsatisfactory job performance. Just before Dominic's termination, his supervisor gave him a negative PA, causing the company to believe that it would have an ironclad defense in an age discrimination suit. At the trial, testimony revealed that the supervisor had lowered Dominic's PA deliberately, without his knowledge, after Dominic complained about age dis-

---

central tendency also occurs when supervisors cannot evaluate employee performance objectively because of a lack of familiarity with the work, lack of supervisory ability, or fear that they will be reprimanded if they evaluate individuals too highly or too strictly.

Leniency Inexperienced or poor supervisors may decide that the easiest way to appraise performance is simply to give everyone a high evaluation, sometimes called the "Lake Wobegone" effect. The supervisor may believe that employees will feel that they have been accurately appraised, or that even if they know they have been inaccurately appraised, it will be to their benefit. Employees will not complain about their appraisals if they all receive high appraisals. However, the best performers in the department will complain about such supervisors because those who are working hard receive no more credit than fellow employees who are not.

Salary considerations will often lead managers to inflate appraisals to justify pay raises for their employees. But truly superior employees who are given glowing reviews receive only modest pay increases because virtually everyone received high evaluations; thus the superior employee becomes unhappy and may leave.[23] Lack of accurate appraisal can lead to turnover among the best employees, who go to organizations that can appraise their performance accurately and give them the recognition they deserve.

Strictness Sometimes supervisors consistently give low ratings even though some employees may have achieved an average or above-average performance level. **Strictness** is the opposite of leniency. The problem of strict-

crimination. Just after Dominic's complaint, the supervisor deluged Dominic with job assignments. The judge let stand a $450,000 verdict against the employer since the jury reasonably believed that the supervisor had set Dominic up for failure.[20]

3. Finally, a Mr. Bals was fired by the Inland Steel Company after receiving several unfavorable PAs from his supervisor. Bals filed a defamation claim against Inland Steel, arguing that information damaging one's reputation within a corporate community is just as devastating to an individual as that communicated to people outside the company. The Indiana Supreme Court held that there *was* "publication" for purposes of defamation in Bals' case. The court said that a person does not, on employment, relinquish his or her right to a good reputation. The court said that "A person's suitability for continued employment and advancement at work may be substantially influenced by the reputation one earns." So, if communications even within a company injure someone's occupational reputation, "the results may be among the most injurious of defamation."[21]

Even though Indiana joined a number of states that allow intracompany communications to form the basis of a defamation suit, it did allow employers to retain a "qualified privilege." To encourage "free and open" intracompany communications and the pursuit of legitimate HR requirements, the court extended a limited privilege to personnel information communicated "in good faith" to persons with a *"legitimate need"* to have the information.[22]

---

ness is not nearly as widespread as the problem of leniency.

Supervisors are often guilty of strictness in ratings because they feel that none of the subordinates is living up to standards of excellence. Unreasonable performance expectations that employees find impossible to achieve can be demoralizing.

Recency When organizations use annual or semiannual PAs, there may be a tendency for supervisors to remember more about what their employees have done just before the appraisal than in prior months. It is human nature for supervisors to remember recent events more clearly than events in the distant past.

To avoid the **recency** error, raters should conduct frequent appraisals—for instance, monthly or quarterly—and/or keep a running log of critical incidents of the employee's be-

haviors and outcomes. The rater can refer to these short notes about these special outcomes and behaviors, good and bad, when performing the typical annual PA. These notes could be kept in a special file or simply on the rater's calendar.

Overall Ratings Many appraisal forms require the supervisor to provide an overall rating of an employee's performance in addition to evaluations of specific performance areas. Often compensation decisions, for example, the amount of pay raises or bonuses, are determined by the employee's overall rating. Often the supervisor must rate the employee as "outstanding," "definitely above average," "doing an average job," "substandard but making progress," or "definitely unsatisfactory." It is difficult for a rater to combine all the separate performance dimensions into one accurate overall rating.[24] Behavioral research indicates that raters are not consistent in this process. Thus, two employees who receive identical evaluations on every specific performance area could nevertheless receive entirely different overall ratings—which most likely will be used for merit and promotion considerations. In addition, employees are often not sure how evaluations of specific areas are weighed to produce an overall evaluation. Some raters may weigh all areas as equal, whereas others may only consider two to three items important in determining an overall rating.[25]

Solutions to appraisal problems focus on two areas: the appraisal system and rater training. Appraisal systems should be based on a job analysis that specifies the content of the job. Specific performance criteria for each content area can then be developed. An employee's job performance is then measured against these criteria. Effectively training the persons, usually supervisors, who perform the appraisal can minimize appraisal problems such as leniency, the halo effects, and recency.[26]

APPRAISAL METHODS AND INSTRUMENTS

The methods chosen, and the instruments (or forms) used to implement these methods, are critical in determining whether the organization manages its performance successfully. The dimensions listed on a PA form often determine which behaviors employees attempt and raters seek, and which are neglected. PA methods and instruments should signal the operational goals and objectives to the individuals, groups, and the organization at large.

Traditionally, PA methods were broken down into two categories based on the standards for success chosen. **Comparative methods**, such as ranking or forced distribution, rate the overall performance of one employee directly against that of other employees. **Absolute standards methods**, such as rating scales or management by objectives (MBO), rate the employee against some objective, selected, or imaginary goal(s).

Due to the expansion of methods used for PA, we believe a more detailed categorization will be helpful, as illustrated by the six systems presented in Figure 8-2.

Work Standards

Work standards are used primarily to measure the performance of clerical and manufacturing employees whose jobs are production or output oriented. Work standards establish the normal or average production output for employees on the job. Standards are set according to the production per hour or the time spent

FIGURE 8-2 Types of performance appraisal systems.

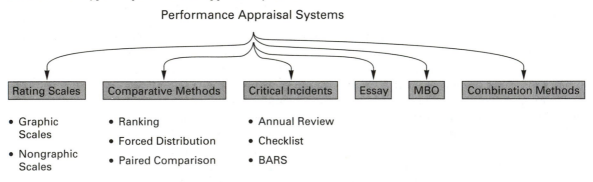

per unit produced or served. This standard allows firms to pay employees on a piece-rate basis. Time-and-motion studies can be used to set output criteria for persons on particular jobs.

Few organizations use work standards as the only PA method. In many cases, production standards are used as part of an appraisal process, especially if the firm pays on a piece-rate basis. Whether rating an individual or a team, quantity of production is only *one* aspect of performance; other aspects (quality, safety, planning, training, maintenance activities, etc.) must be included. An individual's output depends on the performance of others, so it may be unfair to make promotion or pay decisions based solely on the number of units that person completes each hour. Other methods of PA have become more common.

Rating Scales

Graphic Rating Scale   The **graphic rating scale** rates the employee-ratee on some standard or attribute of work. Traditionally, the focus was on personal traits (e.g., friendliness and cooperation), but more recently, it has been on work behaviors and outcomes (e.g., "does job right the first time" and "greets every customer who enters store"). The rating is often done on some 1–3 or 1–5 Likert-type scale, with 1 representing "very unsatisfactory" and 5 representing "excellent." The rating scale is one of the oldest and most common methods, and has survived the many recent innovations in instruments.

As shown in Figure 8-3, graphic rating scales itemize factors, such as attendance and safety (which are factors 2 and 3 under "Behavioral Factors"). The Marley Cooling Tower Company, in Mission, Kansas, has the employee (E) and the supervisor (S) both rate the employee using a 1–5 scale on various factors, including factor 3, "exhibits safe practices in work per-

formance." Marley's PA form also uses the modern approach of self-rating along with supervisor rating on a traditional graphic rating scale form.

Graphic rating scales are popular with managers because they can be filled out quickly and require little training. However, these scales are particularly prone to the rater errors discussed, so some training is required. Courts have sometimes attacked the subjective approach of graphic rating scales. In a wrongful discharge case, one court required that more objective measures be produced even though the graphic rating scales supported the employer.[27]

Nongraphic Rating Scale   Shown in Figure 8-4 is the **nongraphic rating scale**. A nongraphic scale is usually more valid than a graphic scale because the former contains a brief description of each point on a scale rather than simply low and high points of a scale. The rater can give a more accurate description of the employee's behavior on a particular attribute because a description clarifies each level of the rating scale. On the graphic scale, raters arbitrarily decide what various points represent about an attribute; for example, what is "below-average" cooperation?

In general, both graphic and nongraphic rating scales are quick, easy, and less difficult for supervisors to use than many other methods of PA. Also, decision makers find rating scales to be satisfactory for most evaluative purposes because they provide a mathematical evaluation of the employee's performance, which can be used to justify compensation or job changes and to validate selection instruments. For example, if the rating scale contains twenty attributes with a five-point scale for each attribute, employees can receive one hundred points if they perform perfectly. Any percentage of that total can be directly related to a merit increase or promotion probability.

FIGURE 8-3 Graphic rating scale with self and supervisor ratings

Job and Behavioral Summary
Factors Important to MARLEY® Mission and Personal Development

Both [E] employee and [S] supervisor shall answer separately, and record together answers on supervisor's form. Openly discuss variation.

Name: _Pat Dugan_   Date: _5-7-94_

Current Job: _Training Specialist II_   Dept.: _HR_

Job Factors

Mark X at level of current belief   1 2 3 4 5 (high)

#	Factor	E	S	Comment
1	Aim of process is clearly understood	4	3	
2	Role in process is clearly understood	4	4	
3	Information input to job is good	3	4	
4	Training for job is sufficient	2	4	Pat has just entered T & D program
5	Equipment, materials, etc. provided are sufficient	1	3	Budget limits purchases / need supplies
6	Management support is sufficient to accomplish goal(s)	4	4	
7	Expectations of position are realistic	3	4	
8	Team participation is encouraged	3	3	
9	Recognition/reward is a positive factor	5	5	
10	Impact of job on overall system is clear	5	5	

Behavioral Factors

Performance level   1 2 3 4 5 (high)

#	Factor	E	S	Comment
1	Education/experience	5	5	Pat's MBA helps
2	Attendance & punctuality	4	3	We have discussed goals & timetables
3	Exhibits safe practices in work performance	5	5	
4	Personal effort and enthusiasm	5	5	very enthusiatic!
5	Attitude toward mission/vision	4	5	
6	Interest in understanding and delighting customer	5	5	
7	Promotes teamwork in word & action	4	4	
8	Does job right the first time	4	4	
9	Communication skills	5	5	
10	Personal initiative	4	4	
11	Demonstrates tact and diplomacy	4	4	

Include a copy of this page in my personnel file   ☑ yes   ☐ no

I have discussed job factors and behavior with my supervisor:

☑ I agree   ☐ I disagree   ☑ Comments are attached

Employee signature: _Pat Dugan_   Date: _5-7-94_

Supervisor signature: **Mel Fitzpatrick**   Date: **5-7-94**

Used by permission from the Marley Cooling Tower Co.

FIGURE 8-4 An example of the nongraphic form of rating scales.

Name: _____ For period ending: _____

Department: _____ Job title: _____

Instructions:
Listed below are a number of traits, abilities, and characteristics that are important for success. Place an "X" mark on each rating scale, over the descriptive phrase which most nearly describes the person being rated.

ACCURACY is the correctness of work duties performed.

Usually accurate; makes only average number of mistakes	Makes frequent errors	Requires absolute minimum of supervision; is almost always accurate	Requires little supervision; is exact and precise most of the time	Careless; makes recurrent errors

ALERTNESS is the ability to grasp instruction, to meet changing conditions and to solve novel or problem situations.

Requires more than average instructions and explanations	Slow to catch on	Exceptionally keen and alert	Grasps instructions with average ability	Usually quick to understand and learn

CREATIVITY is talent for having new ideas, for finding new and better ways of doing things and for being imaginative.

Continually seeks new and better ways of doing things; is extremely imaginative	Has average imagination; has reasonable number of new ideas	Frequently suggests new ways of doing things; is very imaginative	Rarely has a new idea; is unimaginative	Occasionally comes up with a new idea

FRIENDLINESS is the sociability and warmth which an individual imparts toward customers, other employees, the supervisor, and persons supervised.

Approachable; friendly once known by others	Extremely sociable; excellent at establishing good will	Very distant and aloof	Very sociable and outgoing	Warm; friendly; sociable

PERSONALITY is an individual's behavior characteristics or personal suitability for the job.

Very desirable personality for this job	Personality unsatisfactory for this job	Outstanding personality for this job	Personality satisfactory for this job	Personality questionable for this job

PERSONAL APPEARANCE is the personal impression an individual makes on others. (Consider cleanliness, grooming, neatness, and appropriateness of dress on the job.)

Very untidy; poor taste in dress	Generally neat and clean; satisfactory personal appearance	Unusually well groomed; very neat; excellent taste in dress	Sometimes untidy and careless about personal appearance	Careful about personal appearance; good taste in dress

PHYSICAL FITNESS is the ability to work consistently and with only moderate fatigue. (Consider physical alertness and energy.)

Energetic; seldom tires	Tires easily; is weak and frail	Excellent health; no fatigue	Meets physical and energy job requirements	Frequently tires and is slow

(continued)

FIGURE 8-4 continued

ATTENDANCE is faithfulness in coming to work daily and conforming to work hours.

Always regular and prompt; volunteers for overtime when needed	Often absent without good excuse and/or frequently reports for work late	Very prompt; regular in attendance	Lax in attendance and/or reporting for work on time	Usually present and on time

DEPENDABILITY is the ability to do required jobs well with a minimum of supervision.

Requires close supervision; is unreliable	Requires absolute minimum of supervision	Usually takes care of necessary tasks and completes with reasonable promptness	Requires little supervision; is reliable	Sometimes requires prompting

JOB KNOWLEDGE is the information concerning work duties which an individual should know for a satisfactory job performance

Lacks knowledge of some phases of work	Has complete mastery of all phases of job	Understands all phases of work	Poorly informed about work duties	Moderately informed; can answer most common questions

QUANTITY OF WORK is the amount of work an individual does in a work day.

Volume of work is satisfactory	Very industrious; does more than is required	Does just enough to get by	Superior work production recorded	Does not meet minimum requirements

STABILITY is the ability to withstand pressure and to remain calm in crisis situations.

Thrives under pressure; really enjoys solving crises	Goes "to pieces" under pressure; is "jumpy" and nervous	Tolerates most pressure; likes crises more than the average person	Has average tolerance for crises; usually remains calm	Occasionally "blows up" under pressure; is easily irritated

COURTESY is the polite attention an individual gives other people.

Always very polite and willing to help	Sometimes tactless	Inspiring to others in being courteous and very pleasant	Agreeable and pleasant	Blunt; discourteous; antagonistic

OVERALL EVALUATION in comparison with other employees with the same length of service on this job:

Definitely Unsatisfactory	Substandard but making progress	Doing an average job	Definitely above average	Outstanding

Signature of Supervisor	Date	Signature of Employee	Date
Signature of Reviewing Officer	Date	Signature of Personnel Officer	Date

Remarks:

SOURCE: Kentucky Department of Education, Frankfort, Kentucky. Used by permission.

Rating scales have several disadvantages. Using the scale, raters can easily make halo or central-tendency errors. Since everyone can quickly be rated very high or average on most items, raters who want to use central tendency or leniency in their appraisals can easily do so. Most rating scales also have the disadvantage of not being related to a specific job.

Comparative Methods

A common problem, regardless of the effort spent in developing a PA system, is the appraiser's tendency to assign uniform ratings to employees regardless of performance. One study of over 7000 managerial and professional employees in two large manufacturing firms found that 95 percent of the employees were crowded into only two of up to six rating categories.[28] For whatever reasons, supervisors simply do not (and are not forced to) differentiate between employees despite real differences in performance. **Comparative methods** can be used to tease out differences between employees by providing direct comparisons.

Ranking Ranking employees from most effective to least effective is another appraisal method. Problems of central tendency and leniency are eliminated by forcing raters to evaluate employees over a predetermined range. The ranking method is comparative; supervisors or other raters judge employees' performances in relation to each other instead of against an absolute standard, as is the case with rating scales.

Supervisors usually rank their employees from most effective to least effective in total job performance. This results in as many different rankings as there are departments or areas within the organization, as shown in Figure 8-5.

Some managers try to combine departmental rankings into a ranking for the total organization. Such ranking is very difficult, if not impossible, because employees have not been compared to any common standard. However, when a total organizational ranking is used, employees receiving the highest rankings may receive the highest merit increases or promotion considerations.

The advantage of ranking is that it is fast and easy to complete. A numerical evaluation given to the employees can be directly related to compensation changes or staffing considerations. In addition, ranking completely avoids problems of central tendency or leniency.

There are, however, serious disadvantages. Ranking is seldom developmental because employees do not receive feedback about performance strengths and weaknesses or any future direction. Also, ranking assumes that each department has employees who can be distributed fairly over a range from best to worst. Finally, when ranking is used, there is no common standard of performance by which to compare employees from various departments

FIGURE 8-5 An example of ranking employees by department

Sales	Office	Warehouse	Delivery
1. Dugan	1. Godfrey	1. Lionel	1. Cooper
1. Hansbrough	2. Weber	2. Ellis	2. Grover
3. Douglas	3. Hui	3. Aschbacher	3. Crooker
4. Krug	4. Kelley	4. Ferre	4. Baldwin
5. McCalman	5. Delahanty	5. Futtrell	
	6. Fitzpatrick	6. Wagner	
	7. Hadley		

since employees in each department are compared only with each other. Many employers rank employees and use other PA methods so that they can gain the advantages while avoiding the pitfalls of this method.

Forced Distribution Another comparative method of performance appraisal is called **forced distribution**. Similar to ranking, forced distribution requires that supervisors spread their employee evaluations in a predescribed distribution. As illustrated in Figure 8-6, the supervisor places employees in classifications ranging from poor to excellent. Like ranking, forced distribution eliminates central tendency and leniency biases. However, forced distribution has the same disadvantages as ranking. Often administrators will use forced distribution to compare employees from different departments. However, this is valid only if each department has an equal number of excellent employees, above-average employees, and so on. That assumption is very difficult to make.

Paired Comparison Another comparative method of performance appraisal involves **paired comparison**, in which raters pair employees and choose one as superior in overall job performance. As illustrated in Figure 8-7,

this method results in giving each employee a positive-comparison total and a certain percentage of the total positive evaluation. This percentage of positive comparisons gives paired comparison an advantage over ranking and forced distribution. Paired comparison does not force the distribution of employees in each department. For example, if a department has two outstanding employees and six average employees and paired comparison is correctly used, then those two employees will receive a much higher percentage of positive comparison than the other six. Alternatively, if all employees have about the same performance except for one poor performer, that employee may have a much lower total percentage of positive comparisons than the other employees in the department. Thus, the actual distribution of employees in the department is based on performance.

Like ranking and forced distribution, paired comparison is quick and fairly easy to use if few employees are being rated. In fact, raters may prefer paired comparison to ranking or forced distribution because they compare only two employees at a time rather than all employees to one another.

The number of comparisons required equals $N(N - 1)/2$. Therefore, for 20 employees, 190 comparisons would be necessary $[(20 \times 19)/2$

FIGURE 8-6 An example of forced distribution.

Poor 10%	Below Average 20%	Average 40%	Above Average 20%	Excellent 10%
Fitzpatrick Hadley	Futtrell Crooker Wagner Baldwin	Grover Hansbrough Hui Douglas Aschbacher Krug Kelley Ferre Delahanty McCalman	Dugan Lionel Weber Ellis	Godfrey Cooper

FIGURE 8-7 An example of paired comparison of employees.

Instructions: Assign each employee's name a different capital letter on a separate sheet of paper. Example: A—Smith, B—Jones, etc. Then, develop a chart such as the one below and, for each plotted pair, write in the letter of the employee who, in your opinion, has one the superior job overall.

Example:

	A	B	C	D	E
A		A	A	A	A
B			C	D	E
C				C	E
D					E
E					

To compute employees' positive evaluations:

$$\frac{\text{Number of Positive Evaluations}}{\text{Total Number of Evaluations}} \times 100 = \text{Employee's \% Total Positive Evaluations}$$

Employee A
$$\frac{4}{4} \times 100 = 100\%$$

Employee B
$$\frac{0}{4} \times 100 = 0\%$$

Employee C
$$\frac{2}{4} \times 100 = 50\%$$

Employee D
$$\frac{1}{4} \times 100 = 25\%$$

Employee E
$$\frac{3}{4} \times 100 = 75\%$$

SOURCE: Reprinted with permission from H. J. Bernardin, "Behavioral Expectation Scales versus Summated Scales: A Fairer Comparison," *Journal of Applied Psychology*, 62 (1977): 422–427.

= 190]. Thus, this technique is time-consuming with large numbers of employees.

Another disadvantage of paired comparison is that employees are compared to each other on overall performance rather than on specific job criteria. The advantages of not forcing the employee evaluations into set distributions make paired comparison an attractive alternative to ranking and forced distribution.

Critical Incidents

Several modern PA methods employ the use of **critical incidents** to make the appraisal process more job related than some of the other methods. The critical-incident methods of PA use specific examples of job behavior that have been collected from supervisors or employees or both. Normally, several employees and supervisors compile a list of actual job experiences involving extraordinarily good or bad employee performances. Neither normal procedures nor average work performance is included. Outstandingly good or bad job performances separate the better employees from the average employees and the poor employees from the average employees. Thus, the emphasis is on specific actions as critical examples of excellent or poor behavior. Once a list of critical incidents is finalized, a particular method of using these incidents will be chosen.

Annual Review File or Calendar One form of the method is for the supervisor or appraiser to keep an ongoing record of his or her employees' critical incidents contemporaneously during the period of appraisal. If the review period is one year, the supervisor can keep a file (computer or paper) or calendar in which the outstandingly good or bad examples of subordinates' performance are entered. The supervisor would then make an annual review of this file or calendar before preparing for the PA. Employees who have little or no record during the year are doing their jobs satisfactorily, not performing much above or below job expectations. The advantage of the annual review file is that it is usually very job specific. With specific dates and incidents included in the PA, the supervisor is less affected by bias.

The main disadvantage of using an annual review file is the difficulty of keeping an accurate record. With other interests having a much higher priority, maintaining records for employees is often not given adequate time. Another disadvantage of the annual review is the lack of comparable data on employees; it is very difficult to compare the performances of different employees using records of critical incidents.

Checklist of Critical Incidents Critical incidents may also be used in PA by developing a checklist of critical behaviors related to an employee's performance. Such an appraisal form may have twenty or thirty critical items for one specific job. The supervisor simply checks whether the employee has performed in a superior manner in any one of the incidents. Outstanding employees would receive many checks, indicating that they performed very well during the appraisal period. Average employees would receive few checks because only in a few cases did they perform outstandingly.

The checklist method of critical incidents often involves giving different weights to different items in the checklist to indicate that some are more important than others. The checklist method of critical incidents is fairly fast and easy to use since it can produce a mathematical total for employees. And it is evaluative as well as developmental. But the checklist is time-consuming and expensive to develop since checklists for each job in the organization must be produced.

Behaviorally Anchored Rating Scales (BARS) The most common use of critical-incident performance appraisals is in combination with rating scales. Instead of using broad employee attributes, the points on the rating scale are critical incidents. For example, a **behaviorally anchored rating scale (BARS)** is quick and easy to complete. Such scales are evaluative because mathematical totals can be easily related to merit increases and promotion probability. They are also job related and more developmental than typical rating scales because the items being evaluated are those that are critical to good performance.

The Ohio State Highway Patrol developed a BARS appraisal system consisting of four stages. Stage one involved a detailed task analysis of the job of state troopers. The critical tasks were determined from interviews with troopers and supervisors. Stage two entailed assigning weight to each task according to how critical the task was in relation to the officer's job and how frequently it was required. Descriptions of "excellent," "average," and "poor" performance levels of each task were developed in stage three. The fourth stage included a statistical validation of the appraisal instrument, as discussed in Chapter 5. As an example, the critical task "secure accident scenes" was given the following three levels of evaluation:[29]

1. Uses available equipment and solicits any available assistance to secure scene of accident quickly and efficiently. (Excellent)
2. Generally secures scene adequately before beginning accident investigation. (Average)
3. May fail to secure the scene adequately before beginning accident investigation. (Poor)

BARS systems have been favored by federal agencies and personnel researchers because they are job related. As with the other critical-incident systems, the primary disadvantage of a BARS system is the time and effort involved in adapting critical incidents to a rating-scale format. A BARS system requires a separate rating scale for each job involved in the organization. An example of a BARS for the job dimension "organizational skills" for a college professor is shown in Figure 8-8.

Essay Method

A PA created primarily for employee development is the written essay method. The supervisor or appraiser writes an essay, in narrative style, describing the employee's performance, specifying examples of strengths and weaknesses. Because the essay method forces the supervisor to discuss specific examples of performance, it can also minimize supervisory bias and the halo effect. By asking supervisors to enumerate specific examples of employee

FIGURE 8-8 A BARS for college professors.

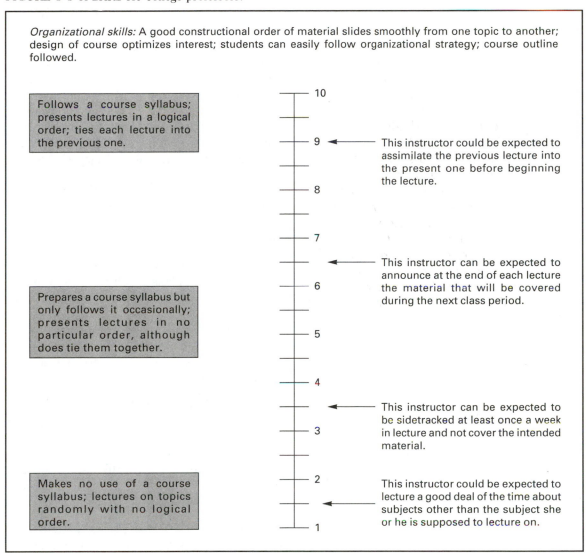

Organizational skills: A good constructional order of material slides smoothly from one topic to another; design of course optimizes interest; students can easily follow organizational strategy; course outline followed.

Follows a course syllabus; presents lectures in a logical order; ties each lecture into the previous one.

Prepares a course syllabus but only follows it occasionally; presents lectures in no particular order, although does tie them together.

Makes no use of a course syllabus; lectures on topics randomly with no logical order.

10 — 9 ← This instructor could be expected to assimilate the previous lecture into the present one before beginning the lecture.

8 — 7

← This instructor can be expected to announce at the end of each lecture the material that will be covered during the next class period.

6 — 5

4 — ← This instructor can be expected to be sidetracked at least once a week in lecture and not cover the intended material.

3 — 2 ← This instructor could be expected to lecture a good deal of the time about subjects other than the subject she or he is supposed to lecture on.

1

SOURCE: Reprinted with permission from H. J. Bernardin, "Behavioral Expectation Scales versus Summated Scales: A Fairer Comparison," *Journal of Applied Psychology*, 62 (1977): 422–427.

behavior, this method also minimizes central tendency and leniency problems because no rating scale is being used.

The essay method often has a distinct disadvantage: the time the supervisors must spend writing separate essays about each employee can be formidable. Also, essays are not very useful for evaluative purposes; 200 essays describing different employees' performances cannot easily be linked to merit increases and promotion because there is no common standard.

Management by Objectives

One of the most widely used performance-appraisal methods is **management by objectives (MBO)**. Although individual approaches may vary somewhat, most MBO programs contain the same essential elements. A description of the typical MBO process is illustrated in Figure 8-9.

Goal Setting   Goal setting lies at the heart of the MBO process. With MBO, the goal-setting process begins with the formulation of long-range objectives and "cascades" through organizational objectives, departmental goals, and finally individual goals.

At the individual goal-setting level, goals are mutually set by the employee and his or her manager. The aspect of participation in goal

setting is one of MBO's major strengths, as there is general agreement that participation in decision making strengthens employee motivation and commitment.

MBO concentrates on setting *measurable* goals as opposed to vague or subjective goals. In the context of MBO, characteristics of good goals include (1) a description of specifically what is to be accomplished and how the accomplishment of a goal will be measured, (2) target dates for goal accomplishment, and (3) the amount of resources (e.g., time, money) to be used in accomplishing the goal (some MBO systems do not include this feature).

For example, an HR manager's goal might be to "create a new employee orientation program by December 31 with an expenditure of no more than 100 staff hours and at a cost in materials and supplies of no more than $5000." In this case the manager knows specifically what his or her expectations are. Compare that goal to being told by the boss to "put together a new employee-orientation program ASAP and spend as little money as possible."

Action Planning   Goals specify *what* is to be achieved; action plans specify *how* goals are to be achieved. In essence, the action plan constitutes a road map for accomplishing the goals. Action plans are important because they provide direction as well as a mechanism (often called *milestones*) for measuring accomplishment toward goals.

Self-Control   A primary assumption of MBO is that employees will accomplish their goals if given management and organizational support. Inherent in this assumption is that those who are being appraised with MBO have a fairly high level of motivation, commitment, and achievement drive.

Periodic Review   Most MBO systems include a mechanism for periodically measuring progress toward goals. A review process is particularly important to discuss problems that an

FIGURE 8-9 The MBO process.

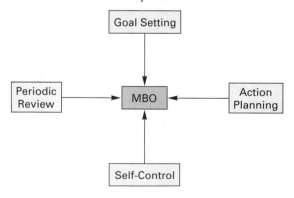

employee may be experiencing in reaching goals; perhaps goals need adjusting to account for problems that could not be forecast during the goal-setting process. In more fortunate situations, exceptional performance may require that goals be adjusted upward. While the actual review periods vary from firm to firm, typical periods are quarterly or monthly. Generally, action plans and the milestones that are often included in them are discussed during the review process.

The advantages of the MBO method are many. Both the supervisor and the employee participate in the appraisal process. The focus of the appraisal process is on specific goals and not on broad personality traits such as "dependability" or "cooperation." What is unique about the MBO procedure is that goals and objectives are determined before the appraisal period begins.[30] Previously discussed methods of appraisal take place after the employees' performance has occurred. Since the MBO process gives employees direction before the appraisal period begins, it is developmental in defining the direction employees should take and the expected level of achievement. The disadvantage of the MBO procedure is the time and effort that must be spent by both the supervisor and the subordinate in the appraisal process.

Numerous studies of organizations' experiences with MBO show that for an MBO program to be successful, several guidelines should be considered before the process begins.[31] First, an independent review committee of management and employees should be set up as an appeals mechanism. Thus, if an employee feels that a supervisor is setting unrealistically high goals or if a supervisor feels that employees are making excuses about goals not met, there is an independent body to which they can appeal for a decision. Second, objectives and goals should be mutually accepted by the employee and supervisor. Generally, four or five specific objectives that are measurable in terms of dollars or units of time should be established. Whenever possible, objectives should be constructed with allowances for individual differences, though they should still be realistic, feasible, but difficult.[32] Third, if possible, there should be a target date for completion of each specific objective. Several target dates for different objectives can be established at the beginning of the appraisal process. Finally, MBO objectives should be specific, giving a time frame, a priority ranking, and a plan of action.[33]

Combination Methods

It has become a common practice to combine two or even three PA methods into an employer's overall PA program. For example, on the form used at Marley (Figure 8-3), there is room to write essay-style comments (they also supply an additional page for this specific purpose, not shown in the figure) along with the graphic rating scales. The essay and MBO approaches can be added to a rating scales approach for a fuller, perhaps more effective, PA system. Team and individual ratings also can be combined to provide a more in-depth appraisal.

Appraisal Schedule

How often to formally appraise employee performance is an important and difficult question. Probably the most common answer fixes a specific interval between formal appraisals, such as one year or six months. The schedule provides consistency in the evaluation process because all employees are evaluated for the same period of time. A variable-interval process can be used when a goal-setting approach establishes specific time periods to achieve certain goals. Thus, at the end of each time period, an appraisal determines the achievement level for a particular goal. When goal achievement does not have to be tied to a specific time period, it can be linked with the company's standard appraisal period in order to maintain appraisal consistency.

WHO SHOULD DO THE RATING?

While the effectiveness of the traditional performance appraisal of individuals has been called into question, employers have been reexamining the question "who should perform the appraisal?" (System and group appraisals will be discussed later in the chapter.) The standard approach has been to have a *single* rater, with the immediate supervisor performing the appraisal as a managerial duty. *Multiple raters* may now be used at a majority of firms. Peer and self evaluations have increased, as have customer or client evaluations. Perhaps the most recent attempts to improve the PA process have included the use of subordinate or reverse ratings and the proliferation of team rating techniques.

Supervisors

The person in the best position to observe the employee's behavior and determine whether the employee has reached specified goals and objectives is the best person to conduct the appraisal. Indeed, EEOC requires the appraiser to observe the employee being rated directly. Traditionally, this has been the supervisor, and in many cases this is still the best choice. Often only the supervisor directly and consistently observes the employee's performance and knows what level of performance should be expected. Supervisors often prefer to avoid the appraisal process because uncomfortable face-to-face confrontations often result. Even so, policymakers should ensure that PAs are conducted in a professional manner because appraisals of subordinates are a legitimate and critical part of supervision.

Peer Evaluations

In some situations, if an employee is working very closely with other employees in a noncompetitive, work group environment, peers may be in the best position to evaluate a coworker's performance. Peers can, in some situations, provide information that the organization could not get from the employee's supervisor due to a lack of direct contact between the supervisor and employee. These subordinates, however, often will not give objective, honest appraisals because of possible retaliation. Further, some research has indicated that factors such as race may have more of a biasing effect when co-workers rate a employee than when a supervisor does the rating.[34]

The technique of allowing a panel of peers to review the behavior of employees, or to review the appraisal itself, may have started at General Electric in the 1980s. GE's **peer review** procedure gives employees the right to have a grievance heard by a panel of three fellow workers and two managers. The panel's decision is final and binding, all proceedings are confidential, and panelists must be trained and be selected randomly from a group of volunteers.[35] Though it started as a union-avoidance technique, GE discovered that as a result of the change to peer review, supervisors now checked policies *before* making decisions, and employees appreciated how tough being fair can be in termination, promotion, demotion, and other such cases. This pushing of decision making further down the organizational ladder also may help keep employers out of court by giving employees a voice in the workplace. Companies like Public Service Company of New Mexico not only allow the outcomes of PAs (like terminations and demotions), to be challenged, but the PAs themselves can be appealed to peer panels.[36]

Customer/Client Evaluations

An increasing number of jobs are now considered service jobs, so evaluations by customers and clients are becoming more valuable as part of the multiple-rater PA process. We are all familiar with customer comment cards located everywhere from banks to restaurants to electronics stores. Specialized customer questionnaires, telephone follow-up surveys, and other techniques are used in addition to comment cards to try to get the customer's evaluation of the employee's performance. However, it would be difficult or impossible for customers and clients to give a total PA because they generally view only part of the employee's performance. For this reason, supervisors generally are still responsible for the overall PA, of which customer input becomes a part.

The reactions of customers is being emphasized even in nonservice jobs, like those in manufacturing. TQM and similar programs, make quality the responsibility of all employees, not just of Quality Inspectors. The end user of each department's output can be thought of as an **internal customer**. When PQ Corporation, a Pennsylvania chemical manufacturer, was converting to a performance-based pay system to fit with its new TQM program, it also adjusted its PA system. To provide support to the TQM principle of pleasing customers first, evaluations from each employee's internal customers were added to those from supervisors. Supervisors now interview their employees' customers, suppliers, peers, and sometimes subordinates to develop a more complete picture of the employees performance.[37]

Self Ratings

Just as customer evaluations are increasing as part of a total PA, a growing number of employers are including **self ratings** — ratings that employees give to themselves. Deane Rothenberg, director of HR in Washington, DC, for The Hay Group, estimated that at the beginning of this decade, 7–10 percent of companies were using self ratings.[38] The appraisal instrument used by Marley (Figure 8-3) formally records the employee's self ratings (E) as well as the ratings given by the supervisor (S) on each factor. According to Marley's PA packet, the rating scales shown are *"for employee and supervisor to answer separately, then meet and dialogue about any perceived differences. It is not to rate or judge the person but to encourage employee development, build genuine

teamwork, and to connect job performance with company goals."*[39] Many personnel consultants believe that effective use of self rating is critical to success in appraising white-collar employees.

Research suggests that supervisors react to employee self ratings. Supervisors who learned that certain employees' self ratings were higher than their own changed their initial ratings. Supervisors generally changed the ratings in a positive direction, gave these employees larger raises, and were less willing to sit down and discuss the appraisal with these high self raters.[40] This finding suggests that some negotiation or posturing may be taking place in such PA procedures. Many employer programs, such as Marley's, encourage discussions of differences on subjective ratings in order to get more involvement from both the supervisor and employee.

Reverse Appraisals

While traditional appraisals have the supervisor rate the employees, in **reverse appraisals**, or upward evaluations, the employees rate the supervisor. As a college student you have probably rated your instructors, and they have graded you. In 1988, Chrysler Corporation began performing appraisals from the bottom up. They gave employees the opportunity to give direct, formal feedback to their supervisors on their managerial performance. Executive development specialist Debra Dubrow said that Chrysler's employees had "felt that management didn't listen as well as it could have and wanted more input into decisions that affected their work."[41] By starting a reverse appraisal process in rating scale form, Chrysler wanted to (1) give employees a more effective voice mechanism; (2) improve managers' supervisory skills; and (3) improve Chrysler's competitive position in the industry (see *HR in the News:* "Rating the Boss" for details on the PA instrument).[42]

Use of reverse rating must be approached with care. "If all you're getting is 'This guy's a

Rating the Boss

A cross section of employees at Chrysler devised a new reverse appraisal process and instrument in late 1988 to improve supervisory skills and strengthen employees' voice at the workplace. The categories that the new reverse appraisal needed to address included

- Teamwork
- Communication
- Quality
- Leadership
- Planning
- Development of the work force[43]

Managers and employees who had taken part in two pilot programs gave input into the reverse appraisal instrument. The questionnaire used rating scales for responses. The 1–5 ratings were *almost never, seldom, occasionally, frequently,* and *almost always.* The following are examples of questions from the categories presented:

- *Teamwork:* "My supervisor promotes cooperation and teamwork within our work group."
- *Communication:* "My supervisor learns current business information and communicates it to our work group."
- *Quality:* "My supervisor demonstrates meaningful commitment to our quality efforts."
- *Leadership:* "My supervisor demonstrates consistency in both words and actions."
- *Planning:* "My supervisor provides reasonable schedules so that my commitments can be met."
- *Development of the work force:* "My supervisor delegates responsibilities and gives me the authority to carry out my job."[44]

Only the individual supervisor and a third party receive the individual appraisals, but the supervisors are expected to present the reverse appraisals in aggregate form to their own managers. Chrysler started with top management being rated by its subordinates, then moved step by step down the organization with the reverse appraisal process.

schmuck,' that's not going to do anything," explained Frank Sadowski, HR and management consultant in Vermont.[43] He states that evaluations must identify particular strengths and weaknesses, rather than consist of vague comments, to be helpful. He also believes that anonymity is necessary unless there is a high level of trust at the workplace. Finally, fear of retaliation must be eliminated for this employee voice mechanism to be effective.

Today, IBM, AT&T, GE Medical Systems, and many other employers are making reverse appraisals part of their appraisal process. A manager at Seventh Generation, a Vermont retailer of consumer products, likes the new supervisor appraisal process. She said, "One of the things for me is, people tell me that they feel I'm too busy to approach, so it's helped me to take a look at my style. . . . It also tells you to spend more time asking people 'how's it going?' "[46]

Team Appraisals

Closely related to peer review is the multiple-rater approach of having a team appraise the performance of individual team members. U.S. employers are not completely following through with the team concept, however. In a survey of 500 organizations, with some 4500 teams operating, only 10–20 percent consider team issues in their PAs. Similarly, 80 percent of their pay systems focus exclusively on individual performance.[47]

At Digital Equipment Corporation, in Colorado, using work groups has led to a more participatory PA system. Digital, like many companies, has been using participative work groups (or self-managed work teams) that include individual contributors and a management consultant. Not only do team members evaluate other team members' performances, but they interview prospective team members and management consultants.[48] Their partnership approach to PAs includes self-appraisals and ratings from all team members. A PA committee develops an extensive document outlining the job description and requirements, and this document sets the group's expectations for individual behavior.

Digital implements its PA using the following process:

1. The employee to be rated is contacted about thirty days before the PA is due. At this time, the ratee chooses a PA chair, usually an advocate of her/his work.

2. The PA chair selects the members of the PA committee, which is comprised of the PA chair, the employee-ratee, the management consultant, and two other coworkers in the group chosen at random.

3. The ratee sends mail to the team members outlining his/her accomplishments and training during the past year.

4. Team members provide input to the PA chair within the next two weeks, a copy of which is forwarded to the ratee.

5. The ratee writes her/his own PA document from the input received from the team and from the self rating. This document is sent to the committee for review.

6. The committee reviews the document for one week and then meets with the ratee. If the PA needs further revision then another meeting is scheduled. If not, a final appraisal is determined based upon the document and the committee jointly sets the goals for the next year.

7. Finally, the PA chair writes a summary of the meeting and attaches the rating and any promotion. The completed document is printed and signed by the entire PA committee. This is forwarded to the personnel department.[49]

While all team appraisal approaches do not have to be as elaborate as this one, team reviews should be considered as a possible improvement at many workplaces. Extensive research has shown that peers and co-workers are more reliable and more valid judges of merit and promotability than are supervisors.[50] Some of the advantages of using a multiple-rater approach are as follows: it reduces the judiciary ("playing God") role and improves the coaching role for supervisors; it exposes some of the rater's errors; it ensures procedural fairness; it standardizes the assessment method; and it increases employees' involvement in their own performance and job.[51]

MONITORING EMPLOYEES ON THE JOB

In 1993 a survey of executives at 301 U.S. companies indicated that 22 percent occasionally used electronic means to monitor employees, usually to investigate suspicions about someone's performance.[52] A 1992 survey of New York employers found that 40 percent monitored their workers' computer keystrokes, using off-the-shelf software programs such as "Peek and Spy."[53]

Employee monitoring at work occurs in many ways. Video surveillance is used to discourage theft and other rules violations. Telephone surveillance of service representatives has been used for a long time to monitor the timing and content of customer contacts. Computer programs can monitor keystrokes to track employee performance, eavesdrop on employee electronic mail (e-mail), and record who accesses which databases at what times. Olivetti, the Italian computer company, has even developed an "active badge." Employees who wear the credit card–sized badge can be located by infrared technology wherever they happen to be in the building.[54] The congressional Office of Technology Assistance estimates that at least 400 million customer-related conversations a year are subject to supervised monitoring. More than 6 million clerical workers and video display terminal operators are also being tallied and electronically

evaluated with computer performance measurement programs.[55]

Many employees object to the increased use of the performance management technology of monitoring. In 1987 nurses at Silver Springs Holy Cross Hospital were "channel surfing" when they found their dressing room live on Channel 16. The hospital explained that the camera was there because of suspicious activity, but soon removed it.[56]

"Many of today's offices have become the equivalent of electronic sweatshops in which production standards constantly are being ratcheted up, and performance evaluations are based solely on meeting some numerical standard established by a computer," according to Illinois Senator Paul Simon.[57] The union 9 to 5 is fighting a syndrome it calls "**techno-stress**," which it says workers suffer from due to the noises of office machines, the blurring of the line between home and office due to modems and faxes, and the psychological pressure from monitoring.[58] Researchers are split on whether monitoring causes such stress. Some studies indicate that stress comes only when performance goals are unreasonable or if the employee is a low performer. Above-average performers even like being monitored.[59] Other research has shown that employee monitoring, if performed in an unbiased and uniform fashion, has a positive influence on employees' perceptions of the employer's fairness.[60]

Not all employee monitoring is high-tech. Forty-three Kmart employees sued the big retailer for spying on them away from work. Undercover investigators were hired to help control thefts, but by befriending employees, these investigators reported such information as off-duty drug use, where workers shopped, and the living arrangements of a female worker. An Illinois judge suggested that the complaint should be filed with the National Labor Relations Board, since this was the first Kmart store to become unionized, and organization by the Teamsters was going on at the time of the investigation.[61]

Employers are attracted to monitoring since technology makes such performance measurement possible and inexpensive. Elan Financial Services, a division of First Wisconsin National Bank, Milwaukee, uses keystroke monitoring as part of its PA system. Workers who do not measure up usually find another position in the organization; rarely are they fired.[62] Objective measures and other proofs gathered through monitoring may supply evidence for the employer to use in defending against the increasing number of wrongful discharge suits.

A speaker for the Communications Workers of America stated that the CWA mostly objects to secret monitoring;[63] employees should be told why monitoring is necessary, and should have a policy stating how monitoring will and will not be conducted. At Sears Teleparts and Service in Tucson, Arizona, employees sign a statement agreeing to be monitored when they are hired. Employees are taped on the telephone on one call every other month, and employee and trainer listen and evaluate the call together.[64]

Legislation to limit employee surveillance has been introduced, such as the "Privacy for Consumers and Workers Act" (HR1218),[65] and clearly this topic will be debated in the future. Meanwhile, video, computer, and telephone surveillance are likely to spread because such monitoring is currently legal, technology is improving, costs are dropping, and demand for such objective performance measurement is growing.

EFFECTIVE PA SYSTEMS

Organizations have traditionally used rating scales instead of job-related PA techniques such as MBO and critical incidents. They have also focused on evaluative rather than developmental objectives. During the 1960s and 1970s there was some movement toward developmental job-related forms, with the introduction of MBO and BARS systems. However,

during the 1980s employers shifted back to the traditional evaluative PA forms, particularly rating scales.[66] Organizations prefer quantitative approaches, and the consistency of using the same rating scales over time for all employees offers a sense of equity and predictability.

In the 1990s the trend has been to continue with instruments that are quantifiable. However, the increase in TQM-type programs has started a shift in philosophy regarding who should be evaluated. TQM programs may allow *individual assessment* of employees, but they are much more interested in a *systems* (or organizational) *assessment*. Effectively meshing this refocus into the PA systems of the future will be a challenge. Many ratings scales no longer measure personality traits, but instead try to measure specific performances, behaviors, and work outcomes. Monitoring technology also allows the use of the work standards approach in today's modern organization. The whole array of PA techniques can now be thought of as options to be included as part of a modern PA system.

PA systems are designed to do more than fulfill some evaluative and developmental objectives. More specifically, HR professionals want PA systems to be designed to (1) help determine merit pay increases and bonuses, (2) comply with the various employment laws, and (3) be easy to administer.[67] The most complete PA instrument can become a total failure if it is too long or too difficult to complete.

Design Input

HR Department Input   In creating or modifying a PA system, employment involvement has become the standard approach, a big change from the past. The traditional approach required the personnel department to write the PA instrument or to use an appropriate one from an HR or other management book or periodical. Employees who would be rated had little or no input into its selection or implementation. HR employees' professional association, the Society for Human Resource Management, (SHRM), reflected the conclusion of HR professional across the nation when it reported that fewer than 10 percent of 3500 companies surveyed felt that their current PA systems were reasonably successful.[68] Management was ready for a fresher approach. HR departments continue to be involved in the PA system, but they no longer dominate the entire process.

Task Team Approach   Technical Services Company, a midwestern professional services firm with 5000 employees worldwide, approached a total performance management system redesign by using employee involvement. TSC significantly improved the management and outcomes of employee performance, resulting in an improvement in the performance of the organization.[69] The company felt that its old, trait-based PA system was not being administered uniformly across its many locations. Worse, there was no link between individual performance objectives and companywide business goals. TSC started with an in-depth assessment followed by a redesign of the performance management system, with employee teams working on each step.

One of the many changes at TSC was a change from rating (or guessing at) the employee's traits to assessing work outcomes. For example, instead of rating a manager on a 1–5 scale on a trait like "leadership," the rater(s) would now respond to an outcome-based statement like this:[70]

> "*Directing:* Provides clear and timely instructions on specific assignments and responsibilities; is accessible to staff and allows ample time to answer questions; provides necessary guidance on other resources; reviews work on a timely basis; provides regular performance feedback to the project team."

Evaluation: _____

_____

The following are suggested steps to involve employees in a PA design or redesign project.[71]

Step 1. Group Formation   A cross-functional team should be assembled similar to the manner in which other *task groups* are chosen. Suggestions for group size range from a maximum of 12–25 employees. The charge to this team from management should be clear. For instance, what are the required outputs, deadlines, and responsibilities, if any, during implementation?

Step 2. Objectives and Concerns   Team members should discuss their own goals and the problems they would like the new PA system to overcome. Employee surveys, customer inputs, and inputs from other sources should be considered at this step. The team should generate a list of desired benefits of PA as well as concerns. It should develop general sections of the PA form that conform to the objectives members have identified. These sections will likely address employee feedback, employee development, work goals, and others.

Step 3. Dimensions of Performance   Next, the team should identify the dimensions of performance that need to be evaluated. Begin with brainstorming up to as many as fifty possibilities. Then trim the list by requiring that each dimension of performance be directly observable, behavioral, and job related. Dimensions that are subjective personality traits, such as "attitude" or "personality," should be eliminated. Working in subgroups, members should then write definitions of each of the final dimensions of performance. These dimensions and definitions will appear on the final PA instrument.

If a rating scale is going to be written, the team must write the statements or questions. Kate Ludeman, president of Worth Training Company in Portoloa Valley, California, has developed software ("M-Prove") to assist in developing PA systems. She also suggests a low-tech approach to writing a PA questionnaire.

Once the dimensions have been identified, Ludeman suggests that the team (assisted by a consultant) write many possible questions on brightly colored cards—using a different color for each dimension. The cards should be *storyboarded,* or taped to the wall in related groups. This step may lead to new dimensions and questions. Team members then walk around the wall and post colored dots on each question that they think should be included. The favored questions will become obvious and can be cleaned up for use in the final questionnaire.[72]

Step 4. Policies and Procedures Finally, the team should prepare guidelines for implementing the new PA system that support the objectives established in Step 2. The team must decide such issues as how often the forms will be completed, who will receive copies, how formal the process will be, and what appeals process will be available, if any. Meetings and training sessions must be discussed. Review and evaluation of the new PA system should also be addressed.

TQM or Systems Approach W. Edwards Deming, the "father" of TQM, lists performance appraisals as one of the "seven deadly diseases" of U.S. management practices. Deming argues that PAs should be completely abandoned. TQM advocates contend that the PA is actually a harmful device because it misdirects managerial attention.[73] Their argument is that PA systems are attempts by management to place blame for poor organizational performance on lower-level, front-line employees. They contend that this is a critical error because TQM should be focused on *system factors* instead of *person factors* of performance.

TQM is founded on the philosophy that quality products are a function of the system in which they are produced. System variables can include anything that influences the final product or service. Availability of raw materials and supplies, the leadership style of supervisors, the culture of the organization, and the efficiency of the manufacturing line are all system variables. TQM should promote a **systems assessment** and should minimize the individual differences between employees that are the focus of traditional PAs.[74]

Many modern organizations are trying to straddle the TQM versus traditional PA argument. While companies have shifted to the continuous improvement and total quality responsibility tenets of TQM, they have sabotaged the success of their TQM programs by continuing their anti-TQM appraisal programs, according to TQM purists. While TQM programs are quick to examine how pay systems should be redesigned, the same programs often overlook appraisals.

One HR vice president described this situation. "We didn't figure this one out until it was time to do the reviews [PAs]. Julie walked out and put a stack of [PAs] on my desk—and I had no supervisors to give them to."[75] After committing to a TQM-team concept, the employer had neglected to reexamine the appraisal system, which apparently had a life of its own. This company, like many modern firms, was faced with the question of who or what to rate. Should employers appraise the entire system or each team within the system? Should they continue to appraise individuals or should they use some combination? A group that advocates trying to get the most out of PAs and TQM systems has the following recommendations:

1. Raters need to be trained in person *and* system factors.

2. Performance ratings should be collected from multiple perspectives and multiple raters.

3. PA interviews should focus on potential barriers (system and person) to individual improvement.

4. Differentiation between employees should be minimized rather than highlighted.

5. The PA system should be aimed at group-based rather than individual-based evaluation.

6. The performance measures should be tailored to the specific needs of the particular organization.[76]

Training Appraisers

Modern Approaches   There is a disagreement about whether effective appraising flows from the appraiser's trained *skill* or natural *ability*.[77] In some ways, this is similar to the continuing argument about whether selection for hiring is a skill or an ability. However, the function of PA involves much more fine tuning than the gross categorization of applicants performed when hiring. For this and other reasons, there is general agreement that training will improve the performance of the rater. Clearly, every rater needs information about the PA system used, the forms and ratings, and the legal issues involved in the PA process. This is especially true for the many employers who are modifying or beginning a formal PA process.

Appraisal processes and techniques are often included in training programs for new supervisors. One-day training seminars sponsored by various personnel and management associations or schools of business are attended by large numbers of supervisors and middle managers. Topics normally included in appraisal training are as follows:

- The purposes of performance appraisal.
- How to avoid problems—halos, bias, central tendency, and so on.
- How to conduct nondiscriminatory appraisals.
- The ethics of appraisals.
- How to conduct effective appraisal interviews.

Raters should be able to eliminate many misunderstandings, and consistency between raters should increase if they receive training. Rater training must provide the knowledge, teach the skills used, and create the attitudes necessary for an effective PA system.[78] Sessions that present information to raters, workbooks, videotapes, and discussions between raters are the traditional training forms. Practice exercises, cases, and role playing can give raters additional insight. Rater errors such as leniency, strictness, central tendency, and especially halo effects can be reduced through proper rater training.[79]

Impression Management   A topic that is often overlooked in training programs on PA systems is the strategy used by the employee-ratee to get a favorable rating. How often does a supervisor hold a PA meeting in which she details seven major performance problems she has observed only to have that subordinate say, *"You are right. I am tardy, sloppy, and unmotivated, and I intend to go on this way as long as I can keep my job!"* In this unrealistic example the subordinate is honest, does not care what the rater thinks, and lets her know it. In reality, employees care very much about what the supervisor and other raters think. For this reason, they disguise their shortcomings and dramatize their strengths— all to create a PA rating higher than their actual performance warrants.

When such employees are managing and disguising the impressions they make, they are engaged in **impression management**. By identifying the shrewd political tools employees use to bias their performance ratings, raters can protect themselves from making inaccurate ratings. The two general strategies employees use are demotion-preventive strategies and promotion-enhancing strategies.[80]

Demotion-preventive strategies seek to minimize responsibility for some negative event or are used to get out of trouble. They include (1) giving accounts or excuses ("I couldn't finish, I was sick"), (2) apologies, and (3) dissociation ("I was the only person on the team who saw the problem coming."). **Promotion-enhancing strategies** seek to gain credit or enhance the employee's viability. They include (1) entitlements ("Perhaps you remember my last suggestion? It's already saved us money!"), (2) enhancements ("Not only is my suggestion saving money, but morale has improved as well."), (3) obstacle disclosure ("I had to overcome reluctant co-workers and red tape to succeed."), and (4) association ("When I was talking with the marketing vice president about this . . .").[81]

Formal and Informal Methods

Many supervisors think about the appraisal process only annually or semiannually—whenever the HR department notifies them that an employee's anniversary date is approaching and the appraisal must be completed. Feeling greatly relieved on completing the mandatory appraisal, some supervisors do not tackle the often painful subject of performance until it is time to complete another appraisal form. This mechanical approach to appraisal may facilitate decision making about pay increases, but it neglects the fact that performance feedback for developmental purposes is a continuous responsibility of supervision. Regular informal appraisal sessions let employees know how they are doing and how they can improve their performances. Good work should not go unnoticed, and frequent supervisory recognition is an important technique for sustaining high levels of employee motivation.

Appraisal System Evaluation

An organization's PA program is generally created and implemented to meet both evaluative and developmental objectives. Many organizations fail to assess periodically whether those objectives are being achieved. Often appraisal programs are set in motion and left to function—sometimes dismally—without a thorough examination of their effectiveness. In extreme cases, ill-conceived and poorly implemented appraisal programs may contribute to negative feelings between employees and management, perceptions of unfairness, hindered career development, and discriminatory (and illegal) employment practices. The periodic evaluation of the organization's PA program indicates good management and makes good sense.

How can an appraisal system be evaluated? One company with approximately 20,000 employees followed these procedures:

- *Interviews* Managers from various departments were interviewed. Discussions focused on strengths and weaknesses of the present system and on recommendations for improving the system.

- *Analysis of employees' records* A random sample of almost 200 PA forms was selected to uncover possible discrimination. The forms were also examined to spot rater errors such as central tendency, leniency, and the halo effect.

- *Analysis of the relationship between the employees and their ratings.* Employee ratings were correlated with certain personal and work factors (such as age, tenure, and race). Employees were asked whether appraisal results were discussed with them.

- *Analysis of PA systems in comparable settings.* The organization's appraisal was compared to the systems used by thirty-nine similar organizations.

One method of evaluating the appraisal system is for upper management to review the appraisals conducted by lower-level managers. Providing feedback to managers about the quality of their performance appraisals has several advantages. It is relatively easy and inexpensive. And because managers are aware that their performance as appraisers will be evaluated, there is a tendency to reduce errors of leniency, strictness, and central tendency. Most important, when managers are shown the ratings of other managers, the leniency error can be significantly reduced in their own ratings. Without such information, managers may not know how lenient or strict they are as raters.[82]

THE APPRAISAL INTERVIEW

One of the final—and most important—steps of the PA process is discussing the appraisal with the employee. Performance-related feedback has been described as one of the most important methods for enhancing employee development and improving individual performance.[83] Most PA administrators require that these interviews take place to provide performance feedback for employees. Thus, employees learn where they stand in the eyes of the organization, and are coached and counseled about how performance may be improved.

Both parties generally perceive the appraisal interview as a stressful event. Even well-constructed, job-related appraisal forms can only reduce what is inherently a stressful process. Important to the success of the interview—that it affect the employee's future behavior—is the supervisor's behavior during the interview. Subordinates carefully evaluate each supervisor's behavior, including oral and written communication, as an index of their own ability and future with the organization.[84] The supervisor seldom has any more enthusiasm for the PA process than the employee. The interview, the most important element of the whole process, sometimes is more effective if the evaluative and developmental aspects are separated. If this is done, the employee feels evaluated fairly on past performance before the focus shifts to specific areas for improvement.[85]

There are three types of information that supervisor-raters generally try to relay in PA interviews: (1) performance improvement feedback, (2) corporate goal feedback, and (3) salary information. Practitioners and researchers argue about whether the "split roles" approach (separating discussions of performance feedback and salary) is helpful or harmful. Some recent research indicates that including salary discussions *helps* the PA interview since it strengthens the motivational utility of performance and enhances employee satisfaction with the interview.[86]

PQ Corporation, mentioned earlier, refers to these interviews as *performance improvement discussions (PIDs)*. These PIDs become central to their TQM approach. Breaking with tradition, during the PID the supervisor acts as a coach and counselor, not as a judge or evaluator.[87] This is the approach that many U.S. employers are attempting to implement in the 1990s.

Problems with the Appraisal Interview

The appraisal interview is a very troublesome and difficult obligation for many managers. Some managers devise ways to avoid the interview even though it may be required by company policy. In other cases, the interview is glossed over or conducted in a mechanical fashion; its value is then highly suspect.

A recent study found that supervisors avoid performing formal PAs for a complex set of reasons. The study identified five *situational* variables that contributed to supervisors' failure to rate subordinates. If the subordinate had worked for the current supervisor for only a short time, if the subordinate had little job experience, if there was little trust between the supervisor and the subordinate, if the supervisor does not initiate a lot of structure for the subordinate, and/or if the subordinate had little confidence in the appraisal system, the supervisor was more likely to avoid performing the appraisal.[88] There are at least four *psychological* variables that are also important to address.

Playing God   In a classic 1957 article, behavioral scientist Douglas McGregor pointed out that many managers who view the appraisal as playing God are uncomfortable in simultaneously playing helper and judge. According to McGregor:[89]

> The modern emphasis upon the manager as a leader who strives to help his subordinates achieve both their own and the company's objectives is hardly consistent with the judicial role demanded by most appraisal plans. If the manager must put on his judicial hat occasionally, he does it reluctantly and with understandable qualms. Under such conditions it is unlikely that the subordinate will be happier with the results than will be the boss. It will not be surprising, either, if he fails to recognize that he has been told where he stands.

The solution to this fear may be found in system and psychological modification. One observer suggests: "Make the manager and employee equals in the appraisal meeting, to eliminate the parent/child relationship. If we don't want employees to act like children, we shouldn't act like parents."[90]

Inability to Give Criticism   Many supervisors have difficulty giving criticism constructively, and many employees have difficulty accepting criticism even though it may be given with sensitivity and diplomacy. One important study showed that defensiveness and poor performance can result from criticism given during the appraisal interview. Further, about half of all employees become defensive when criticized, and a majority of employees feel they performed more favorably than their supervisors' assessments indicate.[91]

Personality Biases   During the appraisal interview, the focus should be on performance and achievement of the goals and objectives, duties, and responsibilities that constitute the employee's job. Some supervisors assume the role of amateur psychologist and attempt to bring about personality changes that may improve job performance. But such an approach is unwise, according to McGregor. In citing the advantages of the objective-oriented appraisal process, whereby the supervisor and subordinate set performance targets, McGregor states:[92]

> Consider a subordinate who is hostile, short-tempered, uncooperative, insecure. The superior may not make any psychological diagnosis. The target setting approach naturally directs the subordinate's attention to ways and means of obtaining better interdepartmental collaboration, reducing complaints, winning the confidence of (his/her employees). Rather than facing the troublesome prospect of forcing his own psychological diagnosis on the subordinate, the superior can, for example, help the individual plan ways of getting "feedback" concerning the impact on his/her associates and subordinates as a basis for self-appraisal and self-improvement.

Inability to Give Effective Feedback   For the appraisal interview to be a truly developmental process, the employee must receive some specific feedback on areas in need of improvement. All too often, supervisors cloak criticism in vague, subjective terms and phrases. Some examples:

- "Your communication skills need improving."
- "Your absenteeism rate is too high."
- "Your output has not been up to par lately."
- "You need to dress a little more conservatively."
- "You need to change your attitude."

Comments such as these provide little basis for positive behavior change; supervisors are responsible for making their expectations clear to employees. For example, do not say, "Your absenteeism rate is too high." It would be much more constructive to state, "You have accumulated six unexcused absences in the past three months and we expect no more than one unexcused absence per month. Can you suggest ways you may be able to achieve this standard in the future?"

Interview Format

The various problems associated with interviews may be minimized by following a planned, standardized approach. Although the precise interview format will vary to some extent from employee to employee, these five steps should be generally covered:

1. *Prepare for the Interview* Preparation is important in a successful appraisal interview. During preparation, the supervisor (or other rater) should gather and review all relevant performance records. These normally include all data regarding work output and quality, absenteeism and tardiness, and so on. For supervisors using an objective-oriented PA system, all performance goals should be reviewed to determine which were met and which were not. The supervisor must be able to support the appraisal with facts. The supervisor may then want to make note of the specific items to be discussed during the interview. Finally, preparation includes setting a date for the appraisal interview that gives the employee lead time to prepare for the interview and develop a list of items to discuss.

2. *State the Purpose of the Interview* The employee should be told if the interview will cover compensation and staffing decisions (merit increase, promotion, transfer, etc.), employee development, or both. Some managers, however, avoid mixing compensation and staffing decisions with employee development issues in the same appraisal interview, contending that this would be "mixing apples and oranges." For example, it may be very difficult to motivate an employee to under-take new responsibilities if he has just been told he is not receiving a salary increase because of the employers' inability to pay due to its poor financial condition.

3. *Indicate Specific Areas of Good Performance and Areas That Need Improvement* Supervisors generally begin the discussion of performance by highlighting areas of good performance. Appreciation and recognition for good work are important parts of the appraisal interview. Areas of performance in need of improvement are discussed next. Again, supervisors must be as specific as possible about performance needing improvement and avoid straying onto personality issues. The focus must remain on job performance.

4. *Invite Participation* In a 1992 broad survey of companies, only 38 percent of employees said that their managers do a good job of seeking their opinions and suggestions. Also, only 29 percent said that their managers do a good job of acting on their suggestions. Worse, both of these percentages have declined since the same study was done in 1989. Perhaps the most serious comment was that only 18 percent of employees felt that their suggestions were not being ignored.[93]

Throughout the appraisal interview, employee should be invited to comment. This enables the employee to "let off steam" and tell why certain performance problems exist. It is also an opportune time to clear up any misunderstandings that may still exist about job expectations. When supervisors have done a good job of communicating job goals, objectives, and standards, employees should not receive any surprises during the interview.

5. *Focus on Development* The next step involves setting up the employee's development program. Employees are much more likely to be committed to develop-

mental programs if they agree with the supervisor that the program is necessary to improve job skills and abilities. Employees who feel that no performance problems exist or that a program of development is unnecessary to promote career goals will be uncommitted to development. Supervisors must clearly show their employees how development is related to job success.

Problem-Solving Interviews

In many cases, a developmental program involves various kinds of on- and away-from-the-job training, development programs, and exercises.

Throughout this chapter, we have emphasized that one of the primary purposes of the PA is to enhance employee development. Most managers and administrators agree that a well-planned and implemented appraisal system can contribute enormously to employees' growth and enhance skills. According to many HR professionals, the **problem-solving interview** lies at the core of the employee development process. To conduct a problem-solving interview successfully, a supervisor must assume a certain role and possess certain attitudes and skills. Table 8-2 illustrates characteristics of the problem-solving method by comparing it to two other popular (but often ineffective) appraisal interviewing techniques.

Violence Related to the Appraisal

Have you ever feared that a PA could stir up a violent reaction?

When HR Vice President Larry Vonderharr arrived at work on the morning of September 14, 1989, the entryway to the office was blocked by security guards. A City of Louisville (Kentucky) SWAT team had just arrived. Workers were being evacuated from the building, jointly occupied by the Standard Gravure printing plant and the Louisville *Courier Jour-*

nal. Vonderharr and a policeman rounded the corner and heard a printing plant employee screaming that someone had been shot, and then saw first one body, and then another and another. There were bodies everywhere, including the now dead gunman.

Seven people had been killed and twelve wounded. The gunman, a printing plant employee, entered the general offices, went to the third floor, and opened fire on managers and fellow employees. In 1991, a survey by the Bureau of Labor Statistics of thirty-one states counted 769 workplace assaults. According to the National Institute for Occupational Safety and Health (NIOSH), 750 people die every year as a result of occupational homicides.

Many observers believe that mergers and the downsizing of work forces place stress on employees that may lead to violence. In one case, John, a poor performer, had been receiving average ratings for years because his supervisor did not want to deal with his unsatisfactory performance. After a merger, the company culture changed. John received a PA that threw him into a panic. The appraisal was so sensitive that the supervisor and the HR manager both attended to lend some objectivity to the event. "He was very controlled but totally devastated by the criticism," said the HR manager. "He was told the people he had to work with found him intimidating."

"Perhaps they know I've been trained to kill," John said. Then he began to attack the supervisor verbally. The HR manager says, "We told him to take the review . . . and think about it, and that we would get him on an improvement program. We didn't specify any date by which his performance needed to improve, and we didn't make any threats."

"On Monday, he called . . . sobbing and hysterical . . . [by] Wednesday, I got a call from the local hospital claims department. He was in the psychiatric unit," the manager said. Though later released by his psychiatrist, he twice failed to show up at work. John later called the HR manager and said, "I can't come

Table 8-2 Characteristics of Three Interviewing Techniques

Characteristic	Tell and Sell	Tell and Listen	Problem-Solving
Objectives	Communicate evaluation Persuade employee to improve	Communicate evaluation Release defensive feelings	Stimulate growth and development in employee
Psychological Assumptions	Employee desires to correct weaknesses if known Any person who desired to do so can improve A superior is qualified to evaluate a subordinate	People will change if defensive feelings are removed	Growth can occur without correcting faults Discussing job problems leads to improved performance
Role of Interviewer	Judge	Judge	Helper
Attitude of Interviewer	People profit from criticism and appreciate help	One can respect the feelings of others if one understands them	Discussion develops new ideas and mutual interests
Skills of Interviewer	Sales ability Patience	Listening and reflecting feelings Summarizing	Listening and reflecting feelings Reflecting ideas Using exploratory questions Summarizing
Reactions of Employee	Suppresses defensive behavior	Expresses defensive behavior Feel accepted	Problem-solving behavior
Employee's Motivation for Change	Use of positive or negative incentives of both Extrinsic: motivation is added to the job	Resistance to change reduced Positive incentive Extrinsic and some intrinsic motivation	Increased freedom Increased responsibility Intrinsic: motivation is inherent in the task
Possible Gains	Success most probable when employee respects interviewer	Develops favorable attitude toward superior, which increases probability of success	Almost assured of improvement in some respect
Risks of Interviewer	Loss of loyalty Inhibition of independent judgment Creates face-saving scenes	Need for change may not be developed	Employee may lack ideas Change may be other than what superior had in mind
Probable Results	Perpetuates existing practices and values	Permits interviewer to change views in light of employee's responses Some upward communication	Both learn, because experience and views are pooled. Change is facilitated

SOURCE: Reprinted from Norman R. F. Maier, *The Appraisal Interview: Three Basic Approaches*. San Diego, CA: University Associates, 1976. Used by permission.

to work because I wouldn't be able to back down from those people; I'd have to hurt somebody."[94]

What can management expect to do to handle violence that can be set off during or after a PA interview? See *HR in the News:* "When Violence Hits Business" for some suggestions.

INTERNATIONAL HR: PERFORMANCE APPRAISAL

In U.S. organizations, PA is a fundamental management tool that can be useful as a basis for such functions as these:

When Violence Hits Business

"We have to react to and deal with the loss that employees feel when they are confronted with great change. It's never one event that pushes someone over the edge; it's a series of things. We can't make things the way they were, but we can help employees to be happier and more comfortable with the way things are." This quote from the HR manager at John's workplace is a challenge to the HR professionals and managers in our 1990s workplace.

Several approaches can be suggested to deal with tough situations similar to John's case.

- *Think about change and how to survive it.* Layoffs, terminations, mergers, and acquisitions are the cause of new performance demands and added stress, according to Jim Francek, whose company, Francek and Associates in Norwalk, Connecticut, has consulted with many companies on the brink of radical change. Francek says that 80 percent of mergers eventually fail because companies do not handle the emotional needs of employees well. "You need to let employees verbalize their concerns and listen—really listen," says Jon Christensen, associate director of the Center for Employee Assistance in Racine, Wisconsin. Christensen recommends that the CEO meet with workers and tell them what is really going on. He believes that an outside employee assistance program (EAP) can be helpful. "Impartial third parties can bring people together and let them ventilate." Beneath the anger, people are frightened and confused.

- *Prevent the stress syndrome.* After an incidence of violence, employees become frightened and may not want to come back to work. Jim Martin, an EAP professional with the Detroit Fire Department, does critical incident debriefing. About forty-six hours after a violent event, he gathers together those who witnessed the incident to talk about their reactions. For those directly involved in the incident, Martin uses a seven-phase process.

- *Develop policies and procedures.* "Every employer should have policies and procedures to address the possibility of employee violence," says Joseph Kinney, executive director of the National Safe Workplace Institute in Chicago. Kinney suggests a "threat assessment team" to manage existing threats and to review policies and programs. Unfortunately, no clear personality or psychological profile of a disaffected employee who is likely to commit violence emerges from what is know about employee violence. So Kinney urges HR professionals to focus on two issues: first, encouraging employees to get the mental health services they require, and second, working to ensure that downsizings and layoffs are handled appropriately.[95] Proper handling of PAs can be key.

- Making administrative decisions regarding personnel actions (e.g., promotions and transfers, and support for taking disciplinary actions or terminations).

- Providing feedback to employees regarding their performance.

- Coaching employees in improving areas of weakness and building upon their areas of strength.

The value of PA can be further increased by linking it to other basic management tools such as performance planning, ongoing performance monitoring, and employee development. Overall, the PA process helps to clarify performance expectations, provide a framework for progress reviews, and identify developmental needs. It would be correct to conclude that for most U.S. employees, PA is an inherently natural management practice— even when it is not well done.

This conclusion may not hold for the manager working in Latin America, the Middle East, or any number of non-Western countries.

Asian companies, for example, use a variety of PA methods much like those used in the United States. In Taiwan and Japan, MBO is often used for evaluating managers. A variation of the critical-incidents method is used for employees in a Chinese company. But in none of these examples is the PA used as evidence for promotion and merit pay decisions. Seniority (time on the job) is considered the most important determinant when it comes to these decisions.[96]

When evaluating employees of the host country, the process can be extremely frustrating to someone who is not familiar with the local culture's expectations for the roles of boss and subordinate. Different cultures have their own ideas and beliefs about work and even about what the culture defines as incompetent, mediocre, and excellent work performance. In the United States it is performance that counts. In Islamic countries, for example, it may be the subordinate's personality and social behavior—not job performance—that matter.[97]

CONCLUSIONS AND APPLICATIONS

- Employees generally dislike and fear PA, and even supervisors find the process stressful. Employees tend to be satisfied with the process if the appraisal interview is constructive and if the chosen method is job related and provides specific direction for future performance.

- The PA process generally has two goals: (1) the evaluation of employees' past performance for salary and selection decisions and (2) the improvement of future performance as a part of career development. The evaluative objective tends to dominate specific organizational uses of appraisal information.

- To pass scrutiny by the EEOC and the courts, the appraisal process should contain certain features. A standardized process should evaluate all employees in a consistent manner. Job analysis should be used in the content development to ensure job relatedness. Supervisors should be trained in the process and should provide employees with direct written feedback from the process.

- Certain rater errors, such as supervisor bias, halo effect, or recency, can only be minimized; others, such as leniency or central tendency, can be eliminated. But forms that eliminate these problems generally contain their own problems. Each appraisal method has unique advantages and disadvantages, but rating scales continue to be used most often by HR managers.

- The appraisal interview is the most important element in the PA process. Supervisors who dislike "playing God" find it hard to act simultaneously as judge and friend. Supervisors need to be trained for and give adequate attention to the appraisal interview. Employee preparation can also help them to provide useful input into the discussion, as well as to be psychologically prepared for any possible negative feedback.

- Organizations can benefit by periodically evaluating their appraisal program. The HR department can provide feedback to supervisors about the quality of their appraisals and check for rater problems, such as the halo effect or leniency. Multiple raters—such as peers, subordinate customers, and team ratings—may be used as information added to supervisors' ratings.

CASE STUDY

Bordon Electric Company

Helen Horn joined the Bordon Electric Company eight months ago as director of human resources. Bordon Electric is a small regional public utility serving 50,000 customers in three communities and the surrounding rural area. Electricity is generated at a central plant, but each community has a substation and its own work crew. The total labor force at the central plant and three substations, exclusive of administrative and clerical personnel, numbers 280 people.

Horn designed and introduced a Performance Evaluation and Review System (PERS) shortly after joining Bordon. This system was based on a similar system she had developed and administered in her prior position with a small company. She thought that the system had worked well and that it could be easily adapted for use at Bordon.

The purpose of PERS, as conceived by Horn, is to provide a positive feedback system for appraising employees that would be uniform for each class of employees. Thus, the system would indicate to employees how they were performing on the job and help them correct any shortcomings. The plant supervisors and field supervisors are responsible for administering the system for the plant workers and the substation crew workers, respectively. The general supervisors are responsible for the plant/field supervisors. Employees get personal PERS reports monthly informing them of their current status, and there is a review and an appraisal every six months.

PERS is based on a point system in an attempt to make it uniform for all workers. There are eight categories for evaluation, with a maximum number of points for each category and a total of 100 points for the system. The eight categories for the plant and crew workers, and the maximum number of points in each category, are as follows:

Categories	Points
1. **Quality of work** Points are deducted if the job must be redone within forty-eight hours of completion.	15

2. **Productivity**   15
   Points are deducted if the work was not completed within the time specified for the type of job.

3. **Safety on the job**   15
   Points are deducted if the employee does not use safe work habits on the job to protect himself or herself and others.

4. **Neatness of work area or repair truck**   15
   Points are deducted if the work area or truck is not clean and neat.

5. **Cooperation with fellow workers**   10
   Points are deducted if an employee does not work well with others.

6. **Courtesy on the job and with the public**   10
   Points are deducted if an employee is rude and unpleasant when there is contact with the public.

7. **Appearance**   10
   Points are deducted if an employee does not wear standard work clothing or if the clothing is sloppy and dirty at the beginning of each day.

8. **Tardiness/excess absenteeism**   10
   Points are deducted if an employee arrives late or is absent for causes other than illness or death in the immediate family.

Total Points   100

The list of categories used to evaluate the plant/field supervisors is slightly different.

Each employee begins the year with 100 points. If an infraction in any of the categories is observed, 1 to 5 penalty points can be assessed for each infraction. Notification is given to the employee indicating the infraction and the points to be deducted. A worker who is assessed 25 points in any one month or loses all the points in any category in one month is subject to immediate review. Similarly, anytime an employee drops below 40 points, a review is scheduled. The general supervisor meets with the employee and the employee's plant/field supervisor at this review.

If an employee has no infractions during the month, up to 12 points can be restored to the employee's point total—2 points each for categories 1 to 4 and 1 point each for categories 5 to 8. However, at no time can a worker have more than the maximum allowed in each category or more than 100 points in total.

When Horn first introduced PERS to the general supervisors, they were not sure that they liked the system. Horn told them how well it had worked where she had used it before. Horn's enthusiasm for the system and her likable personality convinced the general supervisors that the system had merit.

There were a few isolated problems with the system in the first two months. However, Larry Cox, a crew worker, is very unhappy with the new system, as evidenced by his conversation with Bob Cambron, a fellow crew worker.

Cox: "Look at this notice of infraction—I have lost 22 points! Can you believe that?"

Cambron: "How did your supervisor get you for that many points in such a short time?"

Cox: "It's all related to that bad storm we had two weeks ago. He disagreed with me on the work at Del Park and Madeline Court. It was dangerous, and I probably did fly off the handle. It was late at night after I had been working fifteen to sixteen hours straight. Look what he got me for: 5 points for lack of cooperation, 5 points for a dirty uniform, 5 points for a messy truck, including lunch bags and coffee cups in the cab, 4 points for slow work, and 3 points for being ten minutes late the next morning. Can you imagine that—being docked for ten minutes when I worked a double shift the day before? I didn't get home until 1:00 A.M. I even cleaned the truck up after he left that night—on my own time, no less!"

Cambron: "At least you won't get reviewed."

Cox: "Sure, but I bet he planned it to come out less than 25 points."

Cambron: "Boy, we worked ourselves to a frazzle that night and the next two days. You know, one of the guys over in substation 3 told me that his supervisor adds back points to their PERS reports over and above the normal monthly allowances."

Cox: "Well, don't that tell you what a screwy deal this whole PERS system is?"

DISCUSSION QUESTIONS

1. Without regard to Larry Cox's recent experience with the system, evaluate the PERS in terms of its

    a. Design for a performance management and appraisal system.

    b. Value as a motivational device.

2. What problems might occur in the administration of the PERS system, and how might these administrative problems affect employee motivation? Explain your answer.

3. Could a similar PA system be set up to evaluate work crews on a team basis? How?

EXPERIENTIAL EXERCISES

1. Individual: It's Great to Be Loyal—But What Does It Mean?

PURPOSE

To recognize the difficulty of performing a valid PA using a trait-oriented form that includes vague and subjective personal traits.

THE TASK

Listed here are a number of traits taken from PA forms used in a variety of organizations.

A. Write a one-sentence definition for each trait that is related to performing a job. As an example, the first item, "initiative," has been completed. Your instructor may lead a discussion concerning your definitions in class.

1. Initiative: Seeks better ways to do the job without being asked.

2. Cooperation:

3. Judgment:

4. Sensitivity:

5. Effort:

6. Dependability:

7. Attitude:

8. Leadership:

9. Tact:

10. Loyalty:

B. Reword three of these traits in behavioral terms that may be used for a more objective appraisal.

2. Group: Reviewing the President of the United States

PURPOSE

To recognize how multiple raters may rate the same person differently, to experience the difficulty of rating someone whose performance you do not often observe directly, and to practice team appraisal using a rating form.

THE TASK

Return to Figure 8-3, the job and behavioral summary rating form.

1. Use the ten items listed under "Behavioral Factors," starting with "Education/experience," and rate the President of the United States. Remember, the president is a public servant and, therefore, works for us.

2. Form into small groups in class and attempt to reach a consensus on each of the ten rating items. Your goal is to come up with a team rating on which all team members can agree.

3. Each team should report its group rating, and your instructor should list each of the teams' ratings so that a comparison can be made. Discuss whether the teams rated the president similarly and why.

4. Discuss which of the ten items was most difficult to rate. Why did you have difficulty? Was it due to the rating form itself or to some other problem?

5. Discuss whether the rating form covered all of the important aspects of the president's job.

KEY TERMS AND CONCEPTS

Absolute standards methods
Annual review file or calendar
Behaviorally anchored rating scales (BARS)
Central tendency
Comparative methods
Critical incidents
Demotion-preventive strategies
Developmental objectives
Employee monitoring
Essay method
Evaluative objectives
Forced choice
Forced distribution
Graphic rating scale

Halo effects
Impression management
Internal customer
Leniency
Management by objectives (MBO)
Nongraphic rating scale
Overall ratings
Paired comparison
Peer review
Performance appraisal (PA)
Performance management
Problem-solving interview
Promotion-enhancing strategies
Ranking

Recency
Reverse appraisals
Self ratings
Strictness

Supervisory bias
Systems assessment
Techno-stress
Work standards

REVIEW QUESTIONS

1. What are the major purposes and general objectives of PA?

2. How are PA and performance management different?

3. What are the steps in the appraisal process?

4. Describe the major methods used in PA systems.

5. What are the major problems associated with many PA systems?

6. What can raters do to ensure that PA interviews are productive and helpful to both the employee and the organization?

7. Should employers monitor the performance of their employees secretly?

8. What is the best way to perform a PA on a work team or an autonomous work group?

9. What is the system appraisal that many TQM advocates prefer, and how is it different from standard PA programs?

DISCUSSION QUESTIONS

1. Think of two instructors you have had—one very good and one very poor. What specific behaviors distinguish the two instructors? If you were the dean who had to conduct performance appraisals for the instructors, what method would you use to gather performance data?

2. Write five MBO objectives for an individual selling computers at a computer "superstore." How would you weigh each objective in terms of the overall performance of the salesperson?

3. A number of organizations have subordinates rate the performance of their supervisor. What advantages do you see in doing this? What problems may occur?

4. Supervisors may ask employees to furnish a self-rating at the appraisal interview for discussion. What are the benefits and drawbacks of this procedure?

5. What method or methods would you use to appraise the performance of the following kinds of employees: keypunch operator, first-line supervisor in a manufacturing plant, professor of management, airline pilot, office clerk in large government office, and police officer?

6. When the process of evaluating employees is viewed as purely perfunctory, supervisors show little or no interest in completing the forms and conducting the interview. In some cases, the appraisal interview is not conducted. Why do these problems exist? What can be done to reduce them?

7. As an HR administrator who is developing a PA system for department store sales personnel, you have decided to implement the BARS method. Write three behavioral statements that illustrate good performance and three that describe poor or mediocre performance.

8. Should the government pass a law limiting the employer's right to monitor employees? If so, what specifically should such a law prohibit?

9. If a manufacturing employer decided to use multiple raters for PA instead of having only the supervisor perform all of the appraisal, what other raters might be most helpful? What if the employer was a retail store or the state government?

ENDNOTES

Chapter 8

1. Stephen Connock, "The Importance of 'Big Ideas' to HR Managers," *Personnel Management* 24 (June 1992): 25.

2. Cynthia Shanley, "Appraisal Systems Gauge Business, Employees," *Houston Post* (November 4, 1991): F11.

3. James G. Goodale, "Improving Performance Appraisal," *Business Quarterly* 57 (Autumn 1992): 65–66.

4. Ibid.

5. Roy W. Regel and Robert W. Hollmann, "Gauging Performance Objectively," *Personnel Administrator* 32, no. 6 (June 1987): 74–78.

6. Beverly L. Kaye, "Performance Appraisal and Career Development: A Shotgun Marriage," *Personnel* 61, no. 2 (March–April 1984): 57–66.

7. Guvenc Alpander, "Training First-Line Supervisors to Criticize Constructively," *Personnel Journal* 59 (March 1980): 216–21.

8. William L. Shanklin, *Six Timeless Marketing Blunders* (Lexington, MA: Lexington Books, 1989), p. 111.

9. Ibid., p. 112.

10. Tom Peters, "Prometheus Barely Unbound," *Academy of Management Executive* 4 (November 1990): 70–84.

11. "Masters of Innovation," *Business Week* (April 10, 1989): 58–63.

12. William Taylor, "The Business of Innovation: An Interview with Paul Cook," *Harvard Business Review* 68 (March–April 1990): 97–106.

13. For more on performance management techniques in innovative companies, see Ashok K. Gupta and Arvind Singhal, "Managing Human Resources for Innovation and Creativity," *Research Technology Management* 36 (May–June 1993): 41–48.

14. Harold Koontz, "Making Managerial Appraisal Effective," *California Management Review* (Winter 1972): 46–55.

15. "Making a Case for Accurate Appraisals," *Personnel Journal* 71 (November 1992): 116.

16. David I. Rosen, "Appraisals Can Make—or Break—Your Court Case," *Personnel Journal* 71 (November 1992): 113.

17. Ibid., p. 113.

18. Adapted from Rosen, 1992, pp. 113–18.

19. "Making a Case for Accurate Appraisals," p. 116.

20. Ibid.

21. Harry N. Turk, "Questions—and Answers," *Employment Relations Today* 20 (Spring 1993): 133–34.

22. Ibid., p. 134.

23. T. A. Rodman, "Make the Praise Equal the Raise," *Personnel Journal* 63, no. 11 (November 1984): 73–78.

24. P. Slovic, B. Fischoff, and S. Lichenstein, "Behavioral Decision Theory," *Annual Review of Psychology* 28 (1977): 1–39.

25. J. Holson and Frederick W. Gibson, "Capturing Supervisor Rating Policies: A Way to Improve Performance Appraisal Effectiveness," *Personnel Administrator* 29, no. 3 (March 1984): 59–68.

26. Stephen B. Wehrenberg, "Train Supervisors to Measure and Evaluate Performance," *Personnel Journal* 67, no. 2 (February 1988): 77–81.

27. *Brito v. Zia Co.*, 478 F.2d 1200 (10th. Cir. 1973).

28. Kevin J. Murphy, "Performance Measurement and Appraisal: Merck Tries to Motivate Managers to Do It Right," *Employment Relations Today* 20 (Spring 1993): 47.

29. G. Rosinger, L. B. Myers, G. W. Levy, M. Loar, S. A. Mohrman, and J. R. Stock, "Development of a Behaviorally Based Performance Appraisal System," *Personnel Psychology* 35, no. 1 (Spring 1982): 75–88.

30. Dallas de Fee, "Management by Objectives: When and How Does It Work?" *Personnel Journal* 56 (January 1977): 37–39.

31. Jack Bucalo, "Personnel Directors . . . What You Should Know Before Recommending MBO," *Personnel Journal* 56 (April 1977): 176–78.

32. Richard Steers, "Achievement Needs and MBO Goal-Setting," *Personnel Journal* 57 (January 1978): 26–28.

33. Mark McConkie, "A Clarification of the Goal Setting and Appraisal Processes in MBO," *Academy of Management Review* 4, no. 1 (1979): 29–40.

34. Scott H. Oppler, John P. Campbell, Elaine D. Pulakos, and Walter C. Borman, "Three Approaches to the Investigation of Subgroup Bias in

Performance Measurement: Review. Results and Conclusions," *Journal of Applied Psychology* 77 (1992): 201–17.

35. Dick Grote and Jim Wimberly, "Peer Review," *Training* 30 (March 1993): 51–52.

36. Ibid., p. 52.

37. Jeanne C. Poole, William F. Rathgeber III, and Stanley W. Silverman, "Paying for Performance in a TQM Environment," *HRMagazine* 38 (October 1993): 70.

38. Stephen Goldstein, "Some Grade Their Own Work," *The Washington (D.C.) Times* (February 2, 1990): B8.

39. Performance appraisal training packet written by Jim Way, Vice President of Administration, Marley Cooling Tower Co., Mission, KS, January 8, 1993. The appraisal instrument itself was developed by an employee task group.

40. Gerald L. Blakely, "The Effects of Performance Rating Discrepancies on Supervisors and Subordinates," *Organizational Behavior and Human Decision Processes* 54 (1993): 57–80.

41. Joyce E. Santora, "Rating the Boss at Chrysler," *Personnel Journal* 71 (May 1992): 38.

42. Ibid.

43. Joyce E. Santora, "How Chrysler Developed and Implemented Its Reverse-appraisal Program," *Personnel Journal* 71 (May 1992): 42.

44. Ibid.

45. Alex Rothenberg, "Vermont Firms Let Workers Review Bosses" (Barre-Montpeller, VT) *Times-Argus* (May 24, 1992): C7.

46. Ibid.

47. "Work Teams Have Their Work Cut Out for Them," *HR Focus* 70 (January 1993): 10.

48. Carol A. Norman and Robert A. Zawacki, "Team Appraisals—Team Approach," *Personnel Journal* 70 (September 1991): 101.

49. Ibid., pp. 101–02.

50. Mark Edwards, "Symbiotic Leadership: A Creative Partnership for Managing Organizational Effectiveness," *Business Horizons* 35 (May–June 1992): 30.

51. Ibid.

52. According to a Macworld survey, reported by Tom Abate, "More Firms Snooping On Workers," *San Francisco Examiner* (May 21, 1993): D14.

53. Kim Clark, "Who's Watching You?" *Baltimore Sun* (March 21, 1993): B5.

54. Mike Langberg, "High-tech Links to Office Will Reshape the Nature of Work," *San Jose Mercury News* (October 26, 1992): C6.

55. "Debate Is Brewing Over Employees' Right to Privacy," *HR Focus* 70 (February 1993): 1, 4.

56. Clark, "Who's Watching You?", p. B5.

57. "Debate Is Brewing Over Right to Privacy," p. 4.

58. Langberg, "High-tech Links," p. C6.

59. Clark, "Who's Watching You?", p. B6.

60. Brian P. Niehoff and Robert H. Moorman, "Justice As a Mediator of the Relationship Between Methods of Monitoring and Organizational Citizenship Behavior," *Academy of Management Journal* 36 (1993): 527–56.

61. David Dishneau, "Blue Light Spying: Kmart Undercover Security Prompts Worker's Lawsuit," (Charleston, West Virginia) *Gazette-Mail* (January 9, 1994): A1, A4.

62. Erik Gunn, "The Boss Has New Ways to Watch," *Milwaukee Journal* (September 23, 1990): G8.

63. Jennifer J. Laabs, "Surveillance: Tool or Trap?", *Personnel Journal* 71 (June 1992): 96.

64. Kathleen Allen "Firms Using Electronic Monitoring," *Tucson Citizen* (July 26, 1993): A6.

65. Laabs, "Surveillance," p. 96.

66. Robert L. Taylor and Robert A. Zawacki, "Trends in Performance Appraisal: Guidelines for Managers," *Personnel Administrator* 29, no. 3 (March 1984): 71–80.

67. Douglas B. Gehrman, "Beyond Today's Compensation and Performance Appraisal System," *Personnel Administrator* 29, no. 3 (March 1984): 21–33.

68. James G. Goodale, "Improving Performance Appraisal," *Business Quarterly* (Autumn 1992): 65.

69. Sandra O'Neal and Madonna Palladino, "Revamp Ineffective Performance Management," *Personnel Journal* 71 (February 1992): 93. "Technical Services Co." is a disguised name for a company that wished to remain anonymous.

70. Ibid., p. 98.

71. Steps 2, 3, and 4 are adapted

from Goodale, "Improving Performance Appraisal," pp. 65–70.

72. Kate Ludeman, "Upward Feedback Helps Managers Walk the Talk," *HRMagazine* 38 (May 1993): 88.

73. Kenneth P. Carson, Robert L. Cardy, and Gregory H. Dobbins, "Upgrade the Employee Evaluation Process," *HRMagazine* 37 (November 1992): 88.

74. Ibid.

75. John Case, "What the Experts Forgot to Mention," *Inc.* (September 1993): 76.

76. Carson et al., "Upgrade," pp. 89–92.

77. Many studies, unfortunately, have found little or no improvement in selection or PA "skills" as a result of training. This suggests that selection and rating are not based solely on skills that can be improved through traditional training. For a recent example where modern training had little or no effect see Danny L. Balfour, "Impact of Agency Investment in the Implementation of Performance Appraisal," *Public Personnel Management* 21 (Spring 1992): 1–15.

78. Donald Kirkpatrick, "Performance Appraisal: Your Questions Answered," *Training and Development Journal* 40 (1986): 68–71.

79. David E. Smith, "Training Programs for Performance Appraisal: A Review," *Academy of Management Review* 11, no. 1 (January 1986): 22–40.

80. Robert A. Giacalone, "Image Control: The Strategies of Impression Management," *Personnel* 67 (May 1989): 52–55.

81. Ibid.

82. Brian L. Davis and Michael K. Mount, "Design and Use of a Performance Appraisal Feedback System," *Personnel Administrator* 29, no. 3 (March 1983): 47–51.

83. Jane R. Goodson, Gail W. McGee, and Anson Seers, "Giving Appropriate Performance Feedback to Managers: An Empirical Test of Content and Outcomes," *The Journal of Business Communication* 29 (1992): 329.

84. R. H. Finn and P. A. Fontaine, "Performance Appraisal: Some Dynamics and Dilemmas," *Public Personnel Management* 13, no. 3 (Fall 1984): 335–43.

85. H. Kent Baker and Philip I. Morgan, "Two Goals in Every Performance Appraisal," *Personnel Journal* 63, no. 9 (September 1984): 74–78.

86. Goodson, et al., "Giving Appropriate Performance Feedback," p. 331.

87. Poole et al., "Paying for Performance," p. 72.

88. Yitzhak Fried, Robert B. Tiegs, and Alphonso R. Bellamy, "Personal and Interpersonal Predictors of Supervisors' Avoidance of Evaluating Subordinates," *Journal of Applied Psychology* 77 (1992): 462–68.

89. Douglas M. McGregor, "An Uneasy Look at Performance Appraisal," *Harvard Business Review* 35 (May–June 1957): 89–94.

90. Catherine Petrini, "In Practice," *Training and Development* 47 (July 1993): 13 (quoting Dave Lynn of Blessing/While, Inc.).

91. H. H. Meyer et al., "Split Roles in Performance Appraisal," *Harvard Business Review* 43 (January–February 1965): 127.

92. McGregor, "An Uneasy Look at Performance Appraisal," pp. 91–94.

93. Citing The Wyatt Company and The Hay Group in Ludeman, "Upward Feedback," p. 87.

94. The preceding account was adapted from Linda Thornburg, "When Violence Hits Business," *HRMagazine* (July 1993): 40–45, and this author's own memories of the events in Louisville, KY.

95. Ibid.

96. Stephen J. Carroll, "Asian HRM Philosophies and Systems: Can They Meet Our Changing HRM Needs?". In *Readings in Personnel and Human Resource Management*, ed. R. S. Schuler, S. A. Youngblood, and V. L. Huber (St. Paul, MN: West, 1988), p. 448.

97. Lennie Copeland and Lewis Griggs, *Going International* (New York: Random House, 1985), p. 135.

EMPLOYEE TRAINING AND MANAGEMENT DEVELOPMENT

CHAPTER OBJECTIVES

1. To identify the major purposes of training and development (T&D).

2. To recognize the differences and similarities between employee training and management development.

3. To identify the many on-the-job and away-from-the-job T&D techniques.

4. To learn the three phases of training and recognize the importance of each.

5. To identify the different needs for T&D within the modern organization.

6. To understand the principles of learning that apply to T&D programs at the workplace.

Approximately 50 million U.S. workers, representing 42 percent of the work force, need new or significantly expanded skills to keep up with the demands of their jobs. This includes new technology, management, customer service, and basic skills training.[1] Employee training, development, and education programs are big business in corporate America. Recent industry reports indicate that the larger U.S. companies (those with more than 100 employees) budgeted over $43 billion per year for formal training programs, and that approximately 40 million employees receive 1.2 billion hours of formal training each year.[2] Total spending in the United States on employee education is estimated at $200 billion annually, an amount greater than that spent on public education (primary through college). For example, AT&T and IBM each spend over $1 billion on employee training programs, a sum greater than the operating budget of Harvard University.[3]

As the opening *HR in the News* indicates, employee training and development (T&D) is seen as a key factor in meeting the employer's strategic, business, and operational goals. International competition, corporate reorganization, and technological advances, along with social and economic pressures, increase the importance of T&D in U.S. workplaces. HR professionals are not faced with the question of whether there should be training. Instead, the questions facing them (and other managers) are: which employees should be trained, in what area(s), by what method(s), by whom, when or how often, what outcomes should be expected, and what will be the cost?

TRAINING VERSUS DEVELOPMENT

Several terms are used to describe the various training approaches. Increasingly, *employee education* is used to describe basic skills training programs. Labor economists divide training programs into general and specific training programs. *General training* refers to training in which employees gain skills that can be used at most workplaces. Employee education involving basic skills would qualify as general training. For instance, learning how to improve reading and writing would benefit any employer for whom the individual might work. *Specific training* refers to training in which employees gain information and skills that are

Thriving on Chaos

What makes a good training program? In Tom Peters's best-seller, *Thriving on Chaos,* he claims that American investment in training is a "disgrace" and offers ten critical ingredients of successful training for the future.

1. *Focus extensive entry-level training on those skills that "overemphasize" the company's uniqueness.* Grocery-chain owner Stewart Leonard, for example, trains retail clerks in communication and courtesy skills, while most grocers focus their training on the mechanics of operating the cash register.

2. *Treat all employees as potential career employees.* Even in industries where high turnover is the norm, view all employees as career employees and train in the context of career development.

3. *Require regular retraining.* Force everyone into the classroom every year; constant skill broadening should be a goal for all employees.

4. *Spend time and money generously on training.* Give people time off for training regularly and provide generous tuition contributions. Recognize, however, that "throwing money at a problem is unfailingly stupid"; ensure that high-quality, effective training is offered.

5. *OJT is important.* Make sure managers are good coaches and evaluate them on their effectiveness as trainers.

6. *There is no limit to the skills that can be taught.* Many employers have learned that almost everyone can learn relatively complex subjects like statistical process control if the courses are well conceived.

7. *Consider training an important part of the company's strategic thrust.* The strategic planning process of many successful employers, including GE and Hewlett-Packard, has used training to spearhead strategic change.

8. *Emphasize training during a time of crisis.* Resist the normal temptation to cut the training budget during crises; rather, increase it!

9. *Training should be line-driven.* Line managers should be fully involved in planning training and teaching. Without this input, they'll feel little stake in the programs. Training personnel should be considered the experts in organizing training, but line managers should be viewed as the content leaders.

10. *Use training to teach organizational vision and values.* Training is a prime way to teach employees at all levels company values. Make sure top management is involved in training to help transmit the company vision.

tailored specifically to their own workplace. Specific training might involve learning how the specific company's budget system works. Since every firm has its own budget system, this training is directly helpful only to the current employer.

Traditionally, the simple terms **employee training** and **management development** have referred to very different approaches. In this chapter we will examine T&D in a more unified way, generally emphasizing what these approaches have in common. Today's flattening of organizational structures and the corresponding elimination of levels of middle management have blurred some of the traditional boundaries between management and nonmanagement personnel.

Historically, the term **training** has been used to designate the acquisition of technically oriented skills by nonmanagement personnel. The term **management development** has been normally associated with the methods and activities designed to enhance the skills of managers or future managers.

Training and management development have been seen as different in other ways. First, management development activities tend to focus on a broad range of skills, whereas training programs focus on a smaller number of technical skills. For example, a training program for printing press operators would be designed to enable operators to upgrade technical skills such as printing speed and accuracy. In contrast, a development program for printing managers would focus on a wide variety of interpersonal and managerial decision-making skills, such as planning, organizing, leading, communicating, motivating, and scheduling.

Second, management development is usually aimed at the long run, whereas training often concentrates on the short run. Developmental activities should take place continually throughout a manager's career and be an integral, ongoing part of the manager's job.

Traditional Managerial Skills

There is a large movement to redesign jobs that can be seen as an effort to empower employees and to bring the responsibility to the customer down to the lowest levels in the organization. This movement, along with the continuing conversion to team (rather than individual) approaches, is central to total quality management (TQM) concepts. In a sense, some skills of management now reside in employees traditionally considered nonmanagement. T&D programs now need to provide management development to these nonmanagerial employees.

However, many divisions still exist between management and nonmanagement at most workplaces. Other workplaces have made little or no attempt to use TQM concepts. Since there continues to be a narrowing division between these two types of responsibilities, it would be helpful to examine some of the traditional differences a little more closely. Each manager, regardless of the position in the hierarchy, uses a mix of technical, conceptual, and human-relations skills.[4] Figure 9-1 illustrates how the mix of these skills varies according to the level of the traditional management job.

Technical skills include knowledge of equipment, work methods, and work technologies. These skills are much more important for the traditional first-level managers than for middle- and top-level managers. First-level managers often conduct on-the-job training for employees and troubleshoot problems with the organization's technology. In addition, some first-level managers are "working supervisors" and on occasion perform their subordinates' jobs.

Conceptual skill is the ability to view the organization as a whole and to coordinate and integrate a wide array of organizational functions, activities, goals, and purposes. For example, the manager of a large manufacturing plant must integrate production, marketing,

FIGURE 9-1 A different mix of skills traditionally has been required at each level of management.

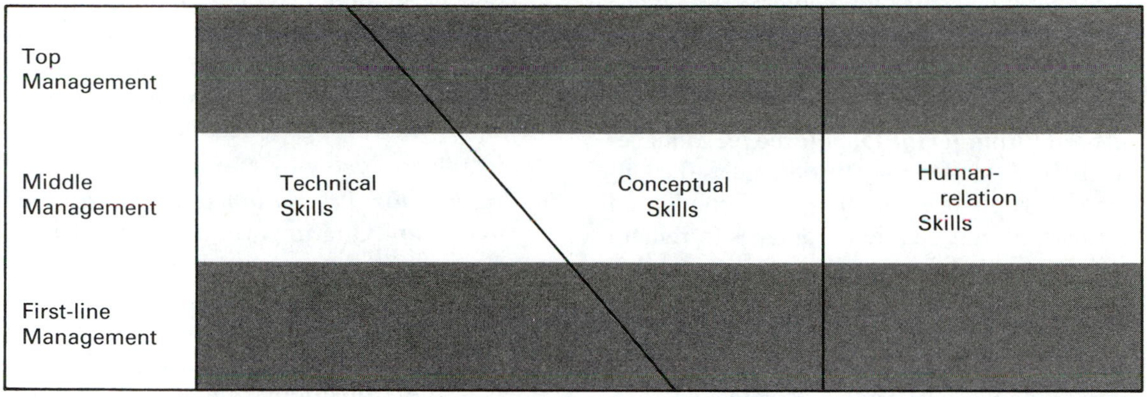

engineering, and financial functions and objectives so that departmental and organizational goals are achieved. The need for conceptual skills, or "vision," becomes increasingly critical as the employee progresses from first-level management to top management.

One popular definition of a manager is "one who accomplishes his or her work through others." In this sense, every manager is a leader, and **human-relations skills** are equally important for managers at all organizational levels. Important human-relations skills include the ability to communicate with employees, to establish strong interpersonal relations, and to build cooperative, satisfying relationships among work-group members.

Purposes of T&D

What are the general purposes of T&D programs for managerial and front-line employees? There are seven major purposes discussed below.

1. *Improve Performance* Employees who perform unsatisfactorily because of a deficiency in skills are prime candidates for training. Although training cannot solve all problems of ineffective performance, a sound T&D program is often instrumental in minimizing those problems.

Sometimes a new or newly promoted employee does not possess the skills and abilities required to be competent on the job. How does this happen? First, no selection device is able to predict success or failure all the time, and training is often necessary to fill the gap between the new employee's predicted and actual performance. Second, managers knowingly hire and promote employees who need training to perform at standard levels. When the number of job openings exceeds the number of applicants, management has little choice but to hire or promote an applicant with few or no job skills and to remedy that lack of skill through training. Third, many times management hires employees who possess the aptitude to learn and then trains them to perform specific tasks. For example, new hires in manufacturing are often given manual dexterity and motor coordination aptitude tests. Based on the results of these aptitude tests, the new workers may undergo company-provided training that may last for periods ranging from a few hours to several days.

2. *Update Employees' Skills* Managers in all areas must always be aware of technological advances that will make their organizations

function more effectively. Technological change means that jobs change. Employee skills must be updated through training so that technological advances are successfully integrated into the organization.

3. *Avoid Managerial Obsolescence* **Managerial obsolescence** may be defined as the failure to keep pace with new methods and processes that enable employees to remain effective. Rapidly changing technical, legal, and social environments have affected the way managers perform their jobs, and management personnel who fail to adapt to these changes become obsolete and ineffective.[5]

4. *Solve Organizational Problems* Managers are expected to attain high goals in spite of personal conflicts, vague policies and standards, scheduling delays, inventory shortages, high levels of absenteeism and turnover, union–management disputes, and a restrictive legal environment. Organizational problems are addressed in many ways. Training is one important way to solve many of those problems. T&D courses may concern human resources, marketing, accounting, finance, manufacturing, purchasing, information systems, and general management. Training personnel, universities, and T&D consultants assist employees in solving problems and performing their jobs more effectively.

5. *Orient New Employees* During the first few days on the job, new employees form their initial impressions of the organization and its managers. These impressions may range from very favorable to very unfavorable, and may influence their job satisfaction and productivity. Therefore, many administrators make an effort to orient new employees to the organization and the job.

   New employees may experience surprise or even shock when events do not conform to their expectations. As a result, they may seek information about organizational realities and their preconceived assumptions. Their immediate need is to reduce any uncertainty about the job and find out how to fit in socially. The orientation process can reduce the difficulties encountered by new employees through effective socialization programs.[6]

6. *Prepare for Promotion and Managerial Succession* One important way to attract, retain, and motivate personnel is through a systematic program of career development. Training enables an employee to acquire the skills needed for a promotion, and it eases the transition from the employee's present job to one involving greater responsibilities. Organizations that fail to provide such training often lose their most promising employees.

7. *Satisfy Personal Growth Needs* For instance, most managers and many front-line employees are achievement oriented and need to face new challenges on the job. T&D can play a dual role by providing activities that result in both greater organizational effectiveness and increased personal growth for all employees.

T&D Priorities Leading to the Twenty-First Century

While priorities change as new issues confront organizations, many observers believe that three issues are receiving the highest priority in the 1990s.

Quality improvement programs have been instituted in response to increasingly higher demands for quality from the customer and the need to be more competitive in a global economy. T&D in leadership, team building, goal setting, problem solving, decision making, and computer modeling is often part of a quality improvement (or TQM) program. Basic skills and other remedial training programs, as discussed in *HR in the News:* "Bridging the Skills Gap" have become a required prerequisite to

Bridging the Skills Gap

What is the gap between the large number of people looking for jobs and the jobs employers are trying to fill?

Skills, according to a recent National Association of Manufacturers (NAM) survey. The study, entitled "Today's Dilemma: Tomorrow's Competitive Edge," found that among the surveyed manufacturers:[7]

- 40% reported serious difficulties in upgrading their *production technology* due to their employees' lack of skills.
- 37% are having serious difficulties *reorganizing jobs* because their employees are having problems learning new skills.
- 25% cannot upgrade the *quality* of their products because their employees have trouble learning statistical process control or other such quality improvement techniques.
- 16% are even having trouble adding *new lines of business* due to such employee inadequacies.

Manufacturers are already short on truly skilled craft workers, and some are having trouble promoting to or hiring for even semiskilled operator jobs. In 1996, shortages are projected to be severe in the areas of technical and professional work.

What are the general skills employees lack? Following are the skill problems manufacturers are encountering with their current and prospective employees (most severe first):[8]

- Inability to adapt to the modern work environment.
- Poor basic reading and writing skills.
- Inadequate calculation and communication skills.

About one-fourth of manufacturers are offering remedial basic skills training to cure these skills problems. However, another one-fourth are simply lowering their promotional and hiring standards or trying to recruit outside their local areas.

Julie Nielsen, speaking for Tower Perrin (who compiled the NAM report), pointed out the irony for manufacturers: "Just as workers' skills are declining, demands from industry have increased due to upgraded technology."[9]

other quality programs due to the skill deficiencies found in the work force.[10]

Technological change–related programs will continue to challenge organizations into and beyond the next century. The rate of advancement of technology continues to accelerate, so employers must continue to offer T&D to keep front-line as well as managerial employees from obsolescence. This has been a training priority since the Industrial Revolution.

Customer service T&D programs are now a top priority for organizations that consider themselves service oriented, an ever-growing group. Financial, banking, insurance, and other such industries clearly have been placing increased emphasis on service to the customer as a possible competitive advantage in their industries. TQM programs in such industries focus on the responsibility that each employee has to the customer or client.[11]

A recent study comparing the priorities in the construction industry found a shift since the late 1980s. At the end of the decade, construction companies saw *leadership* and *supervisory skills* as the top skill priorities. By 1992 the priorities for skills had shifted to *project or team management, scheduling,* and *TQM,* along with leadership and supervisory skills. Further, two-thirds of all contractors felt that for each dollar they spend on managerial/supervisory training, they receive at least a 10 percent return. However, almost one-third of them had no formal T&D function.[12]

SYSTEMS APPROACH TO T&D

The thought of training often brings to mind a trainer, participants, and traditional training techniques: a film being shown, workbooks being completed, or a chalkboard-assisted lecture. But the actual process of training people is only a small part of the training process. Successful T&D involves considerable effort both before and after the trainer and trainees

are brought together. In other words, training is best thought of as a complex *system* that involves a number of distinct but highly interrelated phases.

A **training systems model** is shown in Figure 9-2. The three major phases of training are (1) assessment, (2) training and development, and (3) evaluation.

PHASE 1: NEEDS ASSESSMENT

The first step in the training systems model, needs assessment, may be conducted at three levels: organizational analysis, operations analysis, and person analysis.[13] Not all T&D situations require assessment at each level; however, organizations that face serious, widespread human performance problems would benefit from this approach.

Organizational Analysis

Organizational analysis involves analyzing organizationwide performance criteria (e.g., accidents and injuries, absenteeism, turnover, productivity, quality, labor and operating costs, sexual harassment charges, EEO lawsuits, etc.). The purpose of this analysis is to uncover major problem areas that may indicate a need for training.

Operations Analysis

The purpose of operations analysis, also called *task analysis,* is to determine *how* a job should be performed — the desired level of performance. Through operations analysis, data are collected that enable training personnel to create programs that focus on the right way to perform a job.

Person Analysis

Person analysis focuses on the individual employee and is used to identify employees for training. Specifically, the two purposes of person analysis are to determine (1) who currently needs T&D and (2) what skills, knowl-

FIGURE 9-2 A training systems model.

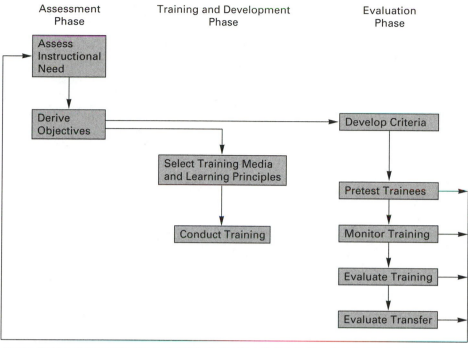

SOURCE: *Training: Program Development and Evaluation.* by I. Goldstein. Copyright © 1974 by Wadsworth Publishing Co. Inc. Reprinted by permission of Brooks/Cole Publishing Company, Pacific Grove, Calif. 93950.

edge, abilities, or attitudes need to be acquired or strengthened. Person analysis is important to ensure that employees who need training are the ones who actually receive it and that programs are designed to fill the gap between actual and desired performance, called the **performance gap**.

There are numerous ways to collect person analysis data. The more common techniques include requests from management, employee interviews, and the following:[14]

- *Advisory Committees* Advisory committees generally comprise various levels of management, and some organizations create multiple committees to represent the various functions, such as production and accounting. Committees often determine whether a particular problem is a T&D problem and establish training priorities. See Table 9-1 for a

comparison of advisory committees with other needs assessment methods.

- *Assessment Centers* Used mostly for management selection and development, the assessment center requires participants to undergo a series of exercises and tests to determine their strengths and weaknesses in performing managerial tasks. Although the assessment center is used primarily to predict success in a managerial role, its use in measuring other training needs is increasing.

- *Attitude Surveys* Attitude surveys are most effective in measuring the general level of job satisfaction, but the data gathered may show various areas where T&D needs exist.

- *Group Discussions* This method generally involves meeting with employees who represent a specific work area. A primary benefit of group discussions is that the employees

Table 9–1 A Comparison of the Various Methods of Needs Assessment Using the Five Selection Criteria

Methods	Criteria				
	Employee Involvement	Management Involvement	Time Required	Cost	Relevant Quantifiable Data
Advisory committees	Low	Moderate	Moderate	Low	Low
Assessment centers	High	Low	High	High	High
Attitude surveys	Moderate	Low	Moderate	Moderate	Low
Group discussions	High	Moderate	Moderate	Moderate	Moderate
Employee interviews	High	Low	High	High	Moderate
Exit interviews	Low	Low	Low	Low	Low
Management requests	Low	High	Low	Low	Low
Observations of behavior	Moderate	Low	High	High	Moderate
Performance appraisals	Moderate	High	Moderate	Low	High
Performance documents	Low	Moderate	Low	Low	High
Questionnaires, surveys, and inventories	High	High	Moderate	Moderate	High
Skills tests	High	Low	High	High	High

SOURCE: Reprinted from J. Newstrom and J. Lilyquist, "Selecting Needs Analysis Techniques," *Training and Development Journal* 33 (1979). Copyright 1979, The American Society for Training and Development. Reprinted with permission. All rights reserved.

are emotionally committed to the training as a result of active participation in the assessment process.

- *Questionnaires* Some organizations use questionnaires to identify T&D needs. The employees themselves are generally the respondents. The questionnaire usually specifies vital skill areas, the importance of the skill, and the employee's perception of training need for each area (see Figure 9-3). The cost of this technique is relatively low because a great deal of data may be collected in a relatively short time.

- *Skills Test* A test of necessary skills, such as typing, computer programming, or driving, may also be used to measure training needs. When using skills tests for needs assessment, it is critical that the tests be job related and

measure those skills and abilities required for successful job performance.

- *Observations of Behavior* Trainers or supervisors may directly observe employees' behavior to identify training needs. This method is generally limited to the assessment of technical skills and behaviors. Its primary drawback is that it is time-consuming and thus costly.

- *Performance Appraisals* A valid, job-related appraisal system will point out strengths and weaknesses in employee performance and may indicate T&D needs. Time and cost are low since the data are regularly gathered. And because both the employee and the supervisor are involved, an emotional commitment to training is often an additional benefit of this method.

FIGURE 9-3 An example of a questionnaire for identifying training needs.

POSITION: Clerical

Employee _____   Department _____

Supervisor _____   Date _____

INSTRUCTIONS

In column A, rate the skill necessary for the employee to perform the job. Use the following ratings: 1—very important; 2—moderately important; 3—not important.

In column B, rate the need for training for each skill area which received a rating of 1 or 2 in column A. In assessing training needs, use the following ratings: 1—no need for training; 2—moderate need for training; 3—immediate, critical need for training.

Skill	A How important is the skill?	B Employee's need for training
Ability to read and comprehend rough-draft material		
Typing speed		
Typing accuracy		
Proofreading skills		
Ability to use office machinery		
Filing skills		
Ability to compose letters and memos		
Oral communications		
Ability to organize daily routine		
Human relations skills		

- *Performance Documents* Most organizations regularly gather data on employee performance, such as productivity, absenteeism, accidents, and turnover. Such information is generally accurate and may be used to point out training needs. A major shortcoming of this approach is that the data simply indicate the existence of a problem and do little to specify its cause. Only a careful analysis will determine whether or not training will solve that problem.

- *Exit Interviews* A high turnover rate may spell organizational problems and a need for training, particularly in the area of supervision of employees. The validity of exit interviews greatly depends on an unbiased and skilled interviewer and on honest answers from the employee who is leaving.

The Special Case of T&D for Managers

Current T&D needs of managers can generally be addressed using the methods outlined earlier. Survey, interview, assessment center, and performance appraisal (PA) data are often used to calculate the current needs of managers. Since current T&D needs are often tied to current performance, the validity of the PA system is very important. HR professionals should be sure that the PA system used for managers contains portions aimed at managerial *development,* not just *evaluation.*

Long-range T&D needs of managers are linked to the HR and strategic planning of the organization. Assessing long-range development needs begins with a forecast of the demand for managers. The HR forecast in the medium-sized company, for example, may show that the size of the management team must increase by 10 percent per year for the next five years to satisfy its optimistic plans for business expansion. To a significant degree, the company's continued growth hinges on its ability to ensure a continual supply of competent managers. The organization may hire new managers from the external labor market. External recruitment may prevent stagnation by bringing fresh, innovative ideas to the company. In addition, recruitment from the outside lessens the need for strong internal management development and its associated operating expenses.

However, if the organization promotes from within, the promotion potential of current managers as well as managerial candidates must be determined. Strengths and weaknesses are closely examined to predict how managers will perform if promoted. During this assessment, managers with many skills and broad experience may be considered promotable without formal development. A certain percentage of managers may have "peaked" in their present jobs and thus may be deemed unpromotable. Others may be judged promotable but only after further preparation. For the last group of managers, an analysis must be made of the specific skills and abilities they will need in order to be successful after being promoted.

Management Succession Chart To assist in making that analysis, some organizations prepare an HR planning tool called a **management** or **executive succession chart.** Succession charts indicate successors for each position in the management hierarchy and often combine current performance data with a judgment of promotion potential. Although the primary focus of a succession chart is on an organization's current structure, the performance and promotion data on the chart are valuable for a growing company in determining promotions in the future. Figure 9-4 illustrates the information normally contained in a management succession chart.

The assessment of development needs—whether to improve current performance or to prepare employees for promotion—should result in a program of T&D approaches somewhat individualized for each manager. No two management jobs are exactly alike, nor is the performance of any two managers identical. An assessment of one plant supervisor may find weaknesses in counseling employees, conducting performance appraisals, and handling diversity issues. Another supervisor may be strong at counseling employees but weak in dealing with PAs, diversity issues, and motivation. The T&D effort should attempt to meet employees where they currently stand and address their individual needs.

Selecting Needs-Assessment Techniques

Several criteria may be used in selecting a needs-assessment method.[15] First, *employee involvement* is important because a feeling of participation in the assessment process enhances employee motivation to undergo T&D. Employee perceptions of a T&D program be-

FIGURE 9-4 A typical management succession chart.

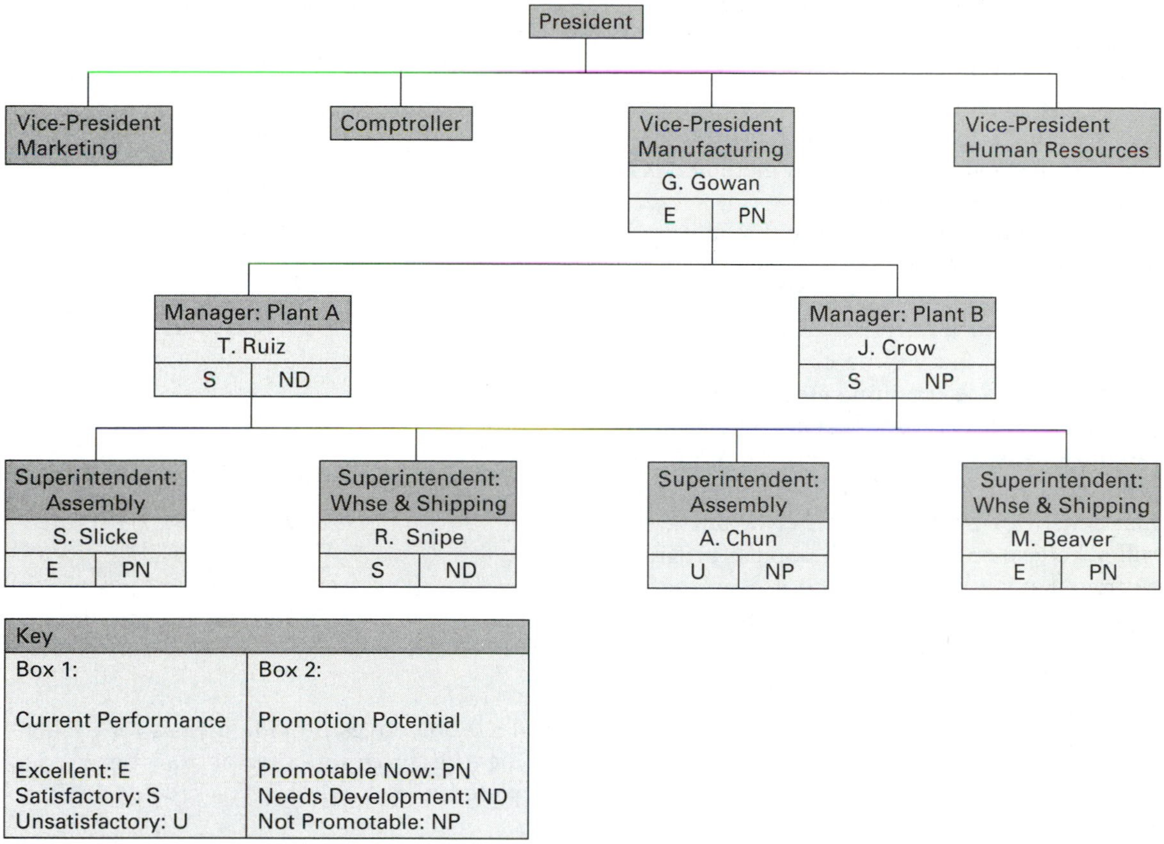

Key

Box 1:	Box 2:
Current Performance	Promotion Potential
Excellent: E	Promotable Now: PN
Satisfactory: S	Needs Development: ND
Unsatisfactory: U	Not Promotable: NP

fore it begins can affect the effectiveness of the training. Many variables are important in achieving training success. Providing a realistic preview of the T&D program can increase commitment to attend and learn. Other research indicates that when employees are given a choice of what training they will receive, they will be more motivated for the training program. However, there is a peril to participation. Employees indicating a choice, but not receiving their choice, have a lower motivational level in the training than those who are never asked about their choice at all.[16]

Second, *management involvement* is important because supervisors generally have accurate information about their employees'

performance and are in an excellent position to assess the need for training in the work group. Third, the *time required* is always important in considering any form of data collection, and needs assessment is no exception. And since time is generally a scarce commodity, trainers often favor methods that do not involve large investments in time. Fourth, the *cost* of the assessment method, in terms of personnel and materials involved, is an important consideration. Training budgets rarely allow the selection of training processes and activities without financial consideration. Fifth, the needs-assessment information must be *relevant* and *quantifiable*. Vague or subjective opinions about training needs will do little to generate the support from top management needed for a successful training program.

How do the various assessment methods measure up to the selection criteria? Table 9-1 shows how each method is evaluated using the five criteria. The table shows that there is no one best method, and that each method has its own strengths and weaknesses.

Finally, you should be aware that many employers perform no formal T&D needs assessment. Employers and some HR departments simply buy into a current fad in training and guess that that fad will be of use to their particular workplace. Training modules in personality (like Myers-Briggs), TQM, management by objectives (MBO), managerial grid, and other concepts have surely helped many organizations. However, many other organizations will purchase or mimic such popular programs without having first identified a need that requires a training intervention. After a workplace need has been identified, training objectives should be specified; only then should a particular program be located or developed. Otherwise, the firm may buy a T&D program that people may enjoy but that provides little objective benefit to the organization.

T&D Objectives

Following an assessment of training needs, **T&D objectives** should be written to reflect what the participant should be able to do on completion of training. T&D objectives indicate the kinds and levels of skills, knowledge, abilities, and attitudes the participant should possess after the program has been completed. Well-written objectives will benefit training in at least three important ways:

1. T&D objectives help determine which methods are appropriate by focusing on the areas of employee performance that need to change.

2. T&D objectives clarify what is to be expected of both the trainer and the participants.

Table 9-2 Three Sample T&D Objectives

Terminal Behavior	Condition	Minimal Achievement
To word process	Given a standard word processing operator's examination	Sixty words per minute, with an error rate no higher than 2 percent
To perform maintenance	Given a standard set of tools	Preventive maintenance on a lathe within thirty minutes according to company standard
To locate and correct errors	Given a business letter containing grammatical errors	Locate 95 percent of all errors after studying the letter for no more than five minutes

3. T&D objectives provide a basis for evaluating the program after it has been completed.

What are the qualities of good T&D objectives? A well-written T&D objective will have three parts: (1) a statement of outcome behavior, that is, what the employee will be able to do on completion of training; (2) a description of the conditions under which the outcome behavior is expected to occur; (3) a statement of the minimum level of achievement that will be accepted as evidence that the employee has accomplished what was required. Table 9-2 shows a few examples of what should be included in written T&D objectives.

PHASE 2: CONDUCTING T&D

After a needs assessment has identified a **performance gap** (the difference between desired and actual performance) or another specific set of developmental needs, and after particular objectives have been set that a T&D approach should accomplish, the organization is ready to seek or design a T&D program. The organization should be careful to select or design a T&D program that will yield verifiable results; otherwise, the large financial investment in training will not pay off. Employers should avoid choosing a popular or entertaining T&D program without having performed either an assessment study, or a reasonable search for a program. The expense of T&D programs should remind employers to use the same business standards for need substantiation and purchasing that they would demand for other business investments.

T&D techniques may be used while employees are either on the job or away from the job. The specific techniques will be briefly discussed, and we will examine some of the advantages and disadvantages of each.

On-the-Job Techniques

On-the-job T&D techniques, commonly referred to as **OJT,** typically involve job instruction given by an employee's supervisor or an experienced co-worker. Many studies indicate that as much as 90 percent of all T&D is performed on the job. OJT may involve learning how to run a machine, complete reports and related computer/paperwork, conduct an interview, or sell a service or product. While employees may say that they learned their jobs "OJT" with a chuckle, learning by doing is a solid educational technique.

OJT is not limited to nonmanagerial or front-line employees. Managers essentially learn by doing. OJT techniques enable managers to practice management skills, make mistakes, and learn from their mistakes under the guidance of an experienced, competent manager. OJT methods include job rotation and lateral promotion, enlarged and enriched job responsibilities, job instruction training, apprentice training, coaching, mentoring, and

committee assignments. (See Figure 9-5 for the assets and liabilities of OJT.)

Job Rotation Also referred to as *cross-training,* **job rotation** involves placing an employee on different jobs for periods of time ranging from a few hours to several weeks. At lower job levels, job rotation normally consumes a short period, such as a few hours or one or two days. At higher job levels, job rotation may consume much larger periods, because staff trainees may be learning complex functions and responsibilities (Figure 9-6). For example, OJT for a bank lending officer may consist of one or two months in each department, including loan operations and collections, bookkeeping, trust operations, data processing, and commercial lending.

Job rotation for managers usually involves temporary assignments that may range from several months to one or more years in various departments, plants, and offices. Job rotation for management trainees usually involves several short-term assignments that teach a variety of skills and give the trainees a greater understanding of how various work areas function. Management trainees are usually college graduates or employees promoted from the blue-collar or clerical ranks into first-level management.

For middle- and upper-level management, job rotation serves a slightly different function. At these levels, job rotation assignments normally involve **lateral promotions,** which may last for one or more years. In contrast to a vertical promotion, in which an employee takes over a supervisor's job, a lateral promotion involves a move to a different work environment so that the manager may develop competence in general management decision-making skills. Much like the short-term job rotation assignment, a lateral promotion allows the manager to be exposed to many organizational operations and management styles.[18]

Although both lateral promotion and short-term job rotation enable employees to broaden

FIGURE 9-5 OJT training techniques: the balance sheet.

The widespread use of OJT training is, no doubt, due to the many benefits it offers. Among the potential assets of this type of training are the following:

- The employee is doing the actual work, not hypothetical or simulated tasks.
- The employee receives instructions from an experienced employee or supervisor who has performed the task successfully.
- The T&D is performed in the actual work environment under normal working conditions and requires no special training facilities.
- The T&D is informal, relatively inexpensive, and easy to schedule.
- The T&D may build cooperative relationships between the employee and the trainer.

Among the potential liabilities of OJT training are the following:[25]

- The trainer may not be motivated to train or to accept the responsibility for T&D; thus, training may be haphazard.
- The trainer may perform the job well but lack the ability to teach others how to do so.
- The trainer may not have the time to train and may omit important elements of the T&D process. While the employee is learning OJT, resources will be inefficiently used, performance (at least initially) will be low, and costly errors may be made.

their organizational knowledge and develop decision-making skills, these methods are not without flaws. First, some organizations need managers with specialized skills in technical areas rather than in general management skills. Second, for upper-level managers, job rotation and lateral promotion often involve an expensive and emotional move to another part of the country. Promotions were accepted with little question years ago, but one study showed that 42 percent of the companies sampled employed managers who had refused transfers.[19] Third, a job rotation or lateral promotion may force employees to take short-term views of their jobs. For example, a plant manager assigned to a facility for a three-year assignment may focus on short-range programs with immediate payoffs, thereby neglecting planning and policy decisions that would not generate benefits for three or four years—long after the manager has been reassigned.

Enlarged and Enriched Job Responsibilities By giving an employee added job duties, and increasing the autonomy and responsibilities associated with the job, the firm allows an

FIGURE 9-6 Dos and don'ts for cross-training.

DO communicate and discuss the cross-training fully with the employee.
DO set up time frames and measurable goals so that cross-training can be evaluated objectively.
DO reward successful completion of cross-training in some way.
DO consider cross-training as a employee benefit and development activity.
DON'T try to cross-train employees for responsibilities that are well beyond their ability and skill levels.
DON'T cross-train strictly for short-term business needs. Make sure that the employee will benefit from cross-training.[17]

employee to learn a lot about the job, department, and organization. Redesigning the job can be seen as a T&D approach since the employee can be stretched and tested in new ways. The "empowerment" philosophy focuses on need satisfaction and motivation, but it can also play a significant role in T&D. Allowing managerial and front-line employees to grow in their jobs, and to take on more personal responsibility and control, is a popular approach in the modern organization. Obviously, some labor agreements and other organizational restrictions may limit the use of job enrichment and enlargement in some situations.

Job Instruction Training Faced with massive training needs during World War II, the federal government developed **job instruction training (JIT)** to enable supervisors to train their employees quickly and effectively. In essence, JIT is a series of steps for supervisors to follow when training their employees. Because of its simplicity and commonsense approach, JIT remains a popular tool for many modern trainers. The simple steps in the JIT system are preparation, presentation, performance tryout, and follow-up.[20]

Apprentice Training A combination of on- and away-from-the-job training, **apprentice training** is widely used in the skilled trades, such as barbering, carpentry, printing, welding, and plumbing. Apprentice training involves cooperation among employees, the government, educational institutions (usually vocational or technical schools), and labor unions. The U.S. Department of Labor regulates apprentice training programs and determines the length of apprenticeships and the minimum requirements for classroom instruction. Certain conditions of employment and training may also be negotiated with individual unions.

Coaching As in athletics, the organizational coach assumes the role of helper and teacher.

The coach—often the new manager's or exceptional employee's boss—achieves developmental objectives by setting goals, by providing assistance in reaching goals, and by giving timely and constructive performance feedback. The coach answers questions, lets the employee participate in making decisions, stimulates the employee's thinking, and helps when problems occur.[21] Trust, cooperation, and mutual respect are imperative for coaching to be helpful. Properly done, **coaching** can be an extremely effective way to develop employee confidence and strong supervisory–subordinate relations.[22]

Coaching, however, is not problem-free. According to psychologist Harry Levinson, coaching will fail unless a rapport conducive to learning is created between the manager and the employee. Levinson suggests that the coach must be willing to give sufficient time to the development process and allow the subordinate to assume some risks and make mistakes.[23]

Mentoring A mentor is an experienced manager who provides guidance to a junior manager or professional and facilitates his or her personal development. **Mentoring** is often used with young professional employees who have high career aspirations. Their mentors are usually eight to fifteen years older and are considered successful managers.

Mentorships are formed in two ways—formally and informally. Since a mentor can "show the ropes" to the protégé, many organizations have set up formal mentor programs, often as part of their affirmative action or orientation efforts. Informal mentoring relationships seem to have always existed, generally based on a judgment by the (senior) mentor that the (junior) employee has promise and that the mentor's advice and counsel will not be wasted. The effectiveness of formal, somewhat artificial, mentoring programs has not been established to be the same as in the traditional informal relationships, where the mentor and protégé are perhaps more genuinely committed to each other.

Possible benefits of mentoring to both the employer and protégé include the following:

- The mentor may advance the career of the protégé by nomination for promotion or sponsorship of membership.
- The mentor may provide the protégé visibility in the organization or profession through joint efforts.
- The mentor may protect the protégé from controversial situations and provide coaching by suggesting work strategies.
- The mentor may provide counseling about work and personal problems.
- There is better job performance and longer service with the organization from protégés who develop more skills and self-confidence.

Recent research indicates that there is now little difference in the mentoring relationships between the genders if males and females have the same education. While there are still relatively few women in top-level management positions, and while cross-gender mentorships can be sensitive, top-performing women are now as likely to be mentored as their male counterparts. Females and males both report receiving more promotions, having higher incomes, and being more satisfied with their pay and benefits than those who experience little or no mentoring.[24]

Committee Assignments A great deal of a manager's time (many think too much) is spent in committees, which permeate all levels of management. Committees are formed to solve current problems, plan for the future, and discuss and act on issues critical to the organization.

Serving on a committee and participating in decision making enable a manager to strengthen a variety of skills. For example, a newly appointed production supervisor may be asked to formulate recommendations to solve a quality-control problem. While working on this **committee assignment**, the supervisor may gain a greater understanding of the issues involved in quality control, meet and discuss the problem with personnel from other departments, and develop an appreciation for good working relationships among quality-control inspectors, production managers, supervisors, and line employees. Junior managers or particular front-line employees can be placed on such committees as regular members or may be sent as substitutes by the regular members.

Away-from-the-Job Techniques

Away-from-the-job T&D includes any form performed away from the employee's immediate work area. Two broad forms of such training programs are the following:

1. In-house programs that are conducted within the organization's own training facility, either by training specialists from the HR department or by external consultants (often a combination of both).
2. Off-site programs held elsewhere and sponsored by an educational institution, a professional association, a government agency, or an independent T&D firm.

A wide range of training methods is employed to train and develop employees away from their jobs. Some methods are used more often in T&D programs for managerial employees, while others are more often used for nonmanagerial employee. However, the differences in responsibilities between these two levels of employees are dissolving in many organizations as TQM and restructuring programs are implemented. This means that a wider range of T&D methods is being made available to all employees.

Videotapes Videotapes bought off the shelf or produced internally are used by 90 percent of organizations, according to a recent survey. New concepts and ideas can be introduced in this convenient format as part of a T&D program. Videotapes can also supplement several of the other techniques to be discussed, especially those showing technical and behavioral skills.[26] See *HR in the News*; "Kodak Develops Employee Humor to Increase Performance" for an unusual use of videotape and other technologies.

Lecture   The **lecture** is the second most popular away-from-the-job T&D technique, with some 85 percent of organizations using this controversial method. Its strength lies in delivering uniform information to a large group of people in a timely manner.[27] Almost all T&D methods contain at least some lecture. Two complaints are often made about this method, however. Behavioral skills seem to be learned more effectively through more interactive methods, such as role playing or case studies. Further, since lectures are one-way communications, participants are often bored and listen ineffectively. As a student, you probably understand the shortcomings of lectures all too well.

The shortcomings of the lecture method may have more to do with the emotional reaction of trainees than with the actual learning. Recent research indicates that trainees react more favorably to an integrative learning (IL)–based training program than to a lecture. IL training creates a relaxed, positive atmosphere and uses a wide range of methods, including discussion, games, stories, poetry, music, and a sophisticated business game. While students at Kodak reacted more positively on T&D reaction forms to IL training, the IL students had the exact same test scores as other students at Kodak who received the same information through traditional lectures.[28]

Conference/Discussion   Many training programs focus on organizational problems, innovative ideas, and new theories and principles. Discussing problems and critical issues in a **conference/discussion** format permits a dialogue between the trainer and trainee, as well

as among the trainees. This two-way communication provides trainees with immediate feedback on their questions and ideas and heightens motivation for the learner.

Vestibule or Simulation   In a training area created to resemble the employee's actual work area, **vestibule** or **simulation** training is performed with the aid of an instructor, who demonstrates on the same kinds of machines and uses processes the trainee will use on the job. Vestibule training has been successfully used for a variety of skilled positions, including retail sales personnel, bank tellers, machine operators, and aircraft pilots.

Technology-Based Systems   The interactive videodisc/CD and other computer-based learning (CBL) techniques are becoming more popular as technology improves and prices decline. CBL and similar **technology-based T&D systems** have taken over what was often called the **programmed instruction** approach. Programmed instruction allows trainees to learn the training information or skill in small segments and at their own pace. As the learner masters one segment, she or he can move on to the next. CBLs are common, and many students are familiar with tutorials that accompany many software programs, such as WordPerfect, Windows, or Quicken.

While some off-the-shelf training CDs and programs are available, most technology-based T&D systems require a great deal of preparation time. Creating enough use to legitimize the expense is crucial for these programs. One study found that it may take 300 hours for a T&D department to create 1 hour of computer-based training.[29]

Satellite linkages and videoconferencing are other technology-based approaches that are becoming popular for organizational communications and training. These techniques can make technology-based programs more cost efficient if used on a large scale since the set costs of the technology can be spread over a greater number of trainees for a lower per-

Kodak Develops Employee Humor to Increase Performance

Surveys of executives show that 96 percent think that people with a sense of humor do better at their jobs than those who seem to lack a funnybone. Kodak decided on an unusual development technique and created a "humor room" to help increase creativity in its manufacturing, research, marketing, and other departments.[30] The humor development room contains the following:

1. A resource library stocked with humorous books, videotapes, and comfortable chairs.

2. Group meeting areas with photos of Charlie Chaplin and Groucho Marx on the wall, where up to twenty can group for problem solving, watching a video, or brainstorming.

3. A "toy store" where punching bags, "boss dolls" (with pull-off arms and legs), rubber eyeballs, and other odd and silly items are free to employees.

4. A high-tech area where computers, or "humor processors," are loaded with software to help employees be more creative in problem solving, speech writing, and generating new ideas.

Kodak is not alone in being serious about humor. Employees at Monsanto Company in St. Louis attended a training session where they were taught a silly exercise of wriggling a nickel stuck on the forehead into a co-worker's cup. This technique is used by their research scientists to loosen up and become more creative.

Tax consultants, stereotyped as serious and stuffy, at Price Waterhouse in New York, attended a humor program where they wrote with pens shaped like vege-

---

trainee cost. Further, linking together multiple sites to receive a single electronic transmission can capture the advantages of immediacy and standardization of training across locations.

Case Study A **case study** is a written description of an organizational problem. The case method was developed at the Harvard Business School in the 1920s and remains a popular teaching technique there and in many other universities, primarily at the graduate level of study. Case studies require participants to identify and analyze specific problems, develop alternative courses of action, and recommend the best alternative.

A case study may be analyzed by individuals or groups. In T&D programs, participants often form teams to study cases and then present their recommendations for discussion and analysis.

The primary purpose of the case study is to

416

tables, wore red clown noses, and gave each other standing ovations for achievements on the job.

At Sun Microsystems in Mountain View, California, elaborate April Fool's hoaxes have become so widely accepted that they are videotaped and shown at other Sun sites. The CEO once came to work to find that his office had been converted into a one-hole, par-four golf course, complete with two sand traps. Sun's co-founder arrived on another April 1 to find his Ferrari on a float in the middle of a fish pond with an "I Break for Pink Flamingos" bumper sticker added.

Improved Performance

Case studies indicate that improved performance results from humor training. At Digital Equipment Corporation, managers who participated in a humor workshop increased their productivity 15 percent and cut their sick days in half in the nine months after the training. Employees who viewed funny training films and went to humor workshops at Colorado Health Sciences Center in Denver had a 25 percent decrease in downtime and a 60 percent increase in job satisfaction. Here is the psychology behind the improvements:

- Humor facilitates camaraderie and teamwork.
- Humor helps people be less rigid and judgmental.
- Humor helps employees accept new ideas more readily.
- Ultimately, humor helps employees enjoy, rather than hate, their workplace.

According to Joel Goodman, founder of the Humor Project in Saratoga Spring, New York, too many people view their jobs as a five-day prison from which they are paroled on Fridays. But, if allowed to have fun, employees generally score higher marks on satisfaction, productivity, creativity, and morale.

Perhaps the shortest distance between two employees is laughter.

---

enhance problem-solving skills.[31] Participants practice defining problems, generating solutions, and deciding on optimal solutions. Working in a group gives members insight into group dynamics and group decision-making processes.

Role Playing During **role playing** (or *reality practice*), participants play the roles of those involved in an organizational problem. Usually there are no scripts, and participants have limited data on which to base their roles. For example, assume that managers are receiving instruction in the use of employee counseling. One member of a group may play the role of an employee who has been tardy and absent several times. Another member plays the role of the employee's supervisor. With as much realism as possible, the two players act out their roles in front of the instructor and other participants. Discussion normally follows role playing, which lasts for only a few minutes.

Role playing may be videotaped and viewed in segments for an in-depth analysis of the roles and how they were acted out.

The primary goals of role playing are to analyze interpersonal problems and develop human-relations skills. Role playing is commonly used to develop skills in interviewing, negotiation, job counseling, disciplining, performance appraisal, sales, and other job duties that involve interpersonal communication.[32] For this technique to be successful, the instructor must attempt to make the situations realistic and ensure that each role player takes his or her role seriously.

Management Games Management games (or *simulations exercises*) are designed to replicate conditions faced by real organizations and usually involve competing teams that both make decisions concerning planning, production, finance, and control of a hypothetical organization.[33] The winner is typically the team that achieves the highest net profit at the completion of the game. More complex games involve the use of a computer.[34] In those games, teams receive a printout detailing the overall impact of their decisions on the effectiveness of the enterprise.

A number of benefits may be derived from playing a management game. First, as a team member, the participant is able to study group dynamics: conflict resolution, communication patterns, and development of interpersonal relationships. Second, the trial-and-error process of game playing enables participants to learn from mistakes without jeopardizing a real organization. Third, participants can examine how various areas of an organization interrelate—how advertising expenditures affect sales volume or how various levels of research affect long-range profits. Finally, participants find that games are fun and interesting. Team players eagerly await the computer printout, which disinterestedly judges the strengths and weaknesses of their collective decision making.[35]

In-basket Exercise An exercise, which is called the **in-basket exercise**, is designed to develop the analytical and problem-solving skills of lower-level managers. The technique centers on a series of hypothetical problems that a supervisor may find in a typical in-basket. Examples of items the in-basket may contain include the following:

- A letter from an EEOC representative who wants to talk about alleged discrimination in the work unit.
- A note from an employee who wants a six-week leave of absence to work in a family business. Without his work, production goals probably would not be met.
- A note from a trusted and valuable employee who will quit if she doesn't get a 10 percent raise.
- A letter from the personnel director stating that he is unable to find qualified candidates for five vacant positions in your work unit.

The in-basket exercise forces the trainee to make immediate decisions and to determine priorities. For this reason, this exercise is often part of an assessment center program. The participant must quickly think through alternative courses of action, select the best solution, and determine how it should be implemented.

Assessment Center The assessment center is a technique that requires managers to participate in activities designed to identify their job-related strengths and weaknesses. It is used primarily as a device to select new managers, but it has seen increasing use as a developmental tool for existing managers.

During an assessment center, which normally lasts for two to three days, a small group (six or seven participants, each from a different department), is observed and evaluated by trained assessors. The participants are evaluated on qualities considered important for effective management. Some of those qualities may include oral and written communication skills, sensitivity, ambition, energy, planning ability, and decision making. Exercises used to measure and evaluate those qualities include interviews, leaderless group discussions, role playing, and in-basket exercises. Following the exercises, participants normally receive detailed, specific feedback about their performance and their developmental and growth needs. Suggestions for T&D may include such away-from-the-job activities as courses, readings, and seminars and such on-the-job activities as task force and committee assignments, coaching, and counseling.[36]

Membership in Professional Organizations One informal way to keep abreast of new theories, principles, methods, and techniques in a field is through membership in a **professional organization**. Hundreds of such associations exist, with memberships varying from a handful to several thousand.

Membership in a professional organization helps develop employees in various ways. During monthly meetings and at conventions, members network with their colleagues, exchange ideas, and discuss common problems. They listen to a variety of speakers and learn about advances in their field. Many companies encourage their managers to join professional organizations and to attend meetings regularly. Often the company pays membership dues and travel expenses to annual meetings. Many professional organizations publish journals for their membership. Examples include the American Society for Training and Development's (ASTD) monthly, *Training and Development* Society for Human Resource Management's HRMagazine, and the American Management Association's *Management Review, Supervisory Management,* and *Personnel.*

Wilderness Training Today more and more managers are swapping business attire for hiking boots with the hope of becoming more motivated and more skilled managers. **Wilderness training** is a generic term to describe any one of a variety of management and executive development programs that take place in outdoor settings and include mountaineering, backpacking, ocean sailing, white-water rafting, canoeing, cross-country skiing, and cycling.[37]

What could a vice-president of finance possibly learn about money markets, bond issues, and the stock market by spending five days challenging the Rocky Mountains in Colorado?

In all probability, nothing. But as with sensitivity training, the purpose of wilderness training is not to develop technical skills, but to develop and hone interpersonal skills such as confidence, self-esteem, teamwork, goal setting, and trust. For example, many wilderness activities require a team effort (e.g., to rappel a 200-foot cliff); such exercises are designed to enable participants to gain an appreciation of the advantages of a team effort versus attempting to achieve a challenging goal alone.

Wilderness programs vary widely. Some are one-day excursions in the woods involving team exercises such as scaling a fourteen-foot wall without ropes or other aids, or using group problem-solving methods to cross a simulated lake or river. Also popular are one-day "ropes courses" where participants, both individually and with the aid of team members, complete a series of exercises high above the ground.

Also popular are **Outward Bound** courses, which generally last for about a week and involve a group of managers who, for example, climb mountains, backpack, or canoe with one or two "facilitators" who not only serve to assist in the physical aspects of the experience but also lead discussions about leadership, teamwork, trust, and other human qualities important for success in the business world.

Does wilderness training work? That depends entirely upon how one defines *work.* Most people who participate in wilderness training speak enthusiastically about the experience, such as the Outward Bound participant who, after successfully rappelling a dangerous cliff, said, "I wouldn't trade this experience for a million dollars. And I wouldn't do it again for two million." But while proponents of wilderness training argue that participants will challenge themselves and uncover hidden potential, they stop short of guaranteeing a "bottom line" impact of spending a few days in the woods.

Behavior Modeling A classroom-oriented technique generally used to teach problem-solving skills to first-level supervisors is called **behavior modeling**. The technique, which utilizes role playing, focuses on individual "skill modules" that address a common problem most supervisors face, such as absenteeism, tardiness, or employee orientation. Each module contains the following elements:[38]

- Trainers introduce the topic (e.g., employee orientation).

- A model of effective supervisory behavior is illustrated, usually by film or videotape. A discussion of key learning points follows the film.

- The training group discusses the model of effective behavior.

- Trainees practice desired behaviors, using role playing, as other trainees observe (each participant acts out the desired behaviors).

- Trainees receive feedback on the effectiveness of their behavior from their fellow observers.

Effectiveness of Behavior Modeling Here are some key findings concerning behavior modeling:[39]

- Instruction is most effective when presented as rule-like learning points.

- The individual used as a model should be someone the participants respect and identify with.

- Videotape demonstrations are less costly, are more convenient, offer greater control and consistency, and are just as effective as live demonstrations.

- Overlearning results in new behaviors that are more likely to be retained in the long run and less likely to break down under stress.

- Posttraining activities, such as follow-up meetings, feedback on progress, and praise and rewards for using new behaviors, are important for sustaining newly learned behaviors.

Studies of the effectiveness of behavior modeling generally show support for the technique. In two studies involving trainees at AT&T and General Electric, supervisors who had received training through behavior modeling performed their jobs significantly better than those who received no training.[40]

Sensitivity Training Through **sensitivity training** (also called *T-group*—*T* for training), individuals become more aware of their feelings and learn how one person's behavior affects the feelings, attitudes, and behaviors of others. In the purest form of sensitivity training, an open and honest "no holds barred, tell it like it is" discussion takes place among participants. Perhaps for the first time, many participants learn how their behavior is perceived by others. For some participants the experience is a tremendous emotional high; others leave the training session depressed, demoralized, and contemplating a lawsuit.

The goals of sensitivity training include the following:

- Becoming more competent in one's personal relationships.

- Learning more about oneself as a person.

- Learning how others react to one's behavior.

- Learning about the dynamics of group formation, group goals, and group growth.

Sensitivity training has many opponents.[41] They argue—justifiably—that there is little or no documentation that performance in the organization improves as a result of participation in sensitivity training. Some opponents assert that one's innermost feelings and beliefs are

HR IN THE NEWS

Diversity T&D Programs—Effective or Destructive?

The joy of creation is in its infinite diversity and in the ways our differences combine to create meaning and beauty.—Mr. Spock, *Star Trek*

No T&D topic has been more popular, or more controversial, in the early 1990s than **diversity training**. The foundation for such training is the gradual demographic shift away from a predominantly white male work force. In 1980 white males represented 51 percent of all workers but will represent only 44 percent in 2005. During the same twenty-five-year period, the proportion of white females will grow from 36 percent to 39 percent, that of blacks will grow from 10 percent to 12 percent, and that of Hispanics, Asians, and other racial groups will grow to 15 percent of all workers.[42]

While diversity was originally discussed in terms of ethnicity, color, and national origin, many have expanded diversity to include issues of gender, physical disabilities, sexual preference, and even profession.[43] A popular approach for T&D is the use of commercially prepared videotapes. Griggs Productions, a video pioneer in the diversity field, offers a "Valuing Diversity" series that includes seven videos:

"Managing Differences"   "Supervising Differences"

"Diversity at Work"   "Champions of Diversity"

"Communicating Across Cultures"   "Profiles in Change"[44]

"You Make the Difference"

Few training programs—whether using videos, external consultants, or internally developed T&D programs—have been more controversial. Objective evaluation of such programs is difficult, and worse, is often not even considered. HR development professionals have been offered some guidelines on how to avoid the common backlash to many diversity T&D programs:

1. Avoid trainers who have a political agenda or support a particular interest group.

2. Integrate any diversity T&D program into the organization's overall approach to diversity.

3. Avoid diversity training too closely linked to a recent EEO investigation or complaint.

4. Differentiate among the concepts of valuing diversity, pluralism, EEO, affirmative action, and managing across cultures.

(continued)

5. Link stereotyping behavior to personal and organizational effectiveness.

6. Avoid basing diversity on the "political correctness" movement.

7. Respect individuals' styles of participation in diversity exercises.

8. Avoid being either too shallow or too deep.

9. Don't pressure only one group to change.

10. All viewpoints should be allowed expression, even concepts like *reverse discrimination.*

11. Trainers should model the behaviors they teach.

12. Trainers should be competent at facilitation and presentation, have credibility with trainees, and be sensitive to diversity issues.[45]

highly personal and that sensitivity training is an invasion of privacy.

Does sensitivity training result in greater managerial effectiveness? Research has proven inconclusive.[46] According to the studies, sensitivity training can produce such behavioral changes as greater openness, trust, and respect for the feelings of others. It has not, however, been demonstrated that behavioral change has led to more effective job performance.

Many diversity training programs are based on sensitivity training in their approach. See *HR in the News:* "Diversity T&D Programs— Effective or Destructive?" for a discussion of this topic.

Packages of T&D Programs   Away-from-the-job T&D programs can come as an integrated package or program of courses. Many such "total" T&D programs are offered as formal courses and seminars, conducted by either in-house or off-site by a university, consulting group, or nonprofit association, such as the American Management Association, American Society for Training and Development, or Society for Human Resource Management.

The length and breadth of these courses vary considerably. A one- or two-day seminar

normally focuses on a specific management technique or problem, such as time management or executive speaking. One- or two-week courses may focus on a wide variety of managerial methods and processes. For example, the American Management Association's popular five-day course "Developing Supervisory Leadership Skills" covers leadership, communication, discipline, employee development, job satisfaction, and morale.

Some universities sponsor advanced management programs that closely resemble a highly concentrated master's degree program in business administration. One of the most popular courses of this nature is the Harvard Business School's Advanced Management Program. Other colleges and universities offering similar programs include the University of Chicago, UCLA, Wharton, Carnegie-Mellon, Indiana University, and Stanford.

Several large, progressive organizations have created in-house educational programs to satisfy their need for skilled management talent. Many corporate programs, which closely resemble those sponsored by universities, offer managers and executives instruction in timely issues and topics involving management theory and practice. Large companies that have established their own management develop-

FIGURE 9-7 Checklist for selecting a training package.

Many employers are interested in purchasing an off-the-shelf training package including a videotape and/or computer programs. The following is a guide to selecting such a package.

1. Do the objectives of the package (behaviors to be learned) match your requirements? How many?

2. Does the content (knowledge and skills) fit your requirements? Does it support the objectives in terms of the knowledge and skills people need to achieve the training objective(s)?

3. Is the package well-organized? Is it packaged in modules to facilitate flexibility in adding or deleting material?

4. Will the supplier/copyright holder permit modification of the package?

5. Will the supplier grant duplicating rights for the courseware (site licensing) and make no participant-based charges?

6. Are the media used of good technical and creative quality? Are they appropriate, current, accurate and believable?

7. Do the approach, strategy and packaging promote ease of use? Do they employ sound principles of adult learning?

8. Is the package structured to provide an integrated skills-building sequence of learning experiences?

9. Does the package provide opportunities for trainees to apply and practice newly acquired knowledge and skills?

10. Are trainer/instructor/facilitator guides and aids provided?

11. Are trainee/participant aids, workbooks and activities included in the package?

12. Was the package developed through a systematic and orderly process? Was it built on a firm foundation of precisely defined job or task performance requirements?

13. Are validation results available?

14. Does the supplier have a good reputation? Is the firm noted for the quality of its products and customer service?

15. Is the package a good value in terms of reasonable per-trainee and total costs?

SOURCE: William R. Tracey "Customizing Off-the-shelf Training Programs," reprinted with the permission of *HRMagazine* (January 1993). Published by the Society for Human Resource Management, Alexandria, Va.

ment centers include IBM, General Motors, Exxon, and General Electric. For information about T&D packages which are primarily video or computer in format, examine Figure 9-7.

OJT or Away-from-the-Job T&D?

A contingency approach is required when deciding which general approach to T&D should be used. In some situations OJT will be a very effective approach, while in others the best T&D program will be available at an external site. See Figure 9-8 for the pros and cons for using away-from-the-job training.

The learning climate of the workplace needs to be taken into account as well. It is impossible to escape job duties when on the property of some employers, while other employers, like Aetna provide an excellent transfer climate. An effective **transfer climate** is one in which the environment—including leadership and rewards and punishments—assists rather than hinders, T&D efforts.[48]

FIGURE 9-8 Away-from-the-job training: the balance sheet.

Among the potential assets of away-from-the-job training are the following:[47]

- Training is cost-efficient because groups rather than individuals are usually trained.
- Trainers, usually full-time instructors or training personnel, are likely to be more competent trainers than on-the-job trainers, who normally spend only a fraction of their time training.
- More planning and organization often go into away-from-the-job training than into on-the-job training.
- Away-from-the-job training enables the trainee to learn in an environment free from the normal pressures and interruptions of the workplace.
- Off-site courses and seminars enable small companies with limited resources to train employees without the formidable expenses of a large training staff and training facilities.

Among the potential liabilities of away-from-the-job training are the following:

- Employees attending away-from-the-job training are not performing their jobs. This is an added expense of training, though training benefits should exceed costs in the long run.
- Away-from-the-job training often has problems of **transfer of learning**. Sometimes this training is of limited practical value to the trainee—particularly when the training is conducted away from the organization. Because it is impossible for the trainer to customize a course for each participant, away-from-the-job programs normally contain limited applications for a trainee's specific problems and situations. This is the greatest potential drawback of away-from-the-job training.

The goals and objectives of the T&D effort need to be identified early in the training process. Wexley and Latham have developed a 3×3 matrix to suggest what type of training might be indicated, depending on the goals sought and strategies favored (see Figure 9-9). Using their figure, if the organization wishes to increase motivation, then an appropriate strategy that is behavior based would involve coaching and behavior modeling (column "Motivation" and row "Behavioral"). Similarly, if the employer wished to increase job skills using a cognitive (or intellectual) approach, then lectures, audiovisual aids, case study, and computer-based training (or learning) would all be reasonable approaches.[49]

Other appropriate considerations relating to the situation are resources and money. Smaller employers, employers who lack **human resource development** (HRD) professionals, and employers who have no appropriate rooms and equipment will generally have to opt for off-site methods for many T&D needs. When budgets shrink, two things happen: employees generally have to perform at higher levels, and staff budgets such as T&D budgets are often cut. Obviously, these two situations work against each other, but the bottom line is usually that OJT methods are preferred since they appear to be free. For the small, financially strapped organization, OJT and low-cost away-from-the-job programs (such as university and government-sponsored courses) are often the only economically feasible training alternatives.

A T&D Plan and Implementation

After identifying T&D needs, setting objectives, and choosing the appropriate methods for training, a **training plan** should be written. The HRD or T&D staff should construct the plan to help schedule and plan what training courses will be offered within a certain time

FIGURE 9-9 Goals and strategies for T&D.

STRATEGIES	Self-Awareness	Job Skills	Motivation
GOALS			
Cognitive	Career development Management role theory Need for achievement Double-loop learning Sensitivity training Self-directed management development Transactional analysis	Orientation training and socialization of new employees Lecture Audiovisual Vroom-Yetton model Case study The incident process Job aids Computer-based training Teleconferencing Corporate classrooms/colleges Seminars and workshops	Role motivation theory Need for achievement Training Survey feedback
Behavioral	Interactive skills training	On-the-job training Apprenticeship Programmed instruction Equipment simulators Computer-assisted instruction Rational manager training Conference discussion Assessment centers Role playing Management games Grid seminars Leader-member exchange Juniors boards Understudy assignments Mentoring	Coaching Behavior modeling
Environmental	Leader match		Job rotation Behavior modification

frame. Many HRD departments offer several courses each week.

The implementation of the T&D program brings trainees, the trainer, and materials together. Careful planning for the sessions themselves must take place, or some important element of the program, like a VCR and a monitor, may be forgotten. Figure 9-10 is an example of a checklist that helps HRD professionals ensure that everything is ready for the training program. It is wise to contact outside training consultants again as the training program draws near in order to take care of any last-minute details. Away-from-the-job training requires many logistical details to be handled by the HRD staff.

FIGURE 9-10 An example of a T&D program checklist.

SEMINAR: _____   DATE(S): _____

SPEAKER: _____   TIME: _____

SPEAKER: _____   FACILITY: _____

NO. OF PARTICIPANTS: _____   MEETING ROOM: _____

                                     LUNCHEON ROOM: _____

LUNCHEON MENU:

1st day: _____

2nd day: _____

3rd day: _____

COFFEE BREAK TIMES AND MENUS:

Registration: _____

Morning break: _____

Afternoon break: _____

AUDIOVISUAL AIDS FOR SPEAKERS: PHYSICAL SETUP:

_____Flip chart and markers   _____Proper posting in lobby

_____Overhead projector   _____Proper storage for equipment

_____35-mm projector   _____Proper lighting

_____Screen   _____No phone calls

_____Computer overhead panel   _____No piped-in music

DIAGRAM OF SEATING ARRANGEMENTS:

MATERIALS FOR PARTICIPANTS:

_____Name tags   _____List of participants

_____Pens   _____Handout material

_____Pencils   _____Textbooks

_____Notebooks   _____Evaluation forms

_____Filler paper   _____Upcoming seminar brochures

_____Legal pads   CONCLUSION OF MEETING:

ADVERTISEMENTS: Collect:

  Publications and dates: _____Evaluation forms

NEWS RELEASES: _____Excess materials

  Publications and dates: _____Audiovisual equipment

  Radio stations and dates:

PHASE 3: EVALUATION

The purpose of T&D evaluation in the training process is to determine whether trainees actually learned new skills and attitudes or a body of knowledge as a result of the T&D program. In the eyes of the trainee, T&D ends when trainer and trainee go their separate ways. On returning to the job duties, the employee hopes to perform more effectively or, perhaps, be better prepared for promotional opportunities. When direct involvement in the program has ended, as far as the employee is concerned, training is over. But though the instruction has ended, the training process has not yet run its full cycle.

One very important question remains: Was the training effective? This often overlooked question involves the third and final phase of T&D —evaluation. Over $100 billion a year is spent nationwide on T&D activities, and the cost of T&D to large organizations can run into the millions of dollars. With T&D costs often consuming a sizable portion of the personnel budget, any prudent manager should ask: Are we getting our money's worth?

There are several strategies that may be used to evaluate training. *Cost-benefit analysis* measures T&D costs against the monetary benefits of T&D. While T&D costs (materials, supplies, lost work time, travel expenses, consultant fees, etc.) are relatively easy to measure, T&D benefits are difficult to translate into economic terms. For example, how does an improvement in communication skills affect the bottom line? While cost-benefit analysis is theoretically appealing, it sees little actual use in practice.

Another strategy for evaluating T&D is to assess the extent to which the objectives were met. As we discussed earlier, T&D objectives define the performance gap between actual and desired performance and may be used to measure training success. Of course, the quality of this strategy is tied to the quality of the objectives, and unfortunately there is little evidence that HRD professionals write high-quality, measurable objectives.

Levels of T&D Evaluation

One popular evaluation strategy includes four different **levels of T&D evaluation**. In fact, it comprises four separate evaluation strategies. The designer of this system, D. L. Kirkpatrick, advocates applying each level of evaluation to a program. He suggests measuring the participants' reaction, participants' learning, change in participants' behavior, and impact of the program on organizational effectiveness.[50]

Level 1: How Did Participants React?
Throughout training, each trainee formulates

opinions and attitudes about the overall effectiveness of the program. Perhaps the trainee is favorably inclined toward the content of the program but thinks that the trainer is too cold or too impersonal. At this level of evaluation, the trainee normally completes a questionnaire about the adequacy of T&D facilities, the skill of the trainer, the quality of the program content, and the relevancy of T&D techniques. After the questionnaires are tabulated and reviewed, the program's quality is judged on the basis of the overall responses.

This first level of evaluation is highly subjective, and training administrators must ensure that the participants are not responding favorably simply because they enjoyed the program or instruction. Figure 9-11 is a questionnaire used for evaluating T&D programs offered through Indiana state government.

Level 2: What Did Participants Learn?
Learning is often assessed by testing a trainee both before and after a program. For example, if a program is designed to teach a word processing program (e.g., WordPerfect), the trainee would be expected to score significantly higher on a test after T&D than before. This second level of evaluation is easily conducted if tests are readily available to measure learning, but the absence of valid tests makes such evaluation difficult to administer. In addition, it is difficult to create a test to measure many behavioral skills, such as communication skills, interpersonal relations, and leadership skills.

Level 3: How Did Participants' Behavior Change?
Participants in T&D are expected to learn a skill or body of knowledge that results in a positive change in job behavior. Learning time management techniques, for example, is purely an academic—and costly—ability unless behavior is changed on the job, that is, unless learning is *applied*. The important question to ask concerning this third level of evaluation is whether learning was transferred from training to the job.

FIGURE 9-11 Evaluation of training.

EVALUATION OF TRAINING
Indiana State Government
State Form 45910 (4-93)

NOTE: Our agency is committed to providing quality training. To assist us in this effort, please complete this evaluation form for both the course content and the course instructor. Doing so will assist us in monitoring our services and enable us to better meet your needs and the needs of other employees.

Your name (optional):	Date: 4-1-95
Course title: **MOTIVATION**	Instructor: **D. McCALMAN**

REGARDING COURSE CONTENT . . .

Did this course meet your expectations?　　　　　Yes ☑　　　No ☐

Was the content of the course logically organized?　Yes ☑　　　No ☐

Was adequate time allowed for the material covered?　Yes ☑　　　No ☐

If you responded "No" to any of the above, please explain: _____

_____

What additional information, if any, would you incorporate into the course?

_____

What information would you remove from the course content? Please explain.

_____

Were the following helpful:

	Yes	No	Some	N/A
Audio visuals	☐	☐	☑	☐
Overhead transparencies	☐	☐	☑	☐
Role plays	☑	☐	☐	☐
Demonstrations	☑	☐	☐	☐
Handouts	☐	☐	☑	☐
Reading Assignments	☐	☐	☐	☑
Discussion	☑	☐	☐	☐
Lecture	☑	☐	☐	☐

Did you have ample time to practice <u>newly acquired</u> skills?　Yes ☑　No ☐

Additional comments:　_we could have used additional time--_

_____enthusiastic Instructor/speaker_____

FIGURE 9-11 (continued)

REGARDING THE INSTRUCTOR . . .

Was the instructor:

Well-informed on the subject	Yes ☒	No ☐
Well prepared/organized	Yes ☒	No ☐
Enthusiastic	Yes ☒	No ☐

Did the instructor:

Encourage participation	Yes ☒	No ☐
Adequately answer questions	Yes ☒	No ☐
Present a professional appearance	Yes ☒	No ☐

Please summarize your <u>overall</u> rating of the instructor:

Knew the material very well

SUMMARY INFORMATION . . .

How will you apply what you have learned in this course to your job?

— gained several ideas on how to motivate my employees

— will re-think my job descriptions for 2 employees.

ADDITIONAL COMMENTS:

Thank you!

Level 4: What Organizational Goals Were Affected?

Ultimately, T&D is expected to result in a more effective organization. The fourth level of evaluation examines the impact of T&D on organizational goals of productivity, quality, and job satisfaction, as well as decreased turnover, accidents, and grievances. Although this level of evaluation is appealing in both theoretical and practical terms, it is not always possible or relevant to do. Where it is difficult to connect acquired skills directly to organizational goals, the administrator must implement a less sophisticated evaluation strategy, that is, one of the other levels.

Applying Evaluation Strategies

T&D effectiveness can be evaluated by the simple and uncomplicated process of measuring participants' reactions or by sophisticated, strategies that compare T&D costs and benefits and measure organizational results. Flexibility should be the key to evaluating T&D programs; T&D personnel should apply the most sophisticated strategy that is both relevant and economically feasible. Combining the four levels of T&D evaluation with a cost-benefit strategy would certainly enable management to ascertain whether a program was contributing to the effectiveness of the organization, but this approach would involve considerable time and money. At the very least, measurable objectives should be written during the assessment phase and evaluated after T&D has been completed.

Costs of T&D Programs and Departments

As we approach the twenty-first century, employers want more from training but are often willing to pay less. The American Society for Training and Development (ASTD) suggests that employers spend 1.5 percent of payroll on T&D. In a recent year, employers spent $30 billion on formal T&D, but of this, $27 billion was paid by only 15,000 employers—less than 1 percent of the employers in the United States.

ASTD reported in its latest benchmarking study, which examined employers with excellent reputations like American Express, Arthur Anderson, AT&T, Chase Manhattan, Dow Chemical, GTE, IBM, Motorola, and Xerox, that T&D investments ranged from $1 million to $1 billion per year, depending on size. The benchmarking study also found that the typical value for T&D expenditures was 3.2 percent of payroll, that employees averaged 3.4 days in training each year, that there was 1 HRD professional for every 150 employees, that external consultants were used in combination with HRD employees, and that $800 to $1000 is spent each year on each employee for T&D.[51]

The amount of formal T&D given to U.S. workers compares disfavorably to the practices of employers in many other countries. New production workers in Japan receive 380 hours of T&D, and new workers in Japanese-owned plants in the United States receive 370 hours. U.S. employers offer only forty-seven hours of T&D to their new employees.[52] Should U.S. employers spend more money on T&D?

Employers should be shrewd shoppers for T&D approaches. For budgeting a T&D project the following equation has been offered: *Cost equals the number of developer hours per hour of T&D, multiplied by the development cost per hour multiplied by the number of hours of T&D.*[53] Of course, if a T&D program cost $10,000 (using the equation) but resulted in $50,000 in savings, what did the T&D really cost? Table 9-3 gives some of the comparative costs of several popular methods of T&D.

PRINCIPLES OF LEARNING

As indicated earlier in this chapter, T&D is a form of education. Whether T&D takes place on or off the job, employees are expected to

Table 9-3 Comparative Training Costs

Medium	Estimated Delivery Cost	Disadvantage	Advantages
Lecture/lab	Usually very high	Difficult scheduling; often boring	Familiar; adaptable
Television	Low trainee time off; hardware is $1,000 to $10,000	Low transfer of training to work; difficult to customize	Familiar
Videotape	Low trainee time off; hardware is $1,000 to $5,000	Little interactivity; difficult to customize	Familiar
Videodisc	Low trainee time off; hardware is $400 to $10,000	High cost for high level of activity; difficult to modify	High interactivity
Computer	Low trainee time off; expensive if hardware is dedicated to training	Can be intimidating	High interactivity; adaptable; excellent; transfer to work
Video-conferencing	Expensive, but low time off	Complex logistics	Social interaction

learn and apply new skills and abilities to benefit both the organization and its employees. Because T&D is a type of learning, trainers can benefit from applying certain principles of learning and learning styles when designing and implementing T&D programs (see *HR in the News:* "What *Learning Style* Do You Use?"). Because neglect or misapplication of principles of learning could easily result in T&D that fails to achieve results, it is important that trainees become familiar with the basics of adult learning.[59]

Motivation

Sometimes the need for T&D is not clear to employees. They may consider it a waste of time and resist being taken away from their jobs. One effective way to motivate trainees is to show them how T&D will help accomplish organizational or personal goals.[60] These goals may include improved job performance and increased opportunities for promotion. Another way is to involve the trainees—either in choosing or planning the T&D.[61]

Participation

Another way to inspire trainees is through active participation in the T&D process. Although direct involvement is an integral part of OJT, away-from-the-job training—especially in the classroom—sometimes fails to consider this important principle of learning. Active participation in the learning process through conferences and discussion enables trainees to become directly involved in the act of learning.

Feedback

Professors sometimes joke that students demand test results before the ink on their papers has dried. Feedback on progress in courses reduces anxiety and lets students know what they must do to improve. Similarly, employees taking part in a T&D program want to know how they are doing and how their progress compares to T&D objectives. Giving the employee feedback is usually an informal part of OJT, and close communication between the trainer and trainee helps the feedback process.[62]

What *Learning Style* Do You Use?

Do you learn more easily from reading, hearing, or seeing information?

Educators, psychologists, and HRD professionals have become very interested in **learning style** theories. There are several learning style approaches, which explain different ways in which individuals learn.

Neurolinguistic programming (NLP) suggests that people have a preferred way of learning and communicating that is tied to the senses. When you want to remember certain information, you try to access a certain "file" in your brain where you have stored the information—either in visual (sights), auditory (sounds), or kinesthetic (physical feelings) form.

Visual learners store information most easily in picture form. You may be a visual learner if you frequently use expressions like "I see" or "I get the picture." In a classroom, visual learners look up (either to the left or right) or keep their eyes unfocused and straight ahead when thinking.[54] T&D programs need to provide images, such as diagrams and models, to help visual learners remember the information.

Auditory learners store information in sound bites. You may be an auditory learner if you frequently use expressions like "I hear you" or "I remember when he said." Auditory learners tend to look directly right or left, or down left, when thinking.[55] T&D programs that focus only on written material, such as used in programmed instruction, need to add elements of the spoken word (like discussion after a tutorial) to assist auditory learners.

Organization

Training must be presented so that segments of materials build on one another; gaps, contradictions, or ambiguities in the material should be avoided. For example, in organizing a course about the operation and maintenance of a large printing press, the safety precautions that must be taken should be presented first. Next, the major parts of the machine and the functions of each should be explained. Then, a competent operator could be observed running the machine, followed by hands-on experience with several uncomplicated tasks, and so on. The final portion of T&D may involve preventive maintenance and minor repairs. In this example, each part of T&D flowed into the next, without inconsistencies or gaps.

Repetition

A wealth of behavioral research shows that frequent practice during T&D helps the learning process. Practice is important whether the skills being learned are technical (e.g., operating a lathe or computer) or behavioral (e.g., communication or interpersonal skills). Including practice sessions in technical training is relatively easy, but practicing interpersonal skills presents challenges to the trainer. Refreshing the training can also help learning. After some time has passed, trainees can be

Kinesthetic learners remember physical sensations associated with their experiences. They talk about "getting a grasp" on things or say things like "I can't seem to get my arms around the problem." Kinesthetic learners look down and to the right when thinking. Experiential exercises, role playing, and simulations are helpful to kinesthetic learners in T&D programs.

The **seven intelligences** provide a different way to understand preferred learning styles. The seven preferences are (1) sequential-linear, (2) verbal, (3) kinesthetic, (4) visual-spatial, (5) musical, (6) interpersonal (between two or more people), and (7) intrapersonal (inside yourself). Educators following the seven intelligences will try to address each type of intelligence within a total T&D or educational unit.[56]

Whole-brain theories emphasize the preference for either the right or left hemisphere. While most of us use both sides of the brain, the right side is considered the seat of creativity and emotion, while the left side is considered the seat of logic and reason.[57] While some whole-brain theories are very complicated, the simplest implications are that a logical approach will work for some persons, while an appeal to emotions may be more successful with others. Men are supposed to have less integration across the hemispheres, resulting in their being influenced exclusively by one side at certain times and by the other side at other times.

Kolb's experiential learning theory suggests that there are four stages of learning, which require four learning abilities. These abilities affect the optimum sequence of learning activities. These abilities are (1) concrete experience, (2) reflective observation, (3) abstract conceptualization, and (4) active experimentation.[58]

---

asked to repeat the behavior or information as a way of recalling and refreshing the prior learning.

Application

Students often complain: "The real world is different from school. I can't apply the theories I learned in class." Similarly, job training is useless unless learning can be applied at work. This **transfer-of-learning** problem is particularly troublesome in off-site instruction. The problem is less severe for technical training (especially with the vestibule technique) because the technology used on the job should be identical to that used during training.

Minimizing transfer-of-learning problems poses a challenge to trainers. The following are specific ways in which a positive transfer may be established:[63]

- Maximize the similarity between the T&D and the job.
- Provide as much experience as possible with the task being taught.
- Provide for a variety of examples when teaching concepts or skills.
- Label or identify important features of a task.
- Make sure that general principles are understood.

- Make sure that the T&D is rewarded on the job.
- Design the T&D so that trainees can see its applicability.
- Use questions to guide trainees' attention.

LEGAL ISSUES

As explained in a previous chapter, various civil rights laws forbid discrimination in terms or conditions of employment because of race, color, religion, sex, national origin, age, or disability. The act covers T&D activities, just as it does any other personnel activity. Anyone involved in training employees must understand how EEOC guidelines, that is, legal issues in T&D, apply. In general, federal employment legislation affects T&D in five ways:[64]

1. T&D required to obtain a job or a promotion must be job related.

2. Selecting employees for a T&D program must not be done in a discriminatory manner.

3. The T&D process itself must not be discriminatory. For example, to comply with federal legislation, AT&T redesigned pole climbing so that women could successfully complete the pole-climbing training course.[65]

4. If career decisions are made by management on the basis of success during T&D, it should be shown that the T&D was job related. For example, if preferred job assignments are given to employees who performed effectively during T&D, a correlation between T&D success and subsequent job success should be shown.

5. Preferential treatment for training minorities is legal if an affirmative action program exists. Such treatment was supported in the Supreme Court case *United Steelworkers* v. *Weber* in 1978. The Court ruled that affirmative action programs involving training *are* legal where evidence of racial imbalance exists. The Court also upheld the use of dual seniority systems for admitting employees to such training programs.[66]

SUCCESSFUL T&D PROGRAMS FOR MANAGERS

Modern facilities, expensive equipment, abundant staff administrators, and an ample training budget will not guarantee the success of T&D efforts. In particular, the success of management development is measured by its ability to produce a steady stream of competent, motivated managers who are able to meet current and future organizational goals. To achieve this end, a number of conditions must be satisfied.

Performance Appraisal
The developmental needs of current managers are most effectively pinpointed through objective, results-oriented appraisal techniques. A vague, subjective appraisal system, such as a graphic rating scale, will offer little help in uncovering specific deficiencies in managerial skills and abilities. Results-oriented systems, such as MBO, remove many of the obstacles in conducting a thorough, valid assessment program.

Long-Range Planning
T&D activities must be based not only on current but also on future needs of managers and on the skills required to fulfill future job responsibilities. For example, potential changes in technology, government legislation, and other internal or external variables must be analyzed and incorporated into T&D activities to prevent managerial obsolescence in the future.

Top Management Support

An organization's T&D activities must receive a strong endorsement from top management. Without this support, T&D programs may be viewed as a form of entertainment or a second-rate, marginally effective activity. Support also means a sufficient budget to carry out a full T&D program. The tendency to slash training budgets during hard times must be avoided.

Support of top management must be earned by demonstrating how programs are contributing to the strategic and operational goals of the organization. Because of the importance of the bottom line, demonstrating the cost effectiveness of T&D may well be the most productive way to gain the support of top management. Unfortunately, that form of evaluation is the most difficult to demonstrate.

What specific skills should HRD professionals possess? One model suggests that HRD professionals acquire four sets of skills: power skills, relationship skills, technical skills, and entrepreneurial skills.[67]

Power skills enable the HRD professional to influence the people he or she interacts with: bosses, subordinates, line managers, and professionals outside the organization. Critically important is the ability to "sell" T&D activities to "clients"—line managers throughout the organization.

Relationship skills enable the development of supportive relationships. These skills include communication, empathy, listening, and team building.

Technical skills pertain to an employee-specific discipline. HRD professionals must maintain state-of-the-art knowledge not only of adult learning but also of related topics, such as productivity improvement and organizational change processes.

Finally, *entrepreneurial skills*—those that include the ability to solve human resource problems creatively and to take calculated risks—are important for contemporary HRD professionals. HRD staff who perceive themselves as entrepreneurs rather than administrators view HRD as a profit center and recognize the strategic link between training and the organization's long-term corporate goals.

Climates for Change

During T&D, managers are often exposed to innovations that may involve unfamiliar techniques or new ways to approach the decision-making process. For T&D to be fully realized, managers must be able to transfer these new skills and abilities to the work environment. Therefore the work environment must be receptive to new ideas and techniques, allowing managers to depart from well-established but ineffective ways. Problems of transfer of learning become significant when managers attempt to apply new ideas in rigid, uncompromising climates. Therefore, the transfer climate in the organization plays an important role in T&D success for managers.

One classic problem of transfer of learning involved a widely used human-relations training program for supervisors. Testing before and after the program revealed that supervisors underwent an attitude change about people-oriented leadership. Supervisors' on-the-job behavior changed, however, only when their new attitude was supported by their bosses.[68]

In the end, the organizational climate and culture has a significant effect on performance. Management development cannot be effective if it conflicts with existing norms, values, beliefs, and customs. In assessing needs and designing activities, staff members must pay close attention to conditions at the workplace and ensure that what is learned can be transformed into on-the-job behavior.

Professional Staff

The contemporary management HRD staff often not only designs but also implements T&D activities. Thus, management HRD professionals must possess strong conceptual skills while being technically able to conduct T&D activities. Training professionals must be familiar with the great variety of T&D activities available and be able to select activities to satisfy myriad development needs.

An organization creates a professional management HRD staff primarily by recruiting and hiring individuals with a proper blend of education and job experience. A sound professional base would be provided by a degree in human resources or a related field. Membership in professional associations such as the American Society for Training and Development and the Society for Human Resource Management helps keep practitioners up to date. Also, short courses and seminars—such as "Train the Trainer" or "Skills and Techniques for the Management Development Specialist"—are particularly important for employees new to management development.

INTERNATIONAL HR: INTERCULTURAL PREPARATION

In their book *Going International,* Lennie Copeland and Lewis Griggs tell how Motorola lost out in France to the Japanese when France's Thomson Group chose the Oki Electric Industry Company to expand the French company's semiconductor business. After working with Motorola for six years, a Thomson Group executive said: "We may just have more in common with the Japanese than we do with the Americans." He explained, "We both attach great importance to form and style."[71]

How can a gap as large as the one between Motorola and Thomson be bridged? And what caused the gap in the first place? The reasons for the gap can be summed up in two words: *cultural ignorance.* Generally speaking, the American manager is hurried, abrupt, direct, and objective. Managers in most other countries have opposite traits. The British and Japanese, for example, pay much more attention to the formalities of communication and interpersonal behavior than Americans do. They are less hurried, more personal, less direct,

more diplomatic, and conscious of form and style as much as substance.

The best solution for closing the gap lies with **intercultural preparation**. The objective is not to make U.S. managers behave like people from other cultures; rather, the objective is to help managers (and other expatriates) cope with unexpected events in a new culture. In Saudi Arabia, for example, it is important for a male to avoid getting into an elevator when it is already occupied by a Saudi female. See *HR in the News:* "T&D South of the Border" for a further discussion of intercultural differences.

While a large number of T&D techniques are available for preparing expatriates for overseas assignments, they can be categorized into five groups:[72]

1. Area studies or documentary programs that expose people to a new culture through written materials on the country's sociopolitical history, geography, economics, and cultural institutions.

2. Cultural assimilator, a programmed instruction method that exposes trainees to specific incidents critical to successful interaction with a target culture.

3. Language preparation.

4. Sensitivity training, in which people's self-awareness is increased.

5. Field experiences, or exposing trainees to minicultures within their own country during short field exercises.

A survey found that of 288 North American companies with international operations, 30 percent provide formal cultural orientation to employees being sent overseas, and an additional 25 percent plan to start such training. Of the companies that do offer cultural orientation, 91 percent include the employee's spouse and 71 percent include the employee's children.[73]

Intel, a high-tech company, integrates intercultural training for front-line supervisors, mid-level managers, and senior managers with

T&D South of the Border

The Americas are getting smaller in many ways. With the passage of the North Atlantic Free Trade Agreement (NAFTA) in 1993 and other such agreements, the trade and employment barriers between the United States and its southern neighbors have fallen significantly. HRD professionals should examine their knowledge of how T&D efforts may need to be adjusted for use in Latin America.

According to Tom Casey, a consultant with Arthur D. Little's North American Management Consulting Directorate, and Ana Maria Groeger, a consultant with the company's Latin American Directorate, Latin Americans respond differently to T&D than do many Europeans and employees in the United States. Casey and Groeger suggest the following ideas for HRD professionals who will design and implement T&D programs in Latin America.[69]

- Be flexible with dates and schedules. Many Latin Americans believe that North Americans are obsessed with time and schedules, and may be somewhat less anxious about time themselves.

- Trainers should focus on presentation rather than facilitation. Trainees prefer to learn from the trainer and less from each other.

- Don't be overly concerned if there is less audience participation in the training than you would expect in the United States; Latin Americans tend to interact less.

- Complaining is done in a more private way. While HRD professionals in the United States are accustomed to outward complaining (and sometimes a lot of it), they will have to listen carefully during coffee breaks and other informal activities to uncover complaints in Latin America.

- Don't be serious all the time. Trainers should include humor and anecdotes to lighten up the T&D program. *Many trainees in the United States wish for the same approach!*

Many of these suggestions agree with the five attitudes for global HRD success:[70]

1. Tolerate ambiguity.
2. Respect the values and practices of other cultures.
3. Be committed to HRD principles and practices.
4. Be persistent and have initiative.
5. Demonstrate a sense of humor.

437

Table 9–4 Line and Staff Responsibilities in the T&D Process

Training Phases	Training Staff's Role	Line Management's Role
Phase 1: Analyzing needs and setting objectives	Conduct actual needs analysis; design tools that may be used to survey needs; determine personnel who need training; write training objectives.	Supply training personnel with necessary performance data; review and approve needs analysis and training objectives.
Phase 2: Designing the program	Determine the type of program and training techniques.	Review and approve training program and techniques; if applicable, perform OJT (or supervise OJT if conducted by a nonsupervisory employee).
Phase 3: Evaluating the program	Perform the evaluation; present findings to line management.	Supply trainer with necessary performance data; review evaluation results.

management topics and business objectives. Intel, which has an internationally diverse work force, offers global training to its foreign-born and other employees in five areas:

- Intercultural awareness.
- Multicultural integration.
- Culture-specific training.
- T&D for international assignments.
- Intact-team training.[74]

The concept of including the team dimension is relatively new in global training. Since Intel forms joint ventures with many non-U.S. companies, its employees must often travel and work as a team unit. Therefore, Intel's T&D efforts develop around the intact-team concept. Like many employers recently engaged in global training, Intel uses mostly external consultants for its intercultural training.[75]

RESPONSIBILITY FOR T&D

Like many staff functions, responsibility for T&D is shared by line management and staff administrators. Effective T&D requires line and staff to work closely together on all phases of the T&D process, and that both parties understand and recognize their shared authority. Trainers or line managers unwilling to approach the T&D process cooperatively find that the process does not help their organizations. Although the responsibility for various functions of T&D will differ from organization to organization, certain responsibilities are usually reserved for either line managers or staff personnel. Table 9-4 illustrates some of the training activities and responsibilities normally carried out by line and staff.

CONCLUSIONS AND APPLICATIONS

- T&D is important in the achievement of organizational objectives. Through training, employees gain skills, abilities, knowledge, and attitudes that help them perform more effectively in present and future jobs. As such, T&D may be considered an investment in human resources that will provide many important benefits and returns to the organization.

- T&D serves the organization by performing a number of important functions: (1) improving performance, (2) updating employee skills, (3) promoting job competency, (4) solving problems, (5) preparing for promotion, and (6) orienting new employees.

- The training process includes three distinct but related phases: needs assessment, the training program itself, and evaluation. Each phase is important for successful T&D, and none can be omitted.

- Effective T&D includes a balance of both on- and away-from-the-job activities. Individual programs should be created, particularly for managers, and should be built on current strengths and weaknesses, career potential, and personal needs.

- T&D administrators should make every effort to evaluate T&D. Only through a sound evaluation will trainers obtain support from top management and show how T&D improves organizational effectiveness. Major T&D efforts should include the following levels of evaluation: reaction, learning, behavior change, and results. Evaluation should focus primarily on how the trainee's performance improves after completion of training.

- Both line and staff trainers must be aware of the legal environment surrounding the T&D function. Race, religion, sex, color, national origin, or age must not be a factor in determining who receives training or who is selected to be developed for promotional opportunities. The only exception to this rule is where an organization has an approved affirmative action program. In this case, preferential treatment for minorities may be legal.

- Technical, conceptual, and human-relations skills provide the foundation for all management jobs, though the mix of the three skills will vary considerably by management level. T&D professionals should become knowledgeable about how the skills and abilities for effective management vary among low-, middle-, and top-management levels.

- All HRD professionals should become familiar with the behavioral patterns of obsolescent managers and determine the extent to which the problem of obsolescence pervades the organization.

- T&D involves close cooperation between line and staff personnel, and each must recognize their shared authority.

- T&D must reflect certain principles of learning to be successful. The following principles hold: the trainee must be motivated, the trainee must get feedback on his or her progress, the material must be well organized, the trainee must be able to practice, and learning must transfer to the job environment.

CASE STUDY

The Walkaround Mall

Melanie Gonzales is the mall manager for the Walkaround Mall, located in Charleston, West Virginia. Walkaround is owned by an investment group, RDH, which owns eleven other malls and two dozen strip shopping centers. Gonzales manages Walkaround on behalf of RDH Investments, and was recently transferred to this mall after achieving notable success at a similar mall in central Indiana. Walkaround features over one hundred stores and businesses, each of which has either a short- or a long-term lease managed by Gonzales. All leases are computed on the basis of a minimum plus a percentage of store (or business) sales dollars.

Two other malls operate in the area, one larger and one smaller. Wal-Mart and Sam's stores moved into the area, in new strip shopping centers, for the first time in 1993. While the population of West Virginia has been decreasing gradually over several years, the population of Charleston is stable. Large employers are located in the area, but the unemployment rate is a little higher than the national average.

Part of Gonzales's role as mall manager is to help develop the overall business of the mall. She was able to show 12 percent total mall sales increases annually during her three years in Indiana. Typically, mall strategy is to focus on three conditions in order to increase mall sales:

1. Increase the occupancy rate with quality stores.
2. Make physical changes that make the mall more attractive.
3. Ensure that the work force within the mall is skilled and motivated.

Gonzales was concerned when Walkaround had only a 4 percent increase in total sales in 1992, so when she moved to Charleston at the beginning of 1993, she focused on the three crucial conditions. During 1993 she lost six shops, but replaced each with a similar store. All four of the "anchors," or large department stores (Sears, Lazarus, Penneys, and Kaufmans), remained on long-term leases. RDH Investments approved a general

facilities "face lift," but there was no new construction, and none was likely during the next two to three years.

Gonzales decided that she needed to move on condition 3 and focus on the managers and sales employees. All employees work for their own stores, not for the mall, but Gonzales met with some of the store managers and developed a T&D plan to help the stores train their employees. The manager of Shoes-Are-You told Gonzales, "If you can help train our employees to be better salespersons, I know we could increase our sales." The T-Shirt World manager suggested that "the store associates who sell the most are those who are pleasant and smile at customers."

By May 1993, Gonzales had scheduled a one-hour training program titled "Increase Your Sales and Smile!" The program would be repeated at various times over a two-month period so that every employee would have a chance to attend. A business professor from a local college presented the program, using a videotape, a brief lecture, and a short role-playing exercise, to emphasize the basics of effective selling. Almost 50 percent of all employee attended the sessions, and many of the trainees said that they really enjoyed the program and that it was helpful. Gonzales made hopeful predictions when talking with RDH managers at their offices that summer.

However, in mid-January 1994, Gonzales was distraught as she set in her office and read the numbers. Overall sales had increased—but only by 4.5 percent. Had the training program, which she had designed with the professor, had only a 0.5 percent effect? She now wonders what she can do to influence the employees working in the mall to help boost sales since her hands are tied on conditions 1 and 2.

She has a meeting scheduled for Monday to discuss the mall performance figures with RDH in Dallas.

QUESTIONS

1. What were the flaws in her training approach?

2. Should she design another training approach to help increase 1994 sales?

3. Did she follow the three phases of an effective T&D plan?

4. What objectives for training would be appropriate for her situation?

5. Is examining the total sales of all mall stores the best, or only, evaluation method available?

6. Can the sluggish sales at Walkaround be solved by an effective T&D program?

EXPERIENTIAL EXERCISES

1. Individual: Supervision—A Basket Case?

PURPOSE

To understand how the in-basket technique for developing managers works by participating in an in-basket exercise.

INTRODUCTION

The in-basket is a simulation consisting of notes, letters, memos, and other information that is typical of the kind of printed material that crosses a manager's desk daily. The term *in-basket* is derived from the fact that supervisors and managers face a constant barrage of written requests, questions, concerns, and problems that must be attended to—the kinds of things that often end up in a manager's in-basket. This management T&D technique forces the manager to make decisions: more specifically, decisions about how to act on (if at all) the things that land in the in-basket. The exercise itself teaches the training participant how to act on a variety of problems that confront managers daily.

THE TASK

Assume that you supervise twenty-five blue-collar employees in a mid-sized manufacturing company (1200 employees) and that you are participating in a management T&D program that uses the in-basket technique. Listed below are brief descriptions of items sitting in your in-basket. For each item, answer the following two questions:

1. How important is this item? (Assign one of the following numbers: 1: not important at all; 2: somewhat important; 3: important; 4: very important; and 5: extremely important.) Be prepared to explain and defend your answer.

2. What specifically should be done with this item? Some options to consider (you may develop others) are: 1: act on the item immediately; 2: postpone acting on it until a later date (specify how much later); 3: delegate the item to someone else to act on (assume you have a secretary or an assistant and that the organization you work for

has a normal line/staff organizational structure with staff assistance from the human resource department, etc); if you chose this option, specify *who* should act on the item; 4: seek more information about the item (specify *what* information you would seek); and 5: do nothing (place the item in the circular file). Be prepared to explain and defend your answer.

In-Basket Items

1. A letter from an employee that requests three days' sick leave to visit a sick aunt in a distant city. Current policies do not provide for sick leave to visit or care for sick relatives. She is, however, an excellent employee.

2. A request from a company to provide a work reference on a former employee you supervised. The employee was a machine operator. He worked for you for about a year and, overall, did satisfactory work, but nothing exceptional.

3. A telephone message to call your spouse immediately.

4. An anonymous letter, signed "concerned female employee," who complains of sexual harassment in your work group. A male employee who is one of your subordinates is named as the harasser.

5. A letter from an excellent employee who wishes to set up an appointment to discuss her future with the company. She states that she is "burned out" in her job and wants a promotion to a more responsible job. She insinuates that she will look for other employment if she is not promoted soon. There are no job opportunities in your work unit and only a handful in other areas of the company.

6. A letter from the HR manager, who expresses concern about the plant's becoming unionized. He wants to meet with you to discuss specifically what you can do to stop "all this talk about a union."

7. A letter from the vice-president of manufacturing, who wants to talk to you about the possibility of using quality circles in the plant to improve product quality. He notes that because you are a recent business school graduate, you "probably know more about quality circles than anyone else at the plant."

8. A letter from an EEOC representative who wants to talk to you about a complaint filed against your company by a former employee. She (a black female) alleges that you fired her not because of poor performance (as you stated to her) but because she was black.

9. An anonymous letter stating that alcohol and illegal drugs are being consumed in cars and vans in the company parking lot during lunch hour.

10. A note from your boss that a supervisory position will be open in a few months. He wants to know who, if anyone, among your current nonsupervisory employees might be a good candidate for the job.

2. Group: Teaching the Teachers

PURPOSE

To experience the work that is required when assessing actual training needs and trying to develop an evaluation method that will provide the information employers really want. Group discussion may expose the student to needs and outcomes that she or he did not think were important.

THE TASK

Perhaps every semester you perform student evaluations on some or all of your instructors. Unless you are guilty of the rater error of leniency, or unless you are taught by an exceptional instructor, you give negative ratings to one or more items describing your instructor.

1. Write down three specific weaknesses of one of your ineffective or mediocre instructors. Do not write down the instructor's name since it is his or her teaching in which we are interested.

2. Form into a small groups, preferably three to six to a group, and discuss your lists. Next, your group should rank-order these identified weaknesses into a group list of at least five weaknesses. Discard any weaknesses that cannot be improved through training.

3. Write training objectives that you would like to see met through some type of T&D program. However, the group should not yet choose what type of training should be conducted.

4. Briefly specify which T&D methods could be used to achieve these objectives.

5. Describe a different evaluation technique for each objective your group specified. Will your evaluation techniques really prove that the weaknesses you originally identified (in step 1) will be corrected after the training?

6. How might you go through these same steps if you were the academic department chair, the academic vice-president, a parent, or a state legislator?

KEY TERMS AND CONCEPTS

Apprentice training
Away-from-the-job training
Behavior modeling
Case study
Coaching
Committee assignments
Conceptual skill
Conference/discussion
Diversity training

Employee training
Human-relations skills
Human Resource Development (HRD)
In-basket exercises
Intercultural preparation
Job instruction training (JIT)
Job rotation
Lateral promotions
Learning styles

Lecture
Levels of T&D evaluation
Management development
Management games
Management (executive) succession chart
Managerial obsolescence
Mentoring
Needs assessment
Neurolinguistic programming (NLP)
On-the-job training (OJT)
Outward Bound
Performance gap
Programmed instruction
Role playing

Sensitivity training
Seven intelligences
T&D evaluation
T&D objectives
Technical skills
Technology-based T&D systems
Training feedback
Training plan
Training systems model
Transfer climate
Transfer of learning
Vestibule/simulation
Whole-brain theories
Wilderness training

REVIEW QUESTIONS

1. What are the major purposes of T&D programs?

2. What are the three levels at which a T&D needs assessment can be made? Describe some of the methods available at the different levels.

3. Name and distinguish the various OJT and away-from-the-job training techniques.

4. When, and in what circumstances, will OJT be more effective than away-from-the-job training techniques? Which approach is more expensive to the organization?

5. How do the training needs of managerial employees differ from the needs of professional nonmanagerial employees, or from those of front-line employees in service or production industries?

6. What are the important principles of learning discussed in this chapter? How should knowing these principles improve the design of a T&D program?

7. How have technology advances changed the T&D methods available to employers? Are high-tech training programs superior to lecture and discussion approaches?

8. Discuss the legal issues that may be involved in T&D. What should an HRD professional do to guard against a complaint or lawsuit involving training?

9. What are the major mistakes employers make in choosing the methods and topics for training programs? Which of the three phases of T&D is most neglected in the workplace?

10. How can an employer enhance the transfer climate of the workplace? What can an organization do at work to help employees learn and remember the training they receive away from the job?

DISCUSSION QUESTIONS

1. Listed are six T&D methods and five situations. From the six T&D selections, select the best answer to the needs in the five situations.

1. Lecture
2. Vestibule
3. OJT instruction
4. College-sponsored seminar
5. Apprentice training
6. Programmed instruction

_____ A. Train thirty new employees to run a large printing press.

_____ B. Small employer needs to familiarize two HR employees with new guidelines on the Americans with Disabilities Act.

_____ C. Office needs to teach one new clerical employee how to run various office machines.

_____ D. Organization of 500 needs training to prepare raters to handle upcoming performance appraisals more effectively.

_____ E. Airline needs to train fifty new pilots.

2. If you were a newly hired T&D director for a medium-sized manufacturing company of 750 employees, how would you communicate the importance of T&D to top management? Could you prove the value of T&D programs in objective terms if necessary?

3. Think of a simple task that can be performed in the classroom, such as how to build a paper airplane. Using JIT, list the steps involved and train a classmate to perform the task and make the same airplane. Ask for feedback from the trainee concerning your effectiveness as a trainer. Create another simple task and switch roles with your classmate.

4. How does operating "lean and mean" after downsizing influence T&D programs in the United States? While it is easy to say that we all need more training, do we really? What proportion of the payroll should be spent on formal T&D programs?

5. Should employers invest in basic skills general training? Who has (or shares) the responsibility for teaching and learning basic reading, writing, and math skills? Will there be a greater need for such basic skills training in the workplace during the next twenty years?

6. Is T&D more important in some industries than in others? Which industries need what kind of T&D programs are involved?

7. What are the problems of people and organizations that cannot be solved with training? List five problems that exist in your workplace (or one you know) that cannot be substantially improved through T&D.

8. It is often very hard to assess the value of a T&D program. What are the problems in evaluating the effects of training?

9. If mentoring can be very helpful to the careers of protégés, what can an employee do to be mentored? Can an employer force a manager to mentor an employee? Do the genders of the mentor and the protégé matter?

10. If you were a top manager and wanted your HRD staff to help your managerial employees become better managers, what five courses would you suggest as part of a managerial T&D program? What topics would be most helpful to managers at various stages of their careers?

ENDNOTES

Chapter 9

1. Carolyn Wiley, "Training for the '90s: How Leading Companies Focus on Quality Improvement, Technological Change, and Customer Service," *Employment Relations Today* 20 (Spring 1993): 79. see also "ASTD Effort Pushes for Better Training of America's Workforce," *Training and Development* 45 (March 1991): 7.

2. "Industry Report: 1992," *Training* 29 (October 1992): 25–26, 28; and "Industry Report: 1991," *Training* 28 (October 1991): 31–33.

3. Wiley, "Training for the '90s," pp. 79–80.

4. E. Mandt, "A Basic Model of Manager Development," *Personnel Journal* 58 (June 1979): 395–400.

5. See Elmer Burack and Gopal Pati, "Technology and Managerial Obsolescence," *MSU Business Topics* (Spring 1970): 49–56; and Herbert Kaufman, *Obsolescence and Professional Career Development* (New York: AMACON, 1974).

6. Gareth R. Jones, "Socialization Tactics, Self-Efficacy, and Newcomers' Adjustments to Organizations," *Academy of Management Journal* 29, no. 2 (June 1986): 262–79.

7. "How Businesses Search for Qualified Applicants: Trying to Bridge the Skills Gap," *Human Resource Measurements*, a supplement to *Personnel Journal* 71 (June 1992): 1–2.

8. Ibid.

9. Ibid.

10. *See* C. Lee, "Who Gets Trained in What," *Training* 28 (October 1991): 47–59; and Wiley, "Training for the '90s," pp. 81–82.

11. Ibid.

12. "Focus Moves from Staffing to Productivity," *Training and Development* 47 (October 1993): 71–72.

13. William McGehee and Paul Thayer, *Training in Business and Industry* (New York: Wiley, 1961), pp. 124–125.

14. J. W. Newstrom and J. M. Lilyquist, "Selecting Needs Analysis Methods," *Training and Development Journal* 33 (1979): 178–82. *See also* K. N. Wexley and G. P. Latham, *Developing and Training Human Resources* (Glenview, IL: Scott, Foresman, 1981), Chapter 3; F. L. Ulschak, *Human Resource Development: The Theory and Practice of Need Assessment* (Reston, VA: Reston, 1983).

15. Newstrom and Lilyquist, "Selecting Needs Analysis Methods," pp. 180–81.

16. Timothy T. Baldwin, Richard J. Magjuka, and Brian T. Loher, "The Perils of Participation: Effects of Choice on Training on Trainee Motivation and Learning," *Personnel Psychology* 44 (1991): 51–65.

17. Adapted from Jim Boucher, "Crosstraining: Just Do It Right," *Training and Development* 47 (September 1993): 10.

18. For a detailed discussion of the advantages and disadvantages of job rotation, see Yoram Ziera, "Job Rotation for Management Development," *Personnel* 71 (July–August 1974): 25–35.

19. See "Taking the Jolts Out of Moving," *Nation's Business* 63 (November 1975): 36–38; and "Moving on Loses Its Glamour for More Employees," *The Wall Street Journal* (August 3, 1976): 1.

20. Methods for modernizing the JIT method are discussed in Fred Wickert, "The Famous JIT Card: A Basic Way to Improve It," *Training and Development Journal* 28 (February 1974): 6–9.

21. A certain amount of risk taking is important for effective management. *See* A. Hill, "How Organizational Philosophy Influences Management Development," *Personnel Journal* 59 (February 1980): 118–20.

22. *See* the Woodlands Group, "Management Development Roles: Coach, Sponsor, Mentor," *Personnel Journal* 59 (November 1980): 918–21; and J. Yeager, "Coaching the Executive: Can You Teach an Old Dog New Tricks?" *Personnel Administrator* 82 (November 1982): 37–42.

23. Harry Levinson, "A Psychologist Looks at Executive Development," *Harvard Business Review* (November–December 1962): 69–75.

24. George F. Dreher and Ronald A. Ash, "A Comparative Study of Mentoring Among Men and Women in Managerial, Professional, and Technical Positions," *Journal of Applied Psychology* 75 (1990): 539–46.

25. For a detailed discussion of the potential pitfalls of OJT, see I. L. Goldstein, *Training: Program Development and Evaluation* (Belmont, CA: Wadsworth, 1974), pp. 142–43.

26. Wiley, "Training for the '90s," p. 83.

27. Ibid.

28. Robert D. Bretz and Robert E. Thompsett, "Comparing Traditional and Integrative Learning Methods in Organizational Training Programs," *Journal of Applied Psychology* 77 (1992): 941–51.

29. Ibid., p. 84.

30. Adapted from Shari Caudron, "Humor Is Healthy in the Workplace," *Personnel Journal* 71 (June 1992): 63–68; and "How Kodak Made Room for Humor," *Personnel Journal* 71 (June 1992): 66.

31. Wexley and Latham, *Developing and Training Human Resources*, p. 193.

32. The various forms of role playing are outlined in W. Rohlsing, "Role Playing" in R. Craig, ed., *Training and Development Handbook* (New York: McGraw-Hill, 1976).

33. C. Craft, "Management Games," in Craig, *Training and Development Handbook*.

34. The distinction between computer-based and manually operated games is discussed in L. Coppard, "Gaming Simulation and the Training Process," in Craig, *Training and Development Handbook*.

35. While interest in management games usually runs high, there is little empirical evidence supporting their effectiveness. See Janet Schriesheim and Chester Schriesheim, "The Effectiveness of Business Games in Management Training," *Training and Development Journal* 28 (May 1974): 14–18; and Wexley and Latham, *Developing and Training Human Resources*, pp. 205–6.

36. W. Byham, "The Assessment Center as an Aid in Management Development," *Training and Development Journal* 25 (December 1971).

37. Berkeley Rice, "Going to the Mountain," *Psychology Today* (December 1979): 65–81; Bruce Knecht, "Executives Go Outward Bound," *Dun's Business Month* (July 1983): 56–58; Janet Long, "The Wilderness Lab," *Training and Development Journal* 41 (March 1987): 30–39.

38. Wexley and Latham, *Developing and Training Human Resources*, p. 178.

39. William M. Fox, "Getting the Most from Behavior Modeling Training," *National Productivity Review* 7 (Summer 1988): 243–44.

40. W. Byham and J. Robinson, "Interaction Modeling: A New Concept in Supervisory Training," *Training and Development Journal* 30 (February 1976): 20–23.

41. For detailed criticisms of this form of training, see John R. Kimberly and Warren R. Nielsen, "Organization Development and Change in Organization Performance," *Administrative Science Quarterly* 20 (June 1975): 191; and Martin Lakin, "Some Ethical Issues in Sensitivity Training," *American Psychologist* 23 (October 1969): 923–28.

42. "White, Male, and Worried," *Business Week* (January 31, 1994): 52–53.

43. David C. Wigglesworth, "Video-ing Diversity: A Review of Training Videos on Workforce Diversity," *Training and Development* 46 (December 1992): 53.

44. Ibid., p. 54.

45. Ideas modified from Michael Mobley and Tamara Payne, "Backlash! The Challenge to Diversity Training," *Training and Development* 46 (December 1992): 45–52.

46. John P. Campbell and Marvin D. Dunnette, "Effectiveness of T-Group Experiences in Managerial Training and Development," *Psychological Bulletin* 64 (August 1968): 73–104; and Robert J. House, "T-Group Education and Leadership Effectiveness: A Review of the Empiric Literature and a Critical Evaluation," *Personnel Psychology* 20 (Spring 1967): 1–32.

47. Wexley and Latham, *Developing and Training Human Resources*, pp. 75–77.

48. For a discussion of the concept of transfer climate, see J. Z. Rouillier and I. L. Goldstein, "Determinants of the Climate for Transfer of Training," presented at the meeting of Society of Industrial/Organizational Psychology (1991), as cited in Scott I. Tannenbaum and Gary Yukl, "Training and Development in Work Organizations," *Annual Review of Psychology* 43 (1992): 399–441.

49. Kenneth N. Wexley and Gary P. Latham, *Developing and Training Human Resources in Organizations*, 2nd ed. (New York: HarperCollins, 1991), p. 6.

50. D. L. Kirkpatrick, "Four Steps to Measuring Training Effectiveness," *Personnel Administrator* 28 (November 1983): 19–26. *See also* K. Bunker and S. Cohen, "The Rigors of Training Evaluation, A Discussion and Field Demonstration," *Personnel Psychology* 30 (1977): 525–41; and K. Bunker and S. Cohen, "Evaluating Organizational Training Efforts: Is Ignorance Really Bliss?" *Training and Development Journal* 32 (1978): 4–11.

51. George Kimmerling, "Gathering the Best Practices," *Training and Development* 47 (September 1993): 29–36.

52. Ray A. Faidley, "Build a Lean, Clean, Training Machine," *Training and Development* 47 (October 1993): 69.

53. James Hassat, "Predicting the Costs of Training," *Training and Development* 46 (November 1992): 42.

54. "Learning-Style Theories," *Personnel Journal* 71 (September 1992): 91. NLP is addressed in Laborde, *Influencing with Integrity*.

55. Ibid.

56. Ibid. The seven intelligences were originally listed in Garner, *Frames of Mind*. (New York: Basic Books, 1983).

57. Ibid.

58. Ibid., citing David A. Kolb's work at Case Western University.

59. An excellent overview of the importance of learning principles is given in Wexley and Latham, *Developing and Training Human Resources*, Chapter 4.

60. The value of goal setting and its impact on motivation is discussed in G. P. Latham and E. A. Locke, "Goal Setting: A Motivational Technique That Works," *Organizational Dynamics* 8 (Autumn 1979): 68–80.

61. Baldwin et al., "The Perils of Participation," pp. 51–65.

62. Research shows that trainees will accept negative feedback as long as it is not seen as punitive. *See* D. R. Illgen, C. O. Fisher, and M. S. Taylor, "Consequences of Individual Feedback on Behavior in Organizations," *Journal of Applied Psychology* 64, no. 4 (May 1982): 349–71.

63. Wexley and Latham, *Developing and Training Human Resources*, pp. 75–77.

64. Ibid., pp. 22–27.

65. E. I. Smith, *Small Climber Development* (Basking Ridge, NJ: AT&T, 1978).

66. For details of the Weber case, see J. Ledvinka, *Federal Regulation of Personnel and Human Resource Management* (Belmont, CA: Wadsworth, 1982), pp. 121–23.

67. Lyle Sussman and Frank

Kuzmits, "The HRD Professional As In-House Consultant," *Personnel* 64 (June 1987): 18–22.

68. Edwin A. Fleishman, "Leadership Climate, Human Relations Training, and Supervisory Behavior," in Edwin A. Fleishman, ed., *Studies in Personnel and Industrial Psychology* (Homewood, IL: Dorsey Press, 1967), pp. 250–63.

69. "Training South of the Border," *Training and Development* 47 (September 1993): 14.

70. Michael J. Marquardt and Dean W. Engel, "HRD Competencies for a Shrinking World," *Training and Development* 47 (May 1993): 60.

71. Lennie Copeland and Lewis Griggs, *Going International* (New York: Random House, 1985), p. xvii.

72. P. Christopher Earley, "Intercultural Training for Managers: A Comparison of Documentary and Interpersonal Methods." *Academy of Management Journal* 30, no. 4 (December 1987): 686.

73. "Preparing Expatriates," *Training and Development* 47 (September 1993): 10.

74. Sylvia Odenwald, "A Guide for Global Training," *Training and Development* 47 (July 1993): 25.

75. Ibid., p. 27.

INTERNAL STAFFING AND CAREER MANAGEMENT

CHAPTER OBJECTIVES

1. To recognize the various kinds of internal-staffing decisions
that have an impact on the HR function and to describe how
these decisions may be effectively made.

2. To discuss the importance of making sound promotion decisions and to describe both effective and ineffective criteria for making these decisions.

3. To understand the inherent dangers in making promotion decisions solely on the basis of past performance.

4. To identify the HR department's role in assisting the laid-off employee to gain employment as quickly as possible.

5. To understand the legal issues that surround the internal staffing process.

6. To explore a career management model and to illustrate the elements necessary for a successful career management function.

7. To examine the problems that typically confront employees when seeking to advance their careers.

8. To identify the problems that women and minorities have when trying to move up the organizational ladder.

The 1990s have been a turbulent time for many organizations and for their employees. Mergers and acquisitions, massive reorganizations, shifts toward service sector jobs, social pressures, demographic changes, and slow economic growth have all lead to downsizing, rightsizing, and layoffs (see the first two *HR in the News*).

The typical organizational chart, with neatly drawn and labeled boxes connected by horizontal and vertical lines, often fails to convey the great amount of movement by personnel that takes place in modern enterprises. People are shifted up, down, across, and out in organizations of all kinds and sizes. These decisions about **internal staffing**, involving promotions, demotions, transfers, and layoffs, represent an important area of HR policy and management. Effective internal-staffing plans, policies, and procedures will promote the achievement of both organizational and personal goals. But mismanagement of internal staffing may result in a great deal of job

dissatisfaction and reduced organizational effectiveness. In this chapter, we will discuss internal-staffing decisions and the issues connected with them. In Chapter 7, the primary concern was with external hiring. The focus here will be on the staffing decisions that affect the firm's internal human resources.

The second part of this chapter concentrates on two special concerns associated with internal staffing: career management and special obstacles to women and minorities. Many contemporary HR professionals have designed programs and procedures that enable employees to progress upward in a planned, systematic way. Successful career management leads to an improved quality of working life and maximum utilization of employee skills.

The last part of the chapter deals with the special problems that women and other minorities face in their careers. While progress has been made in removing obstacles to advancement for these groups in many organizations, a "glass ceiling" may still continue to exist in

The Horizontal Corporation Will Change Careers

Delayered, flattened, squared, or horizontal—however you describe it, the organizational structure of the 1990s has changed. The old hierarchical pyramid structure, managed down by individuals, is rapidly changing into a flattened structure, managed across by teams, in many organizations. While many (perhaps most) employers have downsized during the past decade, many employers have also reorganized according to a different plan that involves more than simply cutting the work force.

AT&T's Network Systems Division reorganized its entire business around processes (rather than tasks) and now sets budgets focused on these processes. Employee bonuses are based on customer evaluations. Eastman Chemical, of Kodak, has over 1000 teams and has eliminated its senior vice-presidents for administration, manufacturing, and R&D, replacing them with self-directed work teams.[1] Many other companies have made similar basic restructuring changes.

Many organizational charts no longer look like pyramids made of boxes and lines. Ernest W. Deavenport, Jr., president of Eastman Chemical, said, "Our organization chart is now called the *pizza chart* because it looks like a pizza with a lot of pepperoni sitting on it." Deavenport, the pepperoni at the center of the pie, explained: "We did it in circular form to show that everyone is equal in the organization. No one dominates the other."[2] Each pepperoni on the pie is a cross-functional team responsible for managing a business, area, or function. PepsiCo's organizational chart is now an inverted pyramid. Other models have included a starburst, to show units splitting off like shooting stars, and a shamrock, whose three leaves (joined at the stem) represent core employees, external contractors, and part-timers.[3]

The objective of the horizontal organization is to get away from the narrow viewpoints of corporate specialists who have spent their careers climbing a vertical hierarchy to the top of their functional area. DuPont's Terry Ennis explained: "Our goals is to get everyone focused on the business as a system in which the functions are seamless." DuPont wanted to get rid of "disconnects" or "handoffs" between departments or functions. Ennis said, "Every time you have an organizational boundary, you get a disconnect. The bigger the organization, the bigger the functions, and the more disconnects you get.[4]

The implications for the careers of millions of employees are not all known. Not all companies will change so radically, but the days of a clear career ladder within a function and predictable job assignments may be fading away.

others. This material will help the student focus on how the old boy network, harmful stereotypes, role conflicts, special pressures of dual-career couples, and special development programs affect the careers of women and minorities.

FACTORS INFLUENCING INTERNAL STAFFING DECISIONS

Figure 10–1 illustrates the important factors that influence internal staffing decisions. These include the following:

Organization Growth Business or government expansion generally results in filling new positions by promoting existing employees. Increases in the number of new positions are particularly common for companies in growth industries. See Figure 10-2 for information on where or-

ganizational and job growth will be in the mid-1990s.

Reorganization A major restructuring of an organization will result in various types of personnel actions. During the 1980s and 1990s, mergers and reorganizations became popular. The purchase or sale of a company or a merger with another company influences a wide range of HR activities, including job design, compensation, benefits, labor relations, and early-retirement programs. Also, a management philosophy of operating with a flatter organizational structure has a wide range of effects on staffing considerations.

General Economic Trends One consequence of major economic downturns is that a significant number of workers will temporarily or permanently lose their jobs. Companies that manufacture durable goods, such as automobiles and home

FIGURE 10-1 Factors influencing internal staffing decisions.

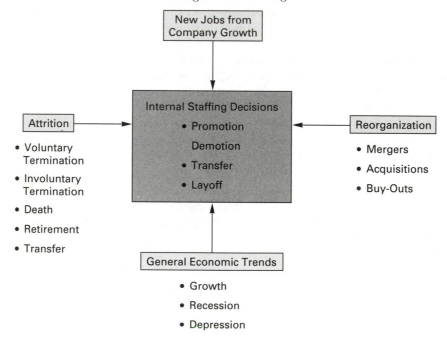

Will Your Own Career Go "Horizontal"?

Tom Peters, in his book *Liberation Management,* observes that due to many factors, people will have to get used to fewer promotions and more lateral (horizontal) career moves. Peters contends that these *horizontal promotions* will (and must) become a common feature "of the new, hierarchy-less, horizontal, project-driven organization."[5]

For most employees, who have been geared to climb the organizational ladder, Peters says there will be no organizational pyramid remaining to climb. "So how will people get their kicks? . . . For hundreds of years we've enjoyed the perks as much as pay increases."[6] Executives have expected the big car, the personal secretary, the club memberships, and all the other trappings. Peters says, "Honestly, now, that's the *real* career progression, isn't it? . . . The secretary gets an attached office. . . . Now add an anteroom. Then on to the executive corridor with a "general pre-anteroom," followed by your own anteroom. Now, add security guards. Joy of joys, the real world never intrudes anymore!"[7]

Parents want their sons and daughters to work for stable, large corporations and proceed up the career ladders they themselves knew (or heard about). Even more frustrating, women and minorities have made progress in moving up those ladders just at the time that Peters sees the ladders beginning to disappear.

Demographic charts show the large group of baby boomers trying to jam into the middle and upper management levels. This overdemand for the traditional spots on the promotion ladder, with the shortening or virtual elimination of the ladder itself, means drastic career consequences for employees. A strong adjustment in realistic expectations will be required. How should employers begin this adjustment?

Peters suggests that they begin with giving recruits straight talk from the beginning, "making it clear that getting ahead means moving laterally, perhaps even downward upon occasion, to build skills and tackle more challenging assignments not necessarily associated with ladder climbing."[8] Peters's solution includes getting new employees directly into a project team. "If steps through (not up) more challenging projects are demonstrably the norm from the start, then the attraction to the trappings of hierarchy never gets established in the first place.[9]

These observations point out the necessity for students to obtain a broad background of educational and work-related experiences to be successful in the twenty-first century.

FIGURE 10-2 Where will job growth occur in the 1990s?

According to Bureau of Labor Statistics, the following employers added the most jobs:[a]

New Jobs

Temporary services	350,000	Up 19.1%
Health care	300,000	Up 3.7%
Construction	200,000	Up 4.2%
Autos & trucks	154,000	Up 4.0%
Financial services	90,000	Up 2.8%

While there has been a mild economic recovery during the early 1990s, job growth has not been part of the mix. The defense industry eliminated 340,000 jobs between 1988 and 1993, and many healthy industries have grown without adding employees. The following list indicates which industries are expected to rise or fall in the mid-1990s.[b] However, the rise of an industry no longer ensures that the number of employees will increase.

Industries to Rise	Industries to Fall
Autos	Defense
Banks	Energy
Computers	Pharmaceuticals
Securities	Transportation
Semiconductors	Utilities

[a]For the period November 1992 to November 1993, as reported in *Business Week* (December, 1993): 34–35.
[b]"It Won't Take Your Breath Away, But . . . The Economy Is Poised for Modest, Steady Growth This Year," *Business Week* (January 10, 1994): 60–61.

appliances, are particularly vulnerable to fluctuations in the business cycle. While some companies that provide services, such as health care and nondurable items, are sometimes said to be "recession proof," the bottom line of most employers is adversely affected by a recession. The slow economic growth experienced during the past few years has led to little, if any, real expansion in the full-time labor force. Economic cycles are clearly an important variable in changes in internal staffing.

Attrition Employee reductions that result from termination, resignation, retirement, transfer out of the business unit, and death are collectively referred to as *attrition*. In particular, early-retirement programs have increased during the downsizing and the recent economic sluggishness, as employers are pressured to trim excess human resources.

PROMOTION

A **promotion** involves the reassignment of an employee to a higher-level job. When promoted, employees generally face increasing demands in terms of skills, abilities, and responsibilities. In turn, employees generally receive increased pay and (sometimes) benefits, as well as greater authority and status.

Promotions serve many purposes and provide benefits to both organizations and employees. First, promotions enable organizations to use their employees' abilities to the greatest extent possible. Second, promotions can encourage excellent performance. Employees generally perform at high levels if they believe that high performance leads to promotion.[10] Third, there is a significant correlation between opportunities for advancement and high levels of job satisfaction.[11]

Recruiting for Promotion

Two main approaches are used to recruit employees for promotion. The more common approach is the **closed promotion system**, which places the responsibility for identifying promotable employees with the supervisor of the job to be filled. In addition to reviewing the past performance and assessing the potential of subordinates, a supervisor may inquire about employees in other departments who may be qualified for the job.

A drawback to the closed promotion system is that many employees who may be qualified and interested in promotion are often overlooked. For example, the vice-president of a large bank with an opening for a commercial loan officer in its home office may be unaware of qualified or interested employees in branch offices. In such cases, the job may be filled by an employee known to the executive but less qualified than other employees.

An approach that generally leads to recruiting the most qualified person from the internal labor pool is known as the **open promotion system**. This approach is also known as *job posting*. With job posting, job vacancies are publicized on bulletin boards and internal communication systems so that all interested employees may apply. Job posting enhances participation and the achievement of equal opportunity goals, but it also increases administrative expenses and takes time. A survey by the Bureau of National Affairs showed that open promotion systems are used mostly at the clerical and blue-collar levels in government and unionized companies, that open and closed systems are used about equally for professional and technical employees, and that closed systems are used almost exclusively for managerial personnel.[12]

Promotion Criteria

For many employees, a promotion is a highly sought prize. Climbing the organizational ladder has long been a part of the American dream. Status, satisfaction, and financial rewards accrue to those who are able to rise in an organization. But frustration, stress, and even severe depression may occur when personal goals of upward mobility are unmet by an organization—particularly when an employee feels passed over for a deserved promotion. Because organizational effectiveness and job satisfaction are influenced by the way in which promotions are made, it is important for organizations to gather reliable data for making decisions about promotions. There are a number of criteria that organizations examine in deciding which candidates to promote.

Seniority Many organizations place significant weight on an employee's seniority or tenure when making a promotion decision. *Seniority* refers to an employee's length of service and has long been important in American industry. For generations, a senior employee has expected and often received a greater share of organizational rewards than a junior employee. Salaries and benefits, such as vacation time and sick leave, are often tied to seniority.

Students of management often think that seniority should be given little or no weight in promotional decisions, holding that seniority is anathema to private enterprise because length of service rather than performance is rewarded. There are, however, sound arguments for using seniority as a criterion in promoting employees. First, seniority avoids the problems of biased managers, who may promote favorite employees. Second, seniority is a quick, easy, and painless way to make a promotion decision. Third, there is often a relationship between seniority and performance: up to a point, employees usually become more competent at their jobs as they gain experience. And fourth, seniority rewards the loyal employee who has perhaps labored for many years to produce the organization's products or services and who has stayed with the employer through good times and bad.

To explore the concept of seniority more fully, it may be helpful to distinguish between unionized and nonunionized employer–employee relationships. Seniority provisions are not required by federal laws, nor is seniority an inherent right of employees. However, seniority is a mandatory bargaining subject in the collective bargaining process. Formal seniority systems are common in virtually all unionized organizations, but are rare among nonunion employers.[13]

Depending on the particular labor agreement, seniority rights are vested within a variety of different employee units. The most common unit is *plantwide seniority,* where an individual employee receives credit that becomes applicable whenever that employee competes with any other employee from another unit for the same position. Other common seniority units include departmental, trade, classification, and companywide. For example, in a *departmental seniority* system, employees accrue seniority according to the amount of time they worked within a particular department, and that seniority credit is valid only within that department.[14] For example, an employee with eleven years of seniority in the shipping department could not compete successfully with an employee with seven years in the maintenance department for an open position in the maintenance department.

In situations involving layoffs, seniority systems often use **bumping**; that is, employees with greater seniority whose jobs have been phased out have the right to displace, or bump, employees with less seniority. Such bumping rights may be limited to departmental or job classification seniority instead of plantwide seniority. In a *combined seniority system,* plantwide seniority is frequently used to determine bumping (sometimes called *rolling*) rights.[15]

Management often disagrees with the use of seniority as the sole determinant of promotion decisions. The Bureau of National Affairs estimates that seniority is a determining factor in promotional policies, as provided by collective bargaining agreements, in 67 percent of labor contracts. However, only 9 percent call for promotion decisions based on seniority as the sole criterion. Another 33 percent provide that the most senior individual will receive promotion if he or she is qualified for the job.[16] In most promotional policies, seniority is treated as a determining factor along with employee skill and ability.

Past and Current Performance   Because of the potential drawbacks in using seniority as the sole promotion criterion, most nonunion organizations strongly consider current performance when promoting employees to jobs of increased responsibility, especially in management and professional jobs. Seniority is given little or no weight in such cases. Instead, a candidate's performance, training and development, education, awards, and other performance data are often used to predict the employee's chances for success in a higher-level job. Using this approach, the chances that the organization will make an effective promotion decision are relatively good when both the candidate's present job and the higher job require similar skills and abilities. Examples of such promotions include the following:

- Receptionist to secretary.
- Police sergeant to police captain.
- Bookkeeper to accounting assistant.
- First-line supervisor to superintendent.
- Regional plant manager to district plant manager.

In these examples, past work performance is a fairly good predictor of future success. But past performance is not always a valid indicator of future performance, particularly when the employee is promoted to a job that requires skills and abilities considerably different from those used in the previous job. A common situation involves the promotion of a lower-level employee to supervisor, such as advancement from assembly-line worker to first-line supervisor. The skills required for effective supervision are almost totally different from those required for successful assembly-line work, and many organizations have committed grave errors by promoting an employee into supervisory ranks solely because of technical expertise.

Employees are often promoted because of talents that bear little resemblance to the talents needed in the new job. Promotion into sales management is another good example. The top salesperson, demonstrating a unique ability to sell effectively, may be promoted to sales manager. Top management may believe that a good salesperson is also a good manager. But the sales manager often becomes frustrated by having to work with subordinates rather than with customers; motivating employees to sell is much different and perhaps much more difficult than persuading customers to buy a product or service. Management and nonmanagement jobs involve different skills, and many employee–job mismatches have resulted from promotions that have ignored this fact.

Assessment Centers In order to improve the chances of making successful promotional decisions—particularly from nonmanagement to management—many organizations are using **assessment centers**. Job candidates are brought to assessment centers for evaluation of their promotability by participating in a series of exercises. These exercises focus on the kinds of skills and abilities required to effectively perform the higher-level jobs that the candidates seek.[17]

American Telephone and Telegraph's (AT&T) assessment-center program is one of the largest and most sophisticated. AT&T set up over fifty assessment centers across the United States. Each assessment center is located in a conference room or seminar area away from the work site.

The primary purpose of the assessment center is to improve an organization's selection of managers, particularly at the first level of man-

agement. A secondary purpose is to increase the pool of employees from which managers are selected. An AT&T employee may ask to attend an assessment center, or a supervisor may feel that an employee is supervisory material and suggest that the employee attend. In either case, the final decision to participate is the employee's.

Roughly a dozen participants together undergo exercises designed to determine their potential as successful managers. Common exercises during the two and one-half day program include the following:[18]

- An in-depth interview concerning career goals and plans.
- A test of general mental ability.
- A test of reasoning ability.
- A test of knowledge about current affairs.
- A series of in-basket exercises.
- A management game involving the start-up and operation of a toy company.
- Role playing.

Throughout the session, six assessors and a director observe and evaluate each participant. They are experienced, successful line managers who volunteered to be trained as assessors.

After the sessions are over, the participants return to work. The assessors pool their evaluations and place each participant into one of the following categories: more than acceptable, acceptable, less than acceptable, and unacceptable. These ratings become important criteria for selecting managers in the future, though they are not the sole criterion used for making a promotion decision.

AT&T participants may request full reports concerning their performances at the assessment center, and about 85 percent of the participants make that request. Receiving a rating of "less than acceptable" or "unacceptable" is not the "kiss of death" for participants. These employees may still get promoted into management with the help of a persuasive supervisor or mentor.[19]

The results of AT&T's studies, and of the studies of many other researchers, show that the assessment center is a more effective selection method than such traditional practices as performance reviews, interviews, and supervisory recommendations.

Although assessment centers vary somewhat from company to company, AT&T's are fairly typical. Generally, smaller organizations do not have enough promotions to justify the expenses of setting up their own center, so they either use one of many external assessment centers or rely on more traditional selection methods.

Studies show that the assessment center approach improves the odds that a correct promotion decision will be made.[20] In comparing the method to traditional methods, one researcher stated that "the average validity of the assessment center is about as high as the maximum validity attained by use of . . . traditional methods."[21]

"Unofficial" Promotion Criteria

A common retort to a presentation of rational criteria used in promotion decisions is this: "Where I work, promotions depend on who you know, not what you do." All too often, a gulf exists between theory and practice when promotions are considered. Criteria such as seniority, performance, and assessment-center ratings may be cast aside for political reasons. Unofficial criteria may influence or even dominate a promotion decision. Such criteria include personal characteristics, nepotism, social factors, and friendships.

Personal Characteristics Together, Title VII of the Civil Rights Act, the Age Discrimination Act, and the Americans with Disabilities Act prohibit discrimination in all terms and conditions of employment on the basis of age, race, color, religion, sex, national origin, or disability. All internal staffing decisions fall under the domain of these acts, just as external recruiting, selection, and placement practices do. Although almost all organizations profess to abide by EEOC guidelines, not all organizations practice what they preach. Certain personal characteristics of the candidate may either help or hinder progression into the upper levels of the organization. Being of the "wrong" sex, race, age, or religion may create a real though unspoken obstacle to advancement. Such practices are not only immoral and unethical but also clearly illegal. Prejudice causes a sizable pool of valuable human talent to be overlooked and wasted.

Nepotism Being of a certain bloodline sometimes helps one's progression to a higher-level job. **Nepotism**, from the Italian *nepotismo* ("favoring of nephews"), is the showing of favoritism or patronage to relatives. Nepotism is often criticized because family members get desirable jobs and promotions primarily by virtue of their lineage.[22] At the highest ranks of the pyramid, nepotism is still practiced at many well-known firms, such as Ford and Toyota motor companies, Brown and Williamson Tobacco Company, IBM, DuPont, and Playboy Enterprises.

Employers have policies that either encourage or discourage nepotism. Courts will generally uphold either approach as long as the policy is clear and consistently applied. Employers may restrict nepotism with a written policy prohibiting the hiring of applicants who are related to current employees. However, the possibility of two employees marrying must also be considered in a nepotism policy. Since such a situation may involve two current, valued employees, it becomes a difficult policy question. A common policy is that if two employees within the same department marry, the junior employee must accept a transfer.

Social Factors Membership in a certain club or political party, graduation from the "right" university, and participation in the "right" sport (traditionally golf, perhaps also jogging, tennis, or racquetball) are important in getting promoted in some organizations, particularly at the upper management and staff levels. One classic account of the importance of these factors in decisions of promotion was published by sociologist Melville Dalton. Dalton conducted in-house research on managerial practices at several large companies, asking, "What are the things that enable men to rise in the plant here?" This response came from a fifty-three-year-old first-line supervisor:[23]

> I'm surprised that anybody who's been around here as long as you have would ask that question. You know as well as I do that getting in and running around with certain crowds is the way to get up. Nearly all the big boys are in the yacht club, and damn near all of 'em are Masons. Hell, these guys all play poker together. Their wives run around together, and they all have their families out to the yacht club hobnobbing together. That's no mystery. Everybody knows it. It's the friendships and connections you make running around in these crowds that makes or breaks you in the plant.

Friendships In organizations of all forms and sizes, strong informal bonds are created between employees who share common interests, ideals, values, beliefs, and attitudes. In turn, such informal bonds between decision makers and candidates for promotion may play a significant role in deciding who gets promoted and who doesn't. Particularly at the top organizational levels, executives prefer to work with people whose thoughts and perceptions mirror their own.

OTHER INTERNAL MOVES

Promotions are not the only way an employee may move in an organization. For many reasons, employees may have to be moved down, over, or even out. Thus, HR professionals must be prepared to deal with demotions, transfers, layoffs, and some less traditional approaches.

Demotion

A **demotion** is the reassignment of an employee to a lower job with less pay, involving fewer skills and responsibilities. Demotions may take place for reasons within or beyond the control of the employees. Typically, there have been five reasons for using the exceptional tool of demotion:

1. A failed promotion.
2. Inability to perform assigned duties.
3. Incapacitation.
4. Downsizing, or the results of a reduction in force.
5. Voluntary request by the employee for personal reasons.[24]

Research indicates that HR directors in manufacturing do not think that demotion is a useful personnel tool (56 percent) and that the incidence of demotion for managers and professionals is extremely low and virtually never used.[25]

Mergers and reorganizations often have resulted in fewer jobs, forcing some employees to accept lower positions. In these cases, both managerial and nonmanagerial employees may be demoted. The common union practice of bumping normally results in the employee with the least seniority being demoted to a lower-paying job. In these cases, the stigma attached to the demotion may be minor. Although employees will no doubt suffer anxiety and frustration over being demoted, they may rationalize the situation by claiming to be "simply in the wrong place at the wrong time—it could have happened to anybody."

However, when demotion is viewed as a devaluation of personal worth, the psychological damage can be significant.

Many managers and HR professionals agree that demotion is not an effective way to handle disciplinary problems. It is extremely unlikely that a demotion will improve the behavior of an employee who has a long record of poor work habits, such as chronic absenteeism or insubordination, or who suffers a chemical dependency. Those problems are most likely to be remedied by using employee assistance programs, supervisory counseling, corrective discipline, and/or employee rehabilitation.

In a small number of situations involving unsatisfactory performance, employees may be the recipients of an aberration of sound HR management: the promotion-demotion. Here employees are "kicked upstairs" to higher-paying jobs that typically involve little authority or responsibility.

Transfer

A **transfer** is the reassignment of an employee to a job with similar pay, status, duties, and responsibilities. Whereas a promotion involves upward movement, a transfer involves horizontal movement from one job to another.[26]

Transfers take place for several reasons. First, because personnel placement practices are not perfect, an employee–job mismatch may have resulted. A transfer moves the employee to a more suitable job. Second, an employee may become dissatisfied with the job for one or a variety of reasons: serious conflicts with co-workers or a supervisor that appear unresolvable, or a dead-end job from which a transfer would advance career goals. Third, organizational needs may require that employees be transferred. Voluntary or involuntary turnover, promotions, demotions, and terminations may result in job vacancies that may be filled most effectively through transfers.

Fourth, as organizations flatten their structures, there is a growing emphasis on lateral transfers for employee development. Having employees hold different jobs within the organization at a given level for a significant period results in a more flexible work force with broader skills, not only for front-line employees on the shop floor, but for managers as well.[27] As Tom Peters points out (*HR in the News:* "Will Your Own Career Go 'Horizontal' "?; see also "The Horizontal Corporation Will Change Careers"), employees need to become willing to accept lateral promotions. Another observer agrees that new ground rules are developing, including the following:

1. The employee can no longer expect to rely on promotions as their primary measure of job success and satisfaction.

2. The old notion that employees who make several lateral moves are dead wood is out; they are dead wood if they do not make enough lateral moves.

3. Learning new skills or getting a MBA will no longer guarantee a promotion.[28]

Layoff

A strong economy has generally meant that business and government expand, sales go up, and jobs become plentiful. As we have discussed, a mild economic recovery (as we have witnessed in the early 1990s) can mean little or no job growth. When the business cycle is in recession, large decreases in the demand for employees increase the unemployment rate.

A **layoff**, sometimes called a *reduction in force,* occurs when an employer cuts jobs from the payroll. If the need for human resources increases after a layoff, some or all of the employees who have been laid off may be *recalled.* If the demand for the organization's products or services does not increase, then the layoff becomes permanent and employees are formally separated from the firm.

Layoffs have become a way of life in the United States today. According to a recent Hewitt Associates survey, 90 percent of the organizations responding had laid off employees between January 1990 and April 1993.[29] Not all of these companies were losing business or operating at lower production levels.

In the past, layoffs typically involved hourly, blue-collar workers in the manufacturing and production centers of the organization. In unionized organizations, layoff and recall procedures are spelled out in great detail in the labor–management agreement. The contract generally specifies the maximum period in which laid-off employees may be recalled and the rights and privileges that employees hold while laid off. Seniority plays a major role in determining the order of layoffs. For example, a contract between Joseph E. Seagram & Sons, Inc., and the Distillery, Rectifying, Wine, and Allied Workers' International Union of America included the following layoff and recall provisions:

> Article XII, section 1
> The employee's length of service for the purpose of determining seniority rights shall be deemed to have commenced on the first day of employment with the employer. In all cases of promotion or recall, seniority rights of employees shall govern. The principle of seniority shall govern in all cases, including the filling of vacancies occurring in shifts or new positions created. If vacancies occur in a higher rated position, seniority including the ability to perform the work shall be the controlling factor in the selection of employees to fill such vacancies.

Production and other front-line employees are usually among the first to be laid off. But managers, staff administrators, and other skilled employees are not immune to layoffs, particularly in an economic age where streamlining and downsizing are common strategies for strengthening productivity. In the past, a layoff at these levels was an admission that an organization was in very serious financial trouble. Administrators generally strive to avoid laying off management and staff employees because the firm has spent a great deal of time and money recruiting them and developing their skills and abilities. However, faced with the realities of survival, management may have little choice. Because managers and staff administrators are not union employees, no formal, written agreement covers the terms and conditions of their layoff. Usually employee performance plays a major role in deciding which upper-level employees to lay off; other criteria include seniority, age, gender, race, family obligations, and political considerations.

Recently, some major corporations have found that the "last hired, first fired" policy is too damaging to minorities and women in their work forces. When AT&T recently cut 58,000 jobs, its proportion of minority supervisors rose from 3 percent to 9 percent and its proportion of women supervisors rose from 2.5 percent to 9 percent. DuPont, Honeywell, and Nynex corporations each had large layoffs in the early 1990s, and their percentages of minorities and women in supervision were basically unchanged.[30] While seniority and performance measures remain as typical guidelines for layoff, some employers are also considering race and gender, since the "last hired" policy would have otherwise created noticeable declines in the percentages reported for minorities and women after the layoffs just cited.

Legal Issues on Layoffs in Union Settings

In the 1970s, a great deal of controversy arose concerning the role of seniority in laying off minority employees under a labor contract. Blacks and women were beginning to make significant gains in many jobs that were highly unionized. As a consequence, most had less seniority than white males. Layoffs of union employees have generally had an adverse impact on minorities. But the federal courts have long upheld the validity of the *bona fide seniority system (BFSS),* holding that it is not illegal to make layoffs using a seniority system unless the seniority system was intentionally designed to discriminate. For example, in 1969 the Crown Zellerbach Company was ordered by the U.S. Court of Appeals to revise its seniority system because labor–management provisions enabled employees to progress only within certain job lines. The effect of this provision was to keep minorities out of departments with high-paying jobs. Crown Zellerbach was ordered to revise its system of promotion and to adopt a plantwide seniority system instead of using what amounted to one seniority system for whites, and another for blacks.

Several court decisions in the early 1980s led to an erosion of the BFSS concept, particularly in government jobs involving police officers, fire fighters, and teachers. A federal judge in 1981 barred the city of Boston from reducing the fire department's 14.7 percent level of minority fire fighters achieved through the city's affirmative action plan. The result was that eighty-three white males with greater seniority were laid off in place of minority workers. Similar court rulings took place in Memphis, Cincinnati, Toledo, and Jackson, Michigan. As might be expected, relations between protected and nonprotected workers have been strained where such rulings have taken place.[31]

The concept and practice of a seniority system was upheld under a precedent-setting 1984 Supreme Court decision, *Firefighters Local 1784* v. *Stotts*.[32] The city agreed to a consent decree to settle charges of race discrimination in the fire department and set a goal of hiring black fire fighters so that the percentage of minority fire fighters reflected the percentage of minorities in the relevant labor market. When the city later responded to a budget crunch by preparing to lay off fire fighters based on their seniority, the district court enjoined any layoffs that would decrease the percentage of blacks in the department.

On appeal, the Supreme Court differed with the district court's ruling. The injunction's interference with a collectively bargained seniority system cannot be justified as an effort to enforce the decree, the Court said, because the decree, to which the union was not a party, mentioned neither layoffs nor an intent to depart from the lawful seniority system. Nor could the district court grant competitive seniority to black employees as a "modification" of its decree, the Court explained, because there was no finding that any of the blacks protected from layoff had themselves been victims of discrimination.[33] Contests between seniority and affirmative action plans seem to require one or the other of these positive con-

cepts to lose out. This is an example of what lawyers mean when they say, "Tough cases make bad law."

Less Traditional Approaches

Telecommuting By 1991 the number of telecommuters and corporate homeworkers totaled over 16 million. Projections indicate that by the year 2000 approximately 25 percent of the entire corporate work force will be telecommuting either full- or part-time.[34] The Travelers Company, in its manual for telecommuters, describes this staffing option: "The definition of **telecommuting** is an individual working at home, supported by appropriate hardware, software, telecommunications, and home management and services."[35] Others may define telecommuting as any staffing arrangement whereby the employee works at home or away from the traditional worksite. At the Apple Computer Company, where Andy Harris pioneered the term, telecommuting has become part of Apple's vision of a "virtual company."[36]

According to a recent study from The Conference Board, management satisfaction with telecommuting is high, with 78 percent satisfied with the job performance aspects, 65 percent satisfied with the administrative costs, and 50 percent satisfied with the ease of supervision.[37] The median profile of a telecommuter is a forty-year-old professional or manager who works between eight and thirty-four hours per week for a very small company. Telecommuters are in all income brackets, 60 percent are women, and the occupations that have seen the greatest recent increases are those of accountant, consultant, lawyer, health care professional, government worker, and salesperson.[38]

Travelers Company and several federal government offices see telecommuting as a competitive edge in recruiting top employees. J.C. Penney uses the concept to tap an underutilized labor pool—educated married women who do not want to leave their children on a regular basis. IBM makes telecommuting an option as part of its work-family initiative and allows long-term leaves. Employees are not required to work during their first year of leave, but may telecommute during a second or third year of family leave.[39] Companies often receive good press for such "employee-friendly" approaches, which aids their retention and recruitment efforts.

The guidelines for managing these "invisible employees" includes the following:[40]

1. Focus on productivity, not presence. Telecommuting often forces managers to set goals and objectives more carefully.

2. Develop policy guidelines. Companies range from informal arrangements between a manager and a telecommuter to using a very specific policy manual. It is wise to clarify who is responsible for expenses (generally the employer furnishes the modem, computer, etc.) and on what basis appraisal will be conducted.

3. Ensure regular time in the office. "Out of sight, out of mind" can destroy the career of a telecommuter, so it helps if the employee comes to the office on a regular basis. Most employers do not hire telecommuters from the outside but use them only as an internal staffing option.

4. Avoid place-based discrimination. There have been a few notable cases in which employees were stripped of their benefit packages when they took telecommuting assignments. The Internal Revenue Service (IRS) rigorously enforces the employee–contractor distinction, so employers cannot generally discriminate in benefits merely on the location of the worksite.

5. Telecommute for appropriate reasons—when beneficial to both the worker and the organization—not because it is a fad.

6. Write down the arrangement. The local supervisor and worker need to negotiate and record the arrangement concerning the length of the assignment, daily schedule requirements, modes of communication, office expectations, and conditions of promotion.

Alternatives to Layoffs One of the most popular cost-cutting HR tools is the offer of early retirement. **Early-retirement programs** give experienced older employees additional benefits for retiring early. Many employers, including GM, IBM, and Polaroid, have offered early retirement as a way to avoid the less desirable options of layoff, termination, and demotion. Generally, an early-retirement package is calculated and offered to employees the organization defines as eligible. There is a wide range of approaches to program design, but most do the following:

1. Strictly define who is eligible for the option, usually with a calculation of years of service and age.

2. Contain a substantially "sweetened" pay or bonus and benefit element.

3. Move forward the date at which the employee can draw the full employer pension benefit.

4. Define a precise "window" of time during which the option can be exercised by the eligible employee (usually brief).

5. Make clear that the choice is voluntary. There can be no coercion or threat because an early retirement program could be a pretext for age discrimination if older employees are told only to "take this option or be terminated."

While early-retirement programs, or *buyouts*, were viewed initially as completely positive, some critical problems have emerged. A recent survey of 1100 HR officials found that 67 percent of companies that offered early-retirement programs saw people leave whom they had hoped to retain. One-half of these companies had to hire replacements for some of these employees within two years.[41] Employers cannot meet cost-cutting goals when they must recruit and train new employees who generally bring less experience to the job. The bill for replacement on a technical or specialized job can be 150 percent of the retiring employee's original salary.[42] Further, if coercion is found later on in the early-retirement offer, the employer's case is worsened if the older worker was replaced with a younger worker, often at lower pay. Finally, the employer plays a guessing game about whether the package is "sweet" enough to achieve the correct number of retirements but not so sweet so as to overshoot the organizational goal.

As an alternative to downsizing, some employers are weaving together several alternatives to layoffs into a comprehensive employee placement package called **HR balancing**. The Loveland, Colorado, Division of Hewlett-Packard had a surplus of 400 employees in the late 1980s when HP made a strategic decision to get out of the fabrication business. Their resources-balancing package gave these employees several options:[43]

- *Regional redistribution,* which allowed surplus employees to move to other divisions within the region.

- *A relocation program,* which gave surplus employees priority over other HP employees for openings in other locations outside the region.

- *A loan program* anywhere a short-term hiring need arose lasting from one day to one year and including *loan conversions,* whenever the short-term loan turned into a permanent offer for the loaned employee.

- *Reclassification* when employees preferred to stay in Loveland in a lower-paid position (10 percent chose this option).

- *An employee draft,* whereby regional HP offices were allocated a certain number of positions for highly skilled employees who matched the needs of the office as closely as possible.

- *Voluntary termination,* which consisted of an early-retirement package and a voluntary severance incentive, each of which amounted to a maximum of one year's salary.

Illinois-based Household International, Inc., won the 1992 Optimas Award for Vision from *Personnel Journal* for Household's program for handling staff reductions with a similar employee placement program. Household had surplus employees in one operation (e.g., a staff position in banking) and a shortage in an entirely different operation (e.g., a line position in insurance). It instituted a hiring freeze and created a *displaced-employee committee* to make transfers and placements throughout the company. Though employees were placed in very different jobs, Household discovered a surprising benefit. After an initial period of learning, many of the formerly displaced employees began to perform beyond expectations. Further, morale throughout the company improved.[44]

Contingency Work Force Called just-in-time employees, throwaway execs, part-timers, freelancers, subcontractors, and independent professionals, these workers illustrate a new philosophy in staffing that has been gathered into the term **contingency work force**. The new staffing strategy is to operate with a core of permanent workers assisted by many workers who are there only when needed. In 1994, Manpower, the temporary-employment agency giant, became the nation's largest private employer, with about 600,000 employees (GM has 400,000).[45] *HR in the News:* "Contingent Workers—Increasing or Not?" provides a detailed discussion of how many employees are now considered contingency workers.

Using temporary workers can result in major tax problems if the IRS determines that

Contingent Workers—
Increasing or Not?

Some experts estimate that one-fourth of all workers are now part of the "new" contingency, or temporary, work force. A few analysts predict that the U.S. workplace will continue to change so rapidly that by the year 2000 half of us will be no longer be considered full-time employees.

Others state that a prediction of 60 million workers being temporary or part-time by 2000 is sheer nonsense.[46] Here are the two sides of the argument.

- ***There's a big trend that will result in half of all workers being temporary***
  Polls of CEOs found that 44 percent increased the use of contingent workers between 1988 and 1993. During the next five years, 44 percent also say, they will increase their use of these temporary workers. Never have so many employees in the United States (6.4 million) said that they are working part-time but really want a full-time job. The 7000 U.S. temporary employment agencies now employ 1.6 million workers, up 240 percent from just under half a million 10 years ago.[47]

  The security and comfort of a regular full-time job with a good employer seems to be fading for many Americans. Boeing CEO Frank Shrontz says, "When it comes to medical help or retirement, contingent workers, who don't usually have benefits, are left hanging. That's not good for society."[48] Other employee qualities like loyalty and commitment may be fading too.

- ***The size of the contingency work force has not gone up, and the discussion is just a faddish obsession with an old situation.*** The alarmists now lump together part-timers and the self-employed. Self-employed workers account for 8.5 percent of the work force, just as they did in 1980. Many of the self-employed are well-paid professionals like doctors and lawyers. Further, when you lump together the part-timers and self-employed ten years ago, 27 percent in the U.S. would qualify. In 1993 the proportion was 26 percent, *down* 1 percent. Ken Nardone, who computes employment figures at the Bureau of Labor Statistics, says, "We hear a lot of anecdotal data about the growth of the contingent work force, but we can't pinpoint the numbers."[49]

  Has there been some massive change, or are we simply now more interested (for some reason) in talking about what has been going on for at least ten years?

these "temporary" workers are really just regular employees. Since the mid-1980s, the IRS has cracked down on employers who have misclassified contingent workers and has collected $678 million in fines and back taxes. Some 439,000 independent contractors have been reclassified as regular full-time employees. When paying employees, employers must use the W-2 form and collect withholding and other employment taxes. When paying independent contractors, employers use the 1099 tax forms and collect neither. The IRS estimates that it is losing $2 billion per year due to incorrect classifications.[50]

Employers should use the 1099 form only for people who truly work *out* of the office. Providing a phone and an office can convert them to employees. Former employees or retirees rehired on contracts are also likely to be viewed as employees. Hiring through an outside agency is a good way to help insulate the employer from misclassifying employees.[51]

INTERNAL STAFFING POLICIES

Sound internal staffing policies and practices will resolve many HR problems for the organization. When employees think that their skills are being disregarded or underused, dissatisfaction is likely to occur. When employees think they are being treated unfairly or discriminated against in promotion, transfer, or layoff decisions, dissatisfaction may result and lead to absenteeism and turnover. An employee who thinks he or she was discriminated against may file a complaint with the EEOC or another equal employment agency. Management may lay off employees with little concern for the workers' interests, creating considerable ill will in the community. Each of these problems reflects a lack of concern for human resources and reduces the organization's overall effectiveness. Therefore, HR professionals must create and implement internal staffing practices that are fair and that make the greatest use of employees' abilities. A discussion of important internal staffing policies follows.

Promotion from Within

The most prudent approach to filling job vacancies is to follow a policy of promotion from within but to maintain enough flexibility to tap the external labor market when employees within the organization are not qualified. To support a policy of promotion from within, HR professionals need tools to predict the promotability of employees, particularly when decisions concern the promotion of personnel from nonmanagement to management positions. In these situations, assessment centers and job-related interviews should prove valuable.

The quality of internal-staffing decisions depends on the quality of the information used to make those decisions. Managers must ensure that their performance appraisal systems generate data that accurately reflect the candidates' achievements. Yet many firms still use vague, subjective, and biased rating systems that provide little meaningful performance information and run the risk of being illegal. Such systems may permit politics to dominate staffing decisions. Results-oriented appraisal systems such as MBO and behavioral systems such as BARS eliminate much of the subjectivity and bias of rating scales and result in better decisions. Assessment centers should also be used by larger firms that make frequent promotion decisions.

Assistance for Laid-Off Employees

Economic misfortunes may cause a firm to lay off great numbers of workers. Layoffs can be professionally managed to reduce the economic strains that laid-off workers and the community face when large numbers of jobs are temporarily or permanently eliminated. Providing assistance to employees during layoffs reflects a genuine concern for the organization's workers and is an act of social responsibility to the community. Laid-off employees can be helped through notification of plant closings, severance pay, supplemental unemployment benefits, and outplacement assistance.

The Worker Adjustment and Retraining Notification Act (WARN) Commonly known as the *Plant Closing Act,* this law covers only employers who have one hundred or more full-time employees (or have one hundred or more employees who together work at least 4000 hours per week, not counting overtime). WARN, which went into effect in 1989, requires these employers to give affected employees sixty days' written notice of anticipated plant closings or large layoffs (generally of fifty or more employees).[52] Employers who violate the law may be required to give back pay to workers laid off without receiving the proper notification and to pay a fine. There are exceptions to WARN. A "faltering company" is exempt if it was seeking money during that time that would have avoided the layoff/closing. "Unforseeable business circumstances" may also provide an exemption to an employer's notification responsibilities. Several state laws place even more responsibilities on an employer who is closing or laying off employees.[53] There was much debate over WARN, which was vetoed by two presidents.

The biggest advantage of notification of an imminent layoff is that workers and communities are given time to prepare for the impending economic hardships. For example, workers would have a chance to find new jobs. But many managers see problems in giving advance notice; they claim that advance notice of a plant closing may hurt their credit ratings and reduce new customer orders. They also worry about employee morale, motivation, and absenteeism as workers look for new jobs.

Supplemental Unemployment Benefits In the 1950s, steel and automobile industry union leaders began negotiating **supplemental unemployment benefits (SUB)** plans. These plans provide additional income to supplement state unemployment benefits to employees who are laid off. Union negotiators understandably contend that state unemployment benefits do not enable the employee to adequately maintain his or her style of living. SUB plans are designed to be directly supplemental; employees receive a certain percentage (e.g., 60

percent) of their gross pay for a maximum number of weeks when unemployed.

Guaranteed Income Stream The relatively high unemployment rate and severe layoffs in the 1970s and 1980s caused job security to become a top priority for union negotiation and members.[54] Several innovative provisions in contracts had the intent of improving employment security. One of the most interesting and most widely publicized is the **guaranteed income stream (GIS)** plan in the auto industry.

The GIS plan is an alternative to the traditional SUB, although the goal of income maintenance for employees is the same. The typical GIS plan differs from SUB plans in three important areas. First, GIS plans furnish benefits to eligible workers until they retire and thus have been called a guaranteed lifetime wage, whereas SUB plans end after a short period of time, usually two years. Second, qualification for a GIS plan is based on earnings and not employment, which encourages laid-off workers to seek other employment. Third, the benefits provided by a GIS plan are only partially offset by outside earnings until a breakeven point is reached. Under most SUB plans, benefits are completely offset by outside earnings—a deterrent to laid-off workers seeking outside jobs. Thus, GIS plans create incentives for laid-off workers, unlike SUB plans, which tie them to their former employer. Both sides may benefit from GIS plans. If laid-off workers find new jobs, the amount of GIS benefits paid by the former employer may be reduced as they are partially offset by the outside income. However, the employer is encouraged to avoid layoffs by the long-term eligibility aspect of a GIS plan. When layoffs are necessary, the employer has an additional financial incentive to help workers find new employment. The GIS plan was thought to eventually replace SUB plans since both management and labor can realize important advantages;[55] however, there has been little expansion of GIS outside of the auto industry in the 1990s.

Severance Pay   Sometimes called *dismissal pay,* **severance pay** is income voluntarily provided to most employees who have been permanently terminated from the job (see Table 10-1). While similar to SUB in its appearance and formula for provision in determining benefits, severance pay is given under quite different circumstances. SUB pay enables the employee who is temporarily laid off to feel a minimum impact from the layoff and to anticipate a return to work and full pay. Employees who receive severance pay, however, realize that they have no hope for future work with the company. No law requires private employers to pay severance pay unless they have agreed to do so. When agreed to, it is not always provided to employees who are terminated for just cause or who quit.

Table 10-1 Terminations Eligible for Severance Pay and Calculation of Payment

Reasons for Termination	% Employers
Discharge for economic reasons	94
Position eliminated	88
"Other" involuntary terminations	51
Poor job performance	42
Disability	8
Resign voluntarily	6
Retire without a pension	6
Retire with a pension	5

Method of Payment	% Employers
One week's pay per year of service	47
Flat payment (e.g., two weeks' pay)	28
"Based on years of service"	10
Two weeks' pay per year	9
Management discretion	5
One month's pay per year	1

SOURCE: David Stier, "Most Pay Severance, Even If Fired," *HR News* (August 1990) 2. Used by permission.

The purpose of severance pay is to cushion the loss of income resulting from plant closing, merger, automation, or subcontracting of work. The amount of severance pay is usually specified by a formula guaranteeing a week of base pay per year of service with the company. To be eligible, employees are normally required to have a minimum number of years of service, usually one, except in a case of disability. In the case of a merger, a plant closing, relocation, or the sale of the company, the liability for severance pay may become a most important issue.

Outplacement Assistance

In contrast to years past, many firms are providing a number of services to laid-off employees that involve job-placement assistance and training for new job skills called **outplacement assistance.** For example, when the Ford Motor Company closed its Milpitas, California, plant, it offered extensive outplacement services to laid-off employees. In cooperation with the United Auto Workers (UAW), Ford assessed the training needs of over 2000 hourly workers, used idle portions of the plant to teach remedial English and math, and offered "vocational exploration" classes that encouraged employees to learn new skills, such as auto upholstery and forklift operations.[56]

What are the components of a model outplacement program? The Illinois AFL-CIO program is often used by employers to guide their efforts in developing programs for the soon-to-be unemployed. The program includes the following:[57]

Advance Notice Advance notice of a plant closing of six months or a year will give "organizations time to organize their outplacement programs and permit employees to adjust their own plans as well as consider the various employment options."[58]

Labor–Management Outplacement Committees A cooperative effort by labor and management, enabling both parties to participate in setting outplacement goals, is believed to be the most effective way to implement outplacement activities.

Job-Search Training Such training is usually helpful, though the success rate is closely tied to the conditions in the labor market.

Job Clubs A job club brings job seekers together, provides a location for job-search training, and reduces the frustration and isolation that generally accompany job-hunting efforts.

Aggressive Job Development These activities include contacting suppliers, customers, and the business community in general in an attempt to place laid-off workers.

Skills Training Research shows that only about 20 or 25 percent of laid-off employees seek skills training, even though it is free. But skills training is important, and many organizations provide this service.

Personnel Assistance During and after a plant closing, a small staff of HR employees should be maintained to assist unemployed workers through counseling, job assistance, and training.

Third Parties Successful programs often include the use of outside consultants who have expertise in creating and implementing outplacement activities.

Industrial Development In most cases, a vacant plant is turned over to industrial real estate personnel, with little or no thought about how the plant could be kept in operation by another company. In several instances, cooperative efforts among management, local governments, federal redevelopment agencies, and labor have resulted in a closed plant being taken over by another firm. In many cases, a significant number of laid-off employees were employed by the new employer.

For managers and staff professionals, outplacement assistance often includes résumé preparation and job counseling. Some firms employ outplacement consultants to help laid-off executives find new jobs. Through counseling, these consultants help individuals gain self-confidence, sharpen interviewing skills, and develop job contacts. Generally, the company that laid off the employee pays the consultant's fee, which may amount to as much as 15 percent of a laid-off executive's annual salary (see *HR in the News:* "Safe Landings for All of AT&T's Workers").

CAREER MANAGEMENT

People have varying expectations about the rewards and satisfactions they seek from their jobs. To some, work is purely a necessary evil, a painful mechanism for earning enough money to support one's self or one's family. These employees do not expect to be fulfilled in their work: they may, in fact, feel that working and enjoyment are totally incompatible. Other employees not only seek good salaries and benefits but also desire to satisfy certain human needs through their work. They want to work with agreeable and friendly co-workers and to receive ego satisfaction from performing their jobs. They may not, however, aspire to middle- or upper-level management or professional positions, feeling that management positions involve stress, too much responsibility, pressure, long hours, and weekends at the office. A good family life with the time to pursue hobbies and other interests may be perceived as being just as important as—or more important than—a high-status, high-paying, high-stress job.

Safe Landings for All of AT&T's Workers

After the breakup of the Bell System in 1984, AT&T laid off more than 100,000 of its 373,000 employees. "Ma Bell" had always taken care of her employees, so a "safe landing" was designed to help employees land safely either inside or outside of AT&T. One of the goals was to help employees stay on their same career tracks. A second, more unusual goal was to focus on HR issues for the survivors of the layoffs, the remaining 273,000 employees.[59] AT&T did some of the traditional outplacement work for laid-off employees, but what it does for the survivors is unique.

The National Personnel Services Organization (NPSO) unit at AT&T was downsized from 901 to 376 employees between 1989 and 1991. Safe landing's "win-win" approach is focused on the individual and the organization. For instance, if survivors find jobs outside the company, safe landing encourages others to support the employees for proceeding on their career track, instead of thinking of them as disloyal or as traitors.

The commitment to the survivors costs big dollars In 1992, AT&T spent $500,000 to train the remaining 376 NPSO employees in new skills that will help them stay on their career tracks—inside or outside of AT&T. The commitment also requires managerial flexibility. Under "Project Exchange," an idea from an employee-involvement meeting, employees can temporarily try another job to see if they like it.

The commitment is also personal There is a periodic review of the surplused individuals. The standard question that has to be answered by managers is "What's being done to help Stacy—or Shannon, or Elsie—to have a safe landing?"[60] The commitment is also successful. Of the 514 NPSO employees surplused, 512 were considered safe landings. Most found jobs inside AT&T, some work for other employers, and some took early retirement.[61]

AT&T was apparently lucky This conclusion is based on some recent research on gender and outplacement. A study found that women often take longer than men to go through their transition, staying in outplacement 38 percent longer. It confirmed that gender bias still exists (even among HR professionals). It also speculated that outplaced women managers and executives require different outplacement support than do men in the same positions. Interestingly, older women often opt out of the corporate world altogether when in outplacement, excited by the prospects of switching over to consulting or starting their own businesses.[62] HR professionals designing or hiring an outplacement program should consider if any special gender sensitivity would be helpful.

For other persons, work is the most significant part of their lives. Totally committed to their jobs, they receive a great deal of personal pride and satisfaction from their work. A vice-presidency or presidency is the pot of gold at the end of the rainbow, and these overachievers are more than willing to invest long hours, weekends, and holidays in pursuit of their dreams. To these employees, the job comes first, and everything else—family, hobbies, social obligations, and other interests—comes second.

On a continuum of career interest, work may be viewed as "just a job" on one end and as a career on the other. In the past, managers did not try to clarify this distinction for their employees. Management has long felt that employees should take personal responsibility for defining their employment goals and aspirations.

HR professionals, however, are playing an increasingly active role in designing and implementing programs that help employees not only focus on career choices and objectives but also achieve the objectives they formulate. Such help originated with a concern for the quality of working life, an eye to EEO legislation, and a need to use the organization's diverse human resources effectively. Programs have been created that draw on both traditional personnel tools and contemporary methods designed specifically for the development of career paths. In general, all these programs fall under the general heading of **career management**. Important terms and concepts in career management are the following:

Career A sequence of jobs held during a person's working life.

Career Management The process of designing and implementing goals, plans, and strategies that enable HR professionals and managers to satisfy work-force needs and allow individuals to achieve their career objectives.

Individual Career Planning The process whereby each employee personally plans career goals.

Organizational Career Planning The process whereby management plans career goals for employees.

Benefits to the Organization

Well-planned and executed career programs will benefit both the organization and employees in a number of ways. These include the following:

Staffing Inventories Effective career management will help ensure a continuous supply of professional, technical, and managerial talent so that future organizational goals may be achieved.

Staffing from Within Because of the many potential advantages of promotion from within, most organizations like to promote employees when positions become available. But recruitment from within requires a strong career management program to guarantee that employees can perform effectively in their new jobs. Promoting employees before they are ready to assume their new jobs will result in unsatisfactory performance, as predicted by the Peter Principle.[63]

Solving Staffing Problems Certain staffing problems may be remedied through effective career management. First, a high rate of employee turnover may be caused, at least in part, by a feeling that little opportunity exists within the organization. Second, recruiting new employees may be easier if applicants realize that the company develops its employees and provides career opportunities.

Satisfying Employee Needs The current generation of employees is very different from those of generations past. Higher levels of education have raised career expectations. And many workers hold their employers responsible for providing opportunities so that those expectations may be realized.

Enhanced Motivation Because progression along the career path is directly related to job performance, an employee is likely to be motivated to perform at peak levels so that career goals may be accomplished.

Equal Employment Opportunity EEO guidelines demand fair and equitable recruiting, selection, and placement policies and the elimination of discriminatory practices concerning promotions and career mobility. Many affirmative action programs contain formal provisions to enhance the career mobility of women and minorities, including the development of career paths and the design of formal T&D activities. Further, several court actions have forced organizations to strengthen such career advancement procedures to remove obstacles to the career progression of minorities.

Successful Career Management Four factors determine the success of an organization's career management efforts. First, career management must be planned; haphazard or ill-conceived attempts to manage careers will fail.[64] Line managers and HR administrators who share the responsibility for effective career management must work together to ensure that line and staff efforts are coordinated.

Second, top management must support career management. Such support comes from a climate that encourages promotion from within, the development of employee skills, and the use of valid performance criteria for promotion decisions.

Third, administrators must not omit or neglect any of career management's many programs and processes. These include organizational career planning, individual career planning, integrating organizational and individual plans, implementation, and evaluation.

A fourth factor, **career match**, has been found to be the most critical factor in career management programs. The program must seek to find a career match between the employer's plans for the employee and the employee's personal aspirations. Programs that simply explain the organization's career plans to the employees, but do not assist them in clarifying their own goals and developing a match between theirs and the organization's, are likely to fail. The employee and employer should negotiate a mutually acceptable outcome. If the employer addresses employees' expectations early in their careers, employees may willingly modify their expectations. However, if differences are ignored, the employee may develop incompatible career plans, which cause undesired turnover when they are not addressed by the employer.[65] In fact, today's workers are more willing to change jobs and even careers if their career objectives are not met.[66]

Organizational Career Planning An important part of the HR planning process involves the forecast of both long- and short-term HR needs. During this process, the major changes the organization is likely to face are predicted (growth, decline, reorganization, new technologies), and their impact on the organization's labor force is assessed. Emphasis is placed on predicting changes in the numbers and kinds of employees that will be needed. But HR plans must be flexible enough to adjust to such contingencies as rapid, unpredicted organizational growth or decline.

Some organizations develop individual career plans for managers and for professional personnel. An executive succession chart is sometimes used as an aid in career planning. Decision makers must develop individual plans based on future organizational needs, the employee's performance and promotability, and EEO considerations.

According to a recent *Wall Street Journal* study, many employers now have developed two career ladders—one the traditional *managerial ladder* and the other on a *professional ladder*. The professional ladder allows employees who have never taken a formal managerial assignment to move up (what's left of) the corporate ladder. For example, to become the department head in customer service, the traditional ladder included three steps up in technical jobs (service representative I, II, and III), then three steps in management (supervisor, manager I and II). The professional ladder may now allow three steps of additional technical or professional jobs (service analyst, service consultant I and II) to substitute for the steps in management. The main reasons given for using this dual ladder approach are these:

- To retain the best professional/technical people.

- To create a career path for those not interested in a career in management.

- To increase the morale of the technical staff.

- To create a more equitable nonmanagement compensation structure.[67]

Individual Career Planning

Today an increasing number of individuals are plotting their own career goals and creating strategies to achieve them. Many books have been published to assist in the planning and integrating of personal, social, family, and work goals.

Many progressive organizations offer counseling on career opportunities as a part of their career management system. Usually, career counseling is voluntary and available to all employees. Typically, career counselors are in the HR department; in smaller firms, an HR professional may conduct career counseling along with other personnel functions.

Whether employees conduct career planning through a course or seminar or through formal career counseling, the first step is the assessment of personal interests, aims, skills, and abilities. It is important that employees find out as much as possible about themselves—their ambitions, needs, values, strengths, and limitations. The second step is the collection of information about existing and future opportunities in an organization. Career counselors are generally prepared to offer this kind of information. Many managers and administrators have also testified to the value of the grapevine in providing career insight. Although many old boy networks have long been closed to women and other minorities, many networking and mentoring systems have been formed to provide minorities with helpful career information.

The final step in the individual planning process is the development of a strategy to achieve career goals. Decisions about such a strategy are often informal, rarely put in writing, and subject to considerable adjustment as an employee progresses through a career. The realities of organizational life demand flexible planning because uncertainty and risk underscore any form of long-range planning. Formal long-term education strategies often include earning an advanced degree such as a master's degree in business administration, health care, management science, or industrial psychology. Short-term educational strategies may include participation in short courses or seminars. Frequently, employers will reimburse some or all of the tuition and other expenses, particularly if the employee's work is related to the additional education.

Integrating Plans

To be effective, career management efforts must strike a workable balance between the organization's HR needs and employees' career goals. In reality, this balance is difficult to achieve. The dynamic nature of organizational life sometimes makes it extremely difficult for each person to carry out career plans within specific time constraints.

To a considerable extent, management can minimize employee frustration and turnover caused by career stagnation through practical career counseling that integrates organizational needs and individual career goals. With the aid of career counselors, employees can realistically appraise career goals and the organization's predicted HR needs. In some cases, overly optimistic personal career goals may have to be trimmed back. In other cases, the counselor may suggest opportunities and, perhaps, alternative career paths to accelerate an employee's career aims.

Implementing Programs

Career development is a long-term process, spanning an employee's entire working career. Although minor (and occasionally major) adjustments in career paths are expected, effective career management enables career progression to proceed with some regularity and predictability. The primary elements in implementing a career management program include the publication of job vacancies, the implementation of employee performance appraisals, the establishment of T&D activities, and the evaluation of career progression.

Job Vacancies Publicizing job vacancies (job posting) is an excellent way to disseminate career information and notify employees who may be qualified for a vacant job. Bulletin boards and internal company news bulletins are normally used in this open promotion system.

Appraisal Data Sound employee PA data are particularly important for career development. Supervisors have the important responsibility of honestly telling employees whether their performance is satisfactory in light of their career goals. Further, HR professionals play an important role by designing and implementing valid PA systems.

T&D Experiences Perhaps the most meaningful aspect of career development is the accumulation of work experiences and away-from-the-job training activities that broaden

employees' skills and abilities. Effective T&D enables the employee to assume increasingly challenging job responsibilities and to perform at higher job levels. Many T&D activities—for example, job rotation, coaching, committee assignments, and away-from-the-job educational strategies—are core components of career management for many organizations.

Career Evaluation The final phase of the career development process is evaluation of an employee's progress toward career goals. (For a lighter look at the implications, see Figure 10-3.) Evaluation usually takes place annually or biannually, possibly during a formal appraisal review. During evaluation, employees review the progress of their careers with supervisors and perhaps career counselors. Particular emphasis is placed on whether career goals and timetables have been reached. If progress has been less than expected, the reasons are explored and discussed. Shortfalls in career progression may be remedied through additional work experiences and away-from-the-job development.

Career Stages HR professionals should recognize that employees generally progress through **career stages**. Each stage represents a unique set of opportunities, problems, and circumstances, and the needs of employees change as they pass from one stage to the next. Research suggests that employees generally advance through four stages:[68]

1. *Establishment* At the beginning of a career, the employee faces anxiety and uncertainty over his or her performance potential and competency. During establishment, a supportive and caring superior is particularly important for assisting the employee to become a productive employee.

2. *Advancement* Next, the employee demonstrates competence and a knowledge of the politics of organizational life. Less guidance and supervision are needed than during the establishment stage. However, coaching,

FIGURE 10-3 Who is *not* having fun at work?

Many employers have bragged about getting "lean and mean," but did you know that the emphasis might have been on "mean"? *Industry Week* compared survey results from 1990 and 1992 and decided that things are getting even less enjoyable at work. Here are some of the results:

	1992	1990
Is it fun where you work?		
No	67%	63%
Yes	33%	37%
Why is there no fun at work?		
We're not a team	61%	49%
Bureaucracy stifles initiative	39%	39%
My efforts aren't recognized	39%	30%
I'm locked into my job	23%	21%
No one tells me anything	21%	16%
"They" want quantity, not quality	21%	18%
Pay stinks	12%	10%
Who's not having fun?		
First-line supervisors	78%	
Nonmanagement	75%	
Middle management	63%	
Vice-presidents	61%	

SOURCE: John S. McLenahan, "On the Job: Lean and Mean" *Industry Week* (November 2, 1992).

counseling, role models, and friendships remain important at this stage.

3. *Maintenance* People generally achieve their highest advancement during the maintenance stage, devoting a considerable amount of their energies to developing and guiding others with less experience. This stage brings a great deal of satisfaction to some—notably those who have achieved their career goals. But others find disappointment and frustration—especially those who have not been particularly effective or have failed to reach career objectives and must consider new directions.

4. *Withdrawal* Withdrawal begins as one retires or moves on to a new career. During this stage, the individual devotes greater time to leisure and to the family. Frustration, stress, and boredom may also characterize this stage because the retiree loses his or her job identity and the social contacts enjoyed at work.

Evaluation of Career Programs

Because career development exists to serve several needs, evaluation must consider a number of different criteria. The degree to which career programs are established to solve staffing problems (e.g., providing a continuous supply of skilled workers or an effective internal promotion system) will influence which criteria are used in the evaluation process. Criteria include internal versus external hiring rates, turnover rates, exit interview results, and analysis of EEOC reports and audits.[69]

Even though a great deal of time and expense are expended on career development programs, few organizations evaluate their efforts formally. One research study involving forty corporations found only fifteen with formal evaluation systems, eight with informal methods, and seventeen with no evaluation whatsoever.[70]

Career Problems Not unlike most large, complex HR programs, career development systems must overcome several obstacles before they become effective. One of the most significant problems involves the question of employee expectations. Some employees think the organization should bear the major responsibility for career development. But most organizations cannot afford the time and cost of planning the career of each employee and expect employees to assume some responsibility for development, such as attending evening graduate programs or funding their own trips to seminars and workshops.

Another problem is the impatience and frustration employees feel when advancement opportunities are limited. Frustration can be minimized through candid career counseling and by telling employees that promotions are not the automatic outcomes of career programs.

The supervisor is the employee's most important career counselor.[71] But an American Management Association study showed that in a sample of 225 companies the majority of supervisors surveyed thought that (1) career planning was a burden, (2) career planning for subordinates was not part of their job, and (3) they were not equipped to assist employees in career planning and counseling.[72] Because of the importance of supervisory participation in the development of careers, it is critical that they receive training in the skills required for career management and that they are rewarded for helping advance the careers of their subordinates.

Issues of an Aging Work Force

One of the growing concerns of today's labor force deals with the career-related problems of an **aging work force**. The 43 million baby boomers born between 1945 and 1950 are now "graying" to the extent that the first boomers turn fifty in 1995. People over fifty will represent 30 percent of the population in 2005. Further, workers fifty-five and older are the fastest-growing sector of the labor force.[73] Management must recognize the shifting age distribution of the labor force and plan HR programs to deal with issues and opportunities the older worker brings to the company.

The graying of the work force is forcing management to examine closely the myths and stereotypes that have long surrounded the older worker. For example, many (perhaps youthful) managers assume that health, productivity, attitudes, and overall usefulness to the organization decline rapidly after age fifty-five or sixty. According to scientific research, however, the truth about the older worker is quite different from commonly held stereotypes:[74]

Physiological Changes While physiological changes take place as one ages, the changes vary markedly in degree among persons of the same age. In the absence of time pressures, the performance of older workers is as good as that of younger employees, and sometimes better.

Work Attitude Research shows that age and job satisfaction are positively related in all sectors of the work force. However, managers should recognize that obsolescence and sudden job changes are major concerns of the older worker, and they should work to minimize these frustrations and fears.

Job Performance According to research, older managers are less willing to take risks, take longer to reach decisions, and are less confident in their decisions. However, older managers are better able to appraise new information and seek to minimize risk by collecting more reliable information. In sales, clerical, and manual labor jobs, age seems to have little effect.

Absenteeism rates do not appear to be significantly affected by age.

Management Action Toward Older Workers While differences between older workers and young workers may not be as pronounced as many believe, management should still be attuned to the unique needs and concerns of older workers. Six areas have been suggested for in preparing for the graying of a company's work force:[75]

1. *Age profile* Age and performance data for jobs throughout the organization should be analyzed to pinpoint problem areas and to suggest alternate career paths for older workers.

2. *Job performance requirements* Organizations should define job requirements precisely and ensure that recruiting and selection procedures are based on critical performance criteria. If selection decisions are based strictly on requisite job skills and abilities, age will not enter into the selection decision.

3. *Performance appraisal* HR managers must closely examine their PA systems to remove any intentional or unintentional biases against the older worker. Progressive employers audit appraisals of older workers to uncover unfair appraisals.

4. *Work force interest surveys* Work force surveys will enable management to get a clear idea of employee needs. Special HR programs can then be created to deal with the needs of various employee groups, including older workers.

5. *Education and counseling* Firms are beginning to counsel older workers on retirement and second-career options following retirement. Special training should also be provided for the older employee who chooses to remain on the job. Programs to avoid mid-career plateauing and obsolescence are particularly important.

6. *Job structure* The older worker raises issues concerning how jobs are structured. Flexibility is important in regard to the work pace, the length of the work day, leaves of absence, and part-time work. In the absence of significant financial rewards, older workers may find job satisfaction resulting largely from intrinsic rewards.

The Plateaued Employee

During the 1990s and beyond, it is predicted that there will be too many managers. When the Depression-era children went to work after World War II, they participated in the longest sustained economic boom America has ever experienced. Companies expanded their work forces, thus creating many rapid promotional opportunities for a relatively small number of people. Moreover, as these conditions continued for about twenty-five years, a career of abnormally swift promotions became the rule rather than the exception. There are now more people in the managerial pool than ever before but fewer opportunities, thanks largely to a slow-growth economy and the baby boom generation. Should the economy boom, the number of ambitious people who regard promotion as the only significant reward will still greatly outnumber the available management opportunities. Sooner or later, inevitably for almost everyone, the process of upward movement ends. When this happens he or she becomes a **plateaued employee**.

Managers are not the only ones experiencing the stress of plateauing. Professionals and employees who find themselves in jobs that offer limited mobility and few opportunities for the expansion of experience feel the same frustration and the stigma of failure. Symptoms include coming late, leaving early, absenteeism, and changes in personality such as irritability and hypersensitivity to criticism. Of course, these symptoms may reflect any number of problems, thus making it difficult for the superior to recognize.

The HR department is often expected to take the lead in addressing and resolving the plateaued employee's frustrations. This may mean encouraging employees at all levels to accept the reality that promotions do not go on forever. It certainly means more lateral assignments within the organization. It may also mean counseling or outplacement services for those who choose to leave. Increasing job mobility is another strategy as long as it is perceived as a positive change.

Dual-Career Couples

Based on Labor Department statistics, about 60 percent of all working women are living with employed husbands. This group represents about 46 million working men and women (out of about 100 million in the U.S. labor force) who are included in a growing segment of today's society: the **dual-career couple**. In the past, organizations largely ignored the problems of the dual-career couple, leaving them to solve the problems that their situation brought about. Faced with a large and growing number of dual-career couples, employers have begun to create policies and services that address their problems. Some of the personal and organizational problems that dual-career couples face include the following:[76]

Conflicting Alternatives Advancing the husband's or the wife's career often means moving in different geographical directions, often resulting in a crisis over whose career is more important. Problems with employing the "trailing spouse" can be difficult.

Reluctance to Approach the Company Many dual-career couples see their employers' policies as rigid and are reluctant to discuss their problems with a boss. They may feel that openness about their career problems may harm their chances of advancement.

Possibility of a No-Career Couple As downsizing continues in the United

States, an increasing number of couples both receive "pink slips" within the same time period, sometimes from the same company. Between 1989 and 1992, the number of unemployed couples in the United States doubled to about 1.75 million, according to the Bureau of Labor Statistics.[77]

Family versus Work Who assumes responsibility for raising the children when both the husband and wife hold professional jobs that may require working evenings and weekends? More specifically, who stays home when the children are sick? Who attends the PTA meetings? Who helps with the homework?

Lack of Experience with Conflict Resolution Many couples lack the skills necessary to solve career-family crises, such as when to begin a family or how to divide the family responsibilities of shopping and cooking.

"Baby Panic" Should the dual-career couple have children, and if so, when? Sometimes referred to as the "thirty-year baby panic," this problem is inevitably faced by professional couples who postpone having children in their twenties for the sake of their careers.

Employers have instituted various programs to help couples with their problems. Authors Francine and Douglas Hall suggest that an effective program will contain the following characteristics:[78]

Dual-Career Audit An audit, performed through a company survey, should be a starting point for a company to recognize the extent of the problem. Areas the audit should address include the number of dual-career employees, the conflicts they face, how effective they perceive present company policies and opportunities to be, and how competent they think they are to manage their careers.

Special Recruiting Techniques By giving a potential employee and his or her spouse a realistic view of the company's work load, travel, and career opportunities, employers may be able to avoid a potentially poor job match. Some companies offer new employees "couple counseling" immediately after hiring to help identify potential problems and conflicts.

Revision of Transfer Policies In many companies, advancement inevitably means a geographical move. But in many cases, relocation results in crises for the dual-career couple. Employers are now finding ways to enhance their employees' careers without permanent geographical transfer. Alternatives include temporary relocation assignments (for two or three months) and more effective use of local T&D activities.

Examination of Nepotism Policies Many employers are revising their policies to allow both spouses to work for the company, as long as an employee does not supervise a relative or participate in decisions concerning the relative's salary, performance, or advancement.

Assistance for Dual-Career Couples Many employers are helping couples learn how to manage their careers. Workshops and seminars enable participants to assess their opportunities, obstacles, potential conflicts, and developmental needs.

WOMEN AND MINORITIES IN MANAGEMENT

Since the beginning of the industrial era, female employees have participated actively in all sectors of the economy. But for decades, women have been restricted almost exclusively to low-paying, monotonous jobs involving little responsibility and few opportunities for advancement. Even though equal employment opportunity and affirmative action programs have led to more women managers, statistics indicate that women are still lower paid and underused in management positions. In 1988 women made up 48 percent of the total labor force. But only 16 percent of all professional employees were women. Statistics for racial minorities are even more discouraging.

Obstacles to Upward Mobility

In 1991, a "glass ceiling" was officially recognized and defined in the U.S. Department of Labor's (DOL) "A Report on the Glass Ceiling Initiative." The report defines the *glass ceiling* "as those artificial barriers based on attitudinal or organizational bias that prevent qualified individuals from advancing upward in their organizations into management level positions." DOL is now conducting reviews according to this report, known as Corporate Management Reviews. DOL is currently focusing on federal contractors, and its reviews of employers focus on whether their organizational practices and corporate cultures impede the advancement of women and minorities.[79] These reviews are not the typical statistical reviews performed on affirmative action plans under E.O. 11246. Rather, they are done to ensure that women and minorities have equal access to the "Pipelines of Progress" (the title of a 1992 Glass Ceiling Commission report).

Employers are advised to conduct a *glass ceiling self-audit* to prepare for a Corporate Management Review and to remove any glass ceiling at their workplace. A self-audit process should follow four steps:

1. Statistical information should be collected on woman and minorities.

2. Both senior management and the corporate culture need to be analyzed as they relate to the opportunities of women and minorities.

3. Barriers to promotion opportunities should be identified.

4. A qualitative analysis of the workplace as it relates to opportunities for women and minorities within the organization should be performed.[80]

There are reasons to believe that women and minorities are continuing to make advances in the workplace. In general, the work force is becoming more diverse, but perhaps not at the pace many observers have expected. In 1980, white males were 51 percent of the work force; in 1993 they remained 47 percent, they are expected to be 44 percent in 2005. The percentages for white females are: 1980, 36 percent; 1993, 38 percent; and 2005, 39 percent. The number of black employees will also grow slowly: 1980, 10 percent; 1993, 11 percent; and 2005, 12 percent. Percentages for Hispanics show the strongest increases: 1980, 6 percent; 1993, 8 percent; and 2005, 11 percent.[81]

Despite only gradual growth in total employment statistics, the percentage of white females in managerial and professional jobs has risen during the period 1983–1993 from 37 percent to 42 percent. The rates of blacks and Hispanics in these positions have improved from 6 percent to 7 percent and from 3 percent to 4 percent during the same time.[82] Over the last twenty years or so, the percentage of women business owners has grown from 5 percent to over 30 percent and is still rising. More people work in companies owned by women than work in the Fortune 500 companies.[83]

Research on the proportion of top management positions filled by women in the Fortune 500 companies has revealed some interesting findings. Between 1980 and 1992, proportionately more women than men were moving into top management, and at a faster rate. This improvement for woman was true when both the man and the woman held MBA degrees.[84]

Persons with disabilities also face major obstacles on the career path. For a brief discussion of their problems and information on the recent Americans with Disabilities Act, read *HR in the News:* "Unintentional Discrimination Against the Disabled".

Stereotypes about Women Managers

One set of obstacles is the stereotypes of women that workers frequently encounter in the world of work. These archaic stereotypes hold that a woman's only place is in the home, and that women lack the mental and physical makeup to perform a management job. Negative stereotypes of working women include the following:[85]

- Women work merely to supplement the family income; they do not need equal pay or benefits because men support families.

- Women do not want to be managers because the extra workload would interfere with family obligations.

- Women are unable to meet certain work demands for emotional toughness and stability because of their psychological makeup. They tend to take things personally, to respond to anger and frustration by crying, and to be insufficiently hard-nosed in making difficult decisions.

There are several strategies for dealing with the negative stereotypes that many female managers must confront. The first is a vocal and assertive stance by top management that recognizes the workplace rights of female employees. Second, T&D for all managers should focus on the legal rights of women, with specific emphasis on the dos and don'ts of managing and promoting women. Third, employees whose antifemale attitudes result in unsatisfactory behavior should be counseled and, if the unsatisfactory performance continues, disciplined. This action sends a message throughout the organization that antifemale stereotypes, or at least the behaviors that often result from them, are inappropriate.

Unintentional Discrimination Against the Disabled?

Most employers geared up to comply with the Americans with Disabilities Act (ADA), which went into effect in 1992. According to the findings of Congress, some 43 million Americans have some disability that affects one or more of their life functions. The ADA protects persons with disabilities from discrimination at the workplace. This was one of the most popular pieces of legislation to pass Congress, but did you know that someone sympathetic to the person with a disability may be the first to discriminate against him or her at work?

According to a couple of recent studies, people making HR decisions often favor a disabled person over a nondisabled person—if the job is "right for them." In the case where a job had duties that kept the worker away from the public (an accounting job with no public duties), the person with disabilities was discriminated *in favor of*. If the same job (accountant) required the person to have the same skills, but to meet the public as part of his/her duties, then the person with disabilities was discriminated *against*.

Further research reveals that the more "social distance" created by the disability itself, the more violent the discrimination. For instance, someone with a hidden disability (heart disease, deafness, etc.) is treated more like a person without disabilities, while a person with an obvious disability (in a wheelchair, blind, etc.) is more likely to be discriminated against.

Well-meaning HR professionals and managers should be very careful if they believe they "have just the job" for a person with disabilities. *All* jobs are available to persons with disabilities. It's the law.

SOURCE: Adapted from Robert D. Hatfield and Chun Hui, "Avoiding Discrimination Suits Under the ADA: An Analysis of When Discrimination Is Most Likely," *Proceedings,* Council on Employee Responsibilities and Rights (June 1992); and Chun Hui and Robert D. Hatfield, "Discrimination Against the Physically Disabled: When Concern for Selection Matters," *Proceedings,* Midwest Division Academy of Management (1992). Used with permission.

The Old Boy Network

Another prevalent obstacle to the development of women and minority managers is the **old boy network**, the informal advice and assistance that often facilitate upward mobility into management ranks. The fast track on which many male managers have swiftly traveled has been greased by membership in an old boy network. For example, at a Rotary Club luncheon, one member may ask another if he is interested in a job opening. By belonging to this club, the aspiring manager becomes privy to inside information: who to know, important positions coming up, job assignments that

481

Diversity or Adversity?

At companies such as IBM, Corning, and Honeywell, **diversity programs** have become part of a broader effort to improve the corporate culture. Instead of focusing only on race and gender issues, as so many diversity programs actually do in effect, these employers are expanding the range of issues, creating a second wave of diversity programs.

They include in diversity concerns about flextime, job sharing, and age- and disability-related issues.[87] Rather than stopping at sensitizing employees to race and gender issues, they are linking diversity more closely to business objectives by holding managers accountable for meeting them. "The diversity of ideas is important, not that you've got a certain ethnicity," according to Barbara C. Williams, vice-president for HR at Pacific Gas and Electric.[88]

There has been some strong opposition to the first wave of diversity programs on the basis that sensitivity techniques were used by instructors with a political axe to grind—against white males (see Chapter 9). Others argued that the first wave of diversity programs simply went nowhere after pointing out that people are different. The second wave of programs, as represented by the employers just cited, is integrating diversity considerations into their organizations.

Here are some suggestions that may help take the adversity out of diversity:[89]

- Adopt a broad definition of diversity. Include work and family issues.
- Stress that managing diversity is more than sensitivity training on race and gender. The organization's talent pool can give it a competitive advantage.
- Hold managers accountable for linking diversity to the company's bottom line.
- Don't stereotype groups like white males; stress respect for individual differences.
- Don't agitate employees with one-shot awareness workshops that pit groups against each other. Instead, try to improve the corporate culture.

---

count, and other valued information that increases both visibility and credibility.

Many women are forming their own career-related information communication systems through **networking**. Networking provides a means to disseminate and collect valued information on jobs available, jobs becoming available, and other information helpful to career-oriented women.

Development for Women and Minorities

Each member of an organization must recognize the responsibility to eliminate inequities that may exist for female and other minority employees. EEO is not solely the HR department's job; it is the responsibility of every worker, regardless of position or level. Management development personnel, however, are in a unique position to push for true EEO opportunities for employees of both sexes and for minorities. Some of the ways management development administrators can facilitate the movement of women and minorities into management ranks include the following:

- Ensure that PA data used for development decisions are free of bias against women and minorities. For example, if a PA includes statements such as "not fit for promotion into management" or "performing unacceptable work as a manager—recommend demotion to a nonsupervisory role," be sure that the reasons for these assessments are valid.

- Include Diversity Training in all developmental programs for new managers and supervisors. Programs should include discussions of relevant EEO guidelines, what discrimination is and how to avoid it, and how to conduct fair and impartial performance appraisals. (For a more specific discussion of diversity training, read *HR in the News:* "Diversity or Adversity?").

- Implement special programs that deal solely with discrimination and EEO. Examples are "Positive Approaches to EEO and Affirmative Action," "What First-Line Supervisors Must Know About EEO," "Developing Minority and Female Employees," and "Managing Diversity."

- Create programs especially for aspiring women and other minority managers. Studies of the problems of these managers suggest that women and minorities would greatly benefit from T&D activities that focus on their particular problems and needs.

One discouraging survey found that women account for just 7 percent of attendees at eight of the most prestigious executive training programs. These executive programs, offered at universities such as Harvard, Dartmouth, and Columbia, require that attendees be at the senior management level. However, since less than 5 percent of these top jobs are held by women, they are actually slightly overrepresented in the executive programs, according to the entrance criteria.[86]

CONCLUSIONS AND APPLICATIONS

- Several factors result in a need for significant internal personnel changes: organizational growth, major reorganizations, changes in general business conditions, resignations, terminations, and retirements. HR administrators should closely monitor these changes to ensure that internal staffing decisions are as planned and orderly as possible, and should strive to integrate both short- and long-range staffing needs.

- Decision makers should look closely at their mechanisms and practices for recruiting promotion candidates. Open promotion systems permit greater use of employee skills and abilities than closed systems.

- Criteria for making promotion decisions should be applied in a manner consistent with the nature of the work force and organizational goals. Seniority is a prime factor in making promotions among unionized employees; performance and promotability are important in promoting nonunionized employees. Political considerations, though impossible to eliminate, should be minimized. Assessment centers are valuable tools for identifying potential managers among nonmanagerial personnel.

- It is important that decision makers write sound HR policies for making internal staffing decisions. An important issue to clarify is whether to promote from within or hire from the outside. Appraisal data for making promotional decisions must be objective and must accurately reflect an employee's performance and promotability. Assistance should be available for laid-off employees. Internal staffing should be consistent with equal opportunity for all employee groups. Long- and short-range planning decisions should be integrated as fully as possible.

- Career management involves integration of organizational staffing needs with the career goals and aspirations of individuals. To be effective, career management should be formal and planned, should receive support from top management, and should be recognized as a process that involves coordination of a number of separate yet interrelated HR tools and techniques.

- Once organizational HR staffing needs and personal career goals have been defined and integrated, a number of personnel practices can start a career in motion. These include job posting, PA, and T&D activities.

- Dual-career couples should be prepared to deal with problems that include potential conflicts over career paths and the division of family responsibilities. Assistance from organizations may include dual-career audits, special recruiting techniques, and special policies for dual-career couples.

- The aging work force requires the HR department to consider policies that meet the unique needs of this growing labor group.

- Historically, women and other minorities have faced formidable obstacles in their advancement into managerial ranks. Management development can play a dual role in removing these obstacles by (1) developing special courses dealing with discrimination in the advancement of women and other minorities and (2) creating management development programs to meet the particular needs of these workers.

CASE STUDY

Assessment Center at Piedmont Insurance

The Piedmont Insurance Company's personnel committee entered the executive conference room, took their seats, drank coffee from Styrofoam cups, and chatted amiably among themselves. Each of the organization's six major departments was represented, typically by the department head. They included Kathy Morris, claims manager; Allen Mazula, manager of personal lines, and Lynn Snead, manager of group insurance. They were waiting for Jerry Smyth, head of Piedmont's HR department and chairman of the personnel committee. The committee members had only a vague notion of what the meeting was about; the memo calling the session spoke sparingly of "problems with promotion decisions" and a need to develop "a system for making more effective promotion decisions."

The Piedmont Insurance Company is a medium-sized, rapidly growing insurance company based in Durham, North Carolina. Piedmont Insurance is one of eighteen insurance companies owned by Tidewater, Inc., a large insurance holding company. Offering a variety of personal, home, and life insurance coverage, Piedmont has recently captured a sizable niche in the group insurance market. Piedmont's labor force totals about 4500 employees, including about 600 line managers and staff administrators.

Smyth, about five minutes late, hurriedly took his chair at the end of the conference table. After uttering a brief apology for his tardiness, he got to the point:

Smyth: "This afternoon we need to discuss a serious personnel problem that we've had in this organization for some time. As I'm sure you are all aware, we have recurring performance problems at the first level of management. Deadlines are frequently missed, and quality control is almost nonexistent. Turnover among the clerical staff and sales personnel is about twice what it should be. And our annual employee attitude surveys show that our supervisors are in dire need of both work-oriented and people-oriented skills. We have much job dissatisfaction at the clerical and salesperson levels, and all fingers point to supervision. Besides, the productivity audit conducted last year by our management consultants, Van Auken and Associates, confirmed that our first level of supervision was one of the organization's weakest links. To make a long story short, we need to consider alternative ways to strengthen our first-line supervision."

Morris: "But Jerry, each new manager is required to attend a forty-hour supervisory training program offered by your department. Isn't the program having any impact?"

Smyth: "Well, we haven't been satisfied with the results of our evaluation studies. Currently we're looking at ways to improve our management training."

Mazula: "Jerry, you don't turn someone into a supervisor in one week. What else are we doing to develop the skills of our new managers?"

Smyth: "Several things. First, we generally pay for an employee to attend a seminar as long as it's related to the job. Second, we reimburse employees for expenses they receive in getting a college degree. And as you know, we also encourage all middle managers to work closely with their supervisors to develop skills through on-the-job coaching."

Snead: "Besides taking a closer look at our T&D programs, what else can we do to improve our supervision?"

Smyth: "I think we need to make some significant changes in the way we make promotion decisions, particularly when promoting a nonmanagement employee into the first level of management. We're currently promoting about seventy-five employees a year into supervision. Historically, we've promoted someone because of a high degree of technical skills. But technical skills play only a minor role in supervision. I'm afraid we've tried to make supervisors out of a good number of people who simply don't have the aptitudes to be successful managers. And we're probably overlooking a lot of employees who have the basic qualities that it takes for successful supervision."

Snead: "And how do we deal with these problems?"

Smyth: "A couple of months ago, I sent each of you a memo and several current journal articles that described the assessment-center concept. I think this is the real key to long-run improvements at our lower management levels. I've been toying with the idea of going ahead with the project for some time and decided to make a formal request to top management. I'm going to propose that we begin an assessment center for selecting first-level managers, and I want to discuss with you several different strategies for getting the program into action.

"One approach is to put our own assessment staff together under my direction. We could study other programs, select our own tests and exercises, train our own assessors, and periodically conduct our own assessment, say every three months or so. Another alternative is to hire an outside consulting firm to come in and do the assessments. And a third approach is to persuade the corporate personnel office at Tidewater to put together a program that could be used by each company. The economies of scale of this approach would be tremendous; with the great number of promotions that are made annually in the Tidewater system, a full-time professional staff would easily keep busy the year around.''

Snead: "Hold on, Jerry. We all realize that a lot of successes have been recorded for the assessment-center concept, but it's not a perfect system. It won't guarantee success. Besides, it's pretty costly. How will we know we're getting our money's worth? To improve the quality of our supervision, maybe we should consider some other alternatives to the assessment center. We could beef up our supervisory training. Or we could make our promotion decisions much more carefully than we do now, perhaps by a formal committee. And to get more candidates, we could use job posting for the first level of supervision. That way all interested personnel would be welcome to apply.

"But if we do finally decide to go with the assessment center, let me strongly encourage that we start slowly at first with a pilot program in one department. That way we can iron out the bugs in the system before we go any further with it.''

QUESTIONS

1. Evaluate the following alternatives for improving Piedmont's first level of supervision: (a) more supervisory training for new supervisors, (b) promotion decisions made by a promotion committee, and (c) implementation of an assessment center.

2. If you recommend an assessment center for Piedmont, who should conduct it—Piedmont's HR department, Tidewater's corporate HR office, or an outside consulting group? Should the program begin on a pilot study basis?

3. Are the training and assessment-center approaches mutually exclusive strategies for improving the quality of supervision? Discuss.

EXPERIENTIAL EXERCISES

1. What Are You Going to Do with Your Life?

PURPOSE

To get you to start thinking about career goals, personal strengths and weaknesses, and strategies for achieving career goals.

THE TASK

Listed here are several areas that are normally the focus of career planning workshops for employees and students. After you complete all questions, your instructor will lead a discussion concerning career planning.

Goal Setting

I. *Career Goals*

Let's begin by outlining a few career goals. How much thought have you given to what you want to be? How much money you want to make? The kind of organization you would like to work for? The industry? Geographical location? Think about these questions, and complete the following section.

A. Job

What *specifically* would you like to be doing in five years?

_____

B. Salary

How much money would you like to be making? (Of course, your salary goals should be tied directly to your job goal.) Be realistic!

$_____ per year

C. What size company would you like to work for?
1. Small (fewer than 300 employees) _____
2. Medium (300 to 1000 employees) _____
3. Large (1000 employees or more) _____

D. Which industry would you prefer to work in?
1. Government
   Local _____
   State _____
   Federal _____
2. Construction _____
3. Mining _____
4. Manufacturing _____ (which kind?—automobile, etc.) _____
5. Agriculture _____
6. Transportation _____
7. Wholesale/retail trade _____
8. Services _____ (which kind?—banking, health care, etc.) _____

E. Where would you like to live?
1. Northeast _____
2. Southeast _____
3. Midwest _____
4. Central Plains _____
5. Southwest _____
6. Northwest _____
7. Doesn't matter _____

II. *Strengths and Weaknesses*

Right now, you have several strengths—knowledge, skills and abilities—that will be assets in achieving your job goal. You will probably also need to acquire *new* skills to realize your job goal. In addition, you may have some weaknesses that you need to overcome before achieving your goals. In relation to your job goal, think about your strengths and weaknesses and complete the following section.

A. Strengths

List your strengths—including all knowledge, skills and abilities, work experience, technical skills such as your college major, and human skills (e.g., communication, leadership, motivation).

B. Skills to develop

Think about the job you would like to have, the skills you currently possess, and the skills you think you'll need to obtain to be competent in the job you want. Needed skills may include decision making, technical, and human-relations skills. List these skills.

C. Obstacles

Now think of all the obstacles that you must overcome to realize your job goal. Obstacles relate less to skill deficiencies (listed before) than to external considerations such as a reluctance to relocate if it is a condition for a promotion or perhaps the difficulties (time and money) you would face in getting an MBA at night.

D. Soul search

Consider all your thoughts thus far: job and salary goals, strengths, areas that need to be developed, and obstacles. In light of your shortcomings and obstacles that need to be overcome, how *realistic* are your job and salary goals? How likely is it that your goals can be achieved? Write a statement about the likelihood of meeting your job goal in five years. Be honest!

2. Designing a Diversity Training Program

PURPOSE

To use role playing and role reversal to become aware of the range of views about the meaning of diversity at the workplace. Students should also gain a clearer understanding of how a diversity of ideas can help an organization become more competitive. Students must approach this exercise with a certain level of maturity but should also be creative.

THE TASK

This is a role reversal exercise that requires students to group by race and/or gender. All students should show respect for all roles. Depending on the size of the class and the composition of the class in terms of race and gender, the instructor may decide to group students in one of the following ways:

1. By gender, with females role-playing males and males role-playing females.

2. By race, with white students role-playing minority students and minority students role-playing white students.

3. By race and gender, with white males role-playing minority females, minority males role-playing white females, and so on.

4. By other categories, which may include age, disability status, and so on.

Step 1:   Your group (role-reversed) should meet and list the elements that you believe should be covered in a diversity training program at a hypothetical large firm in your locale. Emphasize the interests of the gender or racial group you are role-playing.

Step 2: Your class should now return, and the groups should list on the blackboard the ideas generated for the ideal diversity training program. After the lists are written, class members should be encouraged to ask any group to explain why it included certain elements.

Step 3: Your class should draw circles or lines on the board, linking elements

that were common, regardless of the group. This should identify the core elements. Discuss the common, and perhaps the uncommon, elements.

Step 4: What steps, if any, need to be taken at the workplace to remove glass ceilings. Decide whether these core elements (identified in Step 3) of your diversity program will actually help remove these barriers.

Step 5: What did role playing add to the discussions? Discuss how accurate role-players portrayals were.

KEY TERMS AND CONCEPTS

Aging work force
Assessment center
Bumping
Career management
Career match
Career stages
Closed promotion system
Contingency work force
Demotion
Diversity programs
Dual-career couple
Early-retirement programs
Glass ceiling
Guaranteed income stream (GIS)
HR balancing
Individual and organizational career planning

Internal staffing
Layoff
Nepotism
Networking
Old boy network
Open promotion system
Outplacement assistance
Plateaued employee
Promotion
Severance pay
Supplemental unemployment benefits (SUB)
Telecommuting
Transfer
Worker Adjustment and Retraining Act (WARN)

REVIEW QUESTIONS

1. What are the benefits of an effective system for making promotion decisions? What are the various criteria that may be used for making promotion decisions?

2. What are the major causes of employee demotions, transfers, and layoffs?

3. What are some alternatives to layoffs? How effective do you think they can be when an employer is reorganizing?

4. What are some important HR policies and practices that have an impact on internal staffing decisions?

5. What are the benefits that may be gained from a career management program?

6. What are the problems of two-career couples and how may they be overcome?

7. What are the special problems that minorities and women face when trying to move up the corporate ladder?

DISCUSSION QUESTIONS

1. In many organizations, it is customary to place new employees on probation for three to six months. If the new employee does not work out, he or she may be terminated without the right to appeal the firing. Do you think a similar probationary period should be enforced for employees who receive promotions? Can you think of any arguments for and against this proposal?

2. Seniority is a common criterion for deciding who to lay off among the blue-collar work force. Should seniority be the major factor in deciding on white-collar layoffs? Defend your reasoning.

3. Most organizations used closed promotion systems when selecting candidates for promotion to managerial jobs, though it is generally recognized that this minimizes the pool of candidates from which an employee may be selected. Why do organizations continue to use the closed promotion system?

4. An often cited advantage of using seniority as a criterion for making promotions is that it eliminates supervisory bias that may occur. Is there still the possibility of supervisory bias while using performance-related criteria in making promotion decisions?

5. The personnel literature generally holds the assessment center in high regard. Can you think of reasons why an organization would not adopt the assessment center in gathering promotion data?

6. Usually there is a tremendous stigma against an employee who admits that, ''I received a promotion and I am failing on my new job. I would like a job with less authority and responsibility.'' How can this stigma be eliminated?

7. If an employee receives a promotion and fails, whose fault is it—the organization's or the employee's?

8. Do you agree with the requirements of the Plant Closings Act? Why or why not? Would you favor increasing the notification period from 60 days to 120 days?

9. What kind of lateral promotion would you be willing to take?

10. Are women and other minorities really discriminated against at the workplace? How and why?

11. Assuming that you were employed full time, what would you perceive as some of your immediate supervisor's responsibilities in the career management process?

12. How would you evaluate your college's or university's efforts to prepare you for a career in the world of work? Cite your school's strong and weak areas.

ENDNOTES

Chapter 10

1. "The Horizontal Corporation," *Business Week* (December 20, 1993): 78–79.

2. "Congratulations. You're Moving to a New Pepperoni," *Business Week* (December 20, 1993): 80.

3. Ibid., pp. 80–81.

4. "The Horizontal Corporation," p. 79.

5. Tom Peters, "Going 'Horizontal' in Your Career," *Industry Week* (January 4, 1993): 47–50.

6. Ibid.

7. Ibid.

8. Ibid.

9. Ibid.

10. This thesis is supported by the *expectancy theory* of job motivation, which suggests that an employee will be motivated to perform if (a) he or she values a certain outcome or (b) expects that high performance will lead to the outcome. See J. Richard Hackman and Lyman W. Porter, "Expectancy Theory Predictions of Work Effectiveness," *Organizational Behavior and Human Performance* (November 1968): 417–26.

11. See Frederick Herzberg et al., *The Motivation to Work* (New York: Wiley, 1959).

12. Bureau of National Affairs, *Employee Promotion and Transfer Policies*, Personnel Policies Forum survey no. 120 (Washington, DC: Bureau of National Affairs, 1978).

13. Stephen Cabot, *Labor Management Relations Manual* (Boston: Warren, Gorham, Lamont, 1980).

14. Cabot, *Labor Management*.

15. Ibid., chap. 15, pp. 4–5.

16. Bureau of National Affairs (BNA) Editorial Staff, *Grievance Guide* (Washington, DC: Bureau of National Affairs, 1978), p. 173–174.

17. As indicated in a previous chapter, the assessment center may also be used to assess management development needs and strengthen managerial skills. See L. C. Nichols and J. Hudson, "Dual Role Assessment Center," *Personnel Journal* 82 (May 1981): 380–87; and F. Enzs, "Total Development: Selection, Assessment, Growth," *Personnel Administrator* 25 (February 1980).

18. Walter S. Wikstrom, "Assessing Managerial Talent," *The Conference Board Record* (March 1967). Assessment center procedures and exercises are also outlined in C. Jaffee and J. Sefcik, Jr., "What Is an Assessment Center?" *Personnel Administrator* 25 (February 1980): 35–39.

19. Wikstrom, "Assessing Managerial Talent."

20. See F. Frank and J. Preston, "The Validity of the Assessment Center Approach and Related Issues," *Personnel Administrator* 27 (June 1982): 87–94; and C. Millard and S. Pinsky, "Assessing the Assessment Center," *Personnel Administrator* 25 (February 1980): 40–44.

21. S. D. Norton, "The Empirical and Content Validity of Assessment Centers vs. Traditional Methods for Predicting Managerial Success," *Academy of Management Review* 2 (1977): 442–53.

22. This point may be debated. It can be argued, and often is, that the family member is the most qualified person for the job.

23. Dalton Melville, *Men Who Manage* (New York: Wiley, 1959), p. 154.

24. John P. Kohl and David B. Stephens, "Is Demotion a Four-Letter word?" *Business Horizons* 33 (March–April 1990): 74.

25. Ibid.

26. Upper-level transfers (and promotions) sometimes require the professional to relocate to a new area. For a discussion of the problems and coping mechanisms related to the re-

location issue, see the September 1980 and April 1984 issues of *Personnel Administrator*. Both issues are devoted to the topic of employee relocation.

27. Jill Kanin-Lovers, "Pay Dilemma of Lateral Transfers," *Journal of Compensation and Benefits* 55 (May–June 1993): 51.

28. Adapted from John E. Hayes, Jr., "Few Fast Tracks for Tomorrow's Brightest," *HRMagazine* 38 (January 1993): 94.

29. Ceel Pasternak, "HRM Update: Still Losing Jobs," *HRMagazine* 38 (October 1993): 22.

30. Julie Amparano Lopez, "Companies Alter Layoff Policies to Keep Recently Hired Women and Minorities," *The Wall Street Journal* (September 18, 1992): B1, B16.

31. S. Wermiel, "Court Orders That Shield Minorities from Layoffs Generate Bitterness," *The Wall Street Journal* 32 (March 23, 1983): 33.

32. *Firefighters Local 1784* v. *Stotts*, no. 82–206 U.S. (1984).

33. "Blacks Hired Under Consent Decree Subject to Seniority-Based Layoffs." *U.S. Law Week* 52, no. 49 (June 19, 1984): 1193.

34. Barbara J. Farrah and Cheryl D. Dagen, "Telecommuting Policies That Work," *HRMagazine* 38 (July 1993): 64.

35. Ibid., p. 66.

36. Mike Langberg, "High-Tech Link to Office Will Reshape the Nature of Work," *San Jose Mercury News* (October 26, 1992): C6.

37. Kathleen Christensen, "Managing Invisible Employees: How to Meet the Telecommuting Challenge," *Employment Relations Today* 19 (Summer 1992): 136, citing her study *Flexible Staffing and Scheduling in U.S. Corporations*, The Conference Board, Research Bulletin No. 240.

38. Diane Filipowski, "Employees Who Prefer Home Work," *Personnel Journal* 71 (November 1992): 27.

39. Christensen, "Managing Invisible Employees," pp. 137–138.

40. Adapted from Christensen, "Managing Invisible Employees," pp. 139–143.

41. "Early-Retirement Offers Lead to Renewed Hiring," *The Wall Street Journal* (January 26, 1993): B7, citing a study by Rights Associates in Philadelphia.

42. Ibid.

43. Adapted from G. James Francis, John Mohr, and Kelly Anderson, "HR Balancing: Alternative Downsizing," *Personnel Journal* 71 (January 1992): 71–76.

44. Peggy Stuart, "New Internal Jobs Found for Displaced Employees," *Personnel Journal* 71 (August 1992): 50–56.

45. Jaclyn Fierman, "The Contingency Work Force," *Fortune* (January 24, 1994): 30–31.

46. Fierman, "Contingency Work Force," p. 30.

47. Ibid., p. 31.

48. Ibid., p. 32.

49. Ibid., p. 31.

50. Ani Hadjian, "Hiring Temps Full-Time May Get the IRS on Your Tail," *Fortune* (January 24, 1994): 34.

51. Ibid.

52. Paul D. Staudohar, "New Plant Closing Law Aids Workers in Transition," *Personnel Journal* 68 (January 1989): 87–90.

53. Ibid.

54. D. Quinn Mills, "When Employers Make Concessions," *Harvard Business Review* 61 (May–June 1983): 103–13.

55. Peter Cappelli, "Auto Industry Experiments with the Guaranteed Income Stream," *Monthly Labor Review* 107, no. 7 (July 1984): 37–39.

56. "A Ford Plant Closing May Prove a Model of Labor–Management Cooperation," *The Wall Street Journal* (October 11, 1983): 1.

57. W. L. Batt, Jr., "Canada's Good Example with Displaced Workers," *Harvard Business Review* 61 (July–August 1983).

58. G. Shultz and A. Weber, *Strategies for Displaced Workers* (New York: Harper & Row, 1966), p. 190.

59. William J. Barkley, Jr., and Thad B. Green, "Safe Landings for Outplaced Employees at AT&T," *Personnel Journal* 71 (June 1992): 144–47.

60. Ibid.

61. Ibid.

62. Stanlee Phelps and Marguerite Mason, "When Women Lose Their Jobs," *Personnel Journal* 70 (August 1991): 64–69.

63. See L. Peter and R. Hull, *The Peter Principle* (New York: William Morrow, 1969).

64. M. Vosburgh, "The Annual Human Resource Review: A Career Planning System," *Personnel Journal* 59 (October 1980): 830–37.

65. Cherlyn S. Grawrose and James D. Portwood, "Matching Individual Career Plans and Organizational Career Management," *Academy of Management Journal* 30, no. 4 (December 1987): 699–720.

66. M. J. Driver, "Career Concepts—A New Approach to Career Research," in R. Katz, ed., *Career Issues in Human Resource Management* (Englewood Cliffs, NJ: Prentice-Hall, 1982), pp. 23–32.

67. Gilbert Fuchsberg, "Parallel Lines: Companies Create New Ways to Promote Employees—Without Making Them Bosses," *The Wall Street Journal* (April 21, 1993): R4.

68. L. Baird and K. Kram, "Career Dynamics: Managing the Superior/Subordinate Relationship," *Organizational Dynamics* 12 (Spring 1983): 46–64.

69. J. Dowd and J. Sonnenfeld, "A Note on Career Programs in Industry," in J. Sonnenfeld, *Managing Career Systems* (Homewood, IL: Richard D. Irwin, 1984), p. 325.

70. T. Gutteridge and F. Otte, "Organizational Career Development: State of the Practice," unpublished monograph (October 1982), p. 23.

71. J. Walker and T. Gutteridge, "Career Planning Practices: An AMA Report" (New York: AMACOM, 1979).

72. Ibid., p. 13.

73. Michele Galen, "Myths About Older Workers Cost Business Plenty," *Business Week* (December 20, 1993): 83.

74. Jeffrey A. Sonnenfeld, "Dealing with the Aging Workforce," *Harvard Business Review* 56 (November–December, 1978): 54–71.

75. Ibid.

76. F. Hall and D. Hall, "Dual Careers—How Do Couples and Companies Cope with the Problems?" *Organizational Dynamics* 7 (Spring 1978): 57–77.

77. Joann S. Lublin, "Ranks of Unemployed Couples Multiply, Devastating Double-Income Households," *The Wall Street Journal* (May 7, 1993): B1.

78. Hall and Hall, "Dual Careers."

79. Patrick Kelly, "Conduct a Glass Ceiling Self-Audit Now," *HRMagazine* 38 (October 1993): 76–70.

80. Adapted from ibid., pp. 77–79.

81. "White, Male, and Worried," *Business Week* (January 31, 1994): 50–55.

82. Ibid.

83. Joline Godfrey, "If the Dinosaur Won't Change . . ." *Harvard Business Review* 71 (March–April 1993): 20.

84. "The 'Glass Ceiling' That Keeps Women from the Top Ranks of the Corporate World May Have a Few Cracks in It," in footnotes, *Chronicle of Higher Education* 26 (November 24, 1993): A6.

85. Rosalind Loring and Theodora Wells, *Breakthrough: Women into Management* (New York: Van Nostrand Reinhold, 1972), pp. 25–28. See also E. Mirides and A. Cote, "Women in Management: The Obstacles and Opportunities They Face," *Personnel Administrator* 25 (April 1980).

86. Dawn Gunsch, "Women a Rarity in Executive Training Programs," *Personnel Journal* 71 (May 1992): 16.

87. Michele Galen and Ann T. Palmer, "Taking Adversity Out of Diversity," *Business Week* (January 31, 1994): 54–55.

88. Ibid.

89. Liberally adapted from "White, Male, and Worried."

COMPENSATION SYSTEMS

CHAPTER OUTLINE

CHAPTER OBJECTIVES

1. To recognize the relationship between a pay system and the process of attracting and retaining employees.
2. To identify the legal considerations of a pay system.
3. To explain the link between pay, motivation, and performance.
4. To explain the purpose of a wage survey.
5. To develop a time-based pay system using pay grades and steps.

6. To recognize compensation systems that allow workers to increase their pay by taking on new or additional responsibilities.

7. To understand piece-rate incentive systems.

8. To distinguish between individual incentive systems and team-based systems.

9. To recognize the advantages of gainsharing, profit-sharing incentive plans, and ESOPs.

10. To understand executive compensation methods.

11. To explain the current issues of comparable worth and two-tier wage systems.

One of the traditional HR functions is determining employees' compensation. In the modern organization, with a variety of costly employee benefit programs, wage incentive programs, and structured pay scales, the compensation task is even more difficult and challenging for an HR specialist. Employees' compensation affects their productivity and their tendency to stay with the organization. Although managers and researchers do not agree about the degree to which compensation affects productivity, compensation is of great importance. Employees' need for income and their desire to be fairly treated by the organization make developing the compensation program all the more important for the HR department. Yet there is no exact, objective method of determining compensation for any one job or employee. Compensating employees for what they give the organization is to some extent as much an art as a science.

The term *compensation* is often used interchangeably with *wage and salary administration;* however, the term *compensation* actually is a broader concept. Compensation refers not only to *extrinsic rewards* such as salary and benefits but also to *intrinsic rewards* such as achieving personal goals, autonomy, and more challenging job opportunities. The term *wage and salary administration* usually refers strictly to the monetary rewards given to employees. Figure 11-1 is a model of the total compensation system.

The compensation of people at work has become one of the most demanding problems facing management. The effort to control salaries has become a critical problem for companies competing in the global marketplace. In the past, payment for work performed was simple and straightforward. Paying for work not performed, such as paid vacations, was simply unheard of by management. For the most part, the employer displayed a "take it or leave it" attitude when making pay offers for employees. Today the almost-automatic ratcheting up of employee's salaries every 12 months or so is common practice (see *HR in the News:* "Where's My Annual Raise?"). Although things have changed substantially, newer and better ways of compensating people are needed in HR management.[1]

COMPENSATION OBJECTIVES

Organizations have many objectives in designing their compensation systems. The HR specialist must keep in mind the goals of the system and what the organization needs to accomplish to obtain these goals. Primarily,

Where's My Annual Raise?

"How much is our annual raise?" That was the question I heard an employee ask in a social service agency. "But we've always received an annual wage increase," was her next comment.

Employees from hourly workers to CEOs look upon an annual wage increase as a birthright or an entitlement. How, why, and when was the idea of an annual wage increase born?

Annual raises are a relatively new phenomenon. During the depression not only were annual raises rare, it was not uncommon for a boss to tell workers that salaries would be cut.

As I recall, my father received an enormous $5 a week raise after three years without an increase. It called for a family celebration, but nobody suggested that he might get another raise next year or at any time in the foreseeable future. In those days, there was no such thing as a scheduled annual increase.

In the 1950s, when I was working for Underwood (the typewriter company), the corporation was struggling for survival. For two successive years, we signed union contracts without a wage increase; increases for all salaried employees were frozen solid.

At another company, I asked an engineer, during his annual review, what he had done to warrant an increase. "My attendance record is excellent, I've never been late, and I've finished all of my projects on time, if not ahead of schedule."

"If that is what earned you a raise, what was the company paying you for?" was my response. Being at work regularly and on time, and finishing assignments on schedule, is what we are all paid for. Is such performance worthy of an automatic, guaranteed raise?

We seem to believe that the passing of a year entitles us to a raise. Has an assembly-line operator who has served faithfully for another year earned an increase? Has a CEO who has survived another year earned an automatic increase?

Lest I be considered some sort of Neanderthal, let me state that I am not opposed, in any shape, form or manner, to wage increases. However, I just don't recall when all of us started believing that an annual wage increase was something we were entitled to.

Cost of living increases (COLAs) for inflation are one thing, and they should reflect current economic conditions, but not necessarily be granted on a given date, or even annually. And, certainly only when the organization can afford it.

Merit increases should be just that: increase for meritorious performance—not for having survived another year, not for doing what one is being paid to do, but performance above and beyond what one is paid for. That the organization can afford to give merit increases does not mean that every employee is automatically entitled to one.

(continued)

The employees at the social service agency were not getting their expected annual increase (for inflation or performance) because the agency could not afford an increase for anyone, including the executive director.

If that action destroyed the concept of an expected annual increase, so be it. Perhaps during tense, difficult economic times, it is incumbent that we all face the realities of the economic world: There is no such thing as a guaranteed annual wage increase!

SOURCE: Reprinted by permission of *Wall Street Journal* from Harvey Gittler, "Where's My Annual Raise?" *Wall Street Journal,* March 23, 1992:A10. Dow Jones & Company, Inc. All rights reserved worldwide.

the goals of any organization in designing a compensation system should be to attract and retain good employees. Also, the system should motivate employees and comply with all legal requirements. Figure 11-2 shows the objectives of any compensation system and how they are achieved.

Attracting Employees

Although most job applicants are not aware of the exact wages offered by different organiza-

tions for similar jobs within the local labor market, they do compare job offers and pay scales. Job applicants who receive more than one offer will naturally compare monetary offers. Since it is easier to compare dollars, job applicants often will put more weight on the salaries being offered than on other types of compensation, such as benefits and intrinsic rewards. Although one organization may make an offer $2000 a year higher, that organization may provide less take-home pay than a com-

FIGURE 11-1 The total compensation system.

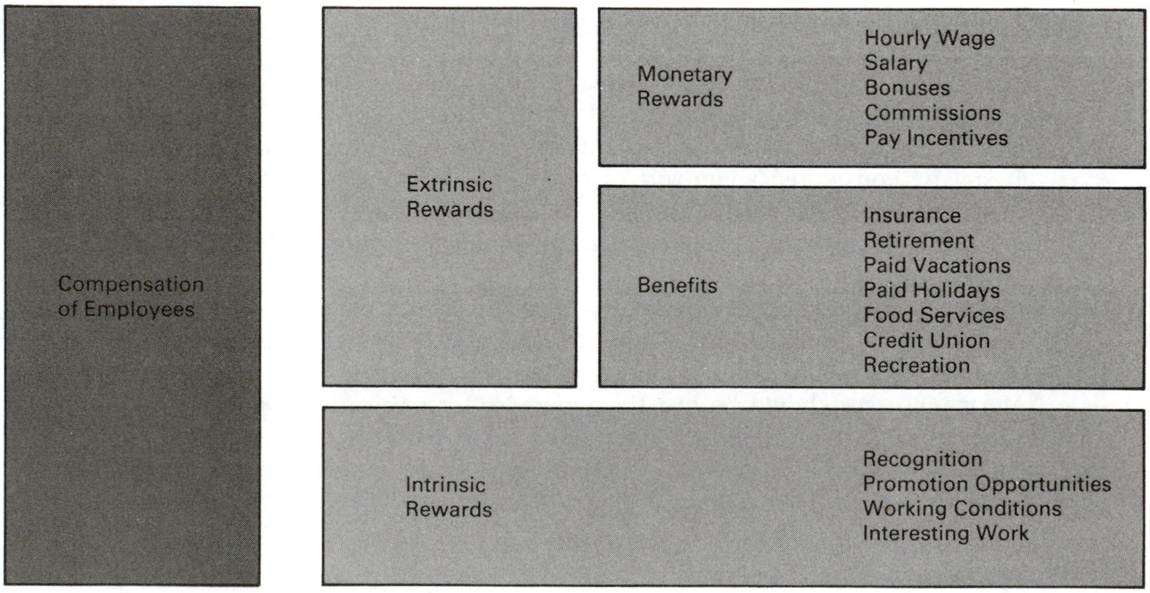

FIGURE 11-2 Objectives of a compensation system.

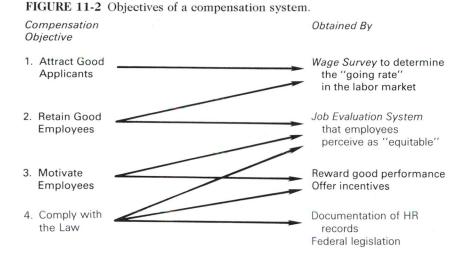

peting organization that pays more of the employee's benefit costs.

Some employers argue that wage level is not the important determinant of job choice; if that were the case, wage levels for similar jobs would be more similar within the same labor market. Employees would readily leave lower-paying organizations and seek out higher-paying organizations. Indeed, job seekers lack a knowledge of the market. Given the limited knowledge job seekers often have about various employers, their general perceptions of the type of work they will perform and the exact salary being offered are the best factors they have to consider.[2]

A **strategic pay** decision by an employer is choosing a general pay level for the organization. In comparison to other employers within the same industry and labor market, management must decide whether to be a high pay-level employer, a low pay-level employer, or a competitive pay-level employer. A *high pay-level strategy* may be chosen because management believes that if it maintains high salaries, the company will attract and retain the best employees within the geographic area, industry, or profession. Sometimes management will expect more from employees because the company pays higher than average salaries. A *low pay-level strategy* may be chosen because management decides to expect and live with the increased turnover and morale problems that may result. The savings in total personnel costs may be estimated to outweigh the disadvantages associated with low morale and high turnover. Employers may choose this strategy simply because the organization cannot afford to pay more. Small employers and those operating in highly competitive markets are likely to choose the low pay-level option. The *competitive pay-level strategy* may be chosen if management believes that the additional costs associated with this strategy cannot be justified or are simply not affordable. At the same time, management may believe that if the company's pay level is competitive within the labor market, the employee problems associated with the low pay-level strategy can be largely avoided.

Most employers will try to remain competitive within the local labor market by offering salaries that are similar to those offered by competing employers. Usually this means determining what the going rate is for jobs within the local labor market. This entails using *wage surveys*, which estimate average salaries for entry-level positions. The employer has two alternatives: the first is for the organization to conduct a wage survey and determine the going rate for jobs in the local labor market; the second is to use published market data.

Conducting a wage survey is a difficult, expensive process for an individual organization. The HR specialist must determine that employers have roughly comparable positions within the local labor market. Job titles are no longer an acceptable means of proving comparability of positions. By comparing brief job descriptions, the specialist must determine if the job is similar to other organizations' positions at a particular wage level.

A further requirement for conducting wage surveys is determining which information about each job is necessary. The wages being paid for each job type included in the survey must be precisely defined. If possible, survey information should include salary ranges, incentives, normal wage changes such as cost of living increases, and specific wage policies and practices within each organization in the survey. Information about seniority provisions, paid vacations, sick leave, and the number of paid holidays per year is helpful. Also, any additional pay, such as a uniform allowance or bonus plan, should be reported. Lastly, a wage survey should include questions concerning unusual working conditions such as high levels of noise or fumes.[3] A typical wage survey data sheet is shown in Figure 11-3.

Organizations have turned more to published wage survey information for a variety of reasons. First, published information can be obtained quickly, at low cost, and with little effort by the organization. Second, conducting wage surveys has become a science in recent years; few organizations have personnel capable of undertaking such a task. Third, using an organization's wage survey may cause problems in court cases. Opposing lawyers will try to prove that the survey caused the organization to perpetuate past discriminatory practices that occurred in the surveyed organizations. Abundance of market data in most large communities has made more effective wage and salary administration possible in most geographic areas; sufficient market data are available to price anywhere from 5 to 50 percent of comparable positions in many organizations. The relative availability of market data today has changed the basic approach to salary classification work. Employers can receive wage survey information from local chambers of commerce, unions, trade services, and the U.S. Department of Labor.

Retaining Good Employees

After the organization has attracted and hired new employees, the compensation system should not hinder efforts to retain productive employees. While many factors may cause employees to leave an organization, inadequate compensation is often the cause of turnover. To retain good employees, the HR manager must make sure that there is compensation equity within the organization.

If employees perceive that they are being treated inequitably by the organization, tension results. The perception of inequity causes an unpleasant emotional state that may cause employees to reduce their future efforts, change their perceptions regarding rewards for their work efforts, or, as often is the case, leave the organization.[4] Research has found that employee perceptions of equitable treatment were affected when an organization altered its pay system to increase the pay of about 50 percent of its employees. But the same employees reported diminished perceptions of inequity nine months after a change in pay systems. This suggests that such perceived inequity is short-term in nature; however, additional perceptions of unfair treatment may cause employees to leave the organization.[5]

Job satisfaction is often considered to be a strong determinant of turnover. However, employee perceptions of inequitable treatment have been found to be even stronger predictors of absence and job turnover than job

FIGURE 11-3 A typical wage survey data sheet.

Name of participating company _____ Code _____

Address _____ Business _____

Survey No. _____ Data furnished by _____ Title _____ Date _____

	Shop	Office	Salary	Incentive
1. Number of employees in your company.	___	___	___	___
2. Minimum hiring rates.	___	___	___	___
3. Do you use training rates for new employees?	___	___	___	___
4. Number of hours worked. per week	___	___	___	___
per year	___	___	___	___
5. What method of progression do you use?				
within the range	___	___	___	___
COLA increase	___	___	___	___
merit increase	___	___	___	___
part COLA—part merit	___	___	___	___
6. Are you granting rest periods? with pay	___	___	___	___
without pay	___	___	___	___
7. Do employees working on holidays receive				
straight hourly rate?	___	___	___	___
time and one-half?	___	___	___	___
double time?	___	___	___	___
other compensation?	___	___	___	___
8. What is the average percentage of base rate paid as supplemental wages?	___%	___%	___%	___%
9. In percent of base rates how much do you pay for a 40-hour workweek?				
afternoon shift	___%	___%	___%	___%
night shift	___%	___%	___%	___%
Saturday	___%	___%	___%	___%
Sunday	___%	___%	___%	___%
holiday	___%	___%	___%	___%
10. Do you supply work clothes and laundry?	___	___	___	___
11. Do you use a single rate (SR) SR	___	___	___	___
or a pay range (RR) for each job? RR	___	___	___	___

12. If you use an incentive plan, briefly explain the incentive method used _____
_____
_____

	Shop	Office	Salary	Incentive
13. What are the average incentive earnings per hour as a percentage of base rate?	___%	___%	___%	___%

(continued)

FIGURE 11-3 continued

14. Do you pay incentive wages?
annual bonus ___ attendance bonus ___ Christmas bonus ___ profit sharing ___
stock purchase plan ___ seniority bonus ___ gainsharing ___
other payments _____

	Shop	Office	Salary	Incentive
15. Are you guaranteeing an annual wage?				
yes	___	___	___	___
no	___	___	___	___

If "yes," please explain amount and number of weeks per year, etc. _____
_____
_____

16. Which of the following holidays do you grant with pay?

	Jan. 1	Feb. 12	Feb. 22	May 30	July 4	Labor Day	Thanksgiving	Dec. 25
Shop	___	___	___	___	___	___	___	___
Office	___	___	___	___	___	___	___	___
Salary	___	___	___	___	___	___	___	___
Incentive	___	___	___	___	___	___	___	___

17. Are vacations granted with pay

	Shop	Office	Salary	Incentive
After 1 year employment	___ wks.	___ wks.	___ wks.	___ wks.
" 2 " "	___ "	___ "	___ "	___ "
" 3 " "	___ "	___ "	___ "	___ "
" 4 " "	___ "	___ "	___ "	___ "
" 5 " "	___ "	___ "	___ "	___ "

18. If you have employee benefit plans, excluding social security and workers compensation, who contributes—

	Company only	Employee only	Both Company	Both Employee
Accident Insurance	_____	_____	_____%	_____%
Life Insurance	_____	_____	_____%	_____%
Hospitalization Insurance	_____	_____	_____%	_____%
Pension	_____	_____	_____%	_____%
Savings	_____	_____	_____%	_____%

19. If sick leave is granted with pay, how is it paid?

	Shop	Office	Salary	Incentive
full pay	___	___	___	___
% of base rate	___%	___%	___%	___%

20. Attached are condensed descriptions of key jobs designated by our job numbers as indicated below. These jobs will also be used in repetitive surveys. Please fill in correct current data.

Job Code No.	Job Code No.	Job Code No.	Job Code No.
_____	_____	_____	_____
_____	_____	_____	_____
_____	_____	_____	_____

SOURCE: Herbert G. Zollitsch and Adolph Langsner, *Wage and Salary Administration* (Cincinnati: South-Western Publishing Co., 1970), pp. 337–38. Used by permission.

satisfaction. If employees perceive that they will be more equitably treated by another organization, the probability of their leaving increases.[6]

To provide for equity among jobs, administrators usually create a systematic relationship among the pay scales for various jobs within an organization. This process is usually called *job evaluation*.

Job evaluation is the systematic determination of the relative worth of jobs within the organization that results in an organization's pay system. Primarily, jobs are compared on the traditional basis of skills required to complete the job, effort required to perform the job, responsibility of the job holder, and working conditions on the job. The primary purpose of job evaluation is to develop a system of compensation that employees will perceive to be equitable. Thus, job evaluation strives to obtain internal consistency among jobs, while wage surveys help the organization to maintain external consistency with other organizations in the local labor market.

No compensation program will keep all employees satisfied all the time. If management is able to minimize turnover and lost production due to perceptions of inequitable compensation, then its goal of retaining good employees has been achieved. Not only must an organization have a very equitable system, but this system must be explained to its employees.

Administrators must tell employees the various wage rates paid for different positions and how those wage levels are determined. Many managers involve employees in job classification and compensation matters. The most equitable compensation system is useless unless employees perceive it to be equitable.

Motivation

Employees expect that their performances will correlate with the rewards received from the organization. Generally, that perceived relationship takes the form exhibited in Figure 11-4. Employees set expectations about rewards and compensation to be received if certain levels of performance are achieved. These expectations determine goals or levels of performance for the future. Employees achieving the desired level of performance expect a certain level of compensation. At some point, management evaluates and rewards the employee's performance. Examples of such rewards include merit increases, promotions, and intrinsic rewards such as goal accomplishment and increased self-esteem. Employees consider the relationship between their performance and the rewards related to that performance and then the fairness of that relationship. The final step in the process involves employees' setting new goals and expectations based on prior experiences within the organization.

FIGURE 11-4 Motivation and performance model.

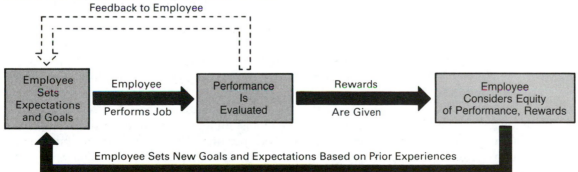

If employees see that hard work and superior performance are recognized and rewarded by the organization, they will expect such relationships to continue in the future. Therefore, they will set higher levels of performance, expecting higher levels of compensation. Of course, if employees see little relationship between performance and rewards, then they may set minimum goals in order to retain their jobs but will not see the need to excel in their positions.

To safeguard this relationship of performance and motivation, which benefits the organization and the employee, the organization must provide the following:

- *Accurate Evaluation.* Management must develop a system of accurate performance appraisal in order to identify those employees who are outstanding, average, and poor performers. Although developing an accurate performance appraisal system is not easy, it is a critical link between employee performance and motivation.

- *Performance Rewards.* Management should identify which rewards relate to performance levels and tell employees that pay, increased benefits, change in hours or working conditions, or recognition will be directly related to high performance.

- *Supervisors' Feedback.* Supervisors must give complete and accurate feedback to employees when appraising their performances. Employees must be told what they are doing well and which performance areas need improvement.

As stated in the discussion on job design, many managers have theories regarding the motivation of employees' performance; some believe that only one motivational theory is enough to develop productive employees. Others may claim that no technique works because employees are born either achievers or loafers. Undoubtedly no single theory will solve all motivational problems; however, something can be learned from each theory.

Legal Considerations

A fourth major objective of the compensation system is to comply with federal legislation. Government has affected compensation by legislating pay levels and nondiscriminatory pay practices. As an employer in competition with private employers, the government also affects pay systems. At any time, government can increase its control over compensation by freezing wages; this occurred during the Korean War and from 1971 to 1974. A governmental *wage freeze* requires that federal regulatory bodies review wage increases. *Wage guidelines* are not strict wage controls but simply requests to employers to comply voluntarily with wage-increase maximums.

Fair Labor Standards Act   The major compensation legislation regulating employers is the **Fair Labor Standards Act (FLSA)** of 1938. This act has been amended by Congress several times to provide higher minimum wage levels. The provisions of this law include the following:

Minimum Wages Under the FLSA, employers must pay an employee at least a minimum wage per hour, as shown in Table 11-1. The minimum wage per hour was $.25 in 1938 and $4.25 in 1994. Exempted from the act are small businesses whose gross sales do not exceed $500,000 (1994). Also exempted are organizations that operate within one state. However, several states have minimum wage laws that parallel the federal minimum wage provisions; some have lower minimum wages.

Child Labor The FLSA prohibits hiring individuals between the ages of sixteen and eighteen for hazardous jobs, or employing individuals under sixteen in interstate commerce except in nonhazardous work for a parent or guardian. The act also requires individuals under eighteen to obtain temporary work permits to be given to their employers.

The declining number of teenagers in the labor force has contributed to a substantial in-

Table 11-1 U.S. Minimum Wage Changes Under the FLSA As Amended (wages per hour)

1938	1945	1950	1956	1962	1967	1974	1978	1979	1980	1985	1990	1991
$.25	$.40	$.75	$1.00	$1.15	$1.40	$2.00	$2.65	$2.90	$3.10	$3.35	$3.80	$4.25

crease in child labor law violations in recent years. The number of citations issued to employers in 1989 was up 250 percent from 1983. The vast majority (78 percent) were in the retail trade industry, which includes fast-food restaurants. Many teachers and parents are concerned that too many students fall asleep in class and do not complete their homework because they are working at part-time jobs. The tragic irony is that corporate America is demanding and often contributing to improvements in American schools—but in some respects may contribute to some teens' poor learning.[7]

Overtime Compensation The FLSA stipulates that certain employees must receive overtime pay of one and one-half times the normal rate when they work over forty hours per week. Certain kinds of employees are *exempt* from the overtime provision of the act.

Under the law, **exempt** most frequently means that a particular individual is exempt from the overtime provision and need not be paid overtime. In and of itself, a job title is not a sufficient basis for exemption. Rather, the actual work performed and the primary duties of the employee are what count. A person with an executive title who does not primarily manage a department or a function may not meet all conditions for exemption.

All workers are **nonexempt** unless proven exempt by the employer. Typically, exemption is determined by referring to a series of salary tests and other requirements that must be met. These are specified for four basic groups of employees: executive, administrative, professional, and outside salespersons. The test for executive, administrative, and professional

employees includes a minimum salary and, most important, a primary duty condition that requires that more than 50 percent of the employee's time used is to "customarily and regularly exercise discretion and independent judgment." In addition, less than 20 percent of their time can be spent on routine, manual, or clerical work.[8]

Some organizations have tried to lower their overtime costs by classifying more employees as exempt, and thus not paying them for hours worked exceeding forty per week. The restaurant, tourist, and medical industries are exempt from the overtime provision, as are agricultural workers. When calculating overtime, a workweek is 168 consecutive hours or seven consecutive days, not necessarily a calendar week. Special provisions allow hospitals to use a fourteen-day period instead of a seven-day period.

The Wage and Hour Division of the U.S. Department of Labor has investigated thousands of cases of possible employer violation of the overtime provision. In 1987 a historic $2 million back pay settlement for hours worked over forty per week was awarded to station managers and assistants of Highway Oil, Inc.[9] The employer claimed that the employees were exempt from the overtime provision of the FLSA and were covered by a commission plan instead. The court disagreed; its decision covered 3300 employees.

While the FLSA has been in existence for fifty years, the U.S. Department of Labor estimates that there are 73,000 compliance investigations annually. About half of them involve the overtime pay provision. In many cases, while the employer and many affected employees are happy with their compensation system, it is found to be in technical violation of the FLSA. Do employees like working overtime? See the *HR in the News:* "America's Love/Hate Relation with Overtime."

Many of the technical violations of the FLSA result from newer compensation plans that include pay incentives such as attendance bonuses, productivity bonuses, and commissions. Employers are often unaware that such bonuses and commissions must be included in the regular rate of pay when computing the overtime rate of pay. As a general rule, the act requires that all compensation be included in the employee's regular rate of pay, with seven specific exceptions:[10]

1. Gifts

2. Christmas bonuses

3. Special occasion bonuses

4. Profit-sharing payments

5. Thrift plan payments

6. Savings plan payments

7. Irrevocable contributions made to a bona fide trust

The most common mistake made by employers is to treat bonuses and commissions as discretionary income and not part of an employee's regular rate of pay, which is used to determine the overtime rate. The Department of Labor's regulations provide that if a bonus or commission is promised to employees by a specific policy or agreement, it is not discretionary income and must be included in the employee's weekly earnings. For example, if employees received a bonus of $100 for a week during which they worked fifty hours, the additional overtime due would be calculated as follows: $100/50 = $2/hour increase in hourly rate; thus, the employees are also due $1 of overtime for each of ten hours, or $10. Employers may choose to base a bonus or commission on a percentage of total earnings if the percentage is increased to one and one-half for all overtime hours.[11]

Overtime Alternatives While most nonexempt employees are paid time-and-a-half, as shown in Table 11-2, employers may legally pay them at a higher rate such as double time or time-and-a-half plus extra days time off for the overtime worked—called **compensatory time.** Many exempt employees also receive "comp time." However, only about 23 percent of all employers award some form of **compensatory time** (paid time off to compensate for overtime hours) mostly to exempt managerial, professional, technical, and sales employees (see Table 11-2). Exempt employees can also be paid their normal pay rate for overtime hours worked.

The Davis-Bacon Act The Davis-Bacon Act of 1931 regulates employers who hold federal government contracts of $2000 or more for federal construction projects. It provides that employees working on these projects must be paid the prevailing wage rate. In most urban areas the union wage is the prevailing wage for that particular geographic area. If the local union wage for plumbers is $10 per hour, then any plumbers hired to work on federal construction projects in the area must be paid $10 per hour. The reasoning behind the Davis-Bacon Act is that often governments will award contracts to the firm submitting the lowest bid

Table 11-2 Overtime (OT) Compensation

Type of Compensation		Workers Receiving OT	
Compensation	%	*Category*	%
Straight time	28	Office/clerical	98
Time-and-a-half	97	Production/service	96
Double time	19	Professional/technical	57
Straight compensatory time	16	First-level supervisors	50
		Sales	29
Other "comp time"	6	Middle management	22

Note: Percentages add up to more than 100 percent because many companies use more than one method.

SOURCE: Bureau of National Affairs.

America's Love/Hate Relation with Overtime

Do you love, or hate, to work overtime and make extra money? Many American workers either love or hate mandatory overtime. Let's look at two:

Last year, Margaret Nix worked an average of 34 out of every 35 days on Boeing Company's aircraft assembly line. She made a lot of money. She also lost a disgruntled husband to divorce, and her teenage daughter suffered a psychological breakdown. When Nix tried to coax her daughter to recall some of their good times, her daughter responded, "Why, you were never home."

Charles Anderson started to work in the Boeing plant only last year. He was badly in debt and volunteered to work far beyond the maximum overtime, some weeks working 40 hours of *overtime* and earning close to $1,000 per week. Anderson is married and the father of a 2 year old daughter. The overtime money enabled him and his wife to buy their first house.

The vast majority of the workers at Boeing, like Margaret Nix, felt exhausted and drenched in guilt and anger. Then in 1989, 57,000 Boeing workers went on strike, demanding stricter limits on overtime at a time when most American workers were concerned about job security. They carried signs saying "Do your children know what you look like?" Boeing agreed to a new limit of 144 hours every three months, an average of 12 hours per week.

American workers are often split on their feelings toward overtime, like Nix and Anderson. The issues of what is a fair and practical HR policy has quickly become critical for many employees who are using overtime as an alternative to hiring additional employees in this era of "lean and mean" business. Overtime has become an important family issue like flextime and child care, because of the disruption it brings to the lives of people like Margaret Nix.

Employers often realize that even paying time-and-a-half wage rates can be cheaper than adding new employees due to the high cost of benefits. Health insurance, for example, does not cost more for the employee working overtime. They also realize that reducing overtime in periods of slow demand is cheaper than paying unemployment benefits to laid-off workers. There are costs, however, in addition to higher wages. Employee fatigue, long-term job burnout, and increased numbers of accidents are often associated with high levels of overtime. These substantial hazards have led some employers, like General Electric Plastics Division in Oxnard, California, to use only voluntary overtime, which means that sometimes the plant shuts down when there aren't enough volunteers.

SOURCE: Adapted from Bob Baker, "The High Price of Overtime," *The Los Angeles Times* (January 16, 1990): A1, 20, 21.

for certain construction specifications. By requiring all employers in construction projects to pay the prevailing wage, the Davis-Bacon Act puts bidders on an equal basis and ensures that craft workers will not be underpaid.

Walsh-Healey Act The Walsh-Healey Act of 1936 covers employers with federal contracts of over $10,000. It requires employers to pay overtime for any hours worked over eight per day at a rate of one and one-half times the normal hourly rate. If an employee works days of more than eight hours within a forty-hour week, he or she will receive greater compensation for the same total hours worked (Figure 11-5).

Federal Wage Garnishment Act In 1970 Congress passed the Federal Wage Garnishment Act to limit the amount individuals can have garnisheed from their paychecks. Employees who do not pay outstanding debts are often taken to court by collection agencies or companies. The court may order their employers to deduct from employee's paychecks a certain amount of money, which is forwarded to the courts and then to the debtor. Under this act, the maximum **garnishment** of an employee's paycheck is 25 percent of take-home pay or thirty times the minimum wage per hour, whichever is less. The act also prohibits employers from firing employees who have had their pay garnished.

JOB EVALUATION

Job evaluation is a process of systematically analyzing jobs to determine the relative worth of jobs within the organization. This analysis is the basis of a job hierarchy and pay ranges. The result is a pay system with the pay rate for each job commensurate with its status within

FIGURE 11-5 Overtime examples under the Walsh-Healey Act.

Example I	Nonexempt employee receives $6.00/hr and works 45 hours in one week.

Hours—Monday through Wednesday = 11 hrs/day
Thursday and Friday = 7 hrs/day

Pay Under Fair Labor Standards Act
Normal Pay =
  40 hrs × $6.00/hr = $240
Overtime Pay =
  5 hrs × $9.00/hr = 45
            = $285

Pay Under Walsh-Healey Act
Normal Pay =
  38 hrs × $6.00/hr = $228
Overtime Pay =
  9 hrs × $9.00/hr = 81
      Total Pay = $309

Difference = $309.00/week − $285.00/week = $24.00/week.

Example II	Nonexempt employee receives $6.00/hr and works 40 hours in one week.

Hours—Monday, Tuesday, Wednesday, Friday = 10 hrs/day

Pay Under Fair Labor Standards Act
Normal Pay =
  40 hrs × $6.00/hr = $240.
    Total Pay = $240.

Pay Under Walsh-Healey Act
Normal Pay =
  32 hrs × $6.00/hr = $192
  8 hrs × $9.00/hr = 72
    Total Pay $264

Difference = $264.00/week − $240.00/week = $24.00/week.

the hierarchy of jobs.[12] Job evaluation should not be confused with performance evaluation, the process of determining how well employees are accomplishing their jobs. Job evaluation does not review the employees within a position but rather assesses the **worth of the position** to the organization. Thus, employees in positions of less worth to the organization are paid less than employees in positions of greater worth. For example, a systems analyst would not receive a higher salary than the director of data processing.

Through job evaluation, management can recruit productive employees to fill positions and maintain internal perceptions of pay equity by paying each position fairly in comparison with all other positions within the organization. Job evaluations may also be used to involve employees in the evaluation process. By understanding how the organization's compensation system is established and maintained, employees can ensure that the system is accurate and complete. Also, employee involvement will help communicate to other employees that the system is equitable.

Job Evaluation Committee

The process of job evaluation is expensive and not completely objective. Primarily a problem-solving, subjective judgmental process, job evaluation requires the best input from individuals within the organization. Because it is impossible for one individual to have adequate knowledge of all the jobs in the organization, a job evaluation committee is necessary. The expertise and varying backgrounds of different committee members contribute to the accuracy of the evaluation process. The members of the committee should have adequate knowledge of all work areas within the organization and a basic familiarity with the jobs within each department. Members should be trained in the basic concept of job evaluation and specifically in the method chosen by the organization to develop job evaluation.[13] Organizations often maintain a permanent job evaluation committee.

Once established, the job evaluation system should be flexible and reviewed periodically. The job evaluation committee can provide this review since those individuals are most familiar with the compensation system. For example, when supervisors ask that a job be reclassified, the committee would be able to make the determination faster and easier than an inexperienced committee made up of new members.

Outside Assistance

The first decision the job evaluation committee makes is whether the organization should produce a job evaluation system or hire outside consultants. Outside consultants offer experience and expertise in the area because they are employed by many firms to produce similar systems year after year. Often faster and more objective than internal employees, outside consultants need substantial internal input to analyze jobs and make difficult comparison decisions. Many decisions critical to the job evaluation process can be made only by individuals familiar with the organization and its basic jobs. While over 70 percent of the organizations in this country are estimated to use job evaluation, less than 20 percent buy packaged evaluation plans from a consultant or other source.[14]

A better alternative is hiring an evaluation consultant to organize the evaluation process and train the job evaluation committee. Once trained, the members do the decision making; the consultant can be brought in at the end of the process to make necessary adjustments.

PAY SYSTEMS

The method by which individuals are paid for performing their job constitutes the pay system of the organization. Generally, people are compensated for the *time* they contribute to the job or the *amount* of work they produce on the job. Time-based systems, the more common type, are used for jobs in which employees are paid by the hours worked (hourly) or by the fraction of an annual rate of pay (salaried), such as a week or month. In general, nonexempt jobs, such as blue-collar and unskilled positions, are hourly so that the employer will comply with the FLSA. Exempt jobs are usually salaried; employees are paid monthly, semimonthly, or weekly. A second method of compensation is paying people for the skills they learn and use. These are generally called *employee-based systems*. Jobs that pay employees according to their performance are often referred to as *performance-based systems* or *incentive pay systems*. They include piece-rate, sales commission, and organizationwide plans.

Most employees in the United States are paid on the basis of time-based systems. Rates of pay are fixed by the hour, day, week, month, or year. Thus, gross pay is calculated by multiplying the rate by the units of time worked. Employers often prefer the time-based system because employee motivation is difficult to predict in a totally performance-based system. Employees often prefer the known pay level they receive in a time-based system, which makes it easier to make house, car, and other fixed monthly payments. But time-based systems have the disadvantage of paying people for unproductive time on the job as well as for productive time. Hard workers can be penalized because greater productivity may not show up in their paychecks.[15]

Time-Based Systems

Most **time-based systems** use a schedule of pay grades and steps such as the one in Table 11-3. The matrix can include hourly rates or annual rates of pay, depending on whether the jobs are hourly or salaried. Jobs are assigned to a particular pay grade, depending on the results of the job evaluation, as discussed earlier in this chapter.

When job evaluation is completed, administrators must determine a final pay system to apply to jobs within the organization. Their decisions involve establishing minimum and maximum pay levels for each pay grade and determining how individuals will advance in pay grades. A standardized pay system must be promulgated and documented in order to maintain internal as well as external *pay equity*. Also, management must be able to document and defend its pay system in court. Administrators have found it advantageous to develop pay grades and steps, or levels, which specify the annual amount paid salaried em-

Table 11-3 A Sample Schedule of Hourly Pay Grades and Steps

Pay Grade	Step 1	Step 2	Step 3	Step 4	Step 5	Step 6	Step 7
1	4.25	4.46	4.68	4.91	5.16	5.42	5.69
2	5.10	5.36	5.63	5.91	6.21	6.52	6.85
3	6.12	6.43	6.75	7.09	7.44	7.81	8.20
4	7.34	7.71	8.10	8.51	8.94	9.39	9.86
5	8.81	9.25	9.71	10.20	10.71	11.25	11.81
6	10.57	11.10	11.66	12.24	12.85	13.49	14.16
7	12.68	13.31	13.98	14.68	15.41	16.18	16.99
8	15.22	15.98	16.78	17.62	18.50	19.43	20.40
9	18.26	19.17	20.13	21.14	22.20	23.31	24.48
10	21.91	23.01	24.16	25.37	26.64	27.97	29.37

ployees in a particular pay grade and step, and to use a monthly or hourly basis for other jobs.

If the organization has undergone a point method of job evaluation, then the pay system can be illustrated on a *scatter diagram* by first plotting the wage rate and pay grade for each current employee. Each employee is then represented by one dot in the diagram. The scatter diagram in Figure 11-6 illustrates the use of equal-interval pay grades. That is, each pay grade has an equal number of points but has an unequal range in terms of the total pay within the pay grade. While the dollar figures in each pay range are not increased equally, the actual

percent increase of pay for each step is 5 percent.

Number of Steps In developing a compensation system, the number of steps within each **pay grade** must be decided. Figure 11-7 illustrates how pay grade 5 is divided into equal increases of approximately 5 percent. Thus employees receive a larger cents-per-hour increase with each step raise, and in the higher pay grades the increases become larger.

Deciding how many **steps** should be included within each pay grade is a difficult decision. If too many steps are included,

FIGURE 11-6 A scatter diagram.

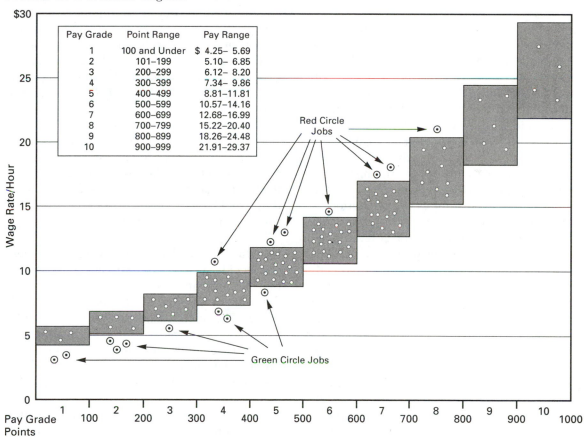

Pay Grade	Point Range	Pay Range
1	100 and Under	$ 4.25– 5.69
2	101–199	5.10– 6.85
3	200–299	6.12– 8.20
4	300–399	7.34– 9.86
5	400–499	8.81–11.81
6	500–599	10.57–14.16
7	600–699	12.68–16.99
8	700–799	15.22–20.40
9	800–899	18.26–24.48
10	900–999	21.91–29.37

FIGURE 11-7 Pay grade 5 with internal steps.

Pay Grade 5		
Step 7	$7.30	TOP LEVEL STEPS
Step 6	7.06	
Step 5	6.81	
Step 4	6.57	MID POINT
Step 3	6.32	ENTRY LEVEL STEPS
Step 2	6.08	
Step 1	5.84	

employees' motivation for good performance will be very small because the increase will be very small. Having few steps in each pay grade creates larger increases and motivates employees to work for merit increases. Employees reach the top of their pay grades more quickly when grades have few steps. Once individuals have reached the top of their pay grades, the practice is usually to keep them at that highest step, to transfer them to jobs in a higher pay grade, or to promote them. Organizations with relatively few opportunities for promotion, or with turnover so low that many individuals stay within one pay grade for several years, find it wise to have many steps and, perhaps, even wider-ranging pay grades.

Figure 11-7 illustrates the practice of using two or more entry-level salaries for jobs within a particular pay grade. The reason for the practice is that while managers wish to be consistent and pay similar wages for similar jobs, allowances must be made for individual differences in job candidates who are hired. Candidates with more experience and skills can be hired in a higher step; a recruit who has just finished school and has no experience would logically be hired at step 1. In most situations this would not violate federal laws: consistency within the pay system could be proved since similar wages were paid for similar work, making allowances for individual differences.

Red Circle Employees   Another decision to be made by the evaluation committee is illustrated in Figure 11-6. Three individuals within the pay grade system have been red-circled or hold **red circle jobs**. A red circle indicates that this individual is currently being paid more than the maximum for that pay grade. Through seniority or for some other reason, the individual is currently being paid more than the organization planned to pay any employee to perform jobs of that pay grade. Red-circled individuals remain at the same pay level until either they are promoted to a higher pay grade or cost-of-living adjustments increase their pay grade salaries to equal or exceed the red circle rate. The Equal Pay Act of 1963 protects individuals from having their pay lowered through the job evaluation process.

Those individuals who are currently paid below the minimum step of their pay grade are in **green circle jobs**. Normally when the pay system is finalized, their pay will be increased to the first step of the pay grade; otherwise, they would be paid less than the minimum worth of the job according to the pay system.

Overlap of Grades   The organization must also decide whether to overlap pay grades so that the maximum of one pay grade is higher than the minimum of the next higher pay grade. The compensation system in Figure 11-6 allows pay grades to overlap. One advantage is that employees can be transferred or promoted from one job to the next without necessarily being given pay increases. For example, an employee paid $10.71 per hour in pay grade 5 could be promoted to a job with a larger point total in pay grade 6 without a large increase in pay.

Management has the option of not paying individuals higher salaries immediately but of offering them higher salaries if they prove themselves and receive merit increases, thus moving up in the pay grade. Another advantage of overlapping pay grades is that this gives grades a greater range with more steps of a meaningful size. Thus, employees are rewarded with merit and seniority increases while they stay in the same job and pay grade.

One disadvantage of overlapping pay grades is that a promotion may not bring a pay increase and could even bring a cut in pay. Also, overlapping grades makes it possible for an individual in a higher pay grade to supervise employees in a lower pay grade who receive higher paychecks than the supervisor. For example, when a new supervisor is placed in a department in which an employee is at the highest step of the next lower pay grade, the employee will receive higher pay than the supervisor. In manufacturing and construction organizations this is not unusual.

Pay Increases

Primarily two types of pay increases are made: *across-the-board increases,* where everyone in the organization receives an equal pay increase, and *merit* or *seniority* increases given to selected individuals.

Across-the-Board Increases These increase the employee's income due to the cost-of-living allowances or in order to make the organization's pay system compatible with the local labor market. An across-the-board **cost-of-living adjustment (COLA)** can be an equal percentage or equal dollars. Managers often prefer to give equal percentage increases because COLAs are related to the cost of living, which is measured in percentages. Hearing that the cost of living has gone up a certain percentage, employees realize that their buying power has decreased. Therefore, they hope to receive a COLA at least equal to the increase in their cost of living.

Using equal percentages can be deceiving since employees must use increased wages and not percentages to purchase goods and services. Using cost-of-living figures can also be misleading because any individual's actual increase in the cost of living depends on spending habits, the cost of major assets such as an automobile and a home, and other factors. The national increase in the cost of living may have little bearing on individual employees' actual bills.

Management often prefers to give across-the-board COLAs in equal percentages. Equal-percentage increases mean that employees in higher pay grades will receive greater actual dollar increases than employees in lower pay grades. An across-the-board percentage increase simply changes the dollar amounts for each grade and step in the compensation system; it does not move any employee or job within the system. Therefore, if a 3 percent cost-of-living pay increase were given to employees in the pay grades and steps in Table 11-3, all of the amounts would change but the pay grades and steps would not. In Figure 11-6, the pay grade configuration would become more sloped as the higher pay grades experienced greater dollar increases than the lower pay grades.

If an equal-dollar across-the-board increase is given as a COLA, the amounts in Table 11-3 would increase an equal dollar figure. In Figure 11-6, the scale on the left side would slide down because individuals in lower pay grades would get a larger percentage increase than individuals in higher pay grades. Individuals in higher pay grades argue that this is unfair because they cannot keep up with the cost of living since their increase is not as great as that of individuals in lower pay grades. In summary, equal-dollar across-the-board COLAs decrease the differentials in pay between jobs and pay grades.

Merit Increases Time-based pay systems are not completely void of a relationship between pay and performance. Instead, many include **merit pay increases** to employees. After a performance appraisal of their work, employees receive increases in pay if their work record is judged meritorious. Merit raises are designed to motivate employees by tying at least part of their pay to their performance.

Merit pay systems rest heavily on three assumptions: (1) employee differences in performance can be accurately measured, (2) employees can effectively perceive pay differences as relating to performance differences, and (3) individuals will improve their future performance to gain more merit increases.[16]

Critics of merit systems, however, point out their frequent problems: (1) there is only a slight relationship between performance appraisals and percentage pay increases, and employees are quick to realize it, (2) supervisor bias remains more important in the appraisal process than employee productivity, and (3) employees simply do not perceive that merit raises are linked to their performance, whether true or not. The opening *HR in the News:* "Where's My Annual Raise?" is typical of the common attitude that it has become an entitlement. Thus management must audit its merit system for these possible problems, and must not simply assume that it is effective because it is well intentioned.[17]

Many managers believe that linking pay increases to performance is effective because behaviors that are rewarded are more likely to be repeated; behaviors that are punished are less likely to be repeated. Also, rewards that are obtained as a result of one's performance will have greater value than rewards that are given to everyone. Thus, a 7 percent merit increase in an organization where the average is 5 percent will be more highly valued than if a 7 percent across-the-board increase was given.[18]

When employees receive merit increases, they do not change pay grades, since a pay grade is based on the point total of their jobs or their classifications. But employees who receive merit increases move up one or more steps within their pay grades. Administrators, for example, may give two-step increases to the top 5 percent of their employees and one-step increases to the next highest 20 percent.

Some organizations give seniority increases to employees who have successfully performed their jobs for a certain length of time. These increases move employees up one or more steps within their pay grades. If the organization of Table 11-3 has merit increases, the dollar amounts in each pay grade would stay the same but employees would move up one step. The same would be true for the organization in Figure 11-6.

Employee-Based Systems

A contemporary compensation question that is often asked by HR professionals is: should organizations pay for the employee or for the job? The latter approaches include performance-based programs, while the former introduce two relatively new ideas—broadbanding and skill-based pay. Employee-based programs allow workers to increase their pay by taking on new or additional activities.

Broadbanding   What is the hottest thing in compensation? Well if you believe Kenan Abosch of Hewitt Associates, compensation consultants, the answer has to be **broadbanding**. It is popping up in conversations all over the country. What it does is to eliminate multiple salary grades in favor of just a few. The idea is to encourage flexibility in moving workers from one job to another without being constrained by narrow salary grades. According to the Hewitt Associates survey data, 60 percent of the participating companies that have implemented or considered bands did so in order to facilitate job transfers, encourage lateral job mobility, and pay for learning individual skills.[19]

Northern Telecom, the Canadian communications company, adopted a broadbanding plan in which fifty-four grades were compressed to thirteen. The fewer bands spanned the pay opportunities formerly covered by most of the old grades. But not all bands are alike. The most obvious differences occur between career bands and traditional bands. *Career bands* serve primarily as a management development compensation strategy. Their objective is to support the contemporary organization—new culture, fewer levels, lateral rather than vertical promotions, and movement away from relying on traditional merit increases. In contrast, *traditional bands* have wide salary ranges too, but the real objective may be a desire to alleviate the "topping-out" problem—a situation of having too many employees who are at, or near, the maximum of their range.

Hewitt's endorsement of broadbanding is not completely shared by other experts. In theory, the plan makes sense. In practice, however, some companies are having second thoughts. Johnson & Johnson implemented broadbanding to foster movement among jobs. After a year the plan was dropped when nearly a third of the 6000 affected employees complained about the lack of a clear path for promotions or because people were not happy about being lumped in a job band with coworkers they had already surpassed. Clearly, broadbanding does not work with traditional organizational hierarchies and may offer only a modest chance of success at companies attempting to support a new culture.[20]

Skill-Based Pay This approach concentrates on paying workers according to their proficiency in learning and using a wide variety of skills that organizations need. It consists of formal systems of cross-training, with financial rewards linked directly to acquiring more knowledge and skills. CPS Corporation, a printing-ink manufacturer in New York State, implemented a skills-based system in 1983 and continues to use it today. They are convinced that the approach encouraged the work force to be more flexible and committed to quality.

Indeed, CPS is not alone. A survey of *Fortune* 1000 companies reported that skill-based pay was being used by 51 percent of their respondents.[21]

At CPS, new employees began cross-training almost immediately after being hired. "In manufacturing, for example, they're expected to learn every piece of equipment," says HR Director Joan Hites, who also has learned to operate the same equipment. "They spend two weeks in the lab, two weeks in shipping and receiving, a week in the office and customer service." Periodically, every employee is evaluated in terms of knowledge and demonstrated competency. Companies such as CPS consider the skills acquired as adding value to the organization, and thus they are prepared to pay for it. It also encourages employees to continue to learn.[22]

Skills-based pay is very different from traditional compensation strategies—and not for the faint of heart. In the majority of pay systems, compensation is linked to hierarchy and time on the job, both very predictable. In the past, employees usually learned new skills anyway if they wanted a promotion or just to keep their job. So why start paying for it now? And traditional companies would have a very hard time accepting an increase in overall compensation costs, which is what typically occurs. Towers Perrin, an HRM consulting firm, said in a report that three out of four companies implementing skills-based systems saw their pay rates exceed applicable market rates.[23]

The rationale for adopting this radical approach is best understood in terms of the concept of what it means to be a manager. The old concept of a manager included span of control, the size of one's budget, controlling people and resources, and so on. Today, the emphasis is more on developing and learning, working in teams, and looking at and understanding strategic business objectives. This differs from the traditional emphasis on specializing in one function or the narrow perspective of protecting one's turf, with little regard to the harm it might cause another department.[24] For an example of companies using skill-based systems, the reader should review the *HR in the News:* "Rewarding 'Renaissance Workers.'"

Performance-Based Systems

Employers today are increasingly considering switching from a straight time-based pay system to a performance-based pay system. The purpose of an incentive or **performance-based system** is to relate employees' pay directly to their performance. As we discussed earlier in this chapter, employees are likely to be more highly motivated, and thus to increase their productivity, if they perceive that there is a direct relationship between their level of performance and the rewards received. Most incentive pay systems provide employees with a base income and the opportunity to earn additional compensation if their productivity exceeds a certain standard.

The use of performance-based systems has seen a resurgence. After critics had convinced many managers that such systems could not be accurate or motivational, some organizations at least have found that Frederick Taylor may have been right all along. Five surveys of over 4700 companies show that after switching from time-based to performance-based pay systems, organizations reported average productivity increases of 29 to 63 percent.[25] IBM, for example, was able to increase labor productivity in typewriter manufacturing by nearly 200 percent over a ten-year period. The reason cited was the use of two policies: (1) pay for productivity, only for productivity, and (2) promote for productivity, only for productivity.[26]

Performance-based systems are not new, however. At Anderson Corporation of Bayport, Minnesota, the nation's largest manufacturer of windows, profit-sharing bonuses have been a tradition since 1914. In 1986, the 3500 workers who produce high-quality, customized products received $72 million in their bonus check—the equivalent of almost nine months'

pay! The Anderson program contains three basic points: (1) produce the best-quality products; (2) hire the best people; and (3) pay the top wages in the industry.[27]

In general, performance-based systems can be divided into three categories: *individual-based incentives systems,* which provide a pay incentive to each worker based on his or her own level of productivity, *team-based incentive systems,* and *organizationwide incentive systems,* which base their rewards on total organizational performance.

Individual Incentive Plans

Many individual incentive systems are *piece-rate* or related plans. Such plans include a guaranteed base rate of pay for individuals who fail to achieve a standard level of production. The guaranteed rate is usually an hourly rate determined through job evaluation. The standard, the output an average employee should be able to produce, is usually determined by industrial engineers using time-and-motion studies. The results, however, are usually open to debate between management and labor.

Piece-Rate Systems Piecework has been around longer than any other individual incentive system. Each worker is quoted a fixed, or standard, rate of pay for each unit of output produced. This is called the **straight piecework plan**. Jobs that are good candidates for piece-rate systems are typically found in manufacturing. Many computer chip manufacturers will pay workers a flat rate—for example, $2 per component. Production standards, usually set by industrial engineers, are stated in terms of expected output per hour or day. In the case of computer chips, a job evaluation may have indicated that forty chips is the typical output over an eight-hour day. If the worker produced the expected output, the total compensation for the day would be $80. If the worker exceeded the standard output by ten, the day's compensation would jump to $100.

Rewarding "Renaissance Workers"

Over the past two years, Steelcase, Inc., an office furniture maker in Grand Rapids, Michigan, has restructured its white-collar work force to eliminate layers of management, broaden the job responsibilities of individual employees and link compensation to each person's increasing knowledge.

"In the old system, we paid a person for the job," said Dan Wiljanen, director of human resources. "We've moved to paying a person for skills and abilities."

Advocates, such as Steelcase, believe that skill-based pay can help companies recreate themselves, particularly encouraging people to become more flexible and to learn more skills. People will be doing less of the same old things and more new things.

Steelcase has made it possible for employees to move laterally, or even downward, and still feel like a success. Under the old system, persuading a grade 18 employee to take a grade 15 job for career development purposes was impossible. Under the new system, employees have already proven they will indeed make the downward jump.

Other companies are praising the concept too. At the Polaroid Corporation, in Cambridge, Mass., where a skill-based system has been in place since 1990, manufacturing employees are operating more efficiently and getting paid more for it.

At Polaroid, the highest one can go as a machine operator is $14 an hour. But employees have the option of redesigning their work and broadening their skills. For example, an operator might begin maintaining equipment, or perform quality inspections, and earn up to 10 percent more pay. But in order to accomplish these tasks, the operator must have an understanding of these functions, including accounting. If the operator wanted to earn even more pay, than it would mean having to learn some supervisory skills.

There are hurdles, however. One is figuring out whether the worker has indeed acquired a new skill. If it was simply operating a new piece of equipment, that would be easy enough, but determining if someone has demonstrated teamwork is quite another matter. And who takes responsibility for deciding? Adding another box in the organization chart is not in keeping with the spirit of skill-based systems. Perhaps the biggest hurdle is paying employees for acquiring skills and the organization not being in a position to immediately utilize them. Craig Schneier, a management consultant, summarized it best.

"Continuous learning is important," Schneier said. "But if the company has no way to apply that learning, I would have trouble paying for it."

SOURCE: Adapted from: "More Firms Trying 'Skill-Based Pay.' " *Omaha World-Herald* (July 11, 1993): G1.

Variations of straight piecework plans include **rising and falling differentials**. With falling piece rates, any gain is shared between the employer and employee. Using the preceding example, instead of the worker collecting an extra $20 for exceeding the standard output by ten chips, the worker and employer would split it according to a previously agreed-on standards. Plans that use a rising piece rate give workers even more incentive for exceeding the standard. Continuing with the example, instead of $2 per chip over forty, the employer agrees to increase it to $2.50 for every chip over forty, thus giving the worker a total daily compensation of $105 (40 × $2 = $80 plus 10 × $2.50 = $25). Why would management agree to a rising piece-rate system? If the higher hourly earnings are sufficiently motivational, the total cost per piece to the company could be lower.

Piece-rate systems have a number of advantages. They are easy to understand, simple to calculate, and effective motivational tools. Nevertheless, they are not implemented as often as one might think. One problem is that most jobs do not have output that can be objectively measured. Another problem is that jobs are becoming more interrelated, which means that one person's output is affected by the output of others. If the other person does not want to make an extra effort, that will destroy whatever motivational force piece-rate systems might have encouraged. But the most often heard complaint is how difficult it is for employers and workers to agree on what is a fair production standard. Unfortunately, some employers have arbitrarily and unilaterally reestablished standards after "concluding" that the old system was tilted too favorably in the workers' direction. An example of how one company confronted this problem is presented in the *HR in the News:* "The Free Ride Is Over for Free Riders."

Standard Hour Plans   *Standard hour plans are similar in concept to piece-rate plans ex-* cept that standard time is set to complete a particular job instead of paying the employee a price per piece. For example, an auto mechanic might be given a standard time of two hours to tune up an eight-cylinder car. If the worker's pay rate is $8.00 per hour and three eight-cylinder tune-ups are finished in six hours, then the employee earns $48.00. If a so-called Halsey 50/50 incentive plan is used, the worker and employer share equally in the time saved by the employee. Thus, if three tune-ups are completed in five hours, then the employee would be paid $52.00 ($48.00 + $4.00 [one-half hour saved at $8.00/hour]), and the employer has an additional hour's work time.

Commissions   An individual incentive system widely used in sales positions is the **commission**. Employees are given a percentage of sales (measured in units or dollars). The percentage may change at predetermined levels in a manner similar to falling or rising piece rates. Employees who are paid on commission generally receive either (1) *straight commission,* which means that their total pay is determined by the commission formula, or (2) *salary-plus-commission,* which combines a monthly salary base with a commission incentive. The salary-plus-commission method has the advantage of providing a minimum income level that employees can count on to pay their living expenses, and provides stability against factors beyond the control of the employee that can affect sales, such as seasonal swings, increased competition, and inventory shortages.

How much of a salary-plus-commission total income should be commission? There is no easy or correct answer to this difficult question. In general, the commission portion is usually 20 to 40 percent of the total. The higher the percentage that is commission, one might argue, the more motivating to the employee. However, one problem with any commission system is determining what is a fair

The Free Ride Is Over for Free Riders

A small manufacturing company observed by one of the authors, which shall remain nameless, introduced a team-based incentive system. Production standards were established on the basis of historical averages. The monetary awards were generous. In fact, each team could conceivably earn enough on top of its total hourly wage to pay each worker a month's rent.

Anyone who has ever worked on a team has probably encountered a **social loafer**. These are the people who work and produce at less than their maximum capability. And when the loafer slacks off more than other team members, yet receives the full benefits of group membership, the member has become a **free rider**. Odd as it may at first seem, social loafing is more of a problem in the United States than in collectivistic societies like Japan and China. Most experts attribute it to our strong belief in individualism.

Soon after the new incentive system was implemented, however, a surprising phenomenon developed: the social pressure on free riders. The pressure was such that they usually quit. The need for supervision became superfluous; the employees essentially supervised themselves for maximum efficiency. Since the incentive reward went to the team, its members requested that those who quit not be replaced. The smaller the team, the greater the reward per member.

One other event worth noting occurred. Happy as the teams were with their monthly bonus, at one point their efforts began to level off—that is, until one worker noted, at a momentous morning meeting, that even better performance was possible if . . . "If what?" the manager demanded. "If management would guarantee that the basis for the incentive, the established standard, would not be raised," the worker blurted out.

Within an hour, the manager posted on the bulletin board and included in every paycheck a notice, signed by the CEO, that as long as he was there, under no circumstances, either now or in the future, would the historical rate on which the incentive bonus was based be changed. The only caveat would be the addition of new equipment or a new process. After that announcement appeared, the company's productivity continued to increase and profits hit all-time highs.

---

percentage of each sale. If the percentage is too low, employees may not find it motivating and may simply rely on their salary; if it is too high, the company may find that it has created some millionaire sales representatives. In one case, the new management of a regional television station substantially increased the commission percentage paid to its sales executives in an effort to increase commercial revenues. The plan worked; after the first quarter revenues were up 40 percent, and the top sales executive had earned more in commissions in one quarter than the station manager earned in a year!

Team-Based Incentive Systems

Organizations are recognizing that some individual incentive systems can do more harm than good, particularly in those situations where teamwork and coordination among workers are becoming more important. For interrelated tasks such as an assembly line, how one worker performs can influence the productivity of everyone else on the line. A pay system that encourages competitive behavior may find that the "competitor" is often a worker's colleague, not an external business competitor. When a situation such as too much competition begins to disrupt operations or when a new team-building program such as TQM is implemented, team-based incentives need to be considered.

Team incentive arrangements differ from traditional incentives in a couple of ways. One difference is that goals and results are clarified and established for teams—not for individuals. Also, teams are evaluated on the degree to which performance targets are met. Goals must be clearly communicated and performance measurably defined—neither of which is an easy task to achieve. A prerequisite is the establishment of a solid communication system, both formal and informal, between management and the team, and within the team as well. And, ideally, teams should not be so large (more than ten) that communication and coordination suffer.

A second difference from traditional systems is that team-based incentive awards are typically more comparable (but not necessarily equal) across participants. Members may be rewarded using a formula based on the final output of the team. Whether it is piece rate or standard hour does not really matter. Most of the evidence supports keeping incentive rewards approximately the same. What does seem to matter is when too much reward disparity occurs among the members. This may breed discontent and undermine the cohesion created.[28]

Yet it is hard to deny the strong, and particularly American, individualistic trait in so many high achievers. One problem with strong individualism within a team is the difficulty of putting the group's needs first. Team members who cannot put the good of the group before their own are called *social loafers* and *free riders* (see *HR in the News:* "The Free Ride Is Over for Free Riders"). Other problems occur when members cannot make a psychological connection between their efforts and some positive team outcome. But it still may be possible for individual performance to play some role. How to strike the right balance between individual performance rewards and team-based rewards is a challenge.

An important measurement tool used in most team-based incentive systems is something called **360 degree feedback**. Pertinent sources for providing constructive feedback are approached and asked to complete an extensive questionnaire. Unlike traditional systems that rely primarily on superior feedback, 360 degree sources include peers, customers, suppliers, other managers, or anyone who is in a position to observe closely the team's or individual's performance. Self-appraisals are also performed. GE Appliances, in Louisville, Kentucky, has been gradually introducing this measurement tool into their teams. Participants are understandably apprehensive the first few times they get feedback from new sources, but they have found the feedback nonthreatening and constructive. One drawback is the time-consuming nature of the questionnaire and the reluctance of busy people to take time to fill it out and return it.

Organizational Incentive Plans

The problems associated with individual incentive systems and the increased designing of more technical and interdependent jobs have led to increased use of organizational incentive plans. Employers want employees to realize the link between a portion of their compensation and the performance of their group or the entire organization. In general, organizational incentive systems fall into two types: profit-sharing plans, which tie employee compensation to the bottom-line profits, and gainsharing plans, which tie compensation to specific productivity measures such as time, materials, or cost savings. Profit-sharing plans focus the incentive on the organization's ability to pay bonuses, and obviously, bonuses are not paid when no profits are earned. Gainsharing plans focus on the contributions to specific productivity target goals.

Gainsharing   The most common types of **gainsharing** incentive plans include the Scanlon, Rucker, and Improshare plans.

Scanlon Plan   The **Scanlon plan** was developed by Joseph Scanlon, an official of the United Steelworkers Union. It has since become a basis for labor–management cooperation above and beyond its use as a group incentive plan. The plan contains two primary features: (1) departmental committees of union and management representatives meet together at least monthly to consider any cost-savings suggestions; and (2) documented cost savings are divided, with 75 percent going to the employees and 25 percent to the company.

The savings under a Scanlon plan are determined by comparing actual labor costs for a month to a standard productivity base, which is determined by reviewing past labor costs during normal operating periods. This formula is expressed as a percentage, and each month the labor costs as a percentage of sales are compared to the formula ratio. A reserve account is created to offset any deficit months, and at the end of the year the reserve account bonuses are paid out.

In Figure 11-8, for example, the standard ratio of labor costs to adjusted production is 30 percent; thus when the actual labor costs were $25,000, a savings of $5000 was created and

available for distribution. In comparison to the other gainsharing plans, the Scanlon plan emphasizes employee participation in developing plans to increase productivity.

After five years with a Scanlon plan, Rocky Mountain Data Systems, a dental profession service company, reported the following:[29]

- Profits were up 22 percent on assets, 11 percent on sales.
- Employee compensation was up 14 percent per year compounded.
- The "peak-out" phenomenon, whereby employees no longer could reach a maximum in their pay grade, was avoided.
- Labor–management hostility subsided as employees realized that they had a stake in the company because they shared in the gains and the losses.

At the Parker Pen Company, the plant manager concluded that the Scanlon plan increased productivity because everyone participated. It generated an atmosphere in which people came forward with good ideas. A union leader at Parker Pen expressed his belief that the plan enabled the company to introduce new equipment without labor opposition and thus beat foreign competition.

Rucker Plan   The **Rucker plan** is similar to the Scanlon Plan except that an additional variable—the dollar value of all materials, supplies, and services used in the production process—is included in the formula. This difference from the Scanlon formula, however, allows workers to benefit from any reduction in materials, supplies, or services used in the production process and thus provides motivation to reduce those costs. The Rucker formula is

$$\frac{\text{Labor costs}}{\text{Value added (production output} - \text{materials, supplies, and services)}}$$

The Rucker concept is often called *value added,* which refers to the difference in the value of the output and the value of the input (material, supplies, services) that has been added to the product by the employees. Employees earn an incentive or bonus in the Rucker plan by improving productivity through a reduction in materials and supplies, customer returns, hours of effort, or a combination of factors that leads to higher output. All savings, regardless of type, increase the value added, and thus a bonus results when the Rucker standard is exceeded (see Figure 11-8). If the Rucker standard is 37.4 percent, then labor receives 37.4 percent of value added. A portion of each monthly bonus is put into a balancing account to offset the deficits of negative months. The balancing account is then closed at the end of the year, with losses absorbed by the company and surpluses paid out as bonuses.[30]

Improshare Improved productivity through sharing (**improshare**) plans are somewhat similar to piecework incentive plans, but with a standard and bonus system applied to all workers within the organization. In effect, improshare is an adaptation of the older individual incentive plans to the realities of today's integrated workplace. Improshare is a bonus system in which the productivity measurement is the labor hours, direct and indirect, needed to produce one unit of product. Gains are hours saved and are equally divided between the employees and the company. The employees' share is converted to a dollar bonus based on their number of hours worked during the period.

For example, as in Figure 11-8, the standard hours needed to produce a unit is calculated to be 1.80, and this is the base productivity factor (BPF). A week's output is counted (20,000 units) and multiplied by the BPF. The result is the improshare hours earned ($36,000 = 20,0001 \times 1.80$). The difference between the improshare hours and the actual hours worked

($36,000$ improshare hours $= 30,000$ actual hours $= 6,000$ hours) is the savings, which is shared 50/50.[31]

Can gainsharing plans work? At the Dana Spicer Heavy Axle Division's facility in Hilliard, Ohio, there are no supervisors or time clocks. After three years of gainsharing the employees (all salaried) are very content, labor efficiency is up 45 percent, and quality problems are down 50 percent. During one six-month period, over 400 productivity ideas were contributed by the employees at Dana, and employees averaged monthly bonuses of 12 to 16 percent. The U.S. General Accounting Office estimates that over 1000 American firms currently use gainsharing.[32]

One widely recognized example of gainsharing is that of the Nucor Corporation. The company reported a staggering growth of 600 percent in sales and 1500 percent in profits over ten years due to a production incentive program. The company actually developed four separate incentive programs: one each for production employees, department heads, professional employees, and senior officers. Their theory was that "money is the best motivation."[33]

Profit-Sharing Plans In a **profit-sharing plan**, employees receive a share of the company's profits. The profit share is paid in addition to employees' regular wages and is generally intended to increase employees' incentive to work.

There are generally three major types of profit-sharing plans:[34]

1. *Distribution plan.* Annual or quarterly payments are paid out in a cash bonus according to a predetermined formula. The payment is made on a quarterly or annual basis as soon as the profit-sharing pool is calculated. This is the most common type of profit-sharing plan.

2. *Deferred plan.* Employees earn profit-sharing credits instead of cash payments, which

FIGURE 11-8 Bonus statements under Scanlon, Rucker, and Improshare Plans.

Scanlon Plan		Rucker Plan		Improshare	
Sales	$ 92,000	Sales	$100,000	Base productivity factor = 1.80	
Inventory increase or decrease	10,000	Less materials, supplies, services	50,000	Production	20,000 units
Production at sales value	$102,000	Value added	$ 50,000	Improshare hours earned:	
Less returns and allowances	2,000	Labor costs	$18,700	20,000 × 1.80 =	36,000
Adjusted production	$100,000	Other costs	$31,300	Actual hours worked	30,000 hours
Allowed labor per ratio*	$30,000			Savings	6,000 hours
Less actual labor	25,000	Rucker standard: $\dfrac{\text{Labor costs}}{\text{Value added}} = \dfrac{\$18,700}{\$50,000} = 37.4\%$		Company share—50%	3,000 hours
Savings or gain	$ 5,000			Employee share—50%	3,000 hours
Less reserve for deficit—10%	500				
For distribution	$ 4,500	Rucker standard—37.4%	$18,700	Bonus hours: $\dfrac{3,000}{30,000} = 10\%$	
Company share—25%	$1,125	Less actual labor cost	16,700		
Employee share—75%	$3,375	Gain	$ 2,000	Sample bonus calculation for one worker:	
Participating payroll (adjusted for new employees, vacation pay, etc.)	$22,500	Balancing account	500	Hours worked	40
		For distribution	$ 1,500	Pay rate	$8.12 per hour
Bonus: $\dfrac{\$3,375}{\$22,500} = \begin{array}{l}\text{15\% paid to each}\\ \text{employee as a percentage}\\ \text{of monthly wages}\end{array}$		Participating payroll	$15,500	Bonus hours (10%)	4.0 hours
		Bonus: $\dfrac{\$1,500}{\$15,500} = \begin{array}{l}\text{9.7\% paid to}\\ \text{participating}\\ \text{employees on}\\ \text{the basis of monthly}\\ \text{earnings}\end{array}$		Bonus: 4.0 hours × $8.12 = $32.48	

*Assumed ratio of labor costs to production

SOURCE: Robert J. Doyle, *Gainsharing and Productivity* (New York: AMACOM, 1983): 10, 14, 15, 17. Used by permission.

are not distributed until disability, death, or retirement. This type of plan is similar to a deferred-income retirement plan.

3. *Combination plan.* This type of plan allows employees to receive a portion of each period's profits in a cash bonus, with the remainder put into a deferred plan.

Use of profit-sharing plans has increased in recent years because management prefers them to increases in salaries or wage rates, which become permanent increases in personnel costs. Profit-sharing bonuses, however, do not automatically carry over to future years. Instead they are paid only in those years in which the company earns a profit.

Profit-sharing plans have also increased in labor agreements.[35] Management favors replacing COLAs with profit sharing as a wage supplement for several reasons: (1) payments are made only if the company makes a profit and thus is usually financially strong; (2) unlike COLAs, payments are not tied to inflation, which is not related to the company's financial status and may require increases during difficult times; (3) workers' pay is linked to their productivity, as well as to the number of hours they work, giving them a direct incentive to make the company more profitable; (4) workers may feel more a part of the company and develop increased interest in reducing waste and increasing efficiency in all areas, as well as in their own jobs.

Examples of successful profit-sharing plans include the following:

- *Ford Motor Company.* In 1990, for example, Ford distributed $153 million in annual profit-sharing checks to its U.S. employees. The average worker received $1025, a decrease from the 1989 average of $2800, when Ford reported higher profits. Peter Pestillo, Ford's personnel chief and chief labor negotiator, noted, "We think it's money well spent. They get more, and they get more

done. We think we get a payback in the cooperation and enthusiasm of the people." The 1984 Ford–United Auto Workers master agreement was the first to contain a profit-sharing provision pushed by management as a means of avoiding the UAW-proposed 3 percent annual raises. The concept of profit sharing within the auto industry is not new, however. Douglas Frasier, former president of the UAW, noted that the union first asked for a profit-sharing plan more than forty years prior to the 1984 agreement and during several other negotiations, but none of the U.S. auto giants was interested until they lost money in the 1980s.[36]

- *Publix Grocery.* At the Florida-based grocer Publix, employees of each store receive a quarterly cash bonus of 20 percent of the store's profits. They also receive 10 percent of the store's profits in a deferred income plan. Publix is also an example of an employee stock ownership plan (ESOP), as employees own 100 percent of the stock.[37]

- *Steelcase.* To survive in the increasingly competitive office-furniture market, Steelcase provides employees profit-sharing bonuses that average up to 60 percent of base pay. In addition, the firm contributes the IRS maximum of 15 percent of total compensation to a deferred income profit-sharing plan for employees.[38]

- *Lincoln Electric.* This Cleveland-based manufacturer of welding machines and motors suffered a 40 percent decline in sales during the 1981–1983 recession. Yet not one employee was laid off. Instead, through the company's Scanlon plan, employees were able to weather the storm and work to bring Lincoln's sales back to normal by 1984. They did suffer a reduction in their profit-sharing bonus during 1981–1983, but in 1984 each employee receives about $15,000 in shared profits.[39]

EMPLOYEE STOCK OWNERSHIP PLANS (ESOPs)

Similar to profit sharing—with many of the same advantages and disadvantages—is stock ownership, sometimes called the **employee stock ownership plan (ESOP)**. Millions of employees are becoming part owners of the companies they work for, and by the year 2000, 25 percent of all U.S. workers may have used an ESOP. The rapid increase is expected as a result of the 1984 Deficit Reduction Act passed by Congress, which provides lucrative tax incentives to employees. In fact, about 70 to 100 failing companies have used ESOPs to avoid hostile takeovers. In one of the most visible cases, the employees at United Airlines (UAL) acquired ownership rather than see the company sold to a rival. It has become America's largest employee-owned company.

A textile manufacturer in Danville, Virginia, Dan River, Inc., has about 8000 employees who own 70 percent of the company's stock through an ESOP. But the union and many employees are not at all happy. Why? They have no voting rights or other control over the operation of the company. Employee ownership is completely under the control of top management and a small group of outside investors. Joseph Blasi, an ESOP expert, calls this type of governance a "feudal culture."[40] He says that this type of company is opposed to any attempt by employee owners to change the company's fundamental organization. Unfortunately, he estimates that 20 to 30 percent of all ESOP companies can be regarded as feudal cultures; for example, the often publicized employee ownership plan at Charles Keating's Lincoln Savings and Loan was a front to convince customers that the institution was safe and sound.

There are other problems as well. In 1983 the employees of Weirton Steel purchased 73 percent of the company. For five years the company appeared to be an employee-owned success story. Employees would break their own work rules—all in the name of running the factory efficiently. Instead of waiting hours for welders, for example, the workers would grab torches and weld ladders and lifting equipment. Today the management–worker teamwork has disintegrated into a war that includes a fight over a public stock offering that would shrink the employees' stake. Fundamentally, the Weirton conflict boils down to money and management control. For capital-intensive industries such as steel and airlines, huge amounts of capital expenditures are periodically needed, which are viewed by workers as draining money away from potential wage increase.[41]

Nevertheless, experts like Blasi believe that employee-ownership plans will continue to grow, with many arrangements being configured more along the lines of participatory governance. Companies like Herman Miller and Proctor and Gamble are success stories and proof that day-to-day employee involvement can be achieved from shareholding. Whether it will save Weirton Steel or even UAL (United Airlines) remains to be seen.

Growth of Incentive Plans

A survey of some 1600 American companies showed that about 10 percent of all employers reported using any incentive system and another 7 percent expect to add systems in the near future. The most popular incentive system was profit sharing, used by 32 percent of the respondents with an incentive system. Lump-sum bonuses not tied directly to profits were reported by 30 percent, individual incentive programs by 28 percent, and gainsharing or small-group incentive plans by 14 percent. The new incentive plans generally replace across-the-board increases.[42]

Just how much can a change from a time-based to a performance-based pay system affect the bottom line of a company? Victor Kiam, chairman of Remington Products, Inc., the shaver company, credits the profit-sharing plan he initiated shortly after purchasing the company with its turnaround from a $5 million-a-year loser to profits of over $10 million a year in ten years. Kiam put "the whole company on incentive, from the maintenance guy to the chief financial officer." The average factory worker at Remington earns one-third of his income in bonuses based on company profits. Kiam also eliminated executive perks including separate washrooms, parking spaces, and dining rooms.[43]

Guidelines for Incentive Plans In his highly acclaimed book *Thriving on Chaos,* Tom Peters states that American productivity and quality problems are directly linked to a failure to involve workers in their jobs and in the success of the organization. Incentive plans can provide that involvement and in general should adhere to the following guidelines:[44]

- *Bold incentives.* Provide bold financial incentives to everyone, from the company president to the janitor. The ultimate recognition should be that their performance is linked to improved company performance. At least 25 percent of base pay should be attainable through incentives.

- *Emphasis on team performance.* Everyone in an incentive program must clearly perceive how they can influence the results. Therefore their additional effort, cost-saving suggestion, or emphasis on quality will affect the bottom line. Group incentive systems should focus on the ten- to thirty-person work group and emphasize team performance. The facility, department, or division, which are the basic building blocks of the organization, should be used to structure the incentive system.

- *Quick feedback.* If possible, at least monthly feedback in terms of group or individual performance and the resulting bonus should be given. The bonus money should be distributed *separately* from the regular paycheck.

- *Above-average base.* In contrast to what may be assumed, base pay should be set above the norm for comparable jobs in the geographic area. With incentives added, total pay will be substantially above the norm.

- *Simple formula.* Keep the formula and process straightforward. People's motivation to increase productivity and profits will not improve if they do not understand the formula. Thus, use numbers like 5 percent instead of 7.33 percent.

Problems with Incentive Plans Incentive or performance-based plans are not without their limitations and potential problems. Individual-based plans are limited to jobs in which the employee can directly increase his or her output without affecting the productivity of others and without having output affected by others. In addition, quality standards must be carefully maintained to ensure that quality is not sacrificed for quantity. In general, individual systems require employees to perform the same job every day, or else their pay is adversely affected. Individual-based systems can also escalate rivalries among employees, which obviously can be counterproductive.

While organizational incentive plans can, if properly designed, avoid the limitations of individual-based plans, they also can cause problems. A major morale problem can occur if employees start to rely on their bonus checks and then receive smaller bonuses due to unanticipated declines in productivity or profits. Employees can also develop a short-term mentality and not make decisions that provide for maximum long-term profits. If plans are poorly designed, they can lead to employee apathy, or even a decrease in productivity if employees perceive that they are being used or mislead. The "peanut-butter approach" of spreading just a thin raise over everyone,[45] for example, can cause employees to believe that the incentive system is just another management program designed to get more work for the same rewards.

If all of the preceding limitations aren't enough, there is the additional problem of different cultural values and beliefs regarding the role of compensation. Performance-based pay is popular in North America and Europe but not in many other nations. In the Far East, for example, seniority, dedication, and loyalty are key compensation criteria.

EXECUTIVE COMPENSATION

In large, established companies, members of top management are paid differently from mid-level and lower-level managers. In general, executive pay comes in four forms: (1) base salary, (2) annual bonus, (3) long-term incentives, and (4) benefits and perquisites ("perks").[46] Base salaries, at the center of executive pay, are generally determined through job evaluation and serve as the basis for the other types of benefits.

Annual bonuses for executives include both cash and stock payments. Bonuses are usually tied to the performance of the company as a whole for the previous year or, for division managers, to their particular area. Although most executive compensation plans design such bonuses to be pay for performance, to some extent executives have come to rely on them to maintain their standard of living.

Long-term incentives are designed to allow the executive to accumulate wealth. The basic philosophy is that these individuals should have a stake in the long-term future of the firm. It is thought that they will make decisions more in line with the company's long-term future if they have a personal stake in that future. Executive benefits and perks range from the traditional executive automobile and dining room to the more unusual country club membership, private use of company airplanes, and personal legal counseling.

Golden Parachutes

A popular long-term incentive is the **golden parachute**. A parachute is a clause in the employment agreement that provides certain compensation if the executive is terminated for certain reasons, such as acquisition, merger, or demotion. Termination due to normal retirement, resignation, or disability is not included in the provision. The compensation that is promised can provide, for example, five years of continued salary, even though the executive is no longer working. The parachute serves two major purposes—to retain key executives and to discourage the takeover of hostile organizations.

Stock Options

Stock options have become extremely important to most executive compensation plans. The gist of the **stock option** is that the executive is given the right to buy the company's stock at an option price up to a fixed future point in time. The option price is usually the current market price. Thus, if an executive is given an option to buy stock at $20 a share and waits five years until the price has risen to $50 a share, then he or she has an unrealized capital gain of $30 a share. Stock option programs are a complex but critical part of executive compensation plans. It is thought that managers should profit from their efforts; if they cause the company's stock price to rise, they should share in the gain.

The most common form of stock option uses the so-called nonqualified approach. The executive is given the right to purchase the company's stock at the current price for up to five or ten years. The company can take a tax deduction on the "spread" between the option price and the current market price when the right is exercised. The tax deduction is taken without incurring a charge to earnings, which is an advantage for the company. But the executive must be able to raise the cash to exercise the option and pay the tax incurred, which is a major drawback for the executive. Stock appreciation rights (SARs) give the executive the right to exercise a nonqualified stock option or receive the spread in cash. The executive thus avoids the need to raise the cash to exercise the option and is not required to hold the stock for any length of time.

Another approach to long-term executive compensation is to tie incentive rewards to corporate performance through performance shares or performance units. With this approach, executives are promised a number of shares of stock or units if the company meets long-term growth targets. Usually the earnings per share of the company are used as the target.

Executive compensation has become a highly complex yet critical aspect of a corporate pay system. Top executive pay packages today usually include traditional base pay and executive benefits supplemented with short-term bonuses, stock options, and performance shares or units. Executives benefit by avoiding some taxes and providing for sizable wealth accumulation; companies are able to focus the executives' decision making on long-term growth and return on investment.

Executive Compensation Reform?

One of the most controversial compensation decisions is determining executive salaries. Michael Eisner, CEO at Walt Disney, received a record $197 million salary in 1993, mostly from cashing in his generous stock options. And it was not one of Disney Corporation's better years (Euro-Disney, outside Paris, saw to that). Eisner was not alone; the average CEO's salary in 1992 climbed faster than at any time since 1988. The William M. Mercer Company, New York compensation consultants, surveyed 350 corporations and found that the median increase in CEOs' annual pay—including salaries and bonuses—was 8.1 percent in 1992,

the highest since the 13.9 percent in 1988. In Mercer's sample, 159 CEOs exercised stock options, for a median gain of $654,431. Median CEO total compensation—including salary, bonuses, long-term incentives, and the value of restricted stock at the time of the grant— came to $1.5 million in 1992.[47]

When corporation after corporation is cutting back, retrenching, and expecting more from their work force, yet compensating their top executives with lucrative stock options and other perks, it is small wonder that their critics are crying foul. Besides the average blue- and white-collar workers and angry stockholders, the critics include some foreign competitors, such as the Japanese, who see these exorbitant salaries as one very good reason why American businesses are not as profitable as they might be. In Japan, the typical CEO makes less than thirty-two times the pay of the average factory worker and twenty-six times what a school teacher earns—not including bonuses that could boost their annual salaries by a third.[48]

In the United States, the gap between top managers and the first-level worker has widened to the point where the average American CEO makes 113 times what a school teacher gets. Compared to the factory worker, the average CEO makes 157 times more. And that gap has been getting progressively worse. In 1960, when U.S. economic power was at its height, CEOs pulled down an average of $190,000. That was only forty-one times a factory worker's average income.[49]

How did these incredible gaps occur in the first place? Usually the CEO appointed a "compensation committee" to study and recommend compensation packages. In most cases, an outside compensation consultant was brought in. *Business Week* (April 26, 1993:64) describes one discouraging scenario:

> The CEO, or the top HR officer, would decide which consultant to hire and what the consultant would study. The report—often a survey of what competitors paid their executives— would then be presented to the compensation

committee as justification for a fatter package for the boss. The CEO was often present in the room as directors discussed and set his pay. It took just a cozy, informal, relatively brief session or two to rubber-stamp the compensation for the CEO and his senior managers.

Reforms are on the way. Directors of compensation committees are beginning to bring in their own independent consultants and often challenging the assumptions that lie behind the old pay packages. Another positive move: more boards of directors are linking CEOs' and other top executives' rewards more closely to performance and shareholders' returns by shrinking salary raises, curbing "give-away" deals, and tying strings around potentially lucrative stock options. In effect, executive compensation will be based more on risk. Some boards are simply requiring their CEOs to buy large chunks of equity to force them to share stockholders' risk and rewards. And, if that doesn't work, the bet is that shareholder activists' groups, along with the public, will force Congress to get involved.

COMPENSATION ISSUES

Several important issues face HR managers in the area of compensation. Inflation constantly decreases employees' disposable income. Social Security and income taxes are taking a bigger bite than ever before. No doubt, employers must be innovative in their approach to compensation problems.

Wage Compression

Wage compression refers to decreasing the differentials between higher and lower pay grades. Faced with high turnover in low-paying jobs and with employees who cannot live within their means, employers have had to give greater increases to lower-paying positions than higher-paying positions. Pay differences between top- and middle-level jobs and between middle- and lower-level jobs are decreasing. With the graduated income tax, salary differences after taxes will probably become even lower in the future.

Compression, however, takes a number of forms. A manager may find that the salary difference after taxes between his or her salary and those of subordinates is insignificant. A similar form of compression occurs when a recent college graduate with no experience finds little difference between his or her pay and that of a qualified, successful graduate with ten years of experience.

When the results of compression are fully perceived, employees complain of pay inequity. Naturally, this results in a loss of morale and a tendency to work less effectively.

Two-Tier Wage Systems

A wage system that pays newly hired workers less than current employees performing the same or similar jobs is called a **two-tier wage system**. Following the institution of the historic first two-tier wage system in 1977 at General Motors' Packard Electric Division in Warren, Ohio, many more union–management negotiations have resulted in similar systems.[50] The basic concept is to provide continued higher wage levels for current employees if the union will accept reduced levels for future employees. Union leaders believe that they must accept the two-tier system or face greater layoffs in the future. Management usually claims that the system is needed to compete with nonunion and foreign competition. The airline, copper, trucking, auto, food, and aerospace industries have negotiated two-tier systems.[51]

While a two-tier system is contrary to the historic union doctrine of equal pay for equal work or pay equity, when the system is first negotiated, the union representatives can claim that they have avoided disaster and have saved the jobs and/or wage levels of current members (who must vote on the contract). It is relatively easy to sell such a concept since no workers at that point are accepting the lower tier. However, five or ten years later, when many workers are being paid lower wages for the same work as their fellow union members, it can become a source of conflict and resentment. In some cases, the lower-paid workers express their feelings with lower product quality and productivity records than their higher-paid counterparts. In these bargaining units, the conflict could present even greater problems to both union and management leaders as the number of lower-tier workers approaches 51 percent of the bargaining unit and they demand equity.[52]

Do employees hired into a lower-tier pay position perceive their treatment as equitable or not? A study of about 2000 employees found that low-tier employees perceived the employer as being significantly lower in pay equity and perceived the union as less useful in obtaining fair pay for its members. In addition, the low-tier employees felt a lower level of commitment to their employer—which might affect their productivity and tenure with the organization. These perception problems may be controlled, the research results suggest, if low-tier employees are assigned to new work locations where there are few high-tier employees and/or if they are hired for part-time instead of full-time work. Employees hired under these conditions do not report equity perception problems.[53] Another method of minimizing the morale problems of low-tier employees is to provide eventual merging of the two tiers for each individual. American Airlines, for example, provides parity for low-tier employees after ten years of service.[54]

Comparable Worth

According to Winn Newman, general council of the Coalition of Labor Union Women, the leading women's economic issue is pay equity, or **comparable worth**. The Equal Pay Act does not always enable women to obtain relief from discrimination because the act guarantees women equal pay with men only on jobs that have the same job classification.

According to the Bureau of Labor Statistics, the gap between the average income for female workers and male workers has slowly narrowed—from 60 percent in 1980 to 72 percent in 1990, with little change since 1986. The gap between young women and men (ages sixteen to twenty-four) narrowed from 77 percent in 1980 to 90 percent in 1990, which provides some encouragement for the future.[55]

Two other factors also contribute to the concerns of women workers; 80 percent of the female work force is employed in only 20 percent of the Labor Department's 427 job classifications, and as the number of women in a job classification increases, the relative wage paid for that work decreases.[56]

The doctrine of comparable worth requires that pay be equal not just for men and women performing the same job but for all jobs requiring comparable skill, effort, responsibility, and working conditions. According to supporters, the doctrine represents the spirit, if not the letter, of the Equal Pay Act. Opponents of comparable worth argue that the large percentage of women in such lower-paying jobs as secretary, nurse, and elementary school teacher is a result of women's attraction to those jobs, and that their pay level is the result of the external marketplace, as verified by wage surveys. Furthermore, opponents argue, the demand for comparable worth is not a demand for equal opportunity but a demand to be protected against one's career choice.[57]

The debate on comparable worth will most likely continue for many years (see Figure 11-9). At stake are billions of dollars in employee wages. It is not an easy issue to decide: what is the worth of a secretary in comparison to a security guard?

In 1985, the EEOC rejected the idea that comparable worth should be instituted as an interpretation of the Civil Rights Act. In a unanimous decision, the commission said that the doctrine should not be recognized as part

FIGURE 11-9 Two opinions in a continuing debate.

Are Comparable Worth Laws Needed? Two Opinions

Yes: Bonnie Erbe, Legal Correspondent, NBC Radio Network

Maybe we should send free-market economists, like my colleague, to work in the pink-collar ghetto to learn a lesson or two. Despite the fact that equal pay for equal work has been the law since 1963, society still segregates women on the job. They are more often seen behind typewriters than wearing hardhats. And we all know why: Secretaries make less than construction workers.

Sex discrimination in the form of lower pay for traditionally female jobs has been rampant for fifty years— ever since women entered the work force in significant numbers. Fifty years ago, women usually worked out of desire, not need. Men made more money because they presumably supported a family while women only supported themselves. This is simply no longer the case, yet the stereotype persists.

A suit last year against the state of California for underpaying women revealed that stenographers (99 percent women) started at $1107 per month, while groundskeepers (96 percent men) started at $1342. Neither job requires a postgraduate education or high-tech skills. What accounts for the difference? The fact that more men are groundskeepers than stenographers.

No: Linda Chavez, Columnist, Canadian Broadcasting Corporation and National Public Radio.

The problem with pay-equity advocates is they don't understand these [sic] basics of a free-market economy. Justice, equity, and intrinsic value have nothing to do with wages and prices. Supply and demand are what matter.

Free-market *inequities* can be eliminated—but at a price most thoughtful people aren't willing to pay. Look at Washington state, where a comparable-worth board has been setting pay for state employees for four years.

State workers in traditionally female jobs, such as secretaries, are earning more. But those in some traditionally male jobs, such as civil engineers, now earn 25 percent less than their counterparts in the private sector. The result is that women are more likely to hold traditionally female jobs now than when pay equity was adopted, and there are vacancies in traditionally male jobs. What's more, the odd pay schedules developed by the board have discouraged women in some categories from seeking promotions to more demanding jobs.

Source: "Equal Pay for Equal Work?" *The San Francisco Chronicle* (August 12, 1990): 2–1.

of the act. The case involved administrative staff workers (85 percent female) and maintenance workers (88 percent male). The commission ruled that no "barriers existed to prevent males and females from moving between job categories—and thus no discrimination."[58]

Also in 1985, the U.S. Court of Appeals for the Ninth Circuit rejected the doctrine of comparable worth, despite a study by a state government that showed that women were paid 20 percent less than men for "jobs requiring the same skills and effort as those held by men." The court held that market factors should determine wage and salary levels.[59]

CONCLUSIONS AND APPLICATIONS

- Organizations use both extrinsic and intrinsic rewards to compensate employees for their time and effort. Pay systems are designed to attract, retain, and motivate employees while complying with state and federal laws.

- Job evaluation is used to evaluate jobs systematically and to assign them to pay grades. The HR specialist strives to maintain a pay system that employees view as equitable both internally and externally. Standard methods of evaluation include ranking, classification, point, and factor comparison. Each offers different advantages to the organization.

- Pay systems are usually designed to compensate people for the amount of work they produce (piecework), the skills they learn and use, or the time they spend on the job (hourly and salaried.) Most employees in the United States are paid through time-based systems because of the complexity of most jobs, which makes a performance-based system impractical.

- Individual-employee, team-based and organizationwide systems such as profit sharing and gainsharing are replacing automatic pay increases to relate pay to performance.

- Executive compensation has become a complex area of HR functions. Top executives often receive compensation in as many as four areas, including salary, bonuses, long-term incentives, and benefits.

- The doctrine of comparable worth became hotly debated in the 1980s. Many supporters of the doctrine believe it is necessary because some new jobs and occupations are low-paying solely because they have historically been filled by women. Opponents argue that EEO laws are changing such disparity and that the marketplace should determine wage levels.

CASE STUDY

Merit Increases

THE TASK

Break into small groups. Read the following incident and discuss each of the questions. Then as a class discuss each group's perceptions of the situation and how they would handle the problem.

INCIDENT: MERIT INCREASES

Dr. Carl Jones is Chairperson of the Department of Management in the College of Business Administration at a large state university in the East. He has been a member of the depart-

ment for fourteen years and a full professor for five years. Last summer he was asked to assume the Chair after a screening committee conducted interviews and reviewed resumes for him and three other candidates.

Carl was very excited about the new challenges and has begun several innovative projects to enhance faculty research and consulting. The teaching function in the Department has always been first-rate, while research has been somewhat weaker. Carl has continued to be very productive as a scholar, publishing three articles, two book chapters, and one proceedings article over the past year. He also made considerable progress on a manage-

SOURCE: Stella M. Nkoma, Myron D. Fottler, and R. Bruce McAfee, *Applications in Personnel/Human Resource Management* (Boston: PWS-Kent Publishing Company, 1988), pp. 139–140. Reprinted by permission.

ment text which he is co-authoring. Finally, he has been active in his professional association, the Academy of Management, where he served as Chair of one of the professional divisions.

The University's policy is that all salary increases are based only on merit. Carl had developed a very sophisticated performance appraisal system for his faculty to help him quantify salary recommendations. His point system considers and weights different items in the areas of teaching, research, and service. Teaching and research were given weights of 40 percent each, with service at 20 percent. For the coming academic year, his recommended salary increases averaged 7 percent and ranged from 3 to 14 percent. Carl felt he had good documentation for all his recommendations.

Carl submitted his recommendations to Dean Edmund Smith and was pleased when all these recommendations were accepted. He then proceeded to schedule appointments to meet with each faculty member to discuss his recommendation, the reasons for the recommendation, and goals for the coming year. While a few of the faculty receiving lower increases indicated dissatisfaction with his weighting system, particularly the emphasis on research, these meetings generally went well.

Carl then submitted his own annual report detailing his accomplishments as Chair, as well as his more personal accomplishments. From his perspective, he felt he deserved at least a 10 percent increase since his department had made major strides in a number of areas while the other departments had been standing still. Moreover, none of the other Chairs were pro-

fessionally active on the national level and none had published in the past year. His teaching evaluations were also in the top 15 percent of faculty in the college.

Dean Smith sent out letters to all the Department Chairs in August. Carl was shocked to learn that his salary increase was just 7 percent. Information he received through the "grapevine" was that all the Chairs had received the 7 percent increase. He also learned from one of the other chairs that the Dean always gave the Chairs equal percentage increases each year. Contrary to the official university policy, there were no distinctions based on merit.

Carl was visibly upset about what he considered to be a major inequity. He then called the Dean's secretary to schedule an appointment to discuss the situation with Dean Smith.

QUESTIONS

1. Are "merit" salary increases always based on merit? Why or why not?

2. Why has Dean Smith had a policy of equal percentage salary increases for all department chairs despite the stated university's policy? Are all the chairs equally meritorious?

3. What should Dr. Jones say to Dean Smith at their meeting? What are the long-range benefits of a true merit program? What are the problems associated with the lack of such a merit system for department chairs? How likely is the discussion to change Dean Smith's decision and future behavior? Why? If the dean does not change his policy, what are the long-run implications for the college?

EXPERIENTIAL EXERCISES

1. How Should These Employees Be Paid?

PURPOSE

To examine the various ways of compensating people using incentive plans.

INTRODUCTION

While most employees are paid a salary for the period of time worked, there is an increasing trend toward a phenomenon known as *pay for performance,* whereby employees, in addition to their normal salary, are paid an incentive for high performance. The increasing use of incentive systems is primarily the result of organizational efforts to increase profits and competitiveness through increased employee productivity. Studies show that incentive plans, if well constructed and implemented, can have a dramatic effect on employee productivity.

CONDITIONS NECESSARY FOR USING INCENTIVE SYSTEMS

In reality, a relatively small percentage of the total labor force is paid on an incentive basis— about 15 percent. Why? Because an incentive pay system is impractical to administer unless certain key conditions can be met. Those conditions include the following:

1. The output must be measurable and suitable for standardization.
2. There must be a consistent relationship between the employee's skill and effort and the employee's output.
3. The output can be measured and credited to the proper individual or group.
4. The incentive system should lead to an increase in productivity.
5. The employees, the union (if one exists), and management must all support the incentive system.

THE TASK

Listed here are several jobs. For each job, complete the questions in the figure provided. Following this exercise, your instructor will lead a discussion on incentive compensation systems. Some jobs are appropriate for incentive compensation systems, while others are more appropriate for a wage or salary system.

Valerie McCloud—Forklift Driver

Valerie McCloud drives a forklift for a small metals manufacturer. She picks up parts that have been boxed and loaded onto pallets and delivers them to the warehouse for shipping. She occasionally also performs odd jobs throughout the day at the request of her supervisor. McCloud is a member of the Teamsters' Union.

Jill Peters—Seamstress

Jill Peters works as a seamstress for a large textile firm in South Carolina. She works independently, using an industrial sewing machine. All day, she sews sleeves and pockets to men's shirts. Her output is tallied twice a day by her supervisor.

William Grant—Assembly-Line Worker

William Grant is an assembly-line worker for a large home appliance manufacturer. He attaches parts to washing machines as they reach his position on the line. Twenty-seven employees work on this particular assembly line in the plant. Daily output for the group is recorded by the employees' supervisor.

Claire Walker—Data Entry Operator

Claire Walker is a data entry operator for a large state government agency. Her work varies from day to day, although much of it is very similar in nature. Weekly, her supervisor receives a computer printout that details each keypuncher's production rate and quality index.

Rick Fernstein—Accounting Instructor

Rick Fernstein is an assistant professor for a large urban university. He is responsible for activities involving teaching, research, and community service. Annually, he prepares a performance report covering all activities for the year. This report includes summaries of student course evaluations, publications, committee work, and other school-related activities. Fernstein's department head closely reviews the report and assigns an overall performance evaluation of "excellent," "good," "satisfactory," "below satisfactory," or "unacceptable."

Dennis Cuestick—Automobile Salesman

Dennis Cuestick is an automobile salesman for a Ford dealer in a midwestern town. Six days a week, he "works the floor." The company's sales personnel have an informal system for taking turns when customers enter the showroom or call to make inquiries about a car. Sales are recorded daily by the sales manager.

Paul McCleskey—Route Salesman

Paul McCleskey is a route salesman for a large cola manufacturer. His route covers a large rural area in central Georgia and consists primarily of servicing small mom-and-pop grocery stores, lounges, and restaurants. At the end of each day, McCleskey turns in a report to his supervisor detailing his sales activity for each account.

Charley Bedeman—Farm Laborer

Charley Bedeman is a farm laborer for the Jiffy Orange Juice Company in Orlando, Florida. He rises daily at 6:00 A.M. and is in the groves picking oranges by 7:00 A.M. Using a centuries-old technology, he carefully places each piece of ripe fruit in the deep "picking bag" slung over his shoulder. He dumps a full bag into a box and starts all over until quitting time at 5:00 P.M.

Kathy Miller—Secretary

Kathy Miller is a secretary to the dean of the Arts and Sciences School at a small, private liberal arts college. She types correspondence and reports, takes dictation, files, maintains the dean's schedule, and so on. Miller's work is evaluated by the dean annually, using a performance evaluation form that includes quantity of work, quality of work, dependability, judgment, communication skills, ability to get along with others, and loyalty. For each of these traits, she is assigned a rating of "very good," "above average," "average," "below average," or "unsatisfactory." One of these ratings is also given to Miller to designate her overall performance for the year.

Sheldon Smedley—Attorney

Sheldon Smedley, a recent graduate of a prestigious eastern law school, works for a reputable Washington law firm specializing in corporate law. Smedley is assigned to the division that handles patent and trademark violations. He works directly with clients, researches cases, writes briefs, and represents clients in court. His performance is reviewed informally about every six months. No special forms are used to conduct these evaluations.

Employee	COMPENSATION PLAN					INCENTIVE PLAN	
	(A) Hourly only	(B) Hourly plus incentive	(C) Salary only	(D) Salary plus incentive	(E) Incentive only	1. If you checked B, D, or E, indicate the appropriate *form* of incentive (piecework, commission, merit increase, bonus, stock option, stock appreciation rights, performance shares, profit sharing, Scanlon plan).	2. If you have recommended some form of incentive, indicate the type of output (net sales, per item manufactured, per set of encyclopedias, etc.) that the incentive should be based on.
Valerie McCloud							
Jill Peters							
William Grant							
Claire Walker							
Rick Fernstein							
Dennis Cuestick							
Paul McCleskey							
Charley Bedeman							
Kathy Miller							
Sheldon Smedley							

2. Nonmonetary Incentives

INTRODUCTION

At some point, unfortunately, every manager will experience the frustration of not having sufficient monetary rewards available for distribution to worthy employees. And, if the manager is responsible for recruiting and motivating volunteers, as would be the case in non-profit sectors like The Red Cross, it becomes an on-going, almost daily challenge.

The Task

Read the following dialogue.

A Red Cross manager, while attending a workshop on how to motivate improved performance, had this to say to the instructor.

> Dr. Smith, I think your ideas on how managers should give merit salary increases to improve individual performance are good, but the reality within my organization is totally different. We are a non-profit agency. Our budgets can barely support our programs much less be used to reward top performance. For us, money is simply unavailable and never will be. For paid employees, salaries are determined by education, position, and seniority. We cannot change this at all. And, for our volunteers there is no money whatsoever, except for administrative expenses and reimburseable items.

At that point, a second participant broke into the discussion and said:

> I also work in a non-profit agency called the St. Vincent de Paul Society. I can't change salaries for our paid staff either—only our Board of Directors can do that. And the vast majority of our employees are volunteers anyway. Had I not been innovative in finding ways to motivate my staff, I would not have any continuity in people or programs. But it can be done and here is how I went about it.

Directions:

Put yourself in the role of the participant from the St. Vincent de Paul Society. The objective of this task is to demonstrate that a manager's hands are not completely tied by a noncontingent pay system. With a bit of creativity and improvisation managers can use elements in the employee's immediate work environment to contingently reward and motivate improved performance.

The class will be divided into teams (4 or 5 members per team). Each team will select a spokesperson. Teams should then prepare a brief presentation to the class with flip charts or transparencies that identify rewards to reinforce improved performance. Each participant should draw upon his or her own experiences, and depend less on theory and dubious assumptions, e.g., thinking of nonprofit organizations as places full of interesting people who work in a loose and nonhierarchical administrative structure. Teams will have 20 minutes to meet and brainstorm.

KEY TERMS AND CONCEPTS

Benchmark jobs
Broadbanding
Classification method
Commission
Comparable worth
Compensable factors
Compensatory time
Cost-of-living adjustment (COLA)
Employee stock ownership plan (ESOP)

Executive compensation
Exempt/nonexempt
Factor-comparison method
Fair Labor Standards Act (FLSA)
Free rider
Gainsharing
Garnishment
Golden handshakes
Golden parachutes

Improshare
Job evaluation
Merit pay increases
Pay grades and steps
Performance-based system
Point method
Profit-sharing plan
Ranking method
Red circle job/green circle job

Rising and falling differentials
Rucker plan
Scanlon plan
Stock options
Straight piecework plan
360 degree feedback
Time-based system
Two-tier wage system

REVIEW QUESTIONS

1. Outline at least four reasons why an organization needs a compensation system.

2. Which jobs might effectively use performance-based pay systems?

3. What steps should an HR specialist take to maximize employee performance motivated by the organization?

4. What is the difference between employee evaluation and job evaluation?

5. When are employees' wages subject to garnishment?

6. In job evaluation, why should a committee be used instead of one person?

7. What are the comparative advantages of each of the four job evaluation methods?

8. Should pay grades be allowed to overlap?

9. What are central arguments in the comparable worth issue?

DISCUSSION QUESTIONS

1. If you were working on an assembly line, would you prefer receiving COLAs or merit increases? Why? If you were a supervisor, would your decision be the same? If you were the owner of a manufacturing plant?

2. You are the head of the newly established HR department for a small company. The owner, who began the firm fifty years ago, refuses to allow employees to discuss their wages—and for good reason. The owner's relatives receive 10 percent more than other employees. Various employees have asked you why salaries have been kept secret, and you say . . .

3. Should federal and state governments be able to legislate minimum wages rather than adopting a laissez-faire attitude that would allow employers operating on a slim profit margin to pay only what they could afford?

4. What arguments would you offer to support the repeal of the Davis-Bacon Act?

5. Which method of job evaluation would you prefer if you were implementing one? What factors would influence your decision?

6. What portion of an employee's annual pay should be due to the employer's profit-sharing plan—25 percent? 50 percent? 100 percent? Why?

NOTES

Chapter 11

1. R. C. Pilenzo, "Compensation: The State of the Art," *Personnel Administrator* (September 1977): 11.

2. L. Dyer, D. P. Schwab, and J. A. Fossum, "Impacts of Pay on Employee Behaviors and Attitudes: An Update," *Personnel Administrator* (January 1978): 51–53.

3. David W. Belcher, *Wage and Salary Administration* (Englewood Cliffs, NJ: Prentice-Hall, 1962), pp. 106–13.

4. J. S. Adams, "Inequity in Social Exchange," in L. Berkowitz, ed., *Advances in Experimental Social Psychology*, vol. 2 (New York: Academic Press, 1965), pp. 422–36.

5. Michael R. Carrell, "A Longitudinal Field Assessment of Employee Perceptions of Equitable Treatment," *Organizational Behavior and Human Performance* 21 (1978): 108–18.

6. John E. Dittrich and M. R. Carrell, "Organizational Equity Perceptions, Employee Job Satisfaction, and Departmental Absence and Turnover Rates," *Organizational Behavior and Human Performance* 24 (1979): 29–40.

7. Christin Klingberg, "Violations of Child Labor Laws Up 250 Percent," *HR News* (March 1990): 9.

8. John A. Dantico, "Wage-hour Law Clarifies Exempt/Nonexempt," *HR News* (January 1990): 3.

9. *Brock* v. *Highway Oil, Inc.*, no. 81-4245 (D. Kan. 1987).

10. Gina Ameci, "Bonuses and Commissions: Is Your Overtime Pay Legal?" *Personnel Journal* 66, no. 1 (January 1987): 107–10.

11. Ibid.

12. Belcher, *Wage and Salary*, pp. 176–77.

13. Richard Henderson, *Compensation Management* (Reston, VA: Reston, 1979), pp. 231–33.

14. *Job Evaluation Policies and Procedures*, Personnel Policies Forum survey no. 113 (Washington, DC.: Bureau of National Affairs, 1976), pp. 1–8.

15. Belcher, *Wage and Salary*.

16. William C. Mihal, "More Research Is Needed; Goals May Motivate Better," *Personnel Administrator* 28, no. 10 (October 1983): 61–67.

17. Frederick S. Hills et al., "Merit Pay: Just or Unjust Desserts?" *Personnel Administrator* 32, no. 9 (September 1987): 53–59.

18. Richard E. Kapeleman, "Linking Pay to Performance Is a Proven Management Tool," *Personnel Administrator* 28, no. 10 (October 1983): 61–68.

19. Carol Braddick, Michael Jones, and Paul Shafer, "A Look at Broadbanding in Practice," *Journal of Compensation and Benefits* (July-August 1992): 28–32.

20. R. Bradley Hill, "Get Off the Broadband Wagon," *Journal of Compensation and Benefits* (January-February 1993): 25–29.

21. Donna Fenn, "Skill-Based Pay Takes Off," *CFO* (January 1993): 57–58.

22. Ibid.

23. Ibid.

24. Robert J. Sahl, "Key Issues for Implementing Skill-based Pay," *Journal of Compensation and Benefits* (May-June 1993): 31–34.

25. C. F. Vough, *Productivity: A Practice Program for Improving Efficiency* (New York: AMACOM, 1979), p. 2.

26. Leonard R. Burgess, *Wages and Salary Administration* (Columbus, OH: Merrill, 1984), p. 242.

27. Tom Peters, *Thriving on Chaos* (New York: Harper & Row, 1987), pp. 403–04.

28. Jill Kanin-Lovers and Marsha Cameron, "Team-Based Reward Systems," *Journal of Compensation and Benefits* (January-February 1993): 56–60.

29. Ibid. p. 251.

30. Robert J. Doyle, *Gainsharing and Productivity* (New York: American Management Association, 1983), pp. 11–19.

31. Ibid.

32. Larry Hatcher, Timothy L. Ross, and Ruth Ann Ross, "Gainsharing: Living Up to Its Name," *Personnel Administrator* 32, no. 6 (June 1987): 153–64.

33. John Savage, "Incentive Programs at Nucor Corporation Boost Productivity," *Personnel Administrator* 22 (August 1981): 33–36.

34. Gary W. Florkowski, "Analyzing Group Incentive Plans," *HR Magazine* 35, no. 1 (January 1990): 36–38.

35. *Basic Patterns in Union Contracts* (Washington, DC: Bureau of National Affairs, 1986), pp. 122–23.

36. "Pay Day: Typical Ford Worker Gets $1,200 for Profit-Sharing," *The Courier Journal* (March 13, 1986), p. B8; "Auto Workers Will Feel Pinch of Lower or No Profits," *The Bakersfield Californian* (February 20, 1990): 87.

37. Speech by Douglas Frasier at the University of Louisville, April 22, 1986.

38. Peters, *Thriving on Chaos*, pp. 402–04.

39. Ibid.

40. Joseph R. Blasi and Douglas L. Kruse, *The New Owners* (New York: HarperBusiness, 1991), pp. 214–38.

41. Robert Rose and Erle Norton, "UAL's New Owners May Face Bumpy Ride If the Past Is a Guide," *The Wall Street Journal* (December 23, 1993): A1.

42. "Non-Traditional Pay Plans Gaining Popularity, Study Shows," *Resource* (December 1986): 1, 6.

43. Speech by Victor Kiam at the University of Louisville School of Business, February 26, 1987.

44. Tom Peters, *Thriving on Chaos*, pp. 398–405.

45. D. Dolan, "Back to Piecework," *Wall Street Journal* (November 15, 1986): 1.

46. William J. Smith, "Executive Compensation After ERTA," *Personnel Administrator* (February 1983): 63–65.

47. "The Boss's Pay," *The Wall Street Journal* (April 21, 1993): R13.

48. Robert Neff, "What Do Japanese CEOs Really Make?" *Business Week* (April 26, 1993): 60–61.

49. "Executive Pay: It Doesn't Add Up," *Business Week* (April 26, 1993): 112.

50. "The Revolutionary Wage Deal at G.M.'s Packard Electric," *Business Week* (August 29, 1983): 54.

51. S. R. Premeaux, R. W. Mondy, and A. L. Bethke, "The Two-Tier Wage Systems," *Personnel Administrator* 31, no. 11 (November 1986): 93–100.

52. Michael R. Carrell and Christina Heavrin, *Collective Bargaining and Labor Relations*, 3d ed. (Columbus, OH: Merrill, 1991), pp. 177–80.

53. James E. Martin and Melanie M. Peterson, "Two-Tier Wage Structures: Implications for Equity Theory," *Academy of Management Journal* 30, no. 2 (June 1987): 297–315.

54. Agis Salpukas, "The Two-Tier Wage System Is Found to Be Two-Edged Sword by Industry," *New York Times* (July 21, 1987): 1, 47.

55. "Earnings Gap Narrowing Faster Between Young Men and Women," *BNAC Communicator* (Winter 1990): 16.

56. Wayne Caseio, *Managing Human Resources: Productivity, Quality of Work Life, Profits* (New York: McGraw-Hill, 1989), p. 56.

57. Robert D. Hershey, "The Wage Gap Between Men and Women Faces a New Assault," *The Louisville Courier-Journal* (November 6, 1983): 1, 4.

58. Pete Yost, "EEOC Rejects Comparable Worth as Means to Judge Discrimination," *The Louisville Courier-Journal* (June 19, 1985): B-1.

59. U.S. Court Says 'No' to Comparable Worth," *Resource* pamphlet (1985).

BENEFITS

CHAPTER OBJECTIVES

1. To understand the growth of employee benefits and their organizational objectives.
2. To cite the benefits required by law.
3. To explain the major elements of pension systems.
4. To identify major paid time-off benefits.
5. To describe alternatives to traditional sick-leave policies.
6. To identify premium pay benefits.
7. To recognize the various methods of providing health-care insurance.

8. To realize the various methods employers may utilize to provide child care.

9. To explain the advantages of flexible benefit plans.

10. To understand the employer's need to publicize the benefit program.

The policy of awarding employee **benefits** increased dramatically in the United States during World War II. As governmental wage controls were imposed, employees and unions looked to benefits as a means of increasing the quality of working life. For many years, benefits were called *fringe benefits*. Today, between 25 and 40 percent of an organization's total payroll costs are usually made up of employees' benefits.

The cost of benefits is high and getting higher. Employers spend an average of 26.7 percent of payroll on such benefits as retirement plans, medical plans, insurance plans, paid leave, and educational assistance. However, variations among industries are substan-

Table 12-1 Estimated Cost of Employee Benefits by Industry

Industries	Cost per Employee per Year
All Industries	**$11,622**
Manufacturing Industries	**13,602**
Food, beverages, and tobacco	8,567
Textile products and apparel	5,361
Pulp, paper, lumber, and furniture	11,214
Printing and publishing	7,820
Chemicals and allied products	12,756
Petroleum	13,285
Rubber, leather, and plastic	15,201
Stone, clay, and glass	8,757
Primary metals	15,147
Fabricated metals (excluding machinery and transportation equipment)	9,604
Machinery (excluding electrical)	11,824
Electrical machinery, equipment, and supplies	10,602
Instruments and miscellaneous manufacturing	11,759
Nonmanufacturing industries	**10,079**
Public utilities	14,368
Department stores	5,767
Trade (wholesale and retail other than department stores)	6,902
Banks, finance companies, and trust companies	8,085
Insurance companies	9,397
Hospitals	8,100
Miscellaneous nonmanufacturing	10,730

SOURCE: Adapted from and with the permission of *Nation's Business*, (February 1988), copyright © 1988, U.S. Chamber of Commerce, and *The Consumer Price Index*, U.S. Department of Labor, 1987–1990.

tial. Business service firms, for instance, spend an average of 18.4 percent of payroll on benefits, while the average in the automotive industry is 35.6 percent.[1] Most of 1992's 5.3 percent hike in benefits cost, compared with a 2.8 percent rise in wages and salaries, came from the health-care tab alone.[2]

Few organizations, however, award benefits based on employee performance; instead, such benefits as paid vacations and pension plans are tied to factors other than performance (e.g., seniority). Benefits have not become a motivational tool because few employees realize the cost of benefits or appreciate many of their benefits until later years.

From 1980 to 1990, the cost of benefits jumped 61 percent, while wages and salaries grew 41 percent. During that time the average cost of benefits per employee increased to $11,626 per year.[3] The U.S. Chamber of Commerce has noted that the costs of benefits vary widely among industries, as shown in Table 12-1. The petroleum, public utility, rubber, and metal industries pay the highest benefits for their employees. The lowest benefits are paid by the textile and apparel industries, department stores, and hospitals. Three benefit areas that have rapidly increased in recent years are medical insurance, pensions, and wages paid for time not worked (Table 12-2).

Table 12-2 Estimated Annual Cost of Benefits per Employee

Benefit	Cost per Employee per Year
Old-age, survivors, disability, and health insurance (FICA)	$ 1,794
Unemployment compensation	291
Workers' compensation	313
State sickness benefits insurance	239
Retirement and savings plans contributions	1,991
Life insurance and death benefits	145
Medical insurance (current employees)	1,813
Medical insurance (retirees)	178
Short-term disability insurance	157
Long-term or salary-continuation insurance	60
Dental insurance	167
Other medically related payments	97
Paid rest periods (coffee and lunch breaks, etc.)	994
Paid vacations, holidays, and sick leave	2,948
Maternity and parental leave	54
Discounts on goods and services	71
Meals furnished	29
Education expenditures	47
Child care	180
Miscellaneous	60
Total benefits costs	**11,622**

SOURCE: Adapted from and with permission of *Nation's Business* (February 1988). Copyright 1988, U.S. Chamber of Commerce; *The Consumer Price Index*, U.S. Department of Labor, 1987–1990.

For example, coffee breaks, rest periods, wash-up time, and any other paid time on the job when the employee does not work, combined with paid vacations, holidays, and sick leave, increased from $1005 in 1971 to $3942 in 1990 (392 percent!).[4]

The amount of increase in benefits differs from one industry to another, but the rapid increase experienced by U.S. companies can be generally attributed to four causes:[5]

1. Federal wage ceilings during World War II and again in the 1970s caused unions and all employees to look to benefits as a means of increasing compensation.

2. Companies use benefits to gain employee compliance and loyalty. When employees have accumulated several years' seniority, they often find that taking a higher-paying job with a different employer would cause a loss of pension and vacation benefits.

3. Most employees' wages satisfy their basic needs; therefore, they have become interested in bargaining for more and greater benefits, especially in the areas of health care and pay for time not worked (vacations, holidays, etc.), which satisfy other needs.

4. Health-care insurance costs have put the United States in the lead in annual percentage increases for over twenty years and are almost out of control (see *HR in the News:* "The Crisis in U.S. Health Care Insurance.")

Government influences employee benefits through regulations concerning employment opportunities, safety, health care, retirement and unemployment compensation, and workers' compensation. Even greater governmental influence is expected in the future. The government appears to be actively transferring the cost of welfare or social programs to private industries in the form of required employee benefits. To stem the tide of the rising costs of benefits, many HR administrators believe that organizations must change their traditional approaches to employee benefits. A few companies, such as IBM (see *HR in the News:* "IBM's New Product: Employee Benefits"), are charging for their services to other IBM units and selling their services to non-IBM clients.

In an effort to contain benefit costs, many employers have instituted a *coordination of benefits (COB) program.* Such programs are primarily established to guard against having to pay duplicate claims when more than one medical policy covers a claimant. The dramatic increase in two-income households has made this type of coverage common. The national average in savings of COB programs is 4 to 5 percent of insurance costs. For example, Borden, Inc., saved over $1,613,000 in the first two years of its COB program simply by self-administration of health care and major medical insurance.[6]

Flexible benefit plans, as discussed later in this chapter, have also been successfully used by employers to contain benefit costs. An employer can set any maximum benefit allowance per employee, requiring the employee to pay any additional costs.

TYPES OF BENEFITS

The various benefits offered by employers can be divided into six types: (1) those that are required by law of the employer, (2) retirement benefits, (3) pay for time not worked, (4) premium pay, (5) insurance, and (6) employee services. Each type presents a different challenge for the HR profession. Skyrocketing costs of insurance and retirement benefits have forced employers to reexamine the usefulness of those benefits and to evaluate whether benefits provided by the government should also be provided by the employer. At the same time, employees are demanding more days away from the workplace with pay.

The Crisis in U.S. Health Insurance

The United States spends $2664 on health care per person—171 percent more than Great Britain; 124 percent more than Japan; 88 percent more than West Germany, and 38 percent more than Canada. Health care represents 11.5 percent of the U.S. gross national product, the largest single category. With all the money we spend, the United States must have the best health care in the world, right? Wrong. The United States ranks twelfth in life expectancy behind Japan, Italy, France, and the Scandinavian countries, and twenty-first in the number of deaths of children under five.* Of all the industrial nations in the world, *only* the United States and South Africa do not provide national health care. Millions of Americans do not have health-care insurance, and the skyrocketing cost increases force more people to go uninsured each year. Thus many people live without adequate health care. Why?

Consumer Reports points to the American Medical Association (AMA). The AMA has fought proposed national health insurance programs, which it terms "socialized medicine," most likely in fear that they would lower the incomes of its 271,000 members. The political clout of the AMA is enormous. In 1990 the AMA ranked second in total spending by political action committees (PACs), according to the Federal Election Commission.** The insurance industry, through its Health Insurance Association of America (HIAA), also fights to maintain the current system of health care.

The American people are increasingly unhappy with the cost and quality of their health care. Unfortunately, President Clinton's plan for universal health care has met with stiff resistance from Congress and many special interest groups. Passage of any substantive health care legislation is going to take a lot of time and compromising. At this time, it is exceedingly doubtful that "real" health care reform will occur anytime soon.

---

*Adapted from "The Crisis in Health Insurance," *Consumer Reports* 55, no. 9 (September 1990): 608–17.
**Ibid, 615.

IBM's New Product: Employee Benefits

One evening in 1991, Walton Burdick, IBM senior vice-president for personnel, was sitting around with a group of fellow managers at company headquarters, when the discussion turned to a pressing issue: how to cut Big Blue's annual $1 billion-plus benefits costs for its 158,000 domestic employees. With health-care costs soaring, the problem had become a familiar one to companies. But out of that session IBM came up with a radical solution: It decided to spin off its huge human resources operation into a separate company called Workforce Solutions, which is now saving IBM millions of dollars annually. Says Burdick: "In retrospect, what we did seems so simple."

Many corporations are finding they can cut overhead and deliver better services to employees by getting out of the benefits business—and handing it over to consultants instead. IBM did them one better. While other businesses let *outsiders* take over key human resource areas such as 401(k) retirement plans, IBM in 1992 set up *Workforce Solutions* to handle everything. And if all goes well, it will soon be a profit center in its own right.

The new outfit still provides all human resources support to IBM's 13 business units, but Workforce Solutions can tailor its services to the units' differing needs. Workforce has eight specialty areas—ranging from occupational health and safety to career development. They allow an IBM unit to put emphasis on building a diverse work force. Customizing benefits is a radical departure from the one-size-fits-all mentality that long prevailed at IBM.

IBM's employees haven't noticed any big changes, which is what IBM intended. "I would say service is a little better," says a worker, adding that she now gets more communications about benefits.

Workforce is trying to forge an identity, picking up accounts outside Big Blue. In 1992, for example, it signed up National Geographic Society. IBM's reputation for excellence and generosity in the benefits area is what appealed to NGS. It turned to IBM—no stranger to downsizing—to help devise a voluntary layoff plan. In all, Workforce has eight HR core competencies—ranging from cultural diversity training to safety and health programs.

Workforce Solutions' early success is focusing attention on the whole idea of marketing internal operations to outsiders. If more companies begin selling their human resources services, there could be revolutionary changes in corporate benefits departments. Long seen as drains on the bottom line, benefits departments could become profit centers. IBM, which hasn't had much to crow about of late, may just be on to something.

SOURCE: Adapted from Tim Smart, "IBM Has a New Product: Employee Benefits," *Business Week* (May 10, 1993): 58.

Finally, employee services, which range from tuition reimbursement to outplacement counseling, have been increasing rapidly.

Required Benefits

Some employee benefits are required by law and therefore do not need to be negotiated with a union. Some benefit plans, such as **supplementary unemployment benefits (SUB)**, are designed to supplement those required by law in order that the employee is guaranteed a greater level of benefit than provided by the government. A few union leaders have expressed opposition to government-imposed benefit programs, such as the Occupational Safety and Health Act of 1970, the Pension Reform Act of 1974, and the Health Maintenance Organization Act of 1973, because the federal government has provided to all employees benefits previously negotiated for union employees. Other union opposition has arisen because such federal legislation has taken from union negotiators the ability to bargain for benefits that might be preferable to those provided by government. Thus, benefits that are provided for all restrict negotiators' ability to bargain for specific programs their membership might prefer.

Unemployment insurance, Social Security, workers' compensation, and *family leave* represent important government-required benefits that are costly to management. **Unemployment insurance** originated in 1938. Government economists realized that unemployment insurance helps maintain the economy by stabilizing purchasing power and also helps workers bridge the gaps between jobs without having a significantly negative impact on their lives.[7] States are able to provide unemployed employees with benefits by imposing unemployment payroll taxes on employers. Normally, the amount paid by employers varies according to the unemployment rate within the state. To receive benefits, unemployed workers must have worked for a certain period

of time and must have registered for employment at a U.S. Employment Office.

In 1935 Congress established the **Social Security system** to provide supplemental income to retired workers. Initially, Social Security was to provide retirees with an income that, when added to their retirement savings, would enable them to live during their retirement years in dignity. The cost of the system is borne by both employers and employees; each group pays an equal amount of taxes into the system, which then uses the funds to pay benefits to currently retired individuals. Technically, Social Security taxes are Federal Insurance Contributions Act (FICA) taxes. It is often noted by management that employees pay half the cost of the system but receive all the benefits. That sentiment ignores the benefits to society that Social Security undoubtedly brings. In addition to Social Security, most labor agreements provide for a separate private pension plan.

The Social Security system is actually two separate systems: one to provide retirement benefits and one to provide disability, survivors', and Medicare benefits. To become eligible, workers must have contributed for ten years or forty quarters in the system.

Since the Social Security Revision Act of 1972, the benefits paid to recipients who are eligible to receive the retirement income increase each year by a percentage equal to the increase in the consumer price index (CPI) if the CPI increases by 3 percent or more. This automatic increase has been one of the causes of the periodic financial troubles of the Social Security system.[8] It also has given employers a strong argument not to provide for increases in employees' private pension dollars. The Social Security tax rate increased from 3.0 percent in 1960 to 7.65 percent in 1993.[9]

Laws requiring **workers' compensation** have been enacted by states to protect employees and their families against permanent loss of income and high medical bills in case of accidental injury or illness occurring on the job. The primary purpose of most state laws is to keep the question of the cause of the accident—whether the employer or employee was at fault—out of the debate. In most cases, the laws provide employees with assured payment for medical expenses or lost income due to injury on the job. Workers' compensation funds are primarily provided through employer contributions to a statewide fund. A state industrial board then reviews cases and determines eligibility for compensation.

Employees are often able to recover total medical expenses and up to two-thirds of lost income due to missed work or disability.[10] States may allow employers to purchase workers' compensation insurance from private insurance companies to augment state funds. Union leaders have played an important role in ensuring that state laws are updated and employees' interests are protected. Their efforts protect the interests not only of union workers but of nonunion workers as well.

A new piece of federal legislation became law in 1993: the **Family and Medical Leave Act (FMLA)**. The law requires employers with at least fifty employees to provide up to twelve weeks of family leave to employees for birth, adoption, or care of a family member who is ill. The law applies to private, not-for-profit, and public employers and to Congress, as well as state and federal workers.

The law guarantees the employee an opportunity to return to the same job or a job with equivalent status and pay. In addition, the employer must continue the employee's health benefits during the leave period. If the employee chooses not to return, other than for health reasons, the employer may recover employer-paid health care premiums.[11]

Up to twelve weeks of leave may be taken. The employer can require the employee to use up all paid vacation, personal, or family leave before taking unpaid leave. Employees planning to take the leave must given the employer 30 days' notice or, if this is not possible, as much notice as is practical. There is no reporting requirement, but records must be kept. Employers who violate the act will be liable for wages and benefits lost plus the risk of being judged not acting in good faith, which can result in the court's doubling the damage awards.

PENSIONS

In the United States, individuals are expected to provide for their retirement through the "three pillars": Social Security, a private pension, and personal savings. Together these three sources of income can replace an employee's preretirement disposable income, and thus can be considered to create the ideal pension system.[12] But today, it is not unusual for someone to have several pensions, 401(k) money from a previous employer that has been rolled into an individual retirement account (IRA), other IRAs, personal savings, assorted annuities, Social Security, and perhaps executive deferred compensation. Planning for retirement can be a highly complicated process because there are so many more financial decisions, as Table 12-3 points out.

The consequences of poor retirement investments can be costly. Plans on how to handle various retirement funds should be prudently thought out and implemented. Most retirees today need to coordinate their decisions to maximize payouts and avoid tax traps. Consequently, getting expert advice is often worth the added expense.

Unfortunately, in a mobile society such as ours, there are thousands of people whose lifestyles and careers involve moving from one job to another and from one company to another, and who may reach the end of the trail prematurely (i.e., via layoffs). For people in their fifties, finding a job is hard, and finding a job with a retirement plan in which they can participate is even harder. Most of these mobile professionals are wise enough to anticipate the dangers. For many, however, planning for re-

Table 12-3 Retirement Savings Glossary

Ever wonder what the differences were between an IRA and an annuity? Don't feel alone; most people never give these alternatives a moment's thought—that is, until the inevitable point arrives and the decisions made early in their careers are the ones they have to live with for the rest of their lives.

Retirement Savings Vehicle	Typical Payout Options at Retirement	Distribution Rules and Tax Consequences
Profit-sharing or 401(k) plan from a recent employer	Lump sum Rollover to IRA* Deferred payout Installment	Withdrawals generally subject to regular income tax; 10% penalty under age 59½; ceiling lowers to age 55 if the person is retiring; 50% penalty if withdrawals not begun by age 70½.
Pension from current and former employers	Annuity Lump sum Rollover to IRA*	May have to begin taking payments at retirement; must begin by age 70½; payments generally subject to regular income tax.
Nonqualified plans for top executives	Annuity Lump sum	Regular income tax on payouts. Must usually be taken at retirement; some allow wait of five years or so.
IRA	Withdrawals (various options)	Must begin by age 70. All deductible contributions and earnings subject to regular income tax; 10% penalty if money taken out before age 59½.
Annuities	Withdrawals Annuity or installment	Surrender penalties may reduce payout. Payments subject to regular income tax; 10% penalty on money taken before age 59½.
Social Security	Monthly check for life	No required date to begin taking payments; can begin at age 62, but monthly payments are greater the longer one waits, until age 70.

*Amounts rolled into IRAs can remain tax deferred until withdrawn

tirement takes second place to paying for their children's education, home, and so on. They anticipate having their forties and fifties, usually the most financially rewarding years, to accrue a sufficient retirement cushion. Perhaps they never work long enough at one company to build vesting benefits, or maybe the company does not have a retirement plan in the first place. For people such as Mel Kalish (see *HR in the News:* "Grapes of Wrath, 1993"), who lose their jobs late in their careers and who do not have any private retirement plan, the penalties can be devastating. These examples are all the more reason to begin investing early, whether in a company retirement plan or independently (through a 401(k) plan), and leave it there. Unless there is no other alternative, don't even think about cashing out of the retirement plan before the age of fifty-nine and one-half.

When employees retire, they usually have lower living expenses than a working family because of the elimination or reduction of commuting costs, mortgage payments, and child-rearing costs. In addition, they gain eligibility for certain tax exemptions, for

Grapes of Wrath, 1993

One year ago, Mel Kalish had the best job of his life. He was an advisory systems analyst at IBM's Santa Clara facility, a job that meant a security clearance and work on Air Force satellites. He was making $59,000 a year—the highest salary of his career—and at age 56, after putting three children through college, he and his wife, Esther, were able to buy their first house.

"Things were going wonderfully. It was like a miracle, in fact," he said. "I don't know how many times I told various levels of managers at IBM that I loved it."

Kalish thought he was with IBM for the long haul. Nearing retirement age, he thought it would be the last job he held in his life. Now his greatest fear is that it was.

After only 18 months at IBM, he saw the beginnings of a cycle that had become all too familiar after a lifetime of working in aerospace and a holder of a Ph.D. Declining sales combined with military budget cuts were squeezing his department.

He hung on for another stressful year before taking a retirement incentive package in July 1992. Called a "bridging leave of absence," it's an agreement that allows him to retain his medical benefits until retirement pay begins in six years, but also requires that he never draw a paycheck again at IBM.

He calls the IBM package "extremely generous," considering the short time he worked for the company. But it has meant financial disaster. Without his weekly paycheck, the Kalishes are on the verge of losing everything: their life savings, their home, their independence.

For a year he has handed his resume to everyone he has met. "I am absolutely terrified that I will, in fact, find nothing," he said. Adding to the problem is a large debt built up paying college tuitions and borrowing to pay bills this year.

"If we lose the house, one of the alternatives—really, the best alternative—is to move 3,000 miles to New Jersey and live with Mel's sister in her basement," Mrs. Kalish said. "I don't know If I could handle that—the idea of being forced to move, the bank taking the house, getting rid of most everything. That's the bottom, and there's not a lot between."

"I feel like it's—'You're 56 and we're done with you, go off in a corner and die,' " he said.

SOURCE: Adapted from "Job Cutbacks Shatter Man's Dreams of Golden Years," *Omaha World-Herald* (September 26, 1993): 11-G.

Medicare, and for other benefits made available to the aged.[13] Thus, retired workers do not normally need 100 percent of their preretirement income but only a portion of it. Employers thus often integrate an employee's pension income with Social Security. Private pension plans also normally provide for early retirement income to employees who lose their jobs because of disability. Approximately two-thirds of private employer pension plans provide immediate disability benefits; the remaining third defer benefits until retirement age. Employees under the latter plans are normally covered by disability insurance until they receive their pension payments.[14]

Early Retirement

Employers often at some point offer an early-retirement *window*. Such a plan is usually characterized by the employer's offering for a specified period of time (usually two to six months) special benefits to eligible employees who choose to retire early. Thus, for a short period, employees have an alternative window to leave their employer. Employers have realized many benefits from early-retirement programs. They can reduce personnel costs and improve the organization's cash flow by replacing retiring employees with lower-paid employees. Employers can even cut the total cost of a vacated position by dividing the retiree's duties among other employees. During hard economic times, severe layoffs and pay cuts may be avoided with early retirements. Eliminating jobs that have become unneeded because of technology is easier if some employees choose early retirement. Younger employees gain from early-retirement programs because new promotion opportunities are created. Participation in an early-retirement program must be voluntary in order to comply with the Age Discrimination in Employment Act, as discussed in Chapter 3.

A major disadvantage of window programs is that highly valued employees may choose to participate. Thus, the program must be carefully designed not to be too attractive to valued employees. Although window programs cost additional dollars to provide incentives for employees to retire early, properly designed programs can provide significant payroll reductions, as well as open up promotion opportunities for deserving younger employees.[15] However, the Age Discrimination Act makes it illegal for an early-retirement program to have as its *sole* purpose the opening of positions for younger employees.

When do most employees choose to retire? This decision has been found to be largely determined by four variables:[16]

1. Changes in the Social Security system and the value of its benefits.

2. Personal health.

3. General economic conditions (people retire earlier during good times).

4. Mandatory retirement laws or policies.

Therefore, the passage of the 1987 Age Discrimination in Employment Act (see Chapter 3), which eliminated employer-mandatory retirement policies, combined with a generally healthier work force and the change in the Social Security retirement age to sixty-seven (with full benefits), will likely cause the average retirement age of employees to increase during the 1990s.[17]

Pension Eligibility

Private pension plans have become one of the most sought-after as well as one of the most expensive employee benefits. But only in the last twenty-five to thirty years have employers felt an obligation to provide income to employees beyond their productive years. This obligation occurred largely as the result of a 1949 decision by the Supreme Court, *Inland Steel Company* v. *NLRB,* in which the Court declared pension plans to be mandatory collective bargaining subjects. In the early stages of the pension movement in the United States, this benefit was recognized as discretionary on the part of an employer and as a source of motivation for senior employees. By 1990 the Bureau of Labor Statistics estimated that 60 percent of all nonfarm employees were covered by a private pension plan. Likewise, the number of private pension plans throughout the United States has increased dramatically since the 1949 decision. Fewer than 1000 private pension plans were in operation in 1940; over 700,000 are in operation today.[18]

Vesting   Vesting refers to an employee's right to receive retirement benefits paid into a plan by an employer. A vested employee can leave an employer and still collect a pension on attaining retirement age. Employees always have a right to the contributions they have made; vesting refers only to the employer's contributions.

The Tax Reform Act of 1986 requires most employers to choose one of two vesting options: (1) 100 percent vesting after five years of service or (2) 20 percent vesting after three years and an additional 20 percent each year, reaching 100 percent after seven years.[19]

Contributing to pension plans does not guarantee benefits. It is estimated that more than 10 million American workers who actively pay into pension plans will never collect from them. For example, one woman worked for more than thirty years for companies with private pension plans. But at the end of that time she was not eligible to receive a single penny in retirement benefits because she had never become vested with an employer for whom she worked. She worked for Liggett & Meyers Tobacco Company in Richmond, Virginia, for twenty-three years, but only seven years counted toward the pension plan by the time the company moved its operation in 1970—not enough to qualify her to meet the minimum requirement of ten years. After several odd jobs, she worked for eight and a half years for the American Tobacco Company in Richmond, but again she had not worked enough years to become eligible to receive

company pension benefits. Therefore, at age fifty-three and after thirty-four years of work, she had no retirement income other than her Social Security.[20]

The reason so many American workers will not receive a private pension when they retire is simply that they leave an organization before becoming vested, that is, before meeting the organization's eligibility requirements. Many employees leave jobs frequently for various reasons during their productive years, and thus they miss being covered by any one company's pension plan. But for many other employees, loss of benefits is the result of a company that shuts down, lays off its workers, or dismisses workers before they become vested (see *HR in the News:* "Grapes of Wrath, 1993). A worker leaving behind a pension may forfeit thousands of dollars of retirement income. Sizable losses in vacation, insurance, and other benefits may also occur.[21]

Pension Plans

Employer-provided pension plans are designed to supplement the employee's Social Security benefits. Pension benefits, when added to Social Security costs, represent for employers the single most costly employee benefit. If an employer's pension plan qualifies under the Internal Revenue Code, the employer may deduct pension costs as a business expense and must meet the standards set by the Employee Retirement Income Security Act of 1974 (ERISA). The nature of a pension plan, or how good a pension plan is for employees, is determined by how the plan addresses several basic pension issues.

Supplemental or Flat Rate   Supplemental pension plans are tied to Social Security benefits. A supplemental pension plan provides retirees with a fixed level of retirement dollars, in addition to Social Security and a private pension. The intention is to have a guaranteed level of retirement benefits created by a pension that augments Social Security benefits.

Therefore, as Social Security benefits increase each year, the amount employers must pay in pension benefits decreases.

Because Social Security benefits rose rapidly in the 1970s and 1980s, *flat-rate pension plans* are becoming more common. The flat-rate pension guarantees employees a certain pension income based on years of service and level of pay. This amount is determined and paid by previous employers, regardless of any other income employees may receive in retirement. The flat-rate system is usually requested by unions.

Financing   Pension benefits received by employees are financed primarily through two plans. Under a **contributory plan** the employee and employer share the cost of pension benefits. The percentage contributed by the employer changes according to the type of contributory plan. A **noncontributory plan** is financed entirely by the employer. Employees and union representatives make strong arguments for noncontributory plans. They argue that because employers incur lower absenteeism and turnover costs with loyal employees who stay with the company due to the pension plan, the employer should pay the pension costs. Also, employers can charge their contributions to pension plans to the cost of doing business; therefore, employers do not pay the tax rate on pension costs that employees must pay. Employers, however, argue for a contributory plan because they feel that employees will value their pension plans more when they contribute something. Small employers believe that they cannot afford to provide pension plans when they must contribute to Social Security.

Funding Methods   There are four general methods of funding pension plans. Each method may provide a particular advantage to management; in general, the methods are trusted plans, current-expenditure plans, insured plans, and profit-sharing plans.

Trusted or **funded plans** are those for which employers have created a separate account for funds and invested dollars annually to provide the future retirement benefits for employees. Employers assume liability for the fund. The fund is usually administered by a bank or separate board, which makes decisions about the investment of the funds and the payment of retirement benefits. Usually, the fund is kept financially sound by an actuarial study of the estimated financial liability of the plan, as well as of its expected value of current assets. If the actuarial study determines that the fund does not have enough money to guarantee benefit payments to both present and past employees who have earned them, then the employer adds the additional money necessary to keep the fund financially sound. This review of actuarial soundness is normally done annually. In some years, if the number of retired employees decreases and the number of new employees changes, it may not be necessary for the employer to add any additional money to the fund; in other years, employers may have to add substantial amounts.

Current-expenditure plans treat the retirement benefits paid to previous employees as a current expense. Therefore, such a plan is known as a **nonfunded** or *pay-as-you-go* plan. Current-expenditure plans are not actuarially sound and guarantee no fund available to current employees for retirement benefits in later years. Yet, for many employers the possibility of funding a trusted plan is very small because such plans usually require a large amount of capital to begin. In the current-expenditure plan, the employer simply meets the yearly retirement benefits due its previous employees as it meets other expenses. The largest nonfunded plan in the world is the U.S. Social Security retirement system.

Insured plans are pension plans provided to employers by insurance companies. The insurance company usually treats the provisions of the pension plan for the employer as it would any other type of collective insurance. That is, the employer is required to pay a premium, for which the insurance company administers the plan, pays out all benefits due, and assumes future payment liability. Although the employer may pay more to the insurance company than might be necessary under a trusted plan, the expertise and experience of the insurance company may be worth the additional fee for the small or medium-sized employer.

Profit-sharing plans are funded pension plans, with the funds provided by a percentage of company profits. A profit-sharing plan is a compromise between a current-expenditure plan and a trusted plan. Management hopes employees will be more interested in the profitability of the company if their pensions share in the risk of doing business. Companies that experience stable profitability and growth will have little trouble funding a pension plan through a profit-sharing approach. But if profits decrease substantially or become nonexistent over several years, the plan may eventually become financially unsound. Sears, Roebuck & Company, as well as other firms in this country, have found profit-sharing pension plans to be quite successful.

Retirement Age   The age at which employees can begin collecting pension benefits is an important aspect of any pension plan. Many plans stipulate that a minimum age must be reached before collecting pension benefits; in most cases it is sixty-five, though sometimes this has been reduced to sixty or even fifty-five. Some companies offer supplemental retirement benefits to encourage early retirement. Others do not set a retirement age but require a specific number of years of service, for example, "twenty and out" or "thirty and out." The advantage of pensions specifying a service requirement is that employees may collect one employer's pension while working for another employer and building up a second retirement income. For example, an employee who begins working for an employer at age twenty may be eligible to collect retirement

benefits at age forty and then begin a second career with a different employer. At retirement from the second job, this employee will receive two full pensions, in addition to Social Security, and is sometimes called a *double dipper*.

Benefit Formula   The many different private pension plans in use can generally be divided into two categories:[22]

1. *Defined benefit plans.* Most retirement plans in the United States are described as **defined benefit retirement plans**. These plans provide a specific monthly benefit determined by a definite formula. The retirement benefit is usually a function of the employee's average earnings over a specific number of years multiplied by the number of years of service (see Figure 12-1).

2. *Defined contribution plans.* In contrast to a defined benefit plan, which provides a known benefit, **defined contribution retirement plans** provide a fixed or known contribution. The contribution is allocated annually to the employee's account, which accrues investment earnings. The account is usually converted into an annuity on the employee's retirement. Employees have limited security because their future benefits are related to the employer's ability to continue making contributions.

Defined contribution plans are always fully funded because they promise only to pay dollars that have accrued in the individual's account including investment gains or losses. Profit-sharing and stock-bonus plans are common examples of defined contribution plans. Defined benefit plans require actuarial calculations to determine what amount the employer needs to contribute to the account to keep it fully funded and thus able to meet promised benefits.

The defined benefit plan is the best means of satisfying the mutual needs of employers and employees, according to Kathleen P. Utzoff, Executive Director of the Pension Benefit

FIGURE 12-1 Determining retirement benefits through a defined benefit plan.

Example I
Base pay = Average pay for last three years worked.
25 years service × $18,000 base pay × 2.0% = $9,000/year or $750/month
Example II
Base pay = Average pay for total years worked.
25 years service × $8,000 base pay × 2.0% = $4,000/year or $333/month
Example III
Base pay = Average pay for total years worked.
35 years service × $6,000 base pay × 2.0% = $3,600/year or $300/month

Guarantee Corporation. The defined benefit plan provides employees a specific retirement income that is protected against the volatility of the investment market, which many people more clearly understand after the stock market fall of October 19, 1987. Also, employees can easily understand and plan on a specified level of income on retirement. With a defined contribution plan, employees cannot easily predict their retirement income and may not realize how susceptible their benefits are to fluctuations in the financial markets.[23]

Every defined benefit plan is based on a formula that determines the benefits employees will receive on retirement. The amount of benefits received by employees is usually determined by multiplying the average pay figure by the years of service and then multiplying that product by a stipulated benefit percentage, such as 2 or 3 percent. Normally, systems use an average of the last three or five years of the employee's career as the average pay figure because inflation substantially lowers the average pay figure and, therefore, retirement benefits. As the years of service increase, the benefit amount increases to a maximum at thirty or thirty-five years of service.

Figure 12-1 illustrates how various average pay figures affect the determination of an individual's retirement benefits. In the first example, the employee's base pay is the average pay for the last three years worked. This amounts to $18,000, not an unusually high salary. An employee with twenty-five years' service and a 2 percent rate is eligible for $9000 a year in retirement benefits, or $750 per month.

If, however, the average pay for total years worked is used, as in the second example, the retirement benefit is substantially changed. Due to inflation, the employee's average pay for a total of twenty-five years is only $8000. Therefore, with the same percentage and service figures, the retirement benefit is only $4000 per year, or $333 per month. If that same employee had worked the previous thirty-five years, the average pay is even lower due to inflation.

Employee Retirement Income Security Act

Prior to 1974, private pension systems were criticized because in too many cases they were not providing employees with sufficient funds to live comfortably in retirement. In addition, many systems were cheating employees out of pension dollars to which they were entitled. Finally, some mismanaged pension systems did not increase the value of their benefit portfolios. In response to these complaints, Congress approved the Pension Reform Act of 1974, officially designated the **Employee Retirement Income Security Act (ERISA)**, or Public Law 93-406. Congress accomplished the most complete overhaul of pension and benefit rules in U.S. history. The reform act affects virtually every pension and benefit plan. Responsibility for administering the complex, new employee benefit program is shared by the U.S. Treasury Department and the U.S. Department of Labor.[24]

The lengthy and complicated law primarily affects the following aspects of pension planning:

1. Employers are required to count toward vesting all service from age eighteen and to count toward earned benefits all earnings from age twenty-one. (Prior to the Retirement Equity Act of 1984, accrual toward vesting began at age twenty-two and toward earnings at age twenty-five.)

2. Employers must choose from among two minimum vesting standards.

3. Each year employers must file reports of their pension plans with the U.S. Secretary of Labor for approval. New plans must be submitted for approval within 120 days of enactment.

4. The Pension Benefit Guarantee Corporation (PBGC) was established within the Department of Labor to encourage voluntary employee pension continuance when changing employment. This is accomplished by providing **portability** — the right of an employee to transfer tax-free pension benefits from one employer to another. In addition, through employer premiums, the PBGC ensures that benefits are paid to participants should a pension plan terminate.

5. Pension plan members are permitted to leave the work force for up to five consecutive years without losing service credit and are allowed up to one year of maternity or paternity leave without losing service credit.[25]

ERISA substantially reduced the number and scope of pension issues. The law has been criticized by employers because it is quite complex and may have encouraged some employers to provide no retirement plan at all.[26]

Unfortunately one risk not included in ERISA occurs when a big corporation, such as

GM (see accompanying *HR In The News:* "Retirees At Risk"), projects high hopes on pension investments that would minimize pension contributions. However, the high returns of the 1980s have disappeared in the 1990s, leaving many pensions woefully underfunded (see *HR in the News:* "Retirees at Risk"). New rules were issued by the Financial Accounting Standards Board to reflect more fully the corporations' financial statements and the costs of pension obligations. One new provision was the requirement that pension funds use "reasonable and acceptable" assumptions for their rate of return on investments. So far, however, many companies have not reduced their overall rate-of-return assumptions.[27]

Unisex Pensions

In July 1983 the U.S. Supreme Court, in a landmark decision, sent shock waves through the insurance and pension industries. The Court ruled that federal laws that prohibit sex discrimination in employment also prohibit sex discrimination in retirement plans. Pension plans must provide equal retirement payments to men and women. The ruling did soften the impact of the Court's decision on pension systems by denying retroactive relief to women currently receiving pensions and allowing for an August 1983 starting date for contributions to retirement plans to provide for equal payments. To comply with the decision, thousands of employers are faced with four options: (1) raise women's benefits to equal men's, (2) reduce men's benefits to equal women's, (3) strike an average between the two, or (4) eliminate lifetime annuities, which guarantee retirees a monthly income for as long as they live and instead give employees their benefits in a lump sum when they retire.

Why had employers previously paid men higher benefits than women? The life expectancy of female employees is longer than that of male employees. Therefore, the insurance companies must pay them retirement benefits for a longer period of time. If, then, male and

Retirees at Risk

Henry Bell can't wait to retire. After 27 years as an assembler as a General Motors Corporation factory in Baltimore, he says he is looking forward to a worry-free life: "I just plan on enjoying my grandchildren and doing work around the house."

But Mr. Bell might feel a bit uneasy if he knew about the gamble GM is taking with his pension money. Like many big companies, GM has been holding down the amount of money it sets aside for retirees by betting that it can reap high rates of return on its pension investments.

In this arcane world of pension accounting, this is the equivalent of driving without a safety belt. And last year, pension funds hit a bump in the road. After years of big profits on their pension investments, low interest rates reduced many pension funds' investment earnings last year to levels far below expectations.

GM officials, for example, concede that they had assumed an 11% rate of return but earned only 6.4%. Moreover, low interest rates are inflating GM's obligations to its retirees. The gap between what the auto maker has promised its retirees and the amount it has set aside for them totals $14 billion, compared with a total obligation valued at $56.84 billion at the end of 1992. And the company says the shortfall could jump to $19 billion this year because of even lower interest rates.

Corporations say their rate-of-return assumptions are long-term estimates that need not reflect day-to-day zigzags in the capital markets and are soundly based on historical experience. Not true, respond critics. "Some pension funds are sticking their heads in the sand and hoping the problem will just go away," says Lawrence Bader, a vice-president at Salomon Brothers. The ability to manipulate their assumptions allows them to avoid properly funding pension plans.

SOURCE: Adapted from Susan Pulliam, "Hopeful Assumptions Let Firms Minimize Pension Contributions," *Wall Street Journal* (September 2, 1993): A1.

---

female employees earn the same total dollar value of benefits, and if female employees will collect those benefits over a longer period of time, their monthly payments must be less. Natalie Norris, however, did not accept this reasoning and time-honored practice—so she sued on the basis of sex discrimination and took her case all the way to the U.S. Supreme Court. Norris believed that since she had made the same monthly payments as her male counterparts, she should not accept a lower monthly benefit simply because she was a female. The U.S. Supreme Court agreed, and millions of American women will benefit from the historic 1983 decision.[28]

Section 401(k) of the Internal Revenue Code

Many small or medium-sized organizations offer **401(k) retirement plans**. Such plans are generally inexpensive and easily understood. Section 401(k) of the Internal Revenue Code first became effective in 1980. It provides for company-sponsored IRS-qualified retirement plans. Usually such plans allow employees to defer a portion of their salary as a payroll deduction and thus reduce federal and state tax liabilities. In addition, most employers increase the incentive for employees to save in 401(k) plans by offering a matching contribution, commonly twenty-five to fifty cents for each employee dollar saved.[29]

The plans have become popular with employees because they can be tailored to meet individual needs. The employee decides how much is deposited in the plan and when to change the level of contributions. Younger employees can use the plan to save for a car or home, whereas older employees can use it as a retirement income supplement. In comparison to traditional savings plans, 401(k) plans allow employees to make pretax instead of after-tax contributions. But access to the funds is limited to age fifty-nine and a half, separation from the employer, or to cover financial hardship. The dollar savings of the pretax 401(k) plan can be substantial but must be weighed against the disadvantage of the limited access.[30]

Under the 1986 Tax Reform Act, the maximum salary deferral to a 401(k) plan is $7000 a year, to be increased as inflation increases. The act also requires 401(k) plans to meet a nondiscrimination test that prohibits highly paid employees from taking substantially greater advantage of this tax shelter than lower-paid employees. Employees' ability to make hardship withdrawals from 401(k) accounts is limited under the 1986 act to their own salary deferrals (not employer contributions), and withdrawals are subject to a 10 percent income tax.[31]

One successful 401(k) plan is in Phoenix, Arizona, at MeraBank. The previous pension plan had been voluntary, but virtually no one participated. The solution was Profit Plus, a new retirement plan. The new 401(k) plan provided quicker vesting, a guaranteed annual employer contribution of 2 percent of wages,

an employer matching contribution of 50 percent of the first 6 percent of employee contribution, and a pretax 401(k) plan match. The 401(k) match was contingent on the firm's return on equity. The employees especially liked the guaranteed 2 percent employer contribution and the fact that they could increase the employer's contribution by increasing their own contribution. MeraBank used written materials, employee meetings, and a video presentation to communicate the new plan. More than 70 percent of the eligible employees enrolled in the new plan, and an opinion survey indicated that they were very satisfied with it. MeraBank reduced the employer's contribution by nearly a million dollars in the first year compared to the previous plan.[32]

PAID TIME OFF

Employees expect to be paid for holidays, vacations, and miscellaneous days they do not work—**paid time off work**. Employers' policies covering such benefits vary greatly. The most common examples of time off with pay are the following:[33]

Holidays	Maternity leave
Vacations	Sick leave
Jury duty	Wellness leave
Election official	Time off to vote
Witness in court	Blood donation
Civic duty	Lunch, rest, and
Military duty	wash-up periods
Funeral leave	Personal leave
Family leave	Sabbatical leave
Marriage leave	

Vacations

Employers have long believed that vacations increase employees' productivity on returning to the job. Employees who take strenuous vacations may not receive physical rest from the job but usually receive a mental break from the workplace. Today virtually all organizations have a schedule of paid vacations based on years of service with the organization. A typical system is shown in Table 12-4.

Employers often require employees to stagger their vacation dates throughout the warmer months to provide the organization with a steady flow of goods or services. Manufacturing and production industries may shut down during the summer, requiring all employees to take their vacations during the shutdown while the company retools or makes necessary repairs within the plant. The steel industry has utilized an unusual form of paid vacation termed a *sabbatical.* Sabbatical vacations are given to employees every five years to provide them with thirteen weeks of continuous paid vacation. Employees may not take second jobs during their thirteen-week vacations. A sabbatical vacation gives employees in particularly unhealthful and tedious work environments time away for a complete rest.

Holidays

Following World War II, unions and employees increased their demands for paid holidays; previously, many holidays were unpaid. The average number of paid holidays in 1950 was three; thirty years later, employees in most organizations received eight holidays. Employees required to work on normal holidays are often given double or triple pay. In the chemical, hotel, and restaurant industries, which operate every day, employees may get double pay for working on holidays, as well as another day off during the following week. Normally,

when a holiday falls during an employee's paid vacation, the employee is scheduled for one extra day's vacation.

The *floating holiday,* which was first provided in the rubber industry, has increased in popularity as an employee demand. Floating holidays allow the selection of the day the holiday is observed to be left to the discretion of the employee or to be mutually agreed on by management and the employee. Employers have resisted the concept of a floating holiday on the theory that there is little difference between a floating holiday and an additional vacation day.

Many employers observe the practice of *Monday holidays* begun by the federal government. The observance of Monday holidays is, in theory, designed to give employees more three-day weekends during the year for additional rest and relaxation. But in practice the Monday holiday has increased the chief administrative problem caused by paid holidays—absenteeism. Employees can easily see that being absent on Friday or Tuesday would provide them a four-day weekend, or almost a complete week's vacation. To minimize this problem and other holiday-related absenteeism problems, a written personnel policy should provide for the following:

- *Eligibility.* Requiring employees to work the last working day before the holiday and the first scheduled working day after the holiday helps to minimize the problem of employees' stretching holiday periods.

- *Holiday rate.* If employees work on what is normally a paid holiday, they should receive premium pay.

- *Paid holidays.* The days determined to be paid holidays should be specified in writing, in advance.

- *Holidays on nonwork days.* If a paid holiday falls on a nonwork day, such as Sunday, for example, will employees be given another day off? If so, which one?

Table 12-4 A Typical Schedule of Paid Vacations

Service	Vacation
1 year	1 week
2–5 years	2 weeks
6–10 years	3 weeks
11–15 years	4 weeks
16–20 years	5 weeks
Over 20 years	6 weeks

Personal Absences

Employees may receive full pay for a number of personal absences, such as a summons by federal, state, or local courts to serve as jurors or witnesses. Employees are not counted absent and are paid during the period covered by the summons. Some employers require that employees reimburse them for any pay received from the court. When a death occurs in the immediate family (spouse, child, parent, sister, brother, or in-laws), employees are eligible to receive three to five days of funeral leave. Usually employees are not charged with vacation or other paid leave, nor do they lose any pay during funeral leave.

Military Leave

Military leave is provided for members of U.S. armed forces reserve units. While most employers do not charge leave time against vacation time, most also do not pay employees for military leave. Some employers do give employees full pay during military leave, and many employers pay the difference between the military pay and the employee's take-home pay.

Sick Leave

Sick leave is generally accrued by employees at a specific rate, for example, one day per month from the first day of employment. Many employers allow unused sick leave to be accumulated without any maximum. A doctor's certificate is usually not necessary for short-term illnesses, but extended sick leave normally requires medical evidence. Sick-leave pay provides income during personal or family illness. Sick leave normally should be taken only for illness; however, it is often used for personal reasons other than illness.

Sick-Leave Plan Alternatives Reducing sick leave has become a high priority to most HR directors. Both the work disruption and the cost of sick leave can be of concern to top management and supervisors. The good intention of a typical sick-leave program often becomes subject to abuse by employees. Paid sick leave is often used for nonillnesses such as personal problems, weather, personal business, child care, hangover, transportation problems, and so on. The costs to the organization that are associated with sick-leave abuse include the following:

- Salary and benefits paid to the absent employee.
- Extra work for other employees who "cover" for the absent employee, or wages paid to temporary or overtime help.
- Loss in productivity caused by less experienced personnel performing the work.
- Lower morale of employees who resent doing the work of others.

To deal with these abuses, employers have developed **sick-leave plan alternatives**. One of the first published alternatives to the traditional sick-leave plan was developed by a hospital. Their *paid-leave plan* combines the vacation days, holidays, and average number of sick days per employee into a total to be used at the discretion of the employee. The hospital's absenteeism was reduced considerably, and hospital employees preferred the paid-leave plan because they had increased control over their work schedules.[34]

Sick-leave banks provide another alternative to traditional programs. This arrangement allows employees to pool some portion of their sick days into a common fund. For example, employees who currently receive ten sick days per year are given only seven days, with the remaining three days placed in a combined employee pool. The use of the pooled sick days is determined by a panel of employees who review requests from employees. Thus employees can be covered against long-term illnesses by the pool, whereas before they would likely have used up most of their personal sick days and been left without income. Peer pressure is used to control abuse by employees. The company benefits because the average number of sick days actually used by employees in a year decreases because the employee panel desires to build up the pool for legitimate needs.

Well-pay programs have become increasingly popular alternatives to the traditional sick-leave plan. The concept is to provide positive reinforcement to employees for not being sick or absent. Employees are either given a bonus in dollars or paid time off for each week or month they are not absent. A typical well-pay program includes the following:

- Discontinuance of sick-leave accrual.
- No pay for the first day of an employee's sick leave.
- A bonus paid to employees not absent at any time for four consecutive weeks, plus additional bonus for consecutive four-week periods without an absence.
- Disability pay for illnesses beyond one day for eligible employees.

Personal leave is an alternative that allows employees fewer days of leave without specifying why they miss work.

Premium Pay

Many employers and virtually all labor agreements provide for special payments to employees for working under undesirable circumstances. The most common **premium pay** is for the Saturday or Sunday hours worked that are not part of the normally scheduled workweek. Other common examples of premium pay include *overtime* rates for time worked over eight hours per day and *shift differentials,* which provide higher hourly rates to employees who work the least desirable hours.

In the manufacturing and construction industries, **reporting pay** is the minimum pay guaranteed employees who report for work even though work is not available. For example, if employees have not been instructed by the company not to report for work within four hours before the start of their shift, they are guaranteed four hours of pay even if work is not available because of equipment failure.

Supplemental pay given to employees called back to work before they were scheduled to report is called *call-in pay.* Thus, employees who do not take their complete rest between scheduled workdays receive a lump-sum bonus for being called in before their next normal reporting time.

Dismissal pay, or *severance pay,* is usually awarded to employees who have been permanently severed from their jobs through no fault of their own. Such premium pay is most common in manufacturing or unionized industries. Dismissal pay includes payments to workers who lose their jobs because of technological change, plant closings, plant mergers, or disability. Employees who quit their jobs or refuse to take other jobs within the company are not covered. Nor does dismissal pay cover employees who are terminated for unsatisfactory performance. The amount of dismissal pay employees receive is determined by their years of service and past salary. The purpose of dismissal pay is to cushion the loss of income of loyal employees.

Insurance

Many employers provide employees with life and medical insurance plans and pay part of the plans' costs. Health insurance packages normally cover group life, accident and illness, hospitalization, and accidental death or dismemberment. The health and life insurance programs are usually part of a **group insurance plan**, which permits the business and the employee to benefit from lower rates based on the total value of the group policy.

Health Insurance

In 1910, Montgomery Ward & Company offered its workers one of the first group health insurance plans—and helped launch a revolu-

Why Some Workers Are Falling Behind in Benefits

Lou Capozzola worked 10 years at *Sports Illustrated,* living the life of a gadfly, jetting from Super Bowls to the Olympics as a lighting specialist. He was on the road 180 days a year, working 15- to 20-hour days.

Bad news came in 1990 when he was told his job was eliminated in an effort to cut costs. However, the company would subcontract the work out to independent contractors and, if he so desired, [he] might want to bid for the work. He did and ended up being selected. As a subcontractor, Capozzola's annual regular wages were cut in half (to $20,000), over-time wages were cut by 66 percent, and benefits were cut 100 percent. The benefits package included medical insurance and retirement and was worth approximately $20,000 per year.

The benefit cuts were the hardest, especially losing retirement and health care coverage. Contract workers like Capozzola have to scramble around to locate health care providers who would cover them and their families.

SOURCE: Adapted from "Workers Are Forced to Take More Jobs with Few Benefits," *The Wall Street Journal* (March 11, 1993): A1.

tion. One of the most common employee benefits available, its purpose is to help covered employees maintain their standard of living when unexpected health-related problems occur. Today, employer-provided insurance dominates American medicine.

Companies are paying more than $200 billion a year to buy care for 150 million workers and their dependents, or 60 percent of the population.[35] The system worked fine until medical costs exploded in the 1980s, forcing employers to tweak and trim benefits in a desperate move to cut their payouts. Many organizations are downsizing and restructuring, letting thousands of people go, to ease their benefit plan burdens. In the United States, most people depend on their employers to make group health insurance available. Unfor-

tunately, some employers are using contract workers, and this group is almost always without health care coverage, as the accompanying *HR in the News:* "Why Some Workers Are Falling Behind in Benefits" illustrates.

A variety of health-care insurance plans covering medical bills and related costs are often provided, in addition to such related health-care benefits as Medicare provided by Social Security, workers' compensation, and in-house medical services. Most employers provide for hospitalization and major medical insurance.[36]

Hospitalization plans normally take one of two forms: commercial insurance or a service plan. *Commercial insurance* involves a contract between an employer and an insurance company that provides fixed cash benefits for hospital room and board, as well as for other hospital charges. The employer agrees to pay the premiums to cover the insurance provided by contract, and the insurance company assumes the liability of those employees who qualify to receive the benefits. Commercial insurance is paid directly to the insured company, which then reimburses the hospital for the cost. Therefore, a plan can be tailored to the needs of the company as specified by an agreement.

Under a **fee-for-service plan**, a nonprofit organization such as Blue Cross–Blue Shield provides coverage for hospital services when needed, including room, board, and other costs. The Blue Cross portion of the plan covers the hospital cost; the Blue Shield portion covers physicians' fees. The primary advantage of a hospital service plan is that hospitals offer lower rates to the Blue Cross system. But such plans are usually less flexible than commercial insurance. The employer and union negotiators must choose from among the options available.[37]

Many health-care plans provide for a $200 deductible to be paid by the employee and a maximum percentage, often 80 percent, to be paid by the employer for major medical expenses. Most plans also provide for a maximum figure. Because such benefits usually overlap with benefits provided by other sources, such as workers' compensation and other insurance, the insurance plan must specify whether benefit payments are made in lieu of any other benefits received or whether benefits received from other plans are to be deducted from the amount the employee is entitled to under the health insurance plan.

Many employers think that health insurance costs are out of control. The biggest supplier to General Motors is not U.S. Steel (now USX) but Blue Cross–Blue Shield. The health-care industry has become a supplier that determines its own supply of doctors, prescribes its own demand for services, and controls its own price levels. Over 50 percent of the nation's total health-care costs are provided through health insurance programs paid for by employers.

Health care reform, at the time of this writing, is still being debated in Congress. It is hard to imagine exactly what the new legislation will look like. Experts are predicting that there will be more "managed competition." It is also expected that consumers will sign up at local "health alliances," large purchasing groups set up by states to negotiate coverage with networks of providers. The new system will, most certainly, involve more government regulation. Critics are concerned that the private sector is better at reining in costs and can do better than the government. And, the critics add, they do not want their employees forced into alliances that have not yet been tested.[38]

Alternatives to Traditional Insurance

More employers each year decide to seek alternatives to the traditional commercial insurance and fee-for-service methods of providing employees' health insurance. Annual double-digit increases in employer premiums and the emergence of sound alternatives have led many employers to consider other ways of providing for health care. In general, these alternatives are called **managed-care systems** in which the employer, directly or through a third party, develops employee health-care delivery systems by contracting directly with doctors, hospitals, and other medical facilities.

The employer can then better manage health-care costs by directly monitoring the services provided employees and their dependents; by requiring higher deductibles, copayments, and second opinions before surgery; and by using outpatient facilities for specified procedures. A large portion of the cost savings is achieved by requiring the use of certain doctors and hospitals that have agreed to provide service at negotiated rates. Thus the employer is able to control health-care costs by decreasing the flexibility in the delivery system and limiting the employees' choice of doctors and facilities to those included in negotiated agreements. As Figure 12-2 indicates, the greatest flexibility is generally found in systems that are the most expensive because individual choice and negotiation of the cost of service are generally more expensive than predetermined costs and larger-quantity services found in managed-care systems. The three most common managed-care methods are self-funding, preferred provider organizations, and health maintenance organizations.

Self-Funding One of the most effective methods of controlling group health costs is employer *self-funding.* Employers who switched from an insurance company to self-funding report, on average, cost savings of about 7 percent.[39] Self-funding allows a company to pay health claims out of its own funds; the employer acts as the insurance company. Improving the cash flow, reducing the costs of premiums and taxes, and eliminating the third party (insurance company) are the primary advantages of self-funding programs, which include the following: (1) the employer pays employees' claims directly from revenues, like

any other expense; (2) a trust is created under Section 501(c)(9) of the Internal Revenue Code. In the latter case, funds held in the trust accumulate tax-free earnings, which are used to pay claims.[40]

Health Maintenance Organizations After years of frustration with typical health insurance plans offered to employers and employees, Congress in 1973 passed the Health Maintenance Organization Act. The act sets standards for private individuals to qualify for federal financial assistance in the creation of a **health maintenance organization (HMO).** The federal government provides financial assistance to establish an HMO as a means of providing employees with an alternative to other health-care delivery systems. Once HMOs are established, they should become self-sufficient through income received from the employees and employers they serve. Generally, HMOs provide employees with more comprehensive care, particularly preventive medicine, which includes normal visits to a physician. This care is not included in most private health-care plans. HMOs are designed to provide total health-care maintenance to the employee and family at a lower annual cost. At first, private insurance companies such as Blue Cross–Blue Shield and Delta Dental were not affected by

FIGURE 12-2 Alternative health-care systems.

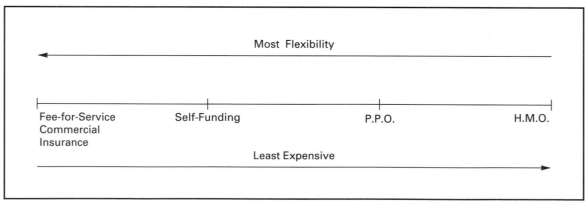

HMOs. However, HMOs are steadily increasing and have made a significant impact in the employee health-care field.

According to the 1973 act, employers with twenty-five or more employees who currently offer a medical benefit plan must offer the HMO option to employees if a federally approved HMO exists in the local area. Primarily a prepaid group health insurance plan, the HMO provides for the family's total health care. An HMO is a local hospital and clinic to which employees may take their families for routine checkups, shots, and treatment for injuries or illnesses. There are a number of advantages to the use of HMOs:[41]

- *Prepayment* for services at a previously negotiated rate.
- *Financial incentives* for providers to deliver care at minimum costs.
- *Preventive care,* including immunizations, well-child care, physical exams, and tests.
- *Administration by the provider* instead of a claim-review process that is common in fee-for-service plans.

HMOs are not without their disadvantages. The major problem in employees' acceptance of HMOs is the limited choice of physicians. Some HMOs require that employees and their families choose HMO member physicians. Many people feel more comfortable with physicians they have known for years and are relatively unwilling to change. Cost is another factor. Many times the monthly HMO premium is more expensive than the cost of a private health insurance plan. While the annual HMO cost of health care to the employee might be less because it provides total health care, some employees think only of the higher monthly premium and are discouraged.

The lack of HMO facilities has also limited employee enrollment. Since HMOs are a relatively new concept in most cities, there are far fewer HMOs than physicians' offices and hospitals. Therefore, HMOs are less convenient because they may not be located in an employee's neighborhood. However, this situation is quickly changing as more HMOs are formed across the United States.

Preferred Provider Organizations   A newer health-care insurance strategy is the **preferred provider organization (PPO)**, which relies on increased competition in the health-care industry. PPOs involve employers, patients, hospitals and other health-care providers, and insurance carriers. The PPO procedure is simple. A contract is negotiated among the employer, insurance carrier, and various health-care providers, such as hospitals, physicians, and dentists. The contract provides for certain services to be delivered at a discount for a guaranteed increase in patients, with rapid repayment of all bills. Employees are given financial incentives to use those specific health-care providers but are not required to do so. This freedom of choice is critical to the success of the PPO. PPOs have generated a great deal of controversy. In general the advantages of PPOs include the following:[42]

- A panel of "preferred" quality doctors and hospitals.
- Negotiated group fees that are lower than normal rates.
- Flexibility in choosing from a list of providers; no "locking in" of employees.
- Financial incentives to employees such as higher deductibles or copayments.
- An out-of-plan option that allows employees, at significant cost, to choose a source outside the preferred panel.

The disadvantages include the following:

- Not as cost-effective as HMOs.
- Not subject to the federal regulatory requirements and checks that HMOs must meet.
- May reduce competition in an area by freezing out nonparticipants.

COBRA

The **Consolidated Omnibus Budget Reconciliation Act (COBRA)** was passed by Congress in 1986. The law provides for the continuation of medical and dental insurance for employees, spouses, and dependents in the event of termination of employment, death of the employee, divorce, legal separation, or reduction of hours, which results in the loss of health-plan eligibility. This coverage must be elected by the employee or dependents, and they must pay the full cost of the plan selected. The intent of this law is to alleviate gaps in health-care coverage by allowing the employee or beneficiary to elect to continue medical and/or dental insurance.

Employers must notify employees and/or spouses of their COBRA rights within 60 days after their employment separation. The extended health coverage must be offered for a maximum of eighteen or thirty-six months, depending on the qualifying circumstances (e.g., reason for separation from employment). The same coverage that the employee and/or dependent received before the employment separation must be offered. If the individual chooses to take extended coverage, he or she must provide 102 percent (2 percent for administrative costs) of the costs.

An employer who fails to inform, in writing, an eligible person of his or her COBRA rights may be liable for resulting medical costs. In one such case, *Gardner* v. *Rainbow Lodge, Inc.* (D.C. Texas, 1990), a judge awarded $10,500 to a waiter who was not informed of his COBRA rights. The waiter had been fired from a restaurant after it was learned that he had AIDS.

Group Dental, Legal, and Vision Insurance

Major group insurance plans are often provided by employers that would not have been provided only a few years ago. Few employers used to provide dental, legal, or auto insurance for employees. Such insurance plans have become common, and they are highly sought by employees. Comprehensive dental benefits have been developed to provide protection against the cost of basic types of dental care. Such plans include (1) schedule plans, (2) comprehensive plans, and (3) combination plans.[43] *Schedule plans* have no deductible and provide specific payments for each procedure covered. *Comprehensive plans* require an initial deductible and then provide a fixed percentage payment of covered expenses. Most *combination plans* provide a fixed fee schedule for routine dental procedures and a deductible on other procedures, with a coinsurance clause requiring the covered employee to pay a percentage of the fee.[44]

The provision of full legal services through negotiated group plans is relatively new. During the early 1970s, prepaid legal services first became common through a Supreme Court decision that upheld such a plan and declared such legal expenses to be nontaxable. Two types of prepaid legal plans are commonly negotiated. One is a so-called open panel, which allows the employee to select any attorney who will perform the service at a stated fee. The other type is a so-called closed panel, which requires employees to use specific attorneys. Most plans require the employee to pay part of the annual fee. Employees usually prefer the open panel because they can use their own attorneys. Companies, however, prefer closed panels, which can be more easily administered.

Routine eye examinations, glasses, and contact lenses are usually included in provisions for vision care. Employees may be given the choice of doctors or may be limited to certain ones who are retained under contract.

EMPLOYEE SERVICES

Employee services include a variety of employee benefits. Organizations vary greatly in the services they offer and the service costs they pay. Employee services have been developed to increase employee loyalty to organizations and decrease absenteeism and turnover.

For example, employees in the greater Los Angeles basin are accustomed to one- to two-hour one-way commutes each day. To help employees ease their "California commuter blues," Cal Comp, a computer graphics manufacturer in Anaheim, offers a unique employee service—an audiocassette program. An extensive library of tapes, from self-help to classic books, is available to employees. Funded by the HR department, the program is managed by an outside firm.[45]

Child-Care Programs

One of the rapidly growing employer services is the provision of child-care programs. (See *HR in the News:* "The Mommy Track.")

The recent growth of employee interest in employer-provided child care is enhanced by Sections 125 and 129 of the Internal Revenue Service Code. Under these sections, employers may provide employees the ability to pay for child care with pretax dollars. This enables employees to save up to 40 percent of their child-care expenses.

The history of employer-sponsored child care (or day care) in the United States began in the nineteenth century. As early as 1854 there was some employer involvement in child care.

The textile industry in the early to mid-1900s sponsored many centers as it greatly expanded its largely female work force.[46] But industrial interest elsewhere did not materialize until the 1940s, when World War II forced millions of married women into the labor force. That period's Lanham Act provided government financial support for over 2800 day-care centers. But when the war ended, so did federal support, forcing the closing of centers; many working wives returned to domestic work.[47] Interest continued to be low until the 1960s, when tax laws and social attitudes made child care appear to be a profitable and responsible employee service. But the 1970s saw many of the new centers of the 1960s close. Reported reasons for closing included high expense (particularly for on-site facilities), administrative problems, and—most important—not enough employee use.[48]

However, by 1985, more than half of all women with a child under age six were working, and the number of employer-sponsored child-care programs is growing to meet the demand. Employers find it increasingly difficult to resist the pressure to implement child-care programs, particularly as more women move into executive and managerial roles and can influence the decision-making process.[49] What are the best employers for working mothers? See Figure 12-3.

FIGURE 12-3 Companies with benefits for working mothers.

Top Ten Companies for Working Mothers (listed alphabetically)

Apple Computer, Cupertino, CA
Beth Israel Hospital, Boston, MA
DuPont, Wilmington, DE
Fel-Pro, Skokie, IL
Hoffmann-La Roche, Nutley, NJ
IBM, Armonk, NY
Merck, Rahway, NJ
Morrison & Foerster, San Francisco
SAS Institute, Cary, NC
Syntex, Palo Alto, CA

Criteria: Salary; advancement opportunity; child care; benefits package, including maternity leave, parental leave, and adoption aid; flexible schedules; part-time work; job sharing; and support for the elderly.

SOURCE: Adapted from *Working Mother* (October 1989).

The Mommy Track

Felice Schwartz, founder of Catalyst, a New York–based research organization, went much further than most supporters of employer-provided child care. Her article, "Management Women and the New Facts of Life," which appeared in *Harvard Business Review,* generated a great deal of controversy by suggesting that (1) the cost of employing women is greater than the cost of employing men because of birth and child raising and (2) employers should provide more flexible employment opportunities. Schwartz further suggested that employers offer women a choice of two tracks; a "fast track" for women who put their career first and a "mommy track" for women who want flexibility in their career to accommodate family needs.[1]

The significant reaction to the Schwartz article from the public and press may have been due to several factors. First, she raised the possibility that career mothers "can't have it all"; second, employers will be forced to make accommodations for career mothers; and third, where is the "daddy track"? Fathers do make significant accommodations in their careers for the best interests of their families—turning down promotions that require travel or relocation, leaving work at 5:00 P.M. but taking home work to do after the children are in bed, scheduling work around family needs, and so on.[2]

Despite growing pressure to provide child-care opportunities, many employees

---

At least five different approaches to child care are offered by employers. Each offers certain advantages and varying costs:[50]

1. *On-site programs.* Large employers, particularly in the health-care industry, can offer to build a facility on the premises or nearby, which allows employees to bring their children to work and visit them during lunch. On-site programs, due to high costs, may only be offered by larger employers. The employer and employee, however, usually share the expense.

2. *Flexible benefits.* Employers will provide, as one flexible benefit option, money to employees to reimburse (voucher systems) existing child-care programs. Employers who do not need child care can spend their dollars on other benefits. This is the fastest-growing approach to child care.

3. *Referral centers.* The employer contracts with a firm that maintains information on child-care facilities and assists employees in finding suitable service. While employers often pay the referral fee, they usually do not pay any of the child-care expenses. This can be the lowest-cost approach.

4. *Consortium of employers.* Several organizations located together (in an industrial park or shopping center) pool their resources to purchase and manage a child-care center for their employees. The advantages are similar to those of an on-site facility.

still believe that they cannot afford to offer the service. A national study by the U.S. Department of Health and Human Services found, however, that the benefits of 95 percent of the child-care programs outweigh the costs. One employer, Union Bank, an employer of 1200 people in Monterey, California, with 170 branches, documented that belief as follows:[3]

- *Start-up costs* Included were $430,000 in an on-site building and fixed assets to be recovered in five years and $105,000 first-year operating subsidy. Direct savings included at least $138,000 due to reduced absenteeism and turnover per year for a payback period of less than four years.

- *Employee morale* Before-and-after surveys indicated reduced tardiness and maternal leave time.

- *Effective recruitment* 61 percent of job applicants cited the on-site center as a reason for accepting the job.

- *Supervisor support* Supervisors reported that their own morale and that of their employees had increased due to the center—and morale was high to begin with.

SOURCES: [1]Felice Schwartz, "Management Women and the New Facts of Life," *Harvard Business Review* (January–February 1989): 65–76.
[2]Douglas T. Hall, "Moving Beyond the 'Mommy Track': An Organization Changes Approach," *Personnel* (December 1989): 23–29.
[3]C. Ransom, P. Aschbacker, and S. Burud, "The Returns in the Child-Care Investment," *Personnel Administrator* 10 (October 1989): 54–58.

5. *Public–private partnership.* Cities and counties have used a wide variety of approaches to the provision of child care but usually require private-sector involvement. San Francisco requires office building and hotel developers either to provide facilities for their employees or contribute to a city fund. Louisville, Kentucky, has provided one-time construction funds to build centers that must then charge parents fees to cover all operating expenses.

Even the smallest employers can usually provide employees a referral service, and more each year are finding that a combination of employee demands and the ability at least to break even on other child-care approaches are causing them to offer a program.

The U.S. Department of Labor estimates that women and minorities will fill 80 percent of the 21 million new jobs that will be created by the year 2000. Employers, however, have been slow to realize that this new work force will demand family care benefits—primarily maternity/paternity leave and day care. "They have been reluctant to venture into this area because family-care changes the whole atmosphere at work—forever," claims Dana Friedman, senior research fellow at the Work and Family Life Center of the Department of Labor. Working women do not want to be forced to choose between a career and raising a family. They want and should be able to choose both, says Friedman. The new breed of fathers also want to help raise their children without fear of losing their jobs.[51]

Elder-Care Programs

The primary care focus today is on child care; however, older Americans represent the fastest-growing segment of the population (see *HR in the News:* "Watch Out! There's a Demographic Time Bomb on the Horizon"). Today's workers are increasingly faced with care problems at both ends of the age spectrum. They might be called the "sandwich generation," according to Robert Beck, executive vice president for corporate human resources at Bank of America. The care issue of the future, according to Beck, will be **elder care**. Research by several large employers, including IBM, Merck, and Corning Glass, indicates that employees with elder-care responsibilities experience work-related problems similar to those of employees with child-care responsibilities. Higher turnover, absenteeism, and health problems, as well as lower productivity, are common problems for employees who must care for older relatives.[52]

A pioneering elder-care project was announced by IBM in 1990. The company provided $3 million for a new IBM Elder Care Project Development Fund. The program provides assistance to employees with elder-care responsibilities. Services include respite-care development, recruitment and training of in-home health and social service workers, and support programs. Why should IBM enter the elder-care field? According to IBM representative Jim Smith, the program represents IBM's continuing response to the changing social environment that affects employees.[53]

Credit Unions

Company credit unions are a long-established employee service that are provided by many organizations. Employees become members by purchasing shares of stock for a small fee. They may then deposit savings that accrue interest at rates higher than those provided by local financial institutions. Employees may apply for loans from their credit union at lower rates than those charged by many financial institu-

tions. Normally administered by a separate board of directors, the credit union is an entity independent of the organization.

Food Services

Most companies provide some type of food facility to minimize the time taken for breaks and lunch periods. Food services vary according to the size of the company and the nature of the work. Some organizations may only provide vending machines and a few tables; others provide complete cafeteria services underwritten by the company. To minimize the time employees spend on coffee breaks, companies have experimented by placing coffee and soft drink stands in each department or by providing mobile coffee stands to bring doughnuts and coffee to individual employees. These alternatives minimize the time employees spend away from their work sites to take coffee breaks.

Education Expenses

Many organizations offer employees partial or total tuition reimbursement. Employees often use this highly sought benefit to prepare themselves for promotion opportunities. Generally, the portion of tuition that organizations reimburse depends on the grades received in the classes taken. For example, the organization may pay 100 percent of the tuition costs for an A, 50 percent for a B, and 25 percent for a C. Employers may also require that employees take career-related courses to receive tuition reimbursement.

Transportation Programs

Higher energy costs have caused employers to consider methods of helping employees get to work. Ride sharing, in use since World War II, is probably still the most common employee **transportation program**. The HR department can assist employees who want to share rides by providing them the names of other employees who live nearby or by working with other employers to involve their employees.

Watch Out! There's a Demographic Time Bomb on the Horizon

Just over the horizon looms a demographic time bomb for the nation's employers, and nobody has figured out yet how to defuse it. What bomb are we taking about? The elder care group is ready to explode.

As the baby boomers get older, and more employees are taking care of their elderly parents and in-laws, study after study is showing strong negative effects on employees and company productivity. A study by Hewitt Associates, benefit consultants, offers these observations. Out of 1,026 employers surveyed in 1992, only 43% offered elder care. That compares to 74% of the respondents offering some kind of child care assistance. That is an improvement over a survey conducted by the Society for Human Resource Management, which showed only 33% offered elder care.

Just how serious is this problem? Experts are saying that the distractions caused by elder care can be more damaging in the workplace than child-care problems. Part of the problem is that the elderly typically live away from their working children, adding to the stress when a crisis occurs. Of course, absenteeism increases. Job performance is impacted in other ways as well. For example, a high percentage of employees drastically change their employment relationship, including changing jobs, quitting or taking several part-time jobs.

But even an employer's best intentions fail. At Remington Products, the company agreed to pay half the cost of respite care for elderly relatives. But only a few signed up, and after a year the company dropped the program. Many employees chose to use their own families as a backup, rather than pay half of the $10 to $15 per hour rate charged by visiting nurses.

Herman Miller, Inc., a Michigan furniture maker, is having more success. They pay for a team of social workers to visit the home of an employee's elderly relative, size up the elder's needs, and help sign up for needed programs.

Unfortunately, the most common method of assisting the elderly goes against the current tax laws, thus making it useless. Tax rules require that for the income to be tax-exempt, the older relative must share a household with the caregiver and depend on the caregiver for more than half of his or her financial support. Few employees take advantage of this company program. Until something is done, the problem is only growing to get worse.

SOURCE: Reprinted by permission of *Wall Street Journal* from Sue Shellenbarger, "Firms Try Harder, But Often Fail, to Help Workers Cope with Elder-Care Problems," *The Wall Street Journal* (June 23, 1993): B1. Dow Jones & Company, Inc. All rights reserved worldwide.

Humana, the international hospital corporation, offers employees at its downtown headquarters the choice of free bus tickets or a parking space. A downtown parking space costs at least $50 a month, while bus fare costs only $25 a month. Additional employer financial gains can be realized through the Environmental Protection Agency's (EPA) *marketable rights system* for pollution controls. The EPA has imposed growth constraints on urban development and thus has created a market for pollution rights generated by an employer's mass-transit subsidy program.[54]

TOTAL BENEFIT PLANNING

With benefit costs requiring to up to 40 percent of total payroll costs, employers are reevaluating their total benefit packages. Many benefit packages have little effect on employee motivation and performance. Since many costly and expensive benefits are tied to seniority, such as vacation and retirement income, employers seldom link benefits to level of performance. Some HR specialists believe that most employees do not truly understand the nature of their benefit packages, nor do they appreciate the total cost of providing them with benefits. When given the choice between additional benefits or disposable income, employees overwhelmingly choose additional disposable income. The organization may find it less expensive and more popular to offer employees fewer benefits and higher wages.

Companies can best use their benefit dollars by assessing employees' needs and determining which benefits are truly demanded. Through meetings with employee representatives and union leaders, employers may find that the employees do not truly desire certain costly benefits and have a greater need for benefits that may be less expensive. The company's total benefit package should be reviewed as a whole and not as separate components.

Flexible Benefit Plans

An alternative to providing employees with a fixed combination of employer-provided benefits is a flexible benefit package. In a typical **flexible benefit plan**, employees are allowed to choose the benefits they believe will best meet their needs from a wide range of benefits. Generally, however, their choices are limited to the total cost the employer is willing to assume. Thus, for example, employees may be given a monthly benefit-dollar figure and told that they can allocate the dollars to the benefits they select from a list of benefits, each of which is a cost to the employees. In many programs employees may exceed their benefit limit, but they pay the difference. At the same time, if employees choose to allocate fewer dollars than their maximum, they may be allowed to keep all or part of the savings as additional monthly income.

Flexible benefit plans have had an on-again–off-again–on-again life. In the 1960s, *cafeteria plans,* which also allowed employees to choose some benefits from a "menu" of benefits, started to spread among employers. However, the cafeteria approach ran into problems. Employees found it confusing and difficult to make decisions, and employers (without today's computer programs) found the administration of the programs expensive and difficult.

In recent years, employers have increasingly implemented flexible benefit plans. A survey of the top 150 *Fortune* 500 companies found that 45 percent either had flexible benefit plans or were considering implementing them.[57] The primary reason employers are switching from fixed to flexible plans, in addition to better meeting employee needs, is to contain their medical costs. In fact, flexible benefit plans may be the most effective means employers have of containing medical costs. A survey of 330 employers with flexible plans found that almost half (49 percent) had achieved their medical cost target, an additional 43 percent reported that it was too soon to tell whether their targets would be met, and only 8 percent reported that they could not meet their target. The survey also reported that more than 87 percent of employers met employees' needs.[58]

Figure 12-4 is an example of a benefits questionnaire in which employees can indicate their preferences. Such a program would be offered by a large company where many

FIGURE 12-4 A sample of an employee benefits questionnaire.

Employee Benefits Questionnaire

1. In the space provided in front of the benefits listed below indicate how important each benefit is to you and your family. Indicate this by placing "1" for the most important, and "2" for the next most important, etc. Therefore, if Life Insurance is the most important benefit to you and your family, place a "1" in front of it.

IMPORTANCE		IMPROVEMENT
(5)	Dental Insurance	(18)
(6)	Disability (Pay while Sick)	(19)
(7)	Educational Assistance. .	(20)
(8)	Holidays	(21)
(9)	Life Insurance	(22)
(10)	Medical Insurance.	(23)
(11)	Retirement Annuity Plan	(24)
(12)	Savings Plan	(25)
(13)	Vacations.	(26)
(14–15)	. . . .	(27–28)
(16–17)	. . . .	(29–30)

Now, go back and in the space provided after each benefit, indicate the priority for improvement. For example, if the Savings Plan is the benefit you would most like to see improved, give it a "1," the next a priority "2," etc. Use the blank lines to add any benefits not listed.

2. Would you be willing to contribute a portion of earnings for new or improved benefits beyond the level already provided by the Company:

(31) ☐ Yes   ☐ No

If yes, please indicate below in which area(s)

(32) ☐ Dental Insurance   (36) ☐ Retirement Annuity
(33) ☐ Disability Benefits   Plan
(34) ☐ Life Insurance   (37) ☐ Savings Plan
(35) ☐ Medical Insurance

3. As you know, in the past the Company has made certain employee benefit improvements each year, in addition to wage and salary adjustments. Which of the following statements reflects your view:

(38) ☐ a. Place more emphasis on improving wages and salaries and less on employee benefits.

☐ b. The current mix of benefit improvements and wage and salary adjustments is about right.

☐ c. Place more emphasis on improving employee benefits and less on wages and salaries.

In order that we may effectively analyze the replies, please check the appropriate boxes.

AGE:
(39) ☐ under 26   ☐ 26–35   ☐ 36–45
     ☐ 46–55   ☐ 56 & over

SEX:
(40) ☐ Male   ☐ Female

MARITAL STATUS:
(41) ☐ Single   ☐ Married   ☐ Other

YEARS OF SERVICE:
(42) ☐ under 1 year ☐ 1–4 years   ☐ 5–9 years
     ☐ 10–14 years   ☐ 15–24 years ☐ 25 & over

PAY GROUP
(43) ☐ Hourly   ☐ Weekly   ☐ Foreman
     ☐ Monthly

DIVISION:
☐ Agricultural   ☐ Central   ☐ Chemicals
                        Research
☐ Corporate HQ   ☐ Cosmetics   ☐ Instrumentation
☐ Metals   ☐ Minerals   ☐ Pharmaceuticals
☐ Toiletries

LOCATION:
(Field Sales employees should check "FIELD" rather than the name of their distribution centers.)

☐ Atlanta   ☐ Boston   ☐ Chicago
☐ Dallas   ☐ Field   ☐ Green Bay
☐ Houston   ☐ Los Angeles   ☐ Manitowoc
☐ Milwaukee   ☐ Newark
☐ New York   ☐ St. Louis

FOR OFFICE USE ONLY Division (44–45)   Location (46–47)

WE'D LIKE TO KNOW . . . If you would like to take this opportunity to explain further any of your answers or comment on any other matter, please use the back of this form.

PLEASE RETURN THIS QUESTIONNAIRE IN THE ENCLOSED PREPAID ENVELOPE
(Compliments: Pfizer, Inc.)

SOURCE: David Thompson, "Introducing Cafeteria Compensation in Your Company." *Personnel Journal* (March, 1977): 128–29. Reprinted with permission of *Personnel Journal*, Costa Mesa, CA. Copyright 1977.

employees are involved and, therefore, where benefits such as a day-care center are practical.

American Can was one of the early major employers to implement a serious flexible benefit plan, starting with 700 participating employees. A survey of the company's 9000 participating employees disclosed that 92 percent thought they had substantially improved their benefits by producing the proper mix of benefits. Pepsi Cola and North American Van Lines were among major firms that followed with their own successful plans. Small firms (eight to twenty employees) have also reported employee and employer satisfaction with flexible plans.[59]

An important feature of a cafeteria plan is the opportunity for each employee to spend employer dollars as personally desired. By contrast, many so-called flexible plans are fixed, offering the employee the opportunity to choose among limited alternatives or offering a "take-it-or-leave" approach. For example, the employer offers to pay a portion of an employee's medical insurance if the employee pays the balance. But if the employee does not choose medical insurance (possibly because of a spouse's coverage), then the employer's contribution is lost. A true flexible plan credits the employee with the employer's share, which could be applied to another benefit.[60]

Types of Flexible Plans   There are at least three major types of flexible employee benefit plans. First, there is the *core cafeteria plan*, which provides employees "core" (minimum) coverage in several areas and allows them to choose either additional benefits or cash, up to a maximum total cost to the employer. In the core cafeteria plan of Figure 12-5, the employee has a choice of items 1 through 6 and cash. This plan strikes a balance between giving the employee complete freedom to choose among benefits and the employer's need to protect employees against poor decisions. Sec-

ond is the *buffet plan*, which starts employees with their exact current benefit coverage and allows them to decrease coverage in some areas (life insurance, medical insurance, etc.) in order to earn credits for other benefits (dental care, day care, etc.). Third is the *alternative dinners plan*, which provides a number of packages ("dinners") to choose from. For example, one package might be aimed at the employee with a nonworking spouse and children, another at the single employee, and a third at an employee with a working spouse and no children. The total cost of each dinner would be approximately the same.[61]

Advantages of Flexible Plans   Originally created as a means of better meeting the needs of employees, flexible plans can often provide a growing number of advantages:

- *Meet diverse needs of employees.* As our work force changes, with an increasing number of single working parents, dual-career couples, second-career retirees, and so forth, flexible plans become increasingly effective as a means of matching employees' needs with their benefit plan.

- *Control benefit costs.* Of employers with flexible plans, 78 percent reported that a major objective in their initiating a plan was to contain rising health-care costs.[60] With health-care costs continuing to rise, this effective containment method is likely to spread among employers. Why does it work? Employers can set the maximum amount of benefit dollars they will spend on employees' benefits as part of their budget process. As the costs of individual health-care options rise, the employee can choose one of several medical plans with varying levels of coverage and different premiums. Employers can avoid automatically absorbing cost increases, which they generally must pay under a fixed benefit plan, or reduce the level of benefits they provide to employees.

FIGURE 12-5 Flexible employee benefits plans.

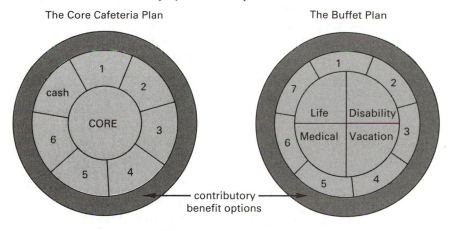

The Core Cafeteria Plan

The Buffet Plan

contributory benefit options

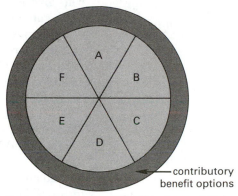

The Alternative Dinners Plan

contributory benefit options

- **Improve benefits offered.** Employers can better meet the needs of their employees by expanding the variety of benefits offered to employees. Since the total cost of all benefits is set by the employer, the cost of adding a new benefit to the package can be minimal. Child care is a good example; employers can pay a portion of or all the cost of providing child care at an off-site facility through a voucher system. In choosing the coverage, employees must either reduce the coverage of another benefit in their plan or have the increased cost deducted from their pay. Employers generally, however, provide a portion of the child care.

- **Attract and retain employees.** The changing work force is causing employers in some industries to consider flexible benefits as a tool in the recruitment and retention of employees. Just as flexible work schedules can be utilized to attract and keep employees, flexible benefit plans can be included in recruitment advertising.[61]

- **Avoid unions.** A flexible benefit plan can provide an effective tool against union organizers.[62] It is far more difficult for a union to promise to increase one or two benefits if employees already have the ability to choose the benefits in a flexible plan.

- *Avoid duplicate coverage.* Another aspect of the changing labor force is the increased number of working married couples with duplicate benefit coverage from separate employers. Flexible benefit plans may allow a married couple to save thousands of dollars in wasted duplicate coverage.

Implementation of Flexible Plans

Companies that have experienced success with flexible benefit plans have begun by "dreaming big but starting small." A small start can be successful if top management is aggressive in adopting the plan and is willing to involve employees.[63] The steps in adopting a cafeteria approach are as follows:

- Review employees' total compensation needs and obtain top management support for the program.

- Develop a timetable for implementation within the benefits section of the HR department.

- Survey employees to determine what their needs and desires are in the benefits area.

- Review the plan with the IRS, appropriate state agencies, and insurance companies.

- Design a data processing system that will minimize additional paperwork and the cost of implementing the program.

- Communicate to employees the need for core coverage, which guarantees certain benefits, such as life insurance and hospitalization, that all employees need unless they have similar coverage elsewhere.

- Implement the program through employee selection, but only after extensive communications through meetings, brochures, and the like, to ensure that employees can make informed choices.

Publicizing Benefits

As employers reexamine benefit programs and question if they are cost-effective, they should determine whether there is a lack of communication with employees concerning the benefit programs. Without such communication, some employees cannot visualize the entire benefit program and its value to them. Since employers must report their pension program to employees under ERISA, the entire benefit program should be communicated.

Studies have demonstrated that employees who give little thought to their benefits may not be able to recall 15 percent of the benefits they receive. Employers might be able to increase the productivity and the advantages of good employee benefits by making employees aware of what the company does for them that does not appear on their paycheck.

An example of one method of providing employees with this information is an **employee earnings and benefits letter**, as shown in Figure 12-6. This letter keeps employees informed and aware of what the company does in terms of benefits. Section A of the letter lists an employee's gross wages and breaks down the various costs of benefits included therein. Section B includes benefits that do not appear on an employee's W-2 earnings statement and, therefore, are not known to employees. Any benefit that does not show up on an employee's paycheck should be included in section B to make the employee aware of benefit costs. Considering companies' investments in providing benefits to employees, it is unusual that more companies do not do a better job of making employees aware of the costs of the benefits. Only when a company translates benefits into dollar values can employees appreciate the magnitude of what their company does for them.

FIGURE 12-6 A sample employee earnings and benefits letter.

Jackson Steel Co.

Employee's Name: William A. Hailey
Address: 1500 North Lake Circle
                 Erie, PA

Dear Mr. Hailey:

Enclosed are your W-2 forms showing the amount of taxable income that you received during 1990. Listed below in Section A are your gross wages and a cost breakdown of various fringe benefit programs that you enjoy. In addition to the money you received as wages, the company paid benefits for you which are not included in your W-2 statement. These are fringe benefits that are sometimes overlooked. In an easy-to-read form, here's what was paid to you in 1990.

SECTION A—PAID TO YOU IN YOUR W-2 EARNINGS

Cost-of-Living Allowance	$ 1,875.
Shift Premium	3,125.
Suggestion Award(s)	0.
Service Awards(s)	1,200.
Vacation Pay	2,400.
Holiday Pay	825.
Funeral Pay	0.
Jury-Duty Pay	0.
Military Pay	0.
Accident & Sickness Benefits	1,956.
Regular Earnings	42,500.
Overtime Earnings	2,450.
Allowances	150.
Gross Wages	56,481.

SECTION B—PAID FOR YOU AND NOT INCLUDED IN YOUR W-2 EARNINGS:

Company Contribution to Stock Purchase & Savings Plan	$ 2,125.
Company Contribution to Pension Plan	2,975.
Company Cost of Your Hospitalization Payments	2,400.
Company Cost of Your Life & Accidental Death Insurance	250.
Company Cost for Social Security Tax on Your Wages	3,251.
Company Cost of the Premium for Your Workers Compensation	300.
Company Cost for the Tax on Your Wages for Unemployment Compensation	150.
Company Cost for Tuition Refund	0.
Company Cost for Safety Glasses	75.
Total Cost of Benefits not Included in W-2 Earnings	$11,526.
Total (A & B) Paid for Your Services in 1990	$68,007.

You have earned the amount on the bottom line, but we wanted to give you a clearer idea of the total cost of your services to the company, and the protection and benefits that are being purchased for you and your family.

Alicia Millsap
HR Director

CONCLUSIONS AND APPLICATIONS

- Employee benefits are not just a fringe cost to employers; they represent a substantial percentage of the total payroll. Benefits are usually awarded equally to all workers or on a seniority basis.
- Certain benefits are required by law, including Social Security, workers' compensation, unemployment insurance, and overtime for nonexempt employees.
- Retirement income is provided through Social Security, private pension plans, and personal savings. Employers believe that they directly or indirectly provide all of these sources—which constitute the single most expensive benefit area.
- Health insurance programs provided by em-

ployers have expanded to include life insurance, dental, legal, and vision care, as well as the traditional medical and hospitalization coverage. Employers are looking to self-funding, HMOs, and PPOs to minimize health insurance rate increases.
- Paid time off from work represents a major benefit cost.
- Flexible benefit plans have received great interest from employers because they help contain benefit costs and provide employees with more individualized benefit programs.
- Changing employee demographics have caused employers to offer child care and elder care programs to help employees meet their family needs.

CASE STUDY

Family Health Insurance

Laura Gains is a confused employee. Washington Electric Company, her employer, is offering a local HMO as an alternative to the company's health insurance plan. Gains attended the employees' meeting, where an HMO official explained the medical services and costs. The official outlined many services, such as dental checkups and flu shots, which would be provided at little cost. Gains knows she spends over $400 a year in these areas alone. The HMO is located about two miles from Gains's home and is always open—something Gains thinks would add to her use of the services. The company will provide the

same dollars for the HMO as it currently does for the employees' health insurance plan. Gains, however, is bothered by the lack of choice of physicians and dentists, though she is not really attached to the ones she is going to now. During this month, Gains must decide whether to change to the HMO for at least a year or else wait until next year's sign-up period.

A widow, Gains is the sole support of her three daughters—Shari, age nine; Amber, age seven; and Tracy, age four. In the past, her annual medical expenses have often exceeded $5000. Whereas the company's health insurance plan does not cover most of her medical expenses, the HMO would cover almost all of them; however, it would cost Gains $80 per month more in premiums. Gains's salary is about $42,000 per year. She prepares her own tax forms and always itemizes deductions.

QUESTIONS

1. How should Gains compare the plans? What quantitative criteria should be considered?

2. What additional information would help Gains make her decision?

3. What would you decide? Why?

EXPERIENTIAL EXERCISES

1. Flexible Benefit Decisions

The purpose of this exercise is to help you gain an understanding of the philosophy behind flexible benefit plans and the individual decision making involved. Management is increasingly striving to negotiate flexible benefit plans as a means of controlling the total cost of employer-paid employee benefits.

If *today* you were given $1000 per month in benefit dollars to allocate among the following, what package of benefits would you choose? Complete the following chart by placing a dollar amount for each benefit you choose in the left column. If your total benefit cost is less than $1000 per month, you will keep half the difference as a monthly cash bonus. You pay any amount over $1000 per month.

Benefit Plan   **Benefit**

_____ Pension plan (matched by employer 50/50 up to $500/month)
_____ Paid vacations ($50/mo. for 2 weeks/year)
_____ Paid holidays ($50/mo. for 10 days/year)
_____ Paid sick leave ($50/mo. for 10 days/year)
_____ Guaranteed maternity or paternity leave ($50/month)
_____ Medical insurance ($250/employee, $350/family/month)
_____ Health maintenance organization health-care option ($200/employee, $250/family/month)
_____ Legal insurance ($50/mo. for 100% legal needs)
_____ Vision care ($50/month for routine checkups and one pair of glasses or contact lenses/year)
_____ Subsidized child care ($60/month per child for on-site care)
_____ Credit union ($25/month)
_____ Subsidized company cafeteria ($50/month for free hot lunches)
_____ Tuition reimbursement ($50/month for 100% tuition)
_____ Funeral leave ($50/month; 3 days/death)
_____ Company-sponsored social events (annual picnic, parties, etc. $25/month)
_____ Life insurance ($50/mo. for $250,000)
_____ Disability insurance ($75/month)
_____ Dental insurance ($50/month for routine checkup and all required care)
_____ Free parking ($50/month—local lots charge $65/month)

_____ Total cost

2. Benefits Survey: Field Research

PURPOSE

To identify, design, and implement benefit programs

TASK

Break into small groups. Each group is to interview the head of a benefits department. Alternatively, if there is no specific benefits department, interview the person who would be responsible for designing and administering the benefits programs. The instructor will inform the class regarding when the project is due.

Each group should plan on giving a short classroom presentation that summarizes their findings.

In preparing their questions, the group should consider the following:

- What demographic changes within the company have influenced the choice of benefit programs?

- What tax changes have taken place that influence specific programs?
- How did the company identify employees' needs?
- How does the company communicate benefit programs?
- Does the company depend on contract workers? If so, what benefits are available to them?
- Assess the company's pension program. How many years does it take to become vested? Is there an employee contribution?
- Does the company offer tuition reimbursement? Do they require employees to pay back any reimbursement if they leave the company?
- What is the company's position on managed health care?
- What future benefits are being considered?
- How does the company measure the effectiveness of their benefit programs?

KEY TERMS AND CONCEPTS

Benefits
Child-care programs
Consolidated Omnibus Budget Reconciliation Act (COBRA)
Contributory/noncontributory retirement plan
Current-expenditure retirement plan
Defined benefit retirement plan
Defined contribution retirement plan
Dismissal pay
Elder care

Employee earnings and benefits letter
Employee Retirement Income Security Act (ERISA)
Fee-for-service plan
Family and Medical Leave Act (FMLA)
Funded retirement plan
401(k) retirement plans
Flexible benefit plans
Funded/nonfunded retirement plan
HMO
Group insurance plan

Insured retirement plan
IRA
Managed-care systems
Maternity and paternity leave
Nonfunded retirement plan
On-call pay
Paid time off work
Portability
Preferred provider organization (PPO)
Premium pay
Profit-sharing retirement plan

Reporting pay
Sick-leave banks
Sick-leave plan alternatives
Social Security system
Supplementary unemployment benefits (SUB)
Transportation programs
Unemployment insurance
Vesting
Workers' compensation
Well-pay programs

REVIEW QUESTIONS

1. How can employee benefits attract, retain, and motivate employees?

2. About how much of the total payroll cost consists of benefits?

3. What factors are important in determining the size of an employee's retirement benefit?

4. Why do some states require employers to pay more unemployment insurance taxes than others?

5. What are the traditional problems with paid sick leave? Solutions?

6. What are the advantages of health insurance self-funding? HMOs? PPOs?

DISCUSSION QUESTIONS

1. If you were establishing your own business, which benefits would you be legally required to pay and which would you choose to offer?

2. Cite examples to prove that the cost of living for retired individuals increases as much as or less than the CPI increases. Therefore, should Social Security increase as the CPI rises?

3. In view of the fact that fewer persons are now working to provide benefits for the Social Security system, would you agree that all state, federal, and local government employees and nonprofit association employees should enter the Social Security system?

4. Do you believe that the government will transfer support of welfare or social programs to private industries in the form of required benefits? If so, how soon?

5. Periodically, pension fund frauds involving the loss of retirement funds for thousands of employees are reported. How can persons and companies that have contributed to the pension fund safeguard their contribution to the future?

6. Should employers provide child care? Elder care? Why?

7. Do you think a national health insurance system is needed?

ENDNOTES

Chapter 12

1. "Benefits Policies and Program," Coopers & Lybrand survey reported in *Ideas & Trends* No. 308 (Chicago: Commerce Clearing House, Inc.), August 18, 1993: 136.

2. "The Scary Math of New Hires," *Business Week* (February 22, 1993): 70–71.

3. Albert G. Holzinger, "The Real Costs of Benefits" *Nation's Business* (February 1988): 30–32; and U.S. Department of Labor, *Consumer Price Index*, 1989, 1990.

4. James R. Morris, "A Brake on Benefits," *Nation's Business* 76, no. 2 (April 1984): 84–86. See also Holzinger, "The Real Costs of Benefits," and U.S. Department of Labor, *Consumer Price Index*, 1990.

5. Richard I. Henderson, *Compensation Management*, (Reston, VA: Reston, 1979), pp. 321–22.

6. Thomas N. and Teresa N. Fannin, "Coordination of Benefits: Uncovering Buried Treasure," *Personnel Journal* 62, no. 5 (May 1983): 386–89.

7. Evan Claque and Leo Kramer, *Manpower Policies and Programs: A Review 1935–1975* (Kalamazoo, MI: Upjohn, 1976), pp. 82–83.

8. Jerry Flint, "The Old Folks," *Forbes* (February 18, 1980): 51–56.

9. Dale Detlefs, *1984 Guide to Social Security* (Louisville, KY: Meidinger and Associates, 1985), pp. 6–9.

10. Michael P. Littea and James E. Inman, *The Legal Environment of Business: Text, Cases and Readings* (Columbus, OH: Grid, 1980), pp. 464–65.

11. "Family and Medical Leave Act of 1993," Society for Human Resource Management (Alexandria, VA: 1993) Report.

12. Kenneth P. Shapiro, "An Ideal Pension System," *Personnel Journal* 60, no. 4 (April 1981): 294–97.

13. Vincent M. Tobin, "What Goes Into a Retirement Income Policy?" *Personnel* 61, no. 4 (July–August 1984): 60–66.

14. Donald Bell and William Wiatrowski, "Disability Benefits for Employees in Private Pension Plans," *Monthly Labor Review* 105, no. 8 (August 1982): 36–40.

15. David H. Gravitz and Frederick W. Rumack, "Opening the Early Retirement Window," *Personnel* 60, no. 2 (March–April 1983): 53–57.

16. Kathryn H. Anderson, Richard V. Burkhauser, and Joseph F. Quinn, "Do Retirement Dreams Come True? The Effect of Unanticipated Events on Retirement Plans," *Industrial and Labor Relations Review* 39, no. 4 (July 1986): 518–26.

17. Michael R. Carrell and Frank E. Kuzmits, "Amended ADEA's Effects on HR Strategies Remain Dubious," *Personnel Journal* 66, no. 5 (May 1987): 111–20.

18. *Basic Patterns in Union Contracts*, 12th ed. (Washington, DC: Bureau of National Affairs, 1989), p. 27.

19. Fredrick I. Schick, "Tax Reform's Impact on Benefit Programs," *Personnel Administrator* 32, no. 1 (January 1987): 80–88.

20. Lawrence Meyer, "Many Workers Lose Retirement Benefits Despite Reform Laws," *Washington Post* (September 7, 1982): 1.

21. Olivia S. Mitchell, "Fringe Benefits and the Cost of Changing Jobs," *Industrial and Labor Relations Review* 37, no. 1 (October 1983): 70–78.

22. Allen Stitler, "Finally, Pension Plans Defined," *Personnel Journal* 66, no. 2 (February 1987): 45–53.

23. Kathleen P. Utzoff, "Defined Benefit Plans: Still a Good Deal?" *Labor Law Journal* 39, no. 7 (July 1988): 444–46.

24. *Pension Reform Act of 1974* (New York: Commerce Clearing House, 1974), p. 2

25. The Retirement Equity Act of 1984.

26. "When Pension Liabilities Dampen Profits," *Business Week* (June 16, 1983): 80–81.

27. Susan Pulliam, "Hopeful Assumptions Let Firms Minimize Pension Contributions," *The Wall Street Journal* (September 2, 1993): A1.

28. Tom Nicholson and Penny Wang, "A Blow to Unisex Pensions," *Newsweek* (July 18, 1983): 66.

29. Trisha Brambley, "The 401(k) Solution to Retirement Planning," *Personnel Journal* 63, no. 12 (December 1984): 66–67.

30. Marcia Lewis and Richard Sears, "How Do 401(k) and Traditional Savings Plans Compare?" *Personnel Administrator* 27, no. 10 (October 1982): 71–76, 92–93.

31. William M. Mercer-Meidinger, Inc., "How Will Reform Tax Your Benefits?" *Personnel Journal* 65, no. 12 (December 1986): 49–57.

32. Adapted from Carroll Roartz, "How MeraBank Lowered Pension Costs Without Lowering Morale," *Personnel Journal* (November 1987): 63–71.

33. Richard I. Henderson, *Compensation Management* (Reston, VA: Reston, 1979).

34. F. C. Joran, "A Fair System for Time Off the Job: Combine Sick Days, Vacation Days and Holidays into Paid Days," *Modern Business Practice* (June, 1974): pp. 113–14.

35. "Health Care Reform: It's Already Here," *Business Week* (June 14, 1993): 114–16.

36. *Employee Benefit Changes Under COBRA 1993* (Chicago: Commerce Clearing House, Issue 308, August 18, 1993): Part 2.

37. Ibid.

38. "Health Care Reform: It's Already Here," *Business Week* (June 14, 1993): 114–16.

39. Ronald Bujan, "A Primer Self-Funding Health Care Benefits," *Personnel Administrator* 28, no. 4 (April 1983): 61–64.

40. Ibid.

41. M. K. Key and D. J. Ottensmeyer, "Managed Healthcare Puts a Clamp on Costs," *Personnel 67*, no. 9 (September, 1990): 29–32.

42. Ibid.

43. Roy M. Hilliard, "Your Dental Plan May Need a Checkup," *HRMagazine* (December 1992): 42–44.

44. Henderson, *Compensation Management*, p. 323.

45. Larry K. Kromling, "Cal Comp Reshapes HR for the Future," *Personnel Journal* 69, no. 1 (January 1990): 59.

46. Sandra E. La Marre and Kate Thompson, "Industry-Sponsored Day Care," *Personnel Administrator* 29, no. 2 (February 1984): 53–65.

47. Thomas I. Miller, "The Effects of Employer Sponsored Child Care on Employee Absenteeism, Turnover, Productivity, Recruitment on Job Satisfaction," *Personnel Psychology* 37, no. 2 (Summer 1984): 277–87.

48. La Marre and Thompson, "Industry-Sponsored Day Care," pp. 53–65.

49. Donald J. Peterson and Douglass Marsengil, "Childcare Programs Benefit Employers, Too," *Personnel* 65, no. 5 (May 1988): 58.

50. "Take Care of Kids and Employees Take Better Care of You," *ABA Banking Journal* (September 1989): 26–28; and Peterson and Marsengill, "Childcare Programs Benefit Employers, Too," pp. 58–62.

51. James Fraze, "Preparing for a Different Future," *Resource* 7, no. 1 (January 1988): 1, 10.

52. Sue Shellenbarger, "Firms Try Harder, But Often Fail, to Help Workers Cope with Elder-Care Problems," *The Wall Street Journal,* (June 23, 1993): B1.

53. Anne Ritter, "Dependent Care Proves Profitable," *Personnel* 67, no. 3 (March 1990): 12–16.

54. Don R. Osborn and Margaret McCarthy, "The Economical and Ecological Advantages of Mass-Transit Subsidies," *Personnel Journal* 66, no. 4 (April 1987): 140–47.

55. Betty A. Iseri and Robert R. Cangemi, "Flexible Benefits: A Growing Option," *Personnel* 3 (March 1990): 30–32.

56. "Flex Plans Lower Health Care Costs: Hewitt Study," *Employee Benefit Plan Review* (July 1989): 19–20.

57. Robert B. Cockrum, "Has the Time Come for Employee Cafeteria Plans?" *Personnel Administrator* 27, no. 7 (July 1982): 66–69.

58. Albert Cole Jr., "Flexible Benefits Are a Key to Better Employee Relations," *Personnel Journal* 62, no. 1 (January 1983): 49–53.

59. Ibid., pp. 51–53.

60. "Flex Plans Lower Health Care Costs: Hewitt Study," p. 19.

61. Elisabeth K. Ryland and Benson Rosen, "Attracting Job Applicants with Flexible Benefits," *Personnel* (March 1988): 71–73.

62. M. Michael Markowich, "United Hospitals Makes Flex Fly," *Personnel Journal* (December 1989): 40–48.

63. David Thompson, "Introducing Cafeteria Compensation in Your Company," *Personnel Journal* (March 1977): 126–28.

CHAPTER **13**

HEALTH AND SAFETY

CHAPTER OBJECTIVES

1. To understand the recent investment of employers in employee wellness programs.
2. To reveal the problems caused by employee alcohol and drug abuse.
3. To discuss policy issues surrounding AIDS in the workplace.
4. To identify the purposes of employee assistance programs.
5. To understand the general provisions of the Occupational Safety and Health Act.
6. To identify the points needed in a comprehensive drug testing policy and the requirements of the Drug-free Workplace Act.
7. To describe the federal right-to-know regulations.
8. To identify job stress warning signs and methods of care.
9. To discuss effective accident prevention programs.

Barbara Butterfield, Vice President for Human Resources, Stanford University: Surviving Burnout

I have been burned out twice—specifically when I was less mature in my career and when there was lots going on.

What have I done to prevent burnout? When I had these two flame-outs (a short-term downer in which I've experienced absolute exhaustion), they lasted about three days. The first day or two, I simply rested, because for me it's almost like the flu, and I said, OK, I've got to get my physical self back in shape first—which does something to get my mental self back in shape. Then I'd do something physical, such as tennis or taking long walks, or just go hiking in the woods. I also touch base with people I care about by phone—to rebuild my contacts. It's also been helpful to have colleagues (not necessarily in HR, but usually in the same workplace) who are close enough to talk with, or who will step in for you for a day or two, and for whom you can return the favor. They should be people with whom you can talk and who will help you put things back in perspective. A lot of folks won't do that. They think they have to pound right through it. I think that's damaging. It's hard to learn when you're first in executive leadership positions because you take all the load on yourself, and you think that if you can't do it all yourself, then something's wrong with you. Instead, what you could do is share the load and support each other. Everybody goes through it. If someone says they haven't, they aren't telling the truth. There are more ways to be tired than by being virally or bacterially ill. Will you take the time out? Will you be as good to yourself as if you just had the 24-hour flu? My work is recreation to me. It's like the toughest tennis game you ever played. For me, it's a lot of fun, a lot of stimulation. Layoffs and big problems actually get me going. I want my work to be like play. That's probably why I don't burn out very often.

SOURCE: Jennifer T. Laabs, "Surviving HR Burnout," *Personnel Journal* (April 1992); 85. Used by permission.

Whether it happens to executives such as Barbara Butterfield in *HR in the News:* "Surviving Burnout" or to a minimum-wage employee working during the hectic Christmas rush season, burnout is a real problem. Some workplace analysts are telling employers that in the 1990s, offices, factories, and stores could become "stress pools" unless management helps workers cope in ways that go beyond the stop-smoking and cardiovascular-fitness programs of the 1970s and 1980s.

But the employees' mental health is just one set of problems. Organizations are also responsible for creating and maintaining a work environment free from unnecessary hazards that can lead to injury, illness, or death. One thing is certain: ignoring the problems will only lead to increased absenteeism, disability claims, health care, recruiting efforts, and training costs.

STRESS

Job stress is considered to be a rising concern in many organizations. The possible causes include increased domestic and foreign competition, which has led to a substantial number of downsizing, layoff, and merger activities; rapidly changing technology; tension among diverse groups of employees; and increased demands for higher quality and service. Organizational managers are interested in maintaining a lower level of job stress for good reasons: high levels of stress can result in low productivity, increased absenteeism and turnover, and an assortment of other employee problems including alcoholism, drug abuse, hypertension, and a host of cardiovascular problems.

Another reason for concern over job stress is that stress-related workers' compensation claims have risen dramatically. About 14 percent of all occupational disease claims are stress related. Stress-related claims, on average, are estimated at $15,000, twice as much

as those for employees with physical injuries.[1] But what exactly is job stress? Unfortunately, it is not easy to define or measure. Various definitions of job stress include the following:[2]

The force or stimulus acting on the individual that results in a response of strain (stimulus definition).

The physical or psychological response an individual makes to an environmental stressor (response definition).

The consequence of the interaction between an environmental stimulus and the idiosyncratic response of the individual (stimulus-response definition).

A comprehensive definition based on the integration of these and other definitions is as follows:[3]

Stress is a discrepancy between an employee's perceived state and desired state, when such a discrepancy is considered important by the employee. Stress influences two behaviors—(1) the employee's psychological and physical well-being, and (2) the employee's efforts to cope with the stress by preventing or reducing it.

Just how common is job stress in the United States? Consider the statistics in Figure 13-1. Over two-thirds of all workers in the United States report that their jobs are either extremely or highly stressful. In addition, one-third seriously consider quitting their jobs each year due to stress. The major factors reported that causes these high stress levels are "too much work," "lack of time for self," and "little control over their jobs."[4]

Just how stressful is your position? Some jobs, such as those in Figure 13-2, consistently have high stress levels due to the nature of the work. Individuals who cannot cope with continuous stress are probably best advised to avoid these careers. The level of stress that exists in any job or organization is not easily determined. The outcomes in high-stress situations are usually high levels of absenteeism, turnover, grievances, accidents, and chemical dependency. Accurately measuring stress levels, however, is not easy. The most common

FIGURE 13-1 Extent of job stress in the United States.

Percent	Stress Issue
66	Employees who report that their jobs are extremely or highly stressful.
34	Employees who seriously thought about quitting their jobs due to stress.
25	Employees reporting stress-related illnesses.
90	Workers who think their employers should act to reduce stress.
40	Workers who feel more stress due to the recession.

Dollars	Stress Issue
$73,270	Average amount corporations sets-aside for stress-related disabilities.
$1,925	Average cost of rehabilitating a stressed employee.

SOURCE: Adapted from Jennifer J. Laabs, "Job Stress," *Personnel Journal* (April 1992): 43.

measurement techniques employ paper-and-pencil tests that ask employees about the existence of stressors in their job environment.

The measurement of employee stress may enable an organization to change its cultural environment and thus lower the level of stress. A good example is the Armstrong Transfer and Storage Company in Memphis, Tennessee. Armstrong suffered a serious problem with stress-related workers' compensation claims and saw its claims rise from $93,000 to $272,000 in just two years. To determine the extent of workplace stress, Armstrong administered questionnaires to its 500 employees. The results showed, for example, that employees were worried about worn-out loading equipment but failed to report it for fear that they would have to pay for it. In response to the survey results, Armstrong's management repaired or replaced broken equipment and held weekly meetings to allow employees to air

FIGURE 13-2 High-stress jobs, warning signs, and ways to cope.

Only recently have consultants and psychologists begun to study workplace tension in depth. They've discovered the most trying professions are those involving danger and extreme pressure—or that carry responsibility without control. The symptoms of stress have been found to range from frequent illness to nervous tics and mental lapses. The most common tips for dealing with it focus on relaxation. But sometimes the only answer is to fight back—or walk away.

10 Tough Jobs	Warning Signs	Ways to Cope
Inner-city high-school teacher	Intestinal distress	Maintain a sense of humor
Police officer	Rapid pulse	Meditate
Miner	Frequent illness	Get a massage
Air-traffic controller	Insomnia	Exercise regularly
Medical intern	Persistent fatigue	Eat more sensibly
Stockbroker	Irritability	Limit intake of alcohol and caffeine
Journalist	Nail biting	Take refuge in family and friends
Customer service/complaint department worker	Lack of concentration	Delegate responsibility
Waitress	Increased use of alcohol and drugs	Quit
Secretary	Hunger for sweets	

SOURCE: Annetta Miller et al., "Stress on the Job," from *Newsweek* (April 25, 1988), copyright 1988, Newsweek, Inc. All rights reserved. Reprinted by permission.

their grievances. Following the stress-reduction program, accidents fell from sixty-five to ten per year, and a follow-up survey showed that perceived stress had dropped significantly.[5]

Controlling Stress

Job stress caused by factors in the workplace is a serious, growing aspect of organizational culture. In general, strategies to control stress focus on organizational-level and individual-based efforts.

Organizational policies and strategies include the following:

- *Preventive management.* With this approach, managers identify potential problems that may become serious stressors and take steps to reduce or eliminate them. Surveys and employee/group interviews are important tools in this process.
- *Maintaining a productive culture.* The development of and adherence to a mission statement that includes the maintenance of a positive organizational environment and satisfied employees sets the right direction. However, following through with programs that actually create and maintain a positive culture is the most important facet of a stress-reduction strategy.
- *Management by objectives.* A management by objectives or similar performance appraisal technique that identifies employees' goals, clarifies roles and responsibilities, and strengthens communication can reduce stress by eliminating uncertainty in critical aspects of employees' jobs.
- *Controlling the physical environment.* Reducing stress in the physical environment requires that management undertake one or two different strategies (or both). The first strategy is to alter the physical environment (reduce noise, institute better control of temperature, etc.). The second strategy is to

protect employees from the environment (with improved safety equipment).

- *Employee fitness facilities.* An increasing number of organizations provide physical fitness facilities to improve employee health and morale and to reduce stress. Many such facilities include exercise equipment and programs such as aerobics, weight training, racquet sports, and running. More sophisticated wellness programs (see the next section) include health testing and counseling by medical professionals.

Personal strategies include the following:

- *Meditation.* While many forms of meditation exist, one of the more popular is transcendental meditation (TM). Using TM, the participant silently utters a mantra—a word or sound that the meditator concentrates on—to enter a state of mental and physical relaxation. While detractors of TM are easily found, research shows that meditation can reduce anxiety and improve work performance and job satisfaction.
- *Exercise.* One of the least expensive and potentially most effective stress-reduction strategies is exercise—jogging, racquet sports, fitness classes, bicycling, and swimming. Research shows that a sound program of physical fitness can improve mental health as well as physical well-being.
- *Removing the cause of stress.* Sometimes one can easily identify the major cause of stress—a confrontational supervisor, difficult support staff, no possibility for advancement, and so on. Thus the key is to remove or lessen the cause. One of the authors of this text recalls working with a woman who, year after year, drove away the best people in her office by making their lives miserable; he avoided all contact with her and, when it was necessary to communicate with her, used written forms to avoid a conversation. This provided a tolerable environment until a new

manager finally removed her and brought peace to the office.

- **Becoming a mentor.** When one has mastered one's own job, helping a junior person learn the job and the organization's culture can reduce excessive stress.

- **Seeking counseling.** Stress is a common psychological problem. Counselors can offer helpful insights and stress-reduction techniques that may alleviate problems. Counseling is also far less expensive than quitting one's job.[6]

- **Extended leave.** Sometimes one can put stress-causing problems into a larger perspective by taking extended leave—such as an extended vacation, sabbatical, or personal leave. On returning, the worker often finds that some problems have resolved themselves and that others simply don't cause the same high levels of stress they did before.

BURNOUT

Job stress and *job burnout* are sometimes used interchangeably or are confused. **Job burnout**, however is more than job stress; it occurs when a person believes that he or she cannot or will not continue to do the job.[7] The difference, according to a physician who has treated both, is that a person who is stressed can take an extended vacation and return rested and ready to get back to work. If that person has experienced burnout, however, within a few days after returning to work he or she will feel as miserable as before the vacation. While stress usually contributes to burnout, it does not explain the whole phenomenon. Burnout, in essence, is the overall perception that one is giving more than one is receiving—in monetary rewards, recognition, support, or advancement. It can occur at all organizational levels, at all pay levels, and in all age groups.[8]

A good example of burnout is Rochelle Ruane, an HR professional. Ms. Ruane, fresh out of college, was hired by a biotechnology company to build its HR department from scratch. It was a job she enjoyed. "I liked the people, I liked the company. It was that wonderful start-up feeling and everybody was working together, and it was a really good atmosphere—a positive culture." The stress and eventual burnout occurred because the more Ruane did, the more she was expected to contribute. "A lot of it was my own fault. . . . It's the classic situation that if the work is getting done, why should they give you any more help? . . . I did far too much and I burned out."[9]

Managers who want to maintain the positive culture Rochelle Ruane mentioned and help employees avoid burnout should first admit that it can and does occur in all organizations—with all levels of employees. Then they should learn to recognize the personal traits or characteristics that may indicate that a person is experiencing burnout (see Figure 13-3).

If one suspects that another person may be experiencing burnout (see Figure 13-4), one can help determine if that may be the situation by asking the person to answer three questions:

1. What do you want from your job?
2. What do you have to do to get what you want?
3. Is it worth it to you to do what is necessary to get what you want?

If the troubled person can answer these questions honestly and is able to get what he or she wants from the job, the person may be rehabilitated. The employee must develop a program of setting and working toward the goals—a key to preventing burnout. These goals provide a reason to continue with the career and an important sense of direction.[10]

FIGURE 13-3 Symptoms of employee burnout.

Physical

A change in physical appearance; decline in grooming or wardrobe.
Complaints such as headaches, backaches, or gastrointestinal problems.
Increased absenteeism for health reasons.
Signs and symptoms of depression, such as a change in weight or eating habits or chronic fatigue.
Frequent infections, especially respiratory infections.

Emotional

Depressed appearance, such as sad expression, slumped posture or rounded shoulders.
Appearing bored or speaking of boredom.
Attitudes of cynicism, resentfulness, apathy or anxiety.
Expressions of frustration and hopelessness.

Behavioral

Decreased productivity, inability to focus on the job or complete a task.
Tardiness.
More frequent absenteeism.
Withdrawal or listlessness.
Expressions of irritability or hostility.
Overworking.
Abuse of drugs, alcohol or caffeine; increased smoking.
Excessive exercise, often to the point of injury.

SOURCE: Hugh F. Stallworth, "Realistic Goals Help Avid Burnout," *HRMagazine* (June 1990): 171. Used by permission.

The organizational culture, no matter how positive and supportive, will most likely be unable to prevent all possible cases of burnout. However, managers can take certain steps to at least mitigate its occurrence:[11]

1. *Acknowledge the problem.* Recognize that burnout can occur. Let employees know, through policy, orientation, and training, that the organization has policies to help them should it occur.

FIGURE 13-4 Are you burned out?

Job Burnout: Five Warning Signs

Employees are vulnerable if they have:

1. Little say about how to do the job
2. Feelings of never being caught up
3. Frequent sickness
4. A desire to quit but fear of doing so
5. Major changes in the work place

SOURCE: Northwestern National Life's Research Report, *Employee Burnout: America's Newest Epidemic.* 1993.

2. *Train managers.* Managers must be trained to recognize the symptoms of employee burnout and refer potential victims to counseling.

3. *Time limits.* Time limits are a key to preventing burnout. Constant excessive overtime is a common cause of stress and burnout.

4. *Recognize people's contributions.* Positive feedback helps people refuel psychologically and improves their self-image.

5. *Provide emotional outlets.* Provide outlets for anger, frustration, helplessness, and depression. Employees must often deal with these emotions alone. Providing a person (often their boss) who can help them cope with such feelings can avoid burnout.

6. *Provide retraining.* Retraining opportunities, even lateral moves for people who feel stuck in a dead-end position, can keep valuable employees motivated and at work.

EMPLOYER HEALTH-CARE PROGRAMS

Employee assistance programs designed to help employees overcome personal crises such as alcoholism, job burnout, or family problems are offered by over 73 percent of large employers.[12] Such programs have proved that valuable, skilled employees who experience problems can be helped. Once they have dealt with their problems, those employees often provide many more productive years of service. In fact, employees may be particularly grateful to employers who have lent them assistance during a time of personal or financial crisis.

General Motors spends more money for employee medical benefits than it spends for steel from its main supplier. Every year in the United States, employee illnesses and injuries cost over $25 billion in lost workdays. The annual rate of disability retirement is 170 percent higher than in the 1950s.[13] Employers pay half of U.S. health-care bills through insurance programs, which equals over 10 percent of the gross national product.[14]

Such statistics alone give employers more than adequate reason to be concerned about employee health and safety. Other reasons include various legal requirements, employer goodwill, and the increased employee productivity and morale that result from health programs. The array of programs available to employers seeking to reduce health-care costs include wellness programs, physical fitness programs, smoking cessation programs, employee assistance programs and substance abuse programs.

Wellness Programs

Employers have tried a number of approaches to address rising health costs and the poor fitness and health of employees. One approach is the establishment of **wellness programs**. The Health Insurance Association of America defines *wellness* as a "freely chosen life-style aimed at achieving and maintaining an individual's good health."[15] From management's perspective, employees are a company's greatest asset, and their state of health affects their contribution to the company in such measurable ways as absenteeism, lowered productivity, fatigue-caused accidents, reduced alertness and creativity, and higher health-care claims and insurance premiums. At the same time, employees indicate, by their high degree of participation, a great interest in wellness programs. Reasons include (1) the presumption that it is a quality program because it is company sponsored, (2) the perception that it is a fringe benefit and thus should be taken advantage of, and (3) the recognition that it is a convenient way to take care of health concerns.[16]

A U.S. Department of Health and Human Services survey confirmed that wellness programs are offered by a majority of American employers. Although such programs were once perceived to be a fad or a frivolous employee benefit, about 66 percent of U.S. employers with over 50 employees offer at least one wellness activity each year. What is the reason for the substantial growth rate in such programs? Employers report that they are an unqualified success. Employees who participate are more likely to have lower health-care costs and generally are healthier. The most common wellness activities offered by employers include the following:

- Smoking cessation (36 percent).
- Health-risk appraisals (30 percent).
- Back care (29 percent).
- Stress management (27 percent).
- Exercise/physical fitness (22 percent).
- Off-the-job accident prevention (20 percent).
- Nutrition education (17 percent).
- Blood pressure checks (17 percent).
- Weight control (15 percent).

One successful corporate wellness program was established by the Mesa Petroleum Company. Their program averaged $173 per participant in medical costs compared to $434 for nonparticipants.[17] General Motors' employee assistance program cut medical benefit payments by 60 percent after one year.[18] The Campbell Soup Company's colon-rectal cancer detection program recorded savings of $245,000 in medical payments.[19] And Burlington Industries reported that absenteeism decreased from 400 to 19 days annually due to its "healthy back" program.[20]

The ability of a wellness program to provide quantifiable savings over several years is still doubted by some people. Adolph Coors Company in Golden, Colorado, however, has carefully developed a wellness program that saves $1.9 million annually in documented savings. Coors estimates that for each dollar spent on their program, the company saves $6.15 in reduced medical costs, reduced sick leaves, reduced workers' compensation stress claims, and increased productivity.[21]

The Coors wellness program has received two national awards and is considered a model program. How does the Coors program work? "By making wellness a part of the corporate culture," says William Coors, chairman and CEO, who pushed the board of directors to build a 25,000-square-foot wellness facility. The facility offers aerobics, strength training, cardiovascular equipment, and an indoor running track. The program is far more than just a facility, however; employees and their spouses can participate in health-risk assessments, nutritional counseling, stress management, smoking cessation programs, on-site mammography and blood pressure screenings, family counseling, and pre- and postnatal education. Each of these components follows the Coors model to achieve behavioral change.[22]

1. *Awareness.* The health hazard appraisal (HHA) gives each employee and spouse personal information about their potential for premature death or disease.
2. *Education.* The HHA counselor describes the variety of on-site fitness activities, as well as programs that can help change employees' behavior. Education is also achieved through brochures, luncheon lectures, and elevator posters, such as the early warning signs of a heart attack.
3. *Incentives.* The company provides the financial incentive of refunding the cost of a program if participants achieve and maintain their personal goals. The programs are held on site.
4. *Programs.* A range of programs is offered, and employees are given a choice of one that interests them and meets their needs. In addition, the company cafeteria provides low-calorie and low-fat food choices.
5. *Self-action.* Programs are made available to all employees and their dependents, since they are included in all medical benefits.

On-site and off-site exercise facilities are also made available, and participants are encouraged to continue a personal exercise program. It is believed that for the program to succeed in the long run, employees must take responsibility for their health.

6. *Follow-up and support.* Follow-up information, such as direct-mail reminders of blood pressure screenings and mammograms, are provided. Periodic follow-up classes are also conducted.

Small Employer Programs   Wellness programs can be successfully implemented by small employers with limited budgets. Sunseeds, Inc., for example, implemented a basic program for its 200 employees at a total cost of only $2000, less than the average cost of one hospital stay.[23] In fact, many of the major benefits of a full-scale program such as the one at Coors can be achieved in a scaled-down program. A number of effective wellness-program activities can be established at a minimum cost, such as awareness brochures and pamphlets on subjects such as smoking, weight loss, stress awareness, and nutrition, on-site annual cholesterol and blood pressure checks by an outside agency; lunchtime walking programs; subsidized fees for smoking cessation and weight-loss programs; and removing cigarette and candy vending machines and replacing them with healthy alternatives.[24]

Companies of all sizes are even more likely to adopt wellness programs as the country's work force ages. With the baby boomers advancing toward their later working years, the average age of employees will increase. Therefore, health problems that occur more often in older workers could be prevented in many cases by an effective wellness program. In addition, the 1986 Age Discrimination in Employment Act amendment prohibits any mandatory retirement age for most workers and requires their employers to continue providing older workers the same health insurance that is offered to younger employees. It is likely, then, that in the future employers will be even more concerned about the health of their employees.

Company Physical-Fitness Programs   One major employer-sponsored method of increasing employees' health is the company **physical fitness program (PFP)**. The National Industrial Recreation Association estimates that over 50,000 firms have PFPs. Such programs are relatively new; more than 70 percent of company PFPs have been started since 1975.[25] A leading authority on PFPs believes that all HR departments should initiate such programs to develop employees mentally and physically. Most employees need up to three years to realize the full benefits from a program.[26]

PFPs vary greatly, from a basketball hoop in the employee parking lot to the Kimberly Clark Company's $2.5 million physical fitness center. According to a survey of 226 program directors, 41 percent of PFPs have gymnasiums and exercise rooms, 34 percent have an entire building used exclusively for physical fitness, 10 percent have company-sponsored teams, and 6 percent use YMCA facilities. In most programs, employees are encouraged to use the facilities and participation is voluntary. In 67 percent of programs, facilities are used on employees' own time; in 33 percent, on company time.[27]

Organizations that support PFPs generally expect them to be attractive to employees, to reduce the impact of stress, and to increase employee productivity. In addition, they are often expected to decrease absenteeism and turnover, as well as accidents and medical claims.[28] Documented improvements by employees who actively participate in a PFP include the following:

- Improved cardiovascular function, decreased body weight, and fat reduction.[29]
- Lower medical claims.[30]
- Smoking reduction and blood pressure normalization.[31]
- General physical fitness.[32]

Hard evidence that PFPs directly cause changes in the corporate bottom line is not readily available. Nevertheless, there continue to be increases in the development of PFPs because many believe that they positively affect both the employees and the organization. Table 13-1 shows the benefits thought to accrue from the establishment of such programs.

Employee Assistance Programs

Employee assistance programs (EAPs) began forty years ago when employers first began recognizing the workplace-related problems associated with alcohol abuse. Today, however, EAPs have a much broader and more comprehensive approach to helping employees identify and solve their personal problems, regardless of the cause. The general philosophy of an EAP is the belief that while the employer has no right to interfere in an employee's personal life, it does have the right to set performance standards and to establish sanctions when those standards are not met. A major cause of the increasing number of EAPs is their success. The recovery rate of participants in EAPs is three times that of the general public. This is likely due to (1) identifying problems early in their development; (2) the use of positive and negative employer reinforcement to motivate EAP patients to continue treatment; and (3)

EAP follow-up monitoring to minimize relapse problems.[33]

But the primary reason company-sponsored EAPs have increased is that they may enhance a company's profitability by reducing absenteeism, turnover, tardiness, accidents, and medical claims. It is estimated that a troubled employee costs the employer at least 5 percent of that employee's annual salary.[34]

A milestone in the growth of EAPs occurred in 1987. Over 800 EAP practitioners applied to take their first professional certification test. The test was developed and sponsored by the Association of Labor–Management Administrators and Consultants on Alcoholism (ALMACA). The certification program was designed to legitimize the EAP profession through standardization. Eventually state or federal laws as well as insurance companies may require EAP certification similar to that required by other professions.[35]

The typical program addresses psychological and physical problems, including job stress, chemical dependency (alcohol and drugs), depression, marital and family problems, financial problems, health, anxiety, and even job boredom. The procedure in virtually all EAPs consists of (1) problem identification, (2) intervention, and (3) treatment and recovery. Program operations generally fall into two

Table 13-1 Benefits of Physical Fitness Programs

Physiological Improvements	Behavior Changes	Benefits to the Organization
Weight and body fat loss	Less absenteeism	Lower medical claims and insurance premiums
Greater strength and endurance	Fewer fatigue-related accidents	Fewer disability claims
Better nutritional habits	Higher productivity	Fewer losses due to accidents
Less smoking	Enhanced mental alertness	Lower workers' compensation costs
Improved blood pressure and cardiovascular function		Higher employee morale and productivity
Stress reduction		Lower overtime and temporary-worker salaries due to absenteeism reduction

categories: internal programs that use a full-time staff of counselors and other employees, and referral centers that use a full-time specialist who identifies the problem and refers the employee to a community agency for treatment.

An example of a successful referral program is the EAP at the Bechtel Power Corporation in San Francisco. When a supervisor believes that an employee's performance has been adversely affected by personal problems, the supervisor phones the EAP office.[36] (An alternative first step is employee self-referral.) Once the supervisor and the EAP specialist discuss the particulars of the situation—such as the employee's performance record, absenteeism, and so on—the supervisor is normally advised to suggest that the employee use the EAP. It is carefully explained to the employee that participation is voluntary and does not affect the discipline process, which may be implemented if required by poor work. Strict confidentiality is guaranteed. At some point the employee may be given the choice of termination or using the EAP.

This critical first step—getting the employee to voluntarily seek assistance from the EAP—can be a difficult process for the supervisor. In general, the supervisor in approaching the employee should do the following:[37]

- Be specific about why the employee's behavior is unacceptable. Do not criticize the person; address only his or her job performance.
- Get a commitment from the employee to meet certain specific work standards that address the performance problem.
- Be consistent and firm in requiring the employee to meet the work standards.
- Resist the urge to diagnose the problem.
- Be prepared to cope with the employee's resistance, defensiveness, and hostility.
- Try to get the employee to acknowledge the problem and then suggest the EAP service, but emphasize that seeking assistance is voluntary.
- Emphasize that if the employee does not seek help, continued employment will depend on the employee's improving his or her performance without help.

When the employee calls the EAP office, a specialist then performs *triage*—the determination of the relative urgency of the case. A case may be (1) a life-threatening emergency such as a suicide attempt; (2) an urgent need such as extreme anxiety or crying; or (3) a routine need. In the first case, the counselor responds immediately; in the second, within hours; in the third, a counseling session is set up within days. At the counseling session, a referral to a local agency is made and the follow-up process is started. Follow-up by the agency is continued for as long as is needed, with particular attention given to the continuance and frequency of the employee's sessions.[38]

Internal programs are usually more expensive and therefore found mostly in larger organizations. Such programs provide a sense of security because the employee is not given a quick diagnosis and sent to an outside source. Instead, sessions with in-house counselors provide the needed treatment in most cases. Exceptions include cases of chemical abuse and various physical problems.[39]

EAP professionals generally agree on what components are essential for a successful program. Essentials for an effective EAP include the following:[40]

- *Confidentiality.* Employees must believe that all information about their problems will be kept confidential by the counselor. Supervisors should only be informed that the employee is continuing to receive assistance.
- *Normal disciplinary procedures.* No employee should receive lenient or harsh treatment due to participation (or lack of it) in an

EAP. Some programs allow the suspension of discipline as an incentive to enter the program. Even in such cases, the employee's work must improve and the problem eventually resolved.

- *Voluntary participation.* Supervisors can strongly urge an employee to participate and even give termination as the alternative, but the employee must seek help voluntarily for any chance of success.

- *Job security.* No employee will be affected by disciplinary or other actions because he or she participated in the program.

- *Insurance coverage.* Both inpatient and outpatient treatment must be covered by insurance.

- *Management support.* Management must provide written assurance that the company is committed to the process.

- *Accessibility.* Employees must know how and for what types of problems they can receive assistance. A broad range of assistance ensures a better image and greater use.

- *Follow-up.* Some problems will take years to correct, though most can be rectified in a number of months. Periodic follow-up, whether by in-house counselors or outside agencies, is critical to a high recovery rate.

- *Separate location.* The program should be located away from the workplace to help ensure privacy.

Substance Abuse in the Workplace

Almost every major change in our society affects the workplace sooner or later. Substance abuse is certainly not an exception. Drug and alcohol abuse in the United States is currently a major contributor to many of society's problems, including the breakup of families, crime, and students' dropping out of school. The National Institute on Drug Abuse estimates that there are over 10.5 million alcoholics in the United States, 5.7 million cocaine users, and 4.3 million marijuana users. And a survey of *Fortune* 1000 company CEOs found that 57 percent consider substance abuse a significant problem in their organization, and they believe that the problem is increasing.[41] The magnitude of the problem has caused many employers to develop policies to deal with employee alcohol and drug abuse.

Alcohol Abuse

One of society's most persistent and devastating ills, alcoholism often leads to severe marital problems, family abuse, estrangement between parents and children, the loss of close friends and acquaintances, emotional illness, and ostracism by society. Statistics show that alcohol and other mood-altering substances increase violent crimes and traffic accidents that result in death. The societal burdens of alcoholism have long been of major concern to professionals in social work, medicine, and psychiatry.

Alcoholism has also received a great deal of attention from both management academicians and HR practitioners. Much of this interest has been created by the publication of data that show that (1) a high percentage of American workers are alcoholics and (2) the alcoholic worker has many more work-related problems than a nonalcoholic worker. How many workers are alcoholics? While the exact numbers are impossible to pin down, most informed sources, including the National Council on Alcoholism (NCA), estimate about 10 percent of the labor force. Alcoholics are in business, government, the professions, sciences, voluntary agencies, and academia on all organizational levels. The National Institute on Alcohol Abuse and Alcoholism (NIAAA) estimates that 25 percent of alcoholic employees are white-collar employees, 30 percent are blue-collar workers, and 45 percent are managers/professionals.[42]

Although some alcoholic employees perform their work satisfactorily and meet job expectations, many cannot. The NCA reports that alcoholic employees are absent an average of two to four times more often than nonalcoholic employees and that on-the-job accidents are two to four times more frequent for alcoholic employees.[43] In addition to these costly problems, alcoholic employees may create other work-related difficulties:

- The alcoholic's negligence may cause accidents and injuries to other employees.
- The alcoholic may disregard job details, use poor judgment, and make bad decisions.
- The alcoholic may perform unevenly in terms of quantity and quality.
- The alcoholic may minimize contact with co-workers and supervisors and exhibit antisocial behavior.

The alcoholic employee's performance, including above-average absenteeism, injuries, accidents, and substandard levels of productivity and quality, represents real costs to the organization. For large organizations, the costs can be staggering. The U.S. Postal Service estimates its losses in productivity from alcoholism at $186 million annually. United California Bank estimates losing $1 million a year to alcoholism among its employees.[44] Nationwide, $25 billion is lost annually due to alcoholics' absenteeism, accidents, sick leave, decreased productivity, and poor work quality. A full-scale attack on alcoholism can be justified not only for social and moral reasons but for economic considerations as well.

What causes alcoholism? There is little agreement about the specific causes. Predicting precisely who will or will not become an alcoholic is impossible. Alcoholism does not discriminate against any particular social or economic class; this disease is as likely to victimize the middle manager as the assembly-line worker.

Nonetheless, researchers have isolated a mix of circumstances that greatly influence problem drinkers. The NCA suggests that the **problem drinker** is one who has the following characteristics:

- Experiences intense relief and relaxation from alcohol.
- Has difficulty in dealing with and overcoming depression, anxiety, and frustration.
- Is a member of a culture in which there is pressure to drink, as well as culturally induced guilt and confusion regarding appropriate drinking behavior.

According to the NCA, when these persons encounter problems with their families, spouses, jobs, loneliness, old age, and so on, their probability of becoming alcoholics increases significantly.

Researchers also recognize the possibility that certain working conditions may lead to alcoholism. In a U.S. Department of Health, Education, and Welfare (HEW) report entitled *Work in America,* the author stated:[45]

> Nonsupportive jobs in which the worker gets little feedback on his performance appear to cause the kind of anxiety that may lead to or aggravate alcoholism. Work addiction, occupational obsolescence, role stress, and unstructured environments (for certain personality types) appear to be other important risk factors for both alcoholism and drug addiction.

The HEW report's suggestion that organizations do have some control over whether an employee becomes a problem drinker is important. Decision makers are faced with a difficult choice involving moral and economic considerations. They may create an environment that produces satisfying human experiences and enhances mental and physical health. Or they may create an environment that leads to frustration, anxiety, and stress—one that compels a certain type of employee to seek relief through alcohol or perhaps other addictive chemicals. Faced with these alternatives, managers have a twofold responsibility: to create programs for employees suffering from alcoholism and to create a work climate that minimizes the conditions and circumstances that pressure an employee to seek relief in excessive drink.

Unlike job attitudes or opinions, alcoholism cannot be measured by traditional HR tools such as surveys or questionnaires. First, many alcoholics are unwilling to admit that they have a problem; thus a general-purpose questionnaire—even though anonymous—would not generate much useful data on alcoholism within the organization. Second, alcoholism can be defined only in the most general terms. For instance, the *American Heritage Dictionary* defines alcoholism as "a chronic pathological condition chiefly of the nervous and gastroenteric systems, caused by habitual excessive alcoholic consumption." In conducting research, it may be difficult to distinguish between heavy or excessive drinking and the various stages of alcoholism. Third, employees may perceive alcoholism as a sensitive personal issue. Many employees would no doubt feel that the collection of information about alcohol abuse is an invasion of privacy.

Even though alcoholism may be difficult to measure quantitatively, persons may determine if they have the symptoms of the problem. Both the NCA and Alcoholics Anonymous (AA) have developed checklists to help individuals decide if they may need help in combating alcohol. Although a checklist is not useful for research purposes, it may be part of an organization's alcoholism education program given to employees who inquire about the organization's rehabilitation services. The AA checklist is shown in Figure 13-5.

Because alcoholism is difficult to measure in an organizational setting, research will be limited. For example, it may be impossible to analyze which employees have the highest rates of alcoholism or what work conditions and environmental settings tend to aggravate the problem.

A researcher may be able to evaluate the organization's rehabilitation efforts with known alcoholic employees and determine how these employees behave differently. By analyzing the work histories of alcoholic employees, it should also be possible to discover how their absenteeism, accidents, injuries, productivity, and work quality differ from organizationwide norms. This information will help call management's attention to the seriousness of the problem.

Reducing Alcoholism Because employee alcoholism may stem from both personal and work factors, the most effective strategy for combating alcoholism is to minimize the potential for alcoholism by keeping stress and anxiety at the lowest possible levels. Rehabilitation programs for employees who are currently suffering from alcoholism should be implemented.

Programs to minimize alcoholism in the workplace may be most difficult for the HR administrator to implement and control. Challenge, stress, and conflict seem to be inevitable in the jobs of many modern managers and administrators. Further, the HR administrator has only moderate control over the work climate and goal-setting process for employees outside of the HR department. Nonetheless, the HR staff can educate top and middle managers about the potentially harmful effects of excessive job stress and anxiety. Through training and development activities, the HR staff can make executives aware that the way people are managed and how their jobs are designed may significantly affect their mental and physical health.

The second strategy to fight alcoholism—the implementation of rehabilitation policies and programs—has become an important personnel responsibility in many larger organizations today. As management and labor con-

FIGURE 13-5 AA's checklist for alcoholism.

One device used in some companies to help alcoholics to appreciate the seriousness of their problem is to ask them to answer 20 questions relating to their drinking pattern. This test has been used, occasionally with modifications, in a number of industrial alcoholism programs.

The test:

		YES	NO
1.	Have you lost time from work due to drinking?	( )	( )
2.	Has drinking made your home life unhappy?	( )	( )
3.	Do you drink because you are shy with people?	( )	( )
4.	Has drinking affected your reputation?	( )	( )
5.	Have you gotten into financial difficulties because of your drinking?	( )	( )
6.	Do you turn to lower companions and an inferior environment when drinking?	( )	( )
7.	Does your drinking make you careless of your family's welfare?	( )	( )
8.	Has your drinking decreased your ambition?	( )	( )
9.	Do you want a drink "the morning after"?	( )	( )
10.	Does your drinking cause you to have difficulty sleeping?	( )	( )
11.	Has your efficiency decreased since drinking?	( )	( )
12.	Has drinking ever jeopardized your job or business?	( )	( )
13.	Do you drink to escape from worries or troubles?	( )	( )
14.	Do you drink alone?	( )	( )
15.	Have you ever had a complete loss of memory as a result of drinking?	( )	( )
16.	Has your physician ever treated you for drinking?	( )	( )
17.	Do you drink to build up self-confidence?	( )	( )
18.	Have you ever been in an institution or hospital on account of drinking?	( )	( )
19.	Have you ever felt remorse after drinking?	( )	( )
20.	Do you crave a drink at a definite time daily?	( )	( )

When they takes the test, the employee is reminded that only they can determine whether or not they are an alcoholic. However, if the employee answers yes to as few as three questions, they can be reasonably certain that alcohol has become, or is becoming, a problem.

SOURCE: Alcoholics Anonymous, *A.A. and the Alcoholic Employee* (New York: Alcoholics Anonymous World Services, Inc., 1962), pp. 12–13.

tinue to accept employee rehabilitation efforts, such programs will, no doubt, continue to expand.

Kemper Insurance Companies, one of the first organizations to implement a formal employee assistance program, has outlined its approach to employee rehabilitation in a pamphlet entitled ***Management Guide on Alcoholism.***[46] Kemper's policies are shown in Figure 13-6.

Do EAPs work? The answer is a qualified yes. The majority of alcoholic employees recover fully as a result of rehabilitation efforts. The NCA reports that business and industry success rates range from 65 to 80 percent and that Air Force and Navy success rates are 70 to 80 percent. A NIAAA research study reported that "72 percent of executives of *Fortune* 500 companies with occupational programs believe their firms have saved money as a result of

FIGURE 13-6 Kemper's policies on employee alcoholism.

Alcoholism Policy. In accordance with our general personnel policies, whose underlying concept is regard for the employee as an individual as well as a worker:

1. We believe alcoholism, or problem drinking, is an illness and should be treated as such.
2. We believe the majority of employees who develop alcoholism can be helped to recover and the company should offer appropriate assistance.
3. We believe the decision to seek diagnosis and accept treatment for any suspected illness is the responsibility of the employee. However, continued refusal of an employee to seek treatment when it appears that substandard performance may be caused by any illness is not tolerated. We believe that alcoholism should not be made an exception to this commonly accepted principle.
4. We believe that it is in the best interest of employees and the company that alcoholism be diagnosed and treated at the earliest possible stage.
5. We believe that the company's concern for individual drinking practices begins only when they result in unsatisfactory job performance.
6. We believe that confidential handling of the diagnosis and treatment of alcoholism is essential.

The objective of this policy is to retain employees who may develop alcoholism by helping them to arrest its further advance before the condition renders them unemployable.

Supervisory Practices. Supervisors are instructed that they should *not* attempt to identify alcoholic employees. Further, supervisors should not discuss "drinking problems" with their employees, except where drinking on the job or an intoxicated employee is observed (the diagnosis of alcoholism is the job of trained professionals). Rather, the supervisor's responsibility is to closely and accurately monitor employee *performance and work habits* and confront the employee whose performance problems persist with the warning that continued poor performance will lead to disciplinary action. . . .

Treatment Facilities. Kemper, as do most companies which conduct employee assistance programs, uses a variety of alcoholism treatment sources. These include both private alcoholism consulting and treatment firms and not-for-profit organizations such as AA and Al-Anon, which provides support and assistance to the family members of an alcoholic.

SOURCE: *Management Guide on Alcoholism* (Long Grove, IL: Kemper Insurance Companies, undated) pp. 6–11. Used by permission.

these programs, and most of the executives are convinced of the effectiveness of the program."[47]

One of the most widely reported company success stories involves Oldsmobile Motor Division's EAP. Oldsmobile's Employee Alcoholism Recovery Program involves a cooperative effort between General Motors and the United Auto Workers. The mechanics of the program are similar to the procedures outlined in Figure 13-6. An evaluation study showed that 117 program participants significantly reduced their absenteeism, accidents, grievances, and disciplinary actions during the year following their participation in the program. Preprogram costs due to lost wages were estimated at $84,616; lost wages were estimated at $43,336 after their involvement in the program. Oldsmobile reported that the economic benefits of the program far exceeded the costs and termed the program both profitable and worthwhile.[48]

Drug Abuse

Employers are increasingly concerned over the rise of drug abuse in the workplace. As a result, testing has moved into almost every industry. In 1987 President Reagan's Commission on Organized Crime requested that all U.S. companies test their employees for drug use. Employee testing, the Commission believed, can create a safer work environment and reduce society's demand for illegal drugs (see *HR in the News:* "Employer Drug Testing Driving Down Use in Society.") How serious

Employer Drug Testing Driving Down Use in Society

The experts say corporate anti-drug campaigns have contributed to an overall decline in casual drug use around the country.

"Corporate programs make drug use more of a hassle and make it seem less socially acceptable," said Dr. Robert B. Millman, the director of alcohol and drug abuse programs at the New York Hospital–Payne Whitney Psychiatric Clinic. "There's no question they have driven down drug use."

Dr. Kent W. Peterson, a vice president of the American College of Occupational and Environmental Medicine and a consultant to companies on drug problems, said there is clearly a "spinoff effect" on the rest of society.

"Company drug policies are often discussed with spouses," Peterson said. "They get communicated to children and they affect one's social and recreational life. They have also sensitized community leaders to the fact that something can be done and that this is not something they have to passively accept."

Two of the largest drug-testing companies, Roche Biomedical Labs and Smith-Kline Beecham Clinical Laboratories, estimate that 15 million Americans are being required to give urine samples for testing annually, up from about half that five years ago, at a cost of $600 million.

Between 5 and 8 percent of those tested by the two big labs are found to have drugs in their system, company officials said. Of those, 40 to 50 percent have

---

are the problems created by a drug user? One company estimated, based on employee records, that the typical drug user, compared to the norm for the work unit:[49]

- Functions at about 67 percent of potential capacity.
- Is 360 percent more likely to be involved in an accident.
- Requires three times the average use of sick leave and benefits.
- Is five times more likely to file a workers' compensation claim.
- Is absent ten more workdays per year.
- Is more likely to file a grievance complaint.

The Drug-free Workplace Act of 1988
Under the 1988 federal **Drug-free Workplace Act**, federal contractors and grantees who receive more than $25,000 in federal grants or contracts must certify that they will maintain a drug-free workplace. Companies must ensure that drug use by employees does not occur in the workplace if they continue to do business with the federal government. The act does not include the use of tobacco or alcohol by employees. The act does require employers to take the following steps to ensure they operate a drug-free workplace:[50]

1. *Policy statement.* Establish and notify all employees of a policy prohibiting the illegal

604

been using marijuana, 20 to 25 percent cocaine, and about 10 percent opiates, mainly codeine, but occasionally heroin.

The rest test positive for either amphetamines; an animal tranquilizer known as PCP, or angel dust; or a variety of mainly prescription drugs that are sometimes abused.

While some surveys show employees strongly support drug testing because it promises greater safety and harmony at work, scores of civil suits in the early and mid-1980s challenged the procedure as an invasion of privacy. The courts, however, have upheld most testing programs, and many fewer suits are being fielded these days. Even the American Civil Liberties Union, which filed many of the suits, acknowledges that drug testing has reduced drug use.

Every company that has instituted drug programs has recorded steep drops in drug incidents. When Pfizer, Inc., the New York based pharmaceutical company, started testing job applicants in 1987, 9.9 percent turned up with evidence of having recently used drugs. But by last year, the percentage had fallen to 3.2.

Hoffmann-Laroche, the big pharmaceutical company, with its U.S. headquarters in New Jersey, and Mobil Corp., which has major offices in New York and New Jersey, found about 7 percent of their job applicants were using drugs when they began testing in the early and mid-1980s. Now, both companies say fewer than 1 percent are testing positive.

Many companies offer counseling and treatment to employees found using drugs and give them a second chance, sometimes even a third. But applicants get no help. They are simply not hired, and many never learn why.

SOURCE: Joseph B. Treasfer, *The New York Times,* as reprinted in the *Omaha World-Herald* (November 21, 1993): 11-G. Used by permission.

use, possession, manufacture, or distribution of controlled substances in the workplace. Warn employees of action that will be taken against violators.

2. *Awareness programs.* Provide a drug-awareness program that educates employees on the dangers of drug abuse. Inform employees of available drug counseling, rehabilitation, and employee assistance programs.

3. *Conditions of employment.* Notify employees that the drug-abuse policy is a condition of employment. Employees must agree to inform the employer of any criminal conviction for a drug-abuse statute violation within five days.

4. *Agency notifications.* The employer must notify the federal contracting agency within ten days of receiving the notice of a conviction from an employee.

5. *Good-faith effort.* The employer must make a good-faith effort to maintain a drug-free workplace.

Supporters of the 1988 act believe that it provides employers with a good incentive to initiate a drug-free program without being subjected to negative public and employee reactions. For an example of how one company does it, see *HR In the News:* "How Motorola Enforces Its Drug-free Policy." Some critics, however, contend the law should have con-

How Motorola Enforces
Its Drug-free Policy

Motorola's drug policy is stated simply: "No use of illegal drugs; no use of legal drugs illegally." To enforce the policy, Motorola instituted a universal drug-testing program on January 1, 1991. HR professionals administer the program.

Every employee becomes a part of the data base, including the CEO and contractors. A specially designed computer program selects from each Motorola site employee names to be tested each day. The computer program ensures that every employee is selected at least once in three years for a drug test. It's possible, however, for some employees to be selected more than once during that period. This is designed to prevent an employee's feeling safe from testing after taking one test.

The HR department informs the employees' supervisors, who are responsible for relaying the information to the employees. The supervisor then has time to plan for the employee's absence. Failure of an employee to report to a designated location may result in disciplinary action.

The collection area prepares split samples for the Motorola employees, allowing for analyses from two different labs if the employees request it. If an employee's test comes out positive, the company's medical-review officer discusses the situation with the employee to determine if there's some legitimate reason—such as a prescription drug that the employee forgot to mention—for a positive result.

If it's determined that a drug-abuse problem exists, the next step for the employee is to report to HR to set up a meeting with an EAP advisor and plan rehabilitation methods. The company pays for the employee's rehabilitation. In the meantime, unless it is some safety-sensitive or security-clearance position, the employee continues working on the job.

After employees complete their rehabilitation programs, their names go into a special random pool. Motorola tests these employees once every 120 days for a one-year period. If during this one-year period an employee again tests positive, the organization terminates him or her. If, however, all tests following rehabilitation come out negative, the employee's name goes back into the three-year pool, and he or she begins the testing process again.

SOURCE: Adapted from Dawn Gunsch, "Training Prepares Workers for Drug Testing," *Personnel Journal* (May 1993): 54.

tained harsh penalties and mandatory drug testing of employees instead of only a policy statement and awareness-program provisions.

Employee Drug Testing Many employers today are less likely to question the need for a drug-testing policy. Instead, the question is what key policy and legal issues should be considered when developing a comprehensive policy.

According to a December 1988 American Management Association survey of more than 1000 companies, 48 percent test employees for drug use, compared to only 21 percent two years earlier (just prior to the commission's report). The survey found that drug-testing programs generally fall into two areas: preemployment testing of new hires and post-employment testing of current employees.[51]

Applicant Testing Employers may require any applicant to submit to a drug-screening test, unless limited by a state law. Employers, in a statement of policy, can express their desire to hire only qualified applicants. Since drug use may adversely affect job performance, they can choose to hire only applicants who pass a drug-screening test.

This concept was generally upheld by a U.S. Supreme Court decision in *New York City Transit Authority* v. *Baeger*.[52] The Court ruled that the safety and efficiency of the public transportation system constituted a valid business necessity and was a justifiable reason to require drug testing of bus driver applicants.

In a landmark 1989 decision, the National Labor Relations Board (NLRB) upheld an employer's right to require applicants to pass a drug test without negotiating the issue with their union. In the case, the *Star Tribune*, a Minneapolis newspaper, denied employment to job applicants who tested positive or refused to take the drug test.[53] The union demanded that the *Star Tribune* bargain over the policy. When management denied the demand, the union filed an unfair labor practice charge based on the refusal to bargain.

The need for drug screening for all job candidates may increase in the future due to several factors:

- Increased drug use in all segments of society.
- Reluctance of previous employers to report suspected or known drug use by former employees for fear of litigation.
- Employer liability for the negligent hiring of employees.

Preemployment drug testing requires the careful consideration of several issues. The following points are contained in the policy developed by the International Business Machine (IBM) Corporation:[54]

1. *Notification.* Notify applicants of the screening on the physical examination questionnaire to minimize claims of invasion of privacy.

2. *No rescheduling of the test.* Do not allow an applicant to reschedule a test after he or she appears at the doctor's office and realizes that it is part of the physical examination. The person may be a substance abuser who could refrain from illegal substance use before the next exam.

3. *Test validity.* In the event of a positive test result, repeat the test using the same sample in order to ensure validity. Ensure that test samples are kept by the doctor's office for 180 days in case of litigation.

4. *Confidentiality.* Maintain confidentiality by recording positive test results only on the doctor's records. On personnel records, use a code if an individual fails the test. Only the applicant should be aware of the test results, and the person can simply be informed that his or her test result was unsatisfactory. This policy holds true for current employees also.

Testing of Current Employees The testing of current employees raises more difficult policy issues, as well as the need to keep up-to-date with court arbitration decisions. Employers usually test employees according to one of three policies:

- ***Random testing.*** All employees are tested at random, periodic intervals or randomly selected employees are tested on predetermined dates.

- ***Probable cause.*** An employee is tested only when his or her behavior causes a reasonable suspicion on the part of supervisors.

- ***After accidents.*** All employees involved are tested after any accident or major incident.

Of the three policies, the use of random testing has raised the strongest criticisms, largely based on an employee's right to privacy. Random testing has been initiated, however, for federal employees.

By Executive Order 12564 (1988), President Reagan provided that federal employees who used illegal drugs—off or on duty—were unfit for federal employment. The executive order provided that random drug testing would be initiated in those federal agencies where the employees' duties involved public safety or law enforcement.

Private-sector employees not involved in public safety should probably not be randomly tested. Instead, there should be a reasonable basis for probable cause before an employee is tested. An important jury decision sent a strong message to employers with random-testing policies. A computer programmer for the Southern Pacific Transportation Company was awarded $485,000 after she was fired for refusing to take a random urinalysis. Her case relied on the general right-of-privacy provisions of the California constitution, which are similar to those found in many states.[55] In general, a random-testing policy will most likely be upheld by a court or arbitrator if it is related to public safety.

Probable Cause A policy of testing employees for drug usage only when there is probable cause will be more readily accepted by employees. Probable-cause testing has also received support from the courts and from arbitrators if the test is given based on a reasonable suspicion of drug use. A supervisor's reasonable suspicion based on an employee's absenteeism, erratic behavior, poor work performance, and the like can generally be accepted as a reason to test.

A major accident involving employees can be considered an immediate probable-cause situation and thus can invoke required testing of all employees involved. The federal government's regulation requiring railroads to test all crew members after major train accidents was upheld by the U.S. Supreme Court in the 1989 *Skinner* case.[56] The Court held that private railroads subject to federal regulations must test all members of a train crew following a major train accident. Both blood and urine tests are required.[57]

There are several policy considerations regarding the probable-cause testing process and the use of test results:

- ***Valid testing procedure.*** The burden of proof is clearly on management regarding the use of confidential, fair, and valid testing procedures. Proper testing procedures include the use of an approved, certified laboratory with state-of-the-art tests. To guard against false-positive results that may lead to unfair discipline or other actions, a second, confirming test should be required.

- ***On-the-job-impairment.*** In cases involving discipline as a result of a positive drug test, an employee or union may contend that the tests prove the presence of a drug in the employee's body but not on-the-job use or impairment. Indeed, in a court case, *Shelby County Health Care Center,* the relevant provision of the contract limited drug- or alcohol-related "major" offenses to drug or alcohol use on the employer's premises or being "under the influence." A fired employee was reinstated because, while his drug test was positive, there was no on-the-job impairment.[58]

There is concern that positive drug tests involving illegal drugs might be used to discipline an employee for the illegal activity involved in obtaining and possessing the drug—regardless of the on-the-job effect. The employer's position is that an employee who engages in such illegal activity is not a fit employee. To date, however, arbitrators and courts have often required a link between the employee's drug use and behavior in the workplace before just cause for discipline is found. Such a relationship should not be difficult to establish in most cases.

- *Refusal to be tested.* An employer can usually sustain the termination of an employee for failure to take a drug test in cases of probable cause. However, just as with other offenses that can lead to termination, the employee should be warned that failure to submit to testing will result in discharge.

- *Supervisor training.* A policy that includes the training of all supervisors to recognize the typical signs of employee drug use is important if probable cause is the basis of testing. The reasonableness of a supervisor's request for a test is more likely to be upheld if the supervisor has participated in an appropriate training program.[59] While many supervisors may be able to detect alcoholic intoxication, behavior caused by drug abuse is more difficult to recognize without training.

How does the general public feel about employee drug testing? A *Newsweek* survey reported very strong public support. Eighty-five percent of those polled supported testing for police officers, 84 percent for airline pilots, 72 percent for professional athletes, 72 percent for government workers, 64 percent for high school teachers, and 50 percent for all workers.[60] Most drug tests are based on analysis of

body fluids; there are other types of drug tests (see Figure 13-7).

Smoking in the Workplace

A 1986 report of the U.S. Surgeon General concluded that sidestream or passive smoking, the involuntary inhaling by nonsmokers of tobacco smoke, is dangerous to their health. The report stated that environmental tobacco smoke (ETS) causes 2400 to 4000 lung cancer deaths annually among nonsmokers. ETS is the combination of sidestream smoke, which comes from burning cigarettes between puffs, and mainstream smoke, which is exhaled by a smoker.[61] In addition, other reports indicate that nonsmokers exposed to ETS have a 1.3 to 3.5 times greater risk of developing lung cancer than unexposed nonsmokers.[62] Tobacco smoke is also a severe problem for allergy sufferers.

Legal restrictions on smoking in the workplace are mostly found at the state and local levels. As of 1986, ten states had enacted laws regulating smoking in the private sector workplace.[63] Many local governments have also passed restrictions. The 1973 federal Rehabilitation Act was applied to workplace smoking in a 1982 court case when an employee successfully claimed that he was handicapped as a result of inhaling the smoke of fellow employees.[64] The court found, however, that the employer only had to make "reasonable accommodations" for the employee and was not required to ban workplace smoking.

Balancing the rights of smokers and nonsmokers is a difficult HR policy issue. However, more employers have continued to develop new policies: 16 percent in 1980 to 84 percent in 1990.[65] In addition to the health considerations of nonsmokers, employers must consider that the employee who smokes costs the employer an average of $400 to $1000 per year more than the nonsmoker in health insurance claims, absenteeism, maintenance, and productivity.[66] But there are conflicting opinions on the specific effects of

FIGURE 13-7 Alternatives to body-fluid testing

Pupillary-Reaction Test

A trained professional may determine if a subject is under the influence of drugs or alcohol by examining the subject's eyes. The pupil will react differently to light (a flashlight is used) if the subject is under the influence of drugs. Follow-up tests by body-fluid testing are usually needed.

Positive features: Noninvasive.
Negative features: Must be administered by a trained professional.
 Some medical conditions may give a false positive result.
 Follow-up tests are needed.

Hair Analysis

Hair samples are examined using radioimmunoassay, then confirmed by gas chromatography or mass spectrometry. The same techniques are used to test urine samples. Chemicals—drugs, legal or illegal—are left behind in hair follicles and provide a record of past drug use. Type of drug, frequency, and duration of use can be determined. Because hair grows about half an inch per month a relatively small sample can provide a long record of drug use.

Positive features: Accepted by courts in criminal trials.
 Detailed record of drug use.
 Cannot be avoided as easily as urinalysis.
 Less embarrassing than urinalysis.
Negative features: Highly invasive.

Video-based Eye-Hand Coordination Test

One company has begun marketing a video-based test of eye-hand coordination. The test takes less than a minute to complete and is self-administered. The test determines only impairment and employees are actually tested against their own normal performance. Lack of sleep, illness, stress, drugs, or alcohol could cause an employee to fail.

Positive features: Can be used immediately before employee begins work.
 Noninvasive. Does not make life-style judgments.
 Self-administered.
 Low cost.
Negative features: So far only implemented at test sites.
 Follow-up tests necessary.

SOURCE: Adapted from "Business Approved Non-invasive Ways to Test Impairment," *HRMagazine* (June, 1990): 65.

employee smoking in the workplace. A non-affiliated research group has published research results indicating that smokers are high achievers and among the most productive employees.[67] Employers have developed a number of policies on workplace smoking:

- **Total ban.** In 1984 the Boeing Company in Seattle announced its intention to provide a smoke-free environment for all employees. With over 85,000 employees, Boeing became the largest U.S. company to ban smoking in the workplace. According to the company's president, Malcolm Stamper, developing a smoke-free environment is an essential ingredient in providing a clean, a safe, and a healthy working environment.[68]

- **Workstation ban.** Restrict smoking to separate, ventilated smoking lounges.

- *Encouragement of no smoking.* A bonus or award may be given to employees who do not smoke. The City Federal Savings and Loan Association of Birmingham, Alabama, for example, awards $20 per month to employees who do not smoke at work.[69]

- *Dangerous area ban.* Allow smoking in all areas except near combustible materials or in other hazardous situations. This policy meets minimum federal Occupational Health and Safety Administration (OSHA) standards.

- *Reasonable accommodation.* Separate employees who complain of smoke from adjacent co-workers who smoke and improve ventilation.

Before establishing one of these policies, an employer should consider the following:

1. All employees, from the president down, must be included in formulating the policy.

2. Disciplinary actions to be invoked when violations occur should be included in any policy.

3. Allow a transition period of several months between the announcement and implementation of the policy. This will give smokers who must quit the time to adjust.

4. Provide smoking cessation classes for smokers if a total ban is imposed.

5. Inform new employees of the policy during the interview process.

"Once adopted, a smoking policy that is properly communicated and fairly enforced can greatly assist employers in protecting the rights of nonsmokers. Such a policy can also help avoid the many legal liabilities which may result from tobacco smoke in the workplace."[70]

The courts have upheld the legal right of employers to prohibit smoking in the workplace, as well as to require job applicants to be nonsmokers. But the U.S. Supreme Court has not yet addressed the issue in a precedent-setting case. HR policymakers have many issues to consider—the rights of smokers and nonsmokers, the health and safety problems that may be caused by smoking in the workplace, and a variety of policy options. The issue will likely continue to be one of the most controversial in the area of employee health and safety.

AIDS in the Workplace

In only a few years AIDS—acquired immune deficiency syndrome—has become a health issue that has captured the attention of all Americans. The reasons are obvious: it is fatal, and the number of cases diagnosed in the United States alone has doubled every year since 1981.[71] The concerns and fears concerning AIDS have spread to the workplace. Issues confronting employers who must deal with **AIDS in the workplace** are complicated.

Employees with AIDS are covered under the 1990 Americans with Disabilities Act (see Chapter 3). The act considers AIDS a physical disability; thus employers cannot discriminate against employees with AIDS with regard to employment decisions or compensation. In addition, the act requires an employer to make "reasonable accommodation" for disabled employees, which may include changes in facilities, hours, and nonessential job duties. The act does not, however, require an employer to hire or continue to employ individuals who cannot perform the essential duties of their jobs.

According to three national surveys, only a minority of all employers have policies covering AIDS. Perhaps the number is small in spite of the national attention focused on the virus because there are major reasons for not issuing AIDS policy statements: (1) there is no need since AIDS should be treated like any other disease or condition; (2) issuing a policy statement may obligate an employer to follow a course of action that may prove unwise; (3) although the facts about AIDS are still rapidly changing, it is generally agreed that the virus cannot be transmitted by normal workplace contacts. The notable exception would occur in organizations where there is a likelihood of blood contact with other persons.[72]

Some employers have, however, issued policies. Bank of America was one of the first U.S. employers to develop a policy on AIDS in the workplace. Their program began with two principles: a safe work environment should be provided to all workers, and an employee's health condition is personal and confidential. The policy treats AIDS in a manner consistent with life-threatening illnesses in that the employer will make reasonable accommodation for employees, which might include a job transfer or disability leave.[73]

The progressive Bank of America policy also stresses education. Employees are told that AIDS is not treated differently from other medical conditions in terms of employee benefits. Employees with questions or concerns about AIDS are directed to AIDS hotlines and community organizations. The policy was also formulated to provide all employees and customers with the facts about AIDS. Medical evidence indicating that AIDS is not spread via casual contact in the workplace is highlighted in regular employee communications. However, if medical research evidence changes, Bank of America would likely change its policy. Nancy Merritt, vice president and program manager of personnel relations, explains: "If we were dealing with a disease that could be transmitted by casual contact in the workplace, we would not permit an affected employee to continue working. Also, if appropriate, we would tell employees what they had been exposed to."[74]

A difficult employment issue is the rights of co-workers of AIDS victims. The Occupational Health and Safety Administration (OSHA) requires every employer to provide a safe and healthy workplace. The Secretary of Labor may take action against employers who fail to provide a safe working environment. Co-workers of an AIDS victim who might seek such action, however, would need to prove that they are at risk of contracting the disease, a difficult task given current medical evidence. Federal OSHA regulations do provide that an employee may refuse to work if "a reasonable person would conclude [that] he faced an immediate risk of death or serious injury." Such action may not be considered reasonable by the Labor Department unless direct contact with blood or other body fluids were required by the job.[75]

SAFETY PROGRAMS

It is estimated that 70 to 95 percent of all injuries resulting from workplace accidents can be attributed directly to employees' engaging in unsafe acts. Therefore, **safety programs** are most effective when they are oriented toward training and motivating employees to adopt safe work habits. Most programs include the logical steps of identifying from safety records the most common unsafe acts that lead to accidents, training employees in proper and safe methods, and then designing a motivational strategy that combines goal setting with feedback or incentives for safe behavior. Employers with safety incentive programs average about $33,000 per year in incentive costs.[76]

Safety-incentive programs usually provide cash rewards or prizes to employees for each week or month on the job without an accident. Even the most successful incentive programs report eventual loss of interest on the part of workers and thus must constantly be replaced with new incentives.

The cost of an effective incentive program, however, will be greatly outweighed by the benefits of a successful program, which includes (1) reduction in insurance premiums; (2) reduction in related legal expenses; (3) savings in wages and benefits paid to injured workers; (4) less overtime and training of new workers to replace injured employees; and (5) greater productivity.[77]

The National Safety Council advises employers to use the **three E's of safety** to prevent accidents: engineering, education, and enforcement of safety rules.[78] Designing safe working conditions is the task of safety engineers, who, for example, design a work station to include adequate lighting, the right tools or equipment for the job, required safety guards and proper electrical grounding for tools and equipment, adequate ventilation, safe storage and usage of chemicals, paints, and so on, and the wearing of safety shoes, clothing, or goggles when necessary. The proper safety training of new employees or all employees given new tools, chemicals, or equipment is a critical part of accident prevention. An employee who is never shown the safe method of operating a machine or pouring a dangerous liquid cannot be expected to avoid an accident. Safety programs for employees can effectively reduce accidents. Such programs often offer monetary rewards, prizes, or paid leave for employees or departments that work without an accident for a specified number of days. The enforcement of safety rules is a critical aspect of accident prevention. Yet, unfortunately, supervisors may be hesitant to discipline employees for not wearing safety goggles or for storing chemicals carelessly. Strong top-management commitment to daily emphasis on employee safety can effectively reinforce strong safety discipline.

Safety engineers encourage the following five steps in designing and maintaining a safe workplace:[79]

1. Eliminate hazards.

2. Use safeguards on equipment.

3. Post warning signs near dangerous chemicals or machinery.

4. Train workers.

5. Require protective clothing, shoes, goggles, hats, and so on.

Participative Safety Management Programs

In recent years, employers have increasingly given employees greater authority and responsibility in job design, work procedures, and decision making concerning their jobs. Generally, as employees have become more self-directed, their motivation has increased, and the result has been improved productivity with lower turnover and absenteeism.

At the General Electric plant in Columbia, Maryland, the concept of greater employee involvement was extended to safety. Management had witnessed the positive effects of General Electric's participative safety management program in the manufacturing operations and decided that the same principles could be applied to promote safety in the workplace. The General Electric plant manufactures electric ranges, thus injuries range from sheet metal cuts and slivers of metal in the eye to carpal tunnel syndrome (repetitive motion trauma). In the past, General Electric had developed an extensive safety program that taught employees how to use tools and equipment properly and designed work stations to fit the person, rather than force the employee to fit the job. It was clear, however, that if employees realized that safety procedures were for their own protection and actively participated in designing the safety program, the program could be improved.[80]

The General Electric participative safety management system began with informal meetings, with staff delivering pep talks and providing safety information and statistics. To encourage workers to take an active role in safety and depend less on supervisory discipline, unique "safety warning cards" were distributed (see Figure 13-8). If an employee witnesses another worker doing something unsafe, the worker silently hands the person the card and walks away. The cards are effective reminders to employees that they are responsible not only for their own safety, but also for the safety of their co-workers. The

FIGURE 13–8 Safety awareness card.

SAFETY AWARENESS
THE BEST ACCIDENT PREVENTION

I JUST NOTICED YOU DOING SOMETHING THAT COULD HAVE CAUSED AN ACCIDENT. THINK ABOUT WHAT YOU'VE DONE IN THE LAST FEW MINUTES AND YOU WILL PROBABLY RECALL WHAT I SAW.

I AM GIVING YOU THIS CARD AS PART OF OUR CAMPAIGN TO MAKE ALL OF US SAFETY CONSCIOUS. KEEP IT UNTIL YOU SEE SOMEONE DOING SOMETHING IN AN UNSAFE WAY AND THEN PASS IT ON.

P.S. I HOPE I DON'T GET IT BACK!

SOURCE: Caras & Associate Inc. Used by permission.

next step was to create safety management teams in each section of the plant. Each team selected its own leader and conducted complete walk-through inspections similar to OSHA inspections. The team noted safety problems, listed corrective actions needed, and assigned the responsibility for those actions to specific individuals. The team monitored the list of items until all have been corrected. The benefits of the program included the following: (1) workers increased their awareness of responsibility for safety and were encouraged by management's willingness to pay for the changes their safety teams requested; (2) a worker MASH (Make Accidents Stop Happening) team reduced the weekly average number of accidents from about 8 to 2.4; and (3) safety team statistics pointed out that the same workers were getting injured each month, fewer than 5 percent of all employees. The safety teams developed a new safety performance policy that includes mandatory training after three injuries in a twelve-month period and a written plan (by the employee) to end the problem. After one additional injury, the "unsafe" employee is placed on "lack of suitable work" status. While the safety team did not call the action termination, it did remove the worker from the workplace, with

normal layoff benefits and no hope of returning to work.[81]

Occupational Injuries and Illnesses

The U.S. Bureau of Labor Statistics reports that each year one in every eleven workers experiences a job-related injury or illness, which translates into 9.4 injuries or illnesses per 100 full-time workers.[82] Many union leaders and activist groups have criticized the federal government for inaction in the area of employee health and safety. They have been concerned about *safety hazards,* those aspects of the workplace that can cause burns, electrical shock, cuts, broken bones, loss of limbs or eyesight, or other impairment of the employee's physical well-being. Of equal concern have been *health hazards,* those aspects of the workplace that can impair an employee's general physical, mental, or emotional well-being, usually including toxic chemicals, dust, noise, or other physical or biological agents. Health hazards cause sicknesses or illnesses that may take a long time to appear. Although states have long had various safety and health laws, the federal government did not establish regulations to protect employees until 1970.

The need for employee safety was first recognized during the Civil War when industries began to manufacture war materials at a fast pace. Rapid industrial expansion forced employers to disregard employee safety in an effort to maintain high output and low cost. In 1869 the first safety law, the Coal Mine Safety Law, was passed. In 1908 the federal government realized the need for workers' compensation for federal employees. The National Safety Council was formed in 1926 to compile injury and accident statistics involving the workplace. Industrial and nonagricultural jobs increased rapidly from the 1920s through the 1960s; the U.S. Department of Labor estimated in 1969 that out of every four workers, one would be affected by an injury or illness before retirement.

The U.S. Public Health Service has estimated that 390,000 new cases of occupational disease appear annually. As many as 100,000 deaths occur each year as a direct or indirect result of occupational disease. Heart disease, a leading cause of death, may well be related to hazardous working environments. Cancer is another leading cause of death in the United States; research in the United Kingdom indicates that more than 80 percent of cancer may be environmentally caused, although how much is due to occupational hazards is not known. Occupational illnesses are concentrated in mining, construction, transportation, and heavy manufacturing; most injuries also occur in these industries.[83]

The U.S. Department of Labor, Bureau of Labor Statistics defines *occupational injuries* on OSHA Form 200 as follows:

Any injury such as a cut, fracture, sprain, amputation, etc. which results from a work accident or from an exposure involving a single accident in the work environment. Note: Conditions resulting from animal bites, such as insect or snake bites, or from a one-time exposure to chemicals are considered to be injuries. And *occupational illness* is any abnormal condition or disorder other than one resulting from an occupational injury, caused by an exposure to environmental factors associated with a person's employment. It includes acute and chronic illnesses or diseases which may be caused by inhalation, absorption, congestion, or direct contact.

The following categories of occupational illnesses and disorders are utilized to classify recordable illnesses:

Code

7a. Occupational Skin Diseases or Disorders
   Examples: Contact dermatitis, eczema, or rash caused by primary irritants and sensitizers or poisonous plants; oil acne; chrome ulcers; chemical burns or inflammations; etc.

7b. Dust Diseases of the Lungs (Pneumoconioses)
   Examples: Silicosis, asbestosis, coal worker's pneumoconiosis, byssinosis, siderosis, and other pneumoconioses.

7c. Respiratory Conditions Due to Toxic Agents
   Examples: Pneumonitis, pharyngitis, rhinitis or acute congestion due to chemicals, dusts, gases, or fumes; farmer's lung; etc.

7d. Poisoning (Systemic Effect of Toxic Materials)
   Examples: Poisoning by lead, mercury, cadmium, arsenic, or other metals; poisoning by carbon monoxide, hydrogen sulfide, or other gases; poisoning by benzol, carbon tetrachloride, or other organic solvents; poisoning by insecticide sprays such as parathion, lead arsenate; poisoning by other chemicals such as formaldehyde, plastics, and resins; etc.

7e. Disorders Due to Physical Agents (Other than Toxic Materials)
   Examples: Heatstroke, sunstroke, heat exhaustion, and other effects of environmental heat; freezing, frostbite, and effects of exposure to low temperatures; caisson disease; effects of ionizing radiation (isotopes, X rays, radium); effects of nonionizing radiation (welding flash, ultraviolet rays, microwaves, sunburn); etc.

7f. Disorders Associated with Repeated Trauma
Examples: Noise-induced hearing loss; synovitis, tenosynovitis, and bursitis; Raynaud's phenomena; and other conditions due to repeated motion, vibration, or pressure.

7g. All Other Occupational Illnesses
Examples: Anthrax, brucellosis, infectious hepatitis, malignant and benign tumors, food poisoning, histoplasmosis, coccidioidomycosis, etc.

Occupational Safety and Health Administration

In 1970 Congress passed the Williams-Steiger Occupational Safety and Health Act (Public Law 91-596). The Williams-Steiger Act was the culmination of years of effort by employee groups, unions, and the National Safety Council to provide safety in the workplace. The act established the **Occupational Safety and Health Administration**, commonly referred to as **OSHA**, within the U.S. Department of Labor, and the **National Institute for Occupational Safety and Health (NIOSH)** within the U.S. Department of Health, Education, and Welfare (now Health and Human Services). NIOSH conducts research and gathers data and statistics relating to the occupational safety and health of employees; it helps determine standards for safety within the workplace by working closely with OSHA.

The Williams-Steiger Act is unique because it not only provides federal occupational safety standards through OSHA but also allows states to administer their own occupational safety and health programs. That provision was a compromise between those who believe that employee safety is a national concern and those who believe that the federal government is infringing on states' rights. A state-run OSHA program must receive federal approval and include federal safety requirements.

The 1970 act requires employers to furnish working environments free from recognized hazards that may cause injury or illness to employees. Employers are required to comply with safety and health standards created by the act or by states that administer their own programs. Employees are also required to comply with health and safety standards and regulations. Laws are enforced through the U.S. Department of Labor or state labor OSHA agencies or both. Regulations cover the use of toxic chemicals; levels of dust, fumes, and noise; the safe use of equipment and tools; and safe work procedures. A sample of OSHA safety and health regulations is shown in Figure 13-9.

Enforcement is provided by inspectors entering the workplace and determining whether employers have violated safety standards. Employers are required to allow the inspectors to enter their workplaces, answer questions, and provide requested data. If the inspector finds a violation of a safety standard, a written citation is issued; inspectors have the authority to determine whether the employer should be fined or warned and given time to correct the unsafe situation. Employers may be assessed a civil penalty of up to $10,000, a criminal penalty of up to $20,000, or a maximum of one year in prison. In most states, however, inspectors try to work with employers to correct the unsafe conditions rather than using penalties. Inspectors may find as many as thirty or forty violations within a work site that has not previously been checked. Thus, the inspector could issue several thousand dollars in fines or instruct the employer to make alterations in order that the standards be met within a reasonable amount of time. Returning to the work site, often without warning, inspectors make sure that those changes have been made. Employers have the right to appeal a citation or fine.

OSHA Penalties Employers in various industries know that OSHA means business. As an example, in 1979 Texaco, Inc., agreed to pay an OSHA penalty that was a record at the

FIGURE 13–9 Sample OSHA safety and health regulations.

§1926.300 General requirements

(a) *Condition of tools.* All hand and power tools and similar equipment, whether furnished by the employer or the employee, shall be maintained in a safe condition.

(b) *Guarding.* (1) When power operated tools are designed to accommodate guards, they shall be equipped with such guards when in use.

(c) Belts, gears, shafts, pulleys, sprockets, spindles, drums, fly wheels, chains, or other reciprocating, rotating or moving parts of equipment shall be guarded if such parts are exposed to contact by employees or otherwise create a hazard. Guarding shall meet the requirements as set forth in American National Standards Institute, B15.1-1953 (R1958), Safety Code for Mechanical Power-Transmission Apparatus.

§1926.301 Hand tools

(a) Employers shall not issue or permit the use of unsafe hand tools.

(b) Wrenches, including adjustable, pipe, end, and socket wrenches shall not be used when jaws are sprung to the point that slippage occurs.

(c) Impact tools, such as drift pins, wedges, and chisels, shall be kept free of mushroomed heads.

(d) The wooden handles of tools shall be kept free of splinters or cracks and shall be kept tight in the tool.

SOURCE: Occupational Safety and Health Standards for the Construction Industry, *Federal Register*, 39 (June 24, 1974), p. 22799

time. Texaco, OSHA, and the Chemical and Atomic Workers Union agreed on a payment of $169,400 as a penalty for OSHA citations issued at Texaco's Port Arthur, Texas, refinery. OSHA had originally recommended penalties totaling $394,000. The citations included six willful, ninety-nine serious, and seven repeated serious violations. A Texaco official stated that payment of the fine was not admission of negligence or a violation of the law in regard to a fire in which eight workers died.[84]

In some instances OSHA recommends criminal prosecution. OSHA law provides that employers who willfully violate standards can be fined not more than $10,000 or be imprisoned for not more than six months if that violation caused an employee's death. In two cases involving workers' deaths, for example, OSHA recommended criminal prosecution. One case involved an explosion at a chemical plant owned by the Rollins Environmental Services Corporation in Bridgeport, New Jersey. That explosion killed six workers and resulted in serious injuries to others. The second case in-

volved an employee who was crushed by an electrical tractor in the Lake County, Indiana, Number 2 Tin Mill of the Youngstown Sheet and Tube Company. Dr. Eula Bingham, who headed OSHA at the time, noted that she was making the announcement of criminal prosecution in the two cases to demonstrate to employers that OSHA will closely examine employees' deaths to determine if they resulted from employers' willful disregard of job safety and health rules.[85]

OSHA Problems OSHA has received numerous criticisms since its inception in 1970. Employers cite the high expenses of meeting regulations and possible lack of actual benefits to employees. The required paperwork has been criticized as being unnecessary and unwieldy. One of the most severe criticisms came from a two-year congressional study of federal regulatory agencies released in 1979. The study concluded that OSHA "has been, at best, a disappointment" and suggested legislation requiring economic impact statements from

Alert at the Switch or Sleeping on the Job?

While visiting a major chemical plant, some colleagues and I were taken to admire its ultra-modern control room. Highly trained technicians watched intricate color graphic displays on computer screens as the plant ran through its continuous processes.

This was high technology at its most impressive. It would, and did, make a wonderful color photograph for the company's annual report.

Because we were doing some training with the night crew, we hung around and chatted with them—about baseball, the weather, their jobs. As night came on and the managers and engineers left, the lights were switched off "to rest the eyes," and we sat there in comfortable chairs, the room lit only by the dim glow of the monitors. The room temperature was also adjusted up a notch as the crew settled down for the night. It was peaceful and quiet (save for the soporific hum of the computers) as the plant smoothly split and purified molecules, filtering and storing them away.

The setting was so cozy that we wondered how the crew managed to stay vigilant through a 12-hour night shift. It didn't; the things the body naturally craves in the middle of the night are things that reduce alertness and bring on sleep. "I just set this baby up, pull my cap down over my eyes, and take in some z's," said an operator. "It wakes me if it needs me."

Did the plant bosses realize they were leaving explosive chemicals and multi-million-dollar equipment in the care of foggy-headed operators? The answer, of

---

OSHA in order to determine if OSHA regulations are desirable when costs are considered. The authors of the report, from the John F. Kennedy School of Government at Harvard University, noted that OSHA's impact on injuries has been minimal. The study's major criticism noted that while human life and health are priceless entities that should not be traded off against dollars, economic comparisons, distasteful as they may be, are inevitable.[86]

Right-to-Know Regulations

OSHA in 1986 began enforcement of a new set of rules formally termed *hazard communication* but popularly known as **right-to-know**

regulations. Unlike most OSHA regulations, right-to-know only requires that employers provide employees with information. Specifically, workers are given the right to know what hazardous substances they may encounter on the job. Common examples of over 1000 hazardous substances include asbestos, cyanide, polychlorinated biphenyls (PCBs), gasoline, acetone, and rosin core solder. The regulations do not require employer testing or study of hazardous substances. Nor do they include "mixed articles" such as automobile tires or vinyl upholstery, which contain hazardous substances that are not released in normal use. The regulations generally apply only when hazardous substances are known to be present

618

course, is that they assumed that the operators would stay alert, not recognizing that they had created a work environment where the operators were bound to fail.

Our society as a whole treats machinery better than the people who run it. Expensive equipment is seldom operated outside of its design specifications. Yet the most sophisticated piece of equipment in that plant—the human operator—is routinely pushed beyond its limits.

Although people don't emit smoke or grind gears, they do show signs of breakdown. People who work in round-the-clock industries suffer a higher rate of illness and death than those who work on straight day shifts. What's more, the major industrial accidents of our time have been rooted in fatigue caused by asking people to perform outside their "design specs." Investigators have concluded that Chernobyl, Three Mile Island, and the Swiss chemical spill that poisoned the Rhine River in 1986 probably would not have happened if those responsible had been alert and well rested. In the Challenger disaster, NASA officials made the ill-fated "go–no go" decision under the stress of staying awake for 20 hours after only 2 or 3 hours' sleep the night before.

But the problem is far broader than just a few notorious accidents. In our finest teaching hospitals, the errors of frazzled interns and residents on 36-hour shifts are publicly acknowledged. On our highways, long-haul truckers work such irregular, sleep-disrupting schedules that accidents in the hours just before dawn climb to 15 times the daytime rate. Fatigue is endemic to our nonstop 24-hour society, in which large sections of the population now work at night or on rotating shifts. And it is only going to get worse.

SOURCE: Adapted from Martin Moore-Ede, "Alert on the Switch," *Technology Review* (October 1993): 53–59.

---

in the workplace and employees can be exposed due to routine operations or a foreseeable emergency. Federal and state hazard communication standards generally require:[87]

- Material safety data sheets (MSDSs) must be maintained for every hazardous substance that employees may be exposed to or handle.

- MSDSs must be kept readily accessible by all affected employees. Many employers keep the MSDSs in three-ring binders and include them in standard operating procedures.

- Labeling must be provided for all types of containers of hazardous substances, including barrels, bags, boxes, cans, cylinders, drums, and tanks.

- A written hazard communication program for employee information and training must be developed. The program should begin with a list of all known hazardous substances in the workplace. Employees should receive training in safe procedures, as well as methods of exposure detection such as distinctive odors, gases, and appearances.

Ergonomic Standards

Workplace injuries from repetitive motions— such as striking computer keys, fileting fish, and checking out groceries—are the most common occupational hazards. All repetitive motion injuries and illnesses taken together account for 48 percent of all employee ill-nesses and injuries. The industry with the highest rate of cumulative trauma disorders caused by repetitive motions is the meat processing industry, where cutting, trimming, and preparing are performed by hand, much the same as they were fifty years ago.

Recent recognition of the extent of cumulative trauma disorders led the U.S. Department of Labor to develop voluntary employer guidelines to reduce their occurrence. Research shows that repetitive-motion problems can be minimized through workplace engineering and job design. The voluntary OSHA guidelines concentrate on four related elements:[88]

1. *Work-site analysis.* Review existing plan layout and identify problems and hazards.
2. *Tools.* Improve the design of the assembly process and tools utilized to minimize hazards.
3. *Medical treatment.* Improve treatment of repetitive-motion ergonomic problems.
4. *Training.* Provide employees with the training needed so that they can protect themselves from repetitive-motion problems.

Shift Work and Safety

More and more companies are operating on a twenty-four-hour-a-day, seven-days-a-week schedule. For many organizations, it is simply good economic sense. A manufacturing facility could increase production without the major expenditure of building a new plant. GM, for example, is going to twenty-four hours-a-day operations at its Ontario, Canada, truck plant. It hopes to hold down investment costs while boosting production of popular models.[89]

While equipment and buildings do not care whether they work twenty-four hours a day, people do. For some workers, adjusting to a new work schedule can be an enormous problem. At GM, workers have complained of disorientation because they work different hours and days each week. People typically do not perform as well at night as they do during the day. Rotating and fixed night-shift workers are not as alert and ready to meet the demands of their job as day workers are, as the *HR in the News:* "Alert at the Switch or Sleeping on the Job?" illustrates.

There are numerous difficulties with shift work, but the most serious concerns are worker health and safety. The natural rhythms of the body must either be adjusted or ignored. Consequently, shift workers have a harder time maintaining good health. One study reported that women regularly working an evening or a night shift while pregnant are more likely to have a miscarriage than women who work the day shift.[90] Eating habits are disrupted, and the food they do eat is not always the healthiest. Regular exercise is a problem, and regular sleep is almost impossible. The odd hours cause friction at home too, where shift workers feel irritable and guilty for having to choose between rest and spending time with their families. And without family support, it is hard to cope effectively with shift work.[91]

While shift work will always pose problems, there are a few steps that HR professionals can take to make life more palatable. Poor shift scheduling design is often part of the problem. Improving shift schedules by offering more flexibility is one option. The most common shift schedule is the eight-hour rotating shift, where workers work seven days, evenings, or nights and then take two days off. However, many employers are moving toward a ten- or twelve-hour shift. Longer shifts require workers to "bite the bullet" and just work, eat, and sleep for three or four days, but then they get three or four days off to spend with their families. Another step that can improve workers' shift lives is to provide counseling—on family-related, work-related, or personal matters.[92] Offering employees and their families more flexibility and counseling is necessary for any long-term shift routines.

CONCLUSIONS AND APPLICATIONS

- Job stress is a pervasive problem in our society. It may result in low productivity, increased absenteeism and turnover, and other employee problems including substance abuse, mental health problems, and cardiovascular illnesses. Strategies to control stress include: Fitness programs, meditation, counseling, and leaves.

- EAPs can help employees overcome serious problems that affect productivity. Employers can retain highly skilled and valuable employees who suffer from alcoholism, drug abuse, depression, family problems, or other common crises. But normal disciplinary procedures should be followed when an EAP is provided. Employee participation may be strongly encouraged, but ultimately the employee must voluntarily seek help.

- OSHA regulations require employees to keep records of employee injuries and illnesses. Employers should ensure that relevant OSHA regulations are met. Organizations can benefit from a safe workplace through reduced insurance premiums, fewer lost worker hours, and fewer accident claims.

- Policies on smoking in the workplace, drug usage, and AIDS are being developed by many employers as these issues generate greater interest in our society. However, while more employers are adopting a smoking ban and testing employees for illegal drugs, few are adopting an AIDS policy.

- Employers today are developing and implementing a drug-free workplace program and a drug-testing policy. The NLRB has upheld policies that require all job applicants to submit to testing. Preemployment testing policies should cover the issues of applicant notification, test validation, rescheduling, and confidentiality.

- The use of random postemployment drug testing has generally been upheld only in cases in which the employer can demonstrate an overwhelming need to protect public safety. Otherwise, the employee's right of privacy may require the employer to demonstrate probable cause before requiring a test. A probable-cause testing policy should provide a valid and confidential testing procedure, job impairment provision, warning of termination for failure to submit to testing, and supervisor training.

CASE STUDY

Designing a Safety Program

Jay Vahaly is the training director of a 1200-employee agricultural products company located in Albuquerque, New Mexico. In the last few months, new equipment has been installed that is expected to increase productivity substantially by minimizing the manual handling of food products in the cleaning, sorting, and packaging processes. The owners, Robert and Juanita Hillard, are concerned about employee safety. In the past, the plant utilized almost no machinery that could pose safety problems for the largely poor and uneducated work force. The Hillards care deeply about their employees; they provide a generous wage and benefit package including a substantial profit-sharing plan. The fifty-year-old firm has had successful employee relations, including high productivity and low absenteeism and turnover.

In the process of evaluating the impact of the new equipment, the Hillards learned that other employers had encountered many start-up accidents because their employees simply did not take seriously the training program in equipment safety that the manufacturer of the new equipment had provided. Several had suffered permanently disabling accidents. The Hillards have contracted with the equipment manufacturer for a six-month extensive employee training program, but they believe that a permanent safety incentive program is needed to keep safety in the minds and actions of their employees. From the an-

ticipated increased revenues, the Hillards have pledged $100,000 annually for prizes and/or cash to be awarded in the safety program. Vahaly has been instructed to have the new program ready in six months, when the training program ends.

QUESTIONS

1. Do you agree with the Hillards' decision? Consider that the firm has already spent millions of dollars on OSHA-approved equipment that includes state-of-the-art safety mechanisms and that the manufacturer has provided a six-month extensive training program.

2. Describe in detail the safety program you would recommend Vahaly implement.

3. Would you anticipate any specific problems that might occur with a safety incentive program that uses prizes or cash as a motivation for safe practices?

4. How should Vahaly evaluate the success of his program?

EXPERIENTIAL EXERCISES

1. What Do You *Really* Know About Drug and Alcohol Abuse?

PURPOSE

To determine what you know and do not know about the use of alcohol and illegal drugs.

THE TASK

Complete the following Security Pacific Corporation drug and alcohol awareness survey. Your instructor will lead a class discussion about the issue.

Drug and Alcohol Awareness Survey

1. What percentage of alcoholics do you believe can return to stable moderate drinking after treatment?
   2% [ ]   12% [ ]   20% [ ]   66% [ ]
   Note: Moderate drinking is less than 7 drinks 4 times a month, and freedom from alcohol related social, legal, or health problems.

2. What is the fastest growing group of new drug users in America?
   Women [ ]   Men [ ]   Age: 18–34 [ ]   35–44 [ ]   45–54 [ ]

3. Compared to others, what risk do children of alcoholics or drug abusing parents have to become alcoholic or drug abusing themselves?
   Twice as much [ ]   Three times as much [ ]   Four times as much [ ]

4. Prolonged use of heroin is less toxic than comparable use of cocaine (as evidenced by lab studies of animals).
   True [ ]   False [ ]

5. How many of your friends', family's or co-workers' lives do you feel have been affected by alcohol or drugs?
   1 in 3 [ ]   1 in 5 [ ]   1 in 7 [ ]   1 in 10 [ ]

6. As a commuter, I have probably seen more alcoholics while traveling to work on the highway than on the streets of skid row.
   Yes [ ]   No [ ]

7. What do you think is the estimate of the percentage of the work force that abuses alcohol, drugs, or both?
   5–10% [ ]   15–25% [ ]   30–35% [ ]   40–45% [ ]

8. Absenteeism, medical expenses, and lost productivity as a result of substance abuse are costing employers, on average, what percentage of their total payroll?
   2% [ ]   3% [ ]   4% [ ]   5% [ ]

9. As a manager/supervisor do you feel you can positively impact on alcoholic or substance abuser if he/she is unwilling to listen?
   Yes [ ]   No [ ]

10. Either job-performance failure or lowered job responsibility always happens before an alcoholic or substance abusing employee is terminated.
    True [ ]   False [ ]

SOURCE: Anthony Kramer, *The Security Pacific Drug and Alcohol Awareness Survey*, Security Pacific Corporation. Used by permission.

2. Are You Burned Out?

PURPOSE

Everyone at some time feels burned out on the job or with life in general. Sometimes a variation, such as a new car, hobby, promotion, or even a serious illness, will revitalize a person and lessen the feeling of burnout.

This exercise can give you an objective appraisal of your degree of burnout *if* you answer it honestly. There are no right or wrong answers, and only you know if your answers are accurate. Once you determine your burnout score, consult the general discussion of what different scores may indicate and decide if any behavioral change is needed in your life, but don't make any major decisions based solely

How Often Do You Have Any of the Following Experiences?

Please use the scale:

1	2	3	4	5	6	7
Never	Once in a great while	Rarely	Sometimes	Often	Usually	Always

_____ 1. Being tired.
_____ 2. Feeling depressed.
_____ 3. Having a good day.
_____ 4. Being physically exhausted.
_____ 5. Being emotionally exhausted.
_____ 6. Being happy.
_____ 7. Being "wiped out."
_____ 8. "Can't take it anymore."
_____ 9. Being unhappy.
_____ 10. Feeling run-down.
_____ 11. Feeling trapped.
_____ 12. Feeling worthless.
_____ 13. Being weary.
_____ 14. Being troubled.
_____ 15. Feeling disillusioned and resentful.
_____ 16. Being weak and susceptible to illness.
_____ 17. Feeling hopeless.
_____ 18. Feeling rejected.
_____ 19. Feeling optimistic.
_____ 20. Feeling energetic.
_____ 21. Feeling anxious.

Computation of score:

Add the values you wrote next to the following items:
1, 2, 4, 5, 7, 8, 9, 10, 11, 12, 13, 14, 15, 16, 17, 18, 21(A) _____.

Add the values you wrote next to the following items:
3, 6, 19, 20(B) _____, subtract B from 32(C) _____.

Add A and C (D) _____.

Divide D by 21 _____. This is your burnout score.

on this test; talk with family, friends, co-workers, or even a counselor first. Wait a week and take the test again if you contemplate any substantial action.

THE TASK

Compute your burnout score by completing the preceeding questionnaire. You can use it to determine how you feel about your work or your life, either today or in general.

Compute your burnout score by completing this questionnaire.

What the Score Means

Of the thousands who responded to this self-diagnosis instrument, none scored either 1 or 7. The reason is obvious. It is unlikely that anyone would be in a state of eternal euphor-

ia implied by the score 1, and it is unlikely that someone who scored 7 would be able to cope with the world well enough to participate in a burnout workshop or a research project.

If your score is between 2 and 3, you are doing well. The only suggestion we make is that you go over your score sheet to be sure you have been honest in your responses. If your score is between 3 and 4, it would be wise for you to examine your work life, evaluate your priorities, and consider possible changes. If your score is higher than 4, you are experiencing burnout to the extent that it is mandatory that you do something about it. A score of higher than 5 indicates an acute state and a need for immediate help.

SOURCE: Adapted from Ayala Pines, Ph.D. and Elliot Aronson, Ph.D., "Why Managers Burn Out," *Sales & Marketing Management* 4 (February 1989): 38.

KEY TERMS AND CONCEPTS

AIDS in the workplace
Drug-free Workplace Act
Employee assistance programs (EAPs)
Ergonomic standards
Health program manager
Job burnout
Job stress
Log and summary of occupational injuries and illnesses
Kemper, *Management Guide on Alcoholism*
National Institute for Occupational Safety and Health (NIOSH)

No-smoking policies
Occupational Safety and Health Administration (OSHA)
Physical fitness program (PFP)
Problem drinker
Right-to-know regulations
Safety programs
Three *E*'s of safety
Wellness programs

REVIEW QUESTIONS

1. Should an employer have an EAP? How should it be established?

2. How can wellness programs be cost-effective?

3. What actions are required of an employer under the Drug-free Workplace Act?

4. How can an employer meet OSHA right-to-know regulations?

5. When is the problem drinker cured?

6. How does the performance of a typical drug user differ from that of other workers?

DISCUSSION QUESTIONS

1. An increasing number of employees are turning to a variety of mood-altering substances to help them get through each day. In most instances, union workers can be dismissed for drinking or taking drugs on the job. If your nonunion company has a pleasant, nonstressful environment, would it be justified in dismissing substance abusers rather than spending the money necessary for rehabilitation?

2. What is a fair and responsible policy on smoking in the workplace?

3. Which common wellness program activities should small employers consider offering to employees? Why?

4. Government officials frequently waver in their enforcement of OSHA. What influences have caused government officials to relax safety rules at times and to create more stringent regulations at others?

5. If supervisors warn their employees about the possible health hazards connected with their jobs and supply safety equipment to the employees, is the company responsible if employees do not use the required safety equipment?

6. How can an employer minimize job stress in the workplace?

7. Is employee drug testing an invasion of privacy? What do you consider a fair and effective drug-testing policy?

ENDNOTES

Chapter 13

1. C. Hymowitz, "Which Corporate Culture Fits You?" *The Wall Street Journal* (July 17, 1989): B1.

2. J. M. Ivancevich and M. T. Matteson, *Stress and Work* (Glenview, IL: Scott, Foresman, 1980), pp. 5–9.

3. Jeffrey R. Edwards, "A Cybernetic Theory of Stress, Coping, and Well-Being in Organization," *Academy of Management Review* 17, no. 2 (1992): 238–74.

4. Jennifer J. Laabs, "Job Stress," *Personnel Journal* (April 1992): 43.

5. Ibid.

6. Thomas L. Brown, "Are You Living in 'Quiet Desperation'?" *Industry Week* (March 16, 1992): 17.

7. Ibid.

8. Harry Levinson, "When Executives Burn Out," *Harvard Business Review* 68 (March–April 1990): 69.

9. Hugh F. Stallworth, "Realistic Goals Help Avoid Burnout," *HRMagazine* (June 1990): 169–71.

10. Jennifer J. Laabs, "Surviving HR Burnout," *Personnel Journal* (April 1992): 82–85.

11. Stallworth, "Realistic Goals," pp. 169–71.

12. Bill Sing, "Corporate Efforts Inching Along," *The Los Angeles Times* (October 14, 1990): D4.

13. John Kondrasuk, "Company Physical Fitness Programs: Salvation or Fad?" *Personnel Administrator* 25, no. 11 (November 1980): 47–50.

14. Stephan W. Hartman and Janet Cozzetto, "Wellness in the Workplace," *Personnel Administrator* 29, no. 8 (August 1984): 108–17.

15. *Your Guide to Wellness at the Worksite* (Washington, DC: Health Insurance Association of America, 1983), p. 3.

16. Hartman and Cozzetto, "Wellness in the Workplace," pp. 108–09.

17. Lynn E. Densford, "Wellness Programs Show Healthy Returns," *Employee Benefit News* 1, no. 8 (November–December 1987): 17–19.

18. "Reduced Costs, Increased Worker Production Are Rationale for Tax-favored Corporate Fitness Plans," *Employee Benefit Plan Review* 37 (November 1983): 21.

19. Charles A. Berry, *An Approach to Good Health for Employees and Reduced Health Care Costs for Industry* (Washington, DC: Health Insurance Association of America, 1981), p. 9.

20. Jane Daniel, "An Offer Your Doctor Can't Refuse," *American Health* (November–December 1982): 82.

21. "Cost-benefit Analysis of the Coors' Wellness Program," University of Oregon Graduate School of Management, Eugene, OR (December 1988).

22. Shari Caudran, "The Wellness Payoff," *Personnel Journal* 69, no. 7 (July 1990): 55–60.

23. Michael Rozek, "A Decrease in Employee Sick Days Is Only One Bonus From Sunseeds' Wellness Program. Morale at the Company Also Has Increased Considerably," *Personnel Journal* 69, no. 7 (July 1990): 60–62.

24. Dennis Thompson, "Wellness Programs Work for Small Employers, Too," *Personnel* 3 (March 1990): 26–28.

25. Jack N. Kondrasuk, "Corporate Physical Fitness Programs: The Role of the Personnel Department," *Personnel Administrator* 29, no. 12 (December 1984): 75–80.

26. R. L. Pyle, "Corporate Fitness Programs—How Do They Shape Up?" *Management Review* 68 (December 1979).

27. Kondrasuk, "Corporate Physical Fitness Programs," pp. 78–79.

28. Loren E. Falkenberg, "Employee Fitness Programs: Their Impact on the Employee and the Organization," *Academy of Management Review* 12, no. 3 (July 1987): 511–22.

29. A. M. Paolone et al., "Results of Two Years of Exercise Training in Middle-Aged Men," *Physicians and Sports Medicine* 4 (December 1976): 77.

30. M. L. Collis, *Employee Fitness* (Ottawa, Canada: Minister of Supplies and Services, 1977), p. 81.

31. L. M. Catheart, "A Four-Year Study of Executive Health Risk," *Journal of Occupational Medicine* (May 1977): 357.

32. Sandra E. Edwards and Larry K. Gettmans, "The Effects of Employee Physical Fitness on Job Performance," *Personnel Administrator* 25, no. 11 (November 1980): 41–44, 60–61.

33. Steven H. Appelbaum and Barbara T. Shapiro, "The ABCs of EAPs," *Personnel* 7 (July 1989): 33–46.

34. William G. Wagner, "Assisting Employees with Personal Problems," *Personnel Administrator* 27, no. 11 (November 1982): 59–64.

35. Virginia K. Tyler, "Growth of EAPs Brings Certification," *Employee Benefit News* 1, no. 4 (May–June 1987): 1.

36. Fred Dickman and William G. Emener, "Employee Assistance Programs: Basic Concepts, Attributes and an Evaluation," *Personnel Administrator* (August 1982): 55–62.

37. Appelbaum and Shapiro, "The ABCs of EAPs," pp. 43–45.

38. Roger K. Good, "What Bechtel Learned Creating an Employee Assistance Program," *Personnel Journal* 63, no. 9 (September 1984): 80–86.

39. Wagner, "Assisting Employees with Personal Problems," pp. 59–64.

40. Donald V. Forrest, "Employee

Assistance Programs in the 1980s: Expanding Career Options for Counselors," *Personnel and Guidance Journal* 62 (October 1983): 105–08.

41. Appelbaum and Shapiro, "The ABCs of EAPs," p. 40.

42. Christine A. Filipowicz, "The Troubled Employee: Whose Responsibility?" *Personnel Administrator* 24 (June 1979): 18.

43. Frank E. Kuzmits and Henry E. Hammons, II, "Rehabilitating the Troubled Employee," *Personnel Journal* 58 (April 1979): 239.

44. Ibid.

45. Filipowicz, "The Troubled Employee," pp. 18–19.

46. The Kemper Insurance Companies publish a number of excellent guidebooks on alcoholism and drug abuse. For information on obtaining these guides, write Public Relations, Kemper Insurance Companies, Long Grove, IL 60049.

47. *Summary of 3rd Report on Alcohol and Health,* (National Institute on Alcohol Abuse and Alcoholism, Washington, DC, 1980) p. 6.

48. Alander Ross and Thomas Campbell, "An Evaluation Study of an Alcohol and Drug Recovery Program—A Case Study of the Oldsmobile Experience," *Human Resource Management* 14 (Spring 1975): 14–18.

49. Ian A. Miners, Nick Nykodym, and Diane M. Samerdyke-Traband, "Put Drug Detection to the Test," *Personnel Journal* 66, no. 8 (August 1987): 92–97.

50. Janet Deming, "Drug-free Workplace Is Good Business," *HRMagazine* 35, no. 4 (April 1990): 61–62.

51. Michael R. Carrell and Christina Heavrin, "Before You Drug Test . . ." *HRMagazine* 35, no. 6 (June 1990): 64–68.

52. *New York City Transit Authority* v. *Beazer,* 440 U.S. 568, 99 S. Ct. 1355, 59L. Ed. 2d 598 (1979).

53. *Minneapolis Star Tribune,* 295, NLRB 63 (1989).

54. David D. Schein, "How to Prepare Company Policy on Substance Abuse Control," *Personnel Journal* 65 (July 1986): 30–38.

55. Katie Hafner and Susan Garland, "Testing for Drug Use: Handle with Care," *Business Week* (March 28, 1988): 65.

56. *Skinner* v. *Railway Labor Executives Association,* 109 D. Vy. 1902 (1989).

57. Ibid.

58. *Shelby County Health Care Center,* 90 LA 1225 (1988).

59. *Consolidated Coal Co.,* 87 LA 111 (1986).

60. Larry Martz et al., "Trying to Say No," *Newsweek* (August 11, 1986): 14–19.

61. *Report of the U.S. Surgeon General* (Washington, DC: Office of the U.S. Surgeon General, 1986).

62. Philip R. Voluck, "Burning Legal Issues of Smoking in the Workplace," *Personnel Journal* 66, no. 6 (June 1987): 140–43.

63. Alaska, Connecticut, Florida, Maine, Minnesota, Montana, Nebraska, New Jersey, Rhode Island, and Utah.

64. *Vickers* v. *Veterans Administration,* 29 FEP Cases 1197 (1982).

65. "ASPA-BNA Survey No. 51, Smoking in the Workplace: 1987 Update," *Bulletin to Management* (Washington, DC: Bureau of National Affairs, November 26, 1987); and J. Carroll Swart, "An Overlooked Cost of Employee Smoking," *Personnel* 67, no. 8 (August 1990): 54.

66. Voluck, "Burning Legal Issues of Smoking in the Workplace," p. 140.

67. Alfred Vogel, *Smoking and Productivity in the Workplace* (Washington, DC: Tobacco Institute, 1985).

68. William L. Weis, "No Smoking," *Personnel Journal* 63, no. 9 (September 1984): 53–58.

69. George Munchus, "An Update on Smoking: Employees' Rights and Employers' Responsibilities," *Personnel* 64 (August 1987): 46–56.

70. R. Craig Scott, "The Smoking Controversy Goes to Court," *Management World* 17, no. 1 (January–February 1988): 14.

71. Frank E. Kuzmits and Lyle Sussman, "Twenty Questions About AIDS in the Workplace," *Business Horizons* 29, no. 4 (July–August 1986): 36–42.

72. Phyllis S. Myers and Donald W. Myers, "AIDS: Tackling a Tough Problem Through Policy," *Personnel Administrator* 32 (April 1987): 95–108, 143.

73. Allan Haleron, "AIDS: The Corporate Response," *Personnel Journal* 65, no. 8 (August 1986): 123–27.

74. "AIDS: Employer Rights and Responsibilities," *Human Resource Management* no. 47 (Chicago: Commerce Clearing House, 1985), pp. 11–24.

75. Lawrence Z. Lorber and J. Robert Kirk, *Fear Itself: A Legal and Personnel Analysis of Drug Testing, AIDS, Secondary Smoke, VDTs* (Washington, DC: ASPA Foundation, 1987), pp. 25–33.

76. Robert A. Reber, Jerry A. Wallin, and David L. Duhan, "Safety Programs That Work," *Personnel Administrator* 34, no. 9 (September 1989): 66–69.

77. D. S. Thelan et al., "Health and Safety in the Workplace: A New Challenge for Business Schools," *Personnel Administrator* 30, no. 10 (October 1985): 38.

78. Lester Bittel, *What Every Supervisor Should Know* (New York: McGraw-Hill, 1974), p. 97.

79. R. L. Barnett and D. B. Breckman, "Safety Hierarchy," *Journal of Safety Research* 17 (1986): 50.

80. John A. Jenkins, "Self-directed Work Force Promotes Safety," *HRMagazine* 35, no. 2 (February 1990): 54–56.

81. Ibid.

82. American Society for Personnel Administration, Berea, OH: *Occupational Safety and Health Review* (March 1985), p. 3.

83. Nicholas A. Ashford, "The Nature and Dimension of Occupational Health and Safety Problems," *Personnel Administrator* 18 (August 1977): 46–48.

84. American Society for Personnel Administration, Berea, OH; *Occupational Safety and Health Review* (March 1979), p. 7.

85. American Society for Personnel Administration, Berea, OH; *Occupational Safety and Health Review* (June 1979), p. 6.

86. American Society for Personnel Administration, Berea, OH; *Occupational Safety and Health Review* (March 1979), p. 4.

87. Bruce D. May, "Hazardous Substances: OSHA Mandates the Right to Know," *Personnel Journal* 65, no. 8 (August 1986):128–30.

88. Oswald Johnston and Bob Baker, "U.S. Takes Initial Steps On Ergonomic Standards," *The Los Angeles Times* (September 1, 1990): D1, 12.

89. Neal Templin, "GM Hopes to Awaken Profits by Operating Plants 24 Hours a Day," *The Wall Street Journal*, (October 6, 1993): A1.

90. Jerry Bishop, "Study Finds Night-Shift Workers More Likely to Have Miscarriages," *The Wall Street Journal* (January 11, 1993): A5.

91. Stephenie Overman, "Not the Usual 9 to 5," *HRMagazine* (January 1993): 47.

92. Jon Pierce and Randall Dunham, "The 12-Hour Work Day: A 48-Hour, Eight-Day Week," *Academy of Management Journal,* 35, no. 5 (1992): 1086–98.

93. Mark Feinberg, "Teaming Up to Save Lives," *Business and Society Review* 71 (Fall 1989): 49–51.

PART **V**

EMPLOYEE
RELATIONS

LABOR UNIONS

1. To identify and discuss the legislation that pertains to labor–management relationships, with emphasis on the legal rights of both unions and management.

2. To describe how unions and their federation—the AFL-CIO—are organized and structured.

3. To understand what takes place during a union organizing drive, with emphasis on the legal dos and don'ts for both labor and management.

4. To explain how management may remain nonunion if it wishes to do so.

5. To discuss why employees may work more effectively in teams and the union response to teams.

6. To identify the stages of the collective bargaining process.

7. To describe the major power tactics used by labor and management.

8. To explain grievance procedures.

9. To cite methods used to end an impasse.

10. To identify the subject areas of labor contracts.

There are many reasons why the study of unions is important for any student of HR management. The presence of a union has significant implications for the structure of an organization and for the management of human resources. For union employees, HR procedures and policies are largely shaped by a written agreement between management and the union. A labor administrator's job in a unionized firm will be markedly different from that same job in a nonunionized firm. And beyond the confines of one organization, the tone of an area's labor relations, whether they are perceived to be good or bad, can have significant impact on the economic health of that area.

A **union** is an organization of workers formed to further the economic and social interests of its members. There are three kinds of unions: industrial unions, trade unions, and employee associations. An **industrial union** is a union composed primarily of semiskilled blue-collar employees in the manufacturing industries, such as automobiles, chemicals, and utilities. A **trade union** (sometimes called a *craft union*) generally includes among its membership skilled employees in a single trade, such as electricians, carpenters, and machinists. An **employee association** (or *fraternal order*) is generally composed of white-collar or professional employees, such as teachers, police officers, and clerical, administrative, technical, and health care employees. **Collective bargaining** is negotiation in good faith between the employer and the union on wages, benefits, hours of work, and other terms and conditions of employment. The result is a written contract specifying the agreements that management and the union have been able to reach.

WHY JOIN A UNION?

Why did workers in many manufacturing industries choose to unionize after the passage of the 1935 Wagner Act? At that time, many of the manufacturing plants were oppressive places of employment. Each morning men lined up at the gate. If there was no work, they were sent home; if they were hired, it was for that day, not continuous employment. They never knew when their workday ended until the whistle blew. One auto worker recalls that some foremen were so intimidating that workers had to do the foremen's yardwork on the weekends and had to bring along their daughters to provide sexual services. The foremen managed by terror and hired prizefighters to keep control. Workers could not talk during lunch and had to raise their hands to go to the bathroom. The bathrooms did not have doors, and foremen followed workers who took a bathroom break to make sure the break was needed. Such indignities, as well as poor wages and unsafe working conditions, made workers ready to join unions.[1]

Today it is unlikely that many managers would consider using the intimidating tactics of the 1930s. In general, however, when workers today choose to unionize, it is due to the same frustration with management over issues such as wages, benefits, or fair treatment that caused their grandfathers to unionize. The labor union developed as a means by which individuals could unite and have the collective power to accomplish goals that could not be accomplished alone. Whether that power is used to increase take-home wages, to ensure job protection, to improve working conditions, or simply to sit across the bargaining table as an equal with the employer, members believe that *in union there is strength!*[2] The most common union means of demonstrating strength has been the strike. But as the chapter-opening *HR in the News:* "UAW–Caterpillar Inc. Strike: Replacement Workers Tri-

umph" illustrates, today unions are less likely to strike for fear of replacement.

A great deal of time and effort have been devoted to the question "Why do employees choose to join a union?" Studies have failed to find a list of reasons that apply to all organizing efforts. But there is general agreement among labor experts that certain issues are likely to lead to an organizing drive by employees. Among them are the following.[3]

Job Security Employees need to have a sense of job security and want to believe that management will not make unfair and arbitrary decisions about their employment. Further, they wish to be protected against layoffs, and may look to the union to ensure that jobs are protected against such technological advances as automation and robotics. For example, the union could request that any employee displaced by an industrial robot be retrained and placed in another job. The most important element in job security is **seniority**, or the length of an employee's service. It is a common practice for HR decisions affecting the union employee—such as layoffs, recall, and promotions—to be made according to seniority.

Wages and Benefits Bread-and-butter economic issues have always been an important concern for employees and are always important in unionization. Specifically, employees want to be paid fairly and receive wages on par with those of other workers in the community. Such benefits as hospitalization insurance, pensions and paid sick leave, vacations, and holidays are also significant issues in employees' decisions to organize. They may think that the union, with its collective power, will be able to achieve a higher level of wages and benefits than could employees acting individually.

Working Conditions Employees want a healthy and safe working environment. Although federal legislation exists to protect health and safety in the workplace, employees

UAW–Caterpillar Inc. Strike: Replacement Workers Triumph

Historically U.S. unions have counted on their ability to put on a successful strike as a means of gaining new wages and benefits at the negotiation table. Employers feared a lengthy strike could cost them substantial market share—or even put them out of business if customers supported the union or simply changed to competitors' products.

The 1981 Air Traffic Controllers Strike, in which President Reagan permanently replaced striking workers with nonunion employees, however, began a new era in labor relations. After the 1981 strike employers began reconsidering their standard practice of only hiring temporary workers during a strike—and then bringing back the union workers once the strike was settled. Instead, they began hiring replacement workers (or threatened to hire them) as soon as a strike was called—often forcing the union to agree to their demands.

Then the UAW demanded that Caterpillar meet the wage package it had negotiated at Deere & Co. This practice of "pattern bargaining" enables a national union to demonstrate to members of various locals that it is representing all of them equally by negotiating similar contracts across an industry. In the 1980s, however, many industrial unions were forced to abandon pattern bargaining due

---

may feel more secure knowing that a union is directly involved in safety and health issues. A good example of a union providing protection is described in *HR in the News:* "Union Nets Largest Child-labor Settlement in U.S. History."

Fair and Just Supervision The day is long gone when supervisors could rule their employees with an iron fist. A significant reason for the general shift in leadership styles from autocratic to people-oriented patterns is the insistence by unions that supervisors treat their employees fairly, justly, and respectfully. Most contracts specify that employees can

only be disciplined for "just cause." A union employee who thinks he or she has been mistreated may file a written *grievance* against the employer, initiating a formal procedure through which the complaint will be heard by both union and management representatives.

Mechanism to Be Heard Employees often complain that they have little or no say in matters that affect their work. They often feel powerless to bring about changes that will benefit them. Through unionization, employees have a powerful collective voice that may be used to communicate to management their dissatisfactions and frustrations. The collective bargain-

to employer economic problems. Caterpillar, like many other employers, was being pressured by a big Japanese competitor, Komatsu Ltd., which had lower labor costs. The confrontation between the UAW and Caterpillar was of national importance because Caterpillar was the last U.S. unionized manufacturer to hold a commanding world-wide market share, over double that of Komatsu, and thus could, thought the UAW, afford to continue the "pattern" settlement negotiated with Deere & Co. The UAW, one of the strongest U.S. unions, was viewed by organized labor as its greatest hope to put on a successful strike.

The UAW called a strike, and Caterpillar responded by advertising for replacement workers. Thousands of would-be strike-breakers responded to an advertisement, and the UAW quickly canceled the strike, without gaining a single concession at the negotiating table and having lost thousands of union jobs. The union also lost the support of many of its members, as one 18 year UAW member explained: "I can't depend on either the union or the company" . . . "The union has saved itself at the expense of the workers."

The reason for this substantial shift in labor relations strategy since the 1981 Air Traffic Controllers Union strike is simple—for too many workers crossing a picket line just doesn't matter today. Fewer Americans today have family or friends in unions and thus are not sympathetic to a union's strike. High levels of unemployment have also caused many to quickly respond to an advertisement for replacement workers. For example, even unemployed UAW workers responded to a Kroger Co. advertisement for replacement workers for its Detroit area supermarkets.

SOURCE: Adapted from Dana Milbank, "Unions' Woes Suggest How the Labor Force in U.S. Is Shifting," *The Wall Street Journal* (May 5, 1992): A1, 4.

---

ing and grievance procedures ensure that union employees will have their wants, needs, and concerns brought before management without retaliation.

Need to Belong The need to belong is strong in all human beings in both their personal and work lives. The union provides a mechanism for bringing people together not only to promote common job-related interests but also to provide programs, activities, and social events that create a strong bond among union members.

Overall, management's failure to include employees as part of the team, involve them in

decision making, or even inform them of the business's status motivates employees to organize. The recent increase in Japanese-owned and -operated businesses in the United States, primarily in the highly unionized automotive industry, has shown a marked contrast in management styles. To increase productivity, Japanese managers cultivate workers' loyalty by shortening or eliminating the distance between them, by giving employees a voice in management, and by minimizing layoffs. Allowing workers to participate in job-related decisions has increased efficiency. Training workers for more than one job cultivates flexibility, job pride, and ultimately more

HR IN THE NEWS

Union Nets Largest Child-labor Settlement in U.S. History

Food Lion, Inc., the supermarket giant, agreed to pay a $16.2 million settlement after the U.S. Department of Labor investigated alleged violations of the child labor and overtime provisions of the 1938 Fair Labor Standards Act. The initial complaint was filed by the United Food and Commercial Workers union, which was involved in an organizing campaign at the company.

The suit involved 30,000 to 40,000 employees of the Salisbury, North Carolina, chain. Workers allegedly were forced to work "off the clock" without pay to complete tasks assigned by the employer. Child-labor violations also included teenagers working around hazardous machinery such as balers used to crush cardboard boxes. Food Lion decided to post the agreement with the Labor Department in its 1,045 stores and hoped the settlement will enable it to refocus on building new stores and improving market share.

Maria Echaveste, the wage and hour administrator involved in the case, noted that "In certain economic times, companies look for ways to cut their labor costs. . . . We're trying to send a signal that everyone needs to play by the same rules."

SOURCE: Adopted from Kevin G. Salwen, "Labor-Law Case Costs Food Lion Big Settlement," *The Wall Street Journal* (August 3, 1993): A3, 5; and Kevin G. Salwen and Glenn Ruffenach, "Food Lion's Big Settlement with U.S. Allows It to Return to Expansion Plans," *The Wall Street Journal* (August 4, 1993): A5.

---

productivity. The relationship at these plants between management and employees represented by a union is good; and at unorganized plants, unions are having difficulties convincing workers that they need a union.[4]

View of Union Members

How do union members believe they benefit from union representation? To answer that question, the Louis Harris Organization conducted a national survey of 1500 union and nonunion workers (see Table 14–1). The following basic questions were asked of individuals of both groups: What conditions in the

Table 14–1 What Union Employees Believe Their Unions Provide Better Compared to Nonunion Employees

Item	Percent Responding
Benefits	67
Pay	62
Job security	56
Fair treatment by supervisors	46
Participation in decision making	38
Health and safety conditions	38

SOURCE: Adapted from Carol Keegan, "How Union Members and Nonunion View the Role of Unions," *Monthly Labor Review* 110, no. 8 (August 1987): 50–51.

638

workplace would change if workers lost their unions? Would conditions get better, worse, or stay the same? The results showed a substantial difference between union and nonunion workers. Union workers responded that conditions would get worse. Of the ten workplace conditions in the survey, they expected the following to worsen: benefits (67 percent of those responding); pay (62 percent); job security (56 percent); treatment by supervisors (46 percent); worker participation in decision making (38 percent); and health and safety conditions (38 percent). Nonunion workers, however, predicted that if they became unionized, they would see pay and benefits "get better" (43 percent) but predicted no change in any nonwage conditions. Therefore, workers who are union members believe unions help them to improve a variety of important economic and noneconomic conditions, while nonunion workers seem unaware of any noneconomic benefit to union representation.[5]

Union Membership

The decline in union membership since the 1940s can be traced to several factors. (See Table 14−2). The number of new workers included in organizational elections each year has declined significantly, as has the success rate of unions trying to win those new workers in organizational elections. Unions have also lost existing members by losing decertification elections. The 1970s were particularly difficult for unions as membership declined in highly unionized manufacturing industries hard hit by recession and foreign competition. Even if these industries had not lost employment, union membership would have declined due to unions' poor performance in certification and decertification elections.[6]

In the traditional union stronghold, production jobs in metropolitan areas, the proportion of union to nonunion employees declined from 73 to 48 percent from 1961 to 1993. This substantial drop in the nation's large cities was not limited to production workers; nonsupervisory office clerical workers in unions also declined.

The construction industry, once one of the strongholds of unions in the United States, has had a decline in union membership from about one-half in 1966 to less than 30 percent thirty years later. Possible reasons for the continued decline include (1) the rising number of union members working for nonunion contractors,

Table 14−2 Union Membership, 1935−1995

Year	Total Membership (thousands)	Percentage of Labor Force	
		Total	Nonagricultural
1935	3,728	6.7	13.2
1940	8,944	15.5	26.9
1945	14,796	21.9	35.5
1950	15,000	22.3	31.5
1955	17,749	24.7	33.2
1960	18,177	23.6	31.4
1965	18,519	22.4	28.4
1970	20,751	22.6	27.3
1975	21,090	20.7	25.5
1980	20,100	18.8	23.0
1985	17,400	17.8	19.1
1990	17,000	16.8	18.5
1995	16,200	15.8	17.2

SOURCE: U.S. Department of Labor.

(2) the gradual narrowing of the union–non-union wage gap, and (3) the disappearance of the union sector's productivity advantage, which had enabled union contractors to pay higher union salaries and still compete with nonunion contractors. The union productivity advantage had been built on the successful recruitment, screening, and training programs in the construction unions. The perceived lack of a productivity advantage in union workers has given owners and contractors a strong incentive to switch from union to less costly non-union labor in the construction industry.[8]

Some people credit an enlightened management for its help in discouraging unionization. Younger workers, women, and minorities have not been courted by labor and now find traditional labor unions unresponsive to their needs, although a U.S. Department of Labor survey confirmed that these workers were as willing as white males to join unions if their job conditions warranted unionization.[9]

Avoiding unionization has become a major task of HR managers in such traditional nonunion areas as health care, financial planning, and insurance companies. But these white-collar workers are obvious targets for organizational campaigns. Their responsibilities and education cause their expectations for respect and participation at their workplace to be higher even than those of assembly-line workers.[10] Clerical employees, the majority of whom are women, are increasingly attracted to organizing, especially when the union organization is a young one geared to their demographic arrangement.[11]

What are the implications if this decline in membership continues? If private sector, nonconstruction union membership remains roughly constant and total U.S. employment continues to expand at the rate of 2.5 percent per year, the unionized share of the work force will not fall below 12 percent before 2000—plenty of time for events to change the current trend. However, an expansion of the unionized share of the work force probably would require both an increased rate of success in new elections and economic improvement in heavily unionized industries.[12]

UNION GOALS

The goals of unions have not changed significantly in almost 200 years. In a broad sense, the primary goal of any union is to promote the interests of its membership. Through collective bargaining and lobbying for labor legislation, union leaders enhance their members' standard of living and improve many conditions that surround their work.

Union Security

Union security, or the ability to grow and prosper in either good or poor economic times, is organized labor's foremost goal. Labor legislation has created the following security provisions (except the closed shop) that organized labor may collectively bargain for the following:

- *Union shop.* All new employees in a union shop must join the union within a specified time, usually thirty days. About twenty states have passed *right-to-work* laws (see Figure 14–2) which prohibit compulsory union membership but allow other forms of unions. Most collective bargaining agreements provide for a union shop.

- *Agency shop.* No employee is required to join a union. However, all nonunion employees must give the union an amount equal to union dues to provide their share of the union's expenses. This arrangement is believed to be reasonable since all employees within the bargaining unit (union and nonunion) receive the same negotiated wages and benefits and are represented by the union in grievance cases.

A landmark 1992 court decision, however, provided that dues collected from nonunion members can only be spent on collective bargaining activities, and not union activities such as political campaigns or lobbying efforts. The National Right to Work Foundation cheered the court decision because it forbids unions to use funds provided by nonunion employees for pro-union political activities.[13]

- *Maintenance-of-membership shop.* Employees are not required to join the union in a **maintenance-of-membership shop**. However, employees who do join must remain in the union until the contract expires or until a designated "escape" period occurs.

- *Closed shop.* The new employee must be a union member at the time of hiring. While the **closed shop** is illegal, it exists in practice, particularly in the construction and printing industries. The practice is promoted by hiring through the union's own placement services and by management's desire to avoid the trouble that may accompany the hiring of nonunion employees.

- *Open shop.* No employee is required to join or contribute money to a labor organization as a condition for employment in an **open shop**.

Job Security

Job security is one of the primary goals of unions. Without jobs, union goals of higher wages and greater benefits are meaningless. Unions provide for job security by negotiating for any of the following contract clauses:

Seniority System   A set of rules governing promotion and layoff/recall opportunities on the basis of service with an employer is called a **seniority system**. It is by far the most commonly negotiated means of measuring service and comparing employees for promotion and employment decisions.

Seniority is perhaps the most important measure of job security to employees, and the issue of seniority is popular among unions and

viewed as critical to job security. Seniority is highly visible because it is so easy to define and measure. Normally, it is calculated in terms of days beginning with the employee's date of hire and, with a few exceptions, continues over the years during the employee's tenure. Union negotiators will vehemently claim that management, in the absence of a job seniority system, will make promotion, layoff, and other decisions based solely on possible short-run cost savings or individual biases rather than the objective criteria that seniority easily provides. These criteria include the employee's loyalty to the company and the skills and productivity that increase with time spent on the job.[14]

Subcontracting   What is subcontracting? It has been termed the "twilight zone" of management rights in collective bargaining, and is considered a headache by both labor and management. Basically, **subcontracting** may be defined as arranging to make goods or perform services with another firm that could be accomplished by the bargaining unit employees within the company's current facilities.[15]

An example of a contract clause limiting the ability of management to subcontract is provided in the agreement between Lithonia Lighting, Inc., and Local Union 613 of the International Brotherhood of Electrical Workers:

SECTION VIII
Subcontracting
The company agrees that wherever possible it will not subcontract work normally performed by members of the bargaining unit while there are employees on layoff capable of performing such work; and in the event work is subcontracted hereunder, such work will not be subcontracted to individuals, firms, or corporations unfair to the IBEW.[16]

Retraining Rights   The need to stay competitive with nonunion and foreign businesses has caused union leaders to accept technology changes as necessary and normal conditions of work. Today, rather than oppose technological change, negotiators anticipate it and bargain for advance notice, **retraining rights**, and outplacement assistance for affected workers.

A total, systematic approach to technological change and worker retraining was developed by the Ford Motor Company and the United Auto Workers (UAW). The decision to close the San Jose, California, plant was announced along with a labor–management initiative to provide assistance to displaced workers. The total program included the following agenda:

- *Orientation and benefits.* All workers were included in meetings that provided them information about available services, company benefits, and personalized information about specific benefits at the time of shutdown.

- *Assessment and testing.* More than 1600 workers participated in retraining programs after taking a skills test administered by the California Employment Department.

- *Basic education and vocational courses.* In-plant courses in basic math, reading, and English enabled 183 workers to pass the General Equivalency Diploma (GED) examination. In addition, Ford personnel taught courses in computers, welding, statistical quality control, auto mechanics, metal repair, electronics, and so on. More than 2100 workers participated.

- *Seminars and programs.* Additional in-plant seminars were offered in small business operation, real estate, armed security, and so forth.

- *Target vocational retraining.* Local technical training institutions taught more than thirty courses in areas such as microwave and machine tool technology and auto service. The courses were paid for by the Ford-UAW "Nickel Fund" for training, the Job Training Partnership Act (JTPA), and the state of California.

- *Job search and placement.* Two-day job search workshops were conducted by California Employment Development Department staff workers.

- *Ford plant relocation.* Under the agreement, 117 San Jose hourly workers chose to relocate to other Ford plants in the United States.[17]

As a result of the program, more than 83 percent of those employees who reentered the labor market (79 percent of all employees) secured employment, and the other 21 percent chose retirement under the agreement's benefit plan. Both labor and management consider the program a model worker retraining program, a workable approach to the challenge of technological change.

Improved Economic Conditions

Economic issues have been a central concern to unions since the beginning of the labor movement. Demands for higher wages are almost certain to be presented during labor–management contract negotiations. During World War II, primarily because of government-imposed wage controls, unions struck for and received liberal benefits packages, including insurance, pensions, and paid holidays and vacations. These benefits remain a high priority today.

Working Conditions

Improvements in working conditions have been important union concerns in recent years. Unions have successfully bargained for better safety programs, shorter workweeks, less mandatory overtime, longer breaks and lunch periods, and a clean, healthy work environment.

Fairness and Justice

Underscoring the union philosophy is the fair and equal treatment of all employees. Without the protection of organized labor, union leaders claim, management will show favoritism by providing to or withholding privileges and benefits from certain workers. Unions hope to minimize the potential for favoritism and unequal treatment by insisting that major personnel decisions, such as in-grade wage increases, job promotions, transfers, layoffs, and other job actions, be made according to seniority. Although the unions' emphasis on seniority can be criticized because the most productive employee may not receive a promotion or may be the first to be laid off, the use of that criterion does constitute an impartial and objective way to make important personnel decisions and is also used in nonunion firms.

Social Action

Today many unions advocate goals that affect society as a whole. These goals are not achieved through the normal collective bargaining process, but by lobbying for federal and state legislation and government-sponsored programs and policies. As the major voice of labor, the AFL-CIO takes a firm stand on social, political, and economic goals. These goals and the strategies for accomplishing them are shown in Figure 14–1.

LABOR–MANAGEMENT LEGISLATION

Beginning in the early 1930s, labor–management relations have been heavily regulated by federal and state legislation. Prior to this period, lawmakers took a laissez-faire attitude toward unions and management and relied primarily on common law to govern labor–management relations. *Common law,* a heritage of the English legal system, is the body of law based on court decisions, custom, and precedent. In contrast, *statute law* is the body of laws established by legislative acts. When enacting the various statutes, Congress was reacting to public opinion and the special needs of labor and management.[18]

Railway Labor Act (1926)

In 1926 the Railway Labor Act gave railroad workers the right to organize and bargain collectively. It prohibited interference by employers. The act was amended in 1934 to include the airline industry. The provisions of the act foreshadowed those of the Wagner Act of 1935.

Norris-LaGuardia Act (1932)

Throughout organized labor's early history, union power was often undercut by *injunctions,* court orders requiring performance or restraint of a particular act. Management frequently obtained a temporary or permanent injunction prohibiting a strike or picketing. In 1932, the Norris-LaGuardia Act expressly forbade the federal courts from issuing injunctions in labor disputes, except to maintain law and order during a union activity. The act also forbade employers from enforcing a *yellow dog contract.* Such a contract stipulated as a condition of employment that an employee was not a union member and would not join a union. (Labor believed only a "yellow dog" would accept a job under such terms.)

National Labor Relations Act (1935)

The 1929 stock market crash plunged the United States into a major depression, the worst in its history. The impact of the Great Depression on workers was devastating. One-third of the country's work force was unemployed. The labor movement made more emphatic efforts to organize and demand recognition and became more politically active. The severity of conditions led to public sympathy for its problems.

Senator Robert Wagner, a champion of labor who had President Roosevelt's support, proposed an act that recognized employees' rights to organize and bargain collectively. A quasi-judicial tribunal with the power and authority to enforce its own orders would be created. While the act purported to protect the

FIGURE 14-1 Social, political, and economic goals of the AFL-CIO.

8-hour Day
Paid Sick Leave
Higher Wages
Health Insurance
Overtime Pay
Pensions
Safer Working Conditions
Paid Holidays
Job Security
Severance Pay
Paid Vacations
Maternity Leave

The preceding was brought to you by the men and women of the Unions of the AFL-CIO who won these benefits at the bargaining table and set the standard for all working Americans.

The new Union Yes "Benefits" commercial premiered nationwide on Solidarity Day, 1991.

SOURCE: AFL-CIO.

public from the disruption of interstate commerce resulting from labor disputes, Senator Wagner stated that it would also give the employee freedom. Labor–management relations generally improved after the passage of this historic act, and union membership rapidly grew to levels previously undreamed of by labor leaders.

The National Labor Relations Act of 1935 is more widely known as the **Wagner Act** because it was sponsored by New York Senator Robert Wagner. The Wagner Act is often called the Magna Carta of organized labor. In essence, the act protects a worker's right to join a union without the employer's interference. Bringing broad powers and sweeping reform to the labor movement, the act encouraged the movement's spectacular growth between 1935 and the early 1950s. Important provisions of the act include the following:

- The employer may not interfere with, restrain, or coerce employees in the exercise of their right to join unions and bargain collectively through representatives of their own choosing.

- The employer may not dominate or interfere with the formation or administration of labor unions.

- The employer may not discriminate against the employee in any condition of employment for taking part in legal union activities.

- The employer may not fire or discriminate against the employee in any condition of employment for taking part in legal union activities.

- The employer may not fire or discriminate against the employee for charging an unfair labor practice against the company.

- The employer may not refuse to bargain collectively with employee representatives in good faith.

National Labor Relations Board The **National Labor Relations Board (NLRB)** was created to administer and enforce the Wagner Act. The National Labor Relations Board is an independent agency of the federal government; members are presidential appointees. The first of the NLRB's two main functions is to investigate charges of **unfair labor practices**. Basically, an unfair labor practice exists when either the employer or the union violates any provision of labor law. For example, a union will likely charge the employer with an unfair labor practice if the employer bribes employees to vote against the union or discriminates against employees who hold prounion sentiments. Examples of activities that may result in a charge of unfair labor practice against a union include instigating violence on a picket line, refusing to bargain in good faith with the employer, charging union employees excessive initiation fees or dues, and featherbedding. If the NLRB finds an employer guilty of a violation and the employer fails to alter certain practices, the board will seek legal action through the U.S. Court of Appeals. Employers may appeal the decisions of the board.

A second function of the board is to conduct certification elections by secret ballot to determine whether employees will be represented by a union. The election process will be discussed later in this chapter.

Labor-Management Relations Act (1947)

While the Wagner Act may be appropriately called prolabor, the Labor-Management Relations Act—more commonly known as the **Taft-Hartley Act**—is decidedly promanagement. Its purpose was to create a balance of power between unions and employers. During the decade following the passage of the Wagner Act in 1935, a feeling developed that unions had grown too big and too influential, that their escalating power had to be brought under control. The act that was sponsored by Senator Robert Taft and Representative Frederick Hartley actually amends the Wagner Act.

Important provisions of the Taft-Hartley Act include the following:

- The union may not coerce or restrain employees from exercising their bargaining rights. For example, the union may not make false statements to employees during organizing drives.

- The union may not cause an employer to discriminate against an employee in order to encourage or discourage union membership.

- The union may not refuse to bargain in good faith with the employer.

- The union may not engage in featherbedding. The U.S. Supreme Court has decided that it is lawful to require employers to pay for **make-work activities** even though they may be inefficient or ineffective.

Section 14b From labor's perspective, a particularly troublesome provision in labor law is Section 14b of the Taft-Hartley Act. This section allows individual states to pass legislation that bars any form of compulsory union membership (union shops); such states are known as **right-to-work** states. Only twenty-one states, mostly located in the South and Southwest (see Figure 14–2), have passed such legislation.

Section 14b has long been a battleground between organized labor and right-to-work advocates. Labor leaders have for years attempted to repeal it. On the other side is the

FIGURE 14-2 Right-to-work states.

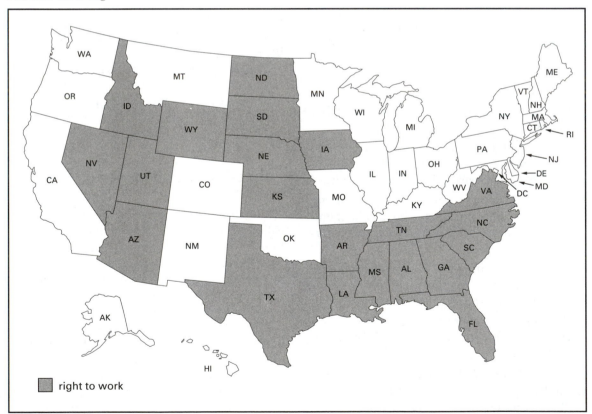

right to work

National Right-to-Work Committee, which works to advance the right-to-work movement and presses for federal right-to-work legislation.

Opponents contend that right-to-work legislation is an attempt to change the bargaining power at the negotiating table in management's favor. In addition, "right-to-work" as a slogan is misleading. Such laws guarantee no one a job and, in their opinion, confer rights only on employers.[19] The phrase implies the union's concomitant right to prevent a person from working. According to union advocates, the requirement of union membership as a condition of employment is no more restrictive of an individual's freedom than the requirement of specific hours of work or of certain minimal job qualifications. Union members contend that employees should support the union primarily because all union and nonunion employees alike receive benefits through collective bargaining agreements.[20]

Proponents of right-to-work legislation believe it affirms the basic right of a person to work for a living whether he or she belongs to a union or not.[21] They contend that no private organization should be able to tax a person and use that money to support causes with which all the members may not agree.

A 1986 right-to-work referendum election was held in Idaho. Both sides waged extensive media campaigns and focused the debate on the issues of lower wages and growth in the Idaho economy. Whether someone should be forced to join a union became a peripheral issue in the campaign. The voters chose to keep the new right-to-work law by a narrow margin—50.2 percent. Idaho had been targeted by the National Right-to-Work Committee since 1976, when it successfully pushed passage of the Louisiana right-to-work law.[22] Right-to-work states have several characteristics that differ from union-shop states. These characteristics include (1) low union membership, (2) little heavy industry, and (3) a high level of agriculture. Idaho shared these characteristics with the twenty right-to-work states.[23]

Labor-Management Reporting and Disclosure Act (1959)

During the 1950s, unionism's reputation was tarnished considerably when a series of exposés uncovered corruption and racketeering in unions, particularly in the Teamsters Union. During 1952 and 1953, the State of New York found widespread racketeering on the New York City waterfront involving the International Longshoremen's Union. The investigation, which uncovered gross mismanagement of the union pension fund, was a principal factor underlying the passage of the Welfare and Pension Plans Disclosure Act of 1958.

The most widely publicized account of union corruption was the investigation held by the McClellan Committee in the U.S. Senate. The committee heard 1526 witnesses in 270 days of hearings. Over half of the testimony was devoted to racketeering and corruption in the Teamsters Union. The committee hearings ultimately led to the expulsion from the AFL-CIO of the Teamsters Union and the Laundry and Bakery and Confectionery Workers Union. The committee hearings influenced the passage of the Labor-Management Reporting and Disclosure Act of 1959, more commonly known as the **Landrum-Griffin Act**. Important provisions of the act include the following:

- *Creation of a "bill of rights" for union members.* The act provided equal rights for union members to attend, participate, and vote in meetings; the right to meet and express any views or opinions about union business and candidates; the right to be free of unreasonably high dues, fees, and assessments; the right to testify against and sue the union for violation of their rights; and the right to inspect copies of collective bargaining agreements.

- *Reporting requirements.* The act requires unions to submit an annual financial report covering assets, liabilities, income, expenses, and so on to the secretary of labor, who must approve the report.

- *Election safeguards.* The act set forth the ground rules for proper union conduct during elections. For example, ballots must be secret and every member in good standing must be allowed a vote.

- *Restrictions on officers.* The act disallows convicted felons from holding union office for five years after conviction. The act also requires union officials to be bonded.

UNION STRUCTURE AND ORGANIZATION

There are approximately 175 national and international unions in America. **National unions** have collective bargaining agreements with different employers in two or more states; *international unions* are headquartered in the United States but have members in Canada. The three largest national unions are those of the teamsters, the auto workers, and the steelworkers.[24]

A union is a private, nonprofit organization whose primary purpose is to advance the interests of its members. In many respects, a union closely resembles the structure and operation of a business firm. Union leaders must plan and organize activities, recruit and hire for union positions, create and manage a budget, influence and motivate other union officials and the rank-and-file membership, see that union goals are met, and be sure that union policies, procedures, and rules are followed. In particular, they must be able to influence and persuade management representatives when a new union contract is being negotiated. A union's function contains basic elements common to all organizations: union goals must be created, jobs must be defined, leaders must be given responsibilities and authority, and departments must be formed. But many real differences exist in the operation and function of a union and a private enterprise. The main differences will now be discussed.[25]

Power Structure In a business firm, leaders are appointed; authority and power flow from the top to the bottom. Union officials are elected by the rank and file or by convention delegates; power flows (at least theoretically) from the bottom to the top.

Ultimate Authority The ultimate authority in business and government organizations is held by top management. It decides the direction the organization will take and determines how to solve critical problems. The rank and file possess ultimate authority in the union, because collective bargaining agreements normally must be ratified (approved by a vote) by the membership. Ratification is not always a rubber-stamp procedure. Union members occasionally send their leaders back to the bargaining table to negotiate for better economic rewards and working conditions.

Tenure At the top of the corporate structure, executives rarely remain in the same position for ten or more years. A certain value is placed on fresh leadership and an orderly system for transferring power to new groups of leaders. Historically, top union leaders have enjoyed tenures of considerable length. For example, John L. Lewis was president of the United Mine Workers for thirty-nine years; Dan Tobin led the Teamsters through its early history for forty-five years. There are few roadblocks to long tenure, because length of service tends to perpetuate itself. The power and charisma of a top union leader often prove to be formidable barriers to the up-and-coming union official, but challenges do occur; see *HR in the News:* "Unions at Crossroads: Cooperation or Confrontation?"

Unions at Crossroads: Cooperation or Confrontation?

The Saturn automobile plant in Spring Hill, Tennessee, produced a high-quality, successful product—often cited as the "crown jewel" in the General Motors line of cars. From its beginning in 1990 the plant was operated with a labor–management partnership that blurred traditional "we vs. they" boundaries. Both the UAW and GM credited much of Saturn's success to its unique consensus style management.

Michael Bennett, the UAW Local 1853 president, however, only narrowly won his first reelection bid, 52% to 48%. The narrow victory was a surprise; incumbent union presidents are usually reelected by overwhelming margins. Bob Haskins, who opposed Bennett, ran on a platform of putting more distance between management and the union and focusing on "bread and butter" issues. For example, he campaigned for traditional overtime pay, which would have added about $60 million to Saturn's annual costs ($200 per car), which management and Bennett said the company could not afford.

After his narrow victory Bennett said, "The partnership is alive and well . . . and we can get on with building world class quality cars."

The 48% who voted for Hoskins, however, may represent millions of other union members who believe that union members of joint labor–management partnerships, which have spread across most industries, may not be able to represent both the company's interests and their personal interests successfully.

SOURCE: Adapted from Neal Templin, "UAW Chief at GM's Saturn Unit Vows to Back Consensus-Management Pact," *The Wall Street Journal* (April 5, 1993): A1.

Local Unions

Most local unions are affiliated with national or international unions. Local unions receive their charters from the national union, which may disband or suspend the local. Less than 2 percent of all local unions are completely independent; they generally serve a single employer or small geographical territory.

Local union leaders are elected by their members, usually for a one-year term. While local union leadership varies by size and union, a typical leadership group consists of a president, vice-president, secretary, and treasurer. In very large locals, union officials work full time for the local union. More often, however, the officials have a full-time job and conduct union affairs on their own time and on time allowed by a company during working hours.

Perhaps the local union's most critical function is to negotiate a contract with employers. The contract is most frequently negotiated by

649

either the president of the local or the business agent; sometimes the contract is negotiated by representatives from the national union. A *business agent* is an elected, full-time, salaried official who represents a large union. The agent may also be heavily involved in handling employee grievances or leading union members during a strike.

Another important local union member is the *shop steward,* sometimes referred to as a *committeeman* or *grievance person.* As the last term suggests, the steward acts as the union representative in processing grievances against management. The handling of grievances will be discussed in detail later in the chapter.

National and International Unions

Like a corporate headquarters with plants and offices scattered throughout the United States, national or international unions direct and support local unions. Direction and support are achieved by creating major policies and maintaining important functions and programs. Some of those policies, functions, and programs include the following:

- Creating uniform contract provisions regarding wages or seniority for local unions in a given area or industry.

- Assisting the local union in contract negotiations.

- Training local union officials in union management and administration.

- Creating and administering strike funds to support local union members on strike.

- Providing data collection services for cost-of-living data, wage data, and so on.

- Increasing union membership by organizing nonunion employees.

National or international unions often employ elected officials and staff specialists appointed by top union leaders. Economists, law-

yers, and public relations specialists are among those who provide valuable services in promoting the union effort.

Independent Unions

The majority of national or international unions are affiliated with the AFL-CIO. Some unions decided at their inception to remain autonomous and thus never joined the AFL or the CIO; they are called **independent unions**. Others, such as the Teamsters in 1957, were expelled from the AFL for corruption; eleven unions were expelled from the CIO. In 1987 the Teamsters rejoined the AFL-CIO, ending one of the deepest rifts in the labor movement.

The AFL-CIO

A single federation of autonomous labor unions, the AFL-CIO influences the activities of its member unions and the labor movement as a whole. Eighty-nine of the national and international unions in the United States are AFL-CIO affiliates. The structure of the AFL-CIO is shown in Figure 14–3.

The national and international affiliates operate autonomously, retaining decentralized decision-making authority over their own affairs. AFL-CIO officials are not authorized to call strikes, influence the negotiating process, or control the behavior of affiliate leaders. Why then have most unions joined the AFL-CIO? According to labor expert Martin Esten, the AFL-CIO provides its members with a number of specialized services.[26]

The plain fact is that the AFL-CIO is not directly involved in the fundamental union function of collective bargaining. For all practical purposes that function is reserved for the national unions and, to a lesser extent, for the locals. The primary role of the federation, instead, may be described as broadly political. The AFL-CIO is to organized labor roughly what the United States Chamber of Commerce is to business; it is engaged in lobbying, public relations, research, and education to present labor's views on countless problems—not only

FIGURE 14-3 The structure of the AFL-CIO.

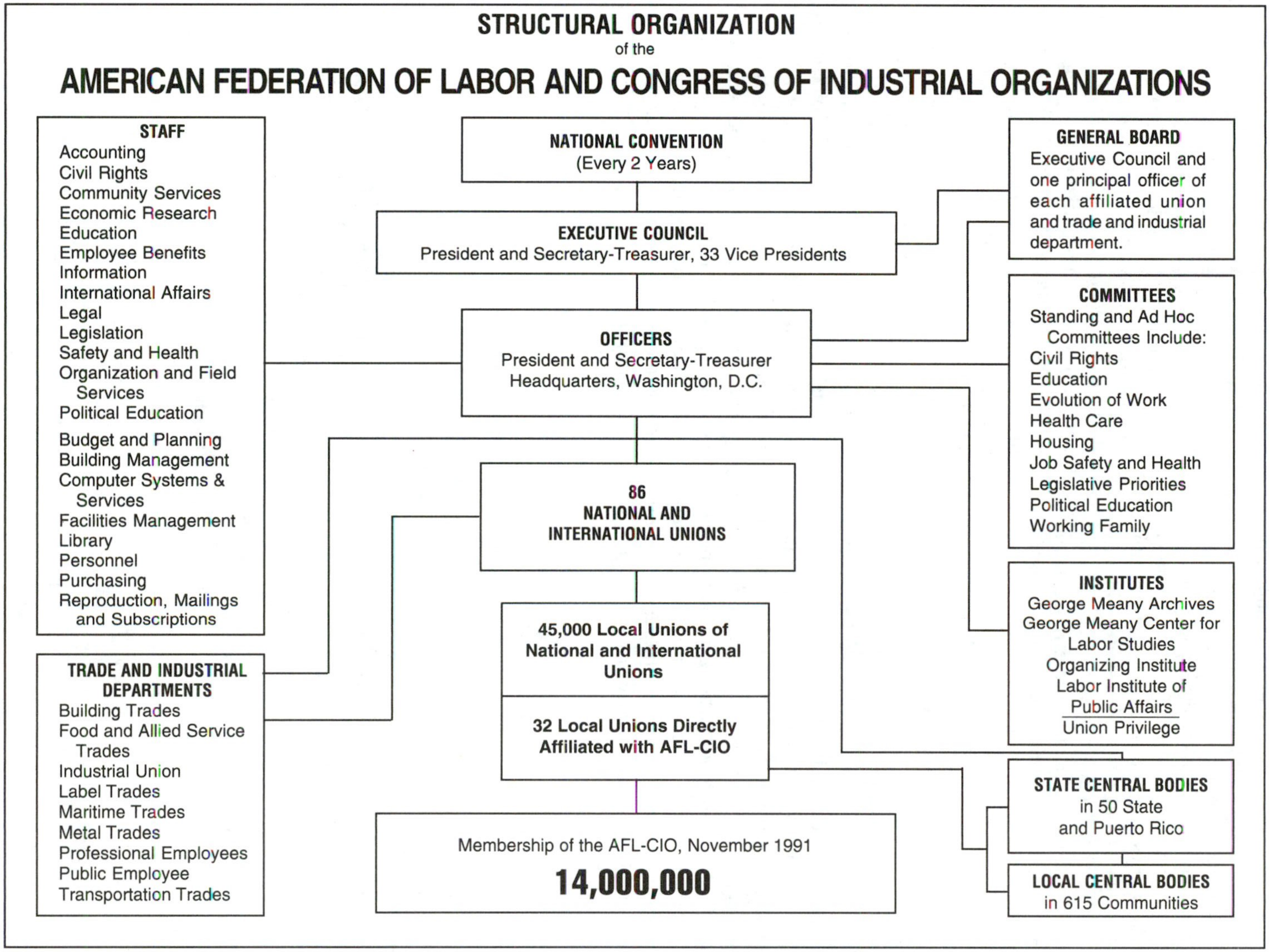

STRUCTURAL ORGANIZATION
of the
AMERICAN FEDERATION OF LABOR AND CONGRESS OF INDUSTRIAL ORGANIZATIONS

NATIONAL CONVENTION
(Every 2 Years)

EXECUTIVE COUNCIL
President and Secretary-Treasurer, 33 Vice Presidents

OFFICERS
President and Secretary-Treasurer
Headquarters, Washington, D.C.

86 NATIONAL AND INTERNATIONAL UNIONS

45,000 Local Unions of National and International Unions

32 Local Unions Directly Affiliated with AFL-CIO

Membership of the AFL-CIO, November 1991

14,000,000

GENERAL BOARD
Executive Council and one principal officer of each affiliated union and trade and industrial department.

COMMITTEES
Standing and Ad Hoc Committees Include:
Civil Rights
Education
Evolution of Work
Health Care
Housing
Job Safety and Health
Legislative Priorities
Political Education
Working Family

INSTITUTES
George Meany Archives
George Meany Center for Labor Studies
Organizing Institute
Labor Institute of Public Affairs
Union Privilege

STATE CENTRAL BODIES
in 50 State and Puerto Rico

LOCAL CENTRAL BODIES
in 615 Communities

STAFF
Accounting
Civil Rights
Community Services
Economic Research
Education
Employee Benefits
Information
International Affairs
Legal
Legislation
Safety and Health
Organization and Field Services
Political Education
Budget and Planning
Building Management
Computer Systems & Services
Facilities Management
Library
Personnel
Purchasing
Reproduction, Mailings and Subscriptions

TRADE AND INDUSTRIAL DEPARTMENTS
Building Trades
Food and Allied Service Trades
Industrial Union
Label Trades
Maritime Trades
Metal Trades
Professional Employees
Public Employee
Transportation Trades

SOURCE: *This Is the AFL-CIO*, Publication no. P-20-1291-15 (Washington, DC: AFL-CIO, 1992), by permission of the AFL-CIO.

on wages, hours, and working conditions, but also on topics ranging from public housing to foreign policy. In addition, the federation performs various necessary functions within the labor movement. It charters new international unions, tries to minimize friction between affiliated unions and settle the disputes which occasionally break out between them, maintains a staff of organizers, and provides research and legal assistance primarily for unions too small to afford their own research staffs.

THE ORGANIZING DRIVE

The impetus to organize employees may come from two sources. First, the workers may be dissatisfied with their pay or work conditions and initiate contact with the union. Such is typically the case. Second, workers may be contacted by a *union organizer,* a full-time, salaried staff member who generally represents a national union. As the job title suggests, the union organizer increases union membership and strength by organizing groups

of workers who are not presently unionized. An organizing drive usually follows the series of events shown in Figure 14–4.

The union's goal is to organize workers and bring them into the union. Labor's strategy is to convince the workers that union membership will bring them benefits they do not presently enjoy. Union organizers may suggest that union representation will result in higher pay, more benefits, better working conditions, and greater fairness in promotions, job transfers, and layoffs. Speaking proudly of the benefits and work improvements they have achieved for other workers, union organizers often cite impressive and convincing statistics about wage gains achieved through collective bargaining. To tell the union side of the story, labor advocates hold formal meetings at the local union hall and encourage supporters to spread the word informally about the benefits a union would bring to the employees' place of work. A new breed of organizers in the 1990s is largely female and minority (see *HR in the News*). Prounion handbills and flyers are often

FIGURE 14-4   The organizing process.

Young and Female: The New Breed of Labor Organizer

Rachel Brickman was once a member of the working class—waiting tables at a country club—and she claims "I never got treated worse in my life." Now she is a graduate of Sarah Lawrence College and an AFL-CIO organizer. Brickman began her union organizing with ten consecutive victories—a perfect record which is unheard of in the 1990s. Why the unusual career choice? Her answer is that it is "a real tangible way to change people's lives."

Ms. Brickman joined her college roommate, Megan Parke, and Katherine Kirsh, a Barnard College graduate, and many others in attending the AFL-CIO Organizing Institute, which began in 1990. Most of the Institute's new breed of organizers are young and female. They are looking for a cause and view organized labor and the AFL-CIO Institute as the Peace Corps of the 1990s. The AFL-CIO recruits the new organizers on college campuses because, according to Richard Bensinger, the Executive Director of the Institute, "Every successful social movement in history, including the civil-rights movement, was run by young people. . . . If the labor movement is going to succeed and grow again they need to be a big part of it."

Brickman's job requires many nights on the road away from home—260 in one year—and her car traveled over 87,000 miles in her first two years. To recruit graveyard shift workers, she often spends her nights in poor neighborhoods to catch tired workers returning home. Her efforts have paid off, however, adding 1,200 new members to the Service Employees International Union in her first two years.

SOURCE: Adapted from "Why Ms. Brickman of Sarah Lawrence Now Rallies Workers," *The Wall Street Journal* (May 25, 1993): A1.

---

passed to workers as they leave work or go to lunch. An example of a handbill is shown in Figure 14–5.

Management's goal is simply to keep the union out of the workplace. Their strategy is to convince the workers that unionization will do them more harm than good. Management may attempt to assure workers that their present pay and benefits are competitive and may show data to prove it. Emphasizing a philosophy of fair dealings with all employees, management may discuss the union's involvement in violent or corrupt activities if such has been the case. Management will also enumerate the costs of union membership, which include initiation fees, dues, and other assessments. The workers will be reminded that wages will be lost should a strike occur. Management may also talk about the loss of freedom and the potential erosion in labor–management relations that unionization might bring.

FIGURE 14-5 An example of a union handbill.

FOLLOW YOUR OWN GOOD JUDGMENT

Remember

Uncle Sam Stands Behind YOU!

Vote ——— Join

International Association of Machinists and Aerospace Workers AFL·CIO

Illegal Activities

Throughout the organizing drive, emotions often run high on both sides, and both union and management supporters often make passionate and dramatic arguments to further their causes. To ensure that both labor and management play fair during the organizing drive, labor legislation has spelled out in detail illegal campaign tactics. During the organizing drive, union representatives or pro-labor employees cannot do the following:[27]

- Solicit employees where they are working unless employees are normally allowed to converse while they work. Oral solicitation is acceptable during breaks and lunch.

- Distribute union literature in work areas; nonwork areas typically include lunch rooms and break areas.

- Offer an employee free union membership before the election unless free membership is granted to everyone who joins the union up to the time the first contract is negotiated.

- Offer excessive attendance prizes to employees who attend a campaign rally. Payment of a sum of money to each participant is an obvious infraction of the rule.

- Make substantial misrepresentations. While both management and labor are allowed a generous amount of puffing (promises and propaganda), the *Hollywood Ceramics* rule forces the election to be set aside if either side makes a "substantial misrepresentation on a material fact made at a time when the other party has inadequate time to respond and correct the misrepresentation."

During the organizing drive, representatives of employers cannot do the following:[28]

- Discipline or threaten employees who engage in lawful solicitation or distribution of union material.

- Prohibit existing employees from legal solicitation and distribution activities at work. Management can, if it desires, prohibit outside union organizers from entering the premises. The only exception to this rule is the rare case when employees are normally inaccessible—such as maritime workers on a ship.

- Engage in antiunion rhetoric before a mass audience twenty-four hours before an election. However, the twenty-four hours rule does not forbid talks to individuals and small groups.

- Speak to employees in "area of management authority" such as the bosses' offices or management conference rooms. Such a setting is thought by the NLRB to be overly intimidating.

- Tell employees that absolutely no good will come if the union gets in. Called the *futility doctrine,* this prohibits the employer from making statements suggesting that it is futile for the employees to unionize.

- Appeal to racial prejudice by pitting black or white workers against one another by suggesting that a certain race would benefit from unionization.

- Promise certain benefits if the union loses. Further, a raise in pay or an increase in benefits cannot be given during the drive unless the increase was planned before the election. Similarly, existing benefits or a planned increase in benefits cannot be rescinded because of the union campaign.

- Keep track of employees' union activities or give the impression that pro-union employees are under surveillance.

Representation Election

Before an election is called by the NLRB, the union must provide a "showing of support" by getting at least 30 percent of the employees to sign **authorization cards** or a *petition*. The card, as shown in Figure 14–6, states that the employee designates the union as the bargaining agent. If more than 50 percent of the employees sign authorization cards, the union may formally request the employer to recognize it as the employees' bargaining agent. The employer still generally refuses to recognize the union; thus the union must then formally petition the NLRB to hold an election.

The NLRB oversees the **representation election** to ensure that at least 30 percent of the employees in the bargaining unit have signed authorization cards and that no illegal campaign activities have taken place. At this time, the NLRB investigator also defines the **bargaining unit**. The bargaining unit is the group of employees the union will represent and bargain for if the election favors the union. Although the NLRB considers several factors in deciding the makeup of the bargaining unit, the most important is the *community of interest principle;* that is, the more employees have in common, the more likely the board is to find that they constitute a valid bargaining unit. Specific factors examined by the board include similarity of work performed, geographical proximity of workers, job integration, similarity of working conditions, prevailing wage rates and benefits, and whether employees work

FIGURE 14-6 A union authorization card.

University of Louisville
American Association of University Professors

I, <u>Frank E. Kuzmits</u>, hereby designate the University of Louisville Chapter of the American Association of University Professors to represent my professional and economic interests in collective bargaining.

Date: <u>4/1/90</u>

Signature

<u>Management</u>
Department

under a common management group. If the union wins the election, all employees within the bargaining unit—both union and nonunion employees—will be represented by the union. Management cannot treat the union employee any differently than the nonunion employee.

Certification and Decertification

The union becomes the official bargaining agent for the employees if it receives over 50 percent of the votes cast in a secret election. If the union does not receive at least 50 percent of the votes cast, it is not allowed to petition the NLRB for another representation election for at least a year.

Under the provisions of the Taft-Hartley Act, an NLRB **certification** is valid only for a one-year period. After that time, employees (but not the employer) within the bargaining unit may petition the NLRB for a **decertification election**. In a process similar to the representation election, the NLRB will conduct a vote if at least 30 percent of the employees sign the petition. If labor fails to receive a majority vote, it loses its bargaining rights, and no additional elections within the bargaining unit may be held for one year. The purpose of the decertification election is to allow employees to rid themselves of a union in which they no longer have faith or confidence. As would be expected, employers will campaign strongly for the defeat of a union, and they may use any lawful method to achieve that end.

Until the 1970s, about 95 percent of all elections were certification—and unions won over 50 percent of all elections. By 1990, however, decertification elections represented 20 percent of all elections—and unions won only 40 percent of all elections. The combined effects of more elections being decertification (thus unions must win just to keep current membership) and their sliding percentage of victories has had a double-barreled effect on union membership.[29]

PREVENTIVE LABOR RELATIONS

There are a number of strategies that businesses may implement to maintain their nonunion status. These strategies are termed **preventive labor relations**. A number of books, journal articles, seminars, and labor consultants offer an increasing number of techniques for keeping an organization union free. The growth in preventive labor relations is, no doubt, due to the desire to keep labor and operating costs as low as possible. In recent years, many firms that aggressively pursued union-free status have experienced considerable success.

Deterring the Organizing Drive

After weighing the advantages and disadvantages of unionization, if the company decides to remain nonunion, management may attempt to prevent the organizing drive from taking place rather than trying to win the representation election once a drive has gotten underway.

In general, the most effective way for a firm to practice preventive labor relations is to give the employees the benefit of unionization without the union. Simply put, if an employer provides the kind of work environment that employees want, they will not seek out a union. Administrators who value their human resources and conduct an effective program of HR management are much less likely to face an organization drive than those who view the employee as simply another factor of production.

Conditions that prevent union drives are generally those that employees have sought since the early stages of the labor movement: a system for resolving employees' complaints, safe working conditions, good wages and benefits, job security, equitable personnel policies, people-oriented supervision, open channels of communication with management, a voice in the decisions that affect their work, and a feeling that management is concerned about their welfare. Inattention to most or all of these job conditions more than likely will bring a union organizer to management's doorstep.

Labor Consultants

Labor consultants provide services in one of two general ways. First, they may consult with an employer during an organizing or decertification drive, advising management on techniques to keep the union out or to get rid of the union. Second, several consulting firms hold seminars on how to maintain a union-free environment. One popular firm regularly conducts seminars entitled "How to Maintain Nonunion Status" and "The Process of Decertification." A brochure published by the firm lists the following topics for the seminar "How to Maintain Nonunion Status":

- Who are the target industries and target employee groups?
- What makes your organization vulnerable?
- How will the union develop its appeals?
- How will the union attempt to organize?
- How to achieve commitment to your nonunion policy.
- How to conduct a nonunion audit.
- How to react when a union threat is anticipated.
- New strategies available in organizing campaigns.
- How to avoid union campaign pitfalls.

WORKING IN TEAMS

A large portion of the work in most organizations occurs within groups. Most jobs do not exist in isolation but instead involve formal work groups (departments, sections, etc.), as well as informal groups of employees whose strong friendships affect their working relationships. The effectiveness of these employee groups or teams can be critical to the success of the entire organization.

In many union and nonunion organizations, formal groups of employees responsible for an identifiable work process, a specific project, or the solution of a problem are called *employee teams* or *labor–management committees*. These groups have been called the productivity breakthrough of the 1990s, even though the first ones, like those at General Foods in Topeka, Kansas, have been in existence for over twenty years.[30] A *Chicago Tribune* survey of the 500 largest companies in the United States found that about 80 percent utilize some form of committees, employee involvement groups, or employee teams.[31] The successful use of teams is a critical element of today's labor–management relationship.

Formal employee teams can generally be divided into three categories: special project teams, problem-solving teams, and self-managed teams (see Figure 14–7). Self-managed teams are characterized as permanent groups of employees who perform all tasks required of one general activity, as well as the supervisory duties related to their work. Special project teams are usually formed by combining labor and management people from different functional areas to design, develop, and produce new products or services. Problem-solving teams usually meet on a regular basis to analyze, recommend, and implement solutions to selected problems. In the 1980s, a handful of U.S. companies began using a new approach to new product development—the project team. *Project teams* most often consist of ten to fifteen people from different functional areas such as research and development, engineering, manufacturing, and marketing brought together to design and develop a new product quickly and successfully. The project team is viewed as an autonomous group operating independently within the organization. Some

FIGURE 14-7 What's a team?

There are several types of teams. Here are three of the most common.

Problem-Solving	**Special-Project**	**Self-Managed**
Usually 5 to 12 members of labor and management who meet a few hours a week to discuss ways of improving quality, efficiency, and work environment.	Usually 10 to 15 people from different functional areas. May design and introduce work reforms or new technology, or meet with suppliers and customers. In union shops, labor and management collaborate at all levels.	From 5 to 15 nonmanagement workers who learn all production tasks and rotate from job to job. Teams do managerial duties such as schedule work and order materials.

SOURCE: Aaron Bernstein, "Putting a Damper on That Old Team Spirit," *Business Week* (May 4, 1992): 60.

early project team successes include the IBM Personal Computer, 3M's Post-It, and Jell-O's Pudding Snacks.[32]

The factors that have caused a growing number of employers to turn to project teams include the following: (1) rising global competition has greatly increased the need to reduce the time required to put a new product on the market; (2) employees today expect and are able to provide more meaningful input into the development of new products; (3) the past successes of project teams, as well as of other employee teams, have convinced more managers to relinquish their authority to project teams; and (4) the synergy factor discussed earlier is believed to be a significant force that drives team members to be more creative, work harder, and achieve greater productivity than they would if they were given only a limited view of the project.

Problem-solving teams have increased in popularity but are generally used to a lesser extent. They can, however, be highly successful groups. Many problem-solving teams have their roots in quality circles and may be characterized as mature, fully empowered quality circles. The creation of permanent problem-solving teams should not be surprising. An American Society for Training and Development survey of organizations with employee teams found that the most common objective of the teams is problem solving (72 percent of those responding listed this as an objective), team building was second (61 percent), and improving quality was third (58 percent).[33] Thus many organizations with positive experiences with quality circles and problem solving as an ongoing concern allowed the evolution of quality circles or similar groups into permanent problem-solving teams.

Self-managed employee teams (also called *employee groups* or *employee involvement groups, autonomous work groups,* or *self-directed teams*) have become common in many American organizations. Special project teams and self-managed teams are the most common and perhaps best-publicized types of employee teams. They have even been called "the new American industrial weapon" in cover stories in *Business Week, Fortune,* and other business publications.[34]

Exactly what are self-managed employee teams? While no universal definition exists, the following is quite good:

A *self-managed team* is a small group of employees responsible for an entire work process or segment. Team members work together to improve their operation or product, plan their work, resolve day-to-day problems, and manage themselves.[35]

Thus self-directed teams are groups of nonmanagement employees who normally work together on an ongoing, day-to-day basis. They are not groups formed to design and develop special projects or new products, or to analyze and solve problems, as discussed in the previous two sections. Their members have not been selected from functional areas to work together as a team. Instead these teams are permanent components within the organization that get the work out on a daily basis. The key difference is that their work is assigned to a team, whereas in traditional organizations it would be assigned to a department with a supervisor or head, who then assigns portions of the work to individuals within the department.

Common characteristics of self-managed teams include the following:[36]

- They plan, control, and make decisions about their work, (they self-manage!).

- Within limits, they set their own productivity goals and inspect their own work.

- They set their own work schedules.

- Members select, appraise, and discipline each other.

- They are responsible for the quality of their work.

Organizations that have chosen to organize work to be performed by self-managed teams may be quite different from traditional organizations with highly specialized jobs. They often have far fewer levels of management. For example, the Nucor Corporation (a highly successful steel manufacturer), which extensively uses teams, has only four levels of management compared to an average of ten in the steel industry. The teams may perform many of the functions normally performed by the additional layers of management—assign work, check to see that it is done properly, discipline people when necessary, hire employees, appraise performance, and so on. Thus, a large amount of savings often occurs from the elimination of many supervisors and managers due to the use of self-managed teams.[37] Another difference is that all members of the teams must learn all the tasks and jobs, not just a single job, as they would in a traditional organization.

The key differences between traditionally designed organizations and self-directed team organizations are summarized in Figure 14–8.

The successful creation and utilization of self-directed teams (both union and nonunion) has been reported by a large number of U.S. companies, including Ford Motor Company, Procter and Gamble, Digital Equipment, IDS, Honeywell, Cummins Engine, General Electric, Boeing, and LTV Steel. In general, these companies all report many positive benefits from their experience with self-directed teams, including higher productivity, improved

FIGURE 14-8 Key differences between traditional organizations and self-directed team organizations.

Element	Traditional Organizations	Self-Directed Teams
Organizational structure	Layered/individual	Flat/team
Job design	Narrow single-task	Whole process/multiple-task
Management role	Direct/control	Coach/facilitate
Leadership	Top-down	Shared with team
Information flow	Controlled/limited	Open/shared
Rewards	Individual/seniority	Team-based/skills-based
Job process	Managers plan, control, improve	Teams plan, control, improve

SOURCE: Richard S. Wellins, William C. Byham, and Jeanne M. Wilson, *Empowered Teams* (San Francisco: Jossey-Bass, 1991): 6. Used by permission.

The Trouble With Teams

The Overly Manufacturing Company is located in western Pennsylvania and, like many aging rust-belt companies in the 1990s, it turned to empowered teams of employees to increase quality, flexibility, productivity, and customer satisfaction. The change was initiated by new owners, brothers Terry and David Reese, when they bought the plant in 1991. The new owners believed Overly's authoritarian "nose-to-the-grindstone" style of management was out of date and not meeting the needs of their workers. Convinced that empowered teams of employees would improve productivity, they provided training to dozens of designers, salespeople, welders, press operators, and plant foreman—and then named teams.

Suddenly everybody had ideas and suggestions, but no one could "tell the troops to knock it off and get back to work." Managers watched the company spiral into self-directed anarchy. Customers' needs could no longer be met because no one had the authority. Gene James, a computer systems manager, summarized the situation: "There's some vague idea that Overly wants to become a democratic organization, empowering people . . . but we've lost the old structure before the new structure is in place."

One team resorted to guerrilla warfare after managers killed its suggestion to stop entering project time data into the computer—the team hid the data cards in a desk—and it was months before management missed the vital data. Union

quality (usually the major goal), improved employee morale, better attendance, and lower turnover.[38]

A national survey by the American Society of Training and Development of companies that use self-directed teams indicated that the following factors had "improved" or "significantly improved":[39]

- Productivity (77 percent of the firms)
- Quality (72 percent)
- Job satisfaction (65 percent)
- Customer service (57 percent)
- Waste reduction (55 percent)

Union Response to Teams

Union leaders and members have varied greatly in their responses to the creation of self-directed employee teams. At a Ford Motor Company assembly plant, the creation of self-directed teams has made the facility "a much better place to work," according to J. R. "Buddy" Hoskinson, union co-chairman of the UAW—Ford Education Development and Training Programs. "In the old days we punched a time card and had no say in what was going on. . . . We'd just do what we had to to get by." But today Hoskinson credits the self-directed teams, which have no direct supervision and devise their own work schedules, with creating "a new sense of pride. . . . We know we're doing the best we can do." The feeling is similar on a project team at the Ford assembly plant. It consists of ten hourly union workers who implemented the plant manager's idea of modifying the Ford Explorer sport util-

leader Tim Crossman, a press operator, said that teamwork was no longer a good idea (after four months) because management was slow to respond to team suggests. Owner Terry Reese, however, still predicts that in ten years "anybody who runs a business on the hierarchical model isn't going to be in business." A more pressing question may be, will Overly still be in business?

Another example of troubled teams occurred at Dow Chemical Co. in Midland, Michigan. Research teams wanted to spend months building a prototype of a new plastic resin while a manufacturing team, wanting a quick startup, preferred a slight variation to an existing product. Neither side budged and the project failed. The members soon realized an important factor—if the team fails, it's *everyone's* fault!

Still another trouble with teams is that, once successful, managers often make lousy team leaders! For example, Bausch & Lomb organized 1,400 workers in its Rochester, New York, plant into 38 self-directed teams. The supervisors were trained to be team leaders. But team members, feeling their new independence, often fought with them, and after three years over half the team leaders had been replaced. The former supervisors had worked their way up by giving orders—and often could not "build consensus and delegate decision-making."

The trouble with empowered teams of employees is that even companies which have successfully changed to a team structure have found that it takes three years, on the average, to complete the change—and some may not have three years to wait.

SOURCE: Adapted from Marc Levinson, "Playing with Fire," *Newsweek* (June 21, 1993): 46–48.

---

ity vehicle for export. Ralph Wiseman, a project team member, noted that in the past, the modification would have been done by an outside firm (a nonunion one, most likely). For the project, the ten members received special training that was unheard of for hourly workers in the past. Wiseman, who bid for a place on the project team, said, "I've never worked so hard, or had a job I liked so much." He emphatically explains his interest in the project: "Our jobs depend on it."[40]

Many other unions, however, view teams as a threat to union strength. They see employee involvement groups and teams as a bridge between management and employees, and once the gap has been bridged, the obvious question may become "Why do we need a union?" Lewis Maltby, Director of the Workplace Task Force of the American Civil Liberties Union, claims that union concerns are justified and that employee teams or involvement groups have no place in a union setting because "employees have already chosen a union to speak for them." Citing this concern over duplication of interest, the United Transportation Union decided that its 8000 Union Pacific members would not participate in Quality Improvement Teams.[41]

The NLRB and the courts have generally agreed with Lewis Maltby and others who have considered employee involvement programs and self-directed work teams as potentially unlawful under Section 8(a)(2) of the Wagner Act. Generally, for a violation to occur, it must be shown that (1) the entity created by the program is a "labor organization" and (2) the employer dominates or interferes with the formation or administration of that labor organization or contributes support to it. A committee or group is generally considered a labor organization if employees participate in it and if at least one purpose is to "deal with" the employer on issues of grievances, labor disputes, wages, work rules, or hours of employment. The dealing must involve give-and-take—as in collective bargaining. If the employer simply says yes or no to employees' proposals (often the case with committee quality circles) or if an employee group can decide such issues by itself (often the case with self-directed teams), then the element of dealing is missing and the group is probably not a labor organization. With regard to the second criterion for violation—employer domination or interference—Section 8(c) of the Wagner Act allows an employer to voice an opinion on labor–management issues but not to create or initiate a labor organization. Thus an employer can suggest the idea of committees or work teams, but employees must be free to adopt or reject (as did the Union Pacific workers) the concept. In cases involving employers suggesting the creation of employee teams, motive may be considered a factor, although Section 8(a)(2) of the Wagner Act does not require the presence of an antiunion motive; it condemns any interference or domination.[42]

The NLRB in two historic decisions has limited the creation of employee committees or teams by its strict interpretation of the Wagner Act, as just described. In the *Electromation*[43] case, the board found that the company had illegally created and dominated a labor organization. The case involved the Electromation Company of Elkhart, Indiana, a non-union electrical parts manufacturer. The employer created six "action committees" to deal with the employer on various issues. The committees contained members of both management and hourly workers and were charged with developing proposals for management's consideration. Issues considered by the action committees included pay, absenteeism, and attendance bonus programs. The Teamsters Union had begun an organizing drive at the company at about the time the committees were created. The NLRB ruled that the company had clearly violated Section 8(a)(2) of the National Labor Relations Act by creating the action committees. The board decided that the committees were formed for the purpose, at least in part, of dealing with the employer on conditions of employment.

In the 1993 landmark *DuPont* case,[44] the NLRB ordered the company to dismantle seven committees of labor and management representatives that had been established to work on safety and recreation issues at its Deepwater, New Jersey, plant. The board ruled that the company had illegally bypassed the plant's union by setting up the committees and thus had violated the Wagner Act. This was the board's first ruling on labor–management committees in a unionized plant.

In the historic 1977 *General Foods* case,[45] employee teams that had authority to make decisions and act without the employer's approval were not found to be illegal labor organizations.

From these cases, it is clear that unions and employers must be cautious when creating employee teams or labor–management committees. Such groups are likely to *not* be considered illegal labor organizations in the following situations:[46]

- They make final decisions, thus acting as management rather than dealing with management. This is true of many self-directed work teams.
- They consist of communication devices such as suggestion boxes or brainstorming meetings.
- They speak only for themselves and clearly are not representatives of other employees.
- They work only on quality and productivity issues and do not consider "wages, pay, hours, working conditions, or grievances";

thus, no mandatory collective bargaining issues are discussed. In the *Electromation* case, the NLRB emphasized that employers could develop committees or teams that deal with managerial issues but not issues of collective bargaining.

- They consist of a majority of supervisors and managers; thus, they are not employee representation committees.

COLLECTIVE BARGAINING

Collective bargaining comprises two broad and highly related processes: contract negotiations and grievance handling. The first process involves activities associated with the creation of the labor–management contract. In essence, the contract spells out the rules of the game: seniority rights, wages, and benefits, work rules (see *HR in the News*, "United Steelworkers/Inland Steel Industries Negotiate Precedent-Setting Contract"), disciplinary procedures, and so on. But rules need interpretation and enforcement; therefore, the collective bargaining process includes a judicial mechanism for handling what are believed to be violations of the labor agreement. These steps, referred to as **grievance procedure**, are an important part of most modern labor–management contracts. The first part of this section discusses the steps involved and the issues related to contract negotiations; the second part examines grievance handling, with attention devoted to how grievances may be kept at a minimum.

CONTRACT NEGOTIATIONS

Unions and employers may conduct contract negotiations within two basic structures: single-employer bargaining and multiple-employer bargaining. Most labor agreements involve a single employer and a single union.

Should a single employer have several plants in various parts of the country, the union usually represents employees at all plants with one master agreement. Certain issues (normally a small number) are left to local negotiation. For example, a basic agreement between the United Auto Workers (UAW) and General Motors covers employees at all GM plants, and each plant negotiates a supplemental agreement with the local union.

A large single employer with diverse activities and manufacturing processes will generally negotiate contracts with more than one union. For example the publishers of the *Louisville Courier-Journal* have contracts with six unions: the Electrical Workers, Graphic Arts, Mailers, Machinists, Printing and Graphic Communications, and Typographical workers. The structures involved in **single-employer bargaining** are shown in Figure 14–9.

In **multiple-employer bargaining**, two or more employers join together to bargain with one or more unions. Two types of multiple-employer bargaining are common today. One involves contract negotiations between an association of two or more employers and a union council representing a group of craft or industrial unions. This bargaining arrangement is common in the construction industry, in which all unionized contractors in a given area will bargain with a variety of craft unions through their building trades council. A second type involves industrywide bargaining, whereby several companies in a given industry bargain with a union through an employers' association. For example, the International Woodworkers of America bargains with the Western States Wood Products Employers' Association, which represents the Crown Zellerbach Corporation, the Georgia-Pacific Corporation, and the Weyerhaeuser Company, among others. The structures involved in multiple-employer bargaining are shown in Figure 14–10.

Both the union and the employer cite advantages to multiple-employer bargaining.

United Steelworkers/Inland Steel Industries Negotiate Precedent-Setting Contract

Faced with tough foreign and nonunion domestic competition, the Inland Steel Industries Corp. and the United Steelworkers negotiated a historic contract. The contract reflects a new attitude by both labor and management. The reason for the new attitudes at the negotiating table?—"We have dragons to slay together and this sets the context for very close company–union cooperation," said Inland President Maurice S. Nelson. The union's chief negotiator, Jack Parton, added: "I think this is the way of the future for the industry and for all industries." The precedent-setting contract provides:

For the union:

- *No-layoff clause.* This provided the union its top priority: job security for its members.

- *Union participation* at all levels of management, including a seat on the board of directors.

- *Wage and benefits increases.* Wages will keep up with inflation during the contract.

For management:

- *Six-year contract* which will provide stability in the labor force and is a record length for steel industry contracts.

- *Most work rule restrictions* were eliminated, enabling management to redesign jobs for greater efficiency.

- *Managed health-care plan* which should enable management to hold the line on cost increases.

- *25% work force reduction,* only through attrition, enabling Inland to become more competitive.

SOURCE: Adapted from Dana Milbank, "Inland Steel Sets Accord with Steelmakers," *The Wall Street Journal* (May 28, 1993): A2.

FIGURE 14-9 The structures involved in single-employer bargaining.

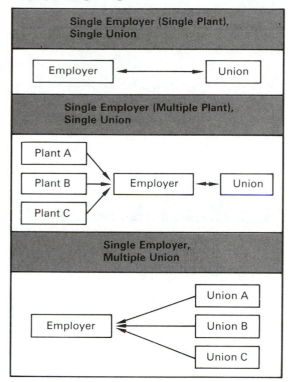

Bargaining with an employers' association is less costly for unions than bargaining individually with several employers. Further, the union favors the creation of uniform wages and work conditions (such as grievance procedures) among unionized firms within a particular industry.

A common wage and benefits package is also advantageous to employers because it eliminates intercompany wage competition and the threat of employees' leaving to work for competitors for higher wages or benefits. Multiple-employer bargaining has also enabled employers to increase bargaining strength and has, perhaps, enabled them to achieve agreements more attractive than those that would be negotiated individually.

On the negative side, multiple-employer bargaining may have drawbacks for the individual employer. First, by negotiating through an association, the employer will lose a certain degree of control over internal operations and affairs. Second, the weaker employers in the association will most likely lose power and prestige to the stronger members.[47]

Prenegotiation

According to the Wagner Act, an employer must recognize and bargain with a union that has been certified by the National Labor Relations Board (NLRB) following a representation election. An employer is also required to bargain with an existing union for a new or modified agreement in order to replace a labor contract about to expire. Both parties are required by law to bargain in good faith, but neither party is compelled to agree or to conclude the negotiation with a contract. In the case of either a newly certified union or an existing union, the collective bargaining process follows three distinct phases: the first is prenegotiation, the second is negotiation, and the third is administering the labor–management agreement.

Labor and management representatives are involved in a great deal of preparation long before they actually sit down at the bargaining table. Local union officials meet with the rank and file to learn what they consider to be major contract issues and problem areas. A questionnaire may be used to help collect information on employee needs. Union officials study the gains made by other unions and familiarize themselves with trends in new benefits packages, shorter workweeks, cost-of-living adjustments, and so on. If possible, they should know the employer's financial status and have an inkling of which concessions the company can and cannot afford. In large national and international unions, full-time staff researchers often assist in these preparations.[48]

FIGURE 14-10 The structures involved in multiple-employer bargaining.

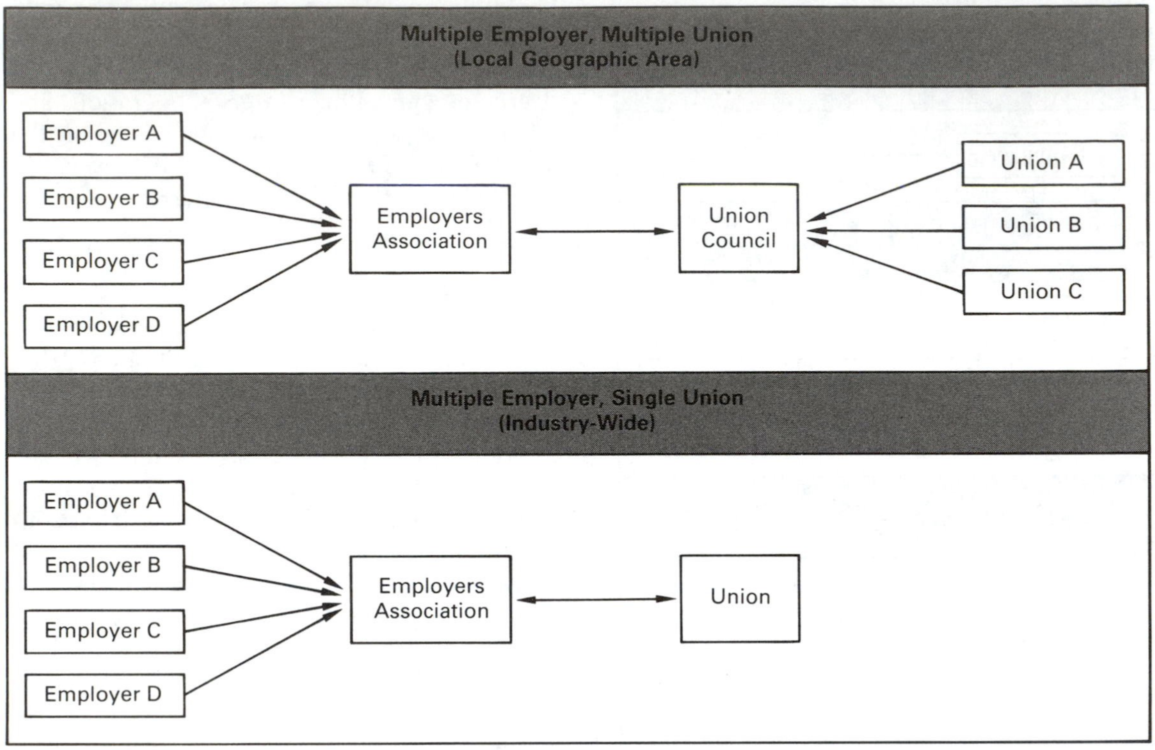

The employer also prepares for the bargaining sessions. Responsibility for doing prenegotiation homework often falls on the HR or industrial relations director and staff. They scrutinize the existing contract, looking for vague contract language or for problem areas that need to be modified. Plant managers and supervisors pinpoint areas of the contract that are difficult to administer.

Negotiation

To begin the actual negotiation process, both management and labor send a team of representatives to bargain at a neutral site — usually a hotel suite. Labor representatives may include the local union president, the business agent, local officers, or perhaps an official from the national union. The employer is typically represented by one or two top manufacturing executives, the HR or industrial relations director, and, perhaps, the company's labor attorney. A company's chief executive will rarely participate in labor negotiations, except when a small firm is involved.

More and more, both labor and management are using computers during contract negotiations to determine the costs of various proposals. Almost instantly, the cost of a proposed pay plan or benefits package may be computed to aid in the negotiation process.[49]

Good Faith   Both sides are legally bound to bargain in good faith, which simply means that labor and management must negotiate with each other and make every reasonable effort to enter into an agreement. **Good-faith bargaining** does not mean that either labor or the employer must agree to the contract terms or that either must make concessions. The stronger party may use its power to obtain a favorable agreement, as long as its representatives show an intent to reach an agreement.

Over the years, the concept of good faith has created a great deal of controversy. Often, when the parties fail to reach an agreement, one side (or both) may claim that the other side is violating the good-faith principle and is acting in bad faith. Labor law enables either labor or management to take their complaints concerning bad-faith bargaining to a labor relations board for adjudication.

One controversial bargaining strategy related to this issue was known as **boulwarism**, after Lemuel R. Boulware, a General Electric Company vice-president during the 1950s. Using boulwarism, GE canvassed first-line supervisors to determine employee needs, and integrated those needs and managerial considerations into a so-called package. The package was publicly announced and backed with a public relations campaign. When collective bargaining was to begin, GE announced that the package was its first and last offer. The union fiercely protested this practice as a gesture of bad faith, and in 1969 boulwarism was found to be in violation of the Wagner Act by a New York circuit court. In essence, the practice was found to constitute bad faith because there was no give-and-take in management's negotiations.[50]

Bargaining Strategies

The actual bargaining process and the events that take place during negotiation depend to a great degree on the relationship between management and the union. Depending on the strength of the employer and the union and on the degree of cooperation that characterizes their relationship, a number of different bargaining strategies may be employed. They include distributive bargaining, integrative bargaining, productivity bargaining, and concession bargaining.

Distributive Bargaining Distributive bargaining, perhaps the most common form of bargaining, takes place when labor and management are in disagreement over the issues in the proposed contract, such as wages, benefits, work rules, and so on. This form of bargaining is sometimes referred to as *win-lose* bargaining, because the gains of one side are achieved at the expense of the other (e.g., a wage increase won by labor may be considered a loss suffered by management). The mechanics of this process are shown in Figure 14–11.

The union's *initial offer* on an issue (such as a wage rate) is generally higher than it expects to receive; the *resistance point* is the minimally acceptable level; the *target point* is realistic and achievable. For the employer, these points are basically reversed. Management's resistance point is a ceiling, or upper limit, on a particular issue; its initial point is the low end of an issue to be used to begin negotiations; its target point is in the general area that management would like to achieve. The *settlement range* lies somewhere between the resistance points of labor and management. If both sides are unable to come to terms on a particular issue or issues, a *bargaining impasse* results. The consequences and possible actions taken by both sides during an impasse will be discussed later in this chapter.

Integrative Bargaining The purpose of **integrative bargaining** is to create a cooperative negotiating relationship that benefits both parties. In this situation, both labor and management win rather than face a win-lose situation. Although integrative bargaining is not nearly as common as the distributive process, signs seem to indicate a steadily growing trend toward this cooperative form of bargaining.

One popular form of integrative bargaining is a jointly sponsored, labor–management quality of working life (QWL) program. An example is the Ford Motor Company–UAW program called *Employee Involvement (EI)*, a QWL program designed to strengthen plant

FIGURE 14-11 The mechanics of distributive bargaining (increase in base wage rate percentage, first year of new contract).

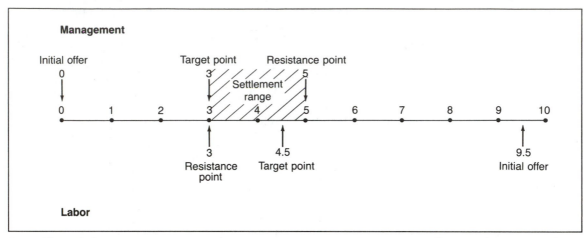

SOURCE: Michael R. Carrell and Christina Heavrin, *Collective Bargaining and Labor Relations,* 3rd ed. (Columbus, OH: Merrill, 1991), p. 139. Used by permission.

productivity and quality through enhanced job satisfaction and cooperative labor–management relationships. At the heart of the EI program are quality circles. By using quality circles, Ford scored a number of impressive improvements in quality and productivity. Some examples of improvements made through EI at the Dearborn plant are shown in Figure 14–12. The improvements in Ford's productivity, partly as a result of the program's effort, have strengthened their competitive position in the national and international automobile and truck markets. The benefits to the UAW membership at Ford are stable employment, job security, and a more satisfying work environment.[51]

When the EI program first began, many union leaders and members were against it because they believed that in the long run it would diminish the role of the UAW. The EI program at Ford, however, has been a success and is now supported by most workers. The reasons for the change in attitudes toward the program can be found in the words of a veteran UAW member: "In my new department there was a strong EI group. People met for an hour on Wednesday afternoons after work in the conference room, and we got paid for it. We talked about all kinds of problems—anything from oil coming out of hoists to bolts not going in, case nuts coming off, bad clips, bad metal. We discussed how the company could improve quality and improve our jobs. In the past nobody was taking care of these problems. It was dog-eat-dog. You came in, you hated your foreman, and your foreman hated you, you did your job, and you hoped they didn't mess with you. . . . Those days are gone, and EI helped get rid of them. You don't see people these days deliberately trying to make life miserable for their foreman. When I'm running EI meetings, I make sure we stay away from contractual issues. EI is not supposed to touch anything that's in the contract. . . . EI is supposed to deal with quality issues—bad parts, bad stock, and other things that get swept under the rug in the rush to keep up production. We're seeing a lot of improvement in the plants today because of EI and because of profit sharing.[52]

FIGURE 14-12 The EI Program was a joint effort between Ford's Dearborn engine plant and UAW local 600.

The Employee Involvement Program

The Dearborn Engine Plant's joint steering committee was formed in March and employee volunteers were chosen by lottery. Problem-solving training started in May and the first employee problem-solving group presentation to the joint steering committee was made in June. Following are some examples of the problems addressed—and the fixes implemented—at this location:

Problem: *Excessive scrap and tool breakage on cylinder head milling machines caused by broken timing belts.*

Solution: Install limit switch to automatically stop the head feed when timing belts break.

Payoff: Reduced scrap and tool breakage . . . improved quality and reduced tool cost.

Problem: *Lack of information about EI activities for employees not participating in problem-solving groups.*

Solution: Install bulletin boards in the plant for posting of EI information. Devote part of the plant newspaper to EI news.

Payoff: Better communication . . . better informed employees.

Problem: *Coolant dripping from parts hung on an overhead conveyor.*

Solution: Install drip pans.

Payoff: Better housekeeping . . . improved work environment.

Problem: *Quality problems and excessive tool breakage on cylinder head transfer machine.*

Solution: Redesign fixture to include set screws to secure locating pins and bushings.

Payoff: Reduced tool breakage and downtime . . . better product quality.

Problem: *Inefficient dust collection on a cutter grinder.*

Solution: Replace fixed exhaust duct with flexible duct to permit operator to adjust duct to most effective position.

Payoff: Improved working conditions . . . better observation of the work in process.

SOURCE: "Employee Involvement . . . It Works." UAW-Ford Committee on Employee Involvement, April 1981.

Productivity Bargaining One of the primary purposes of productivity bargaining is to improve the effectiveness of the organization by eliminating work rules and inefficient work methods that inhibit productivity. Getting labor's agreement to eliminate old, ineffective work habits is not easy. Some unions fear that this form of bargaining will eventually lead to unemployment and a weakening of the union's power base. Despite the reluctance of various unions, many changes have been made to improve productivity, signifying a shift from distributive to productivity bargaining.[53] A primary reason for a union's acceptance of new, improved work methods is a feeling that jobs will become more secure as the employer's productivity strengthens. Some examples of recent changes in work rules in various industries are summarized in Figure 14–13.

An excellent example of labor–management cooperation on the elimination of restrictive work rules in exchange for job security

FIGURE 14-13 Changes in work rules in various industries through productivity bargaining

Area	Changes in Work Rules	Industry
Job assignments	Cutting size of crews, enlarging jobs by adding duties; eliminating unnecessary jobs	Steel, autos, railroads, meatpacking, airlines
Skilled maintenance and construction	Combining craft jobs such as millwright, welder, rigger, and boilermaker; allowing journeymen to perform helpers' duties; permitting equipment operators to run more than one machine	Autos, rubber, steel, petroleum, construction
Hours of work	Giving up relief and wash-up periods; allowing management more flexibility in scheduling daily and weekly hours; working more hours for the same pay	Autos, rubber, steel, meatpacking, trucking, airlines (pilots), textile
Seniority	Restricting use of seniority in filling job vacancies, 'bumping' during layoffs, and picking shifts	Autos, rubber, meatpacking, steel
Wages	Restricting pay to hours worked rather than miles traveled	Railroads, trucking
Incentive pay	Reducing incentives to reflect changing job conditions	Rubber, steel
Team work	Allowing team members to rotate jobs; permitting pay for knowledge instead of function; allowing management to change crew structure to cope with new technology	Autos, auto suppliers, steel, rubber

SOURCE: Reprinted from the May 16, 1983, issue of *Business Week* by special permission; © 1983 by McGraw-Hill, Inc.

involves GE's "factory of the future" in Lynn, Massachusetts. The factory, which employs only about half as many workers as a conventional factory, builds aircraft engine parts and uses robot carts to move engine parts between computer-controlled work centers. GE promised the Electrical Workers that it would maintain a minimum level of jobs for a specified time. GE also promised to spend $450 million to add plant capacity over a period of several years. In return, the Electrical Workers Union agreed to the following work rules:[54]

- To enable the factory to operate twenty-four hours a day, the union agreed that employees will work seven twelve-hour shifts every fourteen days, with four hours' overtime pay for each shift.

- The number of job classifications was to shrink from twelve to three to enable the plant to operate with only 100 employees, who perform a variety of tasks.

- For the first time, the union agreed to let GE set production goals.

A new method of bargaining, **mutual-gains bargaining**, is described in *HR in the News:* "Mutual-Gains Bargaining at Chevron Corporation."

Concession Bargaining The recession in the 1980s saw many companies facing plant closings, mass layoffs, and, in the worst of cases, bankruptcy. To solve their problems, many employers sought agreements from their unions to freeze and in some cases reduce economic rewards such as wages, benefits, and paid vacations, holidays, and sick leave. Unions reluctantly agreed. **Concession** or **giveback** bargaining became common in both manufacturing and services industries but is most prevalent in those industries with the greatest financial difficulties, such as auto and steel.[55]

Union members grant such concessions because they feel they have little choice. For ex-

Mutual-Gains Bargaining
at Chevron Corporation

At the Chevron Corporation's Salt Lake Refinery, past collective bargaining negotiations had left bitter feelings on both sides. Thus the negotiators began exploring alternatives to the old bargaining techniques. During a routine monthly union–management meeting a member of the Oil, Chemical and Atomic Workers' Union (OCAW) described a process called mutual-gains bargaining. Both sides agreed to give it a try and started by listing 56 issues without union or management designation. Then the following mutual-gains process was followed:

1. The union president was placed on a special day-shift assignment during the negotiations, to enhance communication and understanding of the issues.

2. The natural work teams within the refinery addressed the issues within each category.

3. Criteria were developed for each of the work teams to address the issues.

4. We became facilitators for the process, not chief negotiators.

On the lighter side, both the union president and superintendent of HR vowed not to get haircuts until both parties had reached and signed an agreement. The haircut agreement soon became a rallying point for union members and managers.

The following criteria were developed for the work teams:

1. Each team would be represented equally and would select its own representatives.

2. Team members would share information freely, both inside and outside the meetings; weekly communication updates would be posted in the refinery.

3. Any team needing a facilitator could have one.

4. Any issue not resolved would be returned to the Workers' Committee and management for action.

5. If a meeting was scheduled during off time, overtime pay would be received. If a team meeting was scheduled during work time, relief coverage would be provided. Other workers were welcome to attend any meeting, but wouldn't be compensated or relieved.

6. Comprehensive minutes of each meeting would be maintained.

7. The authority of agreements remained with the Workers' Committee and refinery management; team recommendations weren't binding.

8. Teams followed these guidelines:
   - Respect the differences in people and their experience.
   - Avoid confrontation or arguments.

(continued)

- Promote opportunities for all to contribute their ideas and ask questions.
- Recognize that the answer to most questions can be found in the group.
- Don't be afraid to admit that you don't know. Agree to find the answer.
- Pay attention to feelings, both negative and positive.
- Watch for nonverbal signs.
- Be flexible.
- Resist taking things personally.

For three months, seven teams, totaling 40 employees, discussed the 56 issues. The union president and the superintendent of HR attended each meeting, acting as facilitators. The criteria and the group dynamics defined the issue. Teams listed concerns, developed alternatives and made recommendations.

In only three months the teams completed discussions and finalized their recommendations. As expected, some issues weren't resolved. However, the Workers' Committee and refinery management signed a tentative agreement—24 days before the contract expired. On April 15, a near-unanimous union ratification vote finalized the agreement.

The early signing didn't indicate that management had an open checkbook or that the union was a pushover. On the contrary, the final agreement was similar to others found within the industry. The only difference was the *process*—a process emphasizing communication, involvement, trust, and respect. The accomplishment was recognized with a haircut gift certificate for the union president and the superintendent of HR. What was more important, there was a sense of accomplishment felt by all employees—and a sense that we had strengthened our refinery's competitive position.

SOURCE: Dennis Green, Superintendent of Human Resources, Chevron Corporation, and Casey Valdez III, union president, Oil Chemical and Atomic Workers, Local 2-931, "Mutual-Gains Bargaining Assists Contract Negotiations," *Personnel Journal* (August 1993): 60. Used by permission.

---

ample, the employees of the ARCO Metals Company, who were members of the Aluminum, Brick, and Glass Workers unions, agreed to give up $1.40 an hour in pay as well as double-time pay for Sundays. The workers also agreed to begin to contribute $13.50 per worker per month for health benefits. The president of the local union said that he was "not tickled with the contract, but it is the best we could get at this time. It's one of those unfortunate situations where the economy was down and the management took hold of that and beat us."[56]

The historic General Motors–UAW pact signed in 1984 has the characteristics of concession bargaining but also of productivity bargaining. The UAW accepted moderate wage increases in return for several innovative job security measures. With the new agreement, GM agreed not to lay off any worker with at least one year's seniority who was displaced by new technology, plant consolidation, productivity improvement, or the transfer of work to another facility. Instead, these workers were to be placed in a "job opportunity bank" where they would perform a variety of jobs. The plan also included a bonus program for good attendance and profit-sharing payments estimated to be $1000 per worker per year.[57]

The 1990s have witnessed continued concession bargaining, particularly in recession-plagued industries. Northwest Airlines, for example, gained over $1 billion in wage concessions from three unions: the Teamsters, the International Association of Machinists, and the Air Line Pilots Association in 1993. Wage cuts ranged from 6 percent to 12 percent. Teamsters' President Ron Carey, in a letter to 9000 flight attendants, explained the rationale for making the givebacks: "The alternative is obvious . . . you're facing bankruptcy."[58]

Union concessions generally involve wage, benefit, or work-rule changes, with reduced benefits generally more acceptable to employees than wage concessions, although future wage increases may be renegotiated. Often work-rule changes are easier to sell to employees and have a more lasting effect. Employers, however, must expect to pay the price for these concessions through one or more of five areas of negotiation:[59]

1. *Increased job security.* The union will most likely try to extract a promise not to close plants or not to subcontract with non-union producers. Ford Motor Company's provision of a guaranteed income stream will be pursued by many unions. Such restrictions can be very expensive and limiting to employers.

2. *Increased financial disclosure.* The employer will have to make a claim of inability to pay or financial hardship. While the company's financial information normally need not be disclosed in collective bargaining, when the employer puts profitability or financial conditions in contention, the financial data must be provided to substantiate the position.

3. *Profit sharing plans.* Union members generally feel that sharing in austerity now should mean sharing profits in the future. For example, in 1983, Chrysler Corporation's employees demanded a share of the record profits, only three years after the UAW made major concessions to guarantee the federal loan to Chrysler. In 1990, over 160,000 union and nonunion employees of the Ford Motor Company received an average of $1025 as their part of the Ford–UAW profit-sharing plan.[60]

4. *Equality of sacrifice.* Employers must demand the same sacrifices from management and nonunion employees as from union employees. For instance, GM tried to increase its executive bonus program just after the UAW made major concessions in 1982. The UAW and its members demanded, and got, the increases rescinded.

5. *Participation in decision making.* Unions may seek greater participation in various management decisions, including plant closings and the use of new technological methods. If properly used, this concession can help develop greater understanding and improve employee relations.[61]

Bargaining Categories

The NLRB identifies three broad categories of bargaining subjects: mandatory, permissive, and illegal.[62] The parties must negotiate mandatory items if either party requests to do so. Typical **mandatory subjects** include provisions concerning wages, benefits, and working conditions.

Permissive subjects (voluntary) include those not directly related to wages, benefits, conditions of work. If one party desires to bargain over a permissive subject, the other party may agree or refuse to do so. For example, the union may wish to bargain for an increase in the size of the bargaining unit, but the employer could refuse to negotiate this permissive subject if it so desires. Neither side can refuse to sign a contract because the other refuses to discuss a permissive subject.

The inclusion of **illegal subjects** renders an agreement invalid and unenforceable. One example of an illegal item is a provision that permits discrimination on the basis of religion, sex, or national origin or a provision that establishes a closed shop. Any subject that violates any federal, state, or local law is an unlawful bargaining item.

Contract Agreement

After both sides have arrived at an informal agreement, the agreement is taken back to their representatives for final and formal approval. For the employer, top management—often the board of directors—must approve the contract; for labor, the rank and file normally must ratify the contract by a majority vote. Under labor law, union representatives may be given the authority to enter into a contract without ratification. Most unions, however, choose to allow their members to vote on the agreement. Failure to ratify the contract sends union representatives back to the bargaining table to negotiate a revised agreement. Most contracts, however, are ratified on the first vote.

The agreement becomes official once approved, ratified, and signed by labor and management representatives. Once signed, labor and management meet with their respective members to go over the details of the contract. Union members and members of management all receive copies of the agreement. Supervisors and union stewards who have the day-to-day responsibility for administering the contract should be intimately familiar with the agreement so that they may avoid any activity or decision that violates it.

Contract Format

Labor contracts may vary considerably in length and content. Some agreements contain ten or fifteen pages; others, hundreds of pages. The more mandatory and permissive subjects that are negotiated, the lengthier the contract. The order of topics may also vary somewhat, but the following list is fairly representative of most agreements:

- *Union Recognition and Scope of the Bargaining Unit* This section reflects the employer's recognition of the union as the sole bargaining agency for its employees and defines specifically which employees are included within the bargaining unit.

- *Management Rights* This section reflects the union's recognition of the employer's sole and exclusive right to determine the way in which the business shall be managed. Management rights include determining production methods, which products and services to produce, and how products and services should be marketed.

- *Union Security* This section defines the type of union security (union shop, maintenance-of-membership shop, etc.).

- *Strikes and Lockouts* This section outlines the approach each side will take toward strikes and lockouts (a **lockout** is management's refusal to allow employees to work). Typically, this section includes a statement such as "there will be no strikes or lockouts during the term of this agreement" (although a strike may be permitted over certain specific items detailed in the agreement).

- *Job Rights and Seniority* This section defines how transfers, promotions, layoffs, and recalls are to be made. Generally, the contract will stipulate that these decisions are to be made on the basis of seniority.

- *Wages* This section outlines the wage structures and related provisions such as wage adjustments, wage incentives, shift differentials, and bonuses.

- *Benefits and Paid Time Off* This section lists the employee benefits such as hospitalization, pensions, holidays, vacations, sick leave, and rest periods.

- *Safety and Health* This section normally includes statements that underscore both the union's and the employer's desire to maintain safe and healthy working conditions. Many contracts include provisions for the creation of a labor-management safety committee and the administration of a health-and-safety program.

- *Discipline, Suspension, and Discharge* This section outlines the procedures an employer must follow to discipline, suspend, or discharge an employee. Many contracts include provisions for progressive disciplinary systems, whereby additional infractions of a work policy, standards, rules, or regulations result in increasingly serious disciplinary action leading to discharge. Some contracts include a very detailed list of violations and resulting penalties. For example, taking drugs on the job results in immediate dismissal, horseplay results in a verbal warning, and so on.

- *Grievance Handling and Arbitration* This section normally details (1) the steps an employee follows to lodge a formal grievance against the employer and (2) the procedure for bringing in an outside arbitrator if the union and employer are unable to settle the grievance.

BARGAINING IMPASSE

Historically, collective bargaining has proven to be an effective method for settling differences between labor and management. Most negotiations (about 98 percent) end in a signed contract that is agreeable—although not necessarily favorable—to both sides. Management and labor generally recognize that continuous, dispute-free operations are important to preserve harmonious labor relations and maximize the goals of the employee and employer alike.

Serious conflicts do sometimes occur, however, during the course of negotiations. Labor and management may simply be unable to reach accord over certain issues dealing with wages or other contract provisions. When negotiations break down, or when the existing contract expires and the union and employer have been unable to reach an agreement, a bargaining **impasse** results. Should this occur, there are three options. One, the parties may ask for assistance in settling the dispute from an impartial third party called a *mediator*. Two, the union may exert a show of force so that their demands will be accepted. Three, the employer may also show force through one of several pressure techniques. Let us first explore common union strategies for ending the bargaining impasse on their terms.

Union Power Tactics

A union's primary power tactics include calling a strike, waging a corporate campaign, setting up a picket line, or imposing a boycott.

Strike Officially termed a *work stoppage,* the strike is the refusal of union members to work and is recognized as a basic union right. Strike tactics and procedures, however, are subject to considerable regulation by a variety of labor statutes. Various types of strikes are the following:

Economic Strike An **economic strike** is a strike over an economic issue such as wages, benefits, or working conditions (see *HR in the News:* "American Air Strike Strands Thousands"). The employer is free to maintain operations and hire permanent replacements for economic strikers. An employee who is not replaced is entitled to reemployment if the labor dispute is settled.

Often, however, when a strike ends there are only a few jobs left for returning workers. An employer can, therefore, in effect, fire striking workers by hiring permanent replacements during the economic strike. This practice by American employers sharply increased after the 1981 air traffic controllers strike, when President Reagan fired the strikers and hired replacement workers. Prior to 1981, it

American Air Strike Strands Thousands

Perhaps the most successful economic strike of the 1990s was the one by the Professional Flight Attendants against American Airlines. The strike called for an 11-day action over the 1993 Thanksgiving weekend, the busiest of the year for the airlines. The strike was far more successful than management of AMR Corporation (American Airlines) expected and caused hundreds of flights to be canceled and thousands of travelers to be stranded all over the globe. Many travelers, surprised to learn that management had advance notice but did not believe a successful strike could be mounted, vowed to never fly American again.

Union leaders claimed that over 90% of their 21,000 members honored the picket lines and thus American's system was "virtually shut down." AMR management apparently bet that the union could not keep its members out and thousands would cross the picket lines.

The key economic issue which led to the strike was wages. The union rejected American's last, best, and final offer of an immediate 7.8% pay increase, followed by two years of 0% increases, and a 3% raise in the fourth year of a new contract. A second issue of equal importance was job security. AMR Chairman Robert L. Crandell refused to discontinue his plan to dismantle parts of the airline and guarantee job security.

SOURCE: Bridget O'Briars, "American Air Strike Strands Thousands of Fliers," *The Wall Street Journal* (November 19, 1993): B1.

---

was more common for employers to hire only short-term strikebreakers and then bring back striking union members after a settlement was reached.

Before Reagan permanently replaced the striking workers, most large U.S. employers relied on supervisors and temporary workers to keep operating during a strike and then brought back all striking workers once the strike was settled. Since then, however, employers have hired permanent replacement workers with increasing frequency—thus breaking the union. This use of permanent replacement workers has caused a major change in American labor relations, according to U.S. Labor Secretary Robert Reich. The number of major strikes has steadily declined since the 1981 air traffic controllers strike, from a peak in 1974 of 424 to a fifty-year low of 40 in 1991 (see Figure 14–14).[63]

Thus today economic strikes are likely to occur only in cases of severe worker discontent, such as the American Transit Union (ATU) strike. In 1990, 9000 ATU Greyhound drivers struck after hearing of wage-freeze demands by the new owner, Fred Currey. This demand followed sharp wage cuts in their previous two contracts. Greyhound hired replacement drivers as well as several hundred union drivers who crossed the picket lines. Within a year, ridership was 95 percent of the prestrike level. Greyhound was forced to file for bankruptcy, however, to stay in business.[64]

FIGURE 14-14 Number of major U.S. strikes (work stoppages), 1960–1991.

Year	No. of Strikes
1960	222
1965	268
1969	412
1974	424
1979	235
1981	145
1984	62
1989	51
1990	44
1991	40

SOURCE: U.S. Bureau of Labor Statistics, *Compensation and Working Conditions* (Washington, DC: Dept. of Labor, 1993).

Unfair-Labor-Practice Strike An **unfair-labor-practice strike** protests an action by the employer, for example, discrimination against union members because of union activity. A worker who strikes because of an unfair labor practice cannot be permanently replaced.

Sympathy Strike A strike in which other unions agree to a work stoppage, not because of actions by their own employer but to support other union members striking other firms, is called a **sympathy strike**. A common example of the sympathy strike is the refusal of truck drivers to cross a picket line and make deliveries to an employer whose employees are on strike. Legally, the sympathy striker is in violation of a no-strike clause in the agreement unless the contract specifically permits this form of strike activity.

Wildcat Strike An unauthorized work stoppage, the **wildcat strike** is an unlawful activity if the contract contains a no-strike clause; therefore, wildcat strikers are not sanctioned by union leadership. If a wildcat strike does occur, the union must disavow it

or risk being charged with violation of the contract and federal law. The employer may generally take disciplinary action, including suspension and discharge, against wildcat strikers.

Other forms of union pressure include a *sit-down strike,* in which employees strike but remain at their jobs and refuse to work; a *sick out,* in which employees call in sick en masse; and a *slowdown,* in which workers remain at work but cut back their output significantly. Unions, however, usually disapprove of individual worker pressures and support a work stoppage only if it has been formally approved by union leadership. For example, the national union must usually approve a strike by a local affiliate, even after a majority of the local members have approved it.

Picket The **picket**, a line of strikers who patrol the employer's place of business, can be a powerful union pressure tactic. Picketing can help keep a plant or building site closed during a strike. Applicants who cross the picket line to apply for the jobs of striking workers must often confront the jeers and taunts of the picketers. Such strikebreakers, often disparagingly labeled *scabs* because they "close the wound," are held in great contempt by union members and union sympathizers. The courts allow picketing at the primary employer's place of business, or *primary situs picketing,* as long as laws are observed. The picketers must avoid violence, must not mass in large numbers, and must not create physical barriers to the employer's entrance. But the Supreme Court has ruled that *common situs picketing* is illegal. At a common site, employees of several employers work side by side. At a construction site, for example, plumbers, carpenters, masons, electricians, and other skilled workers are represented by different unions and work for different subcontractors. Therefore, one striking union generally cannot picket the entire project; the courts have ruled that each employer at a common situs is a separate employer. If there is only one gate to a construction project, the union may picket there; if there is a special gate reserved for each contractor, the union picket must be confined to that gate.[65]

Boycott A boycott is the refusal to purchase an employer's goods or services. An important distinction must be made between primary and secondary boycotts. A **primary boycott** involves only those parties directly involved in a dispute, such as a large appliance manufacturer and the electrical workers' union. In a primary boycott, the union pressures members (and often the public) to avoid patronizing an employer, even going as far as to levy fines against members who do. Primary boycotts are generally legal. A **secondary boycott** involves a third party not directly involved in a dispute, such as an electrician's union persuading retailers not to buy the manufacturer's products. A secondary boycott is an attempt to increase the power and strength of the union so that the employer is more likely to give in to union demands. Under the Taft-Hartley Act, secondary boycotts are illegal, except in the construction and clothing industries.

The purpose of boycott efforts by picket lines at grocery stores is to urge consumers to avoid buying a particular product, such as grapes or lettuce. This is often referred to as *product picketing*. This is not an illegal secondary boycott because the Supreme Court has ruled that the use of pickets to discourage the purchase of a specific product is not a secondary boycott.

Handbills, or leaflets urging consumers not to purchase a specific product or deal with a company involved in a labor dispute, are legal as long as they are truthful. An example of a handbill is shown in Figure 15–8.

One of the longest successful boycotts was waged by the AFL-CIO against Coors, the Golden, Colorado, beer company. The ten-year boycott ended in 1987 when Coors allowed its employees to seek union representation. The historic boycott began in 1977 when 1500 union workers struck—and Coors hired replacement workers. During the long boycott, Coors lost substantial market share to Budweiser while it started selling in Eastern states for the first time.

Employer Power Tactics

Employers use a number of methods designed to end a bargaining impasse on terms favorable to management. These include the lockout of employees, hiring temporary nonunion employees during a strike, hiring permanent replacement workers, contracting out work, and filing for bankruptcy.[66]

Replacement Workers The most successful strike tactic is to hire permanent **replacement workers** for strikers. According to labor law, an employer may hire permanent replacements for economic strikers but only temporary replacements for unfair-labor-practice strikers. This strategy is not without problems. First, many workers may be extremely hesitant to cross picket lines to be ridiculed by picketers and union sympathizers as scabs. Second, in the case of an unfair-labor-practice dispute, workers may hesitate to accept what is likely to be only short-term employment. Third, this practice is almost sure to seriously damage labor–management relations and lower worker morale if a settlement is reached.

Hiring permanent replacement workers, or threatening to do so, however, has become the employer's most effective power tactic. While the problems just discussed still exist, they are often far outweighed by the advantages. The 1981 historic air traffic controllers strike, in which President Reagan hired replacement air traffic controllers began a new era in labor–management relations. Following the strike, employers quickly realized that public support for the strikers was minimal, and that if highly technical air traffic controllers can be effectively replaced, then almost any strike can be broken by hiring replacement employees. Qualified workers no longer appear to be hesitant to cross the picket lines of striking union workers. A series of strikes, including those of the Eastern Air Lines pilots, machinists, and flight attendants (1989), Greyhound bus drivers (1990), the Kroger Company supermarket employees (1992), and the Caterpillar industrial workers (1992) (see *HR in the News:* "UAW–Caterpillar, Inc., Strike: Replacement Workers Triumph" on page 636.), were successfully broken when management hired replacement employees. The hiring of replacement workers has been so successful that unions have called far fewer strikes in recent years (see Figure 14–14) and blame the tactic, in part, for their continuing membership decline.

Unions argue that their members cannot even consider going out on strike for fear of replacement, thus robbing them of their most effective power tactic and shifting too much power to management. Federal legislation that would ban employers from hiring permanent replacement workers during an economic strike has been introduced several times but has never been passed by Congress. In the 1992 presidential campaign, organized labor made a ban on striker replacement its primary issue. With the election of President Clinton and the support of most Democrats, unions believed they finally had the ability to stop the practice that President Reagan began in 1981. U.S. Labor Secretary Robert Reich predicted that the ban, if passed, would stop management from using replacement workers "as an acceptable way of doing business." The economic strike, claimed Reich, "is a crucial counterweight to the economic powers that business owners and managers bring to the bargaining table." Management and owners, however, believe that the right to hire permanent replacement workers is a needed and logical counter-measure to labor's right to strike. They contend that when a strike is called, hiring replacement workers is often their only method of keeping their business operating.[67]

Lockout   Another tactic, a **lockout**, is the refusal to allow employees to work until an agreement is signed. Because an employer must normally halt operations with this tactic, the lockout sees only limited use. In addition, most contracts contain a no-lockout clause prohibiting a lockout while a contract is in force.

Temporary Nonunion Workers   Should a union strike, the employer may still attempt to maintain operations. One way is for supervisors and other nonunion employees to perform the duties of striking employees. This strategy may be successful where operations are highly automated or routine and where little training is required to perform the strikers' jobs. During a 1983 strike between American Telephone and Telegraph and the Communications Workers of America Union, for example, supervisors and administrators were able to keep phone lines open and force strikers back to work with no pay increase.[68]

Another method of obtaining nonunion workers during a strike is through the resignation of the striking union employees. In a landmark 1985 decision, the U.S. Supreme Court decided that union members have the right to resign from the union during a strike and cross the picket line to return to work.[69] The Court noted that Section 7 of the National Labor Relations Act gives every employee the right to "bargain collectively . . . and . . . the right to refrain from any or all such activities." The decision, however, does not affect union security clauses (union shops), which provide that employees continue to pay dues and fees until they resign under the contractual procedures. The union may suspend or expel an employee who has violated a union rule by resigning. This may become important should the strike end and the union workers return. Employers may inform their employees of their rights under the court decision.[70]

Contracting Out Another technique for maintaining business is to contract out, or arrange for another company to handle the employer's business during a strike. This may be a useful strategy for firms in very competitive fields or those that fear that a strike would damage customer relations. For example, a janitorial service that cleans office buildings may contract out their work until the strike is over. If the subcontractor is unionized, however, its employees may legally refuse to perform work for the struck firm. Courts have ruled that this action does not constitute an illegal secondary boycott.

Bankruptcy In the past, an organization was bound to the terms of the labor agreement, including the level of wages and benefits, until the agreement expired. A Supreme Court decision has changed that interpretation of the law, enabling organizations to use Chapter 11 of the bankruptcy laws to cancel a union contract, cut wages, and lay off workers. In addition, an organization may do this without having to prove that the labor pact would cause the company to go completely broke. The company must only show that "the labor contract burdens its prospects for recovery and that it has made reasonable attempts to bargain with the Union for deferred or smaller wage increases or other money saving measures."[71]

Two major corporations, Wilson Foods and Continental Airlines, chose bankruptcy to void labor contracts and slash wages and benefits. In the case of Wilson Foods, top management decided to file Chapter 11 because of massive losses from sliding revenues and what it claimed was an excessively costly labor contract. Wilson's estimated net worth was $67 million, but the company estimated its losses at $1 million a week. Shortly after filing for bankruptcy, the company terminated its labor contract and cut almost in half the wages for its 6000 union employees. Nonunion employees also faced similar pay cuts. At Continental Airlines, many workers were laid off and pilots' and other staff members' pay was cut by as much as 50 percent after the airline filed Chapter 11.[72]

Labor leaders were distraught over the Supreme Court's decision. The head of the International Association of Machinists called the ruling "outrageous."[73] The president of the UAW forecasted more strikes and less conciliation. On the other hand, employers generally applauded the ruling. The executive of a large airline stated that "the ruling helps us all because it makes it clear to unions that management has other options." The legal counsel for a nationwide building-supply firm was more blunt: "Unions will know and the company will know that the company has an additional weapon."[74]

Successorship Management can decide to sell out to a new owner as a means of ending a labor dispute or ending an existing contract. When there is a change in the ownership of the organization or the union, the courts refer to the collective bargaining situation as a matter of **successorship**. Corporate mergers and acquisitions have occurred much more frequently in recent years and have posed a new threat to the effectiveness of labor unions.

In a recent decision, the U.S. Supreme Court reaffirmed that when a genuine change of employer occurs, the new employer is required to recognize (and negotiate with) the union as the representative bargaining unit of the employees. However, the new employer is not bound by the conditions of any existing labor agreement (even if unexpired).[75] Thus, the new employer may be free to negotiate an entirely new contract with the existing labor unions unless a contract clause binds it to the old contract. If, however, a new owner substantially changes the nature of the business, the successor employer may not be required to recognize the union as the collective bargaining representative of the unit.

Breaking the Impasse

When a bargaining impasse occurs and negotiations stall, labor and management may implement certain techniques to ward off an impending strike or lockout. These techniques, which keep both parties communicating, negotiating, and examining each other's positions, may lead to an eventual resolution of their differences. Each of these methods—mediation, fact-finding, and interest arbitration—requires the involvement of a third party.

Mediation The **mediation** process, in which a neutral third party attempts to bring the union and employer into agreement, follows no particular format. Mediation may, in fact, take place before an impasse occurs. In such cases, labor and management practice *preventive mediation,* requesting that a mediator participate in the negotiations during the early stages. The presence of a mediator during collective bargaining is often instrumental in keeping both parties working toward an agreement and thus avoiding an impasse. In other cases, an impasse may have been reached and a mediator may be called in after negotiations have completely broken off.

The primary role of a mediator is to lead the parties to an agreement by acting as a go-between for the union and the employer. The mediator does not have the authority to impose a decision. After feeling out the parties, the mediator determines which demands are actually firm and which may still be negotiated. The mediator must have the confidence of both sides and be perceived as truly unbiased and impartial.

After an initial joint session with all three parties, labor and management teams are often assembled in separate meeting rooms. The mediator then presents proposals and counterproposals to each side. Although the mediator avoids injecting public opinion or personal feelings into the proceedings, it may become necessary to criticize an extreme demand or unworkable solution presented by either side. Fundamentals that underscore the mediation process and illustrate effective mediator behavior are the following:[76]

- Conveying understanding and appreciation of the problems confronting both parties.
- Conveying to the parties a feeling that the mediator understands their problems.
- Getting the parties to realize that not all of their positions are valid.
- Suggesting alternative approaches that may facilitate agreement.
- Maintaining neutrality.
- Maintaining confidentiality of information disclosed by the parties.

Mediators are often full-time employees of the Federal Mediation and Conciliation Service (FMCS), which was created by the Taft-Hartley Act to help solve labor disputes. Before becoming mediators, most have had experience in labor relations. After formal training in Washington, D.C., mediators are assigned to a regional office to work with experienced mediators.

Fact-Finding Compared to the mediation process, **fact-finding** is rarely used in the private sector. This public sector process is commonly used to settle disputes involving police officers, teachers, and public health employees. The fact-finding board, composed of three nonpartisan individuals, holds a hearing in which each side presents its views regarding the disputed issues. After studying each party's position and arguments, the board publicly announces a recommended settlement, putting pressure on both sides to accept the pact.

Fact-finding appears to be successful in resolving an impasse. It is estimated that 90 percent of the disputes going to fact-finding are resolved and that the fact-finder's reports are responsible for the resolution in 60 to 70 percent of the cases.[77]

Interest Arbitration   This process occurs when an arbitrator (or panel) is called to solve a possible dispute involving issues in a future contract. **Interest arbitration** has seen relatively greater use in the private sector. But unlike mediation and fact-finding, the arbitrator not only studies the dispute but also determines the terms of agreement, which is final and binding on both parties.

Interest arbitration received considerable publicity in labor circles when the United Steelworkers and an employers' association of ten steel companies agreed to submit unresolved issues to an interest arbitration panel in order to avoid a strike or lockout. Although differences were resolved and the panel was not called, the inclusion of the interest arbitration provision in the negotiation agreement (formally termed an *experimental negotiating agreement*) may have helped the parties reach agreement.

Final-Offer Arbitration   The **final-offer arbitration** method requires both parties to submit their final offer to the three-member panel that has the authority to select one of the proposals. Final-offer arbitration gives the parties the motivation to make their final offers reasonable. Both parties realize that an unreasonable offer will have a lower chance of selection. Therefore, they strive to make their offer appear as fair and reasonable as possible. In 1987 Detroit Tiger Jack Morris won a $1.85 million contract dispute through final-offer arbitration. The baseball players' union and major league owners had agreed to begin using the impasse-resolution technique in 1974 to settle salary disputes. When the Tigers and their star pitcher could not reach a salary agreement, they each presented their final offer to an arbitrator, who could only choose one of the two offers and could not choose a compromise. The Tigers' last offer was $1.35 million—$500,000 larger than the previous largest final-offer arbitration award. Morris proposed $1.85 million based on his 123-81 record (most wins in the 1980s) and his performance in the 1984 World Series.[78]

Mediation-Arbitration   Using this combination method, both parties agree to bring in a mediator with authority to arbitrate *any* unresolved issues. Since the parties must agree to abide by the mediator-arbitrator's decision, they will likely agree on the substantive issues as well.

CONTRACT ADMINISTRATION

The signing of the contract spells a new relationship between management and labor because the agreement often reflects significant changes in wages, benefits, work regulations, and other conditions of employment. In effect, the agreement constitutes a new set of work rules, and both management and labor are bound to abide by the new rules. Implementation and enforcement of the agreement, referred to as *contract administration,* represents a critical responsibility for the HR or industrial relations director.

A contract must run for a specific term. Most contracts contain renewal provisions, with prior notice of termination or of a time for reopening negotiations. Contracts can have *openers*—clauses that allow for negotiations to proceed during the terms of the contract on one or more items, generally wages.

A majority of contracts (about 80 percent) contain three-year terms. A movement from one-year to three-year terms was aided by the NLRB in a general ruling that extended the contract bar rule (see the next section) to a three-year period.[79] In recent years, the number of contracts with periods extended to four or five years has increased. The desire by both labor and management to provide greater long-term stability in labor relations has greatly motivated negotiators to work out longer multiyear agreements.[80]

Management Rights

The area of contract administration known as *management rights* has evoked more emotion and controversy than any other single issue. At the core of the debate is the concept of management's right to run the operation versus the union's quest for job security and other protections for its members. Generally, these provisions are found in almost all contracts in a section labeled *management rights;* union rights, however, are usually scattered throughout a contract according to subject matter.[81]

Unquestionably, the question of who controls the workplace is of great interest to both management and labor. **Management rights** generally include decisions governing the working environment of employees, including supervising the work force, controlling production, setting work rules and procedures, assigning duties, and the use of plant and equipment. Management generally believes that if it is to operate efficiently, it must have control over all decision-making factors of the business. Management also contends that any union involvement in the area is an intrusion on its inherent right to manage. Union advocates respond that where the right to manage involves wages, hours, or working conditions, labor has a legal interest under federal law.[82] Arthur Goldberg, former Secretary of the U.S. Department of Labor and U.S. Supreme Court

justice, summarizes the management rights issue:

> . . . Somebody must be boss; somebody has to run the plant. People can't be wandering around at loose ends, each deciding what to do next. Management decides what the employee is to do. However, right to direct or to initiate action does not imply a second-class role for the union. The union has the right to pursue its role of representing the interest of the employee with the same stature accorded it as is accorded management. To assure order, there is a clear procedural line drawn: the company directs and the union grieves when it objects.[83]

A management rights clause often appears at the beginning of a contract following the union recognition and security clauses. An example of a common management rights clause appears in Figure 14–15.

The Grievance Procedure

Regardless of how clearly and objectively a contract is written, disputes will generally arise during its enforcement. Rarely does any agreement run its term completely void of any dispute. For this reason, most contracts contain a contract administration process to solve conflicts. If, for example, management finds that an employee has violated work rules or some aspect of the contract, it may discipline the employee. The employee may be disciplined for any one of many causes: excessive absenteeism, fighting, drinking on the job, verbal abuse, deliberate work slowdown, or disregard for the safety of others. Most disciplinary systems are progressive and contain several separate disciplinary steps, beginning with an oral warning and ending in discharge. The employee may feel that the discipline was unjust and may therefore file a grievance. This sets in motion the contract procedure designed to settle the difference known as the *grievance procedure.*

Exactly what is a grievance? A **grievance** is a formal complaint by an employee concerning

FIGURE 14-15 Management rights provision.

ARTICLE III
Management
The management of the plant and the direction of its working force are vested exclusively in the Company. These functions are broad in nature and include such things as the right to schedule work and shift starting and stopping time, to hire and to discharge for just cause, to transfer or lay off because of work load distribution or lack of work. In the fulfillment of these functions the Company agrees not to violate the following Articles or the intent and purpose of this Contract, or to discriminate against any member of the Union.

SOURCE: Anaconda Company and United Steel Workers of America *Agreement* (Local Union 4612, AFL-CIO, 1980).

a possible violation of the labor contract, an employer's past practice, or a local, state, or federal law. A grievance is not a **gripe**, which is generally defined as a complaint by an employee concerning an action by management that does not violate the contract, past practice, or law. As an example, an employee may only have a gripe if his supervisor speaks to him in a harsh tone, but when the supervisor assigns him work outside of his job classification, he may have a grievance.

Procedural Steps   The procedure for handling grievances varies from agreement to agreement, but most involve four steps.

Step One   In the initial step, the employee generally discusses the grievance with the shop steward. Experienced in grievance matters and familiar with contract terms and provisions, the steward probably has a good idea of how the contract language should be interpreted. In effect, the shop steward screens complaints and often persuades employees to drop those that are insignificant or invalid, but the steward will encourage an employee to pursue a legitimate grievance.

The steward normally investigates the grievance to provide documented facts on the case. The pertinent facts are written on a grievance form such as the one in Figure 14–16. A good rule for remembering the crucial facts in a grievance is the "5 W's":

1. What happened?
2. When did the event take place?
3. Who was involved? (Were there witnesses?)
4. Where did it happen?
5. Why is the complaint a grievance?

The written grievance is delivered to the supervisor, and a meeting of the three parties is held (the shop steward is occasionally accompanied by an HR or industrial relations representative). In discussing the grievance, all the parties make an attempt to settle the matter at that point. Research shows that most grievances are settled at the first step. If the grievance cannot be resolved there, the employee and union may appeal the decision to step two of the process. Figure 14–15 shows that the disposition resulted in management's rejecting the employee's grievance and that the union has decided to refer the grievance to step two.

Step Two   The format for step two is basically the same as for step one: both sides meet to discuss the grievance, with labor representing the employee. Higher-level union and management officials are involved at this step. The union representative may be the steward or business agent; the management representative is often the plant superintendent or plant manager. If the employee and union representatives are not satisfied with management's decision, they may appeal to the next step.

FIGURE 14-16 A standard grievance record form, step 1.

GRIEVANCE NUMBER _82-003_   DATE FILED _4/23/82_   UNION _Local 1233_

NAME OF GRIEVANT(S) _Flacko, George_   CLOCK # _0379_

DATE CAUSE OF GRIEVANCE OCCURRED _4/20/82_

CONTRACTUAL PROVISIONS CITED _Articles III, VII, and others_

STATEMENT OF THE GRIEVANCE:

On April 20, Foreman Pat Zajac asked George Flacko to go temporarily to the Rolling Mill for the rest of the turn. Flacko said he preferred not to, and that he was more senior to others who were available. The foreman never ordered Flacko to take the temporary assignment. He only requested that Flacko do so.

Flacko was improperly charged with insubordination and suspended for three days. The foreman did not have just cause for the discipline.

RELIEF SOUGHT

Reinstatement with full back pay and seniority.

GRIEVANT'S SIGNATURE _George Flacko_ _____ DATE _4/22/82_
STEWARD'S SIGNATURE _Paul Smith_ _____ DATE _4/23/82_

STEP 1

DISPOSITION:

Foreman Zajac gave Flacko clear instructions to report temporarily to the Rolling Mill for the remainder of the shift. Flacko refused to do so and was warned that it could result in discipline. When he again refused the foreman's directive, he was disciplined.

The discipline was for just cause. The grievance is rejected.

SIGNATURE OF EMPLOYER REPRESENTATIVE _J. K. Ellis_ _____ DATE _4/26/82_

_____ Grievance Withdrawn   or   ✔ Referred to Step 2

SIGNATURE OF UNION REPRESENTATIVE _Paul Smith_ _____ DATE _4/28/82_

SOURCE: Donald S. McPherson, _Resolving Grievances: A Practical Approach,_ © 1983, p. 55. Reprinted by permission of Prentice-Hall, Inc., Englewood Cliffs, N.J.

Step Three At this step, the employee is often represented by a plantwide union grievance committee. The plant manager and the industrial-relations director often represent management. Again, management hears the union's case and arguments and then issues its ruling on the matter. If the employee and union are still unsatisfied with the results, they may appeal to a fourth and final step: arbitration.

Step Four The negotiated procedure in which the parties agree to submit an unresolved dispute to a neutral third party for binding settlement is **arbitration**. During the arbitration process, the arbitrator studies the evidence, listens to the arguments on both sides, and renders a decision. The arbitrator's decision, an *award* to one of the sides, is *binding* in that it must be accepted by both sides and cannot be appealed further.

Each arbitration case is unique, and arbitrators can and do vary in their approach to cases. Two national studies of arbitrators concluded that the following eight elements carry the most weight (in order of influence, from most to least critical) in determining the final decision:[84]

1. *Labor contract language.* If the agreement provides clear, specific directives concerning the questions, it is applied.

2. *Past practice.* If the employer and union developed their own interpretation of the contract via a lengthy and consistent past practice, it is accepted.

3. *Judgment of fairness.* The merits of the case, given the grievant's record and the circumstances of the incident, should lead to a fair and reasonable decision.

4. *Future labor relations.* The decision may affect on future labor relations between the employer and the union.

5. *State and federal laws.* While often not a factor, if an action violated a law, it becomes a very important factor.

6. *Outside precedent.* The decisions of other arbitrators in similar cases, while not legally binding, may carry considerable weight.

7. *Social mores and customs.* Changes in society may be integrated into a decision.

8. *Industry practice.* While the parties involved may not have developed a practice relating to the issues, others in the industry may have, which can provide a reasonable guideline.

CONCLUSIONS AND APPLICATIONS

- A union has a major impact on an organization's management. Many HR decisions must be shared with the union, and the labor contract limits management's flexibility for the length of the agreement. Finally, poor relations between management and labor may result in costly and stressful organizational conflict.

- The percentage of the labor force that is organized has slowly declined since the 1950s. Reasons for the decline include the shift from an industrial economy to a service economy; automation, including robotics, and increasing foreign competition, resulting

in unemployment in the United States; and increased manufacturing of goods by the American manufacturers in foreign countries.

- The goals of the unions have not changed dramatically since their beginning. Important union goals include union security, job security, improved wages and benefits, favorable working conditions, and fair and just treatment for their members. The AFL-CIO supports many broad social and political goals.

- Employees working in teams have developed a new spirit that can benefit both employers and unions. Self-directed teams reflect a basic change in organizational structure and increased employee empowerment.

- Relations between organized labor and management are strictly governed by federal legislation. Managers and HR administrators who work in unionized organizations must be intimately familiar with these laws, which include the Wagner Act, the Taft-Hartley Act, and the Landrum-Griffin Act. Knowledge of labor law is also important for managers should an organizing drive take place within the company.

- The heart of the union structure is the local union, though the national union provides important direction and guidance. The local often receives assistance from the national union during the collective bargaining process. Most national unions are affiliated with the AFL-CIO, which provides many support services for its affiliates.

- During the organizing drive, the union attempts to convince workers that they will be better off by organizing. Management tries to convince them that they are better off without the union. Labor legislation provides a number of ground rules, but a considerable amount of campaign "puffing" takes place on both sides.

- There are a variety of different collective bargaining strategies. The most common form involves distributive bargaining, or win–lose bargaining, though this strategy seems to be giving way to more cooperative forms such as integrative bargaining and productivity bargaining. Concessionary bargaining, or give-back bargaining, has increased as a result of nonunion and foreign competition.

- The negotiation process involves a great deal of give and take before an agreement is reached. A bargaining impasse may cause a strike, lockout, or other power tactic. However more often mediation or other third-party technique will be used to end the impasse.

- Grievance handling is a critical part of labor relations. The multi-step procedure usually includes arbitration as a final step. The grievance process can keep minor disagreements from disrupting the workplace unnecessarily.

CASE STUDY

An Unfair Labor Practice?

The company operates about seven hundred convenience stores.

A sales assistant at one of the company's stores was murdered while on duty. The murder was widely publicized, and employees complained of inadequate security measures. As a result of the murder, fifteen sales assistants telephoned the union requesting a union organization effort. The union sent representatives to sixty stores in the area where the murder had occurred and left union authorization cards. Two days later, the company notified the union that an injunction had been issued during a prior union campaign prohibiting solicitation on company property. The next workday, the company had a meeting with the store managers in the area and talked about the need to improve security. The company officials also discussed the union's organization activities, reminded the managers of the "no solicitation" policy, and stated that a union would not necessarily do the employees any good. Later that week, the company had an unprecedented meeting for all sales assistants. Approximately 200 sales assistants attended and were paid for their time. The company officials told the employees that they did not need a union and that the employees from the union could retrieve their authorization cards. The employees were asked their complaints, and they listed the following: getting less than forty hours of work per week; not having breaks; unpaid overtime work; working alone at night; and poor lighting at the stores.

The next day the company sent a memorandum to all regional personnel directing that sales assistants should work a forty-hour workweek; canopy lights were installed at the stores; a policy was adopted that no one would be required to work alone at night; and sales assistants began receiving wages for after-hours overtime work. The company posted "no solicitation" signs in all stores and directed that this policy be enforced; if the employees did not enforce the it, they would lose their jobs.

Later that month the company held further meetings with sales assistants, who again were paid for their time. They were asked to select committee representatives to meet with management to discuss their complaints. Management officials left the room while the employees selected their representatives. The company made a list of the ten most frequently mentioned items from the employees' recommended subjects for the committee to discuss.

Meanwhile, the union filed a representation petition with the NLRB seeking an election in a unit of all Summit, Ohio, sales assistants. The company president told the managers to tell the sales assistants that if they joined the union, the company would close those stores. The first meeting of the employee–management committee was held, and the ten priority items were listed granting employees a new vacation policy, improved health care benefits, sick days, change in holiday hours for pay, recognition of seniority ranks, and improved security systems. Not long after that, the company sent an additional memo around announcing other improvements in life, major medical and accident insurance plans, in addition to death and family benefits, and a revised disciplinary appeal system.

The union charged the company with unfair labor practice for granting benefits to prevent a fair election and for creating an employer-dominated labor union. The company denied that the motivation for the benefits to the employees was to prevent a union; furthermore, the company denied that the employee organization was a labor organization under the act. But even if it was a labor organization, the company denied that it was a company-dominated organization.

QUESTIONS

1. Did the company's actions in forming an employee–management committee interfere with the union's organizational efforts? Explain your answers.

2. Should a company be prevented from instituting necessary employee benefits because of union organizing?

3. Explain why the employee–management committee could be considered a company union.

SOURCE: Adapted from *The Lawson Company, 118 LRRM* (1985) by Michael R. Carrell and Christina Heavrin, *Collective Bargaining and Labor Relations*, 3d ed. (New York: Macmillan, 1991), pp. 29–30.

EXPERIENTIAL EXERCISES

1. Attitudes Toward Unions

PURPOSE

To examine your attitudes toward unions and to recognize the underlying reasons for them.

THE TASK

Complete the following survey. Score it by summing the scores for all items. Following the completion of the survey, your instructor will lead the class in a discussion of attitudes toward unions and labor–management relations.

Directions

The statements in this survey are listed in pairs. Put an "X" next to the statement that you agree with more firmly. If you *strongly* agree with the statement, put *two* "X's" next to it. You may not entirely agree with either of them, but be sure to mark one of the statements. *Do not omit any statement.*

1. a. Unions are an important, positive force in our society.
   b. The country would be much better off without unions.
2. a. Without unions, the state of personnel management would be set back 100 years.
   b. Management is largely responsible for introducing humanistic programs and practices in organizations today.
3. a. Unions help organizations become more productive.
   b. Unions make it difficult for management to produce a product or service efficiently.

4. a. Today's standard of living is largely due to the efforts of the labor movement.
   b. The wealth that people are able to enjoy is largely the result of creativity, ingenuity, and risk taking by management decision makers.
5. a. Most unions are moral and ethical institutions.
   b. Most unions are as corrupt as the Mafia.
6. a. Unions afford the worker protection against arbitrary and unjust management practices.
   b. Managers will treat their employees fairly regardless of whether a union exists.
7. a. Unions want their members to be hardworking, productive employees.
   b. Unions promote job security rather than worker productivity.
8. a. Unions promote liberty and freedom for the individual employee.
   b. With the union, employees lose their individual freedoms.
9. a. Section 14b of the Taft-Hartley Act (which allows individual states to pass right-to-work laws) should be repealed.
   b. Congress should pass federal right-to-work legislation.
10. a. Unions are instrumental in implementing new, efficient work methods and techniques.
    b. Unions resist management efforts to adopt new, labor-saving technology.
11. a. Without unions, employees would not have a voice with management.
    b. Labor–management communication is

strengthened with the absence of a union.

12. a. Unions make sure that decisions about pay increases and promotions are fair.

   b. Union politics often play a role in deciding which union employee gets a raise or gets promoted.

13. a. The monetary benefits that unions bargain for are far greater than the dues the member must pay to the union.

   b. Union dues are usually too high for what the members get through collective bargaining.

14. a. Employee discipline is administered fairly if the organization is unionized.

   b. Union procedures generally make the disciplinary process slow, cumbersome, and costly.

15. a. Without the union, the employee would have no one with whom to discuss work-related problems.

   b. The best and most accessible person for the employee to discuss personal problems with is the immediate supervisor.

16. a. Union officers at all levels carry out their jobs in a competent and professional manner.

   b. Union officers are basically political figures who are primarily interested in their own welfare.

17. a. Most unions seek change through peaceful means.

   b. Most unions are prone to use violence to get what they want.

18. a. Unions are truly democratic institutions with full participation of the rank and file.

   b. Unions are controlled by the top leadership rather than by the rank and file.

19. a. Union members do the real work in our society and form the backbone of our country.

   b. Union employees are basically manual laborers who would flounder without management's direction and guidance.

20. a. Unions are necessary to balance the power and authority of management.

   b. The power and authority of management, guaranteed by the Constitution and the right to own private property, are severely eroded by the union.

2. Negotiation Issues

PURPOSE

To help you become familiar with current labor-relations issues and the general union and management positions on each issue.

THE TASK

Through news articles and other sources, identify ten current collective bargaining issues and summarize each side's general position. Your instructor may divide the class into union and management and require you to negotiate an agreement on these issues.

Example

| Profit-sharing plan | Management will propose to keep long-run wage rates competitive and pay bonuses only when profits are available. | The union will accept only if given job security and wage guarantees. |

Issue	Management	Union
1.		
2.		
3.		
4.		
5.		
6.		
7.		
8.		
9.		
10.		

KEY TERMS AND CONCEPTS

American Federation of Labor and Congress
    of Industrial Organizations (AFL-CIO)
Arbitration
Authorization card
Bargaining unit
Business unionism
Certification/decertification election
Collective bargaining
Economic strike
Employee teams
Grievance procedure
Independent union
Impasse
Landrum-Griffin Act

Lockout
Maintenance-of-membership shop
Management rights
Mediation
National Labor Relations Board (NLRB)
National union
Open shop/closed shop
Retraining rights
Right to work
Seniority system
Subcontracting
Taft-Hartley Act
Unfair labor practices
Wagner Act

REVIEW QUESTIONS

1. Why do workers vote to unionize? Why do they stay unionized?

2. How has union membership changed since the 1940s?

3. What are the primary goals of unions?

4. What are the major labor laws, and what are their key provisions?

5. What are the functions and duties of the national and local unions? What is the AFL-CIO, and what are its functions?

6. What are the major collective bargaining strategies utilized by negotiations?

7. What are the primary events in a union organizing drive?

8. How may a firm remain nonunion if it chooses to do so?

9. What are the possible advantages of employee teams?

10. Why has the number of major strikes declined in recent years?

DISCUSSION QUESTIONS

1. Assume that you are a recent graduate applying for a job as foreman trainee. During a series of interviews, the plant manager says, "Tell me your philosophy toward unions. We are nonunion, and I would specifically like to know how you would feel about this company becoming unionized." How would you respond?

2. Would you prefer to manage union or nonunion workers? Why?

3. Why has organized labor failed to increase its membership significantly in the past two decades? What do you believe must be done to increase union membership?

4. Comment on the following statement: "We live in an age of professional management. The average worker has a safe job, fair wages, good benefits, and competent supervision. Therefore, unions have outlived their purpose."

5. Many organizing campaigns are taking place at colleges and universities to bring their faculties into a union. Do you think that professors should organize? Why or why not?

6. One of the most controversial parts of the Taft-Hartley Act is Section 14b, which enables individual states to ban union and agency shops. Since the passage of the act, labor has lobbied long and hard to repeal Section 14b. On the other hand, many employers feel that a federal right-to-work law should be passed banning union and agency shops throughout the country. Do you believe society would benefit most from the repeal of Section 14b or the passage of a federal right-to-work law? Discuss.

7. Should an employer be legally allowed to hire permanent replacement workers during a strike?

8. If you represented a newly unionized employer, would you agree to binding arbitration of grievances as a provision in your first contract?

ENDNOTES

Chapter 14

1. Richard Feldman and Michael Betzold, *End of the Line: Autoworkers and the American Dream* (New York: Weidenfeld & Nicolson, 1988), p. 6.

2. Albert Rees, *The Economics of Trade Unions* (Chicago: University of Chicago Press, 1977), p. 30.

3. See D. H. Rosenbloom and Jay M. Shafritz, *Essentials of Labor Relations* (Reston, VA: Reston, 1985); P. L. Martin, *Contemporary Labor Relations* (Belmont, CA: Wadsworth, 1979); and J. M. Brett, "Why Employees Want Unions," *Organizational Dynamics* 6 (Spring 1980), pg. 56–67.

4. Aaron Bernstein, "The Difference Japanese Management Makes," *Business Week* (July 14, 1986): 47–50.

5. Carol Keegan, "How Union Members and Nonunion View the Role of Unions," *Monthly Labor Review* 110, no. 8 (August 1987): 50–51.

6. William T. Dickens and Jonathan S. Leonard, "Accounting for the Decline in Union Membership, 1950–1980," *Industrial and Labor Relations Review* 38, no. 3 (April 1985): 323–34.

7. U.S. Bureau of Labor Statistics.

8. Steven G. Allen, "Declining Unionization in Construction: The Facts and the Reasons," *Industrial and Labor Relations Review* 41, no. 3 (April 1988): 343–59.

9. Joseph R. Antos, Mark Chandler, and Wesley Mellow, "Sex Differences in Union Membership," *Industrial and Labor Relations Review* 33, no. 2 (January 1980): 162–69.

10. Daniel C. Stove, Jr, "Can Unions Pick Up the Pieces?" *Personnel Journal* 65, no. 2 (February 1986): 37–40.

11. Amos N. Okafor, "White-Collar Unionization," *Personnel* 62, no. 8 (August 1985): 17–21.

12. Dickens and Leonard, "Accounting for the Decline," pp. 323–

34. See also Howard M. Leftwich, "Organizing in the Eighties: A Human Resources Perspective," *Labor Law Journal* 32, no. 8 (August 1981): 484–91. See also Paula B. Boos, "Union Organizing: Costs and Benefits," *Industrial and Labor Relations Review* 36, no. 4 (July 1983): 576–91.

13. Scott Foster, "Court: VFW Member Dues Cannot Fund Non-Union Work," *The Bakersfield Californian* (May 5, 1992): B1.

14. Carrell and Heavrin, *Collective Bargaining*, p. 249.

15. *Winning at Arbitration* (Columbus, OH: Crain, 1983), p. 20.

16. *Agreement* between Lithonia Lighting Inc. and The International Brotherhood of Electrical Workers Local 613 of Atlanta, Georgia, 1968, p. 4.

17. Gary B. Hansen, "Innovative Approach to Plant Closings: The UAW-Ford Experience at San Jose," *Monthly Labor Review* 108, no. 7 (July 1985): 56–59.

18. For a detailed treatment of labor legislation, see Kenneth L. Sovereign, *Personnel Law*, 2d ed. (Englewood Cliffs, NJ: Prentice-Hall, 1989), chaps. 15 and 16; and Theodore Kheel, *Labor Law* (New York: Matthew Bender, 1988).

19. Norman Hill, "The Double-Speak of Right-to-Work," *AFL-CIO American Federationist* 87 (October 1980): 13–16.

20. Barry T. Hirsch, "The Determinants of Unionization: An Analysis of Interarea Differences," *Industrial and Labor Relations Review* 33, no. 227 (January 1980): 147–61.

21. Kenneth A. Kovach, "National Right-to-Work Law: An Affirmative Position," *Labor Law Journal* 28 (May 1977): 305–14.

22. William A. Wines, "An Analysis of the 1986 'Right-to-Work Referen-

dum in Idaho,' " *Labor Law Journal* 39, no. 9 (September 1988): 622–28.

23. Thomas M. Carroll, "Right to Work Laws Do Matter," *Southern Economic Journal* 5, no. 2 (October 1983): 494–509.

24. *This Is the AFL-CIO*, Publication No. 20 (Washington, DC: AFL-CIO, 1987).

25. Esten, *The Unions*, p. 46.

26. Ibid.

27. Bruce Feldacker, *Labor Guide to Labor Law* (Reston, VA-Reston Pub. Co., 1980), ch. 3 and 4.

28. Ibid.

29. Martin T. Levine, "Double-Digit Decertification Election Activity: Union Organizational Weakness in the 1980s," *Labor Law Journal* 40, no. 5 (May 1989): 311–19.

30. S. Dillingham, "Topeka Revisited," *Human Resource Executive* 4, no. 5 (May 1990): 55–58.

31. Steve Jordan, "Union Defies U.P. Quality Concept," *The Omaha World Herald* (April 6, 1993): M1.

32. Ken Murphy, "Venture Teams Help Companies Create New Products," *Personnel Journal* (March 1991): 60–67.

33. Richard Wellins and Jill George, "The Key to Self-Directed Teams," *Training and Development Journal* 45 (April 1991): 26–29.

34. Frank Shipper and Charles C. Manz, "Employee Self-Management Without Formally Designed Teams: An Alternative Road to Empowerment," *Organizational Dynamics* 20 (Winter 1992): 48–61.

35. Wellins and George, "Self-Directed Teams," p. 27.

36. Richard S. Wellins, William C. Byham, and Jeanne M. Wilson, *Empowered Teams* (San Francisco: Jossey-Bass, 1991), pp. 3–5.

37. Clay Carr, "Managing Self-Managed Workers," *Training and Develop-*

ment Journal 45 (September 1991): 36–42.

38. Shipper and Manz, "Employee Self-Management," p. 48.

39. Wellins and George, "Self-Directed Teams," p. 28.

40. Joe Ward, "It's a New Day on the Assembly Line," *The Courier Journal* (February 7, 1993): J4.

41. Steve Jordan, "Union Defies U.P. Quality Concept": 1M.

42. Harold J. Datz, "Employee Participation Programs and the National Labor Relations Act—A Guide for the Perplexed," presented at the Ninth Annual Labor and Employment Law Institute (1992) at the University of Louisville.

43. *Electromation*, NLRB Case No. 25-CA-19818 (1991).

44. *DuPont*, NLRB Case (1993).

45. *General Foods Corp.*, 231 NLRB 1232, 1235 (1977).

46. James R. Redeker and Daniel P. O'Meara, "Safe Methods of Employee Participation," *HRMagazine* (April 1993): 101–04.

47. In the 1980s, the steel industry saw a disintegration of its bargaining power as members attempted to gain more control over internal affairs and sought ways to be more competitive with nonunion companies. See T. F. O'Boyle and C. Hymouritz, "Steel Industry's Bargaining Group Appears to Be on Verge of Collapse," *The Wall Street Journal* (August 8, 1984): 14.

48. See G. Daniels and K. Gagala, *Labor Guide to Negotiating Wages and Benefits* (Reston, VA: Reston, 1985), pp. 4–10.

49. Ibid., pp. 256–60.

50. D. H. Rosenbloom and J. M. Shafritz, *Essentials of Labor Relations* (Reston, VA: Reston, 1985), pp. 140–41. For a detailed account of boulwarism from the perspective of its creator, see L. R. Boulware, *The Truth about Boulwarism* (Washington, DC: Bureau of National Affairs, 1969).

51. Similar benefits were achieved by the Jones & Laughlin Steel Corporation and the United Steel Workers. See "Steel Listens to Workers and Likes What It Hears," *Business Week* (December 19, 1983): 92–95.

52. Richard Feldman and Michael Betzold, *End of the Line: Autoworkers and the American Dream* (New York: Weidenfeld & Nicolson, 1988), pp. 17–21.

53. See E. Weinberg, "Labor–Management Cooperation: A Report on Recent Initiatives," *Monthly Labor Review* (April 1976): 13–21; R. E. Winter, "Firms' Recent Productivity Drives May Yield Unusually Strong Gains," *The Wall Street Journal* (June 14, 1983): 39; R. Guenther, "Plan for Construction Productivity Stirs Industry, Takes Aim at Unions," *The Wall Street Journal* (April 21, 1983): 33; R. S. Greenberger, "Work Rule Changes Quietly Spread as Firms Try to Raise Productivity," *The Wall Street Journal* (January 25, 1983); and M. H. Schuster, *Union–Management Cooperation* (Kalamazoo, MI: Upjohn Institute, 1984).

54. "Swapping Work Rules for Jobs at GE's 'Factory of the Future,'" *Business Week* (September 10, 1984): 43.

55. See M. H. Dodosh, "Companies Increasingly Ask Labor to Give Back Past Contract Gains," *The Wall Street Journal* (November 27, 1981): 21; and M. Brody, "Union Blues," *Barrons* (January 23, 1984): 22. For a discussion of union resistance to concessions, see R. S. Greenberger, "Resisting a Trend, Machinists Union Continues to Oppose Concessions," *The Wall Street Journal* (September 2, 1983): 13.

56. J. Peters, "Workers Accept ARCO Contract," *The Louisville Courier-Journal* (November 22, 1983): B-5.

57. "The GM Settlement Is a Milestone for Both Sides," *Business Week* (October 8, 1984): 160–62.

58. Robert C. Rose, "Northwest Wins Pay Concessions from Two Unions," *The Wall Street Journal* (May 28, 1993): A2.

59. Michael R. Carrell and Christina Heavrin, *Collective Bargaining and Labor Relations*, 3rd ed. (Columbus, OH: Merrill, 1991), p. 443.

60. "Auto Workers Will Feel Pinch of Lower or No Profits," *The Bakersfield Californian* (February 20, 1990): B-7.

61. Scott A. Kruse, "Giveback Bargaining: One Answer to Current Labor Problems?" *Personnel Journal* 62 (April 1983): 286–89.

62. Carrell and Heavrin, *Collective Bargaining and Labor Relations*, chap. 5.

63. "Reagan Action Altered Landscape," *The Chicago Tribune* (July 11, 1993): 1, 6.

64. Bob Baker, "Workers Fear Losing Jobs to Replacements in Strikes," *The Los Angeles Times* (June 7, 1990): A5; and Scott Forter, "Effects of Strike Overcome, Greyhound Claims," *The Bakersfield Californian* (March 2, 1991): B1, 2.

65. Rosenbloom and Shafritz, *Essentials of Labor Relations*, p. 108.

66. See R. S. Greenberger, "More Firms Get Tough and Keep Operating in Spite of Walkouts," *The Wall Street Journal* (October 11, 1983): 1.

67. Kevin G. Seliven, "Ban on Replacing Strikers Seen Facing Bleak Future as House Prepares to Vote," *The Wall Street Journal* (May 28, 1993): A1.

68. R. S. Greenberger, "AT&T's Managers Weather Strike Despite Long Hours, Tedious Work," *The Wall Street Journal* (August 17, 1983): 26.

69. *Pattern Makers League* v. *NLRB*, 53 U.S.L.W., 4928 (1985).

70. John J. Coleman, "Can Union Members Resign During a Strike?" *Personnel Journal* 65, no. 5 (May 1986): 99–102.

71. "Bankruptcy as an Escape Hatch," *Time* (March 5, 1984): 14.

72. J. S. Lublin, "Conservative Pilots' Union Turns Militant in Response to Fight at Continental Airlines," *The Wall Street Journal* (November 22, 1983): 35.

73. "Bankruptcy as an Escape Hatch."

74. "Unionists Are Alarmed by

High Court Ruling in a Bankruptcy Filing," *The Wall Street Journal* (February 24, 1984): 1.

75. *Fall River Dyeing and Finishing Corp. v. NLRB*, No. 85–1208 (1987).

76. Walter A. Maggiolo, *Techniques of Mediation in Labor Disputes* (Dobbs Ferry, NY: Oceana, 1971), p. 12.

77. Rosenbloom and Shafritz, *Essentials of Labor Relations*, p. 163.

78. Carrell and Heavrin, *Collective Bargaining and Labor Relations*, p. 142.

79. *Basic Patterns in Union Contracts*, 12th ed. (Washington, DC: Bureau of National Affairs, 1989), pp. 1–3.

80. Harold S. Roberts, *Roberts' Dictionary of Industrial Relations*, 3rd ed. (Washington, DC: Bureau of National Affairs, 1986), p. 396.

81. Marvin Hill, Jr., and Anthony V. Sinicrope, *Management Rights* (Washington, DC: Bureau of National Affairs, 1986), p. 3; and *Basic Patterns in Union Contracts*, 1989, pp. 79–81.

82. *Management Rights*, 1986, pp. 4–5.

83. Arthur J. Goldberg, "Management's Reserved Rights: A Labor View," *Proceedings of the 9th Annual Meeting of the National Arbitration Association*, 118 (1956): 120–21.

84. Daniel Jennings and A. Dale Allen, Jr., "How Arbitrators View the Process of Labor Arbitration: A Longitudinal Analysis," *Labor Studies Journal* 31 (Winter 1993): 41–50.

DISCIPLINE AND COUNSELING

CHAPTER OUTLINE

CHAPTER OBJECTIVES

1. To recognize the various sources of poor performance through the illustration and discussion of an unsatisfactory performance model.

2. To explain both good and poor ways to discipline employees, with emphasis on effective disciplinary techniques.

3. To discuss how organizations can manage employees in such a way as to keep disciplinary problems to a minimum.

4. To illustrate a model of positive discipline and describe the procedures for ensuring that discipline achieves its goals.

5. To identify the procedures for carrying out the discharge decision humanely and tactfully.

6. To recognize how the erosion of the employment-at-will concept affects the HR function.

7. To understand what constitutes a defamation action and to identify how employers can minimize their exposure to such cases.

Insubordination—A Cardinal Sin

A basic principle in management–labor relations is management's right to direct the work force, which, of course, involves the concept of authority. The authority to make decisions and run the organization is vested in the owners, who then directly utilize it if they actively manage the organization, or it is delegated to a president, CEO or other top management person who delegates certain authority to others according to their position. Insubordination is a serious workplace disciplinary issue because it involves the authority conferred on someone by the owners. Widespread insubordination could lead to chaos. Thus, it is considered a "cardinal sin" in the workplace and is grounds for immediate discharge in most organizations. Insubordination is a major reason for disciplinary action in organizations, with minor cases leading to lesser penalties. In practice, employees found guilty of insubordination are most often accused of directly refusing to obey an order, using abusive language, committing acts of violence, or not following health and safety rules.

Cases involving insubordination, however, can be complex. For example, is it insubordination if an employee refuses to obey an order issued by someone who is not the immediate supervisor? In general, the courts and arbitrators have said "yes." When does an employee have the right to disobey a command? In most situations, the rule is "obey now, grieve later." This is usually followed because

---

Even in the most sophisticated organizations—those blessed with high-quality HR programs and competent supervisors—a small percentage of employees will be unwilling or unable to achieve a satisfactory level of performance. The percentage of an organization's HR group that may be considered unsatisfactory will vary considerably from firm to firm. No level of the organization—from highest to lowest—can be considered immune to the problems of incompetence. Managers who view the employee as a resource rather than simply a factor of production will take positive steps to maintain high levels of job satisfaction and productivity. But those who view the worker as a necessary evil will, more than likely, show little attention to employee needs and suffer "people problems" and performance shortfalls. Thus, management may choose to minimize performance problems or to accept them. In the end, unsatisfactory performance is a management problem.

PERFORMANCE PROBLEMS

Consider the case of John Bradley, a hypothetical press operator for a large printing company. Both his output and his quality level are consistently below standard. His absenteeism rate is about double the plant average. John is an unsatisfactory performer. But *why* is John an unsatisfactory performer? Is he lazy and shiftless? Is his boss giving him a hard time for no apparent reason? Does he have a substance abuse problem? Was he assigned to a machine

production or customers cannot wait while an issue is settled. Thus, usually employees should follow the order and file a grievance or dispute at a later time. There are, however, exceptions:

- **Health and safety**. If employees genuinely fear for their personal safety (whether or not it is later proven that a danger existed at the time), then arbitrators and courts have often upheld their right to disobey an order.

- **"Shop talk."** While the flagrant use of profanity, epithets, and verbal abuse or threat of physical harm, can easily be judged as insubordination, there is a general exception—"shop talk." Words or gestures which are a common part of the "culture" of the organization can be used by an employee in a noninsubordinate manner. Exactly where the line exists between insubordinate and "shop talk" is not easy to determine and can be the focus of a court case.

- **Violence**. Acts of physical attack such as hitting, pushing, or drawing a knife or other weapons are clearly insubordination. The exception, however, is when witnesses testify that the supervisor taunted or goaded the employee into the act, in which case the supervisor is at least partially to blame. Thus, supervisors are best advised to withdraw from potentially violent situations.

- **Lack of clarity**. If the supervisor was not clear that he/she was issuing an order (not a suggestion or expressed desire) and did not warn the employee of the probably consequences of refusal, then a termination will likely be overturned.

SOURCE: Stanley J. Schwartz, "Insubordination: A Cardinal Sin in the Workplace." *Labor Law Journal* (December 1993): 765–70.

---

that frequently malfunctions? Is he really not sure what the job standards are?[1]

Determining why an employee is performing at an unsatisfactory level is of critical importance because a problem cannot be corrected unless its causes are known. Effective managers not only stay alert for employee performance problems but also recognize that productivity problems stem from a variety of causes. Rather than relying on a gut feeling or hunch, the prudent manager strives to uncover the true causes of performance problems and seeks solutions to eliminate or minimize them.

Performance Analysis

The proper analysis of a performance problem is a critical managerial skill. The model in Figure 15–1 shows the major causes of unsatis-factory performance and the solutions available for solving them. Examination of the components of the **model** is helpful in understanding how managers should treat problems **of poor performance**.

Communication Some managers assume that the employee knows what good performance is and think it unnecessary to state management's expectations. For the new employee or for the experienced employee who receives a promotion or new job assignment, the manager may describe performance standards in vague or subjective terms, leaving the employee to decipher the job standards on his or her own, or perhaps by learning them from other employees. The problem is that an employee's perception of good performance may

FIGURE 15-1 A model for analyzing unsatisfactory performance.

Define and communicate "good" performance

↓

Identify causes of unsatisfactory performance

↓

Lack of skills and abilities   Lack of motivation   Rule breaking   Personal problems

Solutions:
• Train
• Transfer
• Change work environment
• Discipline
• Terminate
• Rehabilitate

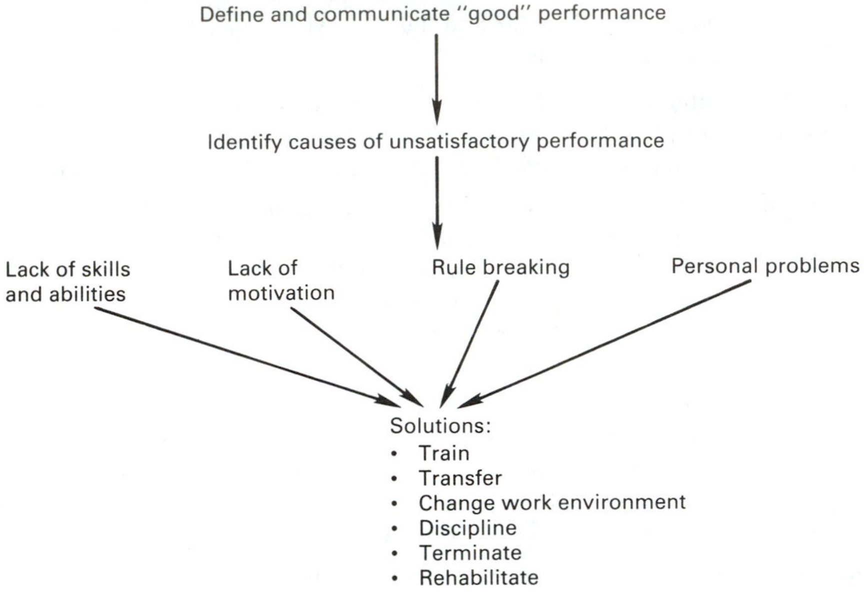

SOURCE: Adapted from F. Kuzmits, R. Herden, and L. Sussman, *Managing the Unsatisfactory Employee* (Homewood, IL: Dow Jones–Irwin, 1984), p. 8.

differ markedly from that of the manager. A well-intentioned, achievement-oriented employee may quickly fall from the manager's grace simply because the employee misunderstood what was expected.

One of the manager's major responsibilities is to define clearly and precisely what good performance means. Managers who neglect this important task are likely to have more than their share of performance problems.

Identifying Causes Recognizing that a gap exists between ideal and actual employee performance brings the supervisor to another issue: what is the cause of the performance shortfall? Without proper analysis of the problem, any solution that is implemented will probably be ineffective, and thus unsatisfactory performance will likely continue. Effective management of unsatisfactory performance greatly depends on selecting the correct solution or solutions to the problem. At least four major causes can be identified:

1. *Lack of skills.* On too many occasions, organizations place an employee in a job for which he or she is unsuited. This difficult problem for management (and for the employee) can normally be remedied in only one of three basic ways: (a) train the employee and remove the skill deficiency; (b) transfer the employee to a job that utilizes the skills the employee does possess; or (c) terminate the employee.

2. *Lack of motivation.* Scores of books and articles have been written on what can be done to motivate employees. A multitude of theories and approaches to employee motivation exists, but most motivational strategies boil down to one seemingly simple axiom: *determine what the employee wants and offer it as a reward for good performance.* Yet as most students of management know, determining the needs of an employee and creating an environment in which those needs are satisfied is one of the

manager's most challenging tasks. In addressing that challenge, decision makers must know the common techniques for motivating the unmotivated:

- *Create meaningful goals and objectives.* Goals should be challenging, attainable, and important to the employees who are expected to achieve them. In addition, goals should be clearly communicated to employees, and supervisors should ensure that employees understand their goals and agree with them. Finally, managers should involve the employees in the goal-setting process by soliciting their feelings and suggestions when creating goals.

- *Invite employee participation.* Employees often have meaningful ideas and suggestions for making their work more productive, satisfying, and interesting. Managers should earnestly solicit these ideas, give serious consideration to them, and implement them whenever possible.

- *Let employees know where they stand.* Employees do not like to be left in the dark; they want to know how their performance and behavior stack up against the supervisor's expectations. Managers should tell employees how well they are doing and discuss any problems they might be having. By being approachable and receptive to discussions about performance problems, supervisors can nip many minor problems in the bud—before they become major crises.

- *Reward good work.* Good work should never go unnoticed. Employees often complain, "When I do something wrong, I'm sure to catch hell. When I do something right, my boss never says a word." Praise for a job well done, given sincerely, is a powerful motivator. Always recognize good work and be generous with praise.

- *Treat employees fairly.* Equity theory provides evidence that fair treatment of employees is a strong determinant of employee behavior and a significant factor influencing employee motivation. In turn, unfair treatment can lead to negative consequences such as employee grievances, absenteeism, and turnover. Employers want to work for supervisors who are fair and just and who give people their due. Playing favorites and giving breaks to friends (such as easy assignments or a promotion) is a sure way to bring about dissatisfaction and low motivation.

- *Make work as interesting as possible.* Many jobs are boring and routine. Jobs are often designed with efficiency in mind, not the needs of the employees who perform them. Managers should do whatever they can to make the work as interesting as possible for employees who seek greater levels of satisfaction from performing their jobs. Strategies for job redesign, discussed in a previous chapter, include job enlargement, in which the number of tasks the employee performs is increased; job rotation, in which the employee swaps jobs with another employee for a period of time; and job enrichment, in which the employee is given more authority to plan and control the work he or she performs.

- *Learn Cultural Differences.* As Chapter 3 discusses in our increasingly diverse work force, understanding, of cultural differences is critical. A logical explanation of unusual behavior may be related to one's culture.

- *Enable employees to grow and develop.* Many employees are not content with "just a job." They want careers with opportunities for growth and promotion. They want to learn new skills and abilities and expect the company to make these opportunities available. The manager plays a role by providing on-the-job training and by setting up off-the-job developmental activities such as seminars and short courses. In addition, the manager should urge employees to develop themselves by attending night school, joining professional organizations, and regularly reading professional journals and books. These opportunities not only motivate employees by helping to satisfy their personal needs but also strengthen the organization's human resources by creating a more competent, motivated work force.

3. *Rule breaking.* A third type of unsatisfactory performance is associated with rule breaking. An example of the rule breaker is the employee who is occasionally absent or late to work, who violates the dress or safety code, who swears at the manager, or who drinks excessively during the lunch period. This employee has the necessary skills and normally does a fair day's work but nevertheless disregards the policies, rules, and regulations of the workplace.

   Although the situation of each rule breaker is different, the most effective approach for dealing with this form of unsatisfactory performance is to apply positive discipline, a technique discussed in detail later in this chapter.

4. *Personal problems.* A final type of unsatisfactory performance is associated with the *troubled employee.* A troubled employee is one whose personal problems are so significant that they prevent the employee from performing satisfactorily at work. Although the troubled employee may suffer from a variety of problems—such as emotional illness, financial crises, drug dependency, chronic physical problems, and family problems—by far the most common ailment of the troubled employee is the abuse of alcohol. Because of the significance and severity of this problem in business and industry today (alcoholism is estimated to cost billions of dollars a year in lost productivity and other expenses), many organizations have created employee assistance programs, a topic discussed in Chapter 13.

DISCIPLINE

The primary objective of discipline is to motivate an employee to comply with the company's performance standards. An employee receives discipline after failing to meet some obligation of the job. The failure to perform as expected could be directly related to the tasks performed by the employee or to the rules and regulations that define proper conduct at work.

A second objective of discipline is to create or maintain mutual respect and trust between the supervisor and employee. Improperly administered, discipline can create such problems as low morale, resentment, and ill will between the supervisor and the employee. In such cases, any improvement in the employee's behavior will be relatively short-lived, and the supervisor will need to discipline the employee again in the near future. The proper administration of discipline will not only improve employee behavior but will also minimize future disciplinary problems through a positive supervisor–subordinate relationship.

In effect, discipline is management's last resort to improve the performance of employees. Generally, discipline for poor task performance should not be applied while employees are being trained and are learning the job. Nor should employees be disciplined for problems beyond their control, for example, failure to meet output standards caused by a lack of raw materials.[2] Discipline should be applied only when it has been determined that the employee is the cause of unsatisfactory performance.

Incorrect Discipline

Just as incorrect disciplinary techniques are applied by parents in supermarkets and shopping centers, they are also applied by managers in organizations. Some of the mistakes associated with the disciplinary process in the work setting include the following:[3]

- *Punitive discipline.* Punitive discipline, sometimes referred to as *negative discipline,* is discipline through fear. Punitive discipline often involves threats, harassment, intimidation, and browbeating. Widespread in the industries of the early twentieth century, punitive discipline is little used today, largely because of union protection and greater acceptance of human-relations techniques. Punitive discipline still exists in some firms, however, particularly among supervisors who prefer to do things the "old way."

- *Negative feedback.* Some supervisors give employees feedback only when unsatisfactory performance occurs and fail to provide positive reinforcement when performance improves or when a job is done well. Feedback should be both positive and negative, depending on the employee's level of performance.

- *Late intervention.* Perhaps best labeled *procrastination discipline,* this form of discipline takes place when supervisors allow a problem to drag on until it reaches a serious level. The problem may begin as a minor one, but the supervisor's inattention to the situation allows the unsatisfactory performance to become habitual and thus difficult to change.

- *Inadequate definition.* During counseling to rectify a performance problem, a supervisor may tell an employee that he or she is "uncooperative," "disloyal," or not a "team player." Couching a performance problem in such vague and ambiguous terms only serves to confuse and frustrate the employee.

- *Labeling employees, not behavior.* Unsatisfactory performance may result in an employee's being labeled "lazy," "shiftless," or a "goof-off" by the supervisor. Such labeling has two major problems. First, the employee may carry the label over to other jobs and work units, and the label may serve as a self-fulfilling prophecy. Second, such descriptions focus on the employee and not on the act of unsatisfactory performance—which is what must be addressed.

- *Misplaced responsibility.* Supervisors often have to realize that they themselves sometimes contribute to the performance problems of their employees. When the entire responsibility for changing behavior falls on the employee and improvement does not occur, the supervisor applies further disciplinary action. But without a change in supervisory behavior, a change in employee behavior is unlikely.

Preventive Discipline

Of all the approaches to discipline, preventive discipline is the most desirable. By **preventive discipline**, people are managed in a way that prevents behaviors that need to be disciplined.[4] Much like the person who eats nutritious food and exercises regularly to avoid health problems, managers and supervisors who practice preventive discipline create an organizational climate conducive to high levels of job satisfaction and employee productivity. In such cases, the need to discipline will be minimal. To create a working environment that supports a preventive discipline approach, managers must do the following:

- Match the employee with the job through effective selection, testing, and placement procedures.

- Properly orient the employee to the job and provide any necessary training.

- Clarify proper employee behavior.

- Provide frequent and constructive feedback to employees on their performance.
- Enable employees to address their problems to management through techniques such as an open-door policy and management–employee group meetings.

Positive Discipline

Positive discipline corrects unsatisfactory employee behavior through support, respect, and people-oriented leadership. The purpose of positive discipline is to help rather than harass the employee. Positive discipline is not an attempt to soft-pedal or sidestep an employee problem. Rather, it is a management philosophy that assumes that improved employee behavior is most likely to be long-lived when discipline is administered without revenge, abuse, or vindictiveness. Positive discipline assumes that most employees are willing to accept personal responsibility for their work problems and, with management's confidence and support, will reverse their unsatisfactory performance. While positive discipline is not a panacea, this process offers a number of advantages over the punitive approach.

Positive discipline is much more than the simple act of a supervisor discussing performance problems with an employee. Rather, it is a process that comprises a series of policies and procedures. Important steps in that process are shown in Figure 15–2.

Clarify Responsibility The question of who should administer discipline is subject to some debate. In theory, the responsibility for discipline should fall on an employee's immediate supervisor. Because the immediate supervisor is responsible for the employee's output, that supervisor should possess the authority to correct the employee's performance problems. Some managers, however, think that decentralizing the responsibility for discipline will result in the inconsistent application of discipline throughout the organization. An equitable and uniformly administered disciplinary

FIGURE 15-2 Steps in the process of positive discipline.

- Clarify Responsibility for Discipline
- Define Expected Employee Behavior
- Communicate Discipline Policy, Procedures, and Rules
- Collect Performance Data
- Administer Progressive Discipline
- Administer Corrective Counseling Techniques

system can take priority over other considerations, and such uniformity may be achieved only by allowing HR department employees to apply the discipline. But this approach also has its drawbacks: the HR staff must spend inordinate amounts of time on disciplinary matters, and the supervisor will lose some control over subordinates.

To overcome the problem of where to place the responsibility for discipline, many organizations give the supervisor authority to administer less severe forms of discipline, such as an oral warning or a written notice. For situations involving suspension or discharge, the supervisor is often required to consult with an HR representative; in some cases the decision is made by an upper-level line manager or HR executive. With this type of approach, consistency in the application of discipline can be achieved while the supervisor retains authority and control over employee behavior.

Define Performance Expectations A central part of every disciplinary process is the definition of behavior that management expects from its employees. Disciplining an employee for unsatisfactory performance is imprudent unless management has clearly defined good performance. Management must ensure that employee standards are consistent with the organization's objectives and that standards are revised as new organizational goals are developed.

It is not only fair to employees but is also a prudent HR practice to provide employees with written principles of behavior such as those in the Lens Lab Company Policy Manual (Figure 15–3).

Communicate Disciplinary Policies, Procedures, and Rules Good communication is of the utmost importance in maintaining satisfactory levels of employee performance. Management is responsible for telling employees precisely what is expected of them and for ensuring that all standards, rules, and regulations are clearly communicated. These expectations may be communicated by the following methods:

- Employee handbooks.
- Orientation programs.

FIGURE 15-3 An expected behavior policy.

Lens Lab Inc.
Personnel Policies
Discipline and Investigations

PRINCIPLES OF BEHAVIOR

It is expected that employees shall be mindful of the following principles in their conduct and behavior. Violations of these principles may constitute grounds for disciplinary action or termination.

11.1(1) Employees, in conducting the business of Lens Lab-Paris Miki, Inc., shall deal with co-workers and the public in a respectful and courteous manner, and act in a manner consistent with the trust inherent in employment relationships.

11.1(2) Employees shall strive to perform their work at a consistently high level of quality.

11.1(3) Employees shall obey and uphold the laws of the United States and the political subdivisions and jurisdictions thereof.

11.1(4) Employees shall follow and promote general standards of safety and health on the job. In keeping with these standards, all employees are required to wear seat belts while operating licensed vehicles owned, leased or rented by Lens Lab-Paris Miki, Inc. and when operating personal vehicles for work-related assignments. Employees are required to carry a valid driver's license when operating any vehicles owned, leased or rented by Lens Lab-Paris Miki, Inc.

11.1(5) Employees shall follow all the rules and regulations established for the department or store in which they have been assigned so long as those rules and regulations do not conflict with Lens Lab-Paris Miki, Inc. Personnel Policies.

11.1(6) Employees shall conduct themselves off the job in a manner which does not cause discredit to Lens Lab-Paris Miki, Inc..

11.1(7) Employees shall report any illegal activity of co-workers or supervisors to their Department Executive or Store Manager.

11.1(8) Employees shall cooperate fully in all hearings and investigations conducted by or authorized by Lens Lab-Paris Miki, Inc..

11.1(9) Employees shall not possess, consume, distribute or be under the influence of alcohol or illegal drugs while on the premises of Lens Lab-Paris Miki, Inc.. Further, employees shall not engage in activities related to these substances which might reflect negatively on Lens Lab-Paris Miki, Inc..

SOURCE: Randy Coe, Lens Lab, Inc., Louisville, Kentucky. Used by permission.

- Union contract.
- Rules and regulations distributed in writing to employees.
- Rules and regulations posted on bulletin boards.
- Supervisor–subordinate discussions of job standards and company policies and procedures.

Some administrators avoid publishing rules and regulations, feeling that such a list is demeaning and condescending to employees. As one executive put it, "We have resisted publishing the whole painful list on the theory that it is more insulting than useful, and that there is going to be some rule overlooked, and if everything is spelled out, then you have no recourse and are in trouble. I speak particularly of the nonunion situation, as evidently unionized companies feel that the contract must be all-inclusive in the matter of behavior."[5] Most firms do formalize their rules for employee conduct. A Bureau of National Affairs survey of 218 companies found that 79 percent put their rules and regulations in writing for nonunion workers. The figure increased to 85 percent for 97 union companies sampled.[6]

Collect Performance Data Before an employee is disciplined, there must be indisputable proof that some standard, rule, or regulation was violated. Discipline should not be a gut reaction by a supervisor. There must be no doubt that unsatisfactory performance has taken place, and the collection of information clearly indicating an employee's wrongdoing makes discipline more effective and easier to administer.[7]

Some performance data are easy to collect; others are difficult. For example, an employee's absenteeism is routinely recorded and rarely subject to misinterpretation. Many companies with computerized absenteeism records furnish their supervisors with weekly or biweekly printouts so that employees requiring discipline for unsatisfactory attendance can be pinpointed. Production and quality statistics are routinely collected—often daily—in many manufacturing companies. Other measures of performance, however, are somewhat subjective and difficult to record. For example, many firms have specific rules against "horseplay," "carelessness," "insubordination," and "abusive or threatening language to supervisors." Inexperienced supervisors may ask: What does "carelessness" mean? How do I know when an employee is "insubordinate"? When is an employee guilty of "horseplay"? Although describing all possible occasions of unsatisfactory performance is impossible, upper-line management should work closely with the training staff to ensure that supervisors are trained to recognize and record unsatisfactory performance in difficult areas.

Concrete, indisputable records of unsatisfactory performance are important for three reasons. First, the burden of proof lies with the employer. This practice is derived from common law, which holds that a person is innocent until proven guilty. Second, an employee is more likely to improve his or her behavior if presented with facts about poor performance. Conflicting, disputable data will not motivate an employee to change. Third, if the unionized employee files a grievance indicating that discipline was unjustly administered and the grievance then reaches arbitration, the arbitrator will look very closely at the data management has collected. If performance data are questionable, or are carelessly or sloppily recorded, the award will most likely go to the employee. The employer is required to document that there is just cause for suspending or discharging an employee.

Workplace Searches/Surveillance Employers, increasingly concerned about employee misconduct, loafing, theft, and other workplace discipline problems, are utilizing sophisticated technology to collect information on employees' performance. **Workplace**

searches/surveillance of employee workstations, electronic surveillance of employee telephone calls, and closed-circuit television monitoring of workstations are common examples.
Employees, however, concerned about their
right of privacy, are challenging HR practices
that invade their "right to be let alone." Statutory laws and court decisions have dealt to a
limited extent with the issue of employees'
workplace privacy rights versus the rights of
employers to monitor workplace activities.
The U.S. Supreme Court has indicated that in
the case of workplace searches, employees'
privacy rights are limited to what are normal
employer practices. Thus, what would otherwise constitute an illegal invasion of privacy
may be permissible. For example, if it is common practice for others to open employees'
desks or files to find needed items or information, then employees should not expect the
contents of their desk and files to be private.
Employers may also retain control over lockers, toolboxes, computer files, and the like by
maintaining master keys and access codes.
Furthermore, the Supreme Court has upheld
an employer's right to conduct searches when
there is "reasonable grounds" for suspecting
employee misconduct or to ensure that weapons, drugs, or alcohol are not brought on the
premises. The Court has noted the employer's
need to maintain "the efficient and proper operation of the workplace" in conducting
such searches. Employers who utilize workplace searches are advised by the Society for
Human Resource Management to consider the
following:[8]

- *Written statement.* Publish a policy in an
  employee handbook or other logical format
  stating the search policy and the conditions
  that would instigate a workplace search.

- *Retain access.* Indicate in the policy that
  desks, files, lockers, computer files, and so
  on are subject to search, and retain master
  keys and access codes. Do not permit employee locks.

- *Conduct random searches.* If the stated
  policy includes random searches, then do so
  regularly or lose the right.

- *No wrongdoing.* Clarify that areas and employees included in a search are not accused
  of any wrongdoing.

- *Search process.* Do not allow personnel to
  touch or search an employee during a
  search. Also, do not prevent an employee
  from leaving the premises if it would normally be permitted.

Electronic devices give employers increased
abilities in workplace searches. The use of
closed-circuit television monitoring of workplace activities is generally not limited by law.
Most devices are used for purposes of security
and preventing theft. However, they can be
used to promote employee efficiency by deter-
ring slack periods or loafing. The Omnibus
Crime Control and Safe Streets Act, however,
does prohibit eavesdropping on employee telephone calls with electronic devices. Individuals violating the law can receive a maximum
fine of $250,000 and five years in prison. The
organization may receive a $500,000 fine as
well. Employers can, however, use telephone-
monitoring devices for purposes of training
employees, evaluating their performance, investigating misconduct, or ensuring the quality
of customer service. In practice it may be difficult to separate monitoring for legitimate
business purposes from eavesdropping on personal telephone calls. Employers should consider the following steps if telephone monitoring devices are used:[9]

- *Inform employees.* Provide written notice to
  employees, in advance, that calls will be
  monitored and state the purposes for the
  monitoring.

- *Restrict monitoring.* Use monitoring only
  for business purposes. Provide separate, un-
  monitored lines for personal calls if they are
  allowed.

- *Announce monitoring.* A beep tone or verbal announcement of monitoring is required in some states.

Administer Progressive Discipline Most companies follow a procedure of **progressive discipline**. Two important characteristics of progressive discipline are (1) a penalty commensurate with the offense and (2) a series of increasingly serious penalties for continued unsatisfactory performance. For nonunion firms, progressive discipline is often discussed in the employee handbook; unionized firms normally include a procedure for progressive discipline in the labor–management agreement.

Administer Corrective Counseling The final step in the process of positive discipline is **corrective counseling**. The purpose of positive discipline is to solve an employee's problems rather than simply to administer penalties and punishment. For corrective counseling to be effective, a supervisor must be genuinely interested in helping an employee overcome problems and must offer support, encouragement, and assistance. Each counseling session will differ somewhat, but there are a number of steps common to every corrective-counseling interview.[10] Figure 15–4 lists the steps and gives examples of how a supervisor might handle an employee being disciplined for excessive absenteeism.

One important way that corrective counseling differs from traditional techniques is that a supervisor avoids telling employees how to solve problems. Supervisors tend to tell employees the "right thing to do." With corrective counseling, however, a supervisor helps employees find solutions. Thus, employees are responsible for determining the most effective way to overcome the problem. With greater problem-solving participation by the employee, the chances for a long-lasting improvement in behavior are greatly increased.[11]

Successful Process General Electric implemented positive discipline in one of its plants with the goal of creating an adult-to-adult problem-solving method that focused on supervisory coaching and individual responsibility. The program included supervisory training, discussions with employees to recognize good performance, and nondisciplinary counseling sessions to bring attention to a problem situation and prevent the need to administer formal discipline. Company representatives claim that the program resulted in improved employee morale, greater supervisory confidence, consistency in the administration of discipline, and fewer disciplinary sessions and terminations. For example, 3565 informal counseling sessions were held by supervisors to discuss the performance-improvement needs during the first year of the program. The success of the counseling sessions was indicated by the need to administer the first level of formal discipline in only 90 cases—a success rate of 97.5 percent. The success rate rose to over 98 percent during the second year of the program.[12]

The Hot-Stove Rule

One effective way to approach the disciplinary process is to follow what is popularly known as the **hot-stove rule**, which suggests that applying discipline is much like touching a hot stove:[13]

- The burn is *immediate;* the cause is clearcut.

- The person had a *warning;* knowing that the stove was hot, the person should have known what would happen if it was touched.

- The burn is *consistent;* all who touch the stove are burned every time it is touched.

- The burn is *impersonal;* the stove will burn anyone, regardless of who he or she is.

Like touching a hot stove, the application of discipline should also be immediate, with

FIGURE 15-4 Steps in a corrective counseling interview, using an example concerning excessive absenteeism.

Step 1: Get the Facts Before Counseling

Make sure you understand the attendance policy.

Closely review the employee's attendance behavior.

Have a copy of absenteeism policies at hand, the employee's attendance record, and any other forms or documents that may be necessary.

Step 2: Discuss in Private

Get away from the work area.

Keep phone calls and interruptions at a minimum.

Hold the discussion as soon as possible but at a time convenient to both of you.

Step 3: Put the Employee at Ease, but Get to the Point

Offer the employee a comfortable seat.

Keep cool. Don't show anger or resentment.

Step 4: Describe the Problem, Using Facts

Emphasize the act, not the employee.

State the problems caused by employee absence.

"Good attendance is really important for us to do a good job and produce a quality product. When people don't come to work, all kinds of problems can occur."

"About two weeks ago, we couldn't start the line in binding on the night shift because of absenteeism. It took us over an hour to get people shifted around and get the line going. A lot of employees really got upset because of all the moving around."

"When I have to replace you, that employee just can't do the job as well as you can. Sometimes I have to spend a half hour or so making sure the replacement employee can do the job, and usually I have to check back every couple of hours or so to make sure everything is going OK. I don't have to do that with you."

"When everybody comes in, it makes my job and everybody else's so much easier."

"Our absenteeism policies contain progressive disciplinary actions that relate to the number of absences an employee accumulates. The first step of the system requires that I discuss attendance with an employee who accumulates three occurrences within a twelve-month period."

Be specific—talk numbers and dates.

"Mary, you were absent on Friday, May 25; Monday, July 29; and Wednesday, August 22. Therefore, I must apply the first disciplinary step."

(continued)

warning, consistent, and impersonal. These guidelines are consistent with the positive approach to discipline. Supervisors who follow these guidelines should experience less tension and anxiety when applying discipline and should learn to view discipline as a supervisory responsibility rather than as a personal dilemma.

Immediate Discipline Some supervisors find it easy to procrastinate about discipline:

"I'm busy today. I'll get to it tomorrow." But putting off discipline until a later date often reduces the impact. The greater the time between the offense and the application of discipline, the less likely it is that the employee will see a direct cause-and-effect relationship between the unsatisfactory performance and the discipline.

Discipline should be administered as soon as it has been determined that unsatisfactory behavior has taken place. Of course, the

FIGURE 15-4 continued

State the consequences of continued unsatisfactory performance.
"If an employee accumulates five occurrences within a twelve-month period, he or she is placed on written probation—step 2. Seven and nine occurrences within a consecutive twelve-month period will result in suspension and discharge, respectively."

Step 5: Get Agreement on the Problem
Make sure the employee understands policies and disciplinary system.
Make sure the employee agrees with the facts (even though he or she may not like the facts).
"Do you have any questions concerning the new policies and disciplinary system?"
"Do my records agree with attendance records that you may be keeping?" (If employees do not keep their own attendance records, suggest that they do.)

Step 6: Involve the Employee in Problem Solving
Get ready to listen.
Get the employee to talk about the problem—particularly work problems.
"What can we do to avoid another absence occurrence?"
"Is there any aspect of your work situation that relates to your absenteeism?"
"What can you do to make sure you are at work on time?"
Avoid offering suggestions unless absolutely necessary.
Discuss the problem until you feel the employee reaches a satisfactory solution.

Step 7: Have Employee Sum Up Problem and Solution
"OK, Marvin, now I would like for you to sum up the problem and tell me how you're going to make sure we don't have to go to the next disciplinary step."

State Goal, End in Positive Note
"Mary, as you know, a calendar month of perfect attendance will remove one occurrence. Will you shoot for this?"
"Barry, when you're here, you do a great job. You get along with the other employees, and we value and appreciate your efforts here. But as I mentioned earlier, good attendance is critical, and we need you here every workday. And please keep in mind I'm here to do whatever I can to make your job as satisfying as possible and one which you want to come to every day. If there's a work problem, let's talk about it."
"OK, Pat, unless you have any questions, I'll let you get back to the press."

supervisor must fully investigate any issue that is not clear-cut. For example, a supervisor may issue an oral warning to an employee for a slowdown of production. A complete investigation of the problem, however, may have shown that a machine malfunction was, in fact, responsible for substandard output. In unionized firms, misapplication of discipline may result in the filing of a formal employee grievance. At best, relations between the supervisor and the employee will be cooled. Gathering the facts as soon as possible—and before disciplining—is a good rule of thumb.

Warn Employees An employee who receives unexpected discipline will more than likely raise cries of unfairness and favoritism. Discipline is more likely to be accepted without resentment if the employee has prior knowledge that certain behavior will result in disciplinary action. Thus, the personnel staff and supervisory team are responsible for ensuring that all employees realize that unsatisfactory behavior will result in discipline.

Even though a disciplinary system is detailed in an employee handbook or labor–management contract, good face-to-face communication between the supervisor and the work group is necessary if all employees are to understand the system and how it works. Too frequently, written communications such as an employee handbook are so quickly glossed over that the message may not be fully understood. Through the spoken word, management can make sure that employees know what is expected of them and are aware of the consequences of unsatisfactory behavior.

Consistent Discipline Employees want to be treated fairly and impartially. Feelings of unfairness may result in low morale, absenteeism, turnover, and grievances.[14] To minimize these problems, management must administer discipline consistently, without bias or favoritism. Consistent discipline means the following:

- Every employee who requires discipline receives it.

- Employees who commit the same offense receive the same discipline.

- Discipline is administered in the same way to all employees. That is, the application of positive discipline to one employee and negative discipline to another is avoided.

Consistent application of discipline is not an easy task because personality issues often interfere. Supervisors are human, and thus they may occasionally overlook the unsatisfactory behavior of likable employees and come down hard on those they dislike. Consistency may also require that discipline be administered at an inconvenient time.

Impersonal Discipline One significant drawback of punitive discipline is that an employee often takes personally the harsh, condescending methods that this technique involves. A supervisor barks at an employee, "This is your third warning, Blanche. If you show up for work stinking like a distillery one more time, it's pink-slip city. This isn't skid row, you know." With this approach, even though she may be guilty of the offense,

Blanche is likely to suffer great personal indignity and to harbor resentment and anger. Perhaps worse, the punitive approach does not find ways to overcome the employee's problems.

When discipline is applied impersonally, the supervisor focuses on the act of unsatisfactory behavior, not the employee as a bad person. The most effective way to achieve this goal is to employ corrective counseling. Using this method, the supervisor places less emphasis on why unsatisfactory performance took place than on how the problem can be solved. With tact and maturity, the supervisor applies discipline in a supportive environment, emphasizing the improvement of performance rather than the infliction of punishment.

An important part of corrective discipline is salvaging the unsatisfactory employee.[15] The primary emphasis is on solving the problem rather than getting rid of the employee. Consistent with good personnel management, this approach documents an organization's social responsibility to its human resources. Nonetheless, administrators will occasionally find necessary the ultimate disciplinary action—discharge.

DISCIPLINARY DISCHARGE

A great deal of colorful jargon describes the act of discharge. Employees talk about getting canned, sacked, booted, axed, pink slipped, and so on. Perhaps the most common lament of the discharged employee is "I got fired."

An employee may be *laid off* because a company has severe financial problems or a plant closes. A *disciplinary discharge* occurs, however, when an employee has committed a serious offense, has repeatedly violated rules and regulations, or has shown a consistent inability to meet performance expectations. For example, in many disciplinary systems, the first offense of intoxication at work, insubordination, theft, willful damage to company property, or falsifying work records will result in discharge.

In past decades, discharge was a relatively infrequent personnel action. Most employees leave an employer voluntarily. The majority of employees perform their jobs satisfactorily; only a small percentage may be labeled unsatisfactory performers. Effective administration of corrective discipline successfully prevents many employees from continually performing at unsatisfactory levels. Other factors also keep the disciplinary discharges at a relatively low level. In recent years, however, corporate downsizing, mergers, and increased competition have caused an increased fear of firing (see *HR in the News*) for many U.S. workers.

Any discharge should be carried out fairly and legally. At worst, a botched discharge can lead to a highly publicized, costly lawsuit and significant damage to the firm's reputation. At best, the disgruntled employee will probably bring disrepute to the company whenever the opportunity arises. A great deal has been written about the consequences of poor discharge procedures and what organizations should do to ensure that their discharges are carried out properly.

Defamation in Employment

More than 1 million employees are disciplined and discharged each year. In almost every case, other employees want to know "why" and "what" about a fellow employee's termination. They will ask questions and rumors will spread—spread on fact or fiction.[16] In some cases, the employer will want to publicize the case—either to make a point about strict enforcement of policy or to notify employees of new policies. The press or potential new employers may also ask exactly why an employee was terminated.

Discharged employees, however, have a right to privacy. They may disagree with the discharge decision and are often angry. Their anger can quickly turn into a **defamation** law-suit—which is occurring with greater frequency in the American workplace.[17]

Exactly what constitutes a defamation action? In the broad legal context, such an action must contain four elements:[18]

1. A false communication (a true communication is an absolute defense).
2. An asserted fact regarding the person.
3. A third person who receives the communications.
4. The communication results in harm to the reputation of the person and thus causes the person to be shunned, avoided, hated, ridiculed, or scorned.

In 1990 the U.S. Supreme Court ruling in *Milkovich* v. *Lorain Journal Co.*[19] substantially altered the scope of defamation cases. Prior to this historic decision, courts had often viewed as different cases in which a person expressed an opinion from those in which he or she made statements of fact. Opinion statements were protected under the free speech clause of the First Amendment. Thus a person who stated, "John Jones is a liar" would be viewed differently from one who said, "In my opinion, John Jones is a liar," the first being stated as a fact, the second as an opinion. In *Milkovich,* however, the Supreme Court ruled that "simply prefacing such statements in terms of an opinion does not negate the underlying implications . . . and can cause much damage to [a] reputation." Thus the *Milkovich* decision clearly ended the opinion defense. In employment situations, employers are entitled to receive information about both the achievements and shortcomings of an employee under what is known as a *qualified privilege*—the subject matter was one about which both the person making the statement and the third party receiving it had a legitimate interest in the communication. Thus communications that arise out of normal employer–employee relationships are easily defended under the qualified privilege principle. In such situations, however, an employee may win a defamation case if he or she can prove that the employer exceeded the qualified privilege by making a statement with *malice* (knowledge that the statement was false) or by communicating it to those who had *no need to know the information.*[20]

The most common defamation claims involve publication of the reasons for an employee's termination. Such cases involve company newsletters or bulletin boards; statements to prospective employers, employment agencies, and outplacement firms; and statements to the press. Generally, employers may communicate (under the need-to-know principle) to managers, supervisors, union officials and employees who work in the same unit as the terminated employee. However, employees who do not work in the same unit and other people outside the organization generally do not need to know why an employee was terminated.[21]

Examples of defamation cases include the following:[22]

- Procter & Gamble was forced to pay $15.6 million in damages to an employee it accused of stealing a $35 company telephone. The

713

company posted notices accusing him of the theft on company bulletin boards to make an example of him. The telephone was found to be the personal property of the employee.

- Contel Corporation was ordered by a jury to pay $7.1 million to an employee fired for "morale and turnover problems in meetings and speeches before employees."

- A jury awarded $670,00 to a former employee of Bell Laboratories. The company claimed she had embezzled or misused company funds, and after an internal investigation the employee was fired and the file was turned over to a county prosecutor's office.

- John Hancock Mutual Life Insurance Company was ordered by a jury to pay $26 million to a former employee whose termination was discussed in a company newsletter. The newsletter stated that the employee was under investigation for giving a client bad advice and for "shady dealings," yet neither claim could be substantiated during the trial.[23]

Defamation suits can be quite costly to employers. In addition to the expense of litigation and sizable potential judgments, the employer often suffers significant lost time by employees involved in a case, reduced morale among many employees who follow the suit, and loss of customers due to the bad publicity generated by the case. To minimize the risk of defamation, HR managers should follow the steps listed in Figure 15–5.[24]

Administering the Discharge Decision

Companies approach the problem of unsatisfactory performance in different ways. Many firms do everything they possibly can to avoid firing employees. Other employers have few or no qualms or regrets about firing employees who have toiled for many years with the company or who are middle or top managers. Some administrators think that the best interests of the company and the employee necessitate a direct approach in discharging an employee who has a minimal or nonexistent chance to perform satisfactorily.

Carrying out the discharge decision should involve tact, maturity, and careful planning. The discharge should be administered so that ill feelings between the employee and the company are minimized. As with the administration of any step in a disciplinary procedure, the discharge should be conducted unemotion-

FIGURE 15-5 Steps to minimize defamation exposure.

1. Limit access to personnel information in cases involving discipline and/or discharge. Supervisors should be directed to not give information about such cases to co-workers.

2. The communication or publication about a disciplined or discharged employee should be limited to persons with a legitimate *need to know.* In such instances, such as reference checks or supervisory inquiries, the communication should be factual, confidential, and with no intent to harm.

3. Allegations of misconduct or of rules violations should be thoroughly investigated and the results documented *before* any statement is made. Accused employees should be permitted to explain their actions, confront their accusers, and contest any allegations before findings are made.

4. If a potentially defamatory statement is published, steps should be taken to prevent further dissemination.

5. Ensure that all responses to reference inquiries are made by a centralized, trained respondent usually someone in the HR field.

6. Reference checkers should only be given factual, documented information, on a need-to-know basis.

ally and without vindictiveness, revenge, or malice.[25]

The final alternative to firing is to **dehire** the employee. A dehired employee is encouraged to quit before being fired. For example, at the end of a performance appraisal session, the employee may be told: "The job isn't right for you. . . . Have you considered other employment? I think it would be in your best interests to find employment more suited to your particular skills and abilities. . . . I like you personally, Fred, but the job isn't working out. You might want to use some of your lunch hours to check into other job opportunities around town."

Why dehire rather than fire an employee? Perhaps the primary advantage of dehiring is that the employee saves face by leaving the company before being fired. Avoiding the disgrace and embarrassment of being discharged, the employee does not have to explain a firing to family members, friends, or prospective employers. The superior may even allow the dehired employee to seek other employment on company time.

Employment at Will

Historically, employers have enjoyed the legal right to discharge an employee for any reason, barring a specific statutory restriction (e.g., Civil Rights Act, ADEA), contractual agreement, or just-cause protection afforded the union employee. Over one hundred years ago, a Tennessee court held that an employee could be fired for "good reason, bad reason, or no reason at all," thus giving rise to the doctrine known as termination at will, or **employment at will**.[26]

A serious erosion of the employment-at-will doctrine has occurred in recent years. In particular, two cases in Michigan and California alarmed employers when the courts allowed discharged employees to present evidence of oral promises of lifetime employment made several years earlier. These and other court cases have weakened the at-will doctrine, which has historically recognized a critical principle of the employment relationship—that neither party is locked into a permanent relationship and that both maintain complete freedom to terminate the relationship when it is no longer satisfactory. A primary advantage of the at-will doctrine is that this freedom enables either party to obtain concessions from the other party or change conditions of employment such as pay, benefits, or working conditions.[27]

The courts have generally recognized three different exceptions to the employment-at-will doctrine:

1. *Public policy.* The first exception occurred in 1959 in the *Peterman* v. *International Brotherhood of Teamsters*[28] case. The California Court of Appeal stated that the right to terminate an employee may be limited by statute or by consideration of public policy.[29] The public policy exception generally applies to the following three categories of situations:[30]

   - *Rights granted by statute.* Employees may be protected from termination if exercising their rights provided by law. Examples include reporting for jury duty, refusing a polygraph test as a condition of employment, and filing a workers' compensation claim. Most legal suits in this area center on whether the employee was terminated for other, legitimate reasons.

   - *Refusal to disobey the law.* Employees may be protected if they refused to violate the law when asked by an employer. Examples include ignoring government regulations (such as those of OSHA) or making false statements (such as lying to a government agency).

   - *Whistle-blowing.* Employees may be protected if they were terminated for reporting a wrongdoing to governmental or other authorities. Examples include reporting violations of discrimination laws, wage and hour laws, and OSHA regulations.

Examples of court decisions in at-will cases include the following:[31]

- International Business Machines (IBM) was ordered to pay $300,000 to a sales manager who was dismissed for dating a former IBM salesman who had gone to work for a competing firm (fair dealing).

- Courts in Indiana and Kentucky have determined that it is against public policy to fire an employee for filing a workers' compensation claim.

- A California court decided that an employer's discharge of an employee for refusing to comply with his employer's order to commit perjury before a state legislative committee was wrongful and contrary to public policy.

2. *Implied contract.* If the employer has made oral or written promises of long-term employment, or has promised to follow certain policies or procedures in written statements, employee handbooks, and so on, and these promises were not kept or policies were not followed, the employee may have a serious case. In a case of terminating those policies and procedures were not followed, the employee may have been wrongfully discharged.

   For example, the Supreme Court of Michigan, in a case involving an employee of Blue Cross–Blue Shield of Michigan, held that the employer's personnel manual clause stating that employees would be discharged only for "cause" created an *implied contractual agreement* between the employer and the employee.

3. *Good faith and fair dealing.* Courts in a minority of states have ruled that an implied covenant of good faith and fair dealing exists between an employee and employer. In essence, this exception to the at-will doctrine requires an employer to "treat employees in a fair and reasonable manner," similar to the "just cause" language found in union contracts. Examples of termination that may not be found to be good faith and fair dealing include firing an employee to avoid paying a Christmas bonus or to prevent the employee from reaching a seniority milestone and thus increasing his or her pension.[32]

The Foley Case A landmark at-will case was decided in 1988. The case, *Foley* v. *Interactive Data Corp.*, may restrict the ability of ex-employees in wrongful-discharge suits. In the case, Daniel Foley was a seven-year employee of Interactive Data Corporation (IDC) who had received numerous commendations and promotions. He was fired two weeks after he questioned the hiring of his supervisor, who Foley suspected was an embezzler. Foley informed IDC of an FBI investigation of his superior, and thus claimed he was wrongfully terminated under the public policy doctrine. The court disagreed because "substantial public" interests were not involved, only private ones. The Foley decision clarified several employment-at-will issues for California employers, as well as for those in other states that are likely to follow the *Foley* reasoning:[33]

- Employers cannot be sued by ex-employees for punitive damages (damages awarded by a court as additional punishment). This decision should reduce awards in future cases. However, they can seek loss of income and benefits until comparable employment is found.

- The question of an employer's ability to terminate at will, or only for good cause, should be based on certain evidence, including personnel policies and practices, the employee's longevity of service, the employer's communications regarding continuance of employment, and industry practice.

- Employment relationships essentially are contracts, with the terms created by the parties. Thus, terminated employees may sue for breach of contract if terminated without good cause.

- At-will employees can sue under the public policy doctrine *if* "substantial public" interests are involved (such as in whistle-blowing cases). Punitive damages may be awarded in public policy cases.

Courts are increasingly deciding that employers should fire "for cause"; thus the traditional employment-at-will concept is weakening. The *Foley* decision opened the door to cases that center on an employer's breach of an implied contract. Many employers are changing HR policies and practices to minimize any implied contract. Some of the steps employers are taking to minimize their risk include the following:

- *At-will policy.* Maintain, in writing, a strict at-will policy that states that employees may leave at any time of their own will and that the employer may ask them to leave under the same conditions.[34]

- *At-will statements.* Many employers have added at-will statements to their employment application forms. Applicants are required to sign the statements to be considered for a position. In general, the statements indicate that the applicant, if hired, will be subject to employment at will and may be terminated with or without cause, at any time, with or without notice. However, a survey of statements used by employers indicates that they vary in level of assertion, some being "strong," others "moderate" or "soft" (see Figure 15–6). All three levels of at-will statements provide (1) that *both* the employee and the employer have the right, at any time, to terminate the employment contract; (2) that the employment situation is for no definite period of time; and (3) that the employment is defined to be at will. Most at-will statements were developed on the advice of legal counsel, according to the survey. Many other employers, however, responded that they decided not to require such statements because they "conflicted with the organization's approach to managing its personnel."[35]

- *Standard revision.* State that the at-will standard can only be modified in writing by the CEO of the company.

- *Termination conduct.* List examples of conduct that may result in immediate termination. Specify, however, that the list is not definitive, but only a list of examples.

- *Progressive discipline.* Utilize progressive discipline and document all steps taken. Do not, however, guarantee continued employment until all steps have been exhausted. Reserve the right to discharge an employee without completing all steps.

- *Probationary periods.* Do not establish probationary periods for a specific length of time, such as ninety days, which may guarantee the employee ninety days of work.[36]

- *Employee handbooks.* Employers are revising employee handbooks for the purpose of removing any reference to "just cause," "fairness," "permanent employee," or "job security." The employee-based book is often considered an implied contract; thus, any policies or procedures that are included must be followed by an employer. For example, in *Pine River State Bank* v. *Mettile,* the Minnesota Supreme Court ruled that a four-step disciplinary procedure included in a handbook created a unilateral contract. Therefore when a bank president unilaterally fired an employee due to fifty-seven serious technical errors, he was guilty of breach of contract because the handbook steps were not followed.[37]

The exact legal limitations on an employer's right to employ at-will will probably not be known until Congress or the U.S. Supreme

FIGURE 15-6 Examples of employment-at-will statements.

Strong

I understand that if I am employed by "XYZ" Company that my employment and compensation can be terminated, with or without cause, and with or without notice at any time, at the option of either the company or myself. I also understand that neither this application for employment nor any present or future employee handbook or personnel policy manual is an employment agreement, either expressed or implied, and that no employee or manager of "XYZ" company except the vice-president of human resources has any authority to enter into any agreement for employment for any specified period of time, or to make any agreement contrary to the foregoing.

I understand that my employment and compensation can be terminated with or without cause, and with or without notice, at any time, at the option of either the employer or myself. I further understand that no representative of the employer other than the employer's president has any authority to enter into any agreement for employment for any specified period, or to make any agreement contrary to the foregoing.

Moderate

I understand that my employment is not governed by any written or oral contract and is considered an "at-will" arrangement. This means that I am free, as is the company, to terminate the employment relationship at any time for any reason, so long as there is no violation of applicable federal or state law.

In the event of employment, I understand that my employment is not for any definite period or succession of periods and is considered an "at-will" arrangement. That means I am free to terminate my employment at any time for any reason, as is the company, so long as there is no violation of applicable federal or state law.

Soft

I understand that, if employed, I may end my employment at any time and that the employer has the same right with any employees. I understand my employment is "at-will," as it is not the practice of the company to enter into employment contracts, express or implied.

I understand that no representative of the company is authorized to state or imply that a contract for permanent employment shall exist between the company and me.

SOURCE: Raymond L. Hilgert, "Employers Protected by At-will Statements," *HRMagazine* (March 1991): 57–60. Used by permission.

Court acts on the issue. However, recent court decisions have indicated that employers no longer have unlimited rights. The HR policies that are adopted by an employer provide an implied contractual agreement between the employee and employer. If employers terminate employees without following the prescribed procedure, they may be breaching that contract. It should be remembered, however, that written disciplinary and discharge procedures can strengthen an employer's case when they are followed in the process. Following the *Foley* case, however, it is less likely that wrongly terminated employees will win large punitive damage awards, except in cases involving public policy whistle-blowing, when the courts might award punitive damages because the public at large was wronged.

Whistle-blower The *Foley* decision may provide additional legal support to employees who make public allegations of organizational wrongdoing. Such employees are commonly referred to as **whistle-blowers**. They may be hailed as public saints, or called squealers or informants. Many social trends, which include greater regulation of employees, erosion of employee loyalty, and changing attitudes toward management, may explain the increased occurrence of whistle-blowing[38] (see Figure 15–7).

One of the most famous whistle-blowing cases in U.S. history involved the *Challenger* space shuttle. In 1986 the *Challenger* exploded shortly after its launch, instantly killing all seven astronauts on board. At the president's commission investigation, three engineers from

FIGURE 15–7 Whistle-blowing hotlines.

In 1979 the U.S. General Accounting Office (GAO) established a whistle-blowing hotline (WBH) to combat fraud, waste, and abuse in the federal government. Since that time, many other governmental agencies and a few private organizations have established whistle-blowing hotlines, not only to catch waste and abuse but also to act as a deterrent once employees know it exists. A random survey of certified internal auditors that measured their attitudes toward hotlines generally found that they believe (and have considerable experience in this area) that employee attitudes in organizations that have hotlines are supportive.

WBH: Employee Attitudes

1. Employees will see whistle-blowing hotlines as a positive action designed to help the company avoid waste and fraud.

| Strongly Agree 13% | Agree 41% | Neutral 17% | Disagree 26% | Strongly Disagree 3% |

2. Employees will see whistle-blowing hotlines mainly as a threat.

| Strongly Agree 5% | Agree 24% | Neutral 23% | Disagree 42% | Strongly Disagree 5% |

3. Employee reactions to a whistle-blowing hotline will depend on the manner in which it is implemented.

| Strongly Agree 40% | Agree 50% | Neutral 8% | Disagree 2% | Strongly Disagree 0% |

4. Whistle-blowing hotlines cause more harm than good in terms of lower employee morale, etc.

| Strongly Agree 3% | Agree 12% | Neutral 34% | Disagree 39% | Strongly Disagree 12% |

5. Whistle-blowing hotlines will cause employees to adopt a defensive style which will reduce innovation.

| Strongly Agree 1% | Agree 17% | Neutral 25% | Disagree 46% | Strongly Disagree 11% |

6. Employees will most often use whistle-blowing hotlines in an unethical manner, e.g., file a dishonest complaint against a co-worker for whom they have a grudge.

| Strongly Agree 2% | Agree 15% | Neutral 24% | Disagree 51% | Strongly Disagree 8% |

7. Most employees are unable to correctly identify waste and fraud, and therefore, will cause many "wild-goose chases."

| Strongly Agree 3% | Agree 25% | Neutral 26% | Disagree 37% | Strongly Disagree 9% |

8 In general whistle-blowing hotlines have more advantages than disadvantages.

| Strongly Agree 15% | Agree 45% | Neutral 24% | Disagree 14% | Strongly Disagree 2% |

SOURCE: Dale L. Flesher and Thomas E. Buttross, "Whistle-blowing Hotlines," *Internal Auditor* (August 1992): 54–58.

Morton Thiokol, Inc., the aerospace company that had developed the rocket's boosters, testified that they had warned that cold temperatures below 53°F—might cause the O-rings to stiffen and render them unable to seal the gases properly. The temperature on the day of the *Challenger* launch was 18°F. Initially, Thiokol's management would not approve a launch below 53°F, but they gave in to pressure from the National Aeronautics and Space Administration (NASA) after the launch had been postponed four times. The engineer who revealed the facts at the investigation was Roger Boisjoly. Boisjoly was later assigned to work on the redesign of the booster seal. But after a few weeks, he was left out of meetings and finally lost his job. Despite a twenty-seven-year career in the industry, he could not find similar work. At later federal investigations, Thiokol President Edwin Garrison testified that he had given an official order to isolate Boisjoly to minimize friction with NASA. This case and others led to passage of the 1989 Whistle-blower Protection Act, but it covers only federal employees.[39]

Should whistle-blowers be protected from retaliation? Most cases concerning whistle-blowers involve an employee who contacts a government agency and provides information essential to protecting the public. Instances such as an employer fixing gasoline prices, delivering stale milk, and manipulating pollution reports are only a few examples of the kind of information provided. Some federal statutes already provide antiretaliation provisions, including the National Labor Relations Act in cases involving union activity and Title VII of the Civil Rights Act in cases involving discrimination.[40] In a landmark decision, the U.S. Supreme Court in *Brock* v. *Roadway Express, Inc.* recognized the interests of a whistle-blower.

In the case, a trucking company employee was discharged for intentionally disabling his truck's lighting system in order to receive additional breakdown pay. He was immediately discharged for dishonesty under the collective bargaining agreement. The driver contended, however, that the discharge was in retaliation for the numerous safety violation complaints he had made against the company. The Supreme Court agreed that the employee was entitled to protection against retaliation under the 1982 Surface Transportation Assistance Act.[41] While most employees do not fall under this federal law, they can receive some protection from the public policy exemption under the *Foley* decision. The extent to which the public policy doctrine covers all cases involving whistle-blowers is not clear, and certainly not all cases that might be in the public's interest are included.

Organization may desire to create a climate in which employees will blow the whistle on fraudulent behavior. They may believe that such an environment would minimize abuses, waste, and fraudulent practices. Normally, employees assume a "don't rock the boat" posture; thus, organizations that want employees to report wrongdoing, either internally or externally, need to develop and communicate clear policies. Research indicates five factors that would encourage an employee to blow the whistle:[42]

- Organizational encouragement and formal channels to report wrongdoing.
- Personal belief that it is a proper action.
- A graduate degree.
- Lack of fear of retaliation.
- Union environment.

Outside Misconduct

When an employer learns that an employee has been involved in a crime outside the workplace, it may be faced with a difficult decision. If the employee is fired, the employer may face a legal suit involving wrongful discharge, discrimination, or defamation—and may lose. However, if no action is taken and the employee commits a wrongful act against a customer or co-worker, the employer may face a legal suit for negligent inaction. Thus, such situations must be handled carefully. The first factor to consider in such a case is whether it is an arrest or a conviction. If an employee is arrested and jailed, he or she can be put on a leave of absence until the outcome is known. If the employee is arrested but is not jailed, the employer may allow the employee to return to work until the issue is resolved. The logical exceptions to this policy involve employees accused of assault, child abuse, rape, or other serious crimes of violence where the effect on co-workers must be considered. Thus, the employee may be put on leave until the case is settled. Once a case is settled, before deciding on a disciplinary action or discharge, the employer should consider several factors:[43]

1. ***The relationship between the job and the misconduct.*** This is probably the most critical factor. Many employers would be on shaky grounds for firing an employee for drunken and disorderly conduct or off-duty use of marijuana, while termination for a crime of violence would usually be on firm ground.

2. ***Tenure.*** A twenty-year veteran may be given a second chance if a lesser crime was committed, while a new hire might be terminated.

3. ***Public interaction.*** Employees who must work with the public—on the employer's premises or elsewhere—can be dismissed if they have committed a crime that indicates that their continued employment might endanger the public or affect the employer's ability to operate the business effectively.

Before finalizing a decision in such a case, the employer should make sure that the decision is consistent with the way others were treated in the past. In addition, the employer should consider that if what occurred outside the workplace has no relationship to the job, then it probably should not be the basis for a disciplinary action.

CONCLUSIONS AND APPLICATIONS

- Many reasons may cause an employee to perform unsatisfactorily. Some of these reasons may be directly attributable to management's shortcomings or to some other problem of the organization. When attempting to determine the cause of poor employee performance, managers should recognize that the employee may not be responsible for the unsatisfactory behavior.

- Discipline should be applied only when it has been determined that the employee is the cause of the unsatisfactory performance. There are different approaches to the disciplinary process; the most effective technique involves administration of *preventive* discipline. If discipline must be administered, the *positive* approach should be used.

- Corrective counseling is a particularly important part of the positive discipline process. It helps build respect and trust between the supervisor and subordinate and encourages the employee to find his or her own solutions to problems. The more the employee participates in the problem-solving process, the greater the chances for a permanent improvement in employee behavior.

- Much of the supervisory resistance to change can be reduced by training supervisors to follow the hot-stove rule. With this technique, discipline is administered immediately, with a warning, consistently, and impersonally. HR managers must ensure that supervisory training programs provide instruction in applying each of the hot-stove rules.

- Discharge can be traumatic and costly for both the dismissed employee and the organization. The discharge should be thoroughly planned and carried out in a professional manner. It is particularly important that the employee be given complete details regarding the discharge, including why it is taking place and how the discharge is to be carried out.

- The doctrine of employment-at-will has eroded considerably in recent years because court decisions have supported employees' claims of unfair and unjust treatment. HR rules, policies, and procedures must be closely examined to ensure that they comply with federal and state laws.

- International managers struggle with the problem of finding good personnel, but a tougher problem is getting rid of employees who do not work out. From Switzerland to Mexico to Indonesia, the unsentimental American "hire and fire" habit seems unnaturally brutal to foreign employees. Foreign personnel are usually more firmly attached to their company and are used to being protected during their working lives. Firing is never abrupt or taken lightly.

- Employees who are disciplined or terminated may file defamation suits against their former employers. HR policies should limit the communication of such actions and only provide information that is factual, on a confidential basis, to those who have a true need to know.

CASE STUDY

Defamation Claim at Milbrae Window Co.

Alexis Rojas was terminated by her supervisor, Colleen Wilson, on Friday, December 23, at 4:30 P.M. She was just putting on her coat when Wilson asked her to step into the office of President Synhorst. She was given no explanation. Rojas had been employed by the Milbrae Window Company for twelve years as an outside sales representative. She had won the company's highest annual sales award in four of the last six years and was generally considered one of the most loyal employees. Thus her abrupt termination came as a shock to her and everyone else. She drove home in a daze but decided to telephone her best friends, Shari Mendoza and Juan Esta-ban, as soon as possible to ask if they knew what had caused her dismissal. Neither of the two had heard a word from anyone and were as puzzled as Rojas.

President Synhorst had made the decision to terminate Rojas on Thursday after receiving substantial evidence from local law enforcement officials and two representatives of major clients that Rojas had accepted kickbacks on large sales orders. Synhorst's attorney recommended the immediate dismissal.

By Monday all of the 300 employees at Milbrae Window Company had heard of the termination. Many were angry and demanded an explanation, but Synhorst refused to comment. Then at 1:00 P.M. almost all of the production and sales employees refused to leave the cafeteria and return to work until Synhorst answered their questions. They began talking about unionizing. Synhorst decided that the situation could become violent and would at least cause major morale problems for several days, and thus walked to the cafeteria at about 1:50 P.M. The employees demanded an explanation, and the following exchange occurred:

Synhorst: Ms. Rojas was terminated for just cause.

Mendoza: And what was the cause?

Synhorst: I can't say.

Mendoza: Why wasn't even Rojas given a reason?

Synhorst: She knows why . . .

Estaban: She says she doesn't!

Synhorst: She knows.

Estaban: She has been a good friend to many of us for years, and she was a good employee. She says she has *no* idea why she was let go . . . and we believe her!

Mendoza: We demand an explanation; is this a racial thing?

Synhorst: (pause) No, she was let go because she took kickbacks, pure and simple. Now get back to work or I'll start docking your pay!

QUESTIONS

1. Rojas, after hearing what occurred, is considering suing Synhorst for defamation. Do you think she has a case? Explain.

2. Would you change your answer to the first question if you knew she was guilty of accepting kickbacks?

3. What could Synhorst have done to possibly avoid the confrontation with the employees?

4. If Rojas was guilty, should she have been terminated for a first offense or given a different disciplinary action?

EXPERIENTIAL EXERCISES

1. Counseling the Troubled Employee

PURPOSE

To show the importance of using correct counseling techniques with the troubled employees.

INTRODUCTION

Disciplining and counseling the troubled employee—the employee who suffers from a personal problem such as alcoholism to the extent that he or she is unable to perform effectively—presents a special challenge to supervisors.

For example, it is not appropriate for the supervisor to discuss drinking or a suspicion of drinking because diagnosis is the job of trained professionals. What is the job of the supervisor?

The supervisor's job is to focus on *job performance* during counseling. The supervisor should confront the employee with specific performance problems in an attempt to motivate the employee to seek treatment and rehabilitation. The supervisor will only aggravate the problem by accusing the employee of having a personal problem such as alcoholism, drug abuse, or emotional instability. In addition, it is the supervisor's job to make it clear to the employee what will happen if the unsatisfactory performance continues. Usually, that means discipline, including the possibility of discharge.

The theory behind this method is simple: if the employee's job is on the line, he or she will likely seek treatment rather than face being fired.

THE TASK

Listed below are several statements that a supervisor made to an employee suspected of excessive drinking. These are actual statements that have been collected anonymously from employees through surveys. Your job is to evaluate the supervisor's statements and, if necessary, to write what the supervisor should have said. After you have completed the exercise, your instructor will lead a discussion on discipline and the troubled employee.

Effective counseling depends very much on saying the right thing to the employee who is suspected of being troubled. Saying the wrong thing will do little to motivate the employee to overcome the problem and could well make matters worse.

Kim, the supervisor of a large group of computer personnel, suspects that Skip, a computer operator, is suffering from alcoholism. At one time, Skip was an excellent employee, but he has recently begun to perform erratically and demonstrates behavioral problems. For example, Skip has made many errors in operating the computer and has experienced several interpersonal problems with Kim and other co-workers. Kim has just begun to talk to Skip in her office. All of Kim's statements are poor and represent the use of improper counseling techniques. Your job is to decide what Kim should have said.

What Kim Said

1. "Skip, I've really been troubled by your performance lately. You've made a lot of computer errors and you haven't gotten along well with the other employees."
2. "Skip, I strongly suspect that problems stem from excessive drinking. It's no secret that you've had drinking problems for some time."
3. "If your performance does not improve, you'll be digging your own grave."

4. (With a heated voice) "Don't disagree with me, Skip. I can back up everything I say. Like it or not, these are the facts."
5. "I have decided that the best thing for you to do is attend AA meetings once a week until your problem clears up."

What Kim Should Have Said

_____
_____
_____

_____
_____
_____

_____
_____
_____
_____
_____
_____
_____
_____

What Kim Said:

6. "The company has special programs available for alcoholic employees."

7. "I heard you were drinking in the men's room this morning. Is that true?"

8. "Look, don't disagree with me. You've got a drinking problem and you know it. All the facts point to it."
9. "You have a real attendance problem and I think I know why. You're on some kind of drug, aren't you? Aren't those needle marks on your arms?"
10. "I know what your problem is, but don't worry; we're not going to fire you if you attend the special program the personnel department has for alcoholics."

What Kim Should Have Said

_____
_____
_____
_____
_____
_____
_____
_____
_____
_____
_____
_____
_____
_____
_____

SOURCE: Adapted from F. Kuzmits, R. Herden, and L. Sussman, *Managing the Unsatisfactory Employee* (Homewood, IL: Dow Jones-Irwin, 1984), pp. 82–83.

2. Cause for Termination?

PURPOSE

An employee's right to privacy outside the workplace is generally protected by law in the United States. However, when an employee's outside activity makes the news, the employer is faced with a difficult decision. In some cases, an employee's criminal activity outside the workplace warrants suspension or termination. In others it may not affect their job at all, and thus no disciplinary action is warranted.

THE TASK

You are the HR director for a 2000-employee retail sales organization. In each of the situations described below, you must choose one of five courses of action: (1) termination; (2) temporary suspension; (3) written warning; (4) notify the employee that he or she is not allowed to return to work (without pay) until the issue is resolved; (5) no disciplinary action.

Situation

1. A sales clerk is convicted of sexually molesting a child.
2. A supervisor is arrested for theft while working on a second job.

Course of Action

1._____
_____
2._____
_____

3. A janitor is one of fifty-six people arrested in a political demonstration.

3. _____

4. A sales supervisor is convicted of tax evasion.

4. _____

5. A window dresser is convicted of drunk driving.

5. _____

6. A maintenance person is arrested in a massage parlor.

6. _____

7. A shift supervisor is given a three-day jail sentence for failing to pay child support.

7. _____

8. A security guard is convicted on charges of grand auto theft.

8. _____

9. A computer technician is arrested in a bar fight.

9. _____

10. A stock clerk is convicted of assaulting a neighbor.

10. _____

KEY TERMS AND CONCEPTS

Corrective counseling
Defamation
Dehire
Employment-at-will
Hot-stove rule
Outside misconduct

Positive discipline
Preventive discipline
Progressive discipline
Punitive discipline
Whistle-blowers
Workplace searches/surveillance

REVIEW QUESTIONS

1. What are the four general causes of unsatisfactory employee performance?

2. Compare and contrast punitive, preventive, and positive discipline.

3. What are the steps involved in the process of positive discipline?

4. How can an employer legally and fairly utilize workplace searches or surveillance of employees?

5. How can employers avoid defamation claims?

6. What is the concept of employment at will, and how can organizations avoid legal problems involving this doctrine?

7. When should an employee be disciplined for actions outside the workplace?

DISCUSSION QUESTIONS

1. In the past, supervisors often used punitive discipline against their employees. What reasons might account for this?

2. With corrective counseling, the supervisor encourages the employee to find solutions to his or her problems. Why might this method be more effective than having the supervisor tell employees how to solve their problems?

3. Assume that you were recently appointed to the job of HR director for a small bank. How would you communicate the company's rules and regulations to employees?

4. If an employee shows up at work intoxicated, what action should the supervisor take? Should the supervisor counsel the employee about the evils of drinking?

5. An employee has repeatedly caused problems with peers and has flaunted his disobeying of work rules until he is terminated through a progressive discipline system. Should the other employees be made aware of this?

6. As HR director you read in the morning newspaper that one of your 20-year employees was arrested for mail fraud. What should you do?

ENDNOTES

Chapter 15

1. Abstracted from F. Kuzmits, R. Herden, and L. Sussman, *Managing the Unsatisfactory Employee* (Homewood, IL: Dow Jones-Irwin, 1984). For a description of other modes of unsatisfactory performance, see D. Laird, *Approaches to Training and Development* (Reading, MA: Addison-Wesley, 1978); R. Mager and P. Pipe, *Analyzing Performance Problems* (Belmont, CA: Pitman Learning, 1970); L. Steinmetz, *Managing the Marginal and Unsatisfactory Performer* (Reading, MA: Addison-Wesley, 1969); and N. F. Elbert and R. Discenza, *Contemporary Supervision* (New York: Random House, 1985).

2. See D. Cameron, "The When, Why, and How of Discipline," *Personnel Journal* 63 (July 1984): 37–39.

3. I. Asherman, "The Corrective Discipline Process," *Personnel Journal* 61 (July 1982): 528–31.

4. Cameron, "The When, Why, and How of Discipline," p. 38. See also J. Belohlav, *The Art of Disciplining Your Employees: A Manager's Guide* (Englewood Cliffs, NJ: Prentice-Hall, 1985).

5. *Employee Conduct and Discipline* (Washington, DC: Bureau of National Affairs, 1973), p. 4.

6. *Employee Discipline and Discharge* (Washington, DC: Bureau of National Affairs, 1985), p. 4.

7. See I. Asherman and S. Vance, "Documentation: A Tool for Effective Management," *Personnel Journal* 60 (August 1981): 641–43.

8. Georgeanna Henshaw and Kernwood C. Youmans, "Employee Privacy in the Workplace and an Employer's Right to Conduct Workplace Searches and Surveillance," SHRM *Legal Report* (Spring 1990): 1–5.

9. Ibid.

10. See H. Le Van, N. Mathys, and D. Drehmer, "A Look at Counseling Practices of Major U.S. Corporations," *Personnel Administrator* 27 (June 1982): 143–46; and P. C. Cairo, "Counseling in Industry: A Selected Review of the Literature," *Personnel Psychology* 36 (March 1983): 1–18.

11. Steinmetz, *Managing the Marginal and Unsatisfactory Performer*, p. 83.

12. A. Bryant, "Replacing Punitive Discipline with a Positive Approach," *Personnel Administrator* 10 (February 1984): 79–87.

13. The originator of the popular hot-stove role remains a mystery, though many ascribe this simple but meaningful axiom to Douglas McGregor, author of the classic management book, *The Human Side of Enterprise*.

14. J. E. Dittrich and M. R. Carrell, "Organizational Equity Perceptions, Employee Job Satisfaction, and Departmental Absence and Turnover Rates," *Organizational Behavior and Human Performance* 24 (April 1979): 29–40.

15. See Steinmetz, *Managing the Marginal and Unsatisfactory Performer*, chap. 5.

16. Marty Denis and Jon Andes, "Defamation—Do You Tell Employees Why a Coworker Was Discharged?" *Employee Relations Law Journal* 16, no. 4 (Spring 1991): 469–79.

17. Ibid.

18. Robert S Soderstrom and James R. Murray, "Defamation in Employment: Suits by "At-Will" Employees," *FICC Quarterly* (Summer 1992): 395–426.

19. *Milkovich* v. *Lorain Journal Co.*, 110 S. Ct. 2695, 111 L. Ed. 2d. 1(1990).

20. Soderstrom and Murray, "Defamation in Employment," p. 399.

21. Ibid., p. 410.

22. Gabriella Stern, "Companies Discover That Some Firings Backfire into Costly Defamation Suits," *The Wall Street Journal* (May 5, 1993): B1.

23. Soderstrom and Murray, "Defamation in Employment," p. 395.

24. Ibid., pp. 424–25.

25. R. F. Westcott, "How to Fire an Executive," *Business Horizons* (April 1976): 34–36.

26. *Payne* v. *Western Atlantic R.R.*, 81 Tenn. 507, 519–20 (1884).

27. Frank Vickory, "The Erosion of the Employment-at-Will Doctrine and the Statute of Frauds: Time to Amend the Statute," *American Business Law Journal* 30 (May 1992): 97–104.

28. 344 P. 2d 25 (Cal. App. 2d Dist. 1959).

29. Stephen M. Reilly, "What Employers Can Do to Correct Imbalance in Employment Contracts," *Defense Counsel Journal* (July 1992): 341–43.

30. Cheryl S. Massingale *At-Will Employment: Going, Going . . .* 24 *University of Richmond Law Review* (June 1990): 187–91.

31. Mark J. Keppler, "Halting Traffic on the Road to Wrongful Discharge," *Personnel* 69, no. 3 (March 1990): 49.

32. Alan B. Krueger, "The Evolution of Unjust-Dismissal Legislation in the United States," *Industrial and Labor Relations Review* 44, no. 4 (July 1991): 644–49.

33. Bill Gore, Douglas A. Kahn, and Stan Shields, "Hiring Ruled Contractual," *Personnel Journal* 68, no. 4 (April 1989): 94–100.

34. Debbie Keary, "Minimize the Risk of Wrongful Discharge," *HR News* (June 1990): 7.

35. Raymond L. Hilgert, "Employers Protected by At-Will Statements," *HRMagazine* (March 1991): 57–60.

36. Keary, "Minimize the Risk of Wrongful Discharge," p. 7.

37. J. D. Cuombe, "Employee Handbooks: Asset or Liability?" *Employee Relations Law Journal* 12 (January 1987): 6–9.

38. John L. Howard, "Current Development in Whistleblower Protection," *Labor Law Journal* 39, no. 2 (February 1988): 67–80.

39. Karen Fitzgerald, "Whistleblowing: Not Always a Losing Game," *IEEE Spectrum* (December 1990): 49–52.

40. Howard, "Whistleblower Protection," pp. 67–80.

41. *Brock* v. *Roadway Express, Inc.*, U.S. 107, S.Ct. 1740 (1987).

42. "Whistle-blowing: Positive or Negative?," *The CPA Journal* (March 1993): 6–7.

43. Steve Bergsman, "Employee Conduct Outside the Workplace," *HRMagazine* (March 1991): 62–64.

PART **VI**

SPECIAL ISSUES

CHAPTER **16**

COMPUTERS, HRISs, AND THE HR DEPARTMENT

CHAPTER OBJECTIVES

1. To trace the evolution of computers in personnel from payroll to human resource information systems (HRIS).

2. To describe the components of a computerized HRIS.

3. To describe the value of an HRIS.

4. To define what the HR staff and others should know about computers.

5. To discuss the important issues in selecting and implementing an HRIS.

6. To identify the categories of computer applications in the HR department.

This chapter discusses the various uses of computers to assist the HR functions. Virtually all employers are using computers to help them in at least some manner. In the 1990s, a small business may own one personal computer (PC), while a global corporate headquarters probably uses a mix of mainframes, local area networks (LANs), and PCs.

Still, there has been a range of use of computerization in HR departments, from those who have not yet "touched keys" to those for whom an HRIS is indispensable. This chapter will explore the possibilities that a **human resource information system (HRIS)** can offer not only to the HR department itself, but to the operation of the entire organization. The strategic role of HRIS emphasizes the increasing importance of HR functions in overall corporate strategy.

History of HR Computerization

From Payroll to HRIS

Usually one of the last areas automated, HR has lagged behind applications in other functions such as accounting, manufacturing, and financial planning. The uneven progress of computers in HR has resulted from the rapid change in technology and the changing role of the HR department.[1]

It was payroll that gave birth to the first personnel data base and, ultimately, to the modern HRIS. It was a long, roundabout process.

Basic payroll information such as name, salary, date of birth, sex, and department code were available to the personnel department for analysis. Business computer languages, COBOL in particular, made possible new accounting application programs that analyzed employee records.

Perhaps the first nonpayroll personnel system appeared in the defense industry. In this system, inventories of skills were compiled—on tapes and cards—and used for bidding on government contracts. Despite the potential benefits, however, the use of computers in HR continued to be the exception rather than the rule. There were too many drawbacks, high costs being the most serious.

Only the bigger companies could afford the luxury of a mainframe computer, along with the frequent downtime for computer maintenance and repairs. Computer technology was so unreliable during its early days that many companies maintained dual systems—manual and automated.

Packaged software was almost nonexistent, which meant that programs had to be written in-house, using sometimes inflexible early computer languages that were difficult to learn and even more difficult to apply.

Programmers were often recruited with backgrounds in engineering and research science. Their interests reflected their backgrounds and their nickname—*number crunchers*. The organization's HR needs, if not ignored, were treated with benign neglect.

What seemed like a sensible idea—tying all the management systems together and cutting

Westin Saves $100,000
with New HRIS

Westin has over 10,000 employees and operates some thirty-five hotels and resorts across the United States. So many different departments had to be contacted each time an employee received a promotion that the opportunity for errors was great. The corporate payroll department had to adjust the pay, the benefits department had to adjust salary-based benefits (life insurance, pension, etc.), the HR records department had to update the personnel files, the compensation department needed to update the data base for compensation analysis, and all personnel changes had to be recorded in general corporate databases.[2]

To add to the confusion, some departments operated on weekly reporting systems, but others reported monthly or semimonthly. It was difficult to reconcile vital records because of the time frame inconsistencies.

In 1989 Westin decided that it would not continue accepting the data and cost inconsistencies. The HRIS manager of Westin, Laura Martin, says, "We were doing the exact opposite of our mission, which is to provide efficient, high-quality, cost-effective service to our hotels."[3]

In 1990 Westin began to implement an HRIS system to integrate the payroll, benefits, HR, and compensation functions. After one year, Westin saved more than $100,000 through the elimination of outside payroll processing fees and the reduction of seven full-time staff positions.

"Although those different departments are still in operation and are accountable to different divisions, today they're able to share one centralized data base," according to Martin.[4]

Selecting the right HRIS package and centralizing the source of data that is used throughout the organization are key components to success stories like Westin's.

---

down on redundancy—seldom moved beyond the planning stage. The idea of the **management information system (MIS)** as a single, completely integrated supersystem, was popular during the late 1960s and early 1970s. But it was an idea whose time had not yet come. It was simply too complicated, given the existing technology, to design one system that could satisfy the variety of organizational needs.

This situation began to change when, in the 1970s, governmental regulatory acts, such as EEO, OSHA, ERISA, and COBRA, required almost every company—large and small, profit and nonprofit—to compile hundreds of statistics on employees and to submit elaborate quarterly and annual reports.

The **microcomputer's** introduction moved control of information systems from data processing to any department that could afford the cost (less than $5000). User-friendly **software** has made the micro easy to master. One personnel computer application soon led to another. Combined with new technology, abundant and affordable software, and lower costs, the microcomputer heralded the coming of the HRIS.

Trend to End-User Independence

While there is resistance from some in MIS departments, the progress in **information technology (IT)** is away from the original model of MIS operations in organizations. With the introduction of inexpensive **personal computers (PCs)** in the 1980s, many non-MIS department employees became computer literate, and at the same time software became user-friendly. These three changes (cost, expertise, and software evolution) combined with the increasing demands for information in motivating employers to take the next step in information systems.

Research indicates that by the end of the 1980s, *users* rather than MIS experts were doing much of their own systems development work.[5] One of the obvious changes that end-user independence precipitates is decentralization of the information system function. The role of MIS is maturing into that of coordination rather than total control. In the 1990s, the increased power of PCs has made it possible for computer-literate employees to use dynamic software to produce extremely sophisticated research and reports. State governments report a continuing increase in the number of PCs used in their organizations, virtually doubling every year since 1984. The proportion of their small computer systems also rose consistently throughout the last decade.[6] Mainframes are still being demanded, however, sparked by the expansion of departmental networks.

Other reasons for the increased demand for end-user independence is due to organizational factors. One study indicates that 75 percent of IT users cited "unsatisfactory performance" by MIS as their top reason for acquiring their own systems.[7] Access and flexibility are additional reasons for users to obtain their own systems.

What Is HRIS?

While some HR professionals are still only beginning to use HRIS as a management decision tool, many have become sophisticated and creative in HRIS use.

HRIS is defined as a computer-based method for collecting, storing, maintaining, retrieving, and validating HR data.[8] More than just a system for preparing standard reports, an HRIS is typically designed and structured to permit the retrieval of user-defined ad hoc reports, comparative analyses, and employee (or applicant) data items.

In addition to employee and applicant information, the HRIS data base contains organizational and job-related data. The creation of the **data base** may be the most important step in implementing the system.[9] Figure 16-1 shows the components of a comprehensive HRIS data base and the organizational concerns it can be used to address.

Large, full-function HRISs can range from $100,000 to $500,000 and track compensation, payroll, benefits, insurance policies, career paths, and employee histories. Many also offer fast ad hoc report generation, background batch operation, platform portability, and customization possibilities.[10] PC versions are currently decreasing the cost and therefore increasing the availability of HRIS to even the smallest employers. This author has seen single-function payroll software packages for $25!

One obvious benefit of having a comprehensive data base is the capacity to answer questions like "what," "how much," and "when." Typically, HRIS accomplishes this function by drawing on standard reports, for instance, salary reviews due next month, EEO-1 reports, work force analysis, or tickler memos.

But the real benefit of an HRIS is that it is a system that goes beyond the "what" questions and uses the computer to answer the "whys" and "what ifs." Sophisticated HRIS systems often include integrated word processing,

FIGURE 16-1 HRIS Data Base Illustration.

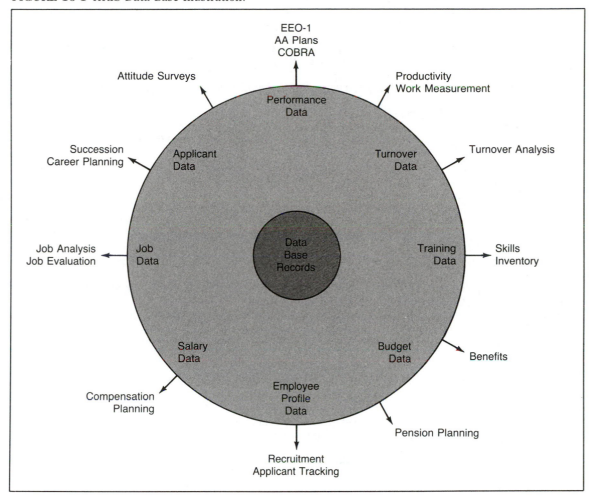

spreadsheet, and data manipulation packages enabling the user to design custom reports.

BASIC COMPUTER INFORMATION

What is often called a **computer** is actually a computer system that includes **hardware**, **software**, a **central processing unit (CPU)**, **peripheral devices** (printer, scanners, disk drives, etc.), and people.[11] The CPU is the brain and is designed to control the interpretation and execution of instructions. It causes data to be read, stored, written, or otherwise processed.[12] Basic computer terminology is provided in Figure 16-2.

The arrangement and speed of the various pieces of equipment that make up the CPU can be grouped into three categories. The largest and most expensive computer configuration is called a **mainframe**. Originally, this term referred to the elaborate array of large rack

FIGURE 16-2 Talking computerese—defining some computer terminology.

Anyone using HRIS or MIS information should be familiar with many of these terms.

Applications software These are the programs which enable the computer to perform particular applied tasks—spreadsheets, word processing, presentational graphics, etc. Software can be developed or purchased commercially.

Artificial intelligence Programming and hardware combined to mimic human intelligence, learning, and decision making.

Backup A copy of information, either on magnetic tape or diskettes, used to protect data.

Baud rate A measure of the speed at which computers can send from one to another through a transmission line (eg., a telephone line via a modem). Speeds may range from 2,400 to 19,200 baud (bits of data per second).

Bit The smallest unit of computer data—one binary digit—recorded as either a 0 or a 1 by the computer.

Byte One byte equals eight bits of data. A single number of letter requires one byte.

CD-ROM Compact disk read-only-media. A laser disk, similar to a music CD, can hold billions of bytes of information. One CD can hold the information contained in an entire encyclopedia. Information on the CD cannot be altered or added by the user.

CAD Computer aided design. Engineers and architects use CAD graphical software packages to design parts, products, and plans in three dimensions.

Chips Electronic circuits in silicon which process or store data. These tiny circuits are found in all "intelligent" electronics.

CPU Central processing unit. The CPU is the brains of the computer, and determines it's processing speed. In a PC the CPU and the microprocessor are the same.

CRT Cathode ray tube. The CRT is the video display hardware—also called a monitor, or VDT (video display terminal).

Data base A collection of information/data which is stored so that it can be retrieved and processed by users. HRIS data bases would include data which can be thought of as personnel file information on all employees.

Disks A hard disk is permanently installed as a drive in the computer. It stores information and allows retrieval. Floppy disks, either at 5¼-inch or 3½-inch size, allow data to be moved from one computer to another.

Download Taking information from a central computer and bringing it into a smaller computer.

Gigaflop One billion instructions or calculations per second. Used to measure the speed of powerful supercomputers.

Hardware The computer and peripherals (printers, modems, monitors, etc.). Everything except the software.

Heat seekers People who feel they need the latest and most powerful computer equipment available.

and panel cabinets that held thousands of vacuum tubes in the early computers.[13] A mainframe will typically serve as the hub of a big company's information systems. The second category of computers is called a **minicomputer** (mini). Although minicomputers may lack the capacity of a mainframe, their particular ability to handle networks and other simultaneous user arrangements at a lower cost, still make them attractive. **Local area networks (LANs),** where many computer stations share the same minicomputer, software, and peripherals simultaneously, have become common in many organizations. However, students should note that LANs can be driven by mainframes or minis as **file servers,** or by PCs as "peer to peer," depending on the applications needed.

FIGURE 16-2 continued

HRIS Human resources information system. These systems are designed to accomplish all the informational needs of an HR department—affirmative action, compensation, planning, etc. Many HRIS programs are available commercially.

Icons Stamp-sized pictures which are used in Windows and Apple program manager screens to represent programs, files, or commands. Icons are an attempt to make switching between software and using programs more intuitive.

ISDN Integrated services digital network. An international telecommunication standard that allows transmissions of voice, video, and data simultaneously.

LAN Local area network. Software that controls the traffic of computers and networks within an office, or building. Users linked into the LAN through hardware and software can share a data base, printer, or other peripherals to create an efficient use of resources.

Megabyte (MB) A unit which quantifies how much information can be stored in RAM or a disk. One meg (megabyte) is approximately one million bytes (exactly 1,048,576 bytes).

Memory The computer's working storage area, which is made up of RAM chips, and disk space. The larger the memory, the more information can be stored and the larger the program which can be run on the computer.

Menus Pull-down or pop-up lists that show options available to the user of a program, used to make the program more user-friendly.

Microcomputer Another name for a PC.

Microprocessor The logic, mathematic, and control functions contained in one chip in PCs, and multiple chips in minicomputers and mainframes.

Minicomputers More powerful computers than PCs since their CPU uses more than one chip.

MIPS One million instructions per second. Pentium chips run at about 100 MIPS.

Modem Hardware which uses software for linking a PC on to a telephone line, to access another computer system/network.

Mouse Hardware held in one hand to point and click on to commands shown on the monitor. A mouse complements the keyboard.

Operating system (OS) Foundational software which defines and controls the basic operations of a PC. DOS and OS/2 provide such a software platform from which other programs operate.

Propeller head A computer programmer; also known as bit brains, Commander Data, or computer nerd.

PC Personal computer. More limited than minicomputers or mainframes only in the sense that PCs have one chip serving as their CPU.

RAM Random access memory. The chips in the computer where application programs are temporarily stored. Graphical programs require 2, 4, or 16 MBs of RAM.

Surge protector Since power supply surges can burn out a computer (or other electrical devices) this hardware is used to protect the computer's circuitry.

Upload Transferring data from a user's own system to a central computer.

The microcomputer, often referred to as a PC, is the smallest and least expensive category of computers. It uses a microprocessor as its CPU (i.e., basic mathematic, logic, and control elements contained on one integrated circuit chip).[14] Evolution in CPUs in IBM-compatibles has gone from the old 8088 chips, quickly through the 286, 386, and 486 Intel series chips, to the Pentium and other advanced chips, which compute at faster and faster speeds. A PC with an advanced CPU, high-capacity random access memory (RAM), and disk drives hard drives, floppy drives, and CD-ROMs), and a revised disk operating system (DOS or OS/2) offers more flexibility than the minicomputer systems of a few years ago. Of course, since minicomputers operate somewhat like a PC, but generally with more than one CPU, they too have gained usefulness through the advances discussed.

In fact, the distinctions between mainframes, minicomputers, and PCs have blurred due to the advances in technology and software. MIPS, meaning one million instructions per second, is the rule for comparing systems. Pentium chips, available on PCs, can run at about 100 MIPS, the same speed as most low-end mainframes.

Users generally *do* distinguish whether or not they are **networked** (or "on line"), through the use of a mainframe, minicomputer, or PC, and whether they can access remote networks through their internal network. This linking of smaller networks is referred to as *wide-area networking*. As an analogy, popular services such as Internet and Bitnet serve as "information super highways" over which a message can travel from within your own city (or work site) to another.

Many organizations have MIS departments that generate, process, and distribute organizational information. Others, who have somewhat decentralized their IT, use MIS departments to coordinate the use of organizational information. The MIS department may also play an advisory role in selecting and implementing an HRIS.

Decision support systems (DSSs) emerged twenty years ago to provide decision-making information to managers. DSSs are used to help managers and groups solve unstructured decision problems.[15] Computer decision modeling continues to be developed for ever more challenging situations.

For instance, the Institute of Manpower Studies uses *projection modeling* to estimate the various impacts of employee turnover. This firm, in the United Kingdom, also is interested in the effect of a company's planned growth or reduction on the future level of recruits and promotions. If current turnover levels remain constant, their model predicts the number of staff vacancies and the related annual costs; the number of promotions available to employees; and the number of trainees who will finish their training in two years. The projection modeling also answers "what?" questions, factoring in different levels of business growth for the company and different business cycle effects.[16] Because so many variables are involved in the calculations, many employers, like the Institute of Manpower Studies, use a DSS staff to build a projection model to predict outcomes. Whether accomplished by a DSS staff or by other persons with modeling expertise, modeling that allows "what if" scenarios is becoming an important strategic management tool.

PCs versus Mainframes

As discussed, organizations are in a state of change regarding how to use which computer options. The 1990s are a pivotal decade in moving away from total reliance on MIS departments and mainframes. Computer mainframes have been used extensively for payroll, various government regulatory requirements (e.g., ERISA, EEO-1), management of benefits and pensions, employee profiles, and historical analysis.[17] PCs and minicomputer networks are aggressively moving into even these traditional mainframe domains.

Organizational strategies and structures have changed and have demanded that IT fit these changes. A typical organization in the 1980s had powerful centralized service and support functions housed in a large corporate headquarters. Resources were dedicated to managing and controlling all aspects of employment. HR departments liked HRISs because they gave them status and allowed them to receive a great deal of information from sites far from the corporate offices. Local line managers had to comply with the information requests but often received little help from the quarterly or annual staffing statistics.[18]

By contrast, organizations in the 1990s are often a collection of small business units linked together by a headquarters that may be little more than a holding company. Downsizing, mergers, and empowerment strategies have created a more decentralized structure. Therefore, modern HRISs must juggle compensation and benefit packages that are different across business units rather than standardized. The "lean and mean" organizational machine demands HR departments that are client-oriented and eager to serve shoulder to shoulder with the front-line managers.[19] In a performance-based, total quality management (TQM)-style company, the information source must serve the front line, not the reverse.

Mainframes and traditional MIS departments fit the organizations of the 1980s, while the addition of PCs and LANs fits the demands of the 1990s. The discussion of software applications in this chapter emphasizes this shift to user-friendly PC HRIS programs.

For companies that still depend on mainframes, the PC tends to use downloaded portions of a centralized data base. This was once a time-consuming and complicated process, but the technology and more sophisticated software have improved the process.[20]

However, even the availability of fast, powerful PCs and the prevalence of the friendly Windows environment does not enable HR departments to utilize PCs fully until the PCs are linked together in a network. A network permits the HR staff to share files and software, as well as provide access to all pertinent information. By 1984 the first PC networks had appeared. Although they were slow by today's standards and very hard to install, they became an overnight success. What makes the system possible is that each networked PC "thinks" it has its own hard disk; in reality, all of the micros are linked to a single disk called a file server. While PCs can accommodate LANs, where several workstations are networked within the same building, minicomputers are being substituted for PCs as the "brains" of these LANs due to their speed and capacity.

WHEN DOES AN HRIS BECOME CRUCIAL TO AN ORGANIZATION?

In strategic analyses of top firms, superior information systems are often identified as distinctive competencies and/or competitive advantages. So, from a competitive viewpoint, HRISs will always be important to any organization large enough to keep records. However, there are critical events in which information systems can directly affect the survival of the firm.

Changes to the organizational structure arguably create the greatest stress on HRISs. Mergers, acquisitions, downsizings, and other restructurings each create opportunities for MISs generally, and HRISs specifically, to either assist or complicate the organizational changes.

When two companies merge, there is generally a hope for the gains of synergy, vertical or horizontal integration, and economies of scale. How do MIS managers do with data bases what the executives did with the boardrooms? Ronald Tober, MIS director for the merged company Outokumpu American Brass, Inc., says, "We did a lot of checking, and then everybody held their breath."[21] When American Brass was purchased by Outokumpu Oy of Finland, the HRIS systems were the typical mix of proprietary software coming from a variety of vendors, with few, if any, standardized codes for information such as payroll, benefits, stock option plans, and other HR systems.

With one system in Buffalo, New York, another in Kenosha, Wisconsin, and yet another in Finland, three options emerged when American Brass tried to integrate its systems. The first option was to purchase a vendor-written conversion program. While these programs have been difficult to find, the most recent HRIS PC packages contain some conversion utilities. The second option was to attempt to convince two operations to simply convert to the system used by the other and have each rekey all of its data. Outokumpu American Brass chose the third option and wrote an in-house conversion program with the help of Software 2000, a Hyannis, Massachusetts, HRIS firm.[22]

Multifoods Corporation, a one-hundred-year-old international food distributor, had a similar situation. Judy Welter, application development manager for Multifoods, witnessed seven *acquisitions* over three years. She recalled, "We've converted data from ADP (Automatic Data Processing, Inc.), CDC (Control Data Corporation), Lawson (Inc.) and some homegrown files into Cyborg (Solution Series)."[23] Problems can occur in the form of the data and even in the terms used. "Somebody calls it 'salary,' another calls it 'pay rate,' or 'pay per period' and another says it's 'annual salary divided out' and that's just for salary. Until there are standards . . . there will be no easy way to do conversions," according to Welter.[24]

During a downsizing effort at a retail electronic company with 4500 employees in sixty stores, an HRIS was used to help eliminate the potential for supervisor bias in the layoffs. While store managers retained the authority to decide which employees to lay off, the HR department generated a staffing analysis on each employee with its HRIS. In keeping with the company's strategic goals and objectives, nonexempt employees were awarded points based on length of service, performance ratings, absenteeism, tardiness, and performance issues. The supervisor also provided a subjective rating. A perfect score totalled one hundred points. With this assistance, decisions were made more consistently, objectively, and quickly.[25]

Integration is not always the goal when mergers and acquisitions occur. Since the flip side of acquisition is divestiture, having individual HR records for each unit can make good business sense. Potential buyers of the unit need to be able to access the makeup of a company and determine the ratio between productivity and people.[26]

Reorganizations involving flattening, decentralizing, or centralizing the organizational structure also put stress on HRISs. A bank with 3200 employees was moving to centralize some of the functions, such as loan processing, which had been delegated to the twenty-eight branches. Since staff would be reassigned or terminated, an HRIS program was used to analyze each position. Reports examining title, salary, skills, department, and location helped to uncover job overlaps and efficient reassignments. At one point, about 200 jobs were open throughout the company. The HRIS allowed immediate, systemwide posting and provided confidential acceptance, reassignment, and termination letters.[27]

COMPUTER APPLICATIONS

Since employees are often the largest corporate expense for most employers, the advantages of a computerized HR department are enormous. In fact, the costs of not computerizing HR departments can be enormous (see *HR in the News:* "New HRIS Demands Created by FMLA").

In 1992 Towers Perrin conducted a study for IBM, "Priorities for Competitive Advantage," in which 3000 HR professionals, line managers, and others from twelve countries were surveyed. The study, which is used as a global benchmark on a number of HR items, identified the top three major current and future benefits of HRIS:

1. Faster information processing and greater information accuracy.

2. Improved planning and program development.

3. Enhanced employee communications.[28]

An "HRM EXPO" was held in San Francisco in 1993. This was a first-time conference to

New HRIS Demands Created by FMLA

When President Clinton signed the Family and Medical Leave Act (FMLA) into law in 1993, HR professionals were already identifying what changes would need to be made in personnel records. Legislation has always driven the need for additional personnel records, and the FMLA is one of several recent laws to affect record keeping. The FMLA is deceptively complex in terms of record keeping, and requires the coordination of the payroll, benefits or HR administration, and perhaps labor relations. The act involves three types of employee issues:

1. Determining eligibility by hours worked, location, and hire date;

2. Tracking the time off that is accrued to family leave; and

3. Administering the continuation of benefits.

If a part-time employee requests a leave for family leave in February and didn't work at least 1,250 hours in the previous twelve-month period then that employee is not eligible, according to the FMLA. However, many payroll systems purge transaction data when they complete year-end closing. The information which HR needs is a rolling twelve-month period, and this simply may not be currently available. An HRIS needs to maintain files like those in payroll (if separate) but for different purposes and time periods.

Total time an employee takes off for FMLA needs to be kept, also on the rolling twelve-month year.

If an organization has not yet purchased and set up an HRIS, then the FMLA provides a good reason to do so. Companies which do use an HRIS may shop for a FMLA module or stand-alone program to handle the new complexities.

Note: For more detailed information about the recordkeeping requirements of the FMLA, see the August 1993 issue of *HR News*.

SOURCE: Adapted from Sandra E. O'Connell, "Implementing FMLA Means Complex Record Keeping," *HRMagazine* 38 (October 1993): 31.

bring together a capacity crowd of HR professionals with over 500 exhibitors offering hardware and software packages.[29] Clearly, there are a myriad of software programs and packages available to start, integrate, or expand an HRIS. Most such programs can be run on modern PCs and minicomputers, many in the Windows environment. While it is impossible to list all such packages (any such list would soon be obsolete), it may be helpful to survey the types of programs available (see *HR in the News:* "HRIS Buyers Guide Listing" for a list of examples) and the newest HR uses on which software companies are focusing.

Computer applications in the HR department can be categorized into three areas—data management, data manipulation, and decision making.[30]

Data Management and Manipulation

The first category, **data management**, is the oldest and most frequently used application. It is a recordkeeping function. Every large company is required by law to maintain employee files that contain information on date of employment, sex, race, work history, and salary level. Usually other types of employee information are added, such as education, job skills, and benefits. Having employee data on computer files speeds up the preparation and increases the accuracy of management reports.

The explosion of HR software has been primarily in the area of **data manipulation** of employment files. For example, the escalating importance of managing health-care costs has resulted in the introduction of many programs to assist employers. Med*E*Calc uses the data you enter, or download from a data management-type data base for each of your indemnity, medical, dental, vision, hearing, HMO, and PPO plans to calculate a value for each.[31] These values are helpful when comparing with other plans with identical coverage, when assessing bids from a new dental or health insurance carrier, and when comparing data at different locations.

While the Med*E*Calc's health-plan evaluation and analysis program is moderately priced, many price tags for software in the early 1990s range from $5000 to more than $30,000.[32] Pricier packages are capable of performing more sophisticated manipulations and analyses. In the area of health-care cost programs, a $12,000 software package may indeed represent significant savings if the return on investment is even 5 percent on an annual insurance bill of $1.5 million. These high-end HR programs do more than review insurance carriers statements item by item; they also perform projections and handle "what if" scenarios;[33] for example, what if the prescription card is dropped from the plan, or what if the employee contribution is increased by 5 percent, or what if other options are added?

Decision Support Systems

It is getting harder to distinguish between data manipulation programs like the insurance programs just discussed and what had been considered decision-making software. Decision support systems (DSS) programs help managers make better decisions. The various packages now available all have in common the ability to take masses of information and rearrange, compile, present and, to some degree, analyze it. A software package called PRIMUS, for example, is designed to assist decision making with regard to career and succession planning by helping the HR user understand how effective recruiting has been (Table 16-1) where to target retention and turnover efforts, whether affirmative action programs are effective, and so on.[34]

Computer-Based Training

Experts have estimated that two out of three U.S. employees are involved in some kind of formal training. Due to technological advances

HRIS "Buyers Guide" Listing.

The number of software packages available to HR departments is exploding in the 1990s.

The following is a list of HRIS software topics featured recently in *HRMagazine*. As many as twelve companies offering various software packages are listed under each of these 59 HR topic areas.

Americans with Disabilities Act
Applicant Tracking
Attendance
Awards and Incentives
Benefit Communication Software
Benefits Administration
Career Development
Certification/Management/Document Imaging
Claims Auditing
COBRA
Compensation Administration
Computer-based Recruiting
Computer-based Testing
Computer-based Training
Data and Survey Analysis
Disability
Employee Assistance Plan Evaluation
EEO and Affirmative Action
Employee Accident/Illness Record Keeping and Analysis
Employee Assessment and Selection
Employee Background Screening
Employee Communications Services
Employment/Recruitment/Assessment
Empowerment Training and Development
Expatriate Management
Flexible Benefits Administration
Group Management
HR/General Business Software
HR Management

HRIS Consulting Services
Interactive Voice Response
Job Analysis
Job Descriptions
Leadership Training
Manuals and Handbooks
Multifunctional HRIS
Nonprofit Educational Trade Association
Organization Development
Organizational Charts
Payroll
Pension Administration
Pension and Profit Sharing Administration
Performance Improvement/Planning
Profit Sharing Administration
Relocation Services
Skills Testing
Spouse Employment Assistance
Stress Management
Substance Abuse
Succession Planning
Surveys
Team Building
Temporary Services Management Testing
Training Administration and Management
Videocassette Training and Education
Wellness Programming

ADAPTED FROM "Buyer's Guide to HRIS," *HRMagazine* 37 (May 1992): 101.

Table 16-1 Computer Usage Is Popular in Recruiting

Application	Percent of Users*
Applicant tracking	74
Correspondence	51
Job posting	44
Management reporting	36
Requisition tracking	31
Government reporting	25
Internal candidate sourcing	21
Hiring cost data and analysis	21
Resume and/or test results storage and retrieval	21

*Survey of 568 randomly selected *Recruitment Today* subscribers.

SOURCE: M. Magnus and M. Grossman, "Using Computers Is Catching On," *Recruitment Today* (Summer 1990): 17.

and job redesigns, workers need continuous and effective training. In order to meet this challenge, the persons responsible for the training function—often HR managers—are seeking instructional methods that are more responsive and adaptive than traditional teacher instruction. Ironically, one promising technique can be found amid the new technologies that created the need—computers.[35]

Computer-based training (CBT) refers to the delivery of instruction through a computer terminal.[36] It can meet a variety of training needs; from robotics maintenance and customer relations to supervisory techniques. CBT is also useful for transferring skills that involve memorization of step-by-step procedures of formulas, such as those found in programming system languages. Even the strongholds of soft training—sales, management, and customer service—are beginning to incorporate extensive CBT applications.

The advantages of CBT are worth noting.[37] Trainees who are geographically dispersed, even worldwide, can still receive CBT as long as they have access to a PC. This creates a number of economic advantages, especially as travel costs, instructor costs, and other training costs continue to escalate. Because it is self-paced, CBT allows trainees to move as slowly (or quickly) as they wish, thus eliminating the need to tailor courses to the learning speed of the weakest students. Further, the quality of instruction is guaranteed to be the same from class to class.[38]

CBT is totally **interactive**, which means that the trainee must respond before the course continues. A trainee who fails a unit test may be "branched" to a remedial module. Usually the trainee must demonstrate mastery of a topic before advancing to the next unit. This approach is enhanced by recent developments in CD-ROM technology.

Adults learn differently than children, in part because of established beliefs, attitudes, values, and habits acquired over the years.[39] When the first steps in learning are relatively easy and nonthreatening, the adult learner will gain confidence. CBT permits the trainee to increase the learning at a gradual rate, rather than overwhelming the learner with complex details. Practice is a basic principle of learning. Numerous studies consistently demonstrate that when people are encouraged to practice what they have learned as soon as they have learned it, their retention rate is higher.[40] CBT provides as many opportunities to practice as trainees need or want. Trainees need help in practicing perfectly—that is, they need accurate and timely feedback that lets them know when they have mastered the skill.[41]

Although CBT users often develop their own courses, this is an expensive undertaking. It is not unusual to take one hundred hours to develop one hour of CBT.[42] However, users are turning to vendors of off-the-shelf or generic software. There are new CBT products every year, ranging in price from less then $100 for simple courses to thousands of dollars for sophisticated CBT applications.[43]

Expert Systems

In the 1980s, only a handful of businesses were using **expert systems**.[44] Expert systems have recently exploded in popularity. They have become the most common commercially available form of artificial intelligence.[45]

Artificial intelligence (AI) is the art of making computers mimic ordinary human abilities. Broadly defined, it includes computerized vision systems that help machines in factories "see" or let computers analyze speech recognition that may result in language translators or electronic typewriters that can take dictation. The biggest AI market is for expert systems: software programs that seek to mimic the reasoning and decision making of specialists in different fields based on rules of thumb and their data bases of knowledge.

OPPORTUNITIES FOR HRIS CAREERS

An emerging field will usually offer many career opportunities. The HRIS field is no different. Over the past few years, recruiters have not looked for HR professionals to program computers; instead, they have hired aspiring computer professionals with the ability and training to design and implement HR applications.

More recently recruiters want people who, at the very least, have the capability to master the standard business software packages already available in most organizations.

SELECTING AND IMPLEMENTING AN HRIS

Converting the HR department's manual system to a computerized system should not be left to chance. Careful and meticulous planning is required. Great care should be taken to make the system accessible and easy to learn. Unlike most MIS systems, the HRIS system will probably be used by more nontechnical workers than any other information system.

Technical assistance in selecting and implementing the system is mandatory. While assistance may come from outside consultants, other HR professionals, or HR technical staff, the group most logically sought is MIS. Occasionally encountered, however, is an adversarial relationship between the HR and MIS staffs.

Managing Conflict and Politics

To paraphrase one HR department head, "to cope with the management of a human resource information system is too important to leave in the hands of data systems professionals."[46] Statements such as this often reflect deep-seated mistrust of **data processors**. Over the past few decades, data processors have grown in power, prestige, and number. This fact has led to their becoming, in some circles, the in-group. Such selective perception by the in-group of out-groups leads to ethnocentrism that, in turn, fosters a distorted reality that can appear as professionalism.[47]

In a few isolated instances, MIS professionals have been guilty of "empire building," using their technical knowledge of the computer system's capabilities. Nevertheless, without data processors—systems analysts, programmers, and operations personnel—there would have been no automated MIS and no HRIS.

MIS and HR professionals need to cooperate to achieve the organization's mission, goals, and objectives. HR departments new at conceptualizing what they need from computerization (see Figure 16-3) can benefit from the experience of most MIS departments. MIS professionals are further along the learning curve not only on computer systems, but also on hardware and vendors.

FIGURE 16-3 Analyzing your HRIS needs

Before purchasing or programming an HRIS there are ten key issues to consider:

1. What documents will be fed into the system?

2. Do these documents need to be modified to fit the system, or to yield better information?

3. What kinds of reports (routine and ad hoc) will be produced?

4. What steps are required to complete the information journey from input to use? Can these paperflow steps be simplified with the new system?

5. Will the HRIS interface (import and export) easily with other systems and other programs?

6. How much capacity is needed on the short- and long-term?

7. Who will need what level of access to the information in the HRIS?

8. What should the new system do that the old system did not?

9. What features are critical to what you hope to accomplish with the HRIS?

10. How can the system be expanded and upgraded in the future?

Evaluating Hardware and Software

Another source of information for HR professionals who want to start or expand an HRIS is other HR professionals who have more experience in computerization. Many local chapters of the Society for Human Resource Management offer special meetings on HRIS and provide an excellent opportunity to assess needs and examine alternatives. More specifically, the Association of Human Resource Systems Professionals (AHRSP), located in Dallas, has 3400 members from many of the top U.S. corporations who trade off-the-record information about HRISs. Membership in this organization, formed in 1980, can provide a buyer with information about which systems have the fewest problems, which are easier to install, which vendors provide the best support, and what should be stressed in requests for proposal (RFPS).[48]

There are many hardware and software alternatives. According to a 1993 FAX poll, all employers responding had computerized some records. One-half had purchased commercial HRIS packages, and one-third use in-house developed systems. However, several of those using in-house systems plan to convert to vendor packages in the near future. Many respondents already automate benefits, compensation, and job descriptions and plan to expand their HRIS automation to other functions. The survey also indicated that 91 percent reported a positive impact on productivity.[49]

Implementing a New or Modified HRIS

HR departments need to engage in a lot of planning when starting or modifying their computer system, called a system **rollout**. Few problems are due to poor computer hardware; most are due to inadequate planning for the system. As discussed, MIS and HR departments should work together in planning the rollout. Another approach is creating a user task group, which is a representative group from the main business and HR areas. In 1992, Prudential Insurance Company's largest operating group put together a **user group** in a series of one-day meetings to do the following:

1. Identify the HR functions needed to support the division's objectives.

2. Identify the processes needed to support the HR functions.

3. Develop a broad-brush picture of where these processes would be undertaken.[50]

This seven-member group helped Prudential focus on what sort of HR department will be appropriate in the future. While the primary benefit of the user group was to ease the HRIS transition, the secondary benefit was the long-term planning, which focused the departments and system on the goals and objectives of the corporation. This approach is in line with the IBM study "Priorities for Competitive Advantage," discussed earlier in the chapter, which charts the future of HR. The study indicates that in the twenty-first century HR will be responsive to a highly competitive marketplace and global business structures, closely linked to business strategic plans, and jointly conceived and implemented by line and HR managers.[51]

Reasonable short-term goals need to be set for the rollout. Typically, the goal is to get the new system ready for user testing in about four months. The employees are then trained, usually in an instructor-led, paper-based workshop that gives hands-on training using test data on computer terminals.[52]

For example, during Westin's conversion (see the *HR in the News* at the beginning of this chapter), the first six months of the rollout were spent on system installation, data conversion, report setup, and employee training.[53] Planning enough time for conversion and training is critical to HRIS success. At Westin, three regional hotel-level training sessions were held to train managers on the new reports and how to interpret them. Corporate-level training sessions for users consisted of two one-week training modules.[54]

Securing the Integrity of HR Data

With the proliferation of inexpensive hardware and software and the increasing access technology makes possible come some risks. Perhaps the biggest risk is to the integrity of the information in the HR files. Similar to other HRIS issues, the issue of keeping records unaltered and safe from tampering is complicated by the issue of which technology is being used. Security dimensions are somewhat different, depending on whether the HRIS is a mainframe, a LAN file server, or a PC system. Since many HR departments use both a mainframe data base and either a minicomputer/LAN or PCs, the security issue becomes even more complicated. Indeed, security has been used as an excuse for some resistance to computerization when the real reason was perceived extra work.[55]

There are two main approaches to maintaining record integrity. The first is *controlling access,* just as MIS departments often did in the past. Employees would fill out a request form for certain information, and this request would be routed and approved through some internal procedure. This procedure defeats the advantages that the latest HRISs offer in terms of communication, speed, and ad hoc analysis.

The second approach is *security technology,* through which a computer user is limited either in (1) what information can be accessed (e.g., payroll files are made unavailable without proper passwords) or (2) type of access. For example, files can be read only, write only, or both. CD-ROMs are currently the ultimate in read-only security, since CD-ROM drives typically cannot write to or alter the data file stored on the CDs. Security devices have been developed in several forms: special hard drives can be removed and secured; "dongles," which prevent computers from being run without a special plug-in unit, can be installed; and security disks that must be inserted before access is given can be used.[56] The possibility of a corruption of programs through a virus also

Kiosks for Wellness and Bars for HR

One of the innovations displayed at the 1993 HRM EXPO in San Francisco was the use of kiosks for HR applications. Kiosks, which are used by banks when they place automatic teller machines (ATMs) inside shopping malls, have been used for several years by many large employers. Cabinets that house a computer, a monitor, and an interactive media system, these kiosks can be used for benefits communication, attitude surveys, and other types of communication activities.

At the HRM EXPO, new technology was demonstrated that allows employees to come to the kiosk to check their blood pressure and take a health-profile test. This "wellness kiosk" was prepared by Computerized Screening, Inc. (CSI), in Dallas CSI demonstrated that clients who take preventive actions have an overall reduction in claims for serious health conditions. Their test takes just minutes, uses a touch screen, and offers a choice of languages to employees.[58]

Stevens Industries, Inc., of Teutopolis, Illinois, has introduced bar-code technology to its HRIS. Employees are given bar-coded badges to identify them in the HR and the payroll systems. Workers "wand" in and out instead of punching in and out. Business Planning and Control System software from System Software Associates, Inc. (Chicago) helps Stevens track hours worked, payroll, accrued vacation, holiday, and sick day information.[59]

---

requires both access and software security attention.

Whatever combination of security approaches is used, many suggest that one person should be responsible for the security of the HRIS. While the inclination has been to tightly limit access as the security approach, how could companies be successful in getting many of their employees to use the wellness kiosk (discussed in *HR in the News:* "Kiosks for Wellness and Bars for HR") with that approach? When a user accesses only the information he or she needs and performs an analysis, wouldn't the employer benefit from maintaining that analysis in a form from which another user could benefit?

The confidentiality of records is also an important consideration. With a combination of more information and more users, the issue of access to particular files becomes a critical issue. Where once such access was written in to in-house programs, PC and other software packages now make access one of their features. For example, HRIS-Pro (Human Resource Microsystems, Inc., San Francisco) allows the system administrator to assign levels of access to different users. Users can be limited to specific functions, modules, screens, reports, utilities, and data fields for which they have a legitimate need. The key to the system is the user's unique password, to which HRIS-Pro attaches defined access parameters.[57]

750

CONCLUSIONS AND APPLICATIONS

- Automation came late to the HR department. And when it did, the system put in place resembled payroll more than personnel.

- During the 1970s, federal and state regulatory agencies required most companies to compile statistics and submit reports on work force composition and wage and hour payments. Report preparation soon gave birth to the computer as an HR management tool.

- The personal computer's (PC) appearance, perhaps more than any other single event, shifted information control away from the data processing/MIS department.

- The computer is becoming an integral part of the HR department. As a tool, it has moved beyond producing simple reports to helping HR managers make complex decisions. Human resource information systems (HRISs) are making this possible. As a whole, HRIS creates more opportunities for the HR profession to influence the company.

- There has been an explosion of PC hardware improvements and software offerings that greatly expand the possibilities of HRIS. Small employers can now benefit by getting the same results on PCs and minicomputers that could only be obtained using mainframes a few years ago.

- The choice between mainframes, minicomputers, and PCs is complicated by the blur-

ring of distinctions between them. Technological improvements are leveling the playing field between competitive technologies, and a likely scenario is that a medium-sized to larger employer will employ a combination of networked computer systems.

- Improvements in computer technology allow more tasks to be accomplished than ever before. Very sophisticated analyses can be performed on an ad hoc basis. Even PC programs allow complicated "what if" questions to be answered. Computers are now used as information service centers for employees, in a move similar to the one made by banks' offering automated teller machines.

- A decision support application that is most promising is computer-based training (CBT). It is a totally interactive system between the trainee and the computer. The trainee must demonstrate adequate progress during each step of the learning module; if this does not occur, the trainee will be branched to a remedial module.

- Modern HRISs place HR professionals in a better position to play a more integral role in the strategic management of today's corporation. Computer technology, which first seemed to divide departments, now serves to bring them closer together as they share information, and more of it, to implement the business strategy.

CASE STUDY

Ward Industries, Inc.

Ward Industries, Inc., wishes the computer had never been invented. One year ago, top management decided to scrap the traditional point method of job evaluation that had been in place for over twenty years. The old method divided jobs into specific factors determined to be critical to the organization.

Under the old method, a job evaluation committee, composed of employees from the affected areas, determined the value (i.e., salary) of new jobs and reevaluated existing jobs. However, as the company grew, new product lines were added that created new job families and occupations. The committees were not only losing control and making inconsistent decisions, they were incorrectly pricing the value of too many new job families.

There were other reasons for changing as well. Managers began complaining that the old job evaluation system was not meeting their needs. With (and without) permission, they began using their own systems. Prior to implementation of the new system, multiple and divergent systems were embedded throughout the company. One division, for example, was simply ranking and pricing jobs in terms of market supply (i.e., how hard it was to recruit).

Perhaps the most serious problem was the backlog of requests for job reclassifications (some requests were over four months old). Another often cited complaint was the bickering between HR and division personnel. The perception among employees was that organizational politics predetermined the outcome.

About one year ago, the HR department purchased an off-the-shelf computerized job analysis/evaluation system. It was believed to

be the best way to lessen human error and minimize alleged charges of favoritism and politics. Indeed, the system offered a number of advantages, namely, objectivity, speed in evaluating jobs, consistency of application, and use of identical compensable factors companywide.

Top management and the HR staff selected about seventy-five jobs that they believed were currently assigned to an appropriate salary grade. These benchmark jobs became the foundation of the computerized system. All incumbents in the benchmark jobs were asked to complete a structured job analysis questionnaire that could be entered directly into the computer. Multiple regression analysis was used to analyze the data, identify those factors that correlated most closely with current salary grade midpoints, and weight the factors appropriately. The end result was similar to a computer-generated point factor plan.

Ward Industries purchased the packaged program because it was easy to implement and could be applied companywide. Employees simply had to complete a structured questionnaire, and the computer provided the answers. It seemed—and was—simple.

But somewhere along the line, this simple system proved to create more problems than it solved. Specifically:

1. The system did not differentiate adequately between technical career steps. The differences between Engineer I and II, for example, were not readily distinguishable using either quantitative or qualitative data.

2. The system was too sensitive to job titles and organizational changes. Simply chang-

ing a job title, and nothing else, could boost an individual into a higher salary grade.

3. The system was insensitive to market changes; for example, the internal rankings produced by the computer for certain high-demand jobs in one year often did not correspond to market realities for the same job two years later.

At this time, there are more complaints than ever. Each division is dead set against the computerized system. There are rumors that managers are circumventing the system with such tactics as fictitious job titles, irrele-

vant compensable factors, and compensable factors that do not exist.

1. Why did the good idea of computerizing the job evaluation system go wrong?

2. What are the advantages of computerizing the system? Disadvantages?

3. What steps should Ward Industries have taken to ensure successful implementation of its computerized job-evaluation process?

4. Should Ward Industries change back to the old system? Explain.

EXPERIENTIAL EXERCISES

1. Shopping for Software

Visit a computer store and examine the software that is new on the racks.

1. What kinds of programs appear to be most popular for general users? What do these non-HRIS packages or programs do that could not be done without a modern computer? Do the programs offer more than speed and convenience?

2. Try to find programs that might be helpful for a small business in performing HR functions. Examine the features of the software. What are the limitations of the package? Are similar packages offered at the same

store? Do you think that the small business owner would save money or increase service by using one of these packages?

3. Look for any security or confidentiality features of the software you have located. Do you think that you, or any friends of yours, could override the security features advertised in the package? Do you know of anyone who did override security features on other, non-HRIS, programs?

4. Write a short set of objectives to use if you were buying and using HRIS programs for your small business.

2. PC-Based HR Applications

Divide the class into small groups and have each group identify several local HR departments in which a PC is used. A member of the

group should contact one or more departments and ask them for permission to visit and learn how the PC and its software are used as a management tool. The group should then arrange a visit to see demonstrations of HR applications being performed on the PC.

Particular attention should be paid to identifying the types of applications—data management, data manipulation, and DSS. Also, does the department use packaged software, or does it create its own application software using spreadsheet analysis, data-based analysis, graphics, word processing, electronic mail, or data retrieval? Does the department link into a mainframe computer? If so, ask how they download data from the mainframe into the PC. Ask how they determined the process and the costs associated with acquiring a PC and related software. Finally, has the introduction of the PC into the HR department saved the company money?

Each group should present to the class its observations and conclusions about the PC's current and potential role in a typical HR department.

KEY TERMS AND CONCEPTS

Artificial intelligence (AI)
Central processing unit (CPU)
Computer
Computer-based training (CBT)
Data base
Data management
Data manipulation
Data processors
Decision Support system (DSS)
Expert systems
File server
Hardware
Human resource information system (HRIS)
Information technology (IT)

Interactive
Local area network (LAN)
Mainframe
Management information system (MIS)
Microcomputer
Minicomputer
Networks
Peripheral
Personal computer (PC)
PROLOG
Rollout
Software
Vendors

REVIEW QUESTIONS

1. How did the PC change the course and growth of MIS?

2. What is the difference between HR computer applications and the HRIS?

3. Why do many HR computer applications still reside on mainframe systems?

4. What are the biggest disadvantages of a PC-based HRIS?

5. Why is HR automation too important to leave totally in the hands of data systems/MIS professionals?

6. When planning an HRIS, why is it more important to spend more time choosing software than hardware?

7. What new services can HR offer due to the improvements in HRIS technology?

DISCUSSION QUESTIONS

1. Assume that new HR systems cannot be justified. The benefits are essentially intangible; they cannot be expressed in hard dollars. Start-up costs are overwhelming. Add to that the problem of payback; HR systems cost a lot, and there is no payback at all. To make matters worse, because of top management's distance from the HRIS function, there is no commitment to costly HR projects. Management has heard plenty about failures with expensive HR systems but not much about successes.

It is your assignment to dispute each of these statements.

2. The PC brings a number of benefits to the HR department; one of the most significant applications is the provision of high-quality training when it is needed. Discuss the different ways in which the PC might become responsive to training and development needs.

3. It would be difficult to design and implement an HRIS without the advice and technical know-how of a professional data processor. Discuss how the HR manager might approach the data processing department with a request for HRIS assistance.

4. Discuss the pros and cons of security on mainframes, minicomputers, and PCs.

5. One emerging trend resulting from the increased use of computers in human resources is the creation of new HRIS jobs. The HR data administrator (HRDA) has been called the newest job in personnel. What might the job description of the HRDA contain, including skills, responsibilities, and educational qualifications?

ENDNOTES

Chapter 16

1. Alfred J. Walker, "Arriving Soon: The Paperless Personnel Office," *Personnel Journal* 61 (July 1980): 559.

2. Joyce E. Santora, "Data Base Integrates HR Functions," *Personnel Journal* 71 (January 1992): 92.

3. Ibid., p. 32.

4. Ibid.

5. Ed Bride, "HRMS Moves to HRIS," *Software News* (January 1986): 47.

6. Ronald R. Gauch, "The Changing Environment in Management Information Systems: New Roles for Computer Professionals and Users," *Public Personnel Management* 21 (Fall 1992): 375.

7. Ibid., p. 374.

8. Alfred J. Walker, *HRIS Development: A Project Team Guide to Building an Effective Personnel Information System* (New York: Van Nostrand Reinhold, 1982), p. 16.

9. Ibid., p. 17.

10. Mel Mandell, "Managing the Human Assets," *Computerworld* 27 (April 6, 1993): 128.

11. Gary Meyer, "What Every Personnel Manager Should Know About Computers," *Personnel Journal* 65 (August 1984): 58.

12. Nicholas Beutell, "Computers and the Management of Human Resources," *Readings in Human Resource Management,* 3rd ed., ed. R. S. Schuler, S. A. Youngblood, and V. L. Huber (St. Paul, MN: West, 1988), p. 86.

13. Donald Spencer, *The Illustrated Computer Dictionary,* 3rd ed. (Columbus, OH: Merrill, 1986), p. 181.

14. Ibid., pp. 188–90.

15. B. C. Romann, "Decision Support Systems: Strategic Management Tools for the Eighties," *Business Horizons* 28 (September–October 1985): 71.

16. Iris Morgan, "The Technology of Information," *Personnel Management* 21 (August 1992): 56.

17. Allen S. Lee, "Despite Microcomputer Proliferation, Mainframes Are Still Preferred," *Computers in Personnel* (Winter 1988): 45–50.

18. Colin Richards-Carpenter, "Loosening the Purse Strings," *Personnel Management* 22 (January 1993): 49.

19. Ibid., p. 49.

20. Stephen G. Perry, "The PC-based HRIS," *Personnel Administrator* 33 (February 1988): 60–63.

21. Bill Sharp, "Managing a Merger: HR Systems Migration," *Datamation* 39 (February 15, 1993): 71.

22. Ibid., p. 72.

23. Ibid.

24. Ibid.

25. Jim Spoor, "HRIS Can Make Downsizing Strategic and Fair," *HR Focus* 68 (August 1991): 7.

26. Jim Spoor, "HRIS and Acquisition: A Smooth Transition," *HR Focus* 69 (January 1992): 17.

27. Ibid., p. 7.

28. Stephenie Overman, "Reaching for the 21st Century," *HRMagazine* 37 (April 1992): 63.

29. Sandra E. O'Connell, "In Search of the Future," *HRMagazine* 38 (July 1993): 33.

30. "Computers in the Executive Suite," *Small Business Report* (November 1984): 74.

31. Leslie Marshall and Nancy Howe, "Evaluate Health Plans," *HRMagazine* 37 (May 1992): 36.

32. O'Connell, "In Search of the Future," p. 35.

33. Ibid., p. 35.

34. For a more complete listing of micro-based HRIS software and software companies, see "Buyer's Guide to HRIS" *HRMagazine* 37 (May 1992): 101ff.

35. Vandra L. Huber and Geri Gay, "Channeling New Technology to Improve Training," *Personnel Administrator* 30 (February 1985): 49.

36. Jeff N. Gee, "Training Program Haute Couture," *Personnel Administrator* 32 (May 1987): 69–72.

37. For a more thorough discussion on the pros and cons of CBT, we recommend William C. Heck, "Computer-based Training—the Choice Is Yours," *Personnel Administrator* (February 1985): 39–46. Also see Stephen Schwade, "Is It Time to Consider Computer-based Training?" *Personnel Administrator* 30 (February 1985): 25–35.

38. Schwade, "Is It Time?" pp. 31–32.

39. Ron Zemke and Susan Zemke, "30 Things We Know for Sure about Adult Learning," *Training/HRD Journal* 18 (June 1981): 45–52.

40. A review of learning theory is found in Craig Schneier, "Training and Development Programs: What Learning Theory and Research Have to Offer," *Personnel Journal* 53 (April 1974): 288–93.

41. Norbert F. Elbert and Richard Discenza, *Contemporary Supervision* (New York: Random House, 1985), pp. 325–49.

42. Heck, "Computer-based Training," p. 39.

43. The *ICP Software Directory,* Microcomputer Series (Autumn 1987), lists CBT courses, ranging from "Conducting Successful Meetings" at $99 to a course called SIMPLER for training course authors at $30,000.

44. Some writers draw a distinction between expert systems and knowledge systems. The more general term *knowledge systems* is applied to systems that employ the same underlying programming technologies as expert systems but are based on

broader "composite" sources of knowledge. In our discussion, we use the term *expert* to include knowledge-based systems. See John P. Gallagher, *Knowledge Systems for Business: Integrating Expert Systems and MIS* (Englewood Cliffs, NJ: Prentice-Hall, 1988), p. 4.

45. Valdis Krebs, "Can Expert Systems Make HR Decisions?" *Computers in Personnel* (Winter 1988): 4–8.

46. Joe Pasqualetto, "Computers: No More Us vs. Them," *Personnel Journal* 66 (December 1987): 61–67.

47. For a complete discussion, see R. Levine and D. Campbell, *Ethnocentrism* (New York: Wiley, 1972); and C. P. Alderfer, "Group and In-

tergroup Relations," in *Improving Life at Work*, ed. J. R. Hackman and J. L. Suttle (Santa Monica, CA: Goodyear, 1977).

48. "Experience Talks," *Computerworld* 25 (April 6, 1992): 128.

49. Sandra E. O'Connell, "Doing More with Less, Part 2," *HRMagazine* 38 (February 1993): 33.

50. Dick Robertson, "A Prudent Review of Data Systems," *Personnel Management* 24 (June 1992): 45.

51. Overman, "Reaching for the 21st Century," p. 63.

52. Barry Walter, "Taking the Byte Out of System Rollouts," *Training and Development* 47 (February 1993): 34.

53. Joyce E. Santora, "Data Base Integrates HR Functions," *Personnel Journal* 72 (January 1992): 93.

54. Ibid., p. 94.

55. Colin Richards-Carpenter, "Loading Security Onto a System," *Personnel Management* 24 (January 1992): 18.

56. Ibid., p. 18.

57. Gary Meyer, "HRIS-Pro Offers Solid HR Support, Plus Adaptability," *HRMagazine* 38 (September 1993): 42.

58. O'Connell, "In Search of the Future," p. 33.

59. "What's Hot in HR?" *Datamation* 39 (February 15, 1993): 72.

HR RESEARCH AND PROBLEM SOLVING

CHAPTER OBJECTIVES

1. To recognize the importance of the HR research function and to cite the individuals and institutions that conduct HR research.

2. To cite the academic and practitioner journals in which personnel and HR research is published.

3. To provide an overview of the major HR research methods.

4. To describe in detail the employee survey process—by far the most common form of HR research.

5. To recognize the importance of conducting—whenever possible—a cost-benefit analysis of HR activities and to provide an example using employee absenteeism.

6. To cite some of the major personnel/HR problems—absenteeism, turnover, job dissatisfaction, and perceptions of unfairness.

For many managers and administrators, people problems rank high among causes of frustration and stress. High levels of absenteeism and turnover, a steady stream of employee grievances, low morale, poor work attitudes, and resistance to change all serve to diminish employee productivity and push up operating costs. But the damage caused by extraordinary human problems often extends beyond the firm's current profit picture. An ineffectual and recalcitrant HR group—together with the absence of sound HR problem-solving techniques—may result in the gradual erosion of an organization's ability to remain competitive in a complex and uncertain business environment.

The ability to conduct research and solve HR problems is critically important to HR professionals and managers (see *HR in the News:* "New Interest in Job Satisfaction at the U.S. Postal Service"). In contrast to years past, the HR staff in many organizations is being called on to play more of a role in the diagnosis of human problems and the creation of policies and programs to solve them. The creation, implementation, and evaluation of many of the HR programs discussed in this book—such as job enrichment, management development, flextime, and training and development (T&D)—usually involve some form of HR research.

The first part of this chapter examines many aspects of HR research: kinds of research, who does it, where the results of research are published, and commonly used research techniques. The second part of the chapter points out four troublesome problems that HR professionals commonly face: absenteeism, turnover, job dissatisfaction, and perceptions of unfairness.

HR RESEARCH

HR research is the collection and investigation of facts related to HR problems in order to eliminate or reduce those problems. Through HR research, managers and administrators are able to substitute facts about human behavior for armchair theorizing, hunches, guesswork, and gut reactions. Specific uses of HR research include the following:[1]

- The measurement and evaluation of present conditions.

- The prediction of conditions, events, and behavioral patterns.

- The evaluation of current policies, programs, and activities.

- The discovery of rational bases for revising current policies, programs, and activities.

- The appraisal of proposed policies, programs, and activities.

Types of Research

Most research can be classified as basic or applied. **Basic research,** sometimes referred to as *pure research,* is undertaken simply to advance knowledge in a particular field or to gather information about a given subject. It is knowledge for the sake of knowledge. The knowledge gained from pure research may not have an immediate application. Most basic research in the HR area is conducted by faculty members of colleges and universities, as well as by private, nonprofit institutions.

Applied research is conducted to solve a particular problem; its results may be put to immediate use. The majority of HR research in business firms and government agencies is of this type. Perhaps the earliest example of sys-

New Interest in Job Satisfaction at the U.S. Postal Service

If there was ever an executive interested in the job satisfaction of employees, it must be Anthony Frank, the postmaster general of the United States. In November 1991 he ordered a survey of his 750,000 employees to learn their attitudes and feelings about their jobs. Earlier that month the country was shocked to learn that Thomas McIlvane, reportedly a disgruntled postal employee, had killed four postal workers and wounded five others.[2]

The McIlvane shooting in Royal Oak, Michigan, was seen as part of a pattern of violence at the U.S. Postal Service. There had been earlier killings that were widely reported—in Ridgewood, New Jersey, in 1991; in Escondido, California, in 1989; and in New Orleans, Louisiana, in 1988. A total of 700 assaults involving supervisors and postal employees were documented between 1986 and 1992.

What is unique about the postal service situation that explains such apparent dissatisfaction? Some observers point out that the actual *rate* of assaults, and even killings, is typical, but is perceived as high since even a low rate of a problem looks big when 750,000 employees are involved. Others suggest that the stress level was ratcheted up when the postal service had its federal funding cut in the 1980s. Since then, the postal service has been expected to turn a profit in an industry where it competes with UPS, Federal Express, and other tough competitors. Still others point to automation, which now requires employees to sort sixty letters a minute in a boring job, monitored closely by computers and sometimes one-way mirrors.

Finally, some question the hiring of younger college-educated supervisors to manage an aging work force during a period of downsizing. Some of these supervisors have been accused of being autocratic and "paramilitary" in style, and some workers feel they are being harassed out of their jobs.

---

tematic, comprehensive applied research is the famous Hawthorne studies, which took place at the Western Electric Company's Hawthorne Works during the late 1920s.[3]

The Researchers

HR research is conducted by individuals and by a variety of public and private organizations. Some 39 percent of HR research is conducted by private research organizations, 34 percent by academic institutions, 22 percent by agencies of the federal government, and 5 percent by business firms.[4]

While it is hard to calculate who is doing HR research, a study in the late 1970s by the Bureau of National Affairs, a private research organization, reported that only about half of the ninety-one organizations surveyed conducted HR research. The most commonly researched areas were effectiveness of training, recruiting

761

sources, performance evaluation, and validation of employee selection systems.[5]

Federal Government Many federal government agencies conduct both basic and applied research. In the HR field, agencies within the Department of Labor, primarily the Bureau of Labor Statistics (BLS), conduct and report research. The Department of Labor's *Monthly Labor Review* contains the results of studies of a wide range of HR topics.

Private Research Organizations Many private organizations have been formed with the sole purpose of conducting pure and applied research in the HR area. Some of these organizations include the National Industrial Conference Board (NICB), the Bureau of National Affairs (BNA), and the Brookings Institution.

Personnel Associations Large national and international personnel associations periodically conduct research concerned with the practices and activities of their members' organizations. Some of these associations include the International Personnel Management Association (IPMA), the Society for Human Resource Management (SHRM), and the American Society for Training and Development (ASTD). The results of these studies are often reported in the associations' journals, such as SHRM's *HRMagazine* and ASTD's *Training and Development*.

Colleges and Universities Institutions of higher learning not only disseminate information but bear an important responsibility for discovering and analyzing information as well. The colleges and universities as a whole represent one of the greatest sources of basic and applied research in the HR field. Many faculty members conduct research as a normal part of their employment responsibilities. In addition, many institutions also operate research centers to conduct both basic and applied research in conjunction with the business community. One of the best-known university research centers is the University of Michigan's Survey Research Center. That center's long-standing work on employee job satisfaction trends remains one of the most sophisticated studies of workers' attitudes to date.

Business Firms Many business firms conduct applied HR research to solve a particular problem or evaluate a present or proposed program or project. Several larger firms, such as General Electric, International Business Machines (IBM), and AT&T, operate full-scale departments of behavioral research. Most firms do not have HR research specialists but require HR professionals to perform research as a normal part of their jobs. Common examples of ongoing research responsibilities of the HR staff may include the following:

- Evaluating T&D programs.
- Conducting periodic wage and salary surveys.
- Predicting future HR staffing requirements.
- Conducting surveys of employee attitudes.
- Performing studies of employee productivity.
- Validating selection and testing instruments.

HR professionals frequently receive requests from line managers to conduct special ad hoc studies of HR problems. These studies are often requested because of some problem the manager is facing. Special studies of this type are an important part of the HR department's service responsibility. Examples of research requests from other departments may include the following:

- Investigation of extraordinarily high employee grievances in a particular manufacturing department.
- A program to reduce absenteeism among clerical personnel.
- Evaluation of changes in a labor–management agreement that may affect employee productivity.

- Development of a special performance appraisal method for sales personnel.

Although line managers may occasionally oversee an HR research project themselves, it is normal for the HR staff to create and implement the project. For any research study to be successful, the HR professional generally needs the cooperation and assistance of the line manager.

HR Research Publications

The results of HR research may be found in a wide variety of printed media. The prudent manager and staff member should keep up-to-date on major research results and use the findings to promote managerial effectiveness, employee productivity, and job satisfaction. A knowledge of important research is one way to keep abreast of the newly developed policies, programs, and techniques that show promise for making organizations function more efficiently.

The most practical and expedient way for HR professionals to keep on top of the research is by regularly reading a selected group of HR journals and magazines and perhaps subscribing to one of many electronic bulletin boards available through Internet. Figure 17-1 contains a list of journals, indexes, and abstracts that frequently report research results in a variety of personnel areas. Journals written primarily for the academician are heavy on technical discussions of research techniques and normally report the results of a research undertaking. Journals written primarily for managers and professionals focus on the application of research and are often written in a "how to" format.

RESEARCH TECHNIQUES

Many different research techniques exist, and the choice of a particular one depends on the purpose of the research and the type of

FIGURE 17-1 Journals, indexes, and abstracts useful to the human resource administrator.

Primarily for the Academician
Academy of Management Journal
Academy of Management Review
Administrative Science Quarterly
Industrial and Labor Relations Review
Journal of Applied Behavioral Science
Journal of Applied Psychology
Organizational Behavior and Human Decision Processes
Personnel Psychology

Primarily for the Manager or Administrator
Academy of Management Executive
Advanced Management Journal
Business Horizons
California Management Review
Harvard Business Review
HRMagazine
Human Resource Management
Labor Law Journal
Management Review
Monthly Labor Review
Organizational Dynamics
Personnel
Personnel Journal
Public Personnel Management
Supervisory Management
Training
Training and Development

Useful Indexes and Abstracts
Business Periodicals Index
Employee Relations Index
Management Abstracts
Personnel Management Abstracts
Psychological Abstracts

problem under study. Familiarity with various research techniques is important for two reasons. First, practitioners encounter a variety of HR problems in the workplace, and the appropriate research technique must be applied to the problem in question. An inappropriate research technique may seriously affect the study's overall validity and usefulness. Second, a broad knowledge of research techniques is necessary in order to read and understand the

Alternative Ways to Gather Opinion

Within the past 3 years, 45 percent of mid-sized and large employers have conducted a written employee survey.[6] New technology—computers, software, faxes, scanners—and new approaches have made it possible to gather employee responses in more flexible, sometimes less expensive, ways.

Generally, the largest expense in using the written survey format is the great hidden cost of employee time spent filling out the questionnaires. Written surveys are also inflexible since there is no way to follow up a response or tailor a question to the individual.

Focus groups are advocated as a way to solve both the cost and flexibility problems. A limited group of employees is gathered to discuss various issues in depth. This method allows the employer to get input on a range of topics without being sidetracked by the complaints of a few disgruntled employees. Fewer employees off the job and short group sessions drastically reduce the expense of this employee voice mechanism.

However, no quantitative data are generated, so this technique is not useful if the employer wants to compare the responses at his or her workplace with those at the workplaces of others. New technology can help solve this problem. "Voting" devices allow participants to give confidential responses to a moderator's questions by pressing buttons on a hand-held panel (similar to those used on some game shows!). A computer processes the responses and presents the results immediately on a monitor, allowing discussion to take place instantly.[7]

---

studies reported by other employers and researchers. The research techniques most often used to conduct HR studies include the survey, interview, historical study, and controlled experiment.

Surveys

The employee survey is the most widely used research technique among HR professionals. The most common surveys include the wage survey and the job satisfaction survey. The job satisfaction survey is often referred to as an *attitude* or *morale survey*. For additional ideas for tapping the responses of employees, see *HR in the News:* "Alternative Ways to Gather Opinion."

Job Satisfaction Survey Although job dissatisfaction has been linked with absenteeism and turnover in many studies, the relationship between job satisfaction and productivity remains controversial. Since morale and job satisfaction have been thought to be important determinants of employee productivity, absenteeism, and turnover, managers have systematically used **job satisfaction surveys** to analyze employee attitudes on important topics.

Many factors contribute to employee job satisfaction. However, the following are the four elements that most surveyed employees reported they like best about their jobs:

1. *The job itself.* Perhaps the most important factor in job satisfaction is the kind of work

PC-based surveys are also popular with employees. Market research indicates that questionnaires on disks mailed to respondents achieve up to twice the response rate of mailed paper-and-pencil surveys (which are used by many employers).[8] Software can generate reliability, validity, and comparison statistics easily and graphically. Other advantages include the possibility of asking a series of questions using a branching technique, which otherwise would seem complicated. Difficult segments can be repeated. The PC's internal clock is also being used for the following purposes:

- To identify employees who have difficulty with the questionnaire.
- To control the length of the questionnaire.
- To determine when to terminate a task.[9]

Interactive telephone surveys, taking advantage of computers and phone mail, are also an efficient survey technique. An employee dials an 800 number and a digitized voice answers, instructing the employee to press numbers on the telephone keypad in response to questions. At the end, the employee is allowed to make any comment he or she would like, and it is recorded. Fast, convenient, and inexpensive, this approach allows employees around the world to take part in a questionnaire. (**Electronic mail surveys** can perform similarly.) Other such "inbound" phone surveys are possible, as are "outbound" surveys, in which the surveyor calls the employee to ask questions.[10]

With these and other new approaches, the key is matching the organizational objectives with the practical considerations at your workplace. Clearly, the days of using only one approach are over.

---

employees perform (especially when it is challenging or interesting) and the freedom they have to determine how the work is done.

2. *Co-worker relations.* The quality of relationships within the work group is very important to employees, especially the extent to which the individual is accepted as part of the work unit and the friendliness and support of his or her fellow employees.[11]

3. *Good supervision.* Job satisfaction is considerably improved when supervisors are perceived to be fair, helpful, competent, and effective. This includes the supervisor's skill as a problem solver, coach, trainer, and listener, and as the timely, authorita-

tive source of key job-related information for employees.

4. *Opportunity to grow.* Employees derive a great deal of job satisfaction from learning new things and from the chance to develop new skills. Advancement opportunity is also very important to them.

On the other hand, the most frequently reported factors that detract from job satisfaction are the following:[12]

1. *Poor supervision.* Insensitive, incompetent, and uncaring supervisors seem to have the most negative effect on employee job satisfaction. This includes unfair, biased treatment by supervisors, failure of

supervisors to listen and respond to employees' problems or concerns, and problems with management communication credibility. Many negative ratings occur on those survey issues that are directly affected by supervisory practices.

2. *Interpersonal conflicts.* Interpersonal conflicts, lack of teamwork, unfriendliness among co-workers, and rivalries among managers and supervisors are reported to have a major negative effect on employee job satisfaction.

3. *Poor work environment.* Dirty, noisy, unsafe, and unhealthy work conditions also are leading detractors from job satisfaction.

4. *Poor pay.* Possibly symptomatic of other problems, low, uncompetitive pay is nonetheless often reported as one of the things that detracted from overall job satisfaction.

On such surveys, pay and promotions are often the lowest-ranked items in terms of job satisfaction.

One of the most widely used job satisfaction surveys is the **Job Descriptive Index (JDI)**. Sample questions on the JDI are shown in Figure 17-2.

Specific-Use Questionnaire Aside from collecting data about job satisfaction, HR researchers often find it useful to gather employees' opinions about specific job-related issues at the workplace. For example, employees may be asked to evaluate the organization's T&D function, orientation program, a proposed flextime, or a job enrichment program. Because these **specific-use questionnaires** focus on an organization's particular problems or issues, they are generally custom-made by members of the HR staff or an outside consultant. Sitespecific, or specific-use, questions are often added to another questionnaire that was developed for more general use. There is an art to wording survey questions, so great care should be exercised when writing them.

Survey Administration The total process of planning, implementing, and analyzing employee surveys and questionnaires includes a number of important elements. Regardless of the type of survey implemented, the following steps must be considered:[13]

Objectives As an initial step, management must identify the objectives of the survey. Common objectives of surveys include the identification of communication problems, excessive turnover, concerns about pay and benefits, T&D needs, predicting unionization efforts, and problems dealing with advancement opportunities and discipline.

Top Management Commitment The support of top management is critical if the survey is to be of benefit to the organization. In particular, management must be willing to share and frankly discuss the outcomes of the survey with the employees.

Survey Development Surveys may either be developed internally or prepared by an outside consulting firm. While management may be inclined to prepare the survey itself, research indicates several advantages to outside development. The outside consultant brings proven competence, experience, and objectivity. Employees are also apt to have more faith in the process when they see the company pay an outside firm to objectively develop and administer the survey.

Announcing the Survey Practitioners differ on whether or not a survey administration should be announced in advance. If the survey is a regularly scheduled event at the workplace, then there may be benefit in sending a letter to employees explaining what is and is not the purpose of the survey. In the case of the performance surveys discussed in *HR in the News:* "Rising Use of 'Performance Surveys' in the 1990's," the cycle for repeating the survey is every four to six months. Everyone is aware that a survey is coming up, so honesty

FIGURE 17-2 Sample questions from the JDI.

Think of the work you do at present. How well does each of the following words or phrases describe your work? **In the blank beside each word below, write**

_____Y_____ for "Yes" if it describes your work
_____N_____ for "No" if it does NOT describe it
_____?_____ if you cannot decide

Work on present job

_____ Routine
_____ Satisfying
_____ Good

Think of the kind of supervision that you get on your job. How well does each of the following words or phrases describe this? **In the blank beside each word below, write**

_____Y_____ for "Yes" if it describes the supervision you get on your job
_____N_____ for "No" if it does NOT describe it
_____?_____ if you cannot decide

Supervision

_____ Impolite
_____ Praises good work
_____ Doesn't supervise enough

Think of the pay you get now. How well does each of the following words or phrases describe your present pay? **In the blank beside each word below, write**

_____Y_____ for "Yes" if it describes your pay
_____N_____ for "No" if it does NOT describe it
_____?_____ if you cannot decide

Present pay

_____ Income adequate for normal expenses
_____ Insecure
_____ Less than I deserve

Think of the majority of the people that you work with now or the people you meet in connection with your work. How well does each of the following words or phrases describe these people? **In the blank beside each word below, write**

_____Y_____ for "Yes" if it describes the people you work with
_____N_____ for "No" if it does NOT describe them
_____?_____ if you cannot decide

SOURCE: "The Job Descriptive Index is copyrighted by Bowling Green State University. The complete forms, scoring key, instructions, and norms can be obtained from Dr. Patricia C. Smith, Department of Psychology, Bowling Green State University, Bowling Green, OH 43403. Used by permission.

Rising Use of "Performance Surveys" in the 1990s

Almost twenty years ago, Edwin Locke estimated that there were at least 3000 articles or studies about job satisfaction of workers. Thousands more have been written solely for internal use. A different survey—a performance survey—is now on the rise in the United States.

These brief, focused **performance surveys** examine key performance issues that are important in reaching the particular business goals of an employer. The following outline demonstrates how this survey is different from the traditional opinion survey. The performance survey has the following characteristics:[41]

- Starts with a series of hypotheses that can be tested empirically.

- Has only twenty-four to thirty-six questions and is limited to three to five specific performance issues.

- Questions are statistically validated as performance indicators before the survey is conducted.

- Is repeated every four to six months rather than every two to three years.

- Unit-level managers receive the results almost immediately.

- Follow-up efforts are targeted to specific items rather than to general/global satisfaction survey items.

- Quick follow-up is required since the next survey takes place very soon.

A *Fortune* 100 company wanted to measure its progress in improving performance in various areas through the eyes of its employees. The company wanted the following information:[42] (1) measurement of changes in employees' perceptions about performance in four key areas—especially *producing quality products;* (2) data on employees' attitudes and changes in them; and (3) identification of other important issues that would need study in later surveys.

To obtain this information, the technique requires six steps:

1. **Select key performance goals** through management and employee meetings. These meetings, and informal feedback from front-line employees, led the

---

and anonymity should be stressed in communications about the survey.

In other circumstances, prior announcements about an upcoming survey can stimulate political or group behavior dysfunctional to the survey. This author discovered that union officials had "suggested" that employees should respond to the questions by giving the same (negative) prearranged answers. This kind of "marshalling" of responses can happen

employer to examine four subjective performance areas—*empowerment, T&D, performance orientation,* and *continuous quality improvement.*

2. **Establish hypotheses**, or statements through which employees can assess performance in each of the performance areas. The employer developed eight hypotheses, two for each of the identified four performance areas. For example:

> *Performance area:*   *Continuous quality improvement*
>   *Hypothesis:*   Employees perceive that the company constantly seeks increases in the quality of the work produced.
>   *Hypothesis:*   Employees perceive that management is open to new ideas about business improvements.[43]

3. **Conduct a pilot survey** to finalize the brief questionnaire. A factor analysis can determine if the questions load on the factors or if they all load on one global factor. The employer had developed thirty-two questions to address the eight hypotheses and found that they loaded into the four performance areas properly.

4. **Conduct a full employee survey** rather than focus on a sample of employees. Since the survey is short, downtime is minimized anyway, and employees feel that they have a voice on these issues.

5. **Analyze the results** to find the strengths and weaknesses on these performance issues. The employer found that the responses were positive overall, but since the performance survey was focused, three potential shortcomings were identified: tolerance of poor performance was seen as high; feedback on performance from the organization was seen as weak; and employees felt that empowerment was a slogan, not a reality.[44]

6. **Provide feedback and develop action plans**. The employer gave employees a written report and held small-group meetings. Managers were trained in a structured process to enable them to develop action plans for their units. They were discouraged from wasting time explaining away results or changing the questionnaire. Obviously, the entire process is repeated in short intervals so that the action plans are instrumental in analyzing changes on the next survey.

---

in other circumstances. In such cases, particularly for a first survey at a workplace, an announcement should be made before the administration of the survey (e.g. on the same day). A great deal of detailed planning should elicit more honest responses than those marshalled by informal leaders.

Implementation Some important considerations for administering the survey are the following: (1) allow employees sufficient time to complete the survey, (2) administer the survey (if possible) to all employees at the same time, and (3) administer the survey on company premises (research shows that only about one-third of the employees who take a survey home will complete and return it (see *HR in the News:* "Alternative Ways to Gather Opinion" for other effective approaches.)

Analysis   Survey results can reflect total organizational results in comparison to individual employee groups (e.g., older vs. younger, male vs. female, long length of service vs. short length of service). Such groups can be identified from the information requested on the cover letter attached to the survey if such information is actually important to the organization). Remember, employees are cautious about identifying themselves on surveys. Based on the results, problem areas may be identified, and recommendations to overcome these problems can later be developed. If an outside firm is not employed, the HR department normally assumes the responsibility. See Figure 17-3 for guidelines on how to tabulate and analyze your own survey results.

Feedback   Survey results should be communicated to the employees soon after they have been tabulated and reviewed by top management. Face-to-face meetings between supervisors and employees are usually most effective for providing survey feedback.

Follow-up   Survey follow-up is important to ensure that good relations are maintained between employees and management and that action is undertaken and completed, if appropriate to the particular survey. Some surveys are general in nature—such as the JDI—and do not call on management directly to "do anything particular in response, other than listen and discuss. Other surveys can operate like a referendum and ask employees what they think should be done. While the advisability of such surveys is questionable, the response from management would obviously need to be direct, since it would be expected to do something about the problem.

Caution   Survey results gain meaning only by virtue of relevant comparisons. Of course, this means that great care should be given to deciding what the goals of the survey are and to asking appropriate questions of the respondents. It further suggests that survey results can be much more useful if there is a large comparative data base collected over a period of time. A one-time survey of worker attitudes, while somewhat useful, can be open to wide interpretation. Surveys gathered over time permit the HR analyst to note trends or if the results are simply related to specific one-time events.

Exit Interviews

Organizations often conduct **exit interviews** with employees who have voluntarily decided to leave. These employees can provide valuable information about the work environment that might not be available through any other source.

The success of the exit interview depends largely on the employees' belief that their responses will not affect the employer's response to future reference requests. Personnel interviewers generally agree that to obtain the employee's cooperation, the interviewer should be someone from the HR department and definitely not the immediate supervisor. The subject matter usually includes the reason for leaving, perceptions of the supervisor, salary, benefits, training, and opportunities for advancement. Questions about the content of the job may help uncover job design or scheduling problems. The employee may provide more candid responses if the interviewer's interest in improving conditions for his or her co-workers is emphasized. Many employees have strong personal friendships with co-workers and are sincerely interested in helping correct any minor or major work environment problems.[14]

FIGURE 17-3 A questionnaire concerning absenteeism.

1. At present, to what extent is employee absenteeism a productivity problem in your work unit?

   Not a problem at all —— A very significant problem

   　　1　　　　　　　　2　　　　　　　　3　　　　　　　　4　　　　　　　　5

2. As a supervisor, about how many hours per week do you feel you spend on problems related to absenteeism (talking with employees who call in to report an absence; calling absent employees; securing, training, and checking the work of replacement employees; counseling chronic absentees, etc.).

   0–1 hours ___　　　2–3 hours ___　　　4–5 hours ___　　　6–7 hours ___　　　8 or more hours ___

3. Overall, I am satisfied with the present absenteeism control system.

   Strongly Agree　　　Agree　　　Neither Agree nor Disagree　　　Disagree　　　Strongly Disagree
   　　1　　　　　　　2　　　　　　　　3　　　　　　　　　4　　　　　　　　5

4. The present system allows employees to be absent and tardy too often.

   Strongly Agree　　　Agree　　　Neither Agree nor Disagree　　　Disagree　　　Strongly Disagree
   　　1　　　　　　　2　　　　　　　　3　　　　　　　　　4　　　　　　　　5

5. The present system has no rewards for employees who come to work regularly.

   Strongly Agree　　　Agree　　　Neither Agree nor Disagree　　　Disagree　　　Strongly Disagree
   　　1　　　　　　　2　　　　　　　　3　　　　　　　　　4　　　　　　　　5

6. The present system is difficult for employees to understand.

   Strongly Agree　　　Agree　　　Neither Agree nor Disagree　　　Disagree　　　Strongly Disagree
   　　1　　　　　　　2　　　　　　　　3　　　　　　　　　4　　　　　　　　5

7. Supervisors in my work area interpret the present system differently.

   Strongly Agree　　　Agree　　　Neither Agree nor Disagree　　　Disagree　　　Strongly Disagree
   　　1　　　　　　　2　　　　　　　　3　　　　　　　　　4　　　　　　　　5

8. The present system allows supervisors to treat employees differently.

   Strongly Agree　　　Agree　　　Neither Agree nor Disagree　　　Disagree　　　Strongly Disagree
   　　1　　　　　　　2　　　　　　　　3　　　　　　　　　4　　　　　　　　5

9. The present system puts supervisors in a difficult position of having to decide when an absence is "acceptable" or "unacceptable."

   Strongly Agree　　　Agree　　　Neither Agree nor Disagree　　　Disagree　　　Strongly Disagree
   　　1　　　　　　　2　　　　　　　　3　　　　　　　　　4　　　　　　　　5

10. What do you consider to be the strong and weak points of the present absenteeism control system?

   _____

   _____

SOURCE: Frank E. Kuzmits, University of Louisville. With permission.

Historical Studies

HR researchers often find that tracking certain data over time helps them gain greater insight into human behavior. By isolating a small number of variables, a **historical study** analyzes patterns over weeks, months, or years. For example, many organizations analyze absenteeism and turnover data to assess whether these problems are increasing, decreasing, or remaining unchanged. One example of a long-standing historical study is a project mentioned earlier—the University of Michigan's Survey Research Center Job Satisfaction Survey. Since 1958, the center has tracked a large sample of employee attitudes concerning overall satisfaction with work. The research indicates that most employees are satisfied in general with their jobs and that workers' attitudes have changed only in certain ways since the study began.

Controlled Experiments

Compared to surveys and interviews, **controlled experiments** are seldom conducted at actual work sites. Unlike the scientist's laboratory or a professor's classroom, where variables are created and controlled with relative ease, the HR researcher in an organization has no such control. Manipulating human or technological factors simply for the sake of experimentation is generally impractical. But there are some occasions when this technique is feasible and may help a research effort.[15] To illustrate the steps involved, a job enrichment pilot study in a large manufacturing plant will be used.

- *Define the problem.* For example: poor productivity, excessive rejects.

- *Evaluate alternatives and select an alternative.* For example: some possible alternatives may be to implement an incentive pay system, introduce new technology, tighten up through closer supervision, and job enrichment. Select job enrichment.

- *State the hypothesis.* For example: six months after the implementation of job enrichment, average employee productivity will have increased by 20 percent and the average rejects per employee will have decreased by 25 percent.

- *Select experimental and control groups.* For example: implement job enrichment in one area; select a similar area to serve as a control group.

- *Measure experimental and control groups prior to the experiment.* For example: collect productivity and quality data for both groups before the experiment begins.

- *Conduct the experiment.* For example: implement job enrichment (experimental group only).

- *Measure experimental and control groups after the experiment.* For example: collect productivity and quality data for six months after the implementation of job enrichment.

- *Analyze data, draw conclusions, report results.* For example: compare before-and-after data, determine the impact of the program, report conclusions to top management.

Human Resource Information System (HRIS)

High-quality research takes a good deal of planning and organizing by a competent researcher.

Extremely important in carrying out high-quality HR research is timely, accurate, and relevant HR information. A sophisticated study of absenteeism, for example, is impossible without relevant absenteeism data broken down by employee, supervisor, department, shift, and, perhaps, by other important categories such as age, sex, and job title. Because of the importance of collecting meaningful information quickly and inexpensively, more and more HR managers have developed and implemented a formal **human resource information system (HRIS)** as discussed in Chapter 16.

Cost-Benefit Analysis

HR activities such as recruiting, selection, training, and labor relations are increasingly being measured and evaluated in economic terms. By attaching dollars-and-cents criteria to HR programs and problems—what is called **cost-benefit analysis**—HR professionals are able to generate support and confidence from top management, who ultimately decide on the size of the HR budget. By analyzing HR activities and problems by cost, HR professionals can not only evaluate proposed programs but can also identify costly personnel problems that require immediate attention. Examples of activities that may be so analyzed include the following:[16]

- *Turnover.* Costs associated with turnover

that may be estimated include separation, replacement, and training costs.

- **Absenteeism.** Costs associated with employee absenteeism include lost salaries (paid sick leave only), benefits payments, supervisors' time spent on absenteeism problems (wages and benefits), and incidental absenteeism costs (e.g., premium for temporary help, overtime premium, quality and productivity problems).

- **Smoking.** Researchers are now attaching cost estimates to the problems associated with smoking. Performance problems for which cost estimates may be made include absenteeism, medical care, insurance, property damage and depreciation, on-the-job time lost (the informal breaks due to lighting and puffing), and passive smoking (the problems suffered by nonsmokers who work around smokers).

- **Employee attitudes.** Dissatisfaction with the job may result in a number of problems. While the strength of the link between job attitudes and performance remains a hotly debated topic among behavioral scientists, there is a significant amount of research to suggest that improved job satisfaction will generally improve employee performance, primarily in the areas of absenteeism, turnover, tardiness, and grievances. To estimate the costs of such employee attitudes researchers must first determine what dimensions of job performance are related to job satisfaction and then attach cost estimates to those dimensions (e.g., absenteeism).

- **Labor contracts.** In many organizations, labor costs are among the largest costs incurred. Thus, in a collective bargaining situation, it is important for management to know how a proposed labor contract will affect the company's financial condition. Many organizations have developed sophisticated techniques (often computerized) for analyzing the cost of a proposed labor contract.

PROBLEM SOLVING AND ANALYSIS

People—with all their problems and promises—will always be the most important resource for any organization, regardless of how sophisticated and advanced technologies become.

One important responsibility of the HR professional is to identify and resolve those HR problems that claim much of management's time and effort. In many organizations, particularly large manufacturing firms and service organizations, a small number of hard-core HR problems require the special attention of line management and HR staff. The most pressing HR problems include absenteeism, turnover, job dissatisfaction, and perceived unfairness.

Absenteeism

The failure to show up for work creates problems of widely varying degrees for managers and administrators. The Monday morning absence of a HR secretary or administrative assistant may not present significant hardships for the boss because the employee's work can often be put off until he or she returns to work. But when 10 to 15 percent of the midnight-to-seven shift of a large manufacturer stays away from work on Friday night, havoc may result. Excessive employee **absenteeism** can significantly drain productivity and profits, creating innumerable problems for supervisors and the employees who work regularly.

Nationwide, the cost of absenteeism in the United States is more than $30 billion annually. Managers consider absenteeism their most serious discipline problem. Absenteeism is not unique to any industry or geographic area. It is a major problem for every organization particularly since downsizing and other "lean and mean" changes have left employers with a smaller work force (see *HR in the News:* "New Concern Over Absenteeism in 1990s"). Decision makers should periodically compute the cost of absenteeism to their organizations. Such data will indicate the severity of the

New Concern Over Absenteeism in the 1990s

Employers are refocusing on their long-time concern with employee absences. In the aftermath of downsizing, layoffs, and an emphasis on work teams, the absence of a worker is more noticeable. Try this "no-fault" multiple choice test:

Of all the workers in the United States, which of the following are most likely to be at work each day?

a. Married women with children younger than six.

b. Married men with children younger than six.

c. Hourly production workers.

d. Executives, administrators, and managers.

e. Low-paid service workers.

According to the Labor Department's Bureau of Labor Statistics, the correct answer is *b*. Married fathers of young children missed an average of 3.3 days in 1992, while married mothers of young children averaged missing 10.5 days.[19] What do these statistics suggest? Are these fathers more ambitious or are the mothers being left with the burden of child care?

"I have great admiration and sympathy for the working woman," said Edward Micek, director of the Occupational Health Center at Philadelphia's Nazareth Hospital. "Working women who have children at home work six to eight hours and then come home to a second job. The husband works, and when he comes home he's finished." The statistics reveal that these mothers are only absent 3.3 days for their own health. The other 7.2 days are due to "other reasons," such as the need to care for a child or an elderly relative.

Among the other groups, low-paid service workers missed an average of 6.2 days, while hourly production workers missed 4.25 days and executives, administrators, and managers missed 3.5 days. (According to the survey).[20]

Employers are reexamining their absentee policies to see if they still fit with their new concepts of operating "lean and mean," and if not, considering what adjustments are possible.

---

problem and the impact of absenteeism on profits; a historical study will indicate whether the total absence-related costs are increasing or decreasing.[18]

Causes of Absenteeism   Although absenteeism is one of today's most complex employee problems, it is possible to isolate the variables that influence employee decisions to attend work. Personal characteristics affect both the employee's motivation and the ability to attend. Put another way, absenteeism results when an employee cannot work (ill, missed the bus, sick child to care for) or does not want to

774

work (job too boring, job too stressful, dislikes co-workers or supervisor, receives no rewards for attendance). These two variables often interact. For example, an employee may not feel good on a Monday morning following a long, wild weekend. An employee may be tired but physically able to go to work. Yet because the job is boring, the boss is hostile, the co-workers are unfriendly, or the union contract includes a liberal provision regarding sick leave, the employee may decide to call in sick.

Measuring Absenteeism Administrators will generally find it useful to compute and analyze these absenteeism measures:

Total Time Lost Total time lost, one of the most popular measures, is used by the BNA to study absenteeism in firms throughout the nation. The computation gives a percentage of total scheduled worktime that is lost to absenteeism. The formula for the measure is:

$$\text{Total Time Lost} = \frac{\text{Days Lost to Absenteeism for a Period}}{\text{Average Number of Employees} \times \text{Total Days in Period}} \times 100$$

Figure 17-4 illustrates BNA absenteeism survey results for one year. (Be aware that several reasons given for missing work are not coded as absent days under the calculations used by BNA which may make these figures seem a little low.)

Absence Occurrences An *absence occurrence* is an absence of any length. For example, an employee absent on Monday collects one absence occurrence. An employee absent Monday, Tuesday, and Wednesday also collects one absence occurrence. A manager must decide which employee would create more problems at work: an employee who is absent twenty times a year for a total of twenty days or an employee who is absent once for twenty days straight. Employees who collect numerous one-day absence occurrences may pre-

FIGURE 17-4 Data collected by the BNA on absenteeism for firms by size, industries, and regions.

Unscheduled Absence
(Average of Monthly Median Rates, in Percent)

All Companies	1.8

Number of Employees

Up to 250	1.5
250-499	1.7
500-999	1.8
1,000-2,499	2.2
2,500 and more	2.0

Industry

Manufacturing	1.8
Non-Manufacturing	1.7
(Finance)	1.7
Non-Business	1.9
Health Care)	1.7

Region

Northeast	1.8
South	1.9
North Central	1.6
West	1.7

SOURCE: Reprinted by permission from *Bulletin to Management, (BNA Policy and Practice Series)* Vol. 42, No. 10, p. 76. Copyright 1994 by The Bureau of National Affairs, Inc.

sent a much greater problem than the employee who may have one or two short-term illnesses.

Tardiness Tardiness is a form of absenteeism that can create work problems, particularly in manufacturing environments where machines and assembly lines are scheduled to start at a specific time. Excessive tardiness disrupts normal working operations, making it difficult for first-level supervisors to synchronize the beginning of a shift operation.

Researching Absenteeism Historical studies are often useful in identifying absence problems. For example, a one-year study of absences may be analyzed by employee, work group, shift, department, and firm to determine which individuals and groups may be major contributors to the problem. In areas of high absence, the results of attitude surveys and exit interviews should be analyzed to locate sources of dissatisfaction that may be partially responsible for the problem. An audit can assess the overall effectiveness of a firm's absenteeism control system.[21] The auditing procedures would involve examining the variables that affect employees' decisions to attend work, including absenteeism policies and goals, discipline and rewards, employee substance abuse, employee selection practices, and supervisory practices.

Reducing Absenteeism Control of absenteeism in large, complex organizations will normally involve multiple strategies that address both the motivation and ability of the employee to attend work. Specific strategies for enhancing motivation include a proper match between employee and job, job enrichment, rewards for good attendance, people-oriented supervision, and clear attendance standards.[22] Strategies for enhancing the ability to attend work include creating a safe and healthy work environment, providing day-care facilities at the workplace, creating programs to assist troubled employees, providing programs for reducing job stress, and providing recreational and exercise facilities.

A research study involving 987 organizations examined a number of methods for controlling absenteeism and management's perception of their effectiveness.[23] Table 17-1 illustrates the ten methods that received the highest ratings from users. The table also shows the percentage of respondents who use each method.

Reasons for the continuance of the problem despite the use of an absence control method include (1) no written absenteeism policy, (2)

Table 17-1 Ten Methods Rated Best in Controlling Absenteeism. Note: The rating for each method is an average of ratings by all firms using that method.

Control Method	Effectiveness (on a scale of 4.0)	Percent of Firms Using
A consistently applied attendance policy	3.47	79%
Termination based on excessive absenteeism	3.47	96%
Progressive discipline for excessive absenteeism	3.43	91%
Identification and discipline of employees abusing attendance policies	3.39	88%
At least monthly analysis of daily attendance information	3.38	57%
Daily attendance records maintained by personnel department	3.36	48%
Employee call-in to give notice of absence	3.35	99%
A clearly written attendance policy	3.33	76%
Daily attendance records maintained by supervisors	3.31	68%
Allow employees to build a paid "absence bank" to be cashed in at a percentage at a later date or added to next year's vacation time	3.28	10%

SOURCE: Adapted from D. Scott and S. Markhaus, "Absenteeism Control Methods: A Survey of Practices and Results," *Personnel Administrator* (June 1982): 76.

inconsistent enforcement, and (3) lack of absence documentation. Effective forms of employer discipline for absenteeism should include the following:[24]

- A written policy statement.

- Distinguishing between absenteeism and other examples of employee misconduct as a reason for discipline.

- Using progressive discipline on the absence record, separate from other misconduct issues.

- Explicit absenteeism standards and a definition of excessive absenteeism.

- Allowing employees to improve their records through good attendance.

- Consistent application of the policy. Lax enforcement by supervisors should result in their discipline.

A relatively recent innovation in the control of absenteeism involves a concept known as **no-fault absenteeism**.[25] Under this approach, there is no distinction between excused and unexcused absenteeism, nor is there a provision for paid sick leave in many cases. The no-fault policy incorporates a point system for various forms of absenteeism and defines the types of absenteeism that are nonchargeable (i.e., without penalty). An example of a no-fault policy is shown in Figure 17-5. By adopting a no-fault policy, a cabinet manufacturer reduced absenteeism by 13 percent, and absenteeism-related grievances fell from an average of fifteen per year to four during the first year with no-fault.[26] Supervisors no longer must "grade" excuses for absences.

Turnover

As noted in Chapter 10, most HR movement takes place through employee promotions, demotions, and transfers. Another form of employee movement involves **turnover**: the movement of employees out of the organization. Turnover results from resignations, transfers out of organizational units, discharges, retirement, and death.

A certain amount of turnover is expected, unavoidable, and considered beneficial to the organization. New employees may inject fresh blood into the firm by introducing new ideas and methods and innovative, more effective ways of doing things. In addition, turnover may help rectify poor hiring and placement decisions. Such turnover is referred to as **functional turnover**. Thus, some turnover renews a stagnating organization. But excessive turnover creates an unstable work force and increases HR costs and organizational ineffectiveness. Turnover that hurts the organization is known as **disfunctional turnover**.[27] The cost of turnover to American industry is estimated to be several billion dollars a year. Examples include the following:

- Increased recruitment, selection, and placement costs.

- Increased T&D costs.

- Lower productivity and more accidents, scrappage, and quality problems.

- Disruption in programs and projects as managers and administrators leave.

Over 1500 scholarly studies of turnover have appeared in this century. The effect that turnover in top management can have on an organization has been of great interest to managers. What is the effect? The results are mixed. For small firms, changes in top management can substantially threaten profits. By contrast, a study of changes in the top management of 167 large corporations over twenty years found little such effect on sales, earnings, or profit margins. The same lack of effect was found in a study of twenty-two National Basketball Association (NBA) teams. However, changes in NBA coaches were found to have a significant effect on subsequent team performance. A similar study of the influence of city mayors found that a change of mayors did not affect budget expenditures or income.

FIGURE 17-5 A no-fault absentee program

As a result of excessive absenteeism and/or tardies, disciplinary action may be required and will be based on frequency of occurrences in accordance with the following:

- Absenteeism is defined as being absent from work on any scheduled workday, whether the absence is excused or unexcused.

- Each period of consecutive absence will be recorded as "one occurrence" regardless of the number of days duration.

- Tardiness will be considered reporting to work within ten (10) minutes of the scheduled starting time. One occasion of tardiness will be charged as one quarter (¼) occurrence of absenteeism.

- Employees who report to work late, as provided for in the reporting regulations, or who leave before the end of the shift (with management's permission) will be charged with one-half (½) of an absence occurrence for either of these occurrences.

- Employees who are absent without call-in will be charged with two occurrences of absence for that occasion.

- Absence due to Funeral Leave, Military Obligation, Jury Duty, or Union Business (each as defined by the Contract), and further including hospital confinement and work-incurred injury will not be recorded as an occurrence of absence for purposes of disciplinary action.

- For each calendar month of perfect attendance, an employee with an absentee record will have one occurrence deducted from his absentee record.

- Absence records will be maintained for a consecutive twelve-month period, starting with the employee's first occurrence of absence. All absence records and warning slips that are one year old, or older, shall not be considered for purposes of disciplinary action under this policy.

Corrective discipline will be administered according to the following:

- Three occurrences or "points," within a twelve-month period—*oral warning*

- Five occurrences, or "points," within a twelve-month period—*written warning*

- Seven occurrences, or "points," within a twelve-month period—*second written warning*

- Twelve occurrences, or "points," within a twelve-month period—*discharge*

The above policy is in addition to action that may be taken: when cumulative time lost from work for any reason substantially reduces the employee's services to the company; or as may be related to provisions of the contract.

Causes of Turnover The causes of turnover are a complex mix of factors both internal and external to the organization. Figure 17-6 shows the various factors that have been determined to affect the turnover rate. General economic conditions have an important bearing on the overall availability of jobs. Thus, turnover closely follows economic swings; turnover is generally high during periods of growth or prosperity (when jobs are plentiful) and low during recessions and low points in the business cycle. Another factor that affects turnover is the local labor market, which is determined by both the local economic conditions and the supply-demand ratio for specific kinds of occupations and professions in that labor market. Personal mobility, or the extent to which one is bound to a particular area because of family or other social ties, is also a factor in deciding whether to leave a particular job. Employees who perceive a low degree of job security in their present jobs may be motivated to seek employment in organizations where they believe a greater degree of security exists. Finally, several demographic factors have been linked to the high turnover. Employees with a

FIGURE 17-6 Factors that affect turnover.

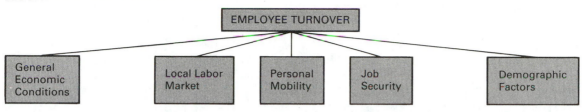

propensity to quit are young employees with little seniority who are dissatisfied with their jobs. A large percentage of voluntary turnover occurs in the first few months of employment. Employees with relatively large families and important family responsibilities tend to remain on the job.[29]

Measuring Turnover Different forms of turnover can be computed for a given period of time. Formulas for three measures of turnover are:

$$\text{Total Separation Rate} = \frac{\text{Separations}}{\text{Average Number of Employees}} \times 100$$

$$\text{Resignation Rate} = \frac{\text{Resignations}}{\text{Average Number of Employees}} \times 100$$

$$\text{Avoidable Turnover Rate} = \frac{\text{Total Separations} - \text{Unavoidable Separations}}{\text{Average Number of Employees}} \times 100$$

While all three formulas may provide important data for decision makers, most organizations measure the total separation rate when computing their own turnover statistics. Recommended by the U.S. Department of Labor, the total separation rate is used by most companies that take part in BNA surveys.[30] When making comparisons across firms, it is important that the same formula be used throughout to avoid mixing apples and oranges. BNA turnover data for firms are shown in Figure 17-7.

Researching Turnover Like absenteeism, turnover may stem from a variety of causes. Therefore, it is generally prudent to research the problem by using a variety of research methods. When researching turnover, management is usually concerned only with learning more about voluntary turnover—the reasons why good employees quit. Those who retire or are terminated for unsatisfactory performance are generally not the focus of research.

Because job dissatisfaction is a significant cause of turnover, researchers often pinpoint specific areas of work that are causing high levels of dissatisfaction. Attitude surveys and interviews can be most useful for this purpose. Exit interviews are particularly valuable in discovering the causes of turnover. In fact, one of the prime reasons for conducting the exit interview is to determine why the employee is quitting.

One interesting way to research turnover is to determine why people stay. Researchers have developed four profiles to describe most employees:[31]

1. *Turnovers.* Highly dissatisfied at work, free of external pressures to stay, and will quit at the first chance.

2. *Turn-offs.* Dislike the job but stay because of pay, benefits, or some other extrinsic job reward.

3. *Turn-ons.* Highly satisfied and motivated at work, but may leave if external pressure becomes significant.

FIGURE 17-7 Turnover rates: 12-month average

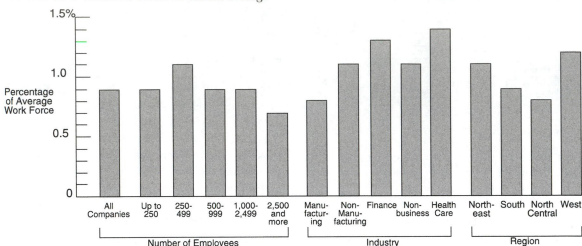

SOURCE: *Bulletin to Management (BNA Policy and Practice Series)*, Vol. 42, No. 10, p. 77. Copyright 1994 The Bureau of National Affairs, Inc.

4. *Turn-ons Plus.* Highly motivated at work and satisfied with the local environment; likely to remain and continue to be productive.

Reducing Turnover   In a meta-analysis on turnover that summarized many studies, several approaches to reduce turnover were reported. The institution of realistic job previews (RJPs) at the workplace reduced turnover rates by an average of 9 percent, while the use of job enrichment approaches reduced turnover rates by an average of 17 percent.[32]

Other programs, policies, and changes that have reduced turnover include the following:[33]

- Programs designed to enhance job satisfaction may reduce turnover because of the link between job dissatisfaction and turnover. Such programs include fair wage and salary structures, competitive benefits packages, T&D, opportunities for advancement, and employee grievance procedures.

- Selection procedures that place the right person in the right job.

- Proper orientation procedures.

- Close contact between the supervisor and the new employee so that the supervisor may iron out early job problems and support the employee.

- Supervisory training and open lines of communication between the supervisor and the employee.

- Explaining benefits to employees and showing how their total wage and benefits package compares favorably to that of other firms in the area.

- Exit interviews and employee surveys to identify areas of discontent.

Job Dissatisfaction

When employees become dissatisfied, costly problems can result. Excessive absenteeism, turnover, and grievances often result when workers experience high levels of **job dissatisfaction**. While it is difficult to put a monetary value on job dissatisfaction, estimates can be made of the economic cost of the results of job dissatisfaction, such as absenteeism, turnover, and employee grievances. As part of their social responsibility, many managers strive to create rewarding and satisfying work environments for their employees.

Causes of Job Dissatisfaction An employee's satisfaction might be defined as the "difference between the amount of some valued outcome a person receives and the amount of that outcome" the person thinks he or she should receive.[34] Thus, an employee becomes dissatisfied when things are not the way they should be. Job satisfaction or dissatisfaction generally depends on pay and benefits, supervision, co-workers, work, and the organization in general.

One of the most fascinating, yet frustrating, studies on job satisfaction was a longitudinal study that followed individuals for thirty years. The high school mood state of an individual (e.g., cheerfulness, irritability, congeniality) recorded by school counselors correlated strongly with satisfaction responses of the same individuals years later. The score from an adolescent at school was one of the best predictors of how that same individual would respond on a job satisfaction survey at work up to thirty years later. This finding may be frustrating to the manager or organization that wants to improve job satisfaction at the workplace for its own sake.[35]

Measuring Job Dissatisfaction Survey techniques are by far the most common and valid method of collecting data on job dissatisfaction. Nonattitudinal organizational data, such as on absenteeism and turnover, are sometimes used as surrogate measures of job satisfaction. But measuring job satisfaction through such indirect means has two pronounced shortcomings. First, job dissatisfaction is unlikely to be the sole cause of an employee's decision to be absent or to quit. Second, measuring job dissatisfaction by analyzing results provides no information about causes. One of the greatest benefits of a well-constructed survey on job satisfaction is that it will cover all significant job dimensions that affect job satisfaction. A valid and reliable paper-and-pencil survey, as illustrated in Figure 17-8, is usually the least costly and most valid way to measure employees' dissatisfaction with their jobs and the conditions that surround their work.

As the questionnaire in Figure 17-8 illustrates, one method for measuring the degree of dissatisfaction is by computing the difference in the score of two questions: How much is there now? How much should there be? If the rating on the second question is greater than the rating on the first, dissatisfaction is presumed to be evident.[36]

Reducing Job Dissatisfaction Survey results that identify only the type and degree of job dissatisfaction still face a difficult challenge. One approach would be to hire people who are less inclined to dissatisfaction. Another, more popular approach is to ask "What do the employees really want and how does management tailor an efficient and effective response?"

One approach that is relatively simple to implement is to include a third question that measures the importance of each potential reward, such as Figure 17-8 depicts. For example, if a group of employees was asked, "How important are flexible benefits?" and responded on the average at 6.5 out of a maximum 7-point importance scale, management would take notice. Combined with data on job dissatisfaction, a ranking of potential rewards can be easily compiled, as illustrated in Table 17-2. Note that in the study of internal auditors, feedback was found to be both high in importance and the second most dissatisfying part of the job. On the other hand, adjustable work schedules were found to be neither important nor a point of dissatisfaction.[37]

Perceptions of Fairness

Most employees expect to be treated fairly and justly in all aspects of their work. Those who think the organization has treated them unfairly may react in one of many ways. Senior employees will often decide that they have

FIGURE 17-8 A questionnaire concerning job dissatisfaction.

	Min						Max
1. Opportunity to help people							
(a) How much is there now?	1	2	3	4	5	6	7
(b) How much should there be?	1	2	3	4	5	6	7
(c) How important is this to me?	1	2	3	4	5	6	7
2. Opportunity to develop friendships							
(a) How much is there now?	1	2	3	4	5	6	7
(b) How much should there be?	1	2	3	4	5	6	7
(c) How important is this to me?	1	2	3	4	5	6	7
3. Opportunity to work in a team-oriented atmosphere							
(a) How much is there now?	1	2	3	4	5	6	7
(b) How much should there be?	1	2	3	4	5	6	7
(c) How important is this to me?	1	2	3	4	5	6	7
4. Feeling of self-esteem							
(a) How much is there now?	1	2	3	4	5	6	7
(b) How much should there be?	1	2	3	4	5	6	7
(c) How important is this to me?	1	2	3	4	5	6	7
5. Prestige within company							
(a) How much is there now?	1	2	3	4	5	6	7
(b) How much should there be?	1	2	3	4	5	6	7
(c) How important is this to me?	1	2	3	4	5	6	7
6. Prestige within community							
(a) How much is there now?	1	2	3	4	5	6	7
(b) How much should there be?	1	2	3	4	5	6	7
(c) How important is this to me?	1	2	3	4	5	6	7
7. Opportunity to display skills and talents							
(a) How much is there now?	1	2	3	4	5	6	7
(b) How much should there be?	1	2	3	4	5	6	7
(c) How important is this to me?	1	2	3	4	5	6	7
8. Opportunity for advancement/promotion recognition							
(a) How much is there now?	1	2	3	4	5	6	7
(b) How much should there be?	1	2	3	4	5	6	7
(c) How important is this to me?							

SOURCE: Norbert F. Elbert, Bellarmine College. With permission.

invested too many years to risk creating a disturbance. Instead, they may perform marginally until retirement. Young employees may feel less inclined to stay with the organization and may quit for better opportunities elsewhere. The union employee may file a grievance and set in motion a time-consuming and potentially costly mechanism to formally address the perceived unfairness.

One helpful way to examine issues of workplace fairness or justice is to look at employees' perceptions of the fairness of the out-

Table 17-2 An Example of How Rewards Can Be Identified Within an Organization

Reward Criteria	Dissatisfaction		Importance	
	Ranking	Mean Score	Ranking	Mean Score
1 Feedback	1	2.03	2	6.34
2 Self-fulfillment	2	2.00	1	6.38
3 Advancement/promotion	3	1.88	4	6.26
4 Mentor/mentee relationship	4	1.76	26	5.61
5 Prestige within company	5	1.69	27	5.48
6 Self-esteem	6	1.61	3	6.30
7 Creativity/innovation	7	1.61	14	5.92
8 Team work environment	8	1.61	19	5.84
9 Salary	9	1.42	5	6.15
10 Participate in goal setting	10	1.42	10	6.03
11 Independent thought	11	1.42	24	5.73
12 Authority	12	1.42	28	5.46
13 Increase technical skills	13	1.38	11	6.03
14 Status symbols	14	1.34	35	3.92
15 Pleasant work environment	15	1.30	15	5.92
16 Impact on operations	16	1.30	23	5.76
17 Risk taking	17	1.30	33	4.72
18 Leisure time	18	1.26	31	5.34
19 Prestige within community	19	1.23	32	4.80
20 Personal initiative	20	1.19	8	6.07
21 Develop friendships	21	1.19	30	5.40
22 Display skills/talents	22	1.15	6	6.15
23 Independence/freedom	23	1.15	20	5.84
24 Increasing challenge	24	1.11	7	6.11
25 Supervisory experience	25	1.11	18	5.88
26 Help others	26	1.07	21	5.80
27 Security	27	1.03	9	6.07
28 Recognized as a professional	28	1.03	16	5.92
29 Written skills	29	1.03	17	5.92
30 Influencing others	30	1.00	29	5.46
31 Oral communication skills	31	0.88	13	5.96
32 Interpersonal skills	32	0.80	12	6.03
33 Adjustable work schedule	33	0.80	25	5.65

SOURCE: Norbert F. Elbert and Tim Swenson, "Motivating Internal Auditors," *Journal of Internal Auditing* (Fall 1990): 26.

comes and their perceptions of the procedure separately. **Procedural justice** examines the fairness of the process: Are decisions made according to clear standards? Can I appeal the decision? Will I get an opportunity to have input? **Distributive justice** examines only the outcome of a decision or policy: Did I receive the promotion? Did I get the raise? Research has indicated that employees often view these two types of workplace justice differently.[39] Further, employers can help ensure that the employee believes that the procedure used is fair and just, even if the employer cannot guarantee that the employee will always get the final outcome that she or he wishes.

The costs of unfair employee treatment are difficult to compute. Research has determined that employees' perceptions of inequitable treatment are very strong predictors of job absence and turnover, two costly employee behaviors. The results of unfair treatment of employees may include lower production quantity, lower production quality, greater absenteeism, greater turnover, less initiative, lower morale, lack of cooperation, spread of dissatisfaction to co-workers, fewer suggestions, and less self-confidence. Each result has a cost, whether direct or indirect.[40]

Measuring Perceptions of Fairness Measuring employee feelings about fair treatment is a complex process. Because the probability of receiving honest answers through interviews and group discussions is low, the most practical alternative is to use anonymous survey techniques. One advantage of using written questionnaires is that the possible sources of perceived inequity can often be identified. Identification can be accomplished by comparing the results of a fairness survey among departments, jobs, and supervisors. See *HR in the News* "Rising Use of 'Performance Surveys' in the 1990s" for a discussion of one survey approach.

Researching Fairness Companies should routinely measure employees' perceptions of

fairness. If the organization waits until a crisis occurs, employees may feel that they are being patronized and may suspect that the organization does not really care about employee feelings. An advantage of conducting a fairness study on an annual basis is that organizations can analyze changes in employee perceptions and possibly identify reactions to organizational changes.

Reducing Unfairness After reviewing the results of a survey of employee perceptions of fairness, management may consider introducing certain changes in the organization. Changes that may reduce perceptions of **unfairness** include the following:

- Reclassify jobs that appear to be inequitably paid (establish internal pay equity).
- Base promotions on objective measures of performance.
- Train supervisors to distribute the workload more fairly.
- Conduct wage surveys of the local labor market to determine compatibility with local firms (establish external pay equity).
- Allow employees to have more involvement in planning and controlling their work.
- Ensure that policies, procedures, rules, and regulations are uniformly administered and enforced.

INTERNATIONAL HR: THE INTERNATIONAL CHALLENGE TO MANAGEMENT RESEARCH

There are many reasons why a better understanding of the international dimensions of management is required. Mr. Fujisawa, the cofounder of the Honda Motor Corporation, once observed that "Japanese and American management is 95 percent the same, and differs in all important aspects." We need a better or more accurate understanding of managerial and organizational differences if we are to compete successfully in a global environment. For example, assuming that Japanese business executives negotiate in the same way as Americans almost guarantees failure. So, too, do we guarantee failure if we send an American-trained plant manager to South America or the Middle East without extensive cross-cultural training. In short, we need to ensure that we have managers who understand the cultural context as a major factor in the business environment.

In addition, cultural differences often define what constitutes legitimate research. For example, several years ago a U.S. manager gave a talk on employee absenteeism to a group of professors in Denmark. After listening pa-tiently to his speech, a senior professor raised his hand and said: "I don't understand why you are studying absenteeism. It is none of your business why people are not at work. That is a personal matter. I assume you are doing this research to further exploit workers and squeeze more productivity out of them." At the same time, in Italy, the government was forming a national commission to study the problem of absence from work. (Unfortunately, the first commission meeting had to be canceled because no one showed up!) In any event, these examples point out how cultural realities serve to encourage or constrain our research on various topics. They define how we do research and how we disseminate the results.[45]

CONCLUSIONS AND APPLICATIONS

- Sound HR research can significantly strengthen an organization's HR program. Some specific uses of research include measurement and evaluation of current personnel policies, programs, and activities and appraisal of proposed polices, programs, and activities.

- Research is generally classified as basic or applied. Most HR research is applied research to solve a particular problem or evaluate a proposed HR program or activity.

- HR research is conducted by a variety of individuals and public and private organizations, including government agencies, private research organizations, personnel associations, colleges and universities, and individual business firms. In a business firm, HR research is usually conducted by a member of the personnel staff. Results are available in a number of journals and other publications.

- Techniques that are frequently used in HR research include surveys, specific-use questionnaires, interviews, and historical studies. The controlled experiment has only limited use because of the difficulties in applying this technique in an organizational setting. The primary uses of surveys, questionnaires, and interviews are to gather employees' feelings and perceptions about areas of job satisfaction and dissatisfaction and to evaluate present and proposed HR programs and policies.

- An important requirement for HR research is a valid HRIS. Without relevant information, it will not only be difficult to carry out meaningful research but will also limit the HR staff's day-to-day effectiveness.

- Whenever possible, HR professionals should analyze HR problems and evaluate their programs, using a cost-benefit analysis. Some problems and activities that lend themselves to this form of analysis are turnover, absenteeism, attitudes, and employee grievances.

- Although HR professionals and line managers must confront a wide array of people problems, a small, hard-core group of problems seem to permeate many organizations and consume an inordinate amount of the time of line and staff decision makers. These problems typically include absenteeism, turnover, job dissatisfaction, and unfairness. For problems such as these, decision makers must, through the use of HR research, systematically analyze the extent of the problem in their organizations, determine where the problems exist, and develop strategies to overcome them.

CASE STUDY

Absenteeism at Digitronics, Inc.

Samuel Godfrey, HR manager for Digitronics, Inc., quickly glanced over his quarterly personnel report. He was due to go over the report with plant manager Jane Newberry in about five minutes. The report contained information on a wide range of HR areas, including direct and indirect labor costs; cost of employee benefits; new hires, transfers, resignations, and discharges; and data on the firm's absenteeism rate.

Digitronics is a medium-sized maker of computer components located in Los Angeles, California. Digitronics sells its parts to large computer manufacturers such as IBM and Honeywell, Inc. The firm has enjoyed relatively peaceful labor relations and is not unionized.

Sam walked a few doors down to Jane's office and took a seat. After exchanging a few pleasantries, they turned their attention to the report.

Newberry: Sam, all the data look pretty good. Our labor costs are in pretty good shape, and our turnover is a little below the industry average. But there seems to be one problem—absenteeism. I see our overall absenteeism rate is 8.5 percent. That's pretty high, I believe. And the quarterly trends are slightly increasing. How do our absenteeism rates compare with industry averages?

Godfrey: Uh, Jane, I'm not sure. It's pretty hard to find comparable absenteeism data. I guess most firms don't want to air their dirty laundry. But I'll check around and see what I can find.

Newberry: Okay. Incidentally, just what does that 8.5 percent absenteeism rate represent? How is it figured? Do you have departmental breakdowns so we can see where the problem is the greatest?

Godfrey: Well, the 8.5 percent figure is for the whole company—all twelve hundred employees. I'm pretty sure it represents the total time lost to all kinds of absenteeism. My assistant prepares the data, and I'm not positive just how the statistic is computed. I'll check when I get back to the office. I don't have any breakdown on that figure, but it shouldn't be too hard to get.

Newberry: I think we'll need some more details on that 8.5 percent figure. We need to compare departments, shifts, and maybe even look at male and female rates. But Sam, the real question is, how can we get that rate down to about 3 or 4 percent?

Godfrey: Well Jane, I'm not sure. You know, absenteeism is a real tough problem, but I don't think there's a whole lot that can be done about it. Maybe we should hire a consultant to look into the problem.

QUESTIONS

1. Could an effective research process help Digitronics reduce its absenteeism? How?

2. Where might Digitronics look for absenteeism data for similar industries?

3. Would you recommend that Digitronics revise its absenteeism information system? If so, how?

EXPERIENTIAL EXERCISES

1. Figuring the Cost of Employee Absenteeism

PURPOSE

To recognize the various cost elements of employee absenteeism and to determine the cost of absenteeism in a hypothetical organization, using commonly accepted HR calculations.

THE TASK

Tables 1 and 2 include cost data for the hypothetical XYZ Corporation. Using the model provided in Figure 1, determine the cost of absenteeism for 1994. Once you have completed Figure 1, your instructor will lead a discussion regarding the purpose of computing absenteeism costs.

Midwest Tube and Tire Company

The Midwest Tube and Tire Company is a medium-sized tube and tire manufacturer located near Indianapolis. The firm employs about 450 operative employees and about 85 managerial, professional, clerical, and administrative personnel. The forty-five-year-old company manufactures primarily tires and tire tubes for large lawnmowers, tractors, and other farm implements. Products are marketed nationwide through a large network of independent dealers.

While Midwest Tube and Tire enjoys considerable success with an excellent product line, it experiences more than its share of personnel problems. Poor labor–management relations (the firm is unionized with the United Auto Workers) have plagued the firm almost from the start. In addition to high levels of grievances and turnover, the firm has suffered excessive absenteeism for several years. Janice Dillon, newly appointed HR manager for the company, has been asked by the plant manager, Wayne Boulton, to determine how much absenteeism cost the firm in 1994. Boulton wanted to use the data to persuade the union of the need for a tougher absenteeism provision in the upcoming labor contract.

Table 1 Total Time Lost, Absenteeism Rates, and Wage/Salary Data per Occupational Group for 1994

	Blue-Collar	Clerical	Management and Professional
Total employees	450	46	39
Total days absent	7,988	564	215
Absenteeism rate	7.1%	4.9%	2.2%
Average hourly wage/salary	$7.47	$6.20	$13.85

Note: Assume that employees received their direct hourly wages/salaries for *all* days absent.

Table 2 Total Benefits Cost for 1994 (Employer's Costs Only)

Legally required payments (old age and survivors insurance, workers' compensation, unemployment compensation)	$ 763,980
Private pensions (employer's share)	163,324
Insurance (life, accident, hospitalization)	955,296
Paid vacations, sick leave, holidays, rest and lunch periods, wash-up time, etc.	1,160,620
Subsidized costs for recreation, cafeteria, education, safety, equipment and clothing	225,984
Other: annual physicals, shift differential, employee discounts	126,345
	$3,395,594

NOTE: Per-employee differences among job classes (e.g., blue-collar vs. clerical vs. managerial) are minor. Assume that employees work 2080 hours per year (52 weeks × 40 hours).

FIGURE 1 Supervisory data related to absenteeism (1994)

Average number of supervisors for the period: 21
Average supervisory salary per hour: $10.05
Total estimated hours lost per supervisor per week to absenteeism: 4

Over the next few weeks, Dillon collected the information shown in Tables 1 and 2 and Figure 1.

Finally, in discussing the problem with plant personnel, it was estimated that annual costs for 1994 due to overtime, production delays, and quality problems related to absenteeism totaled $93,750.

Using Figure 2, determine the total cost of absenteeism for 1994, in addition to the cost of absenteeism per employee.

FIGURE 2 Total estimated cost of employee absenteeism.

1. Total work hours lost to employee absenteeism for the period   _____
2. Weighted average wage/salary per hour per employee   _____
3. Cost of employee benefits per hour per employee   _____
4. Total compensation lost per hour per absent employee
   a. If absent workers are paid (wage/salary plus benefits)
   b. If absent workers are not paid (benefits only)   _____
5. Total compensation lost to absent employees (total worker hours lost
   × 4(a) or 4(b), whichever is applicable)   _____
6. Total supervisory hours lost on employee absenteeism   _____
7. Average hourly supervisory wage, including benefits   _____
8. Total supervisory salaries lost to managing problems of absenteeism
   (hours lost × average hourly supervisory wage—item 6 × item 7)   _____
9. All other costs incidental to absenteeism not included in the preceding
   items   _____
10. Total estimated cost of absenteeism—summation of items 5, 8, and 9   _____
11. Total estimated cost of absenteeism per employee:

$$\frac{\text{(Total Estimated Costs)}}{\text{(Total Number of Employees)}}$$

= $ _____
per employee

2. Stopping Taco Bell Employees from Heading for the Border

PURPOSE

To use role playing to diagnose problems that lead to turnover in one of our largest industries. Students should also be able to understand and set up problem-solving monitoring mechanisms to see if their ideas for improvement are effective.

THE TASK

According to some reports, the turnover rate in the fast-food and hospitality industries can be as high as 200 percent annually. If a fast-food restaurant employs twenty-five people, fifty may have quit or been terminated during the course of a year. It is likely that several students in your class have worked or are working in this or a similar high-turnover workplace. Perhaps you have contributed to the turnover statistics yourself (or maybe look forward to the day when you will). You and your classmates have likely each visited a fast-food restaurant at least twice this week. The problems associated with a high turnover rate seriously affect these businesses.

Step 1: *Preparation*

The class should break up into small groups of about four to seven individuals each. After the groups have formed, the instructor should make the following assignments:

a. Half of the groups should play the role of management. This *management team* is responsible for six fast-food restaurants (Taco Bell or any other single chain named by your instructor) in the vicinity.

b. Half of the groups should play the role of *entry-level fast-food employees* at one of the six locations of the restaurant chain named by your instructor. Some of the employees work full-time; others work part-time.

The management and employee groups should remain separate and not allow the other "side" to hear their discussions.

Step 2:   *Management*

Your role is to address the 200 percent turnover problem that you assume exists at your locations. You have not computed any turnover statistics, but it seems that your turnover is very high.

a. Decide what problem-solving steps you should take to come up with ideas that you can implement. What should you consider first, second, and so on?

b. Decide what the causes of the high turnover are at your locations. So far, you have only been given the worst statistics. Some fast-food restaurants have dramatically lower turnover rates (10–15 percent).

c. Identify tactics and strategies that you will implement to lower the costs of turnover. Of course, you do not want to have a net loss, that is, spend more on a remedy than the turnover costs you.

Step 2:   *Fast-Food Employees*

a. Talk to other members of your group and find out who has worked in fast food or another industry with high turnover. Try to understand what the personal reasons may be on a case-by-case basis. List these causes for quitting and being fired from such jobs.

b. Decide what it would take to keep you working at a fast-food restaurant for at least one year, three years, and ten years or more. What specific steps would the employer have to take or how would the organizations have to change to keep you? List these actions.

Step 3:   *Management versus Fast-Food Employees*

Have each group send one representative to the front of the class—management on one side, employees on the other.

a. Management should present the recommendations they decided on to solve their turnover problems (their Step 2c).

b. The employees should respond to management's set of recommendations. (Management should be allowed to finish its suggestions before the employees respond.)

c. The employees should tell management what it would take to keep them working there for one, three, and ten years.

d. Management should respond to these suggestions after the employees have finished.

e. The class should have an open discussion to assess whether it is any closer to solving the turnover problem in the fast-food industry.

KEY TERMS AND CONCEPTS

Absenteeism
Applied research
Avoidable turnover rate
Basic research
Controlled experiments
Cost-benefit analysis
Costs of absenteeism and turnover
Distributive justice
Dysfunctional turnover
Electronic mail survey
Equity
Exit interviews
Focus groups
Functional turnover

Historical study
HR publications
Human resource information system (HRIS)
Interactive telephone survey
Job Descriptive Index (JDI)
Job dissatisfaction
Job satisfaction survey
No-fault absentee program
PC-based survey
Performance survey
Procedural justice
Specific-use questionnaire
Turnover
Unfairness

REVIEW QUESTIONS

1. Describe the primary uses of HR research.

2. Discuss the areas in which a business firm may find it beneficial to conduct applied research.

3. What are the steps involved in conducting a controlled experiment?

4. What causes employee absenteeism? How may absenteeism be reduced?

5. Is turnover good or bad for the organization? What problems may result from excessive turnover?

6. What is the most effective way to measure job dissatisfaction? In what different ways may job attitudinal data be analyzed?

7. Why may an employee feel that he or she is being treated unfairly? What HR programs may be implemented to reduce employees' feeling of unfairness?

DISCUSSION QUESTIONS

1. Assume that you are the HR manager in a large insurance company. At a luncheon meeting, a sales representative for MUSICO, a firm that sells piped-in music in office buildings, claims, "If you install MUSICO, your clerical employees will be happier and more productive." Could you set up a controlled experiment to determine the effects of

MUSICO on employee morale and productivity? Should your company buy the MUSICO system?

2. In analyzing turnover records, you find that over half of your MBA management trainees leave your large urban bank within one year of being hired. How would you conduct research on this problem? Speculate on some reasons for the turnover problem and offer some alternative solutions to eliminate or reduce these causes.

3. Whose responsibility is it to control employee absenteeism—the line manager's or the HR manager's? Explain how responsibility for controlling this problem might be divided.

4. Many companies employ outside consultants to research an organizational problem and recommend a solution. What are the advantages and disadvantages of using consultants rather than having internal HR staff research a problem?

5. Research shows that the greatest percentage of absenteeism occurs among blue-collar and clerical workers, and that managers and staff professionals are absent very infrequently. What reasons account for this pattern?

6. The Schwartz Company does an attitude survey once a year. The HR manager has found that job satisfaction increased overall among Schwartz employees from 1979 to 1980; the organization has done nothing specifically to improve job satisfaction. What could account for these results?

7. Why is relatively little basic research conducted within the organization by HR researchers?

8. Assume that your company has a significant turnover problem and you want to read about the subject. At the library, (a) find out what organizations regularly publish turnover data, (b) determine how these turnover figures are computed, and (c) gather some recent turnover data and report them to the class.

ENDNOTES

Chapter 17

1. Michael J. Jucius, *Personnel Management* (New York: Irwin, 1971), pp. 534–35.

2. This account was adapted from "Slayings at Michigan Post Office Spur a Review of All Employees," *The New York Times* (November 15, 1991): A8; and "Concerned Over Morale, Post Office Asking 'Why'," *The New York Times* (November 15, 1991): A6.

3. See F. J. Roethlisberger and W. J. Dickson, *Management and the Worker* (Cambridge, MA: Harvard University Press, 1939).

4. William C. Byham, *The Uses of Personnel Research,* Research Study 91 (New York: American Management Association, 1968), p. 8.

5. Bureau of National Affairs, Inc., ASPA-BNA survey no. 37, *Personnel Policies: Research and Evaluation,* Bulletin no. 1516 (March 22, 1979), p. 2.

6. William E. Wymer and Jeanne M. Carsten, "Alternative Ways to Gather Opinion," *HRMagazine* (April 1992): 71, citing *A Survey of Employee Opinion Surveys* by A. Foster Higgins & Co.

7. Ibid., p. 72.

8. Ibid.

9. Ibid.

10. Ibid., pp. 74–76.

11. Louis E. Tagliaferri, "Taking Note of Employee Attitudes," *Personnel Administrator* 33, no. 4 (April 1988): 96–102.

12. Ibid.

13. W. Martin, "What Management Can Expect from an Employee Attitude Survey," *Personnel Administrator* 24 (July 1981). See also W. J. Rothwell, "Conducting an Employee Attitude Survey," *Personnel Journal* 62 (April 1983).

14. Donald A. Drost, Fabius P. O'Brien, and Steve Marsh, "Exit Interviews: Master the Possibilities,"

Personnel Administrator 32, no. 2 (February 1987): 104–10.

15. For details of the various forms of experimental design, see D. T. Campbell and J. C. Stanley, *Experimental and Quasi-Experimental Designs for Research* (Chicago: Rand-McNally, 1963); and T. S. Bateman and G. R. Ferris, *Method and Analysis in Organizational Research* (Reston, VA: Reston, 1984).

16. W. F. Cascio, *Costing Human Resources* (Boston: Kent, 1982).

17. K. Dow Scott, Steven E. Markham, and G. Stephen Taylor, "Employee Attendance: Good Policy Makes Good Sense," *Personnel Administrator* 32, no. 12 (December 1987): 98.

18. F. E. Kuzmits, "How Much Is Absenteeism Costing Your Organization?" *Personnel Administrator* 24 (June 1979): 29–33.

19. "Absenteeism Figures Provoke Questions," *The Philadelphia Inquirer* (June 6, 1993): B1.

20. Ibid.

21. F. E. Kuzmits, "How Good Is Your Absenteeism Control System?" *Advanced Management Journal* 12 (Winter 1980): 4–15.

22. Journal articles on the analysis and control of absenteeism problems abound. See *HR Magazine, Personnel Journal, Personnel, Business Horizons,* and *Supervisory Management.*

23. D. Scott and S. Markham, "Absenteeism Control Methods: A Survey of Practices and Results," 27 *Personnel Administrator* (June 1982): 73–84.

24. Scott et al., "Employee Attendance," pp. 98–106.

25. See F. E. Kuzmits, "Is Your Organization Ready for No-Fault Absenteeism?" *Personnel Administrator* 29 (December 1984): 119–27.

26. Ibid.

27. Dan R. Dalton, David M Krackhardt, and Lyman W. Porter, "Functional Turnover: An Empirical Assessment," *Journal of Applied Psychology* 66 (1981): 716–21.

28. Dan L. Worrell, Wallace N. Davidson III, P. R. Chandy, and Sharon L. Garrison, "Management Turnover Through Deaths of Key Executives: Effects on Investor Wealth," *Academy of Management Journal* 29, no. 4 (December 1986): 674–94.

29. L. W. Porter and R. M. Steers, "Organizational, Work and Personal Factors in Employee Turnover and Absenteeism," *Psychological Bulletin* 80 (1973): 151–76.

30. *Employee Absenteeism and Turnover* (Washington, DC: Bureau of National Affairs, 1974).

31. V. S. Flowers and C. L. Hughes, "Why Employees Stay," *Harvard Business Review* 51 (July–August 1973): 49–60.

32. Wayne F. Cascio and Glen M. McEvoy, "Strategies for Reducing Employee Turnover: A Meta-Analysis," *Journal of Applied Psychology* 70 (1985): 342–53.

33. Personnel and management journals periodically treat issues related to turnover. See the journals listed in note 22; also R. T. Mowday, C. S. Koberg, and A. W. McArthur, "The Psychology of the Withdrawal Process," *Academy of Management Journal* 27 (March 1984): 79–94.

34. M. J. Gannon, *Organizational Behavior* (Boston: Little, Brown, 1979), p. 186.

35. B. M. Staw, N. E. Bell, and J. A. Clausen, "The Dispositional Approach to Job Attitudes: A Lifetime Longitudinal Test," *Administrative Science Quarterly* 31 (1986): 56–77.

36. Norbert F. Elbert and Tim Swenson, "Motivating Internal

Auditors," *Journal of Internal Auditing* 6, no. 2 (Fall 1990): 22–28.

37. Ibid.

38. Ibid.

39. Jerald Greenberg, "Looking Fair vs. Being Fair: Managing Impressions of Organizational Justice," in B. M. Staw and L. L. Cummings, eds., *Research in Organizational Behavior* 12 (Greenwich, Conn.: JAI Press, 1990).

40. R. C. Huseman, J. D. Hatfield and E. W. Miles, "A New Perspective on Equity Theory: The Equity Sensitivity Construct," *Academy of Management Review* 12, no. 2 (June 1987): 222–34.

41. Adapted from Thomas Rollins, "Performance Surveys: Quality Tools Emerging for the 1990s," *Employment Relations Today* (Summer 1992): 119.

42. Ibid., pp. 119–20.

43. Ibid., p. 124.

44. Ibid.

45. Richard M. Steers, "The International Challenge to Management Education," *The Academy of Management Newsletter* 17, no 4 (October 1987): 2–3.

Names Index

CORPORATIONS AND ORGANIZATIONS INDEX

SUBJECT INDEX